# LAROUSSE

## DICTIONARY

**SPANISH-ENGLISH • ENGLISH-SPANISH**
**ESPAÑOL-INGLÉS • INGLÉS-ESPAÑOL**

## DICCIONARIO

LAROUSSE

**Project Management/*Dirección de la Obra***
Sharon J. Hunter

**Editors/*Redacción***
Dileri Borunda Johnston, Claudia Brovetto, Clio E. Bugel
Talia Bugel, Magdalena Coll, Antonio Fortin
José A. Galvez, Rebecca K. Phillips
Carol Styles Carvajal

**Publishing Manager/*Dirección General***
Janice McNeillie

**Design/*Diseño***
Sophie Compagne

**Illustrations/*Illustraciones***
Jean-Pierre Lamerand, Laurent Blondel, Agathe Bouton

**Typesetting/*Composición***
IGS

# Preface

This dictionary is a completely new reference book for students in their first years of learning Spanish. The concept is simple: each word and each different sense of a word has a translation and an example. The layout ensures that entries, as well as the different senses and translations, stand out clearly. Words and senses have been carefully selected to meet the needs of young learners. The wordlist is complemented by instructive notes containing lots of useful information on false cognates, language usage and essential grammar points. As learning a language involves not only learning words but also learning about a different way of life, the dictionary includes boxed notes on Latin American culture.

# Prefacio

Este diccionario es una obra totalmente nueva, dirigida a los jóvenes de los últimos años de enseñanza primaria y los primeros de enseñanza secundaria, que empiezan a aprender inglés. Está basado en un concepto pedagógico simple: a cada palabra o a cada uno de los significados de una palabra se asocian una traducción y un ejemplo. Este concepto se refleja en una presentación clara, en donde las palabras, los sentidos y las traducciones aparecen claramente identificados. Además, esas palabras y sus sentidos fueron cuidadosamente seleccionados, para atender a las necesidades de los jóvenes aprendices. Para completar el léxico, también damos, en formato de notas pedagógicas, una cantidad de información acerca de los falsos amigos, el uso de las palabras y los aspectos gramaticales más difíciles. Finalmente, porque creemos que el aprendizaje de una lengua no se limita a las palabras, sino que pasa también por el conocimiento de una cultura, hemos dedicado recuadros especiales a las particularidades culturales de los Estados Unidos.

# phonetic transcription

## transcripción fonética

| English vowels | | Vocales españolas | |
|---|---|---|---|
| [ I ] | pit, big, rid | [i ] | piso, imagen |
| [ e ] | pet, tend | [e] | tela, eso |
| [ æ] | pat, bag, mad | [a] | pata, amigo |
| [ ʌ ] | run, cut | [o] | bola, otro |
| [ ɒ ] | pot, log | [u] | luz, una |
| [ ʊ ] | put, full | | |
| [ ə ] | mother, suppose | | |
| [ iː ] | bean, weed | | |
| [ ɑː] | barn, car, laugh | | |
| [ ɔː ] | born, lawn | | |
| [ uː] | loop, loose | | |
| [ ɜː ] | burn, learn, bird | | |

### English diphthongs

### Diptongos españoles

| [ eɪ] | bay, late, great | [ei] | ley, peine |
|---|---|---|---|
| [ aɪ] | buy, light, aisle | [ai] | aire, caiga |
| [ ɔɪ] | boy , foil | [oi] | soy, boina |
| [ əʊ] | no, road, blow | [au] | causa, aula |
| [ aʊ] | now, shout, town | [eu] | Europa, deuda |
| [ ɪə] | peer, fierce, idea | | |
| [ eə] | pair, bear, share | | |
| [ ʊə] | poor, sure, tour | | |

### Semi-vowels

### Semivocales

| you, spaniel | [ j ] | hierba, miedo |
|---|---|---|
| wet, why, twin | [ w] | agua, hueso |

### English consonants

### Consonantes españolas

| [ p ] | pop, people | [p ] | papá, campo |
|---|---|---|---|
| [ b ] | bottle, bib | [b ] | vaca, bomba |
| [ t ] | train, tip | [β ] | curvo, caballo |
| [ d ] | dog, did | [t ] | toro, pato |
| [ k ] | come, kitchen | [d ] | donde, caldo |
| [ g ] | gag, great | [k ] | que, cosa |
| [tʃ] | chain, wretched | [g ] | grande, guerra |
| [dʒ] | jet, fridge | [ɣ ] | aguijón, iglesia |
| [ f ] | fib, physical | [tʃ] | ocho, chusma |
| [ v ] | vine, livid | [f ] | fui, afán |

# phonetic transcription

| | |
|---|---|
| [ θ ] | think, fifth |
| [ ð ] | this, with |
| [ s ] | seal, peace |
| [ z ] | zip, his |
| [ ʃ ] | sheep, machine |
| [ ʒ ] | usual, measure |
| [ h ] | how, perhaps |
| [ m ] | metal, comb |
| [ n ] | night, dinner |
| [ ŋ ] | sung, parking |
| [ l ] | little, help |
| [ r ] | right, carry |
| [ ʎ ] | llave, collar |

# transcripción fonética

| | |
|---|---|
| [ θ ] | cera, paz |
| [ ð ] | cada, pardo |
| [ s ] | solo, paso |
| [ z ] | andinismo |
| [ x ] | gemir, jamón |
| [ m ] | madre, cama |
| [ n ] | no, pena |
| [ ŋ ] | banca, encanto |
| [ ɲ ] | caña |
| [ l ] | ala, luz |
| [ ɾ ] | atar, paro |
| [ r ] | perro, rosa |

The symbol [ ' ] indicates that the following syllable carries primary stress and the symbol [ ˌ ] that the following syllable carries secondary stress.

Los símbolos [ ' ] et [ ˌ ] indican que la sílaba siguiente lleva un acento primario o secundario respectivamente.

The symbol [ ʳ ] in English phonetics indicates that the final r is pronounced only when followed by a word beginning with a vowel. Note that it is nearly always pronounced in American English.

El símbolo [ ʳ ] en fonética inglesa indica que la r final de palabra se pronuncia sólo cuando precede a una palabra que comienza por vocal. Adviértase que casdi siempre se pronuncia en inglés americano.

Words considered to be trademarks have been designated in this dictionary by the symbol ®. However, neither the presence nor the absence of such designation should be regarded as affecting the legal status of any trademark.

Los nombres de marca aparecen señalados en este diccionario con el símbolo ®. Sin embargo, ni este símbolo ni su ausencia son representativos de la situación legal de la marca.

# How to use this dictionary

### Entries

The entries in this dictionary are given in alphabetical order and are highlighted in green.

> **astuto** *adjetivo* ■ **shrewd:** eres muy astuto para los negocios you're a very shrewd businessman.

### Parts of Speech

The part of speech is shown after the phonetics (in this case adjetivo).

Some words have more than one part of speech which are shown at the beginning of the entry and are then developed fully one after the other.

> **diferente** *(adjetivo & adverbio)*
> ■ *adjetivo*
> **different:** sus hijos son muy diferentes his children are very different
> ■ *adverbio*
> **differently:** Ana come diferente porque está a dieta Ana is eating differently because she's on a diet.

### Regional variants

In this dictionary we have marked the words which are used in specific Latin American countries only (in this case *Mexico*).

> el **betabel** *Mexico* ■ **beet**.

### Translations

Each translation is given on a new line and is usually followed by an example showing how the word is used.

### Senses

When a word has more than one sense and can be translated in different ways, the translations are numbered.

> el **lavabo**
> 1. **sink:** el lavabo tiene una gotera the sink has a leak
> 2. **restroom:** en la planta baja hay un lavabo there's a restroom on the ground floor.

# How to use this dictionary

## Phrases

Phrases, compounds and constructions are grouped at the end of each part of speech and are preceded by a green arrow.

la **profundidad** ■ depth: a una profundidad de tres metros at a depth of three meters

➤ tiene tres metros de profundidad it's three meters deep

➤ en profundidad in depth: lo estudié en profundidad I studied it in depth.

---

If the plural of a word is irregular it is shown within brackets.

el **balón** (plural los balones) ■ ball

⚠ **Balón** is a false cognate, it does not mean "balloon".

---

The green boxes you see in this dictionary preceded by a warning symbol point out false cognates. These are words that look alike in Spanish and English but have, in fact, different meanings.

Grammatical difficulties are explained in the green boxes.

**tercero** numeral

Tercero becomes **tercer** when it comes before a singular masculine noun:

third: me resultó a la tercera vez I got it the third time around; vive en el tercer piso he lives on the third floor; llegó tercero he came in third; soy el tercero de la lista I'm the third on the list.

---

el **puente**

1. bridge: cruzaron el puente they crossed the bridge
2. long weekend: el puente del primero de noviembre the long weekend for the November first holiday

HACER PUENTE

When a national or religious holiday falls on a Tuesday or a Thursday, it is common practice to **hacer puente**, that is, to have a long weekend by missing work and school on the preceding Monday or the following Friday. While this is not always condoned by the government or employers, people still do it to make the most of their holidays.

On the Spanish-English side of this dictionary you will find green boxes preceded by an open book symbol. These boxes explain certain aspects of Latin American life and culture.

# Cómo usar este diccionario

## Entradas

Las entradas de este diccionario aparecen en orden alfabético, sobre un fondo verde.

## Pronunciación

Entre paréntesis rectos aparece la fonética de cada lema en inglés, mostrando cómo pronunciar correctamente cada palabra.

**berry** ['berɪ] *(plural* berries*) noun* ■ la **baya:** holly has red berries el acebo tiene bayas rojas.

## Plurales

Cuando el plural de una palabra es irregular, lo mostramos entre paréntesis.

Algunas palabras tienen más de una categoría gramatical y esta información aparece al comienzo de la entrada. Después, cada categoría aparece elaborada por completo, una después de la otra.

**cure** [kjʊəʳ] *(noun & verb)*
■ *noun*
el **remedio:** it's a cure for the flu es un remedio para la gripe
■ *verb*
**curar:** the doctor cured him el doctor lo curó.

## Traducciones

Cada traducción aparece en una línea diferente y generalmente va seguida de un ejemplo que muestra cómo se usa la palabra.

**lane** [leɪn] *noun*
1. el **camino:** a country lane un camino campestre
2. el **carril:** this highway has four lanes esta autopista tiene cuatro carriles.

## Sentidos

Cuando una palabra tiene más de un sentido y puede traducirse de diferentes maneras, las traducciones aparecen numeradas.

## Locuciones

Las locuciones, los compuestos y las frases hechas aparecen agrupadas al final de cada categoría gramatical, precedidas por una flecha verde.

**old** [əʊld] *adjective*
1. **viejo:** it's an old house es una casa vieja; he's an old man es un hombre viejo
2. **antiguo:** that's my old school ése es mi antiguo colegio
➤ how old are you? ¿qué edad tienes?
➤ I'm 13 years old tengo trece años
➤ old age la vejez.

# Cómo usar este diccionario

Verbos en inglés con partícula (phrasal verbs)

Los verbos en inglés con partícula, o sea, los verbos seguidos de una preposición como down, in, out, to, up, etc. aparecen en orden alfabético, al final de la entrada.

---

**add** [æd] *verb*

1. **agregar:** add some sugar to the mixture agregar un poco de azúcar a la mezcla
2. **sumar:** she added the numbers together sumó los números

**add up** *phrasal verb* ■ **sumar:** add the numbers up sumar los números.

---

Las dificultades gramaticales aparecen explicadas en recuadros verdes.

---

**everywhere** ['evrɪweəʳ] *adverb*

1. **en todas partes:** I've looked for it everywhere lo busqué en todas partes
2. **dondequiera que:** she follows me everywhere I go ella me sigue dondequiera que vaya

Dondequiera que is followed by a verb in the subjunctive.

---

Las recuadros verdes precedidas por un signo de advertencia señalan falsos cognatos. Son palabras que aunque son parecidas en español y en inglés, tienen significados diferentes.

---

**exit** ['eksɪt] *noun* ■ **la salida**

⚠ Exit es un falso amigo, no significa "éxito".

---

En el lado inglés-español de este diccionario aparecen recuadros verdes precedidas por el dibujo de un libro abierto. Estas cajas explican algunos aspectos de la vida y la cultura de Estados Unidos.

---

**Thanksgiving** ['θæŋks,gɪvɪŋ] *noun* ■ **la Acción de Gracias**

THANKSGIVING

La fiesta de **Thanksgiving**, el cuarto jueves de noviembre, conmemora el establecimiento de los primeros colonos en lo que hoy son los Estados Unidos. La cena en familia que generalmente se celebra ese día consiste en un pavo con salsa de arándanos, acompañado por camotes (batatas) al horno, y el tradicional pay de calabaza (zapallo) como postre.

**a** *preposición*

1. **to:** vamos a una fiesta we're going to a party; dáselo a tu hermano give it to your brother
2. **on:** a la derecha on the right
3. **in:** llegó a México he arrived in Mexico
4. **at:** nos vamos a encontrar en el cine a las cuatro de la tarde we're meeting at the movie theater at four; a cien kilómetros por hora at fifty kilometers per hour.

**abajo** *adverbio*

1. **under:** se escondió abajo de la mesa he hid under the table
2. **downstairs:** mamá está abajo Mom is downstairs
➤ boca abajo face down: se acostó boca abajo she lay face down.

**abandonar** *verbo*

1. **to abandon:** no podemos abandonar a los cachorros, tenemos que alimentarlos we can't abandon the puppies, we have to feed them
2. **to leave:** abandonó su ciudad she left her town
3. **to quit:** no puedo abandonar el trabajo ahora I can't quit my job now
➤ ¡abandonen el barco! abandon ship!

**abarcar** *verbo* ■ **to cover:** el curso de historia abarca desde el siglo XVI hasta el presente the history course covers from the 16th century to the present.

el **abdomen** *(plural* los abdómenes) ■ **abdomen**.

**abdominal** *adjetivo* ■ **abdominal:** tiene dolor abdominal he's suffering from abdominal pain.

los **abdominales** ■ **sit-ups:** hice 50 abdominales I did 50 sit-ups.

el **abecedario** ■ **alphabet**.

la **abeja** ■ **bee**.

la **abertura** ■ **crack:** por la abertura de la puerta se colaba el frío the crack in the door let in a cold draft.

**abierto** *adjetivo* ■ **open:** la puerta está abierta the door is open.

el **abismo** ■ **abyss:** desde el borde de la carretera se ve el abismo you can see the abyss from the edge of the road.

**ablandar** *verbo* ■ **to soften:** el agua ablandó la pasta the water softened the pasta

**ablandarse** *verbo pronominal* ■ **to soften:** la mantequilla se ablandó con el calor the butter softened in the heat.

el **abogado,** la **abogada** ■ **lawyer:** mi madre es abogada my mother is a lawyer.

**abolir** *verbo* ■ **to abolish:** abolieron la pena de muerte they abolished the death penalty.

**abonar** *verbo*

1. **to fertilize:** abonamos la tierra para que la planta crezca fuerte y sana we fertilized the soil so the plant will grow strong and healthy
2. **to pay:** abone en la caja por favor please pay at the register; ayer aboné los primeros cien pesos por la mesa *Mexico* I paid the first 100 pesos for the table yesterday.

el **abono**

1. **fertilizer:** el abono natural no daña el medio ambiente natural fertilizer doesn't damage the environment

**2. season ticket:** tengo un abono para el torneo de básquetbol I have a season ticket for the basketball championships

**3.** *Mexico* **installment:** pagué el primer abono al carpintero I paid the first installment to the carpenter.

**aborrecer** *verbo* ■ **to hate:** mi primo aborrece las espinacas my cousin hates spinach.

**abotonarse** *verbo pronominal* ■ **to button up:** abotónate el abrigo, que te vas a enfriar button up your coat or you'll catch a cold.

**abrazar** *verbo* ■ **to hug:** antes de subir al avión, abrazamos a la familia we hugged our relatives before getting on the plane

**abrazarse** *verbo pronominal*

**1. to hug each other:** los amigos se abrazaron afectuosamente the two friends hugged each other affectionately.

el **abrazo** ■ **hug:** dale un abrazo a tu abuelo give your grandfather a hug.

**abreviar** *verbo*

**1. to abbreviate:** ¿cómo se abrevia "señora"? how do you abbreviate "señora"?

**2. to keep something short:** no hay mucho espacio, intenta abreviar al máximo there's not a lot of space, try to keep it as short as possible.

la **abreviatura** ■ **abbreviation:** "Sr." es la abreviatura de "señor" "Sr." is the abbreviation of "señor".

**abrigar** *verbo*

**1. to wrap up:** abriga bien al niño wrap the baby up warm

**2. to be warm:** estas medias abrigan demasiado these tights are too warm

**abrigarse** *verbo pronominal* ■ **to wrap up:** nos abrigamos con mantas de lana we wrapped ourselves up in wool blankets.

el **abrigo** ■ **coat:** ese abrigo rojo es muy bonito that red coat is very nice.

**abril** *sustantivo masculino* ■ **April:** en abril in April; el próximo abril next April; el pasado abril last April

En inglés los nombres de los meses se escriben con mayúscula.

**abrir** *verbo* ■ **to open:** no puedo abrir esta caja I can't open this box.

**abrocharse** *verbo pronominal* ■ **to fasten:** abróchense los cinturones de seguridad fasten your seat belts.

**absoluto** *adjetivo* ■ **absolute:** un silencio absoluto absolute silence

➤ **en absoluto** not at all: ¿te importa? — en absoluto do you mind? — not at all
no me molestas en absoluto you're not bothering me at all.

**absorber** *verbo* ■ **to absorb:** la tierra seca absorbe rápidamente el agua de la lluvia dry earth quickly absorbs rainwater.

la **absorción** *(plural* las absorciones*)* ■ **absorption:** el algodón es una fibra con alto poder de absorción cotton is a very absorbent fiber.

**abstenerse** *verbo pronominal* ■ **to abstain:** en la votación, 20 legisladores se abstuvieron 20 legislators abstained from voting.

**abstracto** *adjetivo* ■ **abstract:** no entiendo esa idea tan abstracta, dame un ejemplo concreto I don't understand such an abstract concept, give me a concrete example.

**absurdo** *adjetivo* ■ **absurd:** el relato del testigo es absurdo the witness testimony is absurd.

la **abuela** ■ **grandmother**.

el **abuelo** ■ **grandfather**

➤ mis abuelos my grandparents

> ### ABUELOS
>
> People in Latin American countries move around much less than Americans. It is common for someone to live and raise their children in the same town where they themselves were born and raised. Therefore the presence of grandparents in daily life and even in the same house is much more common than in the U.S.

la **abundancia** ■ **abundance:** había comida en abundancia there was an abundance of food
➤ vivir en la abundancia to be well-off.

**abundante** *adjetivo* ■ **plentiful:** la cosecha fue abundante este año the crop was plentiful this year.

**abundar** *verbo* ■ **to abound:** en los pueblos de mar abundan las gaviotas seagulls abound in coastal towns.

**aburrido** *adjetivo* ■ **boring:** la película que vi ayer era muy aburrida the movie I saw yesterday was very boring.

**aburrirse** *verbo pronominal* ■ **to get bored:** nos aburrimos mucho en la fiesta we got really bored at the party.

**abusar** *verbo*
1. **to abuse:** abusó de su posición he abused his position; muchos adultos abusan del alcohol many adults abuse alcohol
2. **to take advantage of:** no quiero abusar de su hospitalidad I don't want to take advantage of your hospitality.

el **abuso**
1. **abuse:** es muy difícil combatir el abuso de las drogas it's very hard to combat drug abuse
2. **outrage:** ¡esto es un abuso! this is an outrage!
3. **imposition:** su acción es un abuso de nuestra generosidad what he did is an imposition on our generosity
➤ el abuso del alcohol alcohol abuse
➤ los precios de este restaurante son un abuso the prices in this restaurant are outrageous.

**acá** *adverbio* ■ **here:** acá están las llaves que buscabas here are the keys you were looking for.

**acabar** *verbo* ■ **to finish:** cuando acabe este capítulo llamaré a mi amiga I'll call my friend when I finish this chapter

**acabarse** *verbo pronominal* ■ **to run out:** se acabó el pan, iré a comprar más we ran out of bread, I'll go buy some more.

la **academia**
1. **academy:** la Real Academia Española se creó en 1713 the Royal Academy of the Spanish Language was founded in 1713
2. **school:** María va tres veces por semana a la academia de danza María goes to dance school three times a week.

**acariciar** *verbo* ■ **to stroke:** al niño le encanta acariciar al gato the boy loves stroking the cat.

**acarrear** *verbo* ■ **to carry:** precisamos ayuda para acarrear estos muebles pesados we need help carrying this heavy furniture.

**acaso** *adverbio*

After acaso in the sense of "maybe", the verb in Spanish has to be in the subjunctive:

**maybe:** acaso tenga frío maybe she's cold
➤ por si acaso just in case: tráete el abrigo, por si acaso bring your coat, just in case.

**acceder** *verbo*
1. **to agree:** al final el maestro accedió al pedido de los alumnos in the end the teacher agreed to the students' request
2. **to obtain:** el estudio permite acceder a mejores puestos de trabajo education can allow you to obtain better jobs.

**accesible** *adjetivo*
1. **approachable:** la nueva maestra es muy accesible the new teacher is very approachable
2. **comprehensible:** la lección de matemática fue accesible gracias a la explicación del profesor the math lesson was made comprehensible thanks to the teacher's explanation.

el **acceso** ■ **access:** éste es el acceso principal al edificio this is the main access to the building.

el **accidente** ■ **accident:** un conductor distraído provocó el accidente a careless driver caused the accident
➤ sufrir un accidente to have an accident.

**3**

la **acción** *(plural* las acciones*)*
1. **action**: estamos listos para entrar en acción, capitán we're ready to go into action, captain
2. **deed**: hizo una buena acción she performed a good deed
➤ **ponerse en acción** to go into action.

**acechar** *verbo* ■ **to lie in wait for**: el gato está siempre acechando al ratón the cat is always lying in wait for the mouse.

el **aceite** ■ **oil**
➤ **aceite de oliva** olive oil.

la **aceituna** ■ **olive**
➤ **aceituna negra** black olive
➤ **aceituna verde** green olive.

la **aceleración** ■ **acceleration**: la aceleración se calcula con una fórmula acceleration is determined by using a formula.

el **acelerador** *(plural* los aceleradores*)*
■ **accelerator**: vas muy rápido, no aprietes más el acelerador you're going too fast, stop pressing the accelerator.

**acelerar** *verbo* ■ **to accelerate**: tendrás que acelerar si lo quieres alcanzar you'll have to accelerate if you want to catch him.

la **acelga** ■ **Swiss chard**.

el **acento**
1. **accent**: "café" lleva acento en la "e" "café" has an accent on the "e"; el acento paraguayo es diferente al acento venezolano the Paraguayan accent is different from the Venezuelan accent
2. **stress**: ¿cuál es la sílaba con acento en la palabra "silla"? what syllable does the stress fall on in the word "silla"?

**acentuar** *verbo*
1. **to accentuate**: el vestido acentuaba su cintura the dress accentuated her waist
2. **to emphasize**: no sé muy bien cuando acentuar las palabras I'm not sure when to emphasize words

**acentuarse** *verbo pronominal* ■ **to be stressed**: "café" se acentúa en la última sílaba "café" is stressed on the last syllable.

**aceptar** *verbo* ■ **to accept**: Juan aceptó el trabajo que le ofrecieron Juan accepted the job they offered him.

la **acera** ■ **sidewalk**.

**acerca de** *adverbio* ■ **about**: la historia es acerca de una familia de extraterrestres the story is about a family of aliens.

**acercar** *verbo* ■ **to move closer**: acerca la silla a la mesa para estar más cómodo move your chair closer to the table, you'll be more comfortable

**acercarse** *verbo pronominal* ■ **to get closer**: me acerqué al fuego para entrar en calor I got closer to the fire to warm up.

el **acero** ■ **steel**
➤ **acero inoxidable** stainless steel.

**acertar** *verbo*
1. **to get right**: acerté sólo cinco preguntas I only got five of the questions right
2. **to guess**: ¿a que no aciertas cuántas páginas tiene este libro? I bet you can't guess how many pages this book has.

**ácido** *adjetivo* ■ **acidic**: los limones son muy ácidos lemons are very acidic.

**acomodar** *verbo* ■ **to arrange**: hay que acomodar estos libros en la estantería these books have to be arranged on the shelves

**acomodarse** *verbo pronominal* ■ **to make yourself comfortable**: la abuela se acomodó en el sofá y se quedó dormida grandma made herself comfortable on the couch and fell asleep.

**acompañar** *verbo*
1. **to go with**: ¿querés acompañarme al supermercado? do you want to go to the supermarket with me?
2. **to keep company**: la acompañé un rato en el hospital I kept her company in the hospital for a while
3. **to accompany**: un pianista lo acompañó en su recital de flauta a pianist accompanied him during his flute recital.

**aconsejar** *verbo* ■ to advise: me aconsejó que aprendiera inglés she advised me to learn English.

el **acontecimiento** ■ event: su llegada fue un gran acontecimiento her arrival was a great event.

**acordar** *verbo* ■ to agree: los enemigos acordaron firmar el tratado de paz the enemies agreed to sign the peace treaty

**acordarse** *verbo pronominal* ■ to remember: siempre me acuerdo de ustedes cuando voy ahí I always remember you when I go there.

el **acordeón** *(plural* los acordeones) ■ accordion.

**acorralar** *verbo* ■ to corner: acorralaron al conejo para meterlo en la jaula they cornered the rabbit to put him in the cage.

**acostar** *verbo* ■ to put to bed: ya es hora de acostar a los niños it's time to put the kids to bed

**acostarse** *verbo pronominal* ■ to go to bed: se acostaron tarde, por eso están tan cansados they went to bed late, that's why they're so tired.

**acostumbrar** *verbo*
➤ acostumbrar a alguien a algo to get someone used to something: hay que acostumbrar al niño a que se duerma temprano you have to get the baby used to going to sleep early

**acostumbrarse** *verbo pronominal* ■ to get used to: al cabo de los años se acostumbraron al frío they got used to the cold after a few years.

el/la **acróbata** ■ acrobat.

la **actitud** ■ attitude.

la **actividad** ■ activity *(plural* activities)
➤ actividades extraescolares extracurricular activities.

**activo** *adjetivo* ■ active.

el **acto**
1. action: los adultos son responsables de sus actos adults are responsible for their actions
2. ceremony: fuimos al acto de inauguración del museo we went to the museum's opening ceremony
➤ en el acto immediately: acudió a mi llamada en el acto he answered my call immediately
se hacen reparaciones en el acto repairs done while you wait.

el **actor** ■ actor.

la **actriz** *(plural* las actrices) ■ actress.

**actual** *adjetivo*
1. current: mi vecina actual no es la misma del año pasado my current neighbor isn't the same one from last year
2. modern: no les gusta mucho la música actual they don't like modern music

⚠ The Spanish word **actual** is a false cognate, it does not mean "actual".

la **actualidad**
➤ en la actualidad currently: en la actualidad, mucha gente usa computadoras currently, a lot of people use computers.

**actualmente** *adverbio* ■ nowadays: actualmente, mucha gente tiene un celular nowadays a lot of people have cell phones

⚠ The Spanish word **actualmente** is a false cognate, it does not mean "actually".

**actuar** *verbo* ■ to act: actuaron rápidamente y evitaron un accidente they acted quickly and avoided an accident; actuó muy mal en las dos últimas películas en que trabajó he acted badly in the last two movies he was in.

la **acuarela** ■ watercolor.

el **acuario**
1. fish tank: me regalaron un acuario para mi cumpleaños I was given a fish tank for my birthday

**2.** aquarium: el domingo fuimos a visitar el **acuario** we went to the aquarium on Sunday.

**acuático** *adjetivo* ■ **aquatic:** en este lago hay muchas plantas acuáticas there are many aquatic plants in the lake.

el **acuerdo** ■ **agreement:** los presidentes firmaron un acuerdo the presidents signed an agreement
➤ estar de acuerdo to agree: **estoy de acuerdo contigo** I agree with you.

**acumular** *verbo* ■ **to accumulate:** las ardillas acumulan frutos secos para el invierno squirrels accumulate nuts for the winter.

el **acusado,** la **acusada** ■ **defendant:** la acusada se declaró culpable the defendant pled guilty.

**acusar** *verbo* ■ **to accuse:** lo acusaron sin razón they accused him for no reason.

**adaptar** *verbo* ■ **to alter:** hay que adaptar esta cortina a la ventana pequeña we'll have to alter this curtain to fit the small window

**adaptarse** *verbo pronominal* ■ **to adapt:** después de varios años, se adaptaron al frío they adapted to the cold after a few years.

**adecuado** *adjetivo* ■ **appropriate:** ese vestido no es adecuado para el funeral that dress isn't appropriate for the funeral.

**adelantar** *verbo*
**1.** to move up: adelantaron la boda un mes they moved the wedding up a month
**2.** to move forward: no adelantes tu ficha, que ahora es mi turno don't move your piece forward, it's my turn
**3.** to make progress: hace dos horas que estás leyendo, ¿cuánto adelantaste? you've been reading for two hours, how much progress have you made?
**4.** to gain time: este reloj adelanta this clock is gaining time
**5.** to pass: "prohibido adelantar" decía ese cartel that sign said "do not pass"

**adelantarse** *verbo pronominal*
**1.** to go ahead: me adelanté para reservar lugar I went ahead to save a place
**2.** to arrive early: este año el invierno se adelantó winter arrived early this year.

**adelante** *adverbio* ■ **forward:** veremos mejor si nos hacemos para adelante we'll see better if we move forward
➤ más adelante *en el tiempo* later
➤ más adelante *en el espacio* further on
➤ adelante de in front of: iba adelante de mí he was in front of me
➤ de ahora en adelante from now on: de ahora en adelante no quiero más discusiones from now on I don't want any more arguments.

**adelgazar** *verbo* ■ **to lose weight:** adelgazó cinco kilos en un mes she lost five kilos in a month.

**además** *adverbio*
**1.** as well as: además de traductora, es intérprete as well as being a translator, she's an interpreter
**2.** in addition: la casa es grande y además tiene un jardín precioso in addition to being very big, the house has a beautiful yard
**3.** besides: además, llegaste tarde besides, you were late.

**adentro** *adverbio* ■ **inside:** fíjate adentro del cajón look inside the drawer.

el **aderezo** *Mexico* ■ **dressing:** no me gusta el aderezo que le pusiste a la ensalada I don't like the dressing you put on the salad.

**adherir** *verbo* ■ **to stick:** asegúrate de adherir bien la estampilla make sure to stick the stamp on well.

**adhesivo** *adjetivo* ■ **adhesive.**

la **adición** *(plural las* adiciones*)* ■ **addition.**

**¡adiós!** *interjección* ■ **goodbye:** dijo "adiós" al despedirse he said goodbye as he was leaving.

la **adivinanza** ■ **riddle**
➤ jugar a las adivinanzas to play at guessing riddles.

**6**

**adivinar** *verbo* ■ **to guess:** ¡adivina lo que tengo para ti! guess what I have for you!

el **adjetivo** ■ **adjective**.

la **administración** *(plural* las administraciones) ■ **management**.

el **administrador,** la **administradora** ■ **manager**
➤ administrador de Web Webmaster.

**administrativo** *adjetivo* ■ **administrative:** se ocupa de las tareas administrativas he's in charge of the administrative work.

la **admiración** ■ **admiration:** se debatía entre la envidia y la admiración he was caught between envy and admiration; tiene gran admiración por su hermano mayor he has a great deal of admiration for his older brother
➤ signo de admiración exclamation mark.

**admirar** *verbo* ■ **to admire:** es la mejor de la clase, todos la admiran everyone admires her, she's the best in the class.

**admitir** *verbo*
1. **to accept:** nos acaban de admitir al club we've just been accepted into the club
2. **to admit:** al final admitió que le gustaba Pedro she finally admitted that she likes Pedro
3. **to allow:** mi madre no admite que le grite my mother doesn't allow me to shout at her.

la **adolescencia** ■ **adolescence**.

**adolescente** *adjetivo* ■ **adolescent**

el/la **adolescente** ■ **teenager**.

**adonde** *adverbio* ■ **where:** adonde vayas, cuídate mucho wherever you go, take care of yourself
➤ adonde fueres, haz lo que vieres when in Rome, do as the Romans do.

**adónde** *adverbio* ■ **where:** ¿adónde vas? where are you going?

Adónde takes an accent in direct and indirect questions.

**adoptar** *verbo* ■ **to adopt:** mis amigos han decidido adoptar un bebé my friends have decided to adopt a baby.

**adorar** *verbo*
1. **to worship:** los mexicas adoraban a Tláloc the Mexicas worshiped Tláloc
2. **to adore:** Juan y María adoran a sus padres Juan and María adore their parents.

**adornar** *verbo* ■ **to decorate:** adornamos la casa para la fiesta we decorated the house for the party.

el **adorno** ■ **decoration:** las calles están llenas de adornos de Navidad the streets are full of Christmas decorations
➤ de adorno just for show: su secretaria no sirve para nada, está de adorno his secretary is useless, she's just for show.

**adquirir** *verbo*
1. **to acquire:** la escuela adquirió más computadoras the school acquired more computers
2. **to gain:** adquirió mucha experiencia trabajando en esa oficina she gained a lot of experience working in that office.

la **adquisición** *(plural* las adquisiciones) ■ **acquisition:** es mi más reciente adquisición it's my most recent acquisition.

**adrede** *adverbio* ■ **on purpose:** no creo que lo haya hecho adrede I don't think she did it on purpose.

la **aduana** ■ **customs** *(plural)*: pasar por la aduana to go through customs.

**adulto** *adjetivo* ■ **adult**

el **adulto** ■ **adult:** los adultos deben responsabilizarse por sus actos adults have to take responsibility for their actions.

el **adverbio** ■ **adverb**

Los adverbios en inglés terminan en general en "-ly", lo que facilita su reconocimiento.

el **adversario,** la **adversaria** ■ **opponent:** mi adversario trató de ganar el primer puesto, pero no lo consiguió my opponent tried to take first place, but failed.

la **advertencia** ■ **warning:** advertencia: no entre a la obra sin casco protector
warning: hard hats must be worn on building
site.

**advertir** *verbo*

1. **to warn:** el maestro advirtió que no tole-
rará tramposos the teacher warned that he
would not put up with cheaters
2. **to be aware:** no advertí la presencia del
ladrón I was not aware of the thief's presence.

**aéreo** *adjetivo* ■ **air**

El adjetivo inglés **air** siempre se usa antes
del sustantivo:

te lo enviaré por correo aéreo I'll send it by
air mail.

los **aerobics** *Mexico* ■ **aerobics:** los martes va a su clase de aerobics she goes to
aerobics class on Tuesday.

el **aeroplano** ■ **airplane**.

el **aeropuerto** ■ **airport**.

el **aerosol** ■ **aerosol:** prefiero usar el
desodorante en aerosol I prefer aerosol
deodorant.

**afectar** *verbo* ■ **to affect:** la violencia
afecta a millones de personas violence affects millions of people.

el **afecto** ■ **affection:** el afecto es muy
importante para la amistad affection is
very important in friendship.

**afeitarse** *verbo pronominal* ■ **to shave:**
mi hermano se afeita todas las mañanas
my brother shaves every morning.

la **afición** *(plural las aficiones)* ■ **hobby:**
Pablo tiene afición por el deporte Pablo's
hobby is sports
➤ **por afición** as a hobby.

el **aficionado,** la **aficionada**
■ **enthusiast:** por aquí hay muchos aficionados al fútbol there are many soccer
enthusiasts around here.

**afilar** *verbo* ■ **to sharpen:** hay que afilar el cuchillo antes de usarlo you should
sharpen the knife before using it.

**afín** *adjetivo* ■ **similar:** Pedro es muy
afín de su hermano Pedro is very similar to
his brother.

**afinar** *verbo* ■ **to tune:** los músicos
afinaron los instrumentos the musicians
tuned their instruments.

la **afirmación** *(plural las afirmaciones)*
■ **statement**.

**afirmar** *verbo*

1. **to state:** Daniela afirmó que le gusta
aprender idiomas Daniela stated that she
likes to learn foreign languages
2. **to steady:** el carpintero afirmó la mesa
con clavos the carpenter steadied the table
with nails.

**afirmativo** *adjetivo* ■ **affirmative**.

**afligir** *verbo* ■ **to be upset:** a Gabriela
le afligen las malas notas que sacó
Gabriela was upset about her bad grades.

**aflojar** *verbo* ■ **to loosen:** no puedo
aflojar este nudo I can't loosen this knot.

**afortunado** *adjetivo* ■ **lucky:** Ana es
muy afortunada Ana is very lucky.

**afuera** *adverbio* ■ **outside:** vamos para
afuera let's go outside
➤ **comer afuera** to eat out.

las **afueras** ■ **outskirts:** las industrias
están en las afueras de la ciudad the factories are on the outskirts of town.

**agacharse** *verbo pronominal*

1. **to bend down:** agáchate y levanta el libro bend down and pick up the book
2. **to crouch down:** me agaché para estar a
la misma altura que los niños I crouched
down to be on the same level as the children.

**agarrar** *verbo*

1. **to catch:** en pocas horas la policía agarró
al ladrón the police caught the thief in just a
few hours

**8**

**2.** to hold: agarra al niño de la mano para cruzar la calle hold the child's hand when you cross the street

**agarrarse** *verbo pronominal*

**1.** to hold on: ¡agárrate bien! hold on tight!

**2.** to catch: abrígate, o te vas a agarrar un resfrío bundle up or you'll catch a cold.

la **agencia** ■ agency (*plural* agencies): compré mi pasaje en la agencia de viajes I bought my ticket at the travel agency.

el/la **agente** ■ agent: la agente de viajes reservó mi pasaje the travel agent reserved my ticket.

**ágil** *adjetivo* ■ agile: las gimnastas son ágiles y flexibles gymnasts are agile and flexible.

**agitar** *verbo* ■ to shake: agita el envase antes de servir el jugo shake the carton before pouring the juice.

la **aglomeración** (*plural* las aglomeraciones) ■ crowd: se produjo una aglomeración a crowd formed.

**agosto** *sustantivo masculino*

En inglés, los meses del año se escriben con mayúscula:

August: en agosto in August; hoy es 28 de agosto today is August 28.

**agotar** *verbo* ■ to use up: agotamos las reservas de agua we've used up our water supplies

**agotarse** *verbo pronominal*

**1.** to become exhausted: mamá se agotó después de tanto esfuerzo Mom was exhausted after all that effort

**2.** to sell out: se agotaron todas las entradas all the tickets are sold out.

**agradable** *adjetivo* ■ pleasant: en primavera, la temperatura es más agradable que en invierno the temperature is more pleasant in the spring than in the winter.

**agradar** *verbo* ■ to like: la obra no me agradó I didn't like the play.

**agradecer** *verbo* ■ to thank: los novios agradecieron los regalos the newlyweds thanked their guests for the presents.

**agrario** *adjetivo* ■ agricultural: el principal producto agrario de Chile son las frutas fruit is Chile's main agricultural product.

**agredir** *verbo* ■ to attack: agredió al árbitro he attacked the referee.

**agregar** *verbo* ■ to add: agrega la leche después de la harina add the milk after the flour.

la **agresividad** ■ aggression.

**agresivo** *adjetivo* ■ aggressive: es muy agresiva she's very aggressive.

el **agricultor,** la **agricultora** ■ farmer: el agricultor trabaja en el campo the farmer works in the fields.

la **agricultura** ■ agriculture
➤ agricultura ecológica organic farming.

**agrio** *adjetivo* ■ sour: la leche está agria the milk turned sour.

el **agua** *sustantivo femenino*

Feminine noun that takes un or el in the singular.

water
➤ agua corriente running water
➤ agua dulce fresh water
➤ agua mineral mineral water
➤ agua potable drinking water
➤ agua salada salt water
➤ agua viva *River Plate* jellyfish.

el **aguacate** ■ avocado.

el **aguacero** ■ downpour.

**aguantar** *verbo*

**1.** to stand: no aguanto más el ruido de esa sirena I can't stand the noise of that siren

**2.** to hold: yo no puedo aguantar la respiración más que 30 segundos I can only hold my breath for 30 seconds

**3.** to take: la bolsa no aguantó el peso de las naranjas the bag couldn't take the weight of the oranges

4. **to last:** no creo que mis zapatos aguanten mucho más I don't think my shoes will last much longer.

**aguardar** *verbo* ■ **to wait for:** aguardaremos cinco minutos el próximo tren we'll wait five minutes for the next train.

**agudo** *adjetivo*

1. **high:** "do" es una nota mucho más aguda que "si" "do" is a higher note than "ti"
2. **sharp:** sentí un dolor agudo en una muela I felt a sharp pain in my tooth.

el **aguijón** *(plural* los aguijones) ■ **sting**.

el **águila** *sustantivo femenino*

> Feminine noun that takes **un** or **el** in the singular.

**eagle**

➤ ¿águila o sol? *Mexico* heads or tails?

el **aguinaldo** ■ **Christmas bonus**

AGUINALDO

In Spanish-speaking countries, workers often receive a year-end bonus known as **aguinaldo**. It is usually paid in December and is generally designated for holiday preparations and for buying presents for Christmas and the Feast of the Epiphany in January.

la **aguja** ■ **needle** : necesitas una aguja e hilo you need a needle and thread

➤ las agujas del reloj the hands of the clock.

la **agujeta** *Mexico* ■ **shoelace:** tienes las agujetas desamarradas your shoelaces are untied.

las **agujetas** ■ tengo agujetas I'm all stiff.

el **agujero** ■ **hole**.

**ahí** *adverbio*

1. *cuando quiere decir 'en o a ese lugar'* **there:** ¿quién está ahí? who's there?; yo ahí no voy I'm not going there
2. *cuando quiere decir 'en ese momento'* **then:** ahí fue cuando me acordé that was when I remembered; de ahí en adelante from then on

3. *cuando quiere decir 'en eso'* **that:** ahí está el problema that's the problem
➤ ahí mismo right there
➤ por ahí *en algún lugar* there somewhere: debe estar por ahí it has to be there somewhere
➤ por ahí *en ese lugar* over there: busquemos por ahí let's look over there
➤ por ahí *aproximadamente* or so: unas 100 personas o por ahí a hundred or so people.

la **ahijada** ■ **goddaughter**.

el **ahijado** ■ **godson:** sus ahijados her godchildren.

**ahogarse** *verbo pronominal*

1. **to drown:** se ahogó en el mar he drowned in the ocean
2. **to suffocate:** me ahogo con tanto humo I'm suffocating with all this smoke.

**ahora** *adverbio* ■ **now:** ahora no está lloviendo it's not raining now
➤ de ahora en adelante from now on: de ahora en adelante él es el jefe from now on he is the boss
➤ ahora mismo right now: ahora mismo no está she's not here right now
➤ hasta ahora so far: hasta ahora todo va bien so far, so good
➤ ¡hasta ahora! see you soon!
➤ por ahora for now.

**ahorita** *adverbio*

1. **now:** ahorita no está lloviendo it's not raining now
2. **in a minute:** ahorita lo hago I'll do it in a minute
3. **a moment ago:** ahorita nomás llamó he called just a moment ago.

**ahorcar** *verbo* ■ **to hang**

**ahorcarse** *verbo pronominal* ■ **to hang oneself:** se ahorcó con un cinturón he hanged himself with his belt.

**ahorrar** *verbo* ■ **to save:** ahorra tiempo y dinero it saves you time and money.

el **aire**

1. **air:** el aire que respiramos the air we breathe

**2. wind:** soplaba un aire frío a cold wind was blowing; **pasan mucho tiempo al aire libre** they spend a lot of time outdoors; **una piscina al aire libre** an outdoor swimming pool

➤ **tomar el aire** to get some fresh air

➤ **aire acondicionado** air conditioning

➤ **al aire libre** outdoors.

**aislar** *verbo*

**1. to isolate:** tuvieron que aislar al enfermo they had to isolate the patient

**2. to insulate:** hay que aislar el techo we need to insulate the roof.

el **ajedrez**

**1. chess:** jugar al ajedrez to play chess

**2. chess set:** el ajedrez está guardado en el cajón the chess set is in the drawer.

**ajeno** *adjetivo* ■ **las cosas ajenas** other people's things; **por razones ajenas a su voluntad** for reasons beyond his control.

el **ají**

**1. chili**

**2.** *Andes* **chili sauce.**

el **ajo** ■ **garlic.**

los **ajustadores** *Cuba* ■ **bra.**

**ajustado** *adjetivo* ■ **tight:** estos pantalones me quedan muy ajustados these pants are too tight on me.

**ajustar** *verbo*

**1. to tighten:** hay que ajustar estos tornillos I have to tighten these screws

**2. to fit:** la tapa no ajusta bien the lid doesn't fit very well

**3. to take in:** la modista ajustó esta falda the seamstress took this skirt in

**ajustarse** *verbo pronominal* ■ **to fasten:** se ajustó el cinturón he fastened his belt.

**al**

> Contraction of **a** and **el.**

➤ a; ➤ el.

el **ala** *sustantivo femenino*

> Feminine noun that takes **un** or **el** in the singular.

**1. wing:** las alas del cóndor the wings of the condor; **el ala izquierda del avión** the plane's left wing

**2. brim:** un sombrero de ala ancha a wide-brimmed hat

➤ **ala delta** hang glider: **hacer ala delta** to hang glide.

el **alacrán** ■ **scorpion.**

la **alambrada** ■ **wire fence.**

el **alambre** ■ **wire**

➤ **alambre de púas** barbed wire.

el **álamo** ■ **poplar.**

**alargar** *verbo*

**1. to lengthen:** quiero alargar estos pantalones I want to lengthen these pants

**2. to extend:** van a alargar las vacaciones they're going to extend their vacation

**alargarse** *verbo pronominal* ■ **to get longer:** en esta época los días se van alargando the days get longer at this time of year.

la **alarma** ■ **alarm:** empezó a sonar la alarma the alarm went off; **dieron la alarma** they sounded the alarm

➤ **alarma antirrobo** antitheft alarm

➤ **alarma contra incendios** fire alarm.

**alarmar** *verbo* ■ **to alarm:** no queremos alarmar a nadie we don't want to alarm anyone

**alarmarse** *verbo pronominal* ■ **to be alarmed:** no hay por qué alarmarse there's no need to be alarmed.

el **alba** *sustantivo femenino*

> Feminine noun that takes **un** or **el** in the singular.

**dawn**

➤ **al alba** at dawn.

el/la **albañil**

**1.** *que construye* **construction worker**

**2.** *que coloca ladrillos* **bricklayer.**

el **albaricoque** ■ apricot.

la **alberca** *Mexico* ■ swimming pool.

el **albergue** ■ hostel
➤ un albergue juvenil a youth hostel.

la **albóndiga** ■ meatball.

el **alboroto** ■ racket: los niños armaron un alboroto the kids made a racket.

el **álbum** ■ album.

la **alcachofa** ■ artichoke.

el **alcalde,** la **alcaldesa** ■ mayor.

el **alcance**
1. reach: no lo dejes al alcance de los niños don't leave it within the children's reach
2. range: un telescopio de largo alcance a long-range telescope.

la **alcancía**
1. moneybox
2. *Uruguay* pencil case.

la **alcantarilla**
1. *para la lluvia* drain
2. *cloaca* sewer.

**alcanzar** *verbo*
1. to reach: no alcanzo el estante de arriba I can't reach the top shelf
2. to catch up with: si te apuras, lo alcanzas if you hurry you can catch up with him
3. to hand: me alcanzó la sal he handed me the salt
4. to be enough: los vasos no alcanzan para todos there aren't enough glasses for everyone.

el **alcaucil** *River Plate* ■ artichoke.

el **alcohol** ■ alcohol
➤ una bebida sin alcohol a non-alcoholic drink.

**alcohólico** *adjetivo* ■ alcoholic

el **alcohólico,** la **alcohólica** ■ alcoholic.

la **aldea** ■ village.

el **aldeano,** la **aldeana** ■ villager.

**alegrar** *verbo* ■ to cheer up: sus nietos siempre lo alegran his grandchildren always cheer him up; me alegró mucho recibir tu carta your letter really cheered me up

➤ me alegra que hayas podido venir I'm so glad you could come

**alegrarse** *verbo pronominal*
1. to cheer up: anda, ¡alégrate! come on, cheer up!
2. to be glad: saqué muy buenas calificaciones — ¡cuánto me alegro! I got very good grades — I'm so glad!
➤ alegrarse de algo to be happy about something: nos alegramos de tu venida we're so happy you're coming
➤ alegrarse por alguien to be happy for someone.

**alegre** *adjetivo*
1. cheerful: es una muchacha muy alegre she's a very cheerful girl; ¡qué alegre estás hoy! you're very cheerful today
2. bright: usa ropa de colores alegres he wears bright clothes.

la **alegría** ■ joy: los niños brincaban de alegría the children jumped for joy
➤ ¡qué alegría! how wonderful!
➤ sentí mucha alegría al verlo I was so happy to see him.

**alejarse** *verbo pronominal* ■ to move away
➤ alejarse de algo to move away from something: aléjense de la orilla move away from the edge
➤ no se alejen demasiado don't go too far.

**alemán, alemana** *adjetivo*

En inglés, los adjetivos que se refieren a un país o una región se escriben con mayúscula:

German: tiene un apellido alemán he has a German last name

el **alemán,** la **alemana**

En inglés, los gentilicios se escriben con mayúscula:

German: los alemanes the Germans.

el **alemán**

En inglés, los idiomas se escriben con mayúscula:

German.

la **alergia** ■ allergy (plural **allergies**)

➤ tener alergia a algo to be allergic to something: **tengo alergia al polen** I'm allergic to pollen.

**alérgico** adjetivo ■ allergic: soy alérgico a los gatos I'm allergic to cats.

la **alerta** ■ alert

➤ dar la alerta to raise the alarm: **alguien dio la alerta** someone raised the alarm

➤ una alerta de bomba a bomb scare.

la **aleta**

1. de pez fin

2. de nadador flipper.

el **alfabeto** ■ alphabet.

el **alfajor** ■ type of snack

> ALFAJOR
>
> In the River Plate area, one of children's favorite snack treats is the **alfajor**: two cookies sandwiched with caramel (**dulce de leche**) and covered with chocolate or meringue. A variation on these is the homemade **alfajor**, with shredded coconut on the edge.

la **alfarería** ■ pottery.

el **alfarero**, la **alfarera** ■ potter.

el **alfiler** ■ pin

➤ alfiler de gancho Andes, River Plate, Venezuela safety pin.

la **alfombra**

1. suelta rug: una alfombra persa a Persian rug

2. grande carpet: una alfombra de pared a pared wall-to-wall carpeting.

el **alga** sustantivo femenino

Feminine noun that takes **un** or **el** in the singular.

seaweed: algunos peces se alimentan de algas some fish eat seaweed

➤ un alga marina seaweed.

el **álgebra** sustantivo femenino

Feminine noun that takes **un** or **el** in the singular.

algebra.

**algo** ( pronombre & adverbio)

■ pronombre

En oraciones afirmativas y en preguntas cuando se espera una respuesta afirmativa **algo** se suele traducir por **something**. En oraciones condicionales y en el resto de las oraciones interrogativas, por lo general se traduce por **anything**:

1. something: compré algo para ti I bought something for you; ¿quieres tomar algo? do you want something to drink?

2. anything: ¿le dijiste algo a la maestra? did you say anything to the teacher?; si algo sale mal, es por su culpa if anything goes wrong it's her fault

➤ o algo así or something like that: su apellido es Laren o algo así her last name is Laren or something like that

■ adverbio

1. rather: es algo difícil de explicar it's rather difficult to explain

2. a little: hablo algo de inglés I speak a little English.

el **algodón** (plural los algodones)

1. cotton: unos calcetines de algodón cotton socks

2. cotton ball: se limpió la herida con un algodón she cleaned her wound with a cotton ball.

**alguien** pronombre

En oraciones afirmativas y en preguntas cuando se espera una respuesta afirmativa **alguien** se suele traducir por **somebody**. En oraciones condicionales y en el resto de las oraciones interrogativas se traduce por **anybody**:

1. somebody: alguien preguntó por ti somebody was asking for you; ¿puede alguien cerrar la puerta? can somebody close the door?

2. anybody: si alguien pregunta, dile que no sabes if anybody asks tell them you don't know; ¿ha llamado alguien? did anybody call?

**algún** adjetivo

Shortened form of **alguno** used before masculine singular nouns.

13

**alguno** (adjetivo & pronombre)

■ adjetivo

En oraciones afirmativas el adjetivo **alguno** se suele traducir por **some**. En preguntas y en oraciones condicionales, por lo general se traduce por **any**:

1. **some:** vinieron algunas amigas some friends came over
2. **any:** ¿haces algún deporte? do you do any sports?; si tienen alguna pregunta, hacerla al final de la clase if you have any questions please ask them at the end of class
➤ ¿has estado alguna vez en España? have you ever been to Spain?
➤ ¿alguna cosa más? anything else?
➤ en alguna parte somewhere

■ pronombre

1. *en singular* **one:** compra alguno barato buy a cheap one; alguna de ellas lo sabe one of them should know
2. *en plural* **some:** algunas tienen techo de madera some of them have wooden roofs.

la **alhaja** ■ piece of jewelry: ¿por qué no le regalas una alhaja? why don't you get her a piece of jewelry?
➤ las alhajas jewelry: su mamá tiene muchas alhajas her mother has a lot of jewelry.

la **alianza**

1. alliance
2. wedding ring.

**aliarse** verbo ■ to form an alliance: se aliaron con los aztecas they formed an alliance with the Aztecs.

el **aliento** ■ breath: tiene mal aliento he has bad breath
➤ llegué arriba sin aliento I was out of breath when I got upstairs
➤ dar aliento a alguien to encourage somebody: lo que dijo nos dio aliento para seguir what he said encouraged us to keep going.

la **alimentación**

1. diet: es importante una alimentación equilibrada a balanced diet is important
2. feeding: yo me hago cargo de la alimentación de mi perro I'm in charge of feeding my dog.

**alimentar** verbo

1. to feed: tienen problemas para alimentar a su familia they are having problems feeding their family
2. to be nutritious: come cosas que no alimentan he eats things that aren't nutritious

**alimentarse** verbo pronominal ■ to eat: deben alimentarse bien you should try to eat well
➤ se alimentan de hierbas they live on plants.

el **alimento** ■ food: alimentos ricos en proteínas foods high in protein
➤ alimento chatarra junk food
➤ alimentos congelados frozen foods.

el **aliño** ■ dressing.

**alistarse** verbo pronominal ■ to get ready: se alistaron para salir they got ready to go out.

**aliviar** verbo
➤ esto te aliviará this will make you feel better
➤ la pastilla me alivió el dolor de cabeza the pill got rid of my headache.

el **alivio** ■ relief
➤ ¡qué alivio! what a relief!: ¡qué alivio sentí cuando lo encontré! what a relief when I found it!

**allá** adverbio ■ over there: allá están los demás the others are over there
➤ ya van para allá they're on their way over
➤ allá arriba up there
➤ allá lejos way over there
➤ allá fuera out there
➤ más allá further over: córranse más allá, por favor move a little further over, please
➤ más allá de beyond
➤ allá tú it's your problem: allá tú si no quieres estudiar it's your problem if you don't want to study.

**allí** adverbio ■ there: estuvieron allí toda la mañana they were there all morning
➤ allí abajo down there
➤ allí mismo right there: allí mismo encontrarán la biblioteca they found the library right there.

el **alma** *sustantivo femenino*

> Feminine noun that takes **un** or **el** in the singular.

**soul:** el cuerpo y el alma body and soul
➤ te lo agradezco en el alma I'm very grateful
➤ siento en el alma no poder ir I'm so sorry I can't go.

el **almacén** *(plural* los almacenes)
1. *de mercancías* **warehouse**
2. *Southern Cone, Peru de comestibles* **grocery store**
3. *Central America, Colombia de ropa* **store**
➤ grandes almacenes department store.

**almacenar** *verbo* ■ **to store**.

el **almacenero,** la **almacenera** *Southern Cone* ■ **grocer**.

la **almeja** ■ **clam**.

la **almendra** ■ **almond**.

el **almíbar** ■ **syrup:** duraznos en almíbar peaches in syrup.

la **almohada** ■ **pillow**.

**almorzar** *verbo*
1. **to have lunch:** almorzamos en el colegio we had lunch at school
2. *Mexico* **to have as mid-morning snack:** almorcé fruta y un pan I had fruit and a roll as a mid-morning snack.

el **almuerzo**
1. **lunch**
2. *Mexico* **mid-morning snack**.

**aló** *Andes, Venezuela interjección* ■ **hello:** ¿aló? ¿con quién hablo? hello! who's this?

el **alojamiento** ■ **accomodations:** encontraron alojamiento en un albergue juvenil they found accomodations at a youth hostel.

**alojarse** *verbo pronominal* ■ **to stay:** nos alojamos en un hotel de lujo we stayed at a luxury hotel.

el **alpinismo** ■ **mountain climbing:** hacer alpinismo to go mountain climbing.

el/la **alpinista** ■ **mountain climber**.

**alquilar** *verbo* ■ **to rent:** le alquila el cuarto a un estudiante she rents the room to a student; alquilé una bicicleta I rented a bicycle
➤ se alquila for rent.

el **alquiler** ■ **rent:** ¿cuánto pagan de alquiler? how much is your rent?
➤ carro de alquiler rental car.

**alrededor** *adverbio* ■ **around:** los niños se sentaron a su alrededor the children sat around him
➤ alrededor de around: corrimos alrededor de la piscina we ran around the pool: estudió inglés alrededor de tres años she studied English for around three years.

los **alrededores** ■ **outskirts:** vive en los alrededores de la ciudad she lives in the outskirts of the city
➤ hay muchas casas en los alrededores del aeropuerto there are a lot of houses in the area around the airport.

el **alta** *sustantivo femenino*
➤ dar de alta a alguien to discharge somebody: lo dieron de alta en el hospital they discharged him from the hospital.

el **altar** ■ **altar**.

**alterar** *verbo*
1. **to change:** tuvimos que alterar los planes we had to change our plans
2. **to disturb:** no debes alterar a la abuela you shouldn't disturb your grandmother

**alterarse** *verbo pronominal* ■ **to upset:** evita que tu padre se altere try not to upset your father.

la **alternativa** ■ **alternative:** no tiene más alternativa que aceptar la propuesta he has no alternative but to accept the offer.

la **altitud** ■ **altitude**.

**alto** *(adverbio & adjetivo)*
■ *adverbio*
1. **high:** es un avión que vuela muy alto it's a plane that flies very high; ponen el volumen muy alto they turn the volume up too high

**2. loud:** no hablen tan alto don't talk so loud
➤ **pasar por alto algo** to overlook something
■ *adjetivo*
**1. high:** una de las montañas más altas del continente one of the highest mountains on the continent
**2. tall:** es muy alto para su edad he's very tall for his age
➤ **alta fidelidad** high fidelity
➤ **en alta mar** on the high seas

el **alto**
➤ tiene dos metros de alto it's two meters high
➤ hicieron un alto para descansar they made a rest stop
➤ pasarse un alto *Mexico* to run a red light
➤ **el alto al fuego** the ceasefire.

el **altoparlante** ■ loudspeaker.

la **altura** ■ **height:** esos aviones pueden volar a mucha altura those planes can fly at great heights
➤ el Aconcagua tiene cerca de 7.000 metros de altura the Aconcagua is nearly 7,000 meters high
➤ **a estas alturas** at this point: a estas alturas no hay nada que podamos hacer at this point there's nothing we can do.

el **alud** ■ avalanche.

**alumbrar** *verbo* ■ **to light:** lleven una linterna para alumbrar el camino take a flashlight to light the way.

el **aluminio** ■ aluminum.

el **alumno,** la **alumna** ■ student.

el **alza** *sustantivo femenino*

> Feminine noun that takes **un** or **el** in the singular.

**increase:** habrá un alza en el precio de las entradas there will be an increase in ticket prices
➤ **en alza** on the rise: el índice de criminalidad está en alza the crime rate is on the rise.

**alzar** *verbo*
**1. to raise:** si quieren hacer una pregunta, alcen la mano raise your hand if you have a question

**2.** *Mexico* **to pick up:** alzamos todos los papeles del suelo we picked all the papers up off the floor
**3.** *Mexico* **to clean up:** antes de salir tengo que alzar mi cuarto I have to clean up my room before I go out
➤ ¡no me alces la voz! don't raise your voice at me!

**amable** *adjetivo* ■ **kind:** la secretaria es muy amable the secretary is very kind
➤ ¿sería tan amable de abrir la ventana? would you be so kind as to open the window?

**amamantar** *verbo*
**1.** *a un bebé* **to nurse**
**2.** *a un animal* **to suckle.**

el **amanecer** ■ dawn
➤ al amanecer at dawn.

**amanecer** *verbo*
**1. to get light:** en esta época amanece más temprano it gets light early at this time of year
**2. to wake up:** amaneció enfermo he woke up sick
➤ hoy amaneció lloviendo it was raining when we got up.

el/la **amante**
**1.** lover
➤ los amantes de la música pop pop music lovers.

la **amapola** ■ poppy *(plural* poppies*).*

**amar** *verbo* ■ **to love.**

**amargado** *adjetivo* ■ **bitter:** es una persona muy amargada she's a very bitter person
➤ están amargados porque perdieron they're sore because they lost.

**amargar** *verbo* ■ **to spoil:** eso nos amargó el paseo it spoiled our outing
➤ le amarga la vida a sus padres he makes his parents' life miserable

**amargarse** *verbo pronominal* ■ **to get upset:** se amarga si me saco malas notas she gets upset if I get bad grades.

**amargo** *adjetivo* ■ bitter.

**amarillo** *adjetivo* ■ **yellow**

el **amarillo** ■ **yellow**.

**amarrar** *verbo* ■ **to tie**: amarró el pe-rro a un árbol he tied the dog to a tree

**amarrarse** *Latin America except River Plate verbo pronominal* ■ **to tie**: se amarró los zapatos he tied his shoelaces.

**Amazonia** *sustantivo femenino* ■ **Ama-zonia**

AMAZONIA

Amazonia is a geographic area covering the 2.5 million square miles of the Amazon River Basin. It in-cludes territories in nine South American countries. It is an area of great natural wealth: it has abundant forests, minerals, plant and animal life, as well as being home to various indigenous tribes. It is the richest reserve of biological diversity on the planet.

la **ambición** (*plural* las ambiciones) ■ **ambition**.

el **ambientador** ■ **air freshener**.

el **ambiente**

1. **atmosphere**: es un ambiente ideal para los niños it's an ideal atmosphere for chil-dren
2. **spirit**: aquí hay un ambiente de camara-dería there's a real spirit of camaraderie here
➤ una fiesta con mucho ambiente a really happening party
➤ abran las ventanas, el ambiente está muy cargado open the windows, it's very stuffy in here
➤ un cambio de ambiente le haría bien a change of scenery will do him good.

**ambos** *adjetivo & pronombre* ■ **both**: los alumnos de ambos colegios the students from both schools; ambos pasaron de cur-so they both passed; los castigaron a ambos they were both punished.

la **ambulancia** ■ **ambulance**.

la **amenaza** ■ **threat**.

**amenazar** *verbo* ■ **to threaten**: me amenazó con dejarme castigado she threatened to ground me.

**ameno** *adjetivo* ■ **enjoyable**: sus clases son muy amenas her classes are very enjoy-able.

**americano** *adjetivo*

En inglés, los adjetivos que se refieren a un continente o a un país se escriben con mayúscula:

1. *de América Latina* **Latin American**
2. *estadounidense* **American**

el **americano**, la **americana**

En inglés los gentilicios se escriben con mayúscula:

1. *de América Latina* **Latin American**
2. *estadounidense* **American**.

la **amígdala** ■ **tonsil**: lo operaron de las amígdalas he had his tonsils removed.

el **amigo**, la **amiga** ■ **friend**: es mi me-jor amigo he's my best friend; son muy amigos they're good friends
➤ hacer amigos to make friends
➤ hacerse amigo de alguien to become friends with somebody.

la **amistad** ■ **friendship**: valoro mucho tu amistad I really value your friendship
➤ las amistades friends: vinieron todas sus amistades all her friends came.

**amistoso** *adjetivo* ■ **friendly**.

el **amo**, la **ama** ■ **owner**: lo abandonó su amo it was abandoned by its owner
➤ una ama de casa homemaker.

**amontonar** *verbo* ■ **to pile up**: amon-tonaron los libros en el piso they piled the books up on the floor.

el **amor** ■ **love**.

**ampliar** *verbo*

1. **to expand**: van a ampliar el gimnasio they're going to expand the gym
2. **to extend**: ampliaron el plazo para la matrícula they extended the registration pe-riod

**17**

**3.** **to enlarge:** quiero ampliar esta foto I want to enlarge this picture.

el **amplificador** ■ amplifier.

**amplio** *adjetivo*

**1.** **spacious:** su casa es bastante amplia their house is pretty spacious
**2.** **wide:** una amplia avenida a wide avenue
**3.** **loose:** prefiere la ropa amplia she prefers loose clothing.

la **ampolla** ■ blister.

la **ampolleta** *Chile* ■ light bulb.

**amueblar** *verbo* ■ to furnish: amueblaron el cuarto they furnished the room
➤ un departamento sin amueblar an unfurnished apartment.

el **analfabetismo** ■ illiteracy.

**analfabeto** *adjetivo* ■ illiterate.

el **analgésico** ■ painkiller.

el **análisis** *(plural los análisis)*

**1.** **analysis:** hicimos un análisis gramatical we did a grammatical analysis
**2.** **test:** un análisis de sangre a blood test.

**analizar** *verbo* ■ to analyze.

el **ananá** ■ *River Plate* pineapple.

la **anatomía** ■ anatomy.

**ancho** *adjetivo*

**1.** **wide:** una avenida muy ancha a very wide avenue
**2.** **loose:** prefiero las camisetas anchas I like loose t-shirts
➤ esta falda me queda ancha this skirt is too big for me
➤ ser ancho de espaldas to have broad shoulders
➤ a lo ancho crosswise

el **ancho** ■ width: mide el ancho de la ventana measure the width of the window
➤ ¿cuánto mide de ancho? how wide is it?
➤ tiene dos metros de ancho it's two meters wide.

la **anchura** ■ width.

la **anciana** ■ elderly woman.

**anciano** *adjetivo* ■ elderly

el **anciano** ■ elderly man
➤ los ancianos the elderly.

el **ancla** ■ anchor

> Feminine word that takes **un** or **el** in the singular.

**anda** *interjección*

**1.** **come on!:** ¡anda! que vamos a llegar tarde come on! we're going to be late
**2.** **hey!:** ¡anda! mira lo que encontré hey! look what I found!

**andar** *verbo*

**1.** **to be:** ando muy ocupado I am very busy; ¿cómo anda tu papá? how is your father?; ando buscando a la profesora I'm looking for the teacher
**2.** **to work:** mi reloj no anda my watch isn't working
**3.** **to walk:** vine andando I walked here
➤ andar en bicicleta to ride a bicycle
➤ andar a caballo to go horseback riding
➤ andar con alguien to go out with someone
➤ anda por los treinta she's about thirty
➤ anda a comprar pan *Colombia, Southern Cone* go buy some bread
➤ hay que andarse con cuidado you should be careful.

el **andén** *(plural los andenes)*

**1.** *en estación* platform
**2.** *Central America, Colombia* acera sidewalk.

el **andinismo** ■ mountain climbing.

el/la **andinista** ■ mountain climber.

**anduve, anduvo, etc** ➤ andar.

la **anécdota** ■ anecdote.

el **ángel** ■ angel.

las **anginas**

**1.** *amigadlitis* tonsillitis
**2.** *Mexico, Venezuela* amígdalas tonsils.

**angosto** *adjetivo*

**1.** **narrow:** un pasillo angosto a narrow hallway.

el **ángulo** ■ angle
➤ un ángulo recto a right angle.

el **anillo** ■ ring
➤ un anillo de bodas a wedding ring
➤ un anillo de compromiso engagement ring.

**animado** *adjetivo*
1. cheerful: ¡qué animado estás hoy! you're very cheerful today!
2. lively: las playas tienen un ambiente muy animado the beaches have a very lively atmosphere.

**animal** *adjetivo* ■ animal: el reino animal the animal kingdom

el **animal** ■ animal: le encantan los animales she loves animals
➤ un animal doméstico a pet.

**animar** *verbo*
1. to cheer up: fuimos para animarlo un poco we went to try to cheer him up a little
2. to cheer on: gritaban para animar al equipo they yelled to cheer on the team
3. to encourage: hay que animarlo para que siga estudiando we have to encourage him to stay in school

**animarse** *verbo pronominal* ■ to cheer up: ¡anda, anímate! come on, cheer up!
➤ animarse a hacer algo to feel like doing something: vamos a nadar ¿quién más se anima? we're going swimming — who else feels like it?
➤ no me animo a decírselo a la profesora I don't dare tell the teacher about it.

**ánimo** *interjección*
➤ ¡ánimo! todo se va arreglar cheer up! it'll all work out
➤ ¡ánimo! que ya casi terminamos come on! we're nearly finished

el **ánimo**
➤ está de muy buen ánimo he's in very good spirits
➤ no tengo ánimos para salir I'm not in the mood to go out
➤ lo que me dijo me dio ánimos what she told me really lifted my spirits
➤ me dieron ánimos para que siguiera estudiando they encouraged me to stay in school.

el **aniversario** ■ anniversary (plural anniversaries): es el aniversario de boda de mis papás it's my parents' wedding anniversary.

**anoche** *adverbio* ■ last night: anoche fuimos al cinema we went to the movies last night.

**anochecer** *verbo* ■ to get dark: en esta época anochece más temprano it gets dark early at this time of year

el **anochecer** ■ nightfall
➤ volvieron al anochecer they came back at nightfall.

**anónimo** *adjetivo* ■ anonymous.

**anotar** *verbo*
1. to write down: anotó las tareas en el cuaderno she wrote down the homework assignment in her notebook
2. to score: anotó el gol ganador she scored the winning goal.

**ante** *preposición*
1. before: tiene que presentarse ante el director she has to appear before the manager
2. facing: estamos ante un grave problema we are facing a serious problem

el **ante** ■ suede: unos guantes de ante suede gloves.

**anteanoche** *adverbio* ■ the night before last.

**anteayer** *adverbio* ■ the day before yesterday.

el **antebrazo** ■ forearm.

los **antecedentes** ■ record: tiene muy buenos antecedentes he has a good record
➤ antecedentes penales police record.

**antemano** *adverbio*
➤ de antemano beforehand: preparé las preguntas de antemano I prepared the questions beforehand.

la **antena** ■ antenna: la antena de la tele está descompuesta the tv antenna is broken
➤ una antena parabólica a satellite dish.

los **anteojos** ■ glasses: lleva anteojos he wears glasses
➤ anteojos de sol sunglasses.

el **antepasado,** la **antepasada** ■ ancestor: estoy orgulloso de mis antepasados I'm proud of my ancestors.

**anterior** adjetivo
ı. previous: mi colegio anterior era mucho mejor my previous school was much better
2. front: las piernas anteriores the front legs.

**anteriormente** adverbio ■ previously.

**antes** adverbio
ı. before: esto lo deberías haber hecho antes you should have done this before
2. first: ella llegó antes she got here first
➤ antes de before: antes de salir, limpiemos la cocina let's clean the kitchen before we go out
➤ antes que nada first of all
➤ cuanto antes mejor the sooner, the better
➤ lo antes posible as soon as possible.

el **antibiótico** ■ antibiotic.

**anticipado** adjetivo
➤ por anticipado in advance.

**anticipar** verbo
ı. to advance: ¿me podría anticipar un 20% de mi sueldo? could you advance me 20% of my salary?
2. to move up: estamos considerando anticipar nuestro viaje we're thinking of moving up our trip

**anticiparse** verbo pronominal ■ to come early: se anticipó el invierno winter has come early
➤ anticiparse a su tiempo to be ahead of one's time: el artista se anticipó a su tiempo the artist was ahead of his time
➤ anticiparse a alguien to get in before somebody: se me anticipó y contestó la pregunta de la profesora she got in before me and answered the teacher's question.

**anticonceptivo** adjetivo ■ contraceptive

el **anticonceptivo** ■ contraceptive.

**anticuado** adjetivo ■ old-fashioned.

el **anticucho** Andes ■ kabob.

el **anticuerpo** ■ antibody.

el **antídoto** ■ antidote.

**antiguamente** adverbio ■ in the old days: antiguamente, todo esto era campo in the old days, this was all countryside.

la **antigüedad** ■ seniority: recibe un plus de antigüedad he gets a seniority bonus

las **antigüedades** ■ antiques
➤ tienda de antigüedades antique store.

**antiguo** adjetivo
ı. antique: un jarrón antiguo an antique vase
2. ancient: las civilizaciones antiguas ancient civilizations
3. old: un antiguo amigo an old friend.

la **antipatía** ■ dislike: no pude disimular mi antipatía hacia ella I couldn't hide my dislike for her.

**antipático** adjetivo ■ unpleasant: ¡que mujer más antipática! what an unpleasant woman!

el **antipático,** la **antipática**
➤ tu jefe es un antipático your boss is very unpleasant.

el **ántrax** ■ anthrax.

**anual** adjetivo ■ yearly: el promedio anual the yearly average.

**anular** verbo
ı. to cancel: no será fácil anular el contrato it won't be easy to cancel the contract
2. to disallow: el árbitro anuló el gol the referee disallowed the goal
3. to overturn: el juez anuló el fallo the judge overturned the verdict.

**anunciar** verbo
ı. to announce: el gobierno anunció una baja de impuestos the government announced a tax cut
2. to advertise: anuncian el producto en televisión the product is advertised on TV.

el **anuncio**
ı. ad: puedes poner un anuncio en el diario you can put an ad in the paper

**2. commercial:** cada día hay más anuncios en la tele there are more commercials on TV every day.

**añadir** *verbo* ■ **to add:** le añadió un poco de pimienta a la salsa he added a little pepper to the sauce.

los **añicos**

➤ el perro hizo añicos tu sombrero the dog tore your hat to shreds

➤ estoy hecho añicos *informal* I'm beat.

el **año**

**1.** *tiempo* **year:** el año que viene next year

**2.** *edad* ¿cuántos años tienes? — tengo 14 años how old are you? — I'm fourteen; cumplo 15 años este marzo I'll be 15 this March

**3.** *curso escolar* **grade:** estoy cursando quinto año I'm in 5th grade

➤ año bisiesto leap year

➤ Año Nuevo New Year: ¡feliz Año Nuevo! happy New Year!

**apagar** *verbo*

**1. to turn off:** apaga la televisión antes de subir turn the TV off before going upstairs

**2. to put out:** se olvidó de apagar las velas he forgot to put out the candles.

**apapachar** *Mexico verbo* ■ **to cuddle.**

el **aparato**

**1. appliance:** aparatos electrodomésticos household appliances

**2. system:** el aparato circulatorio the circulatory system.

**aparecer** *verbo* ■ **to appear.**

**aparentar** *verbo* ■ **to look:** aparenta más de sus 16 años she looks older than 16.

la **apariencia** ■ **appearance:** deberías preocuparte más de tu apariencia you should take more care of your appearance

➤ las apariencias engañan appearances can be deceptive.

**apartado** *adjetivo* ■ **isolated:** vive en un lugar muy apartado he lives in a very isolated place

➤ estar apartado de to be away from: se mantiene apartado de su familia he stays away from his family

el **apartado** ■ **section:** contesta las preguntas en el apartado A answer the questions in section A

➤ apartado postal P.O. Box.

el **apartamento** ■ **apartment.**

**apartar** *verbo*

**1. to move out of the way:** aparta esa basura de ahí move that garbage out of the way

**2. to set aside:** te apartaré un pedazo de pastel I'll set aside a piece of cake for you

**apartarse** *verbo pronominal* ■ **to stand aside:** ¡apártate! stand aside!

**aparte**

■ *adverbio*

**1. to the side:** voy a dejar tus cosas aparte I'll put your things to one side

**2. besides:** y aparte él me dijo que lo hiciera besides, he told me to do it

■ *adjetivo*

**separate:** eso es un caso aparte that's a separate issue.

**apasionar** *verbo* ■ **to be fascinated by**

➤ me apasiona el arte I'm fascinated by art.

la **apatía** ■ **apathy.**

el **apellido** ■ **last name**

APELLIDOS

In the Spanish-speaking world, people commonly use the last names of both their father and their mother (in that order). Thus, if Alejandro Gómez Ortega and Isabel Ruiz Costa have a daughter named María, she will be known as María Gómez Ruiz on all official documents, though in everyday use she might choose to use only her first surname. When a woman gets married, she usually keeps her full maiden name, but she can choose to adopt her husband's first surname as her second, or she can be known by her husband's name. So if María Gómez Ruiz marries Gustavo Núñez Lago, she could either keep her own name, change it to María Gómez de Núñez, or be known as Señora Núñez.

**apenado** *Latin America except Southern Cone adjetivo* ■ **embarrassed**.

**apenarse** *Latin America except Southern Cone verbo pronominal* ■ **to be embarrassed**.

**apenas** *adverbio*
1. **hardly:** apenas podía respirar por el calor I could hardly breathe because of the heat
2. **barely:** hace apenas dos semanas que nos conocemos we met barely two weeks ago
3. **as soon as:** apenas había llegado cuando empezaron con las preguntas they started asking questions as soon as I walked in.

**apestar** *verbo* ■ **to stink:** ¡tu ropa apesta a puros! your clothes stink of cigars!

el **apetito** ■ **appetite**.

**aplastar** *verbo* ■ **to squash:** ¡me estás aplastando! you're squashing me!

**aplaudir** *verbo* ■ **to applaud:** el público aplaudió su discurso the public applauded his speech.

el **aplauso** ■ **applause**.

**aplicar** *verbo*
1. **to apply:** primero, aplicamos la pintura first, we apply the paint
2. **to put into practice:** ahora vamos a aplicar lo que hemos aprendido now we'll put what we've learned into practice
3. *Colombia, Venezuela* **to apply for:** ambos aplicamos al mismo trabajo we both applied for the same job.

**apostar** *verbo* ■ **to bet:** apuesto a que no viene I bet he won't come.

**apoyar** *verbo*
1. **to support:** yo apoyo al candidato progresista I'm supporting the progressive candidate
2. **to rest:** apoya tus piernas en la mesa de centro rest your legs on the coffee table

**apoyarse** *verbo pronominal* ■ **to lean:** se apoyó en la pared he leaned against the wall.

el **apoyo** ■ **support**.

**apreciar** *verbo* ■ **to value:** te aprecio mucho como amigo I really value your friendship.

**aprender** *verbo* ■ **to learn:** hoy aprendí a nadar I learned to swim today

**aprenderse** *verbo pronominal* ■ **to learn:** me aprendí la lección I learned the lesson.

**apretar** *verbo*
1. **to press:** apriete el botón rojo press the red button
2. **to squeeze:** ¡me estás apretando la mano muy fuerte! you're squeezing my hand too tightly!

**aprobar** *verbo*
1. **to approve:** me aprobaron las vacaciones they approved my vacation request
2. **to pass:** me aprobaron en matemática I passed math class.

**aprontarse** *Southern Cone verbo pronominal* ■ **to get ready**.

**apropiado** *adjetivo* ■ **suitable**.

**aprovechar** *verbo* ■ **to make the most of:** aprovéchalo mientras puedas make the most of it while you can.

**apto** *adjetivo* ■ **suitable**
➤ **ser apto para algo** to be suitable for something: **no es apto para niños** it's not suitable for children.

la **apuesta** ■ **bet:** hicimos una apuesta we made a bet.

**apunarse** *verbo pronominal* ■ **to get altitude sickness**.

**apuntar** *verbo*
1. **to write down:** déjame apuntar tu teléfono let me write down your number
2. **to point:** no apuntes con el dedo, que es mala educación don't point, it's rude.

los **apuntes** ■ **notes**
➤ **tomar apuntes** to take notes.

**apurarse** *verbo pronominal* ■ **to hurry up:** ¡apúrate! hurry up!

22

el **apuro** ■ jam: nos vimos en apuros anoche we found ourselves in a jam last night.

**aquel, aquella** *adjetivo* ■ that: está en aquel cajón it's in that drawer; en aquellos días vivía en México in those days he lived in Mexico.

**aquél, aquélla** *pronombre* ■ that one: pásame aquél, por favor pass me that one, please.

**aquello** *pronombre* ■ that: ¿qué fue aquello que me dijiste hace un rato? what was that you told me a while ago?

**aquí** *adverbio* ■ here: no eres de por aquí, ¿verdad? you're not from around here, are you?

la **araña** ■ spider.

**arañar** *verbo* ■ to scratch: el gato arañó la mejilla de la niña the cat scratched the little girl's cheek.

el **árbitro**, la **árbitra**
1. referee: el árbitro le mostró una tarjeta amarilla the referee gave him a yellow card
2. umpire: es árbitra de tenis she's a tennis umpire.

el **árbol** ■ tree
➤ árbol genealógico family tree
➤ árbol de Navidad Christmas tree.

el **arbusto** ■ bush.

**archivar** *verbo* ■ to file: lo voy a archivar en la T I'll file it under "T".

el **archivo**
1. archive: los archivos históricos the historical archives
2. file: este archivo sólo ocupa 30Kb this file is only 30Kb.

el **arco**
1. arch: un arco del triunfo a triumphal arch
2. bow: puso una flecha en el arco he placed an arrow in the bow
3. goal: pateó el balón hacia el arco he kicked the ball toward the goal.

la **ardilla** ■ squirrel.

el **área** *sustantivo femenino*

Feminine noun that takes **un** or **el** in the singular.

area: área metropolitana metropolitan area.

la **arena** ■ sand: hicimos un castillo de arena we built a sand castle
➤ arenas movedizas quicksand.

el **arete** *Colombia, Mexico* ■ earring.

**Argentina** *sustantivo femenino* ■ Argentina.

**argentino** *adjetivo*

En inglés, los adjetivos que se refieren a un país o una región se escriben con mayúscula:

Argentinian: tiene un primo argentino he has an Argentinian cousin

el **argentino**, la **argentina**

En inglés, los gentilicios se escriben con mayúscula:

Argentinian.

la **argolla** ■ ring: una argolla de oro a gold ring.

el **argumento**
1. argument: presentó sus argumentos en contra de la nueva ley he presented his arguments against the new law
2. plot: el argumento de la película the plot of the movie.

la **aristocracia** ■ aristocracy.

el/la **aristócrata** ■ aristocrat.

la **aritmética** ■ arithmetic.

el **arma** *sustantivo femenino*

Feminine noun that takes **un** or **el** in the singular.

weapon
➤ arma de fuego firearm.

**armar** *verbo*
1. to assemble: ayúdame a armar el escritorio help me assemble the desk

**2. to arm:** armaron a la población they armed the population

**armarse** *verbo pronominal* ■ **to arm oneself:** se armaron para la guerra they armed themselves for war.

el **armario** ■ closet
➤ armario empotrado built-in closet.

la **armonía** ■ harmony: estar en armonía to be in harmony.

la **armónica** ■ harmonica.

el **aro**
**1. hoop:** el león pasó por el aro the lion jumped through the hoop
**2.** *Argentina, Chile* **earring:** lleva un aro he wears an earring.

el **aroma**
**1. aroma:** el intenso aroma del café the intense aroma of coffee
**2. scent:** el aroma dulce de las flores the sweet scent of the flowers.

la **arqueología** ■ archaeology.

el **arquero,** la **arquera** ■ goalkeeper: el arquero paró el penal the goalkeeper saved the penalty.

el **arquitecto,** la **arquitecta** ■ architect: mi padre es arquitecto my father is an architect.

la **arquitectura** ■ architecture.

**arrancar** *verbo*
**1. to pull up:** trata de no arrancar las flores try not to pull up the flowers
**2. to tear out:** arranqué todas las páginas del libro I tore out all the pages of the book
**3. to start:** el coche no arranca the car won't start
**4. to leave:** el tren arranca en un minuto the train leaves in one minute.

**arrastrar** *verbo* ■ **to drag:** Pedro arrastró su mochila por el suelo Pedro dragged his backpack on the floor.

**arreglar** *verbo*
**1. to fix:** Bruno arregló mi reloj Bruno fixed my watch

**2. to sort out:** no te preocupes, he arreglado todo don't worry, I've sorted everything out
**3. to prepare:** está arreglando todo para mañana he's preparing everything for tomorrow
**4. to clean up:** arreglemos la casa antes de que lleguen let's clean up the house before they arrive

**arreglarse**
**1. to manage:** yo me las arreglo solo I'll manage on my own
**2. to get ready:** lleva dos horas en el baño arreglándose she's been in the bathroom getting ready for two hours
**3. to get sorted out:** las cosas no se arreglan solas things don't just sort themselves out.

el **arreglo**
**1. repair:** el coche requiere bastantes arreglos the car needs a lot of repairs
**2. arrangement:** tengo un arreglo con uno de los guardias I have a little arrangement with one of the guards
➤ tener arreglo to have a solution: esto no tiene arreglo there's no solution to this problem
➤ arreglo floral flower arrangement
➤ arreglo musical musical arrangement.

**arrendar** *verbo* ■ **to rent:** estoy arrendando mi casa I'm renting my house.

**arrepentirse** *verbo pronominal* ■ **to regret:** me arrepiento de no haberlo hecho antes I regret not having done it sooner.

**arrestar** *verbo* ■ **to arrest:** queda arrestado you're under arrest.

**arriba** *adverbio*
**1. top:** mira en el cajón de arriba look in the top drawer
**2. upstairs:** tu hermano está arriba your brother is upstairs
➤ arriba de above: cuélgalo arriba del otro cuadro hang it above the other painting
➤ hacia arriba upward
➤ más arriba further up
➤ mirar alguien de arriba abajo to look somebody up and down.

**arriesgar** *verbo* ■ **to risk**: arriesgó su vida para salvarme she risked her life to save me

**arriesgarse** *verbo pronominal* ■ **to take risks**: no se arriesgó a provocarla he didn't risk provoking her.

**arrimar** *verbo* ■ **to bring closer**: arrima tu silla para que te pueda ver mejor bring your chair closer so I can see you better.

**arrodillarse** *verbo* ■ **to kneel down**: nos arrodillamos frente al altar we kneeled down in front of the altar.

**arrogante** *adjetivo* ■ **arrogant**: tu esposa es muy arrogante your wife is very arrogant.

**arrojar** *verbo* ■ **to throw**: arrojaron la basura por la ventana they threw the trash out the window.

el **arroyo** ■ **stream**: tomamos agua de un pequeño arroyo we drank water from a small stream.

el **arroz** ■ **rice**
➤ arroz blanco boiled rice
➤ arroz integral brown rice
➤ arroz con leche rice pudding.

la **arruga** ■ **wrinkle**: tiene muchas arrugas en la frente he has a lot of wrinkles on his forehead; su camisa estaba llena de arrugas his shirt was full of wrinkles.

**arrugado** *adjetivo* ■ **wrinkled**: el vestido está muy arrugado this dress is very wrinkled.

**arruinar** *verbo* ■ **to ruin**: la lluvia arruinó la fiesta the rain ruined the party.

el **arte** *(plural* las artes) ■ **art**: el arte moderno modern art
➤ las artes the arts
➤ las artes marciales martial arts.

el **artículo** ■ **article**: tienes que leer este artículo you have to read this article.

**artificial** *adjetivo* ■ **artificial**.

el/la **artista** ■ **artist**: cada cuadro va firmado por el artista each painting is signed by the artist
➤ artista de cine movie star.

**artístico** *adjetivo* ■ **artistic**.

la **artritis** ■ **arthritis**.

la **arveja** ■ **pea**.

el **as** ■ **ace**
➤ el as de picas the ace of spades
➤ ser un as to be brilliant

> The Spanish word as is a false cognate, it does not mean "ass".

el **asa** *sustantivo femenino*

> Feminine noun that takes un or el in the singular.

**handle**: levántalo de las asas lift it by the handles.

**asado** *adjetivo* ■ **roasted**: castañas asadas roast chestnuts

el **asado**
1. **roast**: asado de cordero roast lamb
2. *Southern Cone* **barbecue**: en el verano voy a todos los asados que puedo during the summer I go to as many barbecues as I can.

**asaltar** *verbo*
1. **to hold up**: asaltaron el banco they held up the bank
2. **to mug**: me asaltaron a dos cuadras de mi casa I was mugged two blocks from my house.

el **asalto** ■ **holdup**: ¡esto es un asalto! this is a holdup!

la **asamblea**
1. **assembly**: la asamblea legislativa entra en sesión the legislative assembly is in session
2. **meeting**: resolvieron el problema en asamblea they solved the problem in a meeting.

**asar** *verbo* ■ **to roast**: también voy a asar los pescados I'll roast the fish too

➤ ¡me estoy asando! I'm boiling!

**ascender** *verbo*

1. **to climb:** ascendimos la montaña lentamente we climbed the mountain slowly
2. **to be promoted:** ascendió a gerente he was promoted to manager.

el **ascensor** ■ elevator.

el **asco** ■ me dan asco los cigarros I find cigarettes disgusting
➤ ¡qué asco! how disgusting!

**asear** *verbo* ■ **to clean:** los sábados aseamos la casa on Saturdays we clean the house.

**asegurar** *verbo*

1. **to assure:** le aseguro que no fue así I can assure you that it didn't happen like that
2. **to insure:** aseguré mi casa contra incendios I insured my house against fire
3. **to secure:** mejor asegurarlo con candado it's better to secure it with a padlock

**asegurarse** *verbo pronominal* ■ **to make sure:** asegúrate de que cerraste la puerta make sure you locked the door.

el **aseo** ■ **cleanliness:** el aseo es muy importante cleanliness is very important
➤ aseo personal personal hygiene.

**asesinar** *verbo*

1. *a persona normal* **to murder:** asesinaron al gángster the gangster was murdered
2. *a presidente, rey* **to assassinate:** asesinaron al presidente the presidente was assassinated.

el **asesinato**

1. *de persona normal* **murder**
2. *de presidente, rey* **assassination**.

el **asesino,** la **asesina**

1. *de persona normal* **murderer**
2. *de presidente, rey* **assassin**.

**asfixiar** *verbo* ■ **to suffocate:** casi me asfixio I nearly suffocated.

**así** *adverbio*

1. **like that:** ¡no seas así! don't be like that!
2. **like this:** me dijo que lo hiciera así she told me to do it like this
➤ ¡así de fácil! it's that easy!

➤ **así como así** just like that
➤ **así es** that's right
➤ ¡así me gusta! that's the way I like it!
➤ **así nomás** just like that
➤ **así que** so: así que te habló mal de mí so, he said bad things about me.

el **asiento** ■ **seat:** tome asiento take a seat.

el **asilo**

1. **home:** un asilo de ancianos a retirement home
2. **asylum:** el asilo político political asylum.

**asimilar** *verbo* ■ **to assimilate:** es difícil asimilar tanta información it's hard to assimilate so much information.

el/la **asistente** ■ **assistant:** mandó a su asistente por el café she sent her assistent out for coffee.

**asistir** *verbo*

1. **to attend:** ¿cuántas personas asistieron a la boda? how many people attended the wedding?
2. **to assist:** nos pidió que lo asistiéramos con algo he asked us to assist him with something.

el **asno** ■ **ass**.

la **asociación** *(plural* las asociaciones*)* ■ **association:** estamos trabajando en asociación con la policía we're working in association with the police.

**asociar** *verbo* ■ **to associate:** asocio ese olor con mi niñez I associate that smell with my childhood

**asociarse** *verbo pronominal*

1. **to join:** se asoció al gimnasio she joined the gym
2. **to go into partnership:** estoy pensando asociarme con Juan I'm thinking about going into partnership with Juan.

**asomar** *verbo*

1. **to stick out:** asomó la cabeza por la ventana he stuck his head out of the window
2. **to lean out:** asómate por la ventana para que lo puedas ver lean out the window so you can see it.

**asombrar** *verbo* ■ to astonish: me asombró lo que me dijo I was astonished by what she told me.

el **asombro** ■ astonishment.

el **aspecto**
1. appearance: tiene un aspecto muy refinado he has a very refined appearance
2. aspect: me interesa más el aspecto creativo I'm more interested in the creative aspect.

**áspero** *adjetivo*
1. rough: tengo la piel áspera my skin feels rough
2. harsh: ¡que voz más áspera! what a harsh voice!

la **aspiración** *(plural* las aspiraciones) ■ aspiration: tengo aspiraciones de ser músico my aspiration is to become a musician.

la **aspiradora** ■ vacuum cleaner
➤ pasar la aspiradora to vacuum.

la **aspirina** ■ aspirin.

**asqueroso** *adjetivo* ■ disgusting: es asqueroso cómo come the way he eats is disgusting.

el **asterisco** ■ asterisk.

la **astilla** ■ splinter: tengo una astilla en el dedo I have a splinter in my finger.

la **astrología** ■ astrology.

el/la **astronauta** ■ astronaut: cuando sea grande quiero ser astronauta when I grow up I want to be an astronaut.

la **astronomía** ■ astronomy.

**astronómico** *adjetivo* ■ astronomical: las investigaciones astronómicas son fascinantes astronomical research is fascinating; las cuentas de este mes son astronómicas this month's bills are astronomical.

**astuto** *adjetivo* ■ shrewd: eres muy astuto para los negocios you're a very shrewd businessman.

**asumir** *verbo*
1. to assume: hay que asumir que están bien we have to assume they're fine

2. to take on: asumió el papel de malo he took on the role of bad guy; no quiero asumir esa responsabilidad I don't want to take on that responsibility
3. to deal with: me cuesta asumir que se fue I'm having trouble dealing with her leaving.

el **asunto** ■ matter: estos son asuntos para la policía these are matters for the police
➤ no es asunto suyo it's none of his business.

**asustar** *verbo* ■ to frighten: lo asustaron esos ruidos those noises frightened him

**asustarse** *verbo pronominal* ■ to get scared: si se asusta, llámeme if you get scared, call me.

**atacar** *verbo* ■ to attack: nos atacaron con palos they attacked us with sticks.

el **atajo** ■ short cut: tomamos un atajo we took a short cut.

el **ataque** ■ attack: el ataque nos tomó por sorpresa the attack took us by surprise; le dio un ataque de alergia he had an allergy attack
➤ ataque cardíaco heart attack
➤ tener un ataque de nervios to panic.

**atar** *verbo* ■ to tie: te ves bien con el pelo atado you look good with your hair tied back
➤ átate los zapatos tie your shoelaces.

**atardecer** *verbo* ■ to get dark: apúrate que está atardeciendo hurry up, it's getting dark

el **atardecer** ■ dusk: los mosquitos salen al atardecer mosquitoes come out at dusk.

el **ataúd** ■ coffin.

**atención** *interjección* ■ your attention!
➤ ¡atención, por favor! your attention, please!

la **atención** *(plural* las atenciones)
1. attention: hay que poner atención al maestro you have to pay attention to your teacher

**27**

**2. service:** recibimos excelente atención en el hotel the service at the hotel was excellent
➤ **a la atención de** for the attention of
➤ **llamar la atención** to attract attention
➤ **llamarle la atención a alguien** to reprimand someone
➤ **prestar atención** to pay attention.

**atender** *verbo*
1. **to help:** ¿lo puedo atender? may I help you?
2. **to pay attention:** no me estás atendiendo you're not paying attention to me
3. **to take care of:** atiende muy bien a sus pacientes he takes good care of his patients
4. **to attend to:** ahora tengo que atender a un cliente I have to attend to a client now.

el **atentado**
➤ **un atentado contra el presidente** an assassination attempt on the president
➤ **un atentado terrorista** a terrorist attack.

**atento** *adjetivo*
1. **attentive:** es una estudiante muy atenta she's a very attentive student
2. **thoughtful:** ¡qué atento! that's very thoughtful of you!

el **ateo**, la **atea** ■ atheist.

**aterrar** *verbo* ■ **to terrify:** me aterra con sólo pensar en eso it terrifies me just to think about it.

el **aterrizaje** ■ **landing:** el aterrizaje fue muy suave the landing was very smooth
➤ **aterrizaje forzoso** emergency landing.

**aterrizar** *verbo* ■ **to land:** aterrizaremos en veinte minutos we will be landing in twenty minutes.

**aterrorizar** *verbo* ■ **to terrorize:** esos dos matones aterrorizan a todos los otros niños those two bullies terrorize all the other children.

el **atlas** ■ atlas.

el/la **atleta** ■ athlete.

el **atletismo** ■ **track and field:** soy fanático del atletismo I'm a huge fan of track and field.

la **atmósfera** ■ atmosphere.

**atmosférico** *adjetivo* ■ atmospheric.

**atómico** *adjetivo* ■ atomic.

el **átomo** ■ atom.

**atormentar** *verbo* ■ **to torment:** ¿por qué me estás atormentando con tantas preguntas? why are you tormenting me with all these questions?

la **atracción** *(plural* las attraciones)
■ **attraction:** la atracción entre ellos era obvia the attraction between them was palpable
➤ **atracciones turísticas** tourist attractions.

**atractivo** *adjetivo* ■ **attractive:** el candidato es joven y atractivo the candidate is young and attractive.

**atraer** *verbo*
1. **to attract:** ese bar atrae gente bohemia that bar attracts an artsy crowd
2. **to appeal:** no me atrae para nada el esquí skiing doesn't appeal to me at all.

**atrapar** *verbo* ■ **to catch:** atraparon al fugitivo they caught the fugitive.

**atrás** *adverbio* ■ **back:** hazte para atrás move back
➤ **¡atrás!** get back!
➤ **atrás de** behind: el parque está atrás de ese edificio the park is behind that building.

**atrasado** *adjetivo*
1. **slow:** mi reloj está atrasado diez minutos my watch is ten minutes slow
2. **behind:** va atrasada en la escuela she's behind in school
3. **behind schedule:** el proyecto está atrasado the project is behind schedule
4. **late:** estoy atrasado para mi clase I'm late for my class.

**atravesar** *verbo* ■ **to cross:** el río atraviesa el país entero the river crosses the entire country; atravesamos la calle sin esperar la luz verde we crossed the street without waiting for the light.

**atreverse** *verbo* ■ **to dare:** no me atrevo a decírselo I don't dare tell him.

**atropellar** *verbo* ■ **to run over:** ¡casi me atropellaste! you nearly ran me over.

el **atún** ■ **tuna**
➤ un sandwich de atún a tuna fish sandwich.

**audaz** *(plural* audaces) *adjetivo* ■ **daring:** un piloto audaz a daring pilot.

el **audífono** ■ **hearing aid:** mi abuelo usa audífono my grandfather wears a hearing aid
➤ audífonos headphones.

el **auditorio** ■ **auditorium**.

el **aula** *sustantivo femenino*

> Feminine noun that takes **un** or **el** in the singular.

**classroom**.

el **aullido** ■ **howl:** los aullidos de los perros no me dejaron dormir the dogs' howls kept me awake.

**aumentar** *verbo* ■ **to increase:** me aumentaron el sueldo my salary was increased
➤ aumentar de peso to put on weight.

el **aumento** ■ **increase:** los precios han visto un aumento del 5% prices have increased by 5%.

**aun** *adverbio* ■ **even:** aun así, no lo creo even so, I don't believe it.

**aún** *adverbio*
1. **still:** aún no me dice qué va a hacer she still hasn't told me what she's going to do
2. **yet:** aún no he terminado I haven't finished yet
3. **even:** ¡eres aún más bella de lo que me imaginaba! you're even more beautiful than I imagined!

**aunque** *conjunción*
1. **although:** se me antoja el filete, aunque normalmente no como carne the steak sounds good, although I don't usually eat meat
2. **even though:** te ayudo, aunque estoy agotado I'll help you even though I'm exhausted
3. **even if:** tenemos que ir aunque no quieras we have to go even if you don't want to.

la **ausencia** ■ **absence:** no había cambiado nada en mi ausencia nothing had changed during my absence.

**ausente** *adjetivo*
1. **absent:** has estado ausente demasiadas veces you've been absent too many times
2. **distracted:** te ves ausente hoy you look distracted today

el/la **ausente** ■ **absentee:** hay tres ausentes hoy en esta clase there are three absentees in this class today.

**Australia** *sustantivo femenino* ■ **Australia**.

**australiano** *adjetivo*

> En inglés, los adjetivos que se refieren a un país o a una región se escriben con mayúscula:

**Australian:** el equipo australiano the Australian team

el **australiano,** la **australiana**

> En inglés los gentilicios se escriben con mayúscula:

**Australian:** había dos australianos en la clase there were two Australians in the class.

**auténtico** *adjetivo* ■ **genuine:** un cuadro auténtico an genuine painting.

el **auto** *Southern Cone* ■ **car**.

el **autobús** *(plural* los autobuses) ■ **bus**.

la **autodefensa** ■ **self-defense**.

**automático** *adjetivo* ■ **automatic**.

el **automóvil** ■ **automobile:** la industria del automóvil the automobile industry.

la **autopista** ■ **highway**
➤ autopista de peaje turnpike
➤ autopista de cuota *Mexico* turnpike.

el **autor**, la **autora** ■ author: es la autora del poema she's the author of the poem
➤ el autor de la música the composer
➤ el autor del cuadro the painter
➤ los autores del crimen the perpetrators.

la **autoridad** ■ authority: no tiene ninguna autoridad sobre los alumnos she doesn't have any authority over the students
➤ las autoridades the authorities.

la **autorización** ■ authorization: necesito la autorización del director I need authorization from the manager.

**autorizar** verbo ■ to authorize
➤ autorizar a alguien para que haga algo to authorize someone to do something: nos autorizaron para salir más temprano we were authorized to leave early.

el **auxilio** ■ help: tuvimos que pedir auxilio we had to call for help
➤ ¡auxilio! help!
➤ los primeros auxilios first aid.

**avanzar** verbo
1. to make progress: ha avanzado mucho en sus estudios he has made a lot of progress in school
2. to move forward: la cola avanzaba muy lentamente the line moved forward very slowly.

**avaro** adjetivo ■ miserly

el **avaro**, la **avara** ■ miser.

el **ave** sustantivo femenino

> Feminine noun that takes un or el in the singular.

bird
➤ aves de corral poultry
➤ un ave de rapiña a bird of prey.

la **avellana** ■ hazelnut.

la **avena** ■ oatmeal.

la **avenida** ■ avenue.

**aventar** verbo ■ Colombia, Mexico, Peru to throw: me aventó la pelota she threw me the ball.

el **aventón** (plural los aventones) Mexico ■ ride
➤ darle un aventón a alguien to give somebody a ride: nos dio un aventón al colegio he gave us a ride to school
➤ pedir aventón to hitchhike.

**avergonzar** verbo
1. to embarrass: me avergonzó delante de la clase he embarrassed me in front of the class
2. to be ashamed: ¿no te avergüenza andar con esa ropa? aren't you ashamed to go around dressed like that?

**avergonzarse** verbo pronominal ■ to be ashamed: no tienes por qué avergonzarte you have nothing to be ashamed of
➤ avergonzarse de algo to be ashamed of something: me avergüenzo de haberlo acusado I'm ashamed of accusing him.

la **avería** ■ breakdown: su coche tuvo una avería en el camino their car had a breakdown on the way.

**averiguar** verbo ■ to find out: tengo que averiguar la fecha exacta I have to find out the exact date.

la **aviación**
1. aviation: quiere estudiar aviación civil he wants to study civil aviation
2. air force: es teniente de la aviación he's a lieutenant in the air force
➤ un accidente de aviación a plane crash.

el **avión** (plural los aviones) ■ airplane: le encantan los aviones she loves airplanes
➤ vamos a ir en avión we're flying there
➤ mandé el paquete por avión I sent the package by airmail.

**avisar** verbo
1. to warn: te aviso que vas a tener problemas I'm warning you — you'll have problems
2. to let know: ¿le avisaste que no ibas a ir? did you let her know you weren't going?; avísame con tiempo let me know in advance
➤ siempre llega sin avisar he always comes without calling.

el **aviso**

1. **notice:** el aviso daba información acerca del cambio de dirección the notice informed us of the change of address
2. **commercial:** los avisos de la televisión tv commercials
3. **ad:** puso un aviso en el diario she put an ad in the paper
➤ hasta nuevo aviso until further notice
➤ sin previo aviso without warning.

la **avispa** ▦ wasp.

la **axila** ▦ armpit.

**¡ay!** *interjección*

1. *para expresar dolor* **ouch!:** ¡ay! que me duele ouch! that hurts!
2. *para expresar sorpresa* **oops!:** ¡ay! casi me caigo oops! I nearly fell down
3. *para expresar susto* **oh!:** ¡ay! me asustaste oh! you startled me.

**ayer** *adverbio* ▦ **yesterday:** ayer la vi I saw her yesterday
➤ antes de ayer the day before yesterday
➤ ayer por la mañana yesterday morning
➤ ayer por la noche last night.

la **ayuda** ▦ **help:** ¿necesitas ayuda? do you need help?; me pidió ayuda she asked me for help.

**ayudar** *verbo* ▦ **to help:** me ha ayudado mucho it's helped me a lot
➤ ayudar a alguien a hacer algo to help someone do something: mi papá me ayudó a hacer las tareas my dad helped me do my homework.

el **ayuntamiento** ▦ **City Hall:** un curso organizado por el ayuntamiento a course organized by City Hall; vivo cerca del ayuntamiento I live near City Hall.

la **azafata** ▦ **flight attendant.**

el **azar** ▦ **chance:** me enteré por azar I only found out by chance
➤ al azar at random: escoge una carta al azar pick a card at random.

el/la **azúcar** ▦ **sugar:** no le pongo azúcar al café I don't put sugar in my coffee
➤ azúcar morena o moreno brown sugar.

**azul** *adjetivo* ▦ **blue:** un vestido azul a blue dress; es de color azul it's blue

el **azul** ▦ **blue:** no me gusta el azul I don't like blue; iba vestida de azul she was dressed in blue.

el **azulejo** ▦ **tile.**

el **babero** ▦ **bib.**

la **babosa** ▦ **slug.**

el **bacalao** ▦ **cod.**

el **bache** ▦ **pothole:** hay muchos baches en el camino there are a lot of potholes on this road
➤ están pasando por un mal bache they're going through a bad patch.

el **bachillerato** ▦ **high school course.**

la **bacteria** ▦ **bacteria.**

la **bahía** ▦ **bay.**

**bailar** *verbo* ▦ **to dance:** anoche fuimos a bailar we went out dancing last night
➤ estoy aprendiendo a bailar salsa I'm taking salsa lessons.

el **bailarín**, la **bailarina** ▦ **dancer:** quiere ser bailarina she wants to be a dancer.

el **baile** ▦ **dance:** la rumba es un baile cubano the rumba is a Cuban dance; tiene clases de baile she takes dance lessons; lo van a celebrar con un baile they're going to celebrate with a dance
➤ un baile de etiqueta a ball.

la **baja** ■ drop: una brusca baja de la temperatura a sudden drop in temperature
➤ darse de baja to cancel one's membership: me di de baja en el club I cancelled my club membership.

la **bajada** ■ way down: la bajada es siempre más fácil the way down is always easier
➤ una bajada muy empinada a steep descent.

**bajar** *verbo*
1. to go down: voy a bajar por las escaleras I'll go down the stairs
2. to come down: baja que quiero decirte algo come down here, I need to tell you something; ya bajo I'm coming down
3. to take down: voy a bajar el teléfono a la cocina I'm going to take the phone down to the kitchen
4. to bring down: por favor, bájame un suéter que aquí hace frío please bring me down a sweater — it's cold here
5. to get down: baja el diccionario del estante get the dictionary down from the shelf
6. to lower: han bajado el precio de la entrada they've lowered ticket prices
7. to download: acabo de bajar esta canción I just downloaded this song
8. to turn down: baja la música, por favor please turn down the music
➤ ¡bajen la voz que no puedo estudiar! keep your voices down, I'm trying to study!
➤ bajarse de algo *de un autobús, avión, bicicleta* to get off: nos bajamos juntos del tren we got off the train together
➤ bajarse de *de un coche* to get out of: se bajó de un taxi she got out of a taxi
➤ bajarse de *de un árbol, mesa* to come down from: ¡bájate de ahí que te vas a caer! get down from there before you fall!

**bajo** *(adverbio, preposición & adjetivo)*
■ *adverbio*
low: iba volando muy bajo it was flying very low
➤ hablen más bajo please lower your voices
■ *preposición*
under: escribe bajo un seudónimo she writes under a pseudonym; bajo el gobierno anterior under the previous government

➤ bajo cero below zero: tres grados bajo cero three degrees below zero
➤ bajo tierra underground: estacionamientos construidos bajo tierra underground parking lots
■ *adjetivo*
1. short: José es muy bajo José is very short
2. low: la silla es muy baja the chair is very low; saqué notas muy bajas I got very low grades; las temperaturas no son muy bajas temperatures aren't too low
➤ la planta baja the ground floor
➤ hablaban en voz baja they were talking quietly
➤ pon la música más baja turn the music down
➤ alimentos bajos en calorías low-calorie foods.

la **bala** ■ bullet.

la **balacera** ■ shootout.

la **balanza** ■ scale: me pesé en la balanza del baño I weighed myself on the bathroom scale.

el **balazo** ■ shot: oímos unos balazos we heard some shots
➤ lo mataron de un balazo he was shot to death.

el **balcón** *(plural los balcones)* ■ balcony.

el **balde** ■ bucket: un balde de agua a bucket of water
➤ en balde in vain: hicimos el viaje en balde porque no estaba he was out, so our trip was in vain.

la **baldosa** ■ tile.

la **ballena** ■ whale.

el **balón** *(plural los balones)* ■ ball

⚠ **Balón** is a false cognate, it does not mean "balloon".

la **balsa** ■ raft.

la **banana** *Peru, River Plate* ■ banana.

el **banano** *Central America, Colombia*
1. *árbol* banana tree

**32**

**2.** *fruto* **banana**.

### el banco

**1.** **bank:** depositó el cheque en el banco he deposited the check at the bank

**2.** **bench:** me senté en un banco de la plaza I sat on a bench in the square

➤ los bancos de la iglesia the pews

➤ un banco de sangre a blood bank.

### la banda

**1.** **band:** toca en la banda del colegio she plays in the school band

**2.** **gang:** detuvieron a una banda de ladrones they caught a gang of thieves

**3.** **sash:** llevaba una banda con el nombre de su país she wore a sash with her country's name on it

➤ la banda sonora de la película the movie's soundtrack.

### la bandeja ▪ tray.

### la bandera ▪ flag.

### el banquero, la banquera ▪ banker:
su padre es banquero his father is a banker.

### la banqueta *Mexico* ▪ sidewalk.

### el banquete ▪ banquet: los invitaron a un banquete they were invited to a banquet

➤ el banquete de bodas the wedding reception.

### la bañadera *Argentina* ▪ bathtub.

### bañarse *verbo pronominal*

**1.** *en la tina* **to take a bath**

**2.** *en la ducha* **to take a shower**

**3.** **to swim:** nos bañamos en el mar we swam in the sea.

### el baño

**1.** **bathroom:** ¿dónde está el baño, por favor? can you tell me where the bathroom is, please?; una casa con tres baños a house with three bathrooms

**2.** **bathtub:** llenó el baño de agua she filled the bathtub

➤ darse un baño *en el mar, la piscina* to go for a swim

➤ darse un baño *en la tina* to take a bath

➤ darse un baño *en la ducha* to take a shower

➤ baño público restroom.

### el bar ▪ bar.

### la barata *Mexico* ▪ sale: lo compré en una barata I bought it on sale.

### barato *(adjetivo & adverbio)*

▪ *adjetivo*
**cheap:** ¿cuál es más barato? which one is cheaper?

▪ *adverbio*
**cheaply:** aquí podemos comer barato we can eat cheaply here

➤ el viaje nos costó barato our trip was pretty cheap.

### la barba ▪ beard

➤ dejarse barba to grow a beard: se está dejando barba he's growing a beard.

### la barbacoa

**1.** **barbecue:** hacer una barbacoa to have a barbecue

**2.** *Mexico meat cooked in a hole dug in the ground and lined with red-hot stones.*

### la barbaridad ▪ atrocity: las barbaridades cometidas en la guerra the atrocities committed during the war

➤ no digas tantas barbaridades don't talk such nonsense

➤ tengo una barbaridad de tareas para mañana I've got a load of homework for tomorrow

➤ ¡qué barbaridad! mira qué tarde es oh my God! look how late it is!

### la barbilla ▪ chin.

### la barca ▪ boat: una barca de remos a rowboat.

### el barco

**1.** *grande* **ship**

**2.** *de menor tamaño* **boat**

➤ un barco de guerra a warship

➤ un barco de vela a sailboat.

### la barda *Mexico*

**1.** *de madera* **fence**

**2.** *de ladrillos, cemento* **wall**

➤ una barda de alambre de púas a barbed-wire fence.

### el barniz *(plural los barnices)* ▪ varnish

➤ el barniz de uñas nail polish.

la **barra** ■ bar: una barra de metal a metal bar; una barra de chocolate a chocolate bar; una barra de jabón a bar of soap; tomamos unas bebidas en la barra we had drinks at the bar.

el **barranco** ■ ravine.

**barrer** *verbo* ■ **to sweep**: tengo que barrer el patio I have to sweep the patio

**barrerse** *Mexico verbo pronominal* ■ **to slide**: el portero se barrió para detener la pelota the goalkeeper slid to stop the ball.

la **barrera** ■ barrier
➤ la barrera del sonido the sound barrier.

la **barriga** ■ belly: tiene una tremenda barriga he has a huge belly
➤ me duele la barriga my tummy hurts.

el **barril** ■ barrel: un barril de petróleo an oil barrel.

el **barrilete** *River Plate* ■ **kite**: remontar un barrilete to fly a kite.

el **barrio** ■ neighborhood: un barrio residencial a residential neighborhood; va a un colegio del barrio she goes to a neighborhood school.

el **barro**
1. clay: una olla de barro a clay pot
2. mud: llegó con los zapatos llenos de barro he arrived with his shoes covered in mud.

el **barullo**
1. racket: tenían un barullo en la clase there was a racket in the classroom
2. confusion: en el barullo perdí el libro I lost my book in the confusion
➤ se me armó un barullo con las cuentas the accounts really confused me.

**basarse** *verbo pronominal* ■ **to be based on**: el libro se basa en una historia real the book is based on a true story.

la **báscula** ■ scale.

la **base**
1. base: la base de la pirámide the base of the pyramid; corrió a la tercera base she ran to third base
2. basis: la base de su éxito fue el estudio studying was the basis for his success

➤ lo consiguió a base de esfuerzo he did it through hard work
➤ las bases del concurso the rules of the competition
➤ una base aérea an air base
➤ una base de datos a database.

**básico** *adjetivo* ■ **basic**.

el **básquetbol** ■ basketball.

el **basquetbol** *Mexico* ■ basketball.

**bastante** *(adjetivo & adverbio)*

■ *adjetivo*

> Cuando tiene el sentido de suficiente, el adjetivo **bastante** se traduce por **enough**. Si se refiere a una cantidad o número considerable se traduce por **a lot of**:

1. enough: hay bastante comida para todos there's enough food for everyone; no estudian bastante they don't study enough; ¿queda bastante? is there enough?
2. a lot of: había bastante gente there were a lot of people; mañana tengo bastantes cosas que hacer I have a lot of things to do tomorrow
➤ tengo bastante hambre I'm quite hungry
➤ nos demoramos bastante en llegar we got there pretty late

■ *adverbio*
pretty: son bastante caras they're pretty expensive; habla bastante bien inglés she speaks English pretty well.

el **bastón** ■ cane.

la **basura** *(plural los bastones)* ■ garbage: pasan a recoger la basura los lunes they pick up the garbage on Monday
➤ tirar algo a la basura to throw something in the garbage.

el **basurero**
1. garbage dump: lo encontró en el basurero she found it in the garbage dump
2. *Chile, Mexico recipiente* garbage can: el basurero está debajo del fregadero the garbage can is under the kitchen sink

el **basurero**, la **basurera** ■ garbage collector.

la **bata**
1. **robe:** seguía en bata a las tres de la tarde she was still in her robe at three o'clock in the afternoon
2. **coat:** los doctores usan batas blancas doctors wear white coats
➤ una bata de baño a bathrobe.

la **batalla** ■ battle.

la **batata** ■ sweet potato.

el **bateador,** la **bateadora** ■ batter.

la **batería**
1. **battery:** necesito una nueva batería para mi coche my car needs a new battery
2. **drums:** estoy aprendiendo a tocar la batería I'm learning to play the drums.

**batir** *verbo*
1. **to beat:** bate los huevos ligeramente beat the eggs lightly
2. **to whip:** hay que batir la crema primero you have to whip the cream first
3. **to break:** Woods ha batido todos los récords Woods has beaten all the records.

el **baúl** ■ trunk.

**bautizar** *verbo* ■ **to christen:** la bautizan el sábado she's being christened on Saturday
➤ la bautizaron con el nombre de la abuela she was named after her grandmother.

el **bautizo** ■ christening.

**beber** *verbo* ■ **to drink:** no bebas esa agua don't drink that water
➤ se bebieron todo el vino they drank all the wine
➤ tienes que bebértelo todo you have to drink all of it.

la **bebida** ■ drink.

la **beca**
1. *del gobierno* **grant:** recibimos una beca del gobierno we got a government grant
2. *de universidad, institución privada* **scholarship:** se ganó una beca para asistir a Harvard she won a scholarship to go to Harvard.

el **béisbol** ■ baseball.

el **beisbol** *Mexico* ■ baseball.

la **belleza** ■ beauty.

la **bencina** *Chile* ■ **gasoline:** pusimos bencina en el auto we put gasoline in the car.

la **bencinera** *Chile* ■ gas station.

**bendecir** *verbo* ■ to bless.

la **bendición** *(plural* las bendiciones*)* ■ blessing: el sacerdote realizó la bendición de los anillos the priest performed the blessing of the rings.

**beneficiar** *verbo* ■ **to benefit:** la nueva ley beneficia a todos the new law benefits everybody.

el **beneficio** ■ **profit:** la empresa tuvo un beneficio de 2000 dólares the company made a profit of $2000.

**benéfico** *adjetivo* ■ **benefit:** una cena benéfica a benefit dinner.

**benigno** *adjetivo*
1. **benign:** un tumor benigno a benign tumor
2. **mild:** un clima benigno a mild climate.

la **berenjena** ■ eggplant.

la **berma** *Andes* ■ **shoulder:** el auto se fue a la berma the car went onto the shoulder.

el **berrinche** ■ **rage:** me agarré un berrinche tremendo I flew into a terrible rage.

**besar** *verbo* ■ **to kiss:** se estaban besando they were kissing.

el **beso** ■ **kiss:** le dio un beso he gave her a kiss.

el **betabel** *Mexico* ■ beet.

el **biberón** *(plural* los biberones*)* ■ **bottle:** el bebé está tomando el biberón the baby's taking the bottle.

la **Biblia** ■ Bible.

el **bibliorato** *River Plate* ■ file cabinet.

la **biblioteca** ■ library *(plural* **libraries***)*: la biblioteca de la escuela the school library.

el **bibliotecario,** la **bibliotecaria** ■ librarian.

el **bicho** ■ insect.

la **bicicleta** ■ bicycle
➤ montar en bicicleta to ride a bicycle: **no sabe montar en bicicleta** he doesn't know how to ride a bicycle
➤ bicicleta de montaña mountain bike.

**bien** *adverbio*
1. **good:** me siento bien I feel good
2. **very:** repítelo bien fuerte repeat it very loudly
3. **great:** ¡bien, vamos al cine! great, let's go to the movies!
4. **all right:** está bien: te dejo el coche it's all right: I'm leaving you the car
5. **well:** ¡cierra bien la puerta! close the door well!
➤ la pasamos muy bien we had a good time
➤ ¡bien hecho! well done!
➤ ¿te parece bien? is that OK with you?
➤ ¡qué bien! how wonderful!

el **bien**
1. **good:** el bien y el mal good and evil
2. **well-being:** lo hizo por tu bien she did it for your well-being
➤ los bienes possessions.

la **bienvenida**
➤ dar la bienvenida a alguien to welcome somebody: me dieron la bienvenida they welcomed me.

**bienvenido** *adjetivo* ■ **welcome:** bienvenido a nuestra casa welcome to our home.

el **bife** *River Plate* ■ steak.

el **bigote** ■ mustache.

el **billete**
1. **bill:** un billete de 100 pesos a 100–peso bill
2. **ticket:** un billete de tren a train ticket.

la **billetera** ■ wallet: una billetera de cuero a leather wallet.

la **biografía** ■ biography (*plural* biographies).

la **biología** ■ biology.

**biológico** *adjetivo* ■ biological.

la **birome** *River Plate* ■ pen: una birome azul a blue pen.

el **bis** ■ encore: pidieron un bis en el concierto they asked for an encore at the concert.

la **bisabuela** ■ great-grandmother.

el **bisabuelo** ■ great-grandfather
➤ mis bisabuelos my great-grandparents.

la **bisnieta** ■ great-granddaughter.

el **bisnieto** ■ great-grandson
➤ mis bisnietos my great-grandchildren.

el **bisté** *Mexico* ■ steak.

el **bistec** *Mexico* ■ steak.

**bizco** *adjetivo* ■ **cross-eyed**.

**blanco** *adjetivo* ■ white: una pared blanca a white wall

el **blanco**
1. **white:** el blanco es mi color preferido white is my favorite color
2. **target:** fue el blanco de todas las críticas he was the target of all the criticism; el ciervo fue el blanco de los cazadores the deer was the target of the hunters
➤ dejar algo en blanco to leave something blank: deje esa parte del documento en blanco leave that part of the document blank.

**blando** *adjetivo*
1. **soft:** una superficie blanda a soft surface
2. **indulgent:** es muy blando con sus hijos he's very indulgent with his children.

el **bloque** ■ block: un bloque de cemento a cement block.

**bloquear** *verbo* ■ **to block:** el camión bloqueaba la entrada the truck was blocking the entrance.

el **bloqueo** ■ blockade.

los **blúmers** *Central America, Caribbean* ■ panties.

la **blusa** ■ blouse.

el **bluyín** *Andes, Venezuela* ■ jeans: Juan compró un bluyín Juan bought some jeans.

los **bluyines** *Andes, Venezuela* ■ jeans.

**bobo** *adjetivo* ■ **silly:** es una actitud muy boba it's a very silly attitude

el **bobo,** la **boba** ■ **fool:** Guillermo es un bobo Guillermo is a fool.

la **boca** ■ **mouth:** una boca pequeña a small mouth

➤ **quedarse con la boca abierta** to be dumbfounded

➤ **se me hace agua la boca** my mouth is watering

➤ **boca abajo** face down

➤ **boca arriba** face up.

el **bocado** ■ **bite:** probé un bocado de esa comida I tried a bite of that food.

la **bocina** ■ **horn:** el conductor tocó la bocina the driver honked the horn.

**bocón, bocona** *adjetivo informal* ■ **loud-mouthed:** Pedro es muy bocón Pedro is very loud-mouthed.

la **boda** ■ **wedding.**

la **bodega**

1. **cellar:** una bodega de vino a wine cellar
2. **hold:** el equipaje está en la bodega del barco the luggage is in the ship's hold.

la **bofetada** ■ **slap:** le dio una bofetada fuerte she gave him a hard slap.

el **bóiler** *Mexico* ■ **boiler.**

la **bola** ■ **ball:** pásame la bola pass me the ball

➤ **se corrió la bola** the rumor has spread

➤ **bola de cristal** crystal ball.

**bolear** *Mexico verbo* ■ **to shine:** boleo mis zapatos todas las semanas I shine my shoes every week.

el **bolero,** la **bolera** *Mexico* ■ **shoeshine:** hay muchos boleros en la ciudad there are many shoeshines in the city.

la **boleta**

1. **receipt:** reclama siempre tu boleta de compra always ask for your receipt
2. *Central America, Southern Cone* **fine:** me pusieron una boleta por alta velocidad they gave me a speeding fine.

la **boletería**

1. **box office:** nos vemos en la boletería del cine we'll meet at the box office of the movie theater
2. **ticket office:** la boletería de la estación está cerrada the station's ticket office is closed.

el **boleto** ■ **ticket:** compré un boleto de autobús I bought a bus ticket

➤ **un boleto de lotería** a lottery ticket

➤ **un boleto de ida y vuelta** a round-trip ticket

➤ **un boleto redondo** *Mexico* a round-trip ticket.

el **boliche**

1. **bowling:** le gusta jugar boliche he likes to go bowling
2. *River Plate* **store:** fuimos a tomar algo al boliche de la esquina we went to get a drink at the corner store.

el **bolígrafo** ■ **pen:** marca las correcciones con un bolígrafo rojo mark the corrections with a red pen.

el **bolillo** *Mexico* ■ **roll:** Juan come bolillos todas las mañanas Juan eats rolls every morning.

la **bolita** *Southern Cone* ■ **marble**

➤ **jugar a la bolita** to play marbles: los niños juegan a la bolita en la calle the children play marbles in the street.

**Bolivia** *sustantivo femenino* ■ **Bolivia.**

**boliviano** *adjetivo*

En inglés, los adjetivos que se refieren a un país o una región se escriben con mayúscula:

**Bolivian:** los tejidos bolivianos son de alta calidad Bolivian textiles are high quality

el **boliviano,** la **boliviana**

En inglés, los gentilicios se escriben con mayúscula:

**Bolivian:** los bolivianos the Bolivians.

el **bollo** *Mexico* ■ **roll:** me gustan los bollos calentitos I like hot rolls.

la **bolsa**

1. **bag:** traje las compras en una bolsa de papel I carried the shopping in a paper bag
2. **stock market:** la Bolsa ha subido the stock market has gone up
3. *Mexico* **purse:** mi hermana compró una bolsa roja my sister bought a red purse
➤ una bolsa de agua caliente a hot-water bottle
➤ una bolsa de aire an air pocket
➤ una bolsa de dormir a sleeping bag.

el **bolsillo** ■ **pocket:** este pantalón tiene dos bolsillos these pants have two pockets.

el **bolso** ■ **bag:** un bolso de cuero a leather bag.

la **bomba**

1. **bomb:** estalló una bomba en una tienda a bomb exploded in a store
2. **pump:** usamos una bomba para sacar el agua we used a pump to get the water out
3. *Chile, Ecuador, Venezuela* **gas pump:** dejamos el auto al lado de la bomba we left the car next to the gas pump.

la **bombacha** *River Plate* ■ **panties:** una bombacha blanca a pair of white panties.

**bombear** *verbo* ■ **to pump out:** los voluntarios bombearon el agua del pozo the volunteers pumped out the water from the well.

el **bombero,** la **bombera**

1. **firefighter:** los bomberos apagaron el fuego the firefighters put out the fire
2. *Venezuela* **gas station attendant:** le pedimos al bombero que llenara el tanque we asked the gas station attendant to fill the tank.

la **bombilla**

1. **light bulb:** necesitamos una bombilla para la lámpara we need a lightbulb for the lamp
2. *River Plate* metal tube used to drink **mate**.

el **bombillo** *Central America, Colombia, Mexico* ■ **light bulb**.

la **bombita** *River Plate* ■ **bulb**.

el **boniato** ■ **sweet potato** (*plural* **sweet potatoes**).

**bonito** *adjetivo* ■ **pretty:** esta blusa es muy bonita this blouse is very pretty.

el **bono**

1. **voucher:** me dieron un bono por el 10% de mi compra the gave me a voucher for 10% of my purchase
2. **pass:** Beatriz compró un bono de transporte público Beatriz bought a public transportation pass.

el **bordado** ■ **embroidery**.

el **borde** ■ **edge:** es peligroso asomarse al borde del barranco it's dangerous to get close to the edge of the ravine
➤ estar al borde de algo to be on the verge of something: está al borde de una crisis nerviosa he's on the verge of a nervous breakdown.

**bordo** *sustantivo masculino*
➤ a bordo on board: subimos a bordo de la lancha we got on board the boat.

la **borrachera**
➤ agarrarse borrachera to get drunk: Juan se agarró tremenda borrachera Juan got really drunk.

**borracho** *adjetivo* ■ **drunk:** estaba borracho he was drunk.

el **borrador**

1. **rough draft:** es un borrador it's a rough draft
2. **eraser:** la maestra pidió un borrador nuevo the teacher asked for a new eraser.

**borrar** *verbo* ■ **to erase:** el estudiante borró el pizarrón the student erased the chalkboard.

el **borrego,** la **borrega** ■ **lamb**.

el **borrón** (*plural* los borrones) ■ **smudge:** este trabajo está lleno de borrones this paper is covered with smudges.

**borroso** *adjetivo*

1. **blurred:** una fotografía borrosa a blurred photograph
2. **vague:** un recuerdo borroso a vague memory.

**el bosque**

1. *grande* **forest**
2. *pequeño* **wood**.

**bostezar** *verbo* ■ **to yawn:** Pedro bostezó durante toda la conferencia Pedro yawned during the whole conference.

la **bota** ■ **boot:** compré botas de cuero I bought leather boots.

la **botana** *Mexico* ■ **snack:** es un lugar ideal para comer botanas it's an ideal place to eat snacks.

la **botánica** ■ **botany**.

**botar** *verbo* ■ **to throw:** está prohibido botar papeles al suelo it's prohibited to throw paper on the ground.

**el bote**

1. **can:** compramos un bote de pintura we bought a can of paint
2. **boat:** hay muchos botes en el lago hoy there are lots of boats in the lake today

➤ **pasear en bote** to go sailing.

la **botella** ■ **bottle:** una botella de vidrio a glass bottle.

el **botón** (*plural* los botones) ■ **button:** perdió dos botones de la blusa she lost two buttons off her blouse.

la **bóveda** ■ **vault**.

el **box** *Latin America* ■ **boxing:** el box es un deporte muy rudo boxing is a very rough sport.

el **boxeo** ■ **boxing:** un campeonato de boxeo a boxing championship.

la **brasa** ■ **hot coal:** hay que avivar las brasas we have to stoke the hot coals.

el **brasier** *Colombia, Mexico* ■ **bra**.

**Brasil** *sustantivo masculino* ■ **Brazil**.

**brasileño** *adjetivo*

En inglés, los adjetivos que se refieren a un país o una región se escriben con mayúscula:

**Brazilian:** el equipo brasileño salió campeón the Brazilian team were the champions

**el brasileño, la brasileña**

En inglés, los gentilicios se escriben con mayúscula:

**Brazilian:** los brasileños the Brazilians.

**brasilero** *River Plate adjetivo*

En inglés, los adjetivos que se refieren a un país o una región se escriben con mayúscula:

**Brazilian:** el equipo brasilero salió campeón the Brazilian team were the champions

**el brasilero, la brasilera** *River Plate*

En inglés, los gentilicios se escriben con mayúscula:

**Brazilian:** los brasileros the Brazilians.

el **brassier** *Colombia, Mexico* ■ **bra**.

**bravo** *adjetivo* ■ **brave:** un guerrero muy bravo a very brave warrior

➤ **la situación se puso brava** *River Plate* the situation became very difficult.

**bravo** *interjección* ■ **well done!**

**bravucón, bravucona** *adjetivo* ■ **boastful**.

el **brazo** ■ **arm:** Ricardo se fracturó el brazo Ricardo broke his arm.

el **bretel** *Southern Cone* ■ **strap:** un bretel de mi vestido se rompió a strap on my dress broke; **un vestido sin breteles** a strapless dress.

**breve** *adjetivo*

1. **brief:** una breve pausa a brief pause
2. **short:** un discurso breve a short speech.

el **brevet** *Andes* ■ **license:** saqué el brevet I got out my license.

**brillante** *adjetivo*

1. **shiny:** una superficie brillante a shiny surface
2. **brilliant:** es una estudiante brillante she's a brilliant student

el **brillante** ■ **diamond:** un anillo de brillantes a diamond ring.

**brillar** *verbo*

1. **to shine:** las estrellas **brillan** the stars are shining

2. **to sparkle:** sus ojos **brillaban** his eyes sparkled.

el **brillo**

1. **shine:** el **brillo** del vidrio me ciega the shine from the glass is blinding me

2. **sparkle:** adoro el **brillo** de tus ojos I adore the sparkle of your eyes.

**brilloso** *adjetivo* ▪ **shining:** los zapatos estaban **brillosos** the shoes were shining.

**brincar** *verbo* ▪ **to jump up and down:** el niño **brincaba** de emoción the boy was jumping up and down in excitement.

el **brinco**

➤ pegar un **brinco** to jump: pegó un **brinco** en el aire she jumped in the air.

**brindar** *verbo*

1. **to offer:** te **brindo** mi amor I offer you my love

➤ **brindar** por to drink a toast to: en la fiesta **brindamos** por los novios at the party we drank a toast to the bride and groom

**brindarse** *verbo*

➤ **brindarse** a hacer algo to offer to do something: me **brindé** a lavar los platos I offered to do the dishes.

el **brindis** *(plural* los **brindis)** ▪ **toast:** hagamos un **brindis** por los novios let's drink a toast to the bride and groom.

la **brisa** ▪ **breeze:** hay una **brisa** muy agradable there's a very pleasant breeze.

la **brocha** ▪ **paintbrush.**

el **broche**

1. **fastener:** se rompió el **broche** del collar the fastener of the necklace broke

2. **brooch:** me gusta usar un **broche** en la solapa I like to wear a brooch in my lapel.

la **broma** ▪ **joke:** le gusta hacer **bromas** he likes to make jokes

➤ gastar una **broma** a alguien to play a joke on somebody: gastamos una **broma** a Cristina we played a joke on Cristina

➤ lo decía en **broma** I was just joking.

**bromear** *verbo* ▪ **to joke:** sólo estábamos **bromeando** we were only joking.

el **bromista,** la **bromista** ▪ **joker:** los **bromistas** son personas populares jokers are popular people.

la **bronca**

1. **row:** se armó una **bronca** terrible en el partido there was a terrible row during the game

2. *River Plate*

➤ me da mucha **bronca** it makes me very angry.

**bronceado** *adjetivo* ▪ **tanned:** su piel estaba **bronceada** his skin was tanned

➤ ponerse **bronceado** to get a tan: me pongo **bronceado** después de sólo una hora en el sol I get a tan after only one hour in the sun.

**brotarse** *verbo* ▪ **to break out:** me **broté** con el sol I broke out from the sun.

el **brote** ▪ **sprout:** esta planta tiene **brotes** sanos this plant has healthy sprouts.

la **bruja** ▪ **witch.**

**brujo** *adjetivo* ▪ *Mexico informal* **broke**

➤ estar **brujo** to be broke: a esta altura del mes estamos **brujos** at this point of the month we're broke

el **brujo** ▪ **wizard.**

la **brújula** ▪ **compass.**

la **bruma** ▪ **mist:** hay una espesa **bruma** sobre el mar there's a heavy mist over the sea.

**brusco** *adjetivo* ▪ **sudden:** hizo un movimiento **brusco** he made a sudden movement.

**brutal** *adjetivo* ▪ **brutal:** fue una guerra **brutal** it was a brutal war.

**bruto** *adjetivo*

1. **uncouth:** es un niño muy **bruto** he's a very uncouth boy

2. **gross:** las ganancias **brutas** gross profits.

**bucal** *adjetivo* ▪ **oral:** tienes una infección **bucal** you have an oral infection.

**buen** *adjetivo*

Buen is a shortened form of **bueno** used in front of a masculine singular noun. Example:es un buen año, es un año bueno.

**good:** es un buen principio it's a good beginning.

**bueno** *(adjetivo, adverbio & interjección)*
■ *adjetivo*
**good:** sacó muy buenas notas en el examen he got very good grades on the test
■ *adverbio*
**OK:** bueno, comamos pizza OK, let's eat pizza
■ *interjección*
*Mexico, Colombia al teléfono* **Hello!:** ¡bueno! ¿quién habla? hello! who's speaking?

el **buey** ■ ox *(plural* oxen*)*.

la **bufanda** ■ scarf *(plural* scarves*)*.

el **búho** ■ owl.

el **buitre** ■ vulture.

el **bulbo** ■ bulb.

la **bulla** ■ ruckus: los niños armaron una gran bulla the children raised a terrible ruckus.

el **bullicio** ■ racket: el bullicio de la calle era insoportable the racket of the street was unbearable.

el **bulto**
1. bulge: la billetera te hace un bulto en el bolsillo your wallet makes a bulge in your pocket
2. bag: viajan con cuatro bultos they're traveling with four bags
3. shape: sólo puedo distinguir dos bultos grandes en este cuarto oscuro I can only distinguish two large shapes in this dark room.

el **buque** ■ ship.

la **burbuja** ■ bubble.

la **burguesía** ■ middle class.

la **burla** ■ taunt: las burlas de sus compañeros fueron crueles the taunts of his colleagues were cruel.

**burlarse** *verbo*
➤ burlarse de alguien to make fun of somebody: se burlaron cruelmente del niño they cruelly made fun of the boy.

el **buró** *Mexico* ■ nightstand.

la **burocracia** ■ bureaucracy.

el/la **burócrata** ■ bureaucrat.

**burocrático** *adjetivo* ■ bureaucratic: debemos completar estos trámites burocráticos we have to complete these bureaucratic formalities.

el **burrito** *Central America, Mexico* ■ burrito: se comió dos burritos he ate two burritos.

**burro** *informal adjetivo* ■ stupid: era tan burro que pensaba que el número dos era impar he was so stupid that he thought that two was an odd number

el **burro** ■ donkey.

el **bus** ■ bus: tomamos el bus para ir al museo we took the bus to the museum.

**buscar** *verbo*
1. to look for: estoy buscando trabajo I'm looking for work
2. to pick up: va a buscar a los niños al colegio todos los días she goes to pick up the children from school every day
➤ se busca caniche blanco white poodle wanted
➤ se la está buscando he's looking for trouble.

la **buseta** *Colombia, Costa Rica, Ecuador, Venezuela* ■ bus: voy en buseta a la escuela I go to school by bus.

la **búsqueda** ■ search: la búsqueda de la niña duró dos días the search for the girl lasted two days.

el **busto** ■ bust: inauguraron un busto del famoso poeta they unveiled a bust of the famous poet.

la **butaca** ■ armchair.

el **buzo**
1. *Colombia, Uruguay* jumper: compré un buzo de lana I bought a wool jumper

**41**

**2.** *Argentina* **tracksuit:** uso un buzo para hacer deporte I wear a tracksuit to play sports.

el **buzón** ■ **mailbox:** encontré dos cartas en el buzón I found two letters in the mailbox

➤ eché una carta al buzón I mailed a letter.

la **caballería** ■ **cavalry**.

**caballero** *adjetivo* ■ **gentlemanly:** es muy caballero he's very gentlemanly

el **caballero** ■ **gentleman** (*plural* **gentlemen**): estas cosas no deberían pasar entre caballeros these things shouldn't happen among gentlemen

➤ damas y caballeros ladies and gentlemen.

el **caballo**

**1.** **horse:** el caballo es mi animal favorito the horse is my favorite animal

**2.** **knight:** no te conviene mover el caballo o te haré jaque al rey it's not a good idea for you to move your knight because I'll check your king

➤ andar a caballo to ride.

la **cabaña** ■ **cabin:** fuimos a pasar el fin de semana a la cabaña we went to spend the weekend at the cabin.

**cabecear** *verbo*

**1.** **to nod off:** el viejo cabeceaba frente a la tele the old man was nodding off in front of the TV

**2.** **to head:** el jugador cabeceó y marcó un gol the player headed the ball and scored a goal.

la **cabecera**

**1.** **headboard:** la cabecera de la cama era de madera the headboard of the bed was made of wood

**2.** **head:** el invitado se sentó a la cabecera de la mesa the guest sat down at the head of the table.

el **cabello** ■ **hair:** tiene un cabello suave y brilloso she has smooth, glossy hair.

**caber** *verbo* ■ **to fit:** en esta habitación caben diez personas ten people fit in this room; estos pantalones ya no me caben these pants don't fit me anymore.

la **cabeza**

**1.** **head:** me duele la cabeza I've got a headache

**2.** **person:** corresponden 100 pesos por cabeza it's 100 pesos per person

➤ a la cabeza at the head: el sacerdote iba a la cabeza de la procesión the priest was at the head of the procession

➤ perder la cabeza to lose one's head: perdió la cabeza por esa muchacha he lost his head over that girl

➤ romperse la cabeza to rack one's brains: me rompí la cabeza tratando de entender este ejercicio I racked my brains trying to understand this exercise

➤ cabeza de ajo bulb of garlic

➤ cabeza de familia head of the household.

la **cabina**

**1.** **booth:** hay una cabina telefónica a dos cuadras there's a telephone booth two blocks away

**2.** **cockpit:** se prendió fuego la cabina del avión the airplane's cockpit caught on fire.

el **cabinero,** la **cabinera** *Colombia* ■ **flight attendant:** le pedí agua a la cabinera I asked the flight attendant for water.

el **cable**

**1.** **cable:** se tropezó con un cable he tripped on a cable

**2.** **message:** recibí un cable del exterior I received a message from abroad

**3.** **cable television:** tengo cable en casa I have cable television at home.

el **cabo**
1. **end:** pásame el cabo de la cuerda pass me the end of the rope
2. **corporal:** el sargento ordenó al cabo que saliera the sergeant ordered the corporal to leave
3. **cape:** esta costa tiene muchos cabos this coast has many capes
➤ **llevar a cabo** to carry out: la empresa llevó a cabo un proyecto original the company carried out an original project
➤ **atar cabos** to put two and two together: el inspector ató cabos hasta dar con el asesino the inspector put two and two together and found the murderer.

la **cabra** ▪ goat.

el **cabro** *Bolivia, Chile, Chile informal* ▪ **guy:** conocí a esos cabros en la calle I met those guys on the street.

la **cabuya** *Central America, Colombia, Venezuela* ▪ **rope:** lo atamos con una cabuya we tied it with a rope.

la **caca** *informal* ▪ **poop:** la calle está llena de caca de perro the street is full of dog poop.

el **cacahuate** *Central America, Mexico* ▪ **peanut**.

el **cacao** ▪ cocoa.

el **cacareo** ▪ **crowing:** el cacareo de los gallos era insoportable the crowing of the roosters was unbearable.

la **cacería** ▪ **hunt:** la cacería del zorro fue un éxito the fox hunt was a success.

la **cacerola** ▪ **pan:** puse las verduras crudas en la cacerola I put the raw vegetables in the pan.

**cachar** *Mexico verbo* ▪ **to catch:** caché el llavero en el aire I caught the keyring in the air.

el **cacharro**
1. **junk:** el sótano está lleno de cacharros viejos the basement is full of old junk
2. **pots:** todavía tengo que lavar los cacharros de la comida I still have to wash the pots from dinner.

la **cachetada** ▪ **slap:** le pegó tremenda cachetada she gave him a hard slap.

el **cachete**
1. **cheek:** se le pusieron los cachetes rojos de vergüenza his cheeks turned red in shame
2. **slap:** el padre le pegó un cachete al niño the father gave the boy a slap.

el **cachorro**, la **cachorra**
1. *de perro* **puppy** *(plural* **puppies***)*
2. *de gato* **kitten**
3. *de león, oso* **cub**.

la **cachucha** *Andes, Central America, Mexico* ▪ **cap**.

el **cacique**
1. **chief:** el cacique de la tribu era un hombre de gran sabiduría the chief of the tribe was a man of great wisdom
2. **political leader:** la región está dominada por caciques corruptos the region is dominated by corrupt political leaders.

el **cacto** ▪ **cactus** *(plural* **cacti***)*.

el **cactus** *(plural* los cactus*)* ▪ **cactus** *(plural* **cacti***)*.

**cada** *adjetivo*
1. **each:** cada alumno trajo su propio cuaderno each student brought his own notebook
2. **every:** viene a casa cada quince días he comes home every two weeks
➤ **dices cada cosa** you say the funniest things
➤ **cada vez más** more and more
➤ **cada vez menos** less and less.

el **cadáver** ▪ **corpse**.

la **cadena**
1. **chain:** me regalaron una cadena de plata they gave me a silver chain; el magnate compró una cadena de hoteles the magnate bought a chain of hotels
2. **channel:** una sola cadena de televisión transmitirá el partido only one television channel will show the game
➤ **cadena perpetua** life imprisonment: lo condenaron a cadena perpetua they sentenced him to life imprisonment.

la **cadera** ▪ **hip**.

el **cadete**
1. **cadet:** los cadetes tienen libre el fin de semana the cadets have the weekend free

**43**

**2.** *River Plate* **apprentice:** trabaja de cadete en una oficina he works as an apprentice in an office.

**caducado** *adjetivo* ■ **expired:** estos huevos están caducados these eggs are expired.

la **caducidad** ■ **expiration:** es importante leer la fecha de caducidad de los alimentos it's important to read the expiration date on food.

**caer** *verbo*

**1.** **to fall:** cayó un meteorito a meteorite fell; cayó la dictadura the dictatorship fell; este año el carnaval cae en marzo this year the carnival falls in March

**2.** **to understand:** ahora caigo now I understand

**3.** **to like:** Antonio me cae muy bien I like Antonio very much

➤ **dejar caer** to drop: dejé caer el vaso I dropped the glass

➤ **caer en la cuenta** to realize: caí en la cuenta de que mentía I realized that he was lying

➤ **me cae mal el pescado frito** fried fish disagrees with me

➤ **al caer la noche** at nightfall

**caerse** *verbo* ■ **to fall:** se cayó por la escalera she fell down the stairs.

**café** *adjetivo* ■ **brown:** compré una camisa café I bought a brown shirt

el **café**

**1.** **coffee:** todas las mañanas tomo café I drink coffee every morning

**2.** **café:** me encontré con Juan en el café de la esquina I met Juan at the café on the corner

➤ **café con leche** coffee with milk.

### CAFÉ CON LECHE

Latin America is home to some of the main coffee-producing countries in the world, such as Colombia, Costa Rica and Brazil. Because of this, even children drink coffee - a typical breakfast for many is a **café con leche**, a mug of hot milk with a shot of coffee in it.

la **cafetera**

**1.** *para preparar café* **coffee machine**

**2.** *para servir café* **coffee pot**.

la **cafetería** ■ **café**.

la **caída** ■ **fall:** como consecuencia de una caída, se fracturó una pierna because of a fall, he broke his leg; los precios sufrieron una fuerte caída prices suffered a sharp fall.

el **caimán** (*plural* los caimanes) ■ **alligator**.

la **caja**

**1.** **box:** me regalaron una caja de madera they gave me a wooden box

**2.** **checkout:** tenemos que pagar en la caja we have to pay at the checkout

➤ **caja de ahorros** savings & loan

➤ **caja de cambios** gearbox.

el **cajero**, la **cajera** ■ **cashier:** el cajero me cobró de menos the cashier undercharged me

➤ **un cajero automático** an automatic teller machine.

el **cajón** (*plural* los cajones) ■ **drawer:** guardo las medias en el cajón izquierdo I keep my stockings in the left drawer.

la **cajuela** *Mexico* ■ **trunk:** la cajuela de este carro es muy grande the trunk of this car is very big.

la **cal** ■ **lime**.

el **calabacín** ■ **zucchini**.

la **calabaza** ■ **pumpkin**.

el **calamar** ■ **squid**.

el **calambre** ■ **cramp:** me dio un fuerte calambre en la pierna I got a strong cramp in my leg.

la **calamidad** ■ **disaster:** el accidente fue una gran calamidad the accident was a terrible disaster.

**calar** *verbo* ■ **to soak:** la tormenta nos caló the storm soaked us.

la **calavera** ■ **skull**

las **calaveras** *Mexico* ■ **rear car lights:** no están funcionando bien estas calaveras these rear car lights aren't working well.

el **calcetín** *(plural* los calcetines) ■ **sock**.

el **calcio** ■ **calcium**.

la **calculadora** ■ **calculator**.

**calcular** *verbo*

1. **to calculate:** calcula el monto total y multiplícalo por dos calculate the total amount and multiply it by two
2. **to reckon:** calculo que este trabajo no nos conviene I reckon that this job doesn't suit us.

el **cálculo**

1. **estimate:** hice un cálculo de los costos I made an estimate of the costs
2. **calculus:** el cálculo es realmente difícil calculus is really difficult
3. **calculation:** según mis cálculos, estaremos en la capital antes del mediodía according to my calculations, we will be in the capital before noon
4. **stone:** me operé de unos cálculos en el riñón I was operated on for some kidney stones.

la **caldera**

1. **boiler:** las calderas de la fábrica funcionan todo el día the factory's boilers operate all day
2. **pot:** calentamos agua en una caldera we heated water in a pot.

el **caldo** ■ **broth:** haz el arroz en un caldo de gallina cook the rice in chicken broth.

la **calefacción** ■ **heating:** esta casa tiene muy buena calefacción this house has very good heating.

el **calefón** *(plural* los calefones) *Southern Cone* ■ **water heater:** este calefón tiene una capacidad de 50 litros this water heater has a capacity of 50 liters.

el **calendario**

1. **calendar:** en el calendario solar el año tiene aproximadamente 365 días by the solar calendar the year has approximately 365 days
2. **schedule:** marca los feriados en el calendario mark the holidays on the schedule.

el **calentador** ■ **heater:** el calentador se ha roto the heater has broken.

**calentar** *verbo*

1. **to heat up:** calienta la comida heat up the food
2. **to warm up:** necesito calentar antes del partido I need to warm up before the match.

la **calentura** ■ **fever:** el niño tiene calentura the boy has a fever.

la **caleta** ■ **cove**.

la **calidad** ■ **quality:** este mueble es de muy buena calidad this furniture is very good quality.

**caliente** *adjetivo*

1. **hot:** la plancha está muy caliente the iron is very hot
2. **heated:** es una discusión caliente it's a heated discussion.

la **calificación** *(plural* las calificaciones) ■ **grade:** saqué muy buenas calificaciones en el examen I got very good grades on the test.

**calificar** *verbo*

1. **to describe:** lo calificó de atrevido she described him as daring
2. **to grade:** los profesores calificaron generosamente the professors graded generously.

**callar** *verbo* ■ **to keep quiet:** en estas circunstancias prefiero callar in these circumstances I prefer to keep quiet

**callarse** *verbo* ■ **to stop talking:** todos se callaron cuando el viejo empezó a hablar everybody stopped talking when the old man began to speak

➤ callarse la boca to shut up: ¡cállate la boca! shut up!

la **calle** ■ **street**.

el **callejón** *(plural* los callejones) ■ **alley**.

el **callo**

1. **callus:** tengo un callo en la mano izquierda I have a callus on my left hand
2. **corn:** tengo un callo en el pie derecho I have a corn on my right foot.

la **calma** ■ calm: disfruto mucho la calma del campo I really enjoy the calm of the countryside
➤ mantengan la calma keep calm.

el **calmante**
1. painkiller: tomé un calmante para el dolor de cabeza I took a painkiller for my headache
2. sedative: el té de tilo es un calmante muy eficaz lime tea is a very effective sedative.

**calmar** *verbo*
1. to calm: la niña calmó a su hermano con palabras suaves the girl calmed her brother with gentle words
2. to relieve: la aspirina calma el dolor de cabeza aspirin relieves headaches

**calmarse** *verbo* ■ to calm down: cálmate, que ya vamos a llegar calm down, we'll arrive soon.

el **calor** ■ heat: no aguanto este calor I can't stand this heat
➤ ha hecho mucho calor estos días it's been really hot recently
➤ tengo calor I'm hot.

la **caloría** ■ calorie.

**calvo** *adjetivo* ■ bald.

la **calzada** ■ road.

el **calzado** ■ footwear: aquí el calzado es de muy buena calidad footwear is good quality here.

**calzar** *verbo* ■ to put shoes on: los niños están descalzos, cálzalos the children are barefoot, put shoes on them
➤ ¿cuánto calzas? what size shoe do you wear?

**calzarse** *verbo pronominal* ■ to put one's shoes on: cálzate, que vamos a salir put your shoes on, we're going out.

el **calzón** *(plural los calzones)*
1. *Mexico, River Plate* underwear
2. *Andes* panties.

el **calzoncillo** ■ underwear.

la **cama** ■ bed: hacer la cama to make one's bed.

la **cámara**
1. camera: me voy a comprar una cámara más moderna I'm going to buy myself a more up-to-date camera
2. house: la Cámara de Representantes tiene integrantes de cada estado the House of Representatives has members from every state
3. room: conservan la carne en cámaras frigoríficas they preserve meat in cold-storage rooms.

la **camarera** ■ waitress.

el **camarero** ■ waiter.

el **camarón** *(plural los camarones)* ■ shrimp.

el **camarote** ■ cabin: este barco tiene 400 camarotes this ship has 400 cabins.

**cambiar** *verbo*
1. to trade: te cambio mis medias rojas por las tuyas verdes I'll trade my red stockings for your green ones
2. to change: Pedro cambió mucho desde que llegó aquí Pedro has changed a lot since he arrived here; ayúdame a cambiar las sábanas help me change the sheets
3. to exchange: ¿dónde puedo cambiar dinero? where can I exchange money?
➤ cambiar de idea to change one's mind
➤ cambiar de ropa to change clothes

**cambiarse** *verbo pronominal* ■ to change: este vestido está sucio, me voy a cambiar this dress is dirty, I'm going to change
➤ cambiarse de casa to move: se cambiaron de casa, ya no somos más vecinos they moved, we are no longer neighbors.

el **cambio**
1. change: en las sociedades modernas, los cambios suceden muy rápido in modern societies, changes happen very rapidly; el cajero me dio mal el cambio the cashier gave me the wrong change
2. exchange: no se admiten cambios ni devoluciones exchanges and refunds are not allowed
3. small change: no tengo cambio para el camión I don't have small change for the bus

4. **gearshift:** este coche es automático, no tiene cambios this car is automatic, it doesn't have a manual gearshift
5. **exchange booth:** ¿dónde hay un cambio? preciso comprar dólares where is there an exchange booth? I need to get dollars
➤ **en cambio** on the other hand: a mí me gusta el rojo, en cambio él prefiere el azul I like the red one; on the other hand, he prefers the blue one.

el **camello** ▪ camel.

la **camilla**
1. *en una ambulancia* stretcher
2. *en la consulta* couch.

**caminar** *verbo* ▪ to walk.

el **camino**
1. *de un pueblo a otro* route: tomemos el camino más corto let's take the shortest route
2. *de una casa a otra* path: el camino no es muy ancho the path is not very wide
3. **way:** fuimos a mi casa y por el camino compramos una pizza we went to my house and on the way we bought a pizza.

el **camión** *(plural* los camiones)
1. **truck**
2. *México* bus.

la **camioneta** ▪ van.

la **camisa** ▪ shirt.

la **camiseta**
1. *exterior* T-shirt
2. *interior* undershirt.

el **camisón** *(plural* los camisones) ▪ nightgown.

el **camote** *Andes, Central America, Caribbean, Mexico* ▪ sweet potato *(plural* sweet potatoes).

el **campamento**
1. **camp:** armaron el campamento junto al río they set up camp next to the river
2. **camping:** estuvimos de campamento una semana we went camping for a week.

la **campana** ▪ bell.

la **campanada** ▪ peal: son las dos, acaban de sonar dos campanadas it's two o'clock, two peals just rang out.

la **campaña** ▪ campaign: la campaña contra el tabaquismo durará todo un mes the campaign against tobacco use will last a whole month
➤ una campaña electoral electoral campaign
➤ una campaña publicitaria advertising campaign.

el **campeón**, la **campeona** *(masculine plural* los campeones) ▪ champion.

el **campeonato** ▪ championship.

el **campesino**, la **campesina** ▪ peasant.

el **campo**
1. **country:** mis abuelos viven en el campo my grandparents live in the country
2. **countryside:** el campo está muy bonito en este momento the countryside looks very pretty right now
3. **field:** el campo de deportes está junto a la escuela the playing field is next to the school.

la **cana** ▪ white hair.

**Canadá** *sustantivo masculino* ▪ Canada.

**canadiense** *adjetivo*

En inglés, los adjetivos que se refieren a un país o una región se escriben con mayúscula:

Canadian

el/la **canadiense**

En inglés, los gentilicios se escriben con mayúscula:

Canadian.

el **canal**
1. **channel:** la programación de este canal es muy mala the programming of this channel is very poor
2. **canal**
➤ el Canal de Panamá the Panama Canal.

el **canario** ▪ canary *(plural* canaries).

el **canasto** ▪ basket.

**cancelar** *verbo* ■ to cancel.

el **cáncer** ■ cancer: la lucha contra el cáncer the fight against cancer.

la **cancha**
1. *de fútbol* field
2. *de básquetbol, tenis* court.

la **canción** *(plural* las canciones*)* ■ song.

el **candado** ■ padlock.

el **candelabro** ■ candelabra.

el **candidato,** la **candidata** ■ candidate: ser candidato a la presidencia to be a candidate for the presidency.

la **canela** ■ cinnamon.

el **cangrejo** ■ crab.

el **canguro** ■ kangaroo.

la **canica** ■ marble: la niña tiene muchas canicas the girl has many marbles
➤ jugar a las canicas to play marbles.

la **canilla**
➤ canilla de la pierna shinbone
➤ canilla del brazo armbone.

el **canino** ■ canine tooth *(plural* canine teeth*)*.

la **canoa** ■ canoe.

**canoso** *adjetivo* ■ white-haired.

**cansado** *adjetivo* ■ tired: estoy cansado I'm tired.

el **cansancio** ■ exhaustion
➤ ¡qué cansancio tengo! I'm exhausted!

**cansar** *verbo* ■ to tire: estudiar muchas horas seguidas me cansa studying for many hours in a row tires me
➤ cansarse de algo to get tired of something: me cansé de sus mentiras I got tired of his lies.

el/la **cantante** *sustantivo masculino y femenino* ■ singer.

**cantar** *verbo* ■ to sing.

la **cantidad** *(plural* las cantidades*)*
1. a lot: Luisa tiene una cantidad de fotos Luisa has a lot of photos

2. quantity *(plural* quantities*)*: hay que considerar la calidad más que la cantidad one must consider quality above quantity.

el **canto**
1. singing: María estudia canto, quiere ser soprano María studies singing; she wants to be a soprano
2. song: es hermoso el canto de ese canario that canary's song is beautiful.

la **caña** ■ cane
➤ caña de azúcar sugar cane
➤ caña de pescar fishing rod.

la **cañería** ■ piping: pusimos cañería nueva en la casa we put new piping in the house.

el **caño** ■ pipe: hubo que cambiar el caño roto we had to change the broken pipe.

el **cañón** *(plural* los cañones*)*
1. cannon: en ese fuerte hay varios cañones antiguos in that fort there are several old cannons
2. canyon: hay muchos cañones en esa cordillera there are many canyons in that mountain range
➤ el Gran Cañón the Grand Canyon.

el **caos** ■ chaos: los niños sembraron el caos en casa de sus abuelos the children created chaos at their grandparents' house.

la **capa**
1. cloak: Caperucita llevaba una capa roja Little Red Riding Hood wore a red cloak
2. layer: sacude la capa de polvo que hay sobre los muebles brush off the layer of dust that is on the furniture
➤ la capa de ozono the ozone layer.

la **capacidad**
1. capacity: la capacidad de esta jarra es un litro the capacity of this jar is one liter.
2. talent: tiene mucha capacidad para las ciencias she has a lot of talent for sciences.

el **caparazón** *(plural* los caparazones*)* ■ shell: la tortuga escondió patas y cabeza en su caparazón the turtle hid his feet and head inside his shell.

**capaz** *adjetivo* ■ capable: es un alumno muy capaz he's a very capable student

➤ **ser capaz de algo** to be capable of something: **Pedro no sería capaz de algo así** Pedro wouldn't be capable of something like that.

la **capilla** ■ chapel.

la **capital** ■ capital: **Lima es la capital de Perú** Lima is the capital of Peru.

el **capital** ■ capital: **el capital necesario para abrir una panadería es muy grande** the capital necessary to open a bakery is a lot.

el **capitalismo** ■ capitalism.

el **capitán, la capitana** (masculine plural los capitanes) ■ captain.

el **capítulo** ■ chapter.

el **capricho** ■ whim: **la tía le consiente todos los caprichos** her aunt caters to all her whims.

la **cápsula** ■ capsule: **estas cápsulas son antibióticos** these capsules are antibiotics; **fueron a la luna en una cápsula espacial** they went to the moon in a space capsule.

**captar** verbo
1. **to grasp:** **no capté lo que me dijiste** I didn't grasp what you told me
2. **to receive:** **el televisor está roto, no capta las imágenes** the television is broken; it doesn't receive the pictures.

**capturar** verbo ■ **to capture:** **la policía enseguida capturó a los asesinos** the police immediately captured the murderers.

la **cara**
1. **face:** **ve a lavarte la cara** go wash your face
2. **cheek:** **¡qué cara!** what cheek!
3. **side:** **la otra cara de un problema** the other side of a problem
➤ **cara o cruz** heads or tails
➤ **dar la cara** to face the consequences of one's actions.

el **caracol**
1. animal **snail**
2. concha **snail shell**.

el **carácter** (plural los caracteres)
■ **character:** **una mujer de carácter** a woman of character
➤ **tener buen carácter** to be good-natured
➤ **tener mal carácter** to be bad-tempered.

**característico** adjetivo ■ **characteristic:** **la alegría es un rasgo característico de los optimistas** happiness is characteristic of optimists

la **característica**
1. **characteristic:** **una característica de su escritura es que siempre es muy sencilla** a characteristic of his writing is that it's always very simple
2. **exchange code:** **la característica de Uruguay es 598** the exchange code of Uruguay is 598.

el **caramelo** ■ **candy:** **no comas caramelos antes del almuerzo** don't eat candy before lunch.

el **carbón** ■ **coal**
➤ **carbón de leña** charcoal.

la **carcajada** ■ **loud laugh:** **oímos una carcajada** we heard a loud laugh
➤ **reírse a carcajadas** to roar with laughter: **nos reímos a carcajadas con los cuentos de Pablo** we roared with laughter at Pablo's stories.

la **cárcel** ■ **prison:** **aún no salió de la cárcel** he still hasn't gotten out of prison.

el **cardenal**
1. **cardinal:** **los cardenales eligen al Papa** the cardinals elect the Pope
2. **bruise:** **tuvo un accidente y está lleno de cardenales** he had an accident and is covered with bruises.

**cardiaco** adjetivo ■ **cardiac**
➤ **un paro cardiaco** a cardiac arrest.

**cardinal** adjetivo ■ **cardinal:** **los puntos cardinales** the cardinal points.

la **cardiología** ■ **cardiology**.

el **cardo** ■ **thistle**.

la **carencia** ■ **lack:** **la carencia de alimentos ocasiona debilidad** lack of food causes weakness.

**49**

la **carga**

1. **load:** la carga de manzanas se cayó del camión the load of apples fell from the truck
2. **burden:** puedes quedarte en casa, no eres ninguna carga you can stay in my home, you're not a burden
➤ **carga y descarga** loading and unloading.

el **cargamento** ■ **load:** el camión traía un cargamento de manzanas the truck was carrying a load of apples.

**cargar** *verbo*

1. **to load:** cargamos las valijas en el auto y salimos hacia la estación we loaded the suitcases into the car and left for the station; **cargó el rifle y empezó a disparar** he loaded the rifle and began to shoot
2. **to charge:** preciso cargar la batería del celular I need to charge the cell phone battery.

el **cargo** ■ **position:** la presidencia es el principal cargo de gobierno the presidency is the foremost governmental position.

la **caricia** ■ **caress:** una tierna caricia a gentle caress
➤ **hacerle una caricia a alguien** to caress somebody: **le hizo una caricia a su hijo** she caressed her son.

la **caridad** ■ **charity** (plural **charities**).

la **caries** (plural las caries)

1. **tooth decay:** esta pasta dental previene las caries this toothpaste prevents tooth decay
2. **cavity** (plural **cavities**): voy al dentista, a que me arregle tres caries I'm going to the dentist so he can fill three cavities.

el **cariño**

1. **affection:** había mucho cariño en ese hogar there was a lot of affection in that home
2. **liking:** al cabo de una semana, el perro y el gato se tomaron cariño by the end of one week, the dog and the cat took a liking to each other
3. **Affectionately:** espero tu respuesta. Cariños, Marta I await your reply. Affectionately, Marta
4. *Mexico, Southern Cone* **caress**
➤ **hacerle cariños a alguien** to caress somebody: **siempre está haciéndole cariños al bebé** she's always caressing the baby.

el **carnaval** ■ **carnival**

CARNAVAL

Carnival is celebrated in many Latin American countries, lasting between three days and a week before Ash Wednesday, the beginning of Lent. The festivities include parades, shows, serenades, and water displays. In some regions, indigenous rituals are incorporated into the celebrations. Among the more famous carnivals are the ones in Veracruz, Mexico; Humahuaca in Argentina; and of course, Rio de Janeiro in Brazil.

la **carne** ■ **meat**
➤ **carne de cerdo** pork
➤ **carne de cordero** lamb
➤ **carne molida** ground beef
➤ **carne picada** *River Plate* ground beef
➤ **carne de puerco** *Mexico* pork
➤ **carne de res** *Mexico* beef
➤ **carne de vaca** beef.

el **carnet** ■ **card**
➤ **carnet de manejo** driver's license
➤ **carnet de identidad** identity card.

la **carnicería** ■ **butcher's shop**.

el **carnicero**, la **carnicera** ■ **butcher**.

**caro** *adjetivo, adverbio* ■ **expensive:** siempre compra ropa cara she always buys expensive clothes; **el viaje salió demasiado caro** the trip came out too expensive.

la **carpeta** ■ **folder**.

el **carpintero**, la **carpintera** ■ **carpenter**.

la **carrera**

1. **race:** con mucho esfuerzo gané la carrera with a lot of effort I won the race
2. **degree:** mi hermano está haciendo la carrera de medicina my brother is getting a degree in medicine
3. **career:** mi carrera me es muy importante my career is very important to me.

la **carreta** ■ **cart**.

la **carretera** ■ **road**.

el **carril** ■ **lane**.

el **carro**

1. **cart:** voy a buscar un carro para las valijas I'm going to look for a cart for the suitcases

**2.** *Andes, Caribbean, Central America, Mexico* **car:** compramos un carro nuevo we bought a new car

➤ un carro de bomberos fire truck
➤ un carro de carreras race car
➤ un carro de supermercado grocery cart.

la **carroza**
1. *arrastrada por caballos* **carriage**
2. *en cabalgata* **float**.

el **carrusel** (plural los carruseles) ■ **merry-go-round**.

la **carta**
1. **letter:** recibí una carta de mi prima I received a letter from my cousin
2. **card:** jugamos a las cartas toda la tarde we played cards all afternoon.

el **cartel** (plural los carteles) ■ **sign:** ahí hay un cartel de "Pare" there's a stop sign there.

la **cartelera**
1. **theater section:** no veo esa película en la cartelera de este diario I don't see that movie in the theater section of this newspaper
2. *River Plate* **message board:** fíjate si hay alguna noticia en la cartelera see if there is some information on the message board
➤ la obra estuvo más de un año en cartelera the play ran for more than a year.

la **cartera**
1. *Andes, Caribbean, Central America, Mexico para dinero* **wallet**
2. *River Plate de mujer* **purse**
3. *de colegio* **satchel**.

el **cartero**, la **cartera** ■ **mail carrier**.

el **cartón** (plural los cartones)
1. **cardboard:** preciso una caja de cartón para los zapatos I need a cardboard box for the shoes
2. **carton:** compramos dos cartones de huevos we bought two cartons of eggs.

el **cartucho** ■ **cartridge:** preciso cartuchos para la impresora I need cartridges for the printer.

la **cartulina** ■ **card**.

la **casa** ■ **house:** vive en una casa pequeña she lives in a small house

➤ bienvenido a casa welcome home.

el **casamiento** ■ **wedding:** el casamiento tuvo lugar en una capilla muy bonita the wedding took place in a very pretty chapel.

**casar** *verbo* ■ **to marry:** el sacerdote los casó en una ceremonia rápida the priest married them in a quick ceremony

**casarse** *verbo pronominal* ■ **to get married:** se casaron hace tres años they got married three years ago
➤ casarse con to get married to: Ana se casó con Pedro Ana got married to Pedro.

la **cascada** ■ **waterfall**.

la **cáscara**
1. *de huevo, nuez* **shell**
2. *de limón, naranja* **rind**.

el **casco** ■ **helmet:** siempre lleva casco he always wears a helmet.

la **casera** ■ *Mexico* **landlady** (plural landladies).

**casero** *adjetivo* ■ **homemade:** la comida casera es la más rica homemade food is the most delicious

el **casero** ■ *Mexico* **landlord:** mi casero vino a cobrar el alquiler my landlord came to collect the rent.

el/la **casete** ■ **cassette**.

**casi** *adverbio*
1. **almost:** son casi las once, vamos a dormir it's almost eleven o'clock, let's go to sleep
2. **hardly:** casi no dormí en toda la noche I hardly slept all night.

la **casilla**
1. **box:** complete todas las casillas complete all the boxes
2. **space:** te saltaste una casilla, vuelve para atrás you skipped a space, go back.

el **casillero**
1. **compartment:** en este casillero tengo las cuentas y en aquél las cartas in this compartment I have the bills, and in that one the letters

**51**

2. **locker**: dejó la ropa en un casillero he left his clothes in a locker.

el **caso** ■ case: el caso del asesino en serie fue muy comentado the case of the serial killer was discussed a lot

➤ **hacer caso** to pay attention: hazle caso a tu madre pay attention to your mother: no le hagas caso a tu hermano cuando se burla de ti don't pay attention to your brother when he makes fun of you.

la **caspa** ■ dandruff.

el **castellano**

> En inglés los nombres de los idiomas se escriben con mayúscula:

**Spanish**: estamos aprendiendo castellano we're learning Spanish.

**castigar** verbo ■ to punish: los niños se portaron mal y el padre los castigó the children behaved badly and their father punished them.

el **castigo** ■ punishment: como castigo, lavarás los platos hasta fin de mes as punishment, you will wash the dishes until the end of the month.

el **castillo** ■ castle.

la **casualidad** ■ coincidence: fue una casualidad que nos encontráramos en el parque it was a coincidence that we met in the park

➤ **de casualidad** by coincidence: nos encontramos en el parque de casualidad we met in the park by coincidence

➤ **por casualidad** by chance: ¿por casualidad viste a mi perro? by chance did you see my dog?

la **catarata**

1. **waterfall**: visitamos las cataratas del Iguazú we visited the Iguazú waterfalls

2. **cataract**: a la abuela la operaron de cataratas they operated on my grandmother's cataracts.

la **catástrofe** ■ catastrophe.

la **catedral** ■ cathedral.

la **categoría**

1. **category** (plural **categories**): había tres categorías: principiantes, intermedios y avanzados there were three categories: beginners, intermediate, and advanced

2. **quality**: es un hotel de categoría it's a quality hotel.

**católico** adjetivo

> En inglés las religiones y los miembros de una religión se escriben con mayúscula:

Catholic

el **católico**, la **católica** ■ Catholic.

**catorce** numeral ■ fourteen

➤ hoy es catorce de octubre today is the fourteenth of October.

el **cauce** ■ bed: el cauce del río se secó the river bed dried up.

el **caucho** ■ rubber.

el **caudillo** ■ leader.

la **causa** ■ cause: descubrieron la causa del incendio they discovered the cause of the fire.

**causar** verbo ■ to cause: un cortocircuito causó el incendio a short circuit caused the fire.

**cautivo** adjetivo ■ captive

el **cautivo**, la **cautiva** ■ captive.

**cavar** verbo ■ to dig: cavó varios hoyos para plantar flores he dug several holes to plant flowers.

la **caverna** ■ cavern.

la **caza** ■ hunting: aún hoy se practica la caza even today people go hunting.

**cazar** verbo ■ to hunt.

el **cazo**

1. **saucepan**: calienta el agua en un cazo heat the water in a saucepan

2. **ladle**: sirve la sopa con un cazo serve the soup with a ladle.

la **cazuela**

1. **pan**: pon esa cazuela en el horno put that pan in the oven

**52**

**2. stew:** comimos una cazuela de mariscos deliciosa we ate a delicious seafood stew.

el **CD** *(plural* los CDs) ■ **CD**.

el **CD-Rom** *(plural* los CD-Roms) ■ **CD-Rom**.

la **cebada** ■ **barley**.

**cebar** *River Plate verbo* ■ **to brew:** no todos saben cebar bien el mate not everybody knows how to brew "mate" well.

la **cebolla** ■ **onion**.

la **cebra** ■ **zebra**.

**ceder** *verbo*

**1. to give in:** al final, mi madre cedió y me prestó el coche in the end, my mother gave in and loaned me the car

**2. to give way:** el televisor era demasiado pesado y la mesa cedió the television was too heavy and the table gave way.

la **cédula**
➤ la cédula de identidad identity card.

la **ceguera** ■ **blindness**.

la **ceja** ■ **eyebrow**.

la **celda** ■ **cell**.

**celebrar** *verbo*

**1. to celebrate:** celebró su cumpleaños con una fiesta he celebrated his birthday with a party

**2. to hold:** celebraron la reunión en el salón de actos they held the meeting in the assembly hall.

los **celos** ■ **jealousy:** lo hizo por celos she did it out of jealousy
➤ Pepe tiene celos de su hermana Pepe is jealous of his sister
➤ coquetea con otras mujeres para darle celos he flirts with other women to make her jealous.

**celoso** *adjetivo* ■ **jealous:** es muy celosa she's a jealous person; está celoso de Lupe he's jealous of Lupe.

la **célula** ■ **cell**.

el **celular** ■ **cellular telephone**.

el **cementerio** ■ **cemetery** *(plural* cemeteries)*:* el funeral se celebró en el cementerio the funeral was held at the cemetery
➤ un cementerio de automóviles a junkyard.

el **cemento**
**1.** *material de construcción* **cement**
**2.** *adhesivo* **glue**.

la **cena** ■ **dinner**.

**cenar** *verbo* ■ **to have dinner:** cenamos a las nueve we have dinner at nine o'clock
➤ sólo cené pescado I only ate fish for dinner.

el **cenicero** ■ **ashtray**.

la **ceniza** ■ **ash**.

el **centavo** ■ **cent:** cuesta tres dólares y cuarenta centavos it costs three dollars and forty cents
➤ no tengo ni un centavo I'm broke.

**central** *adjetivo* ■ **central**.

la **central**
**1.** *oficina central* **head office**
**2.** *de energía* **power station**
➤ una central camionera *Mexico* a bus station
➤ una central eléctrica a power plant
➤ una central nuclear a nuclear power plant.

el **centro** ■ **center:** vivo en el centro de Lima I live in the center of Lima
➤ tengo que ir al centro I have to go into town
➤ las tiendas del centro the downtown stores
➤ un centro comercial a shopping mall.

el **ceño** ■ **frown**
➤ frunció el ceño he frowned
➤ lo miró con el ceño fruncido she frowned at him.

**cepillar** *verbo* ■ **to brush**
➤ se cepilló los dientes he brushed his teeth.

el **cepillo** ■ **brush**
➤ el cepillo del pelo the hairbrush
➤ el cepillo de dientes the toothbrush.

la **cera** ■ wax.

la **cerámica** ■ pottery: mi mamá estudia cerámica my mom studies pottery
➤ una cerámica a piece of pottery.

**cerca** *adverbio* ■ close: mi casa está muy cerca my house is very close
➤ ¿hay una farmacia cerca? is there a pharmacy nearby?
➤ queda cerca de la escuela it's near the school
➤ cerca de cien personas around 100 people
➤ me acerqué para verlo de cerca I drew near in order to see it close up
➤ los exámenes ya están cerca exams are already coming up soon

la **cerca**
1. *de madera, alambre* fence
2. *de piedra* wall.

**cercano** *adjetivo*
1. nearby: los pueblos cercanos the nearby towns
2. close: un pariente cercano a close relative; la zona cercana a la estación the area close to the station
➤ una cifra cercana al millón a figure approaching a million.

el **cerdo**
1. *animal* pig: crían cerdos they raise pigs
2. *carne* pork: ayer comimos cerdo yesterday we ate pork
➤ comí como un cerdo *informal* I ate like a pig.

el **cereal** ■ cereal: siempre desayuno cereal I always eat cereal for breakfast.

el **cerebro** ■ brain.

la **ceremonia** ■ ceremony *(plural* ceremonies).

la **cereza** ■ cherry *(plural* cherries).

la **cerilla** ■ match: no juegues con cerillas don't play with matches.

el **cerillo** *Central America, Mexico* ■ match: necesito un cerillo para encender el horno I need a match to light the oven.

el **cero** ■ zero *(plural* zeroes o zeros)
➤ el primer número es cero the first number is zero
➤ cero coma dos zero point two
➤ tenemos dos grados bajo cero it's two degrees below zero
➤ ganaron tres a cero they won three to zero
➤ fue un empate a cero it was a no-score tie
➤ cuarenta cero *en tenis* forty-love
➤ tuvimos que empezar desde cero we had to start from scratch.

el **cerquillo** ■ bangs.

**cerrado** *adjetivo* ■ closed: la tienda estaba cerrada the store was closed
➤ está cerrado con llave it's locked
➤ deja la llave cerrada leave the faucet off
➤ el sobre venía cerrado the envelope came sealed.

la **cerradura** ■ lock.

**cerrar** *verbo*
1. to close: cerró la ventana he closed the window; la biblioteca cierra a las cinco the library closes at five
2. to turn off: cierra bien la llave turn the faucet off completely
➤ ¿cerraste la puerta con llave? did you lock the door?

**cerrarse** *verbo* ■ to close: la ventana se cerró con el viento the window closed with the wind
➤ se me cerraban los ojos I couldn't keep my eyes open.

el **cerro** ■ hill.

el **cerrojo** ■ bolt.

**certificado** *adjetivo* ■ certified: mandé la carta certificada I sent the letter certified.

el **certificado** ■ certificate.

la **cerveza** ■ beer: fueron a tomar unas cervezas they went to have a few beers
➤ cerveza de barril draft beer.

el **césped** ■ lawn
➤ "prohibido pisar el césped" "keep off the lawn".

la **cesta** ■ basket.

el **cesto** ▪ basket
➤ el cesto de los papeles the wastepaper basket.

la **chacra** *Andes, River Plate* ▪ **small farm**.

el **chaleco** ▪ vest
➤ un chaleco salvavidas a lifejacket.

el **chamaco**, la **chamaca** *Mexico* ▪ kid.

la **chamarra** *Mexico* ▪ jacket.

la **chamba**
1. *Mexico, Peru, Venezuela* trabajo informal **work**
2. *Colombia* zanja **ditch**.

el **champán** (plural los champanes) ▪ champagne.

el **champiñón** (plural los champiñones) ▪ mushroom.

el **champú** (plural los champús) ▪ shampoo.

el **chancho**, la **chancha** *Andes, Central America, River Plate* ▪ **pig:** mataron un chancho they killed a pig
➤ comí como chancho *informal* I ate like a pig
➤ carne de chancho *Andes* pork.

la **chancleta** ▪ flip-flop.

el **changador** *River Plate* ▪ **porter**.

el **chantaje** ▪ blackmail: un caso de chantaje a case of blackmail
➤ le hicieron un chantaje they blackmailed him.

**chantajear** *verbo* ▪ to blackmail: lo chantajearon por mucho dinero they blackmailed him for a lot of money.

**chao** *interjección* ▪ bye.

la **chapa**
1. *de metal* **sheet**
2. *cerradura* **lock**
3. *insignia* **badge**
4. *River Plate* de la matrícula **license plate**.

**chaparro** *Central America, Andes, Mexico* adjetivo ▪ **short**.

el **chaparrón** (plural los chaparrones) ▪ downpour.

el **chapopote** *Mexico*
1. *alquitrán* **tar**
2. *asfalto* **asphalt**.

**chapotear** *verbo* ▪ to splash around: los niños chapotearon en la piscina the children splashed around in the swimming pool.

el **chapuzón** (plural los chapuzones) ▪ dip
➤ nos dimos un chapuzón we went for a dip.

la **chaqueta** ▪ jacket
➤ una chaqueta de fuerza a straitjacket.

el **charco** ▪ puddle.

la **charla**
1. **chat:** estaban de charla they were having a chat
2. **talk:** dio una charla sobre el medioambiente she gave a talk about the environment.

**charlar** *verbo* ▪ to chat: charlaron de sus novios they chatted about their boyfriends.

**charlatán**, **charlatana** *adjetivo* ▪ talkative

el **charlatán**, la **charlatana** ▪ chatterbox.

la **charola** *Bolivia, Mexico, Peru* ▪ tray.

el **charro**, la **charra** ▪ *a traditional Mexican horseman or horsewoman*

> **CHARRO**
>
> The **charro** is the traditional Mexican cowboy, who wears embroidered costumes and wide-brimmed hats. **Charreadas** are rodeos where the cowboys rope cows, bulls, and horses. Over centuries of perfecting their skills on ranches, Mexican cowboys have made **charrería** (or rodeo riding) a national institution. Nowadays however, real **charros** no longer exist but can still be found in special clubs that organize **charreadas**.

el **chasco** ▪ disappointment: ¡qué chasco! what a disappointment!

➤ **nos llevamos un chasco** we were disappointed.

la **chatarra** ■ junk.

la **chaucha** *Paraguay, River Plate* ■ green bean.

la **chava** *Mexico*
1. *niña* girl
2. *novia* girlfriend.

el **chavo** *Mexico*
1. *niño* boy
2. *novio* boyfriend.

**checar** *Mexico verbo* ■ to check: **voy a checar si funciona** I'm going to check whether it works
➤ **las fechas no checan** the dates don't check out.

**chele** *Central America adjetivo*
1. *de pelo* blond
2. *de piel* fair.

el **cheque** ■ check
➤ **un cheque de viaje** a traveler's check.

**chévere** *Latin America except Southern Cone adjetivo* ■ excellent.

**chícharo** *Cuba, Mexico sustantivo masculino* ■ pea.

el **chichón** (plural los chichones) ■ bump: **tiene un chichón en la cabeza** he has a bump on his head.

el **chicle** ■ chewing gum: **le gusta mascar chicle** she likes to chew chewing gum
➤ **¿me das un chicle?** may I have a piece of chewing gum?
➤ **chicle de globito** bubble gum.

la **chica** ■ girl: **es una chica muy simpática** she's a very nice girl.

**chico** *adjetivo*
1. *de tamaño* small: **el baño es muy chico** the bathroom is very small; **estos pantalones me quedan chicos** these pants are too small for me
2. *de edad* young: **cuando era chica jugaba con él** when she was young she played with him

el **chico** ■ boy: **es un chico muy simpático** he's a very nice boy
➤ **los chicos del vecino** the neighbor's kids.

el **chile** ■ chili pepper.

**Chile** *sustantivo masculino* ■ Chile.

**chileno** *adjetivo*

> En inglés, los adjetivos que se refieren a un país o una región se escriben con mayúscula:

**Chilean: el paisaje chileno es muy bello** the Chilean landscape is very beautiful

el **chileno, la chilena**

> En inglés, los gentilicios se escriben con mayúscula:

**Chilean: los chilenos** the Chileans.

**chillar** *verbo*
1. *una persona* to scream
2. *un cerdo* to squeal
3. *un ratón* to squeak.

la **chimenea**
1. fireplace: **nos sentamos frente a la chimenea** we sat down in front of the fireplace
2. chimney: **las chimeneas de la fábrica** the factory chimneys.

el **chimpancé** ■ chimpanzee.

el **chinche**
1. *insecto* bedbug
2. *Andes clavito* thumbtack.

la **chinche** *Central America, Mexico, River Plate* ■ thumbtack.

el **chiquero** ■ pigsty: **su casa es un chiquero** his house is a pigsty.

el **chiquillo, la chiquilla** ■ child.

**chirriar** *verbo*
1. *una puerta, bisagra* to squeak
2. *los frenos, neumáticos* to squeal.

el **chisme**
1. gossip: **se pasó dos horas contando chismes** he spent two hours talking gossip
2. *Mexico* thing: **¿para qué sirve este chisme?** what is this thing for?

**chismoso** *adjetivo*
➤ es muy chismoso he's a real gossip.

la **chispa** ■ **spark:** saltaron chispas del fuego sparks popped out of the fire
➤ tiene mucha chispa he's lively
➤ una chispa de sal a pinch of salt.

el **chiste** ■ **joke:** estaban contando chistes they were telling jokes
➤ un chiste colorado *Mexico* a dirty joke
➤ un chiste picante a dirty joke
➤ un chiste verde a dirty joke.

**chistoso** *adjetivo* ■ **funny**.

**chocar** *verbo* ■ **to crash:** chocó contra un árbol he crashed into a tree
➤ choqué con él a la salida I bumped into him on the way out
➤ chocaron de frente they collided head on
➤ me choca el vocabulario que usan the vocabulary that they use shocks me
➤ me choca cuando hace eso *Colombia, Mexico, Venezuela* it bothers me when he does that
➤ ¡chócala! give me five!

el **choclo** *Andes, River Plate* ■ **corn**.

el **chocolate** ■ **chocolate:** me encanta el chocolate I love chocolate
➤ me dio un chocolate she gave me a piece of chocolate
➤ me tomé un chocolate I drank a hot chocolate.

el/la **chofer**
1. *de un coche, camión* **driver**
2. *empleado* **chauffeur**
➤ una limusina con chofer a chauffeur-driven limousine.

el **choque** ■ **crash:** hubo un choque frente al colegio there was a crash in front of the school.

el **chorizo** ■ **pork sausage**.

el **chorro**
1. **stream:** un chorro de agua a stream of water
2. *Central America, Venezuela* **faucet:** tomó agua del chorro she drank water from the faucet
➤ el agua salía a chorros the water was gushing out

➤ un avión a chorro a jet plane
➤ me gusta un chorro ese cantante *Mexico informal* I like that singer a lot.

la **choza** ■ **hut**.

**chueco** *adjetivo* ■ **crooked:** esta raya está chueca this line is crooked; siempre escribo chueco I always write crooked.

la **chuleta**
1. **chop:** una chuleta de cordero a lamb chop
2. *Venezuela* **cheat sheet:** lo sorprendieron copiando de una chuleta they surprised him copying from a cheat sheet.

**chulo** *Mexico informal adjetivo* ■ **cute:** mira, ¡qué vestido tan chulo! look, what a cute dress!
➤ tu hermana es muy chula *Mexico* your sister is very pretty.

**chupar** *verbo* ■ **to suck:** no te chupes el dedo don't suck your finger.

el **chupete**
1. *del bebé* **pacifier**
2. *Andes dulce* **lollipop**
➤ chupete helado *Chile* popsicle.

el **chupón** *(plural los chupones)*
1. *del bebé* **pacifier**
2. *Mexico del biberón* **nipple**.

el **churrasco** ■ **barbecue**.

el **churro** ■ *twisted strip of deep-fried batter sprinkled with confectioner's sugar*.

el **cibercafé** ■ **Internet café**.

la **cicatriz** *(plural las cicatrices)* ■ **scar:** le va a quedar una cicatriz en la frente she's going to have a scar on her forehead.

el **ciclismo** ■ **cycling:** el ciclismo es un deporte bastante popular cycling is a pretty popular sport.

el **ciclo** ■ **cycle:** el ciclo de las estaciones the cycle of the seasons
➤ mi hermana menor está en el primer ciclo my little sister is in the first grade.

el **ciclón** *(plural los ciclones)* ■ **cyclone**.

la **ciclovía** ■ **bicycle path**.

**ciego** *adjetivo* ■ **blind:** es ciega she's blind

➤ se quedó ciego he went blind
➤ es ciego de nacimiento he's blind from birth.

el **cielo**
1. **sky** *(plural* **skies***)*: el cielo estaba despejado the sky was clear
2. **heaven:** dice que su perro está en el cielo she says that her dog is in heaven.

**cien** *numeral* ■ **a hundred:** vinieron cerca de cien personas around a hundred people came; más de cien mil dólares more than a hundred thousand dollars
➤ cien por ciento one hundred percent: es cien por ciento biodegradable it's one hundred percent biodegradable.

la **ciencia** ■ **science:** la ciencia moderna modern science; mañana tengo ciencias tomorrow I have science
➤ ciencia ficción science fiction: una película de ciencia ficción a science fiction movie
➤ ciencias naturales natural sciences.

**científico** *adjetivo* ■ **scientific**

el **científico,** la **científica** ■ **scientist.**

**ciento** *numeral* ■ **a hundred:** ciento cincuenta pesos a hundred and fifty pesos
➤ había cientos de personas there were hundreds of people
➤ por ciento percent: el treinta por ciento de los alumnos thirty percent of the students.

el **cierre**
1. *de collar, pulsera* **clasp**
2. *de un vestido, pantalón* **zipper:** no me puedo subir el cierre I can't zip the zipper
3. *de una fábrica, discoteca* **closing-down.**

**cierto** *adjetivo*
1. **true:** ¡eso no es cierto! that's not true!
2. **certain:** ciertas personas piensan que es culpable certain people think that he's guilty.

el **ciervo,** la **cierva** ■ **deer** *(plural* **deer***).*

la **cifra** ■ **figure:** un número de dos cifras a two-figure number.

el **cigarrillo** ■ **cigarette.**

el **cigarro** ■ **cigar.**

la **cigüeña** ■ **stork.**

la **cima** ■ **top:** subieron hasta la cima they went up to the top.

los **cimientos** ■ **foundations.**

**cinco** *numeral* ■ **five:** tiene cinco hijos she has five children; mi hermana tiene cinco años my sister is five years old
➤ son las cinco it's five o'clock
➤ el cinco de abril the fifth of April.

**cincuenta** *numeral*
1. **fifty:** unas cincuenta personas some fifty people; tiene cincuenta años he's fifty years old.

el **cine**
1. **movie theater:** un cine de barrio a local movie theater
2. **cinema:** el cine mexicano Mexican cinema
➤ fuimos al cine we went to the movies
➤ un artista de cine a movie actor.

**cínico** *adjetivo* ■ **cynical:** es muy cínico he's very cynical

el **cínico,** la **cínica** ■ **cynic.**

la **cinta**
1. **ribbon:** se amarró el pelo con una cinta she tied her hair back with a ribbon
2. **tape:** una cinta virgen a blank tape
➤ cinta adhesiva adhesive tape
➤ cinta Dúrex® Scotch tape®
➤ cinta pegante *Colombia* adhesive tape.

la **cintura** ■ **waist:** me aprieta en la cintura it's too tight in the waist.

el **cinturón** *(plural* los cinturones*)* ■ **belt**
➤ cinturón de seguridad safety belt.

el **circo** ■ **circus.**

el **circuito**
1. *deportes* **track:** una vuelta al circuito a lap around the track
2. *electricidad* **circuit:** circuito cerrado de televisión closed-circuit television.

la **circulación**
1. **traffic:** una calle de mucha circulación a street with a lot of traffic
2. **circulation:** tengo muy buena circulación I have very good circulation.

**58**

**circular** *verbo*

1. *en coche* **to drive:** en ese país circulan por la izquierda in that country they drive on the left side of the road
2. *las personas* **to move about:** podemos circular libremente por el colegio we can move about freely through the school
3. *la sangre, el aire* **to circulate:** abran la puerta para que circule el aire open the window so that the air will circulate
4. *un rumor, una noticia* **to go around:** son rumores que circulan en el colegio they're rumors that go around the school
➤ ¡circulen, por favor! move along, please!

el **círculo** ■ **circle:** dibujamos un círculo we drew a circle; nos sentamos en círculo we sat down in a circle.

la **circunferencia** ■ **circumference**.

la **circunstancia** ■ **circumstance**
➤ bajo ninguna circunstancia under no circumstance
➤ dadas las circunstancias given the circumstances
➤ avísame, si por alguna circunstancia no puedes venir let me know if by some chance you can't come.

la **ciruela** ■ **plum**.

la **cirugía** ■ **surgery:** se hizo la cirugía plástica she had plastic surgery.

el **cirujano**, la **cirujana** ■ **surgeon**.

el **cisne** ■ **swan**.

la **cita**

1. **appointment:** mi mamá tiene una cita con el director my mom has an appointment with the director
2. **date:** tiene una cita con su novio she has a date with her boyfriend
3. **quotation:** una cita de Rubén Darío a quotation from Rubén Darío.

**citar** *verbo* ■ **to quote:** citó un pasaje de la Biblia he quoted a passage from the Bible
➤ la citaron a las nueve they gave her an appointment for nine o'clock
➤ se citaban a escondidas they were meeting secretly.

la **ciudad**

> **City** hace referencia a ciudades grandes y **town** a un pueblo grande o ciudad pequeña.

1. **city** *(plural* **cities***):* en ciudades como Buenos Aires in cities like Buenos Aires
2. **town:** vive en una ciudad de muy pocos habitantes he lives in a town with very few inhabitants
➤ una ciudad balneario a coastal resort
➤ una ciudad perdida *Mexico* a shanty town
➤ la ciudad universitaria the university campus.

el **ciudadano**, la **ciudadana** ■ **citizen:** es ciudadano peruano he's a Peruvian citizen.

**civil** *adjetivo* ■ **civil**
➤ derechos civiles civil rights.

la **civilización** *(plural* las civilizaciones*)* ■ **civilization:** las grandes civilizaciones antiguas the great ancient civilizations.

la **clara** ■ **egg white:** hay que batir las claras you have to beat the egg whites.

**claro** *adjetivo*

1. **clear:** su explicación fue muy clara his explanation was very clear; está claro que miente it's clear that he's lying
2. **light:** prefiere los colores claros she prefers light colors; tiene los ojos verde claro he has light green eyes
➤ no saqué nada en claro con su explicación I didn't get anything clarified by his explanation
➤ dejó en claro que no iba a ir he made it clear that he wasn't going to go

**claro** *adverbio* ■ **clearly:** no lo veo muy claro I don't see it very clearly
➤ tienes que hablarle claro you have to be frank with him
➤ ¡claro! of course!
➤ ¡claro que sí! yes, of course!
➤ ¡claro que no! of course not!

la **clase**

1. **classroom:** los alumnos estaban en la clase cuando llegó el maestro the students were in the classroom when the teacher arrived

**2. class:** esa niña está en mi clase that girl is in my class; hoy tuvimos clase de historia today we had history class

**3. type:** en esta región crecen varias clases de manzana in this region they grow various types of apple

➤ clase baja lower class

➤ clase media middle class

➤ clase alta upper class.

**clásico** *adjetivo* ■ **classical:** le gusta la música clásica she likes classical music

el **clásico** ■ **classic:** Cervantes es un clásico de la literatura Cervantes is a literary classic.

**clasificar** *verbo* ■ **to classify:** en la clase de biología clasificamos varias plantas in biology class we classified a number of plants.

**clavar** *verbo* ■ **to nail:** no permiten clavar nada en estas paredes they don't permit anything to be nailed into these walls

**clavarse** *verbo pronominal* ■ **to prick oneself:** cuidado no vayas a clavarte una espina careful not to prick yourself on a thorn; se clavó una aguja she stuck a needle into herself.

la **clave**

**1. key:** descubrimos la clave del problema we discovered the key to the problem

**2. code:** este mensaje está en clave, por eso no lo entendemos this message is in code; that's why we don't understand it.

el **clavel** ■ **carnation.**

la **clavícula** ■ **collar bone.**

el **clavo** ■ **nail.**

la **clemencia** ■ **clemency.**

el **clero** ■ **clergy.**

el **cliente,** la **clienta** ■ **client.**

el **clima** ■ **climate.**

la **clínica** ■ **clinic.**

el **clip** *(plural* los clips*)* ■ **paper clip.**

el **cloro** ■ **chlorine.**

el **club** *(plural* los clubes*)* ■ **club.**

**coagularse** *verbo pronominal* ■ **to clot:** la sangre se coagula rápidamente blood clots quickly.

**cobarde** *adjetivo* ■ **cowardly**

➤ ¡no seas cobarde! don't be a coward!

la **cobaya** ■ **guinea pig.**

la **cobija** ■ **blanket.**

el **cobrador,** la **cobradora** ■ **collector.**

**cobrar** *verbo*

**1. to charge:** me cobraron 100 pesos por el almuerzo they charged me 100 pesos for lunch

**2. to receive:** cobra 10.000 pesos de sueldo mensual she receives 10,000 pesos as a monthly salary

**3. to collect:** viene todos los meses a cobrar el alquiler he comes every month to collect the rent

➤ se cobra, por favor the bill, please.

el **cobre** ■ **copper.**

la **cocción** ■ **cooking time:** este arroz precisa sólo diez minutos de cocción this rice needs only ten minutes of cooking time.

**cocer** *verbo*

**1. to cook:** cuece el pescado cuarenta minutos en la cacerola you cook the fish forty minutes in the pan

**2. to boil:** cuece las zanahorias quince minutos you boil the carrots fifteen minutes

➤ este arroz tarda sólo diez minutos en cocerse this rice only takes ten minutes to cook.

el **coche**

**1.** *automóvil* car

**2.** *para bebés* carriage.

la **cochera** ■ **garage.**

**cochino** *adjetivo* ■ **filthy:** estás cochino, ¡ve a lavarte! you're filthy, go wash up!

el **cochino** ■ **pig.**

el **cocido** ■ **stew.**

la **cocina**

**1. kitchen:** esta casa tiene una cocina muy amplia this house has a very spacious kitchen

2. **stove:** ayer compramos una cocina nueva yesterday we bought a new stove
➤ un curso de cocina a cooking course
➤ un libro de cocina a cookbook.

**cocinar** verbo ■ **to cook:** voy a cocinar un pollo I'm going to cook a chicken.

el **cocinero,** la **cocinera** ■ cook.

el **coco** ■ coconut.

el **cocodrilo** ■ crocodile.

el **cocotero** ■ coconut palm tree.

la **codicia** ■ greed.

el **código** ■ code
➤ un código de barras a barcode
➤ un código postal a zip code
➤ un código secreto a password.

el **codo** ■ **elbow:** se hizo daño en el codo he hurt his elbow.

la **codorniz** (plural las codornices) ■ **quail.**

**coger** verbo

1. **to get:** cogió sus llaves y salió he got his keys and left
2. **to catch:** la policía cogió al ladrón inmediatamente the police caught the thief immediately
3. **to take:** cogí el autobús para ir al cine I took the bus to go to the movies.

el **cohete** ■ rocket.

**coincidir** verbo ■ **to coincide:** su cumpleaños coincide con Navidad his birthday coincides with Christmas.

**cojear** verbo

1. **to limp:** la vieja cojea mucho the old woman limps a lot
2. **to wobble:** esa mesa cojea that table wobbles.

la **col** ■ cabbage.

la **cola**

1. **tail:** el pavo real tiene una cola hermosa the peacock has a beautiful tail
2. **line:** si llegas temprano, no tendrás que hacer cola if you arrive early, you won't have to get in line

3. **glue:** tengo que pegar estos dos papeles con cola I have to paste these two papers with glue.

**colaborar** verbo ■ **to help:** colabora con la limpieza, no tires papeles al piso help with the cleaning, don't throw paper on the floor.

el **colador** ■ strainer.

**colar** verbo ■ **to strain:** cuela los fideos, mientras yo rallo el queso strain the noodles while I grate the cheese

**colarse** verbo pronominal ■ **to slip into:** presta atención, siempre hay alguien que se cuela en la fila pay attention, there is always somebody who slips into the line.

la **colcha** ■ bedspread.

el **colchón** (plural los colchones) ■ mattress.

la **colección** (plural las colecciones) ■ collection: tiene una colección de estampillas de todo el mundo he has a collection of stamps from all over the world.

**coleccionar** verbo ■ **to collect:** hace muchos años que colecciona sellos he has been collecting stamps for many years.

el **colectivo**

1. Andes **collective taxi**
2. Argentina **bus.**

el/la **colega** ■ colleague.

el **colegial** ■ schoolboy.

la **colegiala** ■ schoolgirl.

el **colegio** ■ school.

la **cólera** ■ anger.

el **cólera** ■ cholera.

**colgar** verbo

1. **to hang:** cuelga tu chaqueta en esa percha hang your jacket on that rack
2. **to hang up:** colgó sin despedirse he hung up without saying goodbye.

el **cólico** ■ colic.

la **coliflor** ■ cauliflower.

la **colina** ■ hill.

el **collar** ■ necklace.

la **colmena** ■ beehive.

el **colmillo** ■ canine tooth (plural **canine teeth**).

el **colmo** ■ height: el colmo de arrogancia the height of arrogance
➤ ¡esto es el colmo! this is the limit!

**colocar** verbo ■ to place: coloca este florero arriba de la mesa place this vase on the table

**colocarse** verbo pronominal ■ to station oneself: colóquense cerca de los árboles station yourselves close to the trees
➤ colóquese en la fila get in line.

**Colombia** sustantivo femenino ■ Colombia.

**colombiano** adjetivo

En inglés, los adjetivos que se refieren a un país o una región se escriben con mayúscula:

**Colombian**

el **colombiano,** la **colombiana**

En inglés los gentilicios se escriben con mayúscula:

**Colombian:** los colombianos the Colombians.

la **colonia**
1. perfume: prefiero las colonias florales I prefer floral perfumes
2. colony (plural **colonies**): España tenía colonias en América y África Spain had colonies in America and Africa
3. Mexico district: viven en la colonia Obregón they live in the Obregón district.

**colonizar** verbo ■ to colonize: los españoles colonizaron una gran parte de América the Spanish colonized a large part of America.

el **color** ■ color.

**colorado** adjetivo ■ red.

**colorear** verbo ■ to color: ahora que dibujaste el paisaje, coloréalo now that you've drawn the landscape, color it.

la **columna**
1. column: la fachada está adornada con columnas the façade is adorned with columns
2. spine: el ortopedista trata los problemas de la columna the orthopedist treats problems of the spine
➤ columna vertebral spinal column.

la **coma**
1. comma: en esa oración no hay que poner coma allí that sentence doesn't require a comma there
2. point: tres coma cinco three point five.

el **coma** ■ coma
➤ estar en coma to be in a coma.

el **combate**
1. battle: el combate fue largo y dejó varios heridos the battle was long and left a number of wounded people
2. fight: hay que empeñarse en el combate a las drogas we have to get involved in the fight against drugs.

**combatir** verbo
1. to fight: estos soldados combatieron en la última guerra these soldiers fought in the last war
2. to combat: es importante combatir la desnutrición it's important to combat malnutrition.

la **combinación** (plural las combinaciones) ■ combination: azul y rojo es una buena combinación de colores blue and red is a good color combination.

el **combustible** ■ fuel: este carro precisa combustible urgentemente this car needs fuel urgently.

la **combustión** ■ combustion: la combustión se estudia en clase de química combustion is studied in chemistry class.

la **comedia**
1. comedy (plural **comedies**): Molière es autor de excelentes comedias Molière is the author of excellent comedies

**2.** *Argentina* **soap opera:** esta comedia empezó hace más de un año this soap opera began more than a year ago.

el **comedor**

**1.** *en casa* **dining room**

**2.** *en colegio* **cafeteria.**

**comentar** *verbo*

**1.** **to discuss:** en clase comentamos los textos que leemos en casa in class we discuss the texts that we read at home

**2.** **to comment:** comentó que hacía mucho frío afuera he commented that it was very cold outside.

**comenzar** *verbo* ■ **to begin:** las clases comienzan a las ocho classes begin at eight o'clock.

**comer** *verbo*

**1.** **to eat:** ¿comiste suficiente? did you eat enough?

**2.** *a mediodía* **to eat lunch:** comemos normalmente a las dos we usually eat lunch at two

**3.** *por la noche* **to eat dinner:** comemos normalmente a las ocho we usually eat dinner at eight

➤ comimos pollo we had chicken for lunch

➤ comimos una pizza we had a pizza for dinner.

el **comercial** ■ **commercial:** no me gusta que interrumpan la película con comerciales I don't like it when the movie is interrupted with commercials.

el/la **comerciante** ■ **merchant.**

el **comercio** ■ **commerce**

➤ comercio electrónico e-commerce.

**comestible** *adjetivo* ■ **edible**

el **comestible** ■ **food:** hay que llevar comestibles para los tres días de campamento we have to take food for the three days of camp

➤ tienda de comestibles grocery store.

la **cometa** ■ **kite.**

el **cometa** ■ **comet.**

**cometer** *verbo*

**1.** **to commit:** cometió muchos crímenes antes de morir he commited many crimes before he died

**2.** **to make:** cometí un error muy grave I made a very serious error.

la **comezón** ■ **itching:** los piquetes de mosquitos dan comezón mosquito bites cause itching.

la **cómica** ■ **comedienne.**

**cómico** *adjetivo* ■ **funny:** la película que vimos ayer era muy cómica the movie we saw yesterday was very funny

el **cómico** ■ **comedian:** Cantinflas fue un cómico muy famoso Cantinflas was a very famous comedian.

la **comida**

**1.** **food:** me gusta preparar la comida con productos frescos I like to prepare the food with fresh products

**2.** **meal:** tomar un comprimido antes de cada comida take one pill before each meal

**3.** *a mediodía* **lunch**

**4.** *por la noche* **dinner**

> **COMIDA**
>
>  In some Spanish-speaking countries (Bolivia, Uruguay, and Venezuela) **comida** can refer to lunch or dinner, while in other places (Chile, Colombia, and Peru) it only refers to dinner. This can lead to confusion, so it's best to make sure you know which meal the speaker is referring to if you are invited to a **comida.**

el **comienzo** ■ **beginning.**

las **comillas** ■ **quotation marks.**

la **comisaría** ■ **police station.**

**como** *(adverbio & conjunción)*

■ *adverbio*

**1.** **like:** tu bicicleta es como la mía your bicycle is like mine

**2.** **as:** eres tan inteligente como ella you're as intelligent as her; como te decía la semana pasada... as I was telling you last week...

**3.** **around:** llegaron como a las diez they arrived around ten o'clock

■ *conjunción*

1. **since**: como llegué tarde, no me dejaron entrar since I arrived late, they didn't allow me to enter

2. **if**: como me desobedezcas, no volverás a salir if you disobey me, you won't go out again

**cómo** *adverbio*

Cómo takes an accent in direct and indirect questions:

**how**: y ahora ¿cómo resuelvo este problema? and now, how do I solve this problem?; no sé cómo resolver este problema I don't know how to solve this problem

➤ ¡cómo no! of course!: ¿me ayudarás? — ¡cómo no! will you help me? — of course!

**cómodo** *adjetivo* ■ **comfortable**.

**comoquiera** *adverbio* ■ **however**: comoquiera que lo hagas, va a salir bien however you do it, it will come out fine.

**compacto** *adjetivo* ■ **compact**.

**compadecer** *verbo* ■ **to sympathize with**: qué difícil ese examen, te compadezco how difficult that test is, I sympathize with you.

el **compañero**, la **compañera**

1. *en la escuela* **classmate**
2. *en el trabajo* **colleague**.

la **compañía** ■ **company** (plural **companies**): trabaja en una compañía francesa she works for a French company; esta noche se presenta una compañía de teatro extranjera tonight a foreign theatrical company is performing tonight; mis amigos me hicieron compañía toda la tarde my friends kept me company all afternoon.

**comparar** *verbo* ■ **to compare**: no le gusta que la comparen con la hermana she doesn't like to be compared with her sister.

el **compartimento** ■ **compartment**: guardemos esto en el compartimento de la izquierda let's keep this in the compartment on the left.

**compartir** *verbo* ■ **to share**: compartió con sus amigos los dulces que le regalaron he shared the candy they gave him with his friends.

el **compás** (*plural* los compases) ■ **rhythm**.

la **compasión** ■ **compassion**.

la **competencia**

1. **rivalry**: hay mucha competencia entre los dos equipos there is a lot of rivalry between the two teams

2. **competition**: la competencia de natación empieza mañana the swimming competition begins tomorrow.

**competente** *adjetivo* ■ **competent**.

**competir** *verbo* ■ **to compete**: esos dos supermercados compiten entre sí those two supermarkets compete against each other; compite mañana por la medalla de oro she competes tomorrow for the gold medal.

**complacer** *verbo* ■ **to please**: es difícil complacer a todo el mundo it's difficult to please everybody; me complace presentarles a este cantante it pleases me to introduce to you this singer.

el **complejo** ■ **complex**: por aquí se va al complejo deportivo de la universidad this is the way to the university's sports complex; tiene complejo porque es muy alto he has a complex because he's very tall.

el **complemento** ■ **complement**: ese verbo no tiene complemento that verb doesn't have a complement
➤ complemento directo direct object
➤ complemento indirecto indirect object.

**completar** *verbo*

1. **to finish**: dentro de un mes completa su carrera he'll finish his studies within a month

2. **to fill in**: complete este formulario, por favor fill in this form, please.

**completo** *adjetivo*

1. **complete**: acabo de comprar las obras completas de Rulfo I just bought the complete works of Rulfo

**2. total:** completo silencio, por favor total silence, please

**3. comprehensive:** ese diccionario es muy completo that dictionary is very comprehensive

**4. filled in:** ¿ese formulario ya está completo? is that form filled in now?

**5. full:** el avión venía completo the airplane was full.

**complicado** *adjetivo* ■ complicated.

el/la **cómplice** *sustantivo masculino y femenino* ■ accomplice.

**componer** *verbo*

**1. to make up:** estos diez jugadores componen el equipo these ten players make up the team

**2. to repair:** este televisor no funciona, hay que componerlo this television doesn't work, we have to repair it

**3. to compose:** Beethoven compuso nueve sinfonías Beethoven composed nine symphonies

➤ el equipo se compone de estos diez jugadores the team consists of these ten players.

la **composición** *(plural* las composiciones) ■ composition: las composiciones de Chopin son muy bellas Chopin's compositions are very beautiful.

el **compositor,** la **compositora** ■ composer.

la **compra**

**1. shopping:** tengo que ir de compras, nos falta comida I have to go shopping, we need food

**2. purchase:** la última compra que hice ayer fue este libro the last purchase that I made yesterday was this book.

**comprar** *verbo* ■ to buy: antes de comprar conviene comparar precios before buying, it's good to compare prices

➤ tienes que comprarte zapatos nuevos you have to buy yourself new shoes.

**comprender** *verbo*

**1. to understand:** no comprendí la lección I didn't understand the lesson

**2. to include:** el curso comprende los más recientes descubrimientos de la astronomía the course includes astronomy's most recent discoveries.

**comprensivo** *adjetivo* ■ understanding: María es una persona muy comprensiva María is a very understanding person.

**comprimir** *verbo* ■ to compress.

**comprobar** *verbo* ■ to check: comprueba que la puerta esté bien cerrada check that the door is closed properly.

**comprometerse** *verbo pronominal*

**1. to promise:** se comprometió a entregar el trabajo mañana he promised to turn in the paper tomorrow

**2. to commit oneself:** no quiso comprometerse, porque no sabía cuándo podría entregar el trabajo he refused to commit himself, because he didn't know when he would be able to turn in the paper.

el **compromiso**

**1. engagement:** no podré verte mañana porque tengo varios compromisos I can't see you tomorrow because I have several engagements

**2. commitment:** es una persona confiable, que respeta sus compromisos she's a trustworthy person who honors her commitments.

**compuesto** *adjetivo* ■ compound: "mediodía" es una palabra compuesta "mediodía" is a compound word.

el **computador,** la **computadora** ■ computer

➤ computadora de mesa desktop computer

➤ computadora personal personal computer

➤ computadora portátil laptop.

**común** *(plural* comunes) *adjetivo*

**1. common:** "Pérez" es un apellido muy común "Pérez" is a very common last name; los alumnos cuentan con una sala de lectura común there is a common reading room for students

2. **normal: es común que haga calor en esta época** it's normal for it to be hot at this time of year

➤ **en común** in common: **tenemos varios intereses en común** we have several things in common.

la **comunicación** (plural las comunicaciones) ■ communication: **un satélite de comunicaciones** a communications satellite

➤ **se cortó la comunicación** we were cut off.

**comunicar** verbo ■ to inform: **nos comunicó su proyecto de casarse** he informed us of his plan to get married

**comunicarse** verbo pronominal

1. **to communicate: las líneas están cortadas, por eso no hemos podido comunicarnos** the lines are down so we haven't been able to communicate with them

2. **to be connected: la habitación se comunica con el baño** the bedroom is connected to the bathroom.

la **comunidad** ■ community: **la comunidad latina es numerosa en esta región** there is a large Latin community in this area.

la **comunión** (plural las comuniones) ■ communion: **primera comunión** first communion.

**con** preposición ■ with: **viajé con mis padres** I traveled with my parents; **rellené las empanadas con queso** I filled the turnovers with cheese

➤ **maneje con prudencia** drive carefully

➤ **con tal de** as long as: **con tal de verte, voy adonde sea** as long as I can see you I'll go anywhere

➤ **con tal de que** in order to: **con tal de que lo aplaudan es capaz de hacer cualquier cosa** he'll do anything in order to get the applause.

**conceder** verbo ■ to grant: **el hada madrina le concedió tres deseos** her fairy godmother granted her three wishes.

la **concentración** ■ concentration: **estudiar requiere mucha concentración** studying requires a lot of concentration.

**concentrarse** verbo pronominal

1. **to concentrate: no logro concentrarme porque están haciendo demasiado ruido** I can't concentrate because you're making too much noise

2. **to gather: varias personas se concentraron en la puerta del teatro** several people gathered at the theater doors.

la **conciencia** ■ conscience: **la voz de la conciencia** the voice of conscience

➤ **no tiene conciencia del daño que le ha hecho** he's not aware of the damage he's done

➤ **tener la conciencia tranquila** to have a clear conscience.

el **concierto** ■ concert: **fuimos a un concierto de rock** we went to a rock concert.

**concluir** verbo

1. **to finish: concluimos el trabajo a tiempo** we finished the work on time

2. **to conclude: concluyo que no te interesa participar en el proyecto** I can only conclude that you're not interested in participating in the project.

la **conclusión** (plural las conclusiones) conclusion.

**concreto** adjetivo ■ specific: **quiero un ejemplo concreto** I want a specific example

el **concreto** ■ concrete.

el/la **concursante** ■ contestant.

**concursar** verbo ■ to be a contestant: **concursó en un programa de preguntas y respuestas** he was a contestant on a quiz show.

el **concurso** ■ contest: **participó en varios concursos de baile** she took part in several dance contests.

la **condena** ■ sentence.

**condenar** verbo ■ to sentence: **lo condenaron a diez años en prisión** he was sentenced to ten years in prison.

la **condición** *(plural* las condiciones)
■ **condition:** te lo presto, con la condición de que me lo devuelvas mañana I'll lend it to you on condition that you give it back to me tomorrow

las **condiciones**
1. **shape:** mi auto está en muy malas condiciones my car is in very bad shape
2. **condition:** la abuela no está en condiciones de hacer un viaje tan largo grandmother is in no condition to make such a long trip.

la **conducta** ■ **behavior**.

el **conductor, la conductora** ■ driver

⚠ The Spanish word **conductor** is a false cognate, it does not mean "conductor".

**conectar** *verbo* ■ **to connect:** esa carretera conecta mi pueblo con la capital this road connects my town to the capital; sólo falta conectar el teléfono we just have to connect the phone.

el **conejo,** la **coneja** ■ **rabbit**.

la **conferencia**
1. **lecture:** voy a dar una conferencia en la facultad de derecho I'm giving a lecture at the law faculty
2. **conference:** fue a una conferencia médica he went to a medical conference.

**confesar** *verbo*
1. **to confess:** el ladrón confesó el crimen the thief confessed to the crime
2. **to admit:** Pablo me confesó que está enamorado de Ana Pablo admitted he's in love with Ana
➤ confesarse to go to confession.

el **confesor** ■ **confessor**.

la **confianza**
1. **trust:** nunca me ha mentido, le tengo total confianza he's never lied to me, I trust him completely
2. **familiarity:** nos trata con confianza porque nos conocemos hace mucho he treats us with familiarity because we've known each other a long time

➤ tenerse confianza to have self-confidence: se tiene confianza y por eso logra sus objetivos she has a lot of self-confidence so she's able to reach her goals.

**confiar** *verbo*
1. **to trust:** confía en su amiga y por eso le presta el coche she trusts her friend so she lets her borrow the car
2. **to entrust:** su padre le confió el cuidado de la tienda his father entrusted him with the running of the store.

la **configuración** *(plural* las configuraciones)* ■ **configuration**.

**configurar** *verbo* ■ **to configure**.

la **confirmación** *(plural* las confirmaciones)* ■ **confirmation:** la confirmación de la reserva the booking confirmation
➤ ya tengo la confirmación de mi vuelo my flight is confirmed.

**confirmar** *verbo* ■ **to confirm:** antes de viajar, es importante confirmar el vuelo it's important to confirm your flights before you travel.

el **conflicto** ■ **conflict**.

**conforme** *adjetivo* ■ **satisfied:** estoy conforme con la decisión que tomaron mis padres I'm satisfied with the decision my parents took.

**conforme** *adverbio* ■ **as:** conforme vayan terminando la prueba, pueden salir you may leave as you finish the test.

**confortable** *adjetivo* ■ **comfortable**.

**confundir** *verbo*
1. **to mix up:** siempre confundo a las dos gemelas I always mix up the twins
2. **to confuse:** con esa jugada lograste confundir a tu rival you managed to confuse your opponent with that move

**confundirse** *verbo pronominal* ■ **to get confused:** me confundí en el camino porque no había señales I got confused on the way because there were no signs.

**67**

la **confusión** (*plural* las confusiones)
■ confusion: en la confusión de la mañana se me olvidaron las llaves I forgot my keys in all the confusion this morning.

**congelado** *adjetivo* ■ frozen.

**congelar** *verbo* ■ to freeze: voy a congelar el pollo que compré I'm going to freeze the chicken I just bought.

el **congreso**
1. conference: fue a un congreso de cirugía en Costa Rica he went to a surgical conference in Costa Rica
2. Congress: lo eligieron para el congreso he was elected to Congress.

la **conjugación** (*plural* las conjugaciones) ■ conjugation.

**conjugar** *verbo* ■ conjugate: estamos aprendiendo a conjugar los verbos irregulares we're learning to conjugate irregular verbs.

la **conjunción** (*plural* las conjunciones)
■ conjunction: "y" es una conjunción "y" is a conjunction.

el **conjunto**
1. band: un conjunto de rock a rock band
2. outfit: compré un conjunto de pantalón y chaqueta I bought an outfit with a jacket and matching pants.

**conmemorar** *verbo* ■ to commemorate.

**conmigo** *pronombre*
1. with me: ayer vino conmigo al cine she went to the movies with me yesterday
2. to me: siempre fue muy buena conmigo she was always very good to me.

**conmover** *verbo* ■ to move: sus lágrimas lo conmovieron her tears moved him.

el **cono** ■ cone
➤ el Cono Sur the Southern Cone.

**conocer** *verbo*
1. to meet: quiero que conozcas a mi hermana I'd like you to meet my sister
2. to know: a Juan lo conozco hace más de diez años I've known Juan for over ten years

➤ no conozco Egipto I have never been to Egypt.

el **conocido**, la **conocida** ■ acquaintance: tiene algunos amigos y muchos conocidos he has some friends and a lot of acquaintances.

el **conocimiento**
1. knowledge: el conocimiento del sistema solar knowledge of the solar system
2. consciousness: perder el conocimiento to lose consciousness
➤ conocimientos knowledge: tiene buenos conocimientos históricos he has a good knowledge of history.

el **conquistador**, la **conquistadora**
■ conqueror.

**conquistar** *verbo*
1. to conquer: conquistamos la cima we conquered the summit
2. to win over: la conquisté con flores I won her over with flowers.

**consciente** *adjetivo*
1. aware: no está consciente de lo que hace he's not aware of what he's doing
2. responsible: deberías ser más consciente you should be more responsible.

el **conscripto**, la **conscripta** ■ draftee.

la **consecuencia** ■ consequence: tendrá que pagar las consecuencias she'll have to pay the consequences
➤ a consecuencia de as a result of: a consecuencia de su ayuda, ganamos we won as a result of his help.

**consecutivo** *adjetivo* ■ consecutive: lo ví durante tres días consecutivos I saw him on three consecutive days.

**conseguir** *verbo*
1. to get: consiguió lo que quería he got what he wanted
2. to achieve: si te dedicas, puedes conseguir cualquier cosa you can achieve anything if you make the effort
➤ finalmente conseguí que me enseñara francés I finally got her to teach me French
➤ ¡lo conseguiste! you did it!

**68**

el **consejo** ■ advice: déjame darte un consejo let me give you some advice.

**consentir** *verbo*

1. to allow: les consienten todo they are allowed to do whatever they want
2. to spoil: su padre siempre la ha consentido her father has always spoiled her.

la **conserva** ■ canned food.

**conservador** *adjetivo* ■ conservative: sus padres son muy conservadores her parents are very conservative.

**conservar** *verbo*

1. to keep: has conservado tu figura you've kept your figure
2. to preserve: quieren conservar sus tradiciones they want to preserve their traditions
➤ conservar la naturaleza to conserve nature.

**considerado** *adjetivo*

1. considerate: debería ser más considerado con nosotros he should be more considerate toward us
2. regarded: está muy bien considerado entre otros músicos he is highly regarded by other musicians.

**considerar** *verbo* ■ to consider: la profesora consideró que valía la pena the teacher considered it worthwhile
➤ considerar los pros y los contras to weigh up the pros and cons
➤ considerar que to take into account that: tenemos que considerar que ha faltado we have to take into account that he's been absent.

**consigo, consigues, etc** *verbo* ➤ conseguir.

**consigo** *pronombre*

1. *con él* with him: Luis llevó su tienda consigo Luis brought his tent with him; habla consigo mismo he talks to himself
2. *con ella* with her: María trajo su traje de baño consigo María brought her bathing suit with her
3. *con usted, ustedes* with you: traiga consigo lo que necesite bring with you whatever you need.

**consistir** *verbo* ■ involve: ¿en qué consiste este juego? what does this game involve?
➤ consistir en to consist of: la obra consiste en dos actos the play consists of two acts.

**consolar** *verbo* ■ to comfort: lo abrazó para consolarlo she comforted him with a hug.

la **consonante** ■ consonant.

**constante** *adjetivo* ■ constant: tengo un dolor de cabeza constante I have a constant headache
➤ ser constante to persevere: para tener éxito hay que ser constante you have to persevere to be successful.

la **constitución** *(plural* las constituciones) ■ constitution.

**constituir** *verbo* ■ to constitute: los dos grupos constituyen una verdadera amenaza the two groups constitute a real threat.

la **construcción** *(plural* las construcciones) ■ construction: hace siete años que está en construcción ese edificio that building has been under construction for seven years; una empresa de construcción a construction company; este sitio está bajo construcción this website is under construction.

**construir** *verbo* ■ to build: construyó su propia casa he built his own house.

**consuelo** *verbo* ➤ consolar.

el **consuelo** ■ consolation: su único consuelo es que no reprobó his only consolation is that he didn't fail the exam.

el/la **cónsul** ■ consul.

el **consulado** ■ consulate.

la **consulta** ■ office: el doctor está en su consulta de 9 a 3 the doctor is in his office from 9 to 3
➤ hacer una consulta a alguien to ask somebody for adivce
➤ consulta a domicilio house call
➤ hacer una consulta to see a patient
➤ horas de consulta office hours.

**consultar** verbo ■ to consult: mejor consulta con el médico you should consult your doctor
➤ consultar un libro to look something up in a book.

el **consumidor,** la **consumidora** ■ consumer: derechos del consumidor consumer rights.

**consumir** verbo ■ to use: su coche consume mucha gasolina his car uses a lot of gas
➤ consumir preferentemente antes de... best before...

el **consumo** ■ consumption: cómprate un coche de bajo consumo buy a car with low gas consumption
➤ el consumo de drogas drug use.

la **contabilidad** ■ accounting: estudiar contabilidad to study accounting.

el **contacto**
1. contact: echo de menos el contacto humano I miss human contact
2. Mexico socket: necesitas más contactos para tanto aparato you need more sockets for all these appliances
➤ ponerse en contacto con alguien to get in touch with someone.

el **contado** ■ cash: pagar al contado to pay in cash.

el **contador,** la **contadora** ■ accountant
➤ contador público certified public accountant.

**contagiar** verbo ■ lávate las manos para que no vayas a contagiar a nadie con tu enfermedad wash your hands so you don't spread your illness to anyone.

**contagioso** adjetivo
1. contagious: esa enfermedad es muy contagiosa it's a very contagious disease
2. infectious: tu risa es muy contagiosa you have an infectious laugh.

la **contaminación** (plural las contaminaciones) ■ pollution: la contaminación del medio ambiente environmental pollution.

**contaminar** verbo ■ to pollute: las fábricas han contaminado el río the factories have polluted the river.

**contar** verbo
1. to count: cuenta hasta diez count to ten
2. to tell: ¿te cuento un cuento? do you want me to tell you a story?
➤ contar con alguien to count on someone
➤ ese gol no cuenta that goal doesn't count.

**contener** verbo ■ to contain: el paquete contiene libros the package contains books

**contenerse** verbo pronominal ■ to contain oneself: no pudo contenerse de alegría she could hardly contain herself she was so happy.

el **contenido** ■ contents: el contenido del sitio web the contents of the website.

**contento** adjetivo ■ happy: está muy contento con sus notas he's very happy with his grades.

**contestar** verbo ■ to answer: contesta el teléfono por favor can you answer the phone, please?

The Spanish word **contestar** is a false cognate, it does not mean "contest".

**contigo** pronombre ■ with you: ¿puedo ir contigo? can I come with you?
➤ contigo mismo with yourself: ¿estás contento contigo mismo? are you happy with yourself?

el **continente** ■ continent.

**continuar** verbo ■ to continue: podemos continuar la discusión después de la comida we can continue this discussion after lunch
➤ no puedes continuar así you can't go on like this.

**contra** preposición ■ against: estoy en contra de la discriminación I'm against discrimination.

el **contrabajo** ■ double bass.

**contradecir** *verbo* ■ **to contradict**: siempre me contradices you're always contradicting me.

la **contradicción** *(plural* las contradicciones)* ■ **contradiction**.

**contradicho, contradigo etc** *verbo* ➤ contradecir.

**contrario** *adjetivo*
1. **opposing**: el equipo contrario no es muy bueno the opposing team isn't very good
2. **opposite**: vamos en sentido contrario we're going in the opposite direction
3. **conflicting**: tienen opiniones contrarias they have conflicting opinions
➤ al contrario on the contrary
➤ de lo contrario otherwise: de lo contrario, te verás en problemas otherwise, you'll be in trouble.

el **contraste** ■ **contrast**: la tele tiene demasiado contraste there's too much contrast on the TV.

el **contrato** ■ **contract**: firmó el contrato ayer she signed the contract yesterday.

la **contribución** *(plural* las contribuciones)*
1. **contribution**: hice una contribución voluntaria I made a voluntary contribution
2. **tax**: la contribución federal federal tax.

el/la **contribuyente** ■ **taxpayer**.

el/la **contrincante** ■ **opponent**: su contrincante es muy diestro his opponent is very skillful.

el **control** ■ **control**: todo está bajo control everything's under control
➤ control de calidad quality control
➤ control de natalidad birth control
➤ control remoto remote control.

**controlar** *verbo*
1. **to control**: deberías aprender a controlarte mejor you should learn to control yourself
2. **to monitor**: estaremos controlando la situación we'll be monitoring the situation.

**convencer** *verbo*
1. **to convince**: su argumento no me convenció his argument didn't convince me

2. **to persuade**: no la pude convencer que viniera I couldn't persuade her to come.

**convencional** *adjetivo* ■ **conventional**: su pensamiento es muy convencional her way of thinking is very conventional.

**conveniente** *adjetivo* ■ **convenient**: no me resulta conveniente it's not convenient for me.

**convenir** *verbo* ■ **to be convenient**: me conviene más a las once eleven o'clock is more convenient for me
➤ no sabes lo que te conviene you don't know what's good for you.

el **convento** ■ **convent**.

la **conversación** *(plural* las conversaciones)* ■ **conversation**: tuvimos una buena conversación we had a good conversation
➤ conversaciones talks: las conversaciones de paz the peace talks.

**convertir** *verbo* ■ **to turn into**: convirtieron la bodega en una discoteca they turned the warehouse into a disco

**convertirse** *verbo pronominal*
1. **to convert**: se convirtió al budismo she converted to Buddhism
2. **to turn into**: se convirtió en un pesado he turned into a jerk.

**convidar** *verbo*
1. **to invite**: ¿vas a convidarlos a la fiesta? are you going to invite them to the party?
2. *Mexico* **to share**: te convido de mi torta I'll share my sandwich with you.

la **cooperación** ■ **cooperation**: la cooperación entre países cooperation between countries.

**cooperar** *verbo* ■ **to cooperate**: esperamos que cooperes con nosotros we hope you'll cooperate with us.

la **cooperativa** ■ **cooperative**.

la **coordenada** ■ **coordinate**: la coordenada "y" the "y" coordinate.

**71**

**coordinar** *verbo* ■ to coordinate: le cuesta coordinar sus movimientos he has trouble coordinating his movements; no sé coordinar la ropa I don't know how to co-ordinate my clothes.

la **copa**
1. glass: ¿quieres una copa de vino? would you like a glass of wine?
2. drink: te invito a una copa I'll buy you a drink
3. cup: ganaron la Copa Mundial they won the World Cup.

la **copia** ■ copy (plural copies): sacó tres copias del artículo she made three copies of the article.

la **copiadora** ■ photocopier.

**copiar** *verbo* ■ to copy.

el **copión**, la **copiona** *informal* ■ copy-cat: ¡José es un copión! José is a copycat!

el **copo** ■ flake: un copo de nieve a snowflake
➤ copos de maíz cornflakes.

**coquetear** *verbo* ■ to flirt: le encanta coquetear she loves to flirt.

el **coraje**
1. courage: hay que tener mucho coraje para hacer eso it takes a lot of courage to do that
2. anger: me da mucho coraje that makes me very angry.

el **corazón** (plural los corazones) ■ heart: el ejercicio es bueno para el co-razón exercise is good for the heart
➤ corazones *en cartas* hearts: la reina de corazones the queen of hearts
➤ Pepe es un hombre de buen corazón Pepe is a kind-hearted man.

la **corbata** ■ tie: lleva corbata he wears a tie
➤ corbata de moño bowtie.

el **corcho** ■ cork.

el **cordel** ■ string: átalo con este cordel tie it with this string.

el **cordero** ■ lamb.

la **cordillera** ■ mountain range: tuvieron que atravesar la cordillera they had to cross the mountain range
➤ la cordillera de los Andes the Andes.

el **cordón** (plural los cordones)
1. shoelace: átate los cordones tie your shoe-laces
2. cord: necesitamos un cordón más fuerte we need a stronger cord.

la **córnea** ■ cornea.

la **corneta**
1. bugle: tocaba la corneta en el ejército he played the bugle in the army
2. cornet: prefiero la trompeta a la corneta I prefer the trumpet to the cornet.

el **coro** ■ choir: Lucía canta en el coro Lucía sings in the choir.

la **corona** ■ crown.

el **coronel**, la **coronela** ■ colonel.

la **corporación** (plural las corporaciones) ■ corporation: las corporaciones multinacionales multinational corpora-tions.

**corporal** *adjetivo* ■ physical: el traba-jo corporal physical labor
➤ el castigo corporal corporal punishment
➤ la temperatura corporal body tempera-ture.

el **corral**
1. pen: hay muchas gallinas en el corral there are a lot of chickens in the pen
2. playpen: a Juanito le encanta el corral Juanito loves his playpen.

la **correa**
1. strap: se me rompió la correa del reloj my watch strap broke
2. leash: ponle la correa al perro put the dog's leash on.

**correcto** *adjetivo*
1. correct: la mayoría de sus respuestas fueron correctas most of her answers were correct
2. polite: es un niño muy correcto he's a very polite boy
➤ ¡correcto! that's right!

el **corredor**[1] ■ corridor: un corredor muy estrecho a very narrow corridor.

el **corredor**[2], la **corredora** ■ runner.

**corregir** *verbo*

1. to correct: me corrigió las faltas de ortografía she corrected my spelling mistakes
2. to grade: estuvo horas corrigiendo los exámenes she spent hours grading tests.

el **correo** ■ mail: mándamelo por correo send it to me by mail
➤ correo aéreo air mail
➤ correo certificado certified mail
➤ correo electrónico e-mail.

**correr** *verbo*

1. to run: corre muy rápido he runs very fast
2. to go fast: no corras tanto que vas a chocar don't go so fast or you'll crash
3. to hurry up: le dije que corriera para no llegar tarde I told him to hurry up so he wouldn't be late
4. to move over: diles que se corran para que nos podamos sentar tell them to move over so we can sit down
➤ el río corre de norte a sur the river runs from north to south.

la **correspondencia**

1. correspondence: no hay correspondencia entre sonidos y letras there is no correspondence between sounds and letters
2. mail: le llega mucha correspondencia he gets a lot of mail.

**corresponder** *verbo* ■ to belong: ponlo donde corresponde put it where it belongs
➤ hacer algo como corresponde to do something properly
➤ le corresponde a él hacerlo it's his job to do it.

la **corrida** ■ bullfight.

**corriente** *(adjetivo & sustantivo)*

■ *adjetivo*
common: un nombre muy corriente a very common name
➤ al corriente up to date
➤ mantenme al corriente de tu situación keep me informed of your situation

■ *sustantivo femenino*

1. draft: cierra la ventana que entra una corriente close the window — there's a draft
2. current: corriente eléctrica electric current
➤ no parece haber corriente there doesn't seem to be any power
➤ se cortó la corriente there was a power cut.

**corromper** *verbo* ■ to corrupt: el poder corrompe power corrupts.

la **corrupción** ■ corruption.

**corrupto** *adjetivo* ■ corrupt: un político corrupto a corrupt politician.

**cortado** *adjetivo*

1. chapped: tengo los labios cortados my lips are chapped
2. closed: la calle está cortada por obras the street is closed due to roadwork
3. curdled: la crema está cortada the cream is curdled.

**cortar** *verbo*

1. to cut: Ana sabe cortar pelo Ana knows how to cut hair; cortaron la escena porque era demasiado violenta they cut the scene because it was too violent
2. to cut off: me cortaron el teléfono the phone was cut off
3. to turn off: corta la luz turn the light off

**cortarse** *verbo pronominal* ■ to cut oneself: me corté con un cuchillo I cut myself with a knife.

el **cortaúñas** *(plural* los cortaúñas*)* ■ nail clippers.

el **corte**[1] ■ cut: tengo un corte en la mano I've got a cut on my hand
➤ un corte de pelo a haircut.

la **corte**[2] ■ court: la corte del rey the royal court
➤ Corte Suprema Supreme Court.

**cortés** *adjetivo* ■ polite: un caballero muy cortés a very polite gentleman
➤ lo cortés no quita lo valiente politeness isn't a sign of weakness.

**73**

la **cortesía** ■ courtesy: **le falta cortesía al manejar** he lacks courtesy when he's driving
➤ **de cortesía** complimentary.

la **corteza**
1. **bark: la corteza del árbol** the tree bark
2. **crust: me gusta la corteza del pan** I like the bread's crust
3. **peel: la corteza del limón** the lemon peel
4. **rind: la corteza del queso** the cheese rind
➤ **corteza cerebral** cerebral cortex.

la **cortina** ■ curtain.

**corto** *adjetivo* ■ **short: te ves bien con el pelo corto** you look good with short hair
➤ **ser corto de vista** to be nearsighted.

la **cosa** ■ **thing: pásame esa cosa verde** pass me that green thing
➤ **cualquier cosa** anything
➤ **no es cosa tuya** it's none of your business
➤ **son cosas de la vida** that's life!

la **cosecha**
1. **harvest: es época de cosecha** it's harvest time
2. **crop: el granizo arruinó la cosecha** hail ruined the crop.

**cosechar** *verbo* ■ to harvest.

**coser** *verbo* ■ **to sew: si supiera coser, te arreglaría la camisa** if I knew how to sew I'd mend your shirt.

el **cosmético** ■ cosmetic.

**cósmico** *adjetivo* ■ cosmic.

las **cosquillas**
➤ **¡no me hagas cosquillas!** stop tickling me!
➤ **tener cosquillas** to be ticklish.

la **costa** ■ **coast: tiene una casa en la costa** he has a house on the coast
➤ **a toda costa** at all costs
➤ **vivir a costa de los demás** to live at other peoples' expense.

el **costado** ■ **side: me gusta dormir de costado** I like to sleep on my side.

**costar** *verbo*
1. **to cost: ¿cuánto cuesta?** how much does it cost?
2. **to take: me costó tres días acabarlo** it took me three days to finish it
➤ **me está costando aprender alemán** I'm finding it hard to learn German.

**Costa Rica** *sustantivo femenino* ■ Costa Rica.

**costarricense** *adjetivo*

En inglés, los adjetivos que se refieren a un país o a una región se escriben con mayúscula:

Costa Rican

el/la **costarricense**

En inglés, los gentilicios se escriben con mayúscula:

Costa Rican: **los costarricenses** the Costa Ricans.

**costarriqueño** *adjetivo*

En inglés, los adjetivos que se refieren a un país o a una región se escriben con mayúscula:

Costa Rican

el **costarriqueño, la costarriqueña**

En inglés, los gentilicios se escriben con mayúscula:

Costa Rican: **los costarriqueños** the Costa Ricans.

la **costera** *Mexico* ■ promenade.

la **costilla** ■ rib.

el **costo** ■ **cost: el costo humano de la guerra** the human cost of war.

la **costra** ■ **scab: no te rasques la costra** don't scratch the scab.

la **costumbre**
1. **habit: una mala costumbre** a bad habit
2. **custom: una costumbre local** a local custom
➤ **como de costumbre** as usual
➤ **no tengo la costumbre** I'm not used to it.

la **costura**
1. **sewing:** a Jimena le gusta la costura Jimena likes sewing
2. **seam:** una costura mal hecha a badly-sewn seam
➤ **alta costura** haute couture.

**cotidiano** *adjetivo* ■ **everyday:** la vida cotidiana everyday life.

el **coyote** ■ coyote.

el **cráneo** ■ skull.

la **creación** *(plural* las creaciones) ■ **creation.**

**crear** *verbo* ■ **to create:** crearon una base de datos they created a database
➤ **crear falsas expectativas** to raise false hopes
➤ **crear problemas** to cause problems.

**crecer** *verbo*
1. **to grow:** has crecido mucho you've grown a lot
2. **to grow up:** creció en Nueva York she grew up in New York
3. **to rise:** ha crecido la inflación y el desempleo inflation and unemployment have risen.

el **crédito**
1. **credit:** le dan crédito en esa tienda he gets credit in that store; **comprar algo a crédito** to buy something on credit
2. **loan:** ¿crees que te darán un crédito? do you think they'll give you a loan?

la **creencia** ■ **belief:** no estoy atacando tus creencias I'm not attacking your beliefs.

**creer** *verbo*
1. **to believe:** no lo puedo creer I can't believe it
2. **to think:** creo que tienes razón I think you're right.

**creído** *adjetivo* ■ **conceited:** José es muy creído José is really conceited.

la **crema** ■ **cream:** la crema le gusta a los gatos cats like cream
➤ **crema ácida** sour cream
➤ **crema de champiñones** mushroom soup
➤ **crema para las manos** hand cream.

**creyendo, creyera, etc** ➤ creer.

el **creyente**, la **creyente** ■ **believer.**

la **cría** ■ una cría de elefante a baby elephant; una cría de león a lion cub.

el **criado**, la **criada** ■ **servant.**

**criar** *verbo*
1. **to bring up:** sus padres la criaron bien her parents brought her up well
2. **to breed:** crían perros they breed dogs
3. **to grow up:** nos criamos juntos we grew up together.

el **crimen** *(plural* los crímenes) ■ **murder:** cometer un crimen to commit murder
➤ **crimen de guerra** war crime
➤ **crimen organizado** organized crime.

el **criminal**, la **criminal** ■ **criminal.**

la **crisis** *(plural* las crisis) ■ **crisis:** una crisis económica an economic crisis
➤ **crisis cardíaca** heart failure
➤ **una crisis nerviosa** a nervous breakdown.

el **cristal** ■ **crystal.**

el **cristiano**, la **cristiana** ■ **Christian.**

**Cristo** *sustantivo masculino* ■ **Christ.**

la **crítica**
1. **criticism:** no aguantó tanta crítica y se fue he couldn't stand so much criticism so he left
2. **review:** voy a escribir una crítica del libro I'm going to write a review of the book.

**criticar** *verbo*
1. **to criticize:** la critica constantemente he's constantly criticizing her
2. **to review:** criticar una película to review a movie.

el **crítico**, la **crítica** ■ **critic**
➤ **un crítico de cine** a movie critic.

el **cronómetro** ■ **stopwatch.**

el **cruce** ■ **crossing:** un cruce fronterizo a border crossing
➤ **un cruce de carreteras** a crossroads.

el **crucigrama** ■ **crossword.**

**crudo** *adjetivo*
1. **raw:** carne cruda raw meat

2. **undercooked:** el pollo está crudo the chicken's undercooked
➤ **estar crudo** *Mexico informal* to be hung over.

**cruel** *adjetivo* ■ **cruel**.

**crujiente** *adjetivo* ■ **crunchy:** una manzana crujiente a crunchy apple.

**crujir** *verbo*

1. **to creak:** la cama crujía cada vez que me movía the bed creaked every time I moved
2. **to rustle:** las hojas secas crujían con el viento the dry leaves rustled in the wind
3. **to grind:** le crujen los dientes he grinds his teeth
4. **to crunch:** la nieve crujía bajos nuestros pies the snow crunched under our feet.

la **cruz** *(plural* las cruces) ■ **cross**.

**cruzar** *verbo* ■ **to cross:** ten cuidado al cruzar la calle be careful when you cross the street
➤ **cruzar los brazos** to fold your arms
➤ **cruzarse con alguien** to run into someone.

el **cuaderno** ■ **notebook:** un cuaderno de espiral a spiral notebook.

la **cuadra** ■ **block:** queda a tres cuadras it's three blocks from here.

**cuadrado** *adjetivo* ■ **square:** una caja cuadrada a square box
➤ **diez kilómetros cuadrados** ten square kilometers
➤ **tu hermano es muy cuadrado** your brother is really square

el **cuadrado** ■ **square**.

**cuadriculado** *adjetivo* ■ **papel cuadriculado** graph paper.

el **cuadro** ■ **painting:** colecciona cuadros she collects paintings.

el **cuadrúpedo** ■ **quadruped**.

**cuál** *pronombre*

1. **what:** ¿cuál es tu nombre? what's your name?
2. **which one:** ¿cuál prefieres? which one do you prefere?

**cual** *pronombre*
➤ **cada cual** everyone: cada cual en su lugar everyone in their place
➤ **sea cual sea** whatever
➤ **sea cual sea el resultado, lo aceptamos** whatever the result is, we'll accept it.

la **cualidad** ■ **quality:** tiene buenas cualidades she has good qualities.

**cualquier** *adjetivo* ➤ cualquiera.

**cualquiera** *adjetivo* ■ **any:** a cualquier hora any time; este examen lo puede aprobar cualquier alumno any student can pass this exam.

**cualquiera** *pronombre*

1. **anyone:** cualquiera puede aprobar el examen si estudia anyone can pass the test if they study
2. **either:** ¿cuál de los dos prefieres? — cualquiera which of the two do you prefer? – either
3. **any of them:** llévate cualquiera take any of them.

**cuándo** *adverbio* ■ **when:** ¿cuándo llegaste? when did you arrive?

**cuando** *conjunción*

1. **when:** ven cuando puedas come when you can
2. **if:** cuando Miguel lo dice, debe ser por algo if Miguel says so it must be for a reason
➤ **cuando menos** at least: necesitarás cuando menos un traje you'll need at least one suit
➤ **de cuando en cuando** every so often.

**cuanto** *adverbio* ■ **as much as:** come cuanto quieras eat as much as you like
➤ **cuanto antes** as soon as possible
➤ **en cuanto** as soon as: nos vamos en cuanto termine de llover we'll go as soon as it stops raining
➤ **en cuanto a** as for: en cuanto a tu salario, lo discutiremos mañana as for your salary, we'll discuss it tomorrow
➤ **cuanto más la conozco, más me gusta** the more I get to know her, the more I like her.

**cuánto** *adjetivo & pronombre*

1. *en singular* **how much:** ¿cuánto pan compro? how much bread do I buy?
2. *en plural* **how many:** ¿cuántos libros tienes? how many books do you have?

**cuarenta** *adjetivo* ■ **forty:** me dio cuarenta dólares he gave me forty dollars; tiene cuarenta años she's forty.

el **cuartel** ■ **barracks**.

**cuarto** *adjetivo* ■ **fourth:** eres la cuarta persona en llegar you're the fourth person to arrive
➤ la cuarta parte a quarter.

el **cuarto**

1. **room:** la casa tiene cinco cuartos the house has five rooms
2. **fourth:** ha hecho tres cuartos de la tarea he's done three fourths of his homework
➤ las diez y cuarto quarter past ten
➤ un cuarto para las diez quarter to ten.

el/la **cuate** *Central America, Mexico*

1. **twin:** sus hijos son cuates her kids are twins
2. *informal* **buddy:** fui al cine con unos cuates I went to the movies with my buddies
3. **guy:** ¿conoces a ese cuate? do you know that guy?

**cuatro** *numeral* ■ **four:** tiene cuatro hijos she has four children
➤ mi hermana tiene cuatro años my sister is four years old
➤ son las cuatro it's four o'clock
➤ el cuatro de abril the fourth of April.

**Cuba** *sustantivo femenino* ■ **Cuba**.

**cubano** *adjetivo*

En inglés, los adjetivos que se refieren a un país o a una región se escriben con mayúscula:

**Cuban**

el **cubano,** la **cubana**

En inglés, los gentilicios se escriben con mayúscula:

**Cuban:** los cubanos the Cubans.

la **cubeta** *Mexico* ■ **bucket**.

**cúbico** *adjetivo* ■ **cubic:** diez metros cúbicos ten cubic meters.

la **cubierta**

1. **cover:** un libro con cubiertas de cuero a book with leather covers
2. **deck:** voy a subir a la cubierta para ver el mar I'm going up on deck to look at the sea.

**cubierto** *verbo* ➤ cubrir.

el **cubierto** ■ **cover charge:** cobran bastante por cada cubierto the cover charge is pretty high
➤ cubiertos cutlery: cubiertos de plata silver cutlery.

el **cubo**

1. **cube:** un cubo de hielo an ice cube
2. **bucket:** un cubo de agua a bucket of water.

**cubrir** *verbo* ■ **to cover:** se cubrió la cara con las manos she covered her face with her hands.

la **cucaracha** ■ **cockroach**.

la **cuchara** ■ **spoon**.

la **cucharada** ■ **spoonful:** una cucharada de azúcar a spoonful of sugar.

la **cucharadita** ■ **teaspoon:** una cucharadita de azúcar a teaspoon of sugar.

el **cucharón** *(plural* los cucharones*)* ■ **ladle**.

**cuchichear** *verbo* ■ **to whisper:** cuchicheó algo al oído de Sonia she whispered something into Sonia's ear.

el **cuchillo** ■ **knife**.

**cuclillas** *adverbio* ■ **tienes que ponerte en cuclillas** you have to squat down.

el **cuello**

1. **neck:** me duele el cuello my neck hurts
2. **collar:** el cuello de la camisa me queda apretado the shirt collar is too tight for me.

la **cuenta**

1. **count:** perder la cuenta to lose count
2. **account:** una cuenta corriente a checking account
3. **bill:** la cuenta del teléfono the phone bill

**4. check:** la cuenta, por favor can I have the check, please
➤ **darse cuenta** to realize: **no me di cuenta de que te habías ido** I didn't realize you'd left
➤ **las cuentas** the accounts
➤ **tomar en cuenta** to take into account.

el **cuento** ■ **story: cuéntame un cuento** tell me a story
➤ **no me vengas con cuentos** I don't want to hear your excuses
➤ **un cuento de hadas** a fairy tale.

la **cuerda**
**1. rope: afloja la cuerda** loosen the rope
**2. string: amarra el paquete con una cuerda** tie the package with some string; **se me rompió una cuerda de la guitarra** I broke a guitar string
➤ **dar cuerda a un reloj** to wind a watch
➤ **saltar la cuerda** to jump rope
➤ **una cuerda floja** a tightrope.

el **cuerno** ■ **horn.**

el **cuero** ■ **leather: guantes de cuero** leather gloves.

el **cuerpo** ■ **body: el cuerpo humano** the human body.

la **cuesta** ■ **slope: esta cuesta es muy empinada** this is a very steep slope
➤ **ir cuesta abajo** to go downhill
➤ **ir cuesta arriba** to go uphill
➤ **me llevó a cuestas** he carried me on his shoulders.

el **cuestionario** ■ **questionnaire.**

la **cueva** ■ **cave.**

**cueza, cuezan, etc** verbo ➤ cocer.

el **cuico,** la **cuica** Chile informal ■ **cop.**

el **cuidado** ■ **care: el cuidado de la piel** skin care
➤ **ten cuidado al cruzar la calle** be careful crossing the street
➤ **con cuidado** carefully
➤ **¡cuidado!** watch out!
➤ **cuidados intensivos** intensive care.

**cuidar** verbo ■ **to take care: deberías cuidar tu salud más** you should take better care of your health

➤ **cuidar de** to look after: **cuida de sus hermanos** she looks after her brothers
➤ **¡cuídate!** take care!

la **culebra** ■ **snake.**

la **culpa**
**1. fault: yo tengo la culpa** it's my fault
**2. blame: me echó la culpa** she put the blame on me.

**cultivar** verbo
**1. to grow: cultiva lechugas en su jardín** she grows lettuce in her garden
**2. to farm: cultivar la tierra** to farm the land
**3. to cultivate: ha estado cultivando amistades** he's been cultivating friendships.

el **cultivo** ■ **farming: el cultivo intensivo** intensive farming.

**culto** adjetivo
**1. educated: una persona muy culta** a well-educated person
**2. formal: usa lenguaje muy culto** she uses very formal language

el **culto** ■ **worship: el culto al sol** sun worship.

la **cultura** ■ **culture: la cultura popular** popular culture.

la **cumbre** ■ **summit.**

el **cumpleaños** (plural los cumpleaños) ■ **birthday: ¡feliz cumpleaños!** happy birthday!

el **cumplido** ■ **compliment: le hice un cumplido** I gave her a compliment.

**cumplir** verbo
**1. to carry out: cumplió con la tarea que le di** he carried out the task I gave him
**2. to keep: no cumple sus promesas** she doesn't keep her promises
**3. to serve: le faltan dos años para cumplir su condena** he has two years left to serve his sentence
**4. to meet: tiene que cumplir los requisitos mínimos** he has to meet the minimum requirements
➤ **cumplir quince años** to turn fifteen years old.

la **cuna** ■ **cradle.**

la **cuñada** ■ **sister-in-law.**

**78**

el **cuñado** ■ brother-in-law.

la **cuota**

1. **fee:** la cuota de socio anual the yearly membership fee
2. **quota:** la cuota de exportación the export quota
3. *Mexico* **toll:** una carretera de quota a toll road.

**cupo** *verbo* ➤ caber.

el **cupón** *(plural* los cupones) ■ **coupon.**

el **cura** ■ **priest.**

la **cura** ■ **cure:** esa enfermedad no tiene cura that illness doesn't have a cure.

**curar** *verbo*

1. **to cure:** saben curar varias formas de cáncer they know how to cure several types of cancer
2. **to treat:** la enfermera me curó la herida the nurse treated my wound

**curarse** *verbo pronominal*

1. **to heal:** se me curó la herida rápidamente my wound healed quickly
2. **to recover:** José tardó dos meses en curarse José took two months to recover.

la **curiosidad** ■ **curiosity.**

**curioso** *adjetivo*

1. **strange:** ¡qué curioso! how strange
2. **inquisitive:** los alumnos son bastante curiosos the students are pretty inquisitive.

la **curita** ■ **Band-Aid®.**

el **currículo** ■ **résumé.**

el **curriculum** *(plural* los curriculums) ■ **résumé.**

el **curso**

1. **class:** estamos en el mismo curso we're in the same class
2. **course:** quiero tomar un curso de francés I want to take a French course
➤ **en el curso de las discusiones** in the course of the discussions.

la **curva** ■ **curve:** esa carretera tiene muchas curvas that road has a lot of curves.

**cuyo** *pronombre* ■ **whose:** el señor cuyo nombre no voy a mencionar the man whose name I won't mention.

el **dado** ■ **dice** *(plural* **dice).**

la **dama** ■ **lady** *(plural* **ladies):** damas y caballeros ladies and gentlemen
➤ **damas** checkers: no sé jugar a las damas I don't know how to play checkers.

la **danza** ■ **dance:** una danza tradicional a traditional dance.

**dañar** *verbo*

1. **to harm:** ¡no dañes al gato! don't harm the cat!
2. **to damage:** dañó la mercancía he damaged the merchandise; el tabaco daña la salud tobacco damages your health.

el **daño** ■ **damage:** el daño que el barco sufrió es leve the damage that the boat suffered is slight
➤ **hacer daño a alguien** to hurt somebody
➤ **hacerse daño** to hurt oneself.

**dar** *verbo* ■ **to give:** le di mi dirección I gave her my address; ¿me da un kilo de papas? could I have a kilogram of potatoes?; me dio permiso para salir he gave me permission to go out
➤ **dar a** to face: el jardín da a la playa the garden faces the beach
➤ **dar las gracias** to thank: ¿le diste las gracias? did you thank him?
➤ **da lo mismo** it doesn't matter
➤ **dar una fiesta** to have a party
➤ **el reloj dio las tres** the clock struck three

➤ **si se entera le va a dar un ataque** if he finds out, he'll have a fit
➤ **dar clases** to teach
➤ **da clases de historia** she teaches history
➤ **me voy a dar un baño** I'm going to have a bath.

el **dato** ■ piece of information: **un dato interesante** an interesting piece of information
➤ **datos** data.

**de** *preposición*
1. **of: una taza de té** a cup of tea; **uno de sus hermanos** one of his brothers
2. **from: Juan es de Guadalajara** Juan is from Guadalajara
3. **in: la montaña más alta del mundo** the highest mountain in the world
4. **by: una película de Spielberg** a movie by Spielberg; **estaba rodeado de admiradores** he was surrounded by fans
5. **than: me demoré más de lo que esperaba** I took longer than I expected; **había más de mil personas** there were more than a thousand people
➤ **esto es de Pepe** this is Pepe's
➤ **la clase de matemáticas** the math class
➤ **salgo de mi casa muy temprano** I leave home very early
➤ **son las tres de la tarde** it's three o'clock in the afternoon
➤ **una pulsera de plata** a silver bracelet.

**dé** *verbo* ➤ dar.

**debajo** *adverbio* ■ under: **ponte algo debajo de la chaqueta** put something on under your jacket
➤ **pasar por debajo** to go under.

el **deber** ■ duty *(plural* **duties**): **es tu deber hacerlo** it's your duty to do it.

**deber** *verbo*
1. **to owe: me debes cien pesos** you owe me a hundred pesos
2. **must: debes pedir perdón** you must ask for forgiveness
➤ **deberías hacerlo** you should do it
➤ **se debe a que no estudias** it's because you don't study.

**débil** *adjetivo* ■ weak.

la **debilidad** ■ weakness: **la debilidad del puente lo hace peligroso** the weakness of the bridge makes it dangerous
➤ **tengo una debilidad por los dulces** I have a weakness for candy.

**debilitar** *verbo* ■ to weaken.

la **década** ■ decade.

**decente** *adjetivo* ■ decent: **es un hombre decente** he's a decent man; **tu casa es bastante decente** his house is pretty decent.

la **decepción** *(plural* las decepciones) ■ disappointment: **el libro fue una decepción** the book was a disappointment

> The Spanish word **decepción** is a false cognate, it does not mean "deception".

**decidido** *adjective* ■ determined: **está decidido a pasar el examen** he's determined to pass the exam; **un hombre muy decidido** a very determined man.

**decidir** *verbo* ■ to decide: **decidió hacerlo después de todo** he decided to do it after all
➤ **¿por cuál te decidiste?** which one did you choose?

**decir** *verbo*
1. **to say: dijo que no** he said no
2. **to tell: dime como te va** tell me how you're doing
➤ **es decir** that is to say: **son buenos, es decir, mejor que los otros** they're good, that is to say, better than the others
➤ **¡no me digas!** no way!
➤ **por así decir** so to speak
➤ **¿que quiere decir esto?** what does this mean?
➤ **¿y ellos, que dicen?** what do they think?

la **decisión** *(plural* las decisiones) ■ decision: **tomó la decisión de irse** he made the decision to leave.

la **declaración** *(plural* las declaraciones)
1. **declaration: una declaración de amor** a declaration of love

**2. statement:** esperamos oír la declaración del presidente we are waiting to hear the president's statement

**3. testimony:** el testigo prestó declaración the witness gave testimony.

**declarar** *verbo*

**1. to announce:** declaró que era inocente he announced he was innocent

**2. to declare:** acaban de declarar la guerra they've just declared war

➤ lo declararon inocente they found him not guilty

➤ se le declaró a María he declared his love to María.

**la decoración** *(plural* las decoraciones*)* ■ **decoration**.

**decorar** *verbo* ■ **to decorate:** decoraron la sala para la Navidad they decorated the room for Christmas.

**la dedicación** ■ **dedication:** si quieres triunfar necesitas dedicación if you want to succeed, you need dedication.

**dedicar** *verbo*

**1. to dedicate:** le dedicó el poema a su hija she dedicated the poem to her daughter

**2. to devote:** deberías dedicar más tiempo al estudio you should devote more time to studying.

**la dedicatoria** ■ **dedication:** le pedí que me escribiera una dedicatoria en su libro I asked him to write a dedication to me in his book.

**el dedo**

**1.** *de la mano* **finger:** se cortó el dedo he cut his finger

**2.** *del pie* **toe:** el dedo gordo del pie the big toe

➤ el dedo gordo de la mano the thumb

➤ hacer dedo to hitch a ride

➤ no levantar un dedo to not lift a finger.

**el defecto**

**1. defect:** tu abrigo tiene un defecto en la manga your coat has a defect on the sleeve

**2. fault:** es un defecto de su personalidad it's a personality fault of his.

**defender** *verbo* ■ **to defend:** ¡siempre lo defiendes a él! you always defend him!

**la defensa** ■ **defense:** salió en mi defensa he came to my defense

➤ defensa personal self-defense.

**deficiente** *adjetivo* ■ **inadequate:** la atención a los pacientes es deficiente the attention to the patients is inadequate

➤ una dieta deficiente en calcio a diet deficient in calcium.

**la definición** *(plural* las definiciones*)* ■ **definition**.

**definir** *verbo* ■ **to define:** ¿cómo defines el amor? how do you define love?

**deformar** *verbo*

**1. to distort:** el espejo deforma la imagen the mirror distorts the image

**2. to deform:** quedó deformado después del accidente he was left deformed after the accident.

**dejar** *verbo*

**1. to leave:** déjalo ahí leave it over there

**2. to let:** lo dejamos entrar we let him in

➤ dejar de hacer algo to stop doing something: ¡deja de molestarme! stop bothering me!: dejar de fumar to give up smoking

➤ ¡déjame en paz! leave me alone!

**del** *preposición*

del is a contraction of de and el.

➤ de.

**delante** *adverbio* ■ **in front:** vaya delante go in front

➤ delante de in front of: se paró delante de mí y no me dejó ver he stopped in front of me and didn't allow me to see.

**delantero** *adjetivo* ■ **front:** la rueda delantera the front wheel.

**el delfín** *(plural* los delfines*)* ■ **dolphin**.

**delgado** *adjetivo* ■ **thin:** estás mucho más delgada que antes you're much thinner than before.

**delicado** *adjetivo*

**1. delicate:** ¡que manos tan delicadas! what delicate hands!

**2. fragile:** estas copas son muy delicadas these glasses are very fragile

3. **sensitive:** tengo la piel muy delicada my skin is very sensitive

4. **tactful:** tienes que aprender a ser más delicado you should learn to be more tactful.

**delicioso** *adjetivo* ■ **delicious**.

la **delincuencia** ■ **crime:** la delincuencia es un problema en este barrio crime is a problem in this area.

el/la **delincuente** *sustantivo masculino y femenino* ■ **criminal**.

el **delito** ■ **crime:** lo que estoy haciendo no es un delito what I'm doing isn't a crime.

la **demanda** ■ **demand:** ese juguete tiene mucha demanda that toy is in great demand

➤ **presentar una demanda contra alguien** to sue somebody: presentamos una demanda contra la compañía we sued the company.

**demandar** *verbo* ■ **to sue:** demandar a alguien to sue somebody

➤ la música demanda mucha práctica music demands a lot of practice.

**demás** *(adjetivo & pronombre)*

■ *adjetivo*
**other:** los demás alumnos entraron por otra puerta the other students came in by another door

■ *pronombre*
➤ **lo demás** the rest: lo demás es para mañana the rest is for tomorrow
➤ **todo lo demás** everything else: estudia esto e ignora todo lo demás study this and ignore everything else
➤ **los demás** the others: los demás no habían estudiado the others hadn't studied.

**demasiado** *(adverbio & adjetivo)*

■ *adverbio*
1. **too:** hablas francés demasiado rápido para mí you speak French too quickly for me
2. **too much:** comes demasiado you eat too much

■ *adjetivo*
1. **too much:** le pusiste demasiada sal you put too much salt on it

2. **too many:** siempre hay demasiada gente there are always too many people.

la **democracia** ■ **democracy** *(plural democracies)*.

**democrático** *adjetivo* ■ **democratic**.

el **demonio** ■ **devil:** estos alumnos son unos pequeños demonios these students are little devils.

la **demora** ■ **delay:** tenemos que hacerlo sin demora we have to do it without delay.

**demorar** *verbo* ■ **to take:** nos estamos demorando mucho we're taking too long.

la **demostración** *(plural las demostraciones)* ■ **demonstration:** tenían varios aparatos de demostración they had several pieces of equipment for demonstration.

**demostrar** *verbo*
1. **to demonstrate:** ahora vamos a demostrar cómo funciona now we shall demonstrate how it works
2. **to show:** demostró interés she showed interest
3. **to prove:** ha demostrado su habilidad she's proven her ability.

la **densidad** ■ **density**.

**denso** *adjetivo*
1. **thick:** un líquido denso a thick liquid
2. **heavy:** un libro denso a heavy book.

la **dentadura** ■ **teeth:** tiene la dentadura muy buena she has very good teeth.

el **dentífrico** ■ **toothpaste**.

el/la **dentista** ■ **dentist**.

**dentro** *adverbio* ■ **inside:** no sé que hay dentro I don't know what's inside; límpialo por dentro clean it on the inside
➤ **ponlo dentro de la caja** put it in the box
➤ **dentro de poco** in a while.

la **denuncia** ■ **report:** voy a tener que hacer una denuncia del robo I'm going to have to file a report about the robbery.

**denunciar** *verbo*
1. **to report:** denunció el crimen a las 3:15 he reported the crime at 3:15

**82**

**2. to condemn:** denunciaron el abuso de poder they condemned the abuse of power.

el **departamento**

1. **apartment**
2. **department:** el departamento de muebles the furniture department
➤ el Departamento de Física the Physics Department.

**depender** verbo ■ **to depend:** ¿puedes venir el martes? — depende can you come on Tuesday? — it depends
➤ **depender de** to depend on: depende de la ayuda de los demás he depends on the help of others.

el **dependiente**, la **dependienta**
■ **salesclerk**.

el **deporte** ■ **sport:** mi deporte preferido es el fútbol my favorite sport is soccer.

el **deportista** ■ **sportsman** (plural sportsmen).

la **deportista** ■ **sportswoman** (plural sportswomen).

**depositar** verbo

1. **to leave:** deposite su basura aquí leave your garbage here
2. **to deposit:** tienes que depositar el dinero antes de las tres you have to deposit the money before three o'clock.

la **depresión** (plural las depresiones)
■ **depression**.

**deprisa** adverbio ■ **quickly:** hazlo deprisa do it quickly.

la **derecha** ■ **right hand**
➤ **a la derecha** to the right: tienes que doblar a la derecha you have to turn to the right: María está sentada a la derecha de Juan María is seated to the right of Juan
➤ **de la derecha** on the right: abre esa puerta, la de la derecha open that door, the one on the right
➤ la derecha política the right.

**derecho** (adverbio & adjetivo)

■ adverbio
**straight:** siéntate derecho sit up straight
➤ **todo derecho** straight ahead

■ adjetivo
**right:** la pierna derecha the right leg

el **derecho**

1. **right:** el derecho a voto the right to vote; los derechos humanos human rights
2. **law:** quiere estudiar derecho she wants to study law.

**derramar** verbo ■ **to spill:** Ana derramó leche sobre su blusa Ana spilled milk on her blouse.

**derretir** verbo ■ **to melt:** derretí el queso I melted the cheese
➤ se derritió el helado the ice-cream melted.

**derribar** verbo

1. **to demolish:** derribaron un edificio viejo they demolished an old building
2. **to knock over:** derribé a otro niño porque no lo vi I knocked down another boy because I didn't see him
3. **to shoot down:** derribaron el avión enemigo they shot down the enemy airplane
4. **to overthrow:** quieren derribar al gobierno they want to overthrow the government.

**derrotar** verbo ■ **to defeat:** logré derrotar a los otros corredores I managed to defeat the other runners.

**derrumbar** verbo ■ **to demolish:** los albañiles derrumbaron la casa vieja the builders demolished the old house.

**desabrochar** verbo ■ **to undo:** tienes los pantalones desabrochados your pants are undone.

**desafiar** verbo

1. **to challenge:** el héroe desafió a su enemigo the hero challenged his enemy
2. **to defy:** los bomberos desafían a la muerte todos los días firefighters defy death every day.

el **desafío** ■ **challenge**.

**desafortunado** adjetivo ■ **unfortunate:** fue un comentario desafortunado that was an unfortunate comment.

**desagradable** *adjetivo* ■ unpleasant: el olor a comida podrida es muy desagradable the smell of rotting food is very unpleasant

➤ ¡no seas tan desagrable! don't be so unpleasant!

**desagradecido** *adjetivo* ■ ungrateful.

el **desagüe** ■ drain: el desagüe está tapado con hojas the drain is clogged with leaves.

**desahogar** *verbo* ■ to vent: Esther desahogó todos sus problemas con su madre Esther vented all her problems to her mother

➤ a veces grita para desahogarse sometimes she screams to let off steam.

**desanimar** *verbo* ■ to discourage: la falta de dinero nos desanimó the lack of money discouraged us.

**desaparecer** *verbo* ■ to disappear: mis llaves han desaparecido my keys have disappeared.

el **desarmador** *Mexico* ■ screwdriver.

**desarmar** *verbo*
1. to take apart: desarmamos el juguete para arreglarlo we took the toy apart in order to fix it
2. to disarm: el policía desarmó con facilidad al pistolero the police officer easily disarmed the gunman.

el **desarme** ■ disarmament.

**desarrollar** *verbo*
1. to develop: desarrolló los músculos de sus brazos he developed his arm muscles
2. to carry out: desarrolla un trabajo indispensable she carries out indispensable work.

el **desarrollo** ■ development: el desarrollo de las niñas comienza antes que el de los niños girls' development begins before that of boys

➤ países en vías de desarrollo developing countries.

el **desastre** ■ disaster: el hundimiento del barco fue un desastre the sinking of the boat was a disaster

➤ ¡eres un desastre! you're hopeless!

➤ vas hecho un desastre you look a mess.

**desatar** *verbo*
1. to untie: desatamos al perro we untied the dog
2. to undo: ayúdame a desatar este nudo help me undo this knot

**desatarse** *verbo pronominal*
1. to come undone: se desató el nudo the knot came undone
2. to break: se desató una tormenta muy violenta a very violent storm broke.

**desayunar** *verbo* ■ to have breakfast: ya es hora de desayunar it's time to have breakfast

➤ desayunar algo to have some breakfast: ¿quieres desayunar algo? would you like to have some breakfast?

el **desayuno** ■ breakfast.

**descalzarse** *verbo pronominal* ■ to take one's shoes off: por favor descálzense antes de entrar please take your shoes off before entering.

**descalzo** *adjetivo* ■ barefoot: me gusta correr descalzo por la playa I like to run barefoot on the beach.

**descansar** *verbo* ■ to rest: descansamos durante las vacaciones we rested during our vacation.

el **descanso**
1. rest: necesito un buen descanso I need a good rest
2. break: vamos a hacer un descanso de diez minutos we're going to take a ten minute break
3. intermission: esta obra de teatro tiene un descanso de cinco minutos this play has a five minute intermission
4. landing: hay una papelera en el descanso de la escalera there is a wastepaper basket on the staircase landing.

**descargar** *verbo*
1. **to unload:** descargaron la mercadería they unloaded the merchandise
2. **to fire:** descargó su arma sobre víctimas inocentes he fired his weapon at innocent victims
3. **to download:** descarga muchos programas de Internet she downloads many programs from the Internet

**descargarse** *verbo pronominal* ■ **to go dead:** se descargó la batería del coche the car battery went dead.

**descender** *verbo*
1. **to go down:** descendió la temperatura the temperature went down
2. **to be relegated:** nuestro equipo descendió de categoría our soccer team was relegated
3. **to be descended:** desciendo de inmigrantes I am descended from immigrants.

el **descenso**
1. **descent:** el descenso de esta montaña es muy peligroso the descent from this mountain is very dangerous
2. **fall:** un fuerte descenso de los precios a sharp fall in prices.

**descifrar** *verbo* ■ **to decipher:** descifró el jeroglífico he deciphered the hieroglyph.

**descolgar** *verbo*
1. **to take down:** descolgamos todos los cuadros we took down all the pictures
2. **to pick up:** descuelga el teléfono pick up the telephone

**descolgarse** *verbo pronominal* ■ **to lower oneself:** las fuerzas especiales se descolgaron por la ventana the special forces lowered themselves through the window.

**descomponer** *verbo*
1. **to decompose:** la comida se descompuso por el calor the food decomposed because of the heat
2. **to break:** ya descompuso su reloj nuevo he already broke his new watch

**descomponerse** *verbo pronominal* ■ *River Plate* **to be sick:** no fui a trabajar porque me descompuse I didn't go to work because I was sick.

la **descompostura** ■ **breakdown:** la descompostura de la televisión no tiene arreglo the television's breakdown is unfixable; me agarré descompostura *River Plate* I had a breakdown.

**desconectar** *verbo* ■ **to disconnect:** desconectemos este cable let's disconnect this cable.

**desconfiar** *verbo* ■ desconfío de sus palabras I distrust his words.

**desconocer** *verbo*
1. **to be unfamiliar with:** desconocen el tema they are unfamiliar with the subject
2. **to not recognize:** la desconocí con esa ropa moderna I didn't recognize her with that trendy clothing.

**desconocido**
1. **unknown:** una actriz desconocida ganó el premio an unknown actress won the award
2. **unrecognizable:** estás desconocido con ese corte de pelo you're unrecognizable with that haircut

el **desconocido, la desconocida**
■ **unknown person** (*plural* **unknown people**): dos desconocidos secuestraron al embajador two unknown people kidnaped the embassador.

el **desconsuelo** ■ **grief**.

**descontar** *verbo* ■ **to deduct:** desconté 100 pesos de la deuda I deducted 100 pesos from the debt.

**descontrolarse** *verbo pronominal* ■ **to lose control:** se descontroló y empezó a gritarme como una loca she lost control and began to shout at me like a crazy woman.

**descortés** *adjetivo* ■ **rude:** su comportamiento fue muy descortés his behavior was very rude.

**describir** *verbo* ■ **to describe:** describí el problema I described the problem.

la **descripción** *(plural* las descripciones) ■ **description:** hizo una detallada descripción de la situación he gave a detailed description of the situation.

**descubierto** *adjetivo* ■ **exposed:** era un lugar descubierto it was an exposed place.

el **descubrimiento** ■ discovery *(plural* discoveries): el descubrimiento de la rueda the discovery of the wheel.

**descubrir** *verbo*
1. **to discover:** descubrieron una isla desierta they discovered a desert island
2. **to uncover:** descubrí el desfalco I uncovered the embezzlement
3. **to unveil:** la novia descubrió su rostro the bride unveiled her face.

el **descuento**
1. **discount:** me hicieron un 15% de descuento they gave me a 15% discount
2. **overtime:** el árbitro agregó cuatro minutos de descuento en la final the referee added four minutes of overtime in the final.

**descuidar** *verbo* ■ **to neglect:** el alumno descuidó sus notas the student neglected his grades.

el **descuido** ■ **oversight:** provocó un accidente por un descuido he caused an accident by an oversight.

**desde** *preposición*
1. **since:** vivo en este país desde 1998 I have lived in this country since 1998
2. **from:** viajamos desde Córdoba a Mendoza we traveled from Córdoba to Mendoza; vi el volcán desde el tren I saw the volcano from the train
➤ vivo aquí desde hace cuatro meses I've lived here for four months
➤ desde entonces since then.

la **desdicha** ■ **unhappiness:** su muerte nos causó una gran desdicha his death caused us great unhappiness.

**desear** *verbo* ■ **to wish:** te deseo toda la suerte del mundo I wish you all the luck in the world; deseo hablar con el encargado I wish to speak with the person in charge.

**desechar** *verbo*
1. **to throw out:** desechamos la ropa vieja we threw out the old clothes
2. **to reject:** deseché la idea de viajar I rejected the idea of traveling.

el **desecho** ■ **waste:** los desechos tóxicos son un problema mundial toxic waste is a worldwide problem.

**desembarcar** *verbo*
1. **to disembark:** los viajeros desembarcaron al llegar al puerto the travelers disembarked upon arriving at the port
2. **to unload:** desembarcaron el equipaje de los pasajeros they unloaded the passengers' luggage.

la **desembocadura** ■ **mouth:** la desembocadura del río queda a dos kilómetros the mouth of the river is two kilometers away.

**desembocar** *verbo*
➤ desembocar en to lead into: esta calle desemboca en la avenida principal this street leads into the main avenue.

**desempeñar** *verbo* ■ **to occupy:** desempeña un cargo ejecutivo she occupies an executive position.

el **desempeño** ■ **performance:** tuvo un excelente desempeño he gave an excellent performance.

el **desempleo** ■ **unemployment:** el desempleo ha aumentado mucho unemployment has increased a lot.

**desencadenar** *verbo* ■ **to set off:** su respuesta desencadenó la burla de los presentes his answer set off the ridicule of those present.

el **desengaño** ■ disappointment.

el **desenlace** ■ **outcome:** el desenlace de los acontecimientos fue inesperado the outcome of the events was unexpected.

**desenredar** *verbo*

1. **to untangle:** me enredo el pelo todas las mañanas I untangle my hair every morning
2. **to unravel:** desenredé el misterio I unraveled the mystery.

**desenvolver** *verbo* ■ **to unwrap:** desenvolvimos los regalos después de la fiesta we unwrapped the gifts after the party

**desenvolverse** *verbo pronominal* ■ **to cope:** se desenvolvió con mucha soltura he coped with ease.

el **deseo**

1. **desire:** mi mayor deseo es hacerte feliz my greatest desire is to make you happy
2. **wish:** pide tres deseos antes de apagar las velitas ask for three wishes before blowing out the candles.

**desértico** *adjetivo* ■ **desert-like:** atravesamos una zona desértica we crossed a desert-like area.

la **desesperación** ■ **despair:** la desesperación lo llevó a la locura despair drove him insane.

**desesperar** *verbo* ■ **to drive crazy:** me desespera la impuntualidad unpunctuality drives me crazy

**desesperarse** *verbo pronominal* ■ **to lose hope:** no te desesperes que aún puedes ganar don't lose hope, you can still win.

la **desestatización** ■ **privatization:** la desestatización de la empresa de teléfonos provocó grandes conflictos the privatization of the telephone company provoked terrible conflicts.

**desestatizar** *verbo* ■ **to privatize:** el nuevo gobierno desestatizó gran parte de las empresas públicas the new government privatized a large number of the public companies.

**desfilar** *verbo*

1. **to parade:** el ejército desfiló ante el Presidente the army paraded before the President

2. **to march:** los escolares desfilaron en el desfile de la victoria the schoolchildren marched in the victory parade.

el **desfile**

1. **review:** el desfile militar duró tres horas the military review lasted three hours
2. **parade:** nos encantó el desfile de Carnaval we loved the Carnival parade
➤ un desfile de modelos a fashion show.

**desgarrar** *verbo*

1. **to tear:** me desgarré un músculo de la pierna I tore a muscle in my leg
2. **to crush:** su muerte desgarró a la familia his death crushed his family.

**desgastar** *verbo* ■ **to wear down:** este conflicto me ha desgastado profundamente this conflict has worn me down terribly

**desgastarse** *verbo pronominal* ■ **to get worn out:** las suelas de las botas se han desgastado the soles of the boots have gotten worn out.

la **desgracia** ■ **tragedy** (*plural* **tragedies**): este accidente fue una verdadera desgracia this accident was a real tragedy
➤ por desgracia unfortunately: por desgracia perdimos el campeonato unfortunately we lost the championship.

**deshabitado** *adjetivo* ■ **uninhabited:** es una casa deshabitada it's an uninhabited house.

**deshacer** *verbo*

1. **to take apart:** deshice el puzzle I took the puzzle apart
2. **to ruin:** el niño deshizo la ropa nueva the boy ruined his new clothes
3. **to pick apart:** el abogado deshizo el tratado the lawyer picked apart the agreement
4. **to unpack:** ya deshice las maletas I've already unpacked the suitcases

**deshacerse** *verbo pronominal*

1. **to melt:** el buen chocolate se deshace en la boca good chocolate melts in your mouth
2. **to come undone:** el nudo se deshizo the knot came undone

**87**

➤ **deshacerse de algo** to get rid of something: **el capitán se deshizo de la carga más pesada** the captain got rid of the heaviest cargo

➤ **deshacerse en elogios** to shower with praise.

**deshidratarse** *verbo pronominal* ■ **to get dehydrated**: **se deshidrató a causa del sol** he got dehydrated because of the sun.

el **desierto** ■ **desert**.

la **desilusión** *(plural* las desilusiones*)* ■ **disappointment**: **me llevé una gran desilusión con su comportamiento** I suffered a terrible disappointment because of his behavior.

**desilusionar** *verbo* ■ **to disappoint**: **me has desilusionado con tus malas notas** you've disappointed me with your bad grades

**desilusionarse** *verbo pronominal* ■ **to be disappointed**: **se desilusionó al ver la reacción de su novio** she was disappointed to see the reaction of her boyfriend.

el **desinfectante** ■ **disinfectant**.

**desinfectar** *verbo* ■ **to disinfect**: **el médico desinfectó la herida** the doctor disinfected the wound.

**desinflar** *verbo* ■ **to deflate**: **desinfló el neumático** he deflated the tire.

**desintegrarse** *verbo pronominal*

1. **to be smashed**: **los vidrios se desintegraron con la explosión** the glass was smashed from the explosion
2. **to split up**: **el grupo musical se desintegró rápidamente** the group split up quickly.

el **desinterés**

1. **lack of interest**: **hay un gran desinterés de los jóvenes por la política** there's a huge lack of interest in politics among young people
2. **unselfishness**: **me ayudó con total desinterés** he helped me with total unselfishness.

**desinteresado** *adjetivo* ■ **impartial**: **te doy un consejo desinteresado** I'll give you an impartial piece of advice.

el **deslave** ■ **landslide**: **el deslave provocó la muerte de muchas personas** the landslide caused the death of many people.

**deslizar** *verbo* ■ **to slip**: **deslizó un billete entre sus manos** he slipped a bill into her hands

**deslizarse** *verbo pronominal* ■ **to slide**: **el auto se deslizó por la pendiente** the car slid down the slope.

**deslumbrante** *adjetivo* ■ **dazzling**: **tuvo una actuación deslumbrante** he gave a dazzling performance.

**deslumbrar** *verbo* ■ **to dazzle**: **me deslumbró con su belleza** she dazzled me with her beauty.

**desmayarse** *verbo pronominal* ■ **to faint**: **se desmayó en medio de la competencia** she fainted in the middle of the competition; **se desmayó de dolor** he fainted from pain.

el **desmayo** ■ **faint**
➤ **le dio un desmayo** she fainted
➤ **sufrió un desmayo** she fainted.

**desnudo** *adjetivo* ■ **naked**: **hay un hombre desnudo en la ventana** there's a naked man in the window.

la **desnutrición** ■ **malnutrition**.

la **desobediencia** ■ **disobedience**.

**desocupar** *verbo*

1. **to vacate**: **desocuparon la casa de al lado** they vacated the house next door
2. **to remove**: **desocupé el mueble de la cocina** I removed the furniture from the kitchen.

el **desorden** *(plural* los desórdenes*)*

1. **mess**: **tienes que acomodar el desorden de tu cuarto** you have to straighten the mess in your room
2. **disturbance**: **cometieron desórdenes públicos** they caused public disturbances.

**desorientar** *verbo*

1. **to disorient:** el fuerte sol los desorientó the strong sunlight disoriented them
2. **to confuse:** me desorientó su actitud his attitude confused me.

**despachar** *verbo*

1. **to attend to:** nos despachó una emplea-da muy amable a very nice clerk attended to us
2. **to deal with:** despachó el tema rápida-mente she dealt with the issue quickly
3. **to sell:** esta tienda despacha productos extranjeros this store sells foreign products
4. **to check:** despachamos cuatro valijas antes de subir al avión we checked four suitcases before getting on the airplane.

el **despacho** ■ **office:** me recibió en su despacho he received me in his office.

**despacio** *adverbio* ■ **slowly:** camina-mos muy despacio we walked very slowly.

**despedir** *verbo*

1. **to fire:** despidieron a cuatro obreros they fired four workers
2. **to see off:** la despedimos esta mañana we saw her off this morning

**despedirse** *verbo pronominal* ■ **to say goodbye:** se despidieron en la estación they said goodbye at the station

➤ **despedirse de alguien** to say goodbye to somebody: **nos despedimos de nuestros padres en el aeropuerto** we said goodbye to our parents at the airport.

**despegar** *verbo* ■ **to take off:** el avión despegó the airplane took off.

**despejado** *adjetivo* ■ **clear:** el cielo está despejado hoy the sky is clear today.

la **despensa** ■ **pantry** (*plural* **pantries**): guardo los dulces en la despensa I keep the candy in the pantry.

**desperdiciar** *verbo* ■ **to throw away:** desperdició muy buenas oportunidades he threw away very good opportunities.

el **desperdicio** ■ **waste:** es un desper-dicio no comer esa carne it's a waste not to eat that meat

➤ no tires los desperdicios don't throw out the trash.

el **desperfecto** ■ **flaw:** este auto tiene algunos desperfectos this car has some flaws.

el **despertador** ■ **alarm clock:** mi des-pertador suena a las seis de la mañana my alarm clock goes off at six in the morning.

**despertar** *verbo*

1. **to wake:** desperté a mi hijo temprano I woke my son early
2. **to arouse:** su actitud despertó sospechas his attitude aroused suspicion

**despertarse** *verbo pronominal* ■ **to wake up:** me desperté con el ruido de la calle I woke up with the noise of the street.

**despierto** *adjetivo*

1. **awake:** no estoy despierto todavía I'm not awake yet
2. **bright:** es una niña muy despierta she's a very bright child.

el **despiole** *River Plate informal* ■ **row:** se armó un gran despiole en la calle there was a big row in the street.

**despistado** *adjetivo* ■ **absent-minded**.

**desplazar** *verbo* ■ **to take the place of:** el avión ha desplazado al barco the airplane has taken the place of the ship

**desplazarse** *verbo pronominal* ■ **to travel:** me desplazo por la ciudad en coche I travel about the city by car.

**desplegar** *verbo* ■ **to unfold:** desple-gó la tela she unfolded the cloth.

**despoblado** *adjetivo* ■ **uninhabited:** atravesamos una zona despoblada we crossed an uninhabited area

el **despoblado** ■ **deserted spot:** deja-mos el coche en un despoblado we left the car in a deserted spot.

**despoblarse** *verbo pronominal* ■ **to be-come depopulated:** el campo se ha des-poblado the countryside has become de-populated.

**despojarse** *verbo* ■ **to remove:** se despojó de la ropa he removed his clothes.

**despreciar** *verbo*
1. **to look down on:** desprecia a sus empleados he looks down on his employees
2. **to despise:** desprecia a su enemigo he despises his enemy
3. **to reject:** despreció la invitación de Ana he rejected Ana's invitation.

**desprender** *verbo* ■ **to give off:** ese calentador desprende gas that heater gives off gas

**desprenderse** *verbo pronominal*
➤ desprenderse de algo to let go of something: no se desprende de sus hijos nunca she will never let go of her children.

**despreocuparse** *verbo pronominal* ■ **to stop worrying:** despreocúpate y descansa un rato stop worrying and rest for a while.

**desprevenido** *adjetivo* ■ **unprepared:** está desprevenido, no va a asimilar lo que le vas a decir he's unprepared, he won't be able to accept what you're going to tell him
➤ la noticia me tomó desprevenida the news took me by surprise.

**desprolijo** *adjetivo* ■ **messy:** sus cuadernos son muy desprolijos his notebooks are very messy.

**después** *adverbio*
1. **afterward:** después, iremos a bailar afterward, we'll go dancing
2. **later:** vino después she came later; un año después retomé mi trabajo a year later I took up my job again
3. **then:** primero le pones la sal, y después le pones la pimienta first you put in the salt and then you put in the pepper
➤ después de after: después de la cena, vamos a hablar after dinner, we're going to talk: después de todo after all
➤ después de Cristo Anno Domini.

**destacar** *verbo* ■ **to emphasize:** destacó sus valores morales he emphasized his moral values

**destacarse** *verbo pronominal* ■ **to stand out:** se destaca por su altura he stands out because of his height.

el **destapador** ■ **bottle opener**.

**destapar** *verbo*
1. **to open:** destapé la gaseosa I opened the soda pop
2. *River Plate* **to unstop:** el plomero destapó el caño the plumber unstopped the pipe.

el **destello** ■ **sparkle:** vi un destello en la oscuridad I saw a sparkle in the darkness.

**destinar** *verbo*
1. **to set aside:** destiné estos ahorros para el futuro I set aside these savings for the future
2. **to assign:** lo han destinado al departamento de contabilidad they have assigned him to the accounting department.

el **destinatario**, la **destinataria** ■ **addressee:** Raúl es el destinatario de esta carta Raúl is the addressee of this letter.

el **destino**
1. **destiny:** mi destino es ayudar a los demás my destiny is to help others
2. **destination:** los pasajeros cuyo destino es Perú deben embarcar a la brevedad the passengers whose destination is Peru must get on board as soon as possible.

la **destreza** ■ **skill:** tiene una destreza increíble con las manos he has incredible skill with his hands.

**destrozar** *verbo*
1. **to destroy:** la explosión destrozó el barrio the explosion destroyed the neighborhood
2. **to ruin:** el perro ha destrozado el sofá the dog has ruined the sofa.

**destructor** *adjetivo* ■ **destructive:** tuvo efectos destructores it had destructive effects.

**destruir** *verbo* ■ **to destroy:** la tormenta destruyó las casas del pueblo the storm destroyed the town's houses.

**desvelar** *verbo*

1. **to keep awake:** el café me desvela coffee keeps me awake
2. **to reveal:** me desveló la verdad he revealed the truth to me
➤ **desvelarse por algo** to be concerned about something: se desvela por nuestra felicidad he's concerned about our happiness.

la **desventaja** ■ **disadvantage**.

la **desviación** *(plural las desviaciones)*

1. **detour:** tuvimos que tomar una desviación en el camino we had to take a detour on the way
2. **deviation:** esta es una desviación de la norma this is a deviation from the norm
➤ **desviación de fondos** diversion of funds.

**desviar** *verbo* ■ **to divert:** desviaron el tránsito they diverted traffic

**desviarse** *verbo pronominal* ■ **to turn off:** nos desviamos de la ruta principal we turned off from the main route.

el **detalle** ■ **detail:** me contó los detalles de la historia he told me the details of the story
➤ ¡qué detalle! how thoughtful!

**detectar** *verbo* ■ **to detect:** el radar detectó el peligro the radar detected the danger.

**detener** *verbo*

1. **to stop:** el conductor detuvo el auto the driver stopped the car
2. **to arrest:** la policía detuvo a los sospechosos the police arrested the suspects

**detenerse** *verbo pronominal* ■ **to stop:** no te detengas, sigue caminando don't stop, keep walking.

**deteriorar** *verbo* ■ **to damage:** el mar deteriora las casas de la costa the sea damages the coastal houses

**deteriorarse** *verbo pronominal* ■ **to deteriorate:** su salud se ha deteriorado rápidamente her health has deteriorated quickly.

**determinado** *adjetivo* ■ **certain:** esta práctica era común en determinada época this practice was common in a certain time period.

**determinar** *verbo*

1. **to determine:** el juez determinó la sentencia de los acusados the judge determined the sentence of the accused
2. **to decide:** determinamos seguir con el viaje we decided to continue with the trip
3. **to state:** la ley determina que tenemos ciertos derechos y obligaciones the law states that we have certain rights and obligations
4. **to bring about:** el excelente trabajo de los empleados determinó el éxito del negocio the excellent work of the employees brought about the success of the business.

**detrás** *adverbio* ■ **at the back:** siéntate detrás sit at the back
➤ **uno detrás de otro** one after another
➤ **detrás de** behind
➤ el gato se escondió detrás de la puerta the cat hid behind the door.

la **deuda** ■ **debt:** tengo una deuda con el banco I owe a debt to the bank.

el **deudor,** la **deudora** ■ **debtor:** los deudores tienen problemas para pagar the debtors are having problems paying.

la **devaluación** *(plural las devaluaciones)* ■ **devaluation:** la devaluación provocó una baja en el consumo interno devaluation caused a decrease in internal consumption.

**devaluar** *verbo* ■ **to devalue:** el Gobierno ya devaluó la moneda dos veces the government has already devalued the currency twice.

la **devoción** ■ **devotion**.

**devolver** *verbo*

1. **to return:** ya he devuelto los libros a la biblioteca I've already returned the books to the library

**2.** **to repay:** le devolveremos el importe we'll repay the amount to him

**3.** **to throw up:** el bebe devolvió la comida the baby threw up the food

**devolverse** *verbo pronominal* ■ *Andes, Central America, Caribbean, Mexico* **to return:** nos devolvimos a los quince días we returned after two weeks.

**devorar** *verbo*

**1.** **to devour:** el jabalí devoró al cordero the wild boar devoured the lamb

**2.** **to consume:** el fuego devoró el depósito the fire consumed the warehouse.

el **día** ■ **day:** los días son más largos en verano the days are longer in the summer; marzo tiene 31 días March has 31 days; los murciélagos duermen de día bats sleep during the day

➤ ¡buenos días! good morning!

➤ ¡buen día! *River Plate* good morning!

➤ hacer buen día to be a fine day

➤ poner al día to catch up: se puso al día con el trabajo he caught up with his work

➤ Día de los Muertos All Souls' Day.

el **diablo** ■ **devil:** el diablo representa el mal the devil represents evil.

el **diagnóstico** ■ **diagnosis:** el médico dio un diagnóstico alentador the doctor gave an encouraging diagnosis.

el **diálogo**

**1.** **dialogue:** el diálogo condujo a una solución pacífica the dialogue led to a peaceful solution

**2.** **conversation:** mantuvimos un diálogo muy interesante we had a very interesting conversation.

el **diamante** ■ **diamond:** me regaló un anillo con un diamante he gave me a diamond ring.

el **diámetro** ■ **diameter:** calcula el diámetro de este círculo calculate the diameter of this circle.

**diario** *adjetivo* ■ **daily:** hago tres comidas diarias I have three meals daily

el **diario**

**1.** **newspaper:** pásame el diario de la mañana pass me the morning newspaper

**2.** **diary** *(plural* **diaries)**: escribo en mi diario todos los días I write in my diary every day.

el/la **dibujante**

**1.** **cartoonist:** el dibujante hizo un oso animado the cartoonist made an animated bear

**2.** **designer:** los dibujantes terminaron el plano the designers finished the plan.

**dibujar** *verbo* ■ **to draw:** dibujó unas figuras preciosas he drew some lovely drawings.

el **dibujo** ■ **drawing:** hizo un dibujo de la madre he did a drawing of his mother.

el **diccionario** ■ **dictionary** *(plural* **dictionaries)**: compró un diccionario ilustrado he bought an illustrated dictionary.

la **dicha** ■ **happiness:** su familia es su mayor dicha his family is his greatest happiness.

el **dicho** ■ **saying:** abusa de los dichos y proverbios she abuses sayings and proverbs

➤ dicho y hecho no sooner said than done.

**dichoso** *adjetivo* ■ **happy:** se siente dichosa con su embarazo she feels happy because of her pregnancy.

**diciembre** *sustantivo masculino*

En inglés los nombres de los meses se escriben con mayúscula:

**December:** en diciembre in December; el próximo diciembre next December; el pasado diciembre last December.

el **dictado** ■ **dictation:** la maestra pone un dictado todas las semanas the teacher assigns a dictation every week.

el **dictador,** la **dictadora** ■ **dictator:** el dictador gobernó por diez años the dictator governed for ten years.

**dictar** *verbo*

**1.** **to dictate:** el jefe le dictó una carta a la secretaria the boss dictated a letter to his secretary

2. **to pronounce:** el juez dictó sentencia the judge pronounced the sentence.

el **diente** ■ **tooth** (plural **teeth**): al bebe le están saliendo los dientes the baby's teeth are coming in; la sierra tiene los dientes gastados the saw's teeth are worn out.

**diestro** adjetivo ■ **skillful:** es muy diestro manejando los caballos he's very skillful at handling the horses.

la **dieta** ■ **diet:** la dieta rioplatense se basa en la carne the River Plate diet is based on meat; el lunes empiezo la dieta Monday I start the diet.

el/la **dietista** ■ **dietician:** el dietista me recomendó que no comiera grasas the dietician recommended that I don't eat fats.

**diez** numeral ■ **ten:** tiene diez hijos she has ten children
➤ mi hermana tiene diez años my sister is ten years old
➤ son las diez it's ten o'clock
➤ el diez de abril the tenth of April.

la **diferencia** ■ **difference:** tiene una gran diferencia de edad con su hermano there's a big age difference between him and his brother; los socios tuvieron graves diferencias the partners had serious differences.

**diferente** ( adjetivo & adverbio)
■ adjetivo
**different:** sus hijos son muy diferentes his children are very different
■ adverbio
**differently:** Ana come diferente porque está a dieta Ana is eating differently because she's on a diet.

**difícil** adjetivo ■ **difficult:** no encuentro salida para esta difícil situación I can't find a way out of this difficult situation.

la **dificultad** ■ **difficulty** (plural **difficulties**): este viaje está lleno de dificultades this trip is full of difficulties.

**dificultar** verbo ■ **to hinder:** la niebla dificulta la visión the fog hinders vision.

**difundir** verbo
1. **to spread:** la luz eléctrica se difundió por todo el mundo electric light spread throughout the whole world
2. **to broadcast:** la televisión difunde las noticias television broadcasts the news.

**digerir** verbo ■ **to digest:** digiere la comida con dificultad he digests food with difficulty.

la **digestión** ■ **digestion**.

el **digitador**, la **digitadora** ■ **keyboarder:** contratamos dos digitadores para entrar los datos en la computadora we hired two keyboarders to enter the data into the computer.

la **dignidad**
1. **dignity:** habla con dignidad he speaks with dignity
2. **honor:** su dignidad le impidió aceptar la oferta deshonesta his honor prevented him from accepting the improper offer.

**digno** adjetivo ■ **worthy:** su trabajo es digno de mención his work is worthy of mention.

**dilatar** verbo
1. **to expand:** el calor dilata los cuerpos heat expands substances
2. **to put off:** dilataron la respuesta intencionalmente they put off the answer intentionally.

**diluir** verbo ■ **to dilute:** diluye estos colores con el blanco dilute those colors with white.

la **dimensión** (plural las dimensiones)
1. **measurement:** las dimensiones del armario son... the measurements of the closet are...
2. **dimension:** es una casa de grandes dimensiones it's a house of large dimensions
3. **scope:** las dimensiones de la catástrofe son incalculables the scope of the catastrophe is incalculable.

**diminuto** adjetivo ■ **tiny:** tiene una cicatriz diminuta she has a tiny scar.

**dinámico** *adjetivo* ■ **dynamic:** es una persona tan dinámica que trabaja 15 horas al día she's such a dynamic person that she works 15 hours a day.

la **dinamita** ■ **dynamite.**

el **dinero** ■ **money:** heredé una fuerte suma de dinero I inherited a large sum of money.

el **dios** ■ **god:** en su religión adoran a más de un dios in their religion they worship more than one god; según la Biblia Dios creó al hombre according to the Bible, God created man
➤ **Dios mediante** God willing
➤ **¡Dios mío!** my God!

la **diosa** ■ **goddess:** la diosa del mar protege a los pescadores the goddess of the sea protects the fishermen.

el **diploma** ■ **diploma.**

la **diplomacia** ■ **diplomacy.**

el **diplomático,** la **diplomática** ■ **diplomat.**

la **dirección** *(plural* las direcciones)
1. **direction:** estamos yendo en dirección norte we are going in a northerly direction; al perdernos pedimos direcciones para volver al camino principal upon getting lost we asked for directions to return to the main road
2. **management:** lo mandaron en castigo a la dirección they sent him to management for punishment
3. **address:** tengo la dirección de la fiesta I have the address of the party
4. **steering:** está fallando la dirección del coche the car's steering is failing.

**directo** *adjetivo*
1. **non-stop:** este es un vuelo directo a Buenos Aires this is a non-stop flight to Buenos Aires
2. **direct:** tengo órdenes directas del jefe I have direct orders from the boss
3. **straight:** fui directo a casa I went straight home

➤ **en directo** live: están transmitiendo el partido en directo they are transmitting the match live.

el **director,** la **directora**
1. **director:** la directora de la empresa prometió llamarnos the director of the company promised to call us
2. **conductor:** el director de la orquesta tiene mucha experiencia the conductor of the orchestra has a lot of experience
3. **principal:** la directora de esa escuela es muy joven the principal of that school is very young
4. **editor:** mi tío es el director de ese periódico my uncle is the editor of that newspaper

el **directorio**
1. **board of directors:** el directorio de la empresa es muy exigente the company's board of directors is very demanding
2. **directory** *(plural* **directories**): tengo muchos directorios en mi computadora I have many directories in my computer
3. *Andes, Central America, Caribbean, Mexico* **directory** *(plural* **directories**): encontré sus datos en el directorio telefónico I found his information in the telephone directory.

**dirigir** *verbo*
1. **to address:** esta carta está dirigida a mi jefe this letter is addressed to my boss
2. **to manage:** el Sr. López dirige esta empresa Mr. López manages this company
3. **to conduct:** el hombre que dirige esta orquesta es muy famoso en Europa the man who conducts this orchestra is very famous in Europe
4. **to direct:** Spielberg ha dirigido muchas películas Spielberg has directed many movies

**dirigirse** *verbo pronominal*
1. **to head towards:** nos dirigimos hacia el oeste we headed towards the west
2. **to address:** se dirigió a los estudiantes he addressed the students.

**discar** *Andes, River Plate verbo* ■ **to dial:** disqué varias veces al banco pero siempre da ocupado I dialed the bank several times but there's always a busy signal.

la **disciplina** ■ discipline: la disciplina es muy importante en esta institución discipline is very important in this institution.

el **discípulo**, la **discípula** ■ student: Carlos es discípulo de un artista famoso Carlos is a student of a famous artist.

el **disco**
1. disk: cortamos esta masa en forma de disco we cut this dough into the shape of a disk
2. record: el disco fue desplazado por el cassette the record was supplanted by the cassette
➤ un disco compacto a compact disc
➤ un disco duro a hard disk.

la **discordia** ■ discord.

la **discreción** ■ discretion: me pidió discreción cuando me reveló su problema he asked me for discretion when he disclosed his problem to me.

**discreto** adjetivo ■ discreet: se viste de manera muy discreta she dresses in a very discreet manner.

la **discriminación** ■ discrimination: discriminación racial racial discrimination.

**discriminar** verbo
1. to discriminate: hay leyes que discriminan según el color de la piel there are laws that discriminate according to skin color
2. to tell the difference: tienes que discriminar entre lo que está bien y lo que está mal you have to tell the difference between what's good and what's bad.

la **disculpa** ■ apology (plural apologies): su disculpa no fue suficiente his apology was not enough
➤ pedirle disculpas a alguien por algo to apologize to somebody for something: te pido disculpas por lo que dije I apologize to you for what I said.

**disculpar** verbo ■ to excuse: te disculpo esta vez I'll excuse you this time
➤ disculpe, ¿podría pasar? excuse me, may I get by?

**disculparse** verbo pronominal ■ to apologize: el profesor se disculpó por haber llegado tarde the professor apologized for having arrived late.

el **discurso** ■ speech: hizo un discurso muy emotivo he gave a very moving speech.

la **discusión** (plural las discusiones)
1. discussion: la discusión sobre el tema se hizo interminable the discussion of the subject became endless
2. argument: tuvimos una discusión con el encargado del restaurante we had an argument with the manager of the restaurant.

**discutir** verbo
1. to discuss: discutimos el tema de la crisis financiera we discussed the subject of the financial crisis
2. to argue: discutieron con el encargado del restaurante they argued with the manager of the restaurant.

**diseñar** verbo ■ to design: el arquitecto diseñó una casa con cuatro dormitorios the architect designed a house with four bedrooms.

el **diseño** ■ design: se encargó del diseño de la próxima colección de vestidos she took charge of the design of the next collection of dresses.

el **disfraz** (plural los disfraces) ■ disguise: el niño se puso un disfraz de pirata the boy put on a pirate disguise.

**disfrazar** verbo ■ to dress up: disfrazó al hijo para el carnaval she dressed her son up for the carnival

**disfrazarse** verbo pronominal
➤ disfrazarse de to dress up as: se disfrazó de vaquero he dressed up as a cowboy.

**disfrutar** verbo ■ to enjoy oneself: disfruté en la fiesta I enjoyed myself at the party
➤ disfrutar de algo to enjoy something: disfruto de las vacaciones en la playa I enjoy vacations at the beach.

**disgustar** *verbo* ▪ **to upset:** a los clientes les disgustan estas respuestas these answers upset the clients

**disgustarse** *verbo pronominal* ▪ **to get upset:** el jefe se disgustó con uno de los empleados the boss got upset with one of the employees.

The Spanish word **disgustar** is a false cognate, it does not mean "to disgust".

el **disgusto**
➤ darle un disgusto a alguien to upset somebody: su respuesta me dio un gran disgusto his answer upset me a lot.

**disimular** *verbo* ▪ **to hide:** disimularon su enojo they hid their anger.

**disminuir** *verbo* ▪ **to decrease:** disminuye la velocidad en la curva decrease your speed on the curve; la inflación disminuyó el 1% inflation decreased by 1%.

**disolver** *verbo*
1. **to dissolve:** tuvimos que disolver la pastilla en el agua we had to dissolve the tablet in the water
2. **to break up:** la policía disolvió la manifestación the police broke up the demonstration

**disolverse** *verbo pronominal* ▪ **to dissolve:** el medicamento se disuelve en el agua the medicine dissolves in water.

**disparar** *verbo* ▪ **to shoot:** la policía disparó sobre los prófugos the police fired on the fugitives.
➤ dispara la fotografía take the picture.

el **disparate** ▪ **nonsense:** lo que dices es un disparate what you're saying is nonsense.

el **disparo** ▪ **shot:** el disparo retumbó en la habitación the shot echoed in the room.

**disponer** *verbo*
1. **to arrange:** dispusimos las sillas junto a las mesas we arranged the chairs close to the tables

2. **to order:** el jefe dispuso que trabajáramos toda la noche the boss ordered us to work all night

**disponerse** *verbo pronominal*
➤ disponerse a to get ready to: nos disponíamos a salir cuando llegó la visita we were getting ready to leave when the visitor arrived.

**disponible** *adjetivo* ▪ **available**.

la **disposición** *(plural* las disposiciones*)*
1. **arrangement:** no me gusta la disposición de las sillas en esta sala I don't like the arrangement of the chairs in this room
2. **aptitude:** no tiene disposición para las matemáticas he has no aptitude for mathematics
3. **provision:** la disposición del gobierno regula el comercio interno the provision of the government regulates internal commerce.

la **distancia** ▪ **distance:** hay una distancia de 100 km entre las dos ciudades there's a distance of 100 km between the two cities
➤ ¿a qué distancia está la tienda? how far away is the store?
➤ a dos millas de distancia two miles away.

**distante** *adjetivo*
1. **far away:** vive en una zona distante de la capital he lives in an area far away from the capital
2. **distant:** tiene una actitud distante con respecto al problema she has a distant attitude regarding the problem.

**distinguir** *verbo*
1. **to distinguish:** no puedo distinguir a un mellizo del otro I can't distinguish one twin from the other
2. **to set apart:** las rayas blancas distinguen a las cebras white stripes set zebras apart
3. **to make out:** no distingue lo que dice aquel cartel he can't make out what that sign says
4. **to honor:** lo distinguieron con el primer premio they honored him with first prize.

**distinto** *adjetivo* ▪ **different:** cada hijo es distinto each child is different.

la **distracción** (plural las distracciones)

1. **lapse of concentration:** una distracción del conductor provocó el accidente a lapse of concentration from the driver caused the accident

2. **pastime:** el cine es una buena distracción movies are a good pastime.

**distraer** verbo

1. **to distract:** el ruido me distrae cuando estudio noise distracts me when I'm studying

2. **to entertain:** las películas me distraen movies entertain me

**distraerse** verbo pronominal

1. **to get distracted:** el niño se distrae fácilmente en clase the boy gets distracted easily in class

2. **to entertain oneself:** me distraigo viendo televisión I entertain myself watching television.

**distribuir** verbo ■ **to distribute:** distribuimos las tareas entre todos we distribute the work between everybody.

el **distrito** ■ **district:** es el encargado de la seguridad del distrito he's the one in charge of the district's safety

➤ **distrito federal** federal district: México es un Distrito Federal Mexico City is a Federal District.

**diurno** adjetivo ■ **day:** me tocó el turno diurno en el trabajo I got the day shift at work.

la **diversidad** ■ **variety:** hay una gran diversidad de artículos en esta tienda there's a wide variety of goods in this store.

la **diversión** (plural las diversiones)

1. **amusement:** le dedica más tiempo a la diversión que al trabajo he dedicates more time to amusement than to work

2. **pastime:** el cine es mi diversión preferida movies are my favorite pastime

⚠ The Spanish word **diversión** is a false cognate, it does not mean "diversion".

**diverso** adjetivo ■ **diverse:** tiene gustos muy diversos he has very diverse tastes.

**divertido** adjetivo ■ **enjoyable:** pasamos un rato muy divertido en la fiesta we had a very enjoyable time at the party.

**divertir** verbo ■ **to amuse:** los payasos no me divierten en absoluto clowns don't amuse me at all

➤ nos divertimos en la fiesta we had fun at the party.

**dividir** verbo

1. **to separate:** un tabique dividía el ambiente en dos a partition separated the room in two

2. **to divide:** divide 464 por cuatro divide 464 by four

3. **to divide up:** dividimos los caramelos entre todos los niños we divided up the candy between all the children.

la **división** (plural las divisiones) ■ **division:** la división de los bienes fue problemática the division of the possessions was problematic; su niño ya hace divisiones en la escuela her son is already doing division at school; su equipo pertenece a la segunda división his team belongs to the second division.

**divorciarse** verbo pronominal ■ **to get divorced:** se divorciaron después de diez años de casados they got divorced after being married for ten years.

el **divorcio** ■ **divorce:** los trámites del divorcio fueron muy costosos the proceedings of the divorce were very costly.

**divulgar** verbo ■ **to spread:** los medios divulgaron la noticia the media spread the news.

**doblar** verbo

1. **to fold:** doblé la ropa antes de guardarla en el ropero I folded the clothes before putting them in the wardrobe

2. **to double:** le doblaron el sueldo they doubled his salary

3. **to turn:** doblamos en la primera esquina we turned at the first corner

4. **to dub:** doblaron la película al español they dubbed the movie into Spanish.

**doble** *(adjetivo & adverbio)*

■ *adjetivo*
**double:** reservé una habitación doble | reserved a double room

■ *adverbio*
**double:** como había perdido la entrada, tuvo que pagar doble since he had lost the ticket, he had to pay double

el **doble**
1. **double:** contrataron un doble para las escenas peligrosas they hired a double for the dangerous scenes
2. **el doble** twice as much; **gana el doble que yo** he earns twice as much as I do.

el **doblez** *(plural los dobleces)* ■ **crease:** el planchado no borró bien los dobleces the ironing didn't completely get the creases out.

**doce** *numeral* ■ **twelve:** tiene doce sobrinos she has twelve nephews
➤ **mi hermana tiene doce años** my sister is twelve years old
➤ **son las doce** it's twelve o'clock
➤ **el doce de abril** the twelfth of April.

el **doctor,** la **doctora**
1. **doctor:** la doctora me dio de alta the doctor pronounced me fit
2. **Doctor of Philosophy** *(plural* **Doctors of Philosophy***)*: únicamente los doctores pueden dar clase en esta universidad only Doctors of Philosophy can teach in this university.

el **documento** ■ **document:** me piden un documento que pruebe mi fecha de nacimiento they are asking me for a document that proves my date of birth
➤ **un documento de identidad** an identity card: **para comprar bebidas alcohólicas necesitas mostrar el documento de identidad** in order to buy alcoholic beverages you need to show your identity card.

el **dólar** ■ **dollar.**

**doler** *verbo*
1. **to ache:** me duelen las muelas my teeth ache
2. **to hurt:** le dolió mucho que la novia lo abandonara it hurt him a lot that his girlfriend left him.

el **dolor** ■ **pain:** la noticia de su muerte le causó mucho dolor the news of his death caused her a lot of pain
➤ **tener dolor de cabeza** to have a headache.

**domesticar** *verbo* ■ **to tame:** consiguieron domesticar un jabalí they managed to tame a wild boar.

**doméstico** *adjetivo* ■ **domestic:** las tareas domésticas domestic chores
➤ **compramos un lavaplatos de uso doméstico** we bought a dishwasher for home use.

el **domicilio** ■ **residence:** escriba su nombre y domicilio en este formulario write your name and address on this form.

**dominar** *verbo*
1. **to rule over:** el ejército enemigo dominaba toda la zona the enemy army ruled over all the area
2. **to control:** domina la pelota de manera increíble he controls the ball in an incredible way.

el **domingo**

En inglés, los días de la semana se escriben con mayúscula:

**Sunday:** hoy es domingo today is Sunday; **el próximo domingo** next Sunday; **el pasado domingo** last Sunday; **el domingo** on Sunday; **te veré el domingo** I'll see you on Sunday; **los domingos** on Sundays; **los domingos vamos al parque** on Sundays we go to the park.

**dominicano** *adjetivo*

En inglés, los adjetivos que se refieren a un país o a una región se escriben con mayúscula:

**Dominican**

el **dominicano,** la **dominicana**

En inglés, los gentilicios se escriben con mayúscula:

**Dominican:** los dominicanos the Dominicans.

el **dominio**

1. **control:** tiene un dominio total de la situación he has total control over the situation
2. **command:** tiene un dominio excelente del español he has an excellent command of Spanish.

el **don**

1. **gift:** tiene un don para los idiomas he has a gift for languages
2. **Mr.:** don Mario López Mr. Mario López.

**donar** *verbo* ■ **to donate:** donó la casa para los más necesitados he donated the house for those most in need.

**donde** *adverbio* ■ **where:** ahí fue donde encontramos la billetera there's where we found the wallet; voy hacia donde tú quieras I'll go wherever you want me to.

**dónde** *adverbio* ■ **where:** ¿dónde estabas ayer a esta misma hora? where were you yesterday at this time?; ¿dónde vas a ir de viaje? where are you going for your trip?; ¿de dónde vienes? where are you from?

la **doña** ■ **Mrs.:** doña Beatriz García Mrs. Beatriz García.

la **dormilona** *Venezuela* ■ **nightgown:** puse a lavar la dormilona nueva I put the new nightgown in the wash.

**dormir** *verbo*

1. **to sleep:** durmió profundamente toda la noche he slept deeply all night
2. **to stay:** dormimos en un hotel 5 estrellas we stayed in a five-star hotel
3. **to anesthetize:** te duermen únicamente la zona que te van a operar they anesthetize only the area they're going to operate on
➤ se me durmió el pie my foot fell asleep.

el **dormitorio** ■ **bedroom:** la casa tiene cuatro dormitorios the house has four bedrooms.

el **dorso** ■ **back:** firme al dorso del documento sign on the back of the document.

**dos** *numeral* ■ **two:** tiene dos hijos she has two children
➤ mi hermana tiene dos años my sister is two years old

➤ son las dos it's two o'clock
➤ el dos de abril the second of April.

la **dosis** *(plural* las dosis) ■ **dose:** le aumentaron la dosis del medicamento they increased his dose of medicine.

el **drama** ■ **drama:** el drama es el género que más me gusta drama is the genre that I like most; la enfermedad de su hijo es un verdadero drama her son's illness is a real drama.

**dramático** *adjetivo*

1. **dramatic:** el accidente tuvo consecuencias dramáticas the accident had dramatic consequences
2. **drama:** este autor se destacó en el género dramático this author stood out in the drama genre.

el **drenaje** ■ **drainage.**

**drenar** *verbo* ■ **to drain:** drenaron la zona después de las inundaciones they drained the area after the floods.

la **droga** ■ **drug:** estos dos medicamentos usan la misma droga these two medicines use the same drug; la cocaína es una droga muy peligrosa cocaine is a very dangerous drug.

la **drogadicción** ■ **drug addiction.**

la **ducha** ■ **shower:** me di una ducha antes de acostarme I took a shower before going to bed; la ducha de este baño es demasiado pequeña the shower in this bathroom is too small
➤ tomar una ducha to take a shower: tomé una ducha después de hacer deporte I took a shower after playing sports.

**ducharse** *verbo pronominal* ■ **to take a shower:** me ducho siempre de mañana I always take a shower in the morning.

la **duda**

1. **doubt:** tengo dudas sobre la honestidad de su respuesta I have doubts about the honesty of his reply
2. **question:** la profesora preguntó si alguien tenía alguna duda sobre el tema the professor asked if anybody had any questions about the topic
➤ tengo la duda de si llamar a Diego o no I don't know whether to call Diego or not.

**99**

**dudar** *verbo*

1. **to doubt:** dudo que venga I doubt that he'll come
2. **to hesitate:** dudo entre ir al cine o ir al teatro I am hesitating between going to the movies and going to the theater
3. **to question:** dudo de sus buenas intenciones I question his good intentions.

el **dueño**, la **dueña** ■ **owner:** es el dueño de un edificio entero he's the owner of a whole building
➤ un dueño de casa a landlord: salió el dueño de casa y nos echó the landlord came out and threw us out.

**dulce** *adjetivo*

1. **sweet:** este postre es muy dulce this dessert is very sweet
2. **gentle:** su hija es la niña más dulce que conozco her daughter is the most gentle girl I know

el **dulce** ■ **sweet:** sus hijos adoran los dulces his children adore sweets.

la **duración** *(plural* las duraciones*)* ■ **length**.

**durante** *preposición*

1. **during:** durmió durante la película he slept during the movie
2. **for:** estudió química durante ocho años she studied chemistry for eight years.

**durar** *verbo*

1. **to last:** estos zapatos nuevos me duraron sólo dos meses these new shoes lasted me only two months
2. **to go on:** este partido de tenis está durando demasiado this tennis match is going on too long.

el **durazno** ■ **peach**.

el **dúrex** *Mexico* ■ **Scotch® tape**.

la **dureza** ■ **hardness:** la dureza de este material es insuperable the hardness of this material is unsurpassable.

**duro** *(adverbio & adjetivo)*

■ *adverbio*
**hard:** estudio duro para el examen I am studying hard for the exam

■ *adjetivo*

1. **hard:** este tipo de madera es más duro que el otro this type of wood is harder than the other
2. **tough:** la carne estaba tan dura que era incomible the meat was so tough that it was inedible
3. **difficult:** ha tenido una vida muy dura she's had a very difficult life
4. **harsh:** el Gobierno dio una dura respuesta a la oposición the government gave a harsh reply to the opposition
➤ a duras penas with great difficulty: a duras penas gana para vivir with great difficulty he makes a living.

el **DVD** *(abreviatura de* Disco Versátil Digital*)* ■ **DVD**.

**e** *conjunción* ■ **and:** María e Inés son compañeras de clase María and Inés are classmates

> e replaces y before words that begin with "i" or "hi".

**ebrio** *adjetivo* ■ **drunk:** una persona ebria no debe conducir a drunk person shouldn't drive.

**echar** *verbo*

1. **to throw:** te eché la pelota I threw you the ball
2. **to throw out:** lo echaron del club they threw him out of the club

3. **to grow:** esta planta ya ha echado raíces this plant has already grown roots

4. **to put:** le eché sal a la sopa I put salt in the soup

➤ **echar de menos** to miss: **te vamos a echar de menos cuando estés de viaje** we're going to miss you when you're on your trip

➤ **echar a perder** to spoil: **vas a echar a perder a la niña con tantos regalos** you're going to spoil the girl with so many gifts

**echarse** *verbo pronominal* ■ **to lie down:** se echó en la cama he lay down on the bed.

el **eclipse** ■ eclipse
➤ **un eclipse de sol** a solar eclipse.

el **eco** ■ echo *(plural* **echoes***)*: en esta cueva hay eco there's an echo in this cave.

la **economía**

1. **economy:** la economía no anda muy bien the economy is not doing very well

2. **economics:** es profesor de economía he's a professor of economics.

**económico** *adjetivo*

1. **economic:** tienen serios problemas económicos they have serious economic problems

2. **inexpensive:** este restaurante es el más económico this restaurant is the most inexpensive

3. **economical:** este carro es más económico que el otro this car is more economical than the other.

el **ecuador** ■ equator.

**Ecuador** *sustantivo masculino* ■ **Ecuador**.

**ecuatoriano** *adjetivo*

En inglés, los adjetivos que se refieren a un país o una región se escriben con mayúscula:

**Ecuadorian:** los tapices ecuatorianos son muy lindos Ecuadorian carpets are very pretty

el **ecuatoriano,** la **ecuatoriana**

En inglés, los gentilicios se escriben con mayúscula:

**Ecuadorian:** los ecuatorianos the Ecuadorians.

la **edad** ■ age: a la edad de tres años at the age of three

➤ **tiene cinco años de edad** he's five years old

➤ **¿qué edad tienes?** how old are you?

el/la **edecán** *(plural* los/las edecanes*) Mexico*
■ **assistant:** su edecán lo acompaña a todas partes his assistant accompanies him everywhere.

el **edificio** ■ building.

la **educación**

1. **education:** el tema de la educación preocupa al Gobierno the topic of education concerns the government

2. **upbringing:** este niño ha tenido una muy buena educación this boy has had a very good upbringing

➤ **educación a distancia** distance education

➤ **educación física** physical education

➤ **educación secundaria** secondary school education.

**educar** *verbo*

1. **to educate:** educaron a sus hijos en los mejores colegios they educated their children in the best secondary schools

2. **to bring up:** no han educado a su hija de una manera muy tradicional they haven't brought up their daughter in a very traditional manner.

**EE.UU.** *(abreviatura de* Estados Unidos*)* *sustantivo masculino plural* ■ **USA**.

el **efectivo** ■ cash: fui a retirar efectivo del banco I went to withdraw cash from the bank.

el **efecto**

1. **effect:** el medicamento me hizo efecto en pocos minutos the medicine took effect on me in just a few minutes

2. **spin:** dio efecto a la pelota he put some spin on the ball

➤ **en efecto** in fact: **en efecto, tienes toda la razón** in fact, you're completely right

➤ **efectos especiales** special effects.

la **eficacia** ■ effectiveness: este medicamento se destaca por su eficacia this medicine stands out for its effectiveness.

**eficaz** *adjetivo*

1. effective: este medicamento es muy eficaz para curar los dolores de cabeza this medicine is very effective in curing headaches.
2. efficient: es un empleado muy eficaz he's a very efficient employee.

la **eficiencia** ■ efficiency: la eficiencia es la mejor de sus virtudes efficiency is the best of his virtues.

el **egoísmo** ■ selfishness: su egoísmo lo ha llevado al aislamiento his selfishness has led to his loneliness.

**egoísta** *adjetivo* ■ selfish: es una de las personas más egoístas que conozco he's one of the most selfish people I know.

el **egresado**, la **egresada** ■ graduate: el número de egresados de la universidad ha aumentado este año the number of university graduates has increased this year.

**egresar** *verbo* ■ to graduate: Francisco egresó de una universidad pública Francisco graduated from a public university.

el **eje**

1. axle: se rompió uno de los ejes de la rueda one of the axles of the wheel broke
2. axis *(plural* axes*)*: el eje de la Tierra es una línea imaginaria the earth's axis is an imaginary line
3. focal point: el eje de sus conversaciones siempre es el dinero the focal point of their conversations is always money.

**ejecutar** *verbo*

1. to carry out: ejecutaron sus órdenes sin protestar the carried out his orders without protesting
2. to execute: ejecutaron a los prisioneros they executed the prisoners.

**ejemplar** *adjetivo* ■ exemplary: comportamiento ejemplar exemplary behavior.

el **ejemplo** ■ example: siguieron el buen ejemplo de su madre they followed the good example of their mother
➤ por ejemplo for example.

el **ejercicio**

1. exercise: la maestra puso varios ejercicios de geometría the teacher assigned several geometry exercises
2. financial year: el ejercicio de la empresa dio números negativos the company's financial year showed negative numbers
➤ hacer ejercicio to exercise: el médico me recomendó que hiciera ejercicio the doctor recommended that I exercise.

**ejercitar** *verbo* ■ to exercise: la cantante ejercita su voz todas las mañanas the singer exercises her voice every morning.

el **ejército** ■ army *(plural* armies*)*: el ejército ocupó la ciudad the army occupied the city.

el **ejote** *Central America, Mexico* ■ green bean.

**el** *artículo* ■ the: el avión sale a las 11 the airplane leaves at 11

> Las partes del cuerpo llevan en español artículo pero deben traducirse al inglés con un pronombre posesivo:

me duele el brazo my arm hurts
➤ el Sr. Macías compró el sombrero Mr. Macías bought the hat
➤ este reloj y el de Roberto son iguales this watch and Robert's are the same
➤ me fascina el chocolate I adore chocolate

> Los nombres abstractos llevan artículo en español pero no en inglés:

➤ la vida es difícil life is difficult

> Para describir el aspecto físico de una persona se usa el artículo en español pero no en inglés:

➤ tiene el pelo rubio he has blond hair.

**él** *pronombre*

1. he: él no vino he didn't come
2. him: este regalo es para él this gift is for him
3. it: se le rompió el bastón y no puede estar sin él his walking stick broke and he can't be without it
➤ él mismo himself: lo hizo él mismo he did it himself

➤ de él his: **éste es el coche de él** this is his car

> In Spanish **él** as a subject is normally omitted unless it's used for emphasis or to contrast with another person.

**elaborar** *verbo*
1. **to produce: elaboran quesos** they produce cheeses
2. **to work out: elaboré un plan de reformas** I worked out a reform plan.

la **elasticidad** ▪ elasticity.

el **elástico** ▪ elastic: **se rompió el elástico de los pantalones** the pants' elastic broke.

la **elección** (*plural* las elecciones)
1. **choice: por lo menos tienes elección** at least you have a choice
2. **election: tuvimos una elección para escoger el presidente del club** we had an election to choose the president of the club.

la **electricidad** ▪ electricity.

**eléctrico** *adjetivo*
1. **electric: compré un cepillo eléctrico** I bought an electric toothbrush
2. **electrical: estudia ingeniería eléctrica** she studies electrical engineering.

la **electrónica** ▪ electronics.

**electrónico** *adjetivo* ▪ **electronic: es un aparato electrónico** it's an electronic device.

el **elefante**, la **elefanta** ▪ elephant.

**elegante** *adjetivo* ▪ **elegant: compró un vestido elegante** she bought an elegant dress.

**elegir** *verbo*
1. **to choose: elegimos esta casa por el precio** we chose this house because of the price
2. **to elect: lo han elegido para el cargo de gerente** they have elected him to the position of director.

**elemental** *adjetivo* ▪ **elementary: este ejercicio es de nivel elemental** this exercise is elementary level.

el **elemento** ▪ element: **su opinión es un elemento esencial en este debate** your opinion is an essential element in this debate.

el **elevador** *Mexico* ▪ **elevator: subimos por el elevador hasta el cuarto piso** we went up in the elevator to the fourth floor.

**eliminar** *verbo*
1. **to eliminate: un equipo rival eliminó a mi equipo de fútbol en la final** a rival team eliminated my soccer team in the finals
2. **to get rid of: el agua ayuda a eliminar las sustancias tóxicas del cuerpo** water helps to get rid of the body's toxic substances.

**ella** *pronombre*
1. **she: ella no está** she's not here
2. **her: me enamoré de ella** I fell in love with her
3. **it: rompí mi pluma y sin ella no puedo escribir la carta** I broke my pen and without it I can't write the letter
➤ **ella misma** herself: **lo hizo ella misma** she did it herself
➤ de ella her: **éste es el apartamento de ella** this is her apartment

> In Spanish **ella** as a subject is normally omitted unless it's used for emphasis or to contrast with another person.

**ello** *pronombre*
➤ por ello that's why: **no estudiamos y por ello perdimos el examen** we didn't study and that's why we failed the exam.

**ellos, ellas** *pronombre*
1. **they: ellos fueron al concierto** they went to the concert
2. **them: salí de noche con ellas** I went out at night with them
➤ **ellos mismos** themselves: **lo hicieron ellos mismos** they did it themselves
➤ de ellos their
➤ **ésta es la casa de ellas** this is their house

> In Spanish **ellos** and **ellas** as a subject is normally omitted unless it's used for emphasis or to contrast with another person.

el **elote** *Central America, Mexico* ▪ **corn**.

**El Salvador** *sustantivo masculino* ■ **El Salvador**.

la **embajada** ■ embassy *(plural* **embassies***)*: la embajada queda en el centro de la ciudad the embassy is in the middle of the city.

el **embajador**, la **embajadora** ■ ambassador.

**embarazada** *adjetivo* ■ **pregnant**: está embarazada de tres meses she's three months pregnant

⚠ The Spanish word **embarazada** is a false cognate, it does not mean "embarrassed".

el **embarazo** ■ pregnancy *(plural* **pregnancies***)*: el embarazo ha sido difícil the pregnancy has been difficult.

la **embarcación** *(plural* las embarcaciones*)* ■ boat.

**emborracharse** *verbo pronominal* ■ to get drunk: el novio se emborrachó durante la fiesta the groom got drunk during the party.

el **embrague** ■ clutch: suelta el embrague despacio let up on the clutch slowly.

**embromado** *Andes, Caribbean, River Plate informal adjetivo* ■ **tricky**: es una situación bien embromada it's a very tricky situation.

**embromar** *Andes, Caribbean, River Plate informal verbo*
1. **to bother**: sus compañeros lo embroman todo el tiempo his classmates bother him all the time
2. **to ruin**: el mal tiempo nos embromó las vacaciones the bad weather ruined our vacation.

**embrujar** *verbo* ■ **to put a spell on**: cree que la han embrujado she believes that they've put a spell on her.

la **emergencia** ■ emergency *(plural* emergencies*)*: llámame si ocurre alguna emergencia call me if there is an emergency.

**emigrar** *verbo*
1. **to emigrate**: mi abuelo emigró de Europa a principios del siglo XX my grandfather emigrated from Europe at the beginning of the 20th century
2. **to migrate**: muchos pájaros emigran al sur antes del invierno many birds migrate to the south before the winter.

**emitir** *verbo*
1. **to emit**: la televisión emitía un sonido raro the television was emitting a strange sound
2. **to issue**: el Gobierno emitirá nuevos billetes the government will issue new bills.

la **emoción** *(plural* las emociones*)* ■ emotion: no puedo expresar la emoción que sentía I can't express the emotion I felt
➤ me dio una gran emoción volver a verte I was very excited to see you again.

**emocionante** *adjetivo* ■ **exciting**: es una noticia realmente emocionante it's really exciting news.

**emotivo** *adjetivo* ■ **moving**: su discurso fue muy emotivo his speech was very moving.

**empacar** *verbo* ■ **to pack**: empacamos nuestras cosas en unos minutos we packed our things in minutes.

la **empanada** ■ turnover: comimos unas ricas empanadas de carne we ate some tasty meat turnovers.

**empañar** *verbo* ■ **to steam up**: se empañaron los vidrios del carro the car windows steamed up.

**empaparse** *verbo pronominal* ■ **to get soaked**: me empapé con el chaparrón I got soaked in the downpour.

**empatar** *verbo* ■ **to tie**: empataron cero a cero they tied zero to zero.

el **empate** ■ tie: hubo un empate en la final de fútbol there was a tie at the soccer finals.

**empeñar** *verbo* ■ **to pawn:** empeñó las joyas de la abuela he pawned his grandmother's jewels

**empeñarse** *verbo pronominal* ■ **to insist**
➤ se empeña en seguir haciendo deporte he insists on continuing to play sports.

el **empeño** ■ **determination:** pone mucho empeño en todo lo que hace he puts a lot of determination into everything he does.

**empezar** *verbo* ■ **to begin:** ya empezó la clase class already began
➤ empezar a to begin to: empiezan a pintar la casa el próximo sábado they'll begin to paint the house next Saturday.

el **empleado**, la **empleada** ■ employee: los empleados de esta oficina trabajan ocho horas the employees of this office work eight hours.

**emplear** *verbo*
1. **to use:** emplean materiales reciclados they use recycled materials
2. **to hire:** la empresa empleó a otro gerente the company hired another manager.

el **empleo**
1. **job:** me ofrecieron empleo en una escuela they offered me a job at a school
2. **employment:** ha bajado el índice de empleo the employment index has gone down.

**emprender** *verbo* ■ **to take on:** emprendieron un nuevo negocio they took on a new business.

la **empresa**
1. **company:** contratamos a una empresa de seguridad we hired a security company
2. **management:** la empresa no se hace responsable por este accidente the management is not responsible for this accident.

la **empresaria** ■ **businesswoman** (*plural* **businesswomen**).

el **empresario** ■ **businessman** (*plural* **businessmen**): es una reunión de empresarios it's a meeting for businessmen.

**empujar** *verbo* ■ **to push:** empujamos el carro unos metros we pushed the car a few meters.

el **empuje**
1. **drive:** siempre tuvo empuje para trabajar he always had the drive to work
2. **push:** le dimos un fuerte empuje a este proyecto we gave this project a strong push.

el **empujón** (*plural* los empujones) ■ **push:** le dieron un empujón tan grande que se cayó por la escalera they gave him such a hard push that he fell down the stairs
➤ se abrió paso a empujones he shoved his way through.

**en** *preposición*
1. **in:** vive en el campo he lives in the country; en el año 2000 in the year 2000; en primavera in spring; pagar en dólares to pay in dollars
2. **by:** viajo frecuentemente en avión I travel frequently by airplane
3. **on:** el sobre está en la mesa the envelope is on the table; el cuadro está en la pared the painting is on the wall
4. **into:** entró en la sala he went into the room
5. **at:** pasé tres horas en la playa I spent three hours at the beach; en casa at home; en el trabajo at work.

**enamorarse** *verbo pronominal* ■ **to fall in love:** se enamora fácilmente she falls in love easily
➤ enamorarse de to fall in love with: se enamoró de Catalina he fell in love with Catalina.

el **enano** *adjetivo* ■ **dwarf:** es una planta enana it's a dwarf plant

el **enano**, la **enana** ■ **dwarf** (*plural* dwarves): soy una enana si me comparo con tu altura I'm a dwarf if I compare myself with your height.

el **encabezado** ■ **headline:** apareció la noticia en todos los encabezados the news appeared in all the headlines.

**encabezar** *verbo*
1. **to head:** encabezo la lista de candidatos I head the list of candidates

**2.** **to lead:** fueron arrestados quienes enca-bezaron los disturbios those who led the riots were arrested.

**encadenar** *verbo* ■ **to chain:** encade-né la bicicleta a un árbol I chained the bi-cycle to a tree.

**encaminar** *verbo* ■ **to guide:** ya enca-minamos el proyecto we're already guiding the project.

**encamotarse** *Andes, Central America informal verbo pronominal* ■ **to fall in love:** se encamotaron they fell in love

➤ encamotarse de to fall in love with: se encamotó de su mejor amigo she fell in love with her best friend.

**encantador, encantadora** *adjetivo* ■ **charming:** tiene tres niñas encantado-ras she has three charming girls.

**encantar** *verbo*
**1.** **to love:** les encanta jugar al fútbol they love to play soccer
**2.** **to enchant:** el hada encantó al príncipe the fairy enchanted the prince.

**encarcelar** *verbo* ■ **to jail:** encarcela-ron a los delincuentes they jailed the crim-inals.

el **encargado,** la **encargada** ■ **man-ager:** hablé con la encargada de la tienda I spoke with the manager of the store.

**encargar** *verbo*
**1.** **to ask:** le encargué que me ingresara estos datos en la computadora I asked him to enter this data into the computer
**2.** **to order:** encargamos dos libros por Internet we ordered two books on the Inter-net

**encargarse** *verbo pronominal*
➤ encargarse de to take care of: el jefe se encarga de estos problemas the boss takes care of these problems: nos estamos encargando del hijo de mi cuñada we're taking care of my sister-in-law's son.

**encender** *verbo*
**1.** **to light:** encendimos la chimenea we lit the chimney
**2.** **to turn on:** encendió la luz he turned on the light
**3.** **to start up:** encendió el motor she started up the engine.

**encerar** *verbo* ■ **to wax:** enceró los pi-sos de la oficina he waxed the office floors.

**encerrar** *verbo* ■ **to shut in:** encerró al perro en el baño she shut the dog in the bathroom

**encerrarse** *verbo pronominal* ■ **to shut oneself away:** se encerró en un convento she shut herself away in a convent.

**enchastrarse** *River Plate informal verbo pronominal* ■ **to get messy:** el bebe se enchastró con el puré the baby got messy with the soup.

la **enchilada** *Mexico* ■ **enchilada**.

**enchilarse** *Mexico informal verbo prono-minal* ■ **to get angry:** se enchiló con sus cuates he got angry with his friends.

**enchufar** *verbo* ■ **to plug in:** enchufó la impresora he plugged in the printer.

el **enchufe** ■ **plug:** compré un enchufe nuevo para la televisión I bought a new plug for the television.

la **enciclopedia** ■ **encyclopedia**.

**encima** *adverbio*
**1.** **on:** siempre llevo encima los documen-tos I always carry the documents on me
**2.** **on top of that:** es feo y encima caro it's ugly and on top of that expensive
➤ ya tenemos encima el período de exámenes the exam period is upon us
➤ por encima de over
➤ encima de on top of: puse la caja más chica encima de la más grande I put the smallest box on top of the largest: encima de pagarle la cena, le dio dinero para un taxi on top of paying for his dinner, I gave him money for a taxi.

**encoger** *verbo* ■ **to shrink:** este pantalón encogió con el lavado these pants shrank when washed

**encogerse** *verbo pronominal*

➤ encogerse de hombros to shrug one's shoulders: se encogió de hombros cuando le di la noticia he shrugged his shoulders when I gave him the news.

la **encomienda** ■ **package:** mandamos una encomienda por avión we're sending a package by air.

**encontrar** *verbo* ■ **to find:** encontramos un reloj en la calle we found a watch in the street

**encontrarse** *verbo pronominal*

1. **to meet:** se encontraron en el parque they met in the park
2. **to be located:** la farmacia se encuentra en esta calle the pharmacy is located on this street

➤ encontrarse con alguien to run across somebody: me encontré con Francisco en el restaurante I ran across Francisco in the restaurant.

el **encuentro**

1. **meeting:** el encuentro de ex-alumnos es el sábado the alumni meeting is Saturday
2. **match:** ayer se realizó el encuentro deportivo más popular del año yesterday the most popular sports match of the year took place.

**enderezar** *verbo* ■ **to straighten:** enderezamos el árbol atándolo a un palo we straightened the tree by tying it to a stick.

**endurecer** *verbo*

1. **to toughen:** la vida lo ha endurecido life has toughened him
2. **to tone:** estos ejercicios endurecen los músculos these exercises tone the muscles

**endurecerse** *verbo pronominal* ■ **to harden:** la masa se endureció demasiado the dough hardened too much.

**enemigo** *adjetivo* ■ **enemy:** el ejército enemigo invadió la ciudad the enemy army invaded the city

el **enemigo, la enemiga** ■ **enemy** (*plural* **enemies**).

la **energía** ■ **energy:** el sol es una fuente importante de energía the sun is an important source of energy

➤ no tengo energías para salir I don't have the energy to go out
➤ energía eólica wind power
➤ energía nuclear nuclear energy
➤ energía solar solar energy.

**enérgico** *adjetivo*

1. **energetic:** tiene una forma de actuar muy enérgica he has a very energetic way of acting
2. **bold:** el gobierno tomó medidas enérgicas frente a la crisis the government took bold measures in facing the crisis.

**enero** *sustantivo masculino*

En inglés los nombres de los meses se escriben con mayúscula:

**January:** en enero in January; el próximo enero next January; el pasado enero last January.

**enfadarse** *verbo pronominal* ■ **to get angry:** se enfadó con los niños por sus travesuras she got angry with the children because of their pranks.

el **énfasis** ■ **emphasis**

➤ poner énfasis en to put emphasis on: puso énfasis en la primera palabra he put emphasis on the first word.

**enfermarse** *verbo pronominal* ■ **to get sick:** me enfermé del estómago I developed stomach problems.

la **enfermedad**

1. **illness:** se recupera de una enfermedad muy grave she's recovering from a very serious illness
2. **disease:** tiene una enfermedad hereditaria he has a hereditary disease.

el **enfermero, la enfermera** ■ **nurse:** los enfermeros de este hospital son excelentes the nurses in this hospital are excellent.

**enfermo** *adjetivo* ■ **ill:** mi maestro estuvo enfermo esta semana my teacher was ill this week; **está gravemente enferma** she's seriously ill

**el enfermo, la enferma**

1. **sick person:** de noche cuida enfermos at night she cares for sick people
2. **patient:** mi médico atiende solo diez enfermos por día my doctor attends only ten patients a day; **un enfermo de asma está esperando al doctor** an asthma patient is waiting on the doctor.

**enfocar** *verbo* ■ **to focus:** enfoquemos en la raíz del problema let's focus on the root of the problem.

**el enfoque** ■ **focus:** cambiemos el enfoque de la investigación let's change the focus of the investigation.

**enfrentar** *verbo* ■ **to face:** enfrenta cargos por difamación he faces charges for slander

**enfrentarse** *verbo pronominal*

1. **to face:** se enfrentó con optimismo a la nueva situación he faced the new situation with optimism
2. **to play against:** el equipo de fútbol local se enfrenta hoy con su tradicional rival the local soccer team is playing against its traditional rival today.

**enfrente** *adverbio* ■ **opposite:** mis amigos estaban sentados enfrente my friends were sitting opposite
➤ **de enfrente** across the way: la oficina de enfrente no atiende público the office across the way doesn't serve the public.

**enfriar** *verbo* ■ **to cool:** esta heladera no enfría bien this refrigerator doesn't cool well
➤ **dejar enfriar** to let cool: dejó enfriar la salsa he let the sauce cool

**enfriarse** *verbo pronominal*

1. **to go cold:** se enfrió la comida the food went cold

2. **to get cold:** te vas a enfriar si no te pones la chaqueta you'll get cold if you don't put on your jacket
3. **to catch a cold:** me enfrié por salir cuando llovía I caught a cold going out while it was raining.

**el enganche** *Mexico* ■ **deposit:** dejamos un cheque por el enganche we left a check for the deposit.

**engañar** *verbo*

1. **to mislead:** me engañaron diciéndome que este producto era de buena calidad they misled me, telling me that this was a high quality product
2. **to deceive:** Sofía engaña a su esposo Sofía is deceiving her husband.

**el engaño**

1. **sham:** el contrato fue un engaño the contract was a sham
2. **deception:** soy víctima de un engaño I'm the victim of a deception.

**engañoso** *adjetivo* ■ **deceitful:** es una persona engañosa he's a deceitful person; **siempre tuvo una conducta engañosa** he always had a deceitful manner.

**engordar** *verbo*

1. **to gain weight:** engordé este mes I gained weight this month
2. **to be fattening:** la mayonesa engorda mayonnaise is fattening.

**la engrampadora** *River Plate* ■ **stapler.**

**engrampar** *River Plate verbo* ■ **to staple:** me pidió que le engrampara estas hojas he asked me to staple these sheets.

**el engranaje** ■ **gear.**

**engrasar** *verbo*

1. **to lubricate:** engrasó el motor he lubricated the motor
2. **to get greasy:** me engrasé la ropa I got my clothes greasy.

**enjabonarse** *verbo pronominal* ■ **to soap:** me enjaboné primero la espalda I soaped my back first.

**enjuagar** *verbo* ■ **to rinse:** enjuagó todos los platos she rinsed all the plates.

el **enlace** ■ link: hay enlace entre los dos crímenes there's a connection between the two crimes; **sigue el enlace para encontrar la otra página web** follow the link to find the other web page.

**enojarse** *verbo pronominal* ■ **to get angry:** se enojó sin razón he got angry for no reason.

el **enojo** ■ anger.

**enorgullecerse** *verbo pronominal* ■ **to be proud:** nos enorgullecemos de nuestros hijos we are proud of our children.

**enorme** *adjetivo* ■ **enormous:** comió un pedazo de torta enorme he ate an enormous piece of cake.

**enredar** *verbo* ■ **to complicate:** su mala actitud enredó más las cosas his bad attitude complicated things more

**enredarse** *verbo pronominal* ■ **to get tangled:** se me enreda el pelo frecuentemente my hair gets tangled frequently.

**enriquecer** *verbo* ■ **to make rich:** el turismo enriqueció a toda la zona tourism made the whole area rich

**enriquecerse** *verbo pronominal* ■ **to get rich:** se enriqueció con su trabajo he got rich with his work.

la **ensalada** ■ salad.

**ensanchar** *verbo* ■ **to widen:** ensancharon la avenida principal they widened the main street.

**ensayar** *verbo* ■ **to rehearse:** ensayó esta obra durante seis meses he rehearsed this piece for six months.

el **ensayo**
1. **rehearsal:** ayer fui al ensayo de un concierto yesterday I went to the concert rehearsal
2. **test:** los ensayos nucleares son altamente peligrosos nuclear tests are extremely dangerous.

**enseguida** *adverbio* ■ **right away:** enseguida comienza la función the performance will begin right away

➤ **enseguida vuelvo** I'll be right back.

la **enseñanza** ■ teaching
➤ **enseñanza primaria** elementary education
➤ **enseñanza secundaria** secondary education
➤ **enseñanza universitaria** university education.

**enseñar** *verbo*
1. **to teach:** en este colegio nos enseñan a razonar at this school they teach us to reason
2. **to show:** me enseñó su computadora nueva he showed me his new computer.

**ensoparse** *Andes, River Plate, Venezuela verbo pronominal* ■ **to get soaked:** me ensopé con la lluvia I got soaked by the rain.

**ensuciar** *verbo* ■ **to dirty:** ensució el mantel con vino he dirtied the tablecloth with wine

**ensuciarse** *verbo pronominal* ■ **to get dirty:** me ensucié en el jardín I got dirty in the garden.

**entender** *verbo* ■ **to understand:** no entiendo lo que dices I don't understand what you're saying
➤ **hacerse entender** to make oneself understood: no se hace entender con claridad he doesn't make himself clearly understood

**entenderse** *verbo pronominal*
1. **to be meant:** ¿qué se entiende por lo que has dicho? what is meant by what you've said?
2. **to get along together:** mi novia y yo nos entendemos muy bien my girlfriend and I get along very well together.

el **entendimiento** ■ understanding: falta entendimiento entre las partes there's a lack of understanding between the parties.

**enterarse** *verbo pronominal*
1. **to find out:** me enteré de que vas a cursar química I found out that you're going to take chemistry
2. **to hear:** no quiero que se enteren de lo nuestro I don't want them to hear about us.

**109**

**entero** *adjetivo* ■ **whole:** tiene una colección entera de figuritas she has a whole collection of figurines.

**enterrar** *verbo* ■ **to bury:** lo enterraron en un cementerio privado they buried him in a private cemetery

➤ me enterré una espina en el pie I got a thorn in my foot.

el **entierro** ■ **burial:** el entierro es hoy a las tres the burial is today at three o'clock.

**entonar** *verbo*

1. **to sing:** entonó una canción he sang a song
2. **to sing in tune:** esta chica entona muy bien this girl sings in tune very well.

**entonces** *adverbio*

1. **then:** hablé con la maestra y entonces me dijo que había perdido el examen I spoke with the teacher and then she told me that I had failed the exam; **para ese entonces ya estará fuera del país** by then he will already be out of the country
2. **so:** entonces lo mejor que puedes hacer es pedir perdón so the best that you can do is to say sorry.

la **entrada**

1. **entrance:** se rompió la puerta de entrada the entrance door broke
2. **admission:** la entrada al concierto fue muy desorganizada admission to the concert was very disorganized
3. **ticket:** compramos cinco entradas para el recital we bought five tickets for the recital
4. **entry** *(plural* **entries)**: este diccionario tiene miles de entradas this dictionary has thousands of entries
5. **appetizer:** de entrada comimos jamón crudo con melón we ate cured ham with melon for an appetizer.

**entrar** *verbo*

1. **to go in:** entraron en la tienda de enfrente they went in the store across the way
2. **to fit:** ya no me entran estos pantalones these pants don't fit me anymore

3. **to begin:** entró en la universidad el año pasado he began at the university last year; **con este vino entramos en calor rápidamente** we got warm quickly with this wine
➤ **entrar en calor** to get warm
➤ **entrar en coma** to go into a coma
➤ **entrar en razón** to see reason
➤ **me entró una pereza terrible** I felt horribly lazy.

**entre** *preposición*

1. **between:** llegará entre las cuatro y las cinco he'll arrive between four and five o'clock; **siempre viaje entre diciembre y febrero** she always travels between December and February; **la escuela queda entre tu casa y la mía** the school is between your house and mine
2. **among:** acampamos entre los árboles we camped among the trees; **siempre están discutiendo entre ellos** they're always arguing among themselves
3. **divided by:** ocho entre cuatro es igual a dos eight divided by four equals two
➤ **entre sí** among themselves: **discutieron entre sí acaloradamente** they argued heatedly among themselves
➤ **entre todos** together: **lo pueden hacer entre todos** together they can do it.

la **entrega**

1. **presentation:** la entrega de premios fue muy emotiva the award presentation was very moving
2. **dedication:** su entrega hacia los demás es totalmente desinteresada her dedication to others is totally unselfish.

**entregar** *verbo*

1. **to deliver:** entregué el paquete al supervisor I delivered the parcel to the supervisor
2. **to hand in:** entregamos los trabajos al profesor we handed in the papers to the professor

**entregarse** *verbo pronominal* ■ **to surrender:** los delincuentes se entregaron a la policía the criminals surrendered to the police.

**entrenar** *verbo* ■ **to train:** entreno todas las mañanas para la competencia I train every morning for the competition.

la **entretención** *Chile* ■ entertainment: la industria de la entretención ha crecido mucho the entertainment industry has grown a lot.

**entretenerse** *verbo pronominal*

1. **to hang around:** me entretuve charlando con unos amigos y llegué tarde a clase I hung around talking with some friends and I arrived late to class

2. **to amuse oneself:** me entretengo mucho con los dibujos animados I amuse myself a lot with cartoons.

el **entretenimiento** ■ entertainment: su entretenimiento favorito es coleccionar sellos his favorite entertainment is collecting stamps.

**entreverar** *Southern Cone verbo* ■ **to mix up:** no entreveres las facturas don't mix up the invoices

**entreverarse** *verbo pronominal* ■ **to get mixed up:** se entreveraron las facturas y ahora tengo que ordenarlas nuevamente the invoices got mixed up and now I have to put them in order again.

la **entrevista** ■ interview: hoy tuve una entrevista de trabajo today I had a job interview.

**entrevistar** *verbo* ■ **to interview:** entrevistamos a cientos de personas para la encuesta we interviewed hundreds of people for the survey.

el **entrometido,** la **entrometida** ■ busybody (*plural* busybodies): es un entrometido insoportable que siempre opina donde no debe he's an intolerable busybody who always gives his opinion when he shouldn't.

el **entusiasmo** ■ enthusiasm: el entusiasmo del público era increíble the enthusiasm of the public was incredible.

**envasar** *verbo*

1. *en cajas, paquetes* **to pack**
2. *en bolsas* **to bag**
3. *en latas* **to can**.

el **envase** ■ container: el envase de esta crema ha cambiado the container of this cream has changed.

**envejecer** *verbo* ■ to age: todos envejecemos tarde o temprano we all age sooner or later.

el **envejecimiento** ■ aging: el envejecimiento es un proceso natural aging is a natural process.

**envenenar** *verbo* ■ to poison: el gas tóxico envenenó a la población the toxic gas poisoned the population.

**enviar** *verbo* ■ to send: enviamos el cheque por correo we sent the check by mail.

la **envidia** ■ envy: la envidia puede destruir una relación envy can destroy a relationship
➤ **tener envidia a** to envy: le tiene envidia a su hermano she envies her brother.

**envidioso** *adjetivo* ■ envious.

el **envío** ■ shipment: aquella oficina se encarga de los envíos de la fábrica that office is in charge of the factory's shipments
➤ envíos a domicilio home delivery
➤ envíos contra reembolso cash on delivery.

la **envoltura** ■ wrapping: se rompió la envoltura del paquete the package's wrapping was torn.

**envolver** *verbo* ■ to wrap: envolvimos el regalo we wrapped the gift.

la **epidemia** ■ epidemic.

el **epílogo** ■ epilogue.

el **episodio** ■ episode: vi únicamente dos episodios de esta serie I saw only two episodes of this series.

la **época** ■ time: es la época más calurosa del año it's the hottest time of the year; estas cosas no pasaban en mi época these things didn't happen in my time.

**equilibrar** *verbo* ■ to balance: equilibró el peso de la estantería he balanced the weight of the shelving.

el **equilibrio** ■ balance: perdió el equilibrio y cayó al piso he lost his balance and fell to the floor.

el **equipaje** ■ luggage: llevo mucho equipaje I'm carrying a lot of luggage.

**equipar** verbo ■ to equip: equiparon la escuela con tecnología moderna they equipped the school with modern technology.

el **equipo**
1. equipment: trajimos el equipo de camping completo we brought the complete set of camping equipment
2. team: los mejores equipos de basquetbol compiten hoy the best basketball teams compete today
➤ equipo de música stereo.

**equitativo** adjetivo ■ fair: repartieron el dinero de manera equitativa they divided up the money in a fair manner.

la **equivalencia** ■ equivalence.

**equivalente** adjetivo ■ equivalent: los significados de estas dos palabras son equivalentes the two words have equivalent meanings

el **equivalente** ■ equivalent: me pagaron el equivalente a dos meses de trabajo they paid me the equivalent of two months of work.

la **equivocación** (plural las equivocaciones) ■ mistake: cometí varias equivocaciones en mi vida I made several mistakes in my life.

**equivocarse** verbo pronominal ■ to make a mistake: debes admitirlo cuando te equivocas you must admit it when you make a mistake
➤ me equivoqué de salida en la autopista I took the wrong exit on the highway.

**erogar** Chile verbo ■ to contribute: erogó una fuerte suma de dinero he contributed a large sum of money.

la **erosión** (plural las erosiones) ■ erosion.

**erradicar** verbo ■ to eradicate: el gobierno intenta erradicar la pobreza the government is trying to eradicate poverty.

**errar** verbo ■ to miss: el delantero erró el penal the forward missed the penalty kick.

**erróneo** adjetivo ■ mistaken: su lógica es errónea his logic is mistaken.

el **error** ■ error: cometió un grave error en el examen he commited a serious error on the exam
➤ por error by mistake: me llevé tu lápiz por error I took your pencil by mistake
➤ un error de imprenta a misprint.

la **erupción** (plural las erupciones)
1. eruption: la erupción del volcán mató a tres personas the eruption of the volcano killed three people
2. rash: le salió una erupción en la cara a rash broke out on his face.

la **escala**
1. stopover: el avión hizo escala en Buenos Aires the airplane had a stopover in Buenos Aires
2. scale: sacó ocho en una escala del uno al diez he got an eight on a scale of one to ten; hicieron el mapa a escala they made the map to scale
➤ a escala to scale.

**escalar** verbo ■ to scale: escalamos una montaña nevada we scaled a snowy mountain.

la **escalera** ■ staircase: la casa tiene una escalera de madera the house has a wooden staircase
➤ una escalera de incendios a fire escape
➤ una escalera de mano a stepladder
➤ una escalera mecánica an escalator.

el **escalofrío** ■ chill: esta gripe me produce escalofríos this flu is making me have chills.

el **escalón** (plural los escalones) ■ step: cuidado con el escalón careful of the step.

la **escama** ■ scale: le sacamos las escamas al pescado we took the scales off of the fish.

el **escándalo**

1. **outrage:** la película provocó un escándalo the movie caused an outrage
2. **scandal:** un escándalo de corrupción a corruption scandal
3. **racket:** ¡dejen de armar tanto escándalo! stop making such a racket!

**escapar** verbo ■ **to escape:** escaparon de la policía they escaped from the police

**escaparse** verbo pronominal ■ **to escape:** se escapó de la cárcel he escaped from prison
➤ se me escapó un grito I let out a scream.

el **escaparate** Mexico ■ **store window.**

**escarbar** verbo ■ **to dig:** el perro escarbaba en el jardín the dog was digging in the garden.

la **escarcha** ■ **frost.**

**escaso** adjetivo

1. **scarce:** el platino es un metal muy escaso platinum is a very scarce metal
2. **meager:** es gente de escasos recursos they're people of meager resources; **siempre anda escaso de tiempo** he is always short of time
➤ escaso de algo short of something.

la **escena** ■ **scene.**

el **escenario** ■ **stage:** los actores salieron al escenario the actors went out on stage.

la **esclavitud** ■ **slavery.**

el **esclavo,** la **esclava** ■ **slave**
➤ no quiero ser esclavo de la moda I don't want to be a slave to fashion.

la **escoba** ■ **broom:** tenemos que comprar una escoba para la cocina we need to buy a broom for the kitchen; **pasó la escoba en la entrada** he swept the entryway
➤ pasar la escoba to sweep
➤ un palo de escoba a broomstick.

**escoger** verbo ■ **to choose:** es difícil escoger entre los dos it's difficult to choose between the two; **hay que escoger uno de este montón** we have to choose one from this pile.

el/la **escolar** ■ **school:** el autobús escolar the school bus

el/la **escolar** ■ **schoolboy, schoolgirl**
➤ la parada estaba llena de escolares the bus stop was full of schoolchildren.

los **escombros** ■ **rubble.**

**esconder** verbo ■ **to hide:** tenemos que esconder los regalos we have to hide the gifts

**esconderse** verbo pronominal ■ **to hide:** se escondió detrás de la puerta he hid behind the door.

las **escondidas**
➤ a escondidas secretly: fuman a escondidas they smoke secretly
➤ jugar a las escondidas to play hide-and-seek.

el **escondite** ■ **hiding place:** el escondite de los ladrones the thieves' hiding place
➤ jugar al escondite to play hide-and-seek.

la **escopeta** ■ **shotgun.**

el **escorpión** (plural los escorpiones) ■ **scorpion.**

**escribir** verbo ■ **to write:** ha escrito varios libros she's written several books; **nos escribe muy seguido** he writes us often
➤ no sabe leer ni escribir he doesn't know how to read or write
➤ ¿cómo se escribe su nombre? how do you spell her name?
➤ han dejado de escribirse they have stopped writing each other.

**escrito** adjetivo ■ **written:** un examen escrito a written test
➤ una nota escrita a mano a hand-written note
➤ por escrito in writing
➤ tienes que pedirlo por escrito you have to request it in writing.

el **escritor,** la **escritora** ■ **writer.**

el **escritorio**

1. **desk:** lo dejé encima del escritorio I left it on the desk

**2. study** *(plural* **studies)**: se encierra a leer en el escritorio he shuts himself up in the study to read.

la **escritura** ■ **writing**: la escritura árabe Arabic writing.

**escuchar** *verbo*

**1. to listen**: ¡escuchen! alguien viene listen! somebody's coming; escuchaban con mucha atención they were listening very attentively

**2. to listen to**: me encanta escuchar música I love to listen to music; tienes que escuchar a la profesora you have to listen to the teacher; no escucha a nadie he doesn't listen to anybody.

el **escudo**

**1. shield**: llevaban escudos para protegerse they carried shields to protect themselves

**2. badge**: una camiseta con el escudo del equipo a shirt with the team badge.

la **escuela** ■ **school**: no pudo ir a la escuela he couldn't go to school

➤ está en la escuela primaria she's in primary school

➤ una escuela de choferes a driving school

➤ una escuela de manejo *Mexico* a driving school.

el/la **escuincle** *Mexico* ■ **kid**.

**escular** *Colombia, Mexico verbo* ■ **to search**: lo escularon antes de subir al avión they searched him before getting on the airplane; escularon el carro en busca de armas they searched the car looking for weapons

➤ no andes esculcando mis cosas don't go through my things.

la **escultura** ■ **sculpture**.

**escupir** *verbo* ■ **to spit**: escupió en el suelo he spit on the floor.

**ese, esa** *adjetivo* ■ **that**: María vive en esa casa María lives in that house; ¿quién es ese muchacho que preguntó por ti? who is that guy who's asking for you?

**ése, ésa** *pronombre* ■ **that one**: me gusta ése I like that one

➤ ése es el que compramos that's the one we bought

➤ ése es el problema that's the problem.

**esencial** *adjetivo* ■ **essential**: la lectura es algo esencial reading is something that's essential

➤ lo esencial the main thing: lo esencial es entender the main thing is to understand.

la **esfera** ■ **sphere**.

el **esfuerzo** ■ **effort**: vas a tener que hacer un esfuerzo you're going to have to make an effort

➤ saltó sin ningún esfuerzo he jumped effortlessly

➤ no lo hacen porque es mucho esfuerzo they don't do it because it takes a lot of effort.

la **esmeralda** ■ **emerald**.

el **esmero** ■ **care**: todo lo hace con mucho esmero she does everything with great care.

el **esmog** ■ **smog**.

**eso** *pronombre* ■ **that**: ¿para qué sirve eso? what is that for?; eso no es cierto that's not true

➤ por eso that's why

➤ por eso llegó tarde that's why she arrived late

➤ pasé de curso y eso que no estudié mucho I passed the course in spite of the fact that I didn't study much

➤ ¡eso es! así es como hay que hacerlo that's it! that's how you have to do it.

**esos, esas** *adjetivo* ■ **those**: esas fotos son mías those photos are mine; ¿de quién son esos cuadernos? whose are those notebooks?

**ésos, ésas** *pronombre* ■ **those**: ésos son más bonitos those are the prettiest.

**espacial** *adjetivo* ■ **space**: construyeron una estación espacial they built a space station

➤ una nave espacial a spaceship.

el **espacio**

**1. room**: no hay suficiente espacio para una cama there's not enough room for a bed; esto ocupa demasiado espacio this takes up too much room

**2. space:** hay que dejar espacio para las **correcciones** you have to leave space for the corrections; **deja un espacio entre las dos palabras** leave a space between the two words

➤ **llena los espacios en blanco** fill in the blanks

➤ **el espacio** space: **el primer hombre en el espacio** the first man in space.

la **espada** ■ sword

⚠ The Spanish word **espada** is a false cognate, it doesn't mean "spade".

la **espalda** ■ back: **me duele la espalda** my back hurts.

el **espantapájaros** (plural los espanta-pájaros) ■ scarecrow.

**espantoso** adjetivo

**1. terrifying:** hubo un choque espantoso there was a terrifying crash; **mostraron unas escenas espantosas** they showed some terrifying scenes

**2.** informal **dreadful:** ¡qué color más espantoso! what a dreadful color!; **se ve espantosa con ese peinado** she looks dreadful with that hairstyle

➤ **tenía un miedo espantoso** she had a great fear

➤ **el calor era espantoso** the heat was terrible.

**España** sustantivo femenino ■ **Spain**.

**español** adjetivo

En inglés, los adjetivos que se refieren a un país o una región se escriben con mayúscula:

**Spanish: tiene un apellido español** he has a Spanish last name

el **español, la española**

En inglés, los gentilicios se escriben con mayúscula:

**Spaniard: los españoles** Spaniards.

el **español**

En inglés, los idiomas se escriben con mayúscula:

**Spanish**.

ESPAÑOL/CASTELLANO

📖 These two words are used inter-changeably in Latin America to refer to the official language of all the countries that were once Spanish colonies. While Spanish is the official language in most countries, a couple of places have more than one official language, such as **Quechua** in Peru and **Guaraní** in Paraguay.

**especial** adjetivo ■ **special: es un precio especial para estudiantes** it's a special price for students; **lo uso sólo en ocasiones especiales** I use it only on special occasions

➤ **la película no tiene nada de especial** the movie is nothing special

➤ **en especial** especially: **son todos inteligentes, en especial Carlos** they're all intelligent, especially Carlos.

la **especialidad** ■ **specialty** (plural specialties).

**especialmente** adverbio ■ **especially**.

la **especie** ■ **species: una especie en vías de extinción** a species in the process of extinction; **llevaba una especie de turbán en la cabeza** he was wearing a type of turban on his head

➤ **una especie de** a type of.

**específico** adjetivo ■ **specific**.

**espectacular** adjetivo ■ **spectacular**.

el **espectáculo**

**1. show: un espectáculo para gente joven** a show for young people

**2. spectacle: un espectáculo muy lamentable** a very pitiful spectacle

➤ **dar un espectáculo** to make a scene: **deja de gritar que estás dando un espectáculo** stop screaming, you're making a scene.

el **espectador, la espectadora**

**1. spectator: un espectador saltó a la cancha** a spectator jumped onto the field

2. **audience member:** hicieron salir del cine a un **espectador** they made an audience member leave
➤ los **espectadores** *en cine, concierto* the audience
➤ los **espectadores** *en estadio* the spectators.

**el** espejo ■ **mirror:** se miró al espejo he looked at himself in the mirror
➤ el **espejo retrovisor** the rearview mirror.

**la** esperanza ■ **hope:** eso me ha dado esperanzas that's given me hope
➤ no tiene ninguna esperanza de salir de vacaciones he doesn't have any hope that he'll go on vacation
➤ no pierdo las esperanzas I don't lose hope.

esperar *verbo*
1. **to wait:** voy a esperar hasta mañana I'm going to wait until tomorrow; **espere en la sala, por favor** wait in the room, please
2. **to wait for:** ¿qué estás esperando? what are you waiting for?; **estoy esperando el tren** I'm waiting for the train; **te espero a la salida** I'll wait for you at the exit
3. **to expect:** espera aprobar el examen she expects to pass the exam; **no esperaba verte aquí** I didn't expect to see you here
4. **to hope:** espero volverlo a ver I hope to see him again; **¿crees que dejará de llover? — espero que sí** do you think it will stop raining? — I hope so
➤ no estudió nada — bueno, eso era de esperar he didn't study at all — well, that was to be expected
➤ está esperando un hijo she's expecting a child
➤ ¡espérate un poco, no seas impaciente! wait a little bit, don't be impatient!

espeso *adjetivo* ■ **thick.**

**la** espina
1. **thorn:** las espinas de los rosales the thorns of the rosebushes
2. **bone:** un pescado con muchas espinas a fish with a lot of bones.

**la** espiral ■ **spiral**
➤ una escalera en espiral a spiral staircase.

**el** espíritu
1. **spirit:** hay que tener espíritu de equipo you have to have team spirit
2. **ghost:** dicen que aquí hay muchos espíritus they say that there are a lot of ghosts here.

**la** esponja ■ **sponge.**

esponjoso *adjetivo* ■ **spongy.**

**la** esposa ■ **wife.**

**el** esposo ■ **husband.**

**la** espuma
1. *del jabón, champú* **foam**
2. *de la cerveza* **froth**
➤ la espuma de las olas the surf.

**el** esqueleto ■ **skeleton.**

**el** esquema
1. **diagram:** les hice un esquema de mi casa I drew them a diagram of my house
2. **outline:** hice un esquema de lo que iba a escribir I made an outline of what I was going to write.

**el** esquí
1. **ski:** un par de esquís a pair of skis
2. **skiing:** el esquí es su deporte favorito skiing is his favorite sport; **hacer esquí acuático** to go water skiing
➤ esquí acuático water skiing.

esquiar *verbo* ■ **to ski:** ¿sabe esquiar? does he know how to ski?

esquimal *adjetivo*

En inglés, los adjetivos que se refieren a un país o una región se escriben con mayúscula:

Inuit

**el/la** esquimal

En inglés, los gentilicios se escriben con mayúscula:

Inuit.

**la** esquina ■ **corner**
➤ está a la vuelta de la esquina it's right around the corner.

esquivar *verbo* ■ **to avoid:** me agaché para esquivar el golpe I ducked to avoid the blow.

**estable** *adjetivo* ■ **stable**.

**establecer** *verbo* ■ **to establish:** han establecido relaciones diplomáticas they've established diplomatic relations; estableció el récord mundial en jabalina he established the world record in the javelin

**establecerse** *verbo pronominal* ■ **to settle:** se establecieron en Ciudad de México they settled in Mexico City.

el **establo** ■ **barn**.

la **estación** *(plural* las estaciones)
1. **season:** la estación de las lluvias the rainy season
2. **station:** se baja en la siguiente estación he gets off at the next station
➤ una estación de esquí a ski resort
➤ una estación de servicio a service station.

el **estacionamiento**
1. **parking:** es una zona de estacionamiento prohibido it's a no parking zone
2. **parking area:** el edificio tiene un estacionamiento subterráneo the building has an underground parking area.

**estacionar** *verbo* ■ **to park:** nunca hay dónde estacionar there's never a place to park

**estacionarse** *verbo pronominal* ■ **to park:** siempre se estaciona en el mismo lugar he always parks in the same place.

la **estadía** ■ **stay:** durante su estadía en esa ciudad during his stay in that city.

el **estadio** ■ **stadium** *(plural* stadia o stadiums).

el **estado** ■ **state:** ¿en qué estado quedó la moto? what state was the motorcycle in?; su estado de salud ha mejorado mucho her state of health has improved a lot
➤ en buen estado in good condition
➤ en mal estado in bad condition
➤ trabaja en una oficina del Estado he works in a government office
➤ estado civil marital status
➤ tiene una beca del Estado she has a scholarship from the state

➤ en uno de los estados del norte in one of the northern states.

los **Estados Unidos** ■ **United States**.

**estadounidense** *adjetivo*

En inglés, los adjetivos que se refieren a un país o una región se escriben con mayúscula:

**American**

el **estadounidense**, la **estadounidense**

En inglés, los gentilicios se escriben con mayúscula:

**American:** los estadounidenses the Americans.

la **estafa** ■ **fraud**.

**estafar** *verbo* ■ **to swindle:** estafaron al banco they swindled the bank
➤ en esa tienda me estafaron they ripped me off in that store.

**estallar** *verbo* ■ **to go off:** un bomba estalló en ese lugar a bomb went off in that place
➤ hacen estallar fuegos artificiales they're setting off fireworks.

el **estambre** *Mexico* ■ **yarn:** me tejió el suéter con estambre de dos colores she made me the sweater with two colors of yarn.

la **estampilla** ■ **stamp**.

la **estancia**
1. *Mexico* **stay:** durante nuestra estancia en el extranjero during our stay out of the country
2. *Southern Cone* **ranch:** tiene dos estancias en la zona he's got two ranches in the area.

el **estanque** ■ **pond**.

el **estante** ■ **shelf**
➤ pusieron unos estantes en la clase they put some shelves in the classroom.

**estar** *verbo*

1.

En términos generales **estar** se traduce por **to be:**

**to be:** está muy cerca it's very close; no ha estado nunca en Cancún she has never been to Cancún; ¿está Pedro? is Pedro there?; hola ¿cómo estás? hello, how are you?; está enfermo he is sick; estoy estudiando I am studying

2. *indicando fechas, precio* ¿a cuántos estamos? what's the date?; estamos a dos it's the second today; ¿a cuánto están los melones? how much are the melons?; estaban a cincuenta pesos el kilo they were fifty pesos per kilogram

➤ está lloviendo it's raining

➤ está muy gorda she looks very fat: Pepe está con paperas Pepe has the mumps

➤ ¡estáte quieto! be still!

la **estatua** ■ statue.

la **estatura** ■ height: es de estatura normal he's of normal height

➤ mide casi dos metros de estatura he's almost two meters tall.

el **este** ■ east: el sol aparece por el este the sun rises in the east; el este de la ciudad the east part of the city

➤ al este to the east

➤ está al este de Lima it's to the east of Lima.

**este, esta** *adjetivo* ■ this: tengo que leer este libro I have to read this book.

**éste, ésta** *pronombre* ■ this one: éste es mejor this one is better

➤ ésta es mi casa this is my house

➤ éste no es el que yo quería this is not the one that I wanted.

**esté, estés etc** *verbo* ➤ estar.

**esterilizar** *verbo* ■ to sterilize.

el **estiércol**
1. *excremento* dung
2. *abono* manure.

**estilarse** *verbo pronominal* ■ to be in fashion

➤ esa clase de peinado ya no se estila that type of hairstyle is no longer in fashion.

el **estilo** ■ style: es típico de su estilo it's typical of his style

➤ salen a caminar, andar en bicicleta y cosas por el estilo they go out for walks, bike rides and that sort of thing

➤ estilo de vida lifestyle.

**estimular** *verbo*
1. to encourage: nos estimulan para que leamos más they encourage us to read more
2. to stimulate: un tónico para estimular el apetito a tonic to stimulate the appetite.

**estirar** *verbo* ■ to strech: salí a estirar las piernas un poco I went out to stretch my legs a little.

**esto** *pronombre* ■ this: ¿para qué sirve esto? what is this for?

➤ todo esto es mío all this is mine.

el **estómago** ■ stomach

➤ me duele el estómago my stomach hurts.

**estorbar** *verbo* ■ to be in the way: estas cajas estorban these boxes are in the way.

el **estorbo** ■ hindrance: estas cosas aquí son un estorbo these things here are a hindrance.

**estornudar** *verbo* ■ to sneeze.

el **estornudo** ■ sneeze.

**estos, estas** *adjetivo* ■ these: tengo que devolver estos libros I have to return these books; ¿de quién son estas llaves? whose keys are these?

**éstos, éstas** *pronombre* ■ these: me quedo con éstos I'm keeping these; éstas son mis compañeras de curso these are my classmates

➤ éstas son las que hay que estudiar these are the ones we have to study

➤ un día de éstos one of these days.

el **estornudo** ■ sneeze.

**estoy** *verbo* ➤ estar.

el **estrecho** strait

➤ el Estrecho de Magallanes the Strait of Magellan.

**estrecho** *adjetivo*
1. narrow: es una calle muy estrecha it's a very narrow street

**2. tight**: le gustan los suéters estrechos she likes tight sweaters.

la **estrella** ■ star
➤ una estrella del cine a movie star
➤ un hotel de tres estrellas a three-star hotel.

**estrenar** *verbo* ■ van a estrenar la película en mayo they're going to release the movie in May; todavía no hemos estrenado la piscina we still haven't used the swimming pool.

el **estreno** ■ première: fui al estreno de la película I went to the première of the movie.

el **estreñimiento** ■ constipation
➤ tener estreñimiento to be constipated.

**estricto** *adjetivo* ■ strict.

**estropear** *verbo*
**1. to break**: si sigues jugando con eso lo vas a estropear if you keep on playing with that you're going to break it
**2. to ruin**: la lluvia nos estropeó el picnic the rain ruined our picnic

**estropearse** *verbo pronominal*
**1. to break**: se nos estropeó la tele our television broke
**2. to spoil**: se estropeó la comida con el calor the food spoiled with the heat.

la **estructura** ■ structure.

el **estuche** ■ case: un estuche para lápices a pencil case.

el/la **estudiante** ■ student.

**estudiar** *verbo* ■ to study: le gustaría estudiar arquitectura she'd like to study architecture.

el **estudio**
**1. study**: ha dedicado su vida al estudio de la fauna he's dedicated his life to the study of animals
**2. studio apartment**: vive en un estudio she lives in a studio apartment
➤ tengo dos horas de estudio entre las clases I have a two-hour study break between classes

➤ dedica muy poco tiempo al estudio she devotes very little time to her studies
➤ un estudio de televisión a television studio

los **estudios** ■ studies: terminó sus estudios a los veinte años he completed his studies when he was twenty
➤ no pudieron darle estudios a su hijo they couldn't give their son a college education.

**estudioso** *adjetivo* ■ studious: mi hermano es muy estudioso my brother is very studious.

la **estufa**
**1. heater**: nos acercamos a la estufa para calentarnos we moved closer to the heater to warm up
**2.** *Colombia, Mexico* **stove**: una olla de agua hervía en la estufa a pot of water boiled on the stove.

**estúpido** *adjetivo* ■ stupid: ¡qué pregunta más estúpida! what a stupid question!

el **estúpido**, la **estúpida** ■ idiot: es un estúpido he's an idiot.

**estuve, estuvo, etc** *verbo* ➤ estar.

la **etapa**
**1. stage**: lo vamos a hacer por etapas we're going to do it in stages
**2. time**: la etapa más feliz de mi vida the happiest time of my life.

**eterno** *adjetivo* ■ eternal.

la **etiqueta** ■ label: una etiqueta adhesiva an adhesive label.

**étnico** *adjetivo* ■ ethnic.

el **euro** ■ euro.

**europeo** *adjetivo*

En inglés, los adjetivos que se refieren a un país o una región se escriben con mayúscula:

**European**

## el **europeo**, la **europea**

En inglés, los gentilicios se escriben con mayúscula:

**European**: los europeos the Europeans.

**evacuar** *verbo* ■ to evacuate.

**evaluar** *verbo* ■ to assess.

**evaporarse** *verbo pronominal* ■ to evaporate: el agua se evaporó con el calor del sol the water evaporated with the heat of the sun.

**evidente** *adjetivo* ■ obvious: es evidente que no ha estudiado it's obvious he hasn't studied.

**evitar** *verbo*
1. to avoid: a esa hora evitamos el tráfico we can avoid traffic at that time
2. to prevent: lo hacen para evitar accidentes they do it to prevent accidents
3. to save: eso nos habría evitado muchas molestias that would have saved us a lot of trouble
➤ no lo pude evitar I couldn't help it.

la **evolución** (*plural* las evoluciones) ■ development: gracias a la evolución de la medicina thanks to medical developments
➤ la teoría de la evolución the theory of evolution.

la **exactitud** ■ precision: la exactitud de un test the precision of a test
➤ no lo recuerdo con exactitud I can't remember precisely.

**exacto** *adjetivo* ■ exact: ¿me puedes dar la hora exacta? can you tell me the exact time?
➤ el avión salió a la hora exacta the plane left right on time.

**exagerar** *verbo* ■ to exaggerate: no exageres don't exaggerate.

el **examen** (*plural* los exámenes) ■ exam: tengo que estudiar para el examen de inglés I have to study for my English exam
➤ un examen de manejar a driving test.

**examinar** *verbo* ■ to examine: este es el médico que me examinó this is the doctor who examined me.

**excavar** *verbo* ■ to dig: hay varios arqueólogos excavando el lugar there are several archaeologists digging on the site.

**excelente** *adjetivo* ■ excellent.

**excéntrico** *adjetivo* ■ eccentric.

la **excepción** (*plural* las excepciones) ■ exception: es una excepción a la regla it's the exception to the rule
➤ hacer una excepción to make an exception: hicieron una excepción con él they made an exception for him
➤ con excepción de except: estudié todo con excepción de esto I studied everything except this.

**excepto** *preposición* ■ except: todos llevaron algo excepto yo everybody except me brought something.

el **exceso** ■ excess: todos los excesos son malos all excesses are bad
➤ en exceso to excess: hay gente que bebe en exceso some people drink to excess
➤ exceso de equipaje excess baggage.

**excitarse** *verbo* ■ to get worked up: se excita mucho cuando discute he gets very worked up when he argues.

la **exclamación** (*plural* las exclamaciones) ■ exclamation
➤ signo de exclamación exclamation mark.

**excluir** *verbo* ■ to exclude: lo excluyeron del equipo he was excluded from the team
➤ fueron todos, excluyendo Pepe they all went except for Pepe.

**exclusivo** *adjetivo* ■ exclusive.

la **excursión** (*plural* las excursiones) ■ trip: hicimos una excursión a un pueblo cercano we made a trip to a nearby town; el martes vamos de excursión con el colegio we're going on a school field trip on Tuesday.

el/la **excursionista** ■ hiker.

la **excusa** ■ excuse.

la **exhibición** *(plural* las exhibiciones)
1. display: tienen reptiles en exhibición they have reptiles on display
2. exhibition: una exhibición de arte africano an exhibition of African art.

**exhibir** *verbo* ■ to show: van a exhibir uno de sus cuadros they're going to show one of his paintings
➤ le encanta exhibirse she loves to show off.

**exigente** *adjetivo* ■ demanding: es una profesora muy exigente she's a very demanding teacher.

**exigir** *verbo* ■ to demand: la profesora nos exige mucho the teacher demands a great deal from us.

el **exiliado**, la **exiliada** ■ exile: un exiliado político a political exile.

**existir** *verbo* ■ to exist: está convencido de que los ovnis existen he's convinced that UFOs exist.

el **éxito** ■ success: el paseo fue un éxito the trip was a success
➤ tener éxito to be successful: su libro ha tenido mucho éxito her book has been very successful

⚠️ The Spanish word **éxito** is a false cognate, it doesn't mean "exit".

**exitoso** *adjetivo* ■ successful.

**exótico** *adjetivo* ■ exotic.

la **expedición** *(plural* las expediciones)
■ expedition.

las **expensas**
➤ han bajado los precios a expensas de la calidad they've lowered prices at the expense of quality
➤ vive a expensas de una tía he lives off his aunt.

la **experiencia** ■ experience: tiene mucha experiencia she has a lot of experience; no es necesario tener experiencia previa no previous experience is necessary
➤ necesitan a una persona con experiencia they need an experienced person.

**experimentar** *verbo*
1. to experiment: experimentan con conejos they experiment on rabbits
2. to experience: nunca había experimentado algo así I'd never experienced anything like it.

el **experimento** ■ experiment.

el **experto**, la **experta** ■ expert: es una experta en computación she's an expert in computers.

la **explicación** *(plural* las explicaciones)
■ explanation: debe haber una explicación para todo esto there has to be an explanation for all of this
➤ pedir explicaciones to demand an explanation.

**explicar** *verbo* ■ to explain: no lo pudo explicar she couldn't explain it; nos explicó cómo lo descubrieron she explained how they discovered it
➤ explicarle algo a alguien to explain something to someone
➤ no sé si me explico bien I don't know if I'm making myself clear
➤ no me lo puedo explicar I can't understand it.

el **explorador**, la **exploradora** ■ explorer.

**explorar** *verbo* ■ to explore.

la **explosión** *(plural* las explosiones)
■ explosion: hubo una gran explosión there was a big explosion
➤ hacer explosión to explode.

el **explosivo** ■ explosive.

la **explotación** ■ exploitation.

**explotar** *verbo*
1. to explode: la bomba va explotar en 10 minutos the bomb will explode in 10 minutes
2. to exploit: han explotado los recursos al máximo they've exploited their resources to the full; dice que la explotan en su trabajo she says they exploit her at work.

**exponer** *verbo*

1. **to exhibit:** van a exponer sus cuadros en una galería they're going to exhibit her paintings in a gallery
2. **to set out:** expuso sus ideas muy claramente she set out her ideas very clearly
➤ exponen su vida para salvar a otros they risk their lives to save others
➤ no deben exponerse demasiado al sol you shouldn't expose yourself to the sun too much.

**exportar** *verbo* ■ to export.

la **exportación** *(plural* las exportaciones *)* ■ export
➤ artículos de exportación export goods.

la **exposición** *(plural* las exposiciones*)*
■ **exhibition:** una exposición de pinturas a painting exhibition
➤ una exposición de perros a dog show.

**expresar** *verbo* ■ to express: le cuesta expresar lo que siente he has trouble expressing his feelings; no sabe expresarse muy bien she's not very good at expressing herself.

la **expresión** *(plural* las expresiones*)*
■ **expression:** tenía una expresión de tristeza en la cara she had a sad expression on her face; canta sin ninguna expresión there's no expression in his singing; es una expresión que se usa en México it's an expression used in Mexico.

**exprimir** *verbo* ■ to squeeze.

**expulsar** *verbo*

1. **to expel:** lo expulsaron del colegio he was expelled from school
2. **to send off:** lo expulsaron en el primer tiempo he was sent off in the first half.

**exquisito** *adjetivo* ■ delicious: nos sirvieron una comida exquisita they served us a delicious meal.

**extender** *verbo*

1. **to spread:** extendió la sábana sobre la cama she spread the sheet on the bed; hay que extender bien el bronceador por el cuerpo you have to spread the tanning lotion all over your body
2. **to extend:** le extendieron la visa por un año her visa was extended for a year; el país se extiende entre los Andes y el Océano Pacífico the country extends from the Andes to the Pacific.

la **extensión** *(plural* las extensiones*)*

1. **expanse:** es dueño de una gran extensión de terreno he owns a vast expanse of land
2. **extension:** ¿sabes el número de su extensión? do you know her extension?; no consiguió la extensión de su visa she didn't get the visa extension.

**extenso** *adjetivo* ■ extensive.

**exterior** *adjetivo*

1. **outside:** hay que subir por la escalera exterior you have to climb up the outside ladder; la parte exterior es más antigua the outside is older
2. **foreign:** el comercio exterior foreign trade

el **exterior** ■ outside
➤ el exterior the outside: pintaron de blanco el exterior de la casa they painted the outside of the house white
➤ el exterior abroad: reportaron las noticias del exterior they reported the news from abroad.

**externo** *adjetivo*

1. **external:** la pomada es de uso externo the ointment is for external use
2. **outside:** la parte externa de una flor the outside of the flower
➤ un colegio sólo para alumnos externos a day school.

la **extinción** *(plural* las extinciones*)*
■ **extinction:** ¿qué provocó la extinción de los dinosaurios? what caused the extinction of dinosaurs?
➤ el viento hizo difícil la extinción del incendio the wind made it difficult to put out the fire
➤ especies en vías de extinción endangered species.

el **extinguidor** ■ fire extinguisher.

**extinguir** *verbo*

1. **to put out:** luchaban por extinguir el fuego they fought to put out the fire

**2. to become extinct:** estas especies se extinguieron hace muchos años these species became extinct many years ago.

| **extra** | adjetivo ■ **extra:** pueden poner una cama extra they can set up an extra bed
➤ **tiempo extra** Central America, Mexico overtime
➤ **trabajar horas extras** to work overtime.

| **extraer** | verbo ■ **to extract:** visitamos los pozos de donde extraen petróleo we visited the wells where they extract the oil.

| **extranjero** | adjetivo ■ **foreign:** un visitante extranjero a foreign visitor

el | **extranjero** | ■ le gustaría viajar por el extranjero she'd like to travel abroad
➤ **ir al extranjero** to go abroad.

el | **extranjero,** la **extranjera** | ■ **foreigner:** muchos extranjeros viven en esta zona a lot of foreigners live in this area.

| **extrañar** | verbo ■ **to miss:** extraña mucho a su familia he misses his family a lot
➤ **me extraña que...** I'm surprised that...: **me extrañó no verte en clases** I was surprised that you weren't in class.

| **extraño** | adjetivo ■ **strange:** una costumbre muy extraña a strange custom
➤ **¡qué cosa más extraña!** how strange!

| **extraordinario** | adjetivo ■ **extraordinary:** hace falta una paciencia extraordinaria it takes extraordinary patience
➤ **no tiene nada de extraordinario** there's nothing unusual about that.

| **extremo** | adjetivo ■ **extreme:** tienen temperaturas extremas en el desierto they have extreme temperatures in the desert
➤ **la extrema derecha** the far right

el | **extremo** | ■ **end:** amarró los dos extremos del cordel he tied the two ends of the rope
➤ **recorrió el país de extremo a extremo** he traveled from one end of the country to the other
➤ **en último extremo** as a last resort.

la | **fábrica** | ■ **factory:** trabaja en una fábrica de automóviles she works in a car factory

⚠ The Spanish word **fábrica** is a false cognate, it doesn't mean "fabric".

| **fabricar** | verbo ■ **to manufacture:** fabrican zapatos de niños they manufacture children's shoes
➤ **fabricado en Corea** made in Korea
➤ **fabricar en serie** to mass-produce.

| **fabuloso** | adjetivo ■ **fabulous.**

la | **facha** | informal ■ **look:** ese muchacho tiene facha de estudiante that guy has the look of a student
➤ **no quiero que nadie me vea en esta facha** I don't want anyone to see me looking like this.

la | **fachada** | ■ **façade:** están pintando la fachada del colegio they're painting the school's façade.

| **fácil** | adjetivo ■ **easy:** una tarea fácil an easy homework assignment; **es muy fácil equivocarse** it's very easy to make a mistake
➤ **es fácil de convencer** he's easy to convince
➤ **lleva paraguas porque es fácil que llueva** bring an umbrella because it could easily rain.

la **facilidad** ■ ease: aprobó los exámenes con facilidad she passed her exams with ease
➤ tiene mucha facilidad para las matemáticas he's good at math
➤ con facilidad easily: ganaron con facilidad they won easily.

el **factor** ■ factor: el clima es un factor importante weather is an important factor.

la **factura**
1. invoice: envíe su factura al finalizar el trabajo send your invoice when the job is finished
2. bill: la factura del teléfono the telephone bill.

la **facultad** ■ faculty: tiene todas sus facultades mentales he's in full possession of his mental faculties
➤ la Facultad de Medicina the medical school
➤ fueron a la misma facultad they were in the same department at school.

el **fajo** ■ wad: un fajo de billetes a wad of cash.

la **falda**
1. skirt: una falda larga a long skirt
2. side: un pueblo en la falda de la montaña a town on the side of the mountain.

la **falla**
1. flaw: devolví el suéter porque tenía una falla I returned the sweater because it had a flaw
2. failure: todo se debió a una falla en el sistema it was all due to a failure in the system
➤ una falla mecánica a break-down
➤ una falla humana human error.

**fallar** verbo ■ to fail: le está fallando la memoria her memory is failing her; le fallaron los frenos his brakes failed
➤ fallar un tiro to miss a shot
➤ cuento contigo, no me vayas a fallar I'm counting on you, don't let me down.

**falsificar** verbo ■ to forge: le falsificó la firma he forged her signature.

**falso** adjetivo
1. false: usaba un nombre falso she was using a false name
2. fake: el pasaporte era falso the passport was fake
➤ un billete falso a counterfeit bill
➤ lo que dijo es falso what he said is false
➤ una falsa alarma a false alarm
➤ falso amigo false cognate: "librería" y "library" son falsos amigos "librería" and "library" are false cognates.

la **falta**
1. lack: por falta de experiencia due to lack of experience
2. foul: el árbitro no marcó la falta the referee didn't call the foul
➤ faltas de ortografía spelling errors
➤ he tenido cuatro faltas en el mes I've been absent four times this month
➤ es por mi falta de costumbre it's because I'm not used to it
➤ es una falta de educación it's bad manners
➤ hace falta más disciplina we need more discipline
➤ me hace falta un buen diccionario I need a good dictionary
➤ sin falta without fail: mañana sin falta lo llamo I'll call him tomorrow without fail.

**faltar** verbo ■ to be missing: a este libro le falta una página this book is missing a page; ¿quién falta? who's missing?
➤ no falta nunca a clases she never misses class
➤ le falta experiencia he lacks experience
➤ va a faltar comida we won't have enough food
➤ a esto le falta sabor it's lacking in taste
➤ falta una semana para mi cumpleaños it's a week till my birthday
➤ falta poco para terminar we're almost finished
➤ ¿te falta mucho? do you have a lot more to do?
➤ sólo me falta poner la fecha I just need to add the date
➤ ¡era lo único que nos faltaba! that's the last thing we need!

la **fama**
1. fame: alcanzó la fama con su primer disco she shot to fame with her first record

**2. reputation:** tiene fama de flojo he has a reputation for being lazy; **tiene muy mala fama** he has a bad reputation.

la **familia** ▬ family: fue a visitar a su familia she went to visit her family
➤ **es de buena familia** he comes from a good family
➤ **celebramos la Navidad en familia** we celebrated Christmas with the family.

**familiar** adjetivo
1. **family:** hay un ambiente familiar en este restaurante this restaurant has a family atmosphere
2. **familiar:** su cara le era familiar her face was familiar to him
➤ **viene en envase familiar** it comes in a family-size pack

el/la **familiar** ▬ relative: vive con un familiar she lives with a relative.

el/la **fan** (plural los/las fans) ▬ fan
➤ **un club de fans** a fan club.

**fanático** adjetivo ▬ fanatical

el **fanático,** la **fanática** ▬ fanatic: es una fanática de la música pop she's a pop music fanatic.

la **fantasía** ▬ fantasy
➤ **un mundo de fantasía** a fantasy world
➤ **joyas de fantasía** costume jewelry.

el **fantasma** ▬ ghost.

**fantástico** adjetivo ▬ fantastic.

la **farmacia** ▬ drugstore.

el **faro**
1. **lighthouse:** podíamos ver el faro en la distancia we could see the lighthouse in the distance
2. **headlight:** encendí los faros del coche I switched on the car's headlights.

el **farol**
1. **streetlight:** los faroles se encendieron al atardecer the streetlights came on as the sun went down
2. **lantern:** un farol alumbraba la entrada a lantern lit up the doorway.

la **farsa** ▬ farce: fuimos al teatro a ver una farsa we went to the theater to see a farce; ¿elecciones con un solo candidato? ¡eso es una farsa! an election with just one candidate? what a farce!

el/la **farsante** ▬ fraud: me ha engañado varias veces, es un farsante he's conned me several times, he's a fraud.

**fascinar** verbo ▬ to fascinate: me fascinan sus pinturas his paintings fascinate me.

la **fase** ▬ phase: las fases de la luna son cuatro the moon has four phases.

**fastidiar** verbo
1. **to annoy:** me fastidia que los vecinos hagan tanto ruido it really annoys me that the neighbors make so much noise
2. **to bother:** no fastidies a tu hermana, que está haciendo su tarea don't bother your sister, she's doing her homework.

el **fastidio** ▬ nuisance: ¡qué fastidio tener que salir con esta lluvia! what a nuisance to have to go out in this rain!

**fatal** adjetivo
1. **fatal:** el accidente fue fatal it was a fatal accident
2. **awful:** hoy fue un día fatal, todo lo que hice me salió mal today was awful — everything I did went wrong.

la **fatiga** ▬ fatigue.

**fatigarse** verbo pronominal ▬ to get breathless: me fatigué al subir las escaleras hasta el septimo piso climbing the stairs to the seventh floor left me breathless.

el **favor** ▬ favor: me han hecho varios favores y por eso les estoy agradecida they've done me a few favors so I'm grateful to them
➤ **a favor de** in favor of: están a favor de la educación bilingüe they're in favor of bilingual education
➤ **por favor** please: cierra la puerta, por favor close the door please.

**favorecer** verbo
1. **to favor:** esa ley favorece a los ricos that law favors the rich

**125**

**2.** **to be flattering: ese color te favorece, deberías usarlo más seguido** that color is very flattering, you should wear it more often.

**favorito** *adjetivo* ■ **favorite**.

el **fax** *(plural los faxes)*

**1.** **fax machine: acabo de instalar el nuevo fax** I just set up the new fax machine

**2.** **fax: llegó un fax con la información que faltaba** we got a fax with the missing information

➤ **mandar algo por fax** to fax something.

la **fe** ■ **faith: la fe religiosa mal entendida provoca guerras terribles** misunderstood religious faith can spark terrible wars; **tengo fe en que todo va a salir bien** I have faith that everything will turn out all right.

la **fealdad** ■ **ugliness**.

**febrero** *sustantivo masculino*

En inglés los nombres de los meses se escriben con mayúscula:

**February: en febrero** in February; **el próximo febrero** next February; **el pasado febrero** last February.

la **fecha** ■ **date**

➤ **fecha de nacimiento** date of birth.

**fecundar** *verbo* ■ **to fertilize**.

la **federación** *(plural las federaciones)* ■ **federation**.

**federal** *adjetivo* ■ **federal**.

la **felicidad** ■ **happiness: el dinero no compra la felicidad** money can't buy you happiness

➤ **es mi cumpleaños — ¡muchas felicidades!** it's my birthday today — happy birthday!

➤ **¡muchas felicidades por el nuevo trabajo!** congratulations on your new job!

las **felicitaciones** ■ **congratulations: los ganadores recibieron las felicitaciones del público** the winners were congratulated by the spectators

➤ **¡felicitaciones!** congratulations!

**felicitar** *verbo* ■ **to congratulate: vamos a felicitarlo por sus buenos resulta-** dos let's congratulate him on his good grades

➤ **llamamos a nuestros amigos para felicitarlos por Navidad** we called our friends to wish them a merry Christmas.

el **feliz** *(plural felices) adjetivo* ■ **happy**

➤ **¡feliz cumpleaños!** happy birthday!

el **felpudo** ■ **doormat**.

**femenino** *adjetivo* ■ **feminine**.

el **fenómeno** ■ **phenomenon**.

**feo** *adjetivo*

**1.** **ugly: ese cuadro no me gusta nada, es muy feo** I don't like that picture at all, it's so ugly

**2.** **unpleasant: esta sopa tiene un sabor muy feo, ¿qué le pusiste?** the soup has an unpleasant flavor — what's in it?

**3.** **not nice: es muy feo mentir, no lo vuelvas a hacer** it's not nice to lie, don't do it again.

el **féretro** ■ **coffin**.

la **feria**

**1.** **fair: me gané el muñeco en la feria** I won the doll at the fair; **mañana se inaugura la feria del juguete** the toy fair opens tomorrow

**2.** *Mexico* **small change: necesito feria para el teléfono** I need some small change for the phone

**3.** *River Plate* **market: fui a la feria a comprar frutas y verduras frescas** I went to the market to buy fresh fruit and vegetables.

el **feriado** ■ **holiday**.

**fermentar** *verbo* ■ **to ferment**.

**feroz** *adjetivo* ■ **fierce**.

la **ferretería** ■ **hardware store**.

el **ferrocarril** ■ **railroad**.

**fértil** *adjetivo* ■ **fertile**.

el **fertilizante** ■ **fertilizer**.

**fertilizar** *verbo* ■ **to fertilize**.

**festejar** *verbo* ■ **to celebrate: el próximo sábado festejo mi cumpleaños** I'm celebrating my birthday next Saturday.

el **festejo** ■ festivity: los festejos de la boda duraron tres días the wedding festivities went on for three days.

el **festival** ■ festival
➤ festival de cine film festival.

la **festividad** ■ festivity: las festividades duraron todo el fin de semana the festivities went on all weekend.

**festivo** *adjetivo* ■ festive.

el **feto** ■ fetus.

el **fiambre** ■ cold cut: de todos los fiambres, el jamón es mi preferido ham is my favorite cold cut.

**fiar** *verbo* ■ to be trustworthy: esa marca de electrodomésticos no es de fiar this brand of appliances isn't very trustworthy

**fiarse** *verbo pronominal*

1. to believe: no te fíes de todo lo que oyes don't believe everything you hear
2. to trust: no te fíes de todos los que vengan a ofrecerte ayuda don't trust everyone that offers to help you.

la **fibra** ■ fiber: el pan integral contiene mucha fibra wholewheat bread contains a lot of fiber; el algodón es una excelente fibra natural cotton is an excellent natural fiber.

la **ficción** *(plural las ficciones)* ■ fiction: sólo escribe ficción she only writes fiction.

la **ficha**

1. card: en esta ficha anotaré tus datos I'll write your details on this card
2. piece: faltan algunas fichas rojas some of the red pieces are missing
➤ ficha médica medical records
➤ una ficha policial a police record.

el **fichero**

1. file: un fichero informático a computer file
2. filing cabinet: guardo los informes en el fichero I keep the reports in the filing cabinet.

la **fidelidad** ■ faithfulness.

el **fideo** ■ noodle: el primer plato es sopa con fideos the appetizer is a noodle soup.

la **fiebre** ■ fever: le dí una aspirina para bajarle la fiebre I gave her an aspirin to lower the fever.

**fiel** *adjetivo* ■ loyal: Juan siempre ha sido fiel a sus amigos Juan has always been loyal to his friends.

la **fiera** ■ wild animal: en este bosque viven varias fieras several wild animals live in this forest
➤ ponerse como una fiera to fly into a rage.

el **fierro** ■ iron.

la **fiesta** ■ party: hicimos una fiesta para su cumpleaños we threw a party for his birthday
➤ estar de fiesta to be celebrating: la familia está de fiesta por el nacimiento del niño the family is celebrating the birth of the baby
➤ fiesta patria independence day

### FIESTAS PATRIAS

Throughout the 19th century, the American colonies began to fight for their independence from Spain. Each country's **fiestas patrias** commemorate the date when the independence movement began or when independence was actually attained, and are celebrated every year. These are official holidays, marked with parades and other displays of patriotism. These are the dates when some Latin American countries achieved independence: Chile and Colombia in 1810, Paraguay and Venezuela in 1811, Argentina in 1816, Central America, Mexico, and Peru in 1821, and Bolivia and Uruguay in 1825.

### FIESTAS RELIGIOSAS

A tradition that Latin America inherited from Spain is that of having holidays honoring the patron saint of each city or country. For example, the patron saint of Mexico is the Virgin of Guadalupe. The festivities include religious processions and folk ceremonies that often combine Catholicism and indigenous rituals.

la **figura** ■ figure: dibujamos figuras de diferentes tamaños we drew different size figures.

**figurar** *verbo* ■ to appear: tu nombre no figura en esta lista your name doesn't appear on this list.

**fijar** *verbo* ■ to set: hay que fijar la fecha de la boda we have to set the date for the wedding

**fijarse** *verbo pronominal*

1. to look carefully: fíjate si tenés las llaves en la cartera look carefully in your purse for the keys

2. to notice: no me fijé que llevaba puesto I didn't really notice what she was wearing.

**fijo** *adjetivo*

1. fixed: la estantería está fija, ya puedes poner tus libros the shelves are fixed to the wall so you can put your books on them

2. set: pagamos una cuota fija todos los meses we pay a set fee every month

3. permanent: todavía no tengo trabajo fijo I don't have a permanent job yet.

la **fila**

1. line: la fila en el banco era larguísima the line at the bank was really long

2. row: conseguimos asientos en tercera fila we got seats in the third row

➤ estacionar en doble fila to double park

➤ ponerse en fila to get in line.

las **Filipinas** ■ the Philippines.

**filmar** *verbo* ■ to film: Pedro filmó el nacimiento de su hijo Pedro filmed the birth of his son.

el **filo** ■ blade: cuidado, no te cortes con el filo del cuchillo careful, don't cut yourself on the knife's blade

➤ sacarle filo a algo to sharpen something: tengo que sacarle filo a este cuchillo I need to sharpen this knife.

la **filosofía** ■ philosophy.

**filtrar** *verbo* ■ to filter: el agua de por aquí no es segura, lo mejor es filtrarla the water here isn't safe to drink, so it's best to filter it

**filtrarse** *verbo pronominal* ■ to leak: se está filtrando agua del techo the roof is leaking.

el **filtro** ■ filter.

el **fin**

1. end: se acerca el fin del año escolar we're approaching the end of the school year

2. purpose: ¿cuál es el fin de tu viaje? what is the purpose of your trip?

➤ "fin" "the end"

➤ a fines de at the end of: viajaremos a fines de diciembre we're going on vacation at the end of December

➤ ¡al fin! finally!: ¡al fin llegaste! you're finally here!

➤ al fin y al cabo after all

➤ en fin well: en fin, ¿qué piensas hacer ahora? well, what are you going to do now?

➤ ¡por fin! finally: ¡por fin terminaste! you finally finished!

➤ el fin de año New Year's Eve

➤ el fin de semana the weekend.

el **final** ■ end: no me gustó el final del cuento I didn't like the end of the story

➤ un final feliz a happy ending: me encantan las películas con final feliz I love movies with a happy ending

la **final** ■ final: México ganó la final Mexico won the final.

**finalizar** *verbo* ■ to finish.

**financiar** *verbo* ■ to finance: el gobierno financió la construcción del puente the government financed the construction of the bridge.

las **finanzas** ■ finances: las finanzas de una empresa a company's finances

➤ Ministerio de Finanzas the Treasury Department.

la **finca** ■ farm.

**fingir** *verbo* ■ to pretend: no finjas que duermes, sé que estás despierta stop pretending you're asleep, I know you're awake.

**fino** *adjetivo*

1. fine: tengo el cabello muy fino I have very fine hair; puse los libros más finos en los estantes de arriba I put the finest books on the top shelves

**2. slender:** la pianista tenía manos largas y dedos finos *the pianist had long hands with slender fingers.*

la **firma** ■ **signature:** aquí está la firma de mi padre *here's my father's signature.*

el **firmamento** ■ **sky.**

**firmar** *verbo* ■ **to sign:** firme aquí, por favor *sign here please.*

**firme** *adjetivo* ■ **steady:** esta mesa es firme, puedes poner el televisor aquí *this table is steady enough to put the TV on.*

el/la **fiscal** ■ **district attorney.**

la **física** ■ **physics.**

**físico** *adjetivo* ■ **physical:** el niño no tiene ningún problema físico *the child has no physical problems*
➤ **educación física** *physical education*

el **físico,** la **física** ■ **physicist.**

**flaco** *adjetivo* ■ **skinny.**

la **flama** ■ *Mexico* **flame.**

**flamante** *adjetivo* ■ **brand-new:** un flamante auto *a brand-new car.*

el **flan** ■ **flan.**

el **flash** ■ **flash:** usa el flash al tomar la foto *use the flash when you take the picture.*

la **flauta** ■ **flute:** toca muy bien la flauta *he plays the flute very well*
➤ **flauta dulce** *recorder.*

la **flecha** ■ **arrow.**

el **fleco**
**1. fringe:** llevaba una chaqueta con fleco *she wore a jacket with fringe on it*
**2.** *Mexico* **bangs:** el fleco le cubría los ojos *her bangs covered her eyes.*

la **flema** ■ **phlegm.**

el **flequillo** ■ **bangs.**

**flexible** *adjetivo* ■ **flexible.**

la **flexión** *(plural* las flexiones) ■ **push-up:** ayer hice 100 flexiones de brazos *I did 100 push-ups yesterday.*

**flexionar** *verbo* ■ **to bend:** al agacharte tienes que flexionar las piernas *you have to bend your legs as you crouch down.*

**flojo** *adjetivo*
**1. loose:** este nudo está muy flojo *this knot is very loose*
**2. weak:** estás flojo en historia *you're history grades are weak*
**3. lazy:** te puedes ir a pie, no seas flojo *you can walk there, don't be lazy.*

la **flor** ■ **flower.**

**florecer** *verbo* ■ **to blossom:** los árboles florecieron temprano este año *the trees blossomed early this year.*

la **florería** ■ **florist.**

el **florero** ■ **vase:** me regalaron un precioso florero de cristal *they gave me a beautiful crystal vase.*

la **flota** ■ **fleet:** la flota pesquera partió antes del amanecer *the fishing fleet left before dawn.*

el **flotador** ■ **rubber ring.**

**flotar** *verbo* ■ **to float:** había muchas hojas flotando en la piscina *there were a lot of leaves floating in the pool.*

**fluir** *verbo* ■ **to flow:** el río fluía rápidamente bajo el puente *the river flowed rapidly under the bridge.*

el **flujo** ■ **flow:** cerraron la compuerta para detener el flujo de agua *they closed the hatch to stop the flow of water.*

**fluorescente** *adjetivo* ■ **flourescent.**

la **foca** ■ **seal.**

el **foco**
**1. spotlight:** el foco brillaba sobre ella *the spotlight shone upon her*
**2. floodlight:** los focos iluminaron el campo *the floodlights lit up the field*
**3. headlight:** encendí los focos al atardecer *I turned on the headlights at dusk*
**4.** *Mexico* **lightbulb:** necesito un foco nuevo para esta lámpara *I need a new lightbulb for this lamp*
➤ **fuera de foco** *out of focus:* esa imagen está fuera de foco *this picture is out of focus.*

el **folleto**
**1.** *de una hoja* **leaflet**
**2.** *como un librito* **brochure.**

el **fondo**

1. **bottom:** están explorando el fondo del mar they are exploring the bottom of the sea
2. **background:** el retrato tenía un fondo azul the portrait had a blue background
3. **end:** el baño está al fondo del corredor the bathroom is at the end of the hall
4. *Mexico* **slip:** se te ve el fondo your slip is showing
➤ **a fondo** in-depth: estudiaron el problema a fondo they did an in-depth study of the problem
➤ **en el fondo** deep down: pelean mucho, pero en el fondo se quieren they fight a lot, but deep down they love each other.

los **fondos** ■ **money:** están recaudando fondos para el hospital they're raising money for the hospital.

el **forastero,** la **forastera** ■ **stranger.**

**forestal** *adjetivo* ■ **forest:** el guardia forestal detectó el incendio the forest ranger spotted the fire.

la **forma**

1. **shape:** encuentra todas las formas circulares find all the circular shapes
2. *Mexico* **form:** llene esta forma y entréguesela a la señorita fill out this form and hand it to the young lady
3. **way:** no me gusta su forma de ser, siempre está de mal humor I don't like the way she acts, she's always in a bad mood; este ejercicio puede resolverse de diferentes formas this problem can be solved several ways
➤ **de cualquier forma** anyway
➤ **de todas formas** anyway: de todas formas tendrás que limpiar tu cuarto you'll have to clean your room anyway
➤ **mantenerse en forma** to stay in shape: Ana camina tres kilómetros por día para mantenerse en forma Ana walks three kilometers a day to stay in shape.

la **formación** ■ **education:** es importante tener una buena formación para conseguir un buen trabajo it's important to have a good education to get a good job.

**formal** *adjetivo*

1. **reliable:** necesitamos trabajadores más formales we need more reliable workers

2. **formal:** nos mandaron una invitación formal they sent us a formal invitation.

**formar** *verbo*

1. **to make:** si unes los puntos formarás la figura de un elefante if you connect the dots you'll make an elephant
2. **to form:** Juan y sus amigos formaron una banda musical Juan and his friends formed a band
3. **to train:** la universidad se ocupa de formar a los profesionales liberales it's the university's job to train professionals.

la **fórmula**

1. **formula:** es difícil recordar todas las fórmulas matemáticas it's hard to remember all the mathematical formulas
2. **set expression:** tienes que empezar la carta con una fórmula de cortesía you should start the letter with a polite set expression; una fórmula mágica a magic formula.

el **formulario** ■ **form.**

**forrar** *verbo* ■ **to cover:** voy a forrar los cuadernos para protegerlos I'm going to cover my notebooks to protect them.

**fortalecer** *verbo* ■ **to strengthen:** el ejercicio físico fortalece los músculos physical exercise strengthens the muscles.

la **fortaleza**

1. **strength:** su fortaleza lo ayudó a recuperarse pronto his strength helped him recover quickly
2. **fortress:** a lo largo de la costa hay varias fortalezas antiguas there are several old fortresses along the coast.

la **fortuna** ■ **fortune:** su fortuna personal es de cerca de diez millones de dólares her personal fortune comes to nearly ten million dollars; tuvo la fortuna de conocer personalmente a su actor favorito he had the good fortune to meet his favorite actor.

**forzar** *verbo* ■ **to force:** el mal tiempo nos forzó a quedarnos en casa todo el fin de semana the bad weather forced us to stay home all weekend.

el **fósforo** ■ **match.**

la **foto** ■ **picture.**

**130**

la **fotocopia** ■ photocopy.

la **fotocopiadora** ■ photocopier.

la **fotografía** ■ photograph
➤ hacer una fotografía de alguien to take a picture of someone.

el **fotógrafo**, la **fotógrafa** ■ photographer.

**fracasar** *verbo* ■ to fail: nuestros planes de viaje fracasaron por falta de dinero our travel plans failed due to lack of money.

el **fracaso** ■ failure: el espectáculo fue un fracaso, no vino nadie the show was a failure, nobody came.

la **fracción** *(plural* las fracciones*)* ■ fraction: en la clase de hoy estudiamos las fracciones we studied fractions in class today.

la **fractura** ■ fracture: la caída le produjo varias fracturas she sustained several fractures from the fall.

**fracturar** *verbo* ■ to fracture: se fracturó la pierna en un accidente de esquí she fractured her leg in a ski accident.

**frágil** *adjetivo* ■ fragile.

**fragmentar** *verbo* ■ to fragment.

el **fragmento** ■ piece: ahora hay que unir los fragmentos y pegarlos now you have to join the pieces and stick them together.

la **frambuesa** ■ raspberry *(plural* raspberries*)*.

**franco** *adjetivo* ■ frank: te voy a ser franco, no confío en él I'll be frank, I don't trust him
➤ para serte franco to be honest.

la **franja** ■ stripe: la bandera uruguaya tiene nueve franjas azules sobre un campo blanco the Uruguayan flag has nine blue stripes on a white background.

la **franqueza** ■ frankness.

el **frasco**
1. bottle: el perfume viene en un frasco muy bonito the perfume comes in a pretty bottle

2. jar: no puedo abrir el frasco de la mayonesa I can't open the mayonnaise jar.

la **frase** ■ sentence.

el **fraude** ■ fraud
➤ un fraude fiscal a tax fraud.

la **frazada** ■ blanket.

la **frecuencia** ■ frequency *(plural* frecuencies*)*: las ondas de una frecuencia tan alta no se oyen you can't hear waves of such a high frequency; ¿con qué frecuencia visitas a tus abuelos? how often do you visit your grandparents?
➤ con frecuencia frequently: somos buenas amigas y nos vemos con frecuencia we're good friends and see each other frequently.

**frecuentar** *verbo* ■ to frequent: le gustaba frecuentar el museo de arte he liked to frequent the art museum.

**frecuente** *adjetivo* ■ frequent.

**freír** *verbo* ■ to fry.

**frenar** *verbo* ■ to brake: no pudo frenar a tiempo y provocó un accidente he couldn't brake in time and caused an accident.

el **freno** ■ brake
➤ el freno de mano the emergency brake

los **frenos** *Mexico* ■ braces.

el **frente** ■ front: el frente de la casa estaba pintado de blanco the front of the house was painted white; vivió experiencias terribles en el frente de batalla he experienced terrible things at the battle front
➤ pasar al frente to go up to the front: la maestra me pidió que pasara al frente para leer mi redacción the teacher asked me to go up to the front of the class to read my essay
➤ de frente head-on: chocaron de frente they had a head-on collision.

la **frente** ■ forehead: era bonita, tenía los pómulos altos y la frente ancha she was pretty, with high cheekbones and a wide forehead.

la **fresa** ■ strawberry.

**fresco** *adjetivo*

1. **cool**: los días están más frescos últimamente the days are growing cooler lately
2. **fresh**: es importante comer verduras y frutas frescas it's important to eat fresh fruit and vegetables
3. **wet**: "cuidado, pintura fresca" "warning: wet paint".

la **frialdad** ■ **coldness**: la frialdad de su mirada the coldness of his look.

la **fricción** *(plural las fricciones)*

1. **friction**: la fricción entre las dos piezas provocó un desgaste friction between the two pieces caused them to wear down
2. **rub**: ¿quieres fricciones en la espalda? do you want a back rub?

el **frigorífico**

1. **cold storage**: la carne para exportación se almacena en frigoríficos the meat that will be exported is kept in cold storage
2. *River Plate* **meat-processing plant**: en los frigoríficos se elaboran los subproductos de la carne meat by-products are produced in meat-processing plants.

el **frijol** ■ *Andes, Caribbean, Central America, Mexico* **bean**.

**frío** *adjetivo* ■ **cold**: la sopa está fría the soup is cold

el **frío** ■ **cold**: hace frío it's cold; tengo frío I'm cold.

**frito** *adjetivo* ■ **fried**: preparé un pescado frito I made some fried fish.

**frontal** *adjetivo* ■ **head-on**: fue un choque frontal it was a head-on crash.

la **frontera** ■ **border**: el estado mexicano de Chihuahua queda en la frontera con Estados Unidos the Mexican state of Chihuahua is on the U.S. border.

**frotar** *verbo* ■ **to rub**: tienes que frotarte las piernas con esta loción you have to rub your legs with this lotion.

la **frustración** *(plural las frustraciones)* ■ **frustration**.

**frustrar** *verbo* ■ **to spoil**: el mal tiempo frustró nuestros planes de viaje the bad weather spoiled our plans

**frustrarse** *verbo pronominal* ■ **to be frustrated**: los niños se frustraron porque el espectáculo se suspendió the children were frustrated because the show was cancelled.

la **fruta** ■ **fruit**
➤ fruta abrillantada *River Plate* crystallized fruit
➤ fruta de estación seasonal fruit
➤ fruta seca nuts and dried fruits.

la **frutería** ■ **fruit store**.

la **frutilla** *River Plate* ■ **strawberry**.

el **fruto** ■ **fruit**: el árbol está cargado de frutos the tree is full of fruit.

el **fuego** ■ **fire**: no consiguieron controlar el fuego they couldn't control the fire
➤ fuegos artificiales fireworks.

la **fuente**

1. **source**: la fuente de este río está en las montañas the source of this river is in the mountains
2. **fountain**: construyeron una hermosa fuente en medio del parque they built a beautiful fountain in the middle of the park
3. **bowl**: ¿tienes una linda fuente para poner la fruta? do you have nice bowl to put the fruit in?
4. **source**: el turismo es la principal fuente de ingresos en esa región tourism is the main source of income in that area.

**fuera** *adverbio* ■ **outside**: el perro duerme fuera de la casa the dog sleeps outside the house.

**fuerte** *adjetivo*

1. **strong**: ese pescado tiene un olor muy fuerte that fish has a very strong smell
2. **loud**: la música está muy fuerte para platicar the music is too loud for conversation
3. **bad**: llegué al dentista con un fuerte dolor de muelas I went to the dentist with a bad toothache
4. **bold**: para la ropa, prefiero los colores fuertes I prefer clothes with bold colors
5. **hard**: se dio un golpe tan fuerte que empezó a llorar he hit himself so hard he started to cry

el **fuerte** ■ **fort**.

la **fuerza**

1. **strength:** vamos a descansar para recuperar fuerzas let's have a break to recover our strength
2. **force:** la fuerza del viento obligó al velero a girar the force of the wind made the sailboat turn around
➤ la fuerza de gravedad gravity
➤ tiene tanta fuerza que partió un ladrillo de un golpe he's so strong he broke a brick with one blow.

la **fuga**

1. **escape:** los prisioneros planearon su fuga the prisoners planned their escape
2. **leak:** encontramos una fuga de gas en la cocina we found a gas leak in the kitchen.

**fugarse** *verbo pronominal* ▪ to escape.

**fugaz** *adjetivo* ▪ fleeting.

**fugitivo** *adjetivo* ▪ fugitive

el **fugitivo, la fugitiva** ▪ fugitive.

**fumar** *verbo* ▪ **to smoke:** fumar en pipa to smoke a pipe
➤ prohibido fumar no smoking.

la **función** *(plural las funciones)*

1. **role:** ¿cuál es tu función en la empresa? what is your role in the company?
2. **showing:** la próxima función empieza a las cinco the next showing starts at five.

**funcionar** *verbo* ▪ **to work:** la licuadora ya no funciona por que es muy vieja the blender doesn't work any more because it's so old.

el **funcionario, la funcionaria** ▪ government employee.

la **funda** ▪ cover.

la **fundación** *(plural las fundaciones)* ▪ **foundation:** desde que se jubiló trabaja como voluntaria en varias fundaciones she's been volunteering at several foundations since she retired.

**fundamental** *adjetivo* ▪ fundamental.

**fundar** *verbo* ▪ **to found:** según la leyenda, Rómulo y Remo fundaron Roma according to legend, Romulus and Remus founded Rome.

**fundir** *verbo*

1. **to melt:** el sol fundió la nieve the sun melted the snow
2. **to smelt:** los altos hornos sirven para fundir metales blast furnaces are used to smelt metal

**fundirse** *verbo pronominal*

1. **to melt:** la manteca se funde si la dejas al calor lard will melt if you leave it out in the heat
2. **to burn out:** el foco de la lámpara se fundió the lightbulb in the lamp burned out
3. **to merge:** durante la crisis económica, varias empresas se fundieron several companies merged during the economic crisis.

**fúnebre** *adjetivo* ▪ funereal.

el **funeral** ▪ funeral.

la **funeraria** ▪ funeral home.

la **furia** ▪ rage.

**furioso** *adjetivo* ▪ furious.

el **fusil** ▪ rifle.

**fusionar** *verbo* ▪ **to merge:** varias pequeñas empresas se fusionaron para lograr mantenerse en el mercado several small companies merged so they could stay in business.

el **fútbol** ▪ **soccer:** un jugador de fútbol a soccer player
➤ fútbol americano football

BABY FÚTBOL

In Latin America, where soccer is the most popular sport, there are **baby fútbol** schools, where children too young to compete in official leagues can train "professionally." The students participate in tournaments with other soccer schools. Many professional young soccer players have gotten their start in these schools.

el/la **futbolista** ▪ soccer player.

**futuro** *adjetivo* ▪ **future:** las generaciones futuras future generations
➤ la futura mamá the mother-to-be

el **futuro** ▪ future.

**133**

la **gabardina** ■ raincoat.

las **gafas** ■ glasses.

la **galaxia** ■ galaxy.

la **galería** ■ gallery: una galería de arte an art gallery
➤ una galería comercial a shopping mall.

el **gallego**, la **gallega** ■ Spaniard

> **GALLEGO**
>
> In South America, the word **ga-llego** is used for all Spaniards, probably because the majority of the Spanish immigrants who arrived in this region during the 19th and 20th centuries came from Galicia. They tended to arrive in the new world with little money and not much education, which is why nowadays the word is used in a pejorative sense for someone who is dumb, clumsy, and ignorant. Many jokes are made about **galle-gos**.

la **galleta** ■ cookie: compré un paquete de galletas I bought a pack of cookies
➤ una galleta salada a cracker.

la **gallina** ■ chicken.

el **gallo** ■ rooster.

el **galpón** *Andes, Caribbean, River Plate* ■ shed: guardamos las herramientas en el galpón we stored the tools in the shed.

la **gamba** ■ shrimp.

la **gana**
➤ muero de ganas de ir al cine I'm dying to go to the movies
➤ pateó la pelota con ganas he kicked the ball hard
➤ tener ganas de hacer algo to feel like doing something: tengo ganas de tomarme un helado I feel like getting an ice cream cone
➤ de buena gana willingly: de buena gana se ofreció a acompañarla he willingly offered to go with her
➤ de mala gana reluctantly: me contestó de mala gana he answered reluctantly
➤ llegamos tarde y nos quedamos con las ganas de ver la película we didn't get to see the movie because we were late.

la **ganadería** ■ ranching.

el **ganadero**, la **ganadera** ■ rancher: los ganaderos de la región están preocupados por la inundación ranchers in the area are worried about the floods.

el **ganado** ■ cattle.

el **ganador**, la **ganadora** ■ winner: la ganadora del concurso es una mujer del campo the contest winner is a woman from the country.

las **ganancias** ■ profits: obtuvimos excelentes ganancias este año we made excellent profits this year.

**ganar** *verbo*
1. to earn: gana seis mil pesos al mes she earns six thousand pesos a month
2. to win: nuestra escuela ganó el campeonato de fútbol our school won the soccer championship
➤ ganarle a alguien to beat someone: la tenista rusa le ganó a la francesa the Russian tennis player beat the French one

**ganarse** *verbo* ■ to earn: se gana la vida como mesero he earns a living as a waiter; se ganó la confianza de todos she earned everybody's trust.

el **gancho**
1. hook: lo colgó de un gancho he hung it on a hook

**2. hanger:** colgamos la ropa en ganchos de plástico we hung up the clothes on plastic hangers

➤ **tener gancho** to be catchy: esta canción tiene gancho that song is very catchy.

el **ganso,** la **gansa** ■ goose.

el **garaje** ■ garage.

la **garantía** ■ guarantee: este equipo de música tiene garantía por un año this stereo system has a one-year guarantee.

**garantizar** verbo ■ to guarantee: garantizan la calidad del producto they guarantee the quality of the product; te garantizo que llegaremos a tiempo I guarantee you we'll get there on time.

la **garganta** ■ throat: me duele la garganta I have a sore throat

➤ **tener buena garganta** to have a good voice: este cantante tiene buena garganta that singer has a good voice.

la **garra**

**1. claw:** el lobo lo lastimó con sus garras the wolf scratched him with his claws

**2. talon:** las garras del cóndor son muy peligrosas the condor's talons are very dangerous

**3. clutches:** cayó en las garras de la mafia she fell into the clutches of the mob.

el **garrote** ■ club: le pegaron con un garrote they beat him with a club.

la **garúa** Andes, Venezuela, River Plate ■ drizzle: caía una garúa finita a fine drizzle was falling.

el **gas** ■ gas: la explosión se produjo por un escape de gas the explosion was caused by a gas leak

los **gases** ■ gas: el niño está con gases the child has a lot of gas.

la **gasolina** ■ gas: tenemos que poner gasolina we need to get gas.

la **gasolinera** ■ gas station: la gasolinera más cercana está a dos cuadras the nearest gas station is two blocks away.

**gastar** verbo

**1. to spend:** gastamos mucho dinero en la reforma de la cocina we spent a lot of money redoing the kitchen

**2. to use:** este coche gasta demasiado this car uses too much gas

**3. to wear out:** este niño gasta mucho la ropa this child really wears out his clothes

**gastarse** verbo ■ to use up: te gastaste todo mi perfume you used up all my perfume.

el **gasto**

**1. expense:** el gasto más importante en nuestra casa es la comida our biggest household expense is on food

**2. waste:** el gasto de energía es exagerado en este país the waste of energy in this country is ridiculous

➤ **gastos de envío** shipping and handling

➤ **gastos de mantenimiento** maintenance costs

➤ **el gasto público** public expenditure.

la **gata** ■ cat

➤ **a gatas** on all fours; caminábamos a gatas en la oscuridad we were going around on all fours in the dark.

**gatear** verbo ■ to crawl: mi hija gatea por toda la casa my daughter crawls all over the house.

el **gato**

**1. cat:** le encantan los gatos she loves cats

**2. jack:** no tenemos un gato para cambiar el neumático we don't have a jack for changing the tire.

la **gauchada** Southern Cone ■ favor

➤ **hacer una gauchada a alguien** to do a favor for someone: me hizo la gauchada de llevarme al aeropuerto he did me the favor of taking me to the airport.

el **gaucho** ■ gaucho

**GAUCHO**

In the River Plate area, **gauchos** are the riders of the pampas, who tend the cattle. The **gaucho** developed in the colonial era, a fusion of the cultures of Spain, the local native peoples, and freed slaves. During the wars for independence, **gauchos** stood out for their bravery.

**135**

la **gema** ■ gem.

**gemelo** *adjetivo* ■ twin: tiene un hermano gemelo she has a twin brother

el **gemelo, la gemela** ■ twin: la maestra confunde a los gemelos de su clase the teacher always confuses the twins in her class.

los **gemelos**
1. cuff links: compré unos gemelos para la camisa I bought some cuff links for the shirt
2. binoculars: observaban los pájaros con unos gemelos they watched the birds through binoculars.

**gemir** *verbo* ■ to whine: el gato del vecino gimió toda la noche the neighbor's cat whined all night long
➤ gemir de dolor to moan with pain: el niño gimió de dolor cuando se lastimó the boy moaned with pain when he hurt himself.

la **generación** (plural las generaciones) ■ generation: somos la segunda generación de inmigrantes en mi familia we're the second generation of immigrants in my family.

el **generador** ■ generator: el hospital compró un nuevo generador the hospital bought a new generator.

**general** *adjetivo* ■ general: hubo una reunión general en la escuela there was a general meeting at the school; por lo general comemos afuera los domingos we generally eat out on Sundays
➤ por lo general generally

el **general** ■ general.

la **generalidad**
1. generality: solo habló de generalidades she only spoke of generalities
2. majority: la generalidad de los maestros gana mal the majority of teachers don't earn a lot.

**generalizar** *verbo*
1. to become widespread: se ha generalizado la pobreza en esta región poverty has become widespread in this region

2. to generalize: la profesora generalizó cuando dijo que todos habíamos copiado the teacher was generalizing when she said we had all cheated.

el **género**
1. genus: estudia el género humano she's studying the human genus
2. gender: género masculino masculine gender; muchos sustantivos de género masculino terminan con la letra o many masculine nouns end in "o"
3. type: también tengo problemas de ese género I also have that type of problem
4. genre: el género policial me gusta mucho I really enjoy the detective genre.

**generoso** *adjetivo* ■ generous: es una persona muy generosa con los demás she's very generous to other people; en este restaurante sirven platos muy generosos the portions are very generous in this restaurant.

**genial** *adjetivo* ■ brilliant: tuvo una idea genial she had a brilliant idea; pocos escritores son tan geniales como él few writers are as brilliant as he is.

el **genio**
1. temper: su esposo tiene buen genio her husband has a good temper
2. genius: fue un verdadero genio de la literatura he was a true literary genius
3. genie: no creo en el genio de la lámpara I don't believe in genies in bottles.

la **gente** ■ people: había mucha gente en la fiesta there were a lot of people at the party
➤ gente bien well-to-do people
➤ gente de bien good people.

**gentil** *adjetivo* ■ kind: es tan gentil que todos lo aprecian mucho everyone is fond of him because he's so kind.

la **geografía** ■ geography.

la **geometría** ■ geometry.

el **gerente, la gerenta** ■ manager.

el **gesto** ■ expression: tiene un gesto de tristeza en la cara she has an expression of sadness on her face

➤ hacer un gesto to gesture: me hizo un gesto para que me acercara he gestured for me to come closer
➤ un gesto simbólico a symbolic gesture.

**gigante** *adjetivo* ■ huge: este apartamento es gigante this apartment is huge

el **gigante** ■ giant: en el cuento el gigante ayudaba a los más pequeños in the story, the giant helped the little people.

la **gimnasia** ■ gymnastics: hacer gimnasia to do gymnastics.

el **gimnasio** ■ gym.

**girar** *verbo*

1. to revolve: la tierra gira alrededor del sol the earth revolves around the sun
2. to turn: giró hacia la derecha he turned to the right
➤ girar en torno a to revolve around: su vida gira en torno al dinero her life revolves around money.

el **giro**

1. turn: un giro a la izquierda a turn to the left; la situación tuvo un giro inesperado the situation took an unexpected turn
2. wire: mandé un giro de 200 dólares I sent a wire for 200 dollars.

el **gis** *Mexico* ■ chalk.

**gitano** *adjetivo* ■ gypsy: tiene alma gitana he has a gypsy soul

el **gitano**, la **gitana** ■ gypsy: una gitana me adivinó el futuro a gypsy woman told my fortune.

el **globo**

1. balloons: trajimos globos de colores para los niños we brought colored balloons for the kids
2. hot-air balloon: mi sueño es viajar en globo my dream is to travel in a hot-air balloon
➤ un globo terráqueo a globe.

**glotón, glotona** *adjetivo* ■ glutton: es tan glotón que en un minuto se comió todo el postre he's such a glutton that he ate all of his dessert in just a minute.

el **gobernador**, la **gobernadora** ■ governor.

el/la **gobernante** ■ leader: los gobernantes de la región están preocupados por la crisis económica the region's leaders are concerned about the economic crisis.

**gobernar** *verbo*

1. to govern: el partido ha gobernado en el país por los últimos 20 años the party has governed the country for the last 20 years
2. to control: este niño es muy difícil de gobernar this kid is very hard to control.

el **gobierno**

1. government: el gobierno tomó drásticas medidas económicas the government took drastic economic measures
2. management: el Presidente anunció su plan de gobierno the President announced his management plan.

el **gol** ■ goal
➤ marcar un gol to score a goal.

el **golfo** ■ gulf.

la **golondrina** ■ swallow.

la **golosina** ■ candy: compré golosinas para los niños I bought some candy for the children.

el **golpe** ■ blow: las bajas calificaciones fueron un golpe para Pedro his low grades were a blow to Pedro
➤ se dio un golpe en la cabeza she bumped her head
➤ lo agarraron a golpes they beat him up
➤ de golpe suddenly: empezó a llover de golpe it suddenly began to rain
➤ un golpe de Estado a coup d'état
➤ un golpe de suerte a stroke of luck
➤ un golpe de vista a glance.

**golpear** *verbo*

1. to knock: golpeamos la puerta porque el timbre no funcionaba we knocked on the door because the doorbell didn't work
2. to beat: lo golpearon y le robaron la cartera they beat him and stole his wallet
3. to hit: se golpeó el codo contra la mesa he hit his elbow on the table.

la **golpiza** ■ beating.

la **goma**

1. rubber: la goma es un material impermeable rubber is a waterproof material

**2. eraser:** necesito una goma para borrar los errores I need an eraser to erase my mistakes

**3.** *Cuba, Southern Cone* **tire:** se pinchó la goma del coche the car got a flat tire

**4. glue:** usa la goma para pegar los dibujos use the glue to stick down the pictures

➤ una goma de borrar an eraser

➤ la goma de mascar chewing gum.

**gordo** *adjetivo*

**1. fat:** José está más gordo que nunca José is fatter than ever

**2. thick:** estoy leyendo un libro muy gordo I'm reading a very thick book

➤ Antonio me cae gordo I can't stand Antonio

el **gordo,** la **gorda**

**1. fat person:** los gordos son discriminados en la sociedad actual fat people are discriminated against in modern society

**2. dear:** ¿cómo estás, gordo? how are you, dear?

la **gorra** ■ **cap:** siempre uso una gorra cuando estoy al sol I always wear a cap in the sun

➤ una gorra de baño a shower cap.

el **gorrión** *(plural* los gorriones) ■ **sparrow**.

el **gorro** ■ **cap**

➤ un gorro de baño a shower cap.

la **gota**

**1. drop:** tienes que tomar cinco gotas de este medicamento you have to take five drops of this medicine

**2. gout:** la gota es una enfermedad muy dolorosa gout is a very painful illness.

**gotear** *verbo* ■ **to drip:** esta llave gotea this faucet drips.

la **grabación** *(plural* las grabaciones) ■ **recording:** hicieron una nueva grabación de la canción they made a new recording of the song.

el **grabado** ■ **engraving:** este grabado reproduce la imagen de una ciudad colonial this engraving shows a colonial city.

**grabar** *verbo*

**1. to engrave:** grabaron sus nombres en los anillos de casamiento they engraved their names on the wedding rings

**2. to record:** acaba de grabar un disco nuevo she just recorded a new album

**3. to tape:** grabé en video la fiesta de cumpleaños I taped the birthday party.

la **gracia**

➤ hacer gracia to amuse: sus chistes me hacen mucha gracia his jokes really amuse me

➤ caerle en gracia a alguien to take a liking to someone: esta niña me cae en gracia I've taken a liking to this girl

➤ dar las gracias a alguien to thank someone: le dimos las gracias a Pedro por su ayuda we thanked Pedro for his help.

**gracias** *interjección* ■ **thanks:** ¡gracias por el regalo! thanks for the present!

➤ gracias — de nada thanks — you're welcome.

**gracioso** *adjetivo* ■ **funny:** contó unos chistes muy graciosos she told some very funny jokes

⚠ The Spanish word **gracioso** is a false cognate, it does not mean "gracious".

la **grada** ■ **step:** nos sentamos en la primera grada we sat on the first step

➤ las gradas the stands: las gradas estaban llenas de espectadores the stands were full of spectators.

el **grado**

**1. degree:** este ángulo tiene 60 grados this is a 60 degree angle

**2. grade:** Ana está en tercer grado Ana is in third grade

➤ a tal grado so: se enojó a tal grado, que acabó a los golpes he got so mad they came to blows

➤ grados bajo cero degrees below zero: hay cinco grados bajo cero it's five degrees below zero.

la **graduación** *(plural* las graduaciones) ■ **graduation**.

**graduado** *adjetivo* ■ **prescription:** uso lentes graduados I wear prescription lenses.

**graduar** *verbo*

1. **to adjust:** gradúa bien el agua caliente antes de meterte en la ducha adjust the hot water carefully before you step into the shower
2. **to calibrate:** el oculista graduó la miopía del niño the optician calibrated the boy's nearsightedness

**graduarse** *verbo* ■ **to graduate:** me gradué el mes pasado y ya estoy trabajando I graduated last month and I'm already working.

la **gráfica** ■ **graph.**

**gráfico** *adjetivo* ■ **graphic:** es un concurso de artes gráficas it's a graphic art contest

el **gráfico** ■ **table.**

la **gramática** ■ **grammar.**

el **gramo** ■ **gram.**

**gran** *adjetivo* ➤ grande

Gran is a shortened form of the word grande. It is used in front of the noun.

**grande** *adjetivo*

1. **big:** su auto es demasiado grande his car is too big
2. **great :** es un gran hombre he's a great man
➤ es un libro para gente grande it's a book for adults.

el **granero** ■ **barn.**

**granizar** *verbo* ■ **to hail:** granizó de madrugada it was hailing at dawn.

el **granizo** ■ **hail:** el granizo estropeó la cosecha the hail ruined the crop
➤ caer granizo to hail: cayó granizo sobre la ciudad it was hailing in the city.

la **granja** ■ **farm.**

el **granjero,** la **granjera** ■ **farmer.**

el **grano**

1. **pimple:** tiene un grano en la nariz she has a pimple on her nose
2. **grain:** se alimenta a base de granos her diet is based on grains; se me metió un grano de arena en el ojo I got a grain of sand in my eye
➤ ir al grano to get to the point: no entiendo lo que me quieres decir, ve al grano I don't understand what you're trying to say, just get to the point.

la **grapa**

1. **staple:** usé una grapa para sujetar estos papeles I used a staple to hold these papers together
2. *Southern Cone* **grappa:** esta grapa es demasiado fuerte para mí this grappa is too strong for me.

la **grasa**

1. **fat:** con alto contenido de grasa high in fat
2. **grease:** las manos del mecánico estaban cubiertas de grasa the mechanic's hands were covered in grease.

**grasoso** *adjetivo* ■ **greasy:** le cae mal la comida grasosa greasy food doesn't agree with him.

**gratis** *adjetivo & adverbio* ■ **free:** tengo dos entradas gratis para el cine I have two free tickets to the movies; los menores entran gratis al concierto children can attend the concert for free.

**gratuito** *adjetivo*

1. **free:** la entrada es gratuita los lunes admission is free on Mondays
2. **gratuitous:** su comentario fue totalmente gratuito her comment was completely gratuitous.

**grave** *adjetivo*

1. **serious:** éste es un problema muy grave this is a very serious problem; cometió un delito grave he committed a serious crime
2. **deep:** el abuelo tiene una voz muy grave grandfather has a very deep voice; tuvo un accidente y está grave he was in an accident and is seriously ill
➤ estar grave to be seriously ill.

la **gravedad**

1. **gravity:** Newton definió las leyes de la gravedad Newton defined the laws of gravity

2. **seriousness:** no nos habíamos imaginado la gravedad del asunto we hadn't realized the seriousness of the situation.

la **grieta** ■ **crack:** hay una grieta en la pared there is a crack in the wall.

el **grifo**

1. **faucet:** el grifo de la izquierda es el del agua caliente the faucet on the left is the hot water

2. *Peru* **gas station:** el próximo grifo queda a tres kilómetros the nearest gas station is three kilometers away.

el **grillo** ■ **cricket.**

**gringo** *peyorativo adjetivo* ■ **gringo:** los productos gringos invadieron el mercado gringo products flooded the market

el **gringo,** la **gringa** ■ **gringo:** los gringos declararon la guerra the gringos declared war.

la **gripa** *Mexico* ■ **flu:** no fui a la escuela por que tenía gripa I didn't go to school because I had the flu.

**gris** *adjetivo* ■ **gray:** compró unos pantalones grises she bought some gray pants

el **gris** ■ **gray:** pinté la pared de gris I painted the wall gray.

**gritar** *verbo* ■ **to shout:** un cliente le gritó al empleado de la tienda a customer shouted at one of the salesclerks

➤ **gritar de alegría** to scream with joy: **grité de alegría cuando me enteré de la noticia** I screamed with joy when I heard the news

➤ **gritar de dolor** to scream with pain: **gritó de dolor cuando se lastimó la mano** he screamed with pain when he hurt his hand.

el **grito** ■ **scream:** el grito de la niña era aterrador the girl's scream was terrifying

➤ **pegarle un grito a alguien** to holler at someone: **le pegó un grito al niño y éste se puso a llorar** he hollered at the boy and made him cry

**EL GRITO**

In Mexico, at 11 o'clock on the night of September 15, the President utters the cry, "¡Mexicanos, vivan los héroes que nos dieron patria! ¡Viva México!" from the balcony of the National Palace. This cry represents the beginning of the fight for Mexico's independence and marks the beginning of the national holiday which honors Miguel Hidalgo, who led the Mexican independence movement in 1810.

la **grosería** ■ **swearword:** le dijo una grosería al conductor del auto he said a swearword to the car driver

➤ **fue una grosería no invitarlo a la fiesta** it was very rude not to invite him to the party.

**grosero** *adjetivo* ■ **rude:** detesto su comportamiento grosero I detest his rude behavior.

la **grúa** ■ **crane:** las grúas del puerto descargan las mercancías de los barcos the port cranes unload the ships' goods.

**grueso** *adjetivo*

1. **thick:** compré una tela gruesa para las cortinas I bought a thick cloth for the curtains

2. **heavyset:** es una mujer gruesa she's a heavyset woman

el **grueso** ■ **major portion:** pagué el grueso de mis deudas I paid the major portion of my debts.

el **gruñido**

1. **growl:** el gruñido del perro me asustó the dog's growl scared me

2. **grunt:** nos contestó con un gruñido he answered us with a grunt.

**gruñón,** **gruñona** *adjetivo*

■ **grumpy:** nos atendió una empleada gruñona a grumpy clerk waited on us.

el **grupo** ■ **group:** formamos un grupo de seis personas we form a group of six people.

la **gruta** ■ **cavern.**

el **guacal**

1. *Central America, Mexico* **pumpkin:** en esta zona plantan guacales in this area they plant pumpkins

2. *Colombia, Mexico* **cage:** pusimos al pájaro dentro del guacal we put the bird inside the cage.

el **guachimán** *(plural* los guachimanes)
*Mexico* ■ **watchman** *(plural* **watchmen**): el guachimán nos avisó del peligro the watchman warned us of the danger.

la **guagua**

1. *Caribbean* **bus:** fuimos a la playa en guagua we went to the beach by bus

2. *Andes* **baby** *(plural* **babies**): tienen dos guaguas preciosas they have two precious babies.

el **guajiro,** la **guajira** *Cuba* ■ **peasant:** muchos guajiros están abandonando el campo many peasants are abandoning the countryside.

el **guajolote** *Central America, Mexico*

1. **turkey:** criamos guajolotes en este terreno we raise turkeys on this land

2. **fool:** estos hombres parecen unos guajolotes these men look like fools.

el **guante** ■ **glove:** uso guantes para lavar los platos I wear gloves to wash the dishes.

**guapo** *adjetivo*

1. **attractive:** es el muchacho más guapo que conozco he's the most attractive guy I know

2. **well-dressed:** iba muy guapa a la fiesta she went to the party very well-dressed.

el **guarache** *Mexico* ■ **sandal.**

el **guaraní** ■ **Guarani**

GUARANÍ

Paraguay is the only Latin American country where an indigenous language, **Guarani**, is used as widely as Spanish. The process of racial mixing between Spaniards and **Guaranis** has resulted in a population that is largely bilingual. Both Spanish and **Guarani** are highly influenced by each other in Paraguay, and are spoken by more than four million inhabitants.

el **guarda**

1. **guard:** los guardas vigilaban la costa the guards were watching the coast

2. *River Plate* **ticket collector:** el guarda nos pidió los boletos del tren the ticket collector asked us for our train tickets.

el/la **guardameta** ■ **goalkeeper:** el guardameta atajó el penal the goalkeeper intercepted the penalty kick.

el **guardapolvo** ■ **overalls:** Lucas se ensució el guardapolvo Lucas got his overalls dirty.

**guardar** *verbo*

1. **to save:** guárdame un poco de cena save me a little supper; les guardamos lugar en el teatro we saved them a place at the theater

2. **to keep:** no guardé el documento necesario I didn't keep the necessary document

3. **to put away:** guardé la ropa en el armario I put the clothes away in the closet

➤ guardar un secreto to keep a secret: no sabe guardar un secreto he can't keep a secret.

el **guardarropa** ■ **cloakroom:** dejamos los abrigos en el guardarropa we left the coats in the cloakroom.

la **guardia**

1. **guard:** la guardia nacional está en estado de alerta the national guard is on a state of alert

2. **shift:** hicimos un turno de guardia nocturna we took a turn on the night shift

➤ estar de guardia to be on duty: está de guardia en el hospital he's on duty at the hospital.

el/la **guardia** ■ **guard:** el guardia disparó al aire the guard fired into the air.

la **guarida**

1. **hideout:** la policía descubrió la guarida de los ladrones the police discovered the thieves' hideout

2. **lair:** los lobos se refugiaron en una guarida the wolves took shelter in a lair.

el **guarura** *Mexico informal* ■ **bodyguard:** anda con dos guaruras día y noche he goes around with two bodyguards day and night.

**Guatemala** *sustantivo femenino* ■ **Guatemala**.

**guatemalteco** *adjetivo*

En inglés, los adjetivos que se refieren a un país o una región se escriben con mayúscula:

**Guatemalan: compré artesanías guatemaltecas** I bought Guatemalan handicrafts

el **guatemalteco**, la **guatemalteca**

En inglés, los gentilicios se escriben con mayúscula:

**Guatemalan: los guatemaltecos** the Guatemalans.

la **guayaba** ■ guava.

la **guayabera** ■ *loose shirt with pockets*.

el **guayabo** ■ guava tree.

el **güero,** la **güera** *Mexico informal* ■ **blond (blonde): me enamoré de un güero** I fell in love with a blond.

la **guerra** ■ war
➤ **declarar la guerra** to declare war.

el **guerrero,** la **guerrera** ■ **warrior**.

la **guerrilla** ■ guerrilla band.

el **guerrillero,** la **guerrillera** ■ **guerrilla: los guerrilleros tomaron la aldea** the guerrillas took the village.

la **guía**
1. guide: **sus enseñanzas son una guía para mí** his teachings are a guide for me
2. guidebook: **compraron una guía de la ciudad** they bought a guidebook to the city
3. directory *(plural* **directories***):* **buscó la información en la guía de la universidad** he looked for the information in the university directory
➤ **una guía telefónica** a telephone directory

el/la **guía** ■ guide: **el guía nos explicó la historia de la catedral** the guide explained the cathedral's history to us.

el **guiar** *verbo* ■ **to guide: José guió a sus amigos por las calles de la ciudad** José guided his friends through the city's streets.

el **guijarro** ■ pebble.

**guiñar** *verbo*
➤ **guiñar el ojo** to wink: **guiñó el ojo mientras me hablaba** he winked while he was talking to me.

el **guiño** ■ wink: **Luis le hizo un guiño a María** Luis gave a wink to María.

el **guión** *(plural* los guiones*)*
1. script: **el guión de la película es excelente** the movie's script is excellent
2. hyphen: **el guión sirve para separar las palabras en sílabas** the hyphen serves to separate words in syllables.

el **guisado** ■ stew.

el **guisante** *Mexico* ■ pea.

**guisar** *verbo* ■ **to cook: guisé el pollo con hierbas** I cooked the chicken with herbs.

el **guiso** ■ stew.

la **guita** *River Plate informal* ■ **money: me quedé sin guita para el alquiler** I didn't have money for the rent.

la **guitarra** ■ guitar.

la **guitarreada** *Southern Cone* ■ **singalong: se armó una linda guitarreada en la fiesta** there was a nice singalong at the party.

la **gula** ■ gluttony.

el **gurí,** la **gurisa** *River Plate informal* ■ **kid: hay demasiados gurises en la clase** there are too many kids in the class.

el **gusano**
1. maggot: **los gusanos me dan asco** maggots disgust me
2. worm: **hay un gusano en la manzana** there's a worm in the apple
➤ **un gusano de seda** a silkworm.

**gustar** *verbo*
1. to like: **a Susana le gusta el cine** Susana likes cinema; **no me gustó que me gritaran** I didn't like them shouting at me; **a Pedro le gusta María** Pedro likes María

**2.** **to be pleasing:** es una música que gusta mucho it's very pleasing music.

el **gusto** ■ **taste:** el gusto es uno de los sentidos más importantes taste is one of the most important senses; **esta leche tiene gusto a podrido** this milk has a spoiled taste; **esta pareja tiene gustos incompatibles** this couple has incompatible tastes
➤ **tener buen gusto** to have good taste: **tienen buen gusto para la decoración** they have good taste in decoration
➤ **tener mal gusto** to have bad taste: **tiene mal gusto para vestirse** he has bad taste in clothes
➤ **mucho gusto** it's a pleasure: **le presento a mi jefe — mucho gusto en conocerlo** allow me to introduce you to my boss – it's a pleasure to meet you.

el **haba** *sustantivo femenino*

Feminine noun that takes **un** or **el** in the singular.

**bean.**

**haber** *verbo* ■ **to have:** han viajado a **Colombia** they have traveled to Colombia
➤ hay *en singular* there is: **hay una sola persona en el cine** there is only one person in the movie theater
➤ hay *en plural* there are
➤ **hay 30 niños en la fiesta** there are 30 children at the party

➤ **hay que** it is necessary: **hay que ayudar a Matilde** it is necessary to help Matilde
➤ **no hay de qué** don't mention it: **gracias - no hay de qué** thanks — don't mention it
➤ **¿qué hay?** how are things?: **¿qué hay? - todo bien, gracias** how are things? — everything's fine, thanks.

la **habichuela** ■ **kidney bean.**

**hábil** *adjetivo* ■ **skillful:** es un carpintero muy hábil he's a very skillful carpenter.

la **habilidad** ■ **skill:** tiene habilidad **para las manualidades** he has skill for handicrafts.

**habiloso** *Chile informal adjetivo* ■ **shrewd:** es un muchacho muy habiloso he's a very shrewd guy.

la **habitación** *(plural* las habitaciones*)* ■ **room:** este departamento tiene cuatro **habitaciones** this apartment has four rooms.

el/la **habitante** ■ **inhabitant.**

**habitar** *verbo* ■ **to live in:** los elefantes **habitan en África y Asia** elephants live in Africa and Asia.

el **hábito** ■ **habit:** tiene el hábito de **acostarse tarde** he has the habit of going to bed late; **pocos sacerdotes usan hábito en la actualidad** few priests wear habits nowadays.

**habitual** *adjetivo* ■ **customary:** esta no es una conducta habitual en él this is not customary behavior for him.

**hablar** *verbo*
**1.** **to talk:** el niño todavía no habla the boy doesn't talk yet
**2.** **to speak:** mis amigos hablan ruso my friends speak Russian; **Roberto y María ya no se hablan** Roberto and María don't speak to each other anymore
➤ **hablar hasta por los codos** to talk too much: **no me gusta Juan porque habla hasta por los codos** I don't like Juan because he talks too much.

el **hacendado, la hacendada** ■ land-owner: **grandes hacendados poseen la mayoría de estas tierras** big landowners own the majority of these lands.

**hacer** *verbo*

1. **to make: las abejas hacen miel** bees make honey
2. **to do: Mariana hace teatro** Mariana does theater; **hacen gimnasia todas las mañanas** they do gymnastics every morning
➤ **hace de la bruja mala** she plays the part of the evil witch
➤ **hace calor** it's hot
➤ **hace dos años que no tomo vacaciones** it's been two years since I took a vacation
➤ **hacer la cama** to make the bed.

el **hacha** *sustantivo femenino*

Feminine noun that takes **un** or **el** in the singular.

**ax**.

**hacia** *preposición*

1. **toward: caminó hacia la salida** he walked toward the exit
2. **around: hacia finales de diciembre terminan las clases** they finish classes around the end of December
➤ **hacia arriba** up: **el globo se fue hacia arriba** the balloon went up
➤ **hacia abajo** down
➤ **tiraron la piedra hacia abajo** they threw the stone down
➤ **hacia delante** forward: **continuaron hacia delante** they continued forward
➤ **hacia atrás** backward: **se cayó hacia atrás** she fell backward.

la **hacienda** ■ **ranch: tenemos muchos animales en la hacienda** we have many animals on the ranch.

**halagar** *verbo* ■ **to flatter: me halagan tus comentarios** your comments flatter me.

**hallar** *verbo* ■ **to find: hallaron un tesoro escondido** they found a hidden treasure

➤ **no hallarse en un lugar** to feel out of place somewhere: **no me hallo en una ciudad tan grande** I feel out of place in such a big city.

la **hamaca**

1. **hammock: estamos descansando en las hamacas** we are resting in the hammocks
2. *River Plate* **swing: a los niños les encantan las hamacas del parque** children love the park swings.

**hamacar** *verbo*

1. **to swing: hamácame más fuerte** swing me harder
2. **to rock: el bebe se durmió mientras su madre lo hamacaba** the baby fell asleep while his mother was rocking him.

el **hambre** *sustantivo femenino*

Feminine noun that takes **un** or **el** in the singular.

**hunger: este niño tiene hambre** this child is hungry
➤ **morirse de hambre** to die of hunger: **es lamentable que todavía haya niños que se mueren de hambre** it's pitiful that there are still children that die of hunger
➤ **pasar hambre** to go hungry: **en el campamento pasamos hambre** at the camp we went hungry
➤ **tener hambre** to be hungry.

la **harina** ■ **flour**.

**hartarse** *verbo pronominal*

1. **to get tired of: me harté de tu mal humor** I got tired of your bad mood
2. **to stuff oneself: se hartaron de dulces** they stuffed themselves with sweets.

**harto** *(adjetivo & adverbio)*

■ *adjetivo*

1. **fed up: estoy harta del estudio** I'm fed up with studying
2. **a lot: tiene harta paciencia** she has a lot of patience; **de este aeropuerto salen hartos aviones** a lot of airplanes depart from this airport
■ *adverbio*
**very: están harto agotados** they're very exhausted.

**hasta** *(preposición & adverbio)*

■ *preposición*

1. **up to:** llene el tanque hasta la mitad fill the tank up to the middle
2. **as far as:** fueron conmigo hasta la playa they went with me as fas as the beach
3. *Central America, Colombia, Ecuador, Mexico* **not before:** pintaremos la casa hasta fin de mes we will not start painting the house before the end of the month
4. **until:** lo cuidó hasta que se curó she took care of him until he got better
➤ **hasta luego** see you later
➤ **hasta mañana** see you tomorrow

■ *adverbio*
**even:** hasta un ignorante puede aprender esto even an ignorant person can learn this.

la **hazaña** ■ **feat**.

el **hecho**

1. **action:** prefiero hechos y no palabras I prefer actions to words
2. **event:** el periodista destacó los hechos más importantes de la semana the reporter highlighted the most important events of the week
➤ **de hecho** in fact: de hecho, los resultados fueron mucho mejor de lo que esperábamos in fact, the results were much better than we had hoped
➤ **es un hombre hecho y derecho** he's a real man.

la **helada** ■ **frost:** anoche cayó una helada last night there was a frost.

la **heladera** ■ **refrigerator**.

**helado** *adjetivo*

1. **freezing:** esta habitación está helada this room is freezing
2. **scared:** nos quedamos helados con la noticia we were scared by the news

el **helado** ■ **ice cream**.

**helarse** *verbo pronominal* ■ **to freeze:** este lago se hiela en invierno this lake freezes in winter.

el **helecho** ■ **fern**.

la **hélice** ■ **propeller**.

el **helicóptero** ■ **helicopter**.

la **hembra** ■ **female:** en algunas especies las hembras son más fuertes que los machos in some species the females are stronger than the males.

el **hemisferio** ■ **hemisphere**.

la **hemorragia** ■ **loss of blood**.

**heredar** *verbo* ■ **to inherit:** heredamos una gran fortuna we inherited a large fortune; Juan heredó el carácter del padre Juan inherited his father's character.

la **heredera** ■ **heiress**.

el **heredero** ■ **heir:** los herederos recibieron una fuerte suma de dinero the heirs received a large sum of money.

la **herencia** ■ **inheritance:** recibió una cuantiosa herencia del tío he received a substantial inheritance from his uncle.

la **herida**

1. **wound:** tiene una herida profunda en la pierna he has a deep wound on his leg
2. **injury** *(plural* **injuries**): sufrió heridas leves he suffered slight injuries
➤ **una herida de bala** a bullet wound.

**herido** *adjetivo*

1. **wounded:** fue herido en la batalla he was wounded in the battle
2. **injured:** resultó herido de gravedad he turned out to be seriously injured

el **herido,** la **herida**

1. **injured person** *(plural* **injured people**): hubo cuatro heridos en el accidente there were four injured people in the accident
2. **wounded person** *(plural* **wounded people**): hubo cien heridos en la batalla there were one hundred wounded people after the battle.

**herir** *verbo*

1. **to injure:** lo hirieron gravemente en la pelea they injured him seriously in the fight
2. **to wound:** la explosión hirió a varias personas the explosion wounded several people

**3. to hurt:** con su negativa lo hirió en lo más profundo with her refusal, she hurt him deeply.

la **hermana** ■ **sister:** tengo una hermana mayor I have an older sister.

el **hermano** ■ **brother:** tengo un hermano menor I have a little brother; **tengo dos hermanos menores, Matías y Ana** I have two younger siblings, Matías and Ana.

**hermoso** *adjetivo* ■ **beautiful:** ¡qué hermoso día! what a beautiful day!

el **héroe** ■ **hero** (plural **heroes**).

**heroico** *adjetivo* ■ **heroic:** su comportamiento heroico me salvó la vida his heroic performance saved my life.

la **heroína** ■ **heroine:** la heroína de la novela the novel's heroin.

la **herramienta** ■ **tool**.

la **herrumbre** ■ **rust**.

**hervir** *verbo* ■ **to boil:** herví las verduras I boiled the vegetables.

**hidratar** *verbo* ■ **to moisturize:** esta crema es ideal para hidratar la piel this cream is ideal to moisturize the skin.

**hidráulico** *adjetivo* ■ **hydraulic:** es un ingeniero hidráulico he's a hydraulic engineer.

la **hiedra** ■ **ivy**.

el **hielo** ■ **ice**
➤ romper el hielo to break the ice: rompió el hielo con un chiste he broke the ice with a joke.

la **hierba**
**1. grass:** tomamos sol en la hierba we sunbathed in the grass
**2. herb:** condimenté el pollo con hierbas I seasoned the chicken with herbs.

el **hierro** ■ **iron**.

el **hígado** ■ **liver**.

la **higiene** ■ **hygiene:** es increíble la falta de higiene de este lugar this place's lack of hygiene is incredible
➤ la higiene corporal personal hygiene
➤ la higiene dental dental hygiene.

la **hija** ■ **daughter:** tienen tres hijas y un hijo they have three daughters and one son.

el **hijo**
**1. son:** tienen tres hijos they have three sons
**2. child:** van a tener un hijo they're going to have a child
➤ un hijo adoptivo an adopted child.

la **hilera**
**1. line:** los niños formaron una hilera the children formed a line
**2. row:** hay una hilera de árboles en la entrada a la casa there's a row of trees at the house's entrance.

el **hilo**
**1. thread:** necesito hilo para coser este dobladillo I need thread in order to sew this hem
**2. trickle:** de su boca salía un hilo de sangre a trickle of blood came out of his mouth
➤ perder el hilo to lose the thread: siempre pierde el hilo de lo que está diciendo he always loses the thread of what he's saying.

el **himno**
**1. hymn**
**2. anthem**
➤ un libro de himnos a hymn book
➤ el himno nacional the national anthem.

**hincarse** *verbo pronominal*
➤ hincarse de rodillas to kneel: se hincó de rodillas cuando entró en la iglesia he kneeled when he went into the church.

**hincharse** *verbo pronominal* ■ **to swell:** se le hinchó la cara después del accidente her face swelled after the accident.

el **hipo** ■ **hiccup**
➤ tener hipo to have the hiccups.

la **hipocresía** ■ **hypocrisy**.

**hipócrita** *adjetivo* ■ **hypocritical:** dio una respuesta hipócrita she gave a hypocritical answer el/la **hipócrita** ■ hypocrite.

**hispánico** *adjetivo*

En inglés los gentilicios se escriben con mayúscula:

**Hispanic.**

**hispano** *adjetivo*

En inglés, los adjetivos que se refieren a un país o una región se escriben con mayúscula:

**Hispanic:** la población hispana the Hispanic population

➤ los países de habla hispana the Spanish-speaking countries

el **hispano**, la **hispana**

En inglés los gentilicios se escriben con mayúscula:

1. *latinoamericano* **Latin American**
2. *residente en EE.UU.* **Hispanic:** los hispanos de ascendencia mexicana the Hispanics of Mexican descent.

**hispanohablante** *adjetivo*
■ Spanish-speaking

el/la **hispanohablante** ■ Spanish speaker.

**histérico** *adjetivo* ■ hysterical.

la **historia**

1. **history** *(plural* **histories***):* estamos estudiando la historia de los antiguos we're studying the history of the ancients
2. **story** *(plural* **stories***):* una historia de amor a love story
➤ déjate de historias y di la verdad stop beating around the bush and tell the truth.

**histórico** *adjetivo*

1. **historic:** un monumento histórico a historic monument
2. **historical:** un personaje histórico a historical character
➤ la llegada a la Luna fue un hecho histórico the trip to the moon was a historical event.

la **historieta** ■ short story *(plural* **short stories***).*

el **hobby** *(plural* los hobbies) ■ hobby *(plural* **hobbies***)*
➤ los colecciona por hobby he collects them as a hobby.

el **hocico**

1. *de puerco* **snout**
2. *de perro* **muzzle***.*

el **hockey** ■ hockey
➤ hockey sobre hielo ice hockey
➤ hockey sobre césped field hockey
➤ hockey sobre pasto *Central America, Mexico* field hockey.

el **hogar** ■ home: tuvo un hogar feliz he had a happy home life
➤ la gente sin hogar the homeless.

la **hoguera** ■ bonfire.

la **hoja**

1. **leaf** *(plural* **leaves***):* las hojas de los árboles the leaves of the trees
2. **sheet:** escríbelo en esta hoja write it on this sheet; una hoja en blanco a blank sheet
3. **page:** está en la hoja siguiente it's on the next page
➤ una hoja de afeitar razor blade
➤ una hoja de cálculo spreadsheet.

la **hojalatería** *Mexico* ■ body shop.

**hola** *interjección* ■ hello: hola ¿qué tal? hello — how are things?

**holgazán, holgazana** *adjetivo*
■ lazy.

el **hombre** ■ man *(plural* **men***):* es un hombre inteligente he's an intelligent man
➤ un hombre de negocios a businessman
➤ un hombre rana a frogman.

el **hombro** ■ shoulder.

el **homenaje** ■ tribute
➤ rendirle homenaje a alguien to pay tribute to somebody: la multitud rindió homenaje a su ídolo the masses paid tribute to their idol

**147**

➤ **en homenaje a** in tribute to: **un concierto en homenaje a las víctimas** a concert in tribute to the victims.

**hondo** *adjetivo* ■ **deep**

➤ **yo no me meto en la parte honda** I don't go in the deep end.

**Honduras** *sustantivo femenino* ■ **Honduras**.

**hondureño** *adjetivo*

En inglés, los adjetivos que se refieren a un país o una región se escriben con mayúscula:

**Honduran**

el **hondureño**, la **hondureña**

En inglés, los gentilicios se escriben con mayúscula:

**Honduran**

➤ **los hondureños** the Hondurans.

la **honestidad** ■ **honesty**: **la honestidad es su mayor virtud** honesty is his greatest virtue

➤ **dímelo con toda honestidad** be completely honest with me.

**honesto** *adjetivo* ■ **honest**.

el **hongo**

1. **fungus**: **es causada por un hongo** it's caused by a fungus
2. **mushroom**: **un hongo comestible** an edible mushroom.

el **honor** ■ **honor**.

la **honradez** ■ **honesty**.

**honrado** *adjetivo* ■ **honest**: **es un hombre honrado** he's an honest man

➤ **se sintió honrado con su visita** he felt honored by his visit.

la **hora**

1. **hour**: **me demoré dos horas en llegar** I took two hours to arrive
2. **time**: **¿qué hora es?** what time it is?; **¿tienes hora?** do you have the time?; **es hora de ir al colegio** it's time to go to school

3. **appointment**: **tengo hora con el oculista** I have an appointment with the eye doctor; **pedí hora en la peluquería** I made an appointment at the hairdresser's

➤ **¿a qué hora empieza el programa?** what time does the program start?

➤ **llegar a la hora** to arrive on time: **nunca llega a la hora** he never arrives on time

➤ **vino a la hora de almorzar** he came at lunchtime

➤ **¿qué haces en tus horas libres?** what do you do in your free time?

➤ **la hora pico** the rush hour.

el **horario** ■ **schedule**: **según mi horario, tengo inglés mañana** according to my schedule, I have English tomorrow; **no sé el horario de los trenes** I don't know the train schedule

➤ **horario de atención al público** opening hours.

**horizontal** *adjetivo* ■ **horizontal**.

el **horizonte** ■ **horizon**: **el sol aparece por el horizonte** the sun appears on the horizon.

la **hormiga** ■ **ant**.

el **hormigón** ■ **concrete**.

el **hormigueo** ■ **tingling**: **tengo un hormigueo en un pie** I have a tingling in one foot.

el **horno** ■ **oven**: **un horno eléctrico** an electric oven

➤ **ser un horno** to be like an oven: **el gimnasio es un horno** the gym is like an oven

➤ **pollo al horno** roasted chicken

➤ **papas al horno** baked potatoes

➤ **un horno microondas** a microwave oven.

el **horóscopo** ■ **horoscope**.

la **horquilla** ■ **bobby pin**: **se sujetó el pelo con horquillas** she secured her hair with bobby pins.

**horrible** *adjetivo* ■ **horrible**: **¡qué lugar tan horrible!** what a horrible place!; **ha hecho un tiempo horrible** the weather has been horrible.

el **horror** ■ **horror**: **escuchó un grito de horror** he heard a scream of horror

**148**

➤ ¡qué horror! how horrible!
➤ una película de horror a horror movie
➤ los horrores de la guerra the horrors of war.

**horroroso** *adjetivo*
1. **horrendous:** ¡qué cuadro más horroroso! what a horrendous painting!
2. **horrifying:** tiene unas escenas horrorosas it has some horrifying scenes
➤ el tiempo estuvo horroroso the weather was awful.

la **hortaliza** ▪ **vegetable.**

**hospedarse** *verbo pronominal* ▪ **to stay:** se hospedaron en albergues juveniles they stayed in youth hostels.

el **hospital** ▪ **hospital:** trabaja en el hospital she works at the hospital; los llevaron al hospital they took them to the hospital.

la **hospitalidad** ▪ **hospitality.**

**hospitalizar** *verbo* ▪ **to hospitalize**
➤ va a tener que hospitalizarse he'll have to be hospitalized.

la **hostia** ▪ **host:** la hostia sagrada the sacred host.

el **hotel** ▪ **hotel.**

**hoy** *adverbio* ▪ **today:** hoy es su cumpleaños today is her birthday; el diario de hoy today's newspaper; la juventud de hoy today's youth
➤ hoy es posible curar muchas enfermedades nowadays it's possible to cure many diseases
➤ de hoy en adelante from now on.

el **hoyo** ▪ **hole:** el perro hizo un hoyo en el jardín the dog made a hole in the garden.

el **huarache** *Mexico* ▪ **sandal.**

**hueco** *adjetivo* ▪ **hollow**

el **hueco**
1. **space:** hay que hacer un hueco para poner este libro we have to make a space for this book
2. **room:** no me queda hueco para comer más I don't have any room to eat more
➤ me hicieron hueco en el taxi they made room for me in the taxi

➤ es difícil encontrar un hueco para estacionarse it's difficult finding a place to park
➤ está muy ocupada pero va a hacer un hueco para recibirme she's very busy but she's going to set aside some time to see me.

la **huelga** ▪ **strike**
➤ están en huelga they're on strike
➤ votaron para ir a la huelga they voted to go on strike
➤ se declararon en huelga they went on strike
➤ una huelga de hambre a hunger strike.

la **huella** ▪ **footprint:** había huellas en la nieve there were footprints in the snow
➤ íbamos siguiendo la huella del jeep we were following the jeep's tracks
➤ desaparecieron sin dejar huella they disappeared without a trace
➤ huellas digitales fingerprints.

**huérfano** *adjetivo* ▪ **orphaned**
➤ quedó huérfano he was orphaned
➤ es huérfano he's an orphan
➤ quieren adoptar a un niño huérfano they want to adopt an orphan

el **huérfano, la huérfana** ▪ **orphan.**

la **huerta**
1. *de legumbres, verduras* **vegetable garden**
2. *de árboles frutales* **orchard.**

el **huerto**
1. *de legumbres, verduras* **vegetable garden**
2. *de árboles frutales* **orchard.**

el **hueso**
1. **bone:** encontraron un hueso de dinosaurio they found a dinosaur bone
2. **pit:** el hueso del durazno the peach pit.

el **huésped, la huésped** ▪ **guest.**

el **huevo** ▪ **egg**
➤ un huevo duro a hard-boiled egg
➤ un huevo estrellado a fried egg
➤ un huevo frito a fried egg
➤ un huevo pasado por agua a soft-boiled egg
➤ un huevo tibio *Colombia, Mexico* a soft-boiled egg
➤ un huevo de Pascua an Easter egg
➤ huevos revueltos scrambled eggs.

**huir** *verbo* ■ **to escape:** varios presos huyeron de la cárcel several prisoners escaped from prison
➤ huyeron cuando vieron que venía la policía they fled when they saw that the police were coming
➤ tuvieron que huir del país they had to flee the country
➤ cuando sonó la alarma salieron huyendo when the alarm went off they ran away.

el **hule**
1. **oilcloth:** un mantel de hule an oilcloth tablecloth
2. *Central America, Mexico* **rubber:** una liga de hule a rubber band.

la **humanidad** ■ **humanity:** fue una gran muestra de humanidad it was a great demonstration of humanity
➤ la humanidad humankind
➤ las humanidades humanities.

**humanitario** *adjetivo* ■ **humanitarian.**

**humano** *adjetivo*
1. **human:** el cuerpo humano the human body
2. **humane:** recibieron un tratamiento muy humano they received very humane treatment.

la **humareda** ■ **cloud of smoke.**

la **humedad**
1. *del aire* **humidity:** el calor y la humedad eran insoportables the heat and humidity were insufferable
2. *del suelo, en las paredes* **moisture:** apareció una mancha de humedad en el techo a moisture spot appeared on the ceiling
➤ no hace mucho calor pero hay mucha humedad it's not very hot but it's very humid.

**humedecer** *verbo* ■ **to dampen.**

**húmedo** *adjetivo*
1. *aire* **humid:** es una ciudad con un clima húmedo it's a city with a humid climate
2. *suelo, paredes* **damp:** esta ropa está húmeda these clothes are damp; la casa es muy húmeda en invierno the house is very damp in the winter.

**humilde** *adjetivo* ■ **humble:** debería ser un poco más humilde he should be a little more humble
➤ alumnos que provienen de zonas humildes students that come from poor areas.

la **humillación** *(plural* las humillaciones) ■ **humiliation.**

**humillar** *verbo* ■ **to humiliate.**

el **humo** ■ **smoke:** el humo de un cigarillo cigarette smoke
➤ el humo de los tubos de escape exhaust fumes
➤ bajarle los humos a alguien to take somebody down a notch: decidimos bajarle los humos we decided to take him down a notch
➤ estaba que echaba humo he was fuming
➤ hacerse humo *informal* to disappear: el libro del profesor se hizo humo the professor's book disappeared.

el **humor**
1. **mood:** el profesor estaba de muy mal humor the professor was in a very bad mood; no estaba de humor para explicar nada she wasn't in the mood to explain anything
2. **humor:** no entiendo esa clase de humor I don't understand that kind of humor
➤ tiene mucho sentido del humor he has a good sense of humor.

**hundirse** *verbo pronominal*
1. **to sink:** el lugar donde se hundió el barco the place where the boat sank
2. **to collapse:** el techo se hundió con el peso de la nieve the roof collapsed with the weight of the snow
➤ se me hundían los pies en el barro my feet sank in the mud.

el **huracán** *(plural* los huracanes) ■ **hurricane.**

**husmear** *verbo*
1. **to sniff:** el perro le husmeaba los zapatos the dog sniffed his shoes
2. **to snoop:** lo encontré husmeando en mi closet I found him snooping in my closet.

**huyendo** *verbo* ➤ huir.

**iba, íbamos etc** *verbo* ➤ ir.

el **icono** ▪ icon: hay que hacer clic en el icono para empezar el programa you have to click on the icon to start the program.

la **ida** ▪ journey out: la ida la hicimos sin problemas we made the journey out without problems
➤ la ida sola sale más cara one-way costs more
➤ es mejor comprar ida y vuelta it's better to buy a round trip
➤ sentimos mucho la ida del profesor de historia we regret a lot the departure of the history professor.

la **idea** ▪ idea: creo que es una buena idea I think it's a good idea
➤ ¿tienes idea de cómo funciona esto? do you have any idea how this works?
➤ no tengo la menor idea I don't have any idea
➤ mi idea era ir al cine my idea was to go to the movies
➤ cambiar de idea to change one's mind: dijo que sí, pero cambió de idea she said yes, but changed her mind.

**ideal** *adjetivo* ▪ ideal: es el lugar ideal para un picnic it's an ideal place for a picnic
➤ lo ideal sería salir bien temprano the ideal thing would be to leave very early

el **ideal** ▪ ideal: mi ideal es tener una carrera y viajar my ideal is to have a career and travel.

**idear** *verbo* ▪ to invent: idearon un sistema diferente they invented a different system
➤ idearon una manera de copiar las respuestas they devised a way to copy the answers.

**idéntico** *adjetivo* ▪ identical: los dos cuadros son idénticos the two paintings are identical
➤ idéntico a algo identical to something: tengo una falda idéntica a la tuya I have a skirt identical to yours
➤ Pedro es idéntico a su padre Pedro's the image of his father.

la **identidad** ▪ identity (*plural* identities).

la **identificación** ▪ identification
➤ es necesario llevar una identificación it's necessary to carry identification.

**identificar** *verbo* ▪ to identify: identificaron al asaltante they identified the attacker
➤ identificarse con alguien to identify with somebody: la gente se identifica con la protagonista people identify with the protagonist.

el **idioma** ▪ language

⚠ The Spanish word **idioma** is a false cognate, it does not mean "idiom".

**idiota** ▪ stupid: ¿por qué eres tan idiota? why are you so stupid?

el/la **idiota** ▪ idiot: no le hagas caso, es una idiota don't pay attention to him, he's an idiot.

el **ídolo** ▪ idol.

la **iglesia** ▪ church: va poco a la iglesia he seldom goes to church
➤ se casaron por la iglesia they got married in the church
➤ la Iglesia Católica the Catholic Church.

la **ignorancia** ▪ ignorance.

**ignorante** *adjetivo* ▪ ignorant: son muy ignorantes they are very ignorant

➤ **soy muy ignorante en ese tema** I'm very uninformed on this topic.

**ignorar** *verbo* ■ **not to know: ignoraba que era cura** she didn't know that he was a priest

➤ **está tratando de molestarte, así que ignóralo** he's trying to bother you, so ignore him.

**igual** *(adjetivo & adverbio) adjetivo*

1. **equal: todos somos iguales ante la ley** we're all equal before the law

2. **same: estos colores son iguales** these colors are the same

➤ **llevaba un suéter igual al mío** he was wearing a sweater similar to mine

➤ **es igual a su padre** he's like his father

➤ **son iguales de largo** they are the same length

➤ **dos por tres es igual a seis** two times three equals six

➤ **van iguales** they're even

➤ **quince iguales** fifteen all

**igual** *adverbio* ■ **the same: los trata igual a todos** he treats everybody the same; **camina igual que tú** he walks the same as you

➤ **igual vino y no estábamos** maybe he came and we weren't there: **me da igual cualquier día** whatever day is fine for me: **todo le da igual** it's all the same to him.

**igualado** *adjetivo*

1. **evenly balanced: fue un partido muy igualado** it was a very evenly balanced match

2. *Mexico informal* **cheeky: despidieron a la muchacha por igualada** they fired the girl for being cheeky.

la **igualdad** ■ **equality: la igualdad ante la ley** equality before the law

➤ **la igualdad de oportunidades** equal opportunity

➤ **la igualdad de sexos** gender equality.

**ilegal** *adjetivo* ■ **illegal**.

**ileso** *adjetivo* ■ **unharmed: todos estaban ilesos** they were all unharmed; **salieron ilesos del accidente** they came out of the accident unharmed.

la **iluminación** ■ **lighting: piden una mejor iluminación de las calles** they are requesting better street lighting.

**iluminar** *verbo* ■ **to light: la luz que ilumina la entrada** the light that lights the entrance

➤ **esta linterna ilumina muy poco** this lantern doesn't give much light

➤ **se le iluminó la cara cuando lo vio** her face lit up when she saw him.

la **ilusión** *(plural* las ilusiones)

1. **hope: empezó con mucha ilusión** he began with a lot of hope

2. **dream: su gran ilusión es ser bailarina** her big dream is to be a dancer

3. **illusion: el color crea la ilusión de que la sala es más grande** the color creates the illusion that the room is bigger

➤ **una ilusión óptica** an optical illusion

➤ **es mejor no hacerse ilusiones** it's best not to get any false ideas.

**ilusionar** *verbo*

➤ **no me ilusiona mucho la idea** the idea doesn't excite me much

➤ **la ilusionaron para después decirle que no** they raised her hopes only to later tell her no

**ilusionarse** *verbo pronominal* ■ **to build up one's hopes: se había ilusionado tanto y todo fracasó** he had built up his hopes so much and everything fell through; **se ilusiona fácilmente con todo** he easily gets excited about everything

➤ **ilusionarse con algo** to get excited about something.

la **ilustración** *(plural* las ilustraciones) ■ **illustration**.

la **imagen** *(plural* las imágenes) ■ **image: es la imagen que la gente tiene de mí** it's the image that people have of me; **el grupo quiere cambiar de imagen** the group wants to change its image

➤ **ser la viva imagen de alguien** to be the spitting image of somebody: **eres la viva imagen de tu tía** you're the spitting image of your aunt.

la **imaginación** (plural las imaginacio-nes) ■ imagination: no tiene imagina-ción para nada he doesn't have any imagi-nation at all; los niños tienen mucha imaginación children have a lot of imagina-tion
➤ ni se me pasó por la imaginación con-társelo it didn't cross my mind to tell him
➤ es pura imaginación tuya it's all in your mind
➤ son imaginaciones tuyas you're imagin-ing things.

**imaginarse** verbo pronominal ■ to imagine: imagínate que estás en una playa desierta imagine that you're on a de-serted beach; me imagino que ya estará en la universidad I imagine that he must be in college now; no te imaginas lo furioso que estaba you can't imagine how furious he was
➤ me lo imaginaba más alto I imagined him to be taller
➤ ¿qué dijo cuando lo supo? — imagína-te what did he say when he found out? — you can imagine.

el **imán** (plural los imanes) ■ magnet.

la **imitación** (plural las imitaciones) ■ imitation: aprenden por imitación they learn by imitation; hay que tener cuidado con las imitaciones you have to be careful with imitations; no es brillante verdadero, es una imitación it's not a real diamond, it's an imitation
➤ le encanta hacer imitaciones he loves to do impressions.

**imitar** verbo
1. to imitate: trata de imitar a su padre he tries to imitate his father; imita a casi todos los profesores he impersonates almost all of the teachers
2. to impersonate
➤ te imita muy bien el acento she imitates your accent very well.

**impaciente** adjetivo ■ impatient: no seas tan impaciente don't be so impatient
➤ estaba impaciente por saber quién ga-nó he was impatient to know who won.

el **impacto** ■ impact.

**impar** adjetivo ■ odd: un número impar an odd number

el **impar** ■ odd number: los impares están a este lado the odd numbers are on this side.

**impedir** verbo
1. to stop: le impidieron la entrada they stopped him from entering; si quieres ir na-die te lo está impidiendo if you want to go nobody is stopping you
2. to block: no impidan el paso do not block the way
3. to prevent: no lo pueden impedir they can't prevent it; la enfermedad le impide ver bien the disease prevents him from see-ing well
➤ impedirle a alguien que haga algo to prevent somebody from doing something: quisieron impedir que reclamáramos they wanted to prevent us from protesting.

**imperfecto** adjetivo ■ imperfect.

el **imperio** ■ empire.

**impermeable** adjetivo ■ waterproof

el **impermeable** ■ raincoat.

**impertinente** adjetivo ■ impertinent.

**imponer** verbo
1. to impose: le impusieron un castigo muy severo they imposed a very severe punish-ment on him
2. to command: el director sabe imponer respeto the director knows how to command respect
➤ le impusieron una multa they imposed a fine on him

**imponerse** verbo pronominal
1. to prevail: es una moda que se impuso en los sesenta it's a fashion that prevailed in the sixties
2. to assert one's authority: la profesora no sabe imponerse the teacher doesn't know how to assert her authority.

la **importación** (plural las importacio-nes) ■ importing: prohibieron la impor-tación de transgénicos they prohibited the importing of genetically modified articles.

la **importancia** ■ importance: la importancia de una buena educación the importance of a good education; un acontecimiento de gran importancia an event of great importance
➤ darle importancia a algo to attach importance to something: le dan mucha importancia a la presentación they attach a lot of importance to presentation
➤ tener importancia to be important: las notas tienen mucha importancia grades are very important
➤ no tiene importancia si no voy it's doesn't matter if I don't go
➤ darse importancia to give oneself airs: se da importancia porque pasó el examen he's giving himself airs because he passed the exam.

**importante** adjetivo ■ important: sus amigos son lo más importante para él his friends are what's most important for him; es una persona muy importante he's a very important person
➤ lo importante es prepararse con tiempo the important thing is to prepare oneself ahead of time.

**importar** verbo
1. to import: tienen que importar muchos productos they have to import many products
2. to matter: no importa si no tienes experiencia it doesn't matter if you don't have experience; eso es lo único que le importa that's the only thing that matters to her
➤ se me rompió — no importa I broke it – it doesn't matter
➤ ¿te importa si se lo cuento? does it matter to you if I tell him?
➤ no me importa caminar hasta el colegio I don't mind walking to school.

**imposible** adjetivo ■ impossible: es imposible estudiar con tanto ruido it's impossible to study with so much noise
➤ es imposible que lo haya sabido it's impossible for him to have found it out
➤ son unos niños imposibles they're impossible children.

el **impostor**, la **impostora** ■ impostor.

la **imprenta**
1. máquina printing press
2. local printer's.

la **impresión** (plural las impresiones) ■ impression: le causó muy buena impresión a la profesora he made a very good impression on the teacher; da la impresión de ser muy estudioso he gives the impression of being very studious
➤ tengo la impresión de haber estado aquí antes I have the feeling that I've been here before
➤ me dio mucha impresión ver tanta pobreza I was shocked to see so much poverty
➤ me ha costado recuperarme de la impresión it's been difficult for me to recuperate from the shock.

**impresionar** verbo
1. to shock: me impresionó ver tanta pobreza it shocked me to see so much poverty
2. to impress: impresionó al público con sus acrobacias he impressed the public with his acrobatics
➤ impresiona lo rápido que aprende it's impressive how fast he learns

**impresionarse** verbo pronominal ■ to be impressed: los niños se impresionan con mucha facilidad children are easily impressed.

**impresionante** adjetivo
1. impressive: tiene una cantidad de videos impresionante he has an impressive number of videos
2. striking: una mujer de una belleza impresionante a woman of striking beauty; el parecido es impresionante the similarity is striking.

la **impresora** ■ printer.

**imprevisible** adjetivo ■ unforeseeable.

**imprevisto** adjetivo ■ unexpected

el **imprevisto**
➤ no pudo ir porque surgió un imprevisto he couldn't go because something unexpected came up

➤ tienen un fondo para **imprevistos** they have a fund for unexpected expenses.

**imprimir** *verbo* ■ **to print**.

**improvisar** *verbo* ■ **to improvise**.

la **imprudencia**

➤ fue una imprudencia manejar de tal manera it was unwise to drive in such a manner

➤ es una imprudencia manejar y hablar por el celular it's unwise to drive and talk on the cell phone.

**imprudente** *adjetivo*

1. **unwise:** sería imprudente tomar una decisión ahora it would be unwise to make a decision now

2. **indiscreet:** es muy imprudente, todo lo cuenta he's very indiscreet, he tells everything

➤ muchos manejan en forma imprudente many people drive in a careless manner

el **impuesto** ■ **tax:** todos deben pagar impuestos everybody has to pay taxes

➤ lo compró en la tienda libre de impuestos he bought it in the duty-free shop.

**impulsar** *verbo* ■ **to drive:** dos motores impulsan el vehículo two motors drive the vehicle; no sabe qué lo impulsó a hacerlo she doesn't know that she drove him to do it.

**impulsivo** *adjetivo* ■ **impulsive**.

el **impulso** ■ **impulse:** mi primer impulso fue esconderme my first impulse was to hide; casi siempre actúa por impulso he almost always acts on impulse

➤ hay que tomar bastante impulso antes de saltar you have to get up enough momentum before jumping.

la **impureza** ■ **impurity** (plural **impurities**).

**inadvertido** *adjetivo*

➤ pasar inadvertido to escape notice: el cantante trató, sin éxito, de pasar inadvertido the singer tried, without success, to escape notice.

**inaguantable** *adjetivo* ■ **unbearable:** este calor es inaguantable this heat is unbearable.

la **inasistencia** ■ **absence:** este trimestre he tenido varias inasistencias this trimester I've had several absences.

la **inauguración** (plural las inauguraciones) ■ **opening:** mañana es la inauguración de la biblioteca tomorrow is the opening of the library; la ceremonia de inauguración the opening ceremony.

**inaugurar** *verbo* ■ **to inaugurate:** mañana inauguran la nueva biblioteca tomorrow they inaugurate the new library.

el/la **inca** *sustantivo masculino y femenino* ■ **Inca**.

la **incapacidad**

1. **inability:** su absoluta incapacidad para expresarse con corrección his absolute inability to express himself correctly

2. **incompetence:** la incapacidad de algunos políticos es impresionante the incompetence of some politicians is amazing

3. *Colombia, Mexico* **sick leave:** el médico le dio una semana de incapacidad the doctor gave him a week of sick leave.

**incapaz, incapaces** *adjetivo* ■ **incapable:** es incapaz de hacer una cosa así he's incapable of doing something like that.

**incendiar** *verbo* ■ **to set fire to:** quisieron incendiar el local they tried to set fire to the place

**incendiarse** *verbo pronominal* ■ **to catch fire:** se le incendió la casa al vecino the neighbor's house caught fire.

el **incendio** ■ **fire:** no pudieron apagar el incendio they couldn't put out the fire

➤ creen que fue un incendio provocado they believe that it was arson.

el **incentivo** ■ **incentive**.

la **incertidumbre** ■ **uncertainty** (plural **uncertainties**).

el **incidente** ■ **incident:** el partido terminó sin incidentes the match ended without incident.

la **inclinación** *(plural* las inclinaciones)
1. **tilt:** la inclinación de la órbita de la tierra the tilt of the earth's orbit
2. **incline:** debido a una inclinación del terreno due to an incline in the land.

**inclinar** *verbo* ■ **to tilt:** inclinó el asiento y estiró las piernas he tilted the seat and stretched his legs

**inclinarse** *verbo pronominal*
1. **to bend down:** se inclinó para recoger el libro he bent down to pick up the book
2. **to lean:** me incliné sobre la cuna para darle un beso I leaned over the cradle to give him a kiss; **inclínate hacia adelante** lean forward.

**incluir** *verbo* ■ **to include:** el premio incluye el viaje de ida y vuelta y la estadía the prize includes the round trip and the stay; **se me olvidó incluirlo en la lista** I forgot to include him on the list.

**inclusive** *adverbio* ■ **including:** hay que estudiar hasta el capítulo tres inclusive we have to study up to and including chapter three; **abren todos los días, inclusive feriados** they're open every day, including holidays.

**incluso** *adverbio* ■ **even:** cualquiera lo puede hacer, incluso un niño anybody can do it, even a child; **incluso nos fue a dejar a la casa** he even left us at the house.

**incoloro** *adjetivo* ■ **colorless.**

**incómodo** *adjetivo* ■ **uncomfortable:** las camas son un poco incómodas the beds are a little uncomfortable
➤ **sentirse incómodo** to feel uncomfortable: **se sentía incómodo con ese traje** he felt uncomfortable in that suit
➤ **es muy incómodo estar sin teléfono** it's very inconvenient to be without a telephone.

**incompatible** *adjetivo* ■ **incompatible.**

**incompetente** *adjetivo* ■ **incompetent.**

**incompleto** *adjetivo* ■ **incomplete.**

**incomprensible** *adjetivo* ■ **incomprehensible.**

**inconcebible** *adjetivo* ■ **unthinkable.**

**inconsciente** *adjetivo*
1. **unconscious:** está vivo pero inconsciente he's alive but unconscious; **cayó inconsciente al suelo** he fell unconscious to the floor
2. **thoughtless:** ¡cómo pueden ser tan inconscientes! how can you be so thoughtless!

el/la **inconsciente**
➤ **son todos unos inconscientes** they're all thoughtless.

el **inconveniente**
1. **problem:** surgieron algunos inconvenientes some problems came up; **el inconveniente es que está en el tercer piso** the problem is that it's on the third floor
2. **disadvantage:** vivir aquí tiene sus conveniente e inconvenientes living here has its advantages and disadvantages
3. **objection:** no nos pusieron muchos inconvenientes they didn't raise many objections
➤ **¿tienes algún inconveniente que lo invite?** do you mind if I invite him?

**incorrecto** *adjetivo* ■ **incorrect:** el uso incorrecto de una palabra the incorrect usage of a word.

**increíble** *adjetivo* ■ **incredible:** nos pasó algo increíble something incredible happened to us.

**inculto** *adjetivo* ■ **ignorant:** es una persona muy inculta he's a very ignorant person.

**incurable** *adjetivo* ■ **incurable.**

**indecente** *adjetivo* ■ **indecent:** un gesto indecente an indecent gesture.

la **indecisión** *(plural* las indecisiones)
■ **hesitation:** el gol se debió a una indecisión del arquero the goal was due to a hesitation of the goalkeeper.

**156**

**indeciso** *adjetivo* ■ **indecisive:** siempre ha sido muy indecisa she's always been very indecisive
➤ está indeciso, no sabe si ir o no he can't make up his mind, he doesn't know whether to go or not.

**indefenso** *adjetivo* ■ **defenseless.**

**indefinido** *adjetivo* ■ **indefinite:** tiene los ojos de un color indefinido his eyes are an indefinite color; se lo prestó por tiempo indefinido she loaned it to him for an indefinite period of time
➤ el artículo indefinido the indefinite article.

la **independencia** ■ **independence.**

la **indemnización** *(plural* las indemnizaciones*)* ■ **compensation.**

**independiente** *adjetivo* ■ **independent.**

**independizarse** *verbo pronominal*
■ **to become independent:** es natural que quieran independizarse de los padres it's natural that they want to become independent from their parents.

**indestructible** *adjetivo* ■ **indestructible.**

**indeterminado** *adjetivo* ■ **indeterminate:** el boleto es válido para un número indeterminado de viajes the ticket is valid for an indeterminate number of trips.

la **indicación** *(plural* las indicaciones*)*
➤ nos hizo una indicación para que nos sentáramos he signaled for us to sit down

las **indicaciones**
1. **instructions:** nunca sigue las indicaciones de los manuales he never follows the manuals' instructions
2. **directions:** me dio un mapa e indicaciones de cómo llegar he gave me a map and directions for how to get there.

**indicar** *verbo*
1. **to indicate:** el barómetro indica mal tiempo the barometer indicates bad weather
2. **to show:** me indicó en el mapa cómo llegar he showed me on the map how to get there
➤ con un gesto nos indicó que nos sentáramos with a gesture he signaled for us to sit down
➤ el médico me indicó que tomara tres al día the doctor advised me to take three a day.

el **indicio** ■ **sign:** la fiebre es un mal indicio fever is a bad sign.

el **índice**
1. **index:** lo busqué en el índice I looked it up in the index
2. **index finger:** lo indicó con el índice he pointed to it with his index finger
3. **rate:** el índice de mortalidad mortality rate.

la **indiferencia** ■ **indifference.**

**indiferente** *adjetivo* ■ **indifferent:** son indiferentes a todo lo que pasa en el mundo they're indifferent to everything that happens in the world
➤ es indiferente que sea blanco o negro it makes no difference whether it's white or black.

**indígena** *adjetivo* ■ **indigenous:** la cultura índígena the indigenous culture

el/la **indígena** ■ **native.**

la **indigestión** ■ **indigestion.**

la **indignación** ■ **anger:** me da mucha indignación cuando veo tanta injusticia I feel a lot of anger when I see so much injustice.

**indignar** *verbo* ■ **to anger:** le indigna que ponga la música tan fuerte it angers him that they play the music so loud

**indignarse** *verbo pronominal* ■ **to get angry:** se indigna cuando le mienten she gets angry when they lie to her.

el **indio,** la **india** ■ **Indian**

En los Estados Unidos se prefiere **Native Americans** para referirse a los indios de ese país.

**157**

la **indirecta** ■ hint: me lanzó una indirecta para que me fuera he dropped a hint that I should leave.

la **indiscreción** (plural las indiscreciones) ■ indiscretion.

**indiscreto** adjetivo ■ indiscreet: fue una pregunta muy indiscreta it was a very indiscreet question

➤ fue muy indiscreto al hacerle esa pregunta he was very tactless to ask her that question.

**indispensable** adjetivo ■ indispensable: es indispensable tener experiencia it's indispensable to have experience

➤ traigan sólo lo indispensable bring only the essentials.

**individual** adjetivo

1. individual: nos sirvieron porciones individuales they served us individual portions

2. single: mi casa tiene un dormitorio individual y dos dobles my house has one single bedroom and two doubles

el **individual** ■ singles: la campeona del individual femenino the champion of the women's singles.

el **individuo** ■ individual: todo individuo tiene derecho a la vida every individual has a right to life.

el **indocumentado,** la **indocumentada** ■ illegal immigrant.

la **industria** ■ industry (plural industries).

**industrial** adjetivo ■ industrial

➤ una zona industrial an industrial area

el **industrial,** la **industrial** ■ industrialist.

**industrializarse** verbo pronominal ■ to become industrialized.

la **inercia** ■ inertia.

**inesperado** adjetivo ■ unexpected.

**inestable** adjetivo

1. unstable: esta mesa es un poco inestable this table is a little unstable

2. changeable: el tiempo ha estado muy inestable the weather has been very changeable.

**inevitable** adjetivo ■ inevitable.

**inexperto** adjetivo ■ inexperienced.

**inexplicable** adjetivo ■ inexplicable.

el **infarto** ■ heart attack: le dio un infarto she had a heart attack.

la **infancia** ■ infancy.

**infantil** adjetivo

1. children's: un cuento infantil a children's story

2. childish: es muy infantil para su edad he's very childish for his age.

la **infección** (plural las infecciones) ■ infection: tiene una infección en la garganta she has a throat infection.

**infectarse** verbo pronominal ■ to become infected: mi computadora se infectó con un virus my computer became infected with a virus; se le infectó la herida his wound became infected.

**infeliz** (plural infelices) adjetivo ■ unhappy: tuvo una niñez muy infeliz he had a very unhappy childhood.

**inferior** adjetivo

1. lower: la parte inferior de la pantalla the lower part of the screen; el párpado inferior the lower eyelid

2. inferior: se siente inferior a su hermano he feels inferior to his brother

➤ productos de calidad inferior inferior-quality products

➤ temperaturas inferiores a lo normal lower than normal temperatures

➤ un número inferior a cincuenta a number below fifty.

el **infierno** ■ hell.

la **infinidad** ■ infinity

➤ tengo una infinidad de cosas que hacer I have an enormous number of things to do

➤ lo ha repetido infinidad de veces he has repeated it countless times.

el **infinitivo** ■ infinitive.

**158**

**infinito** *adjetivo* ■ **infinite:** tiene una paciencia infinita she has infinite patience

el **infinito** ■ **infinity**.

**inflar** *verbo*

1. **to blow up:** hay que inflar los globos you have to blow up the balloons
2. **to inflate:** paramos para inflar una rueda we stopped in order to inflate a tire.

**inflexible** *adjetivo* ■ **inflexible:** el profesor es muy inflexible con los alumnos the professor is very inflexible with the students.

la **influencia** ■ **influence:** tiene mucha influencia sobre los alumnos she has a lot of influence over her students; mi mamá siempre ha sido una gran influencia para mí my mom has always been a big influence for me

➤ una persona de mucha influencia a very influential person.

**influir** *verbo* ■ **to influence:** eso influyó mucho en mi decisión that influenced my decision a lot; las personas que más han influido en mí the people that have influenced me most.

**influyo, influye etc** *verbo* ➤ influir.

la **información** *(plural* las informaciones)

1. **information:** hay mucha información sobre becas there is a lot of information about scholarships
2. **news:** me leí sólo la información internacional I read only the international news
➤ es una información muy valiosa it's a very valuable piece of information
➤ preguntemos en información a qué hora llega let's ask at the information desk when it's arriving
➤ en información te pueden dar el número directory assistance can give you the number.

**informal** *adjetivo*

1. **informal:** un ambiente muy informal a very informal atmosphere
2. **unreliable:** Pepe es muy informal Pepe is very unreliable

3. **casual:** había gente vestida de fiesta y con ropa informal there were people dressed for a party and in casual clothes.

**informar** *verbo* ■ **to inform:** nos informaron que el avión venía atrasado they informed us that the airplane was late
➤ informaron la hora de llegada por los altoparlantes they announced the time of arrival on the loudspeakers
➤ ¿me podría informar sobre el programa de becas? could I get some information about the scholarship program?
➤ me informaron mal they misinformed me
➤ me informé de todo antes del viaje I inquired into everything before the trip.

la **informática** ■ **computing**.

el **informe** ■ **report:** según un informe de la policía according to a police report
➤ pidieron informes sobre su conducta they asked for references regarding his behavior.

la **infracción** *(plural* las infracciones) ■ **offense:** lo multaron por una infracción de tráfico they fined him for a traffic offense.

**ingeniarse** *verbo pronominal* ■ **to come up with:** se ingenió una manera de hacerlo más rápido he came up with a way to do it faster
➤ ingeniárselas to manage: no sé cómo se las ingenia para que nunca lo castiguen I don't know how he manages it so that they never punish him.

la **ingeniería** ■ **engineering**.

el **ingeniero,** la **ingeniera** ■ **engineer:** es ingeniero he's an engineer.

el **ingenio** ■ **ingenuity:** gracias al ingenio de Pepe thanks to Pepe's ingenuity
➤ un ingenio azucarero a sugar refinery.

**ingenioso** *adjetivo*

1. **clever:** es un muchacho muy ingenioso he's a very clever guy; siempre tiene ideas ingeniosas she always has clever ideas
2. **witty:** hizo un comentario muy ingenioso he made a very witty comment.

**ingenuo** *adjetivo* ■ naïve: ¡no seas tan ingenuo! don't be so naïve!

**Inglaterra** *sustantivo femenino* ■ England.

**inglés, inglesa** *adjetivo*

En inglés, los adjetivos que se refieren a un país o una región se escriben con mayúscula:

English

➤ tiene un apellido inglés he has an English last name

el **inglés** *(plural* los ingleses*)*

En inglés, los gentilicios se escriben con mayúscula:

Englishman *(plural* **Englishmen***)*
➤ los ingleses the English.

el **inglés**

En inglés, los idiomas se escriben con mayúscula:

English.

la **inglesa** ■ Englishwoman *(plural* Englishwomen*)*.

el **ingrediente** ■ ingredient.

**ingresar** *verbo*

1. to start: el próximo año ingresa a la universidad he starts college next year

2. to join: me gustaría ingresar al nuevo club de tenis I would like to join the new tennis club

➤ ingresó ayer al hospital he went into the hospital yesterday: lo volvieron a ingresar al hospital they put him back in the hospital.

los **ingresos** ■ income: tienen muy poco ingresos they have very little income.

la **inicial** ■ initial: pon tus iniciales aquí put your initials here.

la **injusticia** ■ injustice: hay muchas injusticias en el mundo there are many injustices in the world; es una injusticia que lo hayan castigado it's an injustice that they've punished him.

**injusto** *adjetivo* ■ unfair: han sido muy injustos con él they've been very unfair to him; es un castigo injusto it's an unfair punishment.

**inmaduro** *adjetivo* ■ immature: es un muchacho muy inmaduro he's a very immature boy.

**inmediato** *adjetivo* ■ immediate: el alivio fue inmediato the relief was immediate

➤ de inmediato immediately: hazlo de inmediato do it immediately.

**inmenso** *adjetivo* ■ immense: tiene un jardín inmenso he has an immense garden

➤ la inmensa mayoría de los estudiantes the vast majority of the students.

la **inmigración** ■ immigration.

el/la **inmigrante** ■ immigrant.

**inmortal** *adjetivo* ■ immortal.

**inmóvil** *adjetivo* ■ motionless: se quedó inmóvil he remained motionless.

**inmune** *adjetivo* ■ immune: con la vacuna estoy inmune al contagio with the vaccine I am immune to the infection.

**innecesario** *adjetivo* ■ unnecessary.

la **inocencia** ■ innocence.

**inocente** *adjetivo*

1. innocent: un niño inocente an innocent child

2. naïve: ¡no seas inocente! don't be naïve!

➤ lo declararon inocente they declared him not guilty

DÍA DE LOS INOCENTES

This is the equivalent of April Fools' Day in Spanish-speaking countries and is celebrated on December 28. On this day people play practical jokes on their friends and try to convince them of the most outrageous hoaxes. Sometimes the media joins in the fun and publishes some incredible news story, such as "Local cookie producers announce they will be giving away their products free for a month."

**inofensivo** *adjetivo* ■ **inoffensive**.

**inolvidable** *adjetivo* ■ **unforgettable**.

**inquieto** *adjetivo*

1. **worried**: están inquietos porque no ha escrito they're worried because he hasn't written

2. **restless**: mi hermano menor es muy inquieto my little brother is very restless.

el **inquilino**, la **inquilina** ■ **tenant**.

**inscribirse** *verbo pronominal* ■ **to enroll**: me inscribí en el curso de inglés I enrolled in the English course.

la **inscripción** *(plural* las inscripciones)

1. **enrollment**: mañana abren la inscripción enrollment starts tomorrow

2. **inscription**: a la entrada hay una inscripción con la fecha at the entrance there is an inscription with the date.

**inscrito** *verbo* ➤ inscribirse.

el **insecticida** ■ **insecticide**.

el **insecto** ■ **insect**.

la **inseguridad** ■ **insecurity** *(plural* insecurities)**: se esfuerza por superar su inseguridad he makes an effort to overcome his insecurity

➤ la inseguridad en el trabajo job insecurity.

**insensible** *adjetivo* ■ **insensitive**: es una persona muy insensible he's a very insensitive person

➤ el brazo derecho le quedó insensible his right arm became numb

➤ son insensibles al frío they're not sensitive to the cold.

**inseparable** *adjetivo* ■ **inseparable**.

**inservible** *adjetivo* ■ **useless**: tiene tantas cosas inservibles en su escritorio he has so many useless things in his desk

➤ lo metió en lavadora y quedó inservible he put it in the washer and it came out unusable.

**insignificante** *adjetivo* ■ **insignificant**.

**insinuar** *verbo* ■ **to hint**: insinuó que le gustaría venir she hinted that she would like to come

➤ insinuó que yo había copiado he insinuated that I had copied.

**insípido** *adjetivo* ■ **insipid**.

**insistir** *verbo* ■ **to insist**: por más que insista no le van a dar permiso however much he insists, they are not going to give him permission

➤ insistir en algo to insist on something: insiste en quiere hacerlo él solo he insists that he wants to do it by himself: insisten en que vaya al dentista they insist that he go to the dentist.

la **insolación** ■ **sunstroke**: le dio una insolación she got sunstroke.

la **insolencia** ■ **insolence**: no sé cómo toleran su insolencia I don't know how they tolerate his insolence

➤ fue una insolencia hablarle así a tu abuela it was rude to speak to your grandmother that way.

**insolente** *adjetivo* ■ **insolent**.

el **insomnio** ■ **insomnia**.

**insoportable** *adjetivo* ■ **unbearable**.

el **inspector**, la **inspectora** ■ **inspector**.

la **inspiración** ■ **inspiration**: mi madre es mi inspiración my mother is my inspiration.

**inspirar** *verbo*

1. **to inspire**: inspira respeto he inspires respect; no me inspira confianza he doesn't inspire my confidence

2. **to inhale**: inspire por favor inhale please.

la **instalación** ■ **installation**: la instalación es gratis installation is free

➤ las instalaciones facilities: las instalaciones deportivas son excelentes the sports facilities are excellent.

**instalar** *verbo* ■ **to install**: instalaron un sistema de seguridad they installed a security system; no puede instalar el programa he can't install the program

**instalarse** *verbo pronominal* ■ **to settle:** se instalaron en el extranjero they settled out of the country.

**instantáneo** *adjetivo* ■ **instantaneous:** la muerte sería instantánea death would be instantaneous
➤ café instantáneo instant coffee.

el **instante** ■ **moment:** en ese mismo instante sonó el teléfono at that same moment the telephone rang; hace un instante estaba aquí he was here a moment ago
➤ a cada instante me preguntaba la hora he was constantly asking me what time it was.

el **instinto** ■ **instinct:** reaccionó por instinto he reacted out of instinct.

la **institución** (*plural* las instituciones) ■ **institution**.

el **instituto** ■ **institute**.

las **instrucciones** ■ **instructions:** tiene instrucciones de no comentarlo con nadie he has instructions to not discuss it with anybody.

**instructivo** *adjetivo* ■ **educational:** es un programa muy instructivo it's a very educational program.

el **instrumento** ■ **instrument**.

**insultar** *verbo* ■ **to insult**.

el **insulto** ■ **insult**.

**intacto** *adjetivo* ■ **intact:** descubrieron un mural maya intacto they discovered an intact Mayan mural; a pesar de los siglos sigue intacto in spite of the centuries it remains intact.

**intelectual** *adjetivo* ■ **intellectual**

el/la **intelectual** ■ **intellectual**.

la **inteligencia** ■ **intelligence**.

**inteligente** *adjetivo* ■ **intelligent**.

la **intemperie**
➤ a la intemperie out in the open: en el campamento tienen que dormir a la intemperie at the camp they have to sleep out in the open.

la **intención** (*plural* las intenciones) ■ **intention:** mi intención no era causar problemas my intention was not to cause problems
➤ con la intención de hacer algo with the intention of doing something: lo hizo con la intención de ayudar he did it with the intention of helping; no tenía la más mínima intención de obedecer he didn't have the least intention of obeying
➤ tenía intenciones de ir mañana I intended to go tomorrow
➤ lo hace con buenas intenciones he does it with good intentions
➤ lo que vale es la intención it's the thought that counts.

**intencionado** *adjetivo* ■ **deliberate:** el cabezazo fue intencionado the headbutt was deliberate
➤ es una persona bien intencionada she's a well-meaning person
➤ no creo que José sea mal intencionado I don't believe that José is malicious.

**intensivo** *adjetivo* ■ **intensive:** ofrecen clases intensivas de inglés they offer intensive English classes.

**intenso** *adjetivo* ■ **intense**.

**intentar** *verbo* ■ **to try:** ya lo ha intentado varias veces he's already tried it several times; intenta concentrarte más en clase try to concentrate more in class; intenta que sea lo más claro posible try to make it as clear as possible
➤ intentar hacer algo to try to do something.

el **intento** ■ **attempt:** pasó el examen al segundo intento he passed the exam on the second attempt.

**intercambiar** *verbo* ■ **to exchange:** intercambiaron direcciones they exchanged addresses.

el **intercambio** ■ **exchange**.

el **interés** (*plural* los intereses) ■ **interest:** tienes que poner más interés en lo que haces you have to take more of an interest in what you do; escuchaba con interés she was listening with interest

➤ **interés en algo** interest in something: **no muestra ningún interés en la lectura** he doesn't show any interest in reading

➤ **sólo lo hace por interés** he only does it for self-interest

➤ **les cobran un interés muy alto** they charge them very high interest.

**interesante** *adjetivo* ■ **interesting**.

**interesar** *verbo* ■ **to interest: siempre me han interesado ese tipo de cosas** that type of thing has always interested me

➤ **le interesa mucho la música** she's very interested in music

➤ **¿te interesaría saber más del tema?** would it interest you to know more on the subject?

**interior** *adjetivo* ■ **interior: en el bolsillo interior de la chaqueta** in the interior pocket of the jacket

➤ **la parte interior es roja** the inner part is red

el **interior** ■ **interior: el interior del país es muy árido** the country's interior is very arid

➤ **lo que ocurre en el interior de la Tierra** what occurs inside the earth

➤ **en su interior estaba muy arrepentido** deep down he was very sorry.

**intermedio** *adjetivo*

1. **intermediate: está en el nivel intermedio** he's at intermediate level

2. **medium: el tamaño intermedio te quedaría mejor** the medium size would fit you better

el **intermedio** ■ **interval**.

**interminable** *adjetivo* ■ **unending**.

**internacional** *adjetivo* ■ **international**.

el **internado** ■ **boarding school**.

**internar** *verbo* ■ **to admit: lo internaron ayer** they admitted him yesterday

➤ **tuvo que internarse para una operación** he had to be admitted for an operation.

el/la **Internet** ■ **Internet: lo encontré en Internet** I found it on the Internet.

**interno** *adjetivo* ■ **internal: son problemas internos del colegio** they are internal problems of the school

➤ **está interna en un colegio de monjas** she's a boarder at a convent school

➤ **si no mejora las notas lo van a poner interno** if he doesn't improve his grades they're going to send him to boarding school.

la **interpretación** *(plural* las interpretaciones)* ■ **interpretation: cada uno le dio una interpretación distinta** each one gave her a different interpretation

➤ **lo que más me gustó fue la interpretación del pianista** what I most liked was the pianist's performance

➤ **interpretación simultánea** simultaneous translation.

**interpretar** *verbo*

1. **to interpret: lo puedes interpretar de diferentes maneras** you can interpret it in different ways

2. **to play: interpretó muy bien el personaje** he played the character very well; **interpretó una pieza al piano** she played a piece on the piano

➤ **me interpretaste mal** you misunderstood me.

el/la **intérprete** ■ **interpreter: quiero ser intérprete** I want to be an interpreter.

**interrogar** *verbo* ■ **to interrogate: la policía lo quiere interrogar** the police want to interrogate him.

**interrumpir** *verbo*

1. **to interrupt: no interrumpas cuando alguien está hablando** don't interrupt when somebody is talking; **no le gusta que lo interrumpan** he doesn't like to be interrupted

2. **to cut short: tuvieron que interrumpir las vacaciones** they had to cut their vacation short

3. **to block: un árbol caído interrumpía el tráfico** a fallen tree was blocking the traffic; **no interrumpas el paso** don't block the way.

la **interrupción** *(plural* las interrupciones)* ■ **interruption: no ha podido estudiar con tanta interrupción** she hasn't been able to study with so much interruption.

el **interruptor** ■ switch.

el **intervalo** ■ interval: a intervalos de diez minutos at ten minute intervals.

el **intestino** ■ intestine.

la **intimidad** ■ privacy: mis hermanos no respetan mi intimidad my brothers don't respect my privacy
➤ celebraron la boda en la intimidad they had a private wedding
➤ lo que pase en la intimidad es cosa de ellos what happens in private is their business.

**íntimo** adjetivo ■ intimate: son amigos íntimos they're intimate friends.

la **intoxicación** (plural las intoxicaciones) ■ poisoning: consejos para evitar intoxicaciones advice to avoid poisoning
➤ intoxicación por alimentos food poisoning.

**intoxicarse** verbo pronominal ■ to be poisoned: se intoxicó con mejillones he was poisoned by mussels.

**intranquilo** adjetivo ■ worried: está muy intranquilo porque ha estudiado muy poco he's very worried because he has studied very little.

la **introducción** (plural las introducciones) ■ introduction.

**introducir** verbo
1. to insert: hay que introducir una moneda en la ranura you have to insert a coin into the slot
2. to introduce: introdujeron el sistema métrico they introduced the metric system; quieren introducir algunos cambios en el horario they want to introduce some changes in the schedule
3. to enter: introdujo los datos en la computadora he entered the data into the computer.

el **intruso**, la **intrusa** ■ intruder.

la **intuición** (plural las intuiciones) ■ intuition: la intuición me dice que no deberíamos tomar ese avión intuition tells me that we shouldn't take that airplane.

la **inundación** (plural las inundaciones) ■ flood: las últimas inundaciones obligaron a evacuar varias casas the last floods forced the evacuation of several houses.

**inundar** verbo ■ to flood: la lluvia inundó las regiones más bajas del pueblo the rain flooded the lowest areas of the town

**inundarse** verbo pronominal ■ to be flooded: las regiones más bajas del pueblo se inundaron con las últimas lluvias the lowest areas of the town were flooded with the last rains.

**inútil** adjetivo ■ useless: su secretaria es inútil his secretary is useless; es inútil, no lo vamos a lograr it's useless, we're not going to manage it

el/la **inútil** (plural los/las inútiles)
➤ eres un inútil, no quiero verte más por aquí you're useless, I don't want to see you around here anymore.

**invadir** verbo ■ to invade: el ejército enemigo invadió la ciudad the enemy army invaded the city.

**inválido** adjetivo ■ disabled: su tío quedó inválido después del accidente his uncle became disabled after the accident

el **inválido**, la **inválida** ■ invalid: los inválidos llegaron en silla de ruedas the invalids arrived in wheelchairs.

la **invasión** (plural las invasiones) ■ invasion.

**invasor** adjetivo ■ invading: el ejército invasor sitió la ciudad the invading army laid siege to the city

el **invasor**, la **invasora** ■ invader: los invasores fueron crueles con los nativos the invaders were cruel to the natives.

**invencible** adjetivo ■ invincible: ese equipo es invencible that team is invincible.

**inventar** verbo
1. to invent: Alexander Graham Bell inventó el teléfono Alexander Graham Bell invented the telephone

2. **to make up:** le gusta inventar historias para entretener a sus hijos he likes to make up stories to entertain his children.

### el **invento**

1. **invention:** el teléfono fue un invento de Alexander Graham Bell the telephone was an invention of Alexander Graham Bell

2. **fabrication:** ya estoy cansada de tus inventos I'm tired of your fabrications.

### el **inventor,** la **inventora** ■ inventor:
el inventor del teléfono fue Alexander Graham Bell the inventor of the telephone was Alexander Graham Bell.

### el **invernadero** ■ greenhouse.

### la **inversión** (plural las inversiones) ■ investment.

### **inverso** adjetivo ■ opposite: en sentido inverso in the opposite direction
➤ a la inversa the other way: yo lo hice así y ellos lo hicieron a la inversa I did it this way and they did it the other way.

### **invertir** verbo

1. **to invest:** hay varios empresarios interesados en invertir en el país there are several businessmen interested in investing in the country

2. **to reverse:** si invertimos el orden de los números, obtendremos otro resultado if we reverse the order of the numbers, we will obtain a different result.

### la **investigación** (plural las investigaciones)

1. **investigation:** al cabo de dos días de investigación policial, capturaron al ladrón at the end of two days of police investigation, they captured the thief

2. **research:** mi amigo se dedica a la investigación en biología my friend is dedicated to research in biology.

### el **investigador,** la **investigadora**

1. **investigator:** los investigadores capturaron al ladrón en un par de días the investigators captured the thief in a couple of days

2. **researcher:** el investigador descubrió una nueva reacción química the researcher discovered a new chemical reaction.

### **investigar** verbo

1. **to investigate:** la policía investiga el caso hace una semana the police have been investigating the case for a week

2. **to research:** los científicos están investigando la nueva enfermedad scientists are researching the new disease.

### el **invierno** ■ winter
➤ en invierno in winter
➤ el próximo invierno next winter.

### **invisible** adjetivo ■ invisible.

### la **invitación** (plural las invitaciones)
■ invitation: no aceptaron mi invitación they didn't accept my invitation.

### el **invitado,** la **invitada** ■ guest.

### **invitar** verbo ■ to invite.

### la **inyección** (plural las inyecciones)
■ injection.

### **ir** verbo

1. **to go:** el nuevo camino irá del pueblo a la ciudad the new road will go from the town to the city; voy al parque todos los domingos I go to the park every Sunday

2. **to be:** la niña iba vestida de rojo the girl was dressed in red

3. **to come:** ¿quieres ir conmigo? do you want to come with me?
➤ ¡vamos! come on!
➤ ¡vámonos! let's go!
➤ voy a comprarlo I'm going to buy it
➤ ¿cómo te va? how's it going?
➤ ¡que le vaya bien! take care!

### **irse** verbo pronominal ■ to leave: nos vamos porque ya es tarde we're leaving because it's late now.

### la **ira** ■ anger: tuvo un arrebato de ira he had a fit of anger.

### **irracional** adjetivo ■ irrational.

### **irreal** adjetivo ■ unreal.

### **irregular** adjetivo ■ irregular: la casa no es segura porque está construida en un terreno irregular the house is not safe because it's constructed on an irregular piece of land.

**irresistible** *adjetivo*

1. **irresistible:** esos chocolates son irresistibles those chocolates are irresistible
2. **unbearable:** el dolor de muelas es irresistible toothache is unbearable.

**irrespetuoso** *adjetivo* ■ **disrespectful**.

la **irresponsabilidad** ■ **irresponsibility:** la irresponsabilidad es su peor defecto irresponsibility is his worst fault.

**irresponsable** *adjetivo* ■ **irresponsible:** ese estudiante es muy irresponsable that student is very irresponsible.

la **irritación** ■ **irritation:** el frío le produjo una irritación en la garganta the cold gave him a throat irritation.

**irritado** *adjetivo*

1. **inflamed:** tiene la piel irritada his skin is inflamed
2. **irritated:** Juan está irritado por la mentira que le dije Juan is irritated because of the lie that I told him.

**irritar** *verbo* ■ **to irritate:** esa crema te está irritando la piel that cream is irritating your skin

**irritarse** *verbo pronominal* ■ **to get irritated:** el vecino se irritó porque los niños rompieron un vidrio the neighbor got irritated because the children broke a window.

**irrompible** *adjetivo* ■ **unbreakable**

la **isla** ■ **island**.

el **itinerario** ■ **itinerary** (*plural* **itineraries**).

la **izquierda** ■ **left hand**
➤ **a la izquierda** to the left: tienes que doblar a la izquierda you have to turn to the left María está sentada a la izquierda de Juan María is seated to the left of Juan
➤ **de la izquierda** on the left: abre esa puerta, la de la izquierda open that door, the one on the left
➤ **la izquierda** *política* the left.

**izquierdo** *adjetivo* ■ **left:** la pierna izquierda the left leg.

el **jabón** (*plural* los jabones) ■ **bar of soap:** compra seis jabones por favor buy six bars of soap please.

**jactarse** *verbo pronominal* ■ **to brag:** se jacta de ser el mejor de la clase he brags about being the best in the class.

**jadear** *verbo* ■ **to gasp for breath:** está jadeando porque corrió mucho she's gasping for breath because she ran a lot.

el **jaguar** (*plural* los jaguares) ■ **jaguar**.

**jalar** *verbo*

1. *Andes, Caribbean, Central America, Mexico* **to pull:** si me jalas el pelo, te pego if you pull my hair, I'll hit you
2. *Mexico* **to pull up:** jala una silla y siéntate pull up a seat and sit down
➤ "jale" "pull": no vi que decía "jale", por eso estaba empujando I didn't see that it said "pull", that's why I was pushing.

la **jalea** ■ **jelly** (*plural* **jellies**).

**jamás** *adverbio* ■ **never:** jamás te mentí I never lied to you.

el **jamón** (*plural* los jamones) ■ **ham**
➤ **jamón cocido** cooked ham.

el **jarabe** ■ **syrup**.

el **jardín** (*plural* los jardines) ■ **garden**
➤ **jardín botánico** botanical garden
➤ **jardín zoológico** zoo.

el **jardinero**, la **jardinera** ■ **gardener**.

la **jarra** ■ jar.

el **jarrón** (plural los jarrones) ■ vase.

la **jaula** ■ cage.

el **jefe**, la **jefa**
1. *en una oficina* **boss**
2. *en un departamento* **head**
3. *de una tribu* **chief**
➤ jefe de estado chief of state.

la **jeringa** ■ syringe.

la **jirafa** ■ giraffe.

el **jitomate** ■ *Mexico* **tomato** (plural to-matoes).

la **joroba** ■ hump: el camello tiene dos jorobas the camel has two humps.

el **jorobado**, la **jorobada** ■ hunchback.

**joven** *adjetivo* ■ **young**: es una abuela muy joven she's a very young grandmother

el/la **joven** (plural los/las jóvenes) ■ **young person** (plural **young people**): los jóvenes exigen cambios en la sociedad young people demand changes in society.

la **joya** ■ jewel.

la **joyería** ■ jewelry.

**jubilado** *adjetivo* ■ **retired**: mi abuelo está jubilado desde hace 15 años my grandfather has been retired for 15 years

el **jubilado**, la **jubilada** ■ **retiree**: muchos jubilados están pasando dificultades económicas many retirees are going through financial difficulties.

**judicial** *adjetivo* ■ **judicial**: el poder judicial es uno de los tres poderes del Estado judicial power is one of the three powers of the State.

el **judo** ■ judo.

el **juego**
1. **game**: tiene muchísimos juegos de computadora he has many computer games
2. **set**: compré un nuevo juego de sábanas I bought a new set of sheets
➤ hacer juego to match: esa corbata te hace juego con la camisa that tie matches your shirt
➤ un juego de mesa a board game

➤ un juego de palabras a word game.

el **jueves** (plural los jueves)

En inglés, los días de la semana se escriben con mayúscula:

**Thursday**: hoy es jueves today is Thursday; el próximo jueves next Thursday; el pasado jueves last Thursday
➤ el jueves on Thursday: te veré el jueves I'll see you on Thursday
➤ los jueves on Thursdays: los jueves vamos al parque on Thursdays we go to the park.

el **juez**, la **jueza**
1. **judge**: cuando el juez entró a la sala todos se pararon when the judge came into the room everybody stood up
2. **referee**: el juez expulsó a dos jugadores en el primer tiempo the referee expelled two players in the first quarter.

el **jugador**, la **jugadora** ■ player.

**jugar** *verbo* ■ **to play**: después de la escuela, los niños juegan en el parque after school, the children play in the park; mi padre juega a la lotería desde hace años my father has been playing the lottery for years.

el **jugo** ■ juice.

el **juguete** ■ toy.

la **juguetería** ■ toy store.

el **juicio** ■ trial: Elena está en medio de un juicio para resolver su divorcio Elena is in the middle of a trial to resolve her divorce
➤ muela del juicio wisdom tooth.

**julio** *sustantivo masculino*

En inglés los nombres de los meses se escriben con mayúscula:

**July**: en julio in July; el próximo julio next July; el pasado julio last July.

la **jungla** ■ jungle.

**junio** *sustantivo masculino*

En inglés los nombres de los meses se escriben con mayúscula:

**June**: en junio in June; el próximo junio next June; el pasado junio last June.

la **junta**

1. **joint:** el motor pierde aceite por esa junta mal apretada the motor is losing oil because of that joint that's not tightened well
2. **meeting:** el presidente está en junta y no puede atenderlo ahora the president is in a meeting and cannot attend to you now.

**juntar** *verbo* ■ **to put together:** junta los pies put your feet together

**juntarse** *verbo pronominal* ■ **to get together:** nos juntamos para celebrar los 80 años del abuelo we got together to celebrate the 80th birthday of our grandfather.

**junto** *adverbio*

➤ junto a next to: como hacía frío, se sentaron junto a la chimenea since it was cold, they sat down next to the fireplace.

**junto** *adjetivo*

1. **close together:** pon los pies juntos put your feet close together
2. **together:** Cecilia y su esposo llegaron juntos a la fiesta Cecilia and her husband arrived together at the party.

el **jurado**

1. **panel:** el jurado del concurso está formado por escritores famosos the competition's panel is made up of famous writers
2. **jury** *(plural* **juries***):* el jurado concluyó que el acusado es culpable del asesinato the jury concluded that the accused is guilty of the murder.

el **juramento** ■ **oath:** los escolares prestaron juramento a la bandera the schoolchildren took the oath to the flag.

**jurar** *verbo* ■ **to swear:** es la verdad, te lo juro it's the truth, I swear it.

la **justicia** ■ **justice:** los manifestantes reclamaban justicia the demonstrators were demanding justice.

**justificar** *verbo* ■ **to justify:** no intentes justificar tu grosería don't try to justify your rudeness.

**justo** *(adverbio & adjetivo)*

■ *adverbio*

1. **right:** llegué justo antes de que el tren se fuera I arrived right before the train left

2. **just enough:** la comida dio justo para todos the food was just enough for everybody

■ *adjetivo*

1. **fair:** tomaron una decisión justa they made a fair decision
2. **tight:** esa blusa te queda demasiado justa that blouse is too tight
➤ aquí tienes 300 pesos justos here you have exactly 300 pesos.

**juvenil** *adjetivo* ■ **teen**
➤ moda juvenil teen fashion.

la **juventud** ■ **youth:** la juventud es la etapa posterior a la adolescencia youth is the stage after adolescence.

el **juzgado** ■ **court**.

**juzgar** *verbo* ■ **to judge:** no juzgues por las apariencias don't judge by appearances; lo juzgaron inocente they judged him innocent.

el **karate** ■ **karate**.

la **kermés** *(plural* las kermeses*) Mexico, Southern Cone* ■ **bazaar**.

el **kerosén** ■ *Andes, River Plate* **kerosene**.

el **kilo** ■ **kilo**.

el **kilogramo** ■ **kilogram**.

el **kilómetro** ■ **kilometer**.

el **kiosco** ■ **newsstand**.

 **la** *(sustantivo femenino & pronombre & artículo)*

■ *sustantivo femenino*
**la:** "la" es la nota anterior a "si" "la" is the note before "ti"

■ *pronombre*
1. **her:** la esperé hasta las nueve de la noche I waited for her until nine o'clock at night
2. **you:** venga por aquí señora, la llevaré a la oficina de su esposo come here madam, I'll take you to your husband's office
3. **it:** esa acuarela no está seca todavía, no la toques that watercolor is not dry yet, don't touch it

■ *artículo*
**the:** la manzana que me comí estaba jugosa the apple I ate was juicy; la profesora compró el sombrero the teacher bought the hat
➤ esta corbata y la de Roberto son iguales this tie and Robert's are the same
➤ se fracturó la pierna he broke his leg
➤ me fascina la pintura I adore painting
➤ la vida es difícil life is difficult

> Los nombres abstractos llevan artículo en español pero no en inglés.

el **laberinto** ■ **labyrinth**.

el **labio** ■ **lip**.

la **labor** *(plural* las labores*)* ■ **work:** siempre está ocupado en sus labores he's always busy with his work
➤ **ocupación:** sus labores occupation: housewife.

**laboral** *adjetivo* ■ **work:** aquí la semana laboral es de cinco días here the work week is five days.

el **laboratorio** ■ **laboratory** *(plural* laboratories*)*.

**laborioso** *adjetivo*
1. **hard-working:** Pedro es un estudiante muy laborioso Pedro is a very hard-working student
2. **difficult:** esta investigación es muy laboriosa this research is very difficult.

el **labrador,** la **labradora** ■ **farmer**.

**lácteo** *adjetivo* ■ **dairy:** los productos lácteos más comunes son la manteca y el queso the most common dairy products are butter and cheese.

**ladear** *verbo* ■ **to tilt:** la torre de Pisa se ha ladeado más y más con el paso de los años the Leaning Tower of Pisa has tilted more and more with the passing of the years.

la **ladera** ■ **hillside**.

**lado** *sustantivo masculino* ■ **side:** me dio un golpe en el lado izquierdo he hit me on the left side; suba por el ascensor del lado derecho go up in the elevator on the right side; el triángulo tiene tres lados the triangle has three sides
➤ **al lado de** beside: ven, siéntate al lado de María come, sit down beside María
➤ **de lado a lado** from one side to the other: con el terremoto, ese muro se abrió de lado a lado with the earthquake, that wall split from one side to the other
➤ **por un lado ..., por otro lado ...** on the one hand..., on the other hand...: por un lado me llevaría éste, pero por otro lado me parece demasiado caro on the one hand I would take this one, but on the other hand it seems too expensive to me
➤ **¿vamos a pasear a algún lado?** are we going to go out somewhere?

**ladrar** *verbo* ■ **to bark**.

el **ladrido** ■ **bark:** a lo lejos se oían los ladridos del perro the dog's barks were heard in the distance.

el **ladrillo** ■ **brick**.

el **ladrón**, la **ladrona**
1. *de carros* thief *(plural* **thieves***)*
2. *de casas* burglar
3. *de bancos* robber.

el **lagarto** ■ lizard.

el **lago** ■ lake.

la **lágrima** ■ tear.

la **laguna** ■ lake.

**lamentar** *verbo* ■ **to be sorry:** lamento que ustedes dos no se entiendan I'm sorry that you two don't understand each other

**lamentarse** *verbo pronominal* ■ **to complain:** perdiste el tren porque te levantaste tarde, ahora no te lamentes you missed the train because you got up late, now don't complain.

el **lamento** ■ **moan:** hay que pedir ayuda, se oyen los lamentos de alguien we have to get help, you can hear somebody's moans.

**lamer** *verbo* ■ **to lick:** la gata lame a sus crías para lavarlas the cat licks her babies to wash them.

la **lámina**
1. **sheet:** con una lámina de madera forramos la mesa we covered the table with a sheet of wood
2. **illustration:** esta enciclopedia tiene unas preciosas láminas de animales this encyclopedia has some beautiful illustrations of animals.

la **lámpara**
1. **lamp:** apaga la lámpara cuando termines de leer turn out the lamp when you finish reading
2. **bulb:** se quemó la lámpara the bulb burned out
➤ una lámpara de mesa a table lamp.

la **lana** ■ **wool:** durante la esquila se les saca la lana a las ovejas during shearing, the wool is taken off of the sheep
➤ pura lana virgen pure new wool.

la **lancha**
1. **boat:** siempre salen con su lancha a hacer esquí acuático they always take their boat out to go water skiing

2. **barge:** vimos varias lanchas auxiliando con los trabajos en el puerto we saw several barges helping with jobs at the port.

el **langostino** ■ king prawn.

el **lanzamiento** ■ **launch:** ayer fue el lanzamiento del nuevo transbordador espacial yesterday was the launch of the new space shuttle.

**lanzar** *verbo*
1. **to throw:** un jugador lanzó una bola que el bateador no pudo responder a player threw a ball that the batter couldn't hit
2. **to let out:** los niños estaban contentos y lanzaban gritos de alegría the children were happy and were letting out shouts of happiness
3. **to launch:** en marzo lanzan el nuevo disco in March they'll launch the new record.

el **lápiz** *(plural* los lápices*)* ■ **pencil:** le escribió una nota a lápiz he wrote her a note in pencil
➤ lápices de colores crayons
➤ un lápiz de labios a lipstick.

el **largo** ■ **length:** el largo de la cuadra es 100 metros the length of the block is 100 meters.

**largo** *adverbio* ■ **at great length:** hacía tiempo que no se veían y hablaron largo it had been a while since they had seen each other and they talked at great length.

**largo** *adjetivo*
1. **long:** caminaron una distancia larga para llegar al pueblo they walked a long distance to arrive at the town
2. **lengthy:** estas conferencias siempre son largas these conferences are always lengthy
➤ a lo largo de throughout: nos encontramos varias veces a lo largo de la semana we ran across each other several times throughout the week
➤ para largo a long time: la conferencia va para largo the conference is going a long time.

**las**
■ *artículo*
1. **the:** las manzanas son rojas the apples are red

**2. your:** lávate las manos wash your hands
➤ nos fuimos a dormir a las diez we went to sleep at ten o'clock
- *pronombre*
1. **them:** compró dos muñecas y se las regaló a sus sobrinas she bought two dolls and gave them to her nieces
2. **you:** ¡las esperé hasta la medianoche! I waited for you until midnight!

la **lástima** ■ **pity:** es una lástima que no hayas podido venir it's a pity that you couldn't come
➤ me da lástima que sufra tanto I feel very sorry that he suffers so much.

**lastimar** *verbo* ■ **to hurt:** ten cuidado, no lastimes a tu hermano be careful, don't hurt your brother

**lastimarse** *verbo pronominal* ■ **to hurt oneself:** se lastimó al caerse de la bicicleta he hurt himself falling off the bicycle.

la **lata**
1. **can:** tenemos varias latas de atún we have several cans of tuna
2. **tin:** hay mucha gente viviendo en casas de lata there are many people living in tin houses.

**lateral** *adjetivo* ■ **side:** el impacto abolló la parte lateral posterior derecha del auto the impact dented the back right side of the car.

el **latido** ■ **beat.**

el **látigo** ■ **whip.**

**Latinoamérica** *sustantivo femenino* ■ **Latin America.**

**latinoamericano, latinoamericana** *adjetivo*

En inglés, los adjetivos que se refieren a un país o una región se escriben con mayúscula:

**Latin American**

el **latinoamericano, la latinoamericana**

En inglés, los gentilicios se escriben con mayúscula:

**Latin American:** los latinoamericanos Latin Americans.

**latir** *verbo* ■ **to beat.**

la **latitud** ■ **latitude:** Buenos Aires está a 37 grados de latitud sur Buenos Aires is at 37 degrees latitude south.

el **laurel** ■ **laurel.**

el **lavabo**
1. **sink:** el lavabo tiene una gotera the sink has a leak
2. **restroom:** en la planta baja hay un lavabo there's a restroom on the ground floor.

el **lavadero**
1. **utility room:** el lavadero está al lado de la cocina the utility room is next to the kitchen
2. *River Plate* **Laundromat:** hay un lavadero a dos cuadras de acá there's a Laundromat two blocks from here.

la **lavadora** ■ **washing machine.**

la **lavandería** ■ **Laundromat.**

**lavar** *verbo* ■ **to wash:** ¿quién va a lavar los platos? who's going to wash the dishes?
➤ lavar a mano to wash by hand
➤ lavar en seco to dryclean

**lavarse** *verbo pronominal*
1. **to wash:** hoy tienes que lavarte el pelo today you have to wash your hair
2. **to brush:** ¿ya te lavaste los dientes? did you already brush your teeth?

el **lazo**
1. **bow:** el paquete tenía un lazo celeste the package had a blue bow
2. **lasso:** el caballo estaba atado a la cerca con un lazo the horse was tied to the fence with a lasso

los **lazos** ■ **ties:** tiene lazos muy estrechos con su familia he has very tight ties with his family.

**le** *pronombre*

1. **him, her:** le dije que me esperara, pero se fue I told him to wait for me, but he left
2. **you:** le pido que me espere aquí unos minutos I'm asking you to wait for me here for a few minutes.

**leal** *adjetivo* ■ **loyal**.

la **lección** (*plural* las lecciones)

1. **lesson:** es mejor que estudies la lección antes de ir a clase it's better for you to study the lesson before going to class
2. **lecture:** esa niña mentirosa se merece una lección that lying child deserves a lecture.

la **leche** ■ **milk**.

la **lechería** ■ **dairy** (*plural* **dairies**).

el **lecho** ■ **bed**.

la **lechuga** ■ **lettuce**.

la **lechuza** ■ **owl**.

el **lector, la lectora** ■ **reader**.

la **lectura** ■ **reading:** todos los días dedica dos horas a la lectura every day he devotes two hours to reading; en esa clase hacemos tres lecturas por semana in that class we do three readings a week.

**leer** *verbo* ■ **to read:** ¿sabes leer? do you know how to read?

**legal** *adjetivo* ■ **legal**.

**legible** *adjetivo* ■ **legible**.

**legislar** *verbo* ■ **to legislate**.

**legislativo** *adjetivo* ■ **legislative**.

**legítimo** *adjetivo* ■ **legitimate**.

la **legumbre**

1. **pulse:** las habas y las lentejas son legumbres beans and lentils are pulses
2. **vegetable:** las lechugas y las papas son legumbres lettuce and tomatoes are vegetables.

**lejano** *adjetivo* ■ **distant:** se fue a vivir a un país muy lejano she went to live in a very distant country.

**lejos** *adverbio* ■ **far:** podemos ir a pie, no es lejos de aquí we can walk, it's not far from here.

la **lengua**

1. **tongue:** el médico me pidió que le mostrara la lengua the doctor asked me to show him my tongue
2. **language:** habla tres lenguas she speaks three languages.

el **lenguado** ■ **sole**.

el **lenguaje** ■ **language**.

la **lente** ■ **lens:** los telescopios funcionan con un sistema de lentes telescopes function with a system of lenses.

la **lenteja** ■ **lentil**.

los **lentes** ■ **glasses:** mi papá usa lentes desde hace años my dad has been wearing glasses for years
➤ **lentes de contacto** contact lenses.

la **lentitud** ■ **slowness:** habla con una lentitud exasperante he speaks with an exasperating slowness.

**lento** *adjetivo* ■ **slow:** es lento y por eso perdió la carrera he's slow and that's why he lost the race.

la **leña** ■ **firewood**.

el **leñador, la leñadora** ■ **lumberjack**.

el **leño** ■ **log:** puse varios leños para avivar el fuego I put on several logs to stoke the fire.

el **león** (*plural* los leones) ■ **lion**.

la **leona** ■ **lioness**.

el **leopardo** ■ **leopard**.

**les** *pronombre*

1. **you:** ¿no me oyeron? les pedí que no hicieran ruido you didn't hear me? I asked you not to make noise
2. **them:** Juan y Ana todavía no llegaron, aunque les pedí que pasaran por aquí a las ocho Juan and Ana still haven't come, even though I asked them to come by here at eight o'clock.

la **lesión** *(plural* las lesiones*)* ■ injury: los accidentados se están recuperando de las lesiones the injured are recuperating from their injuries.

**lesionado** *adjetivo* ■ injured.

la **letra**

1. letter: la "a" es la primera letra del alfabeto "a" is the first letter of the alphabet
2. handwriting: tu letra es ilegible your handwriting is illegible.

el **letrero** ■ sign.

el **levantamiento** ■ revolt: los militares respondieron al levantamiento con violencia the military responded to the revolt with violence.

**levantar** *verbo*

1. to lift: el campeón de pesas levanta 200 kilos the weightlifting champion lifts 200 kilos
2. to pick up: por favor, levanta ese libro que se cayó please, pick up that book that fell
3. to raise: el que esté de acuerdo, que levante la mano those who agree, raise your hands

**levantarse** *verbo pronominal* ■ to get up: al oír el teléfono se levantó de un salto on hearing the telephone he got up with a jump; me levanto a las siete I get up at seven o'clock.

**leve** *adjetivo*

1. light: los pájaros son muy leves y eso les permite volar birds are very light and that allows them to fly
2. slight: tengo una lesión leve I have a slight injury.

la **ley** ■ law: todos los ciudadanos son iguales ante la ley all citizens are equal before the law
➤ la ley de la gravedad the law of gravity
➤ la ley de la oferta y la demanda the law of supply and demand.

la **leyenda** ■ legend: según la leyenda, Rómulo y Remo fundaron Roma according to the legend, Romulus and Remus founded Rome.

el/la **liberal** ■ liberal.

**liberar** *verbo* ■ to free: las autoridades liberaron al acusado the authorities freed the accused.

la **libertad** ■ freedom: tienes total libertad para tomar la decisión que te parezca mejor you have complete freedom to make the decision that seems the best to you
➤ libertad de cultos religious freedom
➤ libertad de expresión freedom of speech
➤ libertad de prensa freedom of the press.

la **libra** ■ pound: una libra equivale aproximadamente a medio quilo one pound equals approximately half a kilo
➤ libra esterlina pound sterling.

**librarse** *verbo pronominal* ■ to get out of: como está enfermo, se libró de limpiar la casa since he's sick, he got out of cleaning the house.

**libre** *adjetivo*

1. free: no aguantaba ver al pájaro en una jaula, así que lo dejé libre I couldn't stand seeing the bird in a cage, so I let it go free
2. available: hace rato que estoy aquí y no hay pasado ni un taxi libre I've been here for a while and not one available taxi has passed by
3. unoccupied: llegamos tarde y ya no había asientos libres we arrived late and there were no longer any unoccupied seats.

la **librería** ■ bookstore

⚠ The Spanish word **librería** is a false cognate, it doesn't mean "library".

el **librero** *Andes, Caribbean, Central America, Mexico* ■ bookcase.

la **libreta** ■ notebook.

el **libro** ■ book: un libro de viajes a travel book
➤ un libro de bolsillo a paperback
➤ un libro de texto a textbook.

la **licencia**

1. permission: a los 16 años le dieron licencia para llegar a medianoche at 16 years old they gave him permission to get home at midnight

**173**

**2.** **license:** para conducir automóviles precisas una licencia in order to drive automobiles you need a license

**3.** *River Plate* **leave:** tengo 20 días de licencia anual I have 20 days of yearly leave

➤ **licencia por enfermedad** sick leave.

el **licenciado, la licenciada** ■ graduate

➤ **mi hermana es licenciada en biología** my sister is a biology graduate

➤ **el licenciado González** *Mexico* Mr. Pérez.

la **licenciatura** ■ **degree:** hizo la licenciatura en la universidad de San Marcos, en Lima he got his degree at the University of San Marcos, in Lima.

**lícito** *adjetivo* ■ **lawful**.

el **licor** *(plural* los licores*)* ■ **liqueur**.

el/la **líder** ■ **leader**.

la **liebre** ■ **hare**.

la **liga**

**1.** **league:** el campeón de la liga de primavera fue el mismo que el año pasado the champion of the spring league was the same as last year's

**2.** **garter:** preciso una liga para la media I need a garter for my stocking.

**ligar** *verbo* ■ **to tie:** los vaqueros le ligaron las patas al caballo the cowboys tied the horse's feet.

**ligero** *adjetivo*

**1.** **light:** la ropa de lino es ligera linen is light

**2.** **quick:** ese caballo es muy ligero that horse is very quick.

**lila** *adjetivo* ■ **lilac**

el **lila** ■ **lilac:** el lila es mi color favorito lilac is my favorite color.

la **lima** ■ **file:** preciso una lima para arreglarme las uñas I need a file to fix my fingernails.

**limitar** *verbo* ■ **to be bounded by:** Costa Rica limita al sur con Panamá y al norte con Nicaragua Costa Rica is bounded on the south by Panama and on the north by Nicaragua

**limitarse** *verbo pronominal* ■ **to limit oneself:** no quiero engordar, por eso me limito a comer frutas y verduras I don't want to get fat, that's why I'm limiting myself to eating fruits and vegetables.

el **límite**

**1.** **boundary** (plural **boundaries**): el balón salió de los límites del campo the ball went out of the field's boundaries

**2.** **limit:** se esforzó hasta el límite para ganar he exerted himself to the limit in order to win

➤ **el límite de velocidad** the speed limit.

el **limón** *(plural* los limones*)*

**1.** *amarillo* **lemon**

**2.** *Mexico, Venezuela verde* **lime**.

la **limonada** ■ **lemonade**.

el **limonero** ■ **lemon tree**.

el **limosnero, la limosnera** ■ **beggar**.

**limpiar** *verbo*

**1.** **to clean:** tú limpia la cocina y yo limpiaré el baño you clean the kitchen and I'll clean the bathroom

**2.** **to wipe:** ¿tienes un trapo para limpiar la mesa? do you have a rag to wipe the table?

➤ **limpiar en seco** to dryclean.

la **limpieza**

**1.** **cleaning:** hoy la limpieza me llevó cuatro horas today the cleaning took me four hours

**2.** **cleanliness:** la limpieza es primordial en los hospitales cleanliness is essential in hospitals.

**limpio** *adjetivo* ■ **clean**.

**lindo** *adjetivo*

**1.** **pretty:** se compró un lindo vestido blanco para la fiesta she bought herself a pretty white dress for the party

**2.** **nice:** es una linda película, vale la pena verla it's a nice film, it's worth seeing.

la **línea** ■ **line:** la distancia más corta entre dos puntos es una línea recta the shortest distance between two points is a straight line; hay varias líneas de ómnibus para ir al centro there are several bus lines that go downtown; había leído apenas diez líneas cuando tuve que interrumpir he had scarcely read ten lines when I had to interrupt

➤ **mantener la línea** to maintain one's figure: **Mónica no come dulces porque quiere mantener la línea** Mónica doesn't eat candy because she wants to maintain her figure

➤ **una línea telefónica** a telephone line.

el **lino** ■ linen.

la **linterna** ■ lantern.

el **lío**
1. **mess:** ¡qué lío hay en esta habitación! what a mess this room is!
2. **row:** si no limpiamos esto antes de que llegué mamá, se va a armar lío if we don't clean this up before Mom arrives, there's going to be a row.

el **líquido** ■ liquid: ese líquido blanco probablemente sea leche this white liquid is probably milk.

**liso** adjetivo
1. **smooth:** la piel de los bebés es lisa y suave babies' skin is smooth and soft
2. **plain:** me gusta más esta blusa lisa que aquella floreada I like this plain blouse more than that flowered one.

la **lista** ■ list: ¿dónde está la lista de invitados? where's the invitation list?
➤ **pasar la lista** to call the roll
➤ **una lista de espera** a waiting list.

**listo** adjetivo
1. **smart:** Marcos es un niño listo, va a tener buenas calificaciones Marcos is a smart boy, he's going to have good grades
2. **ready:** cuando llegué a casa de Marisa, ya estaba lista when I arrived at Marisa's house, she was already ready.

la **literatura** ■ literature.

el **litoral** ■ coast.

el **litro** ■ liter.

**liviano** adjetivo ■ light: este paquete es liviano this package is light.

la **llaga** ■ wound.

la **llama**
1. *de fuego* flame
2. *animal* llama.

la **llamada** ■ call
➤ **una llamada internacional** international call
➤ **una llamada de larga distancia** *River Plate* a long-distance call.

**llamar** verbo
1. **to call:** la mamá de Julio lo llamaba para que entrara a comer Julio's mom was calling him to come in and eat; **mañana te llamo antes de pasar a buscarte** I'll call before coming by to get you; **su nombre es Inés, pero la llaman Ina** her name is Inés, but they call her Ina
2. **to call upon:** el presidente llamó a los ministros para pedirles su opinión the president called upon the ministers to ask them their opinions
3. **to knock:** están llamando a la puerta somebody's knocking at the door

**llamarse** verbo pronominal ■ **to be called:** ¿cómo se llama su último disco? what's his latest record called?
➤ **¿cómo te llamas?** — me llamo Luciana what's your name? — my name is Luciana.

**llamativo** adjetivo ■ flashy: tenía un vestido rojo muy llamativo she had a very flashy red dress.

**llano** adjetivo ■ flat.

la **llanta** ■ tire
➤ **una llanta de refacción** *Mexico* a spare tire.

la **llave**
1. **key:** puedes dejar la llave debajo del felpudo you can leave the key under the doormat
2. **faucet:** cierra la llave para no desperdiciar agua turn off the faucet in order to not waste water
➤ **una llave inglesa** a wrench
➤ **una llave maestra** a skeleton key.

el **llavero** ■ key ring.

**llegar** verbo
1. **to arrive:** llegué en la capital al final del día I arrived in the capital at the end of the day
2. **to reach:** llegar a un acuerdo to reach an agreement

➤ **llegar a ser** to become: **al cabo de los años, llegó a ser un gran pianista** after some years, he became a great pianist.

**llenar** *verbo* ■ **to fill**: **este cajón no cierra porque lo llenas demasiado** this box won't shut because you fill it too full

**llenarse** *verbo pronominal* ■ **to fill up**: **el estadio se llenó de aficionados** the stadium filled up with fans

➤ **no puedo comer más, ya me llené** I can't eat any more, I'm already full.

**lleno** *adjetivo* ■ **full**: **el teatro está lleno, no vamos a poder entrar** the theater is full, we're not going to be able to get in; **estas medias están llenas de agujeros** these stockings are full of holes

➤ **estar lleno** to be full: **no me sirvas más, por favor, estoy lleno** don't serve me more, please, I'm full.

**llevar** *verbo*

1. **to take:** **Elena llevó los platos a la mesa** Elena took the plates to the table
2. **to lead:** **el padre lleva de la mano al niño** the father leads the boy by the hand
3. **to wear:** **lleva un vestido azul** she's wearing a blue dress

➤ **los pacientes llevan una hora esperando al doctor** the patients have been waiting on the doctor for an hour

**llevarse** *verbo pronominal* ■ **to get along**: **los tres hermanos se llevan muy bien** the three brothers get along very well.

**llorar** *verbo* ■ **to cry**.

**llover** *verbo* ■ **to rain**: **está lloviendo a cántaros** it's raining cats and dogs.

la **lluvia** ■ **rain**.

**lo** *(pronombre & artículo)*

■ *pronombre*

1. **it:** **¿tu libro? hace días que no lo veo** your book? I haven't seen it in days
2. **him:** **¿a tu hermano? hace mucho que no lo veo** your brother? I haven't seen him in a long time
3. **you:** **venga conmigo, lo llevaré hasta la oficina de su esposa** come with me, I'll take you to your wife's office

■ *artículo*

➤ **lo bueno es que nos reconciliamos** the good thing is we made up
➤ **prefiero lo dulce** I prefer sweet things
➤ **lo que trajiste del mercado, ponelo en la heladera** put what you brought from the store in the refrigerator.

el **lobo** ■ **wolf**.

el **local** ■ **premises**: **"alquilo local comercial"** "commercial premises for rent".

la **localidad**

1. **town:** **la gente de la localidad es muy simpática** the people in town are very nice
2. **ticket:** **¡qué lástima! ya se agotaron las localidades** what a shame! the tickets are sold out.

**localizar** *verbo* ■ **to find**: **todavía no he logrado localizar los documentos que me pidió el jefe** I haven't been able to find the documents the boss asked me for.

la **loción** *(plural* **las lociones)** ■ **lotion**.

la **loca** ■ **crazy woman**.

el **loco** ■ **crazy man**.

la **locomotora** ■ **locomotive**.

la **locución** *(plural* **las locuciones)** ■ **phrase**.

la **locura** ■ **insanity**: **alegaba que la locura lo llevó a cometer el asesinato** he claimed that insanity led him to commit the murder

➤ **ser una locura** to be crazy: **lo que cobran por esos zapatos es una locura** what they charge for those shoes is crazy.

el **lodo** ■ **mud**.

**lógico** *adjetivo* ■ **logical**.

**lograr** *verbo* ■ **to achieve**: **siempre logra lo que se propone** he always achieves what he sets out to do

➤ **no logro entender este artículo en inglés** I can't seem to understand this article in English.

el **logro** ■ **achievement**: **tiene miedo de volar así que fue un logro subirla al avión** she's afraid of flying so it was quite an achievement to get her on the plane.

la **lombriz** *(plural* las lombrices) ■ earthworm.

la **loma** ■ hill.

el **lomo**
1. back: el lomo de un caballo the back of a horse
2. *carne de cerdo* loin
3. *carne de vaca* fillet
4. spine: en el lomo del libro puedes ver el título you can read the title on the spine of the book.

la **lona** ■ canvas: me compré zapatos azules de lona I bought some blue canvas shoes.

la **longitud**
1. length: la piscina tiene 50 metros de longitud the pool is 50 meters in length
2. longitude: la longitud se mide a partir del meridiano de Greenwich longitude is measured from the Greenwich meridian.

el **loro** ■ parrot.

**los** *(pronombre & articulo)*

■ *pronombre*
1. them: ¿tus zapatos rojos? no, no los vi your red shoes? no, I haven't seen them
2. you: vengan conmigo, los llevaré hasta la oficina de su papá come with me, I'll take you to your father's office

■ *articulo*
the: los melones ya están maduros the melons are ripe now

> Las partes del cuerpo llevan en español artículo pero deben traducirse al inglés con un pronombre posesivo:

lávense los pies antes de meterse en la cama wash your feet before getting into bed

> Para describir el aspecto físico de una persona se usa el artículo en español pero no en inglés:

➤ tiene los ojos castaños she has brown eyes.

la **lotería** ■ lottery.

la **loza** ■ china: lava la loza con cuidado wash the china carefully; hoy usaremos los platos de loza we'll use the china today.

la **lucha** ■ fight.

el **luchador**, la **luchadora**
1. wrestler: los luchadores se enfrentaron en el ring the wrestlers faced off in the ring
2. fighter: Martin Luther King fue un gran luchador Martin Luther King was a great fighter.

**luchar** *verbo*
1. to fight: el regimiento luchó con valentía hasta el fin the regiment fought bravely to the end
2. to struggle: los diputados lucharon por imponer sus ideas the representatives struggled to enforce their ideas.

**lucir** *verbo*
1. to look: trabaja demasiado, por eso luce cansada she works too much, that's why she looks tired
2. to wear: Ana lució con orgullo su vestido nuevo Ana wore her new dress proudly

**lucirse** *verbo pronominal* ■ to excel: Juan se lució en la presentación de fin de año Juan really excelled himself at the end-of-year show.

**luego** *adverbio*
1. then: primero arreglé el jardín y luego me senté a disfrutar del sol first I did the gardening and then sat down to enjoy the sunshine
2. later: el primer grupo irá a las tres y el segundo llegará luego the first group will go at three and the second will arrive later
➤ desde luego of course: ¿quieres venir con nosotros? — ¡desde luego! do you want to come with us? — of course!
➤ hasta luego see you later!

el **lugar**
1. place: queremos comprar una casa en algún lugar con muchos árboles we want to buy a house in a place with a lot of trees
2. seat: llegamos tarde y ya no encontramos lugares we were late and couldn't find seats
3. room: ¿hay lugar para mí en el auto? is there room for me in the car?

el **lujo** ■ luxury: viven rodeados de lujo they live in the lap of luxury

➤ **darse el lujo de algo** to be able to afford something: **no puedo darme el lujo de acompañarte en tu viaje alrededor del mundo** I can't afford to go with you on your trip around the world.

la **lumbre** ■ fire: **no pongas las salchichas directamente en la lumbre que se van a quemar** don't put the hot dogs directly on the fire, they'll burn.

**luminoso** *adjetivo*

1. **bright: la sala es el cuarto más luminoso de la casa** the living room is the brightest room in the house

2. **illuminated: los botones de mi teléfono son luminosos, puedes marcar un número en la oscuridad** the buttons on my phone are illuminated so you can dial in the dark.

la **luna** ■ moon: **una luna llena** a full moon

➤ **estar en la luna** to have your head in the clouds: **¡estás siempre en la luna! tienes que empezar a prestar más atención** you always have your head in the clouds! you need to pay more attention.

el **lunar**

1. **mole: Alicia tiene un lunar en la mejilla izquierda** Alicia has a mole on her left cheek

2. **polka-dot: ayer me compré una blusa roja a lunares** I bought a red polka-dot shirt yesterday.

el **lunes**

> En inglés, los días de la semana se escriben con mayúscula:

**Monday: hoy es lunes** today is Monday; **el próximo lunes** next Monday; **el pasado lunes** last Monday

➤ **el lunes** on Monday: **te veré el lunes** I'll see you on Monday

➤ **los lunes** on Mondays: **los lunes vamos al cine** on Mondays we go to the movies.

el **luto** ■ mourning

➤ **estar de luto** to be in mourning.

la **luz** ■ light: **por favor, apaga la luz** please turn out the light

➤ **dar a luz** to give birth: **Susana dio a luz en su casa** Susana gave birth at home.

la **maceta** ■ flowerpot.

el **macho** ■ male: **el macho es el pez de colores más vivos** the brightly colored fish is the male.

**macizo** *adjetivo* ■ solid: **le regalaron una pulsera de oro macizo** they gave her solid gold bracelet.

la **madera** ■ wood: **esa mesa es de madera maciza, por eso pesa tanto** the table is made of solid wood, that's why it's so heavy.

la **madre** ■ mother: **es madre de dos niños** she's a mother of two

➤ **madre política** mother-in-law.

la **madriguera** ■ warren.

la **madrina** ■ godmother.

la **madrugada** ■ early morning: **siempre se levanta de madrugada para tomar agua** she always gets up early in the morning to drink some water.

**madrugar** *verbo* ■ to get up early: **detesto madrugar** I hate getting up early.

la **madurez** ■ maturity: **es sorprendente la madurez de este niño** the child's maturity is surprising.

**maduro** *adjetivo*

1. **ripe: los duraznos maduros tienen un delicioso perfume** ripe peaches have a delicious scent

2. **mature: su marido es joven, pero muy maduro** her husband is young but very mature

**178**

3. **older:** su padre es un hombre maduro, pero rebosante de salud his father is older, but in very good health.

el **maestro,** la **maestra** ■ teacher.

la **magia** ■ magic: me gustaría mucho aprender a hacer magia I would love to learn how to do magic.

**mágico** adjetivo ■ magic.

el **magisterio** ■ teaching: el magisterio exige mucha paciencia con los alumnos teaching requires a lot of patience with students.

**magnético** adjetivo ■ magnetic.

**magnífico** adjetivo ■ superb.

la **magnitud** ■ magnitude.

el **mago,** la **maga** ■ magician.

el **maíz** ■ corn: desde aquí se ven los campos de maíz you can see the corn fields from here.

**mal** (adjetivo & adverbio)

■ adjetivo
**bad:** nunca entiendo cuando explica, es mal profesor I don't understand his explanations, he's a bad teacher

■ adverbio
1. **bad:** este pescado huele mal this fish smells bad
2. **badly:** mi sobrino sigue portándose mal my nephew is still behaving badly

el **mal**
1. **evil:** las fuerzas del mal the forces of evil
2. **harm:** es incapaz de hacer daño a nadie he's incapable of doing harm to anyone
3. **disease:** lamentablemente todavía existen males incurables unfortunately there are still many incurable diseases.

la **maldición** (plural las maldiciones)
■ **curse:** la maldición del hada mala fue que la princesa dormiría 100 años the evil fairy's curse was that the princess would sleep for 100 years.

**maleducado** adjetivo ■ rude: los niños de los vecinos son muy maleducados the neighbors' children are very rude.

el **malestar** ■ upset: su decisión causó malestar her decision caused upset; tanto chocolate me produjo un malestar estomacal all that chocolate gave me an upset stomach.

la **maleza** ■ undergrowth.

**malhumorado** adjetivo ■ bad-tempered: el dueño de la tienda es un viejo malhumorado the owner of the store is a bad-tempered old man.

**malo** adjetivo
1. **bad:** el pescado estaba malo, tenía un olor insoportable the fish was bad, it really stank; la película estuvo malísima the movie was really bad; es un muchacho malo, que pelea con todo el mundo he's a bad boy, always fighting with everyone
2. **mean:** no seas mala y préstame tu suéter nuevo don't be mean — let me borrow your new sweater.

**maltratar** verbo
1. **to abuse:** el niño había sido maltratado por su padre the boy had been abused by his father
2. **to mistreat:** el sobre llegó roto, sin duda lo maltrataron en el correo the envelope was torn, no doubt it was mistreated in the mail.

**malvado** adjetivo ■ wicked.

la **mamá** ■ mom.

**mamar** verbo
1. **to feed:** el bebé recién nacido mama cada tres horas the newborn feeds every three hours
2. **to suckle:** los gatitos están mamando the kittens are suckling.

el **mamífero** ■ mammal: una característica de los mamíferos es que tienen pelo a characteristic of mammals is that they have hair.

el **manantial** ■ spring.

**manar** verbo ■ to pour: el agua manaba abundantemente de la fuente the water poured freely from the fountain.

**179**

## la mancha

1. **stain:** su blusa tenía una mancha en el cuello her blouse had a stain on the collar
2. **mark:** Paloma tiene una mancha de nacimiento en la mejilla izquierda Paloma has a birthmark on her left cheek
3. **patch:** los dálmatas son perros blancos con manchas negras Dalmatians are white with black patches.

**manchar** *verbo* ■ **to stain:** cuidado, no te vayas a manchar la ropa con grasa be careful not to stain your clothes with grease.

**mandar** *verbo*

1. **to order:** el general mandó que las tropas avanzaran the general ordered the troops to advance
2. **to send:** mi hermana me mandó un paquete por correo my sister sent me a package in the mail
➤ **¿mande?** *Mexico* yes?: disculpe, señorita — ¿mande? excuse me, miss? — yes?

la **mandarina** ■ **tangerine**.

la **mandíbula** ■ **jaw**.

**manejar** *verbo*

1. **to manage:** Alberto maneja la empresa con mucha habilidad Alberto manages the business skillfully
2. **to drive:** mi hija está aprendiendo a manejar my daughter is learning to drive.

la **manera** ■ **way:** Juan tiene una manera de caminar inconfundible Juan has an unmistakeable way of walking
➤ **de ninguna manera** certainly not: ¿quieres que te ayude a preparar la cena? — de ninguna manera do you want me to help you fix dinner? — certainly not
➤ **no hay manera de…** there's no way to…: no hay manera de llegar a nuestro destino antes del anochecer there's no way we'll reach our destination before nightfall.

la **manga** ■ **sleeves:** llevaba una camisa de manga corta he wore a short-sleeved shirt.

el **mango**

1. **handle:** ¡cuidado! el mango de la cacerola está caliente careful! the pan's handle is hot

2. **mango:** cuando están maduros, los mangos son muy perfumados ripe mangoes have a lovely scent.

la **manguera** ■ **hose**.

el **maní** *(plural* los maníes*)* ■ **peanut**.

la **manía** ■ **obsession:** mi hermana tiene la manía de limpiar constantemente my sister has an obsession with cleaning all the time.

el **manicomio** ■ **mental hospital**.

la **manifestación** *(plural* las manifestaciones*)*

1. **sign:** la fiebre es una manifestación de que el cuerpo tiene alguna infección fever is a sign that the body is fighting an infection
2. **demonstration:** hoy habrá una manifestación de los maestros desocupados the unemployed teachers will be holding a demonstration today.

**manifestar** *verbo* ■ **to express:** los obreros manifestaron su acuerdo con la propuesta del Ministerio de Trabajo the workers expressed their agreement with the Labor Department's proposal

**manifestarse** *verbo pronominal*

1. **to become apparent:** las consecuencias de la inundación se manifestaron pocos días después the consequences of the flood became apparent a few days later
2. **to demonstrate:** los maestros se manifestaron contra la guerra the teachers demonstrated against the war.

la **maniobra** ■ **maneuver:** tuvo que hacer varias maniobras para estacionarse en un sitio muy pequeño it took him some maneuvers to get into a tight parking space.

**maniobrar** *verbo* ■ **to maneuver:** un tractor puede maniobrar en terrenos difíciles a tractor can maneuver on difficult terrain.

la **mano**

1. **hand:** lávate las manos wash your hands
2. **coat:** a esta pared le falta una mano de pintura this wall needs a coat of paint

➤ **a mano** by hand: **estos suéters son caros porque se hacen a mano** these sweaters are expensive because they're made by hand

➤ **dar la mano a alguien** to shake hands with someone: **en el mundo hispano, los hombres se dan la mano para saludarse** in the Hispanic world, men greet each other by shaking hands

➤ **dar una mano a alguien** to give someone a hand: **no he terminado de recoger, ¿me das una mano?** I haven't finished cleaning up — can you give me a hand?

el **manojo** ■ **bunch.**

la **mansión** (plural las mansiones) ■ **mansion.**

**manso** adjetivo
1. perro **friendly**
2. caballo **tame.**

la **manta** ■ **blanket.**

la **manteca**
1. **lard: la manteca de cerdo es muy dañina para la salud** lard is very bad for your health
2. River Plate **butter: me encanta el pan con manteca** I love bread and butter.

el **mantel** ■ **tablecloth.**

**mantener** verbo
1. **to support: cuando me case voy a seguir trabajando, no quiero que mi marido me mantenga** I'm going to keep working when I get married, I don't want my husband to have to support me
2. **to keep: con una hora de ejercicio diario se mantiene en forma** he keeps in shape with an hour of exercise a day.

la **mantequilla** ■ **butter.**

el **manto** ■ **cloak.**

**manual** adjetivo ■ **manual: la costura es una actividad manual** sewing is a manual activity

el **manual** ■ **manual: consulté el manual al instalar la computadora** I consulted the manual when I was installing the computer.

el **manubrio** ■ **handlebars.**

**manufacturar** verbo ■ **to manufacture: en el sureste de Asia se manufacturan aparatos electrónicos** electronic appliances are manufactured in Southeast Asia.

la **manzana**
1. **apple: acabo de comerme una deliciosa manzana** I just ate a delicious apple
2. **block: fuimos a dar la vuelta a la manzana** we went for a walk around the block.

la **maña** ■ **habit: tiene la maña de hablar sólo** he has the habit of talking to himself.

**mañana** adverbio ■ **tomorrow: mañana iremos a comprarte ropa** we'll go buy you some clothes tomorrow

➤ **hasta mañana** see you tomorrow

la **mañana** ■ **morning: me levanto todos los días a las siete de la mañana** I get up every day at seven in the morning.

el **mapa** ■ **map: está en el mapa** it's on the map.

**maquillarse** verbo pronominal ■ **to put on make-up.**

la **máquina** ■ **machine.**

la **maquinaria**
1. **machinery: esa fábrica cuenta con maquinaria muy moderna** that factory has very modern machinery
2. **mechanism: la maquinaria de un reloj digital es muy precisa** the mechanism in a digital watch is very precise.

el **mar** ■ **sea**
➤ **el Mar Caribe** the Caribbean Sea.

la **maravilla** ■ **wonder: el faro de Alejandría era una de las siete maravillas del mundo antiguo** the lighthouse at Alexandria was one of the seven wonders of the ancient world

➤ **es una maravilla ...** it's wonderful...: **es una maravilla ver lo rápido que se recuperó después del accidente** it's wonderful to see how quickly he recovered after the accident.

**maravilloso** adjetivo ■ **wonderful.**

la **marca**

1. **mark:** hay varias marcas en la pared, ¿de qué serán? there are several marks on the wall — I wonder what they're from
2. **make:** en cuanto a autos, prefiero las marcas japonesas I prefer Japanese makes when it comes to cars
3. **brand:** ¿qué marca de detergente usas? what brand of detergent do you use?

el **marcador** ■ marker: había dibujado con marcador en la pared she had drawn on the wall in marker.

**marcar** *verbo*

1. **to mark:** marqué todos mis útiles escolares para reconocerlos I marked all my school supplies so I can tell them apart
2. **to dial:** ¿cuál es el número de teléfono que hay que marcar? which phone number do I need to dial?
3. **to score:** mi equipo marcó tres goles my team scored three goals.

la **marcha**

1. **course:** la marcha de los acontecimientos fue inesperada the course of events was unexpected
2. **march:** organizaron una marcha en defensa de la educación pública they organized a march in defense of public education
3. **speed:** aceleraron la marcha porque ya se había hecho tarde they picked up speed because they were running late
➤ **en marcha** running: no puedes bajarte una vez que el tren esté en marcha you can't get off once the train is running
➤ **marcha atrás** reverse.

**marcharse** *verbo pronominal* ■ **to leave:** se marchó del pueblo hace un año he left town a year ago.

**marchitarse** *verbo pronominal* ■ **to wilt:** se marchitaron las flores del jarrón the flowers in the vase wilted.

el **marco**

1. **frame:** el marco de la puerta es de madera the door frame is made of wood
2. **framework:** su comportamiento es inadmisible en un marco legal her behavior is unacceptable in a legal framework.

la **marea** ■ **tide:** la marea está subiendo the tide is rising
➤ **marea alta** high tide
➤ **marea baja** low tide
➤ **marea negra** oil slick.

**marearse** *verbo pronominal* ■ **to get motion sickness:** se marea en los aviones he gets motion sickness on airplanes.

la **margarina** ■ margarine.

el **margen** (plural los márgenes) ■ **margin:** la maestra puso algunos comentarios en el margen the teacher wrote some comments in the margin; nuestro equipo ganó por un amplio margen our team won by a wide margin
➤ **al margen** on the fringes of: se mantuvo al margen de la discusión he stayed on the fringes of the discussion.

el **mariachi** ■ mariachi band

MARIACHI

Mexican mariachi bands may contain from six to eight violinists, two trumpeters, and a guitarist. They are usually hired to serenade someone on special occasions, such as a birthday, an engagement, or Mother's Day. As well as providing the music for songs, mariachi music is a popular form of dance music. Band members wear the typical **charro** outfit: short black jacket, tight pants, and wide-brimmed **sombrero** hat, all with silver trim.

el **marido** ■ husband.

la **marina** ■ navy: entró en la marina el año pasado he joined the navy last year.

el **marinero** ■ sailor.

el **marino** ■ sailor.

la **mariposa** ■ butterfly.

**marítimo** *adjetivo* ■ maritime.

el **mármol** ■ marble.

**marrón** (plural marrones) *adjetivo*
■ **brown:** compré una cartera marrón I bought a brown wallet.

el **martes** ■ **Tuesday:** hoy es martes today is Tuesday; el próximo martes next Tuesday; el pasado martes last Tuesday

➤ el martes **on Tuesday:** te veré el martes I'll see you on Tuesday

➤ los martes **on Tuesdays:** los martes vamos al parque on Tuesdays we go to the park

> En inglés, los días de la semana se escriben con mayúscula.

el **martillo** ■ **hammer.**

**marzo** *sustantivo masculino*

> En inglés los nombres de los meses se escriben con mayúscula:

**March:** en marzo in March; el próximo marzo next March; el pasado marzo last March.

**más** *adverbio*

1. **more:** tiene más juguetes que yo he has more toys than I do; no tengo nada más que decirle I have nothing more to say to him

2. **after:** son más de las tres it's after three

3. **better:** me gusta más nadar que correr I don't like anything better than running

➤ es el edificio más alto de la ciudad it's the tallest building in the city

➤ de más **too much:** pagué 100 pesos de más I paid 100 pesos too much

➤ más bien **rather:** no fue un accidente, más bien lo hizo a propósito it wasn't an accident, rather he did it on purpose

➤ por más que **however much:** por más que intento, no puedo con estos ejercicios however much I try I just can't do these problems.

la **masa**

1. **dough:** esta masa está cruda the dough is raw

2. **mass:** una masa enfurecida tomó las calles a crazed mass of people took to the streets

3. *River Plate* **pastry:** comimos unas masas a la hora del té we ate some pastries at tea time.

el **masaje** ■ **massage:** Pedro le dio un masaje a Adela en la espalda Pedro gave Adela a back massage.

**mascar** *verbo* ■ **to chew.**

la **máscara** ■ **mask.**

la **mascota**

1. **pet:** no se permiten mascotas en este apartamento pets aren't allowed in this apartment

2. **mascot:** la mascota del equipo es un oso the team's mascot is a bear.

**masculino** *adjetivo*

1. **male:** la población masculina ha aumentado en esta ciudad the city's male population has increased

2. **men's:** forma parte del equipo masculino de fútbol he's on the men's soccer team

3. **masculine:** Daniela se viste de manera masculina Daniela dresses in a masculine way.

**masticar** *verbo* ■ **to chew:** es aconsejable masticar bien la comida you should chew your food well.

el **mástil** ■ **mast.**

**matar** *verbo* ■ **to kill:** mataron a personas inocentes they killed innocent people; me mata tener que madrugar it kills me having to get up so early.

**mate** *adjetivo* ■ **matte:** imprimí las fotos en papel mate I printed the pictures on matte paper

el **mate** ■ **maté:** tomamos mate todas las mañanas we drink maté every morning.

las **matemáticas** ■ **mathematics.**

la **materia**

1. **matter:** estudia la transformación de la materia he's studying the transformation of matter

2. **subject:** la materia que más me gusta es química my favorite subject is chemistry

➤ materia gris gray matter

➤ materia prima raw material.

el **material**

1. **material:** trajeron los materiales para construir la casa they brought all the materials for building the house

2. **subject matter:** el material que contiene esta revista es muy interesante the subject matter in this magazine is very interesting.

**maternal** *adjetivo* ■ **maternal:** tiene fuertes sentimientos maternales she has strong maternal instincts.

la **maternidad**
1. **motherhood:** la maternidad es su verdadera vocación motherhood is her true calling
2. **maternity ward:** llegó a la maternidad de madrugada she arrived in the maternity ward at dawn.

**materno** *adjetivo* ■ **maternal:** mi abuelo materno era arquitecto my maternal grandfather was an architect.

el **matiz** (*plural* los matices) ■ **shade:** pintó la habitación con distintos matices de amarillo she painted the room in different shades of yellow.

el **matrimonio**
1. **marriage:** éste es su segundo matrimonio it's his second marriage
2. **couple:** salimos con un matrimonio de ingenieros we went out with a couple who are both engineers
➤ un matrimonio civil a civil wedding
➤ un matrimonio religioso a church wedding.

**matutino** *adjetivo* ■ **morning:** trabajo en horario matutino I work the morning shift.

**máximo** *adjetivo*
1. **maximum:** hay un plazo máximo de tres meses the maximum period is three months
2. **highest:** es el máximo goleador del campeonato he was the highest scorer in the championships.

**mayo** *sustantivo masculino*

En inglés los nombres de los meses se escriben con mayúscula:

**May:** en mayo in May; el próximo mayo next May; el pasado mayo last May.

**mayor** *adjetivo* (*comparative and superlative of* **grande**)
1. **bigger:** la casa nueva tiene un tamaño mayor que la vieja the new house is bigger than the old one

2. **older:** mi hermano mayor es soltero my older brother is single
3. **elderly:** mi abuelo ya es una persona mayor my grandfather is an elderly man
4. **greatest:** es uno de los mayores músicos de su época he's one of the greatest musicians of his era

el/la **mayor**
1. **adult:** es una película para mayores the movie is only for adults
2. **eldest:** es el mayor de todos los hermanos he's the eldest of the brothers; la mayor de las hermanas es ingeniera the eldest of the sisters is an engineer
➤ de mayor when he grows up: de mayor quiere ser doctor she wants to be a doctor when she grows up
➤ ser mayor de edad to be of age: Francisco ya puede votar porque es mayor de edad Francisco can vote because he's of age.

el **mayoreo** ■ **wholesale**
➤ al mayoreo wholesale: aquí venden productos al mayoreo they sell wholesale products here.

la **mayoría** ■ **majority:** la mayoría de los alumnos aprobó el curso the majority of the students passed the course; el partido de derecha obtuvo la mayoría en el parlamento the right-wing party obtained a majority in congress.

**mayúscula** *adjetivo* ■ **capital:** no olvides escribir los nombres propios con letra mayúscula don't forget to write proper nouns with a capital letter

la **mayúscula** ■ **capital:** los nombres propios se escriben con mayúscula proper nouns are written with a capital.

**me** *pronombre* ■ **me:** préstame tu libro lend me your book
➤ me voy a lavar las manos I'm going to wash my hands
➤ me peiné rápidamente I combed my hair quickly
➤ a mí me gusta mucho cantar I really like to sing
➤ me dormí una buena siesta I took a good nap.

la **mecánica** ■ **mechanics:** estudió mecánica he studied mechanics.

el **mecánico** ■ mechanic.

la **medalla**

1. **medallion:** le regalaron una medalla de la Virgen María she was given a medallion of the Virgin Mary
2. **medal:** lo premiaron con una medalla he was rewarded with a medal
➤ **medalla de bronce** bronze medal
➤ **medalla de oro** gold medal
➤ **medalla de plata** silver medal.

la **media**

1. **average:** tienes que calcular la media entre estos números you have to figure out the average of these numbers
2. **pantyhose:** uso medias hasta la cintura I wear pantyhose
3. **sock:** compré tres pares de medias I bought three pairs of socks.

**mediano** adjetivo

1. **medium:** esta caja es de tamaño mediano this is a medium-sized box
2. **average:** es una persona de mediana inteligencia he is a person of average intelligence.

la **medianoche** ■ midnight: llegaron a la medianoche they arrived at midnight.

**mediante** adverbio ■ **by means of:** lograron curar la enfermedad mediante tecnología innovadora they managed to cure the disease by means of a technological innovation.

el **medicamento** ■ medicine.

la **medicina** ■ medicine: estudia medicina she's studying medicine; le recetaron una nueva medicina he was prescribed a new medicine.

**medicinal** adjetivo ■ **medicinal:** esta planta tiene propiedades medicinales this plant has medicinal properties.

el **médico, la médica** ■ doctor.

la **medida**

1. **measurement:** el sastre le tomó las medidas al cliente the tailor took his client's measurements
2. **measure:** la policía tomó estrictas medidas de seguridad the police took strict security measures

➤ **a la medida** custom-made: se mandó hacer un traje a la medida he ordered a custom-made suit
➤ **a medida que** as: a medida que pasaba el tiempo se ponía más guapo he grew more handsome as time went by.

el **medidor** ■ **meter:** el empleado de la electricidad revisó el medidor the man from the electric company checked the meter.

**medio**

■ adjetivo
1. **half:** se tomaron media botella de vino they drank half a bottle of wine
2. **average:** la temperatura media es 25 grados centígrados the average temperature is 25 degrees Celsius
➤ **son las cuatro y media** it's four thirty
■ adverbio
**half:** la niña estaba medio dormida cuando llegamos the little girl was half asleep when we arrived

el **medio** ■ **middle:** hay un monumento en el medio de la plaza there is a monument in the middle of the square
➤ **en medio** between: me senté en medio de mis dos amigas I sat between my two friends
➤ **el medio ambiente** the environment
➤ **los medios de comunicación** the media
➤ **un medio de transporte** a means of transportation.

el **mediodía**

1. **noon:** al mediodía nuestras sombras son pequeñas our shadows are very small at noon
2. **lunchtime:** el cumpleaños comenzó al mediodía the birthday party started at lunchtime

MEDIODÍA

In some Spanish-speaking countries **mediodía** means 12 o'clock noon, while in others it refers to "lunchtime," which can take place anywhere between noon and three o'clock in the afternoon. To avoid confusion, make sure you know what time a person means when you agree to meet them at **mediodía**.

**185**

**medir** *verbo* ■ to measure: medí el tamaño de la cocina I measured the kitchen; la mesa mide más de un metro the table is more than a meter across.

**meditar** *verbo*
1. to meditate: le gusta meditar todas las mañanas he likes to meditate in the morning
2. to think: meditó antes de responder she thought before answering.

la **mejilla** ■ cheek.

**mejor** *(adjetivo & adverbio)*
■ *adjetivo*
*(comparative and superlative of* **bueno***)*
1. better: tiene un auto mejor que el mío she has a better car than I do
2. best: Susana es mi mejor amiga Susana is my best friend
■ *adverbio*
better: Ricardo juega al fútbol mejor que yo Ricardo is better at soccer than I am

el/la **mejor** ■ best: es la mejor de la clase she's the best in the class.

**mejorar** *verbo*
1. to improve: el tiempo mejoró the weather improved
2. to get better: Juan ya se mejoró y hoy vuelve al trabajo Juan has gotten better and is going back to work today.

el **mellizo**, la **melliza** ■ twin.

la **melodía** ■ melody.

la **membrana** ■ membrane.

la **membresía** *Mexico* ■ membership: la membresía de este club es muy cara membership of this club is very expensive.

la **memoria** ■ memory: Augusto tiene una memoria increíble Augusto has an incredible memory; quiero ampliar la memoria de mi computadora I want to expand my computer's memory
➤ saber de memoria to know by heart: sabe de memoria las tablas de multiplicar she knows the multiplication tables by heart.

**memorizar** *verbo* ■ to memorize: memorizó un largo poema he memorized a long poem.

**mencionar** *verbo* ■ to mention: mencionó que iba a llegar tarde she mentioned she would be late.

el **mendigo**, la **mendiga** ■ beggar.

**menear** *verbo* ■ to wag: el perro meneaba la cola the dog was wagging his tail.

**menor** *adjetivo* ■ younger: soy menor de lo que parezco I'm younger than I look
➤ Raúl es el hijo menor de mis tíos Raúl is my aunt and uncle's youngest son
➤ se irrita frente al menor problema she gets upset at the slightest problem
➤ no tengo la menor idea I don't have the slightest clue

el/la **menor** ■ youngest: el menor de los dos hermanos es ingeniero the youngest of the two brothers is an engineer; es la menor de la clase she's the youngest in the class
➤ está prohibida la venta de cigarrillos a menores the sale of cigarettes to minors is against the law
➤ menor de edad minor.

**menos**
■ *adverbio*
1. minus: diez menos cinco es cinco ten minus five is five
2. less: demoré menos de lo que esperaba it took me less time than I thought it would; había menos gente que en la primera función there were less people than at the first show; ¡comé menos, por favor! eat less, please!; es la persona de la oficina que menos trabaja he's the person in the office that does the least work; es la clase con menos alumnos it's the class with the least number of students
➤ al menos at least: había al menos mil personas there were at least 1000 people
➤ de menos too little: me dieron 20 pesos de menos they gave me 20 pesos too little
➤ menos mal just as well: menos mal que dejó de llover just as well it stopped raining
➤ por lo menos at least: pesa por lo menos 80 kilos he weighs at least 80 kilos
■ *preposición*
except: fuimos todos menos Ricardo we all went except for Ricardo

**186**

➤ **son las once menos cinco** it's five to eleven.

el **mensaje** ■ message: **dejé el mensaje en el contestador** I left a message on the answering machine.

el **mensajero**, la **mensajera** ■ messenger: **trabaja de mensajero en una oficina** he works as a messenger in an office.

**menso** *Mexico adjetivo* ■ stupid: **Álvaro es tan menso que me cansa** Álvaro is so stupid it's annoying.

**mensual** *adjetivo* ■ monthly: **es una revista mensual** it's a monthly magazine.

**mental** *adjetivo* ■ mental: **tiene problemas mentales** he has mental problems.

la **mente** ■ mind: **Lucía tiene una mente brillante** Lucía has a brilliant mind
➤ **quedarse la mente en blanco** to go blank: **se me quedó la mente en blanco en medio del examen** my mind went blank in the middle of the test
➤ **tener en mente** to have in mind: **tengo en mente la persona ideal para el trabajo** I have the perfect person in mind for the job.

**mentir** *verbo* ■ to lie: **no me mientas más** don't lie to me anymore.

la **mentira** ■ lie: **lo castigaron por decir mentiras** he was punished for telling lies.

**mentiroso** *adjetivo* ■ **es la persona más mentirosa que conozco** she's the biggest liar I know

el **mentiroso**, la **mentirosa** ■ liar: **detesto a los mentirosos** I hate liars.

el **menú** ■ menu.

**menudeo** *Latin America sustantivo masculino* ■ retail
➤ **al menudeo** retail: **esta tienda vende al menudeo** this is a retail store.

**menudo** *adjetivo* ■ small: **pica la cebolla muy menudita** chop the onion very small
➤ **a menudo** often: **a menudo acompaño a mi abuela a misa** I often go to mass with my grandmother.

el **mercado** ■ market: **hicimos las compras en el mercado** we did our shopping in the market
➤ **el mercado negro** the black market
➤ **el mercado de valores** the stock market.

la **mercancía** ■ goods: **nos vendieron mercancía dañada** they sold us damaged goods.

**merecerse** *verbo pronominal* ■ to deserve: **se merece unas buenas vacaciones** he deserves a good vacation.

**merendar** *verbo* ■ to have an afternoon snack: **merendamos en casa de unos amigos** we had an afternoon snack at our friends' house.

el **meridiano** ■ meridian.

la **merienda** ■ afternoon snack: **tomamos la merienda en casa de unos amigos** we had an afternoon snack at our friends' house.

el **mérito** ■ merit.

el **mes** ■ month: **el mes que más me gusta es diciembre** my favorite month is December; **pagamos un mes por adelantado** we paid a month in advance
➤ **estar de tres meses** to be three months pregnant: **María recién está de tres meses** María is barely three months pregnant.

la **mesa** ■ table: **compré una mesa nueva para el comedor** I bought a new table for the dining room
➤ **poner la mesa** to set the table: **puso la mesa antes de que llegaran los invitados** she set the table before the guests arrived
➤ **¡a la mesa!** dinner is ready!
➤ **la mesa de noche** the nightstand.

la **mesada**
1. allowance: **le dan una buena mesada** he gets a good allowance
2. *River Plate* countertop: **cambiamos la mesada de la cocina** we changed the kitchen countertops.

la **mesera** *Central America, Colombia, Mexico* ■ waitress.

el **mesero** *Central America, Colombia, Mexico* ■ waiter.

la **meseta** ■ plateau.

la **mesonera** *Chile, Venezuela* ■ waitress.

el **mesonero** *Chile, Venezuela* ■ waiter.

**mestizo** *adjetivo* ■ of mixed race: es una persona de origen mestizo he is a person of mixed race

el **mestizo**, la **mestiza** ■ person of mixed race: tradicionalmente los mestizos eran discriminados en la sociedad traditionally, people of mixed race have been discriminated against by society.

la **meta**
1. goal: su meta es hacer mucho dinero his goal is to make a lot of money; metió la pelota en la meta he put the ball in the goal
2. finish line: el deportista colombiano fue el primero en cruzar la meta the Colombian athlete was the first to cross the finish line.

el **metal** ■ metal: el oro es un metal noble gold is a precious metal.

la **metalurgia** ■ metallurgy.

**meter** *verbo*
1. to put: metió toda su ropa en una valija he put all his clothes in a suitcase; metieron al niño en una escuela privada they put the boy in a private school
2. to butt in: no te metas en mi vida don't butt into my life
3. to score: metió el gol ganador she scored the winning goal

**meterse** *verbo pronominal*
1. to go: se metió en el cuarto equivocado she went into the wrong room
2. to go in: no se metan en el agua después de comer don't go in the water after eating
➤ meterse con to pick on: se metieron con Luis en el recreo they picked on Luis at recess.

el **método** ■ method: inventaron un nuevo método de enseñanza de lenguas they invented a new method for teaching languages.

**métrico** *adjetivo* ■ metric: el sistema métrico se usa en la mayor parte del mundo the metric system is used in most places around the world.

el **metro**
1. meter: José mide casi dos metros José is nearly two meters tall
2. subway: tomamos el metro para ir al centro de la ciudad we took the subway into the city
➤ un metro cuadrado a square meter.

**México** *sustantivo masculino* ■ Mexico.

**mexicano** *adjetivo*

En inglés, los adjetivos que se refieren a un continente o a un país se escriben con mayúscula:

Mexican: me interesa mucho la cultura mexicana I'm very interested in Mexican culture

el **mexicano**, la **mexicana**

En inglés los gentilicios se escriben con mayúscula:

Mexican: los mexicanos the Mexicans.

la **mezcla** ■ mix: preparamos una mezcla de aceite y vinagre we made a mix of oil and vinegar.

**mezclar** *verbo* ■ to mix: mezcló los ingredientes en un bol she mixed the ingredients in a bowl
➤ no se mezcló con la gente del lugar he didn't mix with the locals.

**mi** *adjetivo* ■ my: mi casa queda en la playa my house is on the beach.

**mí** *pronombre* ■ me: el regalo es para mí the present is for me
➤ me gusta reflexionar sobre mí misma I like to think about myself.

el **micro** *Argentina, Bolivia, Chile* ■ bus: fuimos en micro al centro de la ciudad we went into the city on the bus.

el **microbio** ■ microbe.

el **micrófono** ■ microphone.

el **miedo** ■ fear: está paralizado por el miedo he's paralyzed by fear
➤ **dar miedo algo a alguien** to scare someone: **me da miedo volar** I'm scared of flying
➤ **tener miedo** to be afraid: **tiene miedo a los perros** he's afraid of dogs.

la **miel** ■ honey.

el **miembro**
1. limb: los miembros inferiores del ser humano son las piernas the legs are a human being's lower limbs
2. member: es miembro de un club deportivo he's a member of a sports club.

**mientras** adverbio ■ while: empezó a llover mientras caminaba it started to rain while she was walking; conserva tu trabajo mientras puedas keep your job while you can
➤ mientras me pondré a estudiar I'll study in the meantime
➤ no vayas mientras no te inviten don't go if you haven't been invited.

el **miércoles** (plural los miércoles)

En inglés, los días de la semana se escriben con mayúscula:

Wednesday: hoy es miércoles today is Wednesday; el próximo miércoles next Wednesday; el pasado miércoles last Wednesday
➤ el miércoles on Wednesday: te veré el miércoles I'll see you on Wednesday
➤ los miércoles on Wednesdays: los miércoles vamos al parque on Wednesdays we go to the park.

la **migración** (plural las migraciones) ■ migration.

**mil** adjetivo ■ thousand: esta camisa cuesta más de mil pesos this shirt costs over a thousand pesos; acudieron miles de personas thousands of people came.

el **milagro** ■ miracle: es un milagro que sobreviviera al accidente it's a miracle she survived the accident
➤ de milagro miraculously: se salvó de milagro she miraculously survived.

la **milanesa** ■ breaded cutlet: preparamos milanesas con papas fritas we made breaded cutlets and french fries.

**militar** adjetivo ■ military: ingresó a la escuela militar he enrolled in military school
el **militar** ■ soldier: mi abuelo era militar my grandfather was a soldier
➤ los militares tomaron el poder the military took power.

el **millón** (plural los millones) ■ million: gastó millones en la reforma de la casa he spent millions on alterations to the house; tengo un millón de problemas I have a million problems.

**mimar** verbo ■ to spoil: todos miman a la pequeña they all spoil the baby girl.

el **mimbre** ■ wicker: compré un canasto de mimbre I bought a wicker basket.

la **mímica** ■ mime.

la **mina**
1. mine: la mina está abandonada the mine is abandoned
2. lead: se me rompió la mina del lápiz the pencil's lead broke.

el **mineral** ■ mineral.

la **minería** ■ mining.

el **minero** ■ miner: los mineros trabajan en condiciones inhumanas miners work in very harsh conditions.

**mínimo** adjetivo
1. minimum: paga la tarifa mínima he pays the minimum fare
2. minute: la distancia entre las dos ciudades era mínima the distance between the two cities was minute
el **mínimo** ■ minimum: quieren reducir los gastos al mínimo they want to cut costs to the minimum.

el **ministerio** ■ department
➤ Ministerio de Defensa Defense Department
➤ Ministerio de Economía Treasury Department
➤ Ministerio de Hacienda Treasury Department.

el **ministro, la ministra**

1. **secretary:** el ministro de Economía se reunió con los empresarios the Treasury Secretary met with the businessmen
2. **minister:** la ministra habló en la ceremonia religiosa the minister spoke at the religious ceremony.

la **minoría** ■ **minority:** una minoría de la población es analfabeta a minority of the population is illiterate; la minoría presentó un proyecto de reforma en el Parlamento the minority presented a reform plan to the congress.

el **minuto** ■ **minute:** espera un minuto, por favor wait a minute, please.

**mío** adjetivo & pronombre ■ **mine:** ese perro es mío that dog is mine; su casa es muy linda pero la mía es más grande her house is very nice, but mine is bigger.

**mirar** verbo

1. **to look:** miraba por la ventana she was looking out the window; mira si tienes dinero suficiente look and see if you have enough money
2. **to check:** me miraron las valijas en la aduana they checked my bags at customs
3. **to peek:** miraron por un agujero they peeked through a hole
4. **to watch out:** ¡mira lo que haces! watch what you're doing!
➤ el jefe miraba cómo trabajaban los empleados the boss watched his employees work
➤ mirar hacia adelante to look in front of you: mira hacia adelante cuando caminas look in front of you when you're walking
➤ mirar hacia arriba to look up: el niño miró hacia arriba en busca de su globo the boy looked up in search of his balloon

**mirarse** verbo pronominal

1. **to look at yourself:** se miró en el espejo del cuarto she looked at herself in the room's mirror
2. **to look at each other:** se miraron con complicidad they looked at each other complicitly.

la **misa** ■ **mass**.

**miserable** adjetivo

1. **stingy:** es la persona más miserable que conozco she's the stingiest person I know
2. **miserable:** vivía en un cuarto miserable he lived in a miserable little room.

la **miseria**

1. **poverty:** vivían en la absoluta miseria they lived in absolute poverty
2. **pittance:** gana una miseria she earns a pittance.

la **misericordia** ■ **mercy**.

la **misión** (plural las misiones) ■ **mission:** el embajador tuvo la misión de continuar el proceso de paz the ambassador's mission was to further the peace process.

**mismo** (adjetivo, pronombre & adverbio)

■ adjetivo
1. **same:** estoy usando la misma camisa que ayer I'm wearing the same shirt I wore yesterday
2. **myself:** yo misma lo vi I saw him myself
3. **exact:** repetí sus mismas palabras I repeated her exact words
■ pronombre
**same:** María ya no es la misma de antes Mariá just isn't the same anymore
➤ terminé el trabajo e hice una copia del mismo I finished the assignment and made a copy of it
■ adverbio
**right:** estacionó delante mismo de mi casa he parked right in front of my house; ahora mismo vuelvo I'll be right back.

el **misterio** ■ **mystery**.

la **mitad** ■ **half:** comimos la mitad del postre we ate half the dessert
➤ a mitad de in the middle of: la carnicería queda a mitad de cuadra the butcher shop is in the middle of the block.

**mixto** adjetivo

1. **mixed:** comí una ensalada mixta I ate a mixed salad
2. **coed:** es una escuela mixta it's a coed school.

la **mochila** ■ **backpack**.

el **moco** ■ **mucus**
➤ limpiate los mocos wipe your nose
➤ tener mocos to have a runny nose.

**el** | mocoso, la mocosa | *Mexico informal*
■ **kid:** los mocosos del barrio rompieron la ventana some neighborhood kids broke the window.

**la** | moda | ■ **fashion:** el mundo de la moda the fashion world

➤ **estar a la moda** to be fashionable: **siempre quiere estar a la moda** she always wants to be fashionable

➤ **ponerse de moda** to come into fashion: **el tango se puso de moda** the tango came into fashion.

**los** | modales | ■ **manners:** tiene muy buenos modales he has very nice manners.

| moderno | *adjetivo* ■ **modern:** vivimos en una casa moderna we live in a modern house.

| modesto | *adjetivo* ■ **modest:** es un hombre modesto que no presume de sí mismo he's a modest man who doesn't show off; **compramos un apartamento modesto** we bought a modest apartment.

| modificar | *verbo*
1. **to alter:** modificamos el frente de la casa we altered the house's façade
2. **to modify:** los adjetivos modifican a los sustantivos adjectives modify nouns.

**el** | modo |
1. **way:** tiene un modo especial de caminar he has a special way of walking
2. **manners:** la empleada de la tienda tiene muy malos modos the salesclerk has very bad manners
3. **mood:** estuvimos practicando el modo subjuntivo en clase de español we practiced the subjunctive mood in Spanish class
➤ **de modo que** so that: **explicó la situación de modo que todos la entendiéramos** he explained the situation so that we would all understand it
➤ **de todos modos** anyway: **de todos modos, tu comportamiento me parece lamentable** anyway, your behavior is deplorable.

| mojar | *verbo*
1. **to wet:** mojé el suelo de la cocina I wetted the kitchen floor
2. **to dunk:** el niño mojó el pan en la sopa the boy dunked his bread in his soup

| mojarse | *verbo pronominal* ■ **to get wet:** nos mojamos con la lluvia we got wet in the rain.

**el** | molcajete | *Mexico* ■ **mortar:** preparó una salsa picante en el molcajete she made a spicy sauce in a mortar.

**el** | molde | ■ **cake pan:** hice la torta en un molde redondo I made the cake in a round cake pan.

| moler | *verbo*
1. **to grind:** molió el grano del café he ground the coffee beans
2. *Mexico informal* **to pester:** este niño malcriado está moliendo a toda la familia that rude child is pestering the whole family.

| molestar | *verbo*
1. **to annoy:** me molesta la impuntualidad de la gente people who aren't punctual annoy me
2. **to bother:** no molesten a Juan mientras está trabajando don't bother Juan while he's working; **¿molesto si fumo?** will it bother you if I smoke?
3. **to hurt:** le molestan los zapatos nuevos his new shoes are hurting him

> The Spanish word **molestar** is a false cognate, it does not mean "to molest".

| molestarse | *verbo pronominal* ■ **to get upset:** Daniela se molestó con Gabriela por lo que le dijo Daniela got upset with Gabriela because of what she said.

**la** | molestia |
1. **hassle:** es una molestia tener invitados en casa having houseguests is a hassle
2. **pain:** siento algunas molestias en la pierna I have some pains in my leg
➤ **no ser ninguna molestia** to be no trouble at all: **no es ninguna molestia prestarte dinero** it's no trouble at all to lend you some money
➤ **tomarse la molestia** to take the trouble: **se tomó la molestia de pasar a visitarme** he took the trouble to stop by and visit me.

| molesto | *adjetivo*
1. **annoying:** es una visita molesta que ya lleva 15 días en casa he's an annoying houseguest who's already been here for two weeks

**2. uncomfortable:** el paciente se siente molesto porque el dolor no cede the patient is uncomfortable because the pain hasn't receded.

el **molino** ■ mill.

**momentáneo** *adjetivo* ■ **momentary:** fue un dolor momentáneo it was just a momentary pain.

el **momento**

**1. moment:** en el momento en que yo salía, ella entraba she walked in the moment I left; fueron momentos de mucha angustia they were very anguished moments

**2. minute:** estaré lista en un momento I'll be ready in just a minute

**3. opportunity:** aproveché el momento para escaparme de la fiesta I took the opportunity to escape from the party

➤ **de momento** for the moment: de momento no necesito nada más for the moment I don't need anything else

➤ **de un momento a otro** any minute now: van a llegar de un momento a otro they'll be here any minute now.

la **monarquía** ■ monarchy.

la **moneda**

**1. coin:** necesito cambio en monedas I need some change in coins

**2. currency:** la moneda de Argentina es el peso the currency of Argentina is the peso.

el **mono, la mona** ■ monkey

el **mono** ■ coveralls: los mecánicos usan un mono azul the mechanics wear blue coveralls.

el **monobloque** *Argentina* ■ apartment building: vive en un monobloque en el centro de la ciudad they live in an apartment building in the middle of the city.

la **monotonía** ■ monotony.

**monótono** *adjetivo* ■ **monotonous:** tengo un trabajo muy monótono I have a very monotonous job.

el **monstruo** ■ monster.

la **montaña** ■ mountain.

**montar** *verbo*

**1. to ride:** montar en bicicleta to ride a bicycle; montamos a caballo durante las vacaciones we went horseback riding during our vacation

**2. to set up:** montó una exposición de arte moderno he set up a modern art exhibition.

el **monte**

**1. mountain:** los montes de la zona son de poca altura the mountains around here aren't very high

**2. scrubland:** el bandido se escondió en el monte the bandit hid in the scrubland.

el **montón** *(plural* los montones)

**1. stack:** en ese montón de fotos debe estar la que busco the picture I'm looking for must be in that stack

**2. load:** había montones de gente en el concierto there were loads of people at the concert

➤ **ser del montón** to be average: es un libro del montón it's just an average book.

el **monumento** ■ monument: levantaron un monumento en honor al poeta they built a monument honoring the poet.

el **moño**

**1. bun:** se peinó con un moño she put her hair in a bun

**2. bow:** ató el paquete con un moño she tied the package with a bow.

**morado** *adjetivo* ■ **purple:** compré una colcha morada I bought a purple bedspread.

la **moral**

**1. moral doctrine:** da clases de religión y moral she teaches religion and moral doctrine

**2. morals:** es una persona de dudosa moral he's a person of questionable morals

**3. morale:** no hay que dejar que decaiga la moral del grupo we have to keep up the group's morale.

**morder** *verbo* ■ **to bite:** el cachorro me mordió el tobillo the puppy bit me on the ankle; me mordí la lengua I bit my tongue.

la **mordida**

**1. bite:** todavía tengo la cicatriz de la mordida del perro I still have a scar from the dog bite

**2.** Central America, Mexico informal **bribe:** tuvimos que darle una mordida para conseguir el permiso we had to give him a bribe to get the permit.

**moreno** adjetivo

**1.** **tan:** mi hermana tiene la piel morena por el sol my sister's skin is tan from the sun

**2.** **dark:** Luis es de piel morena Luis has dark skin

**3.** **brown:** cocino con azúcar morena I cook with brown sugar.

el **moretón** (plural los moretones)
■ **bruise:** me pegué en la frente y me salió un moretón I hit my forehead and got a bruise.

**moribundo** adjetivo ■ **dying:** apareció un perro moribundo en la puerta de la casa a dying dog turned up at our door.

**morir** verbo ■ **to die:** su tío murió en un accidente her uncle died in an accident

➤ **morirse de aburrimiento** to die of boredom: me moría de aburrimiento en la clase I was dying of boredom in class

➤ **morirse de frío** to be freezing: cierra la ventana o me moriré de frío close the window or I'll freeze

➤ **morirse de hambre** to be starving: todavía no comimos y yo me muero de hambre we haven't had lunch yet and I'm starving

➤ **morirse de miedo** to be terrified: se muere de miedo cuando se queda solo en la casa she's terrified when she's alone in the house

➤ **morirse por hacer algo** to be dying to do something: me muero por comer un rico chocolate I'm dying for some nice chocolate.

la **moronga** Central America, Mexico
■ **blood sausage.**

**mortal** adjetivo

**1.** **fatal:** tiene una enfermedad mortal she has a fatal disease

**2.** **mortal:** todos somos seres mortales we're all mortal

**3.** **deadly:** la película es de un aburrimiento mortal the movie was deadly boring.

la **mosca** ■ **fly.**

el **mosquito** ■ **mosquito.**

**mostrar** verbo ■ **to show:** la vendedora nos mostró una camisa carísima the saleswoman showed us a very expensive shirt; un policía me mostró cómo llegar al museo a policeman showed me how to get to the museum.

**motivar** verbo ■ **to motivate:** no se sabe qué lo motivó a tomar esa decisión we don't know what motivated him to make that decision; la maestra motiva a los alumnos a trabajar en clase the teacher motivates her students to work in class.

el **motivo**

**1.** **reason:** la maestra explicó el motivo de su ausencia the teacher explained the reason for her absence

**2.** **motif:** dibujó unos motivos navideños she drew some Christmassy motifs

➤ **con motivo de** for: viajó a Perú con motivo de un congreso he traveled to Peru for a conference

➤ **motivo de divorcio** grounds for divorce.

la **motocicleta** ■ **motorcycle.**

la **motoneta** ■ **scooter:** las motonetas son muy populares entre los jóvenes scooters are very popular among the young.

el **motor** ■ **engine:** se rompió el motor del auto the car's engine died.

**mover** verbo

**1.** **to move:** movió la silla he moved the chair; te toca mover it's your turn to move

**2.** **to put in motion:** empezamos a mover el asunto we put the matter in motion

**3.** **to handle:** mueven grandes cantidades de dinero they handle large sums of money

**moverse** verbo pronominal ■ **to move:** muévete un poco hacia acá move this way a little; el barco se movió durante todo el trayecto the boat swayed during the whole trip.

el **movimiento**

**1.** **movement:** hizo un movimiento con la mano he made a movement with his hand

**2.** **activity:** hay mucho movimiento en la calle there is a lot of activity on the street.

la **moza**

1. **young girl**: una moza del mercado me ayudó con las bolsas a young girl from the market helped me with the bags
2. *Andes, River Plate* **waitress**: la moza me trajo la cuenta the waitress brought me the check.

el **mozo**

1. **young boy**: un mozo del mercado me ayudó con las bolsas a young boy from the market helped me with the bags
2. *Andes, River Plate* **waiter**: el mozo me trajo la cuenta the waiter brought me the check.

la **mucama** | *Andes, River Plate* ■ **maid**: tiene una mucama trabajando en la casa she has a maid at home

➤ **mucama de hotel** chambermaid: las mucamas del hotel eran muy amables the hotel chambermaids were very nice.

el **mucamo** | *Andes, River Plate* ■ **servant**.

el **muchacho**, la **muchacha** ■ **kid**: los muchachos fueron al cine the kids went to the movies

la **muchacha** ■ *Mexico* **maid**: mi casa está hecha un batidero porque estoy sin muchacha my house is a mess because I don't have a maid.

**mucho** | *adjetivo & adverbio*

1. **a lot**: tengo muchos lápices de colores I have a lot of colored pencils; sabe mucho de filosofía he knows a lot about philosophy
2. **much**: no tuvo mucha suerte he didn't have much luck; soy mucho mayor que mi hermana I'm much older than my sister

➤ hoy hace mucho calor it's very hot today
➤ hace mucho tiempo que no lo veo it's been a long time since I've seen him.

**mudarse** | *verbo pronominal*

1. **to move**: se mudaron para la ciudad they moved to the city
2. **to change**: me mudé de ropa antes de salir I changed clothes before going out.

**mudo** | *adjetivo*

1. **mute**: se quedó muda como consecuencia de un golpe en la cabeza she went mute after a blow to the head
2. **silent**: la "h" es la única letra muda del español "h" is the only silent letter in Spanish

el **mudo**, la **muda** ■ **mute**: hay una escuela para mudos en el barrio there is a school for mutes in the neighborhood.

el **mueble** ■ **piece of furniture**: un mueble bonito a very nice piece of furniture; los muebles the furniture; compré muebles nuevos I bought new furniture.

la **muela** ■ **tooth** (*plural* **teeth**): tengo un fuerte dolor de muelas I have a strong toothache

➤ una muela del juicio a wisdom tooth.

el **muelle**

1. **pier**: el barco atracó en el muelle the boat docked at the pier
2. **spring**: compramos un colchón con muelles resistentes we bought a mattress with strong springs.

la **muerte** ■ **death**: muchas personas creen que hay vida después de la muerte many people believe there is life after death; fueron condenados a muerte they were condemned to death.

**muerto** | *adjetivo*

1. **dead**: encontramos un perro muerto en la carretera we found a dead dog on the road; tu teléfono está muerto your phone is dead
2. **beat**: llegué muerto del trabajo I was beat after work

el **muerto**, la **muerta** ■ **dead person**: había un muerto en la acera there was a dead person on the sidewalk

➤ afortunadamente no hubo muertos en el accidente fortunately no one was killed in the accident.

### DÍA DE LOS MUERTOS

November 2 is a religious holiday in all of Latin America. People are off from work and schools are closed, and the day is devoted to remembering friends and family that have passed away. People go to cemeteries to take flowers to their loved ones' graves. In Mexico, families place elaborate altars on the graves, decorated with candles, flowers, and foods prepared specifically for the holiday, such as a special kind of sweet bread (pan de muerto) and little skulls fashioned out of sugar.

la **muestra**

1. **sample:** nos regalaron una muestra de perfume they gave us a perfume sample; se sacó una muestra de sangre they took a blood sample
2. **pattern:** usaron mi vestido como muestra they used my dress as a pattern.

la **mugre** ■ **dirt:** la mugre de esta casa es insoportable the dirt in this house is unbearable.

la **mujer**

1. **woman:** las mujeres de la familia organizaron una fiesta the women in the family organized a party
2. **wife:** Gonzalo me presentó a su mujer Gonzalo introduced me to his wife
➤ una mujer policía a policewoman.

**mulato** adjetivo ■ **of mixed race:** esta zona tiene una población mulata this area has a mixed race population

el **mulato,** la **mulata** ■ **person of mixed race:** los mulatos fueron tradicionalmente discriminados en la sociedad traditionally, people of mixed race were discriminated against by society.

**múltiple** adjetivo ■ **multiple:** ya ha sucedido en múltiples ocasiones it has happened before on multiple occasions.

la **multiplicación,** las **multiplicaciones** ■ **multiplication:** el niño es muy bueno haciendo multiplicaciones the boy is very good at multiplication.

**multiplicar** verbo

1. **to multiply:** multiplica 48 por 2 multiply 48 by 2
2. **to increase exponentially:** se ha multiplicado la pobreza en esta región poverty has increased exponentially in this region.

la **multitud** ■ **crowd:** una multitud de admiradores fue al concierto a crowd of fans attended the concert.

**mundial** adjetivo ■ **world:** una guerra mundial a world war
➤ el hambre es un problema de escala mundial hunger is a problem on a worldwide scale

el **mundial** ■ **world championships:** el mundial de fútbol del 2002 se jugó en Japón y Corea the 2002 soccer world championships took place in Japan and Korea.

el **mundo** ■ **world:** quieren dar la vuelta alrededor del mundo they want to go around the world; me atrae el mundo del deporte I'm attracted by the world of sports
➤ todo el mundo everyone: todo el mundo se enteró del secreto de Adriana everyone found out about Adriana's secret.

la **muñeca**

1. **wrist:** se cayó y se quebró la muñeca derecha she fell and broke her right wrist
2. **doll:** se entretiene todo el día con sus muñecas she's happy playing with her dolls all day.

la **muralla** ■ **wall:** están construyendo una muralla defensiva they're building a defensive wall.

el **murciélago** ■ **bat**.

el **murmullo** ■ **murmur:** a lo lejos se oía el murmullo de las olas you could hear the far-off murmur of the waves.

**murmurar** verbo

1. **to murmur:** se enojó y salió de casa murmurando algo que no entendí he got angry and left the house murmuring something I didn't catch
2. **to gossip:** se pasan el tiempo murmurando de ella they do nothing but gossip about her
➤ se murmura que a fin de año cambiará el director de la escuela it is rumored that they'll change principals at the end of the year.

el **muro** ■ **wall:** los muros de los castillos medievales eran de piedra the walls of medieval castles were made of stone.

el **músculo** ■ **muscle**.

el **museo** ■ **museum**.
➤ museo de ciencias naturales natural history museum.

la **música** ■ **music**.
➤ música clásica classical music
➤ música de fondo background music.

el **músico,** la **música** ■ **musician**.

el **muslo** ■ **thigh**.

**mutuo** *adjetivo* ■ **mutual**.

**muy** *adverbio*

1. **very:** dicen que esa película es muy buena they say the movie is very good
2. **too:** este pantalón no me sirve, es muy corto para mí I can't wear these pants, they're too short for me.

el **nabo** ■ **turnip**.

**nacer** *verbo* ■ **to be born:** Diana nació en 1992 Diana was born in 1992.

el **nacimiento** ■ **birth:** el nacimiento del bebé llenó de alegría a la familia the birth of the baby filled the family with joy
➤ fecha de nacimiento date of birth: ¿cuál es tu fecha de nacimiento? what's your date of birth?

la **nación** *(plural las naciones)* ■ **nation**
➤ Naciones Unidas United Nations.

**nacional** *adjetivo* ■ **national**.

la **nacionalidad** *(plural las nacionalidades)* ■ **nationality:** ¿cuál es tu nacionalidad? what is your nationality?

**nada** *(pronombre & adverbio)*
■ *pronombre*
1. **nothing:** vamos a almorzar afuera porque en casa no hay nada de comer we're going out for lunch because there is nothing to eat at home; ¿qué compraste? — nada what did you buy? — nothing

2. **anything:** ¿no compraste nada? didn't you buy anything?
➤ de nada you're welcome: ¡gracias! — de nada thank you! — you're welcome
■ *adverbio*
**at all:** estoy exhausta, anoche no dormí nada I'm exhausted, I didn't get any sleep at all last night.

**nadar** *verbo* ■ **to swim**.

**nadie** *pronombre*
1. **no one:** ¿ya llegó alguien? — no, nadie is anybody here yet? — no, no one
2. **anybody:** ¿todavía no llegó nadie? has anybody arrived yet?

el **náhuatl** ■ **Nahuatl**

NÁHUATL

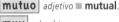 **Náhuatl** is the native language spoken by the Aztecs. It was adopted as a common language at the beginning of Mexico's colonial era until the Spanish Empire decided it was no longer a valid language for common use. Nowadays, there are more than 1,500,000 Nahuatl speakers in the country, and many words commonly used in other languages have Nahuatl roots, such as "chocolate" and "tomato."

la **nalga** ■ **buttock**.

**naranja** *adjetivo* ■ **orange:** llevaba un suéter naranja he wore an orange sweater

el **naranja** ■ **orange:** mi color favorito es el naranja my favorite color is orange.

la **naranja** ■ **orange:** hice jugo de naranja para el desayuno I made orange juice for breakfast.

la **nariz** *(plural las narices)* ■ **nose:** suénate la nariz blow your nose.

**nasal** *adjetivo* ■ **nasal**.

la **natación** ■ **swimming:** me encanta la natación I love swimming.

**nativo** *adjetivo* ■ **native:** Laura es hablante nativa de español Laura is a native Spanish speaker el **nativo**, la **nativa** ■ native: los nativos nos mostraron las herramientas que usan para la agricultura the natives showed us the tools they use for farming.

**natural** *adjetivo* ■ natural.

la **naturaleza** ■ nature: pasamos los fines de semana en el campo, en contacto con la naturaleza we spend weekends in the country, in touch with nature.

el **naufragio** ■ shipwreck.

el **náufrago**, la **náufraga** ■ shipwrecked person.

las **náuseas** ■ tiene náuseas y le duele la cabeza she feels nauseous and has a headache.

**nauseabundo** *adjetivo* ■ nauseating: el olor a huevo podrido es nauseabundo the smell of rotten eggs is nauseating.

la **navaja** ■ penknife.

**naval** *adjetivo* ■ naval.

la **nave** ■ ship
➤ una nave espacial a spaceship.

la **navegación** ■ navigation.

el **navegador** ■ browser: ¿cuál navegador tienes instalado en tu computadora? what browser do you have on your computer?

**navegar** *verbo*
1. to sail: salimos a navegar en su nuevo velero we went sailing on his new sailboat
2. to surf: pasa horas y horas navegando en Internet he spends hours and hours surfing the Internet.

la **navidad** *(plural* las navidades)
■ Christmas: vamos a pasar la navidad en casa de mis abuelos we're spending Christmas at my grandparents' house.

la **neblina** ■ fog.

la **necedad** ■ nonsense: deja ya de decir necedades stop talking nonsense.

**necesario** *adjetivo* ■ necessary: haremos lo que sea necesario we will do whatever is necessary

➤ ser necesario to be necessary: es necesario prepararse para el invierno it's necessary to prepare for winter: no es necesario que traigas tus lápices, podemos dibujar con los míos it's not necessary for you to bring your pencils, we can draw with mine.

**necesitar** *verbo* ■ to need: si somos cuatro para la cena, necesitamos un pollo entero if there's four of us having dinner we'll need a whole chicken.

**necio** *adjetivo* ■ stupid.

**negar** *verbo*
1. to deny: le pregunté si había roto el vidrio y lo negó I asked if he had broken the window and he denied it
2. to refuse: la abuela malcría a los nietos, nunca les niega nada grandma is spoiling her grandchildren, she never refuses them anything

**negarse** *verbo pronominal* ■ to refuse: Juan se negó a que lo ayudara y dijo que él haría la tarea solo Juan refused my help and said he would do his homework by himself.

**negativo** *adjetivo* ■ negative.

**negociar** *verbo* ■ to negotiate: los presidentes se reunieron para negociar un acuerdo the presidents gathered to negotiate an agreement.

el **negocio**
1. business: trabaja en un negocio familiar he works in a family business; mi tío se dedica a los negocios my uncle is a businessman
2. store: vivimos en un barrio residencial donde hay pocos negocios we live in a residential area with few stores.

**negro** *adjetivo* ■ black: hoy me voy a poner el pantalón negro con la blusa roja I'll wear the black pants with the red blouse today

el **negro** ■ black: el negro es mi color favorito black is my favorite color.

la **nena** ■ *River Plate* little girl.

el **nene** ■ *River Plate* little boy.

el **nervio** ■ nerve: el dentista me anestesió los nervios de la muela dañada the dentist numbed the nerves of my damaged tooth

los **nervios** nerves: cálmate, no permitas que los nervios te afecten durante la prueba calm down, don't let nerves get to you during the test.

**nervioso** *adjetivo* ■ nervous: es un niño muy nervioso que distrae a toda la clase he's a nervous boy who distracts the whole class; mamá está nerviosa porque papá tarda en llegar Mom's nervous because Dad is late.

el **neumático** ■ tire.

**neutro** *adjetivo* ■ neutral.

**nevar** *verbo* ■ to snow: hace varios días que nieva sin parar it's been snowing continuously for several days.

**ni** *conjunción*
1. or: no sé coser ni tejer I don't know how to sew or knit
2. nor: no vino ni me llamó he didn't come, nor did he call
➤ ni … ni neither … nor: no quiero ni pollo ni pescado I want neither chicken nor fish; ni mi madre ni mi hermana están en casa neither my mother nor my sister are home
➤ ni siquiera not even: ni siquiera se despidió cuando se fue he didn't even say goodbye when he left.

**Nicaragua** *sustantivo femenino* ■ Nicaragua.

**nicaragüense** *adjetivo*

En inglés, los adjetivos que se refieren a un país o una región se escriben con mayúscula:

**Nicaraguan**

el/la **nicaragüense**

En inglés, los gentilicios se escriben con mayúscula:

**Nicaraguan**

➤ los nicaragüenses the Nicaraguans.

el **nido** ■ nest.

la **niebla** ■ fog.

la **nieta** ■ granddaughter.

el **nieto** ■ grandson.

la **nieve** ■ snow.

**ningún** *adjetivo*

Shortened form of **ninguno** used before masculine singular nouns.

**ninguno** *(adjetivo & pronombre)*
■ *adjetivo*
1. any: no encontramos ninguna película interesante we couldn't find any interesting movies
➤ ningún lado anywhere: no vi a tu hermana por ningún lado I didn't see your sister anywhere
➤ ningún momento never: en ningún momento me dijo que se sentía mal she never said she felt bad
■ *pronombre*
1. none: ninguno de los niños sabía japonés none of the children knew Japanese
2. neither: ninguno de los dos sacó buena nota neither one of them got a good grade.

la **niña** ■ girl: una niña pequeña a small girl.

la **niñera** ■ nanny.

la **niñez** ■ childhood.

el **niño** ■ boy: un niño de cinco años a five year old boy
➤ esa película no la pueden ver los niños this movie isn't for children.

**nítido** *adjetivo* ■ clear.

el **nitrógeno** ■ nitrogen.

el **nivel** ■ level: Montevideo y Buenos Aires están al nivel del mar Montevideo and Buenos Aires are at sea level; el nivel educativo aquí es muy alto the educational level here is very high
➤ el nivel de vida the standard of living.

**no** *adverbio* ■ no: ¿vienes? — no are you coming? — no; ¡he dicho que no! I said no!
➤ no tengo tiempo I don't have time
➤ es cubano, ¿no? he's Cuban, isn't he?

**noble** *adjetivo* ■ noble.

la **noche**

1. **night:** llovió toda la noche it rained all night
2. **dark:** se nos hizo tarde, cuando llegamos ya era noche we were running late and it was dark by the time we arrived
➤ de la noche at night: las ocho de la noche eight o'clock at night
➤ de noche nighttime: cuando en América es de día, en Extremo Oriente es de noche when it's daytime in America it's nighttime in the Far East
➤ en la noche at night: no es sano comer muy pesado en la noche it's not healthy to eat a heavy meal at night.

la **Nochebuena** ■ Christmas Eve.

**nocivo** adjetivo ■ **harmful:** fumar es nocivo para la salud smoking is harmful to your health.

**nocturno** adjetivo

1. **night:** tomaremos el tren nocturno we'll take the night train
2. **nocturnal:** el búho es un ave nocturna owls are nocturnal birds.

**nombrar** verbo

1. **to mention:** no me nombró a su padre en toda la conversación he didn't mention his father in the whole conversation
2. **to appoint:** a mi hermano lo nombraron gerente de ese banco my brother was appointed manager of that bank.

el **nombre**

1. **name:** no sé su nombre, pero su apellido es González I don't know his name, but his last name is González
2. **noun:** palabras como "casa" y "puerta" son nombres words like "house" and "door" are nouns.

el **noreste** ■ northeast.

la **norma** ■ **rule:** para poder cumplir las normas, hay que saberlas you have to know the rules to follow them.

**normal** adjetivo ■ **normal:** es normal que extrañes si es la primera vez que estás lejos de tu familia it's normal to be homesick if it's the first time you've been away from home.

el **noroeste** ■ northwest.

el **norte** ■ north: el norte de la ciudad the north part of the city
➤ al norte to the north: está al norte de Buenos Aires it's to the north of Buenos Aires.

**norteamericano, norteamericana** adjetivo

En inglés, los adjetivos que se refieren a un país o una región se escriben con mayúscula:

**North American**

el **norteamericano,** la **norteamericana**

En inglés, los gentilicios se escriben con mayúscula:

**North American.**

**nos** pronombre

1. **us:** todavía no nos entregaron las notas they haven't given us our grades yet
2. **ourselves:** tuvimos un accidente pero por suerte no nos lastimamos we had an accident but luckily we didn't hurt ourselves
3. **each other:** no nos conocíamos, pero mi hermano nos presentó en la fiesta we didn't know each other but my brother introduced us at the party.

**nosotros** pronombre

1. **we:** ellos quieren helado pero nosotros preferimos fruta they want ice cream but we prefer fruit
2. **us:** los abuelos vinieron al parque con nosotros our grandparents came to the park with us.

la **nota**

1. **note:** vamos a dejarle una nota avisando que fuimos al cine we'll leave her a note to let her know we went to the movies; **"do"** es la primera nota de la escala musical "do" is the first note on the musical scale
2. **grade:** no estoy nada contenta con mis notas este semestre I'm not at all happy with my grades this semester.

**notable** adjetivo ■ **remarkable:** "Rayuela" es la obra más notable de Cortázar "Hopscotch" is Cortazar's most remarkable book.

**199**

**notar** *verbo* ■ **to notice**: ¿notaste que trae un calcetín marrón y otro verde? did you notice she's wearing one brown sock and one green?

**notarse** *verbo pronominal* ■ **to be able to tell**: se nota que estuvo llorando, tiene los ojos irritados you can tell she's been crying, her eyes are all red.

el **notario**, la **notaria** ■ **notary**.

la **noticia** ■ **news**: papá escucha las noticias en la radio todas las mañanas Dad listens to the news on the radio every morning; tengo una noticia para darte: el año que viene no vendré más a esta escuela I have some news for you: I won't be going to this school next year.

la **novedad**

1. **novelty**: como nunca había visto una jirafa, para ella era una novedad since she'd never seen a giraffe before it was quite a novelty for her
2. **latest thing**: ahora la novedad es combinar verde con anaranjado the latest thing is to combine green and orange
3. **news**: al volver de viaje, quiso enterarse de las novedades del país when she returned from her trip she wanted to catch up on the country's news.

la **novela** ■ **novel**.

la **novia**

1. **girlfriend**: ¿tienes novia? do you have a girlfriend?
2. **bride**: la novia estaba elegantísima en su casamiento the bride looked very elegant at the wedding.

**noviembre** *sustantivo masculino*

En inglés los nombres de los meses se escriben con mayúscula:

**November**: en noviembre in November; el próximo noviembre next November; el pasado noviembre last November.

el **novio**

1. **boyfriend**: ¿tienes novio? do you have a boyfriend?

2. **groom**: el novio estaba elegantísimo en su casamiento the groom looked very elegant at the wedding
➤ los novios the bride and the groom.

la **nube** ■ **cloud**.

**nublado** *adjetivo* ■ **cloudy**: está muy nublado hoy it's very cloudy today.

la **nuca** ■ **nape of the neck**.

**nuclear** *adjetivo* ■ **nuclear**.

el **núcleo** ■ **nucleus**: el núcleo de la célula contiene información genética the cell's nucleus contains genetic information
➤ el núcleo familiar the family unit.

el **nudo** ■ **knot**.

la **nuera** ■ **daughter-in-law**.

**nuestro** *(adjetivo & pronombre)*

■ *adjetivo*
**our**: invitamos a nuestros amigos a pasar un día en el campo we invited our friends to spend the day in the country

■ *pronombre*
**ours**: el carro de mis primos es azul y el nuestro es rojo our cousins' car is blue and ours is red.

**nueve** *number* ■ **nine**: tiene nueve hijos she has nine children
➤ mi hermana tiene nueve años my sister is nine years old
➤ son las nueve it's nine o'clock
➤ el nueve de abril the ninth of April.

**nuevo** *adjetivo* ■ **new**: llegó en su coche nuevo she arrived in her new car
➤ de nuevo again; de nuevo me olvidé del libro que me pediste I forgot the book you asked me for again.

la **nuez** *(plural las nueces)* ■ **walnut**.

**numerar** *verbo* ■ **to number**: hay que numerar estas cajas antes de mandarlas al depósito we have to number these boxes before we send them to the warehouse.

el **número**

1. **number**: ¿cuál es tu número favorito? what's your favorite number?; los sustantivos en español tienen género y número in Spanish, nouns have number and gender

**2. size:** ¿qué número calzas? what size shoe do you wear?

**3. issue:** quiero comprar los números atrasados de esa enciclopedia, para tenerla completa I want to buy the back issues of that encyclopedia so I can have the whole set

➤ **un número de fax** a fax number

➤ **un número de identificación personal** a PIN

➤ **un número de matrícula** a license number

➤ **un número de teléfono** a phone number.

**nunca** *adverbio*

**1. never:** nunca me llama he never calls me

**2. ever:** te preciso más que nunca I need you more than ever.

la **nutria** ■ otter.

la **nutrición** ■ nutrition.

el **nutriente** ■ nutrient.

**nutritivo** *adjetivo* ■ **nutritious:** las frutas y verduras son muy nutritivas fruits and vegetables are very nutritious.

**ñato** *adjetivo* ■ **snub-nosed**.

**ñoño** *adjetivo* ■ **spineless**.

**o** *conjunción* ■ **or:** ¿cuáles prefieres: los rojos o los blancos? which ones do you prefer: the red ones or the white ones?

➤ **o ... o ...** either ... or ...: el doctor puede atenderte o mañana o la semana que viene the doctor can see you either tomorrow or next week.

**obedecer** *verbo* ■ **to obey:** generalmente obedezco a mi madre generally I obey my mother.

**obediente** *adjetivo* ■ **obedient**.

la **obesidad** ■ **obesity**.

**objetivo** *adjetivo* ■ **objective:** hizo una presentación objetiva de la situación he gave an objective presentation of the situation

el **objetivo** ■ **objective:** el objetivo de la película es mostrar cómo viven los esquimales the objective of the film is to show how Eskimos live.

el **objeto** ■ **object**

➤ **un objeto volador no identificado** an unidentified flying object.

la **obligación** *(plural* las obligaciones*)* ■ **obligation:** los padres tienen la obligación de cuidar a sus hijos parents have the obligation of caring for their children.

**obligar** *verbo* ■ **to make:** a mi hermano lo obligan a estudiar inglés they make my brother study English.

**obligatorio** *adjetivo* ■ **obligatory:** estudiar lenguas extranjeras no es obligatorio studying foreign languages is not obligatory.

la **obra**

**1. work:** en este museo hay varias obras de Frida Kahlo there are several works by Frida Kahlo in this museum

**2. play:** en ese teatro están dando una obra sensacional they're putting on a sensational play at that theater

**3. construction site:** con el ruido de la obra de al lado, no puedo concentrarme I can't concentrate with the neighboring construction site's noise.

el **obrero,** la **obrera** ■ **worker**

➤ **un obrero calificado** a skilled worker

➤ **un obrero de la construcción** a construction worker.

el **obsequio** ■ **gift**.

la **observación** *(plural* las observaciones*)*

1. **observation:** el paciente está en observación the patient is under observation
2. **comment:** la maestra anotó varias observaciones en mi trabajo the teacher wrote down several comments on my paper.

**observador** adjetivo ■ **observant:** es muy observadora, descubrió todas las diferencias entre las dos figuras she's very observant, she noted all the differences between the two figures.

**observar** verbo

1. **to observe:** se dedicó a observar y estudiar a los monos en la selva he devoted himself to observing and studying monkeys in the jungle
2. **to remark:** este dibujo está excelente, observó la maestra this drawing is excellent, remarked the teacher.

el **obstáculo** ■ **obstacle:** pese a los obstáculos, Javier logró terminar su carrera in spite of the obstacles, Javier managed to finish his studies.

**obstruir** verbo ■ **to obstruct:** no podemos quedarnos aquí, estamos obstruyendo la salida we can't stay here, we're obstructing the exit.

**obtener** verbo

1. **to obtain:** con mucho trabajo, obtuvimos los resultados que queríamos with a lot of work, we obtained the results that we wanted
2. **to get:** obtuvo el primer premio she got first prize.

**obvio** adjetivo ■ **obvious**.

la **ocasión** (plural las ocasiones)

1. **opportunity** (plural **opportunities**): todavía no tuve ocasión de conocerla I still haven't had the opportunity to meet her
2. **occasion:** me prestó el auto en varias ocasiones he loaned me his car on several occasions.

**ocasionar** verbo ■ **to cause:** no te preocupes por mí, no quiero ocasionarte una molestia don't worry about me, I don't want to cause you any trouble.

el **occidente** ■ **west**.

el **océano** ■ **ocean**
➤ el **Océano Atlántico** the Atlantic Ocean
➤ el **Océano Pacífico** the Pacific Ocean.

**ocho** number ■ **eight:** tiene ocho hijos she has eight children
➤ **mi hermana tiene ocho años** my sister is eight years old
➤ **son las ocho** it's eight o'clock
➤ **el ocho de abril** the eighth of April.

el **ocio** ■ **leisure**.

**octubre** sustantivo masculino ■ **October:** en octubre in October; el próximo octubre next October; el pasado octubre last October

En inglés los nombres de los meses se escriben con mayúscula.

el/la **oculista** ■ **eye doctor**.

**ocultar** verbo ■ **to hide:** no me ocultes la verdad don't hide the truth from me; ¿vamos a ocultarnos atrás de la puerta, para darle un susto a papá? are we going to hide behind the door, to scare Dad?

**oculto** adjetivo ■ **hidden:** estuvieron ocultos varios días, hasta que la policía los encontró they were hidden for several days, until the police found them.

la **ocupación** (plural las ocupaciones)

1. **occupation:** ¿qué ocupación tiene tu madre? what is your mother's occupation?
2. **activity** (plural **activities**): nunca está libre, tiene muchísimas ocupaciones he's never free, he has very many activities.

**ocupar** verbo

1. **to take up:** este ropero es muy grande, ocupa todo el cuarto the wardrobe is too big, it takes up the whole room
2. **to occupy:** ¿quién está ocupando ese asiento? who's occupying that seat?
3. **to live in:** nosotros ocupamos el cuarto del fondo, el del frente está libre we live in the room at the back, the one at the front is unoccupied
4. **to take control of:** durante la guerra, el ejército enemigo ocupó la capital during the war, the enemy army took control of the capital

**5.** to employ: **esta fábrica ocupa a cientos de obreros** this factory employs hundreds of workers

**6.** *Mexico* to use: **¿estás ocupando este lápiz?** are you using this pencil?

**ocuparse** *verbo pronominal* ▪ to take care of: **los abuelos se van a ocupar de los niños este fin de semana** their grandparents are going to take care of the children this weekend.

la **ocurrencia** ▪ idea: **¿hacer una fiesta para el cumpleaños del perro? ¡pero qué ocurrencia!** have a party for the dog's birthday? what an idea!

**ocurrir** *verbo* ▪ to happen: **la historia cuenta lo que ocurrió en el pasado** history tells what happened in the past

**ocurrirse** *verbo pronominal* ▪ to occur to: **se me ocurre que no la conozco muy bien** it occurs to me that I don't know her so well

➤ **¿se te ocurre algo para regalarle a mamá el día de su cumpleaños?** can you think of something to give Mom for her birthday?

**odiar** *verbo* ▪ to hate: **¿cuál es la verdura que más odias? — las berenjenas** what is the vegetable that you hate the most? — eggplant.

el **odio** ▪ hatred: **le he tomado odio a la televisión** I've developed a hatred for television

➤ **a los vendedores que llaman por teléfono les tengo odio** I can't stand telemarketers.

**OEA** ▪ Organization of American States

OEA

The **OEA (Organización de Estados Americanos)** was founded in 1948 to promote peace, economic cooperation, and social advancement in the Americas. It has 35 member states and its headquarters are in Washington, DC.

el **oeste** ▪ west: **el sol se oculta por el oeste** the sun sets in the west; **el oeste de la ciudad** the west of the city

➤ **al oeste** to the west: **está al oeste de Lima** it's to the west of Lima.

**ofender** *verbo* ▪ to offend: **es muy grosero y ofende a las personas sin darse cuenta** he's very rude and he offends people without realizing it

**ofenderse** *verbo pronominal* ▪ to be offended: **se ofendió porque no la invitaron a la fiesta** she was offended because they didn't invite her to the party.

la **ofensa** ▪ offense.

la **oferta**

**1.** offer: **recibí dos ofertas de trabajo** I received two job offers

**2.** sale: **decidí aprovechar la oferta de mangos: compré tres por el precio de uno** I decided to take advantage of the sale on mangos: I bought three for the price of one

➤ **en oferta** on sale: **los mangos están en oferta: vendemos tres por el precio de uno** mangos are on sale: we're selling three for the price of one

➤ **hay muchas ofertas de trabajo para los médicos** there are many job openings for doctors.

**oficial** *adjetivo* ▪ official: **la piscina municipal se inaugura mañana con un acto oficial** the city swimming pool will be inaugurated tomorrow with an official ceremony

el **oficial** *(plural* los oficiales*)*

**1.** skilled workman *(plural* **skilled workmen***)*: **en esa obra buscan un oficial** at that construction site they're looking for a skilled workman

**2.** officer: **el oficial vino a ver qué sucedía** the officer came to see what was happening.

la **oficina** ▪ office

➤ **oficina pública** public office.

el **oficio** ▪ trade: **¿qué oficio te gustaría aprender?** what trade would you like to learn?

**ofrecer** *verbo* ■ **to offer:** la vendedora me ofreció varios vestidos y compré el verde the saleswoman offered me several dresses and I bought the green one

**ofrecerse** *verbo pronominal* ■ **to offer to:** el vecino se ofreció para ayudarnos con la mudanza the neighbor offered to help us with the move.

el **oído**
1. **ear:** tengo una infección en el oído derecho I have an infection in my right ear
2. **hearing:** el oído es uno de los cinco sentidos hearing is one of the five senses.

**oír** *verbo*
1. **to hear:** habla más fuerte, no te oigo speak louder, I can't hear you
2. **to listen to:** anoche oí la radio durante dos horas last night I listened to the radio for two hours.

el **ojal** ■ **buttonhole**.

**ojalá** *interjección* ■ **I hope:** ¡ojalá que pare llover! I hope it stops raining!

las **ojeras** ■ **circles under the eyes:** ¿te sientes bien? tienes unas ojeras enormes do you feel well? you have huge circles under your eyes.

el **ojo** ■ **eye:** me entró una basurita en el ojo a piece of dirt got in my eye
➤ ¡ojo! watch out!: ¡ojo al cruzar la calle! watch out crossing the street!

la **ola** ■ **wave**
➤ una ola de calor a heat wave.

**oler** *verbo* ■ **to smell:** acércate y huele las rosas come near and smell the roses
➤ oler a to smell like: huele a perfume, ¿quién estuvo aquí? it smells like perfume, who was here?
➤ oler bien to smell good: ese perfume huele muy bien that perfume smells very good
➤ oler mal to smell bad: esa comida huele mal, no la voy a comer that food smells bad, I'm not going to eat it.

el **olfato** ■ **smell:** el olfato es uno de los cinco sentidos smell is one of the five senses.

la **oliva** ■ **olive**
➤ aceite de oliva olive oil.

la **olla** ■ **pan:** herví el agua en una olla I boiled the water in a pan.

el **olor** ■ **smell:** ¡qué rico olor! what a delicious smell!

**olvidar** *verbo*
1. **to forget:** olvidaste llamar a tu madre you forgot to call your mother
2. **to leave:** olvidé el horno prendido I left the oven on.

el **olvido**
1. **oblivion:** al principio tuvo éxito pero después cayó en el olvido at the beginning he was successful but then he fell into oblivion
2. **oversight:** ¿no felicitaste a tu hijo el día de su cumpleaños? ¡qué olvido imperdonable! you didn't wish your son a happy birthday? what an unforgiveable oversight!

el **ombligo** ■ **navel**.

el **ómnibus** *(plural los ómnibus)* ■ **bus**.

la **onda** ■ **wave**.

**ondulado** *adjetivo* ■ **wavy:** tiene el pelo castaño, ondulado he has brown, wavy hair.

la **opción** *(plural las opciones)* ■ **option:** tienes varias opciones, elige la que te parezca mejor you have several options, choose the one that seems best to you.

la **operación** *(plural las operaciones)* ■ **operation:** por suerte la operación de apéndice de mi hermana salió bien fortunately my sister's appendix operation came out well.

**operar** *verbo* ■ **to operate on:** el oculista la va a operar de cataratas the eye doctor is going to operate on her for cataracts

**operarse** *verbo pronominal* ■ **to have an operation:** mañana se opera de cataratas tomorrow she's having an operation for cataracts.

**opinar** *verbo*
1. **to give one's opinion:** es mejor no opinar cuando uno no conoce el tema it's better to not give one's opinion when one is not familiar with the topic

2. **to think**: ¿qué opinas de los grupos ecológicos? what do you think of ecological groups?

la **opinión** *(plural* las opiniones) ■ **opinion**: ¿cuál es tu opinión sobre los grupos ecológicos? what's your opinion about ecological groups?

**oponerse** *verbo pronominal* ■ **to be opposed**: nuestro grupo se opone a la tala indiscriminada en los bosques our group is opposed to indiscriminate tree felling in the forests.

la **oportunidad** *(plural* las oportunidades) ■ **opportunity** *(plural* **opportunities)**: tuvo la oportunidad de irse a pasar el verano a la playa she had the opportunity to go spend the summer at the beach.

la **oposición** *(plural* las oposiciones) ■ **opposition**: la iniciativa de la maestra se chocó con la oposición de los alumnos the teacher's plans collided with the students' opposition.

la **opresión** ■ **oppression**: la opresión del tirano hizo que estallara la revolución en el país the tyrant's oppression made revolution break out in the country.

**oprimir** *verbo* ■ **to press**: oprima el botón de la derecha press the button on the right.

**optar** *verbo* ■ **to choose**: optaste por quedarte, ahora no te quejes you chose to stay, now don't complain.

**optativo** *adjetivo* ■ **optional**: matemática es obligatoria, pero jardinería es optativa math is obligatory, but gardening is optional.

la **óptica** ■ **optician's**: hoy fui a la óptica a hacerme los anteojos nuevos today I went to the optician's to have my new glasses made.

**optimista** *adjetivo* ■ **optimistic**: Clara es muy optimista Clara is very optimistic.

**opuesto** *adjetivo*

1. **opposing**: Sara y yo tenemos opiniones opuestas Sara and I have opposing opinions

2. **opposite**: vivimos en direcciones opuestas we live in opposite directions.

la **oración** *(plural* las oraciones)

1. **prayer**: algunas personas dicen una oración antes de la comida some people say a prayer before the meal

2. **sentence**: la segunda oración the second sentence.

**oral** *adjetivo* ■ **oral**: al final del curso de inglés tendremos un examen oral at the end of the English course we'll have an oral exam

➤ en la caja de este medicamento dice "administrar por vía oral" on this medicine's box it says "administer orally".

**orar** *verbo* ■ **to pray**.

la **órbita** ■ **orbit**: la Luna describe una órbita ovalada alrededor de la Tierra the moon travels in an oval orbit around the earth.

el **orden**

1. **order**: pónganse en fila, por orden de altura get in line, by order of height; hay que poner un poco de orden en esta oficina we have to put a little order in this office

2. **peace**: la policía es la encargada de preservar el orden the police is in charge of preserving the peace

la **orden** *(plural* las órdenes) ■ **order**: siempre está dando órdenes she's always giving orders

➤ a las órdenes you're welcome: muchas gracias — a las órdenes thank you very much — you're welcome.

**ordenado** *adjetivo*

1. **arranged**: estos libros están ordenados por tema these books are arranged by topic

2. **neat**: es muy ordenada, siempre tiene la casa impecable she's very neat, she always has the house impeccable.

**ordenar** *verbo*

1. **to arrange**: hay que ordenar estos libros we have to arrange these books

2. **to order**: el maestro nos ordenó callarnos the teacher ordered us to be quiet.

**205**

**ordinario** *adjetivo*

1. **ordinary**: esta tela es muy ordinaria, no sirve para un vestido de fiesta this cloth is very ordinary, it won't work for a party dress
2. **vulgar**: no me gustan nada los nuevos vecinos, son muy ordinarios I don't like the new neighbors at all, they're very vulgar.

la **oreja** ■ **ear**.

**orgánico** *adjetivo* ■ **organic**: la materia orgánica se descompone naturalmente con el paso del tiempo organic material decomposes naturally with the passage of time.

el **organismo** ■ **organization**: un organismo internacional an international organization.

la **organización** (plural las organizaciones) ■ **organization**: la organización es importante para poder estudiar con eficiencia organization is important to be able to study efficiently; las organizaciones no gubernamentales surgieron en los últimos veinte años non-governmental organizations appeared in the last twenty years.

**organizar** *verbo* ■ **to organize**: Diego y Rodrigo se encargaron de organizar la fiesta de fin de año Diego and Rodrigo were in charge of organizing the end-of-year party

**organizarse** *verbo pronominal* ■ **to organize oneself**: tienes que hacer un esfuerzo para organizarte you have to make an effort to organize yourself.

el **órgano** ■ **organ**: el corazón es el órgano principal del cuerpo humano the heart is the main organ of the human body; ese músico escribió varias piezas para órgano that musician wrote several pieces for the organ.

el **orgullo** ■ **pride**: siempre habla de su familia con orgullo he always speaks of his family with pride.

**orgulloso** *adjetivo* ■ **proud**: está muy orgulloso de su familia he's very proud of his family.

la **orientación** (plural las orientaciones)

➤ no tiene sentido de la orientación he has no sense of direction
➤ mi ventana tiene orientación hacia el sur my window is facing toward the south
➤ orientación profesional vocational guidance.

**orientar** *verbo* ■ **to direct**: el maestro orientó a sus alumnos en el trabajo the teacher directed her students in their work

**orientarse** *verbo pronominal* ■ **to get one's bearings**: deja que me oriente let me get my bearings.

el **oriente**

1. **east**: esta casa recibe mucho sol porque da al oriente this house gets a lot of sun because it faces the east
2. **East**: el Oriente the East.

el **origen** (plural los orígenes) ■ **origin**: el origen de esta costumbre es un antiguo rito maya the origin of this custom is an ancient Mayan ceremony.

**original** *adjetivo* ■ **original**: éste es el texto original, ¿dónde están las copias? this one is the original text, where are the copies?; es un artista muy original he's a very original artist.

**originario** *adjetivo* ■ **original**: ése no era el plan originario that wasn't the original plan
➤ ser originario de to come from: el maíz es originario de América corn comes from America.

la **orilla**

1. **bank**: las mujeres lavaban la ropa a la orilla del río the women used to wash the clothes at the river bank
2. **shore**: me encanta dar paseos por la orilla del mar I love to take walks on the sea shore.

la **orina** ■ **urine**.

**orinar** *verbo* ■ **to urinate**

**orinarse** *verbo pronominal* ■ **to wet oneself**.

el **oro** ■ **gold**

➤ **bañado en oro** gold-plated: **le regalamos una pulsera bañada en oro** we gave her a gold-plated bracelet

➤ **oro 18 quilates** 18 carat gold: **estas alianzas son de oro 18 quilates** these wedding rings are made of 18 carat gold.

la **orquesta** ■ orchestra.

la **ortografía** ■ spelling: **es importante evitar los errores de ortografía** it's important to avoid spelling errors.

la **oruga** ■ caterpillar.

**osado** *adjetivo* ■ daring: **los miembros del equipo de rescate fueron muy osados, no se detuvieron ante el peligro** the members of the rescue team were very daring, they didn't hesitate in the face of danger.

**osar** *verbo* ■ to dare: **no osé decirle la verdad** I didn't dare tell her the truth.

la **oscilación** (*plural* las oscilaciones) ■ swinging: **la oscilación del péndulo del reloj marca el paso de los segundos** the swinging of the clock's pendulum marks the passing of seconds.

**oscilar** *verbo* ■ to swing: **el péndulo del reloj oscila para marcar el paso de los segundos** the clock's pendulum swings to mark the passing of the seconds.

**oscurecer** *verbo*

1. to get dark: **en invierno, oscurece a las cuatro de la tarde** in the winter, it gets dark at four o'clock in the afternoon
2. to darken: **si no oscureces la habitación no vas a poder dormir la siesta** if you don't darken the room you're not going to be able to take a nap.

la **oscuridad**

1. darkness: **el apagón nos dejó en la oscuridad** the blackout left us in darkness
2. dark: **¿le tienes miedo a la oscuridad?** are you afraid of the dark?

**oscuro** *adjetivo* ■ dark: **aquí está muy oscuro, no puedo leer** it's very dark here, I can't read; **llevaba anteojos oscuros** he was wearing dark glasses

➤ **a oscuras** in the dark; **estábamos a oscuras y empezó a contarme cuentos de ter-** ror we were in the dark and he began to tell me scary stories

➤ **verde oscuro** dark green.

el **oso**, la **osa** ■ bear

➤ **un oso pardo** a brown bear

➤ **un oso de peluche** a teddy bear

➤ **un oso polar** a polar bear.

la **ostra** ■ oyster.

el **otoño** ■ autumn: **el próximo otoño** next autumn

➤ **en otoño** in autumn.

**otorgar** *verbo* ■ to give: **le otorgaron a mi hermano el premio al mejor alumno** they gave the award for the best student to my brother.

**otro** (*adjetivo & pronombre*)

■ *adjetivo*

1. other: **me gustan más las otras clases** I like the other classes more
2. another: **quiero otro pedazo de torta** I want another piece of cake

➤ **yo me refería a otra cosa** I was referring to something else

➤ **si no lo encuentras aquí, debe estar en otra parte** if you don't find it here, it must be somewhere else

■ *pronombre*

1. other one: **éste no me gusta, prefiero el otro** I don't like this one, I prefer the other one
2. others: **no pedí éstos, quiero los otros** I didn't order these, I want the others
3. another one: **¿puedo servirme otro?** can I have another one?

el **óvalo** ■ oval.

la **oveja** ■ sheep (*plural* **sheep**).

el **ovillo** ■ ball: **tengo dos ovillos de lana** I have two balls of wool.

**oxidado** *adjetivo* ■ rusty: **se cortó con una lata oxidada y eso es muy peligroso** she cut herself with a rusty can and that is very dangerous.

**oxidarse** *verbo pronominal* ■ to rust: **el hierro se oxida con la humedad** iron rusts with humidity.

el **oxígeno** ■ oxygen.

la **paciencia** ■ patience.

el/la **paciente** ■ patient: había varios pacientes esperando que llegara el médico there were several patients waiting for the doctor to arrive.

**pacífico** *adjetivo* ■ peaceful: los maestros hicieron una manifestación pacífica the teachers carried out a peaceful demonstration.

el **pacto** ■ pact.

**padecer** *verbo* ■ to suffer: el país está padeciendo una crisis económica the country is suffering an economic crisis.

el **padre** ■ father: Juan salió a pasear con su padre Juan went out for a walk with his father; el párroco de mi iglesia es el padre Luis the parish priest of my church is Father Luis
➤ padre de familia family man
➤ mis padres my parents.

el **padrino** ■ godfather.

la **paga** ■ pay: el día 30 recibo mi paga mensual on the 30th I receive my monthly pay
➤ paga extra salary bonus.

**pagar** *verbo*
1. to pay: me dijeron que no tengo que pagar they told me that I don't have to pay
2. to pay for: tengo que pasar por la caja a pagar esta fruta I have to go by the cash register to pay for this fruit.

la **página** ■ page.

el **pago**
1. payment: tengo que mandarle los pagos al banco cada mes I have to send the payments to the bank every month
2. salary (*plural* salaries): debido a la crisis, los pagos a los funcionarios están atrasados due to the crisis, the employees' salaries are late.

el **país** (*plural* los países) ■ country (*plural* countries).

el **paisaje** ■ landscape.

la **paja** ■ straw.

el **pájaro** ■ bird.

la **pajita** ■ drinking straw.

la **palabra** ■ word
➤ palabra de honor word of honor.

la **palabrota** ■ curse word.

el **palacio** ■ palace.

el **paladar** ■ roof of the mouth.

la **palanca** ■ lever.

la **paleta**
1. palette: el pintor preparó su paleta para empezar a pintar the painter prepared his palette to start painting
2. *Central America, Mexico* popsicle: la paleta de mango que me comí estaba deliciosa the mango popsicle I ate was delicious.

**pálido** *adjetivo* ■ pale: estaba muy pálida la última vez que la vi she was very pale the last time I saw her.

el **palillo**
1. toothpick: te olvidaste de poner los palillos en la mesa you forgot to put the toothpicks on the table
2. drumstick: perdí uno de los palillos y ahora no puedo tocar el tambor I lost one of the drumsticks and now I can't play the drum.

la **paliza**
1. spanking: si su madre se entera le va a dar una paliza if his mother finds out she'll give him a spanking

2. beating: no sólo lo robaron, sino que además le dieron una paliza not only did they rob him, but they also gave him a beating.

la **palma**

1. palm: déjame ver las líneas en la palma de tu mano let me see the lines on the palm of your hand

2. palm tree: el camino a la playa está bordeado de palmas the road to the beach is lined with palm trees.

el **palo**

1. stick: como no tenía bastón, caminaba con la ayuda de un palo since he didn't have a cane, he was walking with the help of a stick

2. suit: los palos de la baraja española son cuatro there are four suits in Spanish cards

3. mast: el palo más alto del barco se quebró durante una tormenta the tallest mast on the boat broke during a storm.

la **paloma** ■ pigeon.

**palpar** verbo ■ to feel: Rosaura palpó la tela para ver si era de fibra natural Rosaura felt the cloth to see if it was made of natural fibers.

la **palpitación** (plural las palpitaciones) ■ palpitation.

**palpitar** verbo

1. to beat: el corazón palpita rápidamente cuando uno está nervioso the heart beats quickly when one is nervous

2. to flutter: Daniel estaba muy nervioso y le palpitaba el estómago Daniel was very nervous and his stomach was fluttering.

la **palta** Andes, River Plate ■ avocado.

la **pampa** ■ prairie.

el **pan**

1. bread: no le gusta comer mucho pan she doesn't like to eat a lot of bread

2. loaf of bread (plural loaves of bread): pasé por la panadería y compré tres panes chicos I went by the bakery and bought three small loaves of bread.

la **pana** ■ corduroy.

la **panadería** ■ bakery (plural bakeries).

el **panadero**, la **panadera** ■ baker.

el **panal** ■ honeycomb.

**Panamá** sustantivo femenino ■ Panama.

el **panameño**, la **panameña**

En inglés los gentilicios se escriben con mayúscula:

Panamanian

**panameño** adjetivo

En inglés, los adjetivos que se refieren a un país o una región se escriben con mayúscula:

Panamanian: los panameños the Panamanians.

la **panceta** ■ bacon.

el/la **panda** ■ panda.

la **pandilla** ■ gang.

el **pánico** ■ panic: los ladrones sembraron el pánico en la ciudad the thieves caused panic in the city.

el **panorama**

1. view: el panorama que se ve desde aquí es muy bonito the view that you can see from here is very pretty

2. scene: el panorama político es desesperanzador the political scene is maddening.

las **pantaletas** ■ Mexico panties.

la **pantalla**

1. screen: como no tenían pantalla, proyectaban la película en una pared blanca since they didn't have a screen, they projected the film onto a white wall

2. shade: hay que ponerle una pantalla a esa lámpara, para que no dé luz directa you have to put a shade on that lamp, so that it doesn't give direct light.

el **pantalón** (plural los pantalones) ■ pants.

el **pantano** ■ swamp.

el **panteón** (plural los panteones)

1. burial plot: a la abuela la enterraron en el panteón familiar they buried their grandmother in the family burial plot

**2.** *Mexico* **cemetery** *(plural* **cemeteries)**: prefirió que la cremaran en vez de que la enterraran en el panteón del pueblo she preferred to be cremated instead of being buried in the town's cemetery.

la **pantera** ■ **panther**.

las **pantimedias** ■ *Mexico* **pantyhose**.

la **pantorrilla** ■ **calf** *(plural* **calves)**: me duelen las pantorrillas después de hacer tanto ejercicio my calves hurt after doing so much exercise.

los **pants** ■ **sweatsuit**.

la **panza** ■ **belly** *(plural* **bellies)**.

el **pañal** ■ **diaper**.

el **paño**
**1.** **cloth**: para las noches frías, tengo un abrigo de paño for the cold nights, I have a cloth blanket
**2.** **rag**: ¿dónde hay un paño para limpiar la mesa? where's a rag to clean the table?

el **pañuelo**
**1.** **handkerchief**: como siempre está resfriada, no va a ningún lado sin un pañuelo since he's always got a cold, he doesn't go anywhere without a handkerchief
**2.** **scarf** *(plural* **scarves)**: había tanto viento, que decidí usar un pañuelo para no despeinarme there was so much wind that I decided to wear a scarf to not mess up my hair.

la **papa** ■ **potato** *(plural* **potatoes)**
➤ papas fritas french fries.

el **papá** ■ **dad**.

el **papalote** ■ **kite**.

la **papaya** ■ **papaya**.

el **papel**
**1.** **paper**: estos cuadernos son de papel reciclado these notebooks are made of recycled paper
**2.** **piece of paper**: saquen un papel y escriban su nombre take out a piece of paper and write your name
**3.** **role**: es el protagonista de la película, tiene el papel principal he's the star of the film, he has the main role

**4.** **document**: piden algunos papeles para hacer el trámite they're asking for some documents to carry out the transaction.

la **papelera** ■ **wastepaper basket**.

la **papelería** ■ **stationer's**.

el **paquete**
**1.** **package**: ¿me podrías traer un paquete de galletitas del supermercado? could you bring me a pack of cookies from the supermarket?
**2.** **parcel**: tengo que pasar por el correo a retirar un paquete I have to go by the post office to get a parcel.

**par** *adjetivo* ■ **even**: 2, 4 y 6 son números pares 2, 4 and 6 are even numbers

el **par**
**1.** **couple**: en un par de horas más termino este trabajo in a couple of hours more I'll finish this paper
**2.** **pair**: necesito un par de medias verdes I need a pair of green stockings.

**para** *preposición*
**1.** **for**: ¿para qué sirve esto? what is this for?
**2.** **to**: me estoy preparando para correr en la maratón I'm getting prepared to run in the marathon
➤ **para siempre** forever: fue a España de paseo y terminó quedándose para siempre she went to Spain for a short time and she ended up staying forever
➤ ¿para cuándo tendrá pronta la traducción? when will he have the translation ready?

el **parabrisas** *(plural* los parabrisas) ■ **windshield**.

el **paracaídas** *(plural* los paracaídas) ■ **parachute**.

la **parada** ■ **stop**: a las dos horas hicimos una parada para descansar after two hours we made a stop to rest
➤ una parada de bus a bus stop
➤ una parada de taxi a taxi stand.

**parado** *adjetivo*
**1.** **standing**: ¿qué haces ahí parada? ven a ayudarme what are you doing standing there? come help me

**2. stopped:** hay un tren parado en el andén, pero no sé si es el que va al centro there's a train stopped at the platform, but I don't know if it's the one that's going downtown.

el **paraguas** *(plural* los paraguas*)* ■ umbrella.

**Paraguay** *sustantivo masculino* ■ Paraguay.

**paraguayo** *adjetivo*

En inglés, los adjetivos que se refieren a un país o una región se escriben con mayúscula:

**Paraguayan**

el **paraguayo,** la **paraguaya**

En inglés los gentilicios se escriben con mayúscula:

**Paraguayan**

➤ los paraguayos the Paraguayans.

el **paraíso** ■ paradise.

**paralelo** *adjetivo* ■ parallel: las ruedas del auto dejaron dos líneas paralelas en la arena the car's wheels left two parallel lines in the sand.

la **parálisis** ■ paralysis.

**paralítico** *adjetivo* ■ paralytic

➤ quedó paralítico a causa del accidente he became paralyzed because of the accident

el **paralítico,** la **paralítica** ■ paralytic: los paralíticos se trasladan en silla de ruedas paralytics get around in wheelchairs.

**paralizar** *verbo* ■ to paralyze: un derrame le paralizó la mitad del cuerpo a hemorrhage paralyzed half of his body.

**parar** *verbo*

**1. to stop:** paré el auto I stopped the car
**2. to end:** la actividad para a las ocho de la noche activity ends at eight o'clock at night
**3. to strike:** los funcionarios paran mañana para reclamar un aumento de salario the employees are striking tomorrow to demand a salary increase

**4. to stay:** cuando viene a la ciudad, para en mi casa when he comes to town, he stays at my house

**pararse** *verbo pronominal*

**1. to stop:** ¿por qué te paraste? sigue caminando why did you stop? keep walking
**2. to stand up:** cuando entró la directora, los músicos se pararon when the conductor came in, the musicians stood up
➤ sin parar nonstop: en esta fábrica trabajan sin parar in this factory they work nonstop.

**parásito** *adjetivo* ■ parasitic: algunas plantas parásitas cuelgan de las ramas de los árboles some parasitic plants hang from the branches of trees

el **parásito** ■ parasite: los parásitos están debilitando al perro, hay que llevarlo al veterinario parasites are weakening the dog, we have to take him to the veterinarian.

el **parche** ■ patch.

**parecer** *verbo*

**1. to look like:** por su aspecto descuidado, parece un vagabundo because of his untidy appearance, he looks like a vagrant
**2. to think:** me parece que su trabajo es de pésima calidad I think that his work is terrible
**3. to seem:** no la conozco, pero parece muy inteligente I don't know her, but she seems very intelligent

**parecerse** *verbo pronominal* ■ to resemble each other: cuando eran chicos, los dos hermanos se parecían mucho when they were little, the two brothers resembled each other a lot.

**parecido** *adjetivo* ■ like: dicen que soy muy parecida a mi mamá they say that I'm very like my mom.

la **pared** ■ wall.

la **pareja**

**1. couple:** Virginia y Antonio hacen una linda pareja Virginia and Antonio make a nice couple
**2. pair:** el tenis se puede jugar en parejas tennis can be played in pairs.

**parejo** *adjetivo* ■ similar: Diego y Andrés son parejos en altura Diego and Andrés are similar in height.

el **paréntesis** *(plural* los paréntesis) ■ parenthesis *(plural* parentheses).

el **pariente,** la **parienta** ■ relative

➤ un pariente cercano a close relative

➤ un pariente lejano a distant relative.

el **parlamento** ■ parliament.

el **parlante** ■ loudspeaker.

el **paro** ■ strike: ayer no fui a la escuela porque había paro de maestros yesterday I didn't go to school because there was a teacher strike.

**parpadear** *verbo*

1. to blink: me entró una basurita en el ojo y por eso parpadeo tanto a piece of dirt got in my eye and that's why I'm blinking so much

2. to flicker: la luz está parpadeando, va a haber un apagón the light is flickering, there's going to be a blackout.

el **párpado** ■ eyelid.

el **parque** ■ park.

la **parra** ■ vine.

el **párrafo** ■ paragraph.

la **parrilla** ■ grill

➤ a la parrilla grilled: prefiero el pollo a la parrilla que hervido I prefer grilled chicken to boiled.

el **párroco** ■ parish priest.

la **parroquia** ■ parish.

la **parte**

1. portion: hay que dividir la torta en ocho partes we have to divide the cake into eight portions

2. side: tenemos que averiguar quién está de nuestra parte we have to find out who's on our side

3. part: vivo en la parte oeste del pueblo I live in the west part of town

➤ en parte partly: todo lo que ha pasado es en parte culpa tuya everything that's happened is partly your fault

➤ de parte de alguien from: mándale saludos a tu mamá de mi parte say hello to your mom from me

➤ ¿de parte de quién? *on the telephone* may I ask who's speaking?

**participar** *verbo* ■ to participate.

el **participio** ■ participle.

**particular** *adjetivo*

1. private: el hotel tiene una playa particular para los huéspedes the hotel has a private beach for the guests

2. special: tiene un talento particular para la pintura he has a special talent for painting.

la **partida**

1. departure: la partida del tren está prevista para las ocho en punto the train's departure is planned for eight o'clock on the dot

2. game: me ganaste dos partidas de póquer you beat me at two games of poker.

el **partido**

1. party *(plural* parties): en política es independiente: no pertenece a ningún partido in politics he's independent: he doesn't belong to any party

2. match: espero que mi equipo gane el partido del domingo I hope that my team wins the match on Sunday.

**partir** *verbo*

1. to divide: mamá partió el pollo en ocho trozos Mom divided the chicken into eight pieces

2. to crack: necesito ayuda para partir este coco I need help to crack this coconut

3. to depart: el tren partió hace cinco minutos the train departed five minutes ago

➤ a partir de starting: a partir del domingo empieza el horario de verano starting on Sunday the summer schedule begins

**partirse** *verbo pronominal* ■ to break in two: el jarrón se cayó de la mesa y se partió the vase fell off the table and broke in two.

la **pasa** ■ raisin.

el **pasado** ■ past: la historia estudia el pasado history studies the past.

**pasado** *adjetivo*

1. **last:** el verano pasado fuimos a la playa y este verano iremos al campo last summer we went to the beach and this summer we'll go to the country

2. **overripe:** ¡qué olor fuerte tienen esos plátanos! deben estar pasadas what a strong smell those bananas have! they must be overripe

el **pasaje**

1. **alleyway:** abrieron un pasaje conectando esas dos calles they opened an alleyway connecting those two streets

2. **ticket:** en estas épocas, conviene comprar los pasajes con anticipación nowadays, it's best to buy tickets ahead of time.

el **pasajero**, la **pasajera** ■ passenger.

el **pasaporte** ■ passport.

**pasar** *verbo*

1. **to go:** ese tren pasa por varias estaciones antes de llegar al centro that train goes through several stations before arriving downtown

2. **to pass:** ¿podrías pasarme el agua, por favor? could you pass me the water, please?

3. **to spend:** durante el verano pasamos unos días en la playa during the summer we spend some days at the beach

4. **to happen:** no sé qué pasó en la clase de ayer I don't know what happened in yesterday's class

5. **to go by:** pasaron 20 minutos y decidí que no esperaba más 20 minutes went by and I decided that I wasn't waiting any more

6. **to be over:** cuando pasó el terremoto, muchas casas estaban destruidas when the earthquake was over, many houses were destroyed

**pasarse** *verbo pronominal*

1. **to go over:** el atleta perdió la competencia porque se pasó de la línea the athlete lost the competition because he went over the line

2. **to get overripe:** hay que comerse estas manzanas antes de que se pasen you have to eat these apples before they get overripe.

**pasear** *verbo*

1. **to take a walk:** después del almuerzo, el abuelo sale a pasear por el jardín after lunch, my grandfather goes out to take a walk through the garden

2. **to go for a ride:** como el día estaba lindo, agarré la bicicleta y salí a pasear since it was a nice day, I got my bicycle and I went for a ride

3. **to go for a drive:** los domingos salimos a pasear con mi tío en el auto on Sundays we go for a drive in the car with my uncle

4. **to walk:** ¿a quién le toca pasear al perro hoy? whose turn is it to walk the dog today?

el **paseo**

1. **walk:** después del almuerzo, el abuelo sale a dar un paseo por el jardín after lunch my grandfather goes out for a walk through the garden

2. **ride:** como el día estaba lindo, agarré la bicicleta y salí de paseo since it was a nice day, I grabbed my bicycle and went out for a ride

3. **drive:** los domingos salimos de paseo con mi tío en el auto on Sundays we go for a drive in the car with my uncle

4. **outing:** dos veces por año toda la escuela hace un paseo twice a year the whole school goes on an outing.

el **pasillo** ■ corridor.

la **pasión** *(plural* las pasiones) ■ passion.

el **paso**

1. **step:** la niña recién aprendió a caminar y da pasos cortos the little girl recently learned to walk and she takes short steps; los pasos en el tango son largos y lentos the steps are long and slow in the tango

2. **way:** hay que ir por otra calle porque aquí está cerrado el paso you have to go by another street because the way is blocked here

➤ "ceda el paso" yield

➤ "prohibido el paso" no entry.

la **pasta**

1. **paste:** usé una pasta para sellar las ventanas I used a paste to seal the windows

2. *Mexico* **dough:** tienes que amasar bien la pasta you have to knead the dough well

3. **pasta:** los ravioles son mis pastas preferidas ravioli is my favorite pasta

➤ **pasta de dientes** toothpaste.

el **pastel**

1. *Mexico* **cake**: a Beatriz le prepararon un pastel de chocolate para su cumpleaños they made a chocolate cake for Beatriz's birthday

2. **pastel**: me gusta pintar con pasteles I like to paint with pastels.

la **pastelería** ▪ **pastry shop**: en la pastelería había dos tartas que se me antojaron at the pastry shop there were two cakes that I wanted.

la **pastilla**

1. **pill**: el médico me recetó unas pastillas para la tos the doctor prescribed me some pills for my cough

2. **bar**: hay que traer seis pastillas de jabón del supermercado you have to bring six bars of soap from the supermarket.

el **pasto** ▪ **grass**.

el **pastor**

1. **shepherd**: el pastor cuida las ovejas the shepherd cares for the sheep

2. **pastor**: el pastor de mi iglesia siempre habla de la caridad the pastor in my church always talks about charity.

la **pastora** ▪ **shepherdess**: la pastora cuida las ovejas the shepherdess cares for the sheep.

la **pata**

1. **paw**: el perro se clavó una espina en la pata the dog got a thorn in his paw

2. **leg**: no te sientes en esa silla, tiene una pata quebrada don't sit in that chair, it has a broken leg

➤ **meter la pata** to put one's foot in it: no sabía que la fiesta para Isabel era una sorpresa, metí la pata cuando le pregunté qué se iba a poner I didn't know that the party for Isabel was a surprise, I put my foot in it when I asked her what she was going to wear

➤ **patas para arriba** upside down: tengo que arreglar la casa antes de que lleguen los invitados, está todo patas para arriba I have to put the house in order before the guests arrive, everything's upside down.

la **patada** ▪ **kick**.

**patear** *verbo* ▪ **to kick**.

**paternal** *adjetivo* ▪ **paternal**.

la **paternidad** ▪ **fatherhood**.

**paterno** *adjetivo* ▪ **paternal**.

la **patilla**

1. **sideburn**: ¿te estás dejando crecer las patillas? are you letting your sideburns grow?

2. **arm**: se me rompió una patilla de los lentes one of the arms on my glasses broke.

el **patín** *(plural los patines)* ▪ **skate**.

el **patinaje** ▪ **skating**

➤ patinaje sobre hielo ice skating.

**patinar** *verbo*

1. **to skate**: patina muy bien she skates very well

2. **to slip**: patiné con una cáscara de plátano y casi me quiebro un brazo I slipped on a banana peel and almost broke my arm.

el **patio**

1. *de una casa* **patio**

2. *de una escuela* **playground**.

el **pato** ▪ **duck**.

la **patria** ▪ **homeland**.

**patrio** *adjetivo* ▪ **home**: al frente de la embajada ondeaba la bandera patria in front of the embassy the home flag was waving.

el/la **patriota** ▪ **patriot**: los patriotas lucharon por la independencia the patriots fought for independence.

**patrocinador** *adjetivo* ▪ **sponsoring**: la institución patrocinadora se encargó de la cena de gala the sponsoring institution took charge of the dinner party

el **patrocinador**, la **patrocinadora** ▪ **sponsor**: los patrocinadores destinaron varios millones de pesos a publicitar el evento the sponsors set aside several million pesos to publicize the event.

el **patrón** *(plural los patrones)*

1. **boss**: el patrón se reunió con los empleados para intentar llegar a un acuerdo the boss met with the employees to try to reach an agreement

**2. pattern:** en esa tienda venden patrones para hacer distintos tipos de vestidos *at that store they sell patterns to make different types of dresses.*

el **patrón,** la **patrona** ■ **patron:** la santa patrona de México es la virgen de Guadalupe *the patron saint of Mexico is the Virgin of Guadalupe.*

la **patrulla** ■ **patrol:** los policías vigilan el barrio en sus patrullas *the police guard watch over the area on their patrols;* una patrulla de vecinos circula por las calles a partir del anochecer *a neighborhood patrol goes throughout the streets starting at nightfall.*

la **pausa**

**1. pause:** después de una pausa dijo: "estoy muy cansado" *after a pause he said: "I'm very tired"*

**2. break:** vamos a hacer una pausa *we're going to take a break.*

**pausado** *adjetivo* ■ **slow:** es fácil entenderla porque tiene una forma de hablar pausada *it's easy to understand her because she has a slow manner of speaking.*

el **pavo** ■ **turkey:** una cena de Navidad con pavo *a Christmas dinner with turkey*
➤ un pavo real *a peacock.*

el **payaso,** la **payasa** ■ **clown.**

la **paz** *(plural* las paces) ■ **peace:** no queremos la guerra, queremos vivir en paz *we don't want war, we want to live in peace*
➤ dejar a alguien en paz *to leave somebody alone:* deja a tu hermano en paz, que está haciendo su tarea *leave your brother alone, he's doing his homework*
➤ hacer las paces *to make peace:* estuvieron peleadas varios días pero al final hicieron las paces *they fought for several days but in the end they made peace.*

el **peaje** ■ **toll:** dentro de un kilómetro está el peaje, ¿tienes dinero a mano? *the toll's coming up in the next kilometer, do you have any money handy?*

el **peatón** *(plural* los peatones) ■ **pedestrian.**

la **peca** ■ **freckle.**

el **pecado**

**1. sin:** la pereza es uno de los siete pecados capitales *laziness is one of the seven deadly sins*

**2. crime:** es un pecado desperdiciar el resto del pollo *it's a crime to throw away the rest of the chicken.*

**pecar** *verbo* ■ **to sin.**

el **pecho** ■ **chest:** Antonio tiene el pecho ancho y fuerte porque nada todos los días *Antonio has a wide, strong chest because he swims every day*
➤ dar el pecho *to breastfeed:* ya es hora de darle otra vez el pecho al bebé *now it's time to breastfeed the baby again.*

la **pechuga** ■ **breast:** ¿qué parte del pollo prefieres: la pata o la pechuga? *what part of the chicken do you prefer: the leg or the breast?*

el **pedal** ■ **pedal.**

el **pedazo** ■ **piece.**

el **pedido** ■ **order:** ya hice el pedido pero todavía no está listo *I already placed the order but it's not ready yet.*

**pedir** *verbo*

**1. to ask:** te pedí que vinieras porque necesito ayuda *I asked you to come because I need help*

**2. to request:** pedí otro tenedor porque éste se me cayó al suelo *I requested another fork because this one fell on the floor*

**3. to order:** pedí dos pollos y ensalada para cinco *I ordered two chickens and salad for five.*

**pegajoso** *adjetivo* ■ **sticky:** tengo las manos pegajosas, me las voy a lavar *I have sticky hands, I'm going to wash them.*

el **pegamento** ■ **glue.**

**pegar** *verbo*

**1. to glue:** pegué la taza rota con pegamento especial para cerámica *I glued the broken cup with special glue for ceramics*

**2. to give:** Susana me pegó su gripe cuando fui a visitarla *Susana gave me her flu when I went to visit her*

**3. to hit:** a ese animal le deben haber pegado mucho, por eso es tan asustadizo they must have hit that animal a lot, that's why it's so skittish

➤ **pegar un salto** to jump: **pegué un salto cuando sonó el teléfono** I jumped when the telephone rang

➤ **pegar un susto a alguien** to scare somebody: **el gato le pegó un susto cuando saltó sobre su falda** the cat scared her when it jumped on her skirt

**pegarse** *verbo pronominal* ■ **to cling:** el cachorro se pegaba a su mamá the puppy clung to his mother.

el **peinado** ■ **hairstyle.**

**peinar** *verbo*
1. *con peine* **to comb**
2. *con cepillo* **to brush.**

el **peine** ■ **comb.**

**pelado** *adjetivo* ■ **peeled:** los plátanos se comen peladas bananas are eaten peeled.

el **pelaje** ■ **coat:** el pelaje de los leopardos tiene manchas negras the leopard's coat has black spots.

**pelar** *verbo*
1. *fruta* **to peel**
2. *nueces* **to shell**

➤ **hacer un frío que pela** to be bitterly cold: **ayer hacía un frío que pelaba** yesterday it was bitterly cold.

el **peldaño** ■ **step.**

la **pelea**
1. **fight:** le quedó un ojo morado después de una pelea en la escuela he had a black eye after a fight at school
2. **argument:** Luisa tuvo otra pelea con el novio Luisa had another argument with her boyfriend.

**pelear** *verbo*
1. **to fight:** los pueblos hispanoamericanos pelearon por conseguir su independencia the Hispanic Americans fought to gain their independence
2. **to argue:** mis hermanos pelean mucho my brothers argue a lot.

la **película** ■ **movie**
➤ **una película de dibujos animados** a feature-length cartoon
➤ **una película de terror** a horror movie.

el **peligro** ■ **danger:** el paciente está fuera de peligro the patient is out of danger
➤ **correr el peligro de** to run the risk of: **corres el peligro de caerte si no tienes cuidado** you run the risk of falling if you aren't careful.

**peligroso** *adjetivo* ■ **dangerous.**

el **pelo** ■ **hair:** me lavo el pelo todos los días I wash my hair every day
➤ **nos salvamos por un pelo** we escaped by the skin of our teeth
➤ **tomar el pelo** to pull somebody's leg: ¡me estás tomando el pelo! you're pulling my leg!

la **pelota** ■ **ball.**

la **pena** ■ **shame:** fue una pena que se muriera la tortuga de Joaquín it was a shame that Joaquín's turtle died
➤ **le da pena hablar en público** he's embarrassed to speak in public
➤ **vale la pena** it's worth it.

**pendiente** *adjetivo* ■ **pending:** hay varios asuntos pendientes there are several matters pending.

la **pendiente** ■ **slope:** bajamos esquiando por la pendiente we went skiing down the slope.

**penetrar** *verbo* ■ **to soak into:** el café penetró el terrón de azúcar the coffee soaked into the lump of sugar.

la **península** ■ **peninsula.**

el **pensamiento** ■ **thought:** yo puedo adivinarte el pensamiento I can guess your thoughts.

**pensar** *verbo*
1. **to think:** pensamos que es un buen candidato a la presidencia we think that he's a good candidate for the presidency
2. **to think about:** voy a pensarlo y mañana te respondo I'm going to think about it and tomorrow I'll give you an answer.

**penúltimo** *adjetivo* ■ **next to last:** el penúltimo corredor the next to last runner

el **penúltimo, la penúltima** ■ **next to last:** es el penúltimo he's next to last.

**peor** *adjetivo & adverbio*

1. **worse:** la película de hoy fue peor que la que vimos ayer today's movie was worse than the one we saw yesterday

2. **worst:** de las tres películas malas que vimos esta semana, la de hoy fue la peor de todas out of the three bad movies we saw this week, today's was the worst of all.

el **pepino** ■ **cucumber**.

**pequeño** *adjetivo*

1. **little:** cuando era pequeña me encantaba jugar con muñecas when I was little I loved to play with dolls

2. **small:** el paquete es pequeño the package is small

el **pequeño, la pequeña** ■ **child** (*plural* **children**): los pequeños llegaron del parque cansadísimos the children arrived back from the park very tired.

la **pera** ■ **pear**.

la **percha** ■ **coat hanger**.

**perdedor** *adjetivo* ■ **losing:** el equipo perdedor salió de la cancha desconsolado the losing team left the field inconsolable

el **perdedor, la perdedora** ■ **loser:** es mal perdedor he's a bad loser.

**perder** *verbo*

1. **to miss:** si no salimos ya mismo, vas a perder el avión if we don't leave right now, you're going to miss the plane

2. **to lose:** perdí las llaves I lost the keys; está triste porque su equipo perdió he's sad because his team lost

➤ perder tiempo to waste time: ponete a trabajar ya, no pierdas más tiempo start working now, don't waste more time

**perderse** *verbo pronominal* ■ **to get lost:** quiero irme antes de que oscurezca, para evitar perderme I want to go before it gets dark, to avoid getting lost.

la **pérdida** ■ **loss:** no ha logrado recuperarse de la pérdida de su madre she hasn't been able to recover from the loss of her mother; por la sequía, los agricultores sufrieron pérdidas graves because of the drought, the farmers suffered severe losses

➤ qué pérdida de tiempo what a waste of time.

el **perdón** (*plural* los perdones) ■ **forgiveness**

➤ pedir perdón to ask for forgiveness: nos pidió perdón por no haber venido a visitarnos he asked for our forgiveness for not having come to visit us

➤ las autoridades otorgaron el perdón al acusado the authorities pardoned the accused man

➤ perdón, ¿me podría decir la hora? excuse me, could you tell me what time it is?

➤ te pisé sin querer, perdón I accidentally stepped on you, I'm sorry.

**perdonar** *verbo*

1. **to forgive:** lo hice sin querer, espero que me perdones I did it unintentionally, I hope that you forgive me

2. **to excuse:** perdóname, te pisé sin querer excuse me, I stepped on you accidentally.

**perecedero** *adjetivo* ■ **perishable:** los alimentos perecederos hay que conservarlos en la heladera you have to keep perishable foods in the refrigerator.

**perecer** *verbo* ■ **to perish:** 20 personas perecieron en el atentado 20 people perished in the attack.

el **peregrino, la peregrina** ■ **pilgrim**.

el **perejil** ■ **parsley**.

la **pereza**

➤ me da pereza ponerme a estudiar I don't feel like starting to study.

**perezoso** *adjetivo* ■ **lazy**.

la **perfección** ■ **perfection:** habla tres idiomas a la perfección she speaks three languages to perfection.

**perfecto** *adjetivo* ■ **perfect**.

el **perfil** ■ profile: los antiguos egipcios pintaban el cuerpo de frente y la cara de perfil the ancient Egyptians painted the body from the front and the face in profile.

el **perfume**

1. perfume: los perfumes franceses son apreciados en todo el mundo French perfumes are esteemed throughout the world

2. scent: me fascina el perfume de los jazmines the scent of jasmine fascinates me.

el **perico** ■ parakeet.

**periódico** adjetivo ■ periodic: es importante hacer visitas periódicas al dentista it's important to make periodic visits to the dentist

el **periódico** ■ newspaper.

el **periodismo** ■ journalism.

el/la **periodista** ■ journalist.

el **periodo** ■ period: el periodo de prueba dura tres meses the test period lasts three months.

**perjudicar** verbo

1. to be harmful to: es mejor que no fumes, el tabaco perjudica la salud it's better that you don't smoke, tobacco is harmful to your health

2. to hurt: esta sequía va a perjudicar a los productores rurales this drought is going to hurt the rural farmers.

**perjudicial** adjetivo ■ harmful: fumar es perjudicial para la salud smoking is harmful to one's health.

el **perjuicio** ■ loss: la sequía trajo graves perjuicios para los productores rurales the drought brought severe losses for the rural farmers.

la **perla** ■ pearl.

**permanecer** verbo ■ to stay.

**permanente** adjetivo ■ permanent.

el **permiso** ■ permission: le dieron permiso para faltar tres días they gave him permission to miss three days

➤ con permiso excuse me: con permiso, ¿puedo pasar? excuse me, can I get by?

**permitir** verbo

1. to permit: un plazo más largo nos permite trabajar con tranquilidad a later deadline permits us to work calmly

2. to allow: no les permitieron entrar porque el concierto ya había empezado they didn't allow them to enter because the concert had already started.

**pero** conjunción

1. but: el modelo de ese vestido es lindo, pero no me gusta el color the style of that dress is pretty, but I don't like the color

2. yet: pero ¿yo no te había dado las instrucciones para llegar a mi casa? yet hadn't I given you directions to get to my house?

el **perro**, la **perra** ■ dog.

la **persecución** (plural las persecuciones) ■ pursuit: la persecución del ladrón duró un par de horas the pursuit of the thief lasted a couple of hours.

**perseguir** verbo ■ to pursue: la policía persiguió al ladrón durante un par de horas the police pursued the thief for a couple of hours.

la **persiana** ■ blind.

la **persona** ■ person (plural people): muchas personas son partidarias del reciclaje many people are in favor of recycling.

el **personaje**

1. character: el personaje principal de una película es el protagonista the main character of a film is the protagonist

2. figure: es un personaje de la política he's a political figure.

el **personal** ■ staff: nos ha ido tan bien con este restaurante que ya necesitamos más personal it's gone so well for us with this restaurant that we already need more staff.

la **personalidad**

1. personality (plural personalities): tiene una personalidad muy abierta she has a very open personality

2. figure: es una personalidad de la política he's a political figure.

**pertenecer** *verbo* ■ to belong: este reloj de bolsillo perteneció a mi abuelo this pocket watch belonged to my grandfather; ¿todavía perteneces al club de coleccionadores de sellos? do you still belong to the stamp collectors club?

la **pertenencia** ■ membership: su pertenencia al club se canceló por falta de pago de la cuota his membership to the club was cancelled for not paying the dues

las **pertenencias** ■ possessions: no quiero que toques mis pertenencias I don't want you to touch my possessions.

**pertinente** *adjetivo* ■ appropriate: hay que tomar las medidas pertinentes para proteger a los menores we have to take the appropriate measures to protect minors.

**perturbar** *verbo* ■ to disturb: tu hermano está descansando, no lo perturbes your brother is resting, don't disturb him.

**Perú** *sustantivo masculino* ■ Peru.

**peruano** *adjetivo*

En inglés los gentilicios se escriben con mayúscula:

Peruvian

el **peruano**, la **peruana**

En inglés, los adjetivos que se refieren a un país o una región se escriben con mayúscula:

Peruvian: los peruanos the Peruvians.

**perverso** *adjetivo* ■ wicked: ese niño perverso metió a un gato en una bolsa con piedras y lo tiró al río that wicked child put a cat in a bag with rocks and threw it into the river.

la **pesadilla** ■ nightmare.

**pesado** *adjetivo* ■ heavy: este baúl es muy pesado this trunk is very heavy; es mejor evitar comidas pesadas antes de irse a dormir it's best to avoid heavy foods before going to sleep

el **pesado**, la **pesada** ■ pain: mi hermano es un pesado my brother is a pain.

**pesar** *verbo* ■ to weigh: el bebé pesa siete kilos the baby weighs seven kilos; por favor, ¿me podría pesar esta bolsa de naranjas? please, could you weigh this bag of oranges for me?; ¿te has pesado? have you weighed yourself?

la **pescadería** ■ fish market.

el **pescado** ■ fish: el pescado asado es mi plato favorito grilled fish is my favorite dish.

el **pescador** ■ fisherman (plural fishermen).

la **pescadora** ■ fisherwoman (plural fisherwomen).

**pescar** *verbo*
1. to go fishing: salimos a pescar con el abuelo we went fishing with our grandfather
2. to catch: en un solo día pescamos 25 truchas in only one day we caught 25 trout
➤ ¡te pesqué con las manos en la masa! I caught you red-handed!

la **peseta** ■ peseta.

**pésimo** *adjetivo* ■ horrible.

el **peso**
1. weight: ¿tiene idea del peso de esa valija? do you have any idea what the weight of that suitcase is?
2. peso: ¿a cuántos pesos chilenos equivale un peso mexicano? how many Chilean pesos equal a Mexican peso?

la **pestaña** ■ eyelash.

la **peste**
1. plague: en Europa hubo varias pestes que diezmaron a la población in Europe there were several plagues that decimated the population
2. stink: ¡qué peste! what a stink!

el **pesticida** ■ pesticide.

el **pétalo** ■ petal.

la **petición** (plural las peticiones)
1. request: hicimos una petición al alcalde we made a request to the mayor

**2. petition:** entregaron una petición al patrón they delivered a petition to the boss.

**petizo** *adjetivo* ■ **short:** mi papá es muy alto y mi mamá es petiza my dad is very tall and my mom is short.

el **petróleo** ■ **petroleum.**

el **pez** *(plural* los peces*)* ■ **fish** *(plural* **fish***)*: hay muchos peces en este río there are many fish in this river
➤ un pez de colores a goldfish.

la **pezuña** ■ **hoof** *(plural* **hooves***)*.

el/la **pianista** ■ **pianist.**

el **piano** ■ **piano.**

la **picadura**

**1.** *de mosquito, serpiente* **bite:** te conviene ponerte repelente, para evitar las picaduras de mosquitos you should put on repellent to avoid mosquito bites
**2.** *de abeja* **sting:** el niño lloraba a causa de una picadura de abeja the boy was crying because of a bee sting.

**picante** *adjetivo* ■ **spicy:** necesito un poco de agua, este pollo está muy picante para mi gusto I need a little water, this chicken is too spicy for my taste

el **picante** ■ **spicy food:** por razones de salud, no puede comer picantes for health reasons, he can't eat spicy food.

**picar** *verbo*

**1. to bite:** estaba en el jardín al anochecer y me picaron los mosquitos I was in the yard at nightfall and the mosquitos bit me; los peces demoraron varias horas en picar the fish took several hours to bite
**2. to chop up:** para esa sopa, hay que picar las verduras en pedazos chicos for that soup, you have to chop up the vegetables into small pieces
**3. to sting:** me pican los ojos my eyes are stinging
➤ ten cuidado, que esta salsa pica mucho be careful, this salsa is very hot.

la **picazón** *(plural* las picazones*)* ■ **itch:** tiene sarampión y eso le provoca una picazón terrible he has the measles and that gives him a terrible itch.

el **picnic** ■ **picnic.**

el **pico**

**1. beak:** la gaviota llevaba en el pico un pez the seagull was carrying a fish in its beak
**2. peak:** quieren llegar al pico del Aconcagua they want to get to the peak of the Aconcagua.

el **picor** ■ **itch.**

el **pie**

**1. foot** *(plural* **feet***)*: a los adolescentes les crecen los pies muy rápido adolescents' feet grow very quickly
**2. base:** pusieron flores al pie de la estatua del héroe they put flowers at the base of the statue of the hero
➤ a pie on foot: como el día estaba lindo, decidimos venir a pie since it was a nice day, we decided to come on foot.

la **piedad** ■ **mercy.**

la **piedra** ■ **stone**
➤ una piedra preciosa a precious stone.

la **piel**

**1. skin:** los bebés tienen la piel suave y delicada babies have soft, delicate skin
**2. leather:** la piel se utiliza para fabricar zapatos leather is used to make shoes
**3. fur:** los abrigos de piel han pasado de moda fur coats have gone out of style.

la **pierna** ■ **leg.**

la **pieza**

**1. piece:** acabo de comprar un rompecabezas de 1.000 piezas I just bought a 1,000 piece puzzle
**2. room:** mis dos hermanos comparten una pieza y mi hermana y yo tenemos otra my two brothers share one room and my sister and I have another
➤ piezas de recambio spare parts.

el/la **pijama** ■ **pijamas.**

la **pila**

**1. battery** *(plural* **batteries***)*: esta radio funciona con electricidad o a pila this radio works with electricity or with batteries
**2. pile:** una pila de libros a pile of books
**3.** *Andes, River Plate* : había una pila de gente a la salida del teatro there were a lot of people at the theater's exit.

el **pilar** ▪ post.

la **píldora** ▪ pill.

la **pileta** *River Plate*

1. **sink:** no acumules platos sucios en la pileta don't pile dirty dishes up in the sink
2. **pool:** en mi escuela hay una pileta there is a pool at my school.

**pillo** *adjetivo* ▪ **naughty**

el **pillo,** la **pilla** ▪ rascal.

el/la **piloto** ▪ pilot.

la **pimienta** ▪ pepper.

el **pimiento** ▪ **pepper:** hay pimientos de color rojo, verde y amarillo there are red, green and yellow peppers
➤ un pimiento morrón a red pepper.

el **pincel** ▪ paintbrush.

el **pingüino** ▪ penguin.

el **pino** ▪ pine tree.

**pintar** *verbo* ▪ **to paint:** le pidieron que pintara un retrato de la familia they asked him to paint a family portrait; si quieres ahorrar plata, podemos pintar nosotros mismos la casa if you want to save money, we can paint the house ourselves

**pintarse** *verbo pronominal* ▪ **to put one's makeup on:** sólo me falta pintarme y estoy lista I just need to put my makeup on and I'll be ready.

el **pintor,** la **pintora** ▪ painter.

la **pintura**

1. **painting:** Irma presentó sus primeras pinturas en una galería de la ciudad Irma showed her first paintings in a gallery in the city
2. **paint:** para pintar toda la casa precisamos muchos tarros de pintura in order to paint the whole house we need a lot of cans of paint
3. **makeup:** no traje mis pinturas, ¿me prestarías delineador negro? I didn't bring my makeup, would you loan me some black eyeliner?

la **pinza**

1. *para ropa* **clothespin**

2. *para pelo* **bobby pin**
3. **tweezers:** con una pinza va a ser más fácil sacarte esa espina it will be easier to get that thorn out for you with tweezers.

la **piña** ▪ pineapple.

la **piñata** ▪ pot of candy

### PIÑATA

In Mexico one of the big attractions at children's parties is the **piñata**, the colorful papier-mâché figure filled with candy, fruit, and small toys. The **piñata** is suspended from a rope and the children line up to take their turn hitting it with a stick while blindfolded, to try to break it open and release its contents. When the **piñata** finally breaks open all the children throw themselves on the contents to get as many treats as possible.

el **piojo** ▪ louse *(plural* lice*)*.

la **pipa** ▪ pipe.

la **pirámide** ▪ pyramid

### PIRÁMIDES MAYAS Y AZTECAS

Aztec and Mayan pyramids are found in central and southern Mexico and in the north of Central America. They were built around 3.000 years ago. They have square bases, some have steps, and some are over 110 feet high. They were used as religious temples or astronomical observatories. The most famous pyramids are the ones found at Chichen-Itzá and Teotihuacán in Mexico and Tikal in Guatemala.

**pirata** *adjetivo* ▪ **pirate:** el mercado de CDs y videos piratas aumenta día a día the pirate CD and video market grows daily

el/la **pirata** ▪ pirate
➤ un pirata informático a hacker.

la **pisada**

1. **footstep:** lo oigo cuando llega porque sus pisadas son muy fuertes I hear him when he arrives because his footsteps are very loud

**2.** **footprint:** en la luna ha habido pisadas humanas desde 1969 there have been human footprints on the moon since 1969.

**pisar** *verbo* ■ **to step in:** mira bien por dónde caminas, no pises los charcos watch carefully where you walk, don't step in the puddles.

la **piscina** ■ **swimming pool**.

el **piso** ■ **floor:** el piso está muy estropeado the floor is badly damaged.

la **pista**

**1.** **trail:** la policía está atrás de la pista del asesino the police are on the trail of the murderer

**2.** **clue:** te voy a dar una pista para ayudarte a encontrar el tesoro escondido I'm going to give you a clue to help you find the hidden treasure

➤ la pista de aterrizaje the runway
➤ la pista de atletismo the running track
➤ la pista de baile the dancefloor
➤ la pista de patinaje the skating rink.

la **pistola** ■ **pistol**.

la **pizarra** ■ **blackboard**.

el **pizarrón** *(plural* los pizarrones) ■ **blackboard**.

la **pizca** ■ **pinch:** creo que le falta algo, agrégale una pizca de sal I think that it's lacking something, add a pinch of salt to it.

la **placa**

**1.** **plate:** desde que se fracturó el cráneo, lleva una placa de metal en la cabeza since he fractured his skull, he has a metal plate in his head

**2.** **plaque:** le entregamos una placa al director, agradeciéndole por su labor we gave a plaque to the director, thanking him for his work

➤ la placa dental plaque.

**placentero** *adjetivo* ■ **pleasant**.

el **placer** ■ **pleasure**.

la **plaga** ■ **plague**.

el **plan** ■ **plan:** no tenemos planes para mañana we don't have any plans for tomorrow.

la **plana** ■ **page:** vi tu foto en primera plana I saw your photo on the front page.

la **plancha**

**1.** **sheet:** compró dos planchas de metal para reforzar la caseta del perro he bought two sheets of metal to reinforce the doghouse

**2.** **iron:** antes las planchas se calentaban con brasas, ahora son eléctricas in the past irons were heated with hot coals, now they're electric

➤ a la plancha grilled: tráigame un bistec a la plancha, por favor bring me a grilled steak, please.

**planchar** *verbo*

**1.** **to do the ironing:** detesto planchar I hate to do the ironing

**2.** **to iron:** ¿quién me va a planchar estas camisas? who is going to iron these shirts for me?

la **planeación** ■ *Mexico* **planning:** la planeación de la fiesta está a cargo de mamá the party planning is up to Mom.

**planear** *verbo* ■ **to plan:** estamos planeando una gran fiesta para fin de año we're planning a big party for the end of the year.

el **planeta** ■ **planet**.

el **plano**

**1.** **plan:** el arquitecto presentó los planos de la casa the architect presented the house plans

**2.** **map:** ¿tienes un plano de la ciudad? do you have a map of the city?

**plano** *adjetivo* ■ **flat**.

la **planta**

**1.** **plant:** tiene muchas plantas que la casa parece una selva en miniatura she has so many plants that her house looks like a miniature jungle; hay varias plantas industriales en las afueras del pueblo there are several industrial plants on the outskirts of town

**2.** **sole:** no me gusta andar descalza porque me da miedo clavarme algo en la planta de un pie I don't like to go barefoot because I'm afraid of something sticking me in the sole of my foot

**3. floor:** el edificio donde trabajo tiene cuatro plantas the building where I work has four floors
➤ la planta baja the first floor.

la **plantación** *(plural* las plantaciones)
■ **plantation:** en América Central hay grandes plantaciones de banano in Central America there are large banana plantations.

**plantar** *verbo* ■ **to plant**.

el **plástico** ■ **plastic:** muchos artículos que antes eran de vidrio hoy son de plástico many things that used to be made of glass are made of plastic nowadays.

la **plata**
**1. silver:** una mina de plata a silver mine
**2.** *Caribbean, Central America, South America* **money:** hay que pagar el almuerzo, ¿trajiste plata? we have to pay for lunch, did you bring money?

la **plataforma**
**1. stage:** el presidente se dirigió al público desde una plataforma the president addressed the public from a stage
**2.** *River Plate* **platform:** los pasajeros estaban en la plataforma esperando el tren the passengers were on the platform waiting for the train
➤ una plataforma petrolera an oil rig.

el **plátano** ■ **banana**.

la **plática** ■ *Mexico* **chat**.

**platicar** *verbo* ■ *Mexico* **to chat**.

el **plato**
**1. plate:** hay que poner cinco platos en la mesa we have to put five plates on the table
**2. course:** de segundo plato había pescado al horno for the second course there was baked fish
**3. dish:** su especialidad son los platos peruanos his specialty is Peruvian dishes
➤ el plato del día the special of the day.

la **playa** ■ **beach:** en esta playa hay que tener cuidado porque las olas son muy grandes you have to be careful because the waves are very big on this beach; el verano pasado fuimos al campo, este verano nos vamos a la playa last summer we went to the country, this summer we're going to the beach.

la **plaza**
**1. square:** la abuela lleva a los nietos a la plaza todas las tardes the grandmother takes her grandchildren to the square every afternoon
**2. bullring:** fuimos a la plaza porque se presentó el torero preferido de mi padre we went to the bullring because my father's favorite bullfighter was fighting.

el **pleito**
**1. lawsuit:** al final ganó el pleito in the end she won the lawsuit
**2. argument:** ya estoy cansada de estos pleitos, no puede ser que dos hermanos se lleven tan mal I'm tired of these arguments, it's not possible that two brothers get along so badly.

**pleno** *adjetivo*
**1. full:** me siento plena de energía I feel full of energy
**2. middle:** en plena actuación, el actor tropezó y se cayó in the middle of the performance, the actor tripped and fell.

el **plomo** ■ **lead**.

la **pluma**
**1. feather:** este bebé es más ligero que una pluma this baby is lighter than a feather
**2.** *Mexico* **pen:** ¿me prestas una pluma para escribir una carta? will you loan me a pen to write a letter?

el **plumaje** ■ **feathers**.

el **plural** ■ **plural**.

la **población** *(plural* las poblaciones)
■ **population:** la población de Uruguay es poco más de tres millones the population of Uruguay is little more than three million.

el **poblado** ■ **town**.

**poblar** *verbo*
**1. to inhabit:** cuando los españoles colonizaron América, los aztecas poblaban lo que hoy es México when the Spanish colonized America, the Aztecs inhabited what is today Mexico

**223**

**2.** to populate: a lo largo de los siglos, diferentes olas de inmigrantes poblaron América through the centuries, different waves of immigrants populated America

**poblarse** *verbo pronominal* ■ to become filled with: con la llegada de la primavera, los campos se poblaron de flores with the arrival of spring, the fields became filled with flowers.

**pobre** *adjetivo* ■ poor: vivíamos en un barrio pobre we used to live in a poor area; el pobre perro tiene frío, hay que hacerlo entrar the poor dog is cold, you have to make him come in.

**la pobreza** ■ poverty.

**poco** *pronombre, adverbio & adjetivo*

**1.** little: ¿quieres flan? queda un poco do you want some custard? there's a little left; estás cansada porque anoche dormiste muy poco you're tired because you slept very little last night; me queda muy poca plata, no va a ser suficiente I have very little money left, it's not going to be enough

**2.** too few: compramos pocas manzanas, vamos a tener que volver y comprar más we bought too few apples, we're going to have to go back and buy more.

**poder** *verbo*

**1.** can: ¿puedo llevarme este libro? — sí, claro can I take this book? — yes, of course

**2.** to be able to: mañana no voy a poder encontrarme contigo tomorrow I'm not going to be able to meet you

➤ puede ser it's possible: ¿te parece que va a aceptar el ofrecimiento? — puede ser do you think he'll accept the offer? — it's possible

**el poder** ■ power: no me interesa el poder, sino el bienestar de mi pueblo power doesn't interest me, but rather the well-being of my people

➤ poder legislativo legislative power.

**poderoso** *adjetivo* ■ powerful.

**podrido** *adjetivo* ■ rotten: había un fuerte olor a fruta podrida there was a strong smell of rotten fruit.

**el poema** ■ poem.

**la poesía**

**1.** poetry: se me hace muy difícil leer poesía I find it very difficult to read poetry

**2.** poem: Laura leyó sus poesías en la fiesta de la escuela Laura read her poems at the school party.

**el/la poeta** ■ poet.

**el policía** ■ policeman (*plural* policemen)

**la policía**

**1.** police: pensamos que había entrado un ladrón y por eso llamamos a la policía we thought that a thief had broken in and that's why we called the police

**2.** policewoman (*plural* policewomen): es policía she's a policewoman.

**político** *adjetivo*

**1.** political: un partido político a political party

**2.** by marriage: la esposa de mi tío es mi tía política my uncle's wife is my aunt by marriage

**el político, la política** ■ politician.

**la pollera** ■ *Andes, River Plate* skirt.

**el pollo** ■ chicken.

**el polo** ■ pole.

**la polución** ■ pollution.

**el polvo** ■ dust: hay que limpiar aquí porque está lleno de polvo you have to clean here because it's covered in dust.

**la pólvora** ■ gunpowder.

**la pomada** ■ ointment.

**el pomelo** ■ grapefruit (*plural* grapefruit).

**el pomo**

**1.** handle: el pomo de esta puerta está pegajoso this door's handle is sticky

**2.** tube: ¿podrías comprar tres pomos de pasta de dientes? could you buy three tubes of toothpaste?

**la pompa** ■ bubble: pompas de jabón soap bubbles.

**el pómulo** ■ cheekbone.

**el poncho** ■ poncho.

**poner** *verbo*

1. **to put:** puse la silla cerca de la ventana para tener más luz I put the chair close to the window to have more light

2. **to set:** hay que poner la mesa para la cena we have to set the table for dinner

3. **to give:** ¿qué nombre le van a poner al bebé? what name are they going to give the baby?

**ponerse** *verbo pronominal*

1. **to put on:** hace mucho frío, es mejor que te pongas algo más abrigado it's very cold, it's best that you put on something warmer

2. **to set:** el sol se pone por el oeste the sun sets in the west.

la **ponzoña** ■ **poison**.

**ponzoñoso** *adjetivo* ■ **poisonous**.

el **popote** *Mexico* ■ **drinking straw**.

**popular** *adjetivo*

1. **popular:** es un cantante muy popular he's a very popular singer

2. **folk:** estudia la cultura popular he studies folk culture.

la **popularidad** ■ **popularity:** su popularidad ha aumentado en los últimos años his popularity has increased in the last few years.

**por** *preposición*

1. **through:** viajamos por varios países we traveled through several countries

2. **because of:** cerraron el aeropuerto por mal tiempo they closed the airport because of bad weather

3. **times:** cinco por cinco es igual a veinticinco five times five equals twenty-five

4. **per:** el límite de velocidad aquí es 100 kilómetros por hora the speed limit here is 100 kilometers per hour

5. **in:** el recorrido es muy largo, hay que hacerlo por etapas the journey is very long, we have to do it in stages

6. **at:** a las cinco paso a buscarte por tu casa at five o'clock I'll come pick you up at your house

➤ **por mí** as far as I'm concerned
➤ **¿por qué?** why?

la **porción** *(plural* las **porciones)** ■ **portion:** estos ingredientes alcanzan para preparar ocho porciones these ingredients will go far enough to make eight portions.

el **poro**

1. **pore:** la piel respira por los poros skin breathes through the pores

2. **leek:** mi tarta favorita es la de poros my favorite kind of tart is leek.

**porque** *conjunción* ■ **because:** no vino porque estaba enfermo he didn't come because he was sick.

el **porqué** ■ **reason:** quiero saber el porqué de este escándalo I want to know the reason for this commotion.

la **porquería**

1. **junk:** estos zapatos son una porquería these shoes are junk

2. *Mexico* **filth:** vive en la porquería he lives in filth.

**portátil** *adjetivo* ■ **portable**.

el **portazo**

➤ **dio un portazo** he slammed the door
➤ **la puerta se cerró de un portazo** the door slammed shut
➤ **desde aquí oí el portazo** I heard the door slam from here.

la **portería**

1. **porter's office:** lo dejé en la portería I left it in the porter's office

2. **goal:** un saque de portería a goal kick.

el **portero,** la **portera**

1. **goalkeeper:** el portero atajó el balón the goalkeeper intercepted the ball

2. **porter:** dejé las llaves con el portero I left the keys with the porter

➤ **el portero eléctrico** the entryphone.

**portorriqueño** *adjetivo*

En inglés, los adjetivos que se refieren a un país o una región se escriben con mayúscula:

**Puerto Rican**

**225**

el **portorriqueño**, la **portorrique-ña**

En inglés, los gentilicios se escriben con mayúscula:

**Puerto Rican:** los portorriqueños the Puerto Ricans.

**portugués** *(plural portugueses)* *adjetivo*

En inglés, los adjetivos que se refieren a un país o una región se escriben con mayúscula:

**Portuguese**

el **portugués**, la **portuguesa**

En inglés, los gentilicios se escriben con mayúscula:

**Portuguese**

➤ los portugueses the Portuguese.

el **portugués** ■ Portuguese.

En inglés, los idiomas se escriben con mayúscula.

la **posada**

1. inn
2. *Mexican Christmas party*

POSADA

A **posada** is a traditional Mexican Christmas party that takes place on one of the nine days before Christmas. At the start of the party, some of the guests go outside to represent Mary and Joseph, and sing a song asking for a room for the night. The guests inside sing the response, inviting them in and the party begins.

la **posibilidad**

1. possibility *(plural possibilities)*: no había pensado en esa posibilidad I hadn't thought about that possibility
2. chance: eso le da la posibilidad de ir a la universidad that gives him the chance to go to college
➤ tener posibilidades de algo to have a good chance of something: tiene muchas posibilidades de llegar a la final he has a good chance of making it to the finals.

**posible** *adjetivo* ■ **possible**: lo siento, pero no es posible I'm sorry, but it's not possible
➤ ¿es posible cambiar los boletos? is it possible to change the tickets?
➤ es posible que se haya perdido it's possible that he got lost
➤ vamos a hacer todo lo posible we're going to do everything possible
➤ lo más pronto posible as soon as possible.

la **posición** *(plural las posiciones)* ■ position: hay que mantenerlo en posición vertical we have to keep it in a vertical position
➤ se clasificó en segunda posición he won second place.

**positivo** *adjetivo* ■ positive
➤ el análisis dio positivo the test was positive.

**posponer** *verbo* ■ to postpone.

la **postal** ■ post card.

el **poste**
1. post: el balón dio en el poste derecho del arco the ball hit the right goal post
2. pole: un poste telegráfico a telegraph pole.

el **póster** *(plural los pósters)* ■ poster.

**postizo** *adjetivo* ■ fake.

el **postre** ■ dessert: ¿qué hay de postre? what is there for dessert?

la **postura** ■ position
➤ tienen dos posturas y ya se rompieron they've been worn twice and they already broke.

**potable** *adjetivo*
➤ agua potable drinking water.

la **potencia** ■ power: un motor de mucha potencia a high power motor
➤ en potencia in the making: es un gran músico en potencia he's a great musician in the making.

**potente** *adjetivo* ■ powerful.

**226**

el **pozo** ■ well: un pozo de petróleo an oil well.

la **práctica** ■ practice: está fuera de práctica he's out of practice
➤ en la práctica in practice: en la práctica la gente confunde esas dos palabras in practice people confuse those two words
➤ poner algo en práctica to put something into practice: puso su idea en práctica he put his idea into practice.

**practicar** verbo ■ to practice: necesitas practicar más tu inglés you need to practice your English more
➤ ¿practicas algún deporte? do you play a sport?

**práctico** adjetivo ■ practical: es una persona muy práctica he's a very practical person.

la **precaución** (plural las precauciones) ■ foresight: tuvo la precaución de dejarlo desenchufado he had the foresight to leave it unplugged
➤ tomar precauciones to take precautions: hay que tomar precauciones cuando tomamos el sol we have to take precautions when we sunbathe.

**precavido** adjetivo ■ well-prepared: como persona precavida, trajo el paraguas like a well-prepared person, she brought the umbrella.

el **precio** ■ price: van a subir los precios otra vez prices are going to go up again
➤ ¿qué precio tienen? how much are they?

la **preciosidad**
➤ los jardines son una preciosidad the gardens are lovely
➤ ¡qué preciosidad de niña! what a lovely girl!

**precioso** adjetivo ■ beautiful.

el **precipicio** ■ cliff: cayó por un precipicio he fell off a cliff.

**precipitarse** verbo pronominal
➤ no se precipiten y elijan con calma don't rush and choose carefully

➤ parece que me precipité al juzgarlo it seems that I was hasty in judging him.

**preciso** adjetivo
1. precise: me dio indicaciones precisas de cómo llegar he gave me precise directions for how to get there
2. accurate: un instrumento muy preciso a very accurate instrument
➤ si es preciso, pide ayuda if necessary, ask for help
➤ no es preciso que te lo aprendas de memoria it's not necessary for you to memorize it.

**predecir** verbo ■ to predict.

**predicar** verbo ■ to preach.

**preescolar** adjetivo ■ preschool.

la **preferencia**
1. preference: dan preferencia a los estudiantes con mejores notas they give preference to the students with better grades
2. right of way: tienen preferencia los que vienen por la derecha the ones that come from the right have the right of way
➤ tiene preferencia por los colores brillantes she prefers bright colors
➤ de preferencia preferably: el martes, de preferencia en la mañana Tuesday, preferably in the morning.

**preferir** verbo ■ to prefer: prefiere estudiar solo en su casa he prefers to study alone in his house
➤ prefiero no saber I'd rather not know.

el **prefijo** ■ prefix.

la **pregunta** ■ question: no contestó mi pregunta he didn't answer my question
➤ me hicieron varias preguntas they asked me several questions.

**preguntar** verbo ■ to ask: pregúntale a la profesora ask the teacher
➤ preguntarle algo a alguien to ask somebody something: le pregunté la hora I asked him what time it was
➤ cuando llegues allá, pregunta por Ana when you get there, ask for Ana
➤ siempre pregunta por él para saber cómo está she always asks about him to know how he is.

el **prejuicio** ■ prejudice
➤ **tener prejuicios** to be prejudiced: **no tiene prejuicios contra nadie** he's not prejudiced toward anybody
➤ **prejuicios raciales** racial prejudices.

**premiar** *verbo*
1. to give an award to: **premiaron al mejor alumno** they gave an award to the best student
2. to reward: **hay que premiar el esfuerzo** we have to reward the effort.

el **premio**
1. prize: **se ganó el primer premio** he won the first prize; **le dieron el Premio Nobel** they gave him the Nobel Prize
2. reward: **en premio a su buen trabajo** in reward for his good work.

la **prenda**
➤ **prenda de vestir** garment
➤ **prendas de lana** woolen garments.

**prender** *verbo*
1. to light: **prendió un cigarrillo** he lit a cigarette
2. to turn on: **prende el televisor** turn on the television; **prendió la luz** he turned the light on
➤ **este carbón no prende** this coal won't light
➤ **prenderle fuego a algo** to set fire to something
➤ **la luces de la calle se prenden al atardecer** the streetlights come on at dusk.

la **prensa** ■ press: **la prensa nacional** the national press
➤ **lo leí en la prensa de hoy** I read it in today's news.

la **preocupación** (*plural* las preocupaciones)
1. worry (*plural* **worries**): **tienen muchas preocupaciones** they have a lot of worries
2. concern: **es un motivo de preocupación para sus padres** it's a cause for concern for his parents.

**preocupar** *verbo* ■ to worry: **no preocupes a tus padres** don't worry your parents; **me preocupa mucho el examen de mañana** tomorrow's exam worries me a lot

**preocuparse** *verbo pronominal* ■ to worry: **no se preocupen** don't worry
➤ **preocuparse por algo** to worry about something: **mi mamá se preocupa por todo** my mom worries about everything
➤ **se preocupa mucho si no llamo** she gets very worried if I don't call.

la **preparación** ■ preparation: **la preparación de los informes lleva tiempo** the reports' preparation takes time
➤ **le falta preparación** he lacks training.

**preparar** *verbo*
1. to prepare for: **el profesor no preparó la clase** the professor didn't prepare for class
2. to prepare: **nos están preparando para el examen de admisión** they're preparing us for the entrance exam
3. to make: **prepara unos postres exquisitos** he makes exquisite desserts; **voy a preparar el té** I'm going to make tea

**prepararse** *verbo pronominal*
1. to get ready: **se preparó para salir** he got ready to leave
2. to prepare: **tienen que prepararse para el examen** they have to prepare for the exam
3. to train: **se están preparando para la maratón** they're training for the marathon
➤ **prepárate para una gran sorpresa** prepare yourself for a big surprise.

los **preparativos** ■ preparations.

la **preposición** (*plural* las preposiciones) ■ preposition.

la **preparatoria** ■ *Mexico* senior high school.

la **presa**
1. dam: **van a construir una presa** they're going to build a dam
2. prey: **tiburones en busca de una presa** sharks in search of prey.

la **presencia** ■ presence: **lo hizo en mi presencia** he did it in my presence.

**228**

la **presentación** *(plural* las presentaciones) ■ **presentation: me puso una
nota por la presentación** he gave me a
grade for the presentation
➤ **hacer las presentaciones** to make the introductions: **mi papá se encargó de hacer
las presentaciones** my father took care of
making the introductions.

el **presentador**

1. **host: el nuevo presentador del programa**
the new host of the program
2. **presenter: el presentador del noticiero
de las seis** the presenter of the six o'clock
news.

la **presentadora**

1. **hostess: la nueva presentadora del
programa** the new program hostess
2. **presenter: la presentadora del noticiero
de las seis** the presenter of the six o'clock
news.

**presentar** *verbo*

1. **to introduce: me presentó a su hermana**
he introduced me to his sister
2. **to hand in: no ha presentado el trabajo**
he hasn't handed in his paper; **el inspector
presentó su renuncia** the inspector handed
in his resignation
3. **to host: presenta el programa de los
martes** he hosts the Tuesday program
4. **to launch: va a presentar su nuevo disco**
he's going to launch his new album
➤ **te presento a mi hermano** this is my
brother

**presentarse** *verbo pronominal*

1. **to turn up: se presentó tarde y sin las tareas** he turned up late and without his homework
2. **to introduce oneself: se presentó como
el nuevo director** he introduced himself as
the new director
➤ **no se presentó al examen** he didn't take
the exam.

**presente** *adjetivo* ■ **present: había sólo tres alumnos presentes** there were only
three students present; **en las presentes
circunstancias** in present circumstances
➤ **tener algo presente** to remember something

➤ **tenía tan presente traerlo y se me olvidó** I had remembered that I was supposed to
bring it, but then I forgot it
➤ **¡presente!** here!

el **presente** ■ **el director se dirigió a
los presentes** the director addressed those
present.

el **presidente,** la **presidenta**

1. *de un país, una empresa* **president: el
Presidente de la República** the President of
the Republic
2. *de una asociación, un jurado* **chairperson: el presidente del club de fútbol** the
chairperson of the soccer club.

la **presión** *(plural* las presiones) ■ **pressure**
➤ **tiene la presión alta** he has high blood
pressure.

**preso** *adjetivo*
➤ **está preso** he's in jail
➤ **se los llevaron presos** they arrested them

el **preso,** la **presa** ■ **prisoner**.

el **préstamo** ■ **loan: pidió un préstamo**
he asked for a loan.

**prestar** *verbo* ■ **to lend: un amigo me
prestó su bicicleta** a friend lent me his bicycle
➤ **¿me prestas los patines?** can I borrow the
skates?
➤ **prestar atención** to pay attention: **presta
más atención a lo que dice la profesora**
pay more attention to what the professor
says.

el **prestigio** ■ **prestige: el prestigio del
primer ministro está cayendo** the prime
minister's prestige is falling
➤ **de prestigio** prestigious.

**presumido** *adjetivo* ■ **vain**.

**presumir** *verbo* ■ **to show off: lo hace
sólo para presumir** he only does it to show
off
➤ **Tito presume de inteligente** Tito thinks
he's really intelligent.

**pretender** *verbo*

1. **to try to achieve:** no sé lo que pretenden con eso I don't know what they're trying to achieve with that
2. **to intend:** pretenden hacernos estudiar más they intend to make us study more
3. **to expect:** no pretenderán que me estudie todo esto they won't expect me to study all this; ¿pretendes que yo te crea? do you expect me to believe you?

⚠ The Spanish word **pretender** is a false cognate: it does not mean "pretend".

la **prevención** ■ **prevention:** la prevención de accidentes accident prevention.

**prevenir** *verbo*

1. **to prevent:** ayuda a prevenir los resfriados it helps to prevent colds
2. **to warn:** me previnieron lo que podría pasar they warned me what could happen
➤ más vale prevenir que curar prevention is better than cure.

**prever** *verbo*

1. **to anticipate:** nadie lo había previsto nobody had anticipated it
2. **to plan:** prevén finalizar las obras este año they plan to finish the repairs this year
➤ prevén un aumento de las temperaturas a nivel mundial they foresee an increase in temperatures worldwide.

**previo** *adjetivo* ■ **previous:** no es necesario tener experiencia previa it's not necessary to have previous experience
➤ sin previo aviso without warning: llegó sin previo aviso he arrived without warning.

**previsto** *(adjetivo & verb part)*

■ *adjetivo*
➤ un cambio que no estaba previsto an unanticipated change
➤ resultó tal como estaba previsto it came out as expected
➤ la salida está prevista a las dos the departure is planned for two o'clock
➤ no tenía previsto gastar tanto he didn't plan to spend so much

➤ tiene prevista la llegada a las dos she's due in at two o'clock
■ *verbo*
➤ prever.

**prieto** *adjetivo*

1. *Mexico informal* **dark:** su hermano es tan prieto como ella her brother is as dark as her
2. **tan:** ¡que prieta estás! ¿estuviste en la playa? how tan you look! were you at the beach?

la **primaria** ■ **elementary school:** este año termina la primaria this year he finishes elementary school.

la **primavera** ■ **spring:** en primavera in spring.

**primer** *adjetivo* ■

Shortened form of **primero** used before masculine singular nouns.

**primero** *adjetivo & pronombre* ■ **first:** en la primera página on the first page; el primer mes del año the first month of the year
➤ en primer lugar, nos dio a todos las gracias first, he thanked all of us
➤ se sienta en la primera fila he sits in the first row
➤ quiere ser la primera de la clase she wants to be at the top of the class
➤ fue el primero en terminar he was the first one to finish
➤ a primera hora de la mañana first thing in the morning
➤ el primer ministro the prime minister
➤ el primero de enero the first of January
➤ primeros auxilios first aid.

**primitivo** *adjetivo* ■ **primitive**.

el **primo**, la **prima** ■ **cousin**
➤ son primas hermanas they are first cousins.

la **princesa** ■ **princess**.

**principal** *adjetivo* ■ **main:** una de las principales causas de accidentes one of the main causes of accidents
➤ lo principal es ser honesto the main thing is to be honest.

el **príncipe** ■ prince.

el/la **principiante** ■ beginner.

el **principio**

1. **beginning:** el principio de la película es muy original the beginning of the movie is very original
2. **principle:** se basa en un principio moral it's based on a moral principle; no tiene principios he doesn't have principles
➤ al principio at first: al principio dijo que no at first he said no
➤ en principio in principle: en principio, parecía bueno in principle, it seemed good
➤ desde un principio no me gustó I didn't like him from the start
➤ a principios de mes at the beginning of the month.

la **prisa** ■ hurry: ¿a qué tanta prisa? what's the hurry?
➤ darse prisa to hurry up: ¡date prisa! hurry up!
➤ correr prisa to be urgent: esto corre prisa this is urgent
➤ tener prisa to be in a hurry.

los **prismáticos** ■ binoculars.

**privado** adjetivo ■ private: un colegio privado a private school; su vida privada his private life
➤ en privado privately: lo celebraron en privado they celebrated it privately.

el **privilegio** ■ privilege: es un gran privilegio it's a great privilege.

la **probabilidad** ■ probability (plural probabilities)
➤ no tiene ninguna probabilidad de ganar he doesn't have any chance of winning
➤ ¿cuáles son las probabilidades? what are the chances?
➤ si no estudian hay menos probabilidades de que aprueben if you don't study there's less chance that you'll pass.

**probable** adjetivo ■ likely: tal vez se perdieron — es muy probable maybe they got lost — it's very likely
➤ me parece muy poco probable it seems very unlikely to me

➤ es probable que se haya olvidado it's likely that he forgot.

el **probador** ■ fitting room.

**probar** verbo
1. **to prove:** puedo probar que miente I can prove that he's lying
2. **to test:** están probando una nueva vacuna they're testing a new vaccine
3. **to taste:** pruébala por si le falta aliño taste it and see if it needs seasoning
4. **to try:** prueba esto, que te va a gustar try this, you'll like it
➤ prueba hacerlo tú mismo try to do it yourself
➤ me probé varias tallas I tried on several sizes.

el **problema** ■ problem: nunca pude resolver el problema I never managed to solve the problem
➤ tiene muchos problemas he has many problems
➤ está viejo y ya empieza a darme problemas it's old and it's now beginning to give me trouble
➤ siempre se está metiendo en problemas he's always getting into trouble
➤ tiene problemas del corazón he has heart problems.

el **procesador** ■ processor
➤ un procesador de palabras word processor
➤ un procesador de textos word processor.

el **proceso** ■ process: el proceso de paz the peace process.

la **producción** (plural las producciones) ■ production.

**producir** verbo
1. **to produce:** la región produce café the region produces coffee
2. **to cause:** el accidente produjo un gran atasco the accident caused a major traffic jam
➤ el polen me produce alergia pollen gives me allergies.

el **producto** ■ product: un producto manufacturado a manufactured product
➤ productos alimenticios foodstuffs.

**231**

la **profesión** *(plural* las profesiones*)* ■ **profession**.

**profesional** *adjetivo* ■ **professional**

el/la **profesional** ■ **professional**.

el/la **profesionista** ■ *Mexico* **professional**.

el **profesor,** la **profesora**
  1. **teacher:** la profesora de inglés the English teacher
  2. **instructor:** la profesora de natación the swimming instructor; **el profesor de manejo** the driving instructor
  ➤ **es profesor universitario** he's a university professor.

la **profundidad** ■ **depth:** a una profundidad de tres metros at a depth of three meters
  ➤ **tiene tres metros de profundidad** it's three meters deep
  ➤ **en profundidad** in depth: lo estudié en profundidad I studied it in depth.

**profundo** *adjetivo* ■ **deep:** la parte más profunda de la piscina the deepest part of the swimming pool
  ➤ **un pozo poco profundo** a shallow well.

el **programa** ■ **program:** un programa informático a computer program
  ➤ **el programa de estudios** the syllabus
  ➤ **no tengo programa para este fin de semana** I don't have plans for this weekend.

el **programador,** la **programadora**
  ■ **programmer**.

**programar** *verbo*
  1. **to program:** por no saber programar el video me perdí el concierto as I didn't know how to program the video recorder, I missed the concert
  2. **to plan:** no he programado nada para el sábado I haven't planned anything for Saturday.

**progresar** *verbo* ■ **to make progress:** ha progresado mucho en los estudios he's made a lot of progress in his studies.

el **progreso** ■ **progress:** el progreso de la ciencia scientific progress; ha hecho progresos en inglés she's made progress in English.

**prohibido** *adjetivo* ■ **forbidden:** eso está absolutamente prohibido that is absolutely forbidden
  ➤ **prohibido fumar** no smoking
  ➤ **prohibida la entrada** no entry
  ➤ **un medicamento prohibido en ese país** a drug banned in that country.

**prohibir** *verbo*
  1. **to ban:** le prohibieron usar el celular en la clase they banned him from using his cell phone in class
  2. **to prohibit:** han prohibido toda publicidad al tabaco they've prohibited all tobacco advertising
  ➤ **le prohibieron los alimentos grasos** they forbade him from eating fatty foods.

**prolongar** *verbo* ■ **to extend:** van a prolongar sus vacaciones they're going to extend their vacations.

el **promedio** ■ **average:** duerme un promedio de siete horas he sleeps an average of seven hours
  ➤ **este año he tenido un buen promedio en los estudios** this year I've had a good grade point average
  ➤ **en promedio, estudia muy poco** on average, he studies very little.

la **promesa** ■ **promise:** siempre cumple sus promesas she always keeps her promises.

**prometer** *verbo* ■ **to promise:** pero si tú prometiste llevarnos al cine but you promised to take us to the movies
  ➤ **prometió estudiar más** he promised to study more
  ➤ **¿me lo prometes?** do you promise?

el **pronombre** ■ **pronoun**.

el **pronóstico** ■ **forecast:** el pronóstico del tiempo the weather forecast.

**pronto** *adverbio* ■ **soon:** va a volver pronto he's going to return soon

➤ ¡hasta pronto! see you soon!

➤ lo más pronto posible as soon as possible

➤ tan pronto como as soon as: llámame tan pronto como llegues call me as soon as you arrive

➤ de pronto oímos un grito all of a sudden we heard a scream.

**pronunciar** *verbo*

1. **to pronounce:** ¿cómo pronuncian la letra z en España? how do they pronounce the letter z in Spain?

2. **to make:** el director pronunció un discurso the director made a speech.

la **propaganda** ■ **advertising:** hay mucha propaganda en la televisión there's a lot of advertising on television

➤ hacerle propaganda a algo to advertise something: le hacen mucha propaganda a ese producto they're advertising that product a lot.

la **propiedad** ■ **property** (*plural* **properties**).

el **propietario,** la **propietaria** ■ **owner**.

la **propina** ■ **tip:** ¿dejaste propina? did you leave a tip?

➤ le di propina la taxista I tipped the taxi driver

➤ ¿cuánto le diste de propina? how much did you tip him?

**propio** *adjetivo*

1. **own:** tengo mi propia computadora I have my own computer

2. **himself (herself):** el propio director me lo dijo the director himself told me

➤ es muy propio de la gente de esa edad it's very typical of people of that age.

**proponer** *verbo*

1. **to suggest:** propuso ir al cine he suggested going to the movies; propongo que nos vayamos I suggest that we leave

2. **to nominate:** lo propusieron para el premio they nominated him for the award

➤ le propuso matrimonio he proposed to her

➤ me propongo escribirles más seguido I plan to write you more often

➤ quiere proponerte algo he wants to propose something to you.

la **proporción** (*plural* **las proporciones**)

■ **proportion:** la cabeza es muy chica en proporción al cuerpo the head is too small in proportion to the body

➤ la proporción es dos por uno the ratio is two to one.

el **propósito** ■ **purpose:** su único propósito es ganar his only purpose is to win

➤ sus propósitos son buenos his intentions are good

➤ creo que lo hizo a propósito I think he did it on purpose

➤ a propósito, si lo ves dile que me llame by the way, if you see him tell him to call me.

la **propuesta** ■ **proposal**.

**próspero** *adjetivo* ■ **prosperous**

➤ les deseamos un próspero Año Nuevo we wish you a Happy New Year.

el/la **protagonista** ■ **main character:** el protagonista muere al final the main character dies at the end.

la **protección** ■ **protection**.

**proteger** *verbo* ■ **to protect:** la sombrilla nos protege del sol the sunshade is protecting us from the sun

➤ ropa para protegerse del frío clothes to shield oneself from the cold.

la **proteína** ■ **protein**.

la **protesta** ■ **protest:** se unieron a la protesta they joined the protest

➤ una manifestación de protesta a protest demonstration.

**protestar** *verbo*

1. **to complain:** lo único que hace es protestar the only thing he does is complain; déjense de protestar por todo y a trabajar quit complaining about everything and get to work

2. **to protest:** protestan por la subida de los precios they're protesting the increase in prices.

**233**

el **provecho**

➤ **sacar provecho de algo** to benefit from something: **no sacó ningún provecho de su estadía en Europa** he didn't benefit at all from his stay in Europe

➤ **¡buen provecho!** have a nice meal!

el **proverbio** ▪ proverb.

la **provincia** ▪ province.

**provisional** *adjetivo* ▪ provisional.

**provisorio** *adjetivo* ▪ provisional.

**provocar** *verbo*

1. **to provoke: déjate de provocar a tu hermano** stop provoking your brother

2. **to cause: las inundaciones han provocado el cierre de varios caminos** the floods have caused the closing of several roads

➤ **no saben lo que provocó el incendio** they don't know what started the fire.

**próximo** *(adjetivo & pronombre)* **next: el próximo lunes tengo una prueba** next Monday I have a test; **invítalo la próxima vez que lo veas** invite him next time you see him

➤ **tome la próxima a la izquierda** take the next left.

**proyectar** *verbo*

1. **to plan: están proyectando viajar a Europa** they're planning to travel to Europe

2. **to show: nos proyectaron una película** they showed us a film

3. **to cast: la casa proyecta su sombra en parte del jardín** the house casts its shadow on part of the yard.

el **proyecto**

1. **plan: están haciendo proyectos para las vacaciones** they're making vacation plans

2. **project: trabaja en un proyecto desarrollo** he works on a development project

➤ **un proyecto de ley** a bill.

el **proyector** ▪ projector.

**prudente** *adjetivo* ▪ sensible: **tienes que ser más prudente** you have to be more sensible

➤ **lo más prudente es no decir nada** the wisest thing is not to say anything.

**prueba, pruebas** *verbo* ➤ probar.

la **prueba**

1. **proof: es prueba de que lo puede hacer** it's proof that he can do it

2. **test: tengo dos pruebas esta semana** I have two tests this week; **le hicieron una prueba de aptitud** they gave him an aptitude test

3. **event: las pruebas de atletismo** the track events

➤ **es una prueba de cariño** it's a token of affection

➤ **una prueba nuclear** a nuclear test

➤ **tienen al jugador a prueba** they have the player on probation

➤ **rímel a prueba de agua** waterproof mascara

➤ **a prueba de balas** bulletproof.

**pruebo** *verbo* ➤ probar.

**publicar** *verbo* ▪ to publish.

la **publicidad**

1. **advertising: una campaña de publicidad** an advertising campaign

2. **publicity: le han dado mucha publicidad al asunto** they've given the matter a lot of publicity; **ha tenido muy mala publicidad** he's had very bad publicity.

**público** *adjetivo* ▪ public: **un colegio público** a public school

el **público**

1. **public: todavía no está abierto al público** it's still not open to the public

2. **audience: el público en el cine empezó a aplaudir** the audience in the movie theater began to applaud

3. **spectators: el público de un estadio** the stadium spectators

➤ **hablar en público lo pone nervioso** speaking in public makes him nervous.

**pude, pudiste etc** *verbo* ➤ poder.

**pudrirse** *verbo pronominal* ▪ to rot.

el **pueblo**

1. *de pocos habitantes* **village**
2. *más grande* **town**
➤ **el pueblo de América Latina** the people of Latin America.

**puedo** *verbo* ➤ poder.

el **puente**

1. **bridge:** cruzaron el puente they crossed the bridge
2. **long weekend:** el puente del primero de noviembre the long weekend for the November first holiday
➤ **hacer puente** to take a long weekend
➤ **el puente aéreo** the shuttle service

HACER PUENTE

When a national or religious holiday falls on a Tuesday or a Thursday, it is common practice to **hacer puente**, that is, to have a long weekend by missing work and school on the preceding Monday or the following Friday. While this is not always condoned by the government or employers, people still do it to make the most of their holidays.

el **puerco**

1. **pig:** crían puercos they raise pigs
2. *Mexico* **pork:** no come puerco she doesn't eat pork.

la **puerta**

1. **door:** la puerta de calle estaba abierta the front door was open
2. **gate:** entró por la puerta del jardín he entered through the garden gate
➤ **llamaron a la puerta** they knocked at the door
➤ **un coche de cuatro puertas** a four-door car
➤ **la puerta de embarque** boarding gate.

el **puerto** ■ port
➤ **llegar a puerto** to come into port
➤ **un puerto deportivo** a marina
➤ **un puerto marítimo** a sea port
➤ **un puerto pesquero** a fishing port.

**Puerto Rico** *sustantivo masculino*
■ Puerto Rico.

**puertorriqueño** *adjetivo*

En inglés, los adjetivos que se refieren a un país o una región se escriben con mayúscula:

**Puerto Rican**

el **puertorriqueño,** la **puertorriqueña**

En inglés, los gentilicios se escriben con mayúscula:

**Puerto Rican:** los puertorriqueños the Puerto Ricans.

**pues** *conjunción*

1. **then:** tengo frío — pues ponte algo más abrigador I'm cold — then put on something warmer
2. **well:** ¿crees que se lo contó? — pues... no sabría decirte do you think that he told her? — well, I couldn't tell you
➤ **¡pues claro que me divertí!** of course I had fun!

la **puesta**
➤ **la puesta de sol** the sunset
➤ **la puesta en libertad de los rehenes** the freeing of the hostages.

el **puesto**

1. **place:** le reservé un puesto en la mesa I saved her a place at the table
2. **stand:** un puesto de fruta a fruit stand
3. **job:** tiene un puesto en la universidad she has a job at the university
➤ **se sacó el primer puesto** he got first place.

la **pulga** ■ flea.

la **pulgada** ■ inch.

el **pulgar** ■ thumb.

**pulir** *verbo* ■ to polish.

el **pulmón** *(plural los pulmones)* ■ lung.

la **pulmonía** ■ pneumonia.

la **pulsera** ■ bracelet: una pulsera de oro a gold bracelet.

el **pulso** ■ pulse: le tomó el pulso she took his pulse

➤ **tiene muy buen pulso** she has very good aim
➤ **levantaron el piano a pulso** they picked up the piano by sheer strength.

el **puma** ◾ puma.

la **punta**
1. **tip:** la punta de la lengua the tip of the tongue
2. **point:** la punta del cuchillo the knife point; se le rompió la punta al lápiz the pencil point broke
3. **end:** la otra punta del cordel the other end of the rope; la punta de la nariz the end of the nose
➤ **la punta de los dedos** the fingertips
➤ **este lápiz no tiene punta** this pencil is not sharpened
➤ **queda en la otra punta de la ciudad** it's at the other end of the city
➤ **recorrió Mexico de punta a punta** he traveled Mexico from one end to the other.

el **puntapié** ◾ kick: le dio un puntapié a la pelota he gave the ball a kick
➤ **le daba puntapiés por debajo de la mesa** he was kicking her underneath the table
➤ **el puntapié inicial** the kickoff.

la **puntería**
➤ **tiene muy buena puntería** she's a good shot.

el **punto**
1. **point:** ganaron por un punto they won by one point; es uno de los puntos que van a tratar it's one of the points that they're going to discuss
2. **dot:** el punto sobre la "i" the dot on the "i"; un punto com a dot com
3. **stitch:** le pusieron cinco puntos en la frente they gave her five stitches on her forehead
4. **period:** hay que terminar la frase con un punto you have to end the sentence with a period
➤ **punto y coma** semicolon
➤ **dos puntos** colon
➤ **puntos suspensivos** ellipsis

➤ **punto de vista** point of view
➤ **estoy a punto de terminar** I'm just about to finish
➤ **estuvo a punto de llorar** he was on the verge of tears
➤ **estuve a punto de decírselo** I nearly told her
➤ **hasta cierto punto eso es verdad** in a way that's true
➤ **son las tres en punto** it's three o'clock on the dot.

el **puñado** ◾ handful: un puñado de tierra a handful of soil.

el **puñal** ◾ dagger.

la **puñalada** ◾ stab
➤ **recibió varias puñaladas** he received several stab wounds
➤ **tiene una puñalada en el pecho** he has a stab wound on his chest.

el **puñetazo** ◾ punch
➤ **le dio un puñetazo en el ojo** he punched him in the eye.

el **puño**
1. **fist:** luchó con los puños he fought with his fists
2. **cuff:** una manga con puño a sleeve with a cuff.

la **pupila** ◾ pupil.

el **puré**
➤ **puré de papas** mashed potatoes.

**purificar** verbo ◾ to purify.

**puro** adjective ◾ pure: es plata pura it's pure silver
➤ **son puras mentiras** they're all lies
➤ **es la pura verdad** it's the absolute truth
➤ **no basta con la pura fuerza** strength alone is not enough
➤ **fue pura coincidencia** it was pure coincidence
➤ **lo hago por puro gusto** I do it just for pleasure

el **puro** ◾ cigar.

el **pus** ◾ pus.

**236**

**mios tiene** the one which has the most awards

En inglés el lenguaje hablado se suele omitir **which** cuando **que** no tiene función de sujeto:

**el disco que compré ayer** the record I bought yesterday; **la clase a la que pertenezco** the class I belong to.

 **qué** *(adjetivo & pronombre)*

1. **what:** ¿**qué día es hoy?** what day is today?; **le voy a preguntar qué quiere hacer** I'm going to ask him what he wants to do
2. **which:** ¿**a qué colegio vas?** which school do you go to?; **no se qué color elegir** I don't know which color to choose
➤ ¿**qué?** what?
➤ ¿**qué tal?** how's it going?
➤ ¿**qué tal te va en el colegio?** how's school going for you?
➤ ¡**qué pena!** what a shame!
➤ ¡**qué casa tan bonita!** what a beautiful house!
➤ ¡**y qué!** so what!

**quebrar** *verbo* ■ **to go bankrupt: han quebrado muchas empresas** many companies have gone bankrupt

**quebrarse** *verbo pronominal* ■ **to break: me caí y me quebré una pierna** I fell and broke a leg; **se le quebró una uña** she broke a nail; **se me han quebrado casi todos los vasos** I've broken almost all the glasses.

el **quechua** ■ Quechua

QUECHUA

**Quechua** is a native American language spoken today by approximately 25% of the population of Bolivia, Ecuador, and Peru, totaling as many as 10 million people in the Andean region. In the pre-Columbian era it was the official language of the Inca Empire, whose capital was the city of Cuzco. Nowadays **quechua** is enjoying a renewed vitality and gaining new speakers.

**quedar** *verbo*

1. **to suit: ese color no le queda bien** that color doesn't suit her

 **que**

■ *(conjunción & pronombre)*

1. **that: dijo que esperaría** he said that he would wait

En inglés en el lenguaje hablado se suele omitir **that**:

**decidió que no quería ir** he decided he didn't want to go

2. **than: tengo mejores notas que tú** I have better grades than you

**Que** no se traduce cuando va precedido de verbos que expresan deseos, ruegos etc. En tales casos en inglés se usa el infinitivo:

➤ **quiero que me ayude** I want him to help me
➤ **le pedí que me llamara** I asked her to call me
➤ ¡**que lo pases bien!** have a good time!
➤ **yo que tú no iría** if I were you I wouldn't go

■ *pronombre*

1. **who: el alumno que sacó mejores notas** the student who made better grades; **el que canta es el menor** the one who's singing is the youngest

En inglés el lenguaje hablado se suele omitir **who** cuando **que** no tiene función de sujeto:

**los amigos que invité a la fiesta** the friends I invited to the party

2. **which: la película que ganó el óscar** the film which won the Oscar; **la que más pre-**

**2. to be left:** no queda leche there's no milk left; **quedan dos limones** there are two lemons left

**3. to be:** el colegio queda muy cerca the school is very close by

➤ quedamos de encontrarnos en el cine we agreed to meet at the movie theater

➤ el postre me quedó muy bueno I really liked the dessert

➤ queda una semana para que empiecen las vacaciones there's one week left before vacation starts

**quedarse** *verbo pronominal*

**1. to stay:** me quedé en el colegio estudiando I stayed at school studying; **se quedó a dormir en mi casa** he stayed at my house to sleep

➤ se quedó callado he stayed quiet

➤ me quedé dormido y llegué tarde I overslept and arrived late

➤ nos quedamos solos we stayed by ourselves

➤ se quedó calvo he went bald

➤ quedarse con algo to keep something.

**quedito** *adverbio Mexico*

**1. quietly:** siempre habla tan quedito he always speaks so quietly

**2. gently:** lo tocó quedito para no despertarlo she touched him gently so as not to wake him.

la **queja** ■ complaint: presentó una queja she made a complaint.

**quejarse** *verbo pronominal* ■ to complain: ¡no te quejes! don't complain!

➤ quejarse de algo to complain about something: se quejó del frío he complained about the cold

➤ quejarse con alguien to complain to somebody: se quejó con la secretaria he complained to the secretary.

la **quemadura** ■ burn: tiene una quemadura en la mano she has a burn on her hand

➤ una crema para las quemaduras de sol a cream for sunburns.

**quemar** *verbo*

**1. to burn:** quemó un montón de hojas he burned a lot of papers

**2. to be boiling hot:** este café quema this coffee is boiling hot

**quemarse** *verbo pronominal*

**1. to burn oneself:** se quemó con la estufa he burned himself on the stove

**2. to get a sunburn:** me quemé en la piscina I got a sunburn at the pool

**3. to tan:** me quemo con facilidad I tan easily

➤ me quemé la mano I burned my hand

➤ se le quemó el arroz he burned the rice

➤ se les quemó la casa their house burned down.

**querer** *verbo*

**1. to want:** ¿qué quieres? what do you want?; **quiero usar el teléfono** I want to use the telephone

**2. to love:** te quiero mucho I love you a lot

➤ ¿quieres tomar algo? would you like a drink?

➤ quisiera saber a qué hora sale el tren I would like to know what time the train leaves

➤ querer que alguien haga algo to want somebody to do something: quiere que vaya a comprar el pan he wants her to go buy the bread

➤ lo hizo sin querer he didn't mean to do it

➤ querer decir to mean: ¿qué quiere decir esta palabra? what does this word mean? no sé qué quiso decir con eso I don't know what he meant by that.

**querido** *adjetivo* ■ dear.

la **quesadilla** ■ *Central America, Mexico folded tortilla with a melted cheese filling.*

el **queso** ■ cheese

➤ queso rallado grated cheese.

**quien** *pronombre* ■ who: la profesora fue quien me lo dijo it was the teacher who told me; **fueron ellos quienes lo rompieron** it was them who broke it; **quien lo haya dicho no importa** who said it is not important

En inglés el lenguaje hablado se suele omitir **who** cuando **quien** no tiene función de sujeto:

la persona con quien hablé the person I spoke with.

**quién** *pronombre* ■ **who:** ¿quién llamó? who called?; no sé quiénes son I don't know who they are
➤ ¿quién es? who's there?
➤ ¿a quién invitaste? who did you invite?
➤ ¿con quién fuiste? who did you go with?
➤ ¿de quién es esto? whose is this?

**quienquiera** *pronombre* ■ **whoever:** quienquiera que sea, dile que no estoy whoever it is, tell him I'm not here.

**quieto** *adjetivo* ■ **still**
➤ ¡quédate quieto! be still!

**químico** *adjetivo* ■ **chemical**

el **químico,** la **química** ■ **chemist:** quiere ser químico he wants to be a chemist.

la **química** ■ **chemistry**.

**quince** *numeral* ■ **fifteen:** tiene quince primos she has fifteen cousins
➤ mi hermana tiene quince años my sister is fifteen years old
➤ el quince de abril the fifteenth of April.

la **quiniela** ■ *Mexico* **lottery**.

**quinientos** *numeral* ■ **five hundred:** tiene quinientas páginas it has five hundred pages.

**quinto** *(adjetivo & pronombre)* **fifth:** fue la quinta persona en entrar he was the fifth person to enter
➤ la quinta parte a fifth

el **quinto** ■ **fifth:** un quinto a fifth
➤ no tienen ni un quinto *Mexico informal* they're broke.

el **quiosco**
1. *de periódicos* **newsstand**
2. *de flores* **flower stand**
3. *de una banda* **bandstand**
4. *de refrescos* **refreshment stand**.

**quisquilloso** *adjetivo*
1. **fussy:** no es quisquilloso, se contenta con poco he's not fussy, anything satisfies him
2. **touchy:** hoy anda muy quisquilloso today he's very touchy.

el **quitamanchas** *(plural* los quitamanchas*)* ■ **stain remover**.

**quitar** *verbo*
1. **to take away:** no le quites el juguete a tu hermano don't take the toy away from your brother
2. **to remove:** hay que quitar esta mancha you have to remove this stain; ¿podrían quitar estas cosas de aquí? could you remove these things from here?

**quitarse** *verbo pronominal* ■ **to take off:** se quitó los zapatos she took off her shoes
➤ quítate de ahí get out of there.

**quizá** *adverbio* ■ **maybe:** quizá vaya al cine maybe I'll go to the movies.

**quizás** *adverbio* ■ **maybe:** quizá vaya al cine maybe I'll go to the movies.

el **rábano** ■ **radish:** no me gusta el rábano I don't like radish
➤ le importa un rábano *informal* he couldn't care less.

la **rabia** ■ **rabies:** lo vacunaron contra la rabia they vaccinated him against rabies
➤ tiene rabia porque lo castigaron he's furious because they punished him
➤ me da rabia que se meta en mis cajones it annoys me that he looks through my drawers

➤ **le tengo rabia** I have a grudge against him
➤ **lloraba de pura rabia** she was crying out of pure rage.

el **rabo** ■ tail.

la **racha**

➤ **están pasando por una buena racha** they're going through a lucky spell
➤ **tuvo una mala racha** he had a piece of bad luck
➤ **una racha de viento** a gust of wind.

**racial** *adjetivo* ■ **racial**.

el **racimo** ■ bunch.

el **racismo** ■ racism.

**racista** *adjetivo* ■ **racist**

el/la **racista** ■ racist.

**racional** *adjetivo* ■ **rational**.

el **radar** ■ radar.

**radiactivo** *adjetivo* ■ **radioactive**.

el **radiador** ■ radiator.

**radiante** *adjetivo* ■ **radiant**: estaba radiante de alegría she was radiant with happiness.

el **radio**

1. *Latin America except Southern Cone* **radio**: prende el radio turn on the radio; me encanta escuchar radio I love to listen to the radio; lo oyó por el radio I heard it on the radio
2. **radius**: estremeció a los edificios en un radio de cinco kilómetros it shook the buildings in a radius of five kilometers
3. **spoke**: el radio de la rueda trasera the spoke of the rear wheel.

la **radiografía** ■ X-ray
➤ **le sacaron una radiografía** they gave her an X-ray.

la **raíz** *(plural* las raíces*)* ■ **root**: un árbol de raíces muy profundas a tree with very deep roots
➤ **a raíz de algo** as a result of
➤ **raíz cuadrada** square root.

la **raja**

1. **crack**: este plato tiene una raja this plate has a crack
2. **slice**: una raja de melón a slice of melon

➤ **una raja de canela** *Mexico* a stick of cinnamon
➤ **rajas de chile** *Mexico* slices of chili.

**rajarse** *verbo pronominal*

1. **to crack**: la pared se rajó the wall cracked
2. **to tear**: se le rajaron los pantalones her pants tore
3. *informal* **to back out**: a último momento se rajó he backed out at the last minute.

el **rallador** ■ grater.

**rallar** *verbo* ■ to grate.

la **rama** ■ branch: las ramas de un árbol the branches of a tree
➤ **irse por las ramas** to beat around the bush.

el **ramo** ■ bouquet: un ramo de rosas a bouquet of roses
➤ **el ramo de la construcción** the construction industry.

la **rana** ■ frog.

el **ranchero**, la **ranchera** ■ *Mexico* peasant.

el **rancho**

1. **shack**: viven en un rancho they live in a shack
2. *Mexico* **ranch**: un rancho ganadero a cattle ranch.

**rancio** *adjetivo* ■ **old**.

la **ranura** ■ slot: mete la moneda en la ranura put the coin in the slot.

la **raqueta** ■ racquet.

**rapar** *verbo* ■ to shave
➤ **le raparon la cabeza** they shaved his head.

**rápido** *(adjetivo & adverbio)*

■ *adjetivo*
**fast**: tu eres más rápido que yo you're faster than me
■ *adverbio*
**quickly**: habla muy rápido he speaks very quickly
➤ **¡rápido!** hurry up!

**raro** *adjetivo*

1. **strange**: me pasó algo muy raro something very strange happened to me; es un poco rara she's a little strange

**2. rare:** es una pieza muy rara y valiosa it's a very rare and valuable piece
➤ ¡qué raro! how strange!
➤ es raro que llegue tan tarde it's strange for him to arrive so late
➤ tiene un sabor un poco raro it has kind of a strange taste to it.

el **rascacielos** (plural los rascacielos)
■ **skyscraper.**

**rascar** verbo ■ **to scratch:** ráscame la espalda scratch my back
➤ no te rasques don't scratch
➤ se rascó la cabeza he scratched his head.

**rasgar** verbo ■ **to tear:** rasgó la tela he tore the cloth
➤ se le rasgó la falda she tore her skirt.

el **rasgo** ■ **feature:** tiene los rasgos muy finos she has very delicate features
➤ lo describió a grandes rasgos he described it briefly.

el **rasguño** ■ **scratch.**

la **rasuradora** ■ Central America, Mexico **electric shaver.**

**rasurarse** verbo pronominal ■ Central America, Mexico **to shave.**

el **rato** ■ **while:** estuve esperando un buen rato I was waiting a good while
➤ al poco rato llegó he arrived shortly after
➤ lo hago para pasar el rato I do it to pass the time
➤ siempre la hace pasar malos ratos he always does it to give her a hard time
➤ el avión viene atrasado así es que tenemos para rato the airplane is late so we still have some time.

el **ratón** (plural los ratones) ■ **mouse** (plural **mice**): la casa está llena de ratones the house is full of mice
➤ haz clic con el ratón sobre este icono click with the mouse on this icon.

la **raya**
**1. line:** haz una raya vertical draw a vertical line
**2. part:** se peina con raya she wears a part in her hair
**3. stripe:** una blusa con rayas azules y blancas a blouse with blue and white stripes

**4. dash:** una raya precedida de un punto a dash preceded by a dot
➤ una falda a rayas a striped skirt
➤ pasarse de la raya to go too far: se pasó de la raya y lo castigaron he went too far and was punished.

**rayar** verbo
**1. to scratch:** no vayas a rayar la mesa con eso don't go and scratch the table with that
**2. to scrawl:** rayaron toda la pared they scrawled all over the wall.

el **rayo**
**1. lightning bolt:** cayó un rayo en el campanario a lightning bolt struck the bell tower
**2. ray:** un rayo de luz a ray of light
**3. spoke:** puso listones de colores en los rayos de su bicicleta she put colored ribbons on the spokes of her bicycle
**4.** Chile, Mexico **highlights:** se hace rayos en el pelo she has highlights in her hair
➤ un rayo láser a laser beam
➤ los rayos ultravioleta ultraviolet rays
➤ los rayos X X-rays.

la **raza**
**1. race:** la raza humana the human race
**2. breed:** no sé de qué raza es su perro I don't know what breed her dog is
➤ es un perro de raza he's a pedigree dog.

la **razón** (plural las razones) ■ **reason:** no hay ninguna razón para que falte a clases there's no reason for him to miss classes
➤ creo que tiene razón I think he's right
➤ no tiene razón he's wrong
➤ vas a terminar por darle la razón you'll end up agreeing with him.

**razonable** adjetivo ■ **reasonable.**

la **reacción** (plural las reacciones) ■ **reaction:** tuvo una reacción alérgica she had an allergic reaction.

**reaccionar** verbo ■ **to react:** reaccionó muy mal he reacted badly.

**real** adjetivo
**1. real:** vive en un mundo que no es real she lives in a world that isn't real
**2. royal:** la familia real the royal family
➤ la novela se basa en un hecho real the novel is based on a true story.

la **realidad** ■ **reality:** una mezcla de realidad y ficción a mix of reality and fiction
➤ en la realidad las cosas son muy distintas in the real world things are very different
➤ en realidad actually: en realidad no sé la respuesta actually, I don't know the answer
➤ mis deseos se hicieron realidad my dreams came true
➤ realidad virtual virtual reality.

**realista** adjetivo ■ **realistic:** seamos más realistas let's be more realistic.

**realizar** verbo ■ **to carry out:** realizaron la operación en un hospital inglés the operation was carried out at an English hospital
➤ han realizado una muy buena tarea they've done a very good job
➤ quiere realizarse como persona she wants to fulfill herself
➤ se le realizaron los sueños his dreams came true.

la **reata** ■ Mexico **rope:** los amarró con una reata he tied them with a rope.

la **rebaja** ■ **discount:** pedí una rebaja I asked for a discount
➤ hacerle una rebaja a alguien to give somebody a discount: me hicieron una rebaja del diez por ciento they gave me a ten percent discount.

**rebajar** verbo ■ **to reduce:** los rebajaron un diez por ciento they reduced them by ten percent
➤ me lo rebajaron a 1000 pesos they brought down the price to 1000 pesos for me.

el **rebaño** ■ **flock**
➤ un rebaño de ovejas a flock of sheep.

**rebasar** verbo ■ Mexico **to pass:** nos rebasó al salir del túnel he passed us as we left the tunnel.

**rebelarse** verbo ■ **to rebel:** se rebelan contra la autoridad they're rebelling against authority.

**rebelde** adjetivo ■ **rebel**

el/la **rebelde** ■ **rebel**.

**rebobinar** verbo ■ **to rewind**.

**rebotar** verbo
1. **to bounce:** la pelota rebotó en la pared the ball bounced against the wall
2. **to ricochet:** una bala rebotó en la pared a bullet ricocheted off the wall.

el **rebozo** ■ **shawl**.

el **recado** ■ **message:** le dejé un recado con la secretaria I left her a message with the secretary.

la **recámara** ■ Mexico **bedroom:** se encerró en su recámara she locked herself in her bedroom.

**recargar** verbo
1. **to refill:** tengo que recargar la pluma I have to refill the pen
2. **to recharge:** tengo que recargar el celular I have to recharge my cell phone
➤ recargarse contra algo Colombia, Mexico to lean against: no se recarguen contra el vidrio don't lean against the glass.

**recaudar** verbo ■ **to collect:** recaudaron fondos para los damnificados they collected money for the victims.

la **recepción** (plural las recepciones) ■ **reception**.

el/la **recepcionista** ■ **receptionist**.

la **receta**
1. **recipe:** ¿me das la receta del postre? will you give me the recipe for the dessert?
2. **prescription:** sólo lo venden con receta it's only available by prescription.

**recetar** verbo ■ **to prescribe:** me recetó unas pastillas para la alergia she prescribed some pills for my allergy.

**rechazar** verbo
1. **to reject:** rechazaron mi idea they rejected my idea
2. **to turn down:** me presenté pero me rechazaron I applied but they turned me down.

el **recibidor** ■ **hall**.

**recibir** verbo
1. **to get:** ¿recibiste mi carta? did you get my letter?

**2. to greet:** salieron a recibirme a la puerta they came to greet me at the door
➤ recibió muchos regalos para su cumpleaños she got a lot of presents for her birthday
➤ todos me recibieron muy bien they all greeted me warmly

**recibirse** *verbo pronominal* ■ **to graduate:** todavía no se ha recibido he hasn't graduated yet
➤ recibirse de algo to get a degree in something: se recibió de arquitecto he got an architecture degree.

**recién** *adverbio* ■ **just:** está recién pintado it's just been painted; está recién llegado de su viaje he's just come back from his trip
➤ recién lo vi I just saw him
➤ un niño recién nacido a newborn baby
➤ los recién casados the newlyweds
➤ "recién pintado" "wet paint".

el **recipiente** ■ **recipient.**

**reclamar** *verbo*

**1. to complain:** déjate de reclamar stop complaining; le reclamé a la profesora por mi nota I complained to the teacher about my grade
**2. to demand:** reclaman una solución a sus problemas they're demanding a solution to their problems.

**recoger** *verbo*

**1. to pick up:** recoja el papel del suelo pick the paper up off the floor; los martes recogen la basura they pick up the trash on Tuesdays; recojan todo antes de irse pick everything up before you leave
**2. to pick:** fuimos a recoger duraznos we went peach picking.

**recomendar** *verbo* ■ **to recommend.**

la **recompensa** ■ **reward:** ofrecen una recompensa they're offering a reward.

**reconocer** *verbo*

**1. to recognize:** no lo reconocí con la barba I didn't recognize him with a beard
**2. to admit:** reconoció que se había equivocado he admitted that he was wrong.

el **récord** *(plural los récords)* ■ **record:** el récord mundial de los 100 metros the 100 meter world record
➤ batió el récord he broke the record
➤ estableció un nuevo récord en la maratón he set a new record for the marathon.

**recordar** *verbo*

**1. to remember:** no recuerdo su nombre I can't remember his name; recuerdo que te lo pedí I remember asking you for it
**2. to remind:** me recuerda a un amigo mío he reminds me of a friend of mine; recuérdame que lo llame remind me to call him.

**recorrer** *verbo*

**1. to travel around:** su sueño es recorrer el mundo his dream is to travel all around the world
**2. to cover:** recorrimos esa distancia en muy poco tiempo we quickly covered that distance
➤ salieron a recorrer la ciudad they went out to see the city.

el **recorrido** ■ **route:** todos los días hace el mismo recorrido he takes the same route every day
➤ hicieron un recorrido por toda Europa they took a trip all around Europe
➤ un tren de largo recorrido a long-distance train.

**recortar** *verbo* ■ **to cut out:** lo recorté del diario I cut it out of the newspaper
➤ hay que recortar los gastos we have to reduce our expenses.

el **recreo** ■ **recess:** tenemos el primer recreo a las diez our first recess is at ten.

la **recta** ■ **straight line:** dibujó una recta he drew a straight line
➤ la recta final the home straight.

el **rectángulo** ■ **rectangle.**

**recto** *adjetivo* ■ **straight:** una línea recta a straight line
➤ unos pantalones rectos straight-legged pants.

el **recuerdo**

**1. memory:** tengo muy buenos recuerdos de mi primer colegio I have very good memories of my first school

**2. souvenir**: es un recuerdo de mi viaje it's a souvenir from my trip
➤ **lo compré de recuerdo** I bought it as a souvenir
➤ **es un recuerdo de familia** it's a family heirloom
➤ **dale muchos recuerdos a tu familia** give my regards to your family.

**recuperar** | *verbo*

**1. to get back**: no pude recuperar mi dinero I couldn't get my money back
**2. to make up**: el sábado vamos a recuperar la clase que no tuvimos we're going to make up the class we missed on Saturday; **tengo que recuperar el tiempo perdido** I have to make up for lost time
**3. to recover**: ya se recuperó de la operación he's already recovered from the operation
➤ **recuperar las fuerzas** to get your strength back: **descansamos un poco para recuperar las fuerzas** we rested a while to get our strength back
➤ **recuperar el conocimiento** to regain consciousness.

la **red**

**1. net**: una red de pesca a fishing net; **la pelota tocó la red** the ball touched the net
**2. network**: una red de carreteras a network of highways
➤ **la Red** the Net.

la **redacción** *(plural* las redacciones)

**1. essay**: tengo que hacer una redacción sobre mis vacaciones I have to write an essay about my vacation
**2. editorial staff**: trabaja en el equipo de redacción de la revista she works on the magazine's editorial staff.

**redactar** | *verbo* ■ **to write**: redactó el discurso inaugural he wrote the inaugural speech; **no saben redactar** they don't know how to write.

**redondo** | *adjetivo* ■ **round**: tiene la cara redonda she has a round face.

**reducir** | *verbo* ■ **to lower**: van a reducir la velocidad máxima permitida they're going to lower the speed limit.

**reduzco** | *verbo* ➤ reducir.

**reemplazar** | *verbo* ■ **to replace**
➤ **reemplazar algo por algo** to replace something with something: **reemplaza esta palabra por una menos formal** replace this word with a less formal one.

la **refacción** *(plural* las refacciones) ■ *Mexico* **spare part**.

**referirse** | *verbo* ■ **to refer**: creo que se refiere a ti I think she's referring to you; **no sé a qué te refieres** I don't know what you're referring to
➤ **¿a qué te refieres con eso?** what do you mean by that?

**reflejar** | *verbo* ■ **to reflect**: la ventana reflejaba su imagen her image was reflected in the window.

el **reflejo** ■ **reflection**: el reflejo del sol en el agua the reflection of the sun in the water

los **reflejos** ■ **reflexes**: tiene muy buenos reflejos he has very good reflexes.

**reflexivo** | *adjetivo* ■ **reflexive**: un verbo reflexivo a reflexive verb.

la **reforma**

**1. reform**: la reforma de la enseñanza educational reform
**2. alteration**: hicieron algunas reformas en su casa they made some alterations to the house
➤ "cerrado por reformas" "closed for alterations".

**reformar** | *verbo*

**1. to change**: van a reformar el sistema educativo they're going to change the educational system
**2. to make alterations to**: están reformando el edificio they're making some alterations to the building

**reformarse** | *verbo pronominal* ■ **to mend one's ways**: se ha reformado y ahora es muy responsable he's mended his ways and is very responsible now.

**refrescar** | *verbo* ■ **to get cool**: en la noche siempre refresca it always gets cool at night

**244**

**refrescarse** *verbo pronominal* ■ **to cool off:** se tiró al agua para refrescarse she jumped into the water to cool off.

el **refresco** ■ **soft drink**.

el **refrigerador** ■ **refrigerator**.

el **refugiado, la refugiada** ■ **refugee**.

**refugiarse** *verbo*

1. **to take shelter:** un lugar para refugiarse del frío a place to take shelter from the cold
2. **to take refuge:** se refugiaron en una iglesia they took refuge in a church.

el **refugio** ■ **shelter:** un refugio para los damnificados a shelter for the victims
➤ un refugio atómico a fallout shelter.

la **regadera**

1. **watering can:** llenó la regadera de agua she filled the watering can with water
2. *Colombia, Mexico, Venezuela* **shower:** siempre canta en la regadera he always sings in the shower.

**regalar** *verbo*

1. **to give:** me regaló un reloj she gave me a watch; no sé qué regalarle para su cumpleaños I don't know what to give him for his birthday
2. **to give away:** me queda chico así es que lo voy a regalar it's too small for me so I'm going to give it away; estaban regalando boletos para el concierto they were giving away tickets for the concert
➤ me regalaron una guitarra para Navidad I was given a guitar for Christmas.

el **regalo** ■ **present:** es un regalo de cumpleaños it's a birthday present
➤ hacerle un regalo a alguien to give somebody a present: me hizo un muy buen regalo he gave me a really good present
➤ una tienda de regalos a gift shop
➤ me lo dieron de regalo al comprar la computadora it was free with the purchase of the computer.

**regañar** *verbo* ■ **to scold:** me regañaron por no hacer las tareas I was scolded for not doing my homework.

el **regaño** ■ **scolding:** le dieron un buen regaño he got a good scolding.

**regar** *verbo* ■ **to water:** voy a regar las plantas I'm going to water the plants.

el **régimen** *(plural* los regímenes*)*

1. **regime:** un régimen democrático a democratic regime
2. **diet:** tiene que seguir un régimen he has to follow a diet; voy a ponerme a régimen I'm going on a diet
➤ **a régimen** on a diet: estoy a régimen I'm on a diet.

la **región** *(plural* las regiones*)* ■ **region**.

**regional** *adjetivo* ■ **regional**.

**registrar** *verbo*

1. **to search:** le registraron el equipaje they searched his luggage; registraron el edificio they searched the building
2. **to register:** los sismógrafos registraron el temblor the seismographs registered the tremor

**registrarse** *verbo pronominal*

1. **to check in:** nos registramos en un hotel we checked into a hotel
2. **to register:** tengo que ir a registrarme en la embajada I have to register at the embassy.

el **registro**

1. **register:** su nombre aparece en el registro de alumnos his name is on the student register
2. **search:** la policía efectuó un registro del edificio the police carried out a search of the building.

la **regla**

1. **ruler:** usó una regla para medir la línea she used a ruler to measure the line
2. **rule:** es una regla en mi colegio it's a rule in my school
3. **period:** tener la regla to have one's period
➤ **en regla** in order: si quiere viajar, tiene que poner en regla sus documentos if you want to travel you'll have to get your papers in order
➤ **por regla general** generally: por regla general, llego al colegio temprano I generally get to school early.

el **reglamento** ■ regulations: el reglamento del colegio the school's regulations.

**regresar** *verbo*

1. **to come back:** tienes que regresar temprano you have to come back early
2. **to go back:** regresaron a su país they went back to their country
3. *Latin America except Southern Cone* **to return:** tengo que regresar el libro a la biblioteca I have to return the book to the library

**regresarse** *verbo pronominal* ■ *Latin America except Southern Cone* **to go back:** me regresé porque se me olvidaron las llaves I went back because I forgot the keys.

el **regreso** ■ **return:** nuestro regreso al colegio se acercaba our return to school was drawing near
➤ **de regreso** on the way back: de regreso paramos en una playa del Caribe on the way back we stopped at a Caribbean beach
➤ el vuelo de regreso the return flight
➤ "no se aceptan regresos sin recibo" "no returns without a receipt".

**regular** *adjetivo* ■ **regular:** viene a intervalos regulares he comes at regular intervals
➤ me pareció una película regular it was a so-so movie
➤ es de tamaño regular it's the regular size
➤ por lo regular usually: por lo regular, me levanto a las siete I usually get up at seven.

el/la **rehén** *(plural* los/las rehenes*)* ■ hostage.

la **reina** ■ queen.

el **reinado** ■ reign.

**reinar** *verbo* ■ to reign.

el **reino** ■ **kingdom**
➤ el reino animal the animal kingdom
➤ el Reino Unido the United Kingdom.

**reír** *verbo* ■ **to laugh:** no me hagas reír don't make me laugh
➤ se echó a reír he burst out laughing

**reírse** *verbo pronominal* ■ **to laugh:** no te rías don't laugh
➤ se ríen de él they're laughing at him
➤ ¿de qué te ríes? what are you laughing at?

la **reja** ■ **grill:** había rejas en todas las ventanas there were grills on all the windows.

la **relación** *(plural* las relaciones*)*

1. **relationship:** tiene una buena relación con los alumnos she has a good relationship with the students
2. **connection:** no hay ninguna relación entre los dos incidentes there's no connection between the two incidents
➤ con relación a with regard to: con relación a tu pregunta with regard to your question
➤ relaciones públicas public relations.

**relajar** *verbo* ■ **to relax:** el sonido del agua me relaja the sound of the water relaxes me
➤ tienes que aprender a relajarte you have to learn to relax.

el **relámpago** ■ **lightning:** ¿viste el relámpago? did you see the lightning?
➤ los relámpagos iluminaron el cielo lightning lit up the sky.

**relativo** *adjetivo*

1. **relating :** le gusta todo lo relativo a la naturaleza she likes everything relating to nature
2. **relative:** todo es relativo it's all relative
➤ lo hizo con relativa facilidad he did it relatively easily.

la **religión** *(plural* las religiones*)* ■ religion.

**religioso** *adjetivo* ■ **religious:** son un pueblo muy religioso they're a very religious people

el **religioso,** la **religiosa** ■ monk, nun.

**rellenar** *verbo*

1. **to stuff:** rellenó los aguacates con camarones she stuffed the avocados with shrimp
2. **to fill:** lo voy a rellenar con crema I'm going to fill it with cream; ¿con qué puedo rellenar esta grieta? what can I fill this crack with?

el **relleno**

1. **stuffing:** el relleno del pollo está delicioso the chicken's stuffing is delicious

**2. filling:** el relleno es de chocolate the filling is chocolate.

el **reloj**

1. *de pared, grande* **clock:** ese reloj está adelantado the clock is fast
2. *en la muñeca* **watch:** mi reloj se atrasa my watch is losing time
➤ **contra reloj** against the clock: **trabajamos contra reloj para poder terminarlo** we worked against the clock to finish it
➤ **un reloj despertador** an alarm clock
➤ **un reloj de pulsera** wristwatch
➤ **un reloj de sol** a sundial.

**remar** *verbo* ■ **to row.**

**remediar** *verbo* ■ **to solve:** así no vas a remediar el problema you're not going to solve the problem like that
➤ **no lo puedo remediar** I can't help it.

el **remedio** ■ **remedy:** un remedio natural a natural remedy; es el mejor remedio para el acné it's the best remedy for acne
➤ **¡tú no tienes remedio!** you're hopeless!
➤ **esto no tiene remedio** this is hopeless
➤ **no tuve más remedio que obedecer** I had no choice but to obey.

el/la **remitente** ■ **sender.**

el **remo**

1. **oar:** perdieron un remo they lost an oar
2. **rowing:** está en el equipo de remo he's on the rowing team.

**remojar** *verbo* ■ **to soak:** hay que remojar las pasas primero you have to soak the raisins first.

el **remolino**

1. *de viento* **whirl**
2. *de agua* **whirlpool**
3. *en el pelo* **cowlick**
4. *Southern Cone de papel* **pinwheel.**

el **remordimiento** ■ **remorse:** no siente el más mínimo remordimiento he doesn't feel a bit of remorse
➤ **estaba lleno de remordimientos** he was full of remorse
➤ **¿no tienes remordimientos de conciencia?** isn't your conscience bothering you?

**remoto** *adjetivo* ■ **remote:** en lugares muy remotos in remote places
➤ **no tiene ni la más remota idea** she doesn't have the slightest idea.

el **renacuajo** ■ **tadpole.**

el **rencor** ■ **anger:** no debe haber rencor entre los hermanos there shouldn't be any anger among siblings
➤ **guardarle rencor a alguien** to hold a grudge against someone: **no le guardes rencor** don't hold a grudge against him.

el **rendimiento** ■ **performance.**

**rendir** *verbo*

1. **to perform well:** no está rindiendo en los estudios she's not doing very well at school
2. **to pay:** le van a rendir un homenaje they're going to pay tribute to him

**rendirse** *verbo pronominal*

1. **to surrender:** se rindieron al enemigo they surrendered to the enemy
2. **to give up:** me rindo ¿cuál es la solución? I give up — what's the answer?

el **renglón** *(plural* los renglones*)* ■ **line.**

la **renta** ■ **rent:** nos van aumentar la renta they're going to raise our rent
➤ **renta de bicicletas** *Mexico* bicycle rental.

**rentar** *verbo* ■ *Mexico* **to rent:** rentamos una casa para las vacaciones we rented a house for the summer; **les renta bicicletas a estudiantes** he rents bicycles to students.

la **renuncia** ■ **resignation:** presentó su renuncia he handed in his resignation.

**renunciar** *verbo*

1. **to quit:** renunció la secretaria the secretary quit
2. **to give up on:** renunciaron a la idea de hacer el viaje they gave up on the idea of making the trip.

**reñir** *verbo* ■ **to quarrel:** ellos siempre riñen entre sí they're always quarreling.

**repartir** *verbo*

1. **to hand out:** la profesora repartió los libros the teacher handed out the books
2. **to deliver:** reparte periódicos he delivers newspapers

3. **to deal:** ¿quién reparte las cartas? who's dealing the cards?
4. **to distribute:** repartieron los juguetes entre todos los niños they distributed the toys among all the children
➤ nos repartimos el dinero entre los cuatro we split the money four ways.

el **reparto**
1. **delivery:** no cobran por el reparto they don't charge for delivery
2. **cast:** tiene un excelente reparto it has an excellent cast
➤ reparto a domicilio delivery service.

**repasar** *verbo*
1. **to review:** están repasando para los exámenes they're reviewing for their exams
2. **to go over:** repasa bien las sumas go over your sums carefully.

el **repaso** ■ **review:** estamos haciendo un repaso de la materia we're doing a review of the material
➤ darle un repaso a algo to review something: tengo que darles un repaso a los verbos I have to review the verbs.

**repente** *adverbio*
➤ de repente suddenly: todo pasó tan de repente it all happened so suddenly.

la **repisa** ■ **shelf:** el diccionario está en la repisa the dictionary is on the shelf
➤ la repisa de la chimenea the mantelpiece
➤ la repisa de la ventana the windowsill.

**repleto** *adjetivo* ■ **packed:** el estadio estaba repleto the stadium was packed.

el **reportaje**
1. **report:** apareció en el reportaje sobre la juventud actual it appeared in the report on today's youth
2. **article:** su reportaje salió publicado en la revista his article was published in the magazine.

el **reporte** ■ *Mexico* **report:** presentó su reporte al jefe he submitted his report to the boss.

el **reportero,** la **reportera** ■ **reporter.**

**reposar** *verbo* ■ **to rest:** se retiró a su habitación para reposar he went to his bedroom to rest.

el **reposo** ■ **rest:** el médico le recomendó que mantuviera reposo the doctor recommended that she get a lot of rest.

la **representación** *(plural las representaciones)* ■ **performance:** hubo quinientas representaciones de la obra there were five hundred performances of the play.

el/la **representante**
1. **representative:** el representante de la empresa the company representative
2. **agent:** el representante de la cantante the singer's agent.

**representar** *verbo*
1. **to represent:** representó a México en las Olimpíadas she represented Mexico in the Olympics
2. **to look:** representa más de su edad he looks older than he is
3. **to perform:** esa obra es muy difícil de representar that play is very difficult to perform
4. **to depict:** vi un dibujo que representa el paisaje mexicano I saw a picture depicting the Mexican countryside
➤ no representa ningún riesgo para mí it doesn't pose any risk to me
➤ representa un 10% del costo total it represents 10% of the total cost.

la **represión** ■ **repression.**

**reprobar** *verbo*
1. **to condemn:** hay que reprobar el uso de las drogas we must condemn the use of drugs
2. **to fail:** si no estudias vas a reprobar el examen if you don't study you'll fail the test.

la **reproducción** *(plural las reproducciones)*
1. **reproduction:** estamos estudiando el proceso de reproducción de las plantas we're studying plant reproduction
2. **copy:** es una reproducción del cuadro original it's a copy of the original painting.

**reproducir** *verbo* ■ **to reproduce:** las fotocopiadoras reproducen textos o dibujos photocopiers reproduce text or graphics.

el **reptil** ■ **reptile.**

la **república** ■ **republic.**

la **República Dominicana** ■ Dominican Republic.

el **repuesto** ■ spare part: ¿venden repuestos para el coche? do you sell spare auto parts?

la **reputación** (plural las reputaciones) ■ reputation: esa tienda tiene mala reputación that store has a bad reputation.

la **resbalada** ■ informal slip: una pequeña resbalada y te puedes hacer daño one small slip and you could hurt yourself.

la **resbaladilla** ■ Mexico slide: los niños se divertían en la resbaladilla the children were having fun on the slide.

**resbalar** verbo ■ to slide: ponle aceite para que resbale mejor put some oil on it so that it slides better

**resbalarse** verbo pronominal ■ to slip: se resbaló en el piso mojado he slipped on the wet floor.

**resbaloso** adjetivo ■ slippery: el piso es muy resbaloso the floor is very slippery.

**rescatar** verbo ■ to rescue: el salvavidas rescató al nadador the lifeguard rescued the swimmer.

el **rescate** ■ rescue: fue un rescate espectacular it was a spectacular rescue.

la **reservación** (plural las reservaciones) ■ reservation: hice una reservación en el restaurante I made a reservation at the restaurant.

**reservar** verbo ■ to reserve: quisiera reservar una mesa para dos I'd like to reserve a table for two.

**resfriado** adjetivo ■ Juan está muy resfriado Juan has a bad cold

el **resfriado** ■ cold: me vas a pegar tu resfriado you're going to give me your cold.

**resfriarse** verbo ■ to catch a cold: te vas a resfriar you're going to catch a cold.

la **residencia** ■ residence: fijó residencia en Veracruz he took up residence in Veracruz

➤ un permiso de residencia a residence permit

➤ una residencia de ancianos a retirement home.

**residente** adjetivo ■ resident: es residente en México he is resident in Mexico

el/la **residente** ■ resident: Rodrigo es un residente de los Estados Unidos Rodrigo is a resident of the United States.

**residir** verbo ■ to live: residió ocho años en el extranjero she lived abroad for eight years.

los **residuos** ■ waste: el procesamiento de residuos nucleares the processing of nuclear waste.

la **resignación** ■ resignation: aceptó su castigo con resignación he accepted his punishment with resignation.

**resignarse** verbo ■ to resign oneself: se resignó a su destino he resigned himself to his fate.

la **resina** ■ resin.

la **resistencia** ■ resistance: no ofreció ninguna resistencia she didn't put up any resistance

➤ tiene gran resistencia física he has great stamina.

**resistente** adjetivo ■ resistant: una tela muy resistente a very resistant fabric.

**resistir** verbo
1. to resist: tienes que resistir la tentación you have to resist temptation
2. to stand: no pudo resistir el frío I can't stand the cold
➤ resistirse a hacer algo to refuse to do something.

la **resolución** (plural las resoluciones) ■ resolution: la resolución del conflicto the resolution of the conflict
➤ una imagen de alta resolución a high-resolution image.

**resolver** verbo ■ to solve: finalmente resolvieron el problema they finally solved the problem.

**resonar** *verbo* ■ **to echo**.

el **resorte**
1. **spring**: un colchón de resortes a spring mattress
2. *Central America, Colombia, Mexico* **elastic**: la falda tiene resorte en la cintura the skirt has an elastic waistband.

la **resortera** ■ *Mexico* **slingshot**.

**respaldar** *verbo*
1. **to support**: decidió respaldar la iniciativa she decided to support the initiative
2. **to back up**: los archivos se pueden respaldar a otro disco duro the files can be backed up on another hard drive.

el **respaldo**
1. **back**: una silla sin respaldo a chair without a back
2. **support**: expresó su respaldo a la idea he expressed his support for the idea
3. **backup**: siempre hay que hacer un respaldo you should always make a backup.

**respetable** *adjetivo* ■ **respectable**: una opinión respetable a respectable opinion.

**respetado** *adjetivo* ■ **respected**: un médico muy respetado a highly-respected doctor.

**respetar** *verbo*
1. **to respect**: respeta las opiniones de los demás respect other people's opinions
2. **to follow**: hay que respetar las reglas you have to follow the rules.

el **respeto** ■ **respect**: trata con respeto a sus mayores he treats his elders with respect.

**respetuoso** *adjetivo* ■ **respectful**: es muy respetuoso de la naturaleza he is very respectful of nature.

la **respiración** ■ **breathing**: tiene la respiración irregular her breathing is irregular.

**respirar** *verbo* ■ **to breathe**.

**respiratorio** *adjetivo* ■ **respiratory**: el aparato respiratorio the respiratory system.

**responder** *verbo*
1. **to answer**: no pudo responder a la pregunta de la maestra she couldn't answer the teacher's question
2. **to reply**: gracias por responder a mi e-mail thank you for replying to my e-mail
3. **to respond**: el enfermo respondió bien al tratamiento the patient responded well to the treatment.

la **responsabilidad** ■ **responsibility** (*plural* **responsibilities**): le han dado mucha responsabilidad they've given her a lot of responsibility.

**responsable** *adjetivo* ■ **responsible**: María es muy responsable María is very responsible
➤ **ser responsable de** to be responsible for: ella es responsable del bienestar de los niños she's responsible for the children's well-being

el/la **responsable** ■ ¿quién es el responsable de esto? who is responsible for this?
➤ Jimena es la responsable del proyecto Jimena is in charge of the project
➤ los responsables de la crisis those responsible for the crisis.

la **respuesta** ■ **reply**: espero tu respuesta I'll await your reply.

la **resta** ■ **subtraction**: haz la resta y dime el resultado do the subtraction and tell me the answer.

**restar** *verbo* ■ **to subtract**: piensa en un número y réstale cinco think of a number then subtract five from it

> ⚠ The Spanish word **restar** is a false cognate, it does not mean "rest".

el **restaurante** ■ **restaurant**.

**restaurar** *verbo* ■ **to restore**.

el **resto** ■ **rest**: deja el resto para mañana leave the rest for tomorrow
➤ yo me como los restos I'll eat the leftovers.

la **restricción** (*plural* las **restricciones**) ■ **restriction**.

**resucitar** *verbo* ■ to revive: los médicos lograron resucitarlo the doctors managed to revive him.

el **resultado**

1. **result**: el resultado del sorteo the results of the drawing
2. **score**: el resultado del partido the game's score.

**resultar** *verbo*

1. **to work out**: no le resultaron sus planes his plans didn't work out
2. **to turn out**: el cuarto resultó ser muy pequeño the room turned out to be very small.

el **resumen** ■ summary: el resumen es demasiado largo the summary is too long
➤ hacer un resumen del texto to summarize the text
➤ en resumen, me gusta más éste in short, I prefer this one.

**resumir** *verbo* ■ to summarize: tuvimos que resumir la película en dos párrafos we had to summarize the movie in two paragraphs
➤ resumiendo in short.

**retar** *verbo* ■ to challenge: lo retó a un partido de tenis she challenged him to a tennis match.

**retardar** *verbo* ■ to delay: el concierto se retardó por media hora the concert was delayed by half an hour.

**retirar** *verbo*

1. **to remove**: por favor retira los platos de la mesa please remove the plates from the table
2. **to withdraw**: fue a retirar su dinero del banco she went to withdraw her money from the bank

**retirarse** *verbo pronominal* ■ to retire.

el **reto** ■ challenge: Juan no pudo resistir el reto de Pablo Juan could not resist Pablo's challenge.

**retocar** *verbo* ■ to touch up: esa foto ha sido retocada that picture has been touched up.

**retorcer** *verbo* ■ to twist: se retorció el tobillo he twisted his ankle.

**retrasado** *adjetivo*

1. **behind**: va un poco retrasado en el colegio he's a little behind in school
2. **slow**: mi reloj está retrasado por cinco minutos my watch is five minutes slow
3. **backward**: una sociedad retrasada a backward society.

**retrasar** *verbo*

1. **to delay**: todos los trenes están retrasados all the trains are delayed
2. **to postpone**: retrasaron la fiesta por una semana they postponed the party for a week
3. **to turn back**: este fin de semana hay que retrasar los relojes we have to turn back the clocks this weekend

**retrasarse** *verbo pronominal* ■ to be late: me retrasé por el tráfico I was late because of traffic.

el **retraso** ■ delay: hubo un retraso de dos horas there was a two-hour delay.

el **retrato** ■ portrait.

**retroceder** *verbo*

1. **to move back**: el coche retrocedió diez metros the car moved back ten meters
2. **to retreat**: los soldados tuvieron que retroceder the soldiers had to retreat.

el **retrovisor** ■ rearview mirror.

**retuerzo** *verbo* ➤ retorcer.

la **reunión** *(plural las reuniones)*

1. **meeting**: la reunión es a las diez the meeting is at ten
2. **get-together**: la reunión en tu casa estuvo muy buena the get-together at your house was a lot of fun.

**reunir** *verbo*

1. **to gather**: reunió todos sus juguetes y los tiró a la basura she gathered all her toys and threw them in the trash
2. **to have**: reúne todas las cualidades necesarias he has all the necessary qualities
➤ se reunieron en su casa they got together at his house
➤ ¿nos reunimos a las tres? shall we meet at three?

la **revancha** ■ rematch: me vas a tener que dar la revancha you're going to have to give me a rematch
➤ Miguel tuvo su revancha después de lo que José le hizo Miguel got his own back after what José did to him.

la **revelación** ■ revelation.

**revelar** verbo
1. to reveal: revelaron todos sus secretos they revealed all their secrets
2. to develop: llevé las fotos a revelar I took the film to be developed.

**reventar** verbo ■ to burst: el globo reventó the balloon burst
➤ su actitud me revienta his attitude really bugs me.

el **reventón** ■ Mexico informal party.

la **reversa** ■ Colombia, Mexico reverse: meter reversa to put the car in reverse.

el **revés**
1. inside: el revés de la chamarra the inside of the jacket
2. back: el revés de la hoja de papel the back of the sheet of paper
3. backhand: tiene un revés muy poderoso she has a very powerful backhand
➤ al revés inside out: tienes el suéter al revés your sweater is inside out
➤ al revés backward: ya no está de moda ponerse la gorra al revés it's not in to wear your cap backward anymore
➤ al revés the other way around: colócalas al revés place them the other way around.

**reviento, revientas etc** verbo ➤ reventar.

**revisar** verbo
1. to check: el maestro revisa diariamente el trabajo de sus alumnos the teacher checks his students' work every day
2. to search: me revisaron las maletas en la aduana they searched my bags at customs.

la **revisión** ■ check: una revisión de calidad a quality check
➤ una revisión médica a check-up.

la **revista** ■ magazine.

**revivir** verbo ■ to refresh: revivió después de la siesta she was completely refreshed after her nap.

la **revolución** (plural las revoluciones) ■ revolution.

**revolucionario** adjetivo ■ revolutionary.

**revolver** verbo
1. to stir: no está revuelto tu café your coffee hasn't been stirred
2. to turn upside down: revolvió toda la casa buscando el libro she turned the house upside down looking for the key.

el **revólver** (plural los revólveres) ■ revolver.

el **rey** ■ king: algún día, el príncipe llegará a ser rey one day, the prince will be king
➤ los reyes de España the King and Queen of Spain
➤ los Reyes Magos the Three Wise Men

**LOS REYES MAGOS**

January 6 is the feast of the Epiphany, honoring the Three Wise Men who visited the baby Jesus bringing gifts of gold, frankincense, and myrrh. It is the favorite religious holiday of many children, who receive presents from the Three Wise Men on the morning of January 6. In some places, children will put out grass and water for the Wise Men's camels, while in others they will leave out a shoe to receive their presents.

**rezar** verbo ■ to pray: siempre rezo por la paz I always pray for peace.

**rico** adjetivo
1. rich: un hombre rico a rich man
2. delicious: ¡que comida más rica! what a delicious meal
➤ un país rico en petróleo a country rich in oil.

**ridículo** adjetivo ■ ridiculous: un ridículo sombrero con plumas a ridiculous feathered hat
➤ hacer el ridículo to make a fool of yourself.

**ríe etc** | *verbo* ➤ reír.

**riego, riegas etc** | *verbo* ➤ regar.

el **riel** | ▪ rail.

el **riesgo** | ▪ risk: tomar un riesgo to take a risk
➤ corres el riesgo de perderlo todo you run the risk of losing it all.

el **rifle** | ▪ rifle.

**rígido** | *adjetivo*
1. rigid: esa barra de metal es muy rígida that metal bar is very rigid
2. strict: la profesora es muy rígida y nos regaña a todos the teacher is very strict and is always scolding us.

la **rima** | ▪ rhyme.

el **rincón** | *(plural* los rincones*)* ▪ corner: había una telaraña en el rincón de mi cuarto there was a spiderweb in the corner of my room.

el **rinoceronte** | ▪ rhinoceros.

el **riñón** | *(plural* los riñones*)* ▪ kidney.

el **río** | ▪ river: en la boca del río at the mouth of the river
➤ río arriba upstream
➤ río abajo downstream.

la **riqueza**
1. wealth: la concentración de la riqueza the concentration of wealth
2. richness: la riqueza de la vegetación the richness of the vegetation.

la **risa** | ▪ laugh: tiene una risa muy contagiosa she has a very infectious laugh
➤ me da risa José José makes me laugh.

el **ritmo**
1. rhythm: el ritmo de la música the rhythm of the music
2. pace: no puedo caminar a tu ritmo I can't walk at your pace.

el **ritual** | ▪ ritual.

el/la **rival** | ▪ rival.

**rizado** | *adjetivo* ▪ curly: el pelo rizado curly hair.

**rizar** | *verbo* ▪ to curl: se rizó el pelo she curled her hair.

el **rizo** | ▪ curl.

**robar** | *verbo*
1. to rob: trataron de robar el banco they tried to rob the bank
2. to steal: me robaron la cartera my wallet was stolen
3. to rip off: si vas a esa tienda te roban you'll get ripped off if you go to that store.

el **robo**
1. robbery: el robo de un banco a bank robbery
2. theft: el robo de una televisión the theft of a TV set
3. burglary: el robo en una casa a burglary
4. rip-off: los precios en esa tienda son un robo the prices at that store are a rip-off.

el **robot** | ▪ robot.

la **roca** | ▪ rock.

la **rodaja** | ▪ slice: ¿me das una rodaja de tu naranja? can I have a slice of your orange?
➤ cebollas cortadas en rodaja sliced onions.

**rodar** | *verbo* ▪ to roll: la pelota rodó por el suelo the ball rolled along the ground.

**rodear** | *verbo* ▪ to surround: los admiradores del cantante lo rodearon the singer's fans surrounded him
➤ le gusta estar rodeado de su familia he likes to be surrounded by his family.

la **rodilla** | ▪ knee
➤ estaba de rodillas he was on his knees.

el **rodillo** | ▪ rolling pin.

**rogar** | *verbo*
1. to beg: me rogó que no me fuera he begged me to stay
2. to ask: les rogamos disculpen estas molestias we ask that you forgive these disruptions
3. to pray: roguemos al Señor let us pray to the Lord.

**rojo** | *adjetivo* ▪ red: un coche rojo a red car

➤ **se puso rojo de pena** he turned red with embarrassment.

el **rollo** ■ roll.

**romántico** *adjetivo* ■ **romantic.**

el **rompecabezas** (*plural* los rompecabezas) ■ **jigsaw puzzle.**

**romper** *verbo*

1. **to break:** rompí un vaso sin querer I accidentally broke a glass
2. **to tear:** rompió el sobre en lugar de cortarlo con cuidado he tore the envelope rather than opening it carefully
➤ **se rompió la tele** the TV is broken
➤ **rompieron después de tres años juntos** they broke up after three years.

el **ron** ■ **rum.**

**roncar** *verbo* ■ **to snore.**

**ronco** *adjetivo*

1. **hoarse:** tengo la voz ronca de tanto gritar my voice is hoarse from screaming so much
2. **husky:** Carlos tiene la voz ronca y grave Carlos has a low, husky voice.

la **ropa** ■ **clothes:** ropa para bebés baby clothes
➤ **la ropa de cama** bedclothes
➤ **la ropa interior** underwear
➤ **la ropa sucia** dirty laundry.

**rosa** *adjetivo* ■ **pink:** una blusa rosa a pink blouse

la **rosa** ■ **rose.**

**rosado** *adjetivo* ■ **pink.**

el **rosal** ■ **rosebush.**

la **rosticería** ■ **rotisserie.**

el **rostro** ■ **face:** tiene el rostro lleno de pecas her face is covered in freckles.

la **rotación** (*plural* las rotaciones) ■ **rotation:** el movimiento de la rotación de la Tierra the Earth's rotation.

**roto** *adjetivo*

1. **ripped:** tienes la camisa rota your shirt is ripped

2. **broken:** este plato está roto this plate is broken
3. **torn:** tus libros siempre están rotos your books are always torn
4. **worn-out:** anda siempre con unos zapatos rotos he always goes around in some worn-out shoes.

**rozar** *verbo*

1. **to brush:** tu beso apenas me rozó la mejilla your kiss barely brushed my cheek
2. **to rub:** los zapatos nuevos me están rozando los talones these new shoes are rubbing against my heels
3. **to scrape:** su brazo rozó contra el tronco del árbol her arm scraped against the tree trunk.

**rubio** *adjetivo* ■ **blond:** tiene el pelo rubio he has blond hair

el **rubio**, la **rubia** ■ **blond (blonde):** llegó con una rubia de ojos azules he arrived with a blue-eyed blonde.

**rudimentario** *adjetivo* ■ **rudimentary.**

**rudo** *adjetivo*

1. **rough:** esta tela es un poco ruda this material is a bit rough
2. **rude:** a veces encuentro que Juan es muy rudo I find Juan very rude at times.

la **rueda** ■ **wheel:** ese vehículo tiene seis ruedas that vehicle has six wheels
➤ **la rueda delantera** the front wheel
➤ **la rueda de la fortuna** the Ferris wheel
➤ **la rueda trasera** the back wheel.

**ruego, ruegas etc** *verbo* ➤ rogar.

el **rugby** ■ **rugby.**

el **rugido** ■ **roar:** el rugido del león the lion's roar.

**rugir** *verbo* ■ **to roar.**

el **ruido** ■ **noise:** eso no es música, es un ruido that isn't music, it's noise.

**ruidoso** *adjetivo* ■ **noisy.**

la **ruina** ■ **ruin**
➤ **la ciudad quedó en ruinas** the city was in ruins

➤ **esa mujer lo llevó a la ruina** that woman ruined him.

la **ruleta** ■ roulette.

el **rumbo** ■ **direction: partió rumbo a la capital** he headed in the direction of the city.

el **rumor**
1. **rumor: han oído algunos rumores acerca de eso** I've heard some rumors about that
2. **murmur: el rumor del gentío** the murmur of the crowd.

**rural** adjetivo ■ rural.

la **ruta** ■ route.

la **rutina** ■ routine.

el **sábado**

En inglés, los días de la semana se escriben con mayúscula:

**Saturday: hoy es sábado** today is Saturday; **el próximo sábado** next Saturday; **el pasado sábado** last Saturday
➤ **el sábado** on Saturday: **te veré el sábado** I'll see you on Saturday
➤ **los sábados** on Saturdays: **los sábados vamos al parque** on Saturdays we go to the park.

la **sabana** ■ savanna.

la **sábana** ■ sheet.

**saber** verbo
1. **to know: ¿sabes cómo se llama?** do you know his name?
2. **to know how to: Rafael no sabe nadar** Rafael doesn't know how to swim
3. **to hear: no supe nada de él por más de un año** I didn't hear from him for over a year
4. **to taste: esta comida sabe muy mal** this food tastes awful
➤ **saberse algo de memoria** to know something by heart

el **saber** ■ knowledge.

la **sabiduría** ■ wisdom.

**sabio** adjetivo ■ **wise: esas son palabras sabias** those are wise words.

el **sabor**
1. **taste: un sabor amargo** a bitter taste
2. **flavor: sabor a manzana** apple flavor.

**saborear** verbo ■ to savor.

**sabré, sabrás etc** verbo ➤ saber.

**sabroso** adjetivo ■ tasty.

el **sacacorchos** (plural los sacacorchos) ■ corkscrew.

el **sacapuntas** (plural los sacapuntas) ■ pencil sharpener.

**sacar** verbo
1. **to take out: ayúdame a sacar la basura** help me take out the garbage; **voy a sacar a pasear al perro** I'm going to take the dog out for a walk
2. **to get: ¿pudiste sacar los boletos?** were you able to get the tickets?
3. **to move: te pedí que sacaras eso de ahí** I asked you to move that out of there
➤ **sacar una foto** to take a picture

**sacarse** verbo pronominal ■ **to take off: sácate el abrigo** take off your coat
➤ **se sacó buenas notas** she got good grades
➤ **se sacó la lotería** she won the lottery.

el **saco**
1. **sack: un saco de carbón** a sack of coal
2. **jacket: un saco sport** a sports jacket
➤ **un saco de dormir** a sleeping bag.

el **sacrificio** ■ sacrifice.

**255**

**sacudir** *verbo*

1. **to shake:** la explosión sacudió mi casa the explosion shook my house
2. *Mexico* **to dust:** sacude los muebles dust the furniture.

**sagrado** *adjetivo*

1. **holy:** la Meca es la ciudad más sagrada del Islam Mecca is the holiest city of Islam
2. **sacred:** la amistad es algo sagrado friendship is sacred.

la **sal** ■ salt.

la **sala**

1. **living room:** la sala de mi casa no es muy grande my living room isn't very large
2. **hall**
➤ sala de conciertos concert hall
➤ sala de conferencias conference hall
➤ sala de embarque departure lounge
➤ sala de espera waiting room
➤ sala de exposiciones gallery
➤ sala de profesores staffroom.

**salado** *adjetivo*

1. **salty:** la comida está demasiado salada the food is too salty
2. **savory:** prefiero la comida salada I prefer savory food.

el **salario** ■ salary: gana un salario enorme he is paid a huge salary
➤ el salario mínimo the minimum wage.

la **salchicha** ■ sausage.

la **salchichonería** ■ *Mexico* deli.

el **saldo** ■ balance: el saldo de esta cuenta es de $5,50 a favor the balance of this account is $5.50 in credit
➤ los saldos empiezan el lunes the sales start on Monday.

**saldré, saldrás etc** *verbo* ➤ salir.

el **salero** ■ salt shaker.

la **salida**

1. **exit:** la salida está por ese pasillo a la derecha the exit is down that corridor on the right
2. **departure:** la hora de salida del tren es a las tres the train's departure time is three o'clock

3. **start:** la salida de la carrera the start of the race
➤ nos vemos a la salida del colegio I'll see you when school lets out
➤ este problema no tiene salida this problem has no solution.

**salir** *verbo*

1. **to leave:** nunca salgo de mi casa sin un paraguas I never leave home without an umbrella; el avión sale a las siete the plane leaves at seven
2. **to come out:** salió demasiado rápido del garage he came out of the garage too quickly; la nueva edición sale el próximo mes the new edition comes out next month
3. **to get out:** ¡sal de mi casa! get out of my house!
4. **to go out:** como castigo no me dejaron salir por un mes I'm not allowed out for a month as punishment
5. **to be on:** salió hoy en las noticias he was on the news today
➤ el sol sale a las 5:30 de la mañana the sun comes up at 5:30 in the morning
➤ el viaje salió muy caro the trip was very expensive
➤ salir con alguien to go out with somebody

**salirse** *verbo pronominal*
➤ me salí en la mitad de la película I left halfway through the movie
➤ se me salen los zapatos my shoes are slipping off
➤ se salió la rueda del coche the car's wheel came off.

la **saliva** ■ saliva.

el **salmón** (*plural* los salmones) ■ salmon.

la **salpicadera** ■ *Mexico* fender.

**salpicar** *verbo* ■ to splash.

la **salsa**

1. **sauce:** la pasta venía en una salsa de vino blanco the pasta came in a white wine sauce
2. *Mexico* **salsa:** esta salsa está muy picante this salsa is really hot
3. **salsa music:** me encanta la salsa I love salsa music.

**256**

**saltar** verbo ■ to jump: no puedo saltar tan alto I can't jump that high

**saltarse** verbo pronominal ■ to skip: no deberías saltarte ninguna comida you shouldn't skip meals
➤ se saltó la cola *Mexico* she cut in line.

el **salto**
1. jump: dio un salto enorme he made a huge jump
2. dive: le gusta saltar al agua she likes diving in the water
➤ salto alto high jump
➤ salto con garrocha pole vault
➤ salto de agua waterfall
➤ salto largo long jump
➤ salto mortal somersault.

**salud** interjección
1. *al brindar* cheers!
2. *después de estornudar* bless you!

la **salud** ■ health: es malo para la salud it's bad for your health.

**saludable** adjetivo ■ healthy.

**saludar** verbo
1. to say hello: ni siquiera me saludó he didn't even say hello to me
2. to wave: lo saludé desde lejos I waved to him from a distance
➤ Lo saluda atentamente Sincerely yours.

el **saludo** ■ regards: les mandó muchos saludos a todos she sends her best regards to everyone
➤ nos recibió con un cálido saludo he greeted us warmly.

**salvadoreño** adjetivo

En inglés, los adjetivos que refieren a un país o a una región se escriben con mayúscula:

**Salvadoran**

el **salvadoreño**, la **salvadoreña**

En inglés, los gentilicios se escriben con mayúscula:

**Salvadoran:** los salvadoreños the Salvadorans.

**salvaje** adjetivo ■ wild: un animal salvaje a wild animal.

**salvar** verbo ■ to save: le salvó la vida su hermano he saved his brother's life
➤ ¡te salvaste! you got out of that!

el **salvavidas** (plural los salvavidas)
1. lifeguard: los salvavidas tienen que saber nadar muy bien lifeguards have to be very good swimmers
2. life preserver.

**salvo** preposición ■ except: todos vinieron salvo Eduardo everyone came except Eduardo
➤ salvo que unless: salvo que se especifique a lo contrario unless otherwise specified.

**San** adjetivo ■ Saint: San Mateo Saint Matthew

San is a shortened form of Santo used before the names of certain saints.

**sanar** verbo
1. to heal: la herida tardó mucho en sanar the wound took a long time to heal
2. to get well: sanará pronto porque su enfermedad no es grave she'll get well soon since the disease isn't serious.

la **sandalia** ■ sandal.

la **sandía** ■ watermelon.

el **sándwich** (plural los sándwiches) ■ sandwich.

**sangrar** verbo ■ to bleed: su herida sangraba mucho her wound was bleeding profusely.

la **sangre** ■ blood.

**sano** adjetivo ■ healthy: es un muchacho fuerte y sano he's a strong and healthy boy; nadar es una actividad sana swimming is a healthy activity
➤ sano y salvo safe and sound.

**santo** adjetivo ■ holy: el santo evangelio the Holy Gospel el **santo** ■ saint's day: mañana es mi santo tomorrow is my saint's day

> Some Spanish speakers celebrate the feast day of the saint they share their first name with.

el **santo**, la **santa** ■ saint: tu hermano es un santo your brother is a saint.

el **sapo** ■ toad.

el **saque** ■ serve: tiene un saque muy poderoso he has a powerful serve.

el **sarampión** (plural los sarampiones) ■ measles.

**sarcástico** adjetivo ■ sarcastic.

la **sardina** ■ sardine.

el **sarro** ■ plaque: el dentista me quitó el sarro de los dientes the dentist removed the plaque from my teeth.

el/la **sartén** (plural los/las sartenes) ■ frying pan.

el **sastre** ■ tailor.

el **satélite** ■ satellite.

la **satisfacción** ■ satisfaction: se notaba su satisfacción con el resultado you could sense his satisfaction with the outcome.

**satisfacer** verbo
1. to satisfy: esa respuesta no me satisface that answer doesn't satisfy me
2. to meet: no satisface los requisitos it doesn't meet the requirements.

**satisfactorio** adjetivo ■ satisfactory: su rendimiento en el examen oral fue satisfactorio his performance on the oral exam was satisfactory.

**satisfecho** adjetivo ■ pleased: la profesora está muy satisfecha con sus alumnos the teacher is very pleased with her students.

el **sauna** ■ sauna.

el **saxofón** (plural los saxofones) ■ saxophone.

**se** pronombre

1.
> Se con sentido reflexivo se traduce por **himself**, **herself**, **itself**, **themselves**, **yourself** o **yourselves**, respectivamente:

se hizo daño con el martillo he hurt himself with the hammer; el radio se apaga solo the radio turns itself off; se declararon ganadores they declared themselves the winners; si quiere, se puede ver en este espejo you can look at yourself in this mirror if you like

2. **each other**: se quieren mucho they love each other very much

3.
> Cuando el verbo con se se refiere a partes del cuerpo o ropa, el inglés usa el artículo posesivo:

se lavó las manos he washed his hands; se amarró los zapatos he tied his shoelaces

4.
> Cuando se va junto a otro pronombre se traduce por **to him**, **to her**, **to them**, **to you**, respectivamente:

se los presté I lent them to him

> En estos casos no se traduce cuando el nombre al que se refiere se repite en la oración:

dáselo a tu hermano give it to your brother; es una sorpresa, no se lo cuentes a Ana it's a surprise so don't tell Ana

5.
> Cuando se tiene un sentido impersonal, generalmente se traduce por **you** o **it**:

se construyó en un año it was built in a year; se puede comprar limones en el mercado you can buy lemons at the market; eso no se hace you shouldn't do that
➤ "se alquila" "for rent"
➤ se está rasurando he's shaving
➤ se quejó del mal servicio he complained about the bad service.

**sé** verbo ➤ saber.

el **secador** ■ blow dryer.

**la secadora**
1. **dryer: pon tu ropa en la secadora** put your clothes in the dryer
2. *Mexico* **blow dryer**
➤ **siempre se seca el pelo con secadora** she always blow dries her hair.

**secar** *verbo* ■ **to dry: ayúdame a secar los platos** help me dry the dishes

**secarse** *verbo pronominal* ■ **to dry oneself: se secó con la toalla** he dried himself with the towel.

**la sección** *(plural* **las secciones)**
1. **section: la oficina está dividida en cinco secciones** the office is divided into five sections
2. **department: trabaja en la sección de muebles** he works in the furniture department.

**seco** *adjetivo*
1. **dry: el desierto es un lugar seco** the desert is a dry place
2. **dried: higos secos** dried figs.

**el secretario, la secretaria** ■ **secretary: trabaja de secretaria en una empresa** she works as a secretary in a company.

**secreto** *adjetivo* ■ **secret: el científico tenía una fórmula secreta** the scientist had a secret formula

**el secreto** ■ **secret: guardó el secreto por varios años** she kept the secret for a few years
➤ **se casaron en secreto** they got married in secret.

**el sector** ■ **sector**.

**la secuencia** ■ **sequence: hay que hacerlo en secuencia para que funcione** you have to do it in sequence for it to work.

**secuestrar** *verbo*
1. **to kidnap: secuestraron a la hija del presidente** the president's daughter was kidnapped
2. **to hijack: secuestraron el avión** they hijacked the plane.

**el secuestro**
1. *de persona* **kidnapping**
2. *de avión* **hijack**.

**secundario** *adjetivo* ■ **secondary**.

**la sed** ■ **thirst: saciar la sed** to quench one's thirst
➤ **tengo sed** I'm thirsty.

**seguido** *(adjetivo & adverbio)*
■ *adjetivo*
**in a row: estornudé cinco veces seguidas** I sneezed five times in a row
■ *adverbio*
**often: voy bastante seguido** I go there pretty often
➤ **lo haré en seguida** I'll do it right away
➤ **vaya todo seguido** keep going straight.

**seguir** *verbo*
1. **to follow: sígueme a mí** follow me
2. **to go along: siga por aquí y luego dé vuelta a la derecha** keep going along here then turn right
3. **to go on: ya no puedo seguir trabajando así** I can't go on working like this
➤ **¿sigues enfermo?** are you still sick?

**según** *(adverbio & preposición)*
■ *adverbio*
**depending on : compraré dos o tres juegos según el dinero que tenga** I'll buy two or three games depending on how much money I have
■ *preposición*
**according to: según Juan, le fue bien en el examen** according to Juan, he did well on the test.

**segundo** *adjetivo* ■ **second: llegó en el segundo tren** she arrived on the second train

**el segundo** ■ **second: 30 segundos** 30 seconds.

**la seguridad**
1. **safety: la seguridad personal** personal safety
2. **security: medidas de seguridad** security measures
➤ **le falta seguridad en sí mismo** he lacks self-confidence
➤ **lo hará con toda seguridad** he'll no doubt do it
➤ **la seguridad social** social security.

**259**

**seguro** *adjetivo*

1. **sure:** ¿estás seguro? are you sure?
2. **safe:** es bastante seguro comprar en Internet it's quite safe to buy on the Internet; no es seguro andar sólo por la noche it's not safe to walk around by yourself at night
3. **certain:** no es seguro que pueda jugar en el partido it's uncertain if he'll be able to play in the game

el **seguro**

1. **insurance:** ¿tienes seguro de casa? do you have home insurance?
2. *Mexico* **safety pin**.

**seis** *numeral* ■ **six:** tiene seis hijos she has six children
➤ mi hermana tiene seis años my sister is six years old
➤ son las seis it's six o'clock
➤ el seis de abril the sixth of April.

**seiscientos** *adjetivo* ■ **six hundred**.

la **selección** *(plural las selecciones)*

1. **selection:** hay una selección de colores enorme there's a great selection of colors
2. **team:** participan las selecciones nacionales de varios países the national teams from several countries are participating.

**seleccionar** *verbo* ■ **to pick:** Felisa seleccionó su vestido más nuevo para ir a la fiesta Felisa picked her newest dress to go to the party.

**sellar** *verbo* ■ **to seal:** sellaron el pozo para evitar accidentes they sealed the well to avoid accidents.

el **sello**

1. **stamp:** un sello de correos a postage stamp
2. **label:** un sello discográfico a record label.

la **selva** ■ **forest**
➤ selva tropical tropical rain forest.

el **semáforo** ■ **traffic light**.

la **semana** ■ **week:** me tardé dos semanas en terminarlo it took me two weeks to finish it
➤ fin de semana weekend: nos vemos los fines de semana we see each other on weekends

➤ **Semana Santa** Holy Week

> **SEMANA SANTA**
>
> **Semana Santa**, or Holy Week, is the week leading up to Easter Sunday and most schools are off for this week. Thursday and Friday are holy days and many people participate in ceremonies and processions. Dried cod is a popular dish at this time.

la **semanada** ■ **weekly allowance**.

**semanal** *adjetivo* ■ **weekly:** es un programa semanal de televisión it's a weekly TV show.

**sembrar** *verbo* ■ **to sow:** sembró las semillas hace unos meses he sowed the seeds a few months ago.

**semejante** *adjetivo*

1. **similar:** descubrieron un sistema solar semejante al nuestro they discovered a solar system similar to ours
2. **such:** no se puede justificar semejante barbaridad you can't justify such an atrocity.

el **semestre** ■ **semester**.

la **semifinal** ■ **semifinal**.

la **semilla** ■ **seed**.

el **senado** ■ **senate**.

el **senador**, la **senadora** ■ **senator**.

**sencillo** *adjetivo* ■ **simple:** la tarea es bastante sencilla the homework is pretty simple

el **sencillo**

1. **single:** el grupo tuvo éxito con ese sencillo the band had a hit with that single
2. **change:** ¿tienes sencillo? do you have any change?

el **sendero** ■ **path**.

la **sensación** ■ **feeling:** una sensación desagradable an unpleasant feeling.

**sensacional** *adjetivo* ■ **sensational:** te ves sensacional you look sensational.

**sensato** *adjetivo* ■ **sensible:** parece ser un chico muy sensato he seems to be a very sensible boy.

**sensible** *adjetivo* ■ **sensitive:** crema para piel sensible cream for sensitive skin; una persona muy sensible a very sensitive person

 The Spanish word **sensible** is a false cognate, it doesn't mean "sensible".

**sentar** *verbo*

1. **to suit:** ese peinado le sienta muy bien that haircut really suits her
2. **to do someone good:** este té te sentará bien this tea will do you good

**sentarse** *verbo pronominal* ■ **to sit down:** siéntate ahí si quieres sit down there if you want.

el **sentido** ■ **sense:** los cinco sentidos the five senses; ¿en que sentido? in which sense?; no tiene sentido del ritmo he has no sense of rhythm
➤ una calle de un solo sentido a one-way street
➤ ir en sentido contrario to go the wrong way
➤ perder el sentido to lose consciousness
➤ sentido común common sense
➤ sentido del humor sense of humor.

**sentimental** *adjetivo* ■ **sentimental.**

el **sentimiento** ■ **feeling.**

**sentir** *verbo*

1. **to feel:** siento un aire frío I feel a cold breeze
2. **to hear:** ¿sentiste ese ruido afuera? did you hear that noise outside?
3. **to smell:** siento un olor a gas I can smell gas
4. **to be sorry:** lo siento mucho I'm really sorry
➤ se siente mal he doesn't feel well
➤ se sintió por lo que dije *Chile, Mexico* she was hurt by what I said.

la **seña** ■ **sign:** te doy una seña cuando esté listo I'll give you a sign when I'm ready
➤ dame tus señas give me your address.

la **señal**

1. **sign:** es una señal positiva it's a positive sign
2. **signal:** la señal es muy débil the signal is very weak
➤ señal de tráfico traffic sign
➤ señal de socorro distress signal.

**señalar** *verbo* ■ **to point:** ¿puedes señalar dónde está? can you point out where it is?
➤ no señales a la gente con el dedo don't point at people.

el **señor**

1. **man:** ese señor te está buscando that man is looking for you
2. **Mr.:** el señor García Mr. García
➤ ¿se le ofrece algo, señor? can I help you, sir?
➤ Muy señor mío... Dear Sir...

 The Spanish word **señor** is a false cognate, it doesn't mean "senior".

la **señora**

1. **lady:** esa señora es mi maestra that lady is my teacher
2. **Mrs.:** la señora García Mrs. García
3. **wife:** le presento a mi señora I'd like you to meet my wife
➤ ¿se le ofrece algo, señora? can I help you, ma'am?

la **señorita**

1. **young lady:** ¡tu hermana ya es una señorita! your sister's a young lady already!
2. **Miss:** todavía me dicen señorita they still call me Miss.

la **separación** *(plural las separaciones)*

1. **separation:** una separación de dos años a two-year separation
2. **gap:** una separación de dos metros a two-meter gap.

**separado** *adjetivo*

1. **separate:** mantén los ingredientes separados keep the ingredients separate
2. **separated:** sus padres están separados his parents are separated
➤ por separado separately.

**separar** *verbo* ■ to separate: separa a los niños, por favor separate the children, please

**separarse** *verbo pronominal* ■ to separate: se separaron después de diez años they separated after ten years.

el **separo** ■ *Mexico* cell: lo pusieron en un separo por 24 horas he was put in a cell for 24 hours.

**septiembre** *sustantivo* *masculino* ■ September: en septiembre in September; el próximo septiembre next September; el pasado septiembre last September

> En inglés los nombres de los meses se escriben con mayúscula.

la **sequía** ■ drought.

**ser** *verbo* ■ to be: Luis es muy inteligente Luis is very intelligent; mi cumpleaños fue ayer my birthday was yesterday; es abogado he's a lawyer; somos veinticinco en la clase there are twenty-five of us in the class
➤ el lápiz es para escribir the pencil is for writing
➤ es la una y media it's half past one
➤ esta bicicleta es de mi hermana this is my sister's bicycle
➤ Rodrigo es de Guadalajara Rodrigo is from Guadalajara
➤ las casas son de adobe the houses are made from adobe
➤ a no ser que unless: a no ser que estudies, te va a ir mal you'll do badly unless you study
➤ o sea so: o sea que mañana no vienes so you're not coming tomorrow

el **ser** ■ being
➤ un ser humano a human being
➤ los seres vivos living things.

la **serie** ■ series: fui a una serie de charlas I went to a series of talks
➤ una serie de televisión a television series.

**serio** *adjetivo* ■ serious: es una persona muy seria he's a very serious person
➤ en serio seriously: no lo puedo tomar en serio I can't take it seriously.

la **serpiente** ■ snake.

el **serrucho** ■ saw.

el **servicio** ■ service: ofrecen un servicio muy bueno they offer very good service
➤ servicio a domicilio delivery service
➤ servicio incluido service is included
➤ servicio militar military service.

la **servilleta** ■ napkin.

**servir** *verbo*
1. to serve: ya sirvieron la cena they've already served dinner
2. to work: la máquina todavía sirve the machine still works
➤ ¿te sirve esta caja? can you use this box?
➤ esto no sirve para nada this is useless
➤ ¿te sirvo más té? can I get you some more tea?

**sesenta** *numeral* ■ sixty.

la **sesión** ■ session: esta sesión termina a las tres this session ends at three o'clock
➤ la última sesión the last showing.

el **seso** ■ brain.

la **seta** ■ mushroom: algunas setas son venenosas some mushrooms are poisonous.

**severo** *adjetivo*
1. harsh: el castigo fue demasiado severo the punishment was too harsh
2. strict: esa profesora es muy severa that teacher is very strict.

**sexista** *adjetivo* ■ sexist.

el **sexo** ■ sex.

**sexto, sexta** *adjetivo y pronombre* ■ sixth.

**sexual** *adjetivo* ■ sexual.

**si** *conjunción*
1. if: si me lo devuelves, te perdono if you give it back to me, I'll forgive you
2. whether: pregúntale si va a venir o no ask her whether she's coming or not
➤ como si no hubiera pasado nada as if nothing had happened

➤ **toma tu medicina porque si no seguirás enfermo** take your medicine or you won't get better.

**sí** (adverbio & pronombre)

■ adverbio
**yes: sí, puedes salir a jugar** yes, you can go out to play
➤ **a él no le gusta, pero a mí sí** he doesn't like it, but I do
➤ **parece que sí** so it seems
■ pronombre

1.

> Sí con sentido reflexivo se traduce por **himself, herself, itself, themselves, yourself** o **yourselves**:

**sabe defenderse a sí misma** she knows how to defend herself; **el cuerpo se repara a sí mismo** the body repairs itself; **debería tener más confianza en sí mismo** he should have more confidence in himself; **están hablando entre sí** they're talking among themselves

2.

> Sí con sentido impersonal se traduce por **yourself**:

**tiene que ver por sí mismo** you have to see for yourself
➤ **en sí** in itself: **el trabajo en sí no me gusta** I don't like work in itself.

**siempre** adverbio ■ **always: esa tienda siempre está cerrada** that store is always closed
➤ **como siempre, hace lo que quiere** as usual, he does what he wants
➤ **seremos amigos para siempre** we'll be friends forever
➤ **siempre y cuando** provided: **sí, siempre y cuando tus notas no bajen** yes, provided your grades don't slip.

la **sierra**
1. herramienta **saw**
2. cordillera **mountain range**.

la **siesta** ■ **nap**
➤ **se fue a dormir la siesta** he went to take a nap
➤ **la hora de la siesta** naptime.

**siete** numeral ■ **seven: tiene siete hijos** she has seven children
➤ **mi hermana tiene siete años** my sister is seven years old
➤ **son las siete** it's seven o'clock
➤ **el siete de abril** the seventh of April.

las **siglas** ■ **abbreviation**.

el **siglo** ■ **century: el siglo XXI** the 21st century
➤ **hace siglos que no escribe** he hasn't written in ages.

el **significado** ■ **meaning**.

**significar** verbo ■ **to mean: ¿qué significa esta palabra?** what does this word mean?
➤ **¿qué significa S.A.?** what does S.A. stand for?
➤ **su amistad significa mucho para mí** her friendship means a lot to me.

el **signo** ■ **sign: el signo de la victoria** the V-sign
➤ **¿de qué signo eres?** what sign are you?
➤ **los signos del zodíaco** the signs of the zodiac.

**siguiente** adjetivo ■ **next: deja todo preparado para el día siguiente** she leaves everything ready for the next day; **debe venir en el siguiente tren** he should be on the next train
➤ **los siguientes alumnos** the following students

el/la **siguiente**
➤ **¡que pase el siguiente!** next!
➤ **esta calle no, la siguiente** not this street, the next one.

la **sílaba** ■ **syllable**.

**silbar** verbo ■ **to whistle**.

el **silbato** ■ **whistle**.

el **silbido** ■ **whistle**
➤ **llamó al perro con un silbido** he called the dog with a whistle.

el **silencio** ■ **silence: necesito silencio para estudiar** I need silence when I study
➤ **¡silencio, por favor!** quiet, please!

**263**

➤ guardaron silencio en señal de respeto they remained silent as a sign of respect

➤ en silencio silently: escuchamos en silencio we listened silently.

la **sinceridad** ■ sincerity.

**sincero** *adjetivo* ■ sincere.

**silencioso** *adjetivo* ■ silent.

el **sindicato** ■ union.

la **silla** ■ chair: se sentó en la silla she sat in the chair

el **síndrome** ■ syndrome.

➤ una silla de montar a saddle

**singular** *adjetivo* ■ singular

➤ una silla de ruedas a wheelchair.

el **singular** ■ singular.

el **sillón** *(plural* los sillones*)* ■ armchair.

**siniestro** *adjetivo* ■ sinister.

**silvestre** *adjetivo* ■ wild: moras silvestres wild berries.

**sino** *conjunción* ■ but: no es actriz sino bailarina she's not an actress but a dancer

la **silueta** ■ silhouette: al fondo vemos la silueta de la catedral at the back we can see the silhouette of the cathedral

➤ no sólo habla inglés, sino también dos idiomas más she not only speaks English, but also two other languages

➤ ejercicios para conservar la silueta exercises for keeping in shape.

➤ no hace sino molestar he doesn't do anything but annoy people

el **símbolo** ■ symbol.

➤ no fue amable, sino todo lo contrario he wasn't nice, but just the opposite.

**simpático** *adjetivo* ■ nice: Ana es muy simpática Ana is very nice

el **sinónimo** ■ synonym.

➤ estuvo muy simpático con nosotros he was very nice to us

**sintético** *adjetivo* ■ synthetic.

➤ me cae simpático I like him

el **sintetizador** ■ synthesizer.

⚠ The Spanish word **simpático** is a false cognate, it doesn't mean "sympathetic".

el **síntoma** ■ symptom.

**sinvergüenza** *adjetivo* ■ shameless: es muy sinvergüenza he's utterly shameless

**simple** *adjetivo* ■ simple: es un ejercicio muy simple it's a very simple exercise

el/la **sinvergüenza** ■ crook: son todos unos sinvergüenzas they're all a bunch of crooks.

➤ no soy más que un simple principiante I'm a mere beginner.

**siquiera** *adverbio*

**simplificar** *verbo* ■ to simplify.

➤ ni siquiera not even: no tiene ni siquiera para sus alimentos he doesn't even have money for food: ni siquiera nos ha llamado she hasn't even called.

**simultáneo** *adjetivo* ■ simultaneous.

**sin** *preposición* ■ without: salió sin paraguas she went out without an umbrella; se fue sin despedirse he left without saying goodbye

la **sirena**
1. *alarma* siren
2. *ser mitológico* mermaid.

➤ sin querer accidentally

el **sirviente, la sirvienta** ■ servant.

➤ estar sin trabajo to be out of work

el **sismo**
1. *temblor* tremor
2. *terremoto* earthquake.

➤ el edificio sigue sin terminar the building remains unfinished

➤ gente sin hogar homeless people

el **sistema** ■ system: un nuevo sistema para enseñar inglés a new system for teaching English

➤ pasó la noche sin dormir she spent a sleepless night.

la **sinagoga** ■ synagogue.

**264**

➤ **el sistema respiratorio** the respiratory system

➤ **el sistema solar** the solar system

---

SISTEMA EDUCATIVO

The educational system in Latin America varies from country to country, but generally it breaks down into about six years of primary education and five or six years at the secondary level. The exception is Argentina, where there are nine years of primary education and three of secondary. Some countries, such as Mexico, Uruguay, and Venezuela, dedicate the last two or three years to preparing students for their future careers. This phase is known as **diversificada** or **preparatoria**. In other countries, such as Peru and Colombia, students who want to attend university take short preparatory courses after finishing their secondary education before taking college entrance exams.

---

el **sitio**

1. **place:** **déjalo en su sitio** leave it in its place; **está en un sitio seguro** it's in a safe place

2. **room:** **no hay suficiente sitio** there's not enough room; **esto ocupa mucho sitio** this takes up a lot of room

➤ **hicieron sitio para que me sentara** they made some room so I could sit down

➤ **cambiaron los muebles de sitio** they moved the furniture around

➤ **en algún sitio debe estar** it has to be around somewhere

➤ **deja sus cosas en cualquier sitio** he leaves his stuff everywhere

➤ **un sitio web** a web site

➤ **un sitio de taxi** *Mexico* a taxi stand.

la **situación** *(plural* las situaciones*)* ■ **situation**.

**situar** *verbo* ■ **to locate:** **¿quién puede situarlo en el mapa?** who can locate it on the map?

➤ **se sitúa entre los cinco mejores tenistas del mundo** she ranks among the five best tennis players in the world.

el **smog** ■ **smog.**

**sobra** *sustantivo femenino* ■ **¿alguien tiene una entrada de sobra?** does anybody

have a spare ticket?; **sabes de sobra que a tu papá eso le molesta** you know well and good that your dad hates that

➤ **de sobra** enough: **tenemos tiempo de sobra** we have enough of time

las **sobras** ■ **leftovers:** **le da las sobras al perro** he gives the leftovers to the dog.

**sobrar** *verbo* ■ **to be left over:** **no sobró nada de comida** there was no food left over

➤ **me sobró algo de dinero** I had some money left over

➤ **aquí sobra una silla** there's one chair too many here.

**sobre** *preposición*

1. **on:** **ponlo sobre la mesa** put it on the table

2. **over:** **volamos sobre la ciudad** we flew over the city

3. **about:** **no sabe nada sobre eso** he doesn't know anything about that; **una película sobre cuatro adolescentes** a movie about four teenagers

➤ **pon uno sobre otro** put them one on top of the other

➤ **sobre todo** above all: **sobre todo, recuerden apagar las luces** above all, remember to turn off the lights

➤ **sobre todo** specially: **una película interesante, sobre todo para los jóvenes** an interesting movie, specially for young people

el **sobre** ■ **envelope:** **un sobre aéreo** an airmail envelope.

**sobrenatural** *adjetivo* ■ **supernatural.**

**sobrepasar** *verbo* ■ **to exceed:** **su población sobrepasa los 17 millones** its population exceeds 17 million people

➤ **nadie lo sobrepasa en altura** no one is taller than him.

**sobresaliente** *adjetivo* ■ **outstanding:** **es un alumno sobresaliente** he's an outstanding student.

**sobresalir** *verbo*

1. **to stand out:** **sobresale entre sus compañeros por su inteligencia** he stands out among his classmates because of his intelligence

**2.** to overhang: había un nido en la cornisa que sobresale de la pared there was a nest on the cornice that overhangs the wall.

el/la **sobreviviente** ■ survivor.

**sobrevivir** *verbo*

**1.** to survive
**2.** to outlive
➤ sobrevivir a algo to survive something: sobrevivieron al accidente they survived the accident
➤ sobrevivir a alguien to outlive somebody: sobrevivió a sus dos hijos he outlived his two sons.

la **sobrina** ■ niece.

el **sobrino** ■ nephew: tiene muchos sobrinos he has many nieces and nephews.

**sociable** *adjetivo* ■ sociable.

**social** *adjetivo* ■ social.

la **sociedad**

**1.** society (*plural* societies): vivimos en una sociedad multicultural we live in a multicultural society
**2.** company (*plural* companies): formaron una sociedad para vender libros por Internet they formed a company to sell books on the Internet.

el **socio, la socia**

**1.** partner: él y mi papá son socios de la empresa he and my father are business partners
**2.** member: soy socio de un club de deportes I'm a member of a sports club
➤ quiero hacerme socio de un club de tenis I want to become a member of a tennis club.

la **sociología** ■ sociology.

el **socorro** ■ help
➤ oímos unos gritos pidiendo socorro we heard some cries for help
➤ ¡socorro! help!

el **sofá** ■ sofa: se sentó en el sofá he sat down on the sofa
➤ un sofá cama a sofa bed.

el **software** ■ software.

el **sol** ■ sun
➤ al sol in the sun: la ropa se secaba al sol the clothes dried in the sun: estaban sentados al sol they were sitting in the sun
➤ hace sol it's sunny
➤ vamos a tomar el sol we're going to sunbathe
➤ al salir el sol at sunrise
➤ al ponerse el sol at sunset.

el/la **soldado** ■ soldier.

**soleado** *adjetivo* ■ sunny.

la **soledad** ■ loneliness: sufren de pobreza y soledad they suffer from poverty and loneliness
➤ no me gusta la soledad I don't like to be alone.

**solicitar** *verbo*

**1.** to apply for: voy a solicitar una beca I'm going to apply for a scholarship
**2.** to request: escribí solicitando información I wrote requesting information.

la **solicitud**

**1.** *de trabajo, de beca* application: rechazaron mi solicitud they rejected my application
**2.** *de información, ayuda* request
➤ presentar una solicitud to put in an application.

la **solidaridad** ■ solidarity: lo hizo en solidaridad con sus compañeros he did it out of solidarity with his companions.

**sólido** *adjetivo* ■ solid.

el/la **solista** ■ soloist.

**solitario** *adjetivo* ■ solitary

el **solitario, la solitaria** ■ loner.

el **solitario** ■ solitaire
➤ le gusta hacer solitarios he likes to play solitaire.

**solo** *adjetivo*

**1.** alone: estaba sola she was alone
**2.** lonely: se siente solo he feels lonely
➤ quiere hablar a solas conmigo he wants to speak to me alone
➤ lo hizo él solo he did it on his own

➤ no tuve ni una sola falta I didn't have a single error

➤ se lo voy a decir una sola vez I'm going to tell him only once

➤ siempre habla solo he always talks to himself

el **solo** ■ solo: un solo de batería a drum solo.

**sólo** adverbio ■ only: sólo quería un vaso de agua I only wanted a glass of water; sólo faltan tres días para mi cumpleaños there are only three days left until my birthday

➤ con sólo pensarlo me da rabia I get angry just thinking about it

➤ no sólo canta sino que también compone he not only sings but he also composes.

**soltar** verbo

1. **to let go of**: no le sueltes la mano don't let go of his hand; ¡suéltame! let go of me!

2. **to release**: soltaron a los sospechosos they released the suspects

3. **to untie**: no puedo soltar este nudo I can't untie this knot

4. **to let out**: soltó al perro he let the dog out

➤ soltó una carcajada she burst out laughing

➤ se soltó el pelo she let her hair down

➤ los tornillos se soltaron the screws came loose.

la **soltera** ■ bachelorette.

**soltero** adjetivo ■ single: es soltero he's single

➤ padres solteros single parents

el **soltero** ■ bachelor.

la **solución** (plural las soluciones) ■ solution.

**solucionar** verbo ■ to solve: no solucionas nada con llorar you don't solve anything by crying

➤ al final todo se solucionó in the end everything was resolved.

la **sombra**

1. **shade**: sentémonos a la sombra let's sit in the shade

2. **shadow**: su sombra se proyectaba en la pared her shadow was cast on the wall

➤ sombra de ojos eyeshadow.

el **sombrero** ■ hat.

la **sombrilla**

1. de mano **parasol**

2. de playa, terraza **sunshade**.

la **sonaja** ■ Mexico rattle.

el **sonajero** ■ rattle.

el **sonámbulo,** la **sonámbula** ■ sleepwalker.

**sonar** verbo

1. timbre, campana **to ring**: el teléfono no ha parado de sonar the telephone hasn't stopped ringing

2. instrumento, voz **to sound**: suena a música de los ochenta it sounds like eighties music

➤ el despertador no sonó the alarm clock didn't go off

➤ esto me suena conocido this sounds familiar

➤ escríbela tal como suena write it just the way it sounds

➤ suénate la nariz blow your nose.

el **sonido** ■ sound.

**sonreír** verbo ■ to smile: me sonrió he smiled at me.

la **sonrisa** ■ smile.

**sonrojarse** verbo pronominal ■ to blush.

**soñar** verbo ■ to dream: soñé que ganábamos el partido I dreamed that we were winning the game

➤ soñar con alguien to dream about somebody: anoche soñé con él last night I dreamt about him

➤ soñar con algo to dream of something: sueña con ser famoso he dreams of being famous.

la **sopa** ■ soup: sopa de pollo chicken soup.

**267**

**soplar** *verbo* ■ **to blow:** está soplando un viento muy frío a very cold wind is blowing

➤ sopla las velas y pide un deseo blow out the candles and make a wish

➤ le soplaron la respuesta they whispered the answer to her.

el **soplido** ■ **blow**

➤ tienes que apagarlas de un soplido you have to blow them out with one blow.

**soportar** *verbo*

1. **to support:** esta columna soporta todo el peso this column supports all the weight
2. **to stand:** apenas puede soportar el dolor he can barely stand the pain

➤ la verdad es que no la soporto the truth is that I can't stand her.

**sorber** *verbo* ■ **to sip**

➤ no sorbas la sopa don't slurp the soup.

el **sorbo** ■ **sip:** apenas le dio un sorbo a la sopa he barely had a sip of the soup

➤ se lo tomó de un sorbo he drank it in one gulp

➤ hay que tomarlo a sorbos you have to sip it.

**sordo** *adjetivo* ■ **deaf:** es sordo he's deaf

➤ se quedó sordo he went deaf.

**sordomudo** *adjetivo* ■ **deaf-mute.**

**sorprendente** *adjetivo* ■ **surprising.**

**sorprender** *verbo* ■ **to surprise:** ya nada me sorprende nothing suprises me these days; no me sorprendería que lo volviera a hacer it would not surprise me if he did it again

➤ lo sorprendieron copiando they caught him copying

➤ se sorprendió de verme he was surprised to see me.

la **sorpresa** ■ **surprise:** quiero que sea una sorpresa I want it to be a surprise

➤ su pregunta me tomó de sorpresa his question took me by surprise

➤ le hicieron una fiesta de sorpresa they gave him a surprise party.

**sortear** *verbo*

1. **to raffle:** sortearon un premio estupendo they raffled a fabulous prize
2. **to avoid:** sortearon los obstáculos con gran habilidad they avoided the obstacles very skillfully.

el **sorteo** ■ **raffle.**

la **sospecha** ■ **suspicion.**

**sospechar** *verbo* ■ **to suspect:** sospecho que mis vecinos lo hicieron I suspect that my neighbors did it

➤ sospechar de alguien to suspect somebody: sospechan del jardinero they suspect the gardener.

**sospechoso** *adjetivo* ■ **suspicious**

el **sospechoso,** la **sospechosa** ■ **suspect.**

el **sostén** *(plural* los sostenes*)* ■ **bra.**

**sostener** *verbo*

1. **to hold:** sostenme la escalera, por favor hold the ladder for me, please
2. **to support:** estas dos vigas sostienen el techo these two beams support the roof
3. **to maintain:** siempre ha sostenido que él no lo hizo she's always maintained that he didn't do it

**sostenerse** *verbo pronominal* ■ **to stand:** el borracho apenas se sostenía en pie the drunk could barely stand.

el **sótano** ■ **basement.**

el **spanglish** ■ **Spanglish**

SPANGLISH

Spanglish is the result of contact between English and Spanish. It contains a blend of both languages spoken by native or heritage Spanish-speakers living in the United States. **Brecas** instead of **frenos** (brakes) and **bloques** instead of **cuadras** (blocks) are some common examples.

**su** *adjetivo*

1. *de él* **his:** vino con su novia he came with his girlfriend

**2.** *de ella* **her:** conozco a su marido I know her husband

**3.** *de una cosa, un animal* **its:** viene en su propia caja it comes in its own box

**4.** *de ellos, ellas, varias cosas* **their:** trajeron sus bicicletas they brought their bicycles; los jóvenes tienen su propio estilo teens have their own style; trae fotos de los pájaros y sus nombres he has pictures of birds and their names

**5.** *de usted, ustedes* **your:** su nombre, por favor your name, please; no dejen sus cosas tiradas don't leave your things lying around.

### suave *adjetivo*

**1.** **soft:** tocaban una música muy suave they were playing very soft music

**2.** **smooth:** es suave al tacto it's smooth to the touch; un aterrizaje suave a smooth landing

**3.** **mild:** tiene un clima suave it has a mild climate

**4.** **gentle:** una champú suave a gentle shampoo.

el **suavizante** ■ fabric softener.

el **subcampeón** *(plural* los subcampeones)* ■ runner-up.

**subdesarrollado** *adjetivo* ■ underdeveloped.

el **subdirector,** la **subdirectora**

**1.** *de colegio* **assistant principal**

**2.** *de empresa* **assistant manager.**

el **subibaja** ■ seesaw.

la **subida**

**1.** **increase:** una subida de la temperatura a temperature increase

**2.** **climb:** iniciaron la subida a la montaña they started the climb up the mountain

**3.** **ascent:** después de la bajada viene una subida empinada after the descent comes a steep ascent.

### subir *verbo*

**1.** **to go up:** subimos a la colina we went up the hill; voy a subir por las escaleras I'm going to go up the stairs

**2.** **to come up:** sube que quiero decirte algo come up, I want to tell you something; ya subo I'm coming up

**3.** **to take up:** voy a subir la televisión a mi cuarto I'm going to take the television up to my room

**4.** **to bring up:** por favor, súbeme el suéter que dejé en la cocina please bring me up the sweater that I left in the kitchen

**5.** **to rise:** ha subido la temperatura the temperature has risen; le subió la fiebre his fever rose

**6.** **to climb:** subió la montaña she climbed the mountain; le cuesta subir las escaleras it's hard for him to climb the stairs

**7.** **to turn up:** sube el volumen, por favor turn up the volume, please

➤ no puedo subirme el cierre I can't get my zipper up

### subirse *verbo pronominal* ■

➤ subirse a algo *a un coche* to get into: se subió a un taxi he got into a taxi

➤ subirse a algo *un autobús, avión, bicicleta* to get on: nos subimos juntos al tren we got on the train together

➤ subirse a algo *a un árbol* to climb: se subió al muro he climbed the wall.

el **subjuntivo** ■ subjunctive.

el **submarino** ■ submarine.

**subrayar** *verbo* ■ to underline.

el **subsidio**

➤ el subsidio de desempleo unemployment compensation.

**subterráneo** *adjetivo* ■ underground.

el **subtítulo** ■ subtitle.

el **suburbio**

**1.** *barrio obrero* **working-class area**

**2.** *barrio de las afueras* **suburb.**

la **suciedad** ■ dirt.

**sucio** *adjetivo* ■ dirty: tienes la cara sucia your face is dirty.

la **sucursal** ■ branch office.

la **sudadera** ■ sweatshirt.

**Sudamérica** *sustantivo*        *femenino*
■ **South America**.

**sudamericano** *adjetivo*

En inglés, los adjetivos que se refieren a un país o una región se escriben con mayúscula:

**South American**

el **sudamericano, la sudamericana**

En inglés, los gentilicios se escriben con mayúscula:

**South American: un sudamericano** a South American; **los sudamericanos** South Americans.

**sudar** *verbo* ■ **to sweat**.

el **sudor** ■ **sweat**.

la **suegra** ■ **mother-in-law** (*plural* **mothers-in-law**).

el **suegro** ■ **father-in-law** (*plural* **fathers-in-law**): **me acompañó mi suegro** my father-in-law came with me
➤ **invitó a sus suegros** she invited her in-laws.

la **suela** ■ **sole**.

el **sueldo**
1. *de un empleado* **salary** (*plural* **salaries**)
2. *de un obrero* **wages**.

el **suelo**
1. *en el exterior* **ground: al salir del cine me caí al suelo** upon leaving the theater I fell to the ground
2. *de una casa, edificio* **floor: un suelo de madera** a wood floor.

**suelto** *adjetivo* ■ **loose: este tornillo está suelto** this screw is loose; **tiene una hoja suelta** it has a sheet loose; **el perro anda suelto** the dog is loose
➤ **andaba con el pelo suelto** she was walking with her hair down
➤ **está prohibido vender cigarrillos sueltos** it's prohibited to sell individual cigarettes

el **suelto** ■ *Mexico* **change: ¿tienes suelto?** do you have any change?

**sueno, suenas etc** *verbo* ➤ sonar.

**sueño, sueñas etc** *verbo* ➤ soñar.

el **sueño**
1. **dream: tuve un sueño muy raro** I had a very strange dream
2. **sleep: es falta de sueño** it's lack of sleep; **necesito nueve horas de sueño** I need nine hours of sleep
➤ **tengo sueño** I'm sleepy
➤ **tiene el sueño muy pesado** he's a heavy sleeper
➤ **ya me caía de sueño** I was so sleepy I could hardly stand.

la **suerte** ■ **luck: deséame suerte** wish me luck; **¡buena suerte!** good luck!
➤ **tener suerte** to be lucky: **tienes mucha suerte** you're very lucky
➤ **tuvo mala suerte** he was unlucky
➤ **por suerte** luckily: **por suerte todo salió bien** luckily everything turned out fine.

el **suéter** ■ **sweater**.

**suficiente** *adjetivo* ■ **enough: no había suficiente comida** there wasn't enough food; **¿hay suficientes sillas?** are there enough seats?

el **sufrimiento** ■ **suffering**.

**sufrir** *verbo* ■ **to suffer: ha sufrido mucho** he has suffered a lot; **no hagas sufrir a tu mamá** don't make your mom suffer
➤ **sufre del corazón** he suffers from a heart condition
➤ **sufre de asma** he suffers from asthma.

la **sugerencia** ■ **suggestion**.

**sugerir** *verbo* ■ **to suggest: sugiero que nos vayamos** I suggest we leave.

**sugiero, sugieres etc** *verbo* ➤ sugerir.

**suicidarse** *verbo* ■ **to commit suicide**.

el **suicidio** ■ **suicide**.

**sujetar** *verbo*
1. **to hold: tienes que sujetarlo con las dos manos** you have to hold it with both hands; **sujétame la escalera** hold the ladder for me
2. **to fix: lo sujetó a la pared con tornillos** he fixed it to the wall with screws

**270**

➤ **sujetó los papeles con un clip** she fastened the papers with a clip

➤ **sujetaba al perro con una cuerda** they held on to the dog with a rope.

el **sujeto** ■ subject.

la **suma**

1. addition: **están haciendo sumas** they're doing addition

2. sum: **la suma de los votos emitidos** the sum of the votes cast

➤ **importantes sumas de dinero** significant sums of money.

**sumar** verbo ■ to add: **hay que sumar estas cantidades** you have to add these numbers

➤ **cuatro y cuatro suman ocho** four plus four equals eight.

**supe** verbo ➤ saber.

**súper** adverbio ■ super: **lo pasé súper bien** I had a super time.

**superar** verbo

1. to overcome: **tiene que superar su timidez** he has to overcome his shyness; **han superado muchos problemas** they have overcome many problems

2. to surpass: **los supera a todos en agilidad** she surpasses them all in agility; **eso supera todas las expectativas** that surpasses all expectations

➤ **superó la marca mundial** he broke the world record

➤ **estudia porque quiere superarse** she studies because she wants to excel.

**superficial** adjetivo ■ superficial.

la **superficie**

1. surface: **la superficie del lago está congelada** the lake's surface is frozen

2. area: **abarca una superficie de cuatro kilómetros cuadrados** it covers an area of four kilometers squared.

el **supermercado** ■ supermarket.

**superior** adjetivo

1. upper: **el incendio empezó en los pisos superiores** the fire started on the upper floors

2. superior: **es de calidad superior** it's of superior quality

➤ **superior a algo** better than something: **este modelo es muy superior al del año pasado** this model is better than last year's

➤ **dame un número superior a diez** give me a number higher than ten.

la **superstición** (plural las supersticiones) ■ superstition.

**supervisar** verbo ■ to supervise.

el/la **suplente**

1. replacement: **entró de suplente en el segundo tiempo** he came in as a replacement in the second half

2. substitute: **es el suplente del profesor de historia** he's the substitute for the history teacher.

**suponer** verbo

1. to suppose: **supongo que no has hecho la tarea** I suppose that you haven't done the homework; **supongo que tienes razón** I suppose you're right

2. to think: **supuse que iba a cambiar de idea** I thought that he was going to change his mind; **supusimos que era para mañana** we thought that it was for tomorrow

3. to mean: **eso supone tener que levantarme más temprano** that means I'll have to get up earlier

➤ **supongo que sí** I suppose so.

**suprimir** verbo ■ to delete: **suprimió varias frases** he deleted several sentences

➤ **van a suprimir parte de la materia del examen** they're going to cut part of the material from the test.

el **supuesto**

➤ **en el supuesto de que no lo supiera** on the assumption that he didn't know

➤ **por supuesto** of course

➤ **por supuesto que no** of course not

➤ **tú das por supuesto que te van a aceptar** you take for granted that they're going to accept you.

el **sur** ■ south: **el sur de la ciudad** the south part of the city

➤ **al sur** to the south: **está al sur de Lima** it's to the south of Lima

➤ **los estados del sur** the southern states.

el **surf** ■ surfing.

el **surfeador**, la **surfeadora** ■ surfer.

**surfear** *verbo* ■ to surf.

el **surfing** ■ surfing.

el/la **surfista** ■ surfer.

**surgir** *verbo* ■ to come up: surgió un problema a problem came up.

**suscribirse** *verbo* ■ to subscribe: me suscribí a una revista I subscribed to a magazine.

la **suscripción** *(plural* las suscripciones) ■ subscription.

**suspender** *verbo*
1. to cancel: suspendieron la fiesta del sábado they canceled Saturday's party; suspendieron las clases por la nieve they canceled classes because of the snow
2. to stop: suspendieron la reunión para almorzar they stopped the meeting to eat lunch
3. to suspend: lo suspendieron por mala conducta they suspended him for bad conduct
➤ suspendieron el partido a causa de la lluvia they postponed the game because of the rain.

el **suspenso** ■ suspense: una historia llena de suspenso a story filled with suspense
➤ una película de suspenso a thriller.

**suspirar** *verbo* ■ to sigh.

el **suspiro** ■ sigh.

la **sustancia** ■ substance.

el **sustantivo** ■ noun.

**sustituir** *verbo* ■ to replace: va a sustituir al director cuando se jubile she's going to replace the director when he retires; Pino sustituyó al arquero en el segundo tiempo Pino replaced the goalkeeper in the second half; van a sustituir a la secretaria porque está enferma they're going to temporarily replace the secretary because she's sick
➤ sustituir algo por algo to substitute something with something: puedes sustituir el azúcar por sacarina you can substitute the sugar with saccharine.

el **sustituto**, la **sustituta**
1. *permanente* replacement
2. *temporal* substitute.

el **susto** ■ scare: me llevé un gran susto I had a bad scare
➤ ¡qué susto me diste! what a scare you gave me!
➤ tener susto to be afraid.

**susurrar** *verbo* ■ to whisper: le susurró algo al oído he whispered something to her.

**sutil** *adjetivo* ■ subtle.

**suyo**
■ *adjetivo & pronombre*
1. *de él* his: fue idea suya it was his idea; no es asunto suyo it's none of his business
2. *de ella* her: no es asunto suyo it's none of her business
3. *de usted, ustedes* your: ¿son estas hijas suyas? are these your daughters?
4. *de ellos, ellas* their: ¿es ésta su calle? — no, la suya es la próxima is this their street? — no, theirs is the next one
■ *pronombre*
1. *de él* his: el suyo es blanco his is white; esta no es su hija, la suya es mucho menor this is not his daughter, his is much younger
2. *de ella* hers: el suyo es rojo hers is red; esta no es su hermana, la suya no vino this is not her sister, hers didn't come
3. *de usted, de ustedes* yours: el rojo es el suyo the red one is yours; éstos no son sus asientos, ésos son los suyos these are not your seats, those are yours
4. *de ellos, ellas* theirs
➤ llegaron con un amigo suyo they arrived with a friend of theirs
➤ estas fotos son suyas these photos are theirs.

el **switch**
1. *Colombia, Mexico* light switch: apaga el switch para cambiar el foco turn off the light switch to change the light bulb
2. *Mexico* ignition switch
➤ dale al switch turn on the ignition.

el **tabaco** ■ tobacco.

la **tabla**

1. **board:** con un par de tablas hizo una mesa with a couple of boards he made a table
2. **table:** las tablas de los verbos the verb tables
➤ las tablas de multiplicar multiplication tables
➤ una tabla de picar a chopping board
➤ la tabla de planchar the ironing board.

el **tablero** ■ **board:** un tablero de damas a checkerboard
➤ el tablero de anuncios the bulletin board.

la **tableta** ■ **tablet**.

la **tablilla** ■ *Mexico* **bar:** una tablilla de chocolate a chocolate bar.

**tacaño** *adjetivo* ■ **stingy**

el **tacaño, la tacaña** ■ **skinflint**.

**tachar** *verbo* ■ **to cross:** taché su nombre de la lista I crossed her name from the list
➤ los tachan de machistas they accused them of being chauvinists.

el **taco**

1. *de tortilla* **taco:** un taco de pollo a chicken taco
2. *de zapato de fútbol* **stud**
3. *comida ligera Mexico* **snack:** echémonos un taco let's have a snack
4. *en el billar* **pool cue**.

el **tacón** *(plural los tacones)* ■ **heel:** se le rompió el tacón her heel broke
➤ zapatos de tacón high-heeled shoes.

la **táctica** ■ **tactics:** van a tener que cambiar de táctica they're going to have to change tactics.

el **tacto**

1. **touch:** es suave al tacto it's soft to the touch
2. **tact:** le falta tacto she's lacking tact
➤ tiene mucho tacto he's very tactful.

**tal** *(adjetivo & adverbio)*

■ *adjetivo*
**such:** lo dijo de tal manera que me ofendió he said it in such a manner as to offend me
➤ nadie esperaba tal cantidad de público nobody expected such a large crowd
➤ un tal Mario preguntó por ti some man named Mario asked for you

■ *adverbio*
➤ ¿qué tal? how's it going?
➤ ¿qué tal estuvo la fiesta? how was the party?
➤ lo hice tal como me lo explicaste I did it exactly like you explained
➤ no todo es tal como lo vemos not everything is just as we see it
➤ te lo presto con tal que me lo devuelvas luego I'll loan it to you provided that you return it to me later
➤ tal vez maybe.

el **taladro** ■ **drill**.

el **talento** ■ **talent:** tiene talento para el dibujo he has a talent for drawing.

la **talla** ■ **size:** ¿qué talla usas? what size do you wear?

**tallar** *verbo*
1. *la madera* **to carve**
2. *una joya, el cristal* **to cut**
3. *Mexico el suelo, una olla* **to scrub**

**tallarse** *verbo pronominal Mexico*
1. **to rub:** se tallaba los ojos she was rubbing her eyes
2. **to scrub:** tállate bien las rodillas scrub your knees well.

los **tallarines** ■ **noodles**.

**273**

el **taller**

1. *de mecánico* **garage**
2. *de artista* **studio**
3. *de carpintero, electricista* **workshop**
➤ un taller de poesía a poetry workshop.

el **tallo** ■ stem.

el **talón** *(plural los talones)*

1. *del pie, de un calcetín* **heel**
2. *de un cheque, recibo* **stub**.

el **tamal** ■ tamale.

el **tamaño** ■ **size**: ¿qué tamaño tiene? what size is he?; son del mismo tamaño they're the same size.

**también** *adverbio* ■ **also**: a mí también me regalaron uno they also gave one to me; canta y también toca el piano he sings and he also plays the piano
➤ Pepe lo sabía — y yo también Pepe knew it — and me too
➤ quiero ir — nosotros también I want to go — we do too.

el **tambor** ■ drum.

**tampoco** *adverbio*

1. **either**: yo tampoco lo sé I don't know either; no estudió ni tampoco hizo la tarea he didn't study and he didn't do his homework either
2. **neither**: no quiero ir ni Pepe tampoco I don't want to go and neither does Pepe; no puedo hacerlo — yo tampoco I can't do it — me neither; no sabía que tenía un hermano — nosotros tampoco she didn't know that he had a brother — neither did we.

el **tampón** *(plural los tampones)* ■ tampon.

**tan** *adverbio*

1. **so**: no comas tan rápido don't eat so quickly; ¡es tan divertido! it's so entertaining!
2. **such**: lo pasamos tan bien we had such a good time; nunca había visto un perro tan grande I had never seen such a large dog
➤ ¡que película tan aburrida! what a boring movie!

➤ lo pusiste tan arriba que no lo puedo alcanzar you put it so high up that I can't reach it
➤ tan...como as...as: no es tan inteligente como su hermano he's not as intelligent as his brother: ven tan pronto como puedas come as soon as you can.

el **tanque** ■ tank.

**tanto** *(adverbio, adjetivo & pronombre)*

■ *adverbio*

1. **so much**: lo quiere tanto she loves him so much; comí tanto que no pude dormir I ate so much that I couldn't sleep
2. **so often**: ya no voy al cine tanto I don't go to the movies so often anymore
➤ no sé por qué se demoró tanto I don't know why he was so late
➤ no debería trabajar tanto she shouldn't work so much
➤ he estudiado tanto como tú I've studied as much as you
➤ tanto Ana como José reprobaron both Ana and José failed
■ *adjetivo & pronombre*

El adjetivo se traduce por **so much** o **so many** según el sustantivo en inglés sea singular o plural respectivamente:

1. **so much**: había tanta comida there was so much food
2. **so many**: me hizo tantas preguntas she asked me so many questions; tengo tanto qué hacer I have so much to do; nunca había visto tanta gente aquí I had never seen so many people here; tengo tantos que no sé qué hacer con ellos I have so many that I don't know what to do with them
➤ he traído tanto dinero como tú I've brought as much money as you
➤ ya no tiene tantos amigos como antes now he doesn't have as many friends as before
➤ no tiene tanta importancia it's not that important
➤ tiene tanta suerte he's so lucky
➤ una mujer de unos veinte y tantos años a woman of twenty-odd years
➤ por lo tanto therefore

el **tanto**

1. **goal**: ganaron un tanto a cero they won, one goal to zero

**2. amount:** hay que pagar un tanto fijo cada mes you have to pay a fixed amount each month

➤ lo puse al tanto de todo I caught him up on everything

➤ te voy a mantener al tanto I'll keep you informed

➤ un tanto por ciento a percentage.

la **tapa**

1. *de olla, caja* **lid**

2. *de libro, revista* **cover:** su nombre estaba en la tapa del libro his name was on the cover of the book

➤ un libro de tapas blandas a paperback book

➤ un libro de tapas duras a hardback book

> ⚠ The Spanish word **tapa** is a false cognate, it doesn't mean "tap".

la **tapadura** ■ *Chile, Mexico* **filling:** se me salió una tapadura one of my fillings came out.

**tapar** *verbo*

1. **to cover:** lo tapó con papel de aluminio she covered it with aluminum foil

2. **to put the lid on:** tienes que tapar la olla you have to put the lid on the pot

3. **to fill:** están tapando los agujeros en la calle they're filling the holes in the street

➤ me taparon una muela *Chile, Mexico* I had a tooth filled

➤ tapa la botella put the cap on the bottle

➤ no me tapes el sol don't block my sunlight

**taparse** *verbo pronominal*

1. **to cover:** se tapó la boca con la mano she covered her mouth with her hand

2. **to get blocked:** se tapó el desagüe the drain got blocked; se me tapa la nariz my nose is blocked

➤ tápate bien wrap yourself up well.

el **tapete**  ■ *Colombia, Mexico* **rug:** un tapete persa a Persian rug

➤ el tapete del baño the bath mat.

la **tapia** ■ **wall:** la pelota se fue por encima de la tapia the ball went over the wall.

el **tapón** *(plural* los tapones*)*

1. *del lavabo, fregadero* **stopper**

2. *de botella* **cork**

3. *para los oídos* **earplug**.

la **taquilla**

1. *de teatro, cine* **box office**

2. *en estación, estadio* **ticket office**.

**tardar** *verbo*

➤ tardaron dos horas en llegar they took two hours to arrive

➤ por favor, no tardes please, don't be late

➤ ¿cuánto tardaste en leerlo? how long did you take to read it?

➤ están tardando en darme los resultados they're taking a while to give me the results

➤ no tardó en darse cuenta he didn't take long to realize

➤ el tren se tarda media hora the train takes half an hour.

**tarde** *adverbio* ■ **late:** ya es demasiado tarde it's too late now

➤ ¡apúrate!, que vamos a llegar tarde hurry! we're going to arrive late

➤ llegué muy tarde anoche I arrived very late last night

➤ más tarde later

➤ tarde o temprano sooner or later

la **tarde**

1. **afternoon:** a las cuatro de la tarde at four o'clock in the afternoon; buenas tardes good afternoon; mañana en la tarde tomorrow afternoon

2. **evening:** a las siete de la tarde at seven o'clock in the evening; buenas tardes good evening; hoy en la tarde this evening.

la **tarea**

1. **task:** tienen la tarea de cuidar los parques they have the task of looking after the parks

2. **homework:** no ha hecho las tareas she hasn't done the homework

➤ las tareas de la casa the chores.

la **tarifa**

1. *de transporte* **fare:** los escolares pagan tarifa reducida the schoolchildren pay a reduced fare

2. *de la luz, del agua* **rate**.

la **tarima** ■ **platform**.

la **tarjeta** ■ card: me mandó una tarjeta para mi cumpleaños he sent me a card for my birthday
➤ una tarjeta de crédito a credit card
➤ una tarjeta de embarque a boarding pass
➤ una tarjeta de Navidad a Christmas card
➤ una tarjeta postal a postcard
➤ una tarjeta telefónica a telephone card.

el **tarro**
1. *de vidrio* jar: un tarro de mermelada a jar of jam
2. *Mexico, Venezuela para el café, té* mug: un tarro de cerveza a beer mug.

**tartamudear** *verbo* ■ to stutter.

**tartamudo** *adjetivo*
➤ es tartamudo he has a stutter.

la **tasa** ■ rate: la tasa de mortalidad the death rate; la tasa de natalidad the birth rate.

el **tatuaje** ■ tattoo.

el **taxi** ■ taxi.

el/la **taxista** ■ taxi driver.

la **taza**
1. cup: me tomé una taza de café I drank a cup of coffee
2. cupful: agregar dos tazas de azúcar add two cupfuls of sugar.

**te** *pronombre*
1. you: te llamó ayer she called you yesterday; te lo dije I told you
2. yourself: sólo si te portas bien only if you behave yourself
➤ ¡no te muevas! don't move!
➤ ponte los zapatos put your shoes on.

el **té** *(plural* los tés*)* ■ tea: ¿quieres té? do you want some tea?
➤ un té con limón a tea with lemon.

el **teatro** ■ theater: fuimos al teatro we went to the theater
➤ no le paso nada, todo es puro teatro *informal* nothing's wrong with him, it's all an act.

el **techo**
1. ceiling: dos lámparas colgaban del techo two light fixtures hung from the ceiling

2. roof: había palomas encima del techo there were pigeons on the roof.

la **tecla** ■ key: las teclas del piano the piano keys.

el **teclado** ■ keyboard.

la **técnica** ■ technique.

**técnico** *adjetivo* ■ technical

el **técnico**, la **técnica**
1. technician: es técnico dental he's a dental technician
2. repairman *(plural* repairmen*)*: el técnico vino a arreglar el televisor the repairman came to fix the television.

la **tecnología** ■ technology *(plural* technologies*)*.

**tejer** *verbo* ■ to sew: esto me lo tejió mi mamá my mom sewed this for me.

el **tejido**
1. *labor* knitting
2. *tela* fabric
3. *del cuerpo humano* tissue.

la **tela** ■ cloth: necesitas un metro de tela you need a meter of cloth
➤ tela de araña spiderweb.

la **telaraña**
1. *nueva* spiderweb: había un insecto atrapado en la telaraña there was an insect trapped in the spiderweb
2. *vieja, con polvo* cobweb: el desván está lleno de telarañas the attic is full of cobwebs.

la **tele** ■ *informal* TV: lo dieron por la tele it was on TV.

el **teleférico** ■ cable car.

el/la **telefonista** ■ telephone operator.

el **teléfono**
1. telephone: no tiene teléfono he doesn't have a telephone
2. telephone number: ¿me das tu teléfono? will you give me your telephone number?
➤ está hablando por teléfono con un amigo he's talking with a friend on the telephone
➤ me llamó por teléfono he called me on the telephone

➤ un teléfono celular a cellphone
➤ un teléfono de tarjeta a card phone.

el **telegrama** ■ telegram.

la **telenovela** ■ soap opera.

la **telera** ■ *Mexico* white bread roll.

el **telescopio** ■ telescope.

el **telespectador**, la**telespectadora** ■ viewer.

el **telesquí** *(plural* los telesquís*)* ■ ski lift.

la **televisión** ■ television: lo vimos por la televisión we saw it on television
➤ la televisión digital digital television.

el **televisor** ■ television set.

el **tema**
1. subject: ¿qué opinas del tema? what's your opinion on the subject?
2. topic: el tema de la conferencia the topic of the conference; el tema de mi proyecto es el medioambiente the topic of my project is the environment
3. theme: un tema musical a musical theme; el tema de la exposición the show's theme
➤ estás cambiando de tema you're changing the subject
➤ los temas de actualidad current affairs.

**temblar** *verbo* ■ to tremble: le temblaban las manos her hands were trembling
➤ estaba temblando de frío he was shivering with cold
➤ temblaba de miedo she was trembling with fear
➤ la explosión hizo temblar el edificio the explosion made the building tremble.

el **temblor** ■ shaking: ¿sentiste el temblor? did you feel the shaking?
➤ un temblor de tierra an earth tremor.

**temer** *verbo*
1. to fear: todos le temen al director everybody fears the director
2. to be afraid: no temas, nada te va a pasar don't be afraid, nothing's going to happen to you; teme que no va ser posible he's afraid that it's not going to be possible

➤ me temo que no es tan simple como crees I'm afraid it's not as simple as you think
➤ temen por su vida they fear for their lives.

el **temor** ■ fear: el temor a lo desconocido the fear of the unknown
➤ por temor a for fear of: no salen de noche por temor a los asaltos they don't go out at night for fear of assault.

el **temperamento** ■ temperament.

la **temperatura** ■ temperature: ¿qué temperatura hace? what's the temperature?; le tomó la temperatura she took his temperature.

la **tempestad** ■ storm.

**templado** *adjetivo*
1. mild: regiones de clima templado mild climate regions
2. warm: un aparato que mantiene la comida templada a device that keeps the food warm; peces de agua templada warm water fish.

el **templo** ■ temple.

la **temporada** ■ season: la temporada de vacaciones the vacation season
➤ está pasando una temporada en Europa he's spending some time in Europe
➤ la temporada alta the high season
➤ la temporada baja the low season.

**temporal** *adjetivo* ■ temporary

el **temporal** ■ storm.

**temprano** *adverbio* ■ early: llegué temprano I arrived early.

**ten** *verbo* ➤ tener.

**tenaz** *(plural* tenaces*) adjetivo* ■ tough.

las **tenazas**
1. *de cangrejo* pincers
2. *utensilio* tongs
➤ recogió las brasas con unas tenazas he picked up the hot coals with some tongs.

la **tendencia**
1. tendency *(plural* tendencies*)*: tiene tendencia a la gordura he has a tendency toward being fat

**277**

**2. trend:** las últimas tendencias en materia de rock the latest trends in rock; **la actual tendencia hacia la globalización** the current trend toward globalization.

**tender** *verbo*

**1.** *la ropa* **to hang out:** la tendió al sol she hung it out in the sun

**2. to lay out:** tendió la toalla en el suelo he laid the towel out on the floor

➤ **tender a** to tend to: **tiende a exagerar** he tends to exaggerate

➤ **le tendieron una trampa** they set a trap for him

**tenderse** *verbo pronominal* ▪ **to stretch out:** se tendió en la arena she stretched out in the sand.

el **tendero,** la **tendera** ▪ shopkeeper.

el **tendón** *(plural* los tendones) ▪ **tendon**

➤ **el tendón de Aquiles** Achilles' heel.

**tendrá, tendré etc** *verbo* ➤ tener.

el **tenedor** ▪ fork.

**tener** *verbo*

**1. to have:** tienen una casa en la playa they have a house on the beach; **tengo muchos amigos** I have many friends; **tiene el pelo corto** she has short hair; **mañana no tenemos clases** we don't have class tomorrow

**2.**

Cuando el verbo tener va seguido de un sustantivo que indica una sensación, el inglés usa **to be** seguido de un adjetivo:

**to be:** tenemos hambre we're hungry; **tengo sed** I'm thirsty; **no tengas miedo** don't be afraid

**3. to hold:** tenme la escalera hold the ladder for me; **¿me puedes tener esto un momento, por favor?** can you hold this for me for a moment, please?

➤ **tengo las manos sucias** my hands are dirty

➤ **¿cuántos años tienes?** how old are you?

➤ **tengo muchas cosas que hacer** I have a lot of things to do

➤ **tiene que ir al dentista** she has to go to the dentist

➤ **tengo que hacer más ejercicio** I have to exercise more

➤ **tengan mucho cuidado** be very careful.

**tengo** *verbo* ➤ tener.

el/la **teniente** ▪ lieutenant.

el **tenis** ▪ tennis.

el/la **tenista** ▪ tennis player.

la **tensión** *(plural* las tensiones)

**1. tension:** había mucha tensión en el ambiente there was a lot of tension in the atmosphere

**2. stress:** durante los exámenes pasamos por un periodo de mucha tensión during the exams we went through a period of a lot of stress

➤ **siempre está en tensión** he's always stressed out.

**tenso** *adjetivo*

**1. tense:** el ambiente estaba muy tenso the atmosphere was very tense

**2. taut:** la cuerda no está suficientemente tensa the cord is not taut enough.

la **tentación** *(plural* las tentaciones) ▪ temptation.

**tentador** *adjetivo* ▪ tempting.

**tentar** *verbo* ▪ **to tempt:** no me tientes con eso don't tempt me with that.

**teñir** *verbo* ▪ **to dye:** tiñó la camiseta de azul she dyed the T-shirt blue; **se tiñe el pelo** she dyes her hair.

la **teoría** ▪ theory *(plural* theories): mi teoría es que copió en el examen my theory is that he copied on the exam

➤ **en teoría** in theory: eso es verdad en teoría pero no en la práctica that is true in theory but not in practice.

**teórico** *adjetivo* ▪ theoretical.

la **terapia** ▪ therapy *(plural* therapies)

➤ **terapia de grupo** group therapy

➤ **terapia intensiva** *Mexico, River Plate* intensive care.

**tercer** *numeral*

Shortened form of **tercero** used before masculine singular nouns.

**tercero** *numeral*

> Tercero becomes **tercer** when it comes before a singular masculine noun:

**third:** me resultó a la tercera vez I got it the third time around; vive en el tercer piso he lives on the third floor; llegó tercero he came in third; soy el tercero de la lista I'm the third on the list
➤ una tercera parte de los estudiantes a third of the students
➤ el tercer mundo the Third World
➤ las personas de la tercera edad senior citizens.

el **tercio** ■ third: un tercio de la población a third of the population.

el **terciopelo** ■ velvet.

**terco** *adjetivo* ■ stubborn.

el **terminal** ■ *informática* computer terminal

la **terminal** ■ terminal: llega a la terminal dos it arrives at terminal two
➤ la terminal de camiones *Mexico* bus station.

**terminar** *verbo*

1. **to finish:** ya terminé las tareas I've already finished my homework
2. **to end:** la clase no ha terminado todavía class hasn't ended yet; ¿a qué hora termina la película? what time does the movie end?
3. **to end up:** terminé aceptando la invitación I ended up accepting the invitation; todos terminamos rendidos we all ended up exhausted
➤ los zapatos terminan en punta the shoes are pointy
➤ terminó con su novio she broke it off with her boyfriend
➤ hay que terminar con la indisciplina you have to stop the lack of discipline

**terminarse** *verbo pronominal*
➤ se nos terminó el dinero we ran out of money
➤ se me terminaron las vacaciones my vacations were over.

el **término** ■ term: es un término técnico it's a technical term

➤ por término medio, duermo ocho horas cada noche on average, I sleep eight hours a night
➤ en términos generales el nivel es muy bajo generally speaking the level is very low
➤ ¿qué término quiere la carne? *Colombia, Mexico* how would you like your meat done?

el **termo** ■ thermos.

el **termómetro** ■ thermometer.

la **ternura** ■ tenderness.

el/la **terrateniente** ■ landowner.

la **terraza**
1. *balcón* balcony (plural balconies)
2. *patio de baldosas* terrace
➤ un bar con terraza a terrace bar.

el **terremoto** ■ earthquake.

el **terreno**
1. **land:** la casa tiene mucho terreno the house has a lot of land; es un terreno muy fértil it's very fertile land
2. **piece of land:** se compraron un terreno en la costa they bought a piece of land on the coast; son dueños de varios terrenos they're owners of several pieces of land
➤ lo vamos a decidir sobre el terreno we're going to decide it on the spot.

**terrible** *adjetivo* ■ terrible: fue un accidente terrible it was a terrible accident
➤ tenía un calor terrible I was terribly hot
➤ tengo un sueño terrible I'm awfully sleepy.

el **territorio** ■ territory (plural territories).

el **terrón** (plural los terrones)
➤ un terrón de azúcar a sugar lump.

el **terror** ■ terror: el temblor causó terror en el pueblo the tremor caused terror in the village
➤ les tiene terror a las arañas she's terrified of spiders
➤ una película de terror a horror movie.

el **terrorismo** ■ terrorism.

**terrorista** *adjetivo* ■ terrorist: un atentado terrorista a terrorist attack

el/la **terrorista** ■ terrorist.

la **tesis** (plural las tesis) ▪ **thesis** (plural **theses**).

el **tesoro** ▪ **treasure:** un tesoro escondido a hidden treasure
➤ ¿cómo estás tesoro? how are you darling?
➤ eres un tesoro you're a real gem.

el **testamento** ▪ **will**
➤ hacer testamento to make one's will.

**testarudo** adjetivo ▪ **stubborn**.

el/la **testigo** ▪ **witness**
➤ fue testigo de la boda de mis papás he was a witness at my parents' wedding
➤ fuimos testigos del accidente we witnessed the accident.

la **tetera**
1. *para servir té* **teapot**
2. *Andes, Mexico para hervir agua* **kettle**.

el **texto** ▪ **text**
➤ un libro de texto a textbook.

**ti** pronombre
1. **you:** lo compré para ti I bought it for you; he estado pensando en ti I've been thinking about you
2. **yourself:** guárdalo para ti keep it for yourself; tienes que pensar más en ti you have to think more about yourself
➤ ¿qué te importa a ti? what does it matter to you?

**tibio** adjetivo ▪ **lukewarm**.

el **tiburón** (plural los tiburones) ▪ **shark**.

el **tic** ▪ **tic:** es un tic nervioso it's a nervous tic.

el **tiempo**
1. **time:** ¿qué haces en tu tiempo libre? what do you do in your free time?; la mayor parte del tiempo most of the time; así ganamos tiempo that way we'll save time
2. **weather:** ¿cómo está el tiempo? what's the weather like?; hace buen tiempo the weather is nice; hace mal tiempo the weather is bad
3. **tense:** tiempo compuesto compound tense
4. **half:** marcaron el gol en el primer tiempo they scored the goal in the first half

➤ a tiempo in time: llegaste justo a tiempo para desayunar you arrived just in time to eat breakfast
➤ llegaron al mismo tiempo they arrived at the same time
➤ no pierdas el tiempo don't waste time
➤ ¿cuánto tiempo hace que esperas? how long have you been waiting?
➤ hace tiempo que no viene he hasn't come for a while
➤ no me llevó mucho tiempo it didn't take me much time
➤ ¡cuánto tiempo sin verte! long time no see!
➤ ¿qué tiempo tiene la niña? how old is the girl?
➤ Ana llegó primero y al poco tiempo Pepe Ana arrived first and Pepe soon after
➤ en esos tiempos la vida era más barata in those days life was less expensive
➤ en los últimos tiempos recently.

la **tienda** ▪ **store:** una tienda de ropa a clothing store
➤ fuimos de tiendas we went shopping
➤ una tienda de abarrotes Andes, Central America, Mexico a grocery store
➤ una tienda de campaña a tent
➤ una tienda de departamentos Mexico a department store.

**tiene etc** verbo ➤ tener.

**tierno** adjetivo ▪ **tender:** la carne estaba muy tierna the meat was very tender; es una persona muy tierna she's a very tender person.

la **tierra**
1. **land:** cultivan la tierra they cultivate the land; un viaje por tierra a journey by land; finalmente llegaron a tierra at last they reached land
2. **soil:** aquí la tierra es muy fértil the soil is very fertile here
➤ extraña su tierra she misses her homeland
➤ la Tierra Earth.

**tieso** adjetivo ▪ **stiff**.

el **tigre** ▪ **tiger**.

las **tijeras** ▪ **scissors:** córtalo con las tijeras cut it with the scissors
➤ necesito unas tijeras I need a pair of scissors.

**280**

los **tiliches** ■ *Mexico informal* **junk:** el cuarto de los tiliches the junk room.

el **timbre**
1. **bell:** sonó el timbre the bell rang
2. *Mexico* **stamp:** colecciona timbres he collects stamps.

**tímido** *adjetivo* ■ **shy.**

la **tina** ■ **bathtub.**

la **tinta** ■ **ink:** una mancha de tinta an ink stain.

el **tinto** ■ **red wine:** se tomó una copa de tinto she had a glass of red wine.

la **tintorería** ■ **dry cleaner's.**

la **tía** ■ **aunt:** la tía Marta Aunt Marta.

el **tío** ■ **uncle:** el tío Juan Uncle Juan.
➤ un regalo de mis tíos a present from my aunt and uncle.

**típico** *adjetivo* ■ **typical:** el típico mexicano the typical Mexican
➤ eso es típico de él that's typical of him
➤ un baile típico del centro del país a traditional dance from the center of the country.

el **tipo**
1. **type:** el tipo de música preferida por los jóvenes the type of music preferred by teens
2. *informal* **guy:** ¿quién es ese tipo? who's that guy?; es un tipo muy divertido he's a very fun guy
3. **figure:** tiene muy buen tipo she has a very good figure
➤ va todo tipo de gente all sorts of people go.

la **tira** ■ **slip:** una tira de papel a slip of paper
➤ una tira cómica a comic strip
➤ la tira *Mexico informal* the cops

el/la **tira** ■ *Chile, Mexico informal* **cop.**

la **tirada** ■ **throw:** sacó dos seises a la primera tirada de los dados he rolled two sixes with the first throw of the dice
➤ de una tirada in one stretch: hicimos el viaje de una tirada we made the trip in one stretch.

el **tiradero** ■ *Mexico* **dump:** un tiradero de basura a garbage dump.

el **tirano, la tirana** ■ **tyrant.**

**tirante** *adjetivo*
1. *cuerda, cable* **tight**
2. *ambiente, situación* **tense**

el **tirante** ■ **strap:** un vestido con tirantes a dress with straps.

los **tirantes** ■ *Mexico, Venezuela* **suspenders.**

**tirar** *verbo*
1. **to throw:** tírame las llaves throw me the keys; les tiraban piedras a los policías they were throwing rocks at the police
2. **to throw away:** deberías tirar esto, ya no sirve you should throw this away, it's no good anymore
3. **to knock down:** van a tirar la pared they're going to knock down the wall
4. **to waste:** que manera de tirar el dinero what a way to waste money
➤ voy a tirar todo esto a la basura I'm going to throw all this in the trash
➤ me empujó y me tiró al suelo he pushed me and knocked me to the ground
➤ tiraron muchas bombas they dropped many bombs
➤ tiré el florero sin querer I accidentally dropped the vase
➤ tiraron con fuerza de la cuerda they tugged hard at the rope
➤ tiene trabajo y van tirando he has work and so they manage

**tirarse** *verbo pronominal*
➤ se tiró al agua she dove into the water
➤ se tiró de cabeza he dove in headfirst
➤ quería tirarse por la ventana he wanted to throw himself out the window
➤ se tiró en la cama he lay down on the bed.

**tiritar** *verbo* ■ **to shiver:** tiritaba de frío he was shivering with cold.

el **tiro** ■ **shot:** disparó un tiro he fired a shot
➤ lo mató de un tiro she shot him to death
➤ le salió el tiro por la culata it backfired on him
➤ tiro al blanco target practice
➤ un tiro libre *en fútbol* a free kick
➤ un tiro libre *en básquetbol* a free throw.

**el tirón** (plural los tirones) ■ **tug:** dale un buen tirón give it a good tug
➤ le dio un tirón de orejas she reprimanded him
➤ leí el libro de un tirón I read the book straight through
➤ dormí doce horas de un tirón I slept twelve hours straight.

**el tiroteo** ■ **shoot-out:** hubo un tiroteo entre la policía y los asaltantes there was a shoot-out between the police and the assailants.

**el títere** ■ **puppet**.

**el titipuchal** ■ Mexico informal
➤ un titipuchal a ton: tenemos un titipuchal de tareas we have a ton of homework
➤ hace un titipuchal de años many years ago.

**el titular** ■ **headline:** viene en todos los titulares it's in all the headlines.

**el/la titular**
1. **holder:** el titular de un pasaporte the holder of a passport
2. **first-team player:** juega de titular he's a first-team player.

**el título**
1. **title:** no me acuerdo del título de la canción I don't remember the title of the song
2. **degree:** acaba de recibir su título universitario she just received her university degree
3. **diploma:** tenía su título colgado en la pared he had his diploma hanging on the wall
➤ tiene título de abogado he's a qualified lawyer.

**la tiza** ■ **chalk**
➤ lo escribió con una tiza she wrote it with a piece of chalk.

**la tlapalería** ■ Mexico **hardware store**.

**la toalla** ■ **towel**
➤ una toalla de manos a handtowel
➤ una toalla femenina Mexico a sanitary napkin
➤ una toalla higiénica a sanitary napkin.

**el tobillo** ■ **ankle**
➤ me torcí el tobillo I twisted my ankle.

**el tobogán** (plural los toboganes) ■ **slide**.

**el tocadiscos** (plural los tocadiscos) ■ **record player**.

**el tocador** ■ **dressing table**.

**tocar** verbo
1. **to touch:** no toques la computadora don't touch the computer; le tocó la mano she touched his hand
2. **to play:** ¿sabes tocar la guitarra? do you know how to play the guitar?; toca el piano muy bien he plays the piano very well
3. **to ring:** tocó el timbre the bell rang
➤ ¿a quién le toca? whose turn is it?
➤ me toca a mí jugar it's my turn to play
➤ le tocó el más grande he got the biggest one.

**el tocino** ■ **bacon**.

**todavía** adverbio
1.

Todavía se traduce por still cuando se trata de oraciones afirmativas o interrogativas:

**still:** todavía la quiere he still loves her; ¿todavía vives en la misma casa? do you still live in the same house?

2.

Todavía se traduce por yet cuando se trata de oraciones negativas:

**yet:** no la he visto todavía I haven't seen her yet; todavía no llega she hasn't arrived yet
3. **even:** ahí hace todavía más calor it's even hotter there.

**todo**
■ adjetivo & pronombre
1. **all:** todo el tiempo all the time; invitó a todas sus amigas she invited all her friends; gente de todo tipo all sorts of people
2. **every:** voy todas las semanas I go every week
3. **whole:** se tomó toda la botella she drank the whole bottle; vino toda su familia his whole family came; toda la verdad the whole truth
➤ ya es todo un hombre now he's every inch a man

➤ **todo el mundo lo sabe** everybody knows
■ *pronombre*

1. **everything:** se lo comieron todo they ate everything; **el dinero no es todo** money is not everything
2. **everybody:** todos vinieron everybody came; **todos lo saben** everybody knows
3. **all:** los vendieron todos they sold them all; **eso es todo, por ahora** that's all, for now
➤ **en esa tienda venden de todo** they sell everything in that store.

### el toldo
1. *de playa* **sunshade**
2. *en tienda, patio* **awning**.

### tolerante *adjetivo* ■ **tolerant**.

### tolerar *verbo* ■ **to tolerate:** no voy a tolerar una cosa así I'm not going to tolerate something like that
➤ **les toleran todo a sus hijos** they put up with everything from their children
➤ **no tolero a la gente mal educada** I can't stand rude people.

### tomar *verbo*
1. **to drink:** no hay que tomar de esa agua you don't have to drink from that water; **¿qué van a tomar?** what are they going to drink?; **se tomaron toda la botella** they drank the whole bottle
2. **to take:** tomamos un taxi we took a taxi; **siempre tomo el mismo tren** I always take the same train; **me voy a tomar el día libre** I'm going to take the day off
➤ **me tomó la mano** he took my hand
➤ **la tomó del brazo** he took her by the arm
➤ **tomé apuntes en la clase** I took notes in class
➤ **tomó nota de todo lo que dijo** he took note of everything she said
➤ **toma la primera calle a la izquierda** take the first street on the left
➤ **toma, se te quedó esto en mi escritorio** here, you left this in my desk
➤ **le tomé cariño** I became fond of him
➤ **te están tomando el pelo** they're pulling your leg
➤ **estuvo tomando el sol** he was sunbathing
➤ **salió a tomar el aire** she went outside to get some fresh air

➤ **se tomó la molestia de venir hasta acá** he took the trouble to come all the way here
➤ **no te lo tomes a mal** don't take it badly
➤ **se lo toma todo en broma** he takes everything as a joke.

### el tomate ■ **tomato** *(plural* **tomatoes**): una ensalada de tomates a tomato salad
➤ **un tomate verde** a green tomato.

### el tomo ■ **volume**.

### la tonelada ■ **ton**.

### el tono
1. **tone:** me di cuenta por el tono de su voz I realized by the tone of his voice
2. **shade:** siempre se viste con tonos claros she always dresses in light shades
➤ **el teléfono no tiene tono** the telephone has no dial tone
➤ **el tono de marcar** the dial tone.

### la tontería
➤ **estás diciendo tonterías** you're talking nonsense
➤ **¡no digas tonterías!** don't talk nonsense!
➤ **pelaron por una tontería** they fought over nothing
➤ **lo que hiciste fue una tontería** what you did was foolish.

### tonto *adjetivo* ■ **silly:** eres muy tonto you're very silly
➤ **¡qué excusa más tonta!** what a stupid excuse!

### toparse *verbo pronominal*
➤ **toparse con alguien** to run into somebody: **me topé con ella a la entrada** I ran into her at the entrance.

### el tope
1. **limit:** le pusieron un tope al número de llamadas que puede hacer they put a limit on the number of calls she can make
2. *Mexico en la calle* **speed bump**
➤ **el estadio estaba lleno hasta los topes** the stadium was completely full.

### el toque ■ **touch:** sólo me falta darle los últimos toques all I have left is to give it the finishing touches
➤ **un toque de queda** a curfew.

### el tórax ■ **thorax**.

**torcer** *verbo*

1. **to twist:** agarra al niño con cuidado, así le estás torciendo un brazo hold the boy carefully, you're twisting his arm; **ayer me torcí un tobillo y hoy lo tengo hinchadísimo** yesterday I twisted my ankle and today it's very swollen
2. **to wring:** antes de colgar la ropa para que se seque, hay que torcerla before hanging the clothes to dry, you have to wring them.

la **tormenta** ■ storm.

el **tornillo** ■ screw.

el **toro** ■ bull.

la **toronja** ■ *Mexico* grapefruit.

**torpe** *adjetivo*

1. **clumsy:** no le des ninguna tarea delicada, es muy torpe don't give him a delicate task, he's very clumsy
2. **awkward:** el bebé todavía tiene un andar torpe y se cae mucho the baby still has an awkward walk and he falls down a lot.

la **torre** ■ tower: el campanario está en la torre más alta de la iglesia the belfry is in the church's highest tower.

el **torso** ■ torso.

la **torta**

1. **pie:** la torta de jamón y queso es mi preferida the ham and cheese pie is my favorite
2. *Southern Cone, Venezuela* **cake:** al final de la fiesta, comimos torta de cumpleaños at the end of the party, we ate birthday cake
3. *Mexico* **sandwich:** no tuve tiempo de sentarme a almorzar, sólo comí una torta I didn't have time to sit down and eat lunch, I only ate a sandwich.

la **tortilla**

1. **omelette:** la tortilla española clásica se prepara con huevos, papas y cebolla the classic Spanish omelette is prepared with eggs, potatoes and onion
2. **tortilla:** en México, la tortilla forma parte de la alimentación básica in Mexico, the tortilla forms part of the essential foods

**TORTILLA ESPAÑOLA**

A **tortilla española** is a type of thick omelette filled with fried onions and potatoes, then sliced into wedges. It is a dish inherited from Spain and in some Latin American countries it is commonly eaten as a "fast food".

la **tortuga** ■ turtle.

la **tos** ■ cough: está resfriada y tiene mucha tos she has a cold and a bad cough.

**toser** *verbo* ■ to cough: estuvo tosiendo toda la noche he was coughing all night.

la **tostada**
➤ una tostada a piece of toast
➤ ¿quieres tostadas? would you like some toast?

la **tostadora** ■ toaster.

**tostar** *verbo* ■ to toast: tostamos varias rebanadas de pan y las comimos con mermelada we toasted several slices of bread and we ate them with jam

**tostarse** *verbo pronominal* ■ to tan: el protector solar ayuda a tostarse sin peligros para la piel sunscreen helps you to tan without danger to your skin.

**total** *(adjetivo & adverbio)*
■ *adjetivo*
**complete:** necesitamos silencio total we need complete silence
■ *adverbio*
**after all:** voy contigo al supermercado, total, no tengo nada que hacer I'm going with you to the supermarket, after all, I don't have anything to do.

el **total** ■ total: el total de sumar 10 más 10 es 20 the total from adding 10 plus 10 is 20.

la **totalidad**
➤ la totalidad de los estudiantes de mi grupo fueron al museo all of the students in my group went to the museum.

**tóxico** *adjetivo* ■ poisonous.

el **trabajador,** la **trabajadora**
■ worker

**284**

**trabajar** *verbo* ■ **to work**: trabajan para una editorial they work for a publishing house

➤ ¿quién trabaja en esa película? who's in that movie?

el **trabajo**

1. **job**: tardó sólo un par de semanas en encontrar trabajo he only took a couple of weeks to find a job
2. **work**: si quieres hablar con ella ahora, puedes llamarla al trabajo if you want to talk with her now, you can call her at work
3. **essay**: ¿cuándo tenemos que entregar el trabajo de historia? when do we have to turn in the history essay?

el **tractor** ■ **tractor**.

la **tradición** (*plural* las tradiciones) ■ **tradition**.

**tradicional** *adjetivo* ■ **traditional**.

la **traducción** (*plural* las traducciones) ■ **translation**.

**traducir** *verbo* ■ **to translate**: hay que traducir estos ejemplos al inglés you have to translate these examples into English.

el **traductor**, la **traductora** ■ **translator**.

**traer** *verbo*

1. **to bring**: tengo frío, por favor tráeme una manta I'm cold, please bring me a blanket
2. **to have**: este diccionario trae muchos ejemplos this dictionary has many examples
3. **to wear**: mi madre trae las sandalias que le regalé my mother is wearing the sandals I gave her.

el **tráfico** ■ **traffic**: por la mala visibilidad, hubo varios accidentes de tráfico because of the poor visibility, there were several traffic accidents.

**tragar** *verbo* ■ **to swallow**.

la **tragedia** ■ **tragedy** (*plural* **tragedies**).

**trágico** *adjetivo* ■ **tragic**: en un trágico accidente perdió a toda su familia he lost his whole family in a tragic accident.

el **trago**

1. **swallow**: tenía mucha sed y se tomó toda el agua de un trago she was very thirsty so she drank all the water in one swallow
2. **sip**: quiero sólo un trago, para probar I only want a sip, just to try it.

el **traje**

1. **suit**: para la entrevista de trabajo, Juan se puso un traje azul for the job interview, Juan put on a blue suit
2. **costume**: mañana es el concurso de trajes típicos regionales tomorrow is the show of typical regional costumes

➤ un traje de baño a bathing suit
➤ un traje de gala an evening dress
➤ un traje de novia a wedding dress.

la **trama** ■ **plot**: ¿podrías contarme la trama de la película? could you tell me the plot of that film?

el **trámite** ■ **procedure**: los trámites se han complicado procedures have become complicated.

el **tramo**

1. **section**: trasladarse será más fácil cuando esté pronto este tramo de la carretera traveling will be easier when this section of highway is done
2. **flight**: la abuela no puede subir más de cuatro tramos de escalera our grandmother can't go up more than four flights of stairs.

la **trampa** ■ **trap**: los cazadores pusieron una trampa para el oso the hunters laid a trap for the bear

➤ hacer trampa to cheat: no me gusta jugar con ella, siempre gana porque hace trampa I don't like to play with her, she always wins because she cheats.

el **trampolín** (*plural* los trampolines) ■ **diving board**.

el **tramposo** *adjetivo* ■ **cheat**: eres un tramposo y por eso siempre ganas you're a cheat and that's why you always win.

**tranquilo** *adjetivo*

1. **calm:** tienes que estar tranquilo para la prueba you have to be calm for the test
2. **peaceful:** después de una fuerte tormenta nocturna, el día amaneció tranquilo after a strong storm in the night, a peaceful day dawned.

**transcurrir** *verbo*

1. **to take place:** la historia de Drácula transcurre en Transilvania the story of Dracula takes place in Transylvania
2. **to pass:** ya transcurrieron dos años desde que llegué a esta ciudad two years have already passed since I arrived in this city.

el/la **transeúnte** ■ **passer-by.**

la **transformación** *(plural las transformaciones)* ■ **transformation:** estudiamos la transformación de la oruga en mariposa we're studying the transformation of the caterpillar into a butterfly.

**transformar** *verbo*

1. **to change:** el mago transformó al conejo en una paloma the wizard changed the rabbit into a dove
2. **to transform:** la tecnología está transformando los métodos educativos technology is transforming educational methods

**transformarse** *verbo pronominal*

1. **to be converted:** en esta represa, la fuerza del agua se transforma en energía eléctrica at this dam, the force of the water is converted into electric energy
2. **to change:** desde la última vez que estuve aquí, este país se ha transformado this country has changed since the last time I was here.

**transgénico** *adjetivo* ■ **genetically modified.**

el **tránsito** ■ **traffic**
➤ accidente de tránsito traffic accident
➤ infracción de tránsito traffic offense.

la **transmisión** *(plural las transmisiones)* ■ **broadcast:** la transmisión del partido de fútbol se interrumpió por el apagón the broadcast of the soccer game was interrupted by the blackout.

**transmitir** *verbo*

1. **to pass on:** le transmitiré a mi familia tus saludos I will pass your greetings on to my family
2. **to broadcast:** la radio acaba de transmitir el alerta the radio just broadcast the alert.

la **transparencia** ■ **transparency** *(plural* **transparencies).**

**transparente** *adjetivo* ■ **transparent.**

la **transpiración** ■ **perspiration.**

**transpirar** *verbo* ■ **to perspire.**

el **transportador** ■ **protractor:** usé el transportador para dibujar este ángulo de 55 grados I used the protractor to draw this 55 degree angle.

**transportar** *verbo* ■ **to transport:** transportaremos la mercadería por barco we'll transport the merchandise by boat.

el **transporte** ■ **transportation:** el sistema de transporte aquí es bastante malo the transportation system here is pretty bad
➤ medio de transporte means of transportation: el tren es mi medio de transporte favorito the train is my favorite means of transportation.

el **trapo** ■ **rag:** ¿dónde hay un trapo para limpiar la mesa? where is there a rag to clean the table?
➤ un trapo de cocina a dishcloth.

la **tráquea** ■ **windpipe.**

**tras** *preposición* ■ **after:** tras los incidentes en el estadio, todos los partidos de la temporada se suspendieron after the incidents in the stadium, all the season's games were canceled
➤ día tras día day after day: regó las plantas día tras día, pero la sequía terminó matándolas he watered the plants day after day, but the drought ended up killing them.

**trasero** *adjetivo* ■ **back:** los niños deben viajar en el asiento trasero del auto children must ride in the back seat of the car

el **trasero** ■ **backside.**

**trasladar** *verbo* ▪ **to move:** hay que trasladar el equipo de música al jardín we have to move the music equipment to the garden; las tortugas se trasladan muy lentamente turtles move very slowly.

**trasplantar** *verbo* ▪ **to transplant.**

el **trasplante** ▪ **transplant.**

el **traste** ▪ *Mexico* **pot:** necesito un traste hondo para este guisado I need a deep pot for this stew.

el **trasto** ▪ **junk:** el sótano está lleno de trastos the basement is full of junk.

**trastornar** *verbo*

1. **to upset:** el accidente lo trastornó the accident upset him
2. **to disturb:** su visita imprevista nos trastornó la rutina semanal her unexpected visit disturbed our weekly routine.

el **tratado** ▪ **treaty** *(plural* **treaties)**.

el **tratamiento** ▪ **treatment:** está haciendo un tratamiento para adelgazar she's doing a treatment to get thinner.

**tratar** *verbo*

1. **to treat:** son excelentes anfitriones, nos trataron muy bien they are excellent hosts, they treated us very well; preciso un médico que me trate esta alergia I need a doctor to treat this allergy for me
2. **to address:** en algunas regiones de América, los amigos se tratan de "vos" in some regions of America, friends address each other as "vos"
3. **to try:** no trates de engañarme porque no tardaré en descubrir la verdad don't try to deceive me because I won't take long to discover the truth.

el **trato** ▪ **deal:** José y Pedro hicieron un trato José and Pedro made a deal.

el **trauma** ▪ **trauma:** el accidente le provocó un trauma tan enorme que desde entonces no ha vuelto a manejar the accident was such a horrible trauma for him that he hasn't driven again since.

**través** *preposición*

➤ a través de through: me enteré a través de una amiga I found out through a friend.

la **travesura** ▪ **prank**
➤ hacer travesuras to play pranks.

**travieso** *adjetivo* ▪ **naughty.**

el **trayecto**

1. **journey:** no paró de hablar en todo el trayecto he didn't stop talking the whole journey
2. **route:** dile al taxista que elija el trayecto más corto tell the taxi driver to choose the shortest route.

la **trayectoria** ▪ **path:** la trayectoria del cometa Halley describe una parábola the path of Halley's comet is a parabola.

**trazar** *verbo* ▪ **to draw.**

el **trazo**

1. **stroke:** está aprendiendo a escribir, sus trazos todavía son inseguros he's learning to write, his strokes are still unsure
2. **mark:** no me gustan los lápices de trazo demasiado fino I don't like pencils with too fine a mark.

el **trébol** ▪ **clover.**

**tremendo** *adjetivo* ▪ **tremendous:** aquí las diferencias entre los pobres y los ricos son tremendas here the differences between the poor and the rich are tremendous.

el **tren** ▪ **train.**

la **trenza** ▪ **braid.**

**trepar** *verbo* ▪ **to climb:** algunos niños tienen miedo de trepar a los árboles some children are afraid of climbing trees.

**tres** *numeral* ▪ **three:** tiene tres hijos she has three children
➤ mi hermana tiene tres años my sister is three years old
➤ son las tres it's three o'clock
➤ el tres de abril the third of April.

el **triángulo** ▪ **triangle.**

la **tribu** ▪ **tribe.**

la **tribuna** ▪ **stands:** toda mi familia estaba en la tribuna my whole family was in the stands.

**el** **tribunal**

1. **court:** terminaron yendo a un tribunal para resolver el conflicto they ended up going to court to resolve the conflict
2. **board of examiners:** el tribunal premió el trabajo dedicado a la preservación ambiental the board of examiners gave an award to the work dedicated to environmental preservation.

**el** **tributo** ■ **tax**.

**el** **triciclo** ■ **tricycle**.

**el** **trigo** ■ **wheat**.

**trinar** *verbo* ■ **to sing:** cuando amaneció los pájaros empezaron a trinar when the day dawned the birds began to sing.

**el** **trineo** ■ **sleigh**.

**triple** *adjetivo* ■ **triple**.

**la** **tripulación** *(plural* las tripulaciones)
■ **crew**.

**triste** *adjetivo* ■ **sad:** está triste porque no lo dejaron ir al circo he's sad because they didn't let him go to the circus; me dijeron que esa película es muy triste they told me that that movie is very sad.

**la** **tristeza** ■ **sadness**
➤ me dio mucha tristeza la muerte de mi perro the death of my dog made me very sad.

**triunfar** *verbo*

1. **to triumph:** en la Segunda Guerra Mundial, los países aliados triunfaron in World War II, the Allied countries triumphed
2. **to succeed:** ¡espero que triunfes en la vida! I hope that you succeed in life!

**el** **triunfo** ■ **victory** *(plural* **victories**): el equipo ganador celebró el triunfo durante varios días the winning team celebrated the victory for several days.

**el** **trofeo** ■ **trophy** *(plural* **trophies**).

**la** **trompa** ■ **trunk**.

**la** **trompada** ■ **punch**.

**tronar** *verbo* ■ **to thunder:** estuvo tronando toda la noche it was thundering all night.

**el** **tronco**

1. **trunk:** una planta trepadora se ha enroscado en el tronco de este árbol a climbing plant has wound itself around the trunk of this tree; en tu dibujo, el tronco del niño ha quedado más largo que las piernas in your drawing, the child's trunk is longer than his legs
2. **log:** puse varios troncos en el hogar para avivar el fuego I put several logs in the fireplace to revive the fire
➤ dormir como un tronco to sleep like a log: estaba tan cansada que dormí como un tronco I was so tired that I slept like a log.

**tropezar** *verbo* ■ **to stumble on:** tropecé con el escalón I stumbled on the stairs.

**el** **tropezón** *(plural* los tropezones)
➤ dio un tropezón he stumbled.

**tropical** *adjetivo* ■ **tropical**.

**el** **trópico** ■ **tropic**
➤ el trópico de Cáncer the Tropic of Cancer
➤ el trópico de Capricornio the Tropic of Capricorn.

**el** **tropiezo** ■ **setback:** si no hay ningún tropiezo, entregaremos el trabajo mañana if there's not a setback, we'll turn in the essay tomorrow
➤ tuvo un tropiezo y se cayó he slipped and fell.

**trotar** *verbo* ■ **to trot**.

**el** **trote** ■ **trot**
➤ ir al trote to trot: mi caballo iba al trote my horse was trotting.

**el** **trozo** ■ **piece:** cuidado, no camines descalza porque puede haber trozos de vidrio en el suelo careful, don't walk barefoot because there might be pieces of glass on the floor.

**el** **truco** ■ **trick:** el mago hizo unos trucos excelentes the magician did some excellent tricks.

**el** **trueno** ■ **thunder**.

**tu** *adjetivo* ■ **your:** quiero que me presentes a tus amigas I want you to introduce me to your friends.

**tú** *pronombre* ■ **you:** haz lo que tú quieras do what you want.

la **tuberculosis** ■ **tuberculosis**.

el **tubo**

1. **pipe:** la iglesia compró un nuevo tubo de órgano the church bought a new pipe organ
2. **tube:** en el baño encontrarás un tubo de crema para las manos in the bathroom you'll find a tube of hand cream.

la **tuerca** ■ **nut**.

**tuerto** *adjetivo* ■ **blind in one eye:** el pirata era tuerto the pirate was blind in one eye.

la **tumba**

1. **grave:** la tumba de mi bisabuela está en Lima my great-grandmother's grave is in Lima
2. **tomb:** las tumbas de los faraones se encuentran en pirámides the pharoahs' tombs are in pyramids.

**tumbar** *Andes, Caribbean, Central America, Mexico verbo* ■ **to knock down:** los ladrones tumbaron la puerta de una patada the thieves knocked down the door with one kick

**tumbarse** *verbo pronominal* ■ **to lie down:** llegó cansadísima y se tumbó en el sofá she arrived extremely tired and lay down on the sofa.

el **túnel** ■ **tunnel**.

**tupido** *adjetivo* ■ **dense:** en la selva, la vegetación es muy tupida in the jungle, the vegetation is very dense.

la **turbina** ■ **turbine**.

**turbio** *adjetivo* ■ **cloudy:** el agua se ve muy turbia the water looks very cloudy.

la **turbulencia** ■ **turbulence:** si mantienes el cinturón ajustado, no correrás peligro cuando haya turbulencias if you keep your seatbelt fastened, you won't be in danger when there's turbulence.

**turbulento** *adjetivo* ■ **turbulent**.

el **turismo** ■ **tourism:** el turismo es la principal fuente de ingresos de la región tourism is the main source of income for the region

➤ **hacer turismo** to travel: vamos a dedicar todo el verano a hacer turismo we're going to dedicate the whole summer to traveling.

el/la **turista** ■ **tourist**.

**turnarse** *verbo pronominal* ■ **to take turns:** cuando la abuela estuvo enferma, nos turnábamos para acompañarla when our grandmother was sick, we took turns keeping her company.

el **turno**

1. **turn:** esperá un poquito, todavía no es tu turno wait a little bit, it's still not your turn
2. **shift:** el turno de la noche empieza a las diez the night shift begins at ten o'clock.

la **tutela** ■ **guardianship:** a la muerte de mis tíos, el juez le dio la tutela de mis primos a mis padres upon the death of my aunt and uncle, the judge gave guardianship of my cousins to my parents.

el **tuteo** ■ *use of the familiar form "tú"*

TUTEO

In Spanish there are two words for the second person singular: one is the informal **tú**, the other is the formal **usted**. **Tuteo** refers to the use of **tú**, which varies greatly from country to country in Latin America. Generally, children and teenagers use **tú** for others their age and **usted** for adults. However, if there is a close relationship with an adult, such as a parent, grandparent, aunt, uncle, or teacher, it is common for the informal **tú** to be used.

el **tutor, la tutora** ■ **guardian:** después de la muerte de mis tíos, mis padres pasaron a ser tutores de mis primos after the death of my aunt and uncle, my parents became guardians of my cousins.

**tuyo** *(adjetivo & pronombre)*

■ *adjetivo*

**yours:** el libro rojo es mío y el azul es tuyo the red book is mine and the blue one is yours

■ *pronombre*

**yours:** este libro es mío, ¿dónde está el tuyo? this book is mine, where's yours?

**u** *conjunción* ■ **or:** pídele a Miguel u Omar que te ayuden ask Miguel or Omar to help you.

la **ubicación** *(plural* las ubicaciones*)*
1. **location:** es una ubicación privilegiada it's a wonderful location
2. **whereabouts:** están trabajando en la ubicación del asesino they're working on the whereabouts of the murderer.

**ubicar** *verbo*
1. **to put:** ubicó a los niños en el asiento trasero she put the children in the back seat
2. **to find:** no logro ubicarlo I can't find him

**ubicarse** *verbo pronominal* ■ **to be situated:** las Américas se ubican entre el océano Pacífico y el Atlántico the Americas are situated between the Pacific and the Atlantic Oceans.

la **úlcera** ■ **ulcer.**

**último** *adjetivo*
1. **last:** es mi último año de estudios it's my last year of studies
2. **top:** viven en el último piso they live on the top floor
3. **back:** se sentó en la última fila she sat down on the back row.

**un, una** *(artículo & numeral)*
■ *artículo*
1. **a, an:** ¿podrías prestarme un paraguas? could you loan me an umbrella?
2. **some:** se fue a la playa con unos amigos he went to the beach with some friends
■ *numeral*
**one:** tiene un hijo she has one son
➤ mi hermana tiene un año my sister is one year old
➤ es la una it's one o'clock.

el **ungüento** ■ **ointment.**

**único** *adjetivo*
1. **only:** es el único par de zapatos que me gusta it's the only pair of shoes that I like
2. **unique:** este pintor es originalísimo, su obra es única this painter is very original, his work is unique.

la **unidad**
1. **unit:** la caja de 20 unidades cuesta el doble que la de 10 the box with 20 units costs twice as much as the one with 10
2. **unity:** es importante que haya unidad entre los miembros de la familia it's important that there be unity among family members
➤ unidad de terapia intensiva *Mexico* intensive care unit.

**unificar** *verbo* ■ **to unite:** después de una larga guerra, el país se unificó after a long war, the country united.

el **uniforme** ■ **uniform:** el uniforme de mi escuela es azul my school uniform is blue.

la **unión** *(plural* las uniones*)* ■ **unity:** es importante que haya unión entre los hermanos it's important that there be unity between the brothers
➤ la Unión Europea the European Union.

**unir** *verbo*
1. **to join:** esta carretera une el pueblo con la capital this highway joins the town with the capital; si unimos estos dos tubos, obtendremos uno más largo if we join these two tubes, we'll get a longer one
2. **to unite:** las dificultades económicas unieron a la familia the economic difficulties united the family; ante las dificultades económicas, la familia se unió confronted with economic difficulties, the family united.

**universal** *adjetivo* ■ **universal:** los derechos humanos son universales human rights are universal.

la **universidad** ■ **university** *(plural* universities*)*.

**universitario** *adjetivo* ■ **university:** un estudiante universitario a university student

➤ después de secundaria haré estudios **universitarios** after high school I'm going to study at the university

**el** universitario, **la** universitaria

1. **university student:** los universitarios estudian muchísimo university students study a lot
2. **university graduate:** un universitario accede a mejor salario que un obrero a university graduate gains a better salary than a worker.

**el** universo ■ **universe.**

uno *(adjetivo & pronombre)*

■ *adjetivo*
**one:** sólo quiero una canasta, no me las des todas I only want one basket, don't give me all of them

■ *pronombre*
**one:** no quiero dos libros, sino sólo uno I don't want two books, only one.

untar *verbo* ■ **to spread:** quiero pan untado con mermelada I want bread spread with jam.

**la** uña ■ **fingernail.**

**el** urbanismo ■ **urban development:** mi papá es arquitecto y se dedica al urbanismo my dad is an architect and he does urban development.

urbano *adjetivo* ■ **urban.**

**la** urbe ■ **metropolis.**

**la** urgencia ■ **emergency** *(plural* **emergencies***)*: los médicos siempre reciben llamadas de urgencia doctors always receive emergency calls

➤ tenía urgencia de ir al banco y salió volando she was in a hurry to go to the bank so she left quickly.

urgente *adjetivo* ■ **urgent:** recibí un llamado urgente, tengo que salir enseguida I received an urgent call, I have to leave immediately.

Uruguay *sustantivo masculino* ■ **Uruguay.**

uruguayo *adjetivo*

En inglés, los adjetivos que se refieren a un país o una región se escriben con mayúscula:

**Uruguayan**

**el** uruguayo, **la** uruguaya

En inglés, los gentilicios se escriben con mayúscula:

**Uruguayan.**

usado *adjetivo*

1. **used:** un auto usado es más barato que uno nuevo a used car is cheaper than a new one
2. **worn:** para estar en casa reservo la ropa más usada I keep my most worn clothes for when I'm at home.

usar *verbo*

1. **to take:** usa las escaleras porque el ascensor está descompuesto take the stairs because the elevator is out of order
2. **to use:** el auto está usando mucho aceite porque tiene una falla the car is using a lot of oil because there's something wrong with it
3. **to wear:** no me gusta usar ropa negra, me parece demasiado triste I don't like to wear black clothes, they seem too gloomy to me

usarse *verbo pronominal* ■ **to be worn:** actualmente el sombrero se usa poco nowadays hats are worn infrequently.

**el** uso

1. **use:** creo que este aparato tiene otros usos, además de abrir latas I think this appliance has other uses, besides opening cans
2. **custom:** se puede aprender mucho de los usos de otras culturas you can learn a lot from the customs of other cultures
3. **wear:** las suelas de estos zapatos están gastadas por el uso the soles of these shoes are worn out from wear.

usted *pronombre* ■ **you:** ¿cómo está usted? how are you?

usual *adjetivo* ■ **normal:** es usual que los adolescentes tengan problemas con sus padres it's normal for teenagers to have problems with their parents.

el **usuario, la usuaria** ▪ user: los usuarios se quejaron por el aumento de tarifas the users complained about the rate increase.

el **utensilio** ▪ utensil: las sartenes y las cacerolas son utensilios de cocina frying pans and the pots are kitchen utensils.

**útil** *adjetivo* ▪ useful

el **útil** ▪ tool.

la **utilidad** ▪ usefulness: no le veo la utilidad a esa cacerola tan grande I don't see the usefulness of this big pot.

la **utilización** ▪ use: la utilización de energía eléctrica trajo grandes progresos the use of electric energy brought great progress.

**utilizar** *verbo* ▪ to use: para preparar el postre utilicé huevos, leche y azúcar to make the dessert I used eggs, milk and sugar.

la **uva** ▪ grape.

la **vaca**

1. **cow**: las vacas comen pasto cows eat grass
2. **beef**.

la **vacación** *(plural* las vacaciones*)* ▪ vacation: en las vacaciones de verano vamos a la playa during summer vacation we go to the beach.

**vaciar** *verbo* ▪ to empty: hay que vaciar estos cajones para limpiarlos bien you have to empty those boxes to clean them well.

**vacilar** *verbo*

1. **to waver**: Gerardo vacila entre estudiar física o química Gerardo wavers between studying physics and chemistry
2. *Caribbean, Central America, Mexico* **to party**: los viernes sale con sus amigos a vacilar Fridays he goes out with his friends to party.

**vacío** *adjetivo* ▪ **empty**: esta botella está vacía, ¿la tiramos? this bottle is empty, should we throw it away?

el **vacío**

1. **space**: en el video vi a los astronautas flotando en el vacío on the video I saw the astronauts floating in space
2. **void**: perdió el equilibrio y cayó al vacío he lost his balance and fell into the void
➤ envasado al vacío vacuum-packed.

la **vacuna** ▪ vaccine: la vacuna antitetánica hay que dársela cada diez años the vaccine against tetanus has to be given every ten years.

la **vacunación** *(plural* las vacunaciones*)* ▪ vaccination: mañana empieza la campaña de vacunación contra la gripe tomorrow the flu vaccination campaign begins.

**vacunar** *verbo* ▪ to vaccinate: hay que vacunar a los perros contra la rabia you have to vaccinate dogs for rabies

**vacunarse** *verbo pronominal* ▪ to get vaccinated: ¿los niños ya se vacunaron contra la poliomielitis? did the children already get vaccinated for polio?

el **vagabundo, la vagabunda** ▪ vagrant: debajo de ese puente viven varios vagabundos several vagrants live underneath that bridge.

**vagar** *verbo*

1. **to wander**: vagando por ese barrio, encontré un museo muy interesante wandering around that neighborhood, I found a very interesting museum

**2. to be lazy:** ya terminé la tarea, voy a vagar un rato antes de cenar I already finished my homework, I'm going to be lazy for a while before eating dinner.

**vago** _adjetivo_

1. **lazy:** no seas vago don't be lazy
2. **vague:** las indicaciones para llegar a su casa eran muy vagas y me perdí the directions to get to your house were very vague and I got lost.

el **vagón** _(plural_ los vagones) ■ **wagon:** los vagones transportaban maquinaria agrícola the wagons carried farm machinery
➤ el vagón restaurante the dining car.

el **vaho**

1. **steam:** el agua hirviendo despide mucho vaho boiling water lets off a lot of steam
2. **breath**
➤ eché vaho en la ventana y se empañó el vidrio I breathed on the window and the glass fogged up.

la **vaina** ■ **pod:** antes de preparar las arvejas, hay que sacarlas de las vainas before preparing the peas, you have to take them out of the pods.

la **vainilla** ■ **vanilla**
➤ helado de vainilla vanilla ice cream.

la **vajilla**

1. **dishes:** entre las tres podemos lavar la vajilla en 15 minutos between the three of us we can wash the dishes in 15 minutes
2. **dinnerware set:** podríamos regalarles una vajilla para el casamiento we could give them a dinnerware set for their wedding.

la **valentía** ■ **bravery:** la valentía del bombero le permitió rescatar a las víctimas the bravery of the firefighter allowed him to rescue the victims.

**valer** _verbo_

1. **to cost:** ¿cuánto vale un kilo de peras? how much does a kilo of pears cost?
2. **to equal:** en matemáticas, dos cuartos valen lo mismo que un medio in mathematics, two fourths equal the same as one half
3. **to be valid:** la prueba no valió porque muchos copiaron the test wasn't valid because many people copied

➤ **valer la pena** to be worth it: voy a comprar las manzanas, a ese precio, vale la pena I'm going to buy the apples, at that price, it's worth it
➤ más vale que te lleves el auto, está lloviendo mucho it's worth taking the car, it's raining a lot.

**valeroso** _adjetivo_ ■ **brave.**

**valiente** _adjetivo_ ■ **brave.**

la **valija** ■ **suitcase:** se iba de viaje por mucho tiempo, llevaba dos valijas llenas he was going off on a trip for a long time, so he was taking two full suitcases.

**valioso** _adjetivo_ ■ **valuable:** le robaron a mamá un valioso anillo they robbed a valuable ring from Mom.

el **valle** ■ **valley.**

el **valor**

1. **value:** Julieta tiene muchos valores, entre ellos, la honestidad Julieta has many values, among them, honesty
2. **importance:** las palabras del abuelo fueron de gran valor para mí the words of my grandfather were of great importance for me
3. **courage:** Luis se lanzó con valor para salvar al niño Luis rushed in with courage to save the child.

la **válvula** ■ **valve.**

la **vanidad** ■ **vanity:** nunca reconoces tus errores, ¡cuánta vanidad! you never acknowledge your mistakes, what vanity!

**vanidoso** _adjetivo_ ■ **vain:** es muy vanidosa she's very vain.

**vano** _adjetivo_ ■ **useless:** los esfuerzos por salvarlo fueron vanos the efforts to save him were useless
➤ en vano in vain: los esfuerzos por salvarlo fueron en vano the efforts to save him were in vain.

el **vapor** ■ **steam:** el vapor del agua caliente empañó los vidrios the steam from the hot water fogged the windows
➤ plancha a vapor steam iron.

la **vaquera** ■ **cowgirl.**

el **vaquero** ■ **cowboy.**

**293**

los **vaqueros** ▪ jeans.

la **vara** ▪ stick.

**variable** *adjetivo* ▪ **changeable:** el clima allí es muy variable the climate there is very changeable.

**variado** *adjetivo* ▪ **varied:** Ana se compró una falda con colores variados Ana bought a skirt with varied colors.

**variar** *verbo* ▪ **to vary:** en la media estación, las temperaturas varían entre 15 y 20 grados during the middle season, the temperatures vary between 15 and 20 degrees.

la **varicela** ▪ **chicken pox**.

la **variedad** ▪ **variety** *(plural* **varieties)**: la variedad de tipos de sangre exige un análisis antes de la transfusión the variety of blood types requires an analysis before the transfusion.

**varios** *adjetivo* ▪ **several:** ¿cuánto hace que no la ves? — varios meses how long has it been since you saw her? — several months.

el **varón** *(plural* los varones*)* ▪ **man** *(plural* **men)**: es un grupo mixto: hay varones y mujeres it's a mixed group: there are men and women.

**varonil** *adjetivo* ▪ **manly:** tiene una voz varonil he has a manly voice.

la **vasija** ▪ **vessel:** ese artesano hace y vende vasijas de barro that artisan makes and sells clay vessels.

el **vaso**
1. **glass:** quiero un vaso de agua, por favor I want a glass of water, please
2. **cup:** para los niños son más prácticos los vasos de plástico plastic cups are more practical for children
3. **vessel:** los vasos sanguíneos forman parte del sistema circulatorio blood vessels form part of the circulatory system

⚠️ The Spanish word **vaso** is a false cognate, it doesn't mean "vase".

el **vecindario** ▪ **neighborhood:** los habitantes del vecindario organizaron una fiesta the residents of the neighborhood organized a party.

el **vecino,** la **vecina**
1. **neighbor:** Susana es mi vecina Susana is my neighbor
2. **resident:** hace muchos años que Pedro es vecino de este pueblo Pedro has been a resident of this town for many years.

la **vegetación** ▪ **vegetation:** la selva tiene una vegetación exuberante the jungle has a lush vegetation.

**vegetal** *adjetivo* ▪ **plant:** estamos estudiando diferentes especies vegetales we're studying different plant species.

el **vegetal** ▪ **vegetable:** los vegetales necesitan agua, luz y tierra para desarrollarse vegetables need water, light and soil to develop.

**vegetariano** *adjetivo* ▪ **vegetarian:** no come carne, adoptó una dieta vegetariana he doesn't eat meat, he adopted a vegetarian diet

el **vegetariano,** la **vegetariana**
▪ **vegetarian:** los vegetarianos no comen carne vegetarians don't eat meat.

el **vehículo** ▪ **vehicle:** el avión, el tren y el automóvil son vehículos modernos the airplane, the train and the automobile are modern vehicles.

la **vejez** ▪ **old age:** el cuidado de la salud es muy importante en la vejez healthcare is very important in old age.

la **vejiga** ▪ **bladder**.

la **vela**
1. **candle:** están de moda las velas perfumadas y de colores colored and scented candles are in fashion
2. **sail:** cerca de la costa se veían las velas de colores near the coast you could see colored sails
➤ barco a vela sailboat
➤ pasar la noche en vela to not sleep all night: el niño tuvo fiebre y los padres pasaron la noche en vela the boy had fever and the parents didn't sleep all night.

**velar** *verbo*

1. **to keep watch over:** la abuelita falleció ayer y la velamos toda la noche our grandmother died yesterday and we kept watch over her all night

2. **to go without sleep:** se quedó velando anoche porque tenía un examen difícil hoy he stayed without sleep last night because he had a difficult exam today

**velarse** *verbo pronominal* ▪ **to blur:** la cámara se abrió accidentalmente y la película se veló the camera opened accidentally and the film blurred.

el **vello** ▪ hair.

el **velo** ▪ veil.

la **velocidad**

1. **speed:** ¿cuál es el límite de velocidad en esta carretera? what's the speed limit on this highway?

2. **gear:** los autos automáticos son más fáciles de manejar que los que tienen velocidades automatics are easier to drive than cars that have gears.

**veloz** *adjetivo* ▪ **fast:** la liebre es más veloz que la tortuga the hare is faster than the turtle.

la **vena** ▪ vein.

el **venado** ▪ deer *(plural* deer*)*.

el **vencedor,** la **vencedora** ▪ winner.

**vencer** *verbo*

1. **to defeat:** el ejército nacional venció a las fuerzas extranjeras the national army defeated the foreign forces

2. **to beat:** el nadador chino venció a los demás en la primera prueba the Chinese swimmer beat the others in the first round

3. **to overcome:** estaba muy cansada y finalmente la venció el sueño she was very tired and finally sleep overcame her

**vencerse** *verbo pronominal*

➤ mañana se vence el plazo para entregar este trabajo tomorrow time's up to turn in this essay.

**vencido** *adjetivo*

1. **defeated:** los jugadores vencidos se retiraron rápidamente the defeated players withdrew quickly

2. **out of date:** tu pasaporte está vencido, tienes que renovarlo your passport is out of date, you have to renew it.

la **venda**

1. **bandage:** llevaba una venda en el brazo lastimado he was wearing a bandage on his injured arm

2. **blindfold:** los secuestradores le pusieron una venda en los ojos the kidnappers put a blindfold over his eyes.

**vendar** *verbo*

1. **to bandage:** le vendaron el tobillo que se torció they bandaged the ankle that he twisted

2. **to blindfold:** los secuestradores le vendaron los ojos the kidnappers blindfolded him.

el **vendedor** ▪ salesman *(plural* salesmen*)*

➤ vendedor ambulante street seller.

la **vendedora** ▪ saleswoman *(plural* saleswomen*)*.

**vender** *verbo* ▪ **to sell:** los vecinos venden su casa the neighbors are selling their house

➤ "se vende" "for sale": "se vende esta casa" "this house is for sale".

el **veneno**

1. **poison:** con este veneno nos libraremos de las ratas with this poison we'll be free of the rats

2. **venom:** hay que inyectarte suero para combatir el veneno de la serpiente we have to inject you with serum to fight the serpent's venom.

**venenoso** *adjetivo* ▪ **poisonous**.

**Venezuela** *sustantivo femenino* ▪ **Venezuela**.

**venezolano, venezolana** *adjetivo* ▪

En inglés, los adjetivos que se refieren a un país o una región se escriben con mayúscula:

**Venezuelan**

el **venezolano**, la **venezolana**

> En inglés, los gentilicios se escriben con mayúscula:

**Venezuelan.**

la **venganza** ■ **vengeance:** las víctimas del estafador prometieron venganza the swindler's victims promised vengeance.

**vengarse** *verbo pronominal* ■ **to take revenge:** las víctimas prometieron que se vengarían del estafador the victims promised that they would take revenge on the swindler.

**venir** *verbo*

1. **to come:** ¿vinieron en auto o en taxi? did they come by car or by taxi?
2. **to be back:** espérame un minutito, ya vengo wait for me just a minute, I'll be back
3. **to be:** la información viene en este manual the information is in this manual
> que viene next: la semana que viene next week.

la **venta** ■ **sale:** las ventas siempre aumentan en diciembre sales always increase in December
> "en venta" "for sale".

la **ventaja** ■ **advantage:** tiene la ventaja de saber inglés y francés she has the advantage of knowing English and French.

la **ventana** ■ **window.**

la **ventilación** ■ **ventilation:** ¡en este cuarto me ahogo! tiene muy poca ventilación I suffocate in this room! It has very little ventilation.

el **ventilador** ■ **fan:** ¡cuidado! no metas los dedos en el ventilador careful! don't put your fingers in the fan.

**ventilar** *verbo* ■ **to ventilate:** antes de limpiar, hay que ventilar bien el cuarto before cleaning, you have to ventilate the room well.

**ver** *verbo*

1. **to see:** no veo bien, necesito lentes I don't see well, I need glasses

2. **to watch:** no es bueno que pases todo el día viendo televisión it's not good that you spend all day watching television
> nos vamos a ver mañana de noche we'll meet tomorrow night
> lo que me contestaste no tiene nada que ver con lo que te pregunté what you answered me doesn't have anything to do with what I asked you

**verse** *verbo pronominal* ■ **to be obvious:** se ve que no sabe nada de inglés it's obvious that he doesn't know any English.

el **verano** ■ **summer**
> en verano in summer
> el próximo verano next summer.

**veras** *adverbio*
> de veras really.

**veraz** *adjetivo* ■ **truthful:** pocos diarios dan información veraz few newspapers give truthful information.

**verbal** *adjetivo* ■ **verbal:** el indicativo y el imperativo son modos verbales the indicative and the imperative are verbal moods.

el **verbo** ■ **verb.**

la **verdad** ■ **truth:** no me gustan las mentiras, quiero la verdad I don't like lies, I want the truth
> de verdad real: me regalaron un auto, pero no es de verdad, sino a control remoto they gave me a car, but it's not real, it's remote control.

**verdadero** *adjetivo* ■ **real:** le dicen María, pero su verdadero nombre es Mariana they call her María, but her real name is Mariana.

**verde** *adjetivo*

1. **green:** me puse la blusa blanca con el pantalón verde I put on the white blouse with the green pants
2. **unripe:** no es saludable comer fruta cuando todavía está verde it's not healthy to eat fruit when it's still unripe.

el **verde** ■ **green:** mi color preferido es el verde my favorite color is green.

la **verdura** ■ vegetable: las lechugas, las espinacas y las cebollas son verduras lettuce, spinach and onions are vegetables.

la **vereda**

1. path: por esa vereda puedes llegar al río you can get to the river on that path
2. *Andes, Caribbean, River Plate* sidewalk: los peatones caminan por la vereda pedestrians walk on the sidewalk.

**vergonzoso** *adjetivo*

1. shy: es muy vergonzosa, no se anima a hablar en público she's very shy, she can't bring herself to speak in public
2. disgraceful: es vergonzoso que haya niños que pasan hambre it's disgraceful that there are children that go hungry.

la **vergüenza** ■ disgrace: ¡cómo le van a pegar así a un niño! ¡es una vergüenza! I can't believe they're going to hit a child like that! it's a disgrace!
➤ volqué todo el café, me dio una vergüenza horrible I tipped over the coffee, I was horribly embarrassed.

**verídico** *adjetivo* ■ true: la película se basa en una historia verídica the film is based on a true story.

**verificar** *verbo* ■ to check: hay que verificar todo antes de entregar la prueba you have to check everything before turning the test in.

**verosímil** *adjetivo* ■ likely: no le creo ni una palabra, esa historia no tiene nada de verosímil I don't believe one word of what he says, that story is not likely at all.

la **versión** *(plural* las versiones*)* ■ version: el testigo dio su versión de los hechos the witness gave her version of the facts.

el **verso** ■ poem: sabe de memoria algunos versos de Neruda he knows some of Neruda's poems by heart.

la **vértebra** ■ vertebra *(plural* vertebrae*)*.

**vertical** *adjetivo* ■ vertical: para formar un cuadrado hay que trazar dos líneas verticales y dos horizontales to form a square you have to draw two vertical lines and two horizontal ones.

el **vértigo** ■ vertigo: no puedo subir muy alto porque tengo vértigo I can't go up very high because I have vertigo
➤ dar vértigo to make dizzy: no puede subir porque la altura le da vértigo he can't go up because heights make him dizzy.

**vespertino** *adjetivo* ■ evening: va a clases en el turno vespertino, de 3 a 8 p.m. he goes to evening classes, from 3 to 8 p.m.

el **vestido** ■ dress: me compré un precioso vestido floreado I bought a lovely flowered dress
➤ vestido de novia wedding dress.

la **vestimenta** ■ clothing: la vestimenta ha cambiado mucho a lo largo de la historia clothing has changed a lot throughout history.

**vestir** *verbo* ■ to dress: Luisa y Juana se entretienen vistiendo a las muñecas Luisa and Juana entertain themselves dressing their dolls

**vestirse** *verbo pronominal* ■ to get dressed: ¿cuánto demoras en vestirte? how long do you take to get dressed?

el **vestuario**

1. *en piscina* locker room
2. *en teatro* dressing room.

el **veterinario,** la **veterinaria** ■ veterinarian.

la **vez** *(plural* las veces*)* ■ time: ya te pedí cien veces que te callaras I already asked you a hundred times to be quiet
➤ a la vez at the same time: escribía una carta a la vez que escuchaba música she was writing a letter at the same time that she was listening to music
➤ a veces sometimes: a veces pienso que no debería haber venido sometimes I think that I shouldn't have come
➤ dos veces twice: nos encontramos dos veces por semana para ir a nadar we meet twice a week to go swimming

➤ **en vez de** instead of: **en vez de ir al parque, podríamos ir a la playa, ¿no?** instead of going to the park, we could go to the beach, don't you think?

➤ **otra vez** again: **no puedo creer que estés aquí otra vez** I can't believe that you're here again

➤ **tal vez** maybe: **tal vez no entiendan inglés** maybe they don't understand English

➤ **una vez** once: **nos encontramos para tomar el té una vez por semana** we meet once a week to have tea.

la **vía**

1. **track**: **las vías del tren son de hierro** the train tracks are made of iron
2. **route**: **en los países con muchos ríos, la vía fluvial es muy utilizada** in countries with many rivers, river routes are often used

➤ **vía aérea** airmail

➤ **vía marítima** sea route.

el **viaducto** ■ **viaduct**.

**viajar** _verbo_ ■ **to travel**: **como no le gusta viajar en avión, usa el tren o el barco** since he doesn't like to travel by plane, he uses the train or the boat.

el **viaje**

1. **trip**: **vamos a hacer un viaje por América del Sur** we're going to take a trip through South America
2. **journey**: **está muy cansada después de tan largo viaje** she's very tired after such a long journey

➤ **viaje de negocios** business trip

➤ **viaje de placer** pleasure trip.

el **viajero, la viajera** ■ **traveler**: **los viajeros llegaron cansados, después de muchas horas de vuelo** the travelers arrived tired, after many hours aboard the plane.

la **víbora** ■ **viper**.

la **vibración** _(plural_ las vibraciones) ■ **vibration**.

**vibrar** _verbo_ ■ **to vibrate**: **los vidrios de las ventanas vibran cuando estalla un trueno** the glass of the windows vibrates when thunder booms.

**viceversa** _adverbio_ ■ **vice versa**.

el **vicio** ■ **vice**: **fumar es un vicio pernicioso para la salud** smoking is a vice that's bad for your health.

la **víctima** ■ **victim**: **la inundación produjo cien víctimas** there were a hundred victims from the flood.

la **victoria** ■ **victory** _(plural_ **victories**): **la victoria fue para el equipo local** the victory went to the local team.

la **vid** ■ **vine**.

la **vida** ■ **life**: **toda su vida la pasó en un pequeño pueblo** she spent all her life in a small town

➤ **vida nocturna** night life.

el **video**

1. **video**: **podríamos alquilar un video para esta noche** we could rent a video for tonight
2. **video cassette player**: **se rompió el video, hay que llevarlo a arreglar** the video cassette player broke, we have to take it to get fixed.

la **vidriera** ■ **store window**: **quiero probarme los zapatos rojos que están en la vidriera** I want to try on the red shoes that are in the store window.

el **vidrio**

1. **glass**: **prefiero las botellas de vidrio a las de plástico** I prefer glass bottles to plastic ones
2. **windowpane**: **se rompió un vidrio de mi cuarto y entra frío** a windowpane in my room broke and the cold comes in.

**viejo** _adjetivo_ ■ **old**: **estos zapatos están muy viejos, tengo que comprar otros** these shoes are very old, I have to buy some others.

la **vieja** ■ **old woman**.

el **viejo** ■ **old man**: **un viejo estaba cruzando la calle** an old man was crossing the road

➤ **aquí los viejos no reciben jubilaciones dignas, viven en la miseria** here the elderly don't get decent retirement pensions, they live in poverty.

el **viento** ■ wind: no hace frío, pero hay mucho viento it's not cold, but there's a lot of wind.

el **vientre** ■ stomach: el fuerte dolor en el vientre resultó ser apendicitis the strong stomach pain ended up being apendicitis.

el **viernes** *(plural* los viernes)

> En inglés, los días de la semana se escriben con mayúscula:

**Friday:** hoy es viernes today is Friday; **el próximo viernes** next Friday; **el pasado viernes** last Friday; **el viernes** on Friday; **te veré el viernes** I'll see you on Friday; **los viernes** on Fridays; **los viernes vamos al parque** on Fridays we go to the park.

el/la **vigilante** ■ security guard: contrataron tres vigilantes para la noche they hired three security guards for the night.

**vigilar** *verbo*

1. **to guard:** varios policías vigilaban a los presos several police officers were guarding the prisoners
2. **to keep an eye on:** hay que vigilar a los niños cuando están en la piscina you have to keep an eye on the children when they're in the pool
3. **to watch:** creo que nos vigilan, cuidado con lo que dices I think they're watching us, careful with what you say.

el **vigor** ■ vitality: los niños suelen tener mucho vigor children often have a lot of vitality.

**vigoroso** *adjetivo* ■ **vigorous:** los niños son muy vigorosos, saltan y corren todo el día children are very vigorous, they jump and run all day.

**vil** *adjetivo* ■ vile.

la **vileza** ■ vile act: golpear a la anciana para robarle fue una vileza hitting the old woman in order to rob her was a vile act.

la **villa**

1. **villa:** se compraron una preciosa villa, construída en un gran terreno they bought a lovely villa, built on a large piece of land

2. **small town:** pasamos el fin de semana en una villa minera, cerca de la capital we spent the weekend in a small mining town, near the capital.

el **villancico** ■ carol.

el **villano,** la **villana** ■ villain: no confíes en él, es un villano don't trust him, he's a villain.

el **vinagre** ■ vinegar.

el **vínculo** ■ bond: tiene un vínculo muy fuerte con su familia he has a very strong bond with his family.

el **vino** ■ wine.

la **viña** ■ vineyard.

el **viñedo** ■ vineyard.

la **violencia** ■ violence: la violencia no es la manera de resolver los conflictos violence is not the way to resolve conflicts.

**violento** *adjetivo* ■ **violent:** anoche oí una discusión muy violenta entre los vecinos last night I heard a very violent argument between the neighbors.

**violeta** *adjetivo* ■ **violet:** me voy a poner la blusa blanca con el pantalón violeta I'm going to put on the white blouse with the violet pants

el **violeta** ■ violet: el violeta es mi color favorito violet is my favorite color.

la **violeta** ■ violet.

el **violín** *(plural* los violines) ■ violin.

el/la **violinista** ■ violinist.

el/la **violonchelista** ■ cellist.

el **violonchelo** ■ cello.

**virgen** *adjetivo* ■ **virgin:** por el bien de todos, es importante preservar la selva virgen for everybody's good, it's important to preserve the virgin jungle
➤ pura lana virgen pure new wool.

la **virgen** *(plural* las vírgenes) ■ **virgin:** la virgen María es la madre de Jesús the Virgin Mary is the mother of Jesus.

**299**

**viril** *adjetivo* ■ **manly:** tiene una voz muy viril: grave y fuerte he has a very manly voice: low and strong.

**virtual** *adjetivo* ■ **virtual**
➤ realidad virtual virtual reality.

la **virtud** ■ **virtue:** la honestidad es una de sus virtudes honesty is one of his virtues.

la **viruela** ■ **smallpox**.

el **virus** *(plural* los virus) ■ **virus:** algunos virus provocan resfríos y gripes some viruses cause colds and the flu.

la **víscera** ■ **entrail:** el corazón y el estómago son vísceras the heart and the stomach are entrails.

la **visera** ■ **visor:** siempre lleva la visera de la gorra para atrás he always wears the visor of his hat backwards.

la **visibilidad** ■ **visibility:** la neblina afecta la visibilidad en la carretera the fog affects visibility on the highway.

**visible** *adjetivo* ■ **visible:** la cerradura tenía marcas visibles: habían tratado de forzarla the lock had visible marks: they had tried to force it.

la **visión** *(plural* las visiones)
1. **eyesight:** fue perdiendo la visión hasta quedar ciego he gradually lost his eyesight until he went blind
2. **vision:** no hay nadie ahí, ves visiones there's not anybody there, you're seeing visions.

la **visita**
1. **visit:** después de la visita de mis sobrinos, la casa es un caos after my nieces' and nephews' visit, the house is chaos
2. **visitor:** anoche las visitas se quedaron hasta tardísimo last night the visitors stayed until very late
➤ horario de visita visiting hours.

el/la **visitante** ■ **visitor:** a los visitantes les encantan las playas de nuestro país visitors love our country's beaches.

**visitar** *verbo* ■ **to visit:** vinieron a visitarnos nuestros parientes españoles our Spanish relatives came to visit us.

el **visor** ■ **viewfinder:** miró por el visor de la cámara y sacó la foto he looked through the camera's viewfinder and took the picture.

la **víspera** ■ **eve:** la víspera del viaje no pude dormir por la emoción I couldn't sleep on the eve of the trip because of the excitement.

la **vista**
1. **sight:** la vista es uno de los cinco sentidos sight is one of the five senses
2. **view:** compramos una preciosa casa con vista al mar we bought a lovely house with a view of the sea.

**vistoso** *adjetivo* ■ **showy:** tenía un vestido muy vistoso, rojo y amarillo she had a very showy dress, red and yellow.

**visual** *adjetivo* ■ **visual:** tiene muy buena memoria visual, siempre recuerda la cara de la gente he has very good visual memory, he always remembers people's faces.

**vital** *adjetivo* ■ **full of vitality:** aún a su edad, la abuela es muy vital, siempre está ocupada con trabajo voluntario even at her age, my grandmother is full of vitality, she's always busy with volunteer work.

la **vitalidad** ■ **vitality:** la abuela tiene una vitalidad increíble, se las arregla sola para todo my grandmother has incredible vitality, she manages on her own.

la **vitamina** ■ **vitamin:** la naranja es una buena fuente de vitamina C oranges are a good source of vitamin C.

la **vitrina** ■ **store window:** quiero probarme los zapatos rojos que están en la vitrina I want to try on the red shoes that are in the store window.

la **viuda** ■ **widow:** las viudas tienen derecho a una pensión widows have a right to a pension.

**viudo** *adjetivo* ■ **widowed:** se quedó viuda pocos meses después del casamiento she became a widow only a few months after the wedding

el **viudo** ■ **widower.**

los **víveres** ■ **supplies:** la lista de víveres para la excursión incluía frutas, carnes frías y agua the list of supplies for the outing included fruits, cold meats and water.

el **vivero** ■ **nursery** (*plural* **nurseries**).

la **vivienda** ■ **dwelling:** han construído muchas viviendas en los suburbios de la ciudad they've built many dwellings in the city's suburbs.

**vivir** *verbo*

1. **to live:** desde muy joven vive de su propio trabajo from very young he's lived by his own labor; vive en un apartamento muy grande, en el centro de la ciudad she lives in a very big apartment, in the middle of the city

2. **to be alive:** el perro quedó malherido, pero aún vive the dog was badly wounded, but he's still alive.

**vivo** *adjetivo*

1. **alive:** ¡no tires esa planta! está viva don't throw that plant out! it's alive

2. **lively:** me gusta decorar la casa con colores vivos I like to decorate the house with lively colors.

el **vocablo** ■ **word.**

el **vocabulario** ■ **vocabulary:** este libro es difícil porque tiene mucho vocabulario técnico this book is difficult because it has a lot of technical vocabulary.

la **vocación** (*plural* las vocaciones) ■ **vocation:** aún no tiene clara cuál es su vocación, no sabe qué va a estudiar she still doesn't have clear what her vocation is, she doesn't know what she's going to study.

**vocal** *adjetivo* ■ **vocal:** no pudo cantar porque tiene las cuerdas vocales inflamadas he couldn't sing because his vocal cords are inflamed.

la **vocal** (*plural* las vocales) ■ **vowel:** "a, e, i, o, u" son las vocales "a, e, i, o, u" are vowels.

el **volante** ■ **steering wheel:** gira un poco el volante a la derecha, para dar vuelta turn the steering wheel a little to the right, in order to turn.

**volar** *verbo* ■ **to fly:** los aviones vuelan a 10.000 metros de altura airplanes fly at an altitude of 10,000 meters.

el **volcán** (*plural* los volcanes) ■ **volcano** (*plural* **volcanoes**).

**volcánico** *adjetivo* ■ **volcanic:** las erupciones son producto de la actividad volcánica eruptions are a product of volcanic activity.

**volcar** *verbo*

1. **to dump:** el camión volcó su carga en el depósito the truck dumped its load at the warehouse

2. **to tip over:** el auto derrapó en la curva y volcó unos metros más adelante the car skidded on the curve and tipped over a few meters further along

3. **to knock over:** me distraje y volqué la taza de café arriba del mantel I got distracted and knocked over the coffee on the tablecloth

**volcarse** *verbo pronominal* ■ **to tip over:** no camines con el vaso lleno, que se te va a volcar el agua don't walk with the glass full, your water will tip over.

**voltear** *verbo*

1. *Andes, Caribbean, Central America, Mexico* **to turn around:** voltea para que pueda verte de espaldas turn around so that I can see your back

2. *Andes, Caribbean, Central America, Mexico* **to turn over:** voltea el vaso para que no le entre polvo turn the glass over so that dirt won't get in

3. *Andes, Mexico, River Plate* **to knock over:** cuidado por donde caminas, vas a voltear la mesita careful where you walk, you're going to knock over the table.

la **voltereta**
1. *en el suelo* **forward roll**
2. *en el aire* **somersault**.

el **volumen** *(plural* los volúmenes) ■ **volume:** la maestra pidió que calculáramos
el volumen de un cubo the teacher asked
us to calculate the volume of a cube; esa novela es muy larga, se publicó en tres volúmenes that novel is very long, it was published in three volumes; ¿podrías bajar el
volumen del radio, por favor? could you
lower the radio's volume, please?

**voluminoso** *adjetivo* ■ **massive:** esa
mesa es tan voluminosa que no pasa por
la puerta that table is so massive that it
doesn't go through the door.

la **voluntad**
1. **will:** con la fuerza de voluntad que tiene,
puede conseguirlo todo with the willpow-
er that he has, he can do anything
2. **volition:** hizo el viaje por su propia voluntad, nadie lo obligó he made the trip of
his own volition, nobody forced him.

**voluntario** *adjetivo* ■ **volunteer:** ese
médico hace trabajo voluntario: atiende
a los pacientes y no les cobra that doctor
does volunteer work: he waits on patients
and doesn't charge them

el **voluntario,** la **voluntaria** ■ **volunteer:** después del terremoto, muchos
voluntarios se ofrecieron para ayudar after the earthquake, many volunteers offered
to help.

**volver** *verbo*
1. **to come back:** espérame un minuto que
enseguida vuelvo wait for me a minute, I'm
coming right back
2. **to go back:** ahora tengo que volver a la
escuela, pero más tarde paso por tu casa
now I have to go back to school, but later I'll
come by your house

**volverse** *verbo pronominal*
1. **to go back:** me volví porque me olvidé de
la llave I went back because I forgot the key
2. **to get:** algo le pasó y se ha vuelto muy
irritable something happened to him and he
got very irritable.

**vomitar** *verbo* ■ **to vomit.**

el **vómito** ■ **vomit.**

la **voracidad** *(plural* las voracidades)
■ **voraciousness.**

**voraz** *adjetivo* ■ **voracious:** mi primo
adolescente tiene un apetito voraz my
teenage cousin has a voracious appetite.

**vos** *pronombre* ■ **you.**

el **voseo** ■ *use of the familiar form "vos"*

**VOSEO**

In some parts of Latin America,
the word **vos** along with **tú** is
used for the second person singular, in the
informal sense. In some countries the two
forms are used interchangeably while in
others vos is considered somewhat less
formal than **tú**. Some of the countries
where **vos** is used are Argentina, Bolivia,
Colombia, Costa Rica, and Uruguay.

**votar** *verbo* ■ **to vote:** aquí se puede
votar a partir de los 18 años here you can
vote starting at 18 years of age.

el **voto** ■ **vote:** en algunos países, el voto es obligatorio in some countries, voting
is obligatory.

la **voz** *(plural* las voces) ■ **voice:** en la
adolescencia, los varones cambian la voz
during adolescence, men's voices change.

el **vuelo** ■ **flight:** es entretenido observar el vuelo de los pájaros it's entertaining
to observe birds' flight.

la **vuelta**
1. **turn:** este paso de baile incluye varias
vueltas this dance step includes several
turns
2. **walk:** ¿vamos a dar una vuelta por el
parque? are we going to go for a walk
around the park?
3. **ride:** salimos a dar una vuelta en el auto
nuevo de mi tío we went out for a ride in my
uncle's new car
➤ dar vuelta la página to turn a page: yo
leo y tú das vuelta la página, ¿está bien?
I'll read and you turn the page, ok?

➤ **dar vuelta** to turn around: **la casa de Ana es allá atrás, ya nos pasamos, tenemos que dar vuelta** Ana's house is back there, we already passed it, we have to turn around

➤ **no comas nada antes de salir, a la vuelta preparamos algo** don't eat anything before leaving, we'll make something when we get back.

**vuestro** *adjetivo* ■ **your: vuestro padre os espera** your father is waiting for you.

**vuestro** *pronombre* ■ **yours: ¿estos jerséis son vuestros?** are these sweaters yours?

**vulgar** *adjetivo*

1. **common: ¿sabes el nombre vulgar de la cefalea?** do you know the common name for a migraine?
2. **coarse: siempre habla a los gritos, es una muchacha muy vulgar** she always shouts, she's a very coarse girl.

la **xenofobia** ■ xenophobia.

el **xilófono** ■ xylophone.

el **walkman**® (*plural* los walkmans) ■ **Walkman**®.

el **waterpolo** ■ water polo.

la **web** ■ website.

el **whisky** (*plural* los whiskys) ■ whisky.

el **windsurf** ■ windsurfing: **me gusta hacer windsurf** I like to windsurf.

**y** *conjunción* ■ **and: acaban de llegar Andrés y su novia** Andrés and his girlfriend just arrived

➤ **¿y qué?** so what?: **el auto no funciona — ¿y qué? podemos ir en taxi** the car's not working — so what? we can go by taxi

➤ **son las ocho y veinte** it's eight twenty.

**ya** *adverbio*

1. **already: ya terminé los deberes** I already finished the assignments
2. **now: engordé y este vestido ya no me sirve** I got heavier and this dress isn't any use to me now

➤ **ya que** since: **ya que vas de compras, trae**

**algo de fruta** since you're going shopping, bring some fruit.

el **yacimiento** ▪ **site**: encontraron aquí un gran yacimiento con restos de dinosaurios they found a huge site here with dinosaur remains.

**yanqui** *adjetivo* ▪ **Yankee**: a las playas de aquí vienen sobre todo turistas yanquis all the Yankee tourists come to the beaches here.

el **yate** ▪ **yacht**.

la **yegua** ▪ **mare**.

la **yema**
1. **yolk**: la yema de huevo tiene una alta concentración de colesterol egg yolk has a high concentration of cholesterol
2. **tip**: en las yemas de los dedos están las huellas dactilares fingerprints are on the tips of the fingers.

la **yerba o yerba mate** ▪ **maté**

> **YERBA MATE**
>
> **Yerba mate** is a plant native to the Southern Cone of South America. When it is prepared as an infusion with boiling water it is called **mate**. It can also be mixed with cold water and lemon leaves, and is then called **tereré**. **Yerba mate** is a stimulant and is thought to be helpful in the digestive process. It is currently exported to Europe and the United States, where it is appreciated for its medicinal effects.

el **yerno** ▪ **son-in-law**.

**yo** *pronombre*
1. **I**: Rosa y yo queremos ser bailarinas Rosa and I want to be dancers
2. **me**: ¿quién quiere ir al parque? — ¡yo! who wants to go to the park? — me!; **soy yo** it's me
➤ **yo que tú** if I were you.

el **yogur** ▪ **yogurt**.

**zafarse** *verbo pronominal* ▪ **to escape**: el prisionero logró zafarse de las ataduras y huyó the prisoner succeeded in escaping the bonds and fled.

el **zaguán** (*plural* los zaguanes) ▪ **hallway**: el zaguán está adornado con muchas plantas the hallway is adorned with many plants.

la **zambullida** ▪ **dive**: su zambullida salpicó a todos los que estaban alrededor de la piscina his dive splashed everybody that was around the pool.

**zambullirse** *verbo pronominal* ▪ **to dive in**: si el agua está fría, es mejor zambullirse que entrar de a poco if the water is cold, it's better to dive in than to enter little by little.

la **zanahoria** ▪ **carrot**.

la **zancadilla**
➤ le hicieron una zancadilla y casi se cayó they tripped him and he almost fell down.

el **zancudo** ▪ **mosquito**.

la **zanja** ▪ **ditch**: como estaba oscuro, no vio la zanja y se cayó since it was dark, he didn't see the ditch and he fell.

el **zapallo** ▪ **pumpkin**.

la **zapatería**
1. **shoe store**: necesito zapatos nuevos, ¿dónde hay una zapatería? I need new shoes, where is a shoe store?
2. **shoe repair shop**: en la zapatería pueden cambiarle la suela a estos zapatos at the shoe repair shop they can change these shoes' soles.

la **zapatilla**

1. **slipper:** la bailarina tenía zapatillas de varios colores the ballerina has several colors of slippers
2. **sneakers:** no puedo salir a correr hoy porque perdí mis zapatillas I can't go running today because I lost my sneakers.

el **zapato** ■ **shoe**

➤ zapato bajo flat shoe
➤ zapato de piso *Mexico* flat shoe
➤ zapato de taco *River Plate* high-heeled shoe.

el **zapote** ■ **plum**.

la **zarpa** ■ **claw:** si te acercas a los gatitos, la gata te mostrará sus zarpas if you get close to the kittens, the mother cat will show you her claws.

**zarpar** *verbo* ■ **to set sail:** el barco zarpa mañana y entonces empieza nuestro viaje the boat sets sail tomorrow and then our trip begins.

el **zarpazo** ■ **scratch:** me acerqué a los gatitos y la gata me dio un zarpazo I got close to the kittens and the mother cat gave me a scratch.

la **zarzamora** ■ **blackberry** *(plural* **blackberries***)*.

el **zigzag** ■ **zigzag**.

la **zona** ■ **zone:** la zona comercial de la ciudad está en el centro the commercial zone of the city is downtown.

**zonzo** *adjetivo* ■ **silly:** no seas zonzo, presta atención a lo que te digo don't be silly, pay attention to what I'm telling you.

el **zoo** ■ **zoo**.

la **zoología** ■ **zoology**.

el **zoológico** ■ **zoo**.

el **zopilote** ■ *Central America, Mexico* **buzzard**.

el **zoquete** ■ *Southern Cone* **sock:** para este pantalón azul, precisas zoquetes celestes for these blue pants, you need sky blue socks.

el **zorrillo** ■ **skunk**.

el **zorro** ■ **fox**.

**zumbar** *verbo* ■ **to buzz:** se oye a las abejas zumbando alrededor de las flores you can hear the bees buzzing around the flowers.

el **zumbido** ■ **buzzing:** se oye el zumbido de las abejas alrededor de las flores you can hear the bees' buzzing around the flowers.

el **zurcido** ■ **patch:** necesitas medias nuevas, las tuyas están llenas de zurcidos you need new stockings, yours are full of patches.

**zurcir** *verbo* ■ **to mend:** tus medias están llenas de agujeros, te las voy a zurcir your stockings are full of holes, I'll mend them for you.

el **zurdo, la zurda** ■ **left-handed person** *(plural* **left-handed people***)*: los zurdos escriben con la mano izquierda left-handed people write with the left hand.

**zurrar** *verbo* ■ **to beat up:** además de robarle, los ladrones lo zurraron in addition to robbing him, the thieves beat him up.

# English-Spanish
## Inglés-Español

**a** [eɪ, ə] *indefinite article* ■ **(an,** ən *antes de una vocal)* **un** *(masculine),* **una** *(feminine)*: **is it a bird or a plane?** ¿es un pájaro o un avión?; **it's an ostrich** es una avestruz

> The indefinite article is not translated in Spanish when you say what somebody's profession or trade is:

**he's an architect** es arquitecto; **she's a doctor** es doctora
➤ **it costs 2 dollars a pound** cuesta 2 dólares la libra
➤ **50 miles an hour** 50 millas por hora
➤ **$10 an hour** $10 por hora
➤ **$7 a head** $7 por persona
➤ **twice a week** dos veces a la semana.

**abbreviation** [ə,briːviˈeɪʃn] *noun*
■ la **abreviatura.**

**abdomen** [ˈæbdəmən] *noun* ■ el **abdomen** *(plural* los **abdómenes).**

**ability** [əˈbɪlɪtɪ] *(plural* abilities) *noun*
■ la **habilidad: children of different abilities** niños con diferentes habilidades.

**able** [ˈeɪbl] *adjective*
➤ **to be able to do something**
1. **poder hacer algo: I'm sure I'll be able to come** estoy seguro de que voy a poder venir
2. **saber hacer algo: I'd like to be able to swim** me gustaría saber nadar.

**aboard** [əˈbɔːrd] *(preposition & adverb)*
■ *preposition*
**abordo de: there are 42 passengers aboard the tren** hay 42 pasajeros abordo del tren
■ *adverb*
**abordo: is everyone aboard?** ¿están todos abordo?

**about** [əˈbaʊt] *(preposition & adverb)*
■ *preposition*
1. **por: his parents worry about him** sus padres se preocupan por él
2. **sobre: I'm reading a book about magic** estoy leyendo un libro sobre magia
■ *adverb*
1. **alrededor de: there were about 50 people** había alrededor de 50 personas; **they'll get here about 5 o'clock** van a llegar aquí alrededor de las 5
2. **de: what are you talking about?** ¿de qué estás hablando?
➤ **just about casi: I'm just about ready** estoy casi listo
➤ **to be about to do something** estar por hacer algo: **he was about to leave when the phone rang** estaba por irse cuando sonó el teléfono
➤ **how about ...? or what about ...?** ¿qué tal si...?
➤ **how about going to the beach?** ¿qué tal si vamos a la playa?

**above** [əˈbʌv] *(preposition & adverb)*
■ *preposition*
1. **encima de: the bathroom is above the kitchen** el baño está encima de la cocina
2. **por encima de: we flew above the clouds** volamos por encima de las nubes
➤ **temperatures above 90 degrees** temperaturas de más de 90 grados
■ *adverb*
1. **de arriba: put it on the shelf above** ponlo en el estante de arriba
2. **más: you can win with a score of 70 or above** puedes ganar con un puntaje de 70 o más
➤ **above all sobre todo: above all, remember to drive on the right!** ¡sobre todo, recuerda manejar por la derecha!

I

**abroad** [ə'brɔːd] *adverb* ■ **en el extranjero: Mary spent a year abroad** Mary pasó un año en el extranjero
➤ **to go abroad** irse al extranjero: **she went abroad** se fue al extranjero.

**absent** ['æbsənt] *adjective*
➤ **to be absent from something** faltar a algo: **Fred was absent from school** Federico faltó a clase.

**absolutely** ['æbsə'luːtlɪ] *adverb* ■ **absolutamente: it's absolutely forbidden** está absolutamente prohibido
➤ **she's absolutely right** tiene toda la razón.

**accelerate** [ək'seləreɪt] *verb* ■ **acelerar: the train is accelerating** el tren está acelerando.

**accent** ['æksent] *noun* ■ **el acento: she has an English accent** tiene acento inglés.

**accept** [ək'sept] *verb* ■ **aceptar: I accept your offer** acepto tu oferta.

**access** ['ækses] *noun* ■ **el acceso**
➤ **to have access to something** tener acceso a algo: **the bedroom has access to a balcony** el cuarto tiene acceso a un balcón.

**accessory** [ək'sesərɪ] *(plural* accessories*) noun* ■ **el accesorio**
➤ **fashion accessories** accesorios.

**accident** ['æksɪdənt] *noun* ■ **el accidente: he had an accident** tuvo un accidente
➤ **by accident**
1. **por casualidad: I met her by accident la conocí por casualidad**
2. **sin querer: I broke the cup by accident rompí la taza sin querer**.

**accommodations** [ə,kɒmə'deɪʃns] *plural noun* ■ **el alojamiento: our travel agent found us accommodations for our trip** nuestro agente de viajes nos encontró alojamiento para el viaje.

**according to** [ə'kɔːdɪŋtuː] *preposition* ■ **según: according to her** según ella

➤ **everything went according to plan** todo salió según lo planeado.

**accordion** [ə'kɔːrdiən] *noun* ■ **el acordeón** *(plural* los **acordeones***).*

**account** [ə'kaʊnt] *noun*
1. **la cuenta: a bank account** una cuenta bancaria
2. **el relato: he gave us an account of his adventures** nos hizo un relato de sus aventuras
➤ **to take something into account** tener en cuenta algo.

**accountant** [ə'kaʊntənt] *noun* ■ **el contador, la contadora: Tanya's father is an accountant** el padre de Tanya es contador.

**accurate** ['ækjʊrət] *adjective* ■ **exacto: it's an accurate description** es una descripción exacta.

**accuse** [ə'kjuːz] *verb* ■ **acusar: she accused him of lying** lo acusó de mentir.

**ace** [eɪs] *noun* ■ **el as: the ace of clubs** el as de trébol.

**ache** [eɪk] *(noun & verb)*
■ *noun*
**el dolor: aches and pains** dolores
■ *verb*
**my head aches** me duele la cabeza.

**achieve** [ə'tʃiːv] *verb* ■ **lograr: he achieved his objectives** logró sus objetivos.

**achievement** [ə'tʃiːvmənt] *noun* ■ **el logro: it's a real achievement** es un verdadero logro.

**acid** ['æsɪd] *noun* ■ **el ácido.**

**acne** ['æknɪ] *uncountable noun* ■ **el acné: Mona has acne** Mona tiene acné.

**acorn** ['eɪkɔːn] *noun* ■ **la bellota.**

**acquainted** [ə'kweɪntɪd] *adjective* ■
➤ **to be acquainted with somebody** conocer a alguien: **are you acquainted with Bob?** ¿conoces a Bob?

**acrobat** ['ækrəbæt] *noun* ■ **el/la acróbata.**

**across** [əˈkrɒs] *(preposition & adverb)*
■ *preposition*
**there's a bridge across the river** hay un puente que atraviesa el río

> When **across** is used with a verb of movement (to walk across, to run across), you can use a verb alone in Spanish to translate it:

**I walked across the street** crucé la calle; **don't run across the road** no cruces la calle corriendo
■ *adverb*
**the river is 1 mile across** el río tiene una milla de ancho.

**act** [ækt] *(noun & verb)*
■ *noun*
1. **el acto: the ghost appears in the second act** el fantasma aparece en el segundo acto
2. **el número: a circus act** un número de circo
■ *verb*
**actuar: we must act quickly** debemos actuar rápidamente; **have you ever acted in a play?** ¿has actuado alguna vez en una obra de teatro?

**action** [ˈækʃn] *noun* ■ **la acción** *(plural* **las acciones)**: **the movie has a lot of action** la película tiene mucha acción
> **we must take action** debemos actuar
> **an action movie** una película de acción.

**active** [ˈæktɪv] *adjective* ■ **activo: he's very active** es muy activo
> **an active volcano** un volcán en actividad.

**activity** [ækˈtɪvətɪ] *(plural* **activities)** *noun* ■ **la actividad: the club offers many outdoor activities** el club ofrece muchas actividades al aire libre.

**actor** [ˈæktər] *noun* ■ **el actor: he's an actor** es actor.

**actress** [ˈæktrɪs] *noun* ■ **la actriz** *(plural* **las actrices)**: **she's an actress** es actriz.

**actual** [ˈæktʃəl] *adjective* ■ **verdadero: what are your actual reasons?** ¿cuáles son tus verdaderas razones?

> **the actual ceremony starts at ten** la ceremonia misma comienza a las 10

⚠ La palabra inglesa **actual** es un falso amigo, no significa "actual".

**actually** [ˈæktʃəlɪ] *adverb*
1. **en realidad: it's not actually raining** en realidad no está lloviendo
2. **de hecho: actually, I do know the answer** de hecho, conozco la respuesta

⚠ La palabra inglesa **actually** es un falso amigo, no significa "actualmente".

**acute** [əˈkjuːt] *adjective* ■ **agudo: an acute pain** un dolor agudo.

**ad** [æd] *(abbreviation of* advertisement*)* *noun* ■ *informal* **el anuncio: I'm calling about the ad in the paper** llamo por el anuncio en el diario
> **the want ads** los anuncios por palabras, los avisos clasificados.

**A.D.** [eɪdiː] *(abbreviation of* Anno Domini*)* **d. de C.** *(abbreviation of* después de Cristo*)* **in 2000 A.D.** en el 2000 d. de C.

**adapt** [əˈdæpt] *verb* ■ **adaptarse: he has adapted well to his new school** se adaptó bien a su escuela nueva.

**add** [æd] *verb*
1. **agregar: add some sugar to the mixture** agregar un poco de azúcar a la mezcla
2. **sumar: she added the numbers together** sumó los números

**add up** *phrasal verb* ■ **sumar: add the numbers up** sumar los números.

**addict** [ˈædɪkt] *noun* ■ **el adicto, la adicta: a therapy for all sorts of addicts** una terapia para toda clase de adictos
> **he's a drug addict** es drogadicto
> **I'm a TV addict** soy fanático de la tele.

**addicted** [əˈdɪktɪd] *adjective* ■ **adicto**
> **to be addicted to something** ser adicto a algo: **she's addicted to cigarettes** es adicta al tabaco.

**addition** [ə'dɪʃn] noun ■ la **suma**
➤ in addition además: **in addition, they of-fer an English course** además, ofrecen un curso en inglés
➤ in addition to además de: **there will be a disco in addition to the band** habrá una discoteca además de la banda.

**address** [ə'dres] noun ■ la **dirección** (plural las **direcciones**): **what's your ad-dress?** ¿cuál es tu dirección?
➤ an address book una libreta de direccio-nes.

**adjective** ['æ, dʒɪktɪv] noun ■ el **adje-tivo**: "happy" and "sad" are adjectives "alegre" y "triste" son adjetivos.

**adjust** [ə'dʒʌst] verb
1. **regular**: he adjusted the volume reguló el volumen
2. **ajustar**: he adjusted the mirror ajustó el retrovisor
3. **adaptarse**: I adjusted to the new situa-tion me adapté a la nueva situación.

**administration** [əd,mɪnɪ'streɪʃn] noun ■ la **administración** (plural las **admi-nistraciones**): the administration of a company la administración de una compa-ñía; the Clinton administration la adminis-tración de Clinton.

**admire** [əd'maɪər] verb ■ **admirar**: he admires his teacher admira a su profesora.

**admission** [əd'mɪʃn] noun ■ la **entra-da**: admission to the museum is free la entrada al museo es libre.

**admit** [əd'mɪt] verb ■ **reconocer**: I ad-mit that I'm wrong reconozco que estoy equivocada
➤ to admit to doing something admitir ha-ber hecho algo: **he admitted to stealing the car** admitió haber robado el auto
➤ he was admitted to the hospital lo ingre-saron en el hospital, lo internaron en el hos-pital Mexico, Southern Cone.

**adopt** [ə'dɒpt] verb ■ **adoptar**: Ed was adopted as a baby Ed fue adoptado cuan-do era bebé.

**adore** [ə'dɔːr] verb ■ **adorar**: she adores her cat adora a su gasto
➤ I just adore chocolate me encanta el cho-colate.

**adult** ['ædʌlt] noun ■ el **adulto**, la **adulta**: he's 21 — he's an adult tiene 21 años — es un adulto.

**advance** [əd'væns] (noun & verb)
■ noun
el **adelanto**: there have been great ad-vances in technology ha habido grandes adelantos en la tecnología
➤ the enemy's advance el avance del enemi-go
➤ in advance con anterioridad: **we reserved our seats in advance** reservamos nuestros asientos con anterioridad
■ verb
**avanzar**: the soldiers are advancing los soldados están avanzando.

**advanced** [əd'vænst] adjective
■ **avanzado**: she's in the advanced math class está en la clase de matemática avanza-da.

**advantage** [əd'væntɪdʒ] noun ■ la **ventaja**: what are the advantages of this method? ¿cuáles son las ventajas de este método?
➤ to take advantage of something
1. **aprovechar algo**: she took advantage of the opportunity aprovechó la oportuni-dad
2. pejorative **aprovecharse de algo**: he took advantage of her ignorance se aprove-chó de su ignorancia.

**adventure** [əd'ventʃər] noun ■ la **aventura**: they had an adventure in Afri-ca tuvieron una aventura en Africa.

**adverb** ['ædvɜːb] noun ■ el **adverbio**: "quickly" is an adverb "rápidamente" es un adverbio

Los adverbios en inglés terminan por lo general en "ly", lo que facilita su recono-cimiento.

**advertise** ['ædvətaɪz] *verb* ■ **anunciar: a lot of companies advertise their products on the Internet** muchas empresas anuncian sus productos en Internet.

**advertisement** [ædvər'taizmənt] *noun* ■ el **aviso: an advertisement for a new brand of make-up** un aviso para una nueva marca de cosméticos.

**advice** [əd'vaɪs] *uncountable noun* ■ a piece of advice un consejo; **it was a good piece of advice** fue un buen consejo
➤ **I asked him for advice** le pedí consejo
➤ **can you give me some advice?** ¿me puedes aconsejar?

**advise** [əd'vaɪz] *verb* ■ **aconsejar: he advised me to wait a while** me aconsejó que esperara un rato

> When using **aconsejar que** remember to put the following verb in the subjunctive.

**aerobics** [eə'rəʊbɪks] *noun* ■ el **aerobic, los aerobics** *Mexico*: **I'm going to my aerobics class** voy a la clase de aerobic.

**aerosol** ['eərəsɒl] *noun* ■ el **aerosol: an aerosol spray** un aerosol.

**affect** [ə'fekt] *verb* ■ **afectar: this problem affects a lot of people** este problema afecta a mucha gente.

**affectionate** [ə'fekʃənət] *adjective* ■ **cariñoso**.

**afford** [ə'fɔːd] *verb*
➤ **I can't afford a new car** no tengo dinero para comprarme un coche nuevo
➤ **we can't afford to go on vacation** no podemos permitirnos el lujo de ir de vacaciones.

**afraid** [ə'freɪd] *adjective*
➤ **to be afraid of something** tenerle miedo a algo: **she's afraid of the dark** le tiene miedo a la oscuridad
➤ **I'm afraid I can't come to your party** me temo que no puedo ir a tu fiesta
➤ **I'm afraid so** me temo que sí.

**Africa** ['æfrɪkə] *noun* ■ el **África** *(feminine)*

> Feminine noun that takes **el** or **un**.

**African** ['æfrɪkən] *(adjective & noun)*
■ *adjective*
**africano**

> Remember not to use a capital letter for the adjective in Spanish.

■ *noun*
el **africano**, la **africana**

> In Spanish, a capital letter is not used for the inhabitants of a country or region.

**after** ['æftər] *(preposition, conjunction & adverb)*
■ *preposition*
**después de: after you!** ¡después de usted!; **we'll leave after breakfast** nos iremos después del desayuno
➤ **it's twenty after three** son las tres y veinte
■ *conjunction*
**después de: after I had spoken to him I left** me fuí después de hablar con él
■ *adverb*
**después: the day after** el día después
➤ **after all** después de todo: **it doesn't really matter after all** la verdad es que después de todo no tiene importancia.

**afternoon** [ˌæftə'nuːn] *noun* ■ la **tarde: I have lessons in the afternoon** tengo clases en la tarde
➤ **I'll see you on Tuesday afternoon** te veo el martes en la tarde
➤ **good afternoon!** ¡buenas tardes!

**afterward, afterwards** ['æftərwərd, 'æftərwərdz] *adverb* ■ **después: they went home afterward** se fueron a su casa después.

**again** [ə'gen] *adverb* ■ **otra vez: try calling him again** prueba a llamarlo otra vez; **I'd like to see you again** me gustaría verte otra vez
➤ **again and again** una y otra vez: **he tried again and again** probó una y otra vez.

**against** [ə'genst] *preposition & adverb*
1. **contra:** she was leaning against the wall estaba apoyada contra la pared
2. **en contra:** they voted against votaron en contra
➤ we're against animal testing estamos en contra de los experimentos con animales.

**age** [eɪdʒ] *noun* ▪ la **edad:** we are the same age tenemos la misma edad; he started school at the age of 5 empezó la escuela a los 5 años de edad
➤ it took ages to download tardó muchísimo en descargar
➤ I haven't seen him for ages hace siglos que no lo veo

AGE

En Estados Unidos uno puede votar a partir de los 18 años. Las personas pueden conducir a los 16, pero para beber bebidas alcohólicas en un bar o comprarlas en una tienda hay que esperar hasta los 21.

**agency** ['eɪdʒənsɪ] *(plural* agencies*)* *noun* ▪ la **agencia**
➤ a travel agency una agencia de viajes
➤ an employment agency una agencia de empleos.

**aggressive** [ə'gresɪv] *adjective*
▪ **agresivo:** city dwellers tend to be very aggressive la gente que vive en ciudades tiende a ser muy agresiva.

**ago** [ə'gəʊ] *adverb*
➤ a long time ago hace mucho tiempo
➤ she left three years ago se fue hace tres años
➤ how long ago did he die? ¿cuánto hace que murió?

**agree** [ə'griː] *verb*
1. **estar de acuerdo:** Jim agrees with me Juan está de acuerdo conmigo
2. **aceptar:** Gabriel agreed to go with them Gabriel aceptó ir con ellos
3. **acordar:** they agreed on a date acordaron una fecha
➤ to agree to do something quedar en hacer algo: I agreed to meet him at the cinema quedé en encontrarme con él en el cine.

**agreement** [ə'griːmənt] *noun* ▪ el **acuerdo:** we've reached an agreement llegamos a un acuerdo.

**ahead** [ə'hed] *adverb*
1. **adelante:** look straight ahead mira hacia adelante; they sent him on ahead to buy the tickets lo mandaron adelante a comprar las entradas
2. **adelantado:** the work is ahead of schedule el trabajo está adelantado respecto de lo previsto.

**aid** [eɪd] *noun* ▪ la **ayuda:** the refugees received aid from the government los refugiados recibieron ayuda del gobierno.

**AIDS, Aids** [eɪdz] *(abbreviation of* acquired immune deficiency syndrome*) noun* ▪ el **sida**.

**aim** [eɪm] *(noun & verb)*
▪ *noun*
el **propósito:** I did it with the aim of saving him lo hice con el propósito de salvarlo
➤ to take aim apuntar
▪ *verb*
1. **apuntar:** she aimed her gun at the tiger apuntó al tigre con su pistola
2. **proponerse:** I aim to help him me propongo ayudarlo.

**air** [eəʳ] *noun* ▪ el **aire:** he threw the ball into the air tiró la pelota al aire; I'm going outside for some fresh air voy a salir a tomar el aire
➤ traveling by air is the fastest way viajar en avión es más rápido
➤ the air force la Fuerza Aérea
➤ an air raid un ataque aéreo
➤ an air terminal una terminal aérea.

**air conditioning** [eəʳkən'dɪʃnɪŋ] *noun* ▪ el **aire acondicionado**.

**airline** ['eəlaɪn] *noun* ▪ la **línea aérea:** I've never flown this airline before nunca había viajado en esta línea aérea.

**airmail** ['eəmeɪl] *noun* ▪ el **correo aéreo:** she sent the package by airmail mandó el paquete por correo aéreo.

**airplane** ['eəpleɪn] *noun* ▪ el **avión** *(plural* los **aviones***)*.

**airport** ['eəpɔːt] *noun* ■ el **aeropuerto**: they met me at the airport me fueron a buscar al aeropuerto.

**aisle** [aɪl] *noun* ■ el **pasillo**: the cereal is located in aisle 5 el cereal está en el pasillo 5.

**alarm** [ə'laːm] *noun* ■ la **alarma**: the fire alarm went off sonó la alarma contra incendios

➤ an alarm clock un despertador: I'll set the alarm for 7 a.m. voy a poner el despertador para las 7 de la mañana.

**album** ['ælbəm] *noun* ■ el **álbum**: Garbage's new album el nuevo álbum de Garbage.

**alcohol** ['ælkəhɒl] *noun* ■ el **alcohol**.

**alike** [ə'laɪk] *adverb*

➤ to be alike ser parecidos: they're very much alike son muy parecidos

➤ to look alike parecerse: they really look alike de verdad se parecen.

**alive** [ə'laɪv] *adjective* ■ **vivo**: is he still alive? ¿aún está vivo?

**all** [ɔːl] *(adjective, pronoun & adverb)*

■ *adjective & pronoun*

**todo**: she laughs all the time se ríe todo el tiempo; they danced all night bailaron toda la noche; he lost all his money perdió todo su dinero; all of the girls were laughing todas las chicas se reían; I've invited all of them los invité a todos; tell me all about it cuéntame todo

■ *adverb*

**todo**: he was all wet estaba todo mojado

➤ all alone completamente solo: the boys are all alone los chicos están completamente solos

➤ not at all nada: I didn't like the play at all no me gustó nada el juego

➤ all over por todas partes: we looked all over for the perfect dress buscamos por todas partes el vestido perfecto

➤ the score is two all van empatados a dos.

**allergic** [ə'lɜːdʒɪk] *adjective* ■ **alérgico**: he's allergic to cat hair es alérgico a los pelos de gato.

**allergy** ['ælədʒɪ] *noun* ■ la **alergia**.

**alley** ['ælɪ] *noun* ■ el **callejón** *(plural* los **callejones**).

**alligator** ['ælɪgeɪtər] *noun* ■ el **caimán** *(plural* los **caimanes**).

**allow** [ə'laʊ] *verb* ■ **permitir**

➤ to allow someone to do something permitirle a alguien hacer algo: are you allowed to go out alone? ¿te permiten salir sola?

**allowance** [ə'laʊəns] *noun* ■ el **dinero de bolsillo**, el **domingo** *Mexico*: I get five dollars a week for my allowance me dan cinco dólares de dinero de bosillo a la semana.

**all right** ['ɔːlraɪt] *adverb*

1. **bien**: it's working all right está funcionando bien; are you all right? ¿estás bien?; she had an accident but she's all right tuvo un accidente, pero está bien

2. **okey**: do you want to go? — all right! ¿quieres ir? ¡okey!

3. **no estar mal**: did you like the movie? — it was all right ¿te gustó la película? no estuvo mal

> Aunque mucha gente usa en el lenguage escrito alright, se considera más correcto all right.

**almond** ['aːmənd] *noun* ■ la **almendra**.

**almost** ['ɔːlməʊst] *adverb* ■ **casi**: I've almost finished this book casi he terminado este libro; I almost missed the train casi pierdo el tren.

**alone** [ə'ləʊn] *adjective & adverb* ■ **solo**: he's all alone está completamente solo; she went out alone salió sola

➤ leave me alone! ¡déjame en paz!

➤ leave my computer alone! ¡no toques mi computadora!

**along** [ə'lɒŋ] *(adverb & preposition)*

■ *adverb*

please move along por favor, córranse; can I come along with you? ¿puedo ir contigo?

➤ all along todo el tiempo: he was in his room all along se pasaba todo el tiempo en su habitación

■ *preposition*
**por:** I walked along the beach caminé por la playa.

**aloud** [ə'laʊd] *adverb* ■ **en voz alta:** he was reading aloud estaba leyendo en voz alta.

**alphabet** ['ælfəbet] *noun* ■ el **alfabeto**.

**alphabetical** [,ælfə'betɪkl] *adjective* ■ **alfabético:** they're in alphabetical order están en orden alfabético.

**already** [ɔːl'redɪ] *adverb* ■ **ya:** he has already left ya se fue.

**also** ['ɔːlsəʊ] *adverb* ■ **también:** he also speaks French también habla francés.

**alternate** ['ɔːltərnət] *adjective* ■ **they** come on alternate days vienen un día sí y otro no.

**alternative** [ɔːl'tɜːnətɪv] *(adjective & noun)*
■ *adjective*
**otro:** there's an alternative route hay otra ruta
➤ alternative medicine la medicina alternativa
■ *noun*
la **alternativa:** I have no alternative no me queda otra alternativa.

**although** [ɔːl'ðəʊ] *conjunction* ■ **aunque:** she went to school although she was sick fue a la escuela aunque estaba enferma.

**altogether** [,ɔːltə'geðər] *adverb*
1. **del todo:** that's not altogether true eso no es del todo cierto
2. **en total:** we spent eighty dollars altogether gastamos ochenta dólares en total.

**aluminum** [ə'luːmɪnəm] *noun* ■ el **aluminio**
➤ aluminum foil el papel de aluminio.

**always** ['ɔːlweɪz] *adverb* ■ **siempre:** she's always late siempre llega tarde.

**am** [æm] ➤ be.

**a.m.** [eɪem] **de la mañana**
➤ at 8 a.m. a las 8 de la mañana.

**amazed** [ə'meɪzd] *adjective* ■ **asombrado:** I was amazed to see her quedé asombrado al verla.

**amazing** [ə'meɪzɪŋ] *adjective* ■ **increíble:** it's an amazing story es una historia increíble.

**ambition** [æm'bɪʃn] *noun* ■ la **ambición** *(plural* las **ambiciones):** her ambition is to be an astronaut su ambición es ser astronauta.

**ambitious** [æm'bɪʃəs] *adjective* ■ **ambicioso:** John is very ambitious Juan es muy ambicioso.

**ambulance** ['æmbjʊləns] *noun* ■ la **ambulancia**.

**America** [ə'merɪkə] *noun*
1. **América** *(feminine):* America is a continent América es un continente
2. **los Estados Unidos:** I'm going to America voy a los Estados Unidos

**AMERICA**
Muchas veces se habla de **America** al referirse a los Estados Unidos de América (**the United States of America**), a pesar de que el término **America** se refiere también al continente americano que incluye Norteamérica (o sea, los Estados Unidos, Canadá, y México) y toda la América Latina. La palabra **America** proviene del nombre del explorador Amerigo Vespucci quien llegara a este continente en 1499.

**American** [ə'merɪkn] *(adjective & noun)*
■ *adjective*

Remember not to use a capital letter for the adjective in Spanish:

**estadounidense:** he has an American accent tiene acento estadounidense
➤ The American Revolution la revolución americana
■ *noun*

In Spanish, a capital letter is not used for the inhabitants of a country or region:

el/la **estadounidense:** a group of Americans un grupo de estadounidenses

8

**among** [ə'mʌŋ] *preposition* ■ **entre**: there are children among the crowd hay niños entre la multitud.

**amount** [ə'maʊnt] *noun* ■ **la cantidad**: there was a large amount of cream in the dessert el postre tenía una gran cantidad de crema.

**amp** [æmp] *noun*
1. el **amplificador**: unplug the amp! ¡desenchufa el amplificador!
2. el **amperio**: a fifteen-amp fuse un fusible de quince amperios.

**amuse** [ə'mju:z] *verb*
1. **hacerle gracia a**: the joke amused Peter el chiste le hizo gracia a Peter
2. **entretener**: the children were very amused by the clown el payaso entretuvo mucho a los niños; she knows how to keep them amused sabe entretenerlos
➤ she amused herself by reading se entretuvo leyendo.

**amusement park** [ə'mju:zmənt-pɑːk] *noun* ■ **el parque de diversiones**.

**an** [ən] *article* ➤ a.

**analyze** ['ænəlaɪz] *verb* ■ **analizar**.

**ancestor** ['ænsestər] *noun* ■ el **antepasado**, la **antepasada**: my ancestors came from Spain mis antepasados eran de España.

**anchor** ['æŋkər] *noun* ■ el **ancla** (*feminine*): they dropped anchor echaron el ancla

Feminine noun that takes **un** or **el** in the singular.

**ancient** ['eɪnʃənt] *adjective* ■ **antigüo**: it's an ancient monument es un monumento antiguo.

**and** [ænd, ənd] *conjunction* ■ **y**: your father and mother tu padre y tu madre; six and a half years seis años y medio
➤ come and see who's here! ¡ven a ver quién está aquí!
➤ he's getting taller and taller está cada vez más alto.

**angel** ['eɪndʒəl] *noun* ■ **el ángel**.

**anger** ['æŋgər] *noun* ■ la **rabia**, el **coraje** *Mexico*: he was shaking with anger temblaba de rabia.

**angle** ['æŋgl] *noun* ■ el **ángulo**: a triangle has three angles un triángulo tiene tres ángulos.

**angry** ['æŋgrɪ] *adjective* ■ **enojado**
➤ to be angry at somebody estar enojado con alguien: Peggy is angry at me Peggy está enojada conmigo
➤ to get angry enojarse: Mrs. Smith got very angry La señora López se enojó mucho.

**animal** ['ænɪml] *noun* ■ el **animal**: wild animals animales salvajes.

**ankle** ['æŋkl] *noun* ■ el **tobillo**: he twisted his ankle se torció un tobillo.

**anniversary** [ˌænɪˈvɜːsərɪ] *(plural anniversaries) noun* ■ el **aniversario**
➤ **wedding anniversary** el aniversario de bodas.

**announce** [əˈnaʊns] *verb* ■ **anunciar**: **they announced the news** anunciaron la noticia.

**announcement** [əˈnaʊnsmənt] *noun* ■ el **anuncio**: **the president made an announcement** el presidente hizo un anuncio.

**annoy** [əˈnɔɪ] *verb* ■ **molestar**: **you're annoying me!** me estás molestando.

**annoyed** [əˈnɔɪd] *adjective* ■ **molesto**: **he's annoyed with me** está molesto conmigo; **I got annoyed with her** me molesté con ella.

**annoying** [əˈnɔɪɪŋ] *adjective* ■ **molesto**: **trying to park here is so annoying** tratar de estacionar aquí es tan molesto.

**annual** [ˈænjʊəl] *adjective* ■ **anual**: **the group is having its annual dinner** el grupo tiene su cena anual.

**anonymous** [əˈnɒnɪməs] *adjective* ■ **anónimo**: **she got an anonymous letter** recibió una carta anónima.

**another** [əˈnʌðəʳ] *adjective & pronoun* ■ **otro**: **would you like another drink?** ¿quieres otra bebida?; **he's looking for another job** está buscando otro trabajo
➤ **one another** el uno a al otro: **they love one another** se aman el uno a al otro.

**answer** [ˈænsəʳ] *(noun & verb)*
■ *noun*
ı. la **respuesta**: **I'm waiting for an answer** estoy esperando una respuesta
2. la **solución** *(plural* las **soluciones**): **there's no easy answer to this problem** no existe una solución fácil para este problema
■ *verb*
**contestar**: **she didn't answer** no contestó
➤ **to answer the phone** contestar el teléfono, atender el teléfono

➤ **to answer the door** abrir la puerta.

**answering machine** [ˈænsərɪŋ məˈʃiːn] *noun* ■ el **contestador automático**.

**ant** [ænt] *noun* ■ la **hormiga**.

**anthem** [ˈænθəm] *noun* ■ el **himno**: **please rise for the national anthem** por favor, pónganse de pie para escuchar el himno nacional.

**antibiotic** [ˌæntɪbaɪˈɒtɪk] *noun* ■ el **antibiótico**: **the doctor gave me an antibiotic for my ear infection** el médico me dio un antibiótico para la infección de oído.

**antique** [ænˈtiːk] *adjective* ■ la **antigüedad**: **the house is full of antiques** la casa está llena de antigüedades.

**anxious** [ˈæŋkʃəs] *adjective* ■ **preocupado**: **she was very anxious about her Spanish test** estaba muy preocupada por su prueba de español
➤ **to be anxious to do something** estar ansioso por hacer algo: **I'm anxious to meet him** estoy ansiosa por encontrarme con él.

**any** [ˈenɪ] *(adjective, pronoun & adverb)*
■ *adjective*
ı.

In questions, negative and conditional sentences **any** is usually not translated:

**are there any famous people here?** ¿hay gente famosa aquí?; **I don't have any money** no tengo dinero; **call me if you need any help** llámame si necesitas ayuda

2.

In questions and negative sentences **any** can be translated as **algún/alguna** or **ningún/ninguna**:

**do you have any friends called Peter?** ¿tienes algún amigo que se llama Pedro?; **do you have any questions?** tienes alguna pregunta?; **I don't have any friends** no tengo ningún amigo; **there aren't any bananas left** no queda ninguna banana

**3.**

In affirmative sentences when **any** means **whichever** it's translated by **cualquier**:

**you can listen to any station you like** puedes escuchar cualquier estación de radio que quieras

■ *pronoun*

**I.**

In questions when **any** refers to a countable noun, it's translated by **alguno/alguna**, when it refers to an uncountable noun, it's not translated:

**I need a clip, are there any left?** necesito un clip ¿queda alguno?; **we're short of bread, did you buy any** nos falta pan ¿compraste?

**2.**

In negative sentences, when **any** refers to a countable noun, it's translated by **ninguno/ninguna**, when it refers to an uncountable noun, it's not translated:

**I don't want any of them** no quiero ninguno; **there isn't any milk** no hay leche

■ *adverb*

Any is not always translated in Spanish:

**is he any better?** ¿está mejor?; **I can't go any faster** no puedo ir más rápido
➤ **any more** más: **do you want any more?** ¿quieres más?; **I don't want any more** no quiero más.

**anybody, anyone** ['enɪˌbɒdɪ, 'enɪwʌn] *pronoun*

I. **alguien: is anybody home?** ¿hay alguien en casa?
2. **nadie: I can't see anybody** no veo a nadie
3. **cualquiera: anybody can do it** cualquiera puede hacerlo.

**anyhow** *adverb* ➤ anyway.

**anymore** ['enɪmɔːʳ] *adverb* ■ **she doesn't live here anymore** ya no vive aquí.

**anyone** *pronoun* ➤ anybody.

**anything** ['enɪθɪŋ] *pronoun*

I. **algo: can I do anything?** ¿puedo hacer algo?
2. **nada: I can't see anything** no veo nada

3. **cualquier cosa: anything can happen** cualquier cosa puede suceder.

**anyway, anyhow** ['enɪweɪ, 'enɪhaʊ] *adverb* ■ **de todos modos: I don't want to go, and anyway it's too late** no quiero ir y de todos modos ya es demasiado tarde.

**anywhere** ['enɪweəʳ] *adverb*

I. **en alguna parte: have you seen John anywhere?** ¿has visto a Juan en alguna parte?
2. **en ninguna parte: I can't find him anywhere** no lo encuentro en ninguna parte
3. **en cualquier parte: put it down anywhere** déjalo en cualquier parte.

**apart** [ə'pɑːt] *adverb* ■ **they are two feet apart** hay 67 centímetros entre los dos
➤ **apart from** aparte de: **apart from that, you're right** aparte de eso, tienes razón.

**apartment** [ə'pɑːtmənt] *noun* ■ **el departamento: she lives in an apartment** vive en un departamento
➤ **an apartment building** un edificio de departamentos.

**apologize** [ə'pɒlədʒaɪz] *verb* ■ **disculparse: she apologized for being late** se disculpó por llegar tarde.

**apology** [ə'pɒlədʒɪ] *noun* ■ **la disculpa: she owes me an apology** me debe una disculpa.

**apostrophe** [ə'pɒstrəfɪ] *noun* ■ **el apóstrofo**.

**apparently** [ə'pærəntlɪ] *adverb* ■ **por lo visto: apparently she doesn't live here anymore** por lo visto, ya no vive aquí.

**appeal** [ə'piːl] *verb*

I. **atraer: to appeal to somebody** atraerle a alguien; **this color appeals to me** este color me atrae
2. **hacer un llamamiento, hacer un llamado: they appealed for help** hicieron un llamamiento pidiendo ayuda.

**appear** [ə'pɪəʳ] *verb*

I. **aparecer: he suddenly appeared** apareció de repente

2. **parecer:** she appears to be sleeping parece que está durmiendo.

**appearance** [əˈpɪərəns] *noun* ■ la **apariencia:** don't judge by appearances no juzgues por las apariencias.

**appetite** [ˈæpɪtaɪt] *noun* ■ el **apetito:** David has a big appetite David tiene mucho apetito.

**applaud** [əˈplɔːd] *verb* ■ **aplaudir:** everyone applauded todos aplaudieron.

**applause** [əˈplɔːz] *uncountable noun* ■ los **aplausos:** the singer was greeted by loud applause recibieron al cantante con fuertes aplausos.

**apple** [ˈæpl] *noun* ■ la **manzana**
➤ an apple pie un pay de manzana
➤ an apple tree un manzano.

**appliance** [əˈplaɪəns] *noun* ■ el **aparato**
➤ domestic appliances los electrodomésticos.

**application** [ˌæplɪˈkeɪʃn] *noun* ■ la **solicitud:** you have to fill out a job application tiene que llenar una solicitud de empleo.

**apply** [əˈplaɪ] *verb*
1. **solicitar:** I applied for a job solicité un empleo
2. **aplicarse:** this rule applies to everybody esta norma se aplica a todo el mundo
3. **aplicar:** apply the cream with your fingers aplicar la crema con los dedos.

**appointment** [əˈpɔɪntmənt] *noun* ■ la **cita:** he has an appointment with the dentist tiene cita con el dentista.

**approach** [əˈprəʊtʃ] *verb*
1. **acercarse:** the enemy is approaching el enemigo se acerca; we approached the summit nos acercamos a la cumbre
2. **abordar:** we must approach the problem in a different way tenemos que abordar el problema de otra manera.

**appropriate** [əˈprəʊprɪət] *adjective* ■ **apropiado:** those shoes aren't appropriate for hiking estos zapatos no son apropiados para el excursionismo.

**approve** [əˈpruːv] *verb* ■ **aprobar:** our project was approved aprobaron nuestro proyecto
➤ I don't approve of his ideas no estoy de acuerdo con sus ideas
➤ they don't approve of me going out with him no les parece bien que yo salga con él.

**approximately** [əˈprɒksɪmətlɪ] *adverb* ■ **aproximadamente:** it costs approximately twenty dollars cuesta aproximadamente veinte dólares.

**apricot** [ˈeɪprɪkɒt] *noun* ■ el **albaricoque,** el **chabacano** *Mexico,* el **damasco** *Southern Cone.*

**April** [ˈeɪprəl] *noun*

> In Spanish the months of the year do not start with a capital letter:

**abril** *(masculine)*: in April en abril; on April 17th el 17 de abril; next April el próximo abril; last April el pasado abril
➤ April Fools' Day el Día de los Inocentes.

**apron** [ˈeɪprən] *noun* ■ el **delantal:** the cook is wearing an apron el cocinero tiene puesto un delantal.

**aquarium** [əˈkweərɪəm] *noun* ■ el **acuario.**

**archeologist** [ˌɑːkɪˈɒlədʒɪst] *noun* ■ el **arqueólogo,** la **arqueóloga:** Paul is an archeologist Pablo es arqueólogo.

**archeology** [ˌɑːkɪˈɒlədʒɪ] *noun* ■ la **arqueología.**

**architect** [ˈɑːkɪtekt] *noun* ■ el **arquitecto,** la **arquitecta:** Sandra is an architect Sandra es arquitecta.

**architecture** [ˈɑːkɪtektʃər] *noun* ■ la **arquitectura.**

**are** [ər, ɑːr] ➤ be.

**area** [ˈeərɪə] *noun*
1. la **zona:** he lives in the Chicago area vive en la zona de Chicago
2. la **superficie:** the room has an area of 200 square feet la habitación tiene una superficie de 200 pies cuadrados

➤ **area code** código de área, clave LADA *Mexico:* **the area code for New York is 212** el código de área de Nueva York es 212.

**aren't** [ɑnt] ➤ are not.

**Argentina** [ˌaːdʒənˈtiːnə] *noun* ■ **Argentina** *(feminine)*.

**Argentinean** [ˌaːdʒənˈtiːnɪən] *(adjective & noun)*
■ *adjective*

> Remember not to use a capital letter for the adjective in Spanish:

**argentino: I like Argentinean beef** me gusta la carne argentina
■ *noun*

> In Spanish, a capital letter is not used for the inhabitants of a country or region:

el **argentino,** la **argentina: he married an Argentinean** se casó con una argentina.

**argue** [ˈɑgjuː] *verb* ■ **discutir: they're always arguing** siempre están discutiendo.

**argument** [ˈɑgjʊmənt] *noun* ■ **la discusión** *(plural* las **discusiones)*: they had an argument** tuvieron una discusión.

**arm** [ɑm] *noun* ■ **el brazo: he put his arm around her shoulders** le puso el brazo alrededor de los hombros.

**armchair** [ˈɑmtʃeəʳ] *noun* ■ **el sillón** *(plural* los **sillones)*.

**armor** [ˈɑməʳ] *noun* ■ **la armadura: a knight in armor** un caballero con armadura.

**army** [ˈɑmɪ] *noun* ■ **el ejército: he's in the army** está en el ejército.

**around** [əˈraʊnd] *(preposition & adverb)*
■ *preposition*
1. **alrededor de: they walked around the lake** caminaron alrededor del lago
2. **por: we were driving around town all afternoon** anduvimos en coche por la ciudad toda la tarde

■ *adverb*
1. **alrededor de: I'll see you around 9 o'clock** te veré alrededor de las 9
2. **alrededor: a yard with a fence all around it** un jardín con una valla a su alrededor
3. **por: he lives around here** vive por aquí
4. **por ahí: she left her clothes laying around everywhere** dejó su ropa tirada por todas partes.

**arrange** [əˈreɪndʒ] *verb*
1. **arreglar: she arranged the chairs around the table** arregló las sillas alrededor de la mesa
2. **organizar: they've arranged a meeting for Monday** organizaron una reunión para el lunes
➤ **to arrange to do something** quedar en hacer algo: **we've arranged to meet at the park** quedamos en encontrarnos en el parque.

**arrangements** [əˈreɪndʒmənts] *plural noun*
1. **los planes: we made arrangements to get a babysitter** hicimos planes para conseguir una babysitter
2. **los arreglos: they made the arrangements for me to travel** hicieron los arreglos para que yo viajara.

**arrest** [əˈrest] *(noun & verb)*
■ *noun*
el **arresto: they made several arrests** hicieron varios arrestos
➤ **you're under arrest** queda arrestado
■ *verb*
**arrestar: the police arrested the thief** la policía arrestó al ladrón.

**arrival** [əˈraɪvl] *noun* ■ **la llegada: what's the arrival time?** ¿cuál es la hora de llegada?

**arrive** [əˈraɪv] *verb* ■ **llegar: Uncle Tony just arrived** el tío Tony acaba de llegar.

**arrow** [ˈærəʊ] *noun* ■ **la flecha: a bow and arrow** un arco y flecha.

**art** [aːt] *noun* ■ **el arte: modern art** el arte moderno; **a work of art** una obra de arte.

**artichoke** [ˈɑːtɪtʃəʊk] *noun* ■ la **alcachofa**, el **alcaucil** *River Plate*.

**article** [ˈɑːtɪkl] *noun* ■ el **artículo**.

**artificial** [ˌɑːtɪˈfɪʃl] *adjective* ■ **artificial**: it's an artificial lake es un lago artificial.

**artist** [ˈɑːtɪst] *noun* ■ el/la **artista**: Teresa is an artist Teresa es artista.

**as** [əz, æz] *conjunction & adverb*
1. **cuándo**: as he walked into the room everyone started clapping cuándo entró en la habitación, todos empezaron a aplaudir
2. **como**: as you can see I'm very busy como puedes ver, estoy muy ocupada; he's late as usual llega tarde, como siempre
➤ as … as **tan … como**: he's as tall as his father es tan alto como su padre
➤ as much as **tanto como**: she doesn't earn as much as I do ella no gana tanto como yo
➤ you can have as many as you like puedes tener tantos como quieras
➤ as soon as possible **lo antes posible**: I'll come as soon as possible vendré lo antes posible
➤ as if or as though **como si**: he acted as if nothing had happened él actuó como si nada hubiera sucedido.

**a.s.a.p.** [eɪeseɪpiː] *(abbreviation of* as soon as possible) **lo antes posible**.

**ash** [æʃ] *noun* ■ la **ceniza**.

**ashamed** [əˈʃeɪmd] *adjective*
➤ to be ashamed of something **estar avergonzado de algo**, **estar apenado de algo** *Latin America except Southern Cone*: he was ashamed of being afraid estaba avergonzado de tener miedo
➤ you should be ashamed of yourself! ¡debería darte vergüenza!

**ashtray** [ˈæʃtreɪ] *noun* ■ el **cenicero**.

**Asia** [ˈeɪʒə] *noun* ■ **Asia** *(feminine)*: Asia is a continent Asia es un continente; Indonesia is in Asia Indonesia está en Asia.

**Asian** [ˈeɪʒn] *(adjective & noun)*
■ *adjective*

> Remember not to use a capital letter for the adjective in Spanish:

**asiático**: an Asian country un país asiático
■ *noun*

> In Spanish, a capital letter is not used for the inhabitants of a country or region:

el **asiático**, la **asiática**.

**aside** [əˈsaɪd] *adverb* ■ **a un lado**: I'll put the book aside for you te dejaré el libro a un lado.

**ask** [æsk] *verb*
1. **preguntar**: I'd like to ask something quisiera preguntar algo
2. **invitar**: he asked me to the party me invitó a la fiesta
3. **pedir**: Fran asked her teacher for help Fran le pidió ayuda a su profesor
➤ to ask somebody to do something **pedirle a alguien que haga algo**: I asked her to wait le pedí que esperara.

**asleep** [əˈsliːp] *adjective* ■ **dormido**: he's already asleep ya está dormido
➤ to fall asleep **quedarse dormido**: she fell asleep se quedó dormida.

**asparagus** [əˈspærəgəs] *uncountable noun* ■ los **espárragos**.

**aspirin** [ˈæsprɪn] *noun* ■ la **aspirina**.

**asset** [ˈæset] *noun*
➤ Fred is an asset to the team Fred es muy valioso para el equipo.

**assignment** [əˈsaɪnmənt] *noun* ■ la **tarea**: he handed in his assignment entregó su tarea.

**assistant** [əˈsɪstənt] *noun* ■ el/la **asistente**: my assistant will call you tomorrow mi asistente lo llamará mañana.

**assume** [əˈsuːm] *verb* ■ **suponer**: I assume you're coming too supongo que tú también vienes.

**assure** [ə'ʃʊəʳ] *verb* ■ **asegurar:** I assure you I'm not lying te aseguro que no estoy mintiendo.

**asterisk** ['æstərɪsk] *noun* ■ el **asterisco.**

**asthma** ['æzmə] *noun* ■ el **asma** *(feminine)*

> Feminine noun that takes **un** or **el** in the singular.

**astonished** [ə'stɒnɪʃt]                *adjective*
■ **pasmado:** I was astonished to hear the news me quedé pasmado al escuchar las noticias.

**astrology** [ə'strɒlədʒɪ] *noun* ■ la **astrología.**

**astronaut** ['æstrənɔːt] *noun* ■ el/la **astronauta.**

**astronomy** [ə'strɒnəmɪ] *noun* ■ la **astronomía.**

**at** [ət, æt] *preposition*
1. *Indicating a place* **en:** the kids are at school los niños están en la escuela; he's at the office está en la oficina; I was at home last night anoche estaba en casa
2. *Indicating a time or a speed* **a:** the movie starts at 8 o'clock la película empieza a las 8; she was driving at 100 miles an hour iba manejando a 130 kilómetros por hora
> **at night** de noche: owls hunt at night los búhos cazan de noche
> we saw her **at Christmas** la vimos para Navidad.

**ate** [eɪt] *past tense* ➤ **eat.**

**athlete** ['æθliːt] *noun* ■ el/la **atleta.**

**atlas** ['ætləs] *noun* ■ el **atlas** *(plural* los atlas): a world atlas un atlas del mundo.

**ATM** *(abbreviation of* Automated Teller Machine) [eɪtiː'em] *noun* ■ el **cajero automático:** I'll get some money from the ATM voy a sacar dinero del cajero automático.

**atmosphere** ['ætmə,sfɪəʳ] *noun*
1. la **atmósfera:** the earth's atmosphere la atmósfera de la Tierra
2. el **ambiente:** there's a good atmosphere in this class hay un buen ambiente en esta clase.

**atom** ['ætəm] *noun* ■ el **átomo.**

**atomic** [ə'tɒmɪk] *adjective* ■ **atómico**
> **atomic energy** energía atómica.

**attach** [ə'tætʃ] *verb*
1. **poner:** he attached the label to his suitcase le puso la etiqueta a la maleta; a notice was attached to the window habían puesto un aviso en la ventana
2. **adjuntar:** I've attached a file to this email he adjuntado un archivo a este email
> **to be attached to someone or something** tenerle cariño a alguien o a algo: she's very attached to her aunt le tiene mucho cariño a su tía.

**attack** [ə'tæk] *(noun & verb)*
■ *noun*
el **ataque:** the enemy attack came at dawn el ataque enemigo ocurrió al amanecer
■ *verb*
**atacar:** the army attacked the fort el ejército atacó el fuerte; her letter attacks the mayor's plan su carta ataca el plan del alcalde.

**attempt** [ə'tempt] *(noun & verb)*
■ *noun*
el **intento:** her last attempt was successful su último intento tuvo éxito
■ *verb*
**tratar**
> **to attempt to do something** tratar de hacer algo: they attempted to steal the diamond trataron de robar el diamante.

**attend** [ə'tend] *verb* ■ **asistir a:** over 100 people attended the meeting unas 100 personas asistieron a la reunión.

**attention** [ə'tenʃn] *noun* ■ la **atención** *(plural* las atenciones): I was trying to catch her attention estaba tratando de atraer su atención
> **pay attention!** ¡presten atención!

**attic** ['ætɪk] *noun* ■ el **desván** (*plural* los desvanes): the attic is full of old junk el desván está lleno de cachivaches viejos.

**attitude** ['ætɪtuːd] *noun* ■ la **actitud**: I don't like her attitude no me gusta su actitud.

**attorney** [ə'tɜːnɪ] *noun* ■ el **abogado**, la **abogada**: my attorney will contact you mi abogado se pondrá en contacto con usted.

**attract** [ə'trækt] *verb* ■ **atraer**: magnets attract iron los imanes atraen el hierro
➤ he's attracted to brunettes le atraen las morena.

**attraction** [ə'trækʃn] *noun* ■ la **attracción** (*plural* las atracciones): a tourist attraction una atracción turística
➤ I don't see the attraction of video games no le veo el atractivo a los videojuegos.

**attractive** [ə'træktɪv] *adjective* ■ **atractivo**: she's a very attractive girl es una chica muy atractiva.

**audience** ['ɔːdjəns] *uncountable noun* ■ el **público**: the audience started clapping el público empezó a aplaudir.

**August** ['ɔːgəst] *noun*

In Spanish the months of the year do not start with a capital letter:

**agosto** (*masculine*): in August en agosto; on August 17th el 17 de agosto; next August el próximo agosto; last August el pasado agosto.

**aunt** [ænt] *noun* ■ la **tía**: aunt Elena la tía Elena.

**Australia** [ɒ'streɪljə] *noun* ■ **Australia** (*feminine*).

**Australian** [ɒ'streɪljən] (*adjective & noun*)
■ *adjective*

Remember not to use a capital letter for the adjective in Spanish:

**australiano**: the Australian bush el bosque australiano

■ *noun*

In Spanish, a capital letter is not used for the inhabitants of a country or region:

el **australiano**, la **australiana**: the singer is an Australian el cantante es australiano.

**author** ['ɔːθər] *noun* ■ el **autor**, la **autora**: J.K. Rowling is my favorite author J.K. Rowling es mi autor favorito.

**autograph** ['ɔːtəgrɑːf] *noun* ■ el **autógrafo**: she collects movie stars' autographs colecciona autógrafos de estrellas de cine.

**automatic** [ˌɔːtə'mætɪk] *adjective* ■ **automático**.

**automatically** [ˌɔːtə'mætɪklɪ] *adverb* ■ **automáticamente**: the door opens automatically la puerta se abre automáticamente.

**automobile** ['ɔːtəməbiːl] *noun* ■ el **coche**, el **carro** *Latin America except Southern Cone*, el **auto** *Southern Cone*.

**autumn** ['ɔːtəm] *noun* ■ el **otoño**.

**available** [ə'veɪləbl] *adjective* ■ **disponible**: he's available on Mondays and Wednesdays está disponible los lunes y los miércoles.

**avalanche** ['ævəlɑːnʃ] *noun* ■ la **avalancha**.

**avenue** ['ævənuː] *noun* ■ la **avenida**.

**average** ['ævərɪdʒ] (*adjective & noun*)
■ *adjective*
**promedio**: that's the average price ése es el precio promedio
■ *noun*
el **promedio**: they studied an average eight hours per week estudian un promedio de ocho horas por semana
➤ on average como promedio: on average, how much TV do you watch every day? como promedio, ¿cuántas horas al día ves la tele?

**avocado** [ˌævə'kɑːdəʊ] *noun* ■ el **aguacate**, la **palta** *Bolivia, Peru, Southern Cone*.

**avoid** [ə'vɔɪd] *verb* ■ **evitar:** let's try to avoid rush hour traffic tratemos de evitar el tráfico de la hora pico.

**awake** [ə'weɪk] *adjective* ■ **despierto:** he's wide awake está completamente despierto.

**award** [ə'wɔːd] *noun* ■ el **premio:** her film won an award su película ganó un premio.

**aware** [ə'weəʳ] *adjective*
➤ to be aware of something ser conciente de algo, estar conciente de algo *Chile, Mexico:* he wasn't aware of the danger no era conciente del peligro.

**away** [ə'weɪ] *adverb* ■ **fuera:** I'll be away for two weeks voy a estar fuera dos semanas
➤ is the beach far away ¿queda muy lejos la playa?
➤ it's two miles away queda a dos millas
➤ tell him to go away dile que se vaya.

**awful** [ˈɔːful] *adjective* ■ **espantoso:** the weather has been awful el clima ha estado espantoso.

**awfully** [ˈɔːflɪ] *adverb*
➤ it's awfully cold today hoy hace un frío espantoso
➤ the book is awfully boring el libro es aburridísimo.

**awkward** [ˈɔːkwəd] *adjective*
1. torpe: he's a slightly awkward child es un niño un tanto torpe
2. incómodo: the handle is awkward to hold el mango es incómodo de tomar; there was an awkward pause in the conversation hubo una pausa incómoda en la conversación.

**ax, axe** [æks] *noun* ■ el **hacha** *(feminine)*

Feminine noun that takes **un** or **el** in the singular.

**baby** [ˈbeɪbɪ] *noun* ■ el/la **bebé,** el bebe, la beba *River Plate,* la **guagua** *Chile*
➤ a baby boy un niño
➤ a baby girl una niña.

**babysit** [ˈbeɪbɪsɪt] *verb* ■ **cuidar niños:** I'll get my neighbor to babysit llamaré a mi vecina para cuide a los niños.

**babysitter** [ˈbeɪbɪˌsɪtəʳ] *noun* ■ el/la **babysitter** *(plural* los/las **babysitters**).

**bachelor** [ˈbætʃələʳ] *noun* ■ el **soltero:** he's a bachelor es soltero.

**back** [bæk] *(noun, adjective, adverb & verb)*
■ *noun*
la **espalda:** my back hurts me duele la espalda
➤ the back of the car la parte de atrás del auto
➤ he's lying on his back está tendido de espaldas
➤ the sweater was at the back of the closet el suéter estaba en el fondo del closet
➤ the back of a chair el respaldo de una silla
■ *adjective*
de atrás: the map is on the back seat el mapa está en el asiento de atrás; the back door was locked la puerta de atrás estaba con llave
■ *adverb*
➤ she took a step back dio un paso hacia atrás
➤ I'll be back at 8 voy a estar de vuelta a las 8

➤ to get back volver: **we got back very late** volvimos muy tarde

➤ to go back volver: **I went back to the store** volví a la tienda

➤ to give back devolver, regresar *Latin America except Southern Cone*: **I have to give this book back** tengo que devolver este libro

➤ to put back volver a poner: **she put the bottle back in the fridge** volvió a poner la botella en el refrigerador

➤ back and forth para atrás y para adelante

**back up** | *phrasal verb*

1. respaldar: **I'll back you up** yo te voy a respaldar

2. hacer un respaldo de: **it's a good idea to back up your files** sería bueno que hicieras un respaldo de tus archivos.

**backbone** | ['bækbəʊn] *noun* ■ la **columna vertebral**.

**background** | ['bækgraʊnd] *noun*

1. el **fondo**: **you can see the mountains in the background** puedes ver las montañas al fondo

2. el **entorno**: **the family background is very important** el entorno familiar es muy importante

➤ he comes from a modest background es de origen modesto.

**backpack** | ['bækpæk] *noun* ■ la **mochila**.

**backward,   backwards** | ['bækwəd, 'bækwərdz] *adverb*

1. atrás: **I took a step backward** di un paso atrás

2. hacia atrás: **move backward** muévanse hacia atrás

3. al revés: **you've got your sweater on backward** tienes puesto el sueter al revés

➤ can you count backward? ¿puedes contar de atrás para adelante?

**backyard** | [ˌbæk'jɑːd] *noun* ■ el **jardín de atrás**, el **fondo** *River Plate*: **we had a barbecue in the backyard** hicimos un asado en el jardín de atrás.

**bacon** | ['beɪkən] *noun* ■ el **tocino**, la **panceta** *River Plate*: **bacon and eggs** huevos con tocino.

**bacteria** | [bæk'tɪərɪə] *plural noun* ■ las **bacterias**.

**bad** | [bæd] *(comparative* **worse***, superlative* **worst***) adjective*

1. malo

> Malo changes to mal before a masculine noun:

**he's a very bad driver** es muy mal conductor; **he's a bad boy** es un niño malo; **did you hear the bad news?** ¿te enteraste de las malas noticias?; **I'm bad at math** soy malo para las matemáticas

2. fuerte: **I was home with a bad cold** estaba en la casa con un fuerte resfriado

3. echarse a perder: **the meat will go bad if it's not in the fridge** la carne se va echar a perder si no está en el refrigerador

➤ not bad no está mal: **new car? — not bad!** ¿auto nuevo? —¡no está mal!

**badge** | [bædʒ] *noun*

1. *of a school* la **insignia**

2. *of metal* la **chapa**, el **botón**, el **pin** *River Plate*

3. *of a policeman* la **placa**.

**badly** | ['bædlɪ] *(comparative* **worse***, superlative* **worst***) adverb*

1. mal: **he plays very badly** toca muy mal

2. gravemente: **he was badly wounded** resultó gravemente herido.

**badminton** | ['bædmɪntən] *noun* ■ el **bádminton**: **to play badminton** jugar bádminton.

**bag** | [bæg] *noun*

1. la **bolsa**: **a paper bag** una bolsa de papel

2. la **maleta**: **I'm packing my bags** estoy haciendo las maletas.

**baggage** | ['bægɪdʒ] *noun* ■ el **equipaje**: **do you have a lot of baggage?** ¿tienes mucho equipaje?

**baggy** | ['bægɪ] *adjective* ■ **ancho**, **guango** *Mexico informal* : **she wore a baggy old sweatshirt** llevaba una sudadera ancha y vieja.

**bake** [beɪk] *verb* ■ **hacer al horno:** are you going to bake it? ¿lo vas a hacer al horno?
➤ I'm baking a cake estoy haciendo un pastel
➤ a baked potato una papa asada.

**baker** ['beɪkər] *noun* ■ el **panadero,** la **panadera.**

**bakery** ['beɪkərɪ] *(plural* bakeries) *noun* ■ la **panadería.**

**balance** ['bæləns] *(noun & verb)*
■ *noun*
el **equilibrio:** I lost my balance perdí el equilibrio
■ *verb*
**hacer equilibrio:** he is balancing on one foot está haciendo equilibrio en un pie.

**balcony** ['bælkənɪ] *(plural* balconies) *noun* ■ el **balcón** *(plural* los **balcones).**

**bald** [bɔːld] *adjective* ■ **calvo:** he's going bald se está quedando calvo.

**ball** [bɔːl] *noun*
1. la **pelota:** a tennis ball una pelota de tenis
2. el **ovillo:** a ball of yarn un ovillo de hilo
3. el **baile:** Cinderella went to the ball Cenicienta fue al baile.

**ballerina** [ˌbælə'riːnə] *noun* ■ la **bailarina:** she's a ballerina es bailarina.

**ballet** ['bæleɪ] *noun* ■ el **ballet** *(plural* los **ballets):** we went to a ballet fue a ver un ballet
➤ a ballet dancer un bailarín de ballet *(feminine* una bailarina de ballet).

**balloon** [bə'luːn] *noun* ■ el **globo:** the children are blowing up the balloons los niños están inflando los globos

 La palabra inglesa **balloon** es un falso amigo, no significa "balón".

**ballpoint pen** ['bɔːlpɔɪntpen] *noun* ■ el **bolígrafo,** la **pluma atómica** *Mexico* la **birome** *River Plate* .

**ban** [bænt] *verb* ■ **prohibir:** they want to ban smoking in restaurants quieren prohibir que se fume en los restaurantes.

**banana** [bənænə] *noun* ■ el **plátano,** la **banana** *River Plate:* a bunch of bananas un racimo de plátanos.

**band** [bænd] *noun*
1. la **banda:** I used to play in a rock band yo tocaba en una banda de rock
2. la **cinta:** there was a band of paper around the flowers había una cinta de papel alrededor de las flores.

**bandage** ['bændɪdʒ] *noun* ■ la **venda:** he has a bandage on his head tiene una venda en la cabeza.

**Band-Aid®** ['bændeɪd] *noun* ■ la **curita.**

**bang** [bæŋ] *(noun & verb)*
■ *noun*
1. la **explosión** *(plural* las **explosiones):** I heard a bang oí una explosión
2. el **golpe:** she got a bang on her head recibió un golpe en la cabeza
■ *verb*
1. **golpear:** somebody's banging on the door alguien está golpeando la puerta
2. **golpearse:** I banged my head me golpée la cabeza.

**bangs** [bæŋz] *plural noun* ■ el **cerquillo,** el **fleco** *Mexico,* la **chasquilla** *Chile:* bangs almost covered her eyes el cerquillo casi le tapaba los ojos.

**bank** [bæŋk] *(noun & verb)*
■ *noun*
1. el **banco:** she has money in the bank tiene dinero en el banco
2. la **orilla:** we walked on the bank of the river caminamos por la orilla del río
➤ a bank account una cuenta bancaria
■ *verb*
**tener una cuenta:** I've been banking here for years tengo una cuenta aquí desde hace años.

**banker** ['bæŋkər] *noun* ■ el **banquero,** la **banquera:** he's a banker es banquero.

**banner** ['bænər] *noun* ■ la **pancarta:** the demonstrators were carrying banners los manifestantes llevaban pancartas
➤ the banner said "Happy Birthday!" el cartel decía "¡Feliz cumpleaños!".

**baptize** ['bæptaɪz] *verb* ■ **bautizar:** she was baptized at St. Peter's la bautizaron en la iglesia de San Pedro.

**bar** [bɑr] *noun*
1. el **barrote:** there were bars on the windows había barrotes en las ventanas
2. el **bar:** we'll meet in the bar at 5 nos encontramos en el bar a las 5
3. la **barra:** they sat at the bar se sentaron en la barra
➤ a candy bar una golosina en barra
➤ a bar of soap una barra de jabón
➤ a bar of chocolate una barra de chocolate, una tableta de chocolate *Mexico*.

**barbecue** ['bɑbɪkjuː] *noun* ■ la **parrillada,** el **asado:** we're having a barbecue estamos haciendo una parrillada.

**barbwire** ['bɑrbwaɪər] *noun* ■ el **alambre de púas**.

**barber** ['bɑbər] *noun* ■ el **peluquero**
➤ a barber shop una barbería.

**bare** [beər] *adjective*
1. **descalzo:** his feet were bare tenía los pies descalzos
2. **desnudo:** all the walls were bare and white todas las paredes eran blancas y estaban desnudas.

**barefoot** [ˌbeəˈfʊt] *(adjective & adverb)*
■ *adjective*
**descalzo:** she was barefoot estaba descalza
■ *adverb*
I love to go barefoot me encanta andar descalzo.

**barely** ['beəlɪ] *adverb* ■ **apenas:** I barely had time to eat apenas tuve tiempo para comer.

**bargain** ['bɑgɪn] *noun* ■ la **ganga:** it's a real bargain es una verdadera ganga.

**bark** [bɑk] *(noun & verb)*
■ *noun*
la **corteza:** the bark of a tree la corteza de un árbol
■ *verb*
**ladrar:** the dog barked at the boy el perro le ladró al niño.

**barn** [bɑːn] *noun* ■ el **granero**.

**bartender** ['bɑːtendər] *noun* ■ el **barman** *(plural* los **barmans***)*, la **cantinera:** she's a bartender es cantinera.

**base** [beɪs] *(noun & verb)*
■ *noun*
la **base:** the base of the pyramid la base de la pirámide; they have their base in L.A. tienen su base en Los Angeles
■ *verb*
**basar:** I base my opinions on hards facts baso mis opiniones en datos concretos
➤ the book is based on his life el libro se basa en su vida
➤ the company is based in Detroit la compañía tiene su sede en Detroit.

**baseball** ['beɪsbɔːl] *noun* ■ el **béisbol,** el **beisbol** *Mexico*: he plays baseball juega béisbol
➤ a baseball cap una gorra de béisbol.

**basement** ['beɪsmənt] *noun* ■ el **sótano:** she went down to the basement bajó al sótano.

**basic** ['beɪsɪk] *adjective*
1. **básico:** I have a basic knowledge of French tengo un conocimiento básico de francés
2. **sencillo:** the food is quite basic la comida es bastante sencilla.

**basically** ['beɪsɪklɪ] *adverb* ■ **básicamente:** basically, he's a good guy es básicamente un buen muchacho.

**basil** ['beɪzl] *noun* ■ la **albahaca**.

**basis** ['beɪsɪs] *(plural* bases ['beɪsiːz]*)* *noun*
1. la **base:** on the basis of the student performance sobre la base del rendimiento del estudiante

2. el **fundamento**: what is the basis of your theory? ¿cuál es el fundamento de tu teoría?
➤ on a monthly **basis** mensualmente
➤ on a regular **basis** regularmente.

**basket** ['baːskɪt] noun ■ la **canasta**: a shopping basket la canasta de las compras
➤ he scored a **basket** metió una canasta.

**basketball** ['baːskɪtbɔːl] noun ■ el **básquetbol**, el **basquetbol** Mexico: they're playing basketball están jugando básquetbol.

**bass** [beɪs] noun ■ el **bajo**: a bass guitar un bajo eléctrico.

**bat** [bæt] (noun & verb)

■ noun
1. el **bate**: a baseball bat un bate de béisbol
2. el **murciélago**: bats come out at night los murciélagos salen de noche

■ verb
**batear**: dad is teaching me to bat mi papá me está enseñando a batear.

**bath** [baːθ] noun ■ el **baño**: to take a bath darse un baño; I'm going to take a bath voy a darme un baño
➤ a bath towel una toalla de baño.

**bathing suit** ['beɪðɪŋsuːt] noun ■ el **traje de baño**, la **malla** River Plate .

**bathrobe** ['baːθrəʊb] noun ■ la **bata de baño**.

**bathroom** ['baːθrʊm] noun ■ el **baño**: where's the bathroom? ¿dónde está el baño?

**bathtub** ['baːθtʌb] noun ■ la **tina**, la **bañera** River Plate.

**battery** ['bætərɪ] (plural batteries) noun
1. la **pila**: these batteries are dead estas pilas están descargadas
2. la **batería**: a car battery una batería de coche.

**battle** ['bætl] noun
1. la **batalla**: a bloody battle una batalla sangrienta
2. la **lucha**: the battle against cancer la lucha contra el cáncer.

**bay** [beɪ] noun ■ la **bahía**: San Francisco bay la bahía de San Francisco.

**B.C.** [biːˈsiː] (abbreviation of before Christ) **a. de C.**: in 200 B.C. en el año 200 a. de C.

**be** [biː] (past tense was, past tense were, past participle been) verb

1.

As a general rule, when be is followed by an adjective, it can be translated into Spanish by ser when it's used to describe permanent or inherent states or by estar when it's used to describe temporary states:

they're happy children son niños felices; I'm very happy in my new school estoy muy contento en mi nuevo colegio; he's fat es gordo; he's so fat I didn't regognize him está tan gordo que no lo reconocí; Anne is French Anne es francesa; the soup is cold la sopa está fría; we are alone estamos solos

2.

Use ser when talking about dates and time:

it's April first today hoy es el primero de abril; it's one o'clock es la una

3.

Use estar when describing where something or someone is:

my school is near the church mi colegio está cerca de la iglesia; where is Alice? ¿dónde está Alice?; they are in Seattle están en Seattle

4.

With certain adjectives that describe how you feel, like "cold", "hot", hungry" or "thirsty", use the verb tener:

I'm cold tengo frío; my hands are cold tengo las manos frías; I'm too hot tengo mucho calor; are you hungry? ¿tienes hambre?

5.

Use tener to say how old somebody is:

how old are you? ¿cuántos años tienes?; I'm thirteen years old tengo trece años

6.

> Use **hacer** to talk about the weather:

it's cold today hace frío hoy; it was very hot hacía mucho calor

7.

> Use **estar** to talk about health and to say how somebody is:

how are you? ¿cómo estás?; I'm very well, thank you estoy muy bien, gracias; Sam is much better Sam está mucho mejor; she's ill está enferma

8.

> Use **estar** in the continuous tense:

I'm working estoy trabajando; what are you doing? ¿qué estás haciendo; it's raining está lloviendo; I was reading when you phoned estaba leyendo cuando llamaste

> The present continuous can also be translated by the simple present tense in Spanish, especially with verbs of movement:

where are you going? ¿adónde vas?; she's leaving se va

9.

> The passive is formed in the same way in Spanish and in English: **ser + past participle**. Remember that in Spanish the past participle must agree in gender (masculine & feminine) and number (singular & plural) with the subject of the verb and is not as common as it is in English. The active construction or a verb with **se** is preferred:

this woman was murdered esta mujer fue asesinada; this method is used by many people muchas personas utilizan este método; I was told to leave me dijeron que me fuera; this is produced in the States esto se produce en los Estados Unidos ➤ **been**.

**beach** [biːtʃ] *noun* ■ la **playa**: they're playing on the beach están jugando en la playa.

**bead** [biːd] *noun* ■ la **cuenta**: a necklace made of glass beads un collar de cuentas de vidrio.

**beak** [biːk] *noun* ■ el **pico**: the pelican has a big beak el pelícano tiene un pico grande.

**beam** [biːm] *noun*
1. el **rayo**: a laser beam un rayo láser
2. la **viga**: wooden beams vigas de madera.

**bean** [biːn] *noun* ■ el **frijol** *Latin America except Southern Cone*, el **poroto** *Southern Cone*
➤ **green beans** las habichuelas verdes, los ejotes *Mexico*, las chauchas *River Plate*, las vainitas *Venezuela*, los porotos verdes *Chile*.

**bear** [beər] *(noun & verb)*
■ *noun*
el **oso**: a polar bear un oso polar
■ *verb*
*(past tense* **bore**, *past participle* **borne***)* **soportar**: I can't bear her no la soporto; I can't bear to see him go no puedo soportar que se vaya.

**beard** [biəd] *noun* ■ la **barba**: my uncle has a beard mi tío tiene barba.

**beat** [biːt] *(noun & verb)*
■ *noun*
el **ritmo**: this music has a strong beat esta música tiene un ritmo marcado
■ *verb*
*(past tense* **beat**, *past participle* **beaten***)* **ganarle a**: we beat the third grade les ganamos a los de tercero; our team beat them 4-2 nuestro equipo les ganó 4 a 2
➤ she beat the world record batió el record mundial

**beat up** *phrasal verb* ■ **darle una paliza a**: he was beaten up le dieron una paliza.

**beautiful** ['bjuːtɪfʊl] *adjective* ■ **precioso**: he has beautiful eyes tiene unos ojos preciosos
➤ a beautiful woman una mujer lindísima.

**beauty** ['bjuːtɪ] *noun* ■ la **belleza**
➤ a beauty parlor un salón de belleza.

**became** [bɪ'keɪm] *past tense* ➤ **become**.

**because** [bɪˈkɒz] *conjunction* ■ **porque**: he went to bed early because he has to get up at 6 se acostó temprano porque tiene que levantarse a las 6
➤ because of por: I can't sleep because of the noise no puedo dormir por el ruido.

**become** [bɪˈkʌm] *(past tense* became, *past participle* become) *verb* ■ **hacerse**: we've become great friends nos hemos hecho muy amigos
➤ it's become fashionable se ha puesto de moda
➤ he's becoming more like his father se parece cada vez más a su padre.

**bed** [bed] *noun* ■ la **cama**: he's in bed está en cama
➤ to go to bed acostarse: I'm going to bed me voy a acostar
➤ to get out of bed levantarse: I got out of bed very early today hoy me levanté muy temprano.

**bedroom** [ˈbedrʊm] *noun* ■ el **dormitorio**, la **recámara** *Mexico*: the house has three bedrooms la casa tiene tres dormitorios.

**bee** [biː] *noun* ■ la **abeja**.

**beef** [biːf] *noun* ■ la **carne de vaca**, la **carne de res** *Central America, Mexico*.

**been** [bɪn] *past participle* ➤ be I have been in this country for three years he estado tres años en este país; he has always been clever siempre ha sido inteligente

When "has been" or "have been" is used as a past participle of **go**, use a conjugated form of **estar** to translate it:

have you ever been to Boston? ¿has estado alguna vez en Boston?

**beer** [bɪər] *noun* ■ la **cerveza**.

**beet** [biːt] *noun* ■ la **remolacha**, el **betabel** *Mexico*, la **betarraga** *Chile*.

**beetle** [ˈbiːtl] *noun* ■ el **escarabajo**.

**before** [bɪˈfɔːr] *(preposition, adverb & conjunction)*

■ *preposition*
1. **antes de**: I'll be back before midnight voy a volver antes de la medianoche
2. **antes que**: I arrived before him llegué antes que él; i comes before e in "believe" la i viene antes que la e en "believe"
3. **ante**: he was brought before the judge lo llevaron ante el juez
■ *adverb*
**antes**: it has never happened to me before no me había pasado nunca antes; I think I've met him before creo que ya lo conocía de antes
■ *conjunction*
**antes de que**: I'll cook dinner before they arrive prepararé la cena antes de que llegaran.

**beg** [beg] *(past tense & past participle* begged) *verb* ■ **mendigar**: he was begging in the street estaba mendigando en la calle
➤ to beg somebody to do something rogarle a alguien que haga algo
➤ I beg you not to tell him te ruego que no se lo digas
➤ I beg your pardon? ¿perdón?

**began** [bɪˈgæn] *past tense* ➤ begin.

**beggar** [ˈbegər] *noun* ■ el **mendigo**, la **mendiga**.

**begin** [bɪˈgɪn] *(past tense* began, *past participle* begun) *verb* ■ **empezar**: my next class begins at noon mi próxima clase empieza al mediodía
➤ to begin to do something empezar a hacer algo: the band began to play la banda empezó a tocar.

**beginner** [bɪˈgɪnər] *noun* ■ el/la **principiante**.

**beginning** [bɪˈgɪnɪŋ] *noun* ■ el **principio**: in the beginning al principio.

**begun** [bɪˈgʌn] *past participle* ➤ begin.

**behalf** [bɪˈhæf] *noun*
➤ on behalf of somebody en nombre de alguien: I'm speaking on behalf of the class hablo en nombre de toda la clase

➤ he called on behalf of a friend llamó de parte de un amigo.

**behave** [bɪ'heɪv] *verb* ■ **portarse:** he behaves badly se porta mal; **the children are behaving themselves** los niños se están portando bien.

**behavior** [bɪ'heɪvjəʳ] *noun* ■ **el comportamiento:** his behavior has improved in the new school su comportamiento en la nueva escuela ha mejorado.

**behind** [bɪ'haɪnd] *(preposition & adverb)*
■ *preposition*
   **detrás de:** he's behind you está detrás de ti; **the switch is behind the door** la llave de la luz está detrás de la puerta
■ *adverb*
➤ he's behind with his work está atrasado con su trabajo
➤ to leave something behind olvidársele algo: **I left my umbrella behind** se me olvidó el paraguas.

**being** ['biːɪŋ] *noun* ■ **el ser:** we are human beings somos seres humanos.

**believe** [bɪ'liːv] *verb* ■ **creer:** I believe you te creo
➤ to believe in something creer en algo: **do you believe in ghosts?** ¿crees en fantasmas?

**bell** [bel] *noun*
1. **el timbre:** somebody rang the bell alguién tocó el timbre
2. **la campana:** the church bells are ringing las campanas de la iglesia están sonando.

**belly** ['belɪ] *(plural* bellies*) noun* ■ **la barriga**
➤ belly button el ombligo.

**belong** [bɪ'lɒŋ] *verb*
➤ to belong to someone pertenecer a alguien: **all this belonged to the same family** todo esto pertenecía a una misma familia
➤ does this pen belong to you? ¿esta lapicera es tuya?
➤ he belongs to the tennis club es socio del club de tenis
➤ put it back where it belongs vuélvelo a poner en su lugar.

**belongings** [bɪ'lɒŋɪŋz] *plural noun* ■ **las pertenencias:** I'll just get my belongings together voy a juntar mis pertenencias.

**below** [bɪ'ləʊ] *(preposition & adverb)*
■ *preposition*
1. **debajo de:** her dress came to below the knee el vestido le llegaba debajo de la rodilla
2. **bajo:** it's 10 below zero hace 10 grados bajo cero
■ *adverb*
   **de abajo:** they live on the floor below viven en el piso de abajo.

**belt** [belt] *noun* ■ **el cinturón** *(plural* los cinturones*)*: **he's wearing a belt** lleva puesto un cinturón
➤ fasten your seat belt ajusten sus cinturones de seguridad.

**bench** [bentʃ] *noun* ■ **el banco:** she sat on a bench in the park se sentó en un banco del parque.

**bend** [bend] *(noun & verb)*
■ *noun*
   **la curva:** there's a bend in the road la calle tiene una curva
■ *verb*
   *(past tense & past participle* bent*)* **doblar:** I can't bend my arm no puedo doblar el brazo; **I bent the wire** doblé el cable

**bend down** *phrasal verb* ■ **agacharse:** he bent down to pick up his book se agachó para recoger el libro.

**bend over** *phrasal verb* ■ **inclinarse:** she bent over to have a closer look se inclinó para mirar más de cerca.

**bent** [bent] *(adjective & verb form)*
■ *adjective*
   **doblado:** a bent nail una uña doblada
■ *past tense & past participle*
   ➤ bend.

**berry** ['berɪ] *(plural* berries*) noun* ■ **la baya:** holly has red berries el acebo tiene bayas rojas.

**beside** [bɪ'saɪd] *preposition* ■ **al lado de:** come and sit beside Bob ven a sentarte al lado de Bob

➤ she's beside herself with joy está fuera de sí de alegría.

**besides** [bɪ'saɪdz] (adverb & preposition)
■ adverb
**además**: besides, I think you're wrong además, creo que estás equivocado
■ preposition
**además de**: besides this book I bought two others además de este libro, me compré dos más.

**best** [best] (adjective, adverb & noun)
■ adjective (superlative of **good**)
**mejor**: he's the best student in the class es el mejor estudiante de la clase; she's my best friend ella es mi mejor amiga
■ adverb (superlative of **well**)
➤ which one do you like best? ¿cuál es el que más te gusta
■ noun
➤ the best el mejor, la mejor: of all the players I know, you're the best de todos los jugadores que conozco, tu eres el mejor
➤ to do one's best hacer todo lo posible: I'll do my best voy a hacer todo lo posible.

**bet** [bet] (noun & verb)
■ noun
**la apuesta**: let's make a bet hagamos una apuesta
■ verb
(past tense & past participle **bet**, present participle **betting**) **apostar**: I bet you can't do it apuesto a que no puedes hacerlo.

**better** ['betər] (adjective & adverb)
■ adjective (comparative of **good**)
**mejor**: this method is better than the other este método es mejor que el otro
■ adverb (comparative of **well**)
**mejor**: she sings better than I do ella canta mejor que yo; I feel much better now ahora me siento mucho mejor
➤ to get better
ı. **mejorar**: the weather is getting better el clima está mejorando
2. **mejorarse**: I hope you get better soon espero que te mejores pronto
➤ I'd better go home me tengo que ir a casa.

**between** [bɪ'twiːn] (preposition & adverb)

■ preposition
**entre**: he's sitting between Greg and Anne está sentado entre Pablo y Mariana; we can split the work between us podemos dividirnos el trabajo entre los dos
■ adverb
➤ in between entre medio: John's sitting in between Juan se sentó entre medio.

**beware** [bɪ'weər] verb ■ **tener cuidado**: beware of pickpockets on the subway tengan cuidado con los carteristas en el metro; "beware of the dog!" ¡cuidado con el perro!

**beyond** [bɪ'jɒnd] preposition ■ **más allá de**: don't go beyond the gate no vayan más allá de la puerta
➤ it's beyond me! ¡no lo puedo entender!

**bicycle** ['baɪsɪkl] noun ■ **la bicicleta**: can you ride a bicycle? ¿sabes andar en bicicleta?
➤ a bicycle path una ciclovía, una bicisenda Southern Cone
➤ a bicycle pump una bomba de bicicleta.

**big** [bɪg] (comparative **bigger**, superlative **biggest**) adjective
ı. **mayor**: my big brother mi hermano mayor
2. **grande**: a big book un libro grande

> Grande changes to gran before singular nouns:

there was a big fire hubo un gran incendio
➤ the Big Apple la Gran Manzana

> **BIG APPLE**
>
> **The Big Apple**, que significa La Gran Manzana, es el apodo de la ciudad de Nueva York. Este nombre lo utilizaron originalmente los músicos de jazz de los años veinte, refiriéndose al éxito que podrían obtener en esta ciudad. Otras ciudades estadounidenses, como Chicago y Detroit, también tienen apodos: **the Windy City**, apodo de la primera, por los fuertes vientos que soplan ahí, y **Motown**, de la segunda, por ser la ciudad del automóvil.

**bike** [baɪk] noun ■ **la bici**: she rides her bike to work va en bici a trabajar.

**bikini** [bɪ'kiːnɪ] *noun* ■ el **bikini** *(feminine)*, la **bikini** *River Plate*: she's wearing a bikini tiene puesto un bikini.

**bilingual** [baɪ'lɪŋgwəl] *adjective* ■ **bilingüe**: a bilingual dictionary un diccionario bilingüe.

**bill** [bɪl] *noun*
1. la **cuenta**: I have a stack of bills to pay tengo una cantidad de cuentas que pagar
2. el **billete**: a ten-dollar bill un billete de diez dólares.

**billboard** ['bɪlbɔːd] *noun* ■ la **valla publicitaria**, el **espectacular** *Mexico*.

**billion** ['bɪljən] *noun* ■ los **mil millones**: three billion dollars tres mil millones de dólares.

**binoculars** [bɪ'nɒkjʊləz] *plural noun* ■ los **binoculares**: a pair of binoculars unos binoculares.

**biology** [baɪ'ɒlədʒɪ] *noun* ■ la **biología**.

**bird** [bɜːd] *noun* ■ el **pájaro**: the birds sing at dawn los pájaros cantan al amanecer
➤ a bird of prey un ave de rapiña.

**birth** [bɜːθ] *noun* ■ el **nacimiento**: what's your date of birth? ¿cuál es tu fecha de nacimiento?
➤ to give birth to dar a luz a: she gave birth to a girl dio a luz a una niña
➤ a birth certificate una partida de nacimiento, un acta de nacimiento *Mexico*.

**birthday** ['bɜːθdeɪ] *noun* ■ el **cumpleaños** *(plural* los **cumpleaños***)*: Gary's birthday is on February 6 el cumpleaños de Gary es el 6 de febrero
➤ happy birthday! ¡feliz cumpleaños!

**bishop** ['bɪʃəp] *noun* ■ el **obispo**.

**bison** ['baɪsn] *noun* ■ el **bisonte**.

**bit** [bɪt] *(noun & verb form)*
■ *noun*
el **pedazo**: a bit of cheese un pedazo de queso

➤ a bit un poco: I'm a bit tired estoy un poco cansada
➤ a bit of un poco de
➤ bit by bit poco a poco
➤ for a bit por un momento
■ *past tense*
➤ bite.

**bite** [baɪt] *(noun & verb)*
■ *noun*
1. la **picadura**: an insect bite una picadura de insecto, un piquete de insecto *Mexico*
2. el **mordisco**: he took a bite of my apple le dio un mordisco a mi manzana
■ *verb*
*(past tense* bit, *past participle* bitten*)*
1. **morder**: the dog bit me el perro me mordió
2. **picar**: I've been bitten by mosquitoes me picaron los mosquitos
➤ to bite one's nails comerse las uñas: he bites his nails se come las uñas.

**bitten** ['bɪtn] *past participle* ➤ bite.

**bitter** ['bɪtəʳ] *adjective*
1. **amargo**: it has a bitter taste tiene un gusto amargo
2. **penetrante**: there's a bitter wind blowing sopla un viento penetrante.

**black** [blæk] *adjective* ■ **negro**: he wore a black hat llevaba puesto un sombrero negro; a black man un hombre negro
➤ I drink my coffee black tomo el café negro
➤ a black eye un ojo morado, un ojo en tinta *Southern Cone*
➤ black and white blanco y negro: a black and white photo una foto en blanco y negro.

**blackberry** ['blækbərɪ] *(plural* blackberries*) noun* ■ la **mora**.

**blackbird** ['blækbɜːd] *noun* ■ el **mirlo**.

**blackboard** ['blækbɔːd] *noun* ■ el **pizarrón** *(plural* los **pizarrones***)*: the teacher is writing on the blackboard el profesor está escribiendo en el pizarrón.

**blade** [bleɪd] *noun* ■ la **hoja**: a razor blade una hoja de afeitar, una navaja de rasurar *Mexico*.

**blame** [bleɪm] *verb*
➤ to blame somebody for something culpar a alguien de algo: **he blames me for his problems** me culpa a mí de sus problemas
➤ **who's to blame?** ¿quién tiene la culpa?: **he's to blame** él tiene la culpa

**blank** [blæŋk] *adjective* ■ **en blanco: a blank sheet of paper** una hoja de papel en blanco
➤ **a blank tape** una cinta virgen
➤ **my mind went blank** me quedé en blanco.

**blanket** ['blæŋkɪt] *noun* ■ **la cobija,** la **frazada: she put a blanket on the bed** puso una cobija en la cama.

**blast** [blɑst] *noun* ■ **el estallido: a bomb blast** el estallido de una bomba.

**bleach** [bliːtʃ] *noun* ■ **la lejía,** el **blanqueador** *Colombia, Mexico,* la **lavandina** *Argentina,* el **agua Jane®** *Uruguay.*

**bleed** [bliːd] *(past tense & past participle* bled [bled]) *verb* ■ **sangrar: my nose is bleeding** me sangra la nariz.

**blender** ['blendər] *noun* ■ **la licuadora: mix the sauce in the blender** mezcle la salsa en la licuadora.

**bless** [bles] *(past tense & past participle* blessed) *verb* ■ **bendecir: the priest blessed him** el sacerdote lo bendijo
➤ **bless you!** ¡salud!

**blew** [bluː] *past tense* ➤ blow.

**blind** [blaɪnd] *(adjective & noun)*
■ *adjective*
**ciego: he's been blind since birth** es ciego de nacimiento
■ *noun*
la **persiana: pull down the blind** baja la persiana.

**blindfold** ['blaɪndfəʊld] *(noun & verb)*
■ *noun*
la **venda sobre los ojos: they put a blindfold on me** me pusieron una venda sobre los ojos
■ *verb*
**vendarle los ojos a: they blindfolded the man** le vendaron los ojos al hombre.

**blink** [blɪŋk] *verb* ■ **parpadear: she blinked when the light came on** parpadeó cuando se prendió la luz.

**blister** ['blɪstər] *noun* ■ **la ampolla: I have a blister on my heel** tengo una ampolla en el talón.

**block** [blɒk] *(noun & verb)*
■ *noun*
1. el **bloque: a block of ice** un bloque de hielo
2. la **manzana: I'll walk around the block** voy a dar la vuelta a la manzana
➤ **it's five blocks from here** queda a cinco cuadras de aquí
■ *verb*
1. **bloquear: a fallen tree was blocking the road** un árbol caído bloqueaba el camino
2. **atascar: something is blocking the sink** algo está atascando el fregadero
➤ **the pipe is blocked** la cañería está tapada.

**blond** [blɒnd] *adjective* ■ **rubio, güero** *Mexico informal* **he has blond hair** tiene el pelo rubio.

**blonde** [blɒnd] *noun* ■ **la rubia,** la **güera** *Mexico informal* **a stunning blonde** una rubia despampanante
➤ **Anne is a blonde** Ana es rubia.

**blood** [blʌd] *noun* ■ **la sangre: he was covered in blood** estaba cubierto de sangre
➤ **blood type** el tipo sanguíneo
➤ **blood pressure** la presión sanguínea.

**blouse** [blaʊs] *noun* ■ **la blusa: she's wearing a pretty blouse** llevaba puesta una blusa muy linda.

**blow** [bləʊ] *(past tense* blew, *past participle* blown) *verb* ■ **soplar: the wind was blowing** soplaba el viento
➤ **to blow a whistle** tocar un silbato: **the referee blew his whistle** el árbitro tocó el silbato
➤ **to blow one's nose** sonarse la nariz

**blow out** *phrasal verb* ■ **apagar: she blew out the candles on the cake** apagó las velitas del pastel.

**blow up** *phrasal verb*
1. **inflar: I'm going to blow up some balloons for the party** voy a inflar unos globos para la fiesta

**2.** explotar: two bombs exploded explotaron dos bombas

**3.** hacer volar: they blew up the bridge hicieron volar el puente

➤ the whole building blew up todo el edificio voló.

**blown** [bləʊn] *past participle* ➤ blow.

**blue** [bluː] *adjective* ■ azul: Cathy has blue eyes Catalina tiene los ojos azules; she's wearing a blue dress lleva puesto un vestido azul.

**blueberry** ['bluːbərɪ] *(plural* blueberries*) noun* ■ el arándano: a blueberry pie un pay de arándano.

**blunt** [blʌnt] *adjective*

**1.** desafilado: the knife is blunt el cuchillo está desafilado

**2.** franco: he's very blunt es muy franco.

**blurred** [blɜːrd] *adjective* ■ borroso: the photo is blurred la foto está borrosa.

**blush** [blʌʃ] *verb* ■ ponerse colorado: you're blushing te estás poniendo colorado; she blushed when I said his name se puso colorada cuando dije su nombre.

**board** [bɔːd] *(noun & verb)*

■ *noun*

**1.** la tabla: a bread board una tabla de cortar el pan

**2.** el pizarrón *(plural* los pizarrones*)*: write the sentence on the board escriba la oración en el pizarrón

**3.** el tablero de anuncios: there are a lot of notices on the board hay muchos avisos en el tablero de anuncios

**4.** el tablero: put the pieces on the board coloca las piezas en el tablero

**5.** la junta: Mr. Owen is on the board of directors el señor Owen está en la junta directiva

➤ board games juegos de mesa

➤ on board a bordo: how many passengers are on board? ¿cuántos pasajeros hay a bordo?

■ *verb*

embarcar, abordar *Mexico*: we'll start boarding in five minutes empezaremos a embarcar en cinco minutos.

**boarding school** ['bɔːdɪŋskuːl] *noun* ■ el internado: he goes to boarding school va a un internado.

**boast** [bəʊst] *verb* ■ alardear: she's boasting about being in the play alardea porque participa en la obra.

**boat** [bəʊt] *noun*

**1.** el barco: we went to Europe by boat fuimos a Europa en barco

**2.** *smaller* la lancha: we're taking the boat out on the lake today vamos a llevar la lancha al lago.

**body** ['bɒdɪ] *(plural* bodies*) noun* ■ el cuerpo: the human body el cuerpo humano.

**bodyguard** ['bɒdɪgɑːd] *noun* ■ el/la guardaespaldas *(plural* los/las guardaespaldas*)*, el/la guarura *Mexico*: he's the president's bodyguard es el guardaespaldas del presidente.

**boil** [bɔɪl] *verb* ■ hervir: the water is boiling el agua está hirviendo

➤ I boiled some potatoes cocí unas papas.

**boiler** ['bɔɪlər] *noun* ■ la caldera, el boiler *Mexico*.

**boiling** ['bɔɪlɪŋ] *adjective* ■ it's boiling hot today hoy hace un calor espantoso.

**bold** [bəʊld] *adjective* ■ osado: it was a bold move for her to change jobs fue muy osado de su parte al cambiar de trabajo

➤ bold type la negrita.

**bolt** [bəʊlt] *(noun & verb)*

■ *noun*

**1.** el tornillo: nuts and bolts tuercas y tornillos

**2.** el cerrojo: there's a bolt on the door hay un cerrojo en la puerta

■ *verb*

echarle el cerrojo a: did you bolt the door? ¿le echaste el cerrojo a la puerta?

**bomb** [bɒm] *(noun & verb)*

■ *noun*

la bomba: a bomb scare una amenaza de bomba

- *verb*
  **bombardear:** the city was bombed continuously bombardearon continuamente la ciudad.

**bone** [bəʊn] *noun* ■ el **hueso:** he gave the dog a bone le dio un hueso al perro.

**bonfire** [ˈbɒnˌfaɪər] *noun* ■ la **fogata:** we sat around the bonfire nos sentamos alrededor de la fogata.

**boo** [buː] *(noun & verb)*
- *noun*
  el **abucheo:** a chorus of boos came from the audience hubo un coro de abucheos del público; they yelled "boo!" to scare us gritaron "¡bu!" para asustarnos
➤ boo! ¡bu!
- *verb*
  **abuchear:** the audience booed el público abucheó.

**book** [bʊk] *(noun & verb)*
- *noun*
  el **libro:** Brian is reading a book Brian está leyendo un libro
➤ a book of tickets un talonario
- *verb*
  **reservar:** I booked two tickets to Buenos Aires reservé dos pasajes para Buenos Aires.

**bookcase** [ˈbʊkkeɪs] *noun* ■ la **estantería,** el **librero** *Mexico:* there's a bookcase in the office hay una estantería en la oficina.

**booklet** [ˈbʊklɪt] *noun* ■ el **folleto:** an instruction booklet el folleto de instrucciones.

**bookmark** [ˈbʊkmɑk] *noun* ■ el **marcador de libros,** el **marcalibros** *Colombia, Southern Cone, Venezuela.*

**bookshelf** [ˈbʊkʃelf] *(plural* bookshelves [ˈbʊkʃelvz]*) noun* ■ la **repisa.**

**bookstore** [ˈbʊkstɔːr] *noun* ■ la **librería:** this is my favorite bookstore esta es mi librería favorita.

**boot** [buːt] *noun* ■ la **bota:** she was wearing red boots llevaba puestas botas rojas.

**booth** [buːð] *noun* ■ la **cabina:** a telephone booth una cabina telefónica.

**border** [ˈbɔːdər] *noun* ■ la **frontera:** the border between the USA and Mexico la frontera entre Estados Unidos y México.

**bore** [bɔːr] *verb* ■ **aburrir:** this really bores me esto me aburre muchísimo
➤ the movie bored me to death me aburrí como ostra con la película.

**bored** [bɔːd] *adjective*
➤ to be bored estar aburrido: I was so bored in that class estaba tan aburrido en esa clase.

**boring** [ˈbɔːrɪŋ] *adjective*
➤ to be boring ser aburrido: this is such a boring book este libro es muy aburrido.

**born** [bɔːn] *adjective*
➤ to be born nacer: where were you born? ¿dónde naciste?: I was born in 1990 nací en 1990.

**borrow** [ˈbɒrəʊ] *verb* ■ **pedir prestado:** he borrowed some money from a friend le pidió prestado dinero a su amigo
➤ can I borrow your pen? ¿me prestas tu lapicera?
➤ I had to borrow the book from the library tuve que sacar el libro de la biblioteca.

**boss** [bɒs] *noun* ■ el **jefe,** la **jefa:** she's my boss es mi jefa.

**bossy** [ˈbɒsɪ] *adjective* ■ **mandón (***feminine* mandona *plural* **mandones):** his sister is very bossy su hermana es muy mandona.

**both** [bəʊθ] *adjective & pronoun* ■ **los/las dos:** both of the girls are Chilean las dos chicas son chilenas; both of them are coming los dos vienen; the girls were both hungry las dos chicas tenían hambre.

**bother** [ˈbɒðər] *verb*
1. **molestar:** I'm sorry to bother you siento molestarte; something is bothering her algo la está molestando
2. **molestarse**
➤ to bother to do something molestarse en hacer algo: he didn't bother to get up no se molestó en ponerse de pie
➤ why bother? ¿para qué molestarse?

**bottle** [ˈbɒtl] *noun* ■ la **botella:** a bottle of milk una botella de leche.

**bottle-opener** ['bɒtl'əʊpnəʳ]   *noun*
■ el **destapador**.

**bottom** ['bɒtəm] *(noun & adjective)*

■ *noun*
1. el **final**: at the bottom of the page al final de la página
2. el **fondo**: it was in the bottom of the box estaba en el fondo de la caja
3. el **pie**: at the bottom of the hill al pie de la colina
4. el **trasero**: she patted his bottom le dio una palmadita en el trasero
➤ she's at the bottom of her class es la última de su clase

■ *adjective*
   de más abajo: it's on the bottom shelf está en el estante de más abajo
➤ he got the bottom grade se sacó la nota más baja.

**bought** [bɔ:t] *past tense & past participle*
➤ buy.

**bounce** [baʊns] *verb*
1. rebotar, botar *Mexico*: the ball bounced twice la pelota rebotó dos veces
2. hacer rebotar, hacer botar *Mexico*: she bounced the ball against the wall hizo rebotar la pelota contra la pared.

**bound** [baʊnd] *adjective* ■ **seguro**: he's bound to win seguro que gana.

**bow** *(noun & verb)*

■ *noun*
   [baʊ]
1. el **arco**: a bow and arrows un arco y flechas
2. el **moño**: she tied the ribbon in a bow hizo un moño con la cinta
➤ a bow tie una corbata de moño

■ *verb*
   [baʊ] hacer una reverencia, hacer una caravana *Mexico*: the actors bowed los actores hicieron una reverencia.

**bowl** [bəʊl] *noun* ■ el **tazón** (plural los tazones): a bowl of milk un tazón de leche
➤ a salad bowl un bol para ensalada.

**bowling** ['bəʊlɪŋ] *uncountable noun*
■ los **bolos**, el **boliche** *Mexico*: bowling is an interesting sport los bolos es un deporte interesante
➤ to go bowling jugar bolos: he goes bowl-

ing with his friends often juega bolos con sus amigos a menudo
➤ a bowling alley un bowling, un boliche *Mexico*.

**box** [bɒks] *noun* ■ la **caja**.

**boxer** ['bɒksəʳ] *noun* ■ el **boxeador**, la **boxeadora**: he's a boxer es boxeador.

**boxer shorts** ['bɒksəʳʃɔ:ts] *plural noun* ■ los **calzoncillos**, los **calzones** *Mexico*: a pair of boxer shorts unos calzoncillos.

**boxing** ['bɒksɪŋ] *uncountable noun* ■ el **boxeo**: he likes to watch boxing le gusta ver boxeo
➤ a boxing match un combate de boxeo
➤ a boxing ring un cuadrilátero.

**boy** [bɔɪ] *noun* ■ el **niño**: a good boy un niño bueno.

**boyfriend** ['bɔɪfrend] *noun* ■ el **novio**.

**bra** [brɑ:] *noun* ■ el **sostén** (plural los sostenes), el **brasier** *Colombia, Mexico*, el **corpiño** *River Plate*.

**braces** ['breɪsɪz] *noun*
1. los **tirantes**: he wears braces usa tirantes
2. el **aparato**, los **brackets** *Mexico*: he has braces on his teeth tiene un aparato en los dientes.

**bracelet** ['breɪslɪt] *noun* ■ la **pulsera**.

**brag** [bræg] *verb* ■ **presumir**: stop bragging! ¡deja de presumir!
➤ he's always bragging about his rich father siempre está presumiendo de tener un padre rico.

**brain** [breɪn] *noun* ■ el **cerebro**
➤ he's got brains es inteligente.

**brainy** ['breɪnɪ] *adjective* ■ **inteligente**.

**brake** [breɪk] *(noun & verb)*

■ *noun*
   el **freno**: the brakes failed fallaron los frenos

■ *verb*
   **frenar**: he braked suddenly frenó de repente.

**branch** [brɑːntʃ] *noun*

**1.** la **rama**: the boy was hanging from a branch el niño estaba colgado de una rama

**2.** la **sucursal**: the bank has a branch in New York el banco tiene una sucursal en Nueva York.

**brand** [brænd] *noun* ■ la **marca**: it's a well-known brand of clothing es una marca de ropa muy conocida.

**brand-new** [brændnjuː] *adjective*
■ **flamante**: I've bought a brand-new computer me compré una computadora flamante.

**brass** [brɑːs] *noun* ■ el **latón**: a brass plate una placa de latón.

**brave** [breɪv] *adjective* ■ **valiente**.

**Brazil** [brəˈzɪl] *noun* ■ **Brasil** (*masculine*).

**Brazilian** [brəˈzɪljən] (*adjective & noun*)
■ *adjective*

> Remember not to use a capital letter for the adjective in Spanish:

**brasileño**: I like Brazilian music me gusta la música brasileña
■ *noun*

> In Spanish, a capital letter is not used for the inhabitants of a country or region:

el **brasileño**, la **brasileña**: a Brazilian sings that song un brasileño canta esa canción.

**bread** [bred] *uncountable noun* ■ el **pan**
➤ a loaf of bread un pan.

**break** [breɪk] (*noun & verb*)
■ *noun*
el **descanso**: they took a break se tomaron un descanso
■ *verb*
(*past tense* **broke**, *past participle* **broken**)

**1.** **romper**: I've broken the radio rompí la radio

**2.** **romperse**: she has broken her leg se rompió la pierna; the glass broke se rompió el vidrio
➤ to break the law violar la ley: she broke the law violó la ley

➤ the TV broke se descompuso la tele
➤ to break a promise romper una promesa: Tom broke his promise Tomás rompió su promesa
➤ to break a record batir un récord: he broke the world record batió el récord mundial

**break down** *phrasal verb*

**1.** **descomponerse**: their car broke down se les descompuso el coche

**2.** **tirar abajo**: the police broke the door down la policía tiró la puerta abajo.

**break in** *phrasal verb* ■ **meterse**: a burglar broke in through the window se metió un ladrón por la ventana.

**break up** *phrasal verb*

**1.** **partir**: they broke it up into five pieces lo partieron en cinco pedazos

**2.** **romper**: he broke up with his girlfriend rompió con su novia

**3.** **terminar**: the meeting broke up at three la reunión terminó a las tres.

**breakdown** [ˈbreɪkdaʊn] *noun* ■ la **avería**, la **descompostura** *Mexico*: we had a breakdown on the highway tuvimos una avería en la carretera
➤ a nervous breakdown una crisis nerviosa.

**breakfast** [ˈbrekfəst] *noun* ■ el **desayuno**
➤ to have breakfast desayunar.

**breast** [brest] *noun* ■ el **pecho**
➤ a chicken breast una pechuga de pollo.

**breaststroke** [ˈbreststrəʊk] *noun* ■ el **estilo pecho**, el **nado de pecho** *Mexico*: she's learning the breaststroke está aprendiendo el estilo pecho
➤ he's swimming breaststroke está nadando pecho.

**breath** [breθ] *noun* ■ el **aliento**: I need to get my breath back necesito recuperar el aliento
➤ he took a deep breath respiró hondo
➤ hold your breath contén la respiración
➤ out of breath sin aliento: I'm out of breath me quedé sin aliento.

**breathe** [briːð] *verb* ■ **respirar**: breathe deeply respira hondo

**breathe in** *phrasal verb* ■ **inhalar**.

**breathe out** *phrasal verb* ■ **exhalar**.

**breed** [briːd] *(verb & noun)*
■ *verb*
*(past tense & past participle **bred**)*
1. **criar:** he breeds ostriches cría avestruces
2. **reproducirse:** rabbits breed very fast los conejos se reproducen muy rápido
■ *noun*
la **raza:** what breed is that dog? ¿de qué raza es ese perro?

**breeze** [briːz] *noun* ■ la **brisa**.

**brick** [brik] *noun* ■ el **ladrillo**.

**bride** [braid] *noun* ■ la **novia:** the bride looked really beautiful la novia se veía muy linda
➤ the bride and groom los novios.

**bridegroom** ['braidgrum] *noun* ■ el **novio**.

**bridesmaid** ['braidzmeid] *noun* ■ la **dama de honor**.

**bridge** [bridʒ] *noun* ■ el **puente:** she walked across the bridge atravesó el puente.

**brief** [briːf] *adjective* ■ **breve:** his speech was very brief su discurso fue muy breve.

**briefcase** ['briːfkeis] *noun* ■ el **maletín** *(plural* los **maletines**), el **portafolios** *(plural* los **portafolios**).

**bright** [brait] *adjective*
1. **brillante:** I like bright colors me gustan los colores brillantes
2. **luminoso:** the room is very bright la habitación es muy luminosa
3. **inteligente:** she's very bright es muy inteligente.

**brilliant** ['briljənt] *adjective* ■ **brillante:** he's a brilliant student es un estudiante brillante.

**bring** [briŋ] *verb* ■ *(past tense & past participle* **brought**) **traer:** I've brought you some flowers te traje flores

**bring back** *phrasal verb*
1. **regresar** *Latin America excluding Southern Cone,* **devolver:** I'll bring your things back tomorrow te voy a regresar tus cosas mañana
2. **traer:** he brought a T-shirt back from Buenos Aires trajo una camiseta de Buenos Aires
3. **llevar:** she brought him back home lo llevó de vuelta a su casa.

**bring up** *phrasal verb*
1. **criar:** he was brought up by his grandparents lo criaron sus abuelos
2. **plantear:** he brought the matter up at the meeting planteó la cuestión en la reunión.

**Britain** ['britn] *noun* ■ **Gran Bretaña** *(feminine)*: I'm going to Britain voy a Gran Bretaña; she lives in Britain vive en Gran Bretaña ➤ Great Britain.

**British** ['britiʃ] *(adjective & noun)*
■ *adjective*

> The Spanish adjective does not start with a capital letter:

**británico:** he's a British actor es un actor británico
■ *noun*

> In Spanish, a capital letter is not used for the inhabitants of a country or region:

➤ the British los británicos
➤ the British Isles las Islas Británicas.

**broad** [brɔːd] *adjective* ■ **ancho:** he has broad shoulders tiene la espalda ancha
➤ in broad daylight a plena luz del día.

**broadcast** ['brɔːdkaːst] *(past tense & past participle* **broadcast**) *(noun & verb)*
■ *noun*
el **programa:** a live TV broadcast un programa de televisión en vivo
■ *verb*
**transmitir:** the program is broadcast on the radio transmiten el programa por radio.

**Broadway** ['brɔːdwei] *noun* ■ *nombre de una calle de Nueva York*

**broccoli** ['brɒkəlɪ] *uncountable noun* ■ el **brócoli**.

**broke** [brəʊk] *(adjective & verb form)*
■ *adjective*
*informal* **quebrado: he's broke** está quebrado
■ *past tense*
➤ break.

**broken** ['brəʊkn] *(adjective & verb form)*
■ *adjective*
**roto: the cup is broken** la copa está rota
➤ **he has a broken bone in his foot** tiene un hueso del pié roto
■ *past participle*
➤ break.

**bronze** [brɒnz] *noun* ■ el **bronce: bronze has many different uses** el bronce tiene usos muy variados
➤ **the Bronze Age** la Edad de bronce
➤ **he won the bronze medal** ganó la medalla de bronce.

**broom** [bruːm] *noun* ■ la **escoba**.

**brother** ['brʌðər] *noun* ■ el **hermano: she has two brothers** tiene dos hermanos.

**brother-in-law** ['brʌðərɪnlɔː] *(plural brothers-in-law) noun* ■ el **cuñado**.

**brought** [brɔːt] *past tense & past participle* ➤ bring.

**brown** [braʊn] *adjective*
1. **marrón (***feminine* **marrón** *plural* **marrones), café** *Central America, Chile, Mexico:* **brown shoes** zapatos marrones
2. **castaño: he has brown hair** tiene el pelo castaño
3. **bronceado: he was very brown after his vacation** estaba muy bronceado después de sus vacaciones

➤ **brown sugar** el azúcar morena.

**brownie** ['braʊnɪ] *noun* ■ el **brownie: he had a brownie for lunch** se comió un brownie de almuerzo.

**browse** [braʊz] *verb*
1. **mirar: he likes browsing that shop** le gusta mirar en esa tienda
2. **hojear: he's browsing through a magazine** está hojeando una revista
3. **navegar: she's browsing the Internet** está navegando en Internet.

**browser** ['braʊzər] *noun* ■ el **navegador: an Internet browser** un navegador de Internet.

**bruise** [bruːz] *(noun & verb)*
■ *noun*
el **moretón** *(plural* los **moretones): he's covered in bruises** está lleno de moretones
■ *verb*
**he bruised his knee** se hizo una magulladura en la rodilla.

**brush** [brʌʃ] *(noun & verb)*
■ *noun*
1. el **cepillo: pass me the brush please, my hair's a mess** pásame el cepillo por favor, que tengo el pelo hecho un desastre; **worn-out brushes don't clean teeth properly** los cepillos gastados no limpian bien los dientes
2. el **pincel: the brush was stiff with dry paint** el pincel estaba duro con la pintura seca
➤ **a hairbrush** un cepillo de pelo
➤ **a paintbrush** un pincel
➤ **a toothbrush** un cepillo de dientes
■ *verb*
1. **cepillar: she brushed the girl's hair** le cepilló el pelo a la niña; **she's brushing her hair** se está cepillando el pelo; **don't forget to brush your teeth!** no olvides de cepillarte los dientes
2. **pasar rozando: she brushed against the table** paso rozando la mesa.

**bubble** ['bʌbl] *(noun & verb)*
■ *noun*
1. la **burbuja: that laundry soap doesn't make enough bubbles** ese detergente no hace suficientes burbujas

**2.** la **pompa**

➤ she was blowing bubbles through her fingers estaba haciendo pompas con los dedos

■ *verb*
**bullir:** the water is beginning to bubble el agua está empezando a bullir.

**buck** [bʌk] *noun* ■ *informal* el **dólar:** it costs ten bucks cuesta diez dólares.

**bucket** ['bʌkɪt] *noun* ■ el **balde,** la cubeta *Mexico.*

**buckle** ['bʌkl] *noun* ■ la **hebilla:** my belt buckle is broken la hebilla de mi cinturón está rota.

**buddy** ['bʌdɪ] *(plural* buddies) *noun* ■ *informal* el **amigo,** la **amiga,** el/la **cuate** *Mexico.*

**buffalo** ['bʌfələʊ] *noun* ■ el **búfalo.**

**bug** [bʌg] *(noun & verb)*

■ *noun*
**1.** el **bicho:** a bug flew in through the window entró un bicho volando por la ventana
**2.** el **virus:** he caught a bug se agarró un virus
**3.** el **error:** there's a bug in the program hay un error el programa

■ *verb*
*informal* **fastidiar:** stop bugging me! ¡deja de fastidiarme!

**build** [bɪld] *(past tense & past participle* built) *verb* ■ **construir:** they're building houses near the school están construyendo casas cerca de la escuela.

**building** ['bɪldɪŋ] *noun* ■ el **edificio**

➤ a building site una obra.

**built** [bɪlt] *past tense & past participle*

➤ build.

**bulb** [bʌlb] *noun* ■ la **bombilla,** el **foco** *Mexico,* el **bombito** *Colombia, Venezuela.*

**bull** [bʊl] *noun* ■ el **toro.**

**bullet** ['bʊlɪt] *noun* ■ la **bala.**

**bullseye** ['bʊlzaɪ] *noun* ■ el **blanco:** she hit the bullseye! ¡dio en el blanco!

**bully** ['bʊlɪ] *(noun & verb)*

■ *noun (plural* bullies)
el **matón** *(plural* los **matones**): he's a real bully es un verdadero matón

■ *verb*
**amedrentar:** she bullies the whole class ella amedrenta a toda la clase.

**bump** [bʌmp] *(noun & verb)*

■ *noun*
**1.** el **golpe:** they felt a bump as the car went over the pothole sintieron un golpe cuando el coche pasó por bache
**2.** el **chichón** *(plural* los **chichones**): I have a bump on my forehead tengo un chichón en la frente

■ *verb*
**golpear:** I bumped my head me golpeé la cabeza

**bump into** *phrasal verb*
**1.** **darse contra:** they bumped into the wall me di contra la pared
**2.** **encontrarse:** I bumped into my old teacher me encontré con una profesora antigua.

**bumpy** ['bʌmpɪ] *adjective*
**1.** **desigual:** it has a bumpy surface tiene una superficie desigual
**2.** **lleno de baches:** the road is bumpy la calle está llena de baches
**3.** **agitado:** we had a bumpy flight tuvimos un vuelo agitado.

**bun** [bʌn] *noun*
**1.** el **bollo:** those buns are too sweet for me esos bollos son demasiado dulces para mí
**2.** el **panecillo,** el **bolillo** *Mexico,* el **pancito** *Chile:* I'm going to heat up the buns for dinner voy a calentar los panecillos para la cena
**3.** el **moño:** Susie wears her hair in a bun Susie lleva el pelo en un moño.

**bunch** [bʌntʃ] *noun*
**1.** el **ramo,** el **bonche** *Mexico:* a bunch of flowers un ramo de flores
**2.** el **racimo:** a bunch of bananas un racimo de bananas
**3.** el **manojo:** a bunch of keys un manojo de llaves.

**burger** ['bɜːgər] *noun* ■ la **hamburguesa.**

**burglar** ['bɜːglər] *noun* ■ el **ladrón**
(*plural* los **ladrones**), la **ladrona**
➤ a burglar alarm una alarma antirrobo.

**buried** ['berɪd] *past tense & past partici-ple* ➤ bury.

**burn** [bɜːn] (*past tense & past participle* burnt o burned) (*verb & noun*)
■ *noun*
la **quemadura: she has a burn on her arm** tiene una quemadura en el brazo
■ *verb*
1. **arder: the house is burning** la casa está ardiendo
2. **quemar: I burned myself** me quemé; **I've burned my hand** me quemé la mano.

**burnt** [bɜːnt] *past tense & past participle* ➤ burn.

**burp** [bɜːp] *verb* ■ *informal* **eructar**.

**burst** [bɜːst] (*past tense & past participle* burst) *verb*
1. **estallar: the bubble burst** la burbuja estalló
2. **reventarse: the balloon burst** se reventó el globo
3. **reventar: he burst the balloon** reventó el globo
➤ to burst into tears ponerse a llorar: **the lit-tle boy burst into tears** el niño se puso a llorar
➤ to burst out laughing echarse a reír: **they all burst out laughing** se echaron a reír.

**bury** ['berɪ] (*past tense & past participle* buried) *verb* ■ **enterrar: my grandmoth-er is buried in Memphis** mi abuela está enterrada en Memphis.

**bus** [bʌs] *noun* ■ el **autobús,** el **camión** *Central America, Mexico,* el **colectivo** *Argenti-na:* **we took the bus into town** tomamos el autobús al centro
➤ a bus stop una parada de autobús.

**bush** [bʊʃ] *noun* ■ el **arbusto**.

**business** ['bɪznɪs] (*plural* businesses) *noun*
1. los **negocios: she's good at business** es buena para los negocios
2. la **empresa: he has a small business** tiene una pequeña empresa

➤ mind your own business! ¡no te metas!

**businessman** ['bɪznɪsmæn] (*plural* businessmen ['bɪznɪsmen]) *noun* ■ el **empresario**.

**businesswoman** ['bɪznɪsˌwʊmən] (*plural* businesswomen ['bɪznɪsˌwɪmɪn]) *noun* ■ la **empresaria**.

**busy** ['bɪzɪ] *adjective*
1. **ocupado: I'm very busy** estoy muy ocupa-do
2. **ajetreado: I have a busy week** tengo una semana ajetreada
3. **de mucho movimiento: New York is a busy city** Nueva York es una ciudad de mu-cho movimiento
➤ I got a busy signal el teléfono me dio ocu-pado.

**but** [bʌt] *conjunction*
1. **pero: I called him but he wasn't there** lo llamé, pero no estaba
2. **sino: she wasn't sad but angry** no estaba triste sino enojada

> **Sino** is used to express a contradiction of a previous negative statement.

**butcher** ['bʊtʃər] *noun* ■ el **carnicero,** la **carnicera: the butcher sold me some good meat** el carnicero me vendió buena carne
➤ the butcher's shop la carnicería.

**butter** ['bʌtər] *noun* ■ la **mantequilla,** la **manteca** *River Plate.*

**butterfly** ['bʌtəflaɪ] (*plural* butter-flies) *noun* ■ la **mariposa**.

**buttocks** ['bʌtəks] *plural noun* ■ las **nalgas**.

**button** ['bʌtn] *noun* ■ el **botón: he lost a button off his shirt** perdió un botón de la camisa; **click on the left mouse button** presiona el botón izquierdo del ratón; **he's wearing a button with a big smiley face on it** lleva puesto un botón con una cara son-riente.

**buy** [baɪ] (*past tense & past participle* bought) *verb* ■ **comprar: I'm going to**

buy some bread voy a comprar pan; she bought him a present le compró un regalo.

**buzz** [bʌz] *verb* ■ **zumbar: the bees were buzzing** las abejas zumbaban.

**by** [baɪ] *preposition*
1. **por: this temple was built by the Romans** este templo fue construido por los romanos
2. **de: a book by Mark Twain** un libro de Mark Twain
3. **en: we went by bus** fuimos en autobús
4. **junto a: he was sitting by the fire** estaba sentado junto al fuego
5. **a más tardar: I'll be there by eight** llegaré a las ocho a más tardar
➤ **by oneself** solo: **I did it all by myself** lo hice yo solo
➤ **by the way** a propósito: **by the way, are you coming tonight?** a propósito, ¿vienes esta noche?

**bye, bye-bye** [baɪ, bə'baɪ] *exclamation* ■ **adiós.**

**cab** [kæb] *noun* ■ **el taxi: I'll take a cab** tomaré un taxi.

**cabbage** ['kæbɪdʒ] *noun* ■ **el repollo.**

**cabin** ['kæbɪn] *noun*
1. **el camarote: her cabin is on the top deck** su camarote está en la cubierta de arriba
2. **la cabaña: he lives in a log cabin** vive en una cabaña de madera.

**cabinet** ['kæbɪnɪt] *noun*
1. **el armario: a bathroom cabinet** un armario de baño
2. **el gabinete: he was in the president's cabinet** estuvo en el gabinete del presidente
➤ **a medicine cabinet** un botiquín.

**cable** ['keɪbl] *noun* ■ **el cable**
➤ **cable television** or **cable TV** televisión por cable: **we have cable television** tenemos televisión por cable.

**cafe, café** ['kæfeɪ] *noun* ■ **el café: we had ice-cream in a café** tomamos helado en un café.

**cafeteria** [ˌkæfɪ'tɪərɪə] *noun* ■ **la cafetería.**

**cage** [keɪdʒ] *noun* ■ **la jaula.**

**cake** [keɪk] *noun* ■ **el pastel,** la **tarta** *River Plate*: **she's making a chocolate cake** está haciendo un pastel de chocolate
➤ **a cake shop** una pastelería, una confitería *River Plate*.

**calculator** ['kælkjʊleɪtər] *noun* ■ **la calculadora.**

**calendar** ['kælɪndər] *noun* ■ **el calendario.**

**calf** [kɑf] *(plural* **calves** [kɑvz]*) noun*
1. **el ternero: a cow and her calf** una vaca y su ternero
2. **la pantorrilla: I've got a pain in my calf** tengo un dolor en la pantorrilla.

**call** [kɔːl] *(noun & verb)*
■ *noun*
**la llamada: I have to make a call** tengo que hacer una llamada
➤ **I'll give you a call** te voy a llamar
■ *verb*
**llamar: we called the police** llamamos a la policía; **everyone calls her Sassy** todos la llaman Sassy; **he called me a liar** me llamó mentiroso
➤ **to be called** llamarse: **what is he called?** ¿cómo se llama?
➤ **what's this called?** ¿cómo se llama esto?
➤ **who's calling?** ¿quién llama?

call back | phrasal verb ■ volver a llamar: I'll call back later volveré a llamar más tarde.

call off | phrasal verb ■ cancelar: they called off the meeting cancelaron la reunión.

call on | phrasal verb ■ pasar a ver: they called on us yesterday nos pasaron a ver ayer.

calm | [kɑm] adjective & verb ■ tranquilo

calm down | phrasal verb ■ calmarse: calm down! ¡cálmate!

calves | plural ➤ calf.

camcorder | ['kæmˌkɔːdər] noun ■ la videocámara.

came | [keɪm] past tense ➤ come.

camel | ['kæml] noun ■ el camello.

camera | ['kæmərə] noun ■ la cámara.

camp | [kæmp] (noun & verb)

■ noun
el campamento: we set up camp near the river armamos campamento cerca del río
➤ a camp site un camping
■ verb
acampar: we camped on the beach acampamos en la playa.

camper | ['kæmpər] noun ■ el/la campista: there are campers near the river hay campistas cerca del río.

camping | ['kæmpɪŋ] uncountable noun
➤ to go camping ir de campamento: we go camping every spring nos vamos de campamento cada primavera
➤ camping is not allowed in that park no está permitido acampar en ese parque.

campus | [campus] noun ■ el campus.

can | (verb & noun)

■ verb
[kən, kæn]
1. (negative can't OR cannot) poder: can I help you with anything? ¿puedo ayudarte en algo?; Peter can't come on Friday Peter no puede venir el viernes; can I speak to Ra-

chel, please? ¿puedo hablar con Rachel, por favor?

When can is used with a verb of perception (like see, hear, feel, understand) it is not translated at all:

I can't see no veo; can you hear me? ¿me oyes?; I can't feel anything no siento nada; he can't understand what you are saying no entiende lo que dices

2.

When can means "know how to":

saber: can you swim? ¿sabes nadar?; I can't drive no sé manejar
■ noun
[kæn] la lata: a can of beer una lata de cerveza
➤ a can opener un abrelatas.

Canada | ['kænədə] noun ■ el Canadá.

Canadian | [kə'neɪdjən] (adjective & noun)
■ adjective

Remember not to use a capital letter for the adjective in Spanish:

canadiense: there is a maple leaf on the Canadian flag la bandera canadiense tiene una hoja de arce
■ noun

In Spanish, a capital letter is not used for the inhabitants of a country or region:

el/la canadiense: many Canadians are bilingual muchos canadienses son bilingües.

canal | [kə'næl] noun ■ el canal.

cancel | ['kænsl] verb ■ cancelar: they canceled the meeting cancelaron la reunión.

cancer | ['kænsər] noun ■ el cáncer.

candidate | ['kændɪdeɪt] noun ■ el candidato, la candidata.

candle | ['kændl] noun ■ la vela.

**candy** ['kændɪ] *uncountable noun* ■ el **dulce**, la **golosina** *River Plate*: he wants a piece of candy quiere un dulce
➤ a candy store una tienda de dulces.

**canned** [kænd] *adjective* ■ **enlatado**: canned sardines sardinas enlatadas.

**cannot** ['kænɒt] *negative* ➤ can.

**canoe** [kə'nuː] *noun* ■ la **canoa**.

**canoeing** [kə'nuːɪŋ] *uncountable noun* ■ el **piragüismo**: she enjoys canoeing le gusta el piragüismo
➤ to go canoeing hacer piragüismo: he goes canoeing every weekend hace piragüismo todos los fines de semana.

**can't** [kɑnt] ➤ cannot.

**cap** [kæp] *noun*
1. la **gorra**: he wears his cap backwards usa su gorra con la visera hacia atrás
2. la **tapa**: take the cap off the bottle sácale la tapa a la botella.

**capable** ['keɪpəbl] *adjective* ■ **capaz**.

**capital** ['kæpɪtl] *noun*
1. la **capital**: Washington is the capital of the United States Washington es la capital de los Estados Unidos
2. la **mayúscula**: write your name in capitals escriba su nombre en mayúscula
➤ a capital city una ciudad capital.

**captain** ['kæptɪn] *noun* ■ el **capitán** (*plural* los **capitanes**), la **capitana**.

**car** [kɑr] *noun*
1. el **coche**, el **auto** *Southern Cone*: he bought a red car se compró un coche rojo; we're going by car vamos en coche
2. el **vagón** (*plural* los **vagones**): this train has ten cars este tren tiene diez vagones
➤ a car crash un choque.

**card** [kɑd] *noun*
1. la **tarjeta**: a birthday card una tarjeta de cumpleaños
2. la **carta**, la **baraja** *Central America, Colombia, Mexico, Argentina*: they're playing cards están jugando a las cartas.

**cardboard** ['kɑdbɔːd] *noun* ■ el **cartón** (*plural* los **cartones**): it's made of cardboard es de cartón.

**care** [keər] (*noun & verb*)
■ *uncountable noun*
el **cuidado**: skin care cuidado de la piel
➤ to take care of cuidar: Jack takes care of the children Jack cuida a los niños
➤ take care! ¡cuídate!
■ *verb*
I don't care no me importa
➤ who cares? ¿y a mí qué?

**care about**  *phrasal verb* ■ **importar**: she doesn't care about her appearance no le importa su aspecto.

**care for** *phrasal verb*
1. **cuidar**: she cares for her elderly parents ella cuida a sus padres ancianos
2. **gustar**: I don't care for his new friends no me gustan sus nuevos amigos.

**career** [kə'rɪər] *noun* ■ la **carrera**.

**careful** ['keəfʊl] *adjective* ■ **cuidadoso**: he's always very careful siempre es muy cuidadoso
➤ be careful! ¡ten cuidado!

**carefully** ['keəfəlɪ] *adverb*
1. **con cuidado**: he drives carefully maneja con cuidado
2. **con esmero**: she did the work carefully hizo el trabajo con esmero.

**careless** ['keəlɪs] *adjective*
1. **descuidado**: Mary is very careless Mary es muy descuidada
2. **poco cuidado**: his work is careless su trabajo es poco cuidado
➤ a careless mistake un descuido.

**Caribbean** [kə'rɪbɪən] (*noun & adjective*)
■ *noun*
the Caribbean el Caribe
■ *adjective*

Remember not to use a capital letter for the adjective in Spanish:

caribeño: I like Caribbean music me gusta la música caribeña
➤ the Caribbean Sea el mar Caribe.

**carnival** ['kɑnɪvl] *noun* ■ el **carnaval**.

**carol** ['kærəl] *noun*

➤ a Christmas carol un villancico.

**carpet** ['kɑpɪt] *noun* ■ la **alfombra: a Persian carpet** una alfombra persa, un tapete persa *Colombia, Mexico;* **a wall-to-wall carpet** una alfombra.

**carried** ['kærɪd] *past tense & past participle* ➤ carry.

**carrot** ['kærət] *noun* ■ la **zanahoria**.

**carry** ['kærɪ] *verb*

ı. **cargar:** she's carrying a large bag está cargando una bolsa grande
2. **llevar:** the bus can carry up to fifty passengers el autobús puede llevar hasta cincuenta pasajeros

**carry on** *phrasal verb* ■ **seguir:** he carried on working siguió trabajando.

**cart** ['kɑt] *noun* ■ el **carro:** the horse was pulling the cart el caballo estaba tirando el carro

➤ a shopping cart un carrito de compras.

**carton** ['kɑtn] *noun* ■ el **cartón: a carton of eggs** un cartón de huevos.

**cartoon** [kɑ'tu:n] *noun*

ı. la **caricatura:** she likes the cartoons in the newspapers le gustan las caricaturas de los diarios
2. el **dibujo animado,** las **caricaturas** *Mexico:* he likes to watch cartoons in the afternoon le gusta ver dibujos animados en la tarde

➤ a cartoon strip una tira cómica, unos monitos *Chile, Mexico.*

**carve** [kɑv] *verb*

ı. **tallar:** he carved a statue out of wood talló una estatua de madera
2. **grabar:** Kevin carved his name on the bench Kevin grabó su nombre en el banco
3. **cortar:** she's carving the chicken está cortando el pollo.

**case** [keɪs] *noun*

ı. el **caso:** in that case I'm not coming en ese caso, no voy; **a case of smallpox** un caso de viruela

2. el **cajón** *(plural* los **cajones):** they bought a case of wine compraron un cajón de vino
3. el **estuche:** she put the camera in its case guardó la cámara en su estuche

➤ in any case en todo caso
➤ in case por si
➤ take your coat in case it rains lléva tu abrigo por si llueve.

**cash** [kæʃ] *uncountable noun* ■ el **dinero en efectivo: I have no cash on me** no tengo dinero en efectivo

➤ to pay cash pagar al contado
➤ a cash machine un cajero automático.

**cashier** [kæ'ʃɪər] *noun* ■ el **cajero,** la **cajera**.

**cash register** ['kæʃ,redʒɪstər] *noun* ■ la **caja registradora**.

**cassette** [kæ'set] *noun* ■ el **cassette**

➤ a cassette player un pasacintas, una casetera *Chile, Mexico.*

**castle** ['kɑsl] *noun* ■ el **castillo**.

**casual** ['kæʒʊəl] *adjective*

ı. **informal:** they were wearing casual clothes llevaban ropa informal
2. **descuidado:** he's very casual about things es muy descuidado con las cosas

> ⚠ La palabra inglesa casual es un falso amigo, no significa "casual".

**casualty** ['kæʒʊəltɪ] *(plural* casualties) *noun* ■ la **víctima**.

**cat** [kæt] *noun* ■ el **gato**.

**catalog** ['kætəlɒg] *noun* ■ el **catálogo**.

**catch** [kætʃ] *(past tense & past participle* caught) *verb*

ı. **atrapar:** he caught a fish atrapó un pescado
2. **agarrar:** she caught the flu the other day se agarró una gripe el otro día, se agarró una gripa el otro día *Mexico*
3. **tomar:** Fred is catching the six o'clock bus Fred va a tomar el autobús de las seis
4. **agarrar:** I caught him smoking lo agarré fumando

5. **oír:** I didn't catch what you said no oí lo que dijiste
6. **pillar:** I caught my finger in the door me pillé el dedo en la puerta

| **catch up** | *phrasal verb*

1. **ponerse al día:** I was away yesterday so I'll have to catch up ayer no estuve, así que tendré que ponerme al día
2. **alcanzar:** you go ahead, I'll catch you up vé adelante, yo te alcanzo.

| **category** | ['kætəgərɪ] *(plural* categories) *noun* ■ la **categoría**.

| **caterpillar** | ['kætəpɪlər] *noun* ■ la **oruga**.

| **cathedral** | [kə'θɪːdrəl] *noun* ■ la **catedral**.

| **Catholic** | ['kæθlɪk] *adjective & noun* ■ **católico**.

| **cattle** | ['kætl] *plural noun* ■ el **ganado**.

| **caught** | [kɔːt] *past tense & past participle* ➤ catch.

| **cauliflower** | ['kɒlɪˌflaʊər] *noun* ■ el **coliflor**.

| **cause** | [kɔːz] *(noun & verb)*

■ *noun*
la **causa:** we don't know the cause of the accident no conocemos la causa del accidente
■ *verb*
**causar:** the storm caused a lot of damage la tormenta causó muchos daños.

| **cautious** | ['kɔːʃəs] *adjective* ■ **cauteloso**.

| **cave** | [keɪv] *noun* ■ la **cueva**.

| **CD** | [ˌsiː'diː] *(abbreviation of* compact disc) *noun* ■ el **CD**
➤ a CD player un reproductor de CD.

| **CD-ROM** | [ˌsiːdiː'rɒm] *(abbreviation of* compact disc read only memory) *noun* ■ el **CD-ROM**.

| **ceiling** | ['siːlɪŋ] *noun* ■ el **techo**.

| **celebrate** | ['selɪbreɪt] *verb* ■ **celebrar:** we're going to celebrate my birthday vamos a celebrar mi cumpleaños; **people are celebrating in the streets** la gente está celebrando en las calles.

| **celebrity** | [sɪ'lebrətɪ] *(plural* celebrities) *noun* ■ la **celebridad**.

| **celery** | ['selərɪ] *noun* ■ el **apio**.

| **cell** | [sel] *noun*

1. la **celda:** the prisoner is in the cell el prisionero está en su celda
2. la **célula:** we have many cells in our bodies tenemos muchas células en el cuerpo.

| **cellar** | ['selər] *noun* ■ el **sótano**.

| **cello** | ['tʃeləʊ] *noun* ■ el **violonchelo**.

| **cemetery** | ['semɪtrɪ] *(plural* cemeteries) *noun* ■ el **cementerio**.

| **cent** | [sent] *noun* ■ el **centavo:** that's five dollars and twenty cents son cinco dólares y veinte centavos.

| **center** | [sentr] *noun* ■ el **centro**
➤ in the center of town en el centro.

| **centigrade** | ['sentɪgreɪd] *adjective* ■ **centígrado:** it's 20 degrees centigrade hace 20 grados centígrados.

| **centimeter** | ['sentɪˌmiːtər] *noun* ■ el **centímetro**.

| **central** | ['sentrəl] *adjective* ■ **central**.

| **century** | ['sentʃʊrɪ] *(plural* centuries) *noun* ■ el **siglo:** in the twentieth century en el siglo XX.

| **cereal** | ['sɪərɪəl] *noun* ■ el **cereal**.

| **ceremony** | ['serɪmənɪ] *(plural* ceremonies) *noun* ■ la **ceremonia**.

| **certain** | ['sɜːtn] *adjective*

1. **seguro:** I'm certain that it's her estoy seguro de que es ella
2. **cierto:** certain people think he's guilty ciertas personas creen que es culpable

➤ **to make certain of something** asegurarse de algo: **he made certain the window was closed** se aseguró de que la ventana estuviera cerrada.

**certainly** ['sɜ:tnlɪ] *adverb* ■ **por supuesto: certainly not!** ¡por supuesto que no!; **I will certainly come** vendré, por supuesto.

**certificate** [sə'tɪfɪkət] *noun* ■ el **certificado**.

**chain** [tʃeɪn] *noun* ■ la **cadena**.

**chair** [tʃeəʳ] *noun* ■ la **silla: a table and chairs** una mesa y sillas.

**chairman** ['tʃeəmən] *(plural* chairmen ['tʃeəmən]*) noun* ■ el **presidente**.

**chairperson** ['tʃeə,pɜ:sn] *(plural* chairpersons) *noun* ■ el **presidente,** la **presidenta**.

**chairwoman** ['tʃeə,wumən] *(plural* chairwomen ['tʃeə,wɪmɪn]*) noun* ■ la **presidenta**.

**chalk** [tʃɔ:k] *uncountable noun* ■ la **tiza,** el **gis** *Mexico:* **a piece of chalk** una tiza.

**challenge** ['tʃælɪndʒ] *(noun & verb)*

■ *noun*
  el **reto**
■ *verb*
  **retar: he challenged me to a game of tennis** me retó a jugar un partido de tenis.

**champagne** [ˌʃæm'peɪn] *noun* ■ el **champán**.

**champion** ['tʃæmpjən] *noun* ■ el **campeón,** la **campeona**.

**championship** ['tʃæmpjənʃɪp] *noun* ■ el **campeonato**.

**chance** [tʃɑːns] *noun*

1. la **posibilidad: he has a good chance of winning** hay buenas posibilidades de que gane
2. la **oportunidad: it gave me a chance to explore the city** me dio la oportunidad de explorar la ciudad

3. la **casualidad: I met him by chance** lo encontré por casualidad
➤ **to take a chance** arriesgarse: **he took a chance and succeeded** se arriesgó y tuvo éxito.

**change** [tʃeɪndʒ] *(noun & verb)*

■ *noun*
  el **cambio: there's been a change of plan** ha habido un cambio de planes; **do you have any change?** ¿tienes algo de cambio?
➤ **a change of clothes** un cambio de ropa
➤ **for a change** para variar: **he's watching TV, for a change** está viendo tele, para variar
■ *verb*
1. **cambiar: he really has changed** ha cambiado muchísimo; **I want to change 200 dollars into euros** quiero cambiar 200 dólares a euros; **she changed before going out** se cambió antes de salir
2. **cambiar de: we have to change buses** tenemos que cambiar de autobús; **he changed into another pair of pants** se cambió los pantalones
➤ **to change one's mind** cambiar de idea: **Richard changed his mind** Richard cambió de idea
➤ **to get changed** cambiarse: **I'm going to get changed** me voy a cambiar.

**channel** ['tʃænl] *noun* ■ el **canal: could you change the channel?** ¿podrías cambiar de canal?

**chapter** ['tʃæptəʳ] *noun* ■ el **capítulo: the hero dies in chapter three** el héroe muere en el capítulo tres.

**character** ['kærəktəʳ] *noun*

1. el **carácter: Jennifer has a very gentle character** Jennifer tiene un carácter muy suave
2. el **personaje: I like the character played by Johnny Depp** me gusta el personaje que hace Johnny Depp.

**charge** [tʃɑːdʒ] *(noun & verb)*

■ *noun*
1. el **costo: there's a delivery charge** hay un costo de transporte
2. el **cargo: he denies the charges** niega los cargos
➤ **it's free of charge** es gratis

➤ to be in charge estar a cargo
➤ I'm in charge of the department estoy a cargo de la sección
■ verb
1. cobrar: they charged me five dollars me cobraron cinco dólares
2. acusar: he has been charged with murder ha sido acusado de asesinato.

**charity** ['tʃærətɪ] (plural charities) noun
1. la organización benéfica (plural las organizaciones benéficas): it's good to donate money to charity es bueno donar dinero a las organizaciones benéficas
2. la caridad: I helped him out of charity lo ayudé por caridad
➤ for charity para un fin benéfico: we raised $100 for charity recaudamos $100 para un fin benéfico.

**charm** [tʃɑːm] noun ■ el encanto: he has a lot of charm tiene mucho encanto.

**charming** ['tʃɑːmɪŋ] adjective ■ encantador.

**chart** [tʃɑːt] noun ■ el gráfico: the chart shows average temperatures el gráfico muestra las temperaturas promedio
➤ the charts la lista de éxitos: her new song is number two on the charts su nueva canción es la número dos en la lista de éxitos.

**chase** [tʃeɪs] (noun & verb)
■ noun
la persecución (plural las persecuciones): a car chase una persecución en coche
■ verb
perseguir: somebody is chasing me alguien me está persiguiendo

**chase after** phrasal verb ■ perseguir: the dog was chasing after me el perro me perseguía.

**chat** [tʃæt] (noun & verb)
■ noun
la conversación, la plática Mexico: we had a long chat tuvimos una conversación larga
➤ a chat room sala de chat
■ verb
1. conversar, platicar Mexico: he was chatting with a friend estaba conversando con un amigo

2. chatear: he likes to chat on the Internet le gusta chatear en Internet.

**cheap** [tʃiːp] adjective ■ barato: it's a cheap dress es un vestido barato.

**cheat** [tʃiːt] (noun & verb)
■ noun
el tramposo, la tramposa: he's a cheat es un tramposo
■ verb
hacer trampa: he cheats at sports hace trampa en el deporte.

**cheater** ['tʃiːtər] noun ➤ cheat.

**check** [tʃek] (noun & verb)
■ noun
1. el control: an identity check un control de identidad
2. la cuenta: can I have the check, please? la cuenta, por favor
3. el cheque: he paid by check pagó con un cheque
■ verb
1. verificar, checar Mexico: the accountant checked the figures el contador verificó los números
2. revisar, checar Mexico: they checked our passports revisaron nuestros pasaportes

**check in** phrasal verb
1. chequear el equipaje, hacer el check-in River Plate: they checked in for their flight chequearon su equipaje para el vuelo
2. registrarse: we checked in at the hotel nos registramos en el hotel.

**check out** phrasal verb
1. dejar: they checked out from the hotel dejaron el hotel
2. informal mirar, checar Mexico: check this out! ¡mira esto!, ¡checa esto! Mexico.

**checkbook** ['tʃekbʊk] noun ■ la chequera.

**checked** [tʃekt] adjective ■ a cuadros: a checked shirt una camisa a cuadros.

**checkers** ['tʃekəz] noun ■ las damas: they're playing checkers están jugando a las damas.

**check-in** ['tʃekɪn] *noun* ■ el **chequeo de equipajes**, el **registro** *Mexico,* el **check-in** *River Plate*: check-in is at six o'clock el chequeo de equipajes es a las seis.

**checkout** ['tʃekaʊt] *noun* ■ la **caja**: a supermarket checkout una caja de supermercado.

**checkup** ['tʃekʌp] *noun* ■ el **chequeo**: he's going to the dentist for a checkup va al dentista para un chequeo.

**cheek** [tʃiːk] *noun* ■ la **mejilla**: she kissed him on the cheek lo besó en la mejilla.

**cheer** [tʃɪər] *(noun & verb)*
■ *noun*
la **ovación** *(plural* las **ovaciones**): there were cheers when he came on stage hubo una ovación cuando subió al escenario
➤ three cheers for Donald! ¡viva Donald!
■ *verb*
**gritar entusiasmadamente**: everyone was cheering todos estaban gritando entusiasmadamente

**cheer up** *phrasal verb*
1. **levantar el ánimo**: I tried to cheer him up traté de levantarle el ánimo
2. **animarse**: he cheered up when his friends came to see him se animó cuando sus amigos vinieron a verlo; cheer up! ¡anímate!

**cheerful** ['tʃɪəfʊl] *adjective* ■ **alegre**.

**cheerleading** ['tʃɪə,liːdɪŋ] *noun* ■ grupo de jóvenes que animan a un equipo deportivo

CHEERLEADING

 En muchas escuelas preparatorias y universidades existe la tradición de las cheerleaders o porristas, grupos de jóvenes que visten atractivos y coloridos trajes que se dedican a animar a los equipos deportivos durante sus partidos y competencias. También los equipos profesionales de fútbol americano y básquetbol suelen tener porristas.

**cheese** [tʃiːz] *noun* ■ el **queso**.

**cheeseburger** ['tʃiːz,bɜːgər] *noun* ■ la **hamburguesa con queso**.

**chef** [ʃef] *noun* ■ el **chef**.

**chemical** ['kemɪkl] *noun* ■ la **sustancia química**.

**chemistry** ['kemɪstrɪ] *noun* ■ la **química**: a chemistry lesson una clase de química.

**cherry** ['tʃerɪ] *(plural* cherries*) noun* ■ la **cereza**
➤ a cherry tree un cerezo.

**chess** [tʃes] *noun* ■ el **ajedrez**: they're playing chess están jugando al ajedrez.

**chest** [tʃest] *noun*
1. el **pecho**: he has a pain in his chest tiene un dolor en el pecho
2. el **baúl**: there's a big chest under the bed hay un baúl grande debajo de la cama
➤ a chest of drawers una cómoda.

**chew** [tʃuː] *verb* ■ **masticar**.

**chewing gum** ['tʃuːɪŋgʌm] *noun* ■ el **chicle**.

**chicken** ['tʃɪkɪn] *noun* ■ el **pollo**: a roast chicken un pollo asado, un pollo rostizado *Mexico*.

**chickenpox** ['tʃɪkɪnpɒks] *noun* ■ la **varicela**: he has chickenpox tiene varicela.

**chief** [tʃiːf] *(noun & adjective)*
■ *noun*
el **jefe**, la **jefa**: he's the chief of an African tribe es el jefe de una tribu africana
■ *adjective*
**principal**: that's the chief problem ése es el problema principal.

**child** [tʃaɪld] *(plural* children ['tʃɪldrən]*) noun* ■ el **niño**, la **niña**: she acts like a child se comporta como una niña.

**childhood** ['tʃaɪldhʊd] *noun* ■ la **infancia**.

**children** *plural* ➤ child.

**Chile** ['tʃɪli] noun ■ Chile (masculine).

**Chilean** ['tʃɪliən] (adjective & noun)
■ adjective

> Remember not to use a capital letter for the adjective in Spanish:

**chileno: Isabel Allende is a famous Chilean writer** Isabel Allende es una famosa escritora chilena
■ noun

> In Spanish, a capital letter is not used for the inhabitants of a country or region:

**el chileno, la chilena: the Chileans export various agricultural products** los chilenos exportan varios productos agrícolas.

**chili** ['tʃɪli] (plural chilies) noun ■ el chile, el ají Andes.

**chill** [tʃɪl] (noun & verb)
■ noun
1. el **resfriado: she caught a chill** pescó un resfriado
2. **fresco: there's a chill in the air** está fresco
■ verb
**enfriar: you should chill the champagne** deberías enfriar el champán.

**chilly** ['tʃɪli] adjective ■ **frío: I feel chilly** me siento frío; **it's chilly** hace frío.

**chimney** ['tʃɪmnɪ] noun ■ la **chimenea**.

**chimpanzee** [tʃɪmpən'ziː] noun ■ el/la **chimpancé**.

**chin** [tʃɪn] noun ■ la **barbilla**, la **pera** Southern Cone.

**china** ['tʃaɪnə] uncountable noun ■ la **porcelana: a china cup** una taza de porcelana.

**chip** [tʃɪp] noun
1. la **papa frita: a packet of chips** un paquete de papas fritas
2. el **chip** (plural los **chips**): **a computer chip** un chip de computadora.

**chocolate** ['tʃɒkələt] noun ■ el **chocolate**
> **a chocolate bar** una barra de chocolate
> **a chocolate cake** una torta de chocolate.

**choice** [tʃɔɪs] noun ■ la **elección** (plural las **elecciones**): **it was a good choice** fue una buena elección.

**choir** ['kwaɪər] noun ■ el **coro**.

**choke** [tʃəʊk] verb
1. **ahogarse: he's choking** se está ahogando
2. **ahogar: you're choking me!** ¡me estás ahogando!

**choose** [tʃuːz] (past tense chose) verb
■ **elegir: she will choose between the two** va a elegir entre los dos.

**chop** [tʃɒp] (noun & verb)
■ noun
la **chuleta**, la **costilla** River Plate: **a pork chop** una chuleta de cerdo
■ verb
1. **cortar: he's chopping wood** está cortando madera
2. **picar: you have to chop the vegetables** tienes que picar las verduras

**chop down** phrasal verb ■ **talar: they chopped the tree down** talaron el árbol.

**chose** [tʃəʊz] past tense ➤ choose.

**chosen** ['tʃəʊzn] past participle ➤ choose.

**christening** ['krɪsnɪŋ] noun ■ el **bautismo**.

**Christian** ['krɪstʃən] adjective & noun ■ **cristiano: she's a Christian** es cristiana.

**Christmas** ['krɪsməs] noun ■ la **Navidad**, la **Pascua** Chile, Peru: **what are you doing at Christmas?** ¿qué vas a hacer para la Navidad?
> **Merry Christmas!** ¡Feliz Navidad!
> **a Christmas card** una tarjeta de Navidad
> **Christmas Day** el día de Navidad
> **Christmas Eve** la Nochebuena

➤ a Christmas tree un árbol de Navidad

## CHRISTMAS

El 25 de diciembre en Estados Unidos la tradicional comida de Navidad incluye pavo al horno acompañado con relleno (**stuffing**) y verduras, junto con **cranberry sauce** o jalea de arándano. Durante la temporada navideña la gente manda **Christmas cards** (tarjetas de Navidad) a todos sus conocidos.

**chunk** [tʃʌŋk] noun ▪ el **pedazo**: a chunk of cheese un pedazo de queso.

**church** [tʃɜːtʃ] noun ▪ la **iglesia**: we go to church on Sundays los domingos vamos a la iglesia.

**cigar** [sɪ'gɑːʳ] noun ▪ el **cigarro**.

**cigarette** [ˌsɪgə'ret] noun ▪ el **cigarrillo**: she's smoking a cigarette está fumando un cigarrillo.

**cinnamon** ['sɪnəmən] noun ▪ la **canela**.

**circle** ['sɜːkl] noun ▪ el **círculo**.

**circulate** ['sɜːkjʊleɪt] verb ▪ **circular**: blood circulates around the body la sangre circula por el cuerpo.

**circumstances** ['sɜːkəmstənsɪz] plural noun ▪ las **circunstancias**: under the circumstances dadas las circunstancias.

**circus** ['sɜːkəs] noun ▪ el **circo**.

**citizen** ['sɪtɪzn] noun ▪ el **ciudadano**, la **ciudadana**: he's a US citizen es ciudadano estadounidense.

**city** ['sɪtɪ] (plural cities) noun ▪ la **ciudad**
➤ city hall el ayuntamiento.

**civil war** ['sɪvl'wɔːʳ] noun ▪ la **guerra civil**
➤ the American Civil War la Guerra de Secesión

## THE AMERICAN CIVIL WAR

En la guerra civil o de secesión, que tuvo lugar entre 1861 y 1865, se enfrentaron los estados del sur, con su economía agrícola basada en gran parte en la esclavitud, y los estados industriales del norte, donde se oponían a la esclavitud. Los estados del norte, con más soldados y armas, ganaron finalmente y se abolió la esclavitud.

**claim** [kleɪm] (verb & noun)
▪ verb
1. **afirmar**: he claims to be famous afirma que es famoso
2. **exigir**: he claimed compensation exigió una indemnización
3. **cobrar**: she claims unemployment benefits cobra subsidio de desempleo
▪ noun
la **demanda**: a wage claim una demanda de aumento salarial.

**clap** [klæp] verb ▪ **aplaudir**: everyone clapped todos aplaudieron.

**clapping** ['klæpɪŋ] uncountable noun ▪ los **aplausos**: the clapping was loud los aplausos eran fuertes.

**clarinet** [ˌklærə'net] noun ▪ el **clarinete**.

**clash** [klæʃ] verb
1. **enfrentarse**: the boss often clashed with his employees el jefe a menudo se enfrentaba con sus empleados
2. **desentonar**: those pink shoes clash with the yellow trousers esos zapatos rosados desentonan con los pantalones amarillos.

**class** [klɑːs] noun ▪ la **clase**: we traveled first class viajamos en primera clase; I have a Spanish class at 11 o'clock tengo una clase de español a las 11.

**classic** ['klæsɪk] (adjective & noun)
▪ adjective
**clásico**: it's a classic design es un diseño clásico
▪ noun
el **clásico**: this film is a classic esta película es un clásico.

**classical** ['klæsɪkl] *adjective* ■ **clásico:** classical music la música clásica.

**classroom** ['klɑːsrʊm] *noun* ■ **la clase, el salón de clases** *Mexico,* **la sala de clases** *Southern Cone.*

**claw** [klɔː] *noun*
1. **la garra:** cats have sharp claws los gatos tienen garras afiladas
2. **la pinza:** crab claws las pinzas del cangrejo.

**clean** [kliːn] *(adjective & verb)*
■ *adjective*
**limpio:** my hands are clean tengo las manos limpias
■ *verb*
**limpiar:** clean the table before you set the places limpia la mesa antes de poner los cubiertos

**clean up** *phrasal verb* ■ **limpiar:** don't forget to clean up before you go no te olvides de limpiar antes de irte.

**cleaner** ['kliːnər] *noun* ■ **el hombre de la limpieza, la mujer de la limpieza:** the cleaner comes twice a week la mujer de la limpieza viene dos veces a la semana
➤ she's a cleaner trabaja haciendo limpieza.

**cleaning** ['kliːnɪŋ] *uncountable noun* ■ **la limpieza:** she's doing the cleaning está haciendo la limpieza.

**clear** [klɪər] *(adjective & verb)*
■ *adjective*
1. **claro:** the instructions are clear las instrucciones son claras; it's clear he has made a mistake está claro que cometió un error
2. **transparente:** it's clear glass es vidrio transparente
3. **despejado:** the road is clear la calle está despejada
■ *verb*
1. **despejar:** they're clearing the road están despejando la calle; can you clear the table? ¿puedes despejar la mesa?
2. **disiparse:** the fog is beginning to clear la niebla está empezando a disiparse

**clear out** *phrasal verb* ■ **ordenar:** I'm going to clear out the cupboards voy a ordenar los armarios.

**clear up** *phrasal verb*
1. **resolver:** he cleared up the problem resolvió el problema
2. **despejar:** it's clearing up outside está despejando.

**clearly** ['klɪəlɪ] *adverb* ■ **claramente:** you've explained it clearly lo has explicado claramente
➤ he's clearly wrong está claro que está equivocado.

**clerk** [klɜːrk] *noun*
1. **el empleado,** la **empleada:** he's a clerk in the toy department es empleado en una tienda de juguetes
2. **el/la oficinista:** he's an office clerk es oficinista.

**clever** ['klevər] *adjective*
1. **inteligente:** Stephen's a clever boy Stephen es un chico inteligente
2. **hábil:** he's clever with his hands es hábil con las manos.

**click** [klɪk] *verb* ■ **hacer click:** click on the icon haz click en el icono.

**client** ['klaɪənt] *noun* ■ **el cliente,** la **clienta.**

**cliff** [klɪf] *noun* ■ **el acantilado.**

**climate** ['klaɪmɪt] *noun* ■ **el clima.**

**climb** [klaɪm] *verb*
1. **subir:** she climbed the stairs subió las escaleras
2. **escalar:** they climbed Everest escalaron el Everest
3. **treparse a:** the boy climbed the tree el chico se trepó al árbol

**climb down** *phrasal verb* ■ **bajarse de:** he climbed down the ladder se bajó de la escalera.

**climb over** *phrasal verb* ■ **trepar por:** he climbed over the fence trepó por la valla.

**climbing** ['klaɪmɪŋ] *uncountable noun* ■ **el montañismo:** climbing in the Rockies is challenging el montañismo en las Rocallosas supone un desafío

➤ **to go climbing** hacer montañismo: **they went climbing in the Alps** fuimos a hacer montañismo en los Alpes.

**cling** [klɪŋ] (past tense & past participle **clung**) verb ■ **agarrarse a: she was clinging to the rope** se agarraba a la soga.

**clip** [klɪp] noun

1. el **clip: I need a clip for these papers** necesito un clip para estos papeles
2. el **pasador,** el **broche** Mexico, Uruguay: **she's looking for a clip for her hair** está buscando un pasador para el pelo.

**clock** [klɒk] noun

1. el **reloj: the clock on my desk is fast** el reloj de mi escritorio está adelantado
➤ **an alarm clock** un despertador
➤ **around the clock** las veinticuatro horas: **this supermarket is open around the clock** este supermercado está abierto las veinticuatro horas.

**clockwise** ['klɒkwaɪz] adverb ■ **en el sentido de las manecillas del reloj.**

**close** (verb, adjective & adverb)

■ verb
[kləʊz]

1. **cerrar: he closed his eyes** cerró los ojos; **the shops close at six o'clock** las tiendas cierran a las seis
2. **cerrarse: the door closed behind him** la puerta se cerró detrás de él

■ adjective
[kləʊs]

1. **cerca: the school's close to the station** la escuela queda cerca de la estación
2. **unido: she's very close to her brother** es muy unida a su hermano
3. **reñido: it's a close contest** es una competencia muy reñida

■ adverb
[kləʊs] **de cerca: I looked at it close up** lo miré de cerca
➤ **close by** cerca: **they live close by** viven cerca.

**closed** [kləʊzd] adjective ■ **cerrado.**

**closely** ['kləʊslɪ] adverb ■ **detenidamente: he looked at it closely** lo miró detenidamente.

**closet** ['klɒzɪt] noun ■ el **armario,** el **clóset** (plural los **clósets**).

**cloth** [klɒθ] noun

1. el **trapo: she wiped the table with a cloth** limpió la mesa con un trapo
2. la **tela: I like this cloth** me gusta esta tela.

**clothes** [kləʊðz] plural noun ■ la **ropa.**

**clothespin** ['kləʊðzpɪn] noun ■ la **pinza.**

**cloud** [klaʊd] noun ■ la **nube.**

**cloudy** ['klaʊdɪ] adjective ■ **nublado: it's cloudy today** hoy está nublado.

**clown** [klaʊn] noun ■ el **payaso.**

**club** [klʌb] noun

1. el **club: she's a member of the chess club** es socia del club de ajedrez
2. la **discoteca: we went to a club last night** anoche fuimos a la discoteca
3. el **garrote: he hit him with a club** le pegó con un garrote
➤ **a golf club** un palo de golf.

**clue** [kluː] noun ■ la **pista: the police are looking for clues** la policía está buscando pistas
➤ **give me a clue!** dame una pista
➤ **I don't have a clue** no tengo ni la menor idea.

**clumsy** ['klʌmzɪ] adjective ■ **torpe.**

**clung** [klʌŋ] past tense & past participle ➤ cling.

**cm** (abbreviation of **centimeter**) noun ■ el **cm.**

**coach** [kəʊtʃ] noun ■ el **entrenador,** la **entrenadora: the team needs a new coach** el equipo necesita un nuevo entrenador.

**coast** [kəʊst] noun ■ la **costa: San Diego is on the coast** San Diego está en la costa.

**coat** [kəʊt] noun

1. el **abrigo: put your coat on** ponte el abrigo
2. la **capa: a coat of paint** una capa de pintura

➤ a coat hanger una percha: **your jacket's on the coat hanger** tu chaqueta está en la percha.

**cobweb** [ˈkɒbweb] *noun* ■ la **telaraña**.

**Coca-Cola®, Coke®** [kəʊkəˈkəʊlə, kəʊk] *noun* ■ la **Coca-Cola®**: **a can of Coke®** una lata de Coca-Cola®.

**cocoa** [ˈkəʊkəʊ] *noun* ■ la **cocoa**

➤ **a cup of cocoa** una taza de cocoa.

**coconut** [ˈkəʊkənʌt] *noun* ■ el **coco**.

**code** [kəʊd] *noun* ■ el **código**: **a secret code** un código secreto; **the message is in code** el mensaje está en código.

**coffee** [ˈkɒfɪ] *noun* ■ el **café**: **a cup of coffee** una taza de café

➤ **a coffee pot** una cafetera

➤ **a coffee shop** una cafetería.

**coffin** [ˈkɒfɪn] *noun* ■ el **ataúd**.

**coin** [kɔɪn] *noun* ■ la **moneda**.

**cold** [kəʊld] *(adjective & noun)*

■ *adjective*
**frío**

➤ **to be cold** tener frío: **I'm cold** tengo frío: **my hands are cold** tengo las manos frías

➤ **it's cold outside** afuera hace frío

■ *noun*

1. el **resfriado**: **he caught a cold** pescó un resfriado

2. el **frío**: **I don't like the cold** no me gusta el frío.

**collapse** [kəˈlæps] *verb* ■ **derrumbarse**: **the whole building collapsed** todo el edificio se derrumbó.

**collar** [ˈkɒlər] *noun*

1. el **cuello**: **his shirt collar is dirty** tiene el cuello de la camisa sucio

2. el **collar**: **the dog is wearing a collar** el perro tiene puesto un collar.

**collect** [kəˈlekt] *verb*

1. **recoger**: **she collected the children from school** recogió a los niños de la escuela; **they're collecting seashells** están recogiendo conchas de mar

2. **coleccionar**: **he collects stamps** colecciona sellos

➤ **a collect call** una llamada de cobro revertido, una llamada por cobrar *Chile, Mexico*: **I'd like to make a collect call** quisiera hacer una llamada de cobro revertido.

**collection** [kəˈlekʃn] *noun*

1. la **colección** *(plural* las **colecciones)*: **his stamp collection** su colección de estampillas

2. la **colecta**: **they took up a collection for the refugees** hicieron una colecta para los refugiados.

**college** [ˈkɒlɪdʒ] *noun* ■ la **universidad**: **she's in college** está en la universidad

➤ school.

**collide** [kəˈlaɪd] *verb* ■ **chocar**: **the cab collided with a truck** el taxi chocó con un camión.

**Colombia** [kəˈlɒmbɪə] *noun* ■ **Colombia** *(feminine)*.

**Colombian** [kəˈlɒmbɪən] *(adjective & noun)*

■ *adjective*

> Remember not to use a capital letter for the adjective in Spanish:

**colombiano**: **I like Colombian coffee** me gusta el café colombiano

■ *noun*

> In Spanish, a capital letter is not used for the inhabitants of a country or region:

el **colombiano**, la **colombiana**: **many Colombians live in the capital** muchos colombianos viven en la capital.

**colon** [ˈkəʊlən] *noun* ■ los **dos puntos**: **you use a colon to introduce a list** para introducir una lista, hay que usar dos puntos.

**colonel** [ˈkɜːnl] *noun* ■ el/la **coronel**.

**color** [ˈkʌlər] *noun* ■ el **color**: **what color is it?** ¿de qué color es?

➤ **a color photo** una foto en colores

➤ **a color television** una televisión en colores.

**colorful** ['kʌləfʊl] *adjective* ■ **de colores muy vivos: a very colorful sweater** un suéter de colores muy vivo.

**column** ['kɒləm] *noun* ■ **la columna: the columns of a Greek temple** las columnas de un templo griego; **the sports column in the newspaper** la columna de deportes del diario.

**comb** [kəʊm] *(noun & verb)*
■ *noun*
**el peine**
■ *verb*
**peinarse: he combed his hair** se peinó.

**come** [kʌm] *(past tense* came, *past participle* come) *verb*
1. **venir: he's coming to the game with us** viene al partido con nosotros; **the bus is coming** viene el autobús
2.

> To say in Spanish what place a person comes from, use **ser de** followed by the name of the place:

**ser de: where do you come from?** ¿de dónde eres?; **I come from Atlanta** soy de Atlanta
➤ **come on!** ¡vamos!, ¡ándale! *Mexico*
➤ **to come true** hacerse realidad: **her dream came true** su sueño se hizo realidad
➤ **I'm coming** ya voy

**come back** *phrasal verb* ■ **volver: I'll come back later** voy a volver más tarde.

**come down** *phrasal verb* ■ **bajar: prices have come down** bajaron los precios
➤ **come down from there!** ¡bájate de ahí!

**come in** *phrasal verb* ■ **entrar: come in!** ¡entre!; **she came in through the kitchen window** entró por la ventana de la cocina.

**come off** *phrasal verb* ■ **caerse: one of my buttons has come off** se me cayó un botón.

**come out** *phrasal verb* ■ **salir: come out with your hands up!** ¡salga con las manos en alto!; **their new album is coming out in May** su nuevo álbum va a salir en

mayo; **this stain won't come out** esta mancha no va a salir.

**come over** *phrasal verb* ■ **venir: come over this evening** ven esta noche.

**come up** *phrasal verb*
1. **acercarse: come up here!** ¡acércate!
2. **salir: the sun has come up** salió el sol
3. **surgir: the problem came up in class** el problema surgió en la clase.

**come up to** *phrasal verb*
1. **llegar a: the mud came up to our knees** el barro le llegaba a las rodillas
2. **acercarse: he came up to me and shook my hand** se me acercó y me dio la mano.

**comedian** [kə'miːdjən] *noun* ■ **el/la humorista**.

**comedy** ['kɒmədɪ] *(plural* comedies) *noun* ■ **la comedia**.

**comfort** ['kʌmfət] *(noun & verb)*
■ *noun*
1. **la comodidad: he likes comfort** le gusta la comodidad
2. **el consuelo: you've been a great comfort to me** has sido un gran consuelo para mí
■ *verb*
**consolar: the policeman comforted the crying girl** el policía consoló a la niña que lloraba.

**comfortable** ['kʌmftəbl] *adjective* ■ **cómodo: it's a very comfortable bed** es una cama muy cómoda; **are you comfortable?** ¿estás cómodo?; **make yourself comfortable** ponte cómodo.

**comic book** ['kɒmɪkbʊk] *noun* ■ **el cómic** *(plural* los **cómics**).

**comic strip** ['kɒmɪkstrɪp] *noun* ■ **la tira cómica**.

**comma** ['kɒmə] *noun* ■ **la coma**.

**command** [kə'maːnd] *(noun & verb)*
■ *noun*
**la orden** *(plural* las **órdenes**): **the captain gave a command** el capitán dio una orden

■ *verb*
**ordenar:** the king commanded him to leave el rey le ordenó marcharse.

**comment** [ˈkɒment] *(noun & verb)*

■ *noun*
el **comentario:** he made some comments on my work hizo algunos comentarios sobre mi trabajo
■ *verb*
**hacer comentarios:** she commented on the news hizo comentarios sobre la noticia.

**commercial** [kəˈmɜːʃl]  *(adjective & noun)*

■ *adjective*
**comercial:** the film is a commercial success la película es un éxito comercial
■ *noun*
el **anuncio,** el **aviso:** he doesn't like TV commercials no le gustan los anuncios de la tele.

**commit** [kəˈmɪt] *verb* ■ **cometer:** he has committed many crimes ha cometido muchos crímenes
➤ to commit suicide suicidarse.

**committee** [kəˈmɪtɪ] *noun* ■ el **comité.**

**common** [ˈkɒmən] *adjective* ■ **común** *(plural* **comunes***):* it's a common expression es una expresión común; the English and the Americans share a common language los ingleses y los americanos tienen un idioma común
➤ in common en común: we have a lot in common tenemos mucho en común
➤ common sense el sentido común: she has a lot of common sense tiene mucho sentido común.

**communicate** [kəˈmjuːnɪkeɪt]  *verb* ■ **comunicarse:** we communicate by e-mail nos comunicamos por correo electrónico.

**communication** [kə,mjuːnɪˈkeɪʃn] *noun* ■ la **comunicación** *(plural* las **comunicaciones***).*

**community** [kəˈmjuːnətɪ]  *(plural* communities*) noun* ■ la **comunidad:** there is a large Hispanic community in

Texas hay una gran comunidad hispana en Texas.

**compact disc** [,kɒmpæktˈdɪsk] *noun* ■ el **disco compacto.**

**companion** [kəmˈpænjən] *noun* ■ el **acompañante,** la **acompañante.**

**company** [ˈkʌmpənɪ] *(plural* companies*) noun* ■ la **compañía:** she works for a Mexican company trabaja para una compañía mejicana
➤ an insurance company una compañía de seguros
➤ to keep somebody company hacerle compañía a alguien: her dog keeps her company su perro le hace compañía.

**compare** [kəmˈpeər] *verb* ■ **comparar**
➤ you can't compare them, they're too different no puedes compararlos, son demasiado diferentes
➤ compared with or compared to comparado con: she's very smart compared to her brother comparada con su hermano, ella es muy inteligente.

**comparison** [kəmˈpærɪsn] *noun* ■ la **comparación** *(plural* las **comparaciones***):* Spain is small in comparison with Australia España es pequeña en comparación con Australia.

**compass** [ˈkʌmpəs] *noun* ■ la **brújula.**

**compete** [kəmˈpiːt] *verb* ■ **competir:** there are ten runners competing in the race hay diez corredores compitiendo en la carrera
➤ to compete against somebody competir contra alguien: she will compete against her brother va a competir contra su hermano
➤ to compete for something competir por algo: they're competing for the gold medal están compitiendo por la medalla de oro.

**competition** [,kɒmpɪˈtɪʃn] *noun*
1. el **concurso:** she entered a beauty competition se presentó en un concurso de belleza
2. la **competencia:** a sporting competition una competencia deportiva.

**competitor** [kəm'petɪtər] *noun* ■ el **competidor**, la **competidora**.

**complain** [kəm'pleɪn] *verb*
1. **quejarse**: he complained about the cold se quejó del frío
2. **reclamar**: if you don't like it you can complain si no te gusta puedes reclamar; I'll complain to the manager voy a reclamarle al gerente.

**complaint** [kəm'pleɪnt] *noun* ■ la **queja**: they received a lot of complaints recibieron muchas quejas
➤ **to make a complaint** quejarse: she made a complaint se quejó.

**complete** [kəm'pliːt] *(adjective & verb)*
■ *adjective*
1. **completo**: the complete works of Shakespeare las obras completas de Shakespeare
2. **total**: there's been a complete change ha habido un cambio total
3. **terminado**: work on the building is complete el trabajo en el edificio está terminado
➤ **I feel like a complete idiot** me siento como un verdadero idiota
■ *verb*
1. **completar**: can you complete this sentence? ¿puedes completar esta oración?
2. **terminar**: I've completed my work terminé mi trabajo.

**completely** [kəm'pliːtlɪ] *adverb* ■ **completamente**.

**complexion** [kəm'plekʃn] *noun* ■ el **cutis**: she has a very good complexion tiene muy buen cutis
➤ **he has a very light complexion** tiene la tez muy clara.

**complicated** ['kɒmplɪkeɪtɪd] *adjective* ■ **complicado**.

**compliment** ['kɒmplɪmənt] *noun* ■ el **cumplido**: she paid me a compliment me hizo un cumplido.

**composer** [kəm'pəʊzər] *noun* ■ el **compositor**, la **compositora**: Gershwin is a famous American composer Gershwin es un famoso compositor estadounidense.

**compulsory** [kəm'pʌlsərɪ] *adjective* ■ **obligatorio**.

**computer** [kəm'pjuːtər] *noun* ■ la **computadora**
➤ **a laptop computer** una computadora portátil
➤ **computer games** los juegos de computadora
➤ **computer science** la informática.

**computing** [kəm'pjuːtɪŋ] *uncountable noun* ■ la **computación**, la **informática**: he works in computing trabaja en computación.

**concentrate** ['kɒnsəntreɪt] *verb* ■ **concentrarse**: I can't concentrate no me puedo concentrar.

**concentration** [,kɒnsən'treɪʃn] *noun* ■ la **concentración**: it requires a lot of concentration requiere mucha concentración.

**concern** [kən'sɜːn] *verb* ■ **concernir**: this concerns us all esto nos concierne a todos
➤ **as far as I'm concerned** en lo que a mí respecta
➤ **to be concerned** estar preocupado: I'm concerned about him estoy preocupado por él.

**concert** ['kɒnsət] *noun* ■ el **concierto**.

**concrete** ['kɒŋkriːt] *noun* ■ el **hormigón**, el **concreto**.

**condition** [kən'dɪʃn] *noun*
1. la **condición** *(plural* las **condiciones)**: he will come with us, but on one condition vendrá con nosotros, pero con una condición
2. el **estado**: it's in good condition está en buen estado.

**conditioner** [kən'dɪʃnər] *noun* ■ el **acondicionador**.

**condom** ['kɒndəm] *noun* ■ el **condón** *(plural* los **condones)**.

**conductor** [kən'dʌktər] *noun*
1. el **director**, la **directora**: an orchestra conductor un director de orquesta

**2.** el **cobrador,** la **cobradora:** a conductor of a train un cobrador de un tren

 La palabra inglesa **conductor** es un falso amigo, no significa "conductor".

**cone** [kəʊn] *noun* ■ *shape* el **cono:** an ice-cream cone un cucurucho, un barquillo *Chile, Mexico.*

**confess** [kən'fes] *verb* ■ **confesar:** he confessed to the murder confesó haber cometido el asesinato.

**confidence** ['kɒnfɪdəns] *noun* ■ la **confianza:** he has no confidence no tiene confianza; I have confidence in you tengo confianza en ti.

**confident** ['kɒnfɪdənt] *adjective*
➤ I'm confident you'll win confío en que vas a ganar
➤ she's very confident es muy segura de sí misma.

**confirm** [kən'fɜːm] *verb* ■ **confirmar:** you must confirm your flight debe confirmar su vuelo.

**confuse** [kən'fjuːz] *verb* ■ **confundir:** don't confuse me! ¡no me confundas!; he confused me with my brother me confundió con mi hermano.

**confused** [kən'fjuːzd] *adjective* ■ **confundido:** I'm confused, can you say all that again? estoy confundido, ¿puedes decir todo eso de nuevo?

**confusing** [kən'fjuːzɪŋ] *adjective* ■ **poco claro:** it's very confusing es muy poco claro.

**confusion** [kən'fjuːʒn] *noun* ■ la **confusión.**

**congratulate** [kən'grætʃʊleɪt] *verb* ■ **felicitar:** they congratulated me on winning the prize me felicitaron por ganar el premio.

**congratulations** [kən,grætʃʊ'leɪʃənz] *plural noun* ■ las **felicitaciones:** congratu-

lations on your success! ¡felicitaciones por tu éxito!

**Congress** ['kɒŋgres] *noun* ■ el **Congreso.**

**connect** [kə'nekt] *verb*
**1.** **conectar:** the bridge connects the two parts of the town el puente conecta las dos partes del pueblo
**2.** **conectarse:** I can't connect to the Internet no puedo conectarme a internet.

**connection** [kə'nekʃn] *noun*
**1.** la **conexión** *(plural* las **conexiones):** I don't want to miss my connection no quiero perder mi conexión; an Internet connection una conexión a internet
**2.** la **relación** *(plural* las **relaciones):** there's no connection between the two events no hay ninguna relación entre ambos acontecimientos.

**conscience** ['kɒnʃəns] *noun* ■ la **conciencia:** he has a guilty conscience le remuerde la conciencia.

**conscious** ['kɒnʃəs] *adjective* ■ **consciente:** I wasn't conscious of what I was doing no era consciente de lo que estaba haciendo, no estaba consciente de lo que estaba haciendo *Chile, Mexico.*

**consciousness** ['kɒnʃəsnɪs] *noun* ■ el **conocimiento:** he lost consciousness perdió el conocimiento.

**consider** [kən'sɪdər] *verb*
**1.** **considerar:** I consider him my friend lo considero mi amigo
**2.** **tener en cuenta:** you must consider the risks debes tener en cuenta los riesgos
➤ she's considering leaving her job está pensando dejar su trabajo.

**considerate** [kən'sɪdərət] *adjective* ■ **considerado.**

**consideration** [kən,sɪdə'reɪʃn] *noun* ■ la **consideración** *(plural* las **consideraciones):** he has no consideration for others no tiene ninguna consideración por los demás

➤ to take something into consideration tener algo en cuenta: I'll take that into consideration lo tendré en cuenta.

**consist** [kən'sɪst] *verb* ■ **consistir**
➤ to consist of consistir en: her baggage consisted of a bag and a guitar su equipaje consistía en una bolsa y una guitarra.

**consonant** ['kɒnsənənt] *noun* ■ la **consonante**.

**constant** ['kɒnstənt] *adjective* ■ **constante**.

**constantly** ['kɒnstəntlɪ] *adverb* ■ **constantemente**.

**constipated** ['kɒnstɪpeɪtɪd] *adjective* ■ **estreñido**: he's constipated está estreñido.

**constitution** [ˌkɒnstɪ'tju:ʃn] *noun* ■ la **constitución** *(plural* las **constituciones***)*: the United States Constitution la Constitución de los Estados Unidos.

**consumer** [kən'sju:məʳ] *noun* ■ el **consumidor**, la **consumidora**.

**contact** ['kɒntækt] *(noun & verb)*
■ *noun*
el **contacto**: we've lost contact with her perdimos contacto con ella
➤ contact lenses lentes de contacto
■ *verb*
**contactar**: I couldn't contact him no pude contactarme con él.

**contain** [kən'teɪn] *verb* ■ **contener**: milk contains calcium la leche contiene calcio.

**container** [kən'teɪnəʳ] *noun* ■ el **recipiente**: I need a bigger container necesito un recipiente más grande.

**contents** ['kɒntents] *plural noun*
1. el **contenido**: he emptied the contents of the box onto the floor vació el contenido de la caja en el suelo
2. el **índice**: the contents are at the front of the book el índice está en la parte de adelante del libro.

**contest** ['kɒntest] *noun* ■ el **concurso**: a beauty contest un concurso de belleza.

**continent** ['kɒntɪnənt] *noun* ■ el **continente**.

**continue** [kən'tɪnju:] *verb* ■ **continuar**: they continued playing continuaron jugando.

**contraceptive** [ˌkɒntrə'septɪv] *noun* ■ el **anticonceptivo**.

**contract** ['kɒntrækt] *noun* ■ el **contrato**.

**contrary** ['kɒntrərɪ] *noun*
➤ on the contrary al contrario.

**contrast** ['kɒntra:st] *noun* ■ el **contraste**.

**contribute** [kən'trɪbju:t] *verb*
1. **contribuir**: he contributed to the success of the project contribuyó al éxito del proyecto
2. **contribuir con**: he contributed a lot of money contribuyó con mucho dinero.

**control** [kən'trəul] *(noun & verb)*
■ *noun*
el **control**: she lost control of her car or her car went out of control perdió el control del coche
➤ we're in control of the situation controlamos la situación
➤ everything's under control todo está bajo control
■ *verb*
**controlar**: who controls the company? ¿quién controla la compañía?; the police can't control the crowd la policía es incapaz de controlar a la muchadumbre
➤ to control oneself controlarse: control yourself! ¡contrólate!

**convenient** [kən'vi:njənt] *adjective*
■ **conveniente**: it's a convenient place to meet es un lugar conveniente para encontrarse
➤ the hotel is convenient to the shops el hotel esta bien ubicado respecto a las tiendas
➤ is Monday convenient for you? ¿te viene bien el lunes?

**conversation** [ˌkɒnvəˈseɪʃn] *noun*
■ la **conversación** *(plural* las **conversaciones***)*.

**convince** [kənˈvɪns] *verb* ■ **convencer: he convinced me to wait** me convenció para que esperáramos.

**cook** [kʊk] *(noun & verb)*
■ *noun*
el **cocinero**, la **cocinera: he's a good cook** es buen cocinero
■ *verb*
1. **cocinar: can you cook?** ¿sabes cocinar?
2. **preparar: I'm cooking breakfast** estoy preparando el desayuno
3. **cocer: cook the potatoes for fifteen minutes** cueza las papas durante quince minutos
➤ **the vegetables are cooked** las verduras están cocidas.

**cookbook** [ˈkʊkˌbʊk] *noun* ■ el **libro de cocina**.

**cookie** [ˈkʊkɪ] *noun* ■ la **galleta**.

**cooking** [ˈkʊkɪŋ] *uncountable noun* ■ la **cocina: I like Mexican cooking** me gusta la cocina mejicana
➤ **I do the cooking** yo cocino.

**cool** [kuːl] *(adjective & verb)*
■ *adjective*
1. **fresco: the water's cool** el agua está fresca; **it's cool tonight** hace fresco esta noche
2. *informal* **buena onda: my Spanish teacher is really cool** mi profesora de español es muy buena onda
➤ **what a cool computer!** ¡qué computadora más genial!
➤ **he stayed cool** no perdió la calma
■ *verb*
**enfriar: leave it to cool** déjelo enfriar

**cool down** *phrasal verb*
1. **enfriarse: the water has cooled down** el agua se enfrió
2. **refrescar: this drink will cool you down** esta bebida te refrescará.

**cope** [kəʊp] *verb* ■ **arreglárselas: I can cope on my own** puedo arreglármelas solo

➤ **I can't cope with so much work** no puedo con tanto trabajo
➤ **he has to cope with lots of problems** tiene que hacer frente a muchos problemas.

**copied** [ˈkɒpɪd] *past tense & past participle* ➤ **copy**.

**copper** [ˈkɒpər] *noun* ■ el **cobre**.

**copy** [ˈkɒpɪ] *(noun & verb)*
■ *noun*
*(plural* **copies***)*
1. la **copia: make a copy of the disk** haz una copia del disco
2. el **ejemplar: they've sold a thousand copies of the book** han vendido mil ejemplares del libro
■ *verb*
**copiar: he copied the poem from the book** copió el poema del libro
➤ **to copy and paste** copiar y pegar: **he copied and pasted the text** copió y pegó el texto.

**corn** [kɔːn] *uncountable noun* ■ el **maíz**
➤ **corn on the cob** la mazorca de maíz, el elote *Mexico*.

**corner** [ˈkɔːnər] *noun*
1. el **rincón** *(plural* los **rincones***)*: **Ron is sitting in a corner** Ron está sentado en un rincón
2. la **esquina: there is a store on the corner** hay una tienda en la esquina
➤ **around the corner** a la vuelta de la esquina: **the store's just around the corner** la tienda está justo a la vuelta de la esquina
➤ **the car took the corner too quickly** el coche tomó la curva muy rápido.

**corpse** [kɔːps] *noun* ■ el **cadáver**.

**correct** [kəˈrekt] *(adjective & verb)*
■ *adjective*
**correcto: that's the correct answer** esa es la respuesta correcta; **you've made the correct decision** tomaste la decisión correcta
➤ **you're completely correct** tienes toda la razón
■ *verb*
**corregir: I corrected the mistake** corregí el error.

**correction** [kə'rekʃn] *noun* ■ la **corrección** *(plural* las **correcciones***)*.

**cosmetics** [kɒz'metɪks] *plural noun* ■ los **cosméticos**.

**cost** [kɒst] *(past tense & past participle* cost*) (verb & noun)*
■ *verb*
**costar: how much does it cost?** ¿cuánto cuesta?; **it costs twenty dollars** cuesta veinte dólares
■ *noun*
el **costo: the cost of living** el costo de vida.

**Costa Rica** ['kɒstəri:kə] *noun* ■ **Costa Rica** *(feminine)*.

**Costa Rican** ['kɒstə'ri:kən] *(adjective & noun)*
■ *adjective*

Remember not to use a capital letter for the adjective in Spanish:

**costarricense: the Costa Rican landscape is beautiful** el paisaje costarricense es precioso
■ *noun*

In Spanish, a capital letter is not used for the inhabitants of a country or region:

el/la **costarricense: the Costa Ricans are relatively prosperous** los costarricenses son relativamente prósperos.

**costume** ['kɒstju:m] *noun* ■ el **disfraz** *(plural* los **disfraces***)*.

**cottage** ['kɒtɪdʒ] *noun* ■ casa pequeña, generalmente en el campo .

**cotton** ['kɒtn] *uncountable noun* ■ el **algodón**
➤ **cotton candy** algodón de azúcar.

**couch** [kaʊtʃ] *noun* ■ el **sofá**.

**cough** [kɒf] *(noun & verb)*
■ *noun*
la **tos**
➤ **to have a cough** tener tos: **I have a cough** tengo tos

■ *verb*
**toser: she's coughing because of the smoke** tose por el humo.

**could** [kʊd] *verb (negative* couldn't*)*
**1. poder: they couldn't stay for dinner** no pudieron quedarse a cenar

When you make a polite request, an offer or a suggestion, "could" is translated by the Spanish verb **poder** in the conditional tense:

**could I speak to Scott please?** ¿podría hablar con Scott, por favor?; **you could wait for him** podría esperarlo; **don't touch it, it could be dangerous** no lo toque, podría ser peligroso

When "could" is used with a verb of perception (see, hear, feel, understand) it is not translated at all:

**I couldn't see anything** no vi nada; **she couldn't hear me** no me oyó; **we could understand what they were saying** entendimos lo que estaban diciendo
**2.** *When "could" means "knew how to"* **saber: she couldn't swim** no sabía nadar; **they couldn't speak English** no sabían hablar inglés.

**couldn't** ['kʊdnt] ➤ could not.

**could've** ['kʊdəv] ➤ could have.

**council** ['kaʊnsl] *noun* ■ el **consejo**.

**count** [kaʊnt] *verb* ■ **contar: he counted sheep to get to sleep** contó ovejas para quedarse dormido
➤ **to count on somebody** contar con alguien: **you can count on me** puedes contar conmigo.

**counter** ['kaʊntər] *noun*
**1.** el **mostrador: the bartender is behind the counter** el barman está detrás del mostrador
**2.** la **ficha: each player has ten counters** cada jugador tiene diez fichas.

**counterclockwise** [,kaʊntə'klɒkwaɪz] *adverb* ■ **en sentido contrario a las agujas del reloj**.

**country** ['kʌntrɪ] *(plural* countries) *noun*

1. el **país:** it's interesting to visit foreign countries es interesante visitar países extranjeros
2. el **campo:** we live in the country vivimos en el campo.

**county** ['kaʊntɪ] *(plural* counties) *noun*
■ el **condado**.

**couple** ['kʌpl] *noun* ■ la **pareja:** a young couple una pareja joven
➤ a couple of un par de: I waited a couple of hours esperé un par de horas.

**courage** ['kʌrɪdʒ] *noun* ■ el **valor:** he got up the courage to go in se armó de valor para entrar.

**course** [kɔːs] *noun*

1. el **curso:** he's taking a Spanish course está haciendo un curso de español
2. el **plato:** the main course of the meal el plato principal de la comida; a five-course meal una comida de cinco platos
3. el **campo**, la **cancha** *Southern Cone:* a golf course un campo de golf
➤ of course por supuesto
➤ of course not por supuesto que no.

**court** [kɔːt] *noun*

1. el **tribunal:** he appeared in court compareció ante el tribunal
2. la **cancha:** a tennis court una cancha de tenis.

**courthouse** ['kɔːthaʊs] *noun* ■ el **juzgado**.

**courtyard** ['kɔːtjaːd] *noun* ■ el **patio**.

**cousin** ['kʌzn] *noun* ■ el **primo**, la **prima**.

**cover** ['kʌvər] *(noun & verb)*

■ *noun*

1. la **tapa:** put the cover on the saucepan ponle la tapa a la olla; there's a dragon on the cover of the book hay un dragón en la tapa del libro
2. la **cobija**, la **frazada:** she put two covers on the bed puso dos cobijas en la cama

➤ to take cover ponerse a cubierto: they're coming, let's take cover ya vienen, pongámonos a cubierto
■ *verb*
**cubrir:** she covered the chair with a sheet cubrió la silla con una sábana
➤ Tom was covered with bruises Tom estaba lleno de moretones.

**cow** [kaʊ] *noun* ■ la **vaca**.

**coward** ['kaʊəd] *noun* ■ el/la **cobarde**.

**cowboy** ['kaʊbɔɪ] *noun* ■ el **vaquero**.

**cozy** ['kəʊzɪ] *adjective* ■ **acogedor:** a cozy bedroom un dormitorio acogedor
➤ it's cozy in here qué bien se está aquí adentro.

**crab** [kræb] *noun* ■ el **cangrejo**, la **jaiba**.

**crack** [kræk] *(noun & verb)*

■ *noun*

1. la **rajadura:** there's a crack in the glass hay una rajadura en el vaso
2. la **grieta:** there are cracks in the wall hay grietas en la pared
■ *verb*
1. **rajar:** I've cracked the glass rajé el vaso
2. **romper:** you have to crack the egg first tienes que romper el huevo primero
3. **rajarse:** the mirror cracked el espejo se rajó
➤ to crack a joke contar un chiste: Lynn cracked a joke Lynn contó un chiste.

**cracked** [krækt] *adjective* ■ **rajado:** the glass is cracked but not broken el vaso está rajado pero no está quebrado.

**cracker** ['krækər] *noun* ■ la **galleta salada:** he's eating a cracker él está comiendo una galleta salada.

**craftsman** ['kraːftsmən] *(plural* craftsmen ['kraːftsmən]) *noun* ■ el **artesano**.

**cranberry** ['krænbərɪ] *(plural* cranberries) *adjective* ■ el **arándano rojo:** cranberry sauce salsa de arándano rojo
➤ Thanksgiving.

**crane** [kreɪn] *noun* ■ la **grúa**: there's a crane on the building site hay una grúa en la obra.

**crash** [kræʃ] *(noun & verb)*
■ *noun*
1. el **accidente**: he was injured in a car crash resultó herido en un accidente automovilístico
2. el **estruendo**: I heard a loud crash escuché un gran estruendo
■ *verb*
1. **chocar**: I'm driving carefully, I don't want to crash estoy manejando con cuidado, no quiero chocar
2. **estrellarse**: the plane crashed el avión se estrelló
➤ to crash into something estrellarse contra algo: they crashed into a wall se estrellaron contra la pared.

**crawl** [krɔ:l] *(verb & noun)*
■ *verb*
**gatear**: the baby is crawling el bebé está gateando
■ *noun*
el **crol**: he's doing the crawl está nadando crol, está nadando de crol *Mexico*.

**crayon** ['kreɪɒn] *noun* ■ la **crayola**.

**crazy** ['kreɪzɪ] *adjective* ■ *informal* **loco**: you're completely crazy! ¡estás completamente loco!; that noise is driving me crazy ese ruido me está volviendo loco.

**cream** [kri:m] *noun* ■ la **crema**: strawberries and cream fresas con crema.

**crease** [kri:s] *(noun & verb)*
■ *noun*
la **arruga**: there's a crease in the paper hay una arruga en el papel
■ *verb*
**arrugar**: try not to crease my dress trata de no arrugarme el vestido.

**create** [krɪ'eɪt] *verb* ■ **crear**: he created a new company creó una nueva compañía.

**creature** ['kri:tʃəʳ] *noun* ■ el **ser**: creatures from outer space seres del espacio exterior.

**credit** ['kredɪt] *noun* ■ el **crédito**
➤ a credit card una tarjeta de crédito.

**creep** [kri:p] *(past tense & past participle crept)* *verb* ■ **entrar sigilosamente**: he crept into the room entró sigilosamente al cuarto.

**creeps** [kri:ps] *plural noun*
➤ to give somebody the creeps darle escalofríos a alguien: the graveyard gives me the creeps el cementerio me da escalofríos.

**crept** [krept] *past tense & past participle*
➤ creep.

**crew** [kru:] *noun*
1. la **tripulación** *(plural* las **tripulaciones***)*: the ship's crew la tripulación del barco
2. el **equipo**: a film crew el equipo de rodaje.

**cricket** ['krɪkɪt] *noun* ■ el **grillo**: I can hear the crickets puedo oír a los grillos.

**cried** [kraɪd] *past tense & past participle*
➤ cry.

**crime** [kraɪm] *noun* ■ el **delito**: theft is a crime el robo es un delito.

**criminal** ['krɪmɪnl] *noun* ■ el/la **delincuente**
➤ to have a criminal record tener antecedentes penales.

**crisis** ['kraɪsɪs] *(plural* crises ['kraɪsɪ:z])* *noun* ■ la **crisis** *(plural* las **crisis***)*.

**critic** ['krɪtɪk] *noun* ■ el **crítico**, la **crítica**: he's a movie critic es crítico de cine.

**criticism** ['krɪtɪsɪzm] *noun* ■ la **crítica**.

**criticize** ['krɪtɪsaɪz] *verb* ■ **criticar**: she's always criticizing me siempre me está criticando.

**crocodile** ['krɒkədaɪl] *noun* ■ el **cocodrilo**.

**crook** [krʊk] *noun* ■ el/la **sinvergüenza**.

**crooked** ['krʊkɪd] *adjective* ■ **torcido, chueco**: the picture's crooked el cuadro está torcido; **he has a crooked nose** tiene la nariz torcida.

**crop** [krɒp] *noun*

1. el **cultivo**: they grow many different crops in this region producen una gran variedad de cultivos en esta región
2. la **cosecha**: we had a good crop of cherries this year tuvimos una buena cosecha de cerezas este año.

**cross** [krɒs] *(adjective, noun & verb)*

■ *adjective*
**enojado**: he's very cross with you está muy enojado contigo

■ *noun*
la **cruz**: there is a cross by the altar hay una cruz junto al altar

■ *verb*
**cruzar**: he crossed the road cruzó la calle; she crossed her legs cruzó las piernas

➤ **let's keep our fingers crossed** crucemos los dedos

**cross off** *phrasal verb* ■ **tachar**: he crossed my name off the list tachó mi nombre de la lista.

**cross out** *phrasal verb* ■ **tachar**: she crossed out the word tachó la palabra.

**cross over** *phrasal verb* ■ **cruzar**: I crossed over the road crucé la calle.

**crossroads** ['krɒsrəʊdz] *(plural* crossroads) *noun* ■ el **cruce**, el **crucero** *Mexico*: turn left at the crossroads doble a la izquierda en el cruce.

**crosswalk** ['krɒswɔːk] *noun* ■ el **paso de peatones**.

**crossword puzzle** ['krɒswɜːd'pʌzl] *noun* ■ el **crucigrama**: he's doing a crossword puzzle está haciendo un crucigrama.

**crow** [krəʊ] *noun* ■ el **cuervo**.

**crowd** [kraʊd] *noun* ■ la **muchedumbre**: there's a huge crowd hay una muchedumbre enorme.

**crowded** ['kraʊdɪd] *adjective* ■ **abarrotado de gente**: the train is crowded el tren está abarrotado de gente.

**crown** [kraʊn] *noun* ■ la **corona**.

**cruel** [krʊəl] *adjective* ■ **cruel**.

**cruise** [kruːz] *noun* ■ el **crucero**: she's going on a Caribbean cruise va a hacer un crucero por el Caribe.

**crumb** [krʌm] *noun* ■ la **miga**.

**crush** [krʌʃ] *(verb & noun)*

■ *verb*
**aplastar**: he crushed a fly aplastó una mosca

■ *noun*
*informal*

➤ **to have a crush on somebody** estar chiflado por alguien: **he's got a crush on my sister** está chiflado por mi hermana.

**cry** [kraɪ] *(past tense & past participle* cried*) verb*

1. **llorar**: don't cry! ¡no llores!
2. **gritar**: "help!" she cried "¡socorro!", gritó

**cry out** *phrasal verb* ■ **gritar**: he cried out in pain gritaba de dolor.

**Cuba** [kuba] *noun* ■ **Cuba** *(feminine)*.

**Cuban** [kuban] *(adjective & noun)*

■ *adjective*

> Remember not to use a capital letter for the adjective in Spanish:

**cubano**: I enjoy Cuban music me gusta la música cubana

■ *noun*

> In Spanish, a capital letter is not used for the inhabitants of a country or region:

el **cubano**, la **cubana**: there are many Cubans in Miami hay muchos cubanos en Miami.

**cube** [kjuːb] *noun* ■ el **cubo**: a dice is a cube un dado es un cubo.

**cuckoo** ['kʊkuː] *noun* ■ el **cucú**.

**cucumber** ['kjuːkʌmbəʳ] *noun* ■ el **pepino**.

**culprit** ['kʌlprɪt] *noun* ▪ el/la **culpable**.

**culture** ['kʌltʃəʳ] *noun* ▪ la **cultura**.

**cup** [kʌp] *noun*
1. la **taza**: she's drinking a cup of coffee está tomando una taza de café
2. la **copa**: Brazil won the cup last year Brasil ganó la copa el año pasado.

**curb** [kɜːb] *noun* ▪ el **bordillo de la acera**, el **borde de la banqueta** *Mexico*, el **cordón de la vereda** *River Plate*, la **cuneta** *Chile*, el **sardinel** *Colombia*.

**cure** [kjʊəʳ] *(noun & verb)*
▪ *noun*
el **remedio**: it's a cure for the flu es un remedio para la gripe
▪ *verb*
**curar**: the doctor cured him el doctor lo curó.

**curious** ['kjʊərɪəs] *adjective* ▪ **curioso**: he's curious to know what happened está curioso por saber qué pasó
➤ to be curious about something tener curiosidad por algo: he's very curious about what's in the box tiene mucha curiosidad por lo que hay en la caja.

**curly** ['kɜːlɪ] *adjective* ▪ **rizado, chino** *Mexico*, **crespo** *Southern Cone*: she has long curly hair tiene el pelo largo y rizado.

**currency** ['kʌrənsɪ] *(plural* currencies) *noun* ▪ la **moneda**: the dollar is the currency of the United States el dólar es la moneda de Estados Unidos.

**current** ['kʌrənt] *(adjective & noun)*
▪ *adjective*
**actual**: the current fashion la moda actual
➤ current affairs asuntos de actualidad: he is interested in current affairs está interesado en asuntos de actualidad
▪ *noun*
la **corriente**: an electric current una corriente eléctrica; he was swimming against the current estaba nadando contra la corriente.

**cursor** ['kɜːsəʳ] *noun* ▪ el **cursor**: move the cursor down mueve el cursor hacia abajo.

**curtain** ['kɜːtn] *noun* ▪ la **cortina**: draw the curtains, it's getting dark corre las cortinas, está oscureciendo.

**curve** [kɜːv] *noun* ▪ la **curva**: there's a curve in the river el río hace una curva.

**cushion** ['kʊʃn] *noun* ▪ el **cojín** *(plural* los cojines).

**custom** ['kʌstəm] *noun* ▪ la **costumbre**: it's an old Mexican custom es una vieja costumbre mejicana.

**customer** ['kʌstəməʳ] *noun* ▪ el **cliente**, la **clienta**.

**customs** ['kʌstəmz] *plural noun* ▪ la **aduana**: we went through customs pasamos por la aduana.

**cut** [kʌt] *(noun & verb)*
▪ *noun*
1. el **corte**, la **cortada** *Colombia, Mexico*: I've got a cut on my arm tengo un corte en el brazo
2. el **corte de pelo**: a cut and blow-dry un corte de pelo y brushing
3. la **reducción** *(plural* las reducciones): a cut in prices una reducción en los precios
▪ *verb*
*(past tense & past participle* cut) **cortar**: he cut the cake into four slices cortó la torta en cuatro trozos
➤ he cut his finger se cortó el dedo

**cut off** *phrasal verb* ▪ **cortar**: he cut off another slice cortó otro trozo; his phone has been cut off le cortaron el teléfono
➤ we were cut off se cortó la comunicación.

**cut out** *phrasal verb* ▪ **recortar**: I cut out the article recorté el artículo.

**cute** [kjuːt] *adjective* ▪ **mono**: the baby's really cute el bebé es realmente mono.

**cyberspace** ['saɪbəspeɪs] *noun* ▪ el **ciberespacio**.

**cycle** ['saɪkl] *noun* ■ el **ciclo**: the cycle of the seasons el ciclo de las estaciones.

**cymbals** ['sɪmblz] *plural noun* ■ los **platillos**: she plays the cymbals toca los platillos.

**dad, daddy** [dæd, 'dædɪ] *noun* ■ el **papá**.

**daffodil** ['dæfədɪl] *noun* ■ el **narciso**.

**daily** ['deɪlɪ] *(adjective & adverb)*
■ *adjective*
**diario**: it's her daily walk es su paseo diario
➤ a daily newspaper un diario
■ *adverb*
**diariamente**: open daily from 8 till 6 abierto diariamente de 8 a 6.

**dairy** ['deərɪ] *adjective* ■ **lácteo**: dairy products productos lácteos.

**daisy** ['deɪzɪ] *(plural daisies) noun* ■ la **margarita**.

**dam** [dæm] *noun* ■ la **presa**: there's a dam across the river hay una presa en el río.

**damage** ['dæmɪdʒ] *(uncountable noun & verb)*
■ *uncountable noun*
el **daño**: the rain caused a lot of damage la lluvia causó muchos daños

■ *verb*
**dañar**: you'll damage the car vas a dañar el coche.

**damp** [dæmp] *adjective* ■ **húmedo**.

**dance** [daːns] *(noun & verb)*
■ *noun*
el **baile**: the rumba is a Cuban dance la rumba es un baile cubano; he invited her to the dance la invitó al baile
■ *verb*
**bailar**: can you dance? ¿sabes bailar?

**dancer** ['daːnsəʳ] *noun* ■ el **bailarín** *(plural* los **bailarines**)*, la **bailarina**.

**dancing** ['daːnsɪŋ] *uncountable noun*
■ el **baile**: he has dancing lessons tiene clases de baile
➤ to go dancing ir a bailar: he goes dancing every Tuesday va a bailar todos los martes.

**dandruff** ['dændrʌf] *uncountable noun*
■ la **caspa**: she has dandruff tiene caspa.

**danger** ['deɪndʒəʳ] *noun* ■ el **peligro**: we're in danger estamos en peligro; you're out of danger now estás fuera de peligro ahora
➤ to be in danger of doing something correr el riesgo de hacer algo: he's in danger of losing all his money corre el riesgo de perder todo su dinero.

**dangerous** ['deɪndʒərəs] *adjective* ■ **peligroso**.

**dare** [deəʳ] *verb*
1. **atreverse**: I daren't tell him no me atrevo a decírselo; I didn't dare to do it or I didn't dare do it no me atreví a hacerlo
2. **desafiar**: I dare you to jump te desafío a saltar.

**daring** ['deərɪŋ] *adjective* ■ **audaz** *(plural* audaces*)*.

**dark** [daːk] *(adjective & noun)*
■ *adjective*
**oscuro**: it's dark in here está oscuro aquí adentro; he has dark hair tiene pelo oscuro; dark blue pants pantalones azul oscuro

■ *noun*
the dark la oscuridad; **she is afraid of the dark** le tiene miedo a la oscuridad
➤ **it's getting dark** está oscureciendo
➤ **it's dark outside** está oscuro afuera
➤ **after dark** de noche: **he never goes out after dark** nunca sale de noche.

**darling** ['daːlɪŋ] *noun* ■ **querido**: hello, darling! ¡hola querido!

**dart** [daːt] *noun* ■ el **dardo**: he's playing darts está jugando a los dardos.

**dash** [dæʃ] *verb*
➤ **he dashed into the room** entró corriendo al cuarto.

**data** ['deɪtə] *uncountable noun* ■ los **datos**: the data is stored on computer los datos están almacenados en la computadora.

**database** ['deɪtəbeɪs] *noun* ■ la **base de datos**.

**date** [deɪt] *noun*
1. la **fecha**: what's your date of birth? ¿cuál es tu fecha de nacimiento?; what's the date today? ¿qué fecha es hoy?
2. la **cita**: let's make a date for lunch hagámos una cita para almorzar
3. el **dátil**: I like dates me gustan los dátiles
➤ **to have a date with somebody** salir con alguien: she has a date with Ken tonight va a salir con Ken esta noche.

**daughter** ['dɔːtəʳ] *noun* ■ la **hija**.

**daughter-in-law** ['dɔːtəʳɪnlɔː] *(plural* daughters-in-law*) noun* ■ la **nuera**.

**dawn** [dɔːn] *noun* ■ el **amanecer**: I got up at dawn me levanté al amanecer.

**day** [deɪ] *noun* ■ el **día**: he took two days off se tomó dos días libres; she comes to see him every day viene a verlo todos los días
➤ **the day before** el día anterior
➤ **the day after** el día después
➤ **the day before yesterday** anteayer
➤ **the day after tomorrow** pasado mañana.

**daylight** ['deɪlaɪt] *noun*
➤ **it's daylight** es de día.

**dead** [ded] *(adjective & adverb)*
■ *adjective*
**muerto**: he's dead está muerto
■ *adverb*
➤ **I'm dead set against it** estoy totalmente en contra de eso
➤ **to stop dead** pararse en seco: she stopped dead se paró en seco.

**deaf** [def] *adjective* ■ **sordo**.

**deal** [diːl] *(noun & verb)*
■ *noun*
el **trato**: I'll make a deal with you haré un trato contigo; it's a deal! ¡trato hecho!
➤ **a good deal** or **a great deal** mucho: I don't have a great deal of time no tengo mucho tiempo
■ *verb*
*(past tense & past participle* dealt*)* **repartir**: he deals the cards reparte las cartas

**deal with** *phrasal verb*
1. **ocuparse de**: I'll deal with it me ocuparé de eso
2. **tratar**: we'll deal with that subject in the next chapter trataremos ese tema en el próximo capítulo.

**dealt** [delt] *past tense & past participle*
➤ deal.

**dear** [dɪəʳ] *(adjective & exclamation)*
■ *adjective*
**querido**: he's a very dear friend es un amigo muy querido; **Dear Mr Jones** Querido señor Jones
■ *exclamation*
oh dear! I've left my homework at home ¡ay, Dios! dejé mi tarea en la casa.

**death** [deθ] *noun* ■ la **muerte**: it's the tenth anniversary of his death es el décimo aniversario de su muerte
➤ **I was bored to death** me aburrí como una ostra
➤ **I'm scared to death** casi me muero del susto.

**debate** [dɪ'beɪt] *noun* ■ el **debate**.

**debt** [det] *noun* ■ la **deuda**: to pay a debt pagar una deuda
➤ **they are in debt** están endeudados.

**decade** ['dekeɪd] *noun* ■ la **década**.

**deceive** [dɪ'siːv] *verb* ■ **engañar**: he deceived his family engañó a su familia.

**December** [dɪ'sembəʳ] *noun* ■

In Spanish the months of the year do not start with a capital letter:

**diciembre** *(masculine)*: **in December** en diciembre; **next December** el próximo diciembre; **last December** el pasado diciembre.

**decent** ['diːsnt] *adjective*
1. **decente**: they gave us a decent meal nos dieron una comida decente; put on something more decent ponte algo más decente
2. **bueno**: he's a decent man es un hombre bueno.

**deception** [dɪ'sepʃən] *noun* ■ el **engaño**

⚠ La palabra inglesa **deception** es un falso amigo, no significa "decepción".

**decide** [dɪ'saɪd] *verb*
1. **decidir**: she decided not to go decidió no ir
2. **decidirse**: I can't decide no me puedo decidir.

**decimal** ['desɪml] *adjective* ■ **decimal**: the decimal system el sistema decimal
➤ a decimal point la coma decimal: don't forget the decimal point when you write the sum no te olvides de la coma decimal cuando escribas el total.

**decision** [dɪ'sɪʒn] *noun* ■ la **decisión** *(plural* las **decisiones***)*: I've made a decision tomé una decisión.

**deck** [dek] *noun*
1. la **cubierta**: they were on the deck of the ship estaban en la cubierta del barco
2. la **baraja**: he bought a deck of cards compró una baraja.

**declare** [dɪ'kleəʳ] *verb* ■ **declarar**: do you have anything to declare? ¿tiene algo que declarar?

**decorate** ['dekəreɪt] *verb* ■ **decorar**: they decorated the Christmas tree decoraron el árbol de Navidad.

**decoration** [ˌdekə'reɪʃn] *noun* ■ el **adorno**: they are putting up the Christmas decorations están colocando los adornos de Navidad.

**decrease** *(noun & verb)*
■ *noun*
['diːkriːs] la **disminución** *(plural* las **disminuciones***)*: there's been a decrease in sales ha habido una disminución de las ventas
■ *verb*
[dɪ'kriːs] **disminuir**: the number of students has decreased el número de estudiantes ha disminuido.

**deep** [diːp] *adjective*
1. **profundo**: the hole is deep el agujero es profundo
2. **grave**: he has a deep voice tiene una voz grave
➤ how deep is the river? ¿qué profundidad tiene el río?

**deeply** ['diːplɪ] *adverb* ■ **profundamente**.

**deer** [dɪəʳ] *(plural* deer*) noun* ■ el **ciervo**.

**defeat** [dɪ'fiːt] *(noun & verb)*
■ *noun*
la **derrota**
■ *verb*
**derrotar**: our team was defeated by two to nothing nuestro equipo fue derrotado dos a cero.

**defend** [dɪ'fend] *verb* ■ **defender**: she tried to defend herself trató de defenderse.

**defense** [dɪ'fens] *noun* ■ la **defensa**: he came to my defense salió en mi defensa.

**definite** ['defɪnɪt] *adjective*
1. **seguro**: is it definite that he's coming? ¿es seguro que viene?; she was quite definite about it estaba bastante segura de eso
2. **definitivo**: we want a definite answer queremos una respuesta definitiva

**3. concreto:** I haven't made any definite plans no tengo planes concretos

**4. claro:** there's a definite improvement hay una clara mejoría.

**definitely** ['defɪnɪtlɪ] *adverb* ■ **sin duda:** he's definitely the smartest es sin duda el más inteligente

➤ I will definitely come es seguro que voy

➤ definitely not! ¡de ninguna manera!

**degree** [dɪ'grɪː] *noun*

**1. el grado:** it was 90 degrees Fahrenheit in the shade hacía 90 grados Fahrenheit a la sombra

**2. el título:** she wants to get a college degree quiere tener un título universitario

➤ she has a degree in English es licenciada en filología inglesa

➤ to a certain degree hasta cierto punto.

**delay** [dɪ'leɪ] *(noun & verb)*

■ *noun*

el **retraso,** la **demora:** there's a two-hour delay hay un retraso de dos horas

➤ without delay inmediatamente, sin demora

■ *verb*

retrasar: he delayed his departure retrasó su partida.

**delete** [dɪ'lɪːt] *verb* ■ **borrar:** I deleted the file borré el archivo.

**deliberate** [dɪ'lɪbərət] *adjective* ■ **intencionado:** that was deliberate! ¡eso fue intencionado!

**deliberately** [dɪ'lɪbərətlɪ] *adverb* ■ **adrede:** he did it deliberately lo hizo adrede

➤ the fire was started deliberately el fuego fue intencionado.

**delicate** ['delɪkət] *adjective* ■ **delicado.**

**delicious** [dɪ'lɪʃəs] *adjective* ■ **delicioso.**

**delighted** [dɪ'laɪtɪd] *adjective* ■ **encantado:** I'm delighted to see you estoy encantada de verte.

**deliver** [dɪ'lɪvəʳ] *verb* ■ **entregar:** when can you deliver the order? ¿cuándo puede entregar el pedido?

➤ to deliver a speech pronunciar un discurso.

**delivery** [dɪ'lɪvərɪ] *(plural* deliveries) *noun* ■ la **entrega:** you pay on delivery usted paga a la entrega

➤ they do free deliveries hacen entregas a domicilio gratis.

**demand** [dɪ'maːnd] *(verb & noun)*

■ *verb*

exigir: I demand an explanation exijo una explicación

■ *noun*

**1. la exigencia:** they won't meet their demands no van a satisfacer sus exigencias

**2. la demanda:** there's a lot of demand for organic produce hay mucha demanda de productos orgánicos.

**democracy** [dɪ'mɒkrəsɪ] *(plural* democracies) *noun* ■ la **democracia:** the United States is a democracy Estados Unidos es una democracia.

**Democrat** ['deməkræt] *noun* ■ el/la **demócrata** ➤ Political parties.

**democratic** [,demə'krætɪk] *adjective* ■ **democrático** ➤ Political parties

➤ the Democratic Party el Partido Demócrata.

**demonstrate** ['demənstreɪt] *verb*

**1. manifestarse:** students are demonstrating in the street los estudiantes se están manifestando en la calle

**2. hacer una demostración de:** he demonstrated how to use the vacuum cleaner hizo una demostración de cómo usar la aspiradora.

**demonstration** [demən'streɪʃn] *noun*

**1. la manifestación** *(plural* las **manifestaciones):** she went on an anti-war demonstration participó en una manifestación contra la guerra

**2. la demostración** *(plural* las **demostraciones):** he gave us a demonstration of the computer's functions nos hicieron una demostración de las funciones de la computadora.

**denied** [dɪ'naɪd] *past tense & past participle* ➤ deny.

**dense** [dens] *adjective* ■ **denso: a dense forest** un bosque denso; **a dense fog** una niebla densa.

**dentist** ['dentɪst] *noun* ■ el/la **dentista**.

**deny** [dɪ'naɪ] *(past tense & past participle* denied*) verb* ■ **negar: don't deny it!** no lo niegues; **he denied taking the money** negó haber tomado el dinero.

**deodorant** [diː'əʊdərənt] *noun* ■ el **desodorante**.

**depart** [dɪ'paːt] *verb* ■ **salir: the train is now departing** el tren está saliendo ahora.

**department** [dɪ'paːtmənt] *noun*
1. la **sección** *(plural* las **secciones**)*: the toy department** la sección juguetería
2. el **departamento: the Spanish department at the university** el departamento de español de la universidad
➤ **a department store** unos grandes almacenes, una tienda de departamentos *Mexico*.

**departure** [dɪ'paːtʃər] *noun* ■ la **salida: the train's departure was delayed** se retrasó la salida del tren.

**depend** [dɪ'pend] *verb* ■ **depender: it depends on you** depende de ti; **it all depends** todo depende.

**deposit** [dɪ'pɒzɪt] *noun* ■ el **depósito: you will get your deposit back when you return the keys** recuperarás tu depósito cuando devuelvas las llaves; **you pay a deposit now and the rest later** deje ahora un depósito y el resto lo paga después
➤ **to make a deposit** hacer un depósito: **he made a deposit at the bank** hizo un depósito en el banco.

**depressed** [dɪ'prest] *adjective* ■ **deprimido**.

**depression** [dɪ'preʃn] *noun* ■ la **depresión** *(plural* las **depresiones**)*.

**depth** [depθ] *noun* ■ la **profundidad: what is the depth of the river?** ¿qué profundidad tiene el río?
➤ **when it comes to programming, I'm out of my depth** tratándose de programación, es muy poco lo que sé.

**describe** [dɪ'skraɪb] *verb* ■ **describir: describe your room** describe tu habitación.

**description** [dɪ'skrɪpʃn] *noun* ■ la **descripción** *(plural* las **descripciones**)*.

**desert** ['dezət] *noun* ■ el **desierto**
➤ **a desert island** una isla desierta.

**deserve** [dɪ'zɜːv] *verb* ■ **merecer: they didn't deserve to win** no merecían ganar
➤ **he got what he deserved** se llevó su merecido.

**design** [dɪ'zaɪn] *(noun & verb)*

■ *noun*
1. el **diseño: it's a car with a completely new design** es un coche con un diseño completamente nuevo
2. el **plano: I like the designs for the new house** me gustan los planos de la nueva casa
3. el **motivo: a carpet with a floral design** una alfombra con un motivo floral

■ *verb*
**diseñar: he designed this bicycle for young children** diseñó esta bicicleta para niños pequeños; **she designs jewelery** diseña joyas.

**designer** [dɪ'zaɪnər] *noun* ■ el **diseñador**, la **diseñadora: he's a big fashion designer** es un gran diseñador de modas
➤ **designer clothes** la ropa de diseño.

**desk** [desk] *noun*
1. el **escritorio: he's sitting at his desk** está sentado en su escritorio
2. el **mostrador: leave your key at the desk in the lobby** deje su llave en el mostrador del vestíbulo.

**desktop** [desktɒp] *noun* ■ el **escritorio: the icon is on the desktop of the computer** el icono está en el escritorio de la computadora
➤ **a desktop computer** una computadora de escritorio.

**desperate** ['desprət] *adjective* ■ **desesperado**

➤ the situation is desperate la situación es deseperada

➤ to be desperate to do something no ver la hora de hacer algo: I was desperate to leave no veía la hora de irme.

**despite** [dɪ'spaɪt] *preposition* ■ **a pesar de**: despite the rain he went out salió a pesar de la lluvia.

**dessert** [dɪ'zɜːt] *noun* ■ el **postre**: what's for dessert? ¿qué hay de postre?

**destroy** [dɪ'strɔɪ] *verb* ■ **destruir**: the bomb destroyed the village la bomba destruyó el pueblo.

**detail** ['diːteɪl] *noun* ■ el **detalle**: the details aren't important los detalles no son importantes

➤ in detail en detalle: he described the island in detail describió la isla en detalle.

**detective** [dɪ'tektɪv] *noun* ■ el/la **detective**: the detective in charge of the investigation el detective a cargo de la investigación

➤ a detective story una novela policíaca

➤ a private detective un detective privado.

**determined** [dɪ'tɜːmɪnd] *adjective* ■ **decidido**: he's determined to go back to Peru está decidido a volver a Perú.

**develop** [dɪ'veləp] *verb*

1. **ampliar**: they're trying to develop the business están tratando de ampliar el negocio

2. **revelar**: they developed my photos quickly revelaron mis fotos rápidamente

3. **desarrollarse**: babies develop very fast los bebés se desarrollan muy rápido

➤ to develop into convertirse en: he developed into a charming young man se convirtió en un joven encantador.

**devil** ['devl] *noun* ■ el **diablo**.

**devote** [dɪ'vəʊt] *verb* ■ **dedicar**: he devoted himself to his studies se dedicó a sus estudios.

**diagram** ['daɪəgræm] *noun* ■ el **diagrama**.

**dial** ['daɪəl] *(verb & noun)*

■ *verb*
**marcar**: she dialed the number marcó el número

■ *noun*
la **esfera**, la **carátula** *Mexico*: a watch with a luminous dial un reloj con una esfera luminosa.

**dial tone** ['daɪəltəʊn] *noun* ■ el **tono de marcar**: there's no dial tone no hay tono de marcar.

**dialog** ['daɪəlɒg] *noun* ■ el **diálogo**.

**diamond** ['daɪəmənd] *noun* ■ el **diamante**: a diamond ring un anillo de diamantes; the ace of diamonds el as de diamantes.

**diaper** ['daɪəpəʳ] *noun* ■ el **pañal**.

**diary** ['daɪərɪ] *(plural diaries)* *noun*

1. el **diario**: she keeps a diary lleva un diario

2. la **agenda**: he wrote down my birthday in his diary anotó mi cumpleaños en su agenda.

**dice** [daɪs] *(plural dice)* *noun* ■ el **dado**: he rolled the dice tiró los dados.

**dictation** [dɪk'teɪʃn] *noun* ■ el **dictado**.

**dictionary** ['dɪkʃənrɪ] *(plural dictionaries)* *noun* ■ el **diccionario**: look it up in the dictionary búscalo en el diccionario.

**did** [dɪd] *past tense* ➤ do.

**didn't** ['dɪdnt] ➤ did not.

**die** [daɪ] *(present participle dying)* *verb* ■ **morir**: he died last year murió el año pasado

➤ to be dying to do something morirse de ganas de hacer algo

➤ I'm dying to see you me muero de ganas de verte

➤ to be dying for something morirse por algo: I'm dying for a drink me muero por una bebida.

**diet** ['daɪət] *noun* ■ **la dieta**: it is important to have a balanced diet es importante tener una dieta equilibrada
➤ **on a diet** a dieta: she's on a diet está a dieta: he went on a diet se puso a dieta.

**difference** ['dɪfrəns] *noun* ■ **la diferencia**: there's a big difference between the two of them hay una gran diferencia entre los dos
➤ it makes no difference da lo mismo.

**different** ['dɪfrənt] *adjective* ■ **diferente**: London is different from New York Londres es diferente de Nueva York
➤ you look different te ves diferente.

**difficult** ['dɪfɪkəlt] *adjective* ■ **difícil**.

**difficulty** ['dɪfɪkəltɪ] *(plural* difficulties) *noun* ■ **la dificultad**: she did it without any difficulty lo hizo sin ninguna dificultad
➤ to have difficulty doing something tener problemas para hacer algo
➤ I had difficulty persuading him tuve problemas para convencerlo.

**dig** [dɪg] *(past tense & past participle* dug) *verb* ■ **cavar**: he's digging a hole está cavando un hoyo
➤ he accidentally dug his nails into her le clavó las uñas sin querer

**dig up** *phrasal verb* ■ **desenterrar**: the dog dug some bones up el perro desenterró unos huesos.

**digital** ['dɪdʒɪtl] *adjective* ■ **digital**
➤ a digital camera una cámara digital
➤ digital television la televisión digital
➤ a digital watch un reloj digital.

**dim** [dɪm] *adjective* ■ **débil**: the light's a little dim la luz está un poco débil.

**dime** [daɪm] *noun* ■ **la moneda de diez centavos**: he put a dime in the machine puso una moneda de diez centavos en la máquina.

**diner** ['daɪnər] *noun* ■ **el restaurante**.

**dining room** ['daɪnɪŋruːm] *noun* ■ **el comedor**.

**dinner** ['dɪnər] *noun* ■ **la cena** *Mexico, River Plate*, **la comida**: he's cooking dinner está preparando la cena
➤ Christmas dinner la cena de Navidad.

**dinosaur** ['daɪnəsɔːr] *noun* ■ **el dinosaurio**.

**dip** [dɪp] *(past tense & past participle* dipped) *verb* ■ **mojar**: she dipped her bread into the soup mojó el pan en la sopa.

**diploma** [dɪ'pləʊmə] *noun* ■ **el diploma**: he has a diploma in computing tiene un diploma en computación.

**direct** [dɪ'rekt] *(adjective & verb)*

■ *adjective*
**directo**: a direct flight between Paris and Athens un vuelo directo entre París y Atenas
■ *verb*
1. **dirigir**: he directs the company dirige la compañía; Spielberg directed the film Spielberg dirigió esta película
2. **indicarle el camino a**: he directed me to the station me indicó el camino para llegar a la estación

**direction** [dɪ'rekʃn] *noun* ■ **la dirección** *(plural* las **direcciones**): we're going in the wrong direction vamos en la dirección equivocada
➤ to ask for directions preguntar cómo llegar: she asked me for directions me preguntó cómo llegar
➤ directions for use modo de empleo: read the directions lea el modo de empleo.

**directly** [dɪ'rektlɪ] *adverb*
1. **directamente**: I went directly to the station fui directamente a la estación
2. **justo**: he was directly behind me estaba justo detrás de mí.

**director** [dɪ'rektər] *noun* ■ **el director, la directora**: he's the director of a big firm es director de una gran compañía; who's the director of this film? ¿quién es el director de esta película?

**directory** [dɪ'rektərɪ] *(plural* directories) *noun*
1. **la guía**: the telephone directory la guía telefónica
2. **el directorio**: save it in that directory guárdalo en ese directorio.

**dirt** [dɜːt] *uncountable noun*

1. la **suciedad**: it's covered in dirt está cubierto de suciedad
2. la **tierra**: put some dirt in the flower pot coloque un poco de tierra en la maceta.

**dirty** ['dɜːtɪ] *adjective* ■ **sucio**: my jeans are dirty mis jeans están sucios
➤ to get something dirty ensuciar algo: I got my shoes dirty me ensucié los zapatos.

**disabled** [dɪs'eɪbld] *adjective* ■ **discapacitado**: she's disabled es discapacitada.

**disadvantage** [ˌdɪsəd'vɑːntɪdʒ] *noun* ■ el **inconveniente**: its main disadvantage is the price su mayor inconveniente es el precio.

**disagree** [ˌdɪsə'griː] *verb* ■ **no estar de acuerdo**: I disagree with you no estoy de acuerdo contigo.

**disappear** [ˌdɪsə'pɪər] *verb* ■ **desaparecer**: the fox disappeared el zorro desapareció.

**disappoint** [ˌdɪsə'pɔɪnt] *verb* ■ **decepcionar**: he really disappointed me realmente, me decepcionó.

**disappointed** [ˌdɪsə'pɔɪntɪd] *adjective* ■ **decepcionado**: I was disappointed with the film quedé decepcionado con la película.

**disappointment** [ˌdɪsə'pɔɪntmənt] *noun* ■ la **decepción** (*plural* las **decepciones**): what a disappointment! ¡qué decepción!

**disapprove** [ˌdɪsə'pruːv] *verb*
➤ she disapproves of smoking está en contra del tabaco
➤ they disapprove of my friends a ellos no les gustan mis amigos.

**disaster** [dɪ'zɑːstər] *noun* ■ el **desastre**: a natural disaster un desastre natural; the meeting was a disaster la reunión fue un desastre.

**discipline** ['dɪsɪplɪn] *noun* ■ la **disciplina**.

**disco** ['dɪskəʊ] (*abbreviation of* discotheque) *noun* ■ la **disco**: they go to a disco on Saturdays van a una disco todos los sábados.

**discount** ['dɪskaʊnt] *noun* ■ el **descuento**: I got a 20% discount on it me hicieron un 20 por ciento de descuento.

**discover** [dɪ'skʌvər] *verb* ■ **descubrir**: she discovered a new chemical element descubrió un nuevo elemento químico.

**discovery** [dɪ'skʌvərɪ] (*plural* discoveries) *noun* ■ el **descubrimiento**.

**discrimination** [dɪˌskrɪmɪ'neɪʃn] *noun* ■ la **discriminación**: racial discrimination la discriminación racial.

**discuss** [dɪ'skʌs] *verb*

1. **discutir**: she discussed the problem with him discutió el problema con él
2. **hablar de**: we discussed the book in class hablamos del libro en clase.

**discussion** [dɪ'skʌʃn] *noun* ■ la **discusión** (*plural* las **discusiones**): they had a long discussion on the subject tuvieron una larga discusión sobre el tema
➤ we had a discussion about the book in class hablamos del libro en clase.

**disease** [dɪ'ziːz] *noun* ■ la **enfermedad**: she caught a rare disease se contagió de una enfermedad poco común.

**disguise** [dɪs'gaɪz] (*verb & noun*)
■ *verb*
**disfrazar**: she disguised herself by dyeing her hair se disfrazó tiñéndose el pelo
■ *noun*
el **disfraz** (*plural* los **disfraces**)
➤ in disguise disfrazado: everyone was in disguise todos estaban disfrazados.

**disgusted** [dɪs'gʌstɪd] *adjective* ■ **indignado**: she was disgusted because of her boyfriend's behavior estaba indignada por el comportamiento de su novio

⚠ La palabra inglesa **disgusted** es un falso amigo, no significa "disgustado".

**disgusting** [dɪs'gʌstɪŋ] *adjective* ■ **repugnante: that smell is disgusting** ese olor es repugnante.

**dish** [dɪʃ] *noun* ■ **el plato: paella is a Spanish dish** la paella es un plato español
➤ **the dishes** los platos, los trates *Mexico*: **he's doing the dishes** or **he's washing the dishes** está lavando los platos.

**dishonest** [dɪs'ɒnɪst] *adjective* ■ **deshonesto**.

**dishwasher** ['dɪʃ,wɒʃəʳ] *noun* ■ **el lavavajillas** *(plural* **los lavavajillas**), la **lavadora de platos**.

**disk** [dɪsk] *noun* ■ **el disco: the hard disk is full** el disco duro está lleno
➤ **save the file on a floppy disk** guarda el archivo en un disquete.

**diskette** [dɪs'ket] *noun* ■ **el disquete**.

**dismiss** [dɪs'mɪs] *verb* ■ **despedir: they dismissed her from her job** la despidieron de su trabajo.

**disorganized** [dɪs'ɔːgənaɪzd] *adjective* ■ **desorganizado: they are very disorganized** son muy desorganizados.

**display** [dɪ'spleɪ] *(noun & verb)*

■ *noun*
1. la **exposición** *(plural* las **exposiciones**): **an art display** una exposición de arte
2. la **exhibición** *(plural* las **exhibiciones**): **an acrobatic display** una exhibición de acrobacias
➤ **on display** en exhibición: **his paintings are on display** sus pinturas están en exhibición

■ *verb*
1. **demostrar: he displayed great courage** demostró un gran coraje
2. **aparecer: the information is displayed on the screen** la información aparece en la pantalla.

**disposable** [dɪ'spəʊzəbl] *adjective*
■ **desechable, descartable** *River Plate*.

**distance** ['dɪstəns] *noun* ■ la **distancia: what's the distance between the two**

**towns?** ¿qué distancia hay entre las dos ciudades?
➤ **in the distance** a la distancia: **I could see her in the distance** la veía a la distancia
➤ **it's within walking distance** se puede ir caminando.

**distant** ['dɪstənt] *adjective* ■ **lejano: in the distant future** en un futuro lejano.

**distinguish** [dɪ'stɪŋgwɪʃ] *verb* ■ **distinguir: he can't distinguish between red and green** no distingue entre el verde y el rojo.

**distort** [dɪ'stɔːt] *verb* ■ **distorsionar: this mirror distorts your face** este espejo distorsiona la cara.

**distract** [dɪ'strakt] *verb* ■ **distraer: you're distracting me from work** me distraes de mi trabajo.

**distribute** [dɪ'strɪbjuːt] *verb* ■ **distribuir: students were distributing flyers** los estudiantes estaban distribuyendo volantes.

**district** ['dɪstrɪkt] *noun* ■ **el distrito**.

**disturb** [dɪ'stɜːb] *verb* ■ **molestar: sorry to disturb you** perdone que lo moleste.

**dive** [daɪv] *(past tense* **dove**, *past participle* **dived**) *verb* ■ **zambullirse, echarse un clavado** *Mexico*: **he dove into the water** se zambulló en el agua.

**divide** [dɪ'vaɪd] *verb*
1. **dividir: she divided the cake into three equal parts** dividió el pastel en tres partes iguales; **14 divided by 2 is 7** 14 dividido entre 2 es igual a 7
2. **repartir: they divided the money between them** se repartieron el dinero entre ellos.

**diving** ['daɪvɪŋ] *noun* ■ **el buceo: he goes diving near the coral reef** hace buceo cerca del arrecife de coral
➤ **a diving board** un trampolín.

**divorced** [dɪ'vɔːst] *adjective* ■ **divorciado: his parents are divorced** sus padres están divorciados

➤ they're getting **divorced** se van a divorciar.

**dizzy** ['dɪzɪ] *adjective*

➤ to feel **dizzy** sentirse mareado: **I'm feeling a bit dizzy** me siento un poco mareado.

**DJ** ['diːdʒeɪ] *(abbreviation of* disc jockey*) noun* ■ el/la **disc jockey** *(plural* los/las **disc jockeys***)*.

**do** [duː] *(past tense* did, *past participle* done*) verb*

1. **hacer: what are you doing?** ¿qué estás haciendo?; **I'm doing my homework** estoy haciendo las tareas; **I've got a lot to do** tengo mucho que hacer; **do as you're told!** ¡haz lo que te digan!

2. **bastar: will 10 dollars do?** ¿bastará con 10 dólares?; **that'll do now!** ¡ya basta!

3. **servir: what does this switch do?** ¿para qué sirve este interruptor?; **this box is too small, the other one will do** esta caja es muy chica, la otra sirve

4.

> Followed by **well** or **badly**:

I'm doing well me va bien; he's doing well at school le va bien en el colegio; she did badly in the exam le fue mal en el examen

5.

> **Do** is not translated when it is used to form a question:

how did you meet Isabela? ¿cómo conociste a Isabela?; does your mother have the keys? ¿tiene las llaves tu mamá?; did Tom call? ¿llamó Tom?

6.

> In negative constructions **do** is not translated, just put **no** before the verb:

I don't want to come no quiero ir; we didn't go out last night no salimos anoche

7.

> In short answers **do** is not translated when it is used to take the place of another verb:

I like reggae — so do I me gusta el reggae — a mí también; do you know how to ski? — no, I don't ¿sabes esquiar? — no, no sé

8.

> In question tags use **¿no?** or **¿verdad?** as a translation:

you know Fran, don't you? conoces a Fran, ¿no?; he doesn't like garlic, does he? no le gusta el ajo, ¿verdad?

9. *In emphatic sentences* **I DO** like him, but I don't want to marry him me gusta, sí, pero no quiero casarme con él; **I DO want to go** sí que quiero ir

10. *In polite requests* **do** sit down siéntese, por favor; **do help yourselves** sírvanse, por favor

➤ how are you doing? ¿cómo te va?

➤ how do you do? mucho gusto

➤ what does your father do? ¿a qué se dedica tu papá?

➤ to do one's hair arreglarse el pelo

**do without** *phrasal verb* ■ **arreglárselas sin: they did without bread** se las arreglaron sin pan.

**doctor** ['dɒktər] *noun* ■ el **médico,** la **médica: I went to the doctor** fui al médico; **she's a doctor** es médica.

**document** ['dɒkjʊmənt] *noun* ■ el **documento.**

**does** [dəz, dʌz] ➤ **do.**

**doesn't** ['dʌznt] ➤ **does not.**

**dog** [dɒg] *noun* ■ el **perro,** la **perra: my dog's name is Lassie** mi perra se llama Lassie.

**doll** [dɒl] *noun* ■ la **muñeca.**

**dollar** ['dɒlər] *noun* ■ el **dólar: it costs twenty dollars** cuesta veinte dólares

➤ a dollar bill un billete de un dólar.

**dolphin** ['dɒlfɪn] *noun* ■ el **delfín** *(plural* los **delfines***)*.

**Dominican Republic** [dəˈmɪnɪkən rɪˈpʌblɪk] *noun* ■ la **República Dominicana.**

**Dominican** [dəˈmɪnɪkən] *(adjective & noun)*

- *adjective*

> Remember not to use a capital letter for the adjective in Spanish:

**dominicano:** Dominican cuisine is different from Mexican cuisine la cocina dominicana es diferente de la mexicana
- *noun*

> In Spanish, a capital letter is not used for the inhabitants of a country or region:

el **dominicano,** la **dominicana:** the Dominicans are usually friendly to tourists los dominicanos suelen ser amables con los turistas

**dominoes** ['dɒmɪnəʊz] *noun* ■ el **dominó:** they're playing dominoes están jugando dominó.

**donate** [də'neɪt] *verb* ■ **donar:** he donated a thousand dollars to charity donó mil dólares para obras de caridad
> to donate blood donar sangre.

**done** [dʌn] *(adjective & verb form)*
- *adjective*
**cocido:** the potatoes aren't done las papas no están cocidas
> are you done with this ¿terminaste con esto?
> I'm nearly done ya casi terminé
- *past participle*
> do.

**donkey** ['dɒŋkɪ] *noun* ■ el **burro.**

**don't** [dəʊnt] > do not.

**donut** ['dəʊnʌt] *noun* ■ el **donut** *(plural* los **donuts),** la **dona** *Mexico.*

**door** [dɔːʳ] *noun* ■ la **puerta:** close the door cierra la puerta; the car door is dented la puerta del coche está abollada.

**doorbell** ['dɔːbel] *noun* ■ el **timbre**
> to ring the doorbell tocar el timbre: somebody rang the doorbell alguien tocó el timbre.

**dormitory** ['dɔːmɪtrɪ] *(plural* dormitories) *noun* ■ la **residencia de estudiantes.**

**dot** [dɒt] *noun* ■ el **punto:** don't forget the dot on the "i" no olvides ponerle el punto a la "i"
> on the dot en punto: at 6 o'clock on the dot a las seis en punto.

**double** ['dʌbl] *(adjective, adverb, noun & verb)*
- *adjective*
1. **doble:** she had a double helping of ice cream se sirvió una porción doble de helado
2. *In phone numbers* double two three five dos, dos tres cinco
> "address" is spelt with a double "d" "address" se escribe con dos des
> a double bed una cama de matrimonio
> a double room una habitación doble
- *adverb*
1. el **doble:** those tickets cost double estas entradas cuestan el doble
2. **doble:** he was seeing double estaba viendo doble
- *noun*
1. el **doble:** the men's doubles el doble caballeros
2. el/la **doble:** she's my double es mi doble
- *verb*
**duplicarse:** prices have doubled los precios se han duplicado.

**double-click** ['dʌbl'klɪk] *verb* ■ **hacer doble clic:** double-click on the icon haz doble clic en el icono.

**doubt** [daʊt] *(noun & verb)*
- *noun*
la **duda:** there is no doubt about it no hay duda acerca de eso
> without doubt sin duda: he's without doubt the champion es, sin duda, el campeón
> to be in doubt dudar: if you're in doubt ask your parents si dudas, pregúntale a tus papás
- *verb*
**dudar:** I doubt it lo dudo; I doubt he'll come dudo que venga

> Use the subjunctive after **dudar que.**

**dough** [dəʊ] *uncountable noun* ■ la **masa:** bread is made from dough el pan se hace con masa.

**70**

**dove** *(noun & verb form)*

■ *noun*

[dʌv] la **paloma: the dove is a symbol of peace** la paloma es un símbolo de paz

■ *past tense*

[dəʊv] ➤ dive.

**down** [daʊn] *(adverb, preposition & adjective)*

■ *adverb*

ı. *With a verb of movement*

> When "down" is used with a verb of movement in English (to come down, to go down, etc.), you often use a verb alone in Spanish to translate it:

**are you coming down?** ¿bajas?; **I'm going down to the shops** voy a las tiendas; **prices have come down** bajaron los precios

2. **abajo: down below** abajo; **she's down in the street** está abajo en la calle; **she cycled all the way down** llegó hasta abajo en bicicleta

➤ **he threw the book down** tiró el libro al suelo

➤ **down there** allá abajo

➤ **can you see that man down there?** ¿ves al hombre allá abajo?

➤ **to fall down** caerse: **I fell down the stairs** me caí por las escaleras

➤ **down there** allá abajo: **can you see that man down there?** ¿ves al hombre allá abajo?

■ *preposition*

ı. *In a prepositional phrase*

> When 'down' is used with a verb of movement in English, even when being used in a prepositional phrase, you often use a verb alone in Spanish to translate it:

**we walked down the street** caminamos por la calle; **they ran down the hill** bajó la colina corriendo

2. **abajo: the bathroom is down the stairs** el baño está abajo

➤ **further down** más abajo: **they live further down the street** viven más abajo, en esta calle

■ *adjective*

*informal* **deprimido: I feel a bit down** estoy un poco deprimido.

**download** [ˌdaʊn'ləʊd] *verb* ■ **descargar: he downloaded the attached file** descargó el archivo adjunto.

**downstairs** [ˌdaʊn'steəz] *(adjective & adverb)*

■ *adjective*

**de abajo: our downstairs neighbors** nuestros vecinos de abajo

■ *adverb*

**abajo: wait for me downstairs** espérame abajo

➤ **to come downstairs or to go downstairs** bajar: **he went downstairs to answer the phone** bajó a contestar el teléfono

➤ **she ran downstairs** bajó corriendo las escaleras.

**downtown** [ˌdaʊn'taʊn] *adverb* ■ **al centro: tomorrow we're going downtown** mañana vamos al centro

➤ **they live in downtown Chicago** viven en el centro de Chicago.

**dozen** ['dʌzn] *noun* ■ **la docena: they cost 50 cents a dozen** cuestan 50 centavos la docena; **she bought a dozen eggs** compró una docena de huevos.

**Dr** *(abbreviation of* Doctor*)* **el Dr., la Dra.**

**draft** [dra:ft] *noun* ■ **la corriente: there's a draft from the window** entra corriente por la ventana.

**drafty** ['dra:ftɪ] *adjective*

➤ **this room is drafty** hay mucha corriente en este cuarto.

**drag** [dræg] *(past tense & past participle* dragged*) verb* ■ **arrastrar: he dragged his bag along the ground** arrastró la bolsa por el suelo.

**dragon** ['drægən] *noun* ■ **el dragón** *(plural* los **dragones***).*

**drain** [dreɪn] *(noun & verb)*

■ *noun*

**el desagüe: the drains are blocked** los desagües están tapados

■ *verb*

**escurrir: you have to drain the vegetables first** tienes que escurrir las verduras primero.

**drama** ['dra:mə] *noun*
1. **el teatro:** he teaches drama enseña teatro
2. **el drama:** the play is a drama la obra es un drama.

**dramatic** [drə'mætɪk] *adjective* ■ **espectacular:** the end of the film is very dramatic el final de la película es muy espectacular.

**drank** [dræŋk] *past tense* ➤ drink.

**draw** [drɔ:] *(verb & noun)*
■ *verb*
*(past tense* **drew***, past participle* **drawn***)*
1. **dibujar:** she drew a tree dibujó un árbol
2. **correr:** she drew the curtains corrió las cortinas
3. **atraer:** we tried to draw his attention tratamos de atraer su atención
■ *noun*
1. **el empate:** the game ended in a draw el partido terminó en un empate
2. **el sorteo:** the lottery draw is tonight el sorteo de la lotería es esta noche.

**drawer** [drɔ:ʳ] *noun* ■ **el cajón** *(plural* los **cajones***),* la **gaveta** *Central America, Mexico*: she took the knife out of the drawer sacó el cuchillo del cajón.

**drawing** ['drɔ:ɪŋ] *noun* ■ **el dibujo:** she did a drawing of a whale hizo un dibujo de una ballena.

**drawn** [drɔ:n] *past participle* ➤ draw.

**dreadful** ['dredfʊl] *adjective* ■ **espantoso:** the weather is dreadful el tiempo está espantoso
➤ **to feel dreadful** sentirse fatal: I feel dreadful me siento fatal
➤ **to look dreadful** verse horrible: you look dreadful in that hat te ves horrible con ese sombrero
➤ **you look dreadful, you should go and lie down** tienes muy mala cara, deberías ir a acostarte.

**dream** [dri:m] *(noun & verb)*
■ *noun*
**el sueño:** I had a strange dream tuve un sueño raro

■ *verb*
*(past tense & past participle* **dreamed** *or* **dreamt***)* **soñar:** I dreamt about you last night anoche soñé contigo; he dreamed he was a prince soñó que era un príncipe.

**dreamt** [dremt] *past tense & past participle* ➤ dream.

**drenched** [drentʃt] *adjective* ■ **estar empapado, estar ensopado** *Colombia, River Plate, Venezuela informal* : I'm completely drenched estoy completamente empapado.

**dress** [dres] *(noun & verb)*
■ *noun*
**el vestido**
■ *verb*
1. **vestirse:** she dresses very elegantly se viste con elegancia
2. **vestir:** she's dressing the children está vistiendo a los niños
➤ **they were dressed in black** estaban vestidos de negro
➤ **to get dressed** vestirse: I got dressed and went out me vestí y salí

**dress up** *phrasal verb*
1. **disfrazarse:** she dressed up as a witch se disfrazó de bruja
2. **ponerse elegante:** she always dresses up to go out siempre se pone elegante para salir.

**dresser** ['dresəʳ] *noun* ■ **la cómoda**.

**drew** [dru:] *past tense* ➤ draw.

**dried** [draɪd] *(adjective & verb form)*
■ *adjective*
**seco:** dried flowers flores secas
■ *past tense & past participle*
➤ dry.

**drill** [drɪl] *(noun & verb)*
■ *noun*
**el taladro**
■ *verb*
➤ **he's drilling a hole** está haciendo un agujero con un taladro.

**drink** [drɪŋk] *(noun & verb)*
■ *noun*
**la bebida:** a cold drink una bebida fría

➤ **we went out for a drink** salimos a tomar algo

➤ **would you like a drink?** ¿quieres tomar algo?

■ *verb*

*(past tense* **drank***, past participle* **drunk***)* **tomar: he's drinking coffee** está tomando café; **they've been drinking** han estado tomando.

**drinking water** ['drɪŋkɪŋ'wɔːtəʳ] *noun* ■ el **agua potable**

> Feminine noun that takes **un** and **el** in the singular.

**drive** [draɪv] *(noun & verb)*

■ *noun*

1. el **paseo en coche: we went for a drive** fuimos a dar un paseo en coche

2. el **viaje en coche: it's a long drive** es un viaje largo en coche

3. el **camino de entrada: we walked up the drive to the house** fuimos caminando por el camino de entrada a la casa

➤ **the disk drive** la unidad de disco

■ *verb*

1. *(past tense* **drove***, past participle* **driven***)* **manejar: can you drive?** ¿sabes manejar?; **he was driving a sports car** manejaba un auto deportivo; **I don't want to drive, I'll take the train** no quiero manejar, voy a tomar el tren

2. **llevar en coche: she drives me to school every day** me lleva en coche al colegio todos los días

➤ **to drive somebody crazy** volver loco a alguien: **you're driving me crazy!** ¡me estás volviendo loca!

**driven** ['drɪvn] *past participle* ➤ drive.

**driver** ['draɪvəʳ] *noun* ■ el/la **chofer: he's a bus driver** es chofer de autobús

➤ **she's a good driver** maneja muy bien

➤ **he's a taxi driver** es taxista

➤ **a driver's license** una licencia de conducir, un registro de conducir *Argentina*, un pase de manejar *Colombia*, un carné de manejar *Chile*, una licencia de manejar *Mexico*, un brevete *Peru*, una libreta de manejar *Uruguay*

➤ **he has a driver's license** tiene licencia de conducir.

**driving** ['draɪvɪŋ] *noun*

➤ **what do you think about Ross' driving?** ¿cómo crees que maneja Ross?

➤ **a driving lesson** una clase de manejar

➤ **a driving test** un examen de manejar, un examen de manejo *Mexico:* **he passed his driving test** aprobó el examen de conducción.

**drop** [drɒp] *(noun & verb)*

■ *noun*

1. la **gota: a few drops of water** unas pocas gotas de agua

2. el **descenso: there's been a drop in the temperature** ha habido un descenso de la temperatura

■ *verb*

*(past tense & past participle* **dropped***)*

1. **dejar: can you drop me off at school?** ¿puedes dejarme en el colegio?

2. **bajar: temperatures have dropped** han bajado las temperaturas

➤ **I dropped the plate** se me cayó el plato

**drop by** *phrasal verb* ■ **pasar: can you drop by tomorrow?** ¿por qué no pasas mañana?

**drought** [draʊt] *noun* ■ la **sequía.**

**drove** [drəʊv] *past tense* ➤ drive.

**drown** [draʊn] *verb* ■ **ahogarse: he drowned in the lake** se ahogó en el lago.

**drug** [drʌg] *noun*

1. el **medicamento: the doctor prescribed drugs** el médico le recetó medicamentos

2. la **droga: opium is a drug** el opio es una droga

➤ **a drug addict** un drogadicto.

**druggist** ['drʌgɪst] *noun* ■ el **farmacéutico,** la **farmacéutica.**

**drugstore** ['drʌgstɔːʳ] *noun* ■ *tienda que vende una gran variedad de artículos como medicamentos, cosméticos, periódicos, comida rápida, etc.*

**drum** [drʌm] *noun* ■ el **tambor: he's beating a drum** está golpeando un tambor

➤ **the drums** la batería: **she plays the drums** toca la batería.

**drummer** ['drʌməʳ] *noun* ■ el/la **baterista**.

**drunk** [drʌŋk] *(adjective & verb form)*
■ *adjective*
**borracho: you're drunk** estás borracho
➤ **to get drunk** emborracharse: **he got drunk** se emborrachó
■ *past participle*
➤ drink.

**dry** [draɪ] *(adjective & verb)*
■ *adjective*
**seco: the ink is dry** la tinta está seca
➤ **it'll be dry tomorrow** no va a llover mañana
➤ **the dry cleaner's** la tintorería
■ *verb*
*(past tense & past participle **dried**)*
1. **secarse: dry yourself** sécate; **she dried her hair** se secó el pelo
2. **secar: he's drying the dishes** está secando los platos; **we need to dry the clothes** tenemos que secar la ropa.

**dryer** ['draɪəʳ] *noun* ■ la **secadora: put the clothes in the dryer** pon la ropa en la secadora.

**duck** [dʌk] *( noun & verb)*
■ *noun*
el **pato: there are some ducks on the river** hay algunos patos en el río
■ *verb*
**agacharse: he ducked as he went through the door** al pasar por la puerta, se agachó.

**due** [dju:] *adjective*
➤ **what time is the train due?** ¿a qué hora llega el tren?
➤ **she's due back soon** va a regresar pronto
➤ **due to** debido a: **he arrived late due to the bad weather** llegó tarde debido al mal tiempo.

**dug** [dʌg] *past tense & past participle*
➤ dig.

**dull** [dʌl] *adjective*
1. **aburrido: the film is very dull** la película es muy aburrida
2. **gris: it's a dull day** hace un día gris.

**dumb** [dʌm] *adjective* ■ **mudo: he was struck dumb** se quedó mudo
➤ **that was a dumb thing to do** eso fue una tontería.

**dump** [dʌmp] *noun* ■ el **basural,** el **tiradero** *Mexico:* **we took the trash to the dump** llevamos la basura al basurero.

**during** ['djuərɪŋ] *preposition* ■ **durante**.

**dusk** [dʌsk] *noun* ■ el **atardecer: we went home at dusk** volvimos a casa al atardecer.

**dust** [dʌst] *(noun & verb)*
■ *noun*
el **polvo: there's a layer of dust on the table** hay una capa de polvo en la mesa
■ *verb*
**quitarle el polvo a, sacudir** *Mexico, Southern Cone:* **he dusted the shelf** le quitó el polvo a la repisa.

**dusty** ['dʌstɪ] *adjective*
1. **polvoriento: a dusty road** un camino polvoriento
2. **lleno de polvo: the furniture is all dusty** los muebles están todos llenos de polvo.

**duty** ['dju:tɪ] *(plural* **duties)** *noun* ■ el **deber: he's doing his duty** cumple con su deber
➤ **on duty**
1. **de guardia: Dr Jones is on duty** **el doctor Jones está de guardia**
2. **de servicio: go and get the police officer on duty** **ve a buscar al policía que está de servicio.**

**DVD** [di:vi:'di:] *(abbreviation of* Digital Video Disc *or* Digital Versatile Disc*)* *noun* ■ el **DVD: I watched the movie on DVD** vi la película en DVD.

**dwarf** [dwɔ:f] *(plural* dwarfs o dwarves [dwɔ:vz]*) noun* ■ el **enano,** la **enana**.

**dye** [daɪ] *(noun & verb)*
■ *noun*
la **tintura**

- *verb*
**teñir: I'm going to dye my jeans** voy a teñir mis jeans
➤ **to dye one's hair** teñirse el pelo: **she dyed
her hair pink** se tiñó el pelo de rosado.

**dying** ['daɪɪŋ]    *present    participle*
➤ die.

**each** [iːtʃ] *(adjective & pronoun)*
- *adjective*
**cada: each time I see that film, I cry** cada
vez que veo esa película, lloro
- *pronoun*
**cada uno** *(feminine* **cada una***):* **they each
have their own room** cada uno tiene su propio cuarto; **each of us had a dessert** cada
uno de nosotros comió un postre; **melons
cost 90 cents each** los melones cuestan 90
centavos cada uno
➤ **each other**

> A reflexive pronoun **se** or **nos** is normally
> used in Spanish to translate "each other":

**they love each other** se quieren: **do you
know each other?** ¿se conocen?: **we write
to each other** nos escribimos.

**eager** ['iːgər] *adjective*
➤ **to be eager to do something** estar impaciente por hacer algo
➤ **she's eager to learn Spanish** está impaciente por aprender español.

**eagle** ['iːgl] *noun* ■ el **águila** *(feminine)*

> Feminine noun that takes **un** and **el** in the
> singular.

**ear** [ɪər] *noun* ■ la **oreja**.

**earache** ['ɪəreɪk] *noun* ■ el **dolor de
oídos**
➤ **to have an earache** tener dolor de oídos.

**early** ['ɜːlɪ] *(adverb & adjective)*
- *adverb*
**temprano: I got up early** me levanté temprano; **you're early** llegas temprano
➤ **he's ten minutes early** llega con 10 minutos de antelación
- *adjective*
➤ **he had an early night** nos acostamos temprano
➤ **she made an early start** salió temprano
➤ **in early spring** a principios de la primavera.

**earn** [ɜːn] *verb* ■ **ganar: she earns 40
dollars an hour** gana 40 dólares por hora.

**earphones** ['ɪəfəʊnz] *plural noun* ■ los
**audífonos**.

**earring** ['ɪərɪŋ] *noun* ■ el **arete**, el **aro**
*Southern Cone*, la **caravana** *Uruguay*.

**earth** [ɜːθ] *noun*
1. la **Tierra: the moon goes around the
earth** la luna gira alrededor de la Tierra

> In Spanish, **Tierra** is written with a capital
> when it means the planet earth.

2. la **tierra: the box was covered with earth**
la caja estaba cubierta de tierra
➤ **what on earth is that?** ¿qué diablos es
eso?

**earthquake** ['ɜːθkweɪk] *noun* ■ el
**terremoto**.

**ease** [iːz] *(noun & verb)*
- *uncountable noun*
la **facilidad**
➤ **with ease** con facilidad: **he passed the
exam with ease** aprobó el examen con facilidad
➤ **at ease** a gusto: **she felt at ease with them**
se sintió a gusto con ellos

■ *verb*
**aliviar**: this ointment will ease the pain
esta pomada te aliviará el dolor.

**easily** ['ɪːzɪlɪ] *adverb*
1. **fácilmente**: I'll easily finish it tonight lo
terminaré fácilmente esta noche
2. **con mucho**: that's easily the best film
I've ever seen ésa es con mucho la mejor película que he visto.

**east** [ɪːst] *(noun, adjective & adverb)*
■ *noun*
el **este**: the sun rises in the east el sol sale
por el este
■ *adjective*
**este**: Boston is on the east coast of America Boston está en la costa este de Estados
Unidos
■ *adverb*
**hacia el este**: we went east fuimos hacia el
este
➤ **east of** al este de: **Louisiana is east of
Texas** Louisiana está al este de Texas.

**Easter** ['ɪːstər] *noun* ■ la **Semana Santa**: I went to see her at Easter fui a visitarla
en Semana Santa
➤ **an Easter egg** un huevo de Pascua.

**eastern** ['ɪːstən] *adjective* ■ **oriental**:
Eastern Europe Europa Oriental.

**easy** ['ɪːzɪ] *adjective* ■ **fácil**: an easy job
un trabajo fácil; it's easy to install this
software es fácil instalar este software
➤ **as easy as pie** pan comido.

**eat** [ɪːt] *(past tense* ate, *past participle*
eaten) *verb* ■ **comer**: she's eating a sandwich está comiendo un sandwich.

**eaten** ['ɪːtn] *past participle* ➤ eat.

**echo** ['ekəʊ] *(plural* echoes) *noun* ■ el
**eco**.

**eclipse** [ɪ'klɪps] *noun* ■ el **eclipse**:
there was an eclipse of the sun hubo un
eclipse de sol.

**ecological** [ɪːkə'lɒdʒɪkl] *adjective*
■ **ecológico**.

**ecology** [ɪ'kɒlədʒɪ] *noun* ■ la **ecolo-
gía**.

**economic** [ɪːkə'nɒmɪk] *adjective*
■ **económico**: an economic crisis una crisis económica.

**economical** [ɪːkə'nɒmɪkl] *adjective*
■ **económico**: this car is very economical
este coche es muy económico.

**economics** [ɪːkə'nɒmɪks] *uncountable*
*noun* ■ la **economía**: she's studying economics estudia economía.

**economy** [ɪ'kɒnəmɪ] *(plural* econom-
ies) *noun* ■ la **economía**: the country's
economy is strong la economía del país es
fuerte.

**Ecuador** ['ekwədɔːr] *noun* ■ **Ecuador**
*(masculine)*.

**Ecuadorian** [ˌekwə'dɔːrɪən] *(adjective
& noun)*
■ *adjective*

Remember not to use a capital letter for
the adjective in Spanish:

**ecuatoriano**: the Ecuadorian landscape
is beautiful el paisaje ecuatoriano es precioso
■ *noun*

In Spanish, a capital letter is not used for
the inhabitants of a country or region:

el **ecuatoriano**, la **ecuatoriana**: some
Ecuadorians live in jungle areas algunos
ecuatorianos viven en regiones selváticas.

**edge** [edʒ] *noun* ■ el **borde**: he's
standing on the edge of the cliff está parado al borde del acantilado.

**edition** [ɪ'dɪʃn] *noun* ■ la **edición** *(plural* las **ediciones**): a new edition of the
dictionary una nueva edición del diccionario.

**educated** ['edʒʊˌkeɪtɪd] *adjective*
■ **culto**: he's not very well educated no es
muy culto.

**education** [ˌedʒʊ'keɪʃn] *noun* ■ la
**educación**: education is important in
early childhood development la educación es importante durante la primera infancia; she works in education trabaja en educación.

**effect** [ɪ'fekt] *noun* ■ el **efecto**: the drug had no effect on him el medicamento no le hizo ningún efecto
➤ special effects los efectos especiales.

**effective** [ɪ'fektɪv] *adjective* ■ **eficaz** *(plural* **eficaces***)*: the treatment is very effective el tratamiento es muy eficaz.

**efficient** [ɪ'fɪʃənt] *adjective* ■ **eficiente**: our secretary is very efficient nuestra secretaria es muy eficiente.

**effort** ['efət] *noun* ■ el **esfuerzo**: make an effort! ¡haz un esfuerzo!

**egg** [eg] *noun* ■ el **huevo**: fried eggs huevos fritos, huevos estrellados *Mexico;* a boiled egg un huevo duro, un huevo cocido *Mexico;* egg yolk yema de huevo.

**eggplant** ['egplɑːnt] *noun* ■ la **berenjena**.

**eight** [eɪt] *number* ■ **ocho**: there are eight boys in the group hay ocho muchachos en el grupo; she's eight tiene ocho años; the film starts at eight la película empieza a las ocho.

**eighteen** [,eɪ'tiːn] *number* ■ **dieciocho**: she's eighteen tiene dieciocho años.

**eighteenth** [,eɪ'tiːnθ] *number* ■ **décimoctavo**
➤ it's her eighteenth birthday cumple dieciocho años
➤ it's May eighteenth es el dieciocho de mayo.

**eighth** [eɪtθ] *number* ■ **octavo**: on the eighth floor en el octavo piso
➤ it's November eighth es el ocho de noviembre.

**eighty** ['eɪtɪ] *number* ■ **ochenta**: she's eighty tiene ochenta años
➤ eighty-one ochenta y uno
➤ eighty-two ochenta y dos.

**either** ['aɪðər, 'iːðər] *(adverb, adjective & pronoun)*
■ *adverb*
**tampoco**: I don't want to go and he doesn't either yo no quiero ir y él tampoco;

I haven't had anything to eat — I haven't either no he comido nada – yo tampoco
■ *adjective*
**cualquiera de los dos**: either team could win cualquiera de los dos equipos podría ganar
➤ there are trees on either side of the road hay árboles a cada lado de la calle
■ *pronoun*
**cualquiera de los dos, ninguno**: you can have either, but not both puedes quedarte con cualquiera de los dos, pero no con ambos; I don't like either no me gusta ninguna
➤ does either of them play the guitar ¿alguno de los dos toca la guitarra?
➤ either ... or ... o ... o ...: you can pay in either euros or dollars puede pagar o en euros o en dólares
either you be quiet, or I'll go home o te quedas callado, o me voy a casa.

**elastic** [ɪ'læstɪk] *adjective* ■ el **elástico**.

**elbow** ['elbəʊ] *noun* ■ el **codo**.

**elder** ['eldər] *adjective* ■ **mayor**: he's my elder brother es mi hermano mayor.

**elderly** ['eldəlɪ] *adjective* ■ **anciano**: she looks after her elderly parents cuida a sus padres ancianos.

**eldest** ['eldɪst] *adjective* ■ **mayor**: she's my eldest sister es mi hermana mayor.

**elect** [ɪ'lekt] *verb* ■ **elegir**: he was elected president lo eligieron presidente.

**election** [ɪ'lekʃn] *noun* ■ la **elección** *(plural* **las elecciones***)*: he won the election ganó la elección

ELECTIONS

Las elecciones presidenciales estadounidenses tienen lugar cada cuatro años. Por ley, el presidente no puede mantenerse en el cargo más de dos periodos consecutivos. Las elecciones se celebran el día después del primer lunes de noviembre.

**electric** [ɪ'lektrɪk] *adjective* ■ **eléctrico**: an electric light una luz eléctrica

➤ **an electric blanket** una cobija eléctrica, una frazada eléctrica

➤ **an electric shock** una descarga eléctrica, un toque eléctrico *Mexico:* **I got an electric shock** me dio una descarga eléctrica.

**electrical** [ɪˈlektrɪkl] *adjective* ■ eléctrico: **an electrical appliance** un aparato eléctrico.

**electrician** [ˌɪlekˈtrɪʃn] *noun* ■ el/la electricista: **he's an electrician** es electricista.

**electricity** [ˌɪlekˈtrɪsətɪ] *noun* ■ la electricidad.

**electronic** [ˌɪlekˈtrɒnɪk] *adjective* ■ electrónico: **electronic mail** correo electrónico.

**elegant** [ˈelɪgənt] *adjective* ■ elegante.

**elementary school** [ˌelɪˈmentərɪskuːl] *noun* ■ la escuela primaria.

**elephant** [ˈelɪfənt] *noun* ■ el elefante.

**elevator** [ˈelɪveɪtər] *noun* ■ el ascensor, el elevador *Mexico.*

**eleven** [ɪˈlevn] *number* ■ once: **there are eleven glasses** hay once vasos; **he's eleven** tiene once años; **I went out at eleven** salí a las once.

**eleventh** [ɪˈlevnθ] *number* ■ onceavo

➤ **it's his eleventh birthday** cumple once años

➤ **it's January eleventh** es el once de enero.

**El Salvador** [ˌelˈsælvədɔːr] *noun* ■ El Salvador.

**else** [els] *adverb* ■ más: **what else?** ¿qué más?; **anyone else?** ¿alguien más?; **nothing else** nada más; **nobody else** nadie más; **I don't want anything else** no quiero nada más

➤ **everyone else** todos los demás: **everyone else had left** todos los demás se habían ido

➤ **someone else** otra persona

➤ **something else** otra cosa

➤ **or else** de lo contrario: **hurry up or else**

**we'll be late** apúrate o de lo contrario vamos a llegar tarde.

**e-mail, email** [ˈiːmeɪl] *(noun & verb)*

■ *noun*

1. el correo electrónico: **what's your e-mail address** ¿cuál es la dirección de tu correo electrónico?

2. el e-mail: **I'll send you an e-mail** te voy a mandar un e-mail

■ *verb*

➤ **to e-mail somebody** mandarle un e-mail a alguien: **he e-mailed me** me mandó un e-mail

➤ **to e-mail something** mandar algo por correo electrónico

➤ **he e-mailed the file to me** me mandó el archivo por correo electrónico.

**embarrassed** [ɪmˈbærəst] *adjective* ■ avergonzado, apenado *Latin America except Southern Cone:* **Laura's very embarrassed** Laura está muy avergonzada

⚠ La palabra inglesa **embarrassed** es un falso amigo, no significa "embarazada".

**embarrassing** [ɪmˈbærəsɪŋ] *adjective* ■ embarazoso, penoso *Latin America except Southern Cone:* **it's very embarrassing** es muy embarazoso.

**embassy** [ˈembəsɪ] *(plural* embassies*)* *noun* ■ la embajada: **the United States embassy** la embajada de Estados Unidos.

**emerald** [ˈemərəld] *noun* ■ la esmeralda.

**emergency** [ɪˈmɜːdʒənsɪ] *(plural* emergencies*)* *(noun & adjective)*

■ *noun*

la emergencia: **this is an emergency!** ¡es una emergencia!

➤ **in an emergency** en caso de emergencia: **in an emergency call the police** en caso de emergencia, llame a la policía

■ *adjective*

emergencia: **the emergency services** los servicios de emergencia

➤ **an emergency exit** una salida de emergencia.

**78**

**emotion** [ɪ'məʊʃn] *noun* ■ la **emoción** (*plural* las **emociones**).

**emotional** [ɪ'məʊʃənl]                  *adjective*
■ **emotivo**: she tends to be an emotional person tiende a ser emotiva.

**emperor** ['empərər] *noun* ■ el **emperador**.

**emphasize** ['emfəsaɪz] *verb* ■ **hacer hincapié en**: he emphasized the importance of physical exercise hizo hincapié en la importancia del ejercicio físico.

**empire** ['empaɪər] *noun* ■ el **imperio**: the Roman empire el imperio romano.

**employ** [ɪm'plɔɪ] *verb* ■ **emplear**: the firm employs 100 people la empresa emplea a 100 personas.

**employee** [ɪm'plɔɪiː] *noun* ■ el **empleado**, la **empleada**.

**employer** [ɪm'plɔɪər]    *noun*    ■    el **empleador**, la **empleadora**.

**employment** [ɪm'plɔɪmənt] *noun* ■ el **empleo**.

**empty** ['emptɪ] (*adjective & verb*)

■ *adjective*
**vacío**
■ *verb*
(*past tense & past participle* **emptied**) **vaciar**: she emptied the drawers vació los cajones
➤ he emptied his pockets se vació los bolsillos.

**encourage** [ɪn'kʌrɪdʒ] *verb* ■ **animar**
➤ to encourage somebody to do something animar a alguien a hacer algo: he encouraged me to work harder me animó a trabajar más duro.

**encyclopedia** [ɪn,saɪklə'piːdjə] *noun* ■ la **enciclopedia**.

**end** [end] (*noun & verb*)

■ *noun*
el **final**: she dies at the end of the film se muere al final de la película; the shop's at the end of the street la tienda está al final de la calle

➤ in the end al final: in the end she said yes al final dijo que sí
■ *verb*
1. **terminar**: the show ends at 11 o'clock el espectáculo termina a las once; how does the story end? ¿cómo termina la historia?
2. **terminar con**: this ended our friendship eso terminó con nuestra amistad

**end up** *phrasal verb* ■ **terminar**: he ended up doing all the work himself terminó haciendo todo el trabajo; he ended up in Spain terminó en España.

**ending** ['endɪŋ] *noun* ■ el **final**: the film has a happy ending la película tiene un final feliz.

**enemy** ['enɪmɪ] (*plural* enemies) *noun* ■ el **enemigo**, la **enemiga**.

**energetic** [,enə'dʒetɪk] *adjective*
1. **lleno de energía**: a very energetic person una persona llena de energía
2. **enérgico**: a very energetic exercise un ejercicio muy enérgico.

**energy** ['enədʒɪ] *uncountable noun* ■ la **energía**.

**engaged** [ɪn'geɪdʒd] *adjective* ■ **comprometido**: they are engaged están comprometidos
➤ to get engaged comprometerse: they have just got engaged acaban de comprometerse.

**engagement** [ɪn'geɪdʒmənt]    *noun*
■ el **compromiso**
➤ engagement ring anillo de compromiso.

**engine** ['endʒɪn] *noun*
1. el **motor**: their car has a powerful engine su coche tiene un motor poderoso
2. la **locomotora**: a steam engine una locomotora a vapor.

**engineer** [,endʒɪ'nɪər] *noun* ■ el **ingeniero**, la **ingeniera**: the engineer that designed the bridge el ingeniero que diseñó el puente.

**England** ['ɪŋglənd] *noun* ■ **Inglaterra** (*feminine*).

**English** [ˈɪŋglɪʃ] *(adjective & noun)*

■ *adjective*

> Remember not to use a capital letter for
> the adjective or the language in Spanish:

**inglés: the English countryside** la campiña
inglesa

■ *noun*
**el inglés: do you speak English?** ¿hablas
inglés?

> In Spanish, a capital letter is not used for
> the inhabitants of a country or region:

➤ **the English** los ingleses.

**Englishman** [ˈɪŋglɪʃmən] *(plural* Englishmen [ˈɪŋglɪʃmən]) *noun* ■ el **inglés**
*(plural* los **ingleses**).

**Englishwoman** [ˈɪŋglɪʃˌwʊmən] *(plural* Englishwomen [ˈɪŋglɪʃˌwɪmɪn]) *noun*
■ la **inglesa**.

**enjoy** [ɪnˈdʒɔɪ] *verb* ■ **disfrutar: she
enjoyed the book** disfrutó el libro; **I enjoy
listening to music** disfruto escuchando música

➤ **to enjoy oneself** divertirse: **I really enjoyed myself at the party** realmente me divertí en la fiesta.

**enormous** [ɪˈnɔːməs]                    *adjective*
■ **enorme**.

**enough** [ɪˈnʌf] *(adjective, adverb & pronoun)*

■ *adjective*
**suficiente: do you have enough money?**
¿tienes suficiente dinero?

■ *adverb & pronoun*
**suficiente: would you like some more or
do you have enough?** ¿quieres más o tienes suficiente?

➤ **that's enough!** ¡basta ya!

**enter** [ˈentəʳ] *verb*

1. **entrar: he knocked on the door and entered** golpeó en la puerta y entró

2. **entrar a: everyone looked at her when
she entered the room** todos la miraron
cuando entró a la habitación

3. **presentarse a: I entered a competition**
me presenté a un concurso

4. **introducir: enter your password and
click on OK** introduzca su clave y haga clic en
OK

➤ **the enter key** la tecla enter.

**entertainment** [ˌentəˈteɪnmənt]
*noun* ■ el **entretenimiento: this film is
good family entertainment** la película es
un buen entretenimiento para toda la familia

➤ **the entertainment business** la industria
del espectáculo.

**enthusiasm** [ɪnˈθjuːzɪæzm] *noun* ■ el
**entusiasmo**.

**enthusiastic** [ɪnˌθjuːzɪˈæstɪk] *adjective* ■ **entusiasta**.

**entire** [ɪnˈtaɪəʳ] *adjective* ■ **entero: he
ate an entire chicken** se comió un pollo
entero.

**entirely** [ɪnˈtaɪəlɪ] *adverb* ■ **completamente: it's entirely my fault** el error es
completamente mío.

**entrance** [ˈentrəns] *noun* ■ la **entrada: wait for me at the school entrance**
espérame en la entrada del colegio

➤ **an entrance exam** un examen de admisión.

**entry** [ˈentrɪ] *noun* ■ la **entrada**

➤ **no entry** prohibida la entrada.

**envelope** [ˈenvələʊp] *noun* ■ el **sobre**.

**environment** [ɪnˈvaɪərənmənt] *noun*

➤ **the environment** el medio ambiente: **we
must protect the environment** debemos
proteger el medio ambiente.

**episode** [ˈepɪsəʊd] *noun* ■ el **episodio**.

**equal** [ˈiːkwəl] *(adjective & verb)*

■ *adjective*
**igual: I divided the cake into two equal
parts** corté el pastel en dos partes iguales

➤ **equal opportunities** igualdad de oportunidades

■ *verb*
**ser igual a: 4 plus 5 equals 9** 4 más 5 es
igual a 9.

**equator** [ɪˈkweɪtərʳ] *noun* ■ el **ecua-dor**.

**equipment** [ɪˈkwɪpmənt] *uncountable noun* ■ el **equipo**: camping equipment equipo de campamento.

**equivalent** [ɪˈkwɪvələnt] *(adjective & noun)*
- *adjective*
  **equivalente**
➤ to be equivalent to something equivaler a algo: this is equivalent to 5 dollars esto equivale a 5 dólares
- *noun*
  el **equivalente**: it costs the equivalent of $50 cuesta el equivalente a 50 dólares.

**eraser** [ɪˈreɪzərʳ] *noun* ■ la **goma**: have you seen my eraser? ¿has visto mi goma?

**error** [ˈerərʳ] *noun* ■ el **error**
➤ a printing error un error de imprenta.

**erupt** [ɪˈrʌpt] *verb* ■ **entrar en erup-ción**: the volcano erupted el volcán entró en erupción.

**escalator** [ˈeskəleɪtərʳ] *noun* ■ la **esca-lera mecánica, la escalera eléctrica** *Mex-ico*.

**escape** [ɪˈskeɪp] *(noun & verb)*
- *noun*
  la **fuga**: the escape of the prisoners la fu-ga de los prisioneros
➤ I had a narrow escape me salvé por un pe-lo
- *verb*
  1. **escaparse**: a monkey escaped from the zoo un mono se escapó del zoológico
  2. **fugarse**: he escaped from prison se fugó de la cárcel.

**especially** [ɪˈspeʃəlɪ] *adverb* ■ **espe-cialmente**: I like all animals, especially horses me gustan todos los animales, espe-cialmente los caballos.

**essay** [ˈeseɪ] *noun* ■ la **redacción** *(plural* las **redacciones***)*: an essay on the envi-ronment una redacción sobre el medio ambiente.

**estimate** [ˈestɪmeɪt] *verb* ■ **calcular**: he estimated the price at 500 dollars cal-culó el precio en 500 dólares.

**EU** [ˈiːjuː] *(abbreviation of* European Union*) noun* ■ la **Unión Europea**.

**euro** [ˈjʊərəʊ] *(plural* euro o euros*) noun* ■ el **euro**: it costs 50 euros cuesta 50 euros.

**Europe** [ˈjʊərəp] *noun* ■ **Europa** *(fem-inine)*.

**European** [ˌjʊərəˈpiːən] *(adjective & noun)*
- *adjective*

  Remember not to use a capital letter for the adjective in Spanish:

  **europeo**: the European continent el conti-nente europeo
➤ the European Union la Unión Europea
- *noun*

  In Spanish, a capital letter is not used for the inhabitants of a country or region:

  el **europeo**, la **europea**: many Europeans travel frequently muchos europeos viajan con frecuencia.

**eve** [iːv] *noun* ■ la **víspera**
➤ Christmas Eve Noche Buena
➤ New Year's Eve Noche vieja.

**even** [ˈiːvn] *(adjective & adverb)*
- *adjective*
  1. **parejo**: the surface is even la superficie es pareja
  2. **par**: four is an even number el cuatro es un número par
➤ their chances are about even tienen casi las mismas posibilidades
➤ to get even with somebody vengarse de alguien
- *adverb*
  1. **incluso**: it has everything, even a tennis court tiene de todo, incluso una cancha de tenis
  2. **aún**: it's even better now ahora está aún mejor; it's even more difficult es aún más difícil

➤ not **even** ni siquiera: **he can't even sing** ni siquiera sabe cantar

> **Aunque** is followed by a verb in the subjunctive in Spanish when it means "even if".

➤ **even if** aunque: **even if he comes it won't make any difference** aunque venga, no habrá ninguna diferencia
➤ **even though** a pesar de que: **he went to school even though he wasn't well** fue al colegio a pesar de que no se sentía bien.

**evening** ['i:vnɪŋ] *noun*

1. *before dark* la **tarde**: **at six in the evening** a las seis de la tarde; **I'm staying at home this evening** esta tarde me quedo en casa; **yesterday evening** ayer en la tarde
2. *after dark* la **noche**: **at ten o'clock in the evening** a las diez de la noche
➤ **good evening!** ¡buenas noches!
➤ **evening classes** clases nocturnas.

**event** [ɪ'vent] *noun*

1. el **acontecimiento**: **it's an important event** es un acontecimiento importante
2. la **prueba**: **he participated in three events at the track meet** participó en tres pruebas en el encuentro de atletismo.

**eventual** [ɪ'ventʃʊəl] *adjective* ■ **final**: **the eventual results will be published** los resultados finales serán publicados.

**eventually** [ɪ'ventʃʊəlɪ] *adverb* ■ **finalmente**: **he left eventually** finalmente, se fue.

**ever** ['evəʳ] *adverb*

1. **nunca**: **nothing ever happens** nunca pasa nada; **I hardly ever watch television** casi nunca veo televisión
2. **alguna vez**: **have you ever been to China?** ¿has estado alguna vez en China?
➤ **as ever** como siempre: **she's as cheerful as ever** está tan alegre como siempre
➤ **for ever** para siempre: **he left for ever** se fue para siempre
➤ **ever since** desde que: **it's been raining ever since I arrived** ha estado lloviendo desde que llegué.

**every** ['evrɪ] *adjective* ■ **todos**

> "Every" + a singular noun is usually translated by **todos los** or **todas las** + a plural noun in Spanish. You can also use **cada** + singular noun, if you want to emphasize that you mean "every single one":

**every student in the class passed the exam** todos los estudiantes de la clase salvaron el examen; **every house in the street has a garden** todas las casas de esta calle tienen un jardín; **every student recited a different poem** cada estudiante recitó un poema diferente
➤ **every day** todos los días
➤ **every other day** un día sí y otro no
➤ **every time** cada vez: **he wins every time** cada vez gana
➤ **every time that** cada vez que: **every time that I go to California, I visit my uncle** cada vez que voy a California, visito a mi tío.

**everybody, everyone** ['evrɪ,bɒdɪ, 'evrɪwʌn] *pronoun* ■ **todos**: **everybody knows him** todos lo conocen; **everyone was enjoying themselves** todos se estaban divirtiendo.

**everything** ['evrɪθɪŋ] *pronoun* ■ **todo**: **do you have everything?** ¿tienes todo?

**everywhere** ['evrɪweəʳ] *adverb*

1. **en todas partes**: **I've looked for it everywhere** lo busqué en todas partes
2. **dondequiera que**: **she follows me everywhere I go** ella me sigue dondequiera que vaya

> **Dondequiera que** is followed by a verb in the subjunctive.

**evidence** ['evɪdəns] *uncountable noun*

1. las **pruebas**: **there's no evidence that he killed her** no hay pruebas de que él la haya matado
2. el **testimonio**: **his evidence was very important in the case** su testimonio era muy importante para el caso.

**evil** ['iːvl]    *(adjective & noun)*
■ *adjective*
   **malvado:** he's an evil man es un hombre malvado
■ *noun*
   **el mal:** to tell good from evil distinguir el bien del mal.

**exact** [ɪg'zækt] *adjective* ■ **exacto.**

**exactly** [ɪg'zæktlɪ] *adverb* ■ **exactamente:** that's exactly what I mean eso es exactamente lo que quiero decir
➤ it's exactly 6 o'clock son las seis en punto.

**exaggerate** [ɪg'zædʒəreɪt]*verb* ■ **exagerar:** don't exaggerate! ¡no exageres!

**exam, examination** [ɪg'zæm, ɪg,zæmɪ'neɪʃn] *noun* ■ el **examen** *(plural* los **exámenes)**: I passed my English exam aprobé el examen de inglés.

**examine** [ɪg'zæmɪn] *verb* ■ **examinar:** he examined the fly through the microscope examinó la mosca por el microscopio.

**example** [ɪg'zaːmpl] *noun* ■ el **ejemplo**
➤ for example por ejemplo.

**excellent** ['eksələnt] *adjective* ■ **excelente.**

**except** [ɪk'sept] *preposition & conjunction* ■ **excepto:** everyone can swim except me todos saben nadar excepto yo
➤ except that salvo que: I don't remember anything except that I was scared no recuerdo nada salvo que tenía miedo.

**exception** [ɪk'sepʃn] *noun* ■ la **excepción** *(plural* las **excepciones)**: it's an exception to the rule es una excepción a la regla
➤ to make an exception hacer una excepción: I'll make an exception for you haré una excepción contigo.

**exchange** [ɪks'tʃeɪndʒ] *(verb & noun)*
■ *verb*
   **cambiar:** she exchanged the CD for a book cambió el CD por un libro
■ *noun*
   I gave him a camera in exchange for a watch le di una cámara a cambio de un reloj

➤ the exchange rate la tasa de cambio.

**excited** [ɪk'saɪtɪd] *adjective* ■ **entusiasmado.**

**exciting** [ɪk'saɪtɪŋ] *adjective* ■ **emocionante.**

**exclamation point** [,eksklə'meɪʃn-pɔɪnt] *noun* ■ el **signo de exclamación.**

**excuse** *(noun & verb)*
■ *noun*
   [ɪk'skjuːs] la **excusa:** that's just an excuse! ¡eso no es más que una excusa!
■ *verb*
   [ɪk'skjuːz] **disculpar:** excuse me! ¡discúlpeme!

**exercise** ['eksəsaɪz] *noun* ■ el **ejercicio:** he doesn't get enough exercise no hace suficiente ejercicio.

**exhausted** [ɪg'zɔːstɪd]    *adjective* ■ **agotado.**

**exhibit** [ɪg'zɪbɪt] *noun* ■ la **exposición** *(plural* las **exposiciones)**: there's a big exhibit in New York hay una gran exposición en Nueva York.

**exist** [ɪg'zɪst] *verb* ■ **existir:** that company doesn't exist anymore esa compañía ya no existe.

**exit** ['eksɪt] *noun* ■ la **salida**

⚠️ Exit es un falso amigo, no significa "éxito".

**exotic** [ɪg'zɒtɪk] *adjective* ■ **exótico.**

**expect** [ɪk'spekt] *verb*
1. **esperar:** I wasn't expecting his visit no esperaba su visita; she's expecting a baby está esperando un bebé

The verb **esperar** is followed by a verb in the subjunctive in Spanish:

I was expecting him to be here esperaba que él estuviera aquí
2. **suponer que:** I expect he has left the country supongo que ha salido del país; I expect so supongo que sí.

**expel** [ık'spel] *(past tense & past participle* expelled*) verb* ■ **expulsar:** they expelled Fred from school expulsaron a Fred del colegio.

**expenses** [ık'spensəz] *plural noun* ■ los **gastos**.

**expensive** [ık'spensıv] *adjective* ■ **caro**.

**experience** [ık'spıərıəns] *noun* ■ la **experiencia:** he has a lot of experience tiene mucha experiencia.

**experiment** [ık'sperımənt] *(noun & verb)*
■ *noun*
el **experimento:** they did an experiment in the laboratory hicieron un experimento en el laboratorio
■ *verb*
**experimentar:** she experimented with drugs experimentó con las drogas.

**expert** ['ekspɜ:t] *noun* ■ el **experto:** he's a computer expert es experto en computadoras.

**explain** [ık'spleın] *verb* ■ **explicar:** can you explain what happened? ¿puedes explicar lo que ocurrió?

**explanation** [ˌeksplə'neıʃn] *noun* ■ la **explicación** *(plural* las **explicaciones)**.

**explode** [ık'spləʊd] *verb*
1. **estallar:** the bomb exploded la bomba estalló
2. **hacer estallar:** the police exploded the bomb la policía hizo estallar la bomba.

**explore** [ık'splɔ:ʳ] *verb* ■ **explorar:** they explored the ruins exploraron las ruinas.

**explorer** [ık'splɔ:rəʳ] *noun* ■ el **explorador,** la **exploradora**.

**explosion** [ık'spləʊʒn] *noun* ■ la **explosión** *(plural* las **explosiones)**.

**export** [ık'spɔ:t] *verb* ■ **exportar:** Brazil exports coffee Brasil exporta café.

**express** [ık'spres] *(adjective & verb)*
■ *adjective*
**expreso:** an express train un tren expreso
■ *verb*
**expresar:** she expressed her feelings expresó sus sentimientos
➤ **to express oneself** expresarse: he expresses himself well in Spanish se expresa bien en castellano.

**expression** [ık'spreʃn] *noun* ■ la **expresión** *(plural* las **expresiones)**: it's a common expression es una expresión común; her expression changed le cambió la expresión.

**extend** [ık'stend] *verb*
1. **prolongar:** I'm going to extend my stay voy a prolongar mi estadía
2. **tender:** he extended his hand tendió su mano
3. **extenderse:** the plain extends to the mountain la llanura se extiende hasta la montaña.

**extension** [ık'stenʃn] *noun*
1. la **ampliación** *(plural* las **ampliaciones)**: we've built an extension hicimos una ampliación
2. la **extensión,** el **anexo** *Chile,* el **interno** *River Plate:* you can call me on extension 429 me puedes llamar a la extensión 429.

**extent** [ık'stent] *noun*
➤ **to a certain extent** hasta cierto punto: **to a certain extent you're right** hasta cierto punto tienes razón.

**exterior** [ık'stıərıəʳ] *adjective* ■ **exterior:** an exterior wall un muro exterior.

**extinct** [ık'stıŋkt] *adjective* ■ **extinct:** dinosaurs are extinct los dinosaurios están extintos
➤ **to become extinct** extinguirse: **that type of whale is becoming extinct** ese tipo de ballenas se está extinguiendo.

**extra** ['ekstrə] *(adjective, adverb & noun)*
■ *adjective*
1. **suplementario:** he's taking extra lessons está tomando clases suplementarias
2. **de más:** I have an extra pencil tengo un lápiz de más

■ *adverb*
**más:** it's worth paying extra for quality vale la pena pagar más para obtener mayor calidad

■ *noun*
1. el **extra:** the price is fixed and there are no **extras** el precio es fijo y no hay extras
2. el/la **extra:** he's an **extra** in the film es un extra en la película.

**extraordinary** [ɪk'strɔːdnɪɪ] *adjective*
■ **extraordinario**.

**extravagant** [ɪk'strævəgənt] *adjective*
1. **derrochador:** he's very extravagant with his money es muy derrochador con su dinero
2. **extravagante:** he wears very extravagant outfits usa ropas muy extravagantes.

**extreme** [ɪk'striːm] *(adjective & noun)*
■ *adjective*
**extremo:** extreme sports deportes extremos
■ *noun*
el **extremo:** she goes from one extreme to another va de un extremo a otro.

**extremely** [ɪk'striːmlɪ] *adverb* ■ **sumamente:** it's an extremely interesting book es un libro sumamente interesante.

**eye** [aɪ] *noun* ■ el **ojo:** she has green eyes tiene ojos verdes
➤ **to keep an eye on something** vigilar algo: can you keep an eye on my luggage? ¿puedes vigilar mi equipaje?

**eyebrow** ['aɪbraʊ] *noun* ■ la **ceja**.

**eyedrops** ['aɪdrɒps] *plural noun* ■ las **gotas para los ojos**.

**eyelash** ['aɪlæʃ] *noun* ■ la **pestaña:** she has long eyelashes tiene las pestañas largas.

**eyelid** ['aɪlɪd] *noun* ■ el **párpado**.

**eyesight** ['aɪsaɪt] *noun* ■ la **vista:** he has good eyesight tiene buena vista.

**fabric** ['fæbrɪk] *noun* ■ el **tela:** cotton fabric tela de algodón

 **Fabric** es un falso amigo, no significa "fábrica".

**fabulous** ['fæbjʊləs] *adjective* ■ **fabuloso**.

**face** [feɪs] *(noun & verb)*
■ *noun*
1. la **cara:** she has a beautiful face tiene una cara hermosa
2. la **mueca:** he made a face hizo muecas
3. la **esfera,** la **carátula** *Mexico*: the clock face is broken la esfera del reloj está rota
■ *verb*
1. **enfrentar:** we must face these problems tenemos que enfrentar estos problemas
2. **dar a:** our house faces the sea nuestra casa da al mar
➤ **face to face** cara a cara
➤ **to face somebody or something** volverse hacia alguien or algo, voltearse hacia alguien or algo *Mexico*

**face up to** *phrasal verb* ■ **enfrontar:** he faced up to the problem enfrontó el problema.

**facilities** [fə'sɪlətɪz] *plural noun* ■ las **instalaciones:** the school has good sports facilities el colegio tiene buenas instalaciones deportivas.

**fact** [fækt] noun
1. el **hecho**: that's a fact es un hecho
2. *(uncountable noun)* la **realidad**: fact and fiction realidad y ficción
➤ in fact de hecho.

**factory** ['fæktərɪ] *(plural* factories*)* noun ■ la **fábrica**.

**fade** [feɪd] verb
1. **desteñirse**: your pants have faded se destiñeron tus pantalones
2. **apagarse**: the color has faded with time el color se ha apagado con el tiempo; the light is fading la luz se está apagando.

**fail** [feɪl] verb
1. **reprobar**: he failed the exam reprobó el examen
2. **fracasar**: I tried to persuade him but I failed traté de convencerlo, pero fracasé
3. **fallar**: the brakes failed los frenos fallaron
➤ the letter failed to arrive la carta no llegó
➤ to fail to do something no lograr hacer algo: I failed to convince him no logré convencerlo.

**failure** ['feɪljər] noun ■ el **fracaso**: it ended in failure terminó en fracaso; she's a failure es una fracasa
➤ a power failure un apagón.

**faint** [feɪnt] *(adjective & verb)*
■ adjective
1. **leve**: there's a faint smell of smoke hay un leve olor a humo
2. **poco visible**: the text is too faint to read el texto es muy poco visible para poder leerlo
3. **débil**: your voice is a bit faint tu voz es un poco débil
4. **tenue**: a faint light una luz tenue
➤ to feel faint sentirse mareado: he suddenly felt faint de pronto, se sintió mareado
■ verb
**desmayarse**: she fainted se desmayó.

**fair** [feər] adjective
1. **justo**: it's not fair! ¡no es justo!
2. **bastante**: she has a fair chance of winning tiene bastantes posibilidades de ganar
3. **rubio, güero** *Mexico*: Donald has fair hair Donald tiene el pelo rubio
4. **blanco**: Carol has fair skin Carol tiene la piel blanca

5. **buen**: the weather is fair hace buen tiempo.

**fairly** ['feəlɪ] adverb
1. **bastante**: it's fairly late es bastante tarde
2. **justamente**: they divided the money fairly repartieron el dinero justamente.

**fairy** ['feərɪ] *(plural* fairies*)* noun ■ el **hada** *(feminine)*
➤ a fairy tale un cuento de hadas.

**faith** [feɪθ] noun
1. la **confianza**: I've lost faith in him le perdí la confianza
2. la **fe**: the Christian faith la fe cristiana.

**faithful** ['feɪθfʊl] adjective ■ **fiel**.

**fake** [feɪk] *(adjective & noun)*
■ adjective
**falso**: these pearls are fake estas perlas son falsas
■ noun
la **falsificación** *(plural* las **falsificaciones***)*: this painting is a fake esta pintura es una falsificación.

**fall** [fɔːl] *(noun & verb)*
■ noun
1. la **caída**: a hard fall una caída dura
2. el **otoño**: in the fall en otoño
■ verb
*(past tense* fell*, past participle* fallen*)*
1. **caerse**: I slipped and fell me resbalé y me caí
2. **bajar**: the temperature has fallen bajó la temperatura
➤ to fall asleep dormirse: she fell asleep se durmió
➤ to fall in love enamorarse: he fell in love with Britney se enamoró de Britney

**fall down** phrasal verb ■ **caerse**: the little girl fell down la niña se cayó.

**fall off** phrasal verb ■ **caerse**: he fell off his bicycle se cayó de la bicicleta.

**fall out** phrasal verb
1. **caerse**: the keys fell out of my pocket se me cayeron las llaves del bolsillo
2. **pelearse**: he's fallen out with his best friend se peleó con su mejor amigo.

**fall over** *phrasal verb*
1. **caerse:** the vase fell over se cayó el jarrón
2. **tropezarse:** he fell over a log se tropezó con un tronco.

**fallen** ['fɔːln] *past participle* ➤ fall.

**false** [fɔːls] *adjective*
1. **falso:** what he said is false lo que dijo es falso
2. **postizo:** he has false teeth tiene la dentadura postiza.

**fame** [feɪm] *noun* ▪ la **fama**.

**familiar** [fə'mɪljəʳ] *adjective* ▪ **familiar:** she has a familiar face tiene una cara familiar.

**family** ['fæmlɪ] *(plural* families*) noun* ▪ la **familia:** the Smith family la familia Smith.

**famous** ['feɪməs] *adjective* ▪ **famoso**.

**fan** [fæn] *noun*
1. el **abanico:** she was holding a fan llevaba un abanico
2. el **ventilador:** an electric fan un ventilador eléctrico
3. el **admirador**, la **admiradora:** she's a fan of the Beatles es admiradora de los Beatles
4. el/la **hincha:** soccer fans hinchas de fútbol.

**fantastic** [fæn'tæstɪk] *adjective* ▪ **fantástico**.

**far** [faːʳ] *(comparative* farther, further, *superlative* farthest, furthest*) (adverb & adjective)*
▪ *adverb*
1. **lejos:** it's not far or it's not far away no queda lejos; Boston isn't far from New York Boston no queda lejos de Nueva York
2. **mucho:** I feel far better me siento mucho mejor
➤ how far is it? ¿a qué distancia estamos?: how far is it to Miami? ¿a qué distancia estamos de Miami?
➤ as far as I know que yo sepa: she's not coming, as far as I know no va a venir, que yo sepa
➤ so far hasta ahora: so far so good hasta ahora, todo bien
➤ that's far too much es demasiado
▪ *adjective*

extremo: the far right la extrema derecha
➤ at the far end of the road al otro extremo de la calle
➤ the Far East el Extremo Oriente
➤ in the far north en el extremo norte.

**fare** [feəʳ] *noun* ▪ la **tarifa:** the bus fare to Chicago la tarifa de autobús a Chicago.

**farm** [faːm] *noun* ▪ la **granja**, el **rancho** *Mexico*.

**farmer** ['faːməʳ] *noun* ▪ el **agricultor**, la **agricultora**, el **ranchero** *Mexico*, la **ranchera** *Mexico*.

**farming** ['faːmɪŋ] *noun* ▪ la **agricultura**.

**farther** ['faːðəʳ] *(comparative of* far*) (adverb & adjective)*
▪ *adverb*
**más lejos:** we have to walk a bit farther tenemos que caminar un poco más lejos
▪ *adjective*
**más alejado:** on the farther side of the room en la parte más alejada de la habitación.

**farthest** ['faːðəst] *(superlative of* far*) (adverb & adjective)*
▪ *adverb*
**lo más lejos:** he went the farthest él fue lo más lejos
▪ *adjective*
**el más alejado:** the farthest tree from the house el árbol más alejado de la casa.

**fascinating** ['fæsɪneɪtɪŋ] *adjective* ▪ **fascinante**.

**fashion** ['fæʃn] *noun* ▪ la **moda:** it's the latest fashion es la última moda
➤ in fashion de moda: this coat is in fashion este abrigo está de moda
➤ it has gone out of fashion pasó de moda: that hairstyle has gone out of fashion este corte de pelo pasó de moda
➤ a fashion show un desfile de modas.

**fashionable** ['fæʃnəbl] *adjective* ▪ **a la moda:** she likes to buy fashionable clothes le gusta comprar ropa a la moda.

**fast** [fɑːst] *(adjective & adverb)*

■ *adjective*
**rápido:** this train is very fast este tren es muy rápido

➤ my watch is fast mi reloj está adelantado; the clock is ten minutes fast el reloj está adelantado por diez minutos

➤ fast food comida rápida

➤ a fast-food restaurant un restaurante de comida rápida

■ *adverb*
**rápido:** he works fast trabaja rápido

➤ to be fast asleep estar profundamente dormido: the baby is fast asleep el bebé está profundamente dormido.

**fasten** ['fɑːsn] *verb*

1. **abrocharse:** fasten your seat belts abróchense el cinturón de seguridad

2. **cerrar:** she fastened her bag cerró su cartera.

**fat** [fæt] *(adjective & noun)*

■ *adjective*
**gordo:** he's very fat es muy gordo

➤ to get fat engordar: she doesn't want to get fat no quiere engordar

■ *noun*
la **grasa:** there's too much fat on this ham este jamón tiene mucha grasa; this yogurt has no fat in it este yogurt no contiene grasa.

**fatal** ['feɪtl] *adjective*

1. **mortal:** he had a fatal accident tuvo un accidente mortal

2. **fatídico:** it was a fatal mistake fue un error fatídico.

**father** ['fɑːðər] *noun* ■ el **padre**

➤ Father's Day el Día del Padre.

**father-in-law** ['fɑːðərɪnlɔː] *(plural fathers-in-law) noun* ■ el **suegro**.

**fault** [fɔːlt] *noun*

1. la **culpa:** whose fault is it? ¿de quién es la culpa?; it's my fault yo tengo la culpa

2. el **defecto:** he has many faults tiene muchos defectos.

**favor** ['feɪvər] *noun* ■ el **favor**

➤ to do somebody a favor hacerle un favor a alguien: can you do me a favor? ¿puedes hacerme un favor?

➤ to be in favor of something estar a favor de algo: we're all in favor of world peace todos estamos a favor de la paz mundial.

**favorite** ['feɪvrɪt] *(adjective & noun)*

■ *adjective*
**favorito:** purple is my favorite color el violeta es mi color favorito

■ *noun*
el **favorito**, la **favorita:** let's listen to this CD, it's my favorite eschuchémos este CD, es mi favorito.

**fax** [fæks] *(noun & verb)*

■ *noun*
el **fax:** he sent me a fax me mandó un fax

➤ a fax machine un fax

■ *verb*
**enviar por fax:** I faxed the letter to Eric le envié la carta a Eric por fax.

**fear** [fɪər] *(noun & verb)*

■ *noun*
el **miedo:** have no fear! ¡no tengas miedo!

■ *verb*
**temer:** she fears nothing no le teme a nada.

**feather** ['feðər] *noun* ■ la **pluma**.

**feature** ['fiːtʃər] *noun*

1. la **característica:** an interesting feature of the landscape una característica interesante del paisaje

2. el **rasgo:** she has fine features tiene rasgos finos.

**February** ['februəri] *noun* ■

In Spanish the months of the year do not start with a capital letter:

**febrero** *(masculine):* in February en febrero; next February el próximo febrero; last February el pasado febrero.

**fed** [fed] *past tense & past participle* ➤ feed.

**fed up** [ˌfedˈʌp] *adjective* ■ *informal*

➤ to be fed up estar harto: I'm fed up! ¡estoy harta!

➤ to be fed up with something estar harto de algo: I'm fed up with waiting estoy harto de esperar.

**feed** [fiːd] *(past tense & past participle* fed*) verb* ■ **alimentar:** she's feeding the dogs está alimentando a los perros.

**feel** [fiːl] *(past tense & past participle* felt*) verb*

1. **sentirse:** how do you feel? ¿cómo te sientes?; I don't feel very well no me siento muy bien; he felt very stupid se sintió muy estúpido

When "feel" is used with certain adjectives (cold, hot, hungry or thirsty), you should translate it with the Spanish verb **tener:**

I feel cold tengo frío; my hands feel cold tengo las manos frías; do you feel hungry? ¿tienes hambre?

2.

When you are describing how something feels to the touch, you should use the verb **ser** or **estar:**

this bed feels very hard esta cama es muy dura; the water feels cold el agua está fría

3. **sentir:** I felt the ground shake sentí la sacudida del suelo

4. **tantear:** he felt his pockets tanteó sus bolsillos

➤ **to feel as if** or **to feel as though** tener la sensación de que: I feel as if I'm going to faint tengo la sensación de que me voy a desmayar

➤ **to feel like doing something** tener ganas de hacer algo: I feel like going to bed tengo ganas de irme a la cama.

**feeling** ['fiːlɪŋ] *noun*

1. el **sentimiento:** a feeling of sadness un sentimiento de tristeza

2. la **sensación** *(plural* las **sensaciones**): I have a funny feeling in my leg tengo una sensación extraña en la pierna.

**feet** *plural* ➤ foot.

**fell** [fel] *past tense* ➤ fall.

**fellow** ['feləʊ] *(adjective & noun)*

■ *adjective*

➤ a fellow countryman un compatriota

➤ a fellow student un compañero de estudios

➤ a fellow worker un compañero de trabajo

■ *noun*

hombre: he's a fine fellow es un hombre bueno.

**felt** [felt] *past tense & past participle* ➤ feel.

**female** ['fiːmeɪl] *(noun & adjective)*

■ *noun*

la **hembra**

■ *adjective*

1. **hembra:** a female kangaroo un canguro hembra

2. **femenino:** I heard a female voice oí una voz femenina

➤ a female student una estudiante.

**feminine** ['femɪnɪn] *adjective* ■ **femenino**.

**fence** [fens] *noun* ■ el **cerco**.

**ferris wheel** ['ferɪswiːl] *noun* ■ la **rueda gigante,** la **rueda de la fortuna** *Mexico,* la **rueda de Chicago** *Chile, Colombia*.

**ferry** ['ferɪ] *(plural* ferries*) noun* ■ el **ferry** *(plural* los **ferrys**).

**festival** ['festəvl] *noun* ■ el **festival**.

**fever** ['fiːvər] *noun* ■ la **fiebre**.

**few** [fjuː] *(adjective & pronoun)*

■ *adjective*

**pocos:** few people come here pocas personas vienen acá

➤ a few unos cuantos: a few people came unas cuantas personas vinieron

➤ I need a few books necesito unos cuantos libros

■ *pronoun*

**pocos:** few of them agree pocos están de acuerdo

➤ a few unos pocos: a few stayed till the end unos pocos se quedaron hasta el final.

**fewer** ['fjuːər] *(adjective & pronoun)*

■ *adjective*

**menos:** we have fewer problems than last year tenemos menos problemas que el año pasado

■ *pronoun*

**menos:** I have a lot fewer than you tengo mucho menos que tú.

**fewest** ['fju:əst] *(adjective & pronoun)*
- *adjective*
➤ **the fewest mistakes possible** el menor número de faltas posibles
- *pronoun*
  **menos: I have the fewest** soy la que menos tengo.

**fiancé** [fɪ'ɒnseɪ] *noun* ▪ el **prometido**.

**fiancée** [fɪ'ɒnseɪ] *noun* ▪ la **prometida**.

**fiction** ['fɪkʃn] *uncountable noun* ▪ la ficción: **he can't distinguish between fact and fiction** no puede distinguir la realidad de la ficción; **he reads a lot of fiction** lee mucha ficción.

**field** [fi:ld] *noun*
1. el **campo: they grow corn in that field** cultivan maíz en ese campo; **she's an expert in that field** es experta en ese campo
2. el **potrero: there are cows in that field** hay vacas en ese potrero
3. la **cancha: they're playing on the baseball field** están jugando en la cancha de béisbol.

**fierce** [fɪəs] *adjective*
1. **fiero: a fierce animal** un animal fiero
2. **violento: it was a fierce battle** fue una batalla violenta.

**fifteen** [fɪf'ti:n] *number* ▪ **quince: fifteen people came to the party** quince personas vinieron a la fiesta
➤ **she's fifteen** tiene quince años.

**fifteenth** [fɪf'ti:nθ] *number* ▪ **decimoquinto: he was the fifteenth person to arrive** fue la decimoquinta persona en llegar
➤ **it's May fifteenth** es el quince de mayo.

**fifth** [fɪfθ] *number* ▪ **quinto: he came fifth** llegó quinto
➤ **it's November fifth** es el 5 de noviembre.

**fifty** ['fɪftɪ] *number* ▪ **cincuenta: there were fifty people in the classroom** había cincuenta personas en la clase
➤ **she's fifty** tiene cincuenta años
➤ **fifty-one** cincuenta y uno
➤ **fifty-two** cincuenta y dos.

**fight** [faɪt] *(noun & verb)*
- *noun*
1. la **lucha: the fight against disease** la lucha contra la enfermedad
2. la **pelea: there was a fight in the street** hubo una pelea en la calle
➤ **to have a fight** tener una pelea: **he had a fight with his wife** tuve una pelea con su esposa
- *verb*
  *(past tense & past participle* **fought***)*
1. **pelear: they were fighting in the street** estaban peleando en la calle
2. **luchar: we must fight against apathy** debemos luchar contra la apatía.

**figure** ['fɪgjər] *(noun & verb)*
- *noun*
1. la **cifra: I added up the figures you gave me** sumé las cifras que me diste
2. la **figura: he's a well-known figure in politics** es una figura muy conocida en política; **she's got a great figure** tiene una estupenda figura
- *verb*
  **figurarse: I figure he'll be late** me figuro que llegará tarde

**figure out** *phrasal verb*
1. **entender: I can't figure out why** no entiendo por qué
2. **calcular: I tried to figure out the total** intenté calcular el total.

**file** [faɪl] *(noun & verb)*
- *noun*
1. el **archivo: there are twenty files on the disk** hay veinte archivos en el disco
2. el **expediente: the police have a file on him** la policía tiene un expediente sobre él
3. la **carpeta: I put my notes in a red file** puse mis notas en una carpeta roja
➤ **a nail file** una lima de uñas
➤ **in single file** en fila india: **we walked in single file** caminamos en fila india
- *verb*
1. **archivar: she's filing her papers** está archivando sus papeles
2. **limarse: she's filing her nails** se está limando las uñas.

**fill** [fɪl] *verb* ▪ **llenar: I filled the bottle with water** llené la botella con agua

**fill in** *phrasal verb* ■ **rellenar:** he filled in the hole rellenó el agujero.

**fill out** *phrasal verb* ■ **rellenar:** she filled out the form rellenó el formulario.

**fill up** *phrasal verb* ■ **llenar:** he filled the tank up with water llenó el tanque con agua.

**filling** ['fɪlɪŋ] *(adjective & noun)*
■ *adjective*
➤ the meal was very filling la comida llenaba mucho
■ *noun*
1. el **empaste,** la **tapadura** *Chile, Mexico*: the dentist gave me a filling el dentista me puso un empaste
2. el **relleno:** this filling is very tasty este relleno es muy sabroso.

**film** [fɪlm] *noun*
1. la **película:** there's a good film on television están dando una buena película en la televisión
2. el **rollo:** I need some more film for my camera necesito otro rollo para mi cámara.

**filthy** ['fɪlθɪ] *adjective* ■ **mugriento.**

**final** ['faɪnl] *(adjective & noun)*
■ *adjective*
1. **último:** this is my final lesson esta es mi última clase
2. **final:** that's my final decision es mi decisión final
■ *noun*
la **final:** the United States is in the finals los Estados Unidos están en la final.

**finally** ['faɪnəlɪ] *adverb*
1. **finalmente:** he has finally arrived finalmente llegó
2. **por último:** finally you add the vanilla por último agregas la vainilla.

**financial** [fɪ'nænʃl] *adjective* ■ **financiero:** they have financial problems tienen problemas financieros.

**find** [faɪnd] *(past tense & past participle found) verb* ■ **encontrar:** I can't find my address book no puedo encontrar mi libreta de direcciones

**find out** *phrasal verb*
1. **averiguar:** I'm going to find out about the concert voy a averiguar sobre el concierto
2. **descubrir:** he found out the truth descubrió la verdad.

**fine** [faɪn] *(adjective, adverb, noun & verb)*
■ *adjective*
1. **excelente:** he did a fine job hizo un trabajo excelente
2. **bien:** how are you? — I'm fine! ¿cómo estás? — ¡bien!
3. **delicado:** she has fine features tiene rasgos delicados
4. **de buen tiempo:** it's a fine day es un día de buen tiempo
➤ the fine arts las bellas artes
■ *adverb*
**bien:** he feels fine se siente bien
■ *noun*
la **multa:** he got a twenty dollar fine le aplicaron una multa de veinte dólares
■ *verb*
**ponerle una multa a:** they fined Peter twenty dollars le pusieron una multa de veinte dólares a Peter.

**finger** ['fɪŋɡər] *noun* ■ el **dedo.**

**fingernail** ['fɪŋɡəneɪl] *noun* ■ la **uña.**

**fingerprint** ['fɪŋɡəprɪnt] *noun* ■ la **huella dactilar.**

**finish** ['fɪnɪʃ] *(verb & noun)*
■ *verb*
**terminar:** she has finished her homework ha terminado su tarea; the movie finishes at 11 o'clock la película termina a las 11 en punto
➤ to finish doing something terminar de hacer algo: I've finished eating he terminado de comer
■ *noun*
1. el **fin:** from start to finish de principio a fin
2. el **final:** we watched the finish of the race vimos el final de la carrera.

**fire** ['faɪər] *(noun & verb)*
■ *noun*
1. el **fuego:** he lit a fire prendió el fuego
2. el **incendio:** they are trying to put out the fire están tratando de apagar el incendio

➤ **on fire** en llamas: **the house is on fire** la casa está en llamas
➤ **to catch fire** prender fuego: **my papers caught fire** mis papeles prendieron fuego
➤ **to set fire to something** prenderle fuego a algo: **they set fire to the house** le prendieron fuego a la casa
➤ **a fire alarm** el alarma contra incendios
➤ **the fire department** el cuerpo de bomberos
➤ **a fire engine** un coche de bomberos
➤ **a fire escape** una escalera de incendios
➤ **the fire exit** la salida de incendios
➤ **a fire extinguisher** un extintor de incendios
➤ **the fire station** la estación de bomberos, el cuartel de bomberos *River Plate*
■ *verb*
1. **disparar: they fired at him** le dispararon; **she fired the gun** disparó la pistola
2. **despedir: he fired the secretary** despidió a la secretaria.

**firefighter** ['faɪəˌfaɪtəʳ] *noun* ■ el **bombero,** la **bombera.**

**fireplace** ['faɪəpleɪs] *noun* ■ la **chimenea.**

**fireworks** ['faɪəwɜːks] *plural noun* ■ los **fuegos artificiales.**

**firm** [fɜːm] *(adjective & noun)*
■ *adjective*
1. **firme: the cushion is firm** el almohadón es firme
2. **estricto: he was firm with me** fue estricto conmigo
■ *noun*
la **empresa: she works for a firm in Seattle** trabaja para una empresa en Seattle.

**first** [fɜːst] *(adjective, adverb & noun)*
■ *adjective*
**primero: it's the first time I've seen him** es la primera vez que lo veo

> **Primer** is used before a masculine singular noun:

**he was the first man to arrive** fue el primer hombre en llegar
■ *adverb*
**primero: I saw it first** yo lo vi primero; **he came first in the race** llegó primero en la

carrera; **I want to have something to eat first** me gustaría comer algo primero
■ *noun*
el **primero,** la **primera: she was the first to leave** fue la primera en irse; **it's May first** es el primero de mayo
➤ **first of all** antes que nada: **first of all tell me your name** antes que nada, dime tu nombre
➤ **at first** al principio: **at first I thought he was mad** al principio pensé que estaba loco
➤ **first aid** los primeros auxilios: **a first-aid kit** un botiquín de primeros auxilios
➤ **first name** el nombre de pila.

**first-class** ['fɜːstˌklɑːs] *adjective*
1. **de primera clase: I bought a first-class ticket** compré un boleto de primera clase
2. **de primera: the food in this restaurant is first class** la comida en este restaurante es de primera.

**fish** [fɪʃ] *(noun & verb)*
■ *noun*
*(plural* **fish)**
1. el **pez** *(plural* los **peces): there are lots of fish in the lake** hay muchos peces en el lago
2. el **pescado: he doesn't like fish** no le gusta el pescado
■ *verb*
**pescar: he was fishing in the river** estaba pescando en el río.

**fishing** ['fɪʃɪŋ] *uncountable noun* ■ la **pesca: to go fishing** irse de pesca
➤ **a fishing boat** un bote de pesca
➤ **a fishing rod** una caña de pescar.

**fist** [fɪst] *noun* ■ el **puño.**

**fit** [fɪt] *(adjective, noun & verb)*
■ *adjective*
**en forma: he tries to keep fit** trata de mantenerse en forma
■ *noun*
1. el **ataque: an epileptic fit** un ataque de epilepsia
2. el **arrebato: a fit of anger** un arrebato de ira
➤ **my mother had a fit when she saw the mess** a mi madre le dio un infarto cuando vio el desorden

■ *verb*
*(past tense, past participle* **fitted***)*

1. **quedar bien: these pants don't fit** estos pantalones no me quedan bien
2. **caber: the pillow doesn't fit in the case** la almohada no cabe en la funda
3. **encajar: he fitted the key into the lock** encajó la llave en la cerradura
4. **instalar: he fitted a radio in his car** instaló un radio en su coche.

**fitting room** ['fɪtɪŋruːm] *noun* ■ el **probador**.

**five** [faɪv] *number* ■ **cinco: there are five pieces of cake** hay cinco pedazos de torta

➤ **she's five** tiene cinco años
➤ **I went out at five** salí a las cinco.

**fix** [fɪks] *verb*

1. **fijar: I fixed the mirror to the wall** fijé el espejo a la pared; **can we fix a date?** ¿podemos fijar una fecha?
2. **arreglar: he's trying to fix the TV** está tratando de arreglar el televisor
3. **preparar: she's fixing us something to eat** nos está preparando algo de comer.

**flag** [flæg] *noun* ■ la **bandera**.

**flame** [fleɪm] *noun* ■ la **llama**: ¡cuidado con la llama! **careful with the flame!**; **the house was in flames** la casa estaba en llamas.

**flan** [flæn] *noun* ■ la **tarta**.

**flap** [flæp] *(past tense & past participle* **flapped***) verb*

1. **batir: the eagle flapped its wings** el águila batió sus alas
2. **agitarse: the flag flapped in the wind** la bandera se sacudía con el viento.

**flash** [flæʃ] *(noun & verb)*

■ *noun*

1. **el destello: the flash blinded me for a few seconds** el destello me deslumbró por unos segundos
2. **el flash: this camera has a flash** esta cámara fotográfica tiene flash
➤ **a flash of lightning** un relámpago
■ *verb*

**prenderse y apagarse: all the lights are flashing** todas las luces se están prendiendo y apagando
➤ **to flash one's headlights** hacer una señal con los faros.

**flashlight** ['flæʃlaɪt] *noun* ■ la **linterna**.

**flat** [flæt] *(adjective & noun) adjective*

1. **plano: a flat surface** una superficie plana
2. **llano: the countryside is flat around our town** el paisaje es llano alrededor del pueblo
➤ **a flat tire** un neumático desinflado, una llanta ponchada *Mexico*.

**flavor** ['fleɪvəʳ] *noun* ■ el **sabor: this soup doesn't have much flavor** este sopa no tiene mucho sabor; **which flavor ice cream do you want?** ¿de qué sabor quieres el helado?

**flea** [fliː] *noun* ■ la **pulga**
➤ **the flea market** el mercado de las pulgas.

**flew** [fluː] *past tense* ➤ **fly**.

**flight** [flaɪt] *noun* ■ el **vuelo: the flight to Rome is at two o'clock** el vuelo a Roma es a las dos en punto
➤ **a flight of stairs** un tramo de las escaleras.

**fling** [flɪŋ] *(past tense & past participle* **flung***) verb* ■ **arrojar, aventar** *Mexico*: **he flung his things on the floor** arrojó sus cosas al piso.

**flipper** ['flɪpəʳ] *noun* ■ la **aleta: seals have flippers** las focas tienen aletas; **the diver's wearing flippers** el buzo está usando aletas.

**float** [fləʊt] *verb* ■ **flotar: a bottle is floating in the water** una botella está flotando en el agua.

**flock** [flɒk] *noun*

1. **la bandada: a flock of birds** una bandada de pájaros
2. **el rebaño: a flock of sheep** un rebaño de ovejas.

**flood** [flʌd] *(noun & verb)*

■ *noun*

1. **la inundación** *(plural* **las inundaciones***):* **there have been floods in this area** ha habido inundaciones en esta zona

**2.** la **avalancha**: we got a flood of letters tuvimos una avalancha de cartas

■ *verb*
**inundarse**: the fields flooded se inundaron los campos.

**floor** [flɔːʳ] *noun* ■ el **piso**: the floor's wet el piso está mojado; which floor do you live on? ¿en qué piso vives?
➤ on the first floor en el primer piso

 **Floor** es un falso amigo, no significa "flor".

**floppy disk** ['flɒpɪdɪsk] *noun* ■ el **disquete**: put the floppy disk into the drive pon el disquete en la disquetera.

**florist** ['flɒrɪst] *noun* ■ el/la **florista**
➤ at the florist's en la florería.

**flour** ['flaʊəʳ] *noun* ■ la **harina**.

**flow** [fləʊ] *verb* ■ **correr**: the water flows through the pipe el agua corre por la cañería.

**flower** ['flaʊəʳ] *(noun & verb)*
■ *noun*
la **flor**: a bunch of flowers un ramo de flores
■ *verb*
**florecer**: these roses are about to flower estas rosas están por florecer.

**flowerpot** ['flaʊəpɒt] *noun* ■ la **maceta**.

**flown** [fləʊn] *past participle* ➤ fly.

**flu** [fluː] *uncountable noun* ■ la **gripe**, la **gripa** *Colombia, Mexico*: she has the flu tiene gripe.

**fluent** ['fluːənt] *adjective* ■ she's fluent in Spanish or she speaks fluent Spanish habla español con fluidez.

**flung** [flʌŋ] *past tense & past participle* ➤ fling.

**flush** [flʌʃ] *verb* ■ **jalarle, tirar la cadena** *Southern Cone*: you didn't flush the toilet! ¡no le jalaste!

**flute** [fluːt] *noun* ■ la **flauta**: he plays the flute toca la flauta.

**fly** [flaɪ] *(noun & verb)*
■ *noun*
*(plural* **flies***)*
**1.** la **mosca**: there's a fly in my soup hay una mosca en mi sopa
**2.** la **bragueta**: your fly is undone tienes la bragueta abierta
■ *verb*
*(past tense* **flew***, past participle* **flown***)*
**1.** **volar**: thousands of birds flew over us miles de pájaros volaron por encima nuestro
**2.** **hacer volar, remontar** *River Plate*: he's flying a kite está haciendo volar una cometa
**3.** **viajar en avión**: he flies often viaja en avión frecuentemente; I'm afraid of flying me da miedo viajar en avión
**4.** **pilotear**: can you fly a plane? ¿sabes pilotar un avión?

**fly away** *phrasal verb* ■ **salir volando**: the bird flew away el pájaro salió volando.

**focus** ['fəʊkəs] *(noun & verb)*
■ *noun*
el **foco**: you have to adjust the focus tienes que ajustar el foco
➤ in focus enfocado: the picture is in focus la foto está enfocada
➤ out of focus fuera de foco: the picture is out of focus la foto está fuera de foco
■ *verb*
**enfocar**: she focused the camera enfocó la cámara fotográfica
➤ to focus on something centrarse en algo: he focused on the importance of education se centró en la importancia de la educación.

**fog** [fɒg] *noun* ■ la **niebla**.

**foggy** ['fɒgɪ] *adjective* ■ it's foggy hay niebla; it was a foggy day era un día de niebla.

**fold** [fəʊld] *verb* ■ **doblar**: I folded the paper in half doblé el papel por la mitad
➤ to fold one's arms cruzarse de brazos: she folded her arms se cruzó de brazos.

**folder** ['fəʊldəʳ] *noun* ■ la **carpeta**: I put my papers in the folder puse mis papeles en la carpeta.

**folding** ['fəʊldɪŋ] *adjective* ■ **plegable**: a folding chair una silla plegable.

**follow** ['fɒləʊ] *verb* ▪ **seguir:** she was following me me estaba siguiendo; follow me! ¡síganme!

**following** ['fɒləʊɪŋ] *adjective* ▪ **siguiente:** it happened the following month sucedió al mes siguiente
➤ the following day al día siguiente.

**fond** [fɒnd] *adjective*
➤ to be fond of somebody or something gustarle alguien o algo: he's very fond of chocolate le gusta mucho el chocolate.

**food** [fuːd] *uncountable noun* ▪ **la comida:** there's enough food for everyone hay comida suficiente para todos.

**fool** [fuːl] *noun* ▪ **el/la idiota:** what a fool! ¡qué idiota!

**foolish** ['fuːlɪʃ] *adjective* ▪ **estúpido:** it was a foolish decision fue una decisión estúpida.

**foot** [fʊt] *(plural* feet [fiːt]*) noun* ▪ **el pie:** I hurt my foot me lastimé el pie; let's go on foot vayamos a pie; he's six feet tall mide seis pies.

**football** ['fʊtbɔːl] *noun*
1. el **fútbol americano,** el **futbol americano** *Mexico*: we went to a football game fuimos a un partido de fútbol americano
2. la **pelota de fútbol americano:** he kicked the football pateó la pelota de fútbol americano
➤ a football team un equipo de fútbol americano.

**footprint** ['fʊtprɪnt] *noun* ▪ **la huella:** we saw footprints in the snow vimos huellas en la nieve.

**footstep** ['fʊtstep] *noun* ▪ **el paso:** I heard footsteps on the stairs oí pasos en las escaleras.

**for** [fɔːʳ] *preposition*
1. **para:** this is for you esto es para ti; a knife for cutting bread un cuchillo para cortar pan
2. **por:** he paid 200 dollars for the car pagó 200 dólares por el coche; thanks for helping me gracias por ayudarme; I'm going to California for two weeks me voy a California por dos semanas; we are going away for the weekend vamos a estar fuera por el fin de semana
3. **hace:** he has lived in France for five years vive en Francia desde hace cinco años; I've been waiting for two hours hace dos horas que estoy esperando

When you are talking about completed actions in the past, you should use a verb in the past tense + **durante:**

she lived in Spain for two years vivió en España durante dos años
➤ **for sale** en venta
➤ **T for Tony** la T de Tony
➤ **we walked for miles** caminamos varias millas
➤ **what for?** ¿para qué?: I need some money — what for? necesito un poco de dinero — ¿para qué?

**forbid** [fə'bɪd] *(past tense* forbade, *past participle* forbidden*) verb* ▪ **prohibir:** I forbid you to go to that party te prohibo que vayas a esa fiesta.

**forbidden** [fə'bɪdn] *adjective* ▪ **prohibido:** smoking is forbidden prohibido fumar.

**force** [fɔːs] *(noun & verb)*
▪ *noun*
la **fuerza:** the ball hit me with great force la pelota me pegó con mucha fuerza
➤ **by force** a la fuerza: they took him away by force se lo llevaron a la fuerza
▪ *verb*
**obligar:** he forced me to tell the truth me obligó a decir la verdad
➤ to **force one's way into something** entrar a la fuerza: he forced his way into the office entró a la oficina a la fuerza.

**forecast** ['fɔːkɑːst] *noun* ▪ **el pronóstico**
➤ **the weather forecast** el pronóstico del tiempo: what's the weather forecast for tomorrow? ¿cuál es el pronóstico del tiempo para mañana?

**forehead** ['fɔːhed] *noun* ▪ **la frente.**

**foreign** ['fɒrən] *adjective* ■ **extranjero:** foreign languages lenguas extranjeras; she lives in a foreign country vive en un país extranjero.

**foreigner** ['fɒrənər] *noun* ■ **el extranjero,** la **extranjera:** he's a foreigner es un extranjero.

**forest** ['fɒrɪst] *noun* ■ **el bosque:** she got lost in the forest se perdió en el bosque.

**forever** [fə'revər] *adverb* ■ **para siempre:** he's gone forever se ha ido para siempre; it won't last forever no va a durar para siempre.

**forgave** [fə'geɪv] *past tense* ➤ forgive.

**forge** [fɔːdʒ] *verb* ■ **falsificar:** she forged her mother's signature falsificó la firma de su madre.

**forgery** ['fɔːdʒərɪ] *(plural* forgeries) *noun* ■ **la falsificación** *(plural* las **falsificaciones):** she was arrested for forgery fue arrestada por falsificación
➤ this passport is a forgery este pasaparte es falso.

**forget** [fə'get] *(past tense* forgot, *past participle* forgotten) *verb* ■ **olvidarse:** I've forgotten your address se me ha olvidado tu dirección; don't forget to call! ¡no te olvides de llamar!; she forgot her purse se le olvidó el monedero.

**forgive** [fə'gɪv] *(past tense* forgave, *past participle* forgiven) *verb* ■ **perdonar:** I forgive you te perdono; I forgave him for not telling the truth lo perdoné por no haber dicho la verdad.

**forgot** [fə'gɒt] *past tense* ➤ forget.

**forgotten** [fə'gɒtn] *past participle* ➤ forget.

**fork** [fɔːk] *noun*
1. el **tenedor:** a knife and fork un cuchillo y un tenedor
2. la **bifurcación** *(plural* las **bifurcaciones):** we came to a fork in the road llegamos a una bifurcación en el camino.

**form** [fɔːm] *(noun & verb)*
■ *noun*
1. la **forma:** there are different forms of life on the planet hay diferentes formas de vida en el planeta
2. el **formulario:** I filled in the form rellené el formulario
■ *verb*
**formar:** the children formed a circle los niños formaron una ronda.

**formal** ['fɔːml] *adjective* ■ **formal:** they made a formal announcement hicieron un anuncio formal.

**former** ['fɔːmər] *adjective*
1. **antiguo:** he's a former student of mine es un antiguo alumno mío
2. **primero:** do you mean the former or the latter? te refieres al primero o al último?

Primer is used before a masculine singular noun:

I'm referring to the former case me refiero al primer caso.

**formula** ['fɔːmjʊlə] *noun* ■ **la fórmula:** they stole the secret formula se robaron la fórmula secreta.

**fort** [fɔːt] *noun* ■ **el fuerte.**

**fortunately** ['fɔːtʃnətlɪ] *adverb* ■ **afortunadamente:** fortunately, everyone is safe afortunadamente, todos están a salvo.

**fortune** ['fɔːtʃuːn] *noun* ■ **la fortuna:** he made his fortune before he was 30 hizo la fortuna antes de cumplir los treinta; he had the good fortune to get an excellent education tuvo la buena fortuna de recibir una excelente educación
➤ to tell somebody's fortune leerle la suerte a alguien.

**forty** ['fɔːtɪ] *number* ■ **cuarenta:** he's forty tiene cuarenta años; forty-one cuarenta y uno; forty-two cuarenta y dos.

**forward,      forwards** ['fɔːwəd, 'fɔːwədz] *adverb* ■ **hacia adelante:** he leaned forward se inclinó hacia adelante
➤ to move forward avanzar: the army is moving forward el ejército está avanzando

➤ to put the clocks forward adelantar los relojes.

**fought** [fɔːt] *past tense & past participle*
➤ fight.

**foul** [faʊl] *adjective* ■ **asqueroso: what a foul smell!** ¡qué asqueroso olor!

**found** [faʊnd] *past tense & past participle*
➤ find.

**fountain** ['faʊntɪn] *noun* ■ **la fuente: I'll see you at the fountain at eight** nos vemos en la fuente a las ocho
➤ a fountain pen una pluma fuente.

**four** [fɔːʳ] *number* ■ **cuatro: they have four children** tienen cuatro hijos; **she's four** tiene cuatro años; **we went out at four** salimos a las cuatro.

**fourteen** [ˌfɔːˈtiːn] *number* ■ **catorce: he's fourteen** tiene catorce años.

**fourth** [fɔːθ] *number* ■ **cuarto: he came fourth** llegó cuarto
➤ it's March fourth es el cuatro de marzo
➤ the Fourth of July el 4 de julio

THE FOURTH OF JULY

El 4 de julio o **Fourth of July**, también llamado **Independence Day**, es una de las fiestas nacionales de mayor importancia en los Estados Unidos; conmemora el momento en que los Estados Unidos declaró su independencia de Inglaterra en el año 1776. Como parte de los festejos se organizan desfiles por las calles, y por la noche se encienden castillos de fuegos artificiales en los que predominan los colores rojo, blanco y azul. Los edificios se decoran con adornos de estos mismos colores o con banderas estadounidenses.

**fox** [fɒks] *(plural* foxes [fɒksɪz]*) noun* ■ **el zorro.**

**fraction** ['frækʃn] *noun* ■ **la fracción** *(plural* las fracciones*)*.

**fragile** ['frædʒaɪl] *adjective* ■ **frágil.**

**frame** [freɪm] *noun* ■ **el marco: I put the photo in a frame** puse la foto en un marco.

**fraternity** [frəˈtɜːrnəti] *noun* ■ *asociación estudiantil*

FRATERNITY

Los clubes de estudiantes masculinos (**fraternities**) son un elemento sobresaliente de la vida social universitaria estadounidense. Cada club posee su propio nombre, constituido por letras del alfabeto griego y tiene su sede en el edificio donde reside la mayoría de sus miembros. Estos clubes realizan trabajos para instituciones de asistencia social, pero también son famosas sus juergas con alcohol y sus ceremonias secretas. Algunas universidades han decidido prohibirlos porque sus ceremonias de iniciación incluían novatadas crueles y peligrosas.

**freckle** ['frekl] *noun* ■ **la peca: Rachel has freckles** Raquel tiene pecas.

**free** [friː] *(adjective & verb)*
■ *adjective*
1. **libre: are you free tonight?** ¿estás libre esta noche?; **is this seat free?** ¿está libre este asiento?
2. **gratis: the tickets are free** los boletos son gratis; **it's free of charge** es gratis
➤ you're free to go puedes irte
■ *verb*
**liberar: they freed the prisoners** liberaron a los prisioneros.

**freedom** ['friːdəm] *noun* ■ **la libertad: freedom of speech** libertad de expresión.

**freeway** ['friːweɪ] *noun* ■ **la autopista.**

**freeze** [friːz] *(past tense* froze*, past participle* frozen*) verb*
1. **congelarse: the lake had frozen overnight** el lago se congeló durante la noche
2. **congelar: I froze the chicken** congelé el pollo.

**97**

**freezer** ['friːzəʳ] *noun* ■ el **congelador:** she put the ice cream in the freezer puso el helado en el congelador.

**freezing** ['friːzɪŋ] *adjective* ■ **helado:** your hands are freezing tienes las manos heladas
➤ I'm freezing me estoy helando de frío
➤ it's freezing today hoy hace un frío espantoso.

**French** [frentʃ] *(adjective & noun)*
■ *adjective*

> Remember not to use a capital letter for the adjective in Spanish:

**francés** (*feminine* **francesa**)**:** I like French cooking me gusta la cocina francesa
➤ French fries papas fritas, papas a la francesa *Colombia, Mexico*
■ *noun*

> In Spanish, a capital letter is not used for the language or the inhabitants of a country or region:

el **francés:** he speaks French habla francés
➤ the French los franceses.

**frequent** ['friːkwənt] *adjective* ■ **frecuente:** accidents are frequent here los accidentes son frecuentes aquí.

**frequently** ['friːkwəntlɪ]          *adverb*
■ **frecuentemente.**

**fresh** [freʃ] *adjective*
1. **fresco:** fresh bread pan fresco
2. **nuevo:** start a fresh page comienza una página nueva
➤ he wants to make a fresh start quiere empezar de nuevo
➤ fresh air aire fresco: let's go and get some fresh air vamos a salir a tomar un poco de aire fresco.

**freshen up** ['freʃnʌp] *phrasal verb*
■ **refrescarse:** I'm just going to freshen up sólo voy a refrescarme.

**Friday** ['fraɪdɪ] *noun* ■ el **viernes** (*plural* los **viernes**)**:** it's Friday today hoy es viernes; next Friday el próximo viernes; last Friday el viernes pasado

➤ on Friday el viernes: I'll see you on Friday te veo el viernes
➤ on Fridays los viernes: Sam goes swimming on Fridays Sam va a nadar los viernes

> In Spanish the days of the week do not start with a capital letter.

**fried** [fraɪd] *(adjective & verb form)*
■ *adjective*
**frito:** fried chicken pollo frito
➤ a fried egg un huevo frito, un huevo estrellado *Mexico*
■ *past participle*
➤ fry.

**friend** [frend] *noun* ■ el **amigo,** la **amiga:** we're friends somos amigos; Sally is my best friend Sally es mi mejor amiga
➤ to make friends hacer amigos: she has trouble making friends tiene problemas para hacer amigos.

**friendly** ['frendlɪ] *adjective* ■ **simpático:** he's very friendly es muy simpático
➤ they gave her a friendly welcome le dieron una cordial bienvenida.

**friendship** ['frendʃɪp] *noun* ■ la **amistad.**

**fries** [fraɪz] *plural noun* ■ las **papas fritas,** las **papas a la francesa** *Colombia, Mexico*: she ordered a burger with fries pidió una hamburguesa con papas fritas.

**fright** [fraɪt] *noun* ■ el **miedo:** she was pale with fright estaba pálida de miedo
➤ to give someone a fright darle un susto a alguien: she gave me a fright me dio un susto.

**frighten** ['fraɪtn] *verb* ■ **asustar:** you frightened me me asustaste.

**frightened** ['fraɪtnd] *adjective*
➤ to be frightened estar asustado: we were cold, frightened and tired teníamos frío y estábamos asustados y cansados.

**frightening** ['fraɪtnɪŋ]          *adjective*
■ **aterrador** (*feminine* **aterradora**)**:** she told us a frightening story nos contó un cuento aterrador.

**frog** [frɒg] *noun* ■ la **rana.**

**from** [frəm, frɒm] *preposition*

1. **de:** I got a letter from my brother recibí una carta de mi hermano; I come from Chicago soy de Chicago; the house is 5 miles from the sea la casa queda a 5 millas del mar

> Remember that de + el = del.

2.

> When you say what country a person is from, you should use an adjective to give the person's nationality in Spanish:

Andy is from Canada Andy es canadiense

3. **desde:** from the bridge you can see the quay desde el puente puedes ver el muelle
> **from now on** a partir de ahora: from now on I'll be working at the other store a partir de ahora trabajaré en la otra tienda
> **from ... to ...** desde ... hasta ...: the bank is open from 9 a.m. to 4 p.m. el banco abre desde las 9 de la mañana hasta las 4 de la tarde.

**front** [frʌnt] *(adjective & noun)*

■ *adjective*

1. **de adelante:** they are playing in the front yard están jugando en el jardín de adelante
2. **primero:** we sat in the front row nos sentamos en la primera fila
> **the front door** la puerta principal

■ *noun*

la **parte delantera:** the front of your shirt is dirty la parte delantera de la camisa está sucia
> **in front of** delante de: George is standing in front of the house George está parado delante de la casa
> **in front** adelante: Bob was walking in front Bob iba caminando adelante.

**frontier** ['frʌn,tɪər] *noun* ■ la **frontera.**

**frost** [frɒst] *noun* ■ la **escarcha:** there was frost on the windows había escarcha en las ventanas.

**frosting** ['frɒstɪŋ] *noun* ■ el **glaseado,** el **betún** *Chile, Mexico:* chocolate frosting glaseado de chocolate.

**frown** [fraʊn] *verb* ■ **fruncir el ceño**

> to frown at someone mirar a alguien con el ceño fruncido: she frowned at me me miró con el ceño fruncido.

**froze** [frəʊz] *past tense* ➤ freeze.

**frozen** [frəʊzn] *(adjective & verb form)*

■ *adjective*

**congelado:** she bought some frozen vegetables compró verduras congelados; my hands are frozen tengo las manos congeladas

■ *past participle*
> freeze.

**fruit** [fruːt] *uncountable noun* ■ la **fruta:** a piece of fruit una fruta
> **fruit juice** jugo de fruta
> **fruit salad** ensalada de frutas.

**fry** [fraɪ] *(past tense & past participle fried) verb* ■ **freír:** he's frying some fish está friendo pescado.

**frying pan** ['fraɪŋ,pæn] *noun* ■ el/la **sartén.**

**ft.** *(abbreviation of foot or feet)* he's 6 ft. tall mide 6 pies de alto.

**fuel** [fjʊəl] *noun* ■ el **combustible:** our fuel supplies are running low nos queda poco combustible.

**full** [fʊl] *adjective*

1. **lleno:** the hotel is full el hotel está lleno; the glass is full of water el vaso está lleno de agua
2. **completo:** please state your full name escriba su nombre completo, por favor
> **a full moon** luna llena: there's a full moon tonight hay luna llena esta noche
> **at full speed** a toda velocidad.

**full-time** ['fʊltaɪm] *(adjective & adverb)*

■ *adjective*

**de tiempo completo:** he has a full-time job tiene un trabajo de tiempo completo

■ *adverb*

**tiempo completo:** he works full-time trabaja tiempo completo.

**fully** ['fʊlɪ] *adverb* ■ **totalmente:** she never fully recovered nunca se recuperó totalmente.

**fun** [fʌn] (adjective & noun )

■ adjective
**divertido: Steve is such a fun guy** Steve es un tipo muy divertido

■ noun
➤ to have fun divertirse: **we had so much fun today** nos divertimos mucho hoy
➤ have fun! ¡que te divertas!
➤ to be fun ser divertido: **this game is a lot of fun** este juego es muy divertido
➤ to make fun of somebody reírse de alguien: **don't make fun of your brother** no te rías de tu hermano.

**funeral** ['fjuːnərəl] noun ■ el **funeral**.

**funny** ['fʌnɪ] adjective
1. **divertido: the movie is very funny** la película es muy divertida
2. **raro: what a funny smell!** ¡qué olor tan raro!

**fur** [fɜːʳ] noun ■ el **pelo: he was stroking the cat's fur** estaba acariciando el pelo del gato
➤ a fur coat un abrigo de piel.

**furious** ['fjʊərɪəs] adjective ■ **furioso: he's furious with me** está furioso conmigo.

**furniture** ['fɜːnɪtʃəʳ] uncountable noun ■ los **muebles: the furniture is very modern** los muebles son muy modernos; **a piece of furniture** un mueble.

**further** ['fɜːðəʳ] (comparative of **far**) (adverb & adjective)

■ adverb
**más lejos: they went a little further** fueron un poco más lejos
➤ is it much further? ¿cuánto falta?
■ adjective
**do you have any further questions?** ¿tienen más preguntas?
➤ until further notice hasta nuevo aviso: **the concert is postponed until further notice** el concierto se posterga hasta nuevo aviso.

**furthest** ['fɜːðɪst] (superlative of **far**) (adverb & adjective)

■ adverb
**más lejos: he walked furthest** fue el que más lejos caminó

■ adjective
**más alejado: the furthest house** la casa más alejada.

**fuse** [fjuːz] noun ■ el **fusible: one of the fuses blew** se fundió uno de los fusibles.

**fuss** [fʌs] noun ■ el **alboroto: what's all the fuss about?** ¿a qué viene tanto alboroto?
➤ to make a fuss armar un escándalo: **please don't make a fuss** por favor, no armen un escándalo.

**fussy** ['fʌsɪ] adjective ■ **quisquilloso: he's such a fussy eater** es tan quisquilloso con la comida.

**future** ['fjuːtʃəʳ] noun ■ el **futuro: we can't predict the future** no podemos predecir el futuro; **I won't help you in future** no te ayudaré en el futuro
➤ the future tense el futuro.

**gadget** ['gædʒɪt] noun ■ el **aparato**.

**gain** [geɪn] verb ■ **conseguir: what do you hope to gain by behaving like this?** ¿qué esperas conseguir comportándote así?
➤ to gain weight engordar: **he gained a lot of weight** engordó mucho
➤ he managed to gain my respect consiguió ganarse mi respeto
➤ what did you gain from your experience? ¿qué provecho sacaste de tu experiencia?

**gallery** ['gælərɪ] (plural **galleries**) noun
■ la **galería**: we visited an art gallery fuimos a una galería de arte; he bought a painting from a gallery compré un cuadro en una galería.

**gallon** ['gælən] noun ■ el **galón** (plural los **galones**).

**gallop** ['gæləp] (noun & verb)
■ noun
el **galope**
■ verb
**galopar**: the horses galloped along the beach los caballos galopaban por la playa.

**gamble** ['gæmbl] verb ■ **jugar**: she gambled 100 dollars jugó 100 dólares.

**gambling** ['gæmblɪŋ] noun ■ el **juego**: gambling is banned in this state el juego está prohibido en este estado.

**game** [geɪm] noun
1. el **juego**: a computer game un juego de computadora
2. el **partido**: what time is the football game? ¿a qué hora es el partido de fútbol?

**gang** [gæŋ] noun ■ la **pandilla**.

**gap** [gæp] noun
1. la **abertura**: they went through a gap in the fence pasaron por una abertura en la valla
2. la **laguna**: there are big gaps in his knowledge tiene grandes lagunas en sus conocimientos
3. la **brecha**: the gap between rich and poor la brecha entre ricos y pobres; there's a large age gap between us hay una gran brecha generacional entre nosotros
➤ she has a gap in her teeth tiene los dientes separados.

**garage** ['gærɑːʒ, 'gærɪdʒ] noun ■ el **garage**: the house has a two-car garage la casa tiene un garage para dos coches.

**garbage** ['gɑːbɪdʒ] noun ■ la **basura**
➤ a garbage can un cubo de la basura, un basurero *Chile, Mexico*, un tacho de la basura *Peru, Southern Cone*, un bote de la basura *Mexico*, una caneca *Colombia*, un tobo de la basura *Venezuela*

➤ a garbage truck el camión de la basura.

**garden** ['gɑːdn] noun ■ el **jardín** (plural los **jardines**).

**gardener** ['gɑːdnər] noun ■ el **jardinero**, la **jardinera**.

**gardening** ['gɑːdnɪŋ] noun ■ la **jardinería**: she loves gardening le encanta la jardinería.

**garlic** ['gɑːlɪk] noun ■ el **ajo**
➤ garlic bread pan de ajo.

**gas** [gæs] noun
1. el **gas**: a gas stove una cocina a gas, una estufa de gas *Colombia, Mexico*
2. la **gasolina**, la **nafta** *River Plate*: my car is almost out of gas casi no le queda gasolina al coche
➤ a gas station una estación de servicio, una estación de nafta *River Plate*, una bomba *Andes, Venezuela*.

**gasoline** ['gæsəliːn] noun ■ la **gasolina**, la **nafta**: it takes unleaded gasoline consume gasolina sin plomo.

**gate** [geɪt] noun
1. el **portón** (plural los **portones**): I opened the gate and walked up the path abrí el portón y caminé por el sendero
2. la **puerta**: we'll be boarding at gate 4 vamos a embarcar por la puerta 4.

**gather** ['gæðər] verb
1. **juntarse**: people are gathering in front of the embassy la gente se está juntando delante de la embajada
2. **recoger**: she's gathering blackberries está recogiendo moras
➤ to gather speed adquirir velocidad: the train was gathering speed el tren iba adquiriendo velocidad.

**gave** [geɪv] past tense ➤ give.

**gaze** [geɪz] verb ■ **mirar**: she's gazing out of the window está mirando por la ventana.

**gear** [gɪər] noun
1. el **cambio**: my bike has ten gears mi bici tiene diez cambios; he changed gear hizo un cambio

2. el **equipo**: he had all his fishing **gear** tenía todo su equipo de pesca.

**geese** *plural* ➤ goose.

**gel** [dʒel] *noun* ▪ el **gel**
➤ hair gel gel para el pelo.

**gem** [dʒem] *noun* ▪ la **gema**.

**gene** [dʒiːn] *noun* ▪ el **gen**.

**general** [ˈdʒenərəl] *(adjective & noun)*
▪ *adjective*
general: it's a general question es una pregunta general
➤ general knowledge cultura general
➤ the general public el público en general
➤ in general en general
▪ *noun*
el/la **general**: he's a general in the army es general del ejército.

**generally** [ˈdʒenərəlɪ] *adverb* ▪ generalmente: they generally go to bed at 10 o'clock generalmente se acuestan a las diez.

**generation** [ˌdʒenəˈreɪʃn] *noun* ▪ la generación *(plural* las **generaciones**): the younger generation la generación más joven.

**generous** [ˈdʒenərəs] *adjective* ▪ generoso: he's very generous es muy generoso.

**genius** [ˈdʒiːnjəs] *noun* ▪ el **genio**: she's a genius es un genio.

**gentle** [ˈdʒentl] *adjective*
1. dulce: he's very gentle with the baby es muy dulce con el bebé
2. suave: there's a gentle breeze hay una brisa suave.

**gentleman** [ˈdʒentlmən] *(plural* gentlemen [ˈdʒentlmən]*) noun* ▪ el **caballero**: come in, gentlemen! ¡entren, caballeros!

**genuine** [ˈdʒenjʊɪn] *adjective*
1. auténtico: it's genuine gold es oro auténtico
2. sincero: she's very genuine es muy sincera.

**geography** [dʒɪˈɒɡrəfɪ] *noun* ▪ la geografía.

**germ** [dʒɜːm] *noun* ▪ el **germen** *(plural* los **gérmenes**).

**gesture** [ˈdʒestʃər] *noun* ▪ el **gesto**.

**get** [get] *(past tense* got, *past participle* gotten) verb
1. *When get means "receive"* recibir: I got a letter from my brother recibí una carta de mi hermano
2. *When get means "achieve"* sacar: she gets good grades saca buenas notas
3. *When get means "find"* conseguir: where did you get that book? ¿dónde conseguiste ese libro?
4. *When get means "buy"* comprar: I'm going to the store to get some milk voy a la tienda a comprar leche; I don't know what to get Harry for his birthday no sé qué comprarle a Harry para su cumpleaños
5. *When get means "bring"* traer: go and get the doctor ve y trae al doctor; can you get my slippers? ¿me puedes traer las zapatillas?
6. *When get means "catch"* agarrar: he got a cold agarré un resfriado; did they get the thief? ¿agarraron al ladrón?
7. *When get means "take"* tomar: let's get a cab to the station tomemos un taxi hasta la estación
8. *When get means "become"*

> When **get** means "become" and is followed by an adjective, it can sometimes be translated by **hacerse** + adjective. You will often find there is a single verb in Spanish that can replace **hacerse** + adjective (to get angry = **enojarse**):

she's getting old se está haciendo vieja; he got angry se enojó; he got married last June se casó en junio pasado; it's getting dark está oscureciendo
9. *When get means "arrive" or "go"* llegar: when did you get here? ¿cuándo llegaron aquí?; how do you get to the station? ¿cómo llegas a la estación?
10. *When get means "understand"* entender: I didn't get the joke no entendí el chiste ➤ have

➤ **to get something ready** preparar algo: he's getting dinner ready está preparando la cena

**get along** *phrasal verb* ■ **llevarse bien:** my brother and I don't get along mi hermano y yo no nos llevamos bien; **I don't get along with Sam** no me llevo bien con Sam.

**get away** *phrasal verb* ■ **escaparse:** the thief got away el ladrón se escapó.

**get back** *phrasal verb*
1. **regresar:** I got back late regresé tarde
2. **devolver:** did you get your money back? ¿te devolvieron el dinero?

**get in** *phrasal verb*
1. **entrar:** they got in through the window entraron por la ventana
2. **entrar a:** get in the car! ¡entren al coche!

**get off** *phrasal verb*
1. **bajarse de:** he got off the bus se bajó del autobús
2. **bajarse:** where do we get off? ¿dónde tenemos que bajarnos?

**get on** *phrasal verb* ■ **subirse a:** they got on the train se subieron al tren.

**get out** *phrasal verb* ■ **salir por:** I got out the window salí por la ventana
➤ she got out of the taxi se bajó del taxi
➤ get out! ¡fuera!

**get up** *phrasal verb* ■ **levantarse:** what time did you get up? ¿a qué hora te levantaste?; Sam gets up at dawn Sam se levanta al amanecer.

**ghost** [gəʊst] *noun* ■ el **fantasma:** do you believe in ghosts? ¿crees en fantasmas?

**giant** ['dʒaɪənt] *noun* ■ el **gigante,** la **giganta.**

**gift** [gɪft] *noun*
1. el **regalo:** I gave her a gift le di un regalo; a gift shop una tienda de regalos
2. el **don:** she has a gift for languages tiene un don para los idiomas.

**gifted** ['gɪftɪd] *adjective* ■ **talentoso:** his son is gifted su hijo es talentoso.

**gigantic** [dʒaɪ'gæntɪk] *adjective* ■ **gigantesco:** they live in a gigantic house viven en una casa gigantesca.

**giggle** ['gɪgl] *verb* ■ **reírse tontamente:** the girls were giggling las niñas se estaban riendo tontamente.

**ginger** ['dʒɪndʒəʳ] *noun* ■ el **jengibre:** there's a bit of ginger in the sauce la salsa tiene un poco de jengibre.

**giraffe** [dʒɪ'raːf] *noun* ■ la **jirafa.**

**girl** [gɜːl] *noun* ■ la **niña:** a little girl una niña pequeña
➤ a Girl Scout una scout.

**girlfriend** ['gɜːlfrend] *noun*
1. la **novia:** Bob has a new girlfriend Bob tiene una novia nueva
2. la **amiga:** she went out with her girlfriends salió con sus amigas.

**give** [gɪv] *(past tense* gave, *past participle* given*) verb*
1. **dar:** to give something to somebody darle algo a alguien; give me the book dame el libro; give it to me! ¡dámelo!; he gave them some money les dio algo de dinero
2. **regalar:** she gave him a CD for his birthday le regaló un CD para su cumpleaños
➤ to give somebody a present hacerle un regalo a alguien
➤ to give something back to somebody devolverle algo a alguien, regresarle algo a alguien *Latin America except Southern Cone:* he gave the book back to me me devolvió el libro

**give up** *phrasal verb*
1. **rendirse:** it's too hard, I give up es muy difícil, me rindo
2. **dejar de:** he gave up smoking dejó de fumar.

**given** ['gɪvn] *past participle* ➤ give.

**glad** [glæd] *adjective* ■

Alegrarse de que is followed by a verb in the subjunctive:

➤ **to be glad** alegrarse: **I'm glad you came** me alegro de que hayas venido.

**glamor** ['glæmə<sup>r</sup>] *noun* ■ el **glamour**: **the glamor of Hollywood** el glamour de Hollywood.

**glamorous** ['glæmərəs] *adjective*

1. **glamoroso**: **she's very glamorous** es muy glamorosa
2. **atractivo**: **she has a glamorous job** tiene un trabajo atractivo.

**glance** [gla:ns] *(noun & verb)*
■ *noun*
la **mirada**: **have a quick glance at this** échale una mirada rápida a esto
➤ **at first glance** a primera vista
■ *verb*
➤ **to glance at something** echarle una mirada a algo: **he glanced at his watch** le echó una mirada a su reloj.

**glass** [gla:s] *noun*
1. el **vaso**: **can I have a glass of water?** ¿me podrías dar un vaso de agua?
2. el **vidrio**: **it's made of glass** es de vidrio.

**glasses** ['gla:sɪz] *plural noun* ■ los **anteojos**: **I can't see without my glasses** no veo sin mis anteojos.

**glide** [glaɪd] *verb* ■ **deslizarse**: **they glided around the dance floor** se deslizaban por la pista de baile.

**glitter** ['glɪtə<sup>r</sup>] *(verb & noun)*
■ *noun*
la **diamantina**, los **brillantes** *Argentina*, la **brillantina** *Uruguay*
■ *verb*
**brillar**: **the diamond glittered in the light** el diamante brillaba en la luz.

**global** ['gləʊbl] *adjective* ■ **global**
➤ **global warming** calentamiento global.

**globe** [gləʊb] *noun* ■ el **globo terráqueo**.

**gloomy** ['glu:mɪ] *adjective*
1. **lúgubre**: **this is such a gloomy house** ésta es una casa tan lúgubre
2. **triste**: **you look gloomy today** te ves triste hoy.

**glorious** ['glɔ:rɪəs] *adjective* ■ **espléndido**: **what a glorious day!** ¡qué día tan espléndido!

**glove** [glʌv] *noun* ■ el **guante**: **he was wearing black gloves** usaba guantes negros.

**glow** [gləʊ] *(noun & verb)*
■ *uncountable noun*
la **luz**: **the fire gave off a warm glow** el fuego daba una luz cálida
■ *verb*
**brillar**: **the fire was glowing** el fuego brillaba.

**glue** [glu:] *(noun & verb)*
■ *noun*
la **goma**: **use some glue to stick the pieces back together** usa un poco de goma para pegar los pedazos
■ *verb*
**pegar**: **he glued the two pieces together** pegó los dos pedazos
➤ **to be glued to something** estar pegado a algo: **we were glued to the TV all day** estuvimos pegados a la tele todo el día.

**go** [gəʊ] *verb (past tense* **went***, past participle* **gone***)*
1. **ir**: **I'm going to Australia** voy a Australia; **we went for a walk** fuimos a dar un paseo; **how's it going?** ¿cómo va todo?
2. **salir**: **the train has already gone** el tren ya salió; **we're going on vacation** vamos a salir de vacaciones
3. **irse**: **she left home** se fue de la casa; **I must be going now** ya tengo que irme; **let's go!** ¡vámonos!
4. **pasar**: **time goes quickly** el tiempo pasa rápido
5. **resultar**: **the party went well** la fiesta resultó bien
6. **andar**: **the car won't go** el coche no anda
➤ **to be going to** ir a: **it's going to rain** va a llover
**what are you going to do?** ¿qué vas a hacer?
**I'm going to call my parents** voy a llamar a mis papás
➤ **he went crazy** se volvió loco
➤ **her hair has gone white** se la ha puesto el pelo blanco

➤ ready, set, go! ¡preparados, listos, ya!

**go away** *phrasal verb* ■ **irse:** she went away se fue
➤ go away! ¡vete!

**go back** *phrasal verb* ■ **volver:** I went back to the store volví a la tienda
➤ to go back to sleep volverse a dormir: I couldn't go back to sleep no pude volverme a dormir.

**go down** *phrasal verb* ■ **bajar:** she has gone down to the cellar bajó al sótano; we went down the hill bajamos el cerro; prices have gone down bajaron los precios.

**go in** *phrasal verb* ■ **entrar:** Sam knocked on the door and went in Sam golpeó en la puerta y entró.

**go off** *phrasal verb*
1. explotar: the bomb went off la bomba explotó
2. sonar: the alarm clock went off at 6 a.m. el despertador sonó a las 6 de la mañana
3. irse: she went off without me se fue sin mí
4. apagarse: the heating went off se apagó la calefacción.

**go on** *phrasal verb*
1. seguir: they went on talking siguieron hablando
2. pasar: what's going on? ¿qué pasa?

**go out** *phrasal verb* ■ **salir:** I'm going out tonight voy a salir esta noche; he's going out with Tina está saliendo con Tina.

**go up** *phrasal verb* ■ **subir:** they went up the hill subieron el cerro; prices have gone up subieron los precios.

**goal** [gəʊl] *noun*
1. el objetivo: our goal is to succeed nuestro objetivo es triunfar
2. el gol: he scored the winning goal marcó el gol de la victoria.

**goalkeeper, goalie** ['gəʊlˌkiːpəʳ, gəʊli] *noun* ■ el **arquero,** la **arquera.**

**goat** [gəʊt] *noun* ■ la **cabra.**

**god** [gɒd] *noun* ■ el **dios:** she believes in God cree en Dios

➤ oh my God! ¡Dios mío!

**goddess** ['gɒdɪs] *noun* ■ la **diosa.**

**godfather** ['gɒdˌfɑːðəʳ] *noun* ■ el **padrino.**

**godmother** ['gɒdˌmʌðəʳ] *noun* ■ la **madrina.**

**goes** [gəʊz] ➤ go.

**goggles** ['gɒglz] *plural noun* ■ los **anteojos**
➤ safety goggles anteojos protectores
➤ swimming goggles anteojos de natación.

**gold** [gəʊld] *uncountable noun* ■ el **oro:** it's made of gold es de oro; he gave her a gold ring le regaló un anillo de oro
➤ a gold medal una medalla de oro.

**golden** ['gəʊldən] *adjective* ■ **dorado.**

**goldfish** ['gəʊldfɪʃ] *(plural* goldfish) *noun* ■ el **pez de colores** *(plural* los **peces de colores).**

**goldmine** ['gəʊldmaɪn] *noun* ■ la **mina de oro.**

**golf** [gɒlf] *noun* ■ el **golf:** he plays golf juega golf
➤ a golf ball una pelota de golf
➤ a golf club un club de golf
➤ a golf course un campo de golf.

**gone** [gɒn] *past participle* ➤ go.

**good** [gʊd] *(adjective & noun)*
■ *adjective*
**bueno**

> Bueno becomes buen before a masculine noun:

it's a really good book es un libro realmente bueno; did you have a good vacation? ¿tuvieron unas buenas vacaciones?; have a good day! ¡que tengas un buen día!; that cake looks good la pastel parece bueno; exercise is good for you el ejercicio es muy bueno
➤ be good! ¡portarte bien!
➤ they were very good to me se portaron muy bien conmigo

➤ **to have a good time** pasarlo bien, pasarla bien *Mexico:* **did you have a good time?** ¿lo pasaste bien?

➤ **good morning!** ¡buenos días!

➤ **good afternoon!** ¡buenas tardes!

➤ **good evening!** ¡buenas tardes!

➤ **good night!** ¡buenas noches!

■ *noun*

el **bien:** **good and evil** el bien y el mal

➤ **it'll do you good** te va a hacer bien

➤ **it's no good crying** de nada sirve llorar

➤ **for good** para siempre: **she left for good** se fue para siempre.

**goodbye** [ˌgʊd'baɪ]  *exclamation*
■ ¡adiós!

**good-looking** [gʊd'lʊkɪŋ]  *adjective*
■ **buenmozo, guapo** *Mexico:* **he's very good-looking** es muy buenmozo.

**goose** [guːs] *(plural* **geese** [giːs]*) noun*
■ el **ganso.**

**gorgeous** ['gɔːdʒəs] *adjective*

1. **precioso: what a gorgeous hat!** ¡qué sombrero tan precioso!

2. **guapísimo: she's gorgeous** es guapísima.

**gorilla** [gə'rɪlə] *noun* ■ el/la **gorila.**

**gossip** ['gɒsɪp] *(noun & verb)*

■ *noun*

1. los **chismes: that's just gossip** son sólo chismes

2. el **chismoso,** la **chismosa: she's a real gossip** es muy chismosa

➤ **a piece of gossip** un chisme

■ *verb*

**chismear**

➤ **to gossip about somebody** chismear sobre alguien.

**got** [gɒt] *past tense & past participle*
➤ get.

**gotten** ['gɒtn] *past participle* ➤ get.

**government** ['gʌvnmənt] *noun* ■ el **gobierno.**

**grab** [græb] *(past tense & past participle* grabbed) *verb* ■ **agarrar: he grabbed the rope** agarró la cuerda.

**graceful** ['greɪsfʊl] *adjective* ■ **lleno de gracia: the dancer's movements are graceful** los movimientos de la bailarina son llenos de gracia.

**grade** [greɪd] *noun*

1. la **nota: she always gets good grades** siempre saca buenas notas

2. el **año: what grade are you in?** ¿en qué año estás?

➤ **grade school** escuela primaria.

**gradually** ['grædʒʊəlɪ] *adverb* ■ **poco a poco: things gradually got better** las cosas mejoraron poco a poco.

**graduate** ['grædʒʊət] *(noun & verb)*

■ *noun*

el **licenciado,** la **licenciada: she's a university graduate** es licenciada universitaria

■ *verb*

**recibirse: I graduated in 1997** me recibí en 1997

### GRADUATE SCHOOL

Muchos estudiantes universitarios en Estados Unidos continúan sus estudios en una **graduate school** tras alcanzar la licenciatura. Allí pueden obtener primero la maestría y después el doctorado. Para ingresar a la graduate school hay que presentar el GRE, un examen que requieren las universidades para admisión a los programas de posgrado. Aunque continuar los estudios puede resultar muy caro, el título de posgrado casi se ha convertido en requerimiento para trabajar en ciertos campos.

**graffiti** [grə'fiːtɪ] *noun* ■ las **pintadas: there's some graffiti on the wall** hay unas pintadas en la pared.

**grain** [greɪn] *noun*

1. el **grano: a grain of sand** un grano de arena

2. el **cereal: this bread contains several grains** este pan contiene varios cereales.

**gram** [græm] *noun* ■ el **gramo: there are 1000 grams in a kilo** un kilo tiene 1000 gramos.

**grammar** ['græmə<sup>r</sup>] noun ■ la **gramática**.

**grandchild** ['græntʃaɪld] *(plural* grandchildren ['græntʃɪldrən]*)* noun ■ el **nieto**, la **nieta**: Mrs. Evans has four grandchildren la señora Evans tiene cuatro nietos.

**granddaughter** ['græn,dɔːtə<sup>r</sup>] noun ■ la **nieta**.

**grandfather** ['græn,faːðə<sup>r</sup>] noun ■ el **abuelo**.

**grandma** ['grænmaː] noun ■ *informal* la **abuelita**.

**grandmother** ['græn,mʌðə<sup>r</sup>] noun ■ la **abuela**.

**grandpa** ['grænpaː] noun ■ *informal* el **abuelito**.

**grandparents** ['græn,peərənts] *plural noun* ■ los **abuelos**.

**grandson** ['grænsʌn] noun ■ el **nieto**.

**granny** ['grænɪ] *(plural* grannies ['græniːz]*)* noun ■ *informal* la **abuelita**.

**grant** [graːnt] *(noun & verb)*
■ *noun*
la **beca**: they have a research grant tienen una beca de investigación
■ *verb*
**conceder**: he granted us permission to enter nos concedió permiso para entrar.

**grape** [greɪp] noun ■ la **uva**
➤ a bunch of grapes un racimo de uvas.

**grapefruit** ['greɪpfruːt] noun ■ la **toronja** *Latin America except Southern Cone,* el **pomelo** *Southern Cone.*

**graph** [graːf] noun ■ el **gráfico**: the graph shows the company's profits el gráfico muestra las ganancias de la empresa.

**grasp** [graːsp] *verb* ■ **agarrar**: he grasped my hand me agarró la mano.

**grass** [graːs] noun ■ el **pasto**.

**grasshopper** ['graːs,hɒpə<sup>r</sup>] noun ■ el **saltamontes** *(plural* los **saltamontes**), el **chapulín** *(plural* los **chapulines** *Mexico ).*

**grate** [greɪt] *verb* ■ **rallar**: can you grate some cheese on the pasta? ¿podrías rallar un poco de queso en la pasta?

**grateful** ['greɪtfʊl] *adjective* ■ **agradecido**: I'm very grateful to you estoy muy agradecido de ti.

**grave** [greɪv] noun ■ la **tumba**: I placed some flowers on the grave puse unas flores en la tumba.

**graveyard** ['greɪvjaːd] noun ■ el **cementerio**.

**gravity** ['grævətɪ] noun ■ la **gravedad**: the force of gravity la fuerza de la gravedad.

**gravy** ['greɪvɪ] noun ■ la **salsa**.

**gray** [greɪ] *adjective* ■ **gris**: the sky is gray el cielo está gris
➤ she has gray hair tiene el pelo canoso.

**grease** [griːs] noun ■ la **grasa**: the mechanic's hands are covered in grease las manos del mecánico están llenas de grasa.

**greasy** ['griːzɪ] *adjective*
1. **graso**: her hair was greasy tenía pelo graso
2. **grasiento**: a greasy rag un trapo grasiento.

**great** [greɪt] *adjective*
1. **grande**

> Grande becomes gran before a masculine singular noun:

it's a great success es un gran éxito
2. *informal* **sensacional**: he's a great guy es un tipo sensacional; what a great view! ¡que vista tan sensacional!
➤ I feel great me siento estupendo
➤ a great deal of mucho: he has a great deal of money tiene mucho dinero.

**Great Britain** ['greɪt'brɪtn] *noun* ■ **Gran Bretaña** *(feminine).*

**greedy** ['griːdɪ] *adjective*
1. **glotón** *(plural* **glotones**), **glotona**: I want some more cake — don't be greedy! quiero un poco más de pastel – ¡no seas glotón!

2. **codicioso**: a greedy businessman un hombre de negocios codicioso.

**green** [griːn] *adjective* ■ **verde**: she has green eyes tiene los ojos verdes
➤ a green light una luz verde
➤ a green salad una ensalada verde.

**greenhouse** ['griːnhaʊs] *noun* ■ el **invernadero**.

**greet** [griːt] *verb* ■ **saludar**: I greeted him with a wave lo saludé con la mano.

**greeting card** ['griːtɪŋkɑːd] *noun* ■ la **tarjeta de felicitación**.

**grew** [gruː] *past tense* ➤ grow.

**grief** [griːf] *noun* ■ el **dolor**.

**grill** [grɪl] *(noun & verb)*
■ *noun*
la **parrilla**: he cooked the fish on the grill hizo el pescado en la parrilla
■ *verb*
**asar a la parrilla**: I grilled the chicken asé el pollo a la parrilla.

**grin** [grɪn] *(noun & verb)*
■ *noun*
la **sonrisa**: he had a big grin on his face tenía una gran sonrisa en la cara
■ *verb*
**sonreír**: she was grinning at me me estaba sonriendo.

**grind** [graɪnd] *(past tense & past participle* grind*)* *verb* ■ **moler**: it's for grinding spices sirve para moler especias.

**grip** [grɪp] *(past tense & past participle* gripped*)* *verb* ■ **agarrar**: I gripped his arm le agarré el brazo; she was gripping my hand tightly me agarraba la mano con fuerza.

**groan** [grəʊn] *(noun & verb)*
■ *noun*
el **gemido**: I could hear the patient's groans oía los gemidos del paciente
■ *verb*
**gemir**: he groaned with pain gemía de dolor.

**groceries** ['grəʊsəriz] *noun* ■ los **comestibles**: she's gone to get groceries fue a comprar comestibles.

**grocery store** ['grəʊsərɪ,stɔːr] *noun* ■ la **tienda de comestibles**, la **tienda de abarrotes** *Andes, Central America, Mexico*, el **almacén** *(plural* los **almacenes***) Southern Cone*: I'm going to the grocery store voy a la tienda de comestibles.

**groom** [gruːm] *noun* ■ el **novio**
➤ the bride and groom la novia y el novio.

**gross** [grəʊs] *adjective*
1. **grosero**: his behavior is really gross su comportamiento es realmente grosero
2. **bruto**: his gross income su ingreso bruto.

**ground** [graʊnd] *(adjective & noun)*
■ *adjective*
**molido**: ground coffee café molido
➤ ground beef carne molida, carne picada *River Plate*
■ *noun*
1. el **suelo**: I dug a hole in the ground hice un hoyo en el suelo
2. el **terreno**: a camping ground un terreno de camping
➤ on the ground en el suelo: I was sitting on the ground estaba sentada en el suelo
➤ the ground floor la planta baja: I took the elevator to the ground floor tomé el ascensor hasta la planta baja.

**group** [gruːp] *noun* ■ el **grupo**: a large group of tourists un grupo grande de turistas.

**grow** [grəʊ] *(past tense* grew*, past participle* grown*)* *verb*
1. **crecer**: these plants grow quickly estas plantas crecen rápido; she has really grown ha crecido mucho
2. **aumentar**: the number of net users has grown ha aumentado el número de usuarios de la red
3. **cultivar**: we grow a lot of vegetables cultivamos muchas verduras
4. **dejarse crecer**: she's growing her hair se está dejando crecer el pelo
➤ to grow bigger crecer
➤ to grow old envejecer: he's growing old está envejeciendo

**grow up** phrasal verb ■ **criarse:** I grew up in Kansas me crié en Kansas
➤ I want to be a pilot when I grow up cuando sea grande, quiero ser piloto.

**growl** [graʊl] verb ■ **gruñir:** the dog growled el perro gruñió.

**grown** [grəʊn] past participle ➤ grow.

**grown-up** ['grəʊnʌp] (adjective & noun)
■ adjective
adulto: my little girl is all grown-up mi pequeña ya es toda una adulta
■ noun
la **persona mayor:** you're a grown-up now ya eres una persona mayor.

**growth** [grəʊθ] noun ■ **el crecimiento:** economic growth crecimiento económico.

**grumble** ['grʌmbl] verb ■ **quejarse:** she's always grumbling about something siempre está quejándose de algo.

**grumpy** ['grʌmpɪ] adjective ■ **gruñón** (plural **gruñones**), **gruñona:** a grumpy old man un viejo gruñón.

**grunt** [grʌnt] verb ■ **gruñir:** the pigs were grunting los cerdos estaban gruñendo.

**guarantee** [ˌgærən'tɪː] (noun & verb)
■ noun
la **garantía:** it has a five-year guarantee tiene garantía por cinco años
■ verb
garantizar: I can't guarantee I'll come no puedo garantizar que vaya a venir
➤ my watch is guaranteed mi reloj tiene garantía.

**guard** [gɑːd] (noun & verb)
■ noun
el/la **guardia:** he's a prison guard es guardia de prisión
➤ to be on guard estar de guardia
➤ a guard dog un perro guardián
■ verb
vigilar: the soldiers are guarding the building los soldados están vigilando el edificio.

**guava** ['gwɑːvə] noun ■ la **guayaba**.

**guess** [ges] (noun & verb)
■ noun
la **suposición** (plural las **suposiciones**): it's just a guess es solo una suposición
➤ to take a guess adivinar
■ verb
1. **adivinar:** I couldn't guess the answer no pude adivinar la respuesta; guess what I did! ¡adivina qué hice!
2. **suponer:** I guess so supongo que sí.

**guest** [gest] noun
1. el **invitado,** la **invitada:** we're having guests for dinner tenemos invitados a cenar
2. el/la **huésped:** the hotel has over 100 guests el hotel tiene más de cien huéspedes.

**guide** [gaɪd] (noun & verb)
■ noun
el/la **guía:** he's a tour guide es guía de turismo
➤ a guide book una guía
➤ a guide dog un perro lazarillo
■ verb
guiar: he guided us to the castle nos guió hasta el castillo.

**guilty** ['gɪltɪ] adjective ■ **culpable:** he's not guilty of murder no es culpable de asesinato; I feel guilty about lying to her me siento culpable por haberle mentido.

**guinea pig** ['gɪnɪpɪg] noun ■ el **conejillo de Indias**.

**guitar** [gɪ'tɑːʳ] noun ■ la **guitarra:** I'm learning to play guitar estoy aprendiendo a tocar guitarra.

**gum** [gʌm] noun ■ el **chicle:** a stick of gum un chicle.

**gums** [gʌmz] plural noun ■ la **encía**.

**gun** [gʌn] noun
1. el **revólver:** he has a gun in his hand tiene un revólver en la mano
2. el **fusil:** he bought a gun for hunting compró un fusil para cazar.

**gunfire** ['gʌnfaɪəʳ] *uncountable noun* ■ los **disparos**: we could hear gunfire escuchábamos disparos.

**gutter** ['gʌtəʳ] *noun* ■ la **canaleta**.

**guy** [gaɪ] *noun* ■ el **tipo**: he's a nice guy es un tipo simpático.

**gym** [dʒɪm] *noun*
1. el **gimnasio**: I go to the gym on Mondays voy al gimnasio los lunes
2. la **gimnasia**: we have gym class after lunch tenemos clase de gimnasia después de almuerzo.

**gypsy** ['dʒɪpsɪ] *(plural* gypsies ['dʒɪp-si:z]*) noun* ■ el **gitano**, la **gitana**.

**habit** ['hæbɪt] *noun* ■ la **costumbre**: she has some bad habits tiene algunas malas costumbres
➤ I've gotten into the habit of exercising me he acostumbrado a hacer ejercicio.

**hacker** ['hækəʳ] *noun* ■ el **pirata informático**, la **pirata informática**.

**had** [hæd] *past tense & past participle*
➤ have.

**hadn't** ['hædnt] ➤ had not.

**hail** [heɪl] *(noun & verb)*
■ *noun*
el **granizo**

■ *verb*
1. **granizar**: it's hailing está granizando
2. **hacerle señas a**: he hailed a cab le hizo señas a un taxi.

**hair** [heəʳ] *noun* ■ el **pelo**: she has black hair tiene el pelo negro; there's dog hair everywhere hay pelos del perro por todas partes; there's a hair in my soup hay un pelo en la sopa
➤ to do one's hair peinarse: she's doing her hair se está peinando.

**hairbrush** ['heəbrʌʃ] *noun* ■ el **cepillo**.

**haircut** ['heəkʌt] *noun* ■ el **corte de pelo**: she has a great haircut tiene un corte de pelo sensacional.

**hairdresser** ['heə,dresəʳ] *noun* ■ el **peluquero**, la **peluquera**: she's a hairdresser es peluquera
➤ we're going to the hairdresser vamos a la peluquería.

**hairdryer** ['heə,draɪəʳ] *noun* ■ el **secador de pelo**, la **secadora de pelo** *Mexico*.

**hairspray** ['heəspreɪ] *noun* ■ la **laca**.

**hairstyle** ['heəstaɪl] *noun* ■ el **peinado**: she hasn't changed her hairstyle in years hace años que no cambia de peinado.

**hairy** ['heərɪ] *adjective* ■ **peludo**: he has hairy arms tiene los brazos peludos.

**half** [hæf] *(noun & adverb)*
■ *noun*
1. la **mitad**: he ate half the cake se comió la mitad del pastel
2. *In time expressions* an hour and a half una hora y media; half an hour media hora; it's half past three son las tres y media; two and a half years dos años y medio
3. el **tiempo**: the first half of the game el primer tiempo del partido
➤ to cut something in half partir algo por la mitad
■ *adverb*
**medio**: she's half asleep está medio dormida
➤ he's half Spanish, half English es mitad español, mitad inglés.

**halftime** ['haːf,taɪm] *noun* ■ **el descanso**, el **medio tiempo**: he came back after halftime volvió después del descanso.

**halfway** [haːf'weɪ] *adverb* ■ **a mitad de camino**: halfway between San Francisco and Seattle a mitad de camino entre San Francisco y Seattle
➤ halfway through the movie en la mitad de la película.

**hall** [hɔːl] *noun*
1. el **vestíbulo**: he hung his coat up in the hall colgó el abrigo en el vestíbulo
2. la **sala**: there's a large hall where meetings take place hay una amplia sala donde tienen lugar las reuniones.

**Halloween** [,hæləʊ'iːn] *noun* ■ **Halloween** *(masculine)*

HALLOWEEN

Se pensaba que el 31 de octubre, víspera del Día de Todos los Santos, los espíritus de los muertos venían a visitar a los vivos. Hoy en día, los niños se disfrazan de brujas y fantasmas y van de puerta en puerta, llamando "trick or treat!" para pedir golosinas.

**hallway** ['hɔːlweɪ] *noun* ■ **el vestíbulo**.

**halt** [hɔːlt] *noun*
➤ to come to a halt **detenerse**: the car came to a halt el coche se detuvo.

**ham** [hæm] *noun* ■ **el jamón** *(plural los jamones)*: a ham sandwich un sandwich de jamón.

**hamburger** ['hæmbɜːgər] *noun*
1. la **hamburguesa**: Mom's making hamburgers for dinner mamá está preparando hamburguesas para la cena
2. la **carne molida**, la **carne picada** *River Plate*: the recipe calls for a pound of hamburger la receta lleva una libra de carne molida.

**hammer** ['hæmər] *noun* ■ **el martillo**.

**hamster** ['hæmstər] *noun* ■ **el hámster** *(plural los hámsters)*.

**hand** [hænd] *(noun & verb)*
■ *noun*
1. la **mano**: he writes with his left hand escribe con la mano izquierda
2. la **manecilla**: the hands of a clock las manecillas de un reloj
➤ to hold hands **ir de la mano**: they were holding hands iban de la mano
➤ to give somebody a hand **echarle una mano a alguien**: he gave me a hand with my suitcases me echó una mano con las maletas
■ *verb*
**pasar**: can you hand me a pencil? ¿pudes pasarme un lápiz?

**hand in** *phrasal verb* ■ **entregar**: they handed in their homework entregaron las tareas.

**hand out** *phrasal verb* ■ **repartir**: the teacher handed out the papers la profesora repartió los trabajos.

**hand over** *phrasal verb* ■ **entregar**: I handed the money over to her le entregué el dinero.

**handcuffs** ['hændkʌfs] *plural noun* ■ **las esposas**.

**handkerchief** ['hæŋkətʃɪf] *noun* ■ **el pañuelo**.

**handle** ['hændl] *(noun & verb)*
■ *noun*
1. la **manija**: he turned the door handle giró la manija de la puerta
2. el **asa** *(feminine)*

Although **asa** is a feminine noun, it takes **un** or **el** in the singular.

hold the cup by the handle agarra la taza del asa
3. el **mango**: the handle of the broom is broken el mango de la escoba está roto
■ *verb*
1. **manejar**: he handled the crisis well manejó bien la crisis
2. **tratar**: he knows how to handle people sabe tratar a las personas.

**handlebars** ['hændlbaːz] *plural noun* ■ **el manubrio**.

**handmade** [ˌhænd'meɪd]      *adjective*
■ **hecho a mano**.

**handrail** ['hændreɪl] *noun* ■ **el pasa-manos** *(plural* los **pasamanos)*: hold on to the handrail agárrense del pasamanos.

**handsome** ['hænsəm]                *adjective*
■ **buen mozo, guapo** *Mexico*: he's very handsome es muy buen mozo.

**handy** ['hændɪ] *adjective*
1. **práctico**: it's a handy little tool es una pequeña herramienta muy útil
2. **a mano**: I always have extra batteries handy siempre tengo pilas de más a mano.

**hang** [hæŋ] *(past tense & past participle* hung) *verb*
1. **colgar**: he hung the picture on the wall colgó el cuadro en la pared
2. *(past tense & past participle* **hanged)** **ahorcar**: they hanged the murderer ahorcaron al asesino
➤ the picture is hanging on the wall el cuadro está colgado en la pared

**hang on** *phrasal verb* ■ *informal* **esperar**: can you hang on a minute? ¿puedes esperar un minuto?

**hang up** *phrasal verb* ■ **colgar**: hang up your coat cuelga tu abrigo; they hung the decorations up colgaron los adornos; after the phone call he hung up después de la llamada telefónica, colgó.

**hanger** ['hæŋəʳ] *noun* ■ **la percha, el gancho**: put your jacket on the hanger cuelga tu chaqueta en la percha.

**happen** ['hæpən] *verb* ■ **pasar**: what happened? ¿qué pasó?; it happened last week pasó la semana pasada; guess what happened to me! ¡adivina lo que me pasó!; what's happening? ¿qué pasa?

**happier** ['hæpɪəʳ]      *comparative*  ➤ happy.

**happiest** ['hæpɪəst]    *superlative*  ➤ happy.

**happiness** ['hæpɪnɪs]           *uncountable noun* ■ **la felicidad**.

**happy** ['hæpɪ] *adjective* ■ **contento**:
I'm very happy to see you estoy muy contento de verte; Karen looks happier today Karen se ve más contenta hoy
➤ Happy birthday! ¡Feliz cumpleaños!
➤ Happy New Year! ¡Feliz Año Nuevo!

**harbor** ['hɑːbəʳ] *noun* ■ **el puerto**: the ships are in the harbor los barcos están en el puerto.

**hard** [hɑːd] *(adjective & adverb)*
■ *adjective*
1. **duro**: the bed is very hard la cama es muy dura
2. **difícil**: that's a hard question ésa es una pregunta difícil
➤ she's very hard on him es muy dura con él
➤ the hard disk el disco duro
■ *adverb*
**duro**: she works hard trabaja duro
➤ to try hard esforzarse: I tried very hard to succeed me esforcé mucho para lograrlo.

**hard-boiled** [hɑːd'bɔɪld] *adjective*
➤ a hard-boiled egg un huevo duro.

**hardly** ['hɑːdlɪ] *adverb* ■ **apenas**: I hardly know him apenas lo conozco
➤ hardly ever casi nunca: he hardly ever phones casi nunca llama por teléfono.

**hardware** ['hɑːdweəʳ] *noun* ■ **el hardware**: we're getting all new hardware for the office estamos consiguiendo todo el hardware nuevo para la oficina
➤ a hardware store una ferretería.

**hare** [heəʳ] *noun* ■ **la liebre**.

**harm** [hɑːm] *(noun & verb)*
■ *noun*
**el daño**: it won't do him any harm no le hará ningún daño
■ *verb*
1. **hacerle daño a**: he wouldn't harm a fly no le haría daño ni a una mosca
2. **dañar**: the gases could harm the environment los gases podrían dañar el medio ambiente.

**harmful** ['hɑːmfʊl] *adjective* ■ **perjudicial**: the harmful effects of smoking los efectos perjudiciales de fumar.

**harmless** ['ha:mlɪs] *adjective* ■ **ino-fensivo**: these animals are harmless estos animales son inofensivos.

**harmonica** [ha:'mɒnɪkə] *noun* ■ **la armónica**: he plays the harmonica toca la armónica.

**harsh** [ha:ʃ] *adjective* ■ **severo**: it's a harsh punishment es un castigo severo.

**harvest** ['ha:vɪst] *noun* ■ **la cosecha**: there's a lot of work at harvest time hay mucho trabajo en la época de la cosecha.

**has** [həz, hæz] ➤ **have**.

**hasn't** ['hæznt] ➤ **has not**.

**hat** [hæt] *noun* ■ **el sombrero**: she's wearing a big hat lleva puesto un sombrero grande.

**hate** [heɪt] *verb* ■ **odiar**: I hate liver odio el hígado
➤ to hate doing something odiar hacer algo: he hates getting up early odia levantarse temprano.

**hatred** ['heɪtrɪd] *noun* ■ **el odio**.

**haunted** ['hɔːntɪd] *adjective* ■ **embrujado**: this house is haunted esta casa está embrujada.

**have** [hæv] *(past tense & past participle had) verb*
1. **tener**: I have a dog called Sammy or I've got a dog called Sammy tengo un perro que se llama Sammy; do you have any brothers? or have you got any brothers? ¿tienes hermanos?; Rosie has blue eyes or Rosie has got blue eyes Rosie tiene los ojos azules; they didn't have time no tenían tiempo
2.

> When "have" is used with certain nouns, you can use a single verb in Spanish to translate "have" + noun:

I'm going to have a shower voy a ducharme; I'll have some coffee tomaré café; we had sandwiches for lunch almorzamos sandwiches; let's have dinner cenemos

3. **pasar**: we had a nice evening pasamos una tarde agradable; I hope you have a good time espero que la pases bien
4. *In the perfect tenses* **haber**: have you seen my glasses? ¿has visto mis anteojos?; she had forgotten to phone se había olvidado de llamar; he has become very rich se ha hecho muy rico
5.

> "Have to" and "have got to" are translated by **tener que** + infinitive:

I have to leave or I've got to leave tengo que irme; he had to go to the dentist tuvo que ir al dentista

> To say you "don't have to", use the construction **no tener que** + infinitive:

you don't have to come no tienes que venir
➤ to have something done hacer hacer algo: I'm going to have the rugs cleaned voy a hacer limpiar las alfombras
➤ to have a party tener una fiesta
➤ I'm having a party on Friday tengo una fiesta el viernes.

**haven't** ['hævnt] ➤ **have not**.

**hay** [heɪ] *uncountable noun* ■ **el heno**: the cows are eating hay las vacas están comiendo heno
➤ hay fever fiebre del heno: she has hay fever tiene fiebre del heno.

**hazardous** ['hæzədəs] *adjective* ■ **peligroso**.

**hazelnut** ['heɪzl,nʌt] *noun* ■ **la avellana**.

**he** [hiː] *personal pronoun* ■ **él**

> In Spanish, he is not usually translated:

he's named John se llama John; he came to see me vino a verme

> Use él for emphasis or to avoid ambiguity:

he did it él lo hizo; he doesn't know it but she does él no lo sabe pero ella sí
➤ there he is! ¡ahí está!

**head** [hed] *noun*

1. la **cabeza**: my head hurts me duele la cabeza
2. el **jefe**, la **jefa**: he's the head of state es el jefe de Estado
➤ heads or tails? ¿cara o cruz?, ¿águila o sol? *Mexico*

**head for** *phrasal verb* ■ **dirigirse hacia**: they're heading for the exit se dirigen hacia la salida.

**headache** ['hedeɪk] *noun* ■ el **dolor de cabeza**: she has a headache tiene dolor de cabeza.

**headlight** ['hedlaɪt] *noun* ■ el **faro**: the driver put the headlights on el chofer encendió los faros.

**headline** ['hedlaɪn] *noun* ■ el **titular**: to read the headlines leer los titulares.

**headphones** ['hedfəʊnz] *plural noun* ■ el **auricular**: she put on her headphones to listen to the music se puso los auriculares para escuchar música.

**heal** [hiːl] *verb*

1. **cicatrizar**: the wound is healing la herida está cicatrizando
2. **curar**: this will heal your wounds esto curará tus heridas.

**health** [helθ] *uncountable noun* ■ la **salud**: he's in good health tiene buena salud.

**healthy** ['helθɪ] *adjective*

1. **sano**: she's very healthy es muy sana; he leads a healthy life lleva una vida sana
2. **saludable**: a healthy diet una alimentación saludable.

**heap** [hiːp] *noun* ■ el **montón** *(plural los montones)*: a heap of leaves un montón de hojas; his clothes are lying in a heap su ropa está tirada en un montón.

**hear** [hɪəʳ] *(past tense & past participle heard [hɜːd]) verb*

1. **oír**: she heard a noise oyó un ruido; I heard him laughing lo oí reírse
2. **saber**: have you heard the news? ¿supiste lo que pasó?; I heard he was sick supe que estaba enfermo

**hear from** *phrasal verb* ■ **tener noticias de**: I haven't heard from her for ages hace años que no tengo noticias de ella.

**hear of** *phrasal verb* ■ **oír hablar de**: I've never heard of him nunca he oído hablar de él.

**heart** [haːt] *noun* ■ el **corazón** *(plural los corazones)*: my heart missed a beat me dio un vuelco el corazón
➤ by heart de memoria: I know the poem by heart me sé el poema de memoria
➤ a heart attack un ataque al corazón
➤ the ace of hearts el as de corazones.

**heat** [hiːt] *(noun & verb)*

■ *noun*
el **calor**: I don't like the heat no me gusta el calor

■ *verb*
**calentar**: heat the water for ten minutes caliente el agua durante diez minutos

**heat up** *phrasal verb*

1. **calentar**: I heated the pizza up in the oven calenté la pizza en el horno; I heated up the milk calenté la leche
2. **calentarse**: the water is heating up el agua se está calentando.

**heater** ['hiːtəʳ] *noun* ■ el **calentador**: he turned the heater on prendió el calentador.

**heating** ['hiːtɪŋ] *noun* ■ la **calefacción**: he put the heating on prendió la calefacción.

**heaven** ['hevn] *noun* ■ el **cielo**: will he go to heaven? ¿se irá al cielo?

**heavy** ['hevɪ] *(comparative heavier, superlative heaviest) adjective*

1. **pesado**: my luggage is very heavy mi equipaje está muy pesado
2. **grueso**: a heavy coat un abrigo grueso
➤ the traffic is heavy at weekends los fines de semana hay mucho tráfico
➤ I had a heavy week tuve una semana muy ocupada.

**he'd** [hiːd] ➤ he had; he would.

**hedge** [hedʒ] *noun* ■ el **seto**: there's a hedge around the yard hay un seto alrededor del jardín.

**hedgehog** ['hedʒhɒg] *noun* ■ el **erizo**.

**heel** [hiːl] *noun*

1. el **talón** *(plural* los **talones***)*: these socks have a hole on the heel estas medias tienen un agujero en el talón

2. el **tacón** *(plural* los **tacones***),* el **taco** *Southern Cone*: her shoes have very high heels sus zapatos tienen los tacones muy altos.

**height** [haɪt] *noun*

1. la **altura**: what is the height of the wall? ¿qué altura tiene la pared?

2. la **estatura**: she's of average height es de estatura mediana.

**heir** [eəʳ] *noun* ■ el **heredero**, la **heredera**.

**held** [held] *past tense & past participle* ➤ hold.

**helicopter** ['helɪkɒptəʳ] *noun* ■ el **helicóptero**.

**hell** [hel] *noun* ■ el **infierno**: heaven and hell el paraíso y el infierno.

**he'll** [hiːl] ➤ he will.

**hello** [həˈləʊ] *exclamation*

1. **hola**: hello, how are you? hola, ¿cómo estás?

2. **¿aló?, ¿bueno?** *Mexico,* **¿hola?** *River Plate*: hello, this is Paul speaking ¿aló?, habla Paul.

**helmet** ['helmɪt] *noun* ■ el **casco**: you should wear a helmet when you ride your bike deberías usar un casco cuando andas en bicicleta.

**help** [help] *(noun, exclamation & verb)*

■ *noun*
la **ayuda**: do you need any help? ¿necesitas ayuda?; he asked for help pidió ayuda

■ *exclamation*
**socorro**: help, I'm drowning! ¡socorro! ¡que me ahogo!

■ *verb*
**ayudar**: can I help you? ¿te ayudo?; can you help me with my homework? ¿me ayudas con mis tareas?; I helped her wash the car la ayudé a lavar el coche

➤ I can't help it no puedo evitarlo

➤ help yourself! ¡sírvete!: can I have some water? — help yourself! ¿puedo tomar agua? — ¡sírvete!

➤ I helped myself to some cheese me serví un poco de queso.

**helpful** ['helpfʊl] *adjective*

1. **servicial**: he's always very helpful siempre es muy servicial

2. **útil**: your advice was helpful tu consejo fue útil.

**helping** ['helpɪŋ] *noun* ■ la **porción** *(plural* las **porciones***)*: I had a big helping of rice me serví una buena porción de arroz

➤ to have a second helping servirse otra porción: would you like to have a second helping of cake? ¿quieres servirte otra porción de torta?

**hen** [hen] *noun* ■ la **gallina**.

**her** [hɜːʳ] *(pronoun & adjective)*

■ *personal pronoun*

1. *Direct object* **la**: can you see her? ¿la ves?; call her! ¡llámala!; I didn't see her no la vi; he had always loved her siempre la ha amado

2. *Indirect object* **le**: I gave her the flowers le dí flores

> Use **se** instead of **le** when **her** is used with a direct object pronoun:

give them to her! ¡dáselas!

3. *After a preposition* **ella**: these chocolates are for her estos chocolates son para ella; I'm taller than her soy más alto que ella

■ *possessive adjective*
**su**

> In Spanish the possessive adjective agrees in number (singular or plural) with the noun that follows:

her father is a doctor su padre es médico; her car won't start su coche no arranca; she lent me her books me prestó sus libros

Use the definite article (**el, la, los** or **las**), not the possessive adjective, with parts of the body:

she raised her hand levantó la mano; **I'm brushing my teeth** me estoy cepillando los dientes.

**herb** [ɜːrb] *noun* ■ la **hierba**.

**herd** [hɜːd] *noun* ■ el **rebaño: a herd of sheep** un rebaño de ovejas.

**here** [hɪər] *adverb* ■ **aquí: come here!** ¡ven aquí!
➤ **here is** or **here's** aquí está: **here's Jenny** aquí está Jenny
➤ **here are** aquí están: **here are your keys** aquí están tus llaves.

**hero** ['hɪərəʊ] *(plural* heroes) *noun* ■ el **héroe: he's my hero** es mi héroe.

**heroin** ['herəʊɪn] *noun* ■ la **heroína: heroin is a dangerous drug** la heroína es una droga peligrosa.

**heroine** ['herəʊɪn] *noun*
1. la **heroína: she's my heroine** es mi heroína
2. la **protagonista: who is the heroine of the book?** ¿quién es la protagonista del libro?

**herring** ['herɪŋ] *noun* ■ el **arenque**.

**hers** [hɜːz] *possessive pronoun*
1. **el suyo**

In Spanish the possessive pronoun agrees in gender (masculine or feminine) and number (singular or plural) with the noun it replaces:

my blouse is blue, hers is red mi blusa es azul, la suya es roja
2. **suyo: that book's not hers** ese libro no es suyo; **she's a friend of hers** es una amiga suya.

**herself** [hɜːˈself] *pronoun*
1. **se: she's washing herself** se está lavando; **she enjoyed herself** se divirtió
2. **ella misma: she made it herself** ella misma lo hizo
➤ **she's pleased with herself** está satisfecha consigo misma

➤ **by herself** sola: **Amy is all by herself** Amy está completamente sola.

**he's** [hiːz]
1. ➤ he is; ➤ he has.

**hesitate** ['hezɪteɪt] *verb* ■ **dudar: I hesitated for a moment** dudé por un momento; **don't hesitate to call me!** ¡no dudes en llamarme!

**hi** [haɪ] *exclamation* ■ *informal* **hola: hi, how are you?** hola, ¿qué tal?

**hiccup** ['hɪkʌp] *noun* ■ el **hipo: I've got the hiccups** tengo hipo.

**hid** [hɪd] *past tense* ➤ hide.

**hidden** ['hɪdn] *past participle* ➤ hide.

**hide** [haɪd] *(past tense* hid, *past participle* hidden) *verb*
1. **esconder: hide the presents!** ¡esconde los regalos!
2. **esconderse: she hid behind the sofa** se escondió detrás del sofá.

**hide-and-seek** [haɪdəndˈsiːk] *noun* ■ las **escondidas: they're playing hide-and-seek** están jugando a las escondidas.

**high** [haɪ] *adjective*
1. **alto: this fence is very high** esta valla es muy alta; **prices are high in New York** los precios son altos en Nueva York
2. **agudo: she has a high voice** tiene una voz aguda
➤ **how high is the tower?** ¿qué altura tiene la torre?
➤ **it's 6 feet high** tiene 6 pies de alto
➤ **the high jump** el salto alto
➤ **at high speed** a alta velocidad: **the train travels at high speed** el tren anda a alta velocidad.

**higher** ['haɪər] *(comparative* high) **más alto: Harry can jump higher than me** Harry salta más alto que yo; **a higher number** un número más alto.

**highlight** ['haɪlaɪt] *(noun & verb)*
■ *noun*
**lo más destacado: the speech was the highlight of the evening** el discurso fue lo más destacado de la noche

■ *verb*

1. marcar con rotulador, marcar con plumón *Chile, Mexico*: **I've highlighted the important words in the book** marqué con rotulador las palabras importantes del libro

2. destacar: **double-click on a word to highlight it** haga doble clic sobre una palabra para destacarla.

**highlighter** ['haɪlaɪtəʳ] *noun* ■ el rotulador, el plumón *(plural* los plumones *Chile, Mexico)*.

**high school** ['haɪskuːl] *noun* ■ la secundaria, la preparatoria *Mexico*, el liceo *Southern Cone, Venezuela*: **he's still in high school** todavía está en la secundaria.

**high-tech, hi-tech** [haɪ'tek] *adjective* ■ de alta tecnología: **it's a high-tech computer** es una computadora de alta tecnología

➤ **a high-tech industry** una industria de alta tecnología.

**highway** ['haɪweɪ] *noun* ■ la autopista.

**hijack** ['haɪdʒæk] *verb* ■ secuestrar: **a plane has been hijacked** secuestraron un avión.

**hike** [haɪk] *noun* ■ la caminata: **we went on a hike in the morning** hizo una caminata en la mañana.

**hiking** ['haɪkɪŋ] *noun* ■ el excursionismo: **do you want to go hiking?** ¿quieres hacer excursionismo?

**hilarious** [hɪ'leərɪəs] *adjective* ■ divertidísimo: **the show was hilarious** el programa fue divertidísimo.

**hill** [hɪl] *noun* ■ la colina: **there's a house on the top of the hill** hay una casa en la cumbre de la colina; **they walked up the hill** subieron la colina caminando.

**him** [hɪm] *personal pronoun*

1. *Direct object* **lo: I can't see him** no lo veo; **find him!** ¡encuéntralo!; **I saw him** lo vi

2. *Indirect object* **le: she gave him a kiss** le dio un beso; **tell him to come** dile que venga

> Use **se** instead of **le** when **him** is used with a direct object pronoun:

**give them to him!** dáselos

3. *After preposition* **él: these CDs are for him** estos CDs son para él; **I'm taller than him** soy más alta que él.

**himself** [hɪm'self] *pronoun*

1. se: **he's washing himself** se está lavando; **he cut himself** se cortó

2. él mismo: **he made it himself** lo hizo él mismo

➤ **Jack's very pleased with himself** Jack está muy satisfecho consigo mismo

➤ **by himself** solo: **he's all by himself** está completamente solo

**he did it by himself** él solo lo hizo.

**hip** [hɪp] *noun* ■ la cadera.

**hippopotamus, hippo** [ˌhɪpə'pɒtəməs, 'hɪpəʊ] *noun* ■ el hipopótamo.

**hire** ['haɪəʳ] *verb* ■ contratar: **the factory hired 20 new workers** la fábrica contrató a 20 nuevos trabajadores.

**his** [hɪz] *(adjective & pronoun)*

■ *possessive adjective*
   su

> In Spanish the possessive adjective agrees in number (singular or plural) with the noun that follows:

**his brother is named Dan** su hermano se llama Dan; **his car won't start** su coche no arranca; **his parents are away** sus padres salieron

> Use the definite article (**el, la, los** or **las**), not the possessive adjective, with parts of the body:

**he raised his hand** levantó la mano; **he's washing his face** se está lavando la cara

■ *possessive pronoun*
1. **el suyo**

> In Spanish the possessive pronoun agrees in gender (masculine or feminine) and number (singular or plural) with the noun it replaces:

**my shirt is green, his is blue** mi camisa es verde, la suya es azul
2. **suyo: it's his** es suyo; **he's a friend of his** es un amigo suyo.

**hiss** [hɪs] *verb* ■ **silbar: the snake hissed** la serpiente silbó.

**history** ['hɪstərɪ] *noun* ■ **la historia: they're studying American history** están estudiando la historia de Estados Unidos.

**hit** [hɪt] ( *noun & verb*)

■ *noun*
**el éxito: her book was a big hit** su libro fue un gran éxito

■ *verb*
(*past tense & past participle* **hit**)
1. **golpear: she hit him** lo golpeó
2. **chocar: the car hit a tree** el coche chocó contra un árbol
3. **atropellar: she was hit by a car** la atropelló un coche
4. **golpearse: I hit my knee on the table** me golpeé la rodilla en la mesa
5. **dar en: the bullet hit the target** la bala dio en el blanco.

**hitchhike** ['hɪtʃhaɪk] *verb* ■ **hacer dedo, ir de aventón** *Mexico*: **she hitchhiked to Denver** hizo dedo hasta Denver.

**hi-tech** *adjective* ➤ **high-tech.**

**hoarse** [hɔːs] *adjective* ■ **ronco: my voice is hoarse** tengo la voz ronca.

**hobby** ['hɒbɪ] (*plural* hobbies ['hɒbɪz]) *noun* ■ **el hobby** (*plural* **los hobbies**)**: do you have any hobbies?** ¿tienes algún hobby?

**hockey** ['hɒkɪ] *noun* ■ **el hockey sobre hielo: they're playing hockey** están jugando hockey sobre hielo.

**hold** [həʊld] (*past tense & past participle* held) *verb*

1. **tener: I was holding the key in my hand** tenía la llave en la mano
2. **tener capacidad de: the bottle holds a quart of water** la botella tiene una capacidad de un cuarto de galón de agua
3. **celebrar: we're holding a meeting tomorrow** vamos a celebrar una reunión mañana
➤ **to hold your breath** contener la respiración: **how long can you hold your breath?** ¿cuánto tiempo puedes contener la respiración?
➤ **please hold the line!** no cuelgue, por favor
➤ **hold it!** ¡espera!
➤ **to get hold of something** conseguir algo: **I couldn't get hold of his address** no pude conseguir su dirección

**hold on** *phrasal verb*
1. **esperar: hold on a minute!** ¡espera un minuto!
2. **agarrarse: hold on tight!** ¡agárrate fuerte!
➤ **to hold onto something** agarrarse a algo: **hold onto the strap** agárrate a la correa.

**hold out** *phrasal verb* ■ **tender: he held out his hand** le tendió la mano.

**hold up** *phrasal verb*
1. **levantar: she held up her hand** levantó la mano
2. **retrasarse: we were held up in a traffic jam** nos retrasamos debido a un embotellamiento
3. **atracar: three men held up the bank** tres hombres atracaron el banco.

**holdup** ['həʊldʌp] *noun*
1. **el atraco: there was a holdup at the bank** hubo un atraco en el banco
2. **el retraso: what's the holdup?** ¿cuánto es el retraso?

**hole** [həʊl] *noun* ■ **el agujero: the puppy was digging a hole** el cachorro estaba haciendo un agujero.

**holiday** ['hɒlɪdeɪ] *noun* ■ **el día feriado: July 4th is a holiday** el 4 de julio es un día feriado
➤ **the holidays** las vacaciones: **what are you doing for the holidays** ¿qué vas a hacer para las vacaciones?

**hollow** ['hɒləʊ] *adjective* ■ **hueco:** the tree trunk is hollow el tronco del árbol está hueco.

**Hollywood** ['hɒlɪwʊd] *noun* ■ **Hollywood** *(masculine)*

HOLLYWOOD

Hollywood es una zona de Los Angeles, California, donde se produce la mayor parte de las películas estadounidenses desde hace casi un siglo, y donde viven muchas celebridades. Las primeras productoras cinematográficas se establecieron allí en 1908, donde el clima privilegiado permitía rodar en exteriores todo el año. Los años 30s y 40s fueron la edad dorada de Hollywood.

**holy** ['həʊlɪ] *adjective* ■ **santo.**

**home** [həʊm] *(noun & adverb)*
■ *noun*
la **casa:** you have a lovely home tienes una casa preciosa
➤ a **home page** una página de inicio
■ *adverb*
**casa:** she took me home me llevó a mi casa
➤ at **home** en la casa: I stayed at home today hoy me quedé en la casa
➤ make yourself at home! ¡siéntete como en tu casa!
➤ to go home irse a casa: I want to go home quiero irme a casa
➤ James got home late James llegó a casa tarde.

**homeless** ['həʊmlɪs] *noun*
➤ to be homeless estar sin hogar
➤ the homeless los sin techo.

**homemade** [,həʊm'meɪd] *adjective*
■ **casero:** they served homemade bread sirvieron pan casero.

**homesick** ['həʊmsɪk] *adjective*
➤ she was homesick for most of the trip extrañó a su familia durante la mayor parte del viaje.

**homework** ['həʊmwɜːk] *uncountable noun* ■ las **tareas:** do you have any homework? ¿tienes tareas?; have you done your homework ¿hiciste las tareas?

**honest** ['ɒnɪst] *adjective*
1. **honrado:** she's a very honest person es una persona muy honrada
2. **sincero:** be honest with me sé sincero conmigo.

**honesty** ['ɒnɪstɪ] *noun* ■ la **honradez:** honesty is the best policy la honradez es la mejor política.

**honey** ['hʌnɪ] *noun* ■ la **miel:** she put some honey in her tea le puso un poco de miel a su té.

**honeymoon** ['hʌnɪmuːn] *noun* ■ la **luna de miel:** they spent their honeymoon in Cancún pasaron su luna de miel en Cancún.

**honor** ['ɒnəʳ] *noun* ■ el **honor.**

**hood** [hʊd] *noun*
1. la **capucha:** put the hood of your coat up súbete la capucha del abrigo
2. el **capó,** el **cofre** *Mexico:* the hood of the car el capó del coche.

**hoof** [huːf, hʊf] *(plural* hoofs o hooves [huːvz]) *noun*
1. el **casco:** horses have hooves los caballos tienen cascos
2. la **pezuña:** cows and sheep have hooves las vacas y las ovejas tienen pezuñas.

**hook** [hʊk] *noun*
1. el **gancho:** the picture is hanging on a hook la foto está colgada de un gancho
2. el **anzuelo:** he caught the fish on a hook pescó el pescado con un anzuelo
➤ the phone is off the hook el teléfono está descolgado.

**hooray** ➤ hurray.

**hop** [hɒp] *(past tense & past participle* hopped) *verb*
1. **brincar:** he hopped over the ditch brincó por encima de la zanja
2. **subirse:** she hopped in the car and drove off se subió al coche y se fue.

**hope** [həʊp] *(noun & verb)*
■ *noun*
la **esperanza:** the news gave me hope la noticia me dio esperanzas

■ *verb*

**esperar: I hope she succeeds** espero que lo logre; **he was hoping for an answer tonight** esperaba tener una respuesta esta noche; **I hope to see you soon** espero verte pronto
➤ **I hope so** espero que sí
➤ **I hope not** espero que no.

**hopeful** ['həʊpʊl] *adjective*

1. **esperanzado: everybody is hopeful** todos están esperanzados
2. **alentador: the news is hopeful** la noticia es alentadora.

**hopefully** ['həʊpfəlɪ] *adverb* ■ **es de esperar que: hopefully, it will be sunny tomorrow** es de esperar que mañana haga sol

> **Es de esperar que** is followed by a verb in the subjunctive.

**hopeless** ['həʊplɪs] *adjective*

1. **desesperado: the situation is hopeless** la situación es desesperada
2. **negado: he's hopeless at sports** es negado para los deportes.

**horizon** [həˈraɪzn] *noun* ■ **el horizonte: I can see a ship on the horizon** veo un barco en el horizonte.

**horn** [hɔːn] *noun*

1. **el cuerno: bulls have horns** los toros tienen cuernos
2. **la claxon: he honked the horn** tocó el claxon.

**horoscope** ['hɒrəskəʊp] *noun* ■ **el horóscopo.**

**horrible** ['hɒrəbl] *adjective* ■ **horrible: what a horrible place!** ¡qué lugar tan horrible!

**horror** ['hɒrəʳ] *noun* ■ **el horror**
➤ **a horror film** una película de terror.

**horse** [hɔːs] *noun* ■ **el caballo: can you ride a horse?** ¿sabes andar a caballo?
➤ **horse racing** carreras de caballos.

**horseback** ['hɔːsbæk] *noun*
➤ **on horseback** a caballo

➤ **horseback riding** la equitación: **she loves to go horseback riding** le encanta hacer equitación.

**horseshoe** ['hɔːsʃuː] *noun* ■ **la herradura: horseshoes bring good luck** las herraduras traen buena suerte.

**hose** [həʊz] *noun* ■ **la manguera: a garden hose** una manguera de jardín.

**hospital** ['hɒspɪtl] *noun* ■ **el hospital: they took him to the hospital** lo llevaron al hospital
➤ **in the hospital** en el hospital: **she's in the hospital** está en el hospital.

**host** [həʊst] *noun* ■ **el anfitrión** *(plural* **los anfitriones): Gary is a very gracious host** Gary es un anfitrión muy amable.

**hostage** ['hɒstɪdʒ] *noun* ■ **el rehén** *(plural* **los rehenes): they have 12 hostages in there** tienen 12 rehenes allí dentro; **she was taken hostage** fue tomada como rehén.

**hostess** ['həʊstes] *noun* ■ **la anfitriona.**

**hot** [hɒt] *adjective*

1. **caliente: the water's hot** el agua está caliente
2. **picante, picoso** *Mexico*: **he likes hot food** le gusta la comida picante
➤ **a hot sauce** una salsa picante, una salsa picosa *Mexico*
➤ **I'm hot** tengo calor
➤ **it's hot today** hoy hace calor
➤ **a hot dog** un hot dog, un pancho *River Plate*.

**hotel** [həʊˈtel] *noun* ■ **el hotel.**

**hour** ['aʊəʳ] *noun* ■ **la hora: I waited for two hours** esperé dos horas
➤ **an hour and a half** una hora y media
➤ **half an hour** media hora
➤ **a quarter of an hour** un cuarto de hora.

**house** [haʊs] *noun* ■ **la casa: he lives in a small house** vive en una casa pequeña; **you can stay at my house** puedes quedarte en mi casa; **I went to her house** fui a su casa
➤ Senate, Congress, Political Parties
➤ **the House of Representatives** la Cámara de Representantes

La Cámara de Representantes (**House of Representatives**) constituye, junto con el Senado, el organismo legislativo estadounidense. Cada dos años se elige a sus 435 miembros, cuyo número es proporcional con la población de cada estado. De esta manera, el estado de Delaware tiene sólo 2 representantes mientras que California tiene 52. Todas las leyes nuevas deben ser ratificadas por ambas cámaras del Congreso.

**housewife** ['haʊswaɪf] (plural housewives ['haʊswaɪvz]) noun ■ el **ama de casa** (plural las **amas de casa**)

Feminine noun that takes **un** or **el** in the singular.

**housework** ['haʊswɜːk] uncountable noun ■ los **quehaceres domésticos**: he hates doing the housework odia los quehaceres domésticos.

**how** [haʊ] adverb

1. **cómo**: how are you? ¿cómo estás?; how was the test? ¿cómo estuvo la prueba?; tell me how you did it cuéntame cómo lo hiciste
2. With "much" and "many" how much is it? ¿cuánto es?; how much money do you have? ¿cuánto dinero tienes?; how many continents are there? ¿cuántos continentes hay?
3. In exclamations **qué**: how pretty you look! ¡qué linda te ves!; how kind! ¡qué amable!

➤ to know how to do something saber hacer algo: I don't know how to drive no sé manejar: do you know how to ski? ¿sabes esquiar?
➤ how long will it take? ¿cuánto tiempo va a tardar?
➤ how long is the rope? ¿qué largo tiene la cuerda?
➤ how old are you? ¿cuántos años tienes?

**however** [haʊˈevəʳ] adverb ■ **sin embargo**: she worked hard; however, she failed the final exam trabajó duro, sin embargo, no aprobó el examen final.

**howl** [haʊl] verb ■ **aullar**.

**hug** [hʌg] (noun & verb)
■ noun
el **abrazo**: she gave me a big hug me dio un gran abrazo
■ verb
**abrazar**: I hugged him lo abracé.

**huge** [hjuːdʒ] adjective ■ **enorme**: elephants are huge animals los elefantes son animales enormes; a huge building un edificio enorme.

**hum** [hʌm] verb
1. **tararear**: he was humming a tune estaba tarareando una melodía
2. **zumbar**: we could hear the bees humming oíamos zumbar las abejas.

**human** ['hjuːmən] adjective ■ **humano**: we're all human todos somos humanos
➤ a human being un ser humano.

**humid** ['hjuːmɪd] adjective ■ **húmedo**: it's very humid está muy húmedo.

**humor** ['hjuːməʳ] noun ■ el **humor**: Suzanne has a good sense of humor Suzanne tiene un buen sentido del humor.

**hump** [hʌmp] noun ■ la **joroba**: a camel with two humps un camello con dos jorobas.

**hundred** ['hʌndrəd] number ■

Use **cien** before a noun:

a hundred dollars cien dólares; a hundred people cien personas; she's a hundred years old tiene cien años

When **hundred** is preceded by another number, use the compound form **doscientos, trescientos etc**, which must agree with the noun:

three hundred trescientos; two hundred people doscientas personas; three hundred and one trescientos uno

But use **cien** when **hundred** is followed by **thousand** or **million**:

one hundred thousand dollars cien mil dólares; one hundred million euros cien millones de euros
➤ there were hundreds of people at the party había cientos de personas en la fiesta.

**hung** [hʌŋ] *past tense & past participle*
➤ hang.

**hunger** ['hʌŋgəʳ] *noun* ■ el **hambre**

Feminine noun that takes **un** or **el** in the singular.

**hungry** ['hʌŋgrɪ] *adjective*
➤ to be hungry tener hambre: I'm hungry tengo hambre; are you very hungry? ¿tienes mucha hambre?

**hunt** [hʌnt] *verb*
1. cazar: they hunt deer cazan ciervos
2. buscar: the police are hunting the murderer la policía está buscando al asesino
➤ to hunt for something buscar algo: he's hunting for his keys está buscando sus llaves.

**hunter** ['hʌntəʳ] *noun* ■ el **cazador,** la cazadora: he's a hunter es cazador.

**hunting** ['hʌntɪŋ] *noun* ■ la **caza**.

**hurl** [hɜːl] *verb* ■ **tirar, aventar** *Colombia, Mexico, Peru*: she hurled the ball through the window tiró la pelota por la ventana.

**hurray, hooray** [hʊ'reɪ] *exclamation*
■ **hurra**.

**hurricane** ['hʌrɪkən] *noun* ■ el **huracán** (*plural* los **huracanes**).

**hurry** ['hʌrɪ] (*noun & verb*)
■ *noun*
➤ to be in a hurry tener prisa, estar apurado: she's always in a hurry siempre tiene prisa

take your time, I'm not in a hurry tómate tu tiempo, no tengo prisa
➤ to do something in a hurry hacer algo a toda prisa, hacer algo a las apuradas *River Plate*: she did her homework in a hurry hizo las tareas a toda prisa
■ *verb*
(*past tense & past participle* **hurried**) apurarse: she hurried to catch the bus se apuró para tomar el autobús

**hurry up** *phrasal verb* ■ **apurarse:** hurry up! ¡apúrate!

**hurt** [hɜːt] (*adjective & verb*)
■ *adjective*
1. herido: he's badly hurt está gravemente herido
2. dolido: she's hurt that you didn't invite her está dolida porque no la invitaste
■ *verb*
(*past tense & past participle* **hurt**)
1. doler: ouch, that hurts! ¡ay! eso duele; my head hurts me duele la cabeza
2. hacer daño: stop it, you're hurting me basta ya, me estás haciendo daño
3. herir: what he said hurt me me hirió lo que dijo
➤ to hurt someone's feelings herir los sentimientos de alguien: I didn't mean to hurt your feelings no quise herir tus sentimientos
➤ I hurt her leg me hice daño en la pierna
➤ to hurt yourself lastimarse: did you hurt yourself? ¿te lastimaste?

**husband** ['hʌzbənd] *noun* ■ el **marido**: she met her husband in college conoció a su marido en la universidad.

**hut** [hʌt] *noun* ■ la **choza**, el **jacal** *Mexico*: the tribes live in huts las tribus viven en chozas.

**hymn** [hɪm] *noun* ■ el **himno**.

**hyphen** ['haɪfn] *noun* ■ el **guión** (*plural* los **guiones**): "e-mail" is written with a hyphen "e-mail" se escribe con un guión.

**icicle** ['aɪsɪkl] *noun* ▪ el **carámbano**: there are icicles hanging from the trees hay carámbanos colgando de los árboles.

**icing** ['aɪsɪŋ] *noun* ▪ el **glaseado**: a cake with pink icing un pastel con glaseado rosado.

**icon** ['aɪkɒn] *noun* ▪ el **icono,** el **ícono**: click on the icon to open the program haga clic sobre el icono para abrir el programa.

**icy** ['aɪsɪ] *adjective*
1. **helado**: an icy wind un viento helado
2. **cubierto de hielo**: be careful, the road is icy ten cuidado, la calle está cubierta de hielo.

**I'd** [aɪd]
➤ I had; ➤ I would.

**ID** [aɪdiː] *(abbreviation of* identification*) noun* ▪ el **documento de identidad**: do you have any ID? ¿tienes algún documento de identidad?

**idea** [aɪ'dɪə] *noun* ▪ la **idea**: that's a good idea es una buena idea; where is he? — I have no idea ¿dónde está? — no tengo idea.

**ideal** [aɪ'dɪəl] *adjective* ▪ **ideal**: it's an ideal place for a party es un lugar ideal para hacer una fiesta.

**identical** [aɪ'dentɪkl] *adjective* ▪ **idéntico**
➤ identical twins gemelos idénticos.

**identification** [aɪ,dentɪfɪ'keɪʃn] *noun* ▪ la **identificación** *(plural* las **identificaciones**): do you have any identification? ¿tienes alguna identificación?

**identify** [aɪ'dentɪfaɪ] *(past tense & past participle* identified*) verb* ▪ **identificar**: they've identified the body han identificado el cuerpo.

**identity** [aɪ'dentətɪ] *(plural* identities*) noun* ▪ la **identidad**: he revealed the murderer's identity reveló la identidad del asesino.

**I** [aɪ] *pronoun* ▪ **yo**: she and I went dancing ella y yo fuimos a bailar

I is usually not translated:

I live in Mexico vivo en México; I went to see him fui a verlo

Use yo for emphasis or to avoid ambiguity:

I did it yo lo hice; he doesn't know it but I do él no lo sabe pero yo sí
➤ here I am! ¡aquí estoy!

**ice** [aɪs] *noun* ▪ el **hielo**: the children are skating on the ice los niños están patinando sobre el hielo; there's ice on the road hay hielo en la calle; do you want ice in your drink? ¿quieres hielo en la bebida?
➤ an ice cube un cubo de hielo
➤ ice hockey hockey sobre hielo.

**iceberg** ['aɪsbɜːg] *noun* ▪ el **iceberg** *(plural* los **icebergs**).

**ice cream** [,aɪs'kriːm] *noun* ▪ el **helado**: do you want some ice cream? ¿quieres helado?

**ice skate** [aɪsskeɪt] *noun* ▪ el **patín para el hielo** *(plural* los **patines para el hielo**).

**ice skating** [aɪs'skeɪtɪŋ] *noun* ▪ el **patinaje sobre hielo**
➤ we're going ice skating in the park vamos a patinar sobre hielo en el parque.

**idiom** ['ɪdɪəm] *noun* ■ el **modismo**

 La palabra inglesa **idiom** es un falso amigo, no significa "idioma".

**idiot** ['ɪdɪət] *noun* ■ el/la **idiota**: what an idiot! ¡qué idiota!

**if** [ɪf] *conjunction* ■ **si**: you can come if you want puedes venir si quieres; if I knew the answer I'd tell you si supiera la respuesta, te la diría; I dont' know if she's back no sé si ha vuelto

➤ if not si no: I must go, if not, I'll be late tengo que irme, si no, llegaré tarde

➤ if only ojalá: if only I could go! ¡ojalá pudiera ir!

Ojalá is followed by a verb in the subjunctive.

**ignore** [ɪg'nɔːʳ] *verb* ■ **ignorar**: he ignored my advice ignoró mi consejo; I saw her in the street but she ignored me la vi en la calle, pero me ignoró.

**ill** [ɪl] *adjective* ■ **enfermo**: he's very ill está muy enfermo.

**I'll** [aɪl] ➤ I will or I shall.

**illegal** [ɪ'liːgl] *adjective* ■ **ilegal**: it's illegal to drive through a red light es ilegal pasarse un semáforo en rojo.

**illness** ['ɪlnɪs] *noun* ■ la **enfermedad**: leukemia is a serious illness la leucemia es una enfermedad grave.

**illustration** [ˌɪlə'streɪʃn] *noun* ■ la **ilustración** (*plural* las **ilustraciones**): there are many illustrations in the book hay muchas ilustraciones en el libro.

**I'm** [aɪm] ➤ I am.

**image** ['ɪmɪdʒ] *noun* ■ la **imagen** (*plural* las **imágenes**): the company has changed its image la compañía ha cambiado de imagen.

**imaginary** [ɪ'mædʒɪnrɪ] *adjective* ■ **imaginario**: she has an imaginary playmate tiene un compañero de juegos imaginario.

**imagination** [ɪˌmædʒɪ'neɪʃn] *noun* ■ la **imaginación** (*plural* las **imaginaciones**): the boy had a great imagination el niño tenía mucha imaginación.

**imagine** [ɪ'mædʒɪn] *verb* ■ **imaginar**: imagine a princess beside a lake imagina a una princesa junto a un lago; I imagine he's happy me imagino que es feliz.

**imitation** [ˌɪmɪ'teɪʃn] *noun* ■ la **imitación** (*plural* las **imitaciones**).

**immediate** [ɪ'miːdjət] *adjective* ■ **inmediato**: I need an immediate answer necesito una respuesta inmediata.

**immediately** [ɪ'miːdjətlɪ] *adverb* ■ **inmediatamente**: tell him to see me immediately dígale que me venga a ver inmediatamente.

**immigrant** ['ɪmɪgrənt] *noun* ■ el/la **inmigrante**.

**impatient** [ɪm'peɪʃnt] *adjective* ■ **impaciente**: he's impatient to leave está impaciente por irse

➤ to get impatient impacientarse: she's beginning to get impatient está empezando a impacientarse.

**import** [ɪm'pɔːt] *verb* ■ **importar**: they import goods from China importan mercancías de China.

**importance** [ɪm'pɔːtns] *noun* ■ la **importancia**: it's a matter of great importance es un asunto de gran importancia.

**important** [ɪm'pɔːtnt] *adjective* ■ **importante**.

**impossible** [ɪm'pɒsəbl] *adjective* ■ **imposible**: this word is impossible to pronounce esta palabra es imposible de pronunciar; it's impossible to get tickets for the concert es imposible conseguir entradas para el concierto.

**impression** [ɪm'preʃn] *noun* ■ la **impresión** (*plural* las **impresiones**): she made a good impression on them les causó una buena impresión.

**improve** [ɪm'pruːv] *verb* ■ **mejorar:** she wants to improve her Spanish quiere mejorar su español; **the weather's improving** el tiempo está mejorando.

**improvement** [ɪm'pruːvmənt] *noun* ■ **la mejora:** this model is an improvement on the previous one este modelo es una mejora con respecto al anterior

➤ there's been an improvement in his work su trabajo ha mejorado.

**in** [ɪn] *(preposition & adverb)*

■ *preposition*

1. **en:** there's a desk in my room hay un escritorio en mi cuarto; **put this photo in an envelope** mete esta foto en un sobre; **Lisa lives in Ireland** Lisa vive en Irlanda; **it's written in Spanish** está escrito en español

2. **a:** they arrived in Mexico this morning llegaron a México esta mañana; **they sat in the sun** se sentaron al sol

3. **dentro de:** in two weeks dentro de dos semanas; **she'll be back in an hour** va estar de vuelta dentro de una hora

4. *In time expressions, seasons* **en:** my birthday's in May mi cumpleaños es en mayo; **he was born in 1932** nació en 1932; **I woke up in the night** me levanté en la noche; **the film starts in 10 minutes** la película empieza en 10 minutos; **in the nineties** en los noventa; **in winter** en invierno

5. *With morning, afternoon, evening* **I went for a walk in the afternoon** salí a caminar en la tarde; **I'll call you in the morning** te voy a llamar en la mañana; **it's three o'clock in the morning** son las tres de la mañana

6. *With superlatives* **de:** Everest is the tallest mountain in the world el Everest es la montaña más alta del mundo; **she's the best student in the class** es la mejor alumna de la clase

➤ we were caught in the rain nos agarró la lluvia

➤ she's dressed in black está vestida de negro

➤ he spent all day in his pajamas pasó todo el día en piyama

■ *adverb*

1. **en la casa:** we had a night in pasamos la noche en la casa

2. *informal* **de moda:** are hats in? ¿están de moda los sombreros?

➤ is Dan in? ¿está Dan?

➤ he's not in today hoy no está

➤ nobody was in no había nadie

➤ the tide's in la marea está alta

➤ in writing por escrito

**inch** [ɪntʃ] *noun* ■ **la pulgada.**

**include** [ɪn'kluːd] *verb* ■ **incluir:** I wasn't included in the team no me incluyeron en el equipo

➤ service is included el servicio está incluido.

**including** [ɪn'kluːdɪŋ] *preposition*

➤ everyone's coming, including Thomas vienen todos, incluyendo Thomas

➤ that's twenty dollars including service son veinte dólares con el servicio incluido.

**income** ['ɪnkʌm] *uncountable noun* ■ **los ingresos:** a source of income una fuente de ingresos

➤ income tax impuesto sobre la renta.

**increase** *(noun & verb)*

■ *noun*

['ɪnkriːs] el **aumento:** there's been an increase in the price ha habido un aumento del precio

■ *verb*

[ɪn'kriːs] **aumentar:** the number of users is increasing está aumentando el número de usuarios; **they've increased the price** aumentaron el precio.

**incredible** [ɪn'kredəbl] *adjective* ■ **increíble.**

**indecisive** [ˌɪndɪ'saɪsɪv] *adjective* ■ **indeciso.**

**indeed** [ɪn'diːd] *adverb*

1. **realmente:** I'm very tired indeed estoy realmente cansado

2. **efectivamente:** indeed there is a problem efectivamente, hay un problema

➤ thank you very much indeed muchísimas gracias.

**independence** [ˌɪndɪ'pendəns] *noun* ■ **la independencia**

➤ **Independence Day** el Día de la Independencia.

**independent** [ˌɪndɪ'pendənt] *adjective* ■ **independiente**.

**index** ['ɪndeks] *noun* ■ el **índice**: look it up in the index búscalo en el índice
➤ **the index finger** el dedo índice.

**indicate** ['ɪndɪkeɪt] *verb* ■ **indicar**: he indicated the quickest route nos indicó el camino más rápido.

**indigestion** [ˌɪndɪ'dʒestʃn] *uncountable noun* ■ la **indigestión**: he has indigestion tiene indigestión.

**individual** [ˌɪndɪ'vɪdʒʊəl] *(adjective & noun)*
■ *adjective*
**individual**: an individual room una habitación individual
■ *noun*
el **individuo**.

**indoor** ['ɪndɔːr] *adjective*
1. **de interior**: indoor plants plantas de interior
2. **bajo techo**: indoor sports deportes bajo techo
➤ **an indoor pool** una piscina cubierta, una alberca cubierta *Mexico*.

**indoors** [ˌɪn'dɔːz] *adverb* ■ **adentro**: they're indoors están adentro
➤ **to go indoors or to come indoors** entrar: come indoors, it's raining entra, está lloviendo.

**industrial** [ɪn'dʌstrɪəl] *adjective* ■ **industrial**: an industrial zone una zona industrial.

**industry** ['ɪndəstrɪ] *(plural industries)* *noun* ■ la **industria**: he works in the film industry trabaja en la industria cinematográfica.

**infection** [ɪn'fekʃn] *noun* ■ la **infección** *(plural las infecciones)*
➤ **a throat infection** una infección de garganta.

**infinitive** [ɪn'fɪnɪtɪv] *noun* ■ el **infinitivo**.

**inflatable** [ɪn'fleɪtəbl] *adjective* ■ **inflable**: an inflatable toy un juguete inflable.

**influence** ['ɪnflʊəns] *(noun & verb)*
■ *noun*
la **influencia**: she has a lot of influence on her brother tiene mucha influencia sobre su hermano
■ *verb*
**influir**: don't let him influence you no dejes que te influya.

**inform** [ɪn'fɔːm] *verb* ■ **informar**: I informed him I was leaving le informé que me iba.

**informal** [ɪn'fɔːml] *adjective*
1. **informal**: an informal atmosphere una ambiente informal; wear informal clothes usen ropa informal
2. **familiar**: an informal expression una expresión familiar.

**information** [ˌɪnfə'meɪʃn] *uncountable noun* ■ la **información** *(plural las informaciones)*: I'd like some information about train times quisiera información sobre horarios de trenes
➤ **the information desk** el mostrador de información
➤ **the information superhighway** la autopista de la información
➤ **information technology** la informática.

**ingredient** [ɪn'griːdjənt] *noun* ■ el **ingrediente**: mix the ingredients together in a bowl mezcle los ingredientes en un tazón.

**inhabitant** [ɪn'hæbɪtənt] *noun* ■ el/la **habitante**: our town has 100,000 inhabitants nuestra ciudad tiene 100.000 habitantes.

**inherit** [ɪn'herɪt] *verb* ■ **heredar**: he inherited some money from his great-aunt heredó dinero de su tía abuela.

**initials** [ɪ'nɪʃlz] *plural noun* ■ la **inicial**: his initials are GWS sus iniciales son GWS.

**injection** [ɪn'dʒekʃn] *noun* ■ la **inyección** (*plural* las **inyecciones**): **the doctor gave him an injection** el médico le puso una inyección.

**injure** ['ɪndʒər] *verb* ■ **lesionar**: **he has injured his leg** se lesionó la pierna.

**injured** [ɪn'dʒəd] *adjective* ■ **lesionado**.

**injury** ['ɪndʒərɪ] (*plural* **injuries**) *noun* ■ la **lesión** (*plural* las **lesiones**): **he has serious injuries** tiene lesiones graves.

**ink** [ɪŋk] *noun* ■ la **tinta**.

**innocent** ['ɪnəsənt] *adjective* ■ **inocente**: **he was found innocent** fue declarado inocente.

**inquire** [ɪn'kwaɪər] *verb* ■ **pedir información**
➤ **to inquire about something** pedir información sobre algo: **he inquired about the departure times** pidió información sobre los horarios de partida.

**inquiry** [ɪn'kwaɪərɪ] (*plural* **inquiries**) *noun* ■ la **investigación** (*plural* las **investigaciones**).

**insane** [ɪn'seɪn] *adjective* ■ **loco**: **she is insane** está loca
➤ **to go insane** volverse loco: **he has gone insane** se ha vuelto loco.

**insect** ['ɪnsekt] *noun* ■ el **insecto**.

**inside** [ɪn'saɪd] (*preposition, adverb, adjective & noun*)
■ *preposition*
**dentro**: **the keys are inside the car** las llaves están dentro del auto
■ *adverb*
**adentro**: **I've put them inside** las puse adentro
➤ **to come inside** or **to go inside** entrar: **come inside!** ¡entra!; **let's go inside** entremos
■ *adjective*
**interior**: **the inside pages of the book** las páginas interiores del libro

■ *noun*
el **interior**: **the inside of the box** el interior de la caja
➤ **inside out** al revés: **your shirt is inside out** tienes la camisa al revés.

**insist** [ɪn'sɪst] *verb* ■ **insistir**: **Ann insisted on coming** Ann insistió en venir.

**inspect** [ɪn'spekt] *verb* ■ **examinar**: **they want to inspect our passports** quieren examinar nuestros pasaportes.

**inspector** [ɪn'spektər] *noun* ■ el **inspector**, la **inspectora**: **he's a police inspector** es inspector de policía.

**inspire** [ɪn'spaɪər] *verb* ■ **inspirar**: **the music inspired me** la música me inspiró.

**install** [ɪn'stɔ:l] *verb* ■ **instalar**: **click on the icon to install the program** haga clic en el ícono para instalar el programa.

**instance** ['ɪnstəns] *noun*
➤ **for instance** por ejemplo.

**instant** ['ɪnstənt] *adjective*
1. **inmediato**: **the album was an instant success** el disco fue un éxito inmediato
2. **instantáneo**: **I don't like instant coffee** no me gusta el café instantáneo.

**instead** [ɪn'sted] *adverb* ■ **en vez**: **I don't eat meat, I'll have vegetables instead** no como carne, pero voy a comer verduras en vez
➤ **instead of** en lugar de: **instead of helping us, he got in the way** en lugar de ayudarnos, se nos puso en el camino
➤ **instead of somebody** en lugar de alguien: **Jenny's going to the meeting instead of me** Jenny va a ir a la fiesta en mi lugar.

**instructions** [ɪn'strʌkʃnz] *plural noun* ■ las **instrucciones**: **follow my instructions** sigan mis instrucciones; **read the instructions before you use the camera** lea las instrucciones antes de usar la cámara.

**instructor** [ɪn'strʌktər] *noun* ■ el **instructor**, la **instructora**: **he's a driving instructor** es instructor de manejo.

**instrument** ['ɪnstrʊmənt] *noun* ■ el **instrumento**: she plays an instrument toca un instrumento.

**insult** *(verb & noun)*
■ *verb*
[ɪn'sʌlt] **insultar**: he insulted his teacher insultó a su profesor
■ *noun*
['ɪnsʌlt] el **insulto**: the crowd was shouting insults la multitud estaba gritando insultos.

**insurance** [ɪn'ʃʊərəns] *noun* ■ el **seguro**: I took out some fire insurance saqué un seguro contra incendio
➤ an insurance policy una póliza de seguros.

**insure** [ɪn'ʃʊəʳ] *verb* ■ **asegurar**: she insured her car against theft aseguró su automóvil contra robos.

**intelligent** [ɪn'telɪdʒənt] *adjective* ■ **inteligente**.

**intend** [ɪn'tend] *verb* ■ **tener la intención de**: I intend to go to Australia tengo la intención de ir a Australia.

**intensive** [ɪn'tensɪv] *adjective* ■ **intensivo**
➤ in intensive care en cuidado intensivo.

**interest** ['ɪntrəst] *(noun & verb)*
■ *noun*
el **interés** *(plural* los **intereses***)*: what are your interests? ¿cuáles son tus intereses?; they charge 10% interest cobran un 10% de interés
➤ to take an interest in something interesarse por algo: she takes an interest in other people se interesa por las personas
➤ to lose interest in something perder interés en algo
➤ to be in one's best interest convenir: it's in your best interest to finish your degree te conviene terminar tus estudios de grado
■ *verb*
**interesar**: archeology interests me la arqueología me interesa.

**interested** ['ɪntrəstɪd] *adjective* ■ **interesado**: he seems interested parece estar interesado
➤ to be interested in tener interés por: **Toby is interested in motorbikes** Toby tiene interés por las motos
➤ I'm not interested in that eso no me interesa.

**interesting** ['ɪntrəstɪŋ] *adjective* ■ **interesante**.

**interfere** [ˌɪntə'fɪəʳ] *verb* ■ **entrometerse**: to interfere in somebody's business entrometerse en los asuntos de alguien
➤ don't interfere! ¡no te metas!

**intermediate** [ˌɪntə'mɪːdjət] *adjective* ■ **de nivel intermedio**: he's in the intermediate class está en la clase de nivel intermedio.

**internal** [ɪn't3:nl] *adjective* ■ **interno**: an internal modem un módem interno.

**international** [ˌɪntə'næʃənl] *adjective* ■ **internacional**.

**Internet, internet** ['ɪntənet] *noun* ■ el/la **Internet**: you'll find the information on the Internet encontrarás la información en Internet
➤ an Internet café un cibercafé
➤ an Internet Service Provider un proveedor de servicios de Internet.

**interpreter** [ɪn't3:prɪtəʳ] *noun* ■ el/la **intérprete**: she's an interpreter es intérprete.

**interrupt** [ˌɪntə'rʌpt] *verb* ■ **interrumpir**: she interrupted the teacher interrumpió a la profesora.

**interruption** [ˌɪntə'rʌpʃn] *noun* ■ la **interrupción** *(plural* las **interrupciones***)*.

**intersection** [ˌɪntə'sekʃn] *noun* ■ el **cruce**: turn left at the intersection dobla a la izquierda en cruce.

**interview** ['ɪntəvjuː] *(noun & verb)*
■ *noun*
la **entrevista**: he has a job interview tiene una entrevista de trabajo

■ verb
entrevistar: he interviewed the President entrevistó al presidente.

**into** ['ɪntʊ] preposition

1. en: he put the book into his bag puso el libro en su bolso; he cut the cake into three pieces cortó la torta en tres pedazos
2. a: she translated the letter into Spanish tradujo la carta al español; he got into bed se metió a la cama.

**introduce** [,ɪntrə'djuːs] verb

1. presentar: she introduced me to her mother me presentó a su madre; let me introduce you to Brian déjame presentarte a Brian
2. introducir: he introduced a new fashion introdujo una nueva moda.

**introduction** [,ɪntrə'dʌkʃn] noun
■ la introducción (plural las introducciones): the book has a good introduction el libro tiene una buena introducción.

**invade** [ɪn'veɪd] verb ■ invadir: tourists invaded the town los turistas invadieron la ciudad.

**invasion** [ɪn'veɪʒn] noun ■ la invasión (plural las invasiones).

**invent** [ɪn'vent] verb ■ inventar: who invented the telephone? ¿quién inventó el teléfono?

**invention** [ɪn'venʃn] noun ■ el invento.

**inventor** [ɪn'ventər] noun ■ el inventor, la inventora.

**investigate** [ɪn'vestɪgeɪt] verb ■ investigar: they're investigating the accident están investigando el accidente.

**investigation** [ɪn,vestɪ'geɪʃn] noun
■ la investigación (plural las investigaciones): a police investigation una investigación policial.

**invisible** [ɪn'vɪzɪbl] adjective ■ invisible.

**invitation** [,ɪnvɪ'teɪʃn] noun ■ la invitación (plural las invitaciones): an invitation to a party una invitación a una fiesta.

**invite** [ɪn'vaɪt] verb ■ invitar: I invited Tara to my party invité a Tara a mi fiesta.

**involve** [ɪn'vɒlv] verb

1. significar: it involves a lot of work significa mucho trabajo
2. involucrar: he's involved in some nasty business está involucrado en asuntos desagradables
3. envolver: I'm not involved in the project no estoy envuelto en el proyecto
4. afectar: it involves us all nos afecta a todos.

**Ireland** ['aɪələnd] noun ■ Irlanda (feminine).

**Irish** ['aɪrɪʃ] (adjective & noun)

■ adjective

> Remember not to use a capital letter for the adjective or the language in Spanish:

irlandés: Sinéad is an Irish name Sinéad es un nombre irlandés

■ noun
el irlandés: he speaks Irish habla irlandés

> In Spanish, a capital letter is not used for the inhabitants of a country or region:

➤ the Irish los irlandeses.

**iron** ['aɪən] (noun & verb)

■ noun

1. (uncountable) el hierro: it's made of iron es de hierro
2. la plancha: the iron is too hot la plancha está demasiado caliente

■ verb
planchar: he's ironing his shirt está planchando su camisa.

**ironing** ['aɪənɪŋ] noun ■ el planchado: she's doing the ironing está haciendo el planchado
➤ an ironing board una tabla de planchar, un burro de planchar Mexico.

**irregular** [ɪ'regjʊlər] adjective ■ irregular.

**irritating** ['ɪrɪteɪtɪŋ] *adjective* ■ **irritante**.

**is** [ɪz] ➤ **be**.

**island** ['aɪlənd] *noun* ■ **la isla**.

**Islamic** [ɪz'læmɪk] *adjective* ■ **islámico**.

**isle** [aɪl] *noun* ■ **la isla**.

**isn't** ['ɪznt] ➤ **is not**.

**issue** ['ɪʃuː] *noun*
1. **el número**: it's the first issue of the magazine es el primer número de la revista
2. **el asunto**: it's an important issue es un asunto importante.

**it** [ɪt] *pronoun*
1. *Subject pronoun*

In Spanish, **it** is not usually translated:

where's my book? — it's over there ¿dónde está mi libro? — está ahí; **do you like my dress?** — yes, it's lovely ¿te gusta mi vestido? — sí, es precioso
2. *Direct object pronoun*

Use **lo** when "it" stands for a masculine noun and **la** for a feminine noun:

I've got an extra ticket, do you want it? tengo una entrada de más, ¿la quieres?; **I've lost my dog, have you seen it?** perdí mi perro, ¿lo has visto?
3. *Indirect object pronoun*

Use **le** when "it" represents an indirect object:

give it a push dale un empujón
➤ it's raining está lloviendo
➤ it's hot today hoy hace calor
➤ what time is it? ¿qué hora es?
➤ it's ten o'clock son las diez
➤ it's me! ¡soy yo!

**IT** *(abbreviation of* information technology*) noun* ■ **la informática**: she works in IT trabaja en informática.

**Italian** [ɪ'tæljən] *(adjective & noun)*
■ *adjective*

Remember not to use a capital letter for the adjective or the language in Spanish:

**italiano**: I like Italian ice cream me gusta el helado italiano
■ *noun*
1. **el italiano**: she speaks Italian habla italiano

In Spanish, a capital letter is not used for the inhabitants of a country or region:

2. **el italiano, la italiana**: Italians are known for their good food los italianos son famosos por su buena comida.

**italic** [ɪ'tælɪk] *noun* ■ **la cursiva**: in italics en cursiva.

**itch** [ɪtʃ] *verb* ■ **picar**: my arm itches me pica el brazo; **I itch all over** me pica todo.

**itchy** ['ɪtʃɪ] *adjective*
➤ my nose is itchy me pica la nariz
➤ this hat is itchy este sombrero pica.

**it'd** ['ɪtəd]
➤ **it had**; ➤ **it would**.

**it'll** [ɪtl] ➤ **it will**.

**its** [ɪts] *possessive adjective* ■ **su**

In Spanish the possessive adjective agrees in number (singular or plural) with the noun that follows:

put the camera back in its case guarda la cámara en su estuche; **the woman handed me her shoes** la mujer me alcanzó sus zapatos.

**it's** [ɪts]
➤ **it is**; ➤ **it has**.

**itself** [ɪt'self] *pronoun*
1. **a sí mismo**: the cat is washing itself el gato se está lavando a sí mismo
2. **en sí**: the town itself is not very big la ciudad en sí no es muy grande
➤ **by itself** solo: the door closed by itself la puerta se cerró sola.

**I've** [aɪv] ➤ I have.

**ivory** ['aɪvərɪ] *noun* ■ el **marfil**.

**ivy** ['aɪvɪ] *noun* ■ la **hiedra**

### IVY LEAGUE

 El término **Ivy League** se utiliza en Estados Unidos para referirse al colegio universitario de Dartmouth y a las universidades de Brown, Columbia, Cornell, Harvard, Pensilvania, Princeton y Yale, que son algunos de los centros académicos más antiguos del país. El nombre de la liga alude a la hiedra, **ivy**, que suele trepar por las paredes de los añosos edificios que albergan estas universidades. Un título de la Ivy League es un aval para el éxito profesional.

**jacket** ['dʒækɪt] *noun* ■ la **chaqueta**.

**jail** [dʒeɪl] *(noun & verb)*

■ *noun*
la **cárcel**: they sent him to jail lo mandaron a la cárcel

■ *verb*
**encarcelar**: they jailed the suspect immediately encarcelaron al sospechoso inmediatamente.

**jam** [dʒæm] *noun*

1. la **mermelada**: raspberry jam mermelada de frambuesa

2. el **embotellamiento**: a traffic jam un embotellamiento

➤ to be in a jam estar en apuros.

**jammed** [dʒæmd] *adjective* ■ **atascado**: the drawer's jammed el cajón está atascado.

**janitor** ['dʒænɪtər] *noun* ■ el/la **conserje**: Mr Freeman is a janitor el señor Freeman es conserje.

**January** ['dʒænjʊərɪ] *noun*

In Spanish the months of the year do not start with a capital letter:

**enero** *(masculine)*: in January en enero; next January el enero próximo; last January el enero pasado.

**Japanese** [ˌdʒæpə'niːz] *(adjective & noun)*

■ *adjective*

Remember not to use a capital letter for the adjective or the language in Spanish:

**japonés** *(feminine* **japonesa)**: I like Japanese cooking me gusta la comida japonesa
■ *noun*
el **japonés**: they speak Japanese hablan japonés

In Spanish, a capital letter is not used for the inhabitants of a country or region:

➤ the Japanese los japoneses.

**jar** [dʒaːr] *noun* ■ el **tarro**: a jar of jam un tarro de mermelada.

**jaw** [dʒɔː] *noun* ■ la **mandíbula**: Dan has a square jaw Dan tiene la mandíbula angular.

**jazz** [dʒæz] *noun* ■ el **jazz**.

**jealous** ['dʒeləs] *adjective* ■ **celoso**.

**jeans** [dʒiːnz] *plural noun* ■ los **vaqueros**: a pair of jeans un par de vaqueros; he's wearing jeans lleva puestos unos vaqueros.

**Jell-O**® ['dʒeləʊ] *noun* ■ la **gelatina**: the children had Jell-O® for dessert los niños comieron gelatina de postre.

**jellyfish** ['dʒelɪfɪʃ] (plural jellyfish)
noun ■ la **medusa,** el **aguamala** *Mexico,* el **aguaviva** *River Plate.*

**jet** [dʒet] noun

1. **chorro:** a water jet un chorro de agua
2. **el avión** (plural los **aviones**): she took a jet to America tomó un avión a los Estados Unidos
➤ jet lag jet lag: he's suffering from jet lag está padeciendo de jet lag.

**Jew** [dʒuː] noun ■ el **judío,** la **judía.**

**jewel** ['dʒuːəl] noun ■ la **joya.**

**jeweler** ['dʒuːələʳ] noun ■ el **joyero,** la **joyera**
➤ the jeweler's la joyería.

**jewelry** ['dʒuːəlrɪ] noun ■ las **alhajas:** that actress has a lot of jewelry esa actriz tiene muchas alhajas; gold jewelry alhajas de oro.

**Jewish** ['dʒuːɪʃ] adjective

The Spanish adjective does not start with a capital letter:

**judío:** a Jewish tradition una tradición judía
➤ a Jewish man un judío.

**jigsaw, jigsaw puzzle** ['dʒɪgsɔː, 'dʒɪgsɔː'pʌzl] noun ■ el **rompecabezas** (plural los **rompecabezas**): he's doing a jigsaw puzzle está armando un rompecabezas.

**job** [dʒɒb] noun ■ el **trabajo:** he has a job in a bookstore tiene un trabajo en una librería; you've done a good job has hecho un buen trabajo.

**jobless** ['dʒɒblɪs] adjective ■ **desempleado:** he's jobless está desempleado.

**jog** [dʒɒg] (past tense & past participle jogged) verb ■ **correr:** I jog once a week corro una vez por semana.

**jogging** ['dʒɒgɪŋ] noun ■ hacer **jogging:** I go jogging every day hago jogging todos los días.

**join** [dʒɔɪn] verb

1. **unir:** you have to join the two ends together tienes que unir las dos puntas
2. **sentarse con:** can I join you? ¿puedo sentarme contigo?
3. **hacerse socio de:** Sally joined the judo club Sally se hizo socia del club de judo
➤ to join the army alistarse en el ejército

**join in** phrasal verb

1. **participar:** Charlie wanted to join in Charlie quería participar
2. **participar:** everyone joined in the conversation todos participaron en la conversación.

**joint** [dʒɔɪnt] (noun & adjective)

■ noun
la **articulación** (plural las **articulaciones**): my joints ache in the winter en invierno, me duelen las articulaciones

■ adjective
**conjunto:** they have a joint account tienen una cuenta conjunta.

**joke** [dʒəʊk] (noun & verb)

■ noun
1. el **chiste:** he told us a joke nos contó un chiste
2. la **broma:** they played a joke on Simon le hicieron una broma a Simón

■ verb
**bromear:** are you joking? ¿estás bromeando?

**journalist** ['dʒɜːnəlɪst] noun ■ el/la **periodista:** she's a journalist es periodista.

**journey** ['dʒɜːnɪ] noun

1. el **viaje:** they went on a long journey hicieron un viaje largo; it's an hour's journey on the bus es un viaje de una hora en autobús
2. el **camino:** the journey to school el camino a la escuela.

**joy** [dʒɔɪ] noun ■ la **alegría:** the children are jumping for joy los niños están saltando de alegría.

**joystick** ['dʒɔɪstɪk] noun ■ el **joystick.**

**judge** [dʒʌdʒ] (noun & verb)

■ noun
el/la **juez** (plural los/las **jueces**): he's a judge es juez

■ *verb*

**juzgar**: they will judge the defendant to-morrow van a juzgar al acusado mañana.

**judo** ['dʒuːdəʊ] *noun* ■ el **judo**: he does judo hace judo.

**juggle** ['dʒʌgl] *verb* ■ **hacer malabarismo**: do you know how to juggle? ¿sabes hacer malabarismo?

**juice** [dʒuːs] *noun* ■ el **jugo**: orange juice jugo de naranja.

**juicy** ['dʒuːsɪ] *adjective* ■ **jugoso**.

**July** [dʒuːˈlaɪ] *noun*

In Spanish the months of the year do not start with a capital letter:

**julio** *(masculine)*: in July en julio; next July el julio próximo; last July el julio pasado.

**jump** [dʒʌmp] *(noun & verb)*

■ *noun*

el **salto**: the high jump el salto alto

■ *verb*

**saltar**: she jumped out of the window saltó por la ventana

➤ you made me jump me asustaste.

**June** [dʒuːn] *noun*

In Spanish the months of the year do not start with a capital letter:

**junio**: in June en junio; next June el junio próximo; last June el junio pasado.

**jungle** ['dʒʌŋgl] *noun* ■ la **selva**.

**junior** ['dʒuːnjər] *(adjective & noun)*

■ *adjective*

1. **subalterno**: he's a junior employee es un empleado subalterno
2. **menor**: the junior tennis championship el campeonato de tenis de menores

■ *noun*

➤ a junior un estudiante de tercer año

➤ junior high school escuela secundaria.

**junk** [dʒʌŋk] *uncountable noun*

1. los **trastos**: the house is full of junk la casa está llena de trastos
2. *informal* la **basura**: it's a piece of junk! ¡es basura!

➤ junk food la comida chatarra.

**jury** ['dʒʊərɪ] *(plural juries) noun* ■ el **jurado**: Mrs Davies is on the jury la señora Davies está en el jurado.

**just** [dʒʌst] *adverb*

1. **justo**: it happened just after midnight ocurrió justo después de la medianoche; we have just enough time tenemos el tiempo justo; you're just in time! ¡estamos justo a tiempo!; that's just what I need eso es justo lo que necesito
2. **sólo**: she's just seven sólo tiene siete años; just add water sólo agregue agua
➤ I was just about to leave estaba a punto de irme
➤ it's just about ready está casi pronto
➤ just a minute! ¡espere un minuto!

**justice** ['dʒʌstɪs] *noun* ■ la **justicia**.

**kangaroo** [ˌkæŋgəˈruː] *noun* ■ el **canguro**.

**karate** [kəˈraːtɪ] *noun* ■ el **karate**: he does karate hace karate.

**keep** [kiːp] *(past tense & past participle* kept) *verb*

1. **quedarse con**: keep the change quédese con el vuelto
2. **guardar**: can you keep a secret? ¿puedes guardar un secreto?

3. **mantener:** we must keep calm debemos mantener la calma; **he kept his promise** mantuvo su promesa

4. **tener:** they keep chickens tienen pollos

➤ **to keep doing** or **to keep on doing** seguir: **I kept on working** seguí trabajando **she keeps calling me** me sigue llamando

➤ **to keep somebody from doing something** impedir que alguien haga algo: **nothing will keep me from going** nada impedirá que me vaya

➤ **to keep somebody waiting** hacer esperar a alguien: **I'm sorry to keep you waiting** lamento hacerte esperar

➤ **to keep fit** estar en forma

➤ **to keep quiet** callarse la boca: **they kept quiet** se callaron la boca

➤ **keep quiet!** ¡quédate callado!

**keep off** *phrasal verb* ■ **keep off the grass** prohibido pisar el pasto.

**keep out** *phrasal verb* ■ **keep out!** prohibido entrar.

**keep up** *phrasal verb* ■ **seguir el ritmo:** **don't go so fast, I can't keep up** no vayas tan rápido, no puedo seguirte el ritmo.

**kept** [kept] *past tense & past participle* ➤ keep.

**ketchup** ['ketʃəp] *uncountable noun* ■ el **ketchup:** **do you want some ketchup?** ¿quieres ketchup?

**key** [kiː] *noun*

1. la **llave:** **I've lost my keys** perdí mis llaves

2. la **tecla:** **the computer keys are dirty** las teclas de la computadora están sucias

➤ **a key ring** un llavero.

**keyboard** ['kiːbɔːd] *noun* ■ el **teclado:** **we need a new keyboard for the computer** necesitamos un nuevo teclado para la computadora.

**keyhole** ['kiːhəʊl] *noun* ■ la **cerradura**.

**khaki** ['kaːkɪ] *adjective* ■ el **caqui**.

**kick** [kɪk] *(noun & verb)*

■ *noun*

la **patada:** **he gave me a kick** me dio una patada

■ *verb*

1. **patear:** **he kicked me** me pateó; **she kicked the ball** pateó la pelota

2. **patalear:** **stop kicking!** ¡deja de patalear!

**kid** [kɪd] *informal (noun & verb)*

■ *noun*

1. el **niño,** el **chavo** *Mexico,* el **pibe** *Argentina:* **there are twenty kids in the class** hay veinte niños en la clase

2. el **hijo:** **they have four kids** tienen cuatro hijos

➤ **he's my kid brother** es mi hermano pequeño

■ *verb*

**bromear:** **I'm only kidding!** ¡sólo estoy bromeando!

**kidnap** ['kɪdnæp] *(past tense & past participle* kidnapped*) verb* ■ **secuestrar:** **they kidnapped the rich man for his money** secuestraron al hombre rico por su dinero.

**kidney** ['kɪdnɪ] *noun* ■ el **riñón** *(plural* los **riñones***)*.

**kill** [kɪl] *verb* ■ **matar:** **he killed a bear** mató un oso.

**kilo** ['kiːləʊ] *(abbreviation of* kilogram*) noun* ■ el **kilo**.

**kilogram** ['kɪləgræm] *noun* ■ el **kilogramo**.

**kilometer** [kɪ'lɒmɪtər] *noun* ■ el **kilómetro**.

**kind** [kaɪnd] *(adjective & noun)*

■ *adjective*

**amable:** **that's very kind of you** es muy amable de tu parte

■ *noun*

el **tipo:** **it's a kind of bird** es un tipo de pájaro; **I like all kinds of music** me gusta todo tipo de música

➤ **what kind of plant is it?** ¿qué especie de planta es?

**kindergarten** ['kɪndə,gaːtn] *noun* ■ el **kindergarten:** **she goes to kindergarten** va al kindergarten.

**kindness** ['kaɪndnɪs] *noun* ■ la **amabilidad**.

**king** [kɪŋ] *noun* ■ el **rey**: King Harold el rey Harold.

**kingdom** ['kɪŋdəm] *noun* ■ el **reino**: the United Kingdom el Reino Unido; the animal kingdom el reino animal.

**kiss** [kɪs] *(noun & verb)*

■ *noun*

el **beso**: she gave her father a kiss le dio un beso a su padre

➤ love and kisses besos y cariños

■ *verb*

1. **besar**: she kissed me on the cheek me besó en la mejilla

2. **besarse**: they kissed and said goodbye se besaron y se despidieron.

**kit** [kɪt] *noun*

➤ a first-aid kit un botiquín de primeros auxilios

➤ a tool kit una caja de herramientas.

**kitchen** ['kɪtʃɪn] *noun* ■ la **cocina**.

**kite** [kaɪt] *noun* ■ la **cometa**.

**kitten** ['kɪtn] *noun* ■ el **gatito**.

**knee** [niː] *noun* ■ la **rodilla**: he was on his knees estaba de rodillas.

**kneel** [niːl] *(past tense & past participle* knelt [nelt] *past tense & past participle* kneeled [niːld]) *verb* ■ **arrodillarse**: he knelt down se arrodilló.

**knelt** [nelt] *past tense & past participle*
➤ kneel.

**knew** [njuː] *past tense* ➤ know.

**knife** [naɪf] *(plural* knives [naɪvz]) *noun* ■ el **cuchillo**: a bread knife un cuchillo para cortar pan.

**knight** [naɪt] *noun* ■ el **caballo**: the knight is a piece used in a game of chess el caballo es una pieza del ajedrez.

**knit** [nɪt] *(past tense & past participle* knitted) *verb* ■ **tejer**: I knitted a scarf tejí una bufanda.

**knives** [naɪvz] *plural* ➤ knife.

**knob** [nɒb] *noun*

1. la **perilla**: turn the knob to the right gira la perilla hacia la derecha

2. el **pomo**: a door knob el pomo de una puerta.

**knock** [nɒk] *(noun & verb)*

■ *noun*

el **golpe**: I heard a knock at the door oí un golpe en la puerta

■ *verb*

1. **golpear**: somebody's knocking at the door alguien está golpeando en la puerta

2. **golpearse**: I knocked my head on the shelf me golpeé la cabeza con el estante

3. **clavar**: he knocked the nail into the wall clavó el clavo en la pared

**knock down** *phrasal verb*

1. **derribar**: they knocked that building down derribaron ese edificio

2. **atropellar**: he was knocked down by a car lo atropelló un coche.

**knock out** *phrasal verb*

1. **dejar sin sentido**: the thief knocked the guard out el ladrón dejó sin sentido al guardia

2. **eliminar**: México knocked Argentina out of the tournament Mexico eliminó a Argentina del torneo.

**knock over** *phrasal verb* ■ **tirar**: I knocked the glass over tiré el vaso.

**knot** [nɒt] *noun* ■ el **nudo**: he tied a knot in the string hizo un nudo en la cuerda.

**know** [nəʊ] *(past tense* knew, *past participle* known) *verb*

Use the verb **saber** for knowing facts. Use the verb **conocer** for knowing people or places:

1. **saber**: I know you're right sé que tienes razón; he's Italian — yes, I know es italiano — sí, lo sé; I don't know where he is no sé dónde está; she doesn't know any English no sabe nada de inglés

2. **conocer**: do you know Vanessa? ¿conoces a Vanessa?; I'm slowly getting to know

him lo estoy conociendo de a poco; **I don't know London very well** no conozco muy bien Londres
➤ **how should I know?** ¿cómo quieres que sepa?
➤ **to know how to do something** saber hacer algo: **do you know how to swim?** ¿sabes nadar?

**know about** *phrasal verb*

1. **saber de: do you know about the accident?** ¿sabes del accidente?
2. **saber sobre: he knows all about computers** sabe todo sobre las computadoras.

**know-how** [nəʊhaʊ] *noun* ▇ los **conocimientos y experiencia: he doesn't have the know-how** no tiene los conocimientos y experiencia.

**knowledge** ['nɒlɪdʒ] *uncountable noun*
▇ el **conocimiento: she has a good knowledge of English** tiene un buen conocimiento del inglés.

**known** [nəʊn] *past participle* ➤ know.

**lab** [læb] *(abbreviation of* laboratory*)*
*noun* ▇ *informal* el **laboratorio: a chemistry lab** un laboratorio de química.

**label** ['leɪbl] *noun* ▇ la **etiqueta**.

**labor** ['leɪbəʳ] *noun* ▇ la **mano de obra: skilled labor** mano de obra especializada
➤ **Labor Day** el Día de los Trabajadores
➤ **a labor union** un sindicato de trabajadores

**laboratory** ['læbrəˌtɔːrɪ] *(plural* laboratories) *noun* ▇ el **laboratorio**.

**lace** [leɪs] *noun*
1. el **cordón** *(plural* los **cordones**), la **agujeta** *Mexico*: **he tied his laces** se amarró los cordones
2. el **encaje: a lace tablecloth** un mantel de encaje.

**lack** [læk] *(noun & verb)*
▇ *noun*
la **falta: through lack of experience** por falta de experiencia
▇ *verb*
**carecer de: she lacks confidence** carece de confianza.

**ladder** ['lædəʳ] *noun* ▇ la **escalera**.

**lady** ['leɪdɪ] *(plural* ladies) *noun* ▇ la **señora: there's a lady waiting to see you** hay una señora esperando para verte
➤ **ladies' clothes** ropa de mujer
➤ **Ladies and Gentlemen!** ¡señoras y señores!
➤ **the ladies' room** el baño de señoras: **where is the ladies' room?** ¿dónde está el baño de señoras?

**laid** [leɪd] *past tense & past participle*
➤ lay.

**laid-back** [leɪdbæk] *adjective* ▇ *informal* **tranquilo: people are very laid-back in California** la gente de California es muy tranquila.

**lain** [leɪn] *past participle* ➤ lie.

**lake** [leɪk] *noun* ▇ el **lago**.

**lamb** [læm] *noun* ▇ el **cordero**.

**lame** [leɪm] *adjective* ▇ **cojo: his horse is lame** su caballo está cojo.

**lamp** [læmp] *noun* ▇ la **lámpara**.

**land** [lænd] *(noun & verb)*
- *noun*

  la **tierra**: this land is very fertile esta tierra es muy fértil
- ➤ a piece of land un terreno
- *verb*

  **aterrizar**: the plane lands at 6 o'clock el avión aterriza a las seis.

**landing** ['lændɪŋ] *noun*
1. el **aterrizaje**: the pilot made an emergency landing el piloto hizo un aterrizaje forzoso
2. el **rellano,** el **descanso** *Southern Cone*: the bathroom is on the landing el baño está en el rellano.

**landscape** ['lændskeɪp] *noun* ■ el **paisaje**: the fields and woods of the American landscape los prados y bosques del paisaje estadounidense.

**lane** [leɪn] *noun*
1. el **camino**: a country lane un camino campestre
2. el **carril**: this highway has four lanes esta autopista tiene cuatro carriles.

**language** ['læŋgwɪdʒ] *noun*
1. la **lengua**: can you speak a foreign language? ¿sabes alguna lengua extranjera?
2. el **lenguaje**: legal language el lenguaje legal.

**lap** [læp] *noun*
1. la **falda**: the baby is sitting on her lap el bebé está sentado en su falda
2. la **vuelta**: the runners did two laps los corredores dieron dos vueltas.

**laptop** ['læptɒp] *noun* ■ el/la **laptop**: he wants a laptop quiere un laptop.

**large** [lɑːdʒ] *adjective*
1. **grande**: Houston is a very large city Houston es una ciudad muy grande
2. **importante**: a large sum una cantidad importante.

**laser** ['leɪzər] *noun* ■ el **láser**: a laser beam un rayo láser.

**last** [lɑːst] *(adjective, adverb, noun & verb)*
- *adjective*
1. **último**: that's the last time I listen to you! ¡es la última vez que te hago caso!
2. **pasado**: it happened last week ocurrió la semana pasada; Greg arrived last Tuesday Greg llegó el martes pasado
- ➤ last name apellido: what is your last name? ¿cuál es tu apellido?
- *adverb*
1. **último**: she came last fue la última en venir
2. la **última vez**: I last saw her in Boston la última vez que la vi fue en Boston
- *noun*

  el **último**, la **última**: he's the last in the class es el último de la clase
- *verb*

  **durar**: the movie lasted two hours la película duró dos horas
- ➤ last night anoche: I saw him last night lo vi anoche
- ➤ the year before last hace dos años
- ➤ the next to last penúltimo
- ➤ at last por fin: we're home at last ¡por fin llegamos a casa!

**late** [leɪt] *adjective & adverb* ■ **tarde**: I'm sorry I'm late perdón por llegar tarde; he arrived late llegó tarde; it's too late es demasiado tarde; I went to bed late me acosté tarde; he arrived two hours late llegó dos horas tarde
- ➤ in late June a fines de junio.

**lately** ['leɪtlɪ] *adverb* ■ **últimamente**: have you seen him lately? ¿lo has visto últimamente?

**later** ['leɪtər] *(comparative of late) adverb* ■ **después**: I'll do it later lo haré después
- ➤ see you later! ¡hasta luego!

**latest** ['leɪtɪst] *(superlative of late) adjective* ■ **último**: here are the latest news esta son las últimas noticias
- ➤ at the latest a más tardar: it will be ready by tomorrow at the latest estará listo mañana, a más tardar.

**Latin** ['lætɪn] *(adjective & noun)*
- *adjective*

Remember not to use a capital letter for the adjective or the language in Spanish:

**latino**
➤ **Latin America** América Latina: **Peru is in Latin America** Perú está en América Latina
➤ **Latin American** latinoamericano
■ *noun*
el **latín: he's studying Latin** está estudiando latín.

**laugh** [lɑːf] *(noun & verb)*
■ *noun*
la **risa**
➤ **for a laugh** para divertirse: **we did it for a laugh** lo hicimos para divertirnos
➤ **to have a good laugh** divertirse mucho
■ *verb*
**reírse: the audience was laughing** el público se estaba riendo; **she burst out laughing** se echó a reír

**laugh at** *phrasal verb* ■ **reírse de: he was laughing at me** se estaba riendo de mí.

**laughter** [ˈlɑːftər] *uncountable noun* ■ la **risa: I can hear laughter** oigo risas.

**Laundromat®** [ˈlɔːndrəmæt] *noun* ■ la **lavandería**.

**laundry** [ˈlɔːndrɪ] *uncountable noun* ■ la **ropa sucia: put the laundry in the basket** coloca la ropa sucia en la canasta
➤ **to do the laundry** lavar la ropa sucia.

**lavatory** [ˈlævətrɪ] *(plural lavatories) noun* ■ el **baño: where is the lavatory?** ¿dónde está el baño?

**law** [lɔː] *noun*
1. la **ley: we must obey the law** debemos obedecer la ley; **to break the law** violar la ley
2. el **derecho: he's studying law** estudia derecho
➤ **it's against the law** va contra la ley
➤ **law and order** la ley y el orden.

**lawn** [lɔːn] *noun* ■ el **pasto: she's mowing the lawn** está cortando el pasto.

**lawnmower** [ˈlɔːnˌməʊər] *noun* ■ la **máquina de cortar pasto**.

**lawyer** [ˈlɔːjər] *noun* ■ el **abogado, la abogada: Cheryl's a lawyer** Cheryl es abogada.

**lay** [leɪ] *(verb & verb form)*
■ *verb*
*(past tense & past participle laid)* **poner: he laid his hand on my shoulder** me puso la mano sobre el hombro
➤ **to lay an egg** poner un huevo: **the hen laid an egg** la gallina puso un huevo
■ *past tense*
➤ **lie**.

**layer** [ˈleɪər] *noun* ■ la **capa: there's a thick layer of snow on the roof** hay una gruesa capa de nieve sobre el techo.

**lazy** [ˈleɪzɪ] *adjective* ■ **perezoso**.

**lead**¹ [liːd] *(verb, noun & adjective)*
■ *verb*
*(past tense & past participle led)*
1. **llevar: this path leads to the village** este sendero lleva al pueblo; **he leads a busy life** lleva una vida muy ajetreada
2. **ir ganando por: Brazil is leading 3 goals to 2** Brasil va ganando por 3 goles a 2
➤ **to lead the way** mostrar el camino
■ *noun*
➤ **to be in the lead** llevar la delantera: **Shadowfax is in the lead** Shadowfax lleva la delantera
■ *adjective*
**principal: he's the lead trumpet of the orchestra** es el trompetista principal de la orquesta.

**lead**² [led] *noun*
1. el **plomo: the pipes are made of lead** las cañerías son de plomo
2. la **mina: the lead in a pencil** la mina de un lápiz.

**leader** [ˈliːdər] *noun*
1. el/la **líder: the leader of our party** el líder de nuestro partido; **the leader of the gang** el líder de la pandilla
2. el **presidente: the leader of the country** el presidente del país.

**leaf** [liːf] *(plural leaves [liːvz]) noun* ■ la **hoja: the trees are losing their leaves** los árboles están perdiendo sus hojas.

**league** [liːg] *noun* ∎ **la liga:** our team is at the top of the league nuestro equipo encabeza la liga.

**leak** [liːk] *(noun & verb)*

∎ *noun*

**el escape:** there has been a gas leak ha habido un escape de gas

∎ *verb*

1. **gotear:** the bucket is leaking el balde está goteando

2. **dejar pasar el agua:** the boat's leaking el barco está dejando pasar el agua.

**lean** [liːn] *verb*

1. **apoyar:** I leaned the ladder against the wall apoyé la escalera contra la pared; my bike is leaning against the wall mi bicicleta está apoyada contra la pared

2. **apoyarse:** she leaned on the door se apoyó en la puerta

3. **inclinarse:** he leaned forward se inclinó hacia delante

**lean out** *phrasal verb* ∎ **asomarse:** she leaned out the window se asomó por la ventana.

**lean over** *phrasal verb* ∎ **inclinarse:** he leaned over to speak to me se inclinó para hablarme.

**leap** [liːp] *(past tense & past participle* leapt o leaped*) verb* ∎ **saltar, brincar** *Mexico*: the cat leaped on the mouse el gato saltó sobre el ratón; she leapt out of bed saltó de la cama

➤ to leap to one's feet ponerse de pie de un salto.

**leapt** [lept] *past tense & past participle* ➤ leap.

**leap year** [liːpjɪəʳ] *noun* ∎ **el año bisiesto:** there's a leap year every four years hay un año bisiesto cada cuatro años.

**learn** [lɜːn] *verb* ∎ **aprender:** we're learning English estamos aprendiendo inglés; she's learning to swim or she's learning how to swim está aprendiendo a nadar.

**learner** [ˈlɜːnəʳ] *noun* ∎ **el/la estudiante**.

**least** [liːst] *(superlative of* little*) (adjective, adverb & pronoun)*

∎ *adjective*

➤ the least: he has the least money es el que menos dinero tiene

I don't have the least idea no tengo la menor idea

∎ *adverb*

➤ the least *With verbs* el que menos: I like those ones the least esos son los que menos me gustan

➤ the least *With adjectives and nouns* menos: the least expensive restaurant el restaurante menos caro: the least funny joke la broma menos graciosa

∎ *pronoun*

➤ the least menos: Sarah ate the least Sarah es la que menos comió

➤ at least al menos: it'll cost at least $100 costará al menos 100 dólares

➤ at least por lo menos: she's never met him, at least that's what she says no lo conoce, por lo menos eso es lo que dice

➤ it's the least I can do es lo menos que puedo hacer.

**leather** [ˈleðəʳ] *noun* ∎ **el cuero**.

**leave** [liːv] *(noun & verb)*

∎ *noun*

**la licencia:** the secretary has two days' leave la secretaria tiene dos días de licencia

∎ *verb*

*(past tense & past participle* left*)*

1. **irse:** I'm leaving tomorrow me voy mañana; she has already left ya se fue

2. **dejar:** she left the country this morning dejó el país esta mañana; I left the door open dejé la puerta abierta; leave me alone! ¡déjame en paz!; leave the book at home deja el libro en casa

**leave out** *phrasal verb* ∎ **omitir:** you've left a word out omitiste una palabra.

**leaves** *plural* ➤ leaf.

**lecture** [ˈlektʃəʳ] *noun*

1. **la charla:** he gave a lecture on rock-climbing dio una charla sobre la escalada en roca

**2.** la **clase:** he missed his history lecture se perdió la clase de historia

⚠️ **Lecture** es un falso amigo, no significa "lectura".

**led** [led] *past tense & past participle*
➤ **lead**.

**left** [left] *(adjective, adverb, noun & verb form)*
■ *adjective*
**izquierdo:** he took it with his left hand lo tomó con su mano izquierda
■ *adverb*
**izquierdo:** turn left at the end of the road dobla a la izquierda al final de la calle
■ *noun*
la **izquierda:** look to the left mira hacia la izquierda; you drive on the left in Britain en Gran Bretaña, se maneja por la izquierda
■ *past tense & past participle*
➤ **leave**
➤ to be left quedar: do you have any money left? ¿te queda algo de dinero?
there's none left no queda nada.

**left-hand** ['lefthænd] *adjective* ■ **de la izquierda:** the left-hand drawer el cajón de la izquierda
➤ on the left-hand side del lado izquierdo.

**left-handed** [ˌleft'hændɪd] *adjective*
■ **zurdo:** he's left-handed es zurdo.

**leftovers** ['leftəʊvəʳz] *plural noun* ■ las **sobras:** I threw away the leftovers tiré las sobras.

**leg** [leg] *noun* ■ la **pierna:** Colin has broken his leg Colin se quebró una pierna
➤ to pull somebody's leg tomarle el pelo a alguien: he's pulling your leg te está tomando el pelo
➤ a leg of lamb una pierna de cordero
➤ a chicken leg un muslo de pollo.

**legal** ['liːgl] *adjective* ■ **legal**.

**legend** ['ledʒənd] *noun* ■ la **leyenda:** he became a legend se convirtió en una leyenda.

**leisure** ['liːʒər] *uncountable noun* ■ el **ocio**

➤ leisure time tiempo libre: what do you do in your leisure time? ¿qué haces en tu tiempo libre?

**lemon** ['lemən] *noun* ■ el **limón** *(plural* los **limones):** a slice of lemon una rodaja de limón
➤ lemon juice jugo de limón.

**lemonade** [ˌleməˈneɪd] *noun* ■ la **limonada**.

**lend** [lend] *(past tense & past participle* lent) *verb* ■ **prestar**
➤ to lend something to somebody prestarle algo a alguien: can you lend me your pencil? ¿puedes prestarme el lápiz?

**length** [leŋθ] *noun*
**1.** el **largo:** what length is it? ¿cuánto tiene de largo?; it's five inches in length tiene cinco pulgadas de largo
**2.** la **duración:** the length of a prison sentence la duración de la pena de prisión.

**lens** [lenz] *noun*
**1.** el **lente:** the lens of a camera el lente de la cámara
**2.** el **cristal:** my glasses have thick lenses mis lentes tienen cristales gruesos
**3.** el/la **lente de contacto:** she wears contact lenses usa lentes de contacto.

**lent** [lent] *past tense & past participle*
➤ **lend**.

**Lent** [lent] *noun* ■ la **Cuaresma**.

**leopard** ['lepəd] *noun* ■ el **leopardo**.

**less** [les] *(comparative of* little) *adjective, adverb & pronoun* ■ **menos:** I have less money than you tengo menos dinero que tú; you should eat less deberías comer menos; it's less serious than I thought es menos grave de lo que pensaba; the more I see him, the less I like him cuanto más lo veo, menos me gusta; he'll be here in less than two hours estará aquí en menos de dos horas; he has less than me tiene menos que yo.

**lesson** ['lesn] *noun*
**1.** la **lección** *(plural* las **lecciones):** we will study that lesson in the book tomorrow estudiaremos esa lección del libro mañana

**2.** la **clase: she's taking English lessons** está tomando clases de inglés

➤ **that'll teach him a lesson!** ¡eso le servirá de lección!

**let** [let] *(past tense & past participle* let*) verb*

**1.** *In suggestions* **let's go!** ¡vamos!; **let's go to the movies tonight** ¿vamos al cine esta noche?

**2.** **dejar: to let somebody do something** dejar a alguien hacer algo; **my parents won't let me go out** mis padres no me van a dejar salir; **let me explain** déjame que te explique

➤ **to let go of somebody or something** soltar a alguien o algo: **let me go!** ¡suéltame!

➤ **to let somebody know something** avisarle a alguien: **I'll let you know what time I arrive** te avisaré a qué hora llego

➤ **let us know** avísanos

**let down** *phrasal verb* ■ **fallar: she let me down at the last minute** me falló en el último momento.

**let in** *phrasal verb* ■ **dejar entrar: he went to the door and let them in** fue hasta la puerta y los dejó entrar; **they wouldn't let us in the club** no nos van a dejar entrar al club.

**let off** *phrasal verb* ■ **perdonar: I'll let you off this time, but don't do it again** te perdono esta vez, pero no lo vuelvas a hacer.

**let's** [lets] ➤ let us.

**letter** ['letər] *noun*

**1.** la **carta: I sent him a letter** le mandé una carta

**2.** la **letra: the letters of the alphabet** las letras del abecedario.

**lettuce** ['letɪs] *noun* ■ la **lechuga: she bought a head of lettuce** compró una lechuga.

**level** ['levl] *(noun & adjective)*

■ *noun*
el **nivel: they're on the same level** están al mismo nivel

■ *adjective*

**1.** **plano: the ground is level** el terreno es plano

**2.** **derecho: the pictures aren't level** los cuadros no están derechos.

**lever** ['levər] *noun* ■ la **palanca**.

**liar** ['laɪər] *noun* ■ el **mentiroso,** la **mentirosa: he's a liar** es un mentiroso.

**liberal** ['lɪbərəl] *adjective* ■ **liberal**.

**liberty** ['lɪbətɪ] *noun* ■ la **libertad**.

**librarian** [laɪ'breərɪən] *noun* ■ el **bibliotecario,** la **bibliotecaria**.

**library** ['laɪbrərɪ] *(plural* libraries*) noun* ■ la **biblioteca**

➤ **a library book** un libro de la biblioteca

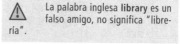 La palabra inglesa **library** es un falso amigo, no significa "librería".

**license** ['laɪsəns] *noun* ■ la **licencia**

➤ **a license plate** una placa de la matrícula, una patente *Southern Cone*.

**lick** [lɪk] *verb* ■ **lamer**

➤ **the cat's licking its paws** el gato se está lamiendo las patas.

**lid** [lɪd] *noun* ■ la **tapa: put the lid back on the saucepan** ponerle la tapa a la olla.

**lie** [laɪ] *(noun & verb)*

■ *noun*
la **mentira: it's all lies!** ¡son todas mentiras!

➤ **to tell lies** decir mentiras: **he's telling lies** está diciendo mentiras

■ *verb*

**1.** *(past tense & past participle* lied, *present participle* lying*)* **mentir: you're lying** estás mintiendo; **she lied to me** me mintió

**2.** *(past tense* lay, *past participle* lain, *present participle* lying)* **acostarse: he lay on the grass** se acostó en el pasto

**lie down** *phrasal verb* ■ **acostarse: I want to lie down on the bed** quiero acostarme en la cama; **go and lie down** anda y acuéstate

➤ **to be lying down** or **to be lying** estar acostado: **Marcus was lying down** Marcus estaba acostado
**she's lying on the sofa** está acostada en el sofá.

**life** [laɪf] *(plural* lives [laɪvz]*) noun* ■ la vida: you saved my life! ¡me salvaste la vida!; that's life! ¡así es la vida!
➤ a life preserver un salvavidas.

**lifeboat** ['laɪfbəʊt] *noun* ■ el bote salvavidas.

**lifeguard** ['laɪfgɑːd] *noun* ■ el/la salvavidas *(plural* los/las **salvavidas**).

**lift** [lɪft] *(noun & verb)*

■ *noun*
➤ to give somebody a lift llevar a alguien, darle un aventón a alguien *Mexico:* she gave me a lift to school me llevó a la escuela
can I give you a lift? ¿quieres que te lleve a algún lado?

■ *verb*
levantar: this suitcase is too heavy, I can't lift it la valija es muy pesada, no la puedo levantar.

**light** [laɪt] *(adjective, noun & verb)*

■ *adjective*
1. ligero, liviano: it's as light as a feather es tan ligero como una pluma; we had a light meal comimos una comida ligera
2. claro: he's wearing a light green shirt tiene puesta una camisa verde claro

■ *noun*
1. la luz *(plural* las **luces**): there's not enough light to read by no hay suficiente luz para leer; can you switch the light on? ¿puedes prender la luz?; the driver put his lights on el chofer encendió las luces
2. el fuego: have you got a light? ¿tienes fuego?
➤ a traffic light un semáforo: the traffic light is red el semáforo está en rojo
➤ a light bulb una bombilla, una ampolleta *Chile*, un foco *Mexico*, una bombita *River Plate*

■ *verb*
*(past tense & past participle* lit) prender: she lit the candle prendió la vela.

**lighter** ['laɪtər] *noun* ■ el encendedor: a cigarette lighter un encendedor.

**lighthouse** ['laɪthaʊs] *noun* ■ el faro.

**lightning** ['laɪtnɪŋ] *uncountable noun*
■ los relámpagos: there was thunder and lightning había truenos y relámpagos
➤ a flash of lightning un relámpago: I saw a flash of lightning vi un relámpago
➤ as quick as lightning como un rayo
➤ the barn was struck by lightning cayó un rayo en el granero.

**like** [laɪk] *(preposition & verb)*

■ *preposition*
como: their house is like ours su casa es como la nuestra
➤ what's he like? ¿cómo es él?
➤ what's the weather like? ¿cómo está el tiempo?
➤ to look like somebody parecerse a alguien: she looks like her sister se parece a su hermana
➤ do it like this hazlo como este

■ *verb*

> In Spanish, the verb **gustar** is used for expressing likes and dislikes. When you use this verb, don't forget that the object liked or disliked becomes the subject of the sentence, since **gustar** literally means "to be pleasing to":

I like music me gusta la música; she doesn't like sardines no le gustan las sardinas; do you like dancing? ¿te gusta bailar?

> To ask someone if he or she would like to do something, or if he or she would like something, you often use the verb **gustar** in the conditional. You can also use the verb **querer** in the indicative or in the past subjunctive. This also applies to you stating your own desires:

➤ if you like si quieres
➤ I would like *or* I'd like quisiera
➤ I'd like a cup of tea quisiera una taza de té
➤ would you like some more cake? ¿te gustaría un poco más de pastel?
➤ I'd like to me gustaría: I'd like to go to Egypt me gustaría ir a Egipto.

**likely** ['laɪklɪ] *adjective* ■ probable: that's not very likely eso no es muy probable
➤ it's likely to rain probablemente llueva.

**lilac** ['laɪlək] *noun* ■ el lila.

**lime** [laɪm] *noun* ■ la lima: lime juice jugo de lima.

**limit** ['lɪmɪt] *(noun & verb)*

■ *noun*
el **límite**: he knows his limits conoce sus límites
■ *verb*
**limitar**: we have to try and limit our expenses tenemos que tratar de limitar nuestros gastos.

**limp** [lɪmp] *(verb & noun)*

■ *verb*
**cojear**: she's limping está cojeando
■ *noun*
➤ to have a limp **cojear**.

**line** [laɪn] *(noun & verb)*

■ *noun*
1. la **línea**: draw a straight line traza una línea recta; **all the lines to New York are busy** todas las líneas a Nueva York están ocupadas
2. la **fila**: there was a long line of cars había una larga fila de coches
➤ to stand in line **hacer cola**
➤ to drop somebody a line **escribirle unas líneas a alguien**
➤ I dropped her a line **le escribí unas líneas**
■ *verb*
1. **bordear**: trees lined the avenue los árboles bordeaban la avenida
2. **forrar**: a coat lined with silk un abrigo forrado de seda

**line up** *phrasal verb* ■ **formar fila**: the children are lining up los niños están formando fila.

**link** [lɪŋk] *(noun & verb)*

■ *noun*
la **conexión** *(plural* las **conexiones)**: there's a link between the two events hay una conexión entre los dos hechos
■ *verb*
1. **conectar**: the two towns are linked by rail los dos pueblos están conectados por ferrocarril
2. **relacionar**: the two events are linked los dos acontecimientos están relacionados.

**lion** ['laɪən] *noun* ■ el **león** *(plural* los **leones)**: the lion roared el león rugió.

**lioness** ['laɪənes] *noun* ■ la **leona**.

**lip** [lɪp] *noun* ■ el **labio**: I bit my lip me mordí el labio.

**lipstick** ['lɪpstɪk] *noun* ■ el **lápiz de labios**.

**liquid** ['lɪkwɪd] *noun* ■ el **líquido**.

**liquor** ['lɪkər] *noun* ■ el **alcohol**
➤ a liquor store una tienda de vinos y licores, una vinatería *Mexico*, una botillería *Chile*.

**list** [lɪst] *(noun & verb)*

■ *noun*
la **lista**: her name is on the list su nombre está en la lista; **make a list** hacer una lista
■ *verb*
**hacer la lista**: I've listed the presents to buy hice la lista de los regalos que comprar.

**listen** ['lɪsn] *verb* ■ **escuchar**: she's listening to the music está escuchando música.

**lit** [lɪt] *past tense & past participle* ➤ **light**.

**liter** ['liːtər] *noun* ■ el **litro**.

**literature** ['lɪtrətʃər] *noun* ■ la **literatura**.

**little** ['lɪtl] *(adjective & adverb)*

■ *adjective*
1. **pequeño**: a little boy un niño pequeño
2. **poco**: there's very little hope hay muy poca esperanza
➤ her little sister su hermanita
■ *adverb*
**poco**: he eats very little come muy poco
➤ a little un poco de: I'm a little hungry tengo un poco de hambre
➤ a little bit un poquito
➤ little by little poco a poco.

**live** *(verb & adjective)*

■ *verb*
[lɪv] **vivir**: he lives with his father vive con su padre; **Martha lives in Chicago** Marta vive en Chicago
■ *adjective*
[laɪv]
1. **en vivo**: the broadcast is live el programa es en vivo

**2. vivo:** experiments on live animals experimentos con animales vivos.

**lively** ['laɪvlɪ] *adjective*
1. **lleno de vida:** she's very lively está llena de vida
2. **animado:** a lively place un lugar animado.

**liver** ['lɪvəʳ] *noun* ■ el **hígado**.

**lives** *plural* ➤ life.

**living** ['lɪvɪŋ] *noun*
➤ to earn a living ganarse la vida
➤ what do you do for a living? ¿en qué trabajas?

**living room** ['lɪvɪŋruːm] *noun* ■ la **sala**.

**lizard** ['lɪzəd] *noun* ■ el **lagarto**.

**llama** ['lɑːmə] *noun* ■ la **llama**.

**load** [ləʊd] *(noun & verb)*
■ *noun*
la **carga:** a heavy load una carga pesada
➤ **loads of** *informal* un montón de: he's got loads of money tiene un montón de dinero
■ *verb*
**cargar:** they loaded the luggage into the car cargaron el equipaje en el auto; he loaded the gun cargó el arma
➤ to load a camera ponerle rollo a la cámara.

**loaf** [ləʊf] *(plural* loaves [ləʊvz]*) noun*
■ el **pan**, el **pan de caja** Mexico: a loaf of bread un pan.

**loan** [ləʊn] *(noun & verb)*
■ *noun*
el **préstamo:** the bank gave him a loan el banco le dio un préstamo
■ *verb*
**prestar:** he loaned me his camera me prestó su cámara.

**loaves** *plural* ➤ loaf.

**lobby** ['lɒbɪ] *(plural* lobbies*) noun* ■ el **vestíbulo:** he's waiting for me in the lobby of the hotel me está esperando en el vestíbulo del hotel.

**lobster** ['lɒbstəʳ] *noun* ■ la **langosta**.

**local** ['ləʊkl] *adjective*
1. **local:** a local newspaper un diario local

**2. de la zona:** the local inhabitants los habitantes de la zona.

**locally** ['ləʊkəlɪ] *adverb* ■ **en la zona:** she lives locally vive en la zona.

**location** [ləʊ'keɪʃn] *noun* ■ la **ubicación** *(plural* las **ubicaciones**): the house is in a beautiful location la casa tiene una ubicación preciosa.

**lock** [lɒk] *(noun & verb)*
■ *noun*
la **cerradura:** she put the key in the lock metió la llave en la cerradura
■ *verb*
**cerrar con llave:** she locked the door cerró la puerta con llave

**lock in** *phrasal verb* ■ **encerrar:** they locked her in her room la encerraron en su cuarto.

**lock out** *phrasal verb* ■ **quedarse afuera sin llave:** I've locked myself out me quedé afuera sin llave.

**locker** ['lɒkəʳ] *noun* ■ el **locker** *(plural* los **lockers**), el **casillero** Chile, Mexico: he keeps his books in his locker guarda sus libros en el armario
➤ the locker room el vestuario, el vestidor Chile, Mexico.

**log** [lɒg] *(noun & phrasal verb) noun* ■ el **tronco:** put a log on the fire poner un tronco en el fuego
➤ a log cabin una cabaña de madera

**log in, log on** *phrasal verb* ■ **entrar en el sistema**.

**log off, log out** *phrasal verb* ■ **salir del sistema**.

**logical** ['lɒdʒɪkl] *adjective* ■ **lógico**.

**lollipop** ['lɒlɪpɒp] *noun* ■ el **pirulí**, la **paleta** Mexico.

**lonely** ['ləʊnlɪ] *adjective*
1. **solo:** she feels lonely or she's lonely se siente sola
2. **solitario:** a lonely beach una playa solitaria.

**long** [lɒŋ] *(adjective & adverb)*

■ *adjective*

**largo:** her skirt is too long su falda es demasiado larga

➤ the fence is ten meters long la valla tiene diez metros de largo

➤ the concert is three hours long el concierto dura tres horas

➤ a long time mucho tiempo

➤ I've been waiting a long time hace mucho tiempo que espero

➤ it takes a long time lleva mucho tiempo

➤ it's a long way queda lejos

■ *adverb*

**tiempo:** I didn't wait long no esperé mucho tiempo

➤ I won't be long no voy a demorar

➤ how long will it take? ¿cuánto tiempo te llevará?: how long will you be? ¿cuánto tiempo estarás?

how long have you been here? ¿hace cuánto que estás aquí?

> When "as long as" means "provided that" the verb that follows must be in the subjunctive:

➤ as long as el tiempo que sea, mientras

➤ I'll wait as long as you like esperaré todo el tiempo que quieras

➤ as long as you are here, you're safe mientras estés aquí, estás a salvo

➤ so long! adiós.

**look** [lʊk] *(noun & verb)*

■ *noun*

la **mirada:** he gave me a funny look me miró de un modo gracioso

➤ to have a look at something echar un vistazo a algo: can I have a look? ¿puedo echar un vistazo?

■ *verb*

1. **mirar:** don't look! ¡no mires!

2. **parecer:** you look tired te pareces cansado

➤ it looks as if it's going to snow parece que va a nevar

➤ to look like somebody parecerse a alguien: Felicia looks like her mother Felicia se parece a su madre

**look after** *phrasal verb* ■ **cuidar:** he's looking after his little brother está cuidando a su hermano menor.

**look around** *phrasal verb*

1. **mirar alrededor:** he looked around when I called him miró alrededor cuando lo llamé

2. **mirar:** I'm just looking around sólo estoy mirando

3. **recorrer:** let's look around the museum vamos a recorrer el museo.

**look at** *phrasal verb* ■ **mirar:** he looked at her él la miró.

**look for** *phrasal verb* ■ **buscar:** I'm looking for my keys estoy buscando mis llaves.

**look forward to** *phrasal verb*

1. **desear:** I'm really looking forward to Christmas estoy deseando que llegue Navidad

2. **esperar:** I look forward to hearing from you espero tener noticias tuyas.

**look out** *phrasal verb* ■ **tener cuidado:** look out! ¡cuidado!

**look up** *phrasal verb*

1. **ir a ver:** I looked up when he came in lo fui a ver cuando vino

2. **buscar:** look the word up in a dictionary busca la palabra en el diccionario.

**loose** [luːs] *adjective* ■ **flojo:** loose clothes ropa floja

➤ to come loose aflojarse: the knot has come loose el nudo se aflojó.

**lord** [lɔːd] *noun* ■ **el señor:** he lives like a lord vive como un rey.

**lose** [luːz] *(past tense & past participle* lost*) verb* ■ **perder:** I've lost my ticket perdí mi entrada; the team lost by three goals to one el equipo perdió por tres goles a uno

➤ to lose one's way perderse: he lost his way se perdió.

**loser** [ˈluːzər] *noun*

1. **perdedor:** he's a bad loser es un mal perdedor

2. *informal* **fracasado:** he's a real loser es un verdadero fracasado.

**loss** [lɒs] *noun* ■ **la pérdida.**

**lost** [lɒst] *(adjective & verb form)*

■ *adjective*
**perdido**
➤ **to get lost** perderse: **I got lost in the woods** me perdí en el bosque
➤ **the lost-and-found** los objetos perdidos
■ *past tense & past participle*
➤ lose.

**lot** [lɒt] *noun*

➤ **a lot** mucho: **he eats a lot** come mucho
➤ **thanks a lot!** ¡muchas gracias!
➤ **he has a lot of friends** tiene muchos amigos
➤ **lots** *informal* un montón de: **she has lots of money** tiene un montón de dinero.

**lotion** ['ləʊʃn] *noun* ■ la **loción** *(plural* las **lociones)**
➤ **suntan lotion** el bronceador.

**lottery** ['lɒtərɪ] *noun* ■ la **lotería**.

**loud** [laʊd] *adjective & adverb* ■ **fuerte:** **the music's too loud** la música está muy fuerte; **can you speak a bit louder?** ¿puedes hablar un poco más fuerte?
➤ **out loud** en voz alta: **he spoke out loud** habló en voz alta
**to read out loud** leer en voz alta.

**lousy** ['laʊzɪ] *adjective informal*

1. **pésimo, asqueroso:** **this book's lousy** el libro es pésimo; **the food's lousy** la comida es asquerosa
2. **horrible:** **the weather's lousy** el tiempo está horrible.

**love** [lʌv] *(noun & verb)*

■ *noun*
el **amor**
➤ **a love song** una canción de amor
➤ **to be in love** estar enamorado: **he's in love with her** él está enamorado de ella
➤ **to fall in love** enamorarse: **she fell in love with him** se enamoró de él
➤ **give her my love** darle mi amor
■ *verb*
1. **amar:** **I love you** te amo
2. **encantar:** **I'd love to come to your party** me encantaría ir a tu fiesta; **he loves chocolate** le encanta el chocolate; **I love dancing** me encanta bailar.

**lovely** ['lʌvlɪ] *adjective*

1. **precioso:** **that's a lovely dress** es un vestido precioso; **you look lovely, Claire!** Claire, ¡te ves preciosa!
2. **encantador:** **he's a lovely man** es un hombre encantador
3. **delicioso:** **this tastes lovely** esto está delicioso
➤ **we had a lovely time** lo pasamos muy bien
➤ **what lovely weather!** ¡qué buen tiempo que hace!

**low** [ləʊ] *(adjective & adverb)*

■ *adjective*
**bajo:** **the ceiling is very low** el techo es muy bajo
■ *adverb*
**bajo:** **the plane is flying low** el avión está volando bajo.

**low-fat** [ləʊfæt] *adjective* ■ **de bajo contenido graso:** **low-fat yogurt** yoghurt de bajo contenido graso.

**luck** [lʌk] *uncountable noun* ■ la **suerte:** **you're in luck** estás de suerte
➤ **good luck!** ¡buena suerte!
➤ **bad luck!** ¡mala suerte!

**lucky** ['lʌkɪ] *adjective*

➤ **to be lucky** tener suerte: **she's very lucky** tiene mucha suerte
➤ **to be lucky** dar suerte: **horseshoes are lucky** las herraduras dan suerte
➤ **a lucky charm** un amuleto.

**lump** [lʌmp] *noun*

1. el **terrón** *(plural* los **terrones):** **a lump of sugar** un terrón de azúcar
2. el **chichón** *(plural* los **chichones):** **she has a lump on her forehead** tiene un chichón en la frente.

**lunch** [lʌntʃ] *noun* ■ el **almuerzo,** la **comida** *Mexico:* **what did you have for lunch?** ¿qué almorzaste?
➤ **to have lunch** almorzar, comer *Mexico*
➤ **we have lunch at one o'clock** almorzamos a la una
➤ **the lunch hour** la hora del almuerzo, la hora de la comida *Mexico*.

**lunchtime** ['lʌntʃtaɪm] *noun* ▪ la **hora del almuerzo, la hora de la comida** *Mexico*: it's nearly lunchtime es casi la hora del almuerzo.

**lung** [lʌŋ] *noun* ▪ el **pulmón** (*plural* los **pulmones**).

**luxury** ['lʌkʃərɪ] *noun* ▪ el **lujo**: she lives in luxury vive con lujo
➤ a luxury hotel un hotel lujoso.

**lying** ['laɪɪŋ] ➤ lie.

**lyrics** ['lɪrɪks] *plural noun* ▪ la **letra**.

**machine** [mə'ʃiːn] *noun* ▪ la **máquina**: a sewing machine una máquina de coser
➤ a machine gun una ametralladora.

**mad** [mæd] *adjective*
1. **loco**: he's mad está loco; you must be going mad debes estar volviéndote loco
2. **enojado**: I'm mad at him estoy enojado con él.

**madam** ['mædəm] *noun* ▪ la **señora**: can I help you, madam? ¿qué desea, señora?

**made** [meɪd] *past tense & past participle*
➤ make.

**magazine** [ˌmægə'ziːn] *noun* ▪ la **revista**: a fashion magazine una revista de modas.

**magic** ['mædʒɪk] (*noun & adjective*)
▪ *noun*
la **magia**: he likes to do magic le gusta hacer magia
▪ *adjective*
**mágico**: a magic wand una varita mágica
➤ a magic trick un truco de magia.

**magician** [mə'dʒɪʃn] *noun* ▪ el **mago**, la **maga**.

**magnet** ['mægnɪt] *noun* ▪ el **imán** (*plural* los **imanes**).

**magnetic** [mæg'netɪk] *adjective*
▪ **magnético**.

**magnificent** [mæg'nɪfɪsənt] *adjective*
▪ **magnífico**.

**magnifying glass** ['mægnɪfaɪɪŋglɑːs] *noun* ▪ la **lupa**.

**maid** [meɪd] *noun* ▪ la **sirvienta,** la **mucama** *Colombia, Peru, River Plate*, la **empleada** *Southern Cone*.

**maiden name** ['meɪdn neɪm] *noun* ▪ el **apellido de soltera**.

**mail** [meɪl] (*noun & verb*)
▪ *noun*
1. la **correspondencia**: has the mail arrived? ¿ha llegado la correspondencia?; you have mail tienes correspondencia
2. el **correo**: I'll send it by mail te lo mandaré por correo
▪ *verb*
**mandar por correo**: to mail a letter to somebody mandarle una carta a alguien por correo.

**mailbox** ['meɪlbɒks] *noun* ▪ el **buzón** (*plural* los **buzones**).

**mailman** ['meɪlmən] (*plural* mailmen ['meɪlmən]) *noun* ▪ el **cartero**.

**main** [meɪn] *adjective* ▪ **principal**
➤ the main course el plato principal
➤ a main road una carretera principal.

**mainly** ['meɪnlɪ] *adverb* ▪ **principalmente**.

**major** ['meɪdʒəʳ] *(adjective & noun)*

■ *adjective*

**muy importante:** it's a major event es un acontecimiento muy importante
➤ a major road una carretera principal
➤ it's of major importance esto es de enorme importancia

■ *noun*

la **asignatura principal:** my major is physics mi asignatura principal es física.

**majority** [məˈdʒɒrətɪ] *(plural majorities) noun* ■ la **mayoría:** he won by a big majority ganó por una amplia mayoría
➤ the majority of people la mayoría de las personas.

**make** [meɪk] *(verb & noun)*

■ *verb*

*(past tense & past participle **made**)*

1. **hacer:** I made this vase myself yo mismo hice este jarrón; have you made the bed? ¿hiciste la cama?
2. **fabricar:** these cars are made in Germany fabrican estos coches en Alemania
3. **preparar:** to make a meal preparar una comida
4. **ganar:** he makes a lot of money gana mucho dinero
➤ to be made of ser de: this ring is made of gold este anillo es de oro
  what is it made of? ¿de qué está hecho esto?
➤ to make somebody do something hacer a alguien hacer algo: she made me laugh me hizo reír
  he made her open the safe la hizo abrir la caja fuerte
➤ the film made me sad la película me puso triste
➤ to make do arreglárselas: we'll have to make do vamos a tener que arreglárnoslas; to make do with something conformarse con algo; they made do with the leftovers se conformaron con las sobras
➤ make yourself at home siéntete como en tu casa
➤ 3 and 4 make 7 3 y 4 son 7

■ *noun*

**marca:** what make of car is that? ¿qué marca de coche es esa?

**make out** *phrasal verb*

1. **descifrar:** I can't make out what the inscription says no puedo descifrar lo que dice la inscripción
2. **entender:** I can't make out what they are saying no puedo entender lo que dicen
3. **pretender:** she's not as rich as she makes out no es tan rica como pretende.

**make up** *phrasal verb*

1. **inventar:** he made up an excuse inventó una excusa
2. **reconciliarse:** they had an argument, but they've made up now discutieron, pero ahora se reconciliaron
➤ to make up one's mind decidirse.

**make up for** *phrasal verb*

1. **compensar:** to make up for a loss compensar una pérdida
2. **recuperar:** we must make up for lost time debemos recuperar el tiempo perdido.

**make-up** [meɪkʌp] *uncountable noun*
■ el **maquillaje**
➤ a make-up bag una bolsa del maquillaje
➤ to wear make-up maquillarse: Susan doesn't wear make-up Susan no se maquilla.

**male** [meɪl] *(noun & adjective)*

■ *noun*

el **varón** *(plural* los **varones**)

■ *adjective*

1. **macho:** a male hamster un hámster macho
2. **masculino:** I heard a male voice escuché una voz masculina
➤ a male nurse un enfermero
➤ a male student un estudiante varón.

**mall** [mɔ:l] *noun* ■ el **centro comercial,** el **shopping** *(plural* los **shoppings**) *River Plate,* el **mall** *(plural* los **malls**) *Chile:* a shopping mall un centro comercial.

**mammal** ['mæml] *noun* ■ el **mamífero**.

**man** [mæn] *(plural* men [men]) *noun* ■ el **hombre:** men's clothes ropa de hombre
➤ he's an old man es un viejo
➤ a young man un joven

➤ **the men's room** el baño de hombres: **where is the men's room?** ¿dónde está el baño de hombres?

**manage** ['mænɪdʒ] *verb*

1. **poder: I can manage by myself** puedo solo

2. **dirigir: he manages a big company** dirige una gran empresa

➤ **to manage to do something** arreglárselas para hacer algo: **how did you manage to carry your suitcase?** ¿cómo te las arreglaste para acarrear tu maleta?

**management** ['mænɪdʒmənt] *noun*

■ **la dirección: the management does not accept responsibility** la dirección no asume responsabilidad

➤ **management studies** administración de empresas.

**manager** ['mænɪdʒər] *noun*

1. **el/la gerente: the bank manager** el gerente del banco

2. **el encargado, la encargada: a store manager** un encargado de la tienda

3. **el/la manager** *(plural* **los/las managers***):* **he's the team manager** es el manager del equipo.

**mango** ['mæŋɡəʊ] *noun* ■ **el mango**.

**Manhattan** ['mæn͵hætən]        *noun*

■ **Manhattan** *(masculine):* **Edward lives in Manhattan** Edward vive en Manhattan

---

**MANHATTAN**

Manhattan es el distrito central de la ciudad de Nueva York. Se divide en los tres barrios llamados **Downtown, Midtown** y **Uptown.** Allí se encuentran lugares tan conocidos como **Central Park, la Quinta Avenida, Broadway, la Estatua de la Libertad** y **Greenwich Village,** así como los famosos edificios el **Empire State Building** y el **Chrysler Building.** La **Manhattan Skyline** es la vista famosa de Nueva York dominada por los rascacielos que incluían las torres gemelas del World Trade Center, hasta la destrucción de éstas en los ataques terroristas del 11 de septiembre del 2001.

---

**mankind** [mæn'kaɪnd] *noun* ■ **la humanidad**.

**man-made** [mænmeɪd] *adjective*

1. **artificial: a man-made lake** un lago artificial

2. **sintético: a man-made fabric** una tela sintética.

**manner** ['mænər] *noun* ■ **la manera: she treated me in a decent manner** me trató de manera amable.

**manners** ['mænərz] *plural noun* ■ **los modales: he has very good manners** tiene muy buenos modales.

**mansion** ['mænʃn] *noun* ■ **la mansión** *(plural* **las mansiones***).*

**manual** ['mænjʊəl] *noun* ■ **el manual: an instruction manual** un manual de instrucciones.

**many** ['menɪ] *(adjective & pronoun)*

■ *adjective*

**muchos: she has many friends** tiene muchos amigos

➤ **were there many people at the match?** ¿había mucha gente en el partido?

■ *pronoun*

**muchos: don't eat all the chocolates, there aren't many left** no te comas todos los chocolates, no quedan muchos

➤ **how many?** ¿cuántos?: **how many are there?** ¿cuántos hay?: **how many presents did you get?** ¿cuántos regalos recibiste?

➤ **too many** demasiados: **I ate too many chocolates** comí demasiados chocolates

➤ **there are too many people here** hay demasiada gente aquí

➤ **as many** tantos como: **I don't have as many CDs as my brother** no tengo tantos CDs como mi hermano

➤ **take as many as you like** toma tantos como quieras, toma todos los que quieras.

**map** [mæp] *noun*

1. **el mapa: a map of Argentina** un mapa de Argentina

2. **el plano: a map of New York** un plano de Nueva York.

**maple** ['meɪpl] *noun* ■ el **arce**, el **maple** *Mexico*

➤ **maple syrup** jarabe de arce, miel de maple *Mexico*.

**marathon** ['mærəən] *noun* ■ el/la **maratón** *(plural* los/las **maratones***)*.

**marble** ['maːbl] *noun*

1. el **mármol**: a marble statue una estatua de mármol
2. la **canica**: they're playing marbles están jugando a las canicas.

**march** [maːtʃ] *verb* ■ **marchar**: the soldiers were marching los soldados marchaban; **forward march!** ¡adelante, marchen!

**March** [maːtʃ] *noun*

In Spanish the months of the year do not start with a capital letter:

**marzo**: in March en marzo; next March el próximo marzo; last March el pasado marzo.

**margarine** [ˌmaːgəˈriːn] *noun* ■ la **margarina**.

**margin** ['maːdʒɪn] *noun* ■ el **margen** *(plural* los **márgenes***)*: he wrote something in the margin escribió algo en el margen.

**mark** [maːk] *(noun & verb)*
■ *noun*
la **mancha**: there's a mark on your T-shirt tienes una mancha en la camiseta; there are marks all over his body tiene manchas en todo el cuerpo
■ *verb*
**marcar**: X marks the spot el lugar está marcado con una X.

**market** ['maːkɪt] *noun* ■ el **mercado**: I'm going to the market voy al mercado.

**marriage** ['mærɪdʒ] *noun* ■ el **matrimonio**: this is her second marriage éste es su segundo matrimonio.

**married** ['mærɪd] *adjective* ■ **casado**: are you married? ¿eres casado?

➤ to get married casarse: they're getting married se van a casar.

**marry** ['mærɪ] *(past tense & past participle* married*) verb* ■ **casarse con**: she married Ian Jones se casó con Ian Jones; will you marry me? ¿te quieres casar conmigo?

**marvelous** ['maːvələs] *adjective* ■ **maravilloso**.

**masculine** ['mæskjʊlɪn] *adjective* ■ **masculino**.

**mashed potatoes** [mæʃtpəˈteɪtəʊz] *plural noun* ■ el **puré de papas**.

**mask** [maːsk] *noun* ■ la **máscara**: he's wearing a mask tiene puesta una máscara.

**mass** [mæs] *noun*

1. el **montón** *(plural* los **montones***)*: a mass of papers un montón de papeles
2. la **misa**: Catholics go to mass on Sunday los católicos van a misa los domingos.

**massage** [məˈsaːʒ] *noun* ■ el **masaje**.

**massive** ['mæsɪv] *adjective* ■ **masivo**.

**master** ['maːstər] *noun* ■ el **dueño**: the master of the house el dueño de casa.

**masterpiece** ['maːstəpiːs] *noun* ■ la **obra maestra**.

**mat** [mæt] *noun*

1. la **colchoneta**: an exercise mat una colchoneta para hacer gimnasia
2. el **felpudo**, el **tapete** *Colombia, Mexico*: wipe your feet on the mat before you come in límpiate los pies en el felpudo antes de entrar
➤ a place mat un mantel individual.

**match** [mætʃ] *(noun & verb)*
■ *noun*
1. el **partido**: a tennis match un partido de tenis
2. el **fósforo**, el **cerillo** *Mexico*: a box of matches una caja de fósforos
➤ a boxing match un combate de boxeo
■ *verb*
1. **hacer juego con**: that tie doesn't match your shirt esa corbata no hace juego con tu camisa
2. **hacer juego**: those socks don't match esos calcetines no hacen juego.

**matchbox** ['mætʃbɒks] *noun* ■ **la caja de fósforos, la caja de cerillos** *Mexico*.

**matching** ['mætʃɪŋ] *adjective* ■ **haciendo juego:** matching dress and shoes vestido y zapatos haciendo juego.

**material** [mə'tɪərɪəl] *noun*
1. el **material:** building materials materiales de construcción
2. la **tela:** she bought some curtain material compró tela para hacer cortinas
➤ raw materials materia prima.

**math** [mæθ] *(abbreviation of mathematics) uncountable noun* ■ *informal* **las matemáticas:** I like math me gustan las matemáticas; math is difficult las matemáticas son difíciles.

**mathematics** [ˌmæθə'mætɪks] *uncountable noun* ■ **las matemáticas.**

**matter** ['mætər] *(noun & verb)*
■ *noun*
el **asunto:** it's a delicate matter es un asunto delicado
➤ it's a matter of time es cuestión de tiempo
➤ as a matter of fact de hecho
➤ what's the matter? ¿qué pasa?
➤ what's the matter with her? ¿qué le pasa?
➤ there's nothing the matter no pasa nada
■ *verb*
**importar:** it doesn't matter no importa.

**mattress** ['mætrɪs] *noun* ■ el **colchón** *(plural* los **colchones)**.

**mature** [mə'tjʊər] *adjective* ■ **maduro:** he's very mature for his age es muy maduro para su edad.

**maximum** ['mæksɪməm] *(adjective & noun)*
■ *adjective*
**máximo:** what's the maximum speed? ¿cuál es la velocidad máxima?
■ *noun*
el **máximo:** there'll be a maximum of twenty habrá un máximo de veinte.

**may** [meɪ] *verb*

1. *Possibility*

> In Spanish, when "may" is used with another verb to say something is possible, you can translate it using the expression **puede que** followed by a verb in the subjunctive:

we may come puede que vengamos; it may rain puede que llueva; she may have called puede que haya llamado
2. *Asking and giving permission* **poder:** may I open the window? ¿puedo abrir la ventana?; you may sit down pueden sentarse.

**May** [meɪ] *noun*

> In Spanish the months of the year do not start with a capital letter:

mayo: in May en mayo; next May el próximo mayo; last May el pasado mayo
➤ May Day el primero de mayo.

**maybe** ['meɪbɪ] *adverb* ■ **quizás**

> Quizás must be followed by a verb in the subjunctive:

maybe I'll come quizás venga; maybe you're right quizás tengas razón
➤ maybe not quizás no.

**mayonnaise** [ˌmeɪə'neɪz] *noun* ■ la **mayonesa.**

**mayor** [meər] *noun* ■ el **alcalde,** la **alcaldesa:** he's the mayor of New York es el alcalde de Nueva York.

**maze** [meɪz] *noun* ■ el **laberinto:** this building is a real maze este edificio es un verdadero laberinto.

**me** [miː] *personal pronoun*
1. *Direct and indirect object* **me:** she doesn't know me no me conoce; can you hear me? ¿puedes oírme?; give it to me! ¡dámelo!
2. *After prepositions* **mí:** is that for me? ¿eso es para mí?; she left without me se fue sin mí

> In Spanish, "with me" has a special form:

come with me ven conmigo

**3.** *In comparisons* **yo:** he's taller than me es más alto que yo.

**meal** [miːl] *noun* ■ la **comida:** she made a big meal preparó una gran comida
➤ enjoy your meal! ¡buen provecho!

**mean** [miːn] *(adjective & verb)*

■ *adjective*
**malo:** he's always mean to his sister siempre es malo con su hermana

■ *verb*
*(past tense & past participle* **meant***)*
**1.** **significar:** what does this expression mean? ¿qué significa esta expresión?; it doesn't mean anything esto no significa nada
**2.** **querer decir:** what do you mean? ¿qué quieres decir?; that's not what he meant eso no es lo que quería decir
**3.** **querer:** I mean to leave at six o'clock quiero irme a las seis en punto; I didn't mean to hurt you no quise herirte
➤ I meant it lo dije en serio
➤ to be meant for ser para: this present is meant for your sister este regalo es para tu hermana.

**meaning** [miːnɪŋ] *noun* ■ el **significado:** what's the meaning of this word? ¿cuál es el significado de esta palabra?

**means** [miːnz] *noun* ■ el **medio:** it's a means to get what he wants es un medio para obtener lo que quiere
➤ by means of por medio de: they communicate by means of a variety of sounds se comunican por medio de una variedad de sonidos
➤ the thief got in by means of a ladder el ladrón entró usando una escalera
➤ a means of transport un medio de transporte.

**meant** [ment] *past tense & past participle*
➤ mean.

**meantime** [miːnˌtaɪm] *noun*
➤ in the meantime mientras tanto.

**meanwhile** [miːnˌwaɪl] *adverb*
■ **mientras tanto:** meanwhile, I was out with my friends mientras tanto, yo estaba afuera con mis amigos.

**measles** [miːzlz] *noun* ■ el **sarampión:** she has measles tiene sarampión.

**measure** [meʒər] *verb* ■ **medir:** she measured the chair with a tape measure midió la silla con una cinta métrica; the room measures 2 feet by 3 feet la habitación mide 2 pies por 3 pies.

**measurement** [meʒəmənt] *noun* ■ la **medida:** he took my measurements me tomó las medidas

MEASUREMENTS

En Estados Unidos no se usa comúnmente el sistema métrico, sino que se emplean las medidas del antiguo sistema inglés. Las unidades más comunes son: **inches** - pulgadas; **feet** - pies; **yards** - yardas; **miles** - millas; **ounces** - onzas; **pounds** - libras; **degrees Fahrenheit** - grados Fahrenheit. 1 inch = 2.54cm, 1 foot = 30.48cm, 1 yard = 91.44cm, 1 mile = 1.6km, 1 ounce = 28.35g, 1 pound = 0.453kg, 1 degree Fahrenheit = -17.22 degrees Celsius.

**meat** [miːt] *noun* ■ la **carne:** she doesn't like meat no le gusta la carne.

**Mecca** [mekə] *noun* ■ la **Meca.**

**mechanic** [mɪkænɪk] *noun* ■ el **mecánico, la mecánica.**

**mechanical** [mɪkænɪkl] *adjective*
■ **mecánico.**

**medal** [medl] *noun* ■ la **medalla:** she won a gold medal ganó una medalla de oro.

**media** [miːdjə] *noun*
➤ the media los medios de comunicación: the event was reported in the media el acontecimiento fue divulgado por los medios de comunicación.

**medical** [medɪkl] *adjective* ■ **médico:** medical treatment tratamiento médico
➤ a medical student un estudiante de medicina.

**medicine** ['medsɪn] *noun*

1. la **medicina**: Andrew's studying medicine Andrés está estudiando medicina
2. el **medicamento**: I must take my medicine debo tomar mi medicamento.

**medium** ['mɪːdjəm] *adjective* ■ **mediano**: he's of medium height es de estatura mediana.

**medium-sized** ['mɪːdjəmsaɪzd] *adjective* ■ **tamaño mediano**: a medium-sized town una ciudad de tamaño mediano.

**meet** [mɪːt] *(past tense & past participle* met) *verb*

1. **conocer**: have you met Lisa's brother? ¿conoces al hermano de Lisa?
2. **encontrarse**: we met by chance in the street nos encontramos por casualidad en la calle; let's meet in front of the movie theater encontrémonos frente al cine
3. **reunirse**: the board met today el consejo se reunió hoy
4. **buscar**: I'm going to meet them at the airport at 3 o'clock voy a buscarlos al aeropuerto a las 3 en punto
➤ I met Sue outside the store me encontré con Sue afuera de la tienda
➤ pleased to meet you encantado de conocerlo.

**meeting** ['mɪːtɪŋ] *noun*

1. la **reunión** *(plural* las **reuniones)**: I have a meeting today tengo una reunión hoy
2. el **encuentro**: this was our first meeting éste era nuestro primer encuentro.

**megabyte** ['megəbaɪt] *noun* ■ el **megabyte**.

**melody** ['melədɪ] *(plural* melodies) *noun* ■ la **melodía**.

**melon** ['melən] *noun* ■ el **melón** *(plural* los **melones)**.

**melt** [melt] *verb* ■ **derretirse**: the ice is melting el hielo se está derritiendo.

**member** ['membər] *noun* ■ el **socio**, la **socia**: Rita's a member of the chess club Rita es socia del club de ajedrez

➤ a Member of Congress un miembro del congreso.

**memorial** [mɪ'mɔːrɪəl] *noun* ■ el **monumento**: a war memorial un monumento a los caídos

MEMORIAL DAY

**Memorial Day** es el día en que se conmemoran a todos los soldados que participaron y murieron en las guerras. Hay desfiles de soldados y veteranos y las calles y las casas se decoran con banderas y listones de los colores nacionales: rojo, blanco y azul. Memorial Day se celebra el último lunes de mayo y se considera el comienzo informal del verano.

**memorize** ['meməraɪz] *verb* ■ **memorizar**: you must memorize your password debes memorizar tu contraseña.

**memory** ['memərɪ] *(plural* memories) *noun*

1. la **memoria**: she has a good memory tiene buena memoria; the new computer has a lot of memory la nueva computadora tiene mucha memoria
2. el **recuerdo**: I have good memories of that evening tengo buenos recuerdos de esa noche.

**men** *plural* ➤ man.

**mend** [mend] *verb* ■ **remendar**: I'm going to mend this shirt voy a remendar esta camisa.

**mental** ['mentl] *adjective* ■ **mental**.

**mention** ['menʃn] *verb* ■ **mencionar**: he mentioned your name mencionó tu nombre

➤ thank you! —don't mention it! ¡gracias! — ¡no hay de qué!

**menu** ['menjuː] *noun* ■ el **menú** *(plural* los **menús)**: what's on the menu? ¿qué hay en el menú?; choose Print from the File menu elija Imprimir en el menú Archivo.

**mercy** ['mɜːsɪ] *noun* ■ la **piedad**: he showed no mercy no tuvo piedad.

**mermaid** ['mɜːmeɪd] *noun* ■ la **sirena**.

**merry** ['merɪ] *adjective*
➤ Merry Christmas! ¡Feliz Navidad!

**merry-go-round** ['merɪgəʊraʊnd] *noun* ■ el **carrusel**.

**mess** [mes] *uncountable noun* ■ el **desorden**: what a mess! ¡qué desorden!
➤ to make a mess dejar un desastre: **the workmen made a mess** los obreros dejaron un desastre

**mess around** | *phrasal verb informal*
1. **perder el tiempo**: stop messing around! ¡deja de perder el tiempo!
2. **hacer tonterías**: the children are messing around in the yard los niños están haciendo tonterías en el jardín
➤ don't mess around with my guitar ¡deja mi guitarra tranquila!

**mess up** | *phrasal verb informal*
1. **desordenar**: he's messed up the kitchen desordenó la cocina
2. **estropear**: that's messed up my plans eso estropeó mis planes
3. **echar a perder**: I really messed up my work realmente eché a perder mi trabajo.

**message** ['mesɪdʒ] *noun* ■ el **mensaje**.

**messenger** ['mesɪndʒəʳ] *noun* ■ el **mensajero**, la **mensajera**.

**messy** ['mesɪ] *adjective* ■ **desordenado**: my room is very messy mi cuarto está muy desordenado; you're very messy eres muy desordenado
➤ it's a messy job es un trabajo sucio.

**met** [met] *past tense & past participle*
➤ meet.

**metal** ['metl] *noun* ■ el **metal**.

**meter** ['miːtəʳ] *noun*
1. el **medidor**: a water meter un medidor de agua
2. el **metro**: it's two meters long tiene dos metros de largo
➤ a parking meter un parquímetro.

**method** ['meθəd] *noun* ■ el **método**: we must change our methods debemos cambiar nuestros métodos.

**metric** ['metrɪk] *adjective* ■ **métrico**: the metric system el sistema métrico.

**Mexican** ['meksɪkn] *(adjective & noun)*
■ *adjective*

Remember not to use a capital letter for the adjective in Spanish:

**mejicano**: I like Mexican food me gusta la comida mejicana
■ *noun*

In Spanish, a capital letter is not used for the inhabitants of a country or region:

el **mejicano**, la **mejicana**: the Mexicans are famous for their cuisine los mejicanos son famosos por su cocina.

**Mexico** ['meksɪkəʊ] *noun* ■ **México** *(masculine)*.

**mice** *plural* ➤ mouse.

**microphone** ['maɪkrəfəʊn] *noun* ■ el **micrófono**.

**microscope** ['maɪkrəskəʊp] *noun* ■ el **microscopio**.

**microwave** ['maɪkrəweɪv] *noun* ■ el **microondas**.

**midday** [mɪd'deɪ] *noun* ■ el **mediodía**: she went out at midday salió al mediodía.

**middle** ['mɪdl] *(adjective & noun)*
■ *adjective*
**del medio**: he sat in the middle chair se sentó en la silla del medio
➤ the Middle Ages la Edad Media
➤ the Middle East el Medio Oriente: she lives in the Middle East vive en el Medio Oriente
➤ middle name segundo nombre: what is your middle name? ¿cuál es tu segundo nombre?
■ *noun*
el **medio**: the table's in the middle of the room la mesa está en el medio de la habitación

➤ it happened in the middle of the night ocurrió en la mitad de la noche.

**middle-aged** [ˈmɪdleɪdʒd] *adjective*
■ **de mediana edad: she's middle-aged** ella es de mediana edad.

**middle-class** [ˈmɪdlklɑːs] *adjective*
■ **de clase media: he's very middle-class** es muy de clase media.

**midnight** [ˈmɪdnaɪt] *noun* ■ **la medi-noche: he came back at midnight** volvió a medianoche.

**might** [maɪt] *verb*

> In Spanish, you can use the expression **puede que** followed by a verb in the subjunctive to translate "might":

**they might be away** puede que se hayan ido; **it might snow** puede que nieve; **she might have gotten lost** puede que se haya perdido.

**mighty** [ˈmaɪtɪ] *adjective* ■ **poderoso:** he was a mighty king fue un rey poderoso.

**mike** [maɪk] *(abbreviation of* micro-phone*) noun* ■ *informal* el **micrófono: he was talking into the mike** estaba hablando por el micrófono.

**mild** [maɪld] *adjective* ■ **templado:** the climate is very mild el clima es templado.

**mile** [maɪl] *noun* ■ **la milla: she was driving at 50 miles an hour** iba manejando a 50 millas por hora; **I walked for miles** caminé millas y millas.

**military** [ˈmɪlɪtrɪ] *adjective* ■ **militar:** a military band una banda militar.

**milk** [mɪlk] *noun* ■ **la leche: a glass of milk** un vaso de leche
➤ **milk chocolate** chocolate con leche
➤ **a milk shake** un batido con leche, una merengada *Venezuela*.

**millennium** [mɪˈlenɪəm] *(plural* mil-lennia [mɪˈlenɪə]*) noun* ■ el **milenio: it's the new millennium** es el nuevo milenio.

**millimeter** [ˈmɪlɪˌmiːtər] *noun* ■ el **milímetro**.

**million** [ˈmɪljən] *noun* ■ el **millón** *(plural* los **millones***):* **three million** tres millones; **a million dollars** un millón de dólares.

**millionaire** [ˌmɪljəˈneər] *noun* ■ el **millonario,** la **millonaria**.

**mind** [maɪnd] *(noun & verb)*

■ *noun*
la **mente: he has a very agile mind** tiene una mente muy ágil
➤ **it never crossed my mind** ni se me pasó por la cabeza
➤ **to have something on one's mind** tener algo en mente: **she has something on her mind** tiene algo en mente
➤ **to make one's mind up** decidirse: **I haven't made up my mind yet** no me he decidido todavía
➤ **to change one's mind** cambiar de opinión: **she's changed her mind** cambió de opinión
■ *verb*
➤ **I don't mind** no me importa: **I don't mind waiting** no me importa esperar
➤ **I'm sorry about the noise — oh, I don't mind** perdón por el ruido — ah, no me molesta
➤ **do you mind if I open the window?** ¿te importa si abro la ventana?
➤ **never mind!** ¡no importa!
➤ **I wouldn't mind a coffee** me tomaría un café
➤ **mind your own business!** ¡no te metas en lo que no te importa!

**mine** [maɪn] *(pronoun & noun)*

■ *possessive pronoun*
**mío**

> In Spanish the possessive pronoun agrees in gender (masculine or feminine) and number (singular or plural) with the noun it replaces:

**his computer's a PC, mine is a Mac** su computadora es un PC, la mía es una Mac; **her dress is blue, mine is red** su vestido es azul, el mío es rojo; **his books are on the table, mine are on the shelf** sus libros están sobre la mesa, los míos están en el estante; **is this glass mine?** ¿es mío este vaso?; **he's a friend of mine** es un amigo mío

■ *noun*
la **mina**: a coal mine una mina de carbón;
the tank hit a mine el tanque chocó contra
una mina.

**miner** ['maɪnə<sup>r</sup>] *noun* ■ el **minero, la
minera**: he's a miner es minero.

**mineral   water** ['mɪnərəl'wɔːtə<sup>r</sup>]
*noun* ■ el **agua mineral**

> Feminine noun that takes **un** or **el** in the
> singular.

**miniature** ['mɪnətʃə<sup>r</sup>] *adjective* ■ **en
miniatura**.

**minimum** ['mɪnɪməm] *(noun & adjective)*

■ *noun*
el **mínimo**: you have to pay a minimum
of $50 tienes que pagar un mínimo de $50
■ *adjective*
**mínimo**: what's the minimum wage?
¿cuál es el salario mínimo?

**miniskirt** ['mɪnɪskɜːt] *noun* ■ la **mini-
falda**.

**minister** ['mɪnɪstə<sup>r</sup>] *noun* ■ el **pastor,
la pastora**: he's a minister in the church
es pastor de la iglesia.

**minivan** ['mɪnɪvæn] *noun* ■ la **furgoneta, la vagoneta**.

**minor** ['maɪnə<sup>r</sup>] *adjective* ■ **menor**: it's
a minor problem es un problema menor.

**minority** [maɪ'nɒrətɪ] *(plural* minor-
ities*) noun* ■ la **minoría**: we're in the minority estamos en minoría.

**mint** [mɪnt] *noun*
1. la **menta**: he likes mint tea le gusta el té de
menta
2. la **pastilla de menta**: would you like a
mint? ¿quieres una pastilla de menta?

**minus** ['maɪnəs] *preposition* ■ **menos**:
20 minus 7 equals 13 20 menos 7 es igual a
13
➤ it's minus three degrees hace tres grados
bajo cero
➤ the minus sign el signo de menos.

**minute** ['mɪnɪt] *noun* ■ el **minuto**: he
left five minutes ago se fue hace cinco minutos; wait a minute! ¡espera un minuto!
➤ stop this minute! ¡para ahora mismo!

**mirror** ['mɪrə<sup>r</sup>] *noun*
1. el **espejo**: he was looking at himself in
the mirror se estaba mirando en el espejo
2. el **espejo retrovisor**: look in your mirror
before you pass that car mira por el espejo
retrovisor antes de adelantar a ese coche.

**misbehave** [,mɪsbɪ'heɪv] *verb* ■ **portarse mal**: they always misbehave in
class siempre se portan mal en clase.

**mischief** ['mɪstʃɪf] *uncountable noun*
■ la **travesura**: he's always up to mischief siempre está haciendo travesuras.

**miser** ['maɪzə<sup>r</sup>] *noun* ■ el **avaro, la
avara**.

**miserable** ['mɪzrəbl] *adjective*
1. **deprimido**: he looks miserable se ve deprimido
2. **deprimente**: the weather's miserable el
tiempo es deprimente.

**misery** ['mɪzərɪ] *noun* ■ la **desdicha**:
it'll bring nothing but misery no traerá
más que desdichas.

**miss** [mɪs] *verb*
1. **perder**: I missed the train perdí el tren
2. **perderse**: the film was terrible, you
didn't miss anything la película fue espantosa, no te perdiste nada
➤ I miss you te extraño
➤ it's a big house, you can't miss it es una
casa grande, la vas a ver enseguida.

**Miss** [mɪs] *noun* ■ **señorita**: can I help
you, Miss? ¿qué desea, señorita?; Miss
Janet Brown la señorita Janet Brown.

**missing** ['mɪsɪŋ] *adjective* ■ **desaparecido**: a missing person una persona desa-
parecida
➤ to be missing **faltar**: how many pieces
are missing? ¿cuántas piezas faltan?
there's something missing falta algo
my watch is missing falta mi reloj

➤ fill in the missing words llene las palabras que faltan.

**mission** ['mɪʃn] *noun* ■ la **misión, las misiones:** our mission is to find him nuestra misión es encontrarlo.

**mist** [mɪst] *noun* ■ la **neblina**.

**mistake** [mɪ'steɪk] *(noun & verb)*

■ *noun*
1. la **equivocación** *(plural* las **equivocaciones)**: it was a big mistake fue una gran equivocación
2. el **error:** a spelling mistake un error de ortografía
➤ to make a mistake cometer un error: I made a mistake by telling him cometí un error al decírselo; I made a lot of mistakes in my essay cometí muchos errores en mi trabajo escrito
➤ to make a mistake equivocarse: I'm sorry, I must have made a mistake perdón, debo haberme equivocado
anyone can make a mistake cualquiera puede equivocarse
➤ by mistake por equivocación: he took my pencil by mistake tomó mi lápiz por equivocación
■ *verb*
*(past tense* **mistook,** *past participle* **mistaken)**
➤ to mistake someone for somebody else confundir: I mistook you for your brother te confundí con tu hermano.

**mistaken** *past participle* ➤ mistake.

**mistletoe** ['mɪsltəʊ] *noun* ■ el **muérdago:** to kiss under the mistletoe besarse bajo el muérdago.

**mistook** *past tense* ➤ mistake.

**misunderstand** [,mɪsʌndə'stænd]
*(past tense & past participle* misunderstood [,mɪsʌndə'stʊd])* verb* ■ **entender mal:** I misunderstood you te entendí mal.

**misunderstanding** [,mɪsʌndə'stændɪŋ]
*noun* ■ **malentendido:** there's been a misunderstanding hubo un malentendido.

**misunderstood** *past tense & past participle* ➤ misunderstand.

**mix** [mɪks] *(noun & verb)*
■ *noun*
la **mezcla:** it's a mix of two cultures es una mezcla de dos culturas
➤ a cake mix *un preparado para hacer pasteles*
■ *verb*
**mezclar:** mix all the ingredients together mezcle todos los ingredientes juntos

**mix up** *phrasal verb*
1. **confundir:** he mixed me up with my brother me confundió con mi hermano; you're mixing me up me estás confundiendo
2. **desordenar:** he's mixed up all the photos desordenó todas las fotos
➤ I'm getting mixed up me estoy confundiendo.

**mixed** [mɪkst] *adjective*
1. **surtido:** a bag of mixed candy una bolsa de dulces surtidos
2. **mixto:** it's a mixed school es una escuela mixta.

**mixture** ['mɪkstʃər] *noun* ■ la **mezcla:** it's a mixture of rap and jazz es una mezcla de rap y jazz.

**mix-up** [mɪksʌp] *noun* ■ la **confusión:** there's been a mix-up ha habido una confusión.

**moan** [məʊn] *verb* ■ **quejarse:** the patient moaned el paciente se quejó.

**model** ['mɒdl] *noun*
1. el **modelo:** it's the latest model es el último modelo
2. el/la **modelo:** she's a model es modelo
3. la **maqueta:** a model plane una maqueta de avión.

**modem** ['məʊdem] *noun* ■ el **módem** *(plural* los **módems).**

**modern** ['mɒdən] *adjective* ■ **moderno**
➤ modern languages lenguas modernas.

**modest** ['mɒdɪst] *adjective* ■ **modesto:** Fred's very modest Fred es muy modesto.

**moldy** ['məʊldɪ] *adjective* ■ **mohoso**.

**mole** [məʊl] *noun*
1. el **lunar**: she has a mole on her arm tiene un lunar en el brazo
2. el **topo**: moles live under the ground los topos viven debajo de la tierra.

**mom** [mɒm] *noun* ■ *informal* la **mamá**: hi, mom! ¡hola, mamá!; his mom's a nurse su mamá es enfermera.

**moment** ['məʊmənt] *noun* ■ el **momento**: he's not here at the moment no está aquí en este momento
➤ wait a moment! ¡espera un momento!

**mommy** ['mɒmɪ] *noun* ■ *informal* la **mami**.

**monastery** ['mɒnəstrɪ] *(plural* mon-asteries) *noun* ■ el **monasterio**.

**Monday** ['mʌndɪ] *noun*

In Spanish the days of the week do not start with a capital letter:

el **lunes** *(plural* los **lunes**): it's Monday today hoy es lunes; next Monday el próximo lunes; last Monday el lunes pasado
➤ on Monday el lunes: I'll see you on Monday nos vemos el lunes
➤ on Mondays los lunes: he does judo on Mondays hace judo los lunes.

**money** ['mʌnɪ] *uncountable noun* ■ el **dinero**: I don't have any money no tengo dinero.

**monk** [mʌŋk] *noun* ■ el **monje**: he's a monk es un monje.

**monkey** ['mʌŋkɪ] *noun* ■ el **mono,** la **mona**.

**monster** ['mɒnstər] *noun* ■ el **monstruo**.

**month** [mʌnθ] *noun* ■ el **mes**: this month este mes; next month el mes próximo; last month el mes pasado; we see each other twice a month nos vemos dos veces al mes.

**monument** ['mɒnjʊmənt] *noun* ■ el **monumento**: it's a historic monument es un monumento histórico.

**moo** [muː] *(past tense & past participle* mooed [muːd]) *verb* ■ **mugir**: I can hear the cows mooing oigo las vacas mujiendo.

**mood** [muːd] *noun* ■ el **humor**: she's in a good mood está de buen humor; I'm in a bad mood estoy de mal humor.

**moody** ['muːdɪ] *adjective*
1. **malhumorado**: you're very moody today hoy estás muy malhumorado
2. **temperamental**: she's a moody person es muy temperamental.

**moon** [muːn] *noun* ■ la **luna**: there's a full moon tonight esta noche hay luna llena.

**moonlight** ['muːnlaɪt] *noun* ■ la **luz de la luna**: I went for a walk in the moonlight salí a caminar a la luz de la luna.

**moped** ['məʊped] *noun* ■ la **bicimoto**: she rides a moped to work va a trabajar en bicimoto.

**moral** ['mɒrəl] *(adjective & noun)*
■ *adjective*
**moral**: we're here for moral support estamos aquí para dar apoyo moral
■ *noun*
la **moraleja**: what's the moral of the story? ¿cuál es la moraleja de la historia?

**morale** [məˈrɑːl] *noun* ■ la **moral**: we have to boost their morale tenemos que levantarles la moral.

**more** [mɔːr] *(adjective, adverb & pronoun)*
■ *adjective*
*(comparative of* many, much *and* a lot of)
**más**: there are more trains in the morning hay más trenes en la mañana; he has more money than me tiene más dinero que yo; there isn't any more bread no hay más pan; I need three more tickets necesito tres boletos más; would you like some more cake? ¿quieres un poco más de pastel?; do you have any more questions? ¿tienes más preguntas?

■ *adverb*

**más**: it's **more expensive** es más caro; **she's more intelligent than him** ella es más inteligente que él; **Tom reads more than me** Tom lee más que yo; **she doesn't live here any more** no vive más aquí; **you have to work more** debes trabajar más

➤ **once more** otra vez

■ *pronoun*

*(comparative of* **many**, **much** *and* **a lot***)* **más**: **it costs more than $100** cuesta más de $100; **he eats more than I do** come más que yo; **there aren't any more** no hay más; **I need more of them** necesito más; **I like this cake, can I have some more?** me gusta este pastel, ¿puedo comer más?

➤ **more and more** cada vez más: **she travels more and more** viaja cada vez más
**more and more people are taking up yoga** cada vez más gente empieza a hacer yoga

➤ **more or less** más o menos: **the new program does more or less the same as the old one** el nuevo programa hace más o menos lo mismo que el viejo.

**morning** ['mɔːnɪŋ] *noun* ■ la **mañana**: **he's not going to school this morning** no va a ir a la escuela esta mañana; **she works in the morning** trabaja en la mañana; **at six o'clock in the morning** a las seis de la mañana; **I'll do it in the morning** lo haré en la mañana; **she stayed in bed all morning** se quedó en la cama toda la mañana

➤ **every morning** todas las mañanas

➤ **yesterday morning** ayer en la mañana

➤ **tomorrow morning** mañana en la mañana.

**mosque** [mɒsk] *noun* ■ la **mezquita**: **they go to the mosque on Fridays** van a la mezquita los viernes.

**mosquito** [mə'skiːtəʊ] *noun* ■ el **mosquito**: **I'm covered in mosquito bites** estoy lleno de picaduras de mosquito.

**most** [məʊst] *(adjective, adverb & pronoun)*

■ *adjective*

ı. la **mayoría de**: **most tourists visit the Empire State Building** la mayoría de los turistas visitan el edificio del Empire State

**2.** **más**: **she has the most money** es la que tiene más dinero

■ *adverb*

**más**: **he's the most experienced player on the team** es el jugador con más experiencia del equipo; **it's the most beautiful city in the world** es la ciudad más linda del mundo; **we got the most expensive tickets** conseguimos los boletos más caros

■ *pronoun*

la **mayor parte**: **most of the tourists are American** la mayor parte de los turistas son norteamericanos; **I spent most of the day in bed** me pasé la mayor parte del día en cama; **most of them left early** la mayor parte se fue temprano

➤ **Paul ate the most** Pablo fue el que más comió.

**mostly** ['məʊstlɪ] *adverb* ■ **en su mayoría**: **there were lots of customers, mostly young people** había muchos clientes, en su mayoría gente joven.

**motel** [məʊ'tel] *noun* ■ el **motel**: **we stopped at a motel for the night** paramos en un motel para pasar la noche.

**moth** [mɒθ] *noun* ■ la **polilla**.

**mother** ['mʌðəʳ] *noun* ■ la **madre**

➤ **Mother's Day** el Día de la Madre.

**mother-in-law** ['mʌðəʳɪnlɔː] *noun* ■ la **suegra**.

**motivated** ['məʊtɪveɪtɪd] *adjective* ■ **motivado**: **my students are very motivated** mis estudiantes están muy motivados.

**motivation** [ˌməʊtɪ'veɪʃn] *noun* ■ la **motivación** *(plural* las **motivaciones***)*: **he seems to lack motivation** parece que le falta motivación.

**motive** ['məʊtɪv] *noun* ■ el **motivo**: **what was the motive for the crime?** ¿cuál fue el motivo del crimen?

**motor** ['məʊtəʳ] *noun* ■ el **motor**: **an electric motor** un motor eléctrico.

**motorboat** ['məʊtəbəʊt] *noun* ■ la **lancha a motor**.

**motorcycle** ['məʊtə,saɪkl] *noun* ■ la **motocicleta**: let's go for a ride on your motorcycle vamos a dar una vuelta en tu motocicleta.

**motorcyclist** ['məʊtə,saɪklɪst] *noun* ■ el/la **motociclista**.

**motto** ['mɒtəʊ] *noun* ■ el **lema**: our motto is "quality above all" nuestro lema es "calidad por encima de todo".

**mount** [maʊnt] *(verb & noun)*
■ *verb*
1. **montarse en**: Dan mounted his horse Daniel se montó en el caballo
2. **aumentar**: the construction costs are mounting los costos de la construcción están aumentando
■ *noun*
el **monte**
➤ Mount Rushmore el Monte Rushmore

> **MOUNT RUSHMORE**
>
> Se trata de un gigantesco relieve de los bustos de los presidentes estadounidenses Washington, Jefferson, Lincoln y Theodore Roosevelt, excavado en un lado del monte Rushmore (Dakota del Sur). Es un monumento nacional y una popular atracción turística. Los bustos se esculpieron utilizando taladros neumáticos y miden 28 metros de altura.

**mountain** ['maʊntɪn] *noun* ■ la **montaña**: they set out to climb the mountain salieron para escalar la montaña
➤ a mountain bike una bicicleta de montaña.

**mouse** [maʊs] *(plural* mice [maɪs])* *noun* ■ el **ratón** *(plural* los **ratones**)*: a mouse ran across the room un ratón atravesó la habitación
➤ use the mouse to move around the screen usa el ratón para moverte por la pantalla
➤ a mouse pad una almohadilla para el ratón, un tapete para el ratón *Mexico*.

**mousse** [muːs] *noun* ■ el/la **mousse**: chocolate mousse mousse de chocolate.

**mouth** [maʊθ] *noun* ■ la **boca**: don't talk with your mouth full! ¡no hables con la boca llena!; he didn't open his mouth no abrió la boca.

**move** [muːv] *(noun & verb)*
■ *noun*
1. el **paso**: selling that stock was a wise move vender esas acciones fue un paso acertado
2. *In games* la **jugada**: that was a very good move ésa fue una excelente jugada
3. la **mudanza**: the vase broke during the move el florero se rompió durante la mudanza
➤ it's your move te toca a ti jugar
■ *verb*
1. **mover**: I can't move my arm no puedo mover el brazo
2. **moverse**: don't move no te muevas; come on, get moving! ¡vamos, muévete!
3. **correr**: we have to move the furniture to paint the room tenemos que correr los muebles para pintar el cuarto
4. **avanzar**: the expedition moved slowly la expedición avanzó lentamente
5. **mudarse**: they're moving next week se mudan la semana que viene; we're moving to Florida nos mudamos a Florida
6. **conmover**: his speech really moved me su discurso verdaderamente me conmovió; she was very moved estaba muy conmovida

**move forward** *phrasal verb* ■ **avanzar**: the soldiers are moving forward los soldados están avanzando.

**move in** *phrasal verb* ■ **mudarse**: the new tenant just moved in el nuevo inquilino acaba de mudarse.

**move off** *phrasal verb* ■ **ponerse en marcha**: the convoy moved off la caravana se puso en marcha.

**move out** *phrasal verb* ■ **mudarse**: he moved out last month se mudó el mes pasado.

**move over** *phrasal verb* ■ **correrse**: move over, I don't have enough room córrete, no tengo suficiente espacio.

**movement** ['mu:vmənt] *noun* ■ el **movimiento**: she made a sudden movement hizo un movimiento repentino.

**movie** ['mu:vɪ] *noun* ■ la **película**: let's go see a movie vayamos a ver una película
➤ the movies el cine: I went to the movies with a friend fui al cine con un amigo
➤ a movie theater un cine.

**mow** [məʊ] (*past tense* mowed [məʊd], *past participle* mowed o mown [məʊn]) *verb* ■ **cortar, podar** *Mexico*: she's mowing the lawn está cortando el pasto, está cortando la grama *Central America, Venezuela*.

**mower** ['məʊəʳ] *noun* ■ la **máquina de cortar pasto**, la **podadora** *Mexico*, la **cortagrama** *Central America, Venezuela*.

**mown** *past participle* ➤ mow.

**Mr.** ['mɪstəʳ] *noun*
1. el **señor**: Mr. Smith is here el señor Smith está aquí
2. *In correspondence* **Sr.** (*masculine*)

**Mrs.** ['mɪsɪz] *noun*
1. la **señora**: Mrs. Smith is here el señora Smith está aquí
2. *In correspondence* **Sra.** (*feminine*)

**Ms.** [mɪz] *noun*
1. la **señora**: Ms. Brown is here to see you la señora Brown está aquí para verlo
2. *In correspondence* **Sra.** (*feminine*)

**much** [mʌtʃ] (*comparative* more, *superlative* most) (*adjective, pronoun & adverb*)
■ *adjective*
**mucho**: I don't have much time no tengo mucho tiempo
■ *pronoun*
**mucho**: I don't want much no quiero mucho
■ *adverb*
**mucho**: she doesn't go out much no sale mucho; thank you very much muchas gracias
➤ how much cuánto: how much does it cost? ¿cuánto cuesta?
how much money do you have? ¿cuánto dinero tienes?

➤ too much demasiado: she talks too much habla demasiado
there's too much sugar in my coffee hay demasiada azúcar en mi café
➤ so much tanto: I missed you so much te eché tanto de menos
he got into so much trouble at school se metió en tantos problemas en la escuela
➤ have as much as you like toma todo lo que quieras
➤ he doesn't have as much time as I do no tiene tanto tiempo como yo.

**mud** [mʌd] *noun* ■ el **barro**: the car is covered in mud el coche está cubierto de barro.

**muddy** ['mʌdɪ] *adjective*
1. **embarrado**: the ground is very muddy el suelo está muy embarrado
2. **lleno de barro**: my hands are all muddy tengo las manos llenas de barro.

**mug** [mʌg] (*noun & verb*)
■ *noun*
la **taza alta**, el **tarro** *Mexico*: a mug of coffee un taza alta de café
■ *verb*
**asaltar**: she was mugged in the street la asaltaron en la calle.

**mugger** [,mʌgəʳ] *noun* ■ el/la **asaltante**: the police caught the mugger la policía atrapó al asaltante.

**multimedia** [,mʌltɪ'mi:djə] *noun* ■ el/la **multimedia**: a multimedia display una presentación multimedia.

**multiple-choice test** [,mʌltɪpl-'tʃɔɪstest] *noun* ■ la **prueba de opción múltiple**.

**multiplication** [,mʌltɪplɪ'keɪʃn] *noun* ■ la **multiplicación** (*plural* las **multiplicaciones***): to do a multiplication hacer una multiplicación
➤ multiplication sign signo de multiplicar
➤ multiplication table tabla de multiplicar.

**multiply** ['mʌltɪplaɪ] (*past tense & past participle* multiplied) *verb* ■ **multiplicar**: what's 3 multiplied by 7? ¿cuánto es 3 multiplicado por 7?

**murder** ['mɜːdər] (noun & verb)

■ noun

el **asesinato**: he was accused of murder lo acusaron de asesinato

■ verb

**asesinar**: somebody was murdered near the station asesinaron a alguien cerca de la estación.

**murderer** ['mɜːdərər] noun ■ el **asesino**, la **asesina**.

**muscle** ['mʌsl] noun ■ el **músculo**: the stomach muscles los músculos del estómago.

**museum** [mjuːˈzɪːəm] noun ■ el **museo**: we're going to the art museum vamos al museo de arte.

**mushroom** ['mʌʃrʊm] noun ■ el **champiñón** (plural los **champiñones**)

➤ mushroom soup sopa de champiñones.

**music** ['mjuːzɪk] noun ■ la **música**: he's listening to music está escuchando música.

**musical** ['mjuːzɪkl] (adjective & noun)

■ adjective

➤ a musical instrument un instrumento musical: she plays a musical instrument toca un instrumento musical

■ noun

el **musical**: we're going to see a musical vamos a ver un musical.

**musician** [mjuːˈzɪʃn] noun ■ el **músico**, la **música**: she's a musician es música.

**Muslim** ['mʊzlɪm] (adjective & noun)

■ adjective

Remember not to use a capital letter for the adjective or the noun in Spanish:

**musulmán**

■ noun

el **musulmán** (plural los **musulmanes**), la **musulmana**.

**mussel** ['mʌsl] noun ■ el **mejillón** (plural los **mejillones**), el **choro** Chile, Peru.

**must** [mʌst] verb ■ **deber**

You can use the verb **deber** + infinitive to translate "must," or you can use the impersonal construction **hay que** + infinitive. You can also use **tener que** + infinitive:

you musn't tell anyone no debes contárselo a nadie; you must always read the instructions siempre hay que leer las instrucciones; I must go tengo que irme; you must come and see us tienes que venir a vernos

To make deductions, you use the verb **deber** in Spanish:

he must be English debe ser inglés; she must have gotten lost debe haberse perdido.

**mustache** ['mʌstæʃ] noun ■ el **bigote**: he has a mustache tiene bigote.

**mustard** ['mʌstəd] noun ■ la **mostaza**.

**mustn't** [mʌsnt] ➤ must not.

**must've** ['mʌstəv] ➤ must have.

**mutton** ['mʌtn] noun ■ la **carne de oveja**: we never eat mutton nunca comemos carne de oveja.

**my** [maɪ] possessive adjective ■ **mi**

In Spanish the possessive adjective agrees in number (singular or plural) with the noun that follows:

my dog is called Spike mi perro se llama Spike; my car won't start mi coche no arranca; my parents are on vacation mis padres están de vacaciones

Use the definite article (**el**, **la**, **los** or **las**), not the possessive adjective, with parts of the body:

I broke my leg me quebré la pierna; I'm going to wash my hair voy a lavarme el pelo.

**myself** [maɪˈself] pronoun

1. **me**: I'm washing myself me estoy lavando

**2. yo mismo:** I asked him myself yo mismo le pregunté

**3. mí mismo:** I often talk about myself a menudo hablo de mí mismo

➤ **I'm enjoying myself** estoy disfrutando

➤ **by myself** solo: **I did it by myself** lo hice solo.

**mysterious** [mɪ'stɪərɪəs] *adjective* ■ **misterioso**.

**mystery** ['mɪstərɪ] *(plural* **mysteries)** *noun* ■ **el misterio:** it's a real mystery es un verdadero misterio

➤ **a murder mystery** una novela policíaca.

**myth** [mɪθ] *noun* ■ **el mito:** the Greek myths los mitos griegos.

**mythology** [mɪ'θɒlədʒɪ] *noun* ■ **la mitología:** Greek mythology la mitología griega.

**nag** [næg] *(past tense & past participle* **nagged)** *verb* ■ **fastidiar, dar la lata** *informal*: **stop nagging me** deja de fastidiarme, deja de darme la lata.

**nail** [neɪl] *(noun & verb)*

■ *noun*

**1. el clavo:** he hammered a nail into the wall puso un clavo en la pared

**2. la uña:** he bites his nails se come las uñas

➤ **a nail file** una lima de uñas

➤ **nail polish** el esmalte de uñas

■ *verb*

**clavar:** she nailed the sign to the door clavó el cartel en la puerta.

**naked** ['neɪkɪd] *adjective* ■ **desnudo:** he was completely naked estaba completamente desnudo.

**name** [neɪm] *noun* ■ **el nombre:** he has a foreign name tiene un nombre extranjero

➤ **what's your name?** ¿cómo te llamas?

➤ **my name is Paul** me llamo Paul.

**nap** [næp] *noun* ■ **la siesta:** I took a nap me eché una siesta.

**napkin** ['næpkɪn] *noun* ■ **la servilleta:** a paper napkin una servilleta de papel.

**narrow** ['næroʊ] *adjective* ■ **angosto:** this street is very narrow esta calle es muy angosta.

**nasty** ['nɑːstɪ] *adjective*

**1. muy desagradable:** this cheese has a nasty taste este queso tiene un sabor muy desagradable

**2. malo:** she was nasty to him fue muy mala con él.

**nation** ['neɪʃn] *noun* ■ **la nación** *(plural* **las naciones)**.

**national** ['næʃənl] *adjective* ■ **nacional**

➤ **the national anthem** el himno nacional.

**nationality** [,næʃə'nælətɪ] *(plural* **nationalities)** *noun* ■ **la nacionalidad:** what nationality are you? ¿de qué nacionalidad eres?

**native** ['neɪtɪv] *(adjective & noun)*

■ *adjective*

**1. natal:** Chile is his native country Chile es su país natal

**2. materno:** English is my native language el inglés es mi lengua materna

➤ **a native English speaker** una hablante nativo de inglés

■ *noun*

➤ **she is a native of Mexico** es originaria de México

## NATIVE AMERICAN

Las tribus de aborígenes americanas que poblaban Estados Unidos antes de la llegada de los europeos reciben el nombre de **native american**. Cada una poseía su propia lengua y modo de vida. Muchos indios murieron combatiendo a los colonos europeos o bien por haber contraído alguna de las enfermedades que estos trajeron a América. Otros muchos fueron obligados a vivir en reservas, territorios apartados especialmente para ellos. A lo largo del siglo XX, el gobierno estadounidense ha procurado conceder más derechos a los grupos étnicos nativos de Estados Unidos; también ha ido mostrando cada vez mayor interés por su historia y su cultura tradicional.

**natural** ['nætʃrəl] *adjective* ■ **natural: I like to wear natural fibers** me gusta vestirme con fibras naturales; **it's natural to feel that way** es natural que te sientas así.

**naturally** ['nætʃrəlɪ] *adverb*

1. **naturalmente: naturally, I was angry** naturalmente, estaba enojado
2. **por naturaleza: she's naturally generous** es generosa por naturaleza.

**nature** ['neɪtʃəʳ] *noun* ■ **la naturaleza: I'm a real nature lover** soy un verdadero amante de la naturaleza; **he has a very kind nature** es amable por naturaleza
➤ **a nature reserve** una reserva natural.

**naughty** ['nɔːtɪ] *adjective* ■ **travieso: he's a naughty boy** ¡es un niño travieso!
➤ **they've been very naughty** se han portado muy mal.

**navy** ['neɪvɪ] *(noun & adjective)*

■ *noun*
**la marina: he's in the navy** está en la marina

■ *adjective*
**azul marino** *(plural* **azul marino***): she's wearing a navy skirt** tiene una falda azul marina
➤ **navy blue** azul marino.

**near** [nɪəʳ] *(adjective, adverb & preposition)*

■ *adjective*
**cercano: where is the nearest hospital?** ¿dónde está el hospital más cercano?
➤ **the nearest thing** lo más cercano: **she's the nearest thing to a mother I ever had** es lo más cercano a una madre que yo he tenido
➤ **in the near future** en el futuro próximo: **we're going to buy a house in the near future** vamos a comprar una casa en un futuro próximo
➤ **his story is nearer to the truth** su historia se acerca más a la verdad

■ *adverb*
**cerca: the station is very near** la estación está muy cerca

■ *preposition*
**cerca de: there's a supermarket near the school** hay un supermercado cerca de la escuela; **is there a restaurant near here?** ¿hay un restaurante cerca de aquí?
➤ **near to** cerca de.

**nearby** [nɪə'baɪ] *(adjective & adverb)*

■ *adjective*
**cercano: there was a fire in a nearby town** hubo un incendio en un pueblo cercano

■ *adverb*
**cerca: there's a school nearby** hay una escuela cerca.

**nearly** ['nɪəlɪ] *adverb* ■ **casi: it's nearly 8 o'clock** son casi las 8; **I nearly started laughing when she said that** casi me pongo a reír cuando dijo eso.

**nearsighted** [,nɪə'saɪtɪd] *adjective* ■ **corto de vista: she's nearsighted** es corta de vista.

**neat** [niːt] *adjective*

1. **ordenado: the house is very neat** la casa es muy ordenada
2. *informal* **fantástico, padre** *Mexico:* **that was a neat movie!** ¡ésa fue una película fantástica!

**neatly** ['niːtlɪ] *adverb* ■ **cuidadosamente: she writes very neatly** escribe cuidadosamente.

**necessary** ['nesəsrɪ] *adjective* ■ **necesario: I'll make the necessary arrangements** haré los arreglos necesarios.

**neck** [nek] *noun* ■ el **cuello**: she has a scarf around her neck tiene una bufanda alrededor del cuello.

**necklace** ['neklɪs] *noun* ■ el **collar**: she's wearing a gold necklace tiene puesto un collar de oro.

**nectarine** ['nektərɪn] *noun* ■ la **nectarina**.

**need** [niːd] *(noun & verb)*
■ *noun*
la **necesidad**: there is no need to go no hay necesidad de ir
➤ to be in need of something necesitar algo: the children are in need of medical attention los niños necesitan atención médica
■ *verb*
1. necesitar: he needs a new bike necesita una bicicleta nueva; I need to get some sleep necesito dormir un poco
2. *When need means "have to"*

> You can use the constructions **tener que** or **hay que** + infinitive to translate "need":

I need to leave right away tengo que irme ahora mismo; do we need to show our passports? ¿hay que mostrar los pasaportes?

> To translate "to not need to do something", you can use the Spanish construction **no tener que hacer algo** or the impersonal constructions **no es necesario que** or **no hace falta que**:

you don't need to wait no tienes que esperar; we don't need to pick him up no es necesario que lo pasemos a buscar.

**needle** ['niːdl] *noun* ■ la **aguja**: I can't find a needle to sew on the button no puedo encontrar una aguja para coser el botón.

**negative** ['negətɪv] *(adjective & noun)*
■ *adjective*
negativo: we got a negative answer nos dieron una respuesta negativa

■ *noun*
el **negativo**: he printed a photo from the negative sacó una copia de una foto usando el negativo.

**neigh** [neɪ] *verb* ■ **relinchar**: the horse neighed el caballo relinchó.

**neighbor** ['neɪbər] *noun* ■ el **vecino**, la **vecina**: he doesn't like his neighbors no le gustan sus vecinos.

**neighborhood** ['neɪbəhʊd] *noun* ■ el **barrio**: there are a lot of restaurants in the neighborhood hay muchos restaurantes en este barrio.

**neither** ['naɪðər, 'niːðər] *(conjunction, adjective & pronoun)*
■ *conjunction*
1. ni: it's neither good nor bad no es ni bueno ni malo; he's neither English nor American no es inglés ni americano
2. tampoco: he doesn't know and neither does she él no sabe y ella tampoco; she can't swim — neither can I ella no sabe nadar — yo tampoco
■ *adjective & pronoun*
ninguno: neither book is any good ninguno de los libros es bueno; neither of them came ninguno de ellos vino; which dress do you want? — neither ¿qué vestido quieres? — ninguno.

**neon** ['niːɒn] *noun* ■ el **neón**
➤ neon lights luces de neón.

**nephew** ['nefjuː] *noun* ■ el **sobrino**.

**nerve** [nɜːv] *noun*
1. el **nervio**: it's a disease that attacks the nerves es una enfermedad que ataca los nervios; she had an attack of nerves before the show tuvo un ataque de nervios antes del espectáculo
2. el **valor**: he didn't have the nerve to tell her the truth no tuvo el valor de decirle la verdad
3. el **descaro**: she had the nerve to come without being invited tuvo el descaro de venir sin ser invitada
➤ to get on somebody's nerves sacar de quicio a alguien: that guy really gets on my nerves ese tipo realmente me saca de quicio.

**nervous** ['nɜːvəs] *adjective* ■ **nervioso:** going to the dentist makes me nervous me pone nervioso ir al dentista; **she's a nervous driver** es un conductor nervioso

➤ **to be nervous** estar nervioso: **actors are often nervous before they go on stage** los actores generalmente están nerviosos antes de entrar al escenario

➤ **I'm nervous about speaking in public** me pone nervioso hablar en público

➤ **a nervous breakdown** una crisis nerviosa.

**nest** [nest] *noun* ■ **el nido: a bird's nest** un nido de pájaros.

**net** [net] *noun*

1. la **red**
2. **the Net** la red; **she spends hours surfing the Net** pasa horas navegando en la red

➤ **a fishing net** una red de pescar.

**network** ['netwɜːk] *noun* ■ **la red: a computer network** una red de computadoras.

**never** ['nevəʳ] *adverb*

1. **nunca: he never drinks** no toma nunca; **I've never been to Rome** no he estado nunca en Roma

> If **nunca** is used before the verb it is not necessary to use "no":

**I've never spoken with her** nunca he hablado con ella

2. **jamás: will you tell me your secret? — never!** ¿me dirás tu secreto? — ¡jamás!

➤ **all I can say about jogging is, never again!** todo lo que puedo decir sobre hacer "jogging" es ¡nunca más!

**new** [njuː] *adjective* ■ **nuevo: this is my new address** ésta es mi nueva dirección; **Harriet has a new boyfriend** Harriet tiene un novio nuevo; **there's a new moon tonight** hay luna nueva esta noche

➤ **I've got a brand new bike** tengo una bicicleta flamante

➤ **what's new?** ¿qué hay de nuevo?

**newborn** ['njuːbɔːn] *adjective* ■ **recién nacido: a newborn baby** un bebé recién nacido.

**newcomer** ['njuːˌkʌməʳ] *noun* ■ **el recién llegado, la recién llegada: we'd like to welcome any newcomers** quisiera darles la bienvenida a los recién llegados.

**news** ['njuːz] *noun*

1. **la noticia: do you have any news from him?** ¿tienes alguna noticia de él?; **I have some good news** tengo buenas noticias; **what bad news!** ¡qué mala noticia!
2. **las noticias: he's listening to the news on the radio** está escuchando las noticias en la radio

➤ **a piece of news** una noticia.

**newspaper** ['njuːzˌpeɪpəʳ] *noun* ■ **el periódico: I read the newspaper over breakfast** leí el periódico durante el desayuno.

**newsstand** ['njuːzstænd] *noun* ■ **el kiosco de periódicos**.

**New Year** [njuːˈjɪəʳ] *noun* ■ **I'll see you in the new year** te veré en el Año Nuevo

➤ **Happy New Year!** ¡Felíz Año Nuevo!

➤ **New Year's Day** el día de Año Nuevo

➤ **New Year's Eve** la noche de Fin de Año.

**New Zealand** [njuːˈziːlənd] *noun* ■ **Nueva Zelandia** *(feminine)*: **they're going to New Zealand** se van a Nueva Zelandia; **David lives in New Zealand** David vive en Nueva Zelandia.

**New Zealander** [njuːˈziːləndəʳ] *noun* ■

> In Spanish, a capital letter is not used for the inhabitants of a country or region:

**el neocelandés, la neocelandesa**.

**next** [nekst] *(adjective & adverb)*

■ *adjective*

1. **próximo: the big game is next week** el gran partido es la próxima semana; **I'll see you next Tuesday** te veré el próximo martes; **we're going to Jamaica next year** vamos a Jamaica el próximo año

**2.** **siguiente:** it's on the next page está en la página siguiente; **next, please!** ¡el siguiente, por favor!; **the next day was a holiday** el día siguiente era feriado

➤ **the next day she came to see me** al día siguiente vino a verme

**3.** **de al lado:** who's in the next room? ¿quién está en el cuarto de al lado?

➤ **next door** la puerta de al lado: **they live next door** viven al lado

➤ **our next-door neighbors** nuestros vecinos de al lado

➤ **next to** al lado: **the bank is next to the bookstore** el banco está al lado de la librería

➤ **next to nothing** casi nada: **it cost next to nothing** no costó casi nada

■ *adverb*

**después:** what happened next? ¿qué pasó después?

➤ **when I see him next I'll tell him** la próxima vez que lo vea se lo voy a decir.

**nice** [naɪs] *adjective*

**1.** **simpático:** Mrs. Thompson is very nice la Sra. Thompson es muy simpática

**2.** **bonito:** that's a nice dress ese es un vestido bonito

**3.** **lindo:** it's a nice day hace un lindo día

**4.** **agradable:** we had a very nice day pasamos un día muy agradable

**5.** **bueno:** dinner was nice la cena estuvo buena

➤ **have a nice time!** ¡que lo pases bien!

**nicely** ['naɪslɪ] *adverb*

**1.** **bien:** she was nicely dressed estaba bien vestida

**2.** **con buenos modales:** ask nicely! ¡pide con buenos modales!

**nickel** ['nɪkl] *noun* ■ el **níquel: a nickel is worth five cents** un níquel vale cinco centavos.

**nickname** ['nɪkneɪm] *noun* ■ el **apodo: his nickname is "Killer"** su apodo es "Killer".

**niece** [niːs] *noun* ■ la **sobrina**.

**night** [naɪt] *noun* ■ la **noche: did you have a good night?** ¿pasaste una buena noche?; **we danced all night** bailamos toda la noche

➤ **last night** anoche: **it happened last night at 8 o'clock** pasó anoche a las 8

**what did you do last night?** ¿qué hiciste anoche?

➤ **at night** de noche: **badgers come out at night** los tejones salen de noche

➤ **good night!** ¡buenas noches!

**nightclub** ['naɪtklʌb] *noun* ■ el **club nocturno: the band is playing at a nightclub** la banda toca en un club nocturno.

**nightgown** ['naɪtɡaʊn] *noun* ■ el **camisón** *(plural* los **camisones**).

**nightmare** ['naɪtmeəʳ] *noun* ■ la **pesadilla: I had a terrible nightmare** tuve una pesadilla espantosa.

**nighttime** ['naɪttaɪm] *noun* ■ la **noche: it's very noisy at nighttime** hay mucho ruido de noche.

**nine** [naɪn] *number* ■ **nueve: there are nine girls in the group** hay nueve niñas en el grupo; **Bill is nine** Bill tiene nueve años; **she went out at nine** salió a las nueve.

**nineteen** [ˌnaɪn'tiːn] *number* ■ **diecinueve: Lisa is nineteen** Lisa tiene diecinueve años.

**nineteenth** [ˌnaɪn'tiːn] *number* ■ **decimonoveno: it's her nineteenth birthday** es su decimonoveno cumpleaños

➤ **it's May nineteenth today** hoy es el 19 de mayo.

**ninety** ['naɪntɪ] *number* ■ **noventa: she's ninety** tiene noventa años

➤ **ninety-two** noventa y dos.

**ninth** [naɪnθ] *number* ■ **noveno: on the ninth floor** en el noveno piso

➤ **it's October ninth today** hoy es el 9 de octubre.

**no** [nəʊ] *(adverb & adjective)*

■ *adverb*

**no: do you like seafood? — no, I don't** ¿te gustan los mariscos? — no; **no, thank you** no, gracias

- *adjective*

> In Spanish **no** is not used before the noun but before the verb:

**she has no money** no tiene dinero; **there are no buses on Sundays** no hay autobuses los domingos; **there's no hope** no hay esperanza.

**nobody, no one** ['nəʊbədɪ, nəʊwʌn] *pronoun* ■ **nadie: nobody came** no vino nadie

> If **nadie** is used before the verb it is not necessary to use "**no**":

**nobody saw me** nadie me vio; **who did you see? — nobody!** ¿a quién viste? — a nadie; **there's no one in here** no hay nadie aquí adentro.

**nod** [nɒd] *(past tense & past participle* nod**ded**) *verb*
1. **asentir con la cabeza: I asked him if he was coming and he nodded** le pregunté si vendría y asintió con la cabeza
2. **saludar con la cabeza: he didn't say hello, but he nodded to me** no dijo "hola", pero me saludó con la cabeza.

**noise** [nɔɪz] *uncountable noun* ■ **el ruido: you're making too much noise** estás haciendo mucho ruido.

**noisy** ['nɔɪzɪ] *adjective* ■ **ruidoso: your computer is very noisy** tu computadora es muy ruidosa.

**none** [nʌn] *pronoun*
1. **ninguno: how many cards do you have left? — none** ¿cuántas cartas te quedan? — ninguna; **none of the pictures is for sale** ninguno de los cuadros está a la venta; **none of us won** ninguno de nosotros ganó.
2. *With uncountable nouns* **nada: do you have any money? — no, none at all** ¿tienes dinero? — no, no tengo nada; **there's none left** no queda nada.

**nonsense** ['nɒnsəns] *noun* ■ **las tonterías: you're talking nonsense** estás hablando tonterías

> **nonsense!** ¡tonterías!

**nonsmoker** [,nɒn'sməʊkə<sup>r</sup>] *noun* ■ **el no fumador, la no fumadora**.

**nonstop** [,nɒn'stɒp] *(adjective & adverb)*
- *adjective*
**sin escalas: we took a nonstop flight** tomamos un vuelo sin escalas
- *adverb*
**sin parar: I'm working nonstop** estoy trabajando sin parar.

**noodles** ['nuːdlz] *plural noun* ■ **los fideos**
> **egg noodles** fideos de huevo.

**noon** [nuːn] *noun* ■ **el mediodía: we're meeting at noon** nos vamos a encontrar al mediodía.

**no one** *pronoun* ➤ **nobody**.

**nor** ['nɔː<sup>r</sup>] *conjunction* ■ **ni: neither Fred nor Lucy is coming** ni Fred ni Lucy vienen.

**normal** ['nɔːml] *adjective* ■ **normal: that's quite normal** eso es bastante normal
> **we'll meet at the normal time** nos encontraremos a la hora de siempre.

**normally** ['nɔːməlɪ] *adverb* ■ **normalmente: I normally get up at 7 o'clock** normalmente me levanto a las 7.

**north** [nɔːθ] *(noun, adjective & adverb)*
- *noun*
**el norte**
- *adjective*
**norte** *(plural* **norte**): **she lives on the north coast** vive en la costa norte
> **North America** América del Norte: **Mexico is in North America** México está en América del Norte
> **the North Pole** el Polo Norte
- *adverb*
**norte: we are going north** vamos hacia el norte
> **north of something** al norte de algo: **Boston is north of New York** Boston está al norte de Nueva York.

**northeast** [ˌnɔːθəˈriːst] *noun* ■ el **nores-te: we headed northeast** nos dirigimos hacia el noreste; **the new train line runs through the Northeast** la nueva vía del tren va a través del noreste
➤ **the Northeast** el noreste.

**northern** ['nɔːðən] *adjective* ■ **del norte: Northern Europe** Europa del Norte.

**northwest** [ˌnɔːθəˈwest] *noun* ■ el **noroeste: we live in the northwest of the country** vivimos en el noroeste del país.

**nose** [nəʊz] *noun* ■ la **nariz** *(plural* las **narices)*: he has a big nose** tiene la nariz grande
➤ **to blow your nose** sonarse la nariz: **blow your nose!** ¡suénate la nariz!

**nosebleed** ['nəʊzbliːd] *noun*
➤ **she had a nosebleed after falling down** le sangró la nariz después de caerse.

**nosey** ➤ nosy.

**nostril** ['nɒstrəl] *noun* ■ la **fosa nasal**.

**nosy, nosey** ['nəʊzɪ] *adjective* ■ **entrometido: our neighbors are so nosy** nuestros vecinos son tan entrometidos
➤ **don't be so nosy!** ¡no seas tan entrometido!

**not** [nɒt] *adverb* ■ **no: he's not coming** no viene

> Por lo general **not** se usa en la forma contraída "-n't", en cuyo caso va unida al verbo que la precede:

**I don't think so** no lo creo; **Hank didn't come** Hank no vino; **are you coming or not?** ¿vienes o no?; **do you go out on Saturday nights? — not always** ¿sales los sábados de noche? — no siempre
➤ **I'm afraid not** me temo que no
➤ **not really** en realidad no: **do you want to come? — not really** ¿quieres venir? — en realidad no
➤ **not yet** todavía no: **are you ready? — not yet** ¿estás listo? — todavía no.

**note** [nəʊt] *(noun & verb)*
■ *noun*
la **nota: she's taking notes** está tomando nota; **I sent him a note** le mandé una nota

■ *verb*
**notar: please note that some products are out of stock** sírvase notar que algunos productos están agotados

**note down** *phrasal verb* ■ **anotar: she noted down the phone number** anotó el número de teléfono.

**notebook** ['nəʊtbʊk] *noun* ■ el **cuaderno**.

**notepad** ['nəʊtpæd] *noun* ■ el **bloc de notas** *(plural* los **blocs de notas)*.

**nothing** ['nʌθɪŋ] *pronoun* ■ **nada: I've got nothing to do** no tengo nada que hacer; **she has nothing left** no le queda nada; **did you see anything? — no, nothing!** ¿viste algo? — ¡no, nada!
➤ **I didn't pay for it, I got it for nothing** no lo pagué, lo conseguí gratis.

**notice** ['nəʊtɪs] *(noun & verb)*
■ *noun*
el **letrero: they put up a notice on the door** pusieron un letrero en la puerta
➤ **to take no notice of someone** no hacerle caso a alguien: **he took no notice of her** no le hizo caso

> ⚠ La palabra inglesa **notice** es un falso amigo, no significa "noticia"

■ *verb*
**darse cuenta: I didn't notice you standing there** no me di cuenta de que estabas parado ahí.

**noun** [naʊn] *noun* ■ el **sustantivo:** "dog," "London," and "happiness" are all nouns "perro", "Londres" y "felicidad" son todos sustantivos.

**novel** ['nɒvl] *noun* ■ la **novela: Katie is reading a novel** Katie está leyendo una novela.

**novelist** ['nɒvəlɪst] *noun* ■ el/la **novelista: Agatha Christie is a famous novelist** Agatha Christie es una famosa novelista.

**November** [nə'vembər] *noun*

In Spanish the months of the year do not start with a capital letter:

noviembre (*masculine*): **in November** en noviembre; **next November** el próximo noviembre; **last November** el pasado noviembre.

**now** [naʊ] *adverb* ■ **ahora: what shall we do now?** ¿qué haremos ahora?

➤ **from now on** de ahora en adelante: **I'll be more careful from now on** tendré más cuidado de ahora en adelante

➤ **any time now** en cualquier momento: **I'm expecting her any time now** la espero en cualquier momento

➤ **right now** ahora mismo: **get over here right now!** ¡ven aquí ahora mismo!

➤ **he should be here by now** ya tendría que estar aquí

➤ **now and then** de vez en cuando: **I still see him now and then** todavía lo veo de vez en cuando.

**nowadays** ['naʊədeɪz] *adverb* ■ **hoy en día: a lot of people work on computers nowadays** hoy en día mucha gente trabaja con computadoras.

**nowhere** ['nəʊweər] *adverb* ■ **where are you going? — nowhere** ¿adónde vas? — a ningún lugar; **there's nowhere to sit down** no hay ningún lugar para sentarse

➤ **nowhere near** lejísimos: **Seattle is nowhere near Atlanta** Seattle queda lejísimos de Atlanta.

**nuclear** ['njuːklɪər] *adjective* ■ **nuclear**

➤ **a nuclear bomb** una bomba nuclear

➤ **nuclear power** poder nuclear

➤ **a nuclear power station** una estación nuclear.

**nude** [njuːd] (*adjective & noun*)

■ *adjective*
**desnudo: they were completely nude** estaban completamente desnudos

■ *noun*
➤ **in the nude** desnudo: **she poses in the nude** posa desnuda.

**nudge** [nʌdʒ] *verb* ■ **codear: she nudged me** me codeó.

**nuisance** ['njuːsns] *noun* ■ **el pesado, la pesada: my little brother is such a nuisance** mi hermanito es un pesado.

**numb** [nʌm] *adjective* ■ **dormido: my hand has gone numb** tengo la mano dormida.

**number** ['nʌmbər] *noun* ■ **el número: what's your telephone number?** ¿cuál es tu número de teléfono?; **we live at number 210** vivimos en el número 210; **odd numbers and even numbers** números pares y números impares; **a large number of people** un gran número de personas; **your password should contain letters and numbers** tu pasaporte debe tener letras y números; **the numbers on the keyboard** los números en el teclado.

**numeral** ['njuːmərəl] *noun* ■ **el número: Roman numerals** números romanos.

**nun** [nʌn] *noun* ■ **la monja: she's a nun** es monja.

**nurse** [nɜːs] *noun* ■ **el enfermero, la enfermera: Sue is a nurse** Sue es enfermera.

**nursery** ['nɜːsərɪ] (*plural* **nurseries**) *noun*

1. **el vivero: I bought the plants at a nursery** compré las plantas en el vivero

2. **la guardería: there's a nursery for employees' children** hay una guardería para los hijos de los empleados

3. **el cuarto de los niños: the baby sleeps in the nursery** el bebé duerme en el cuarto de los niños

➤ **a nursery rhyme** una canción infantil

➤ **nursery school** kindergarten, jardín de niños *Mexico,* jardín de infantes *River Plate*

➤ **Amy goes to nursery school** Amy va al kindergarten.

**nut** [nʌt] *noun*

1. **la nuez** (*plural* **las nueces**): **the cake was topped with nuts** el pastel tenía nueces encima

**2.** la **tuerca**: the table is assembled with nuts and bolts la mesa está armada con tuercas y tornillos.

**nylon** ['naɪlɒn] *noun* ■ el **nylon**: a nylon shirt una camisa de nylon.

**oak** [əʊk] *noun* ■ el **roble**: an oak tree un roble; an oak table una mesa de roble.

**oar** [ɔːʳ] *noun* ■ el **remo**.

**oasis** [əʊ'eɪsɪs] *(plural* oases [əʊ'eɪsiːz]*) noun* ■ el **oasis** *(plural* los **oasis**).

**oatmeal** ['əʊtmiːl] *noun* ■ la **avena en copos**: I had oatmeal for breakfast desayuné avena en copos.

**oats** [əʊts] *plural noun* ■ la **avena**.

**obedient** [ə'biːdjənt] *adjective* ■ **obediente**: Fido's a very obedient dog Fido es un perro muy obediente.

**obey** [ə'beɪ] *verb* ■ **obedecer**: she has always obeyed her parents siempre ha obedecido a sus padres; you must obey the rules debes obedecer las reglas.

**object** ['ɒbdʒɪkt] *noun*

**1.** el **objeto**: what is that strange object? ¿qué es ese objeto raro?

**2.** el **objetivo**: the object of the game is to get rid of all your cards el objetivo del juego es deshacerse de todas las cartas.

**oblong** ['ɒblɒŋ] *adjective* ■ **alargado**: an oblong table una mesa alargada.

**oboe** ['əʊbəʊ] *noun* ■ el **oboe**: she plays the oboe toca el oboe.

**observation** ['aːbzər'veɪʃən] *noun* ■ la **observación** *(plural* las **observaciones**): the doctors are keeping her for observation los médicos la dejaron en observación; he made some intelligent observations hizo algunas observaciones inteligentes.

**observe** [əb'zɜːv] *verb* ■ **observar**: he carefully observed the procedure observó el procedimiento cuidadosamente.

**obsessed** [əb'sest] *adjective* ■ **obsesionado**: she's obsessed with the idea está obsesionada con la idea.

**obstacle** ['ɒbstəkl] *noun* ■ el **obstáculo**

➤ an obstacle race una carrera de obstáculos.

**obtain** [əb'teɪn] *verb* ■ **obtener**: he obtained permission to leave obtuvo permiso para irse.

**obvious** ['ɒbvɪəs] *adjective* ■ **obvio**: it was obvious that he was nervous era obvio que estaba nervioso.

**obviously** ['ɒbvɪəslɪ] *adverb*

➤ she's obviously right es obvio que tiene razón

➤ obviously he's not coming está claro que no va a venir.

**occasion** [ə'keɪʒn] *noun* ■ la **ocasión** *(plural* las **ocasiones**): he's been here on several occasions ha estado aquí en varias ocasiones; it's an important occasion es una ocasión importante.

**occasionally** [ə'keɪʒnəlɪ] *adverb* ■ **ocasionalmente**: I see her occasionally ocasionalmente la veo.

**occupation** [,ɒkjʊ'peɪʃn] *noun* ■ la **ocupación** *(plural* las **ocupaciones**): what is his occupation? ¿cuál es su ocupación?

**occur** [ə'kɜːr] *(past tense & past participle* occurred) *verb*
1. **ocurrir: the incident occurred yesterday** el incidente ocurrió ayer
2. **ocurrirse: it never occurred to me to call** nunca se me ocurrió llamar.

**ocean** ['əʊʃn] *noun* ■ el **océano: the Atlantic Ocean** el Océano Atlántico.

**o'clock** [ə'klɒk] *adverb* ■ **it's three o'clock** son las tres.

**October** [ɒk'təʊbər] *noun*

In Spanish the months of the year do not start with a capital letter:

**octubre** *(masculine)*: **in October** en octubre; **next October** el próximo octubre; **last October** el pasado octubre.

**octopus** ['ɒktəpəs] *noun* ■ el **pulpo**.

**odd** [ɒd] *adjective*
1. **raro: that's very odd** eso es muy raro
2. **impar: five is an odd number** el cinco es un número impar.

**of** [əv, ɒv] *preposition*
1. **de: in the middle of the street** en el medio de la calle; **he ate half of the cake** se comió la mitad del pastel; **there are thousands of people** hay miles de personas; **a pound of apples** una libra de manzanas; **a cup of coffee** una taza de café; **the ring is made of silver** el anillo es de plata
2. *Giving the date* **the 4th of July** el 4 de julio
➤ **some of them left early** algunos se fueron temprano
➤ **how many cups are there? — there are seven of them** ¿cuántas tazas hay? — hay siete
➤ **there are four of us** somos cuatro.

**off** [ɒf] *(adjective, adverb & preposition )*
■ *adjective*
1. **apagado: the lights are off** las luces están apagadas; **is the TV off?** ¿está apagada la tele?
2. **suspendido: the game is off** el partido está suspendido
➤ **he's off this week** tiene esta semana libre

■ *adverb*
**he took a week off** se tomó una semana libre; **it's my day off** es mi día libre; **he turned the light off** apagó la luz; **turn the tap off** cierra la llave; **the jeans are $10 off** los jeans tienen $10 de descuento
■ *preposition*
**he got off the train** se bajó del tren; **she took the book off the shelf** tomó el libro de la repisa; **the island is just off the coast** la isla está a poca distancia de la costa; **he's off work** no está en el trabajo.

**offend** [ə'fend] *verb* ■ **ofender: I didn't mean to offend you** no quise ofenderte.

**offense** [ə'fens] *noun* ■ la **infracción** *(plural* las **infracciones**): **he committed an offense** cometió una infracción
➤ **to take offense** ofenderse: **I think he took offense at what I said** creo que se ofendió por lo que dije.

**offer** ['ɒfər] *(noun & verb)*
■ *noun*
1. el **ofrecimiento: I appreciate the offer** aprecio el ofrecimiento
2. la **oferta: they made me a good offer** me hicieron una buena oferta
■ *verb*
**ofrecer: I offered her something to drink** le ofrecí algo para tomar
➤ **she offered to come with me** se ofreció a acompañarme.

**office** ['ɒfɪs] *noun* ■ la **oficina: Bill's office is down the hall** la oficina de Bill está por el pasillo; **he's at the office** está en la oficina
➤ **an office building** un edificio de oficinas.

**officer** ['ɒfɪsər] *noun* ■ el/la **oficial: he's an officer in the army** es un oficial de la armada
➤ **a police officer** un agente de policía.

**official** [ə'fɪʃl] *adjective* ■ **oficial: an official announcement** un anuncio oficial.

**offline** [,ɒf'laɪn] *adjective* ■ **fuera de línea: I'm working offline** estoy trabajando fuera de línea.

**often** ['ɒfn, 'ɒftn] *adverb* ■ **a menudo:** she often plays tennis juega tenis a menudo

➤ how often? ¿con qué frecuencia?: how often do you see her? ¿con qué frecuencia la ves?

**oil** [ɔɪl] *noun*

1. el **aceite:** tuna in oil atún en aceite; I'm having the car's oil changed le estoy haciendo un cambio de aceite a mi auto

2. el **petróleo:** they've found oil in the area encontraron petróleo en la zona

➤ an oil slick una mancha de petróleo

➤ an oil well un pozo petrolero.

**ointment** ['ɔɪntmənt] *noun* ■ **la pomada:** put this ointment on your skin ponte esta pomada en la piel.

**OK, okay** [,əʊ'keɪ] *adjective*

1. **okey:** do you want to come? — OK! ¿quieres venir? — ¡okey!; I'll see you tomorrow, OK? te veo mañana, ¿okey?

2. **bien:** how are you? — I'm OK! ¿cómo estás? — ¡estoy bien!

➤ is that OK with you? ¿te parece bien?

➤ how was the movie? — it was OK ¿qué tal la película? - no estuvo mal.

**old** [əʊld] *adjective*

1. **viejo:** it's an old house es una casa vieja; he's an old man es un hombre viejo

2. **antiguo:** that's my old school ése es mi antiguo colegio

➤ how old are you? ¿qué edad tienes?

➤ I'm 13 years old tengo trece años

➤ old age la vejez.

**older** [əʊldəʳ] *adjective* ■ (comparative of old) **mayor:** she's my older sister es mi hermana mayor; she's older than me es mayor que yo; he's three years older than me es tres años mayor que yo.

**oldest** [əʊldəst] *adjective (superlative of old)*

1. **mayor:** she's the oldest daughter in the family es la hija mayor de la familia

2. **más antigua:** it's the oldest church in the town es la iglesia más antigua del pueblo.

**old-fashioned** [,əʊld'fæʃnd] *adjective*

1. **pasado de moda:** she wore an old-fashioned coat usó un abrigo pasado de moda

2. **chapado a la antigua:** his parents are very old-fashioned sus padres son muy chapados a la antigua.

**olive** ['ɒlɪv] *noun* ■ **la aceituna**

➤ olive oil aceite de oliva

➤ an olive tree un olivo.

**Olympic** [ə'lɪmpɪk] *adjective* ■ **olímpico:** an Olympic champion un campeón olímpico

➤ the Olympics las Olimpíadas.

**omelette, omelet** ['ɒmlɪt] *noun* ■ **la omellete** *(plural* las **omelletes***).*

**on** [ɒn] *(adjective, adverb & preposition)*

■ *adjective*

1. **encendido:** the lights are on las luces están encendidas; the dryer is on la secadora está encendida

■ *adverb*

put the lid on ponle la tapa; I'm going to put a sweater on me voy a poner el sweater; what's on at the Ritz? ¿qué hay dan en el Ritz?; put the radio on prende la radio

■ *preposition*

1. **en:** he sat on a chair se sentó en una silla; the map is on the table el mapa está en la mesa; the information is on disk la información está en el disco duro; there's a picture on the wall hay un cuadro en la pared; she has a ring on her finger tiene un anillo en el dedo; what's on TV? ¿qué hay en la tele?

2. **a:** we went on foot fuimos a pie; my house is on the left mi casa está a la izquierda

3. *In time expressions*

When talking about days and dates, instead of a preposition use **el** or **los:**

I'm coming on Thursday vengo el jueves; she goes swimming on Tuesdays hace natación los martes; he left on May 17th se fue el 17 de mayo

4. **sobre:** it's a book on Australia es un libro sobre Australia

➤ I don't have money on me no llevo dinero encima

➤ **she's on the phone** está hablando por teléfono

➤ **I'm having a party on my birthday** voy a dar una fiesta para mi cumpleaños.

**once** [wʌns] *adverb*

1. **una vez:** once a day una vez al día

2. **antes:** this part of the city was once a village esta parte de la ciudad era antes una aldea

➤ **once more** una vez más: **I'd like to go once more** me gustaría ir una vez más

➤ **once and for all** de una vez por todas: **we'll have to solve this problem once and for all** tenemos que resolver este problema de una vez por todas

➤ **once in a while** de vez en cuando: **he comes to see me once in a while** viene a verme de vez en cuando

➤ **once upon a time** había una vez: **once upon a time there was a beautiful princess** había una vez una hermosa princesa

➤ **at once** enseguida: **I must leave at once** tengo que irme enseguida

➤ **at once** a la vez: **don't all speak at once** no hablen todos a la vez.

**one** [wʌn] *(number & pronoun)*

■ *number*
**uno**

**Uno** becomes **un** before masculine nouns:

**one day** un día; **chapter one** el capítulo uno; **one, two, three, go!** ¡uno, dos y tres!; **we have one dog and two cats** tenemos un perro y dos gatos; **there's only one plate** hay un plato solamente

➤ **one hundred** cien

■ *pronoun*

1. **uno, una:** one of those books is mine uno de esos libros es mío; **one of the girls is Mexican** una de las chicas es mexicana; **do you need a stamp? — no, I've got one** ¿necesitas un clip? - no, ya tengo uno; **I have two caps, you can have one** tengo dos gorras, puedes quedarte con una

2. *Referring to a particular person or thing* **which one?** ¿cuál?; **this one, not that one** éste, no aquél; **this bike is better than the old one** esta bici es mejor que la vieja

3. *Impersonal pronoun* **uno:** one never knows uno nunca sabe

➤ **they love one another** se aman el uno al otro.

**oneself** [wʌn'self] *pronoun*

1. **se:** to wash oneself lavarse; **to enjoy oneself** divertirse

2. **uno mismo:** to do something oneself hacer algo uno mismo

3. **sí mismo:** to talk about oneself hablar de sí mismo

➤ **by oneself** solo.

**one-way** [ˌwʌn'weɪ] *adjective*

➤ **a one-way street** una calle de un solo sentido

➤ **a one-way ticket** un boleto de ida, un boleto sencillo *Mexico*.

**onion** ['ʌnjən] *noun* ■ la **cebolla**.

**online, on-line** ['ɒnlaɪn] *(adjective & adverb)*

■ *adjective*
**en línea:** online help ayuda en línea; **she's online** está en línea

■ *adverb*
**en línea:** I love to shop online me encanta comprar en línea

➤ **to go online** conectarse.

**only** ['əʊnlɪ] *(adjective & adverb)*

■ *adjective*
**único:** he's the only friend I have es el único amigo que tengo

➤ **an only child** hijo único: **Susan is an only child** Susan es hija única

■ *adverb*
**sólo:** she only reads science-fiction sólo lee ciencia ficción; **there are only three seats left** sólo quedan tres sillas; **how much do you have left? — only twenty dollars** ¿cuánto dinero te queda? - sólo veinte dólares

➤ **not only** no sólo: **he's not only tall but he's good-looking too** no sólo es alto sino que también es buen mozo.

**onto** ['ɒntuː] *preposition* ■ he slammed his books down onto the table tiró los libros sobre la mesa; **he jumped onto the horse** se subió al caballo de un salto; **the house looks onto the park** la casa da al parque.

**174**

**onward** ['ɒnwəd] *adverb* ■ **en adelante**: read from page 50 onward lean de la página 50 en adelante.

**open** ['əʊpn] *(adjective, noun & verb)*

■ *adjective*
**abierto**: the door's open la puerta está abierta

➤ **wide open** abierto de par en par: **he left the window wide open** dejó la ventana abierta de par en par

■ *noun*
➤ **out in the open** al aire libre: **we slept out in the open** dormimos al aire libre

■ *verb*
1. **abrir**: I opened the door abrí la puerta; open the window! ¡abran la ventana!; the stores open at 9 o'clock las tiendas abren a las nueve
2. **abrirse**: the door opened and I walked in la puerta se abrió y entré.

**opera** ['ɒpərə] *noun* ■ **la ópera**.

**operate** ['ɒpəreɪt] *verb*
1. **hacer funcionar**: he can't operate the VCR no puede hacer funcionar el video
2. **operar**: the doctors operated on him but couldn't save him los doctores lo operaron pero no pudieron salvarlo.

**operation** [,ɒpə'reɪʃn] *noun* ■ **la operación** *(plural* **las operaciones***)*
➤ **to have an operation** operarse: **I'm going to have an operation on my knee** me voy a operar de la rodilla.

**operator** ['ɒpəreɪtər] *noun*
1. **el operador, la operadora**: I dialed the operator for assistance llamé al operador para que me ayudara
2. **el operario, la operaria**: he's a fork-lift operator es operario de carretilla elevadora
➤ **a switchboard operator** un telefonista de conmutador.

**opinion** [ə'pɪnjən] *noun* ■ **la opinión** *(plural* **las opiniones***)*: it's a matter of opinion es una cuestión de opinión
➤ **what's your opinion on this matter?** ¿tú qué opinas sobre este tema?
➤ **in my opinion** en mi opinión: **in my opinion, you should ask her to leave** en mi opinión, deberías pedirle que se fuera

➤ **an opinion poll** una encuesta de opinión.

**opponent** [ə'pəʊnənt] *noun* ■ **el/la oponente**: he's facing a tough opponent se enfrenta a un duro oponente.

**opportunity** [,ɒpə'tjuːnətɪ] *(plural* **opportunities***) noun* ■ **la oportunidad**: it will give you the opportunity to travel te dará la oportunidad de viajar.

**opposed** [ə'pəʊzd] *adjective*
➤ **to be opposed to something** estar en contra de algo: **she's opposed to nuclear weapons** está en contra de las armas nucleares.

**opposite** ['ɒpəzɪt] *(adjective, noun & preposition)*

■ *adjective*
**opuesto**: he went in the opposite direction se fue en la dirección opuesta
➤ **the bank is on the opposite side of the street** el banco está al otro lado de la calle
➤ **the opposite sex** el sexo opuesto
■ *noun*
**lo contrario**: the opposite of sad is happy lo contrario de triste es contento; **he always does the opposite of what he is told** siempre hace lo contrario de lo que le dicen
■ *preposition*
**frente a**: the school is opposite the station la escuela está frente a la estación.

**optician** [ɒp'tɪʃn] *noun* ■ **el óptico, la óptica**: she's an optician es óptica.

**optimistic** [,ɒptɪ'mɪstɪk] *adjective* ■ **optimista**: I'm not very optimistic no soy muy optimista.

**option** ['ɒpʃn] *noun* ■ **la opción** *(plural* **las opciones***)*: I have no other option no tengo otra opción.

**optional** ['ɒpʃənl] *adjective* ■ **optativo**: the German class is optional la clase de alemán es optativa.

**or** [ɔːr] *conjunction*
1. **o**: do you want tea or coffee? ¿quieres té o café?; are you coming or not? ¿vienes o no?; hurry up or we'll miss the train apúrate o vamos a perder el tren

**2. ni:** I can't come today or tomorrow no puedo venir hoy ni mañana; **he couldn't eat or sleep** no podía comer ni dormir.

**oral** [ˈɔːrəl] *adjective* ■ **oral**
➤ an oral exam un examen oral.

**orange** [ˈɒrɪndʒ] *(noun & adjective)*
■ *noun*
la **naranja**
➤ orange juice jugo de naranja
➤ an orange tree un naranjo
■ *adjective*
**naranja:** Bob's wearing an orange shirt Bob tiene puesta una camisa naranja.

**orchard** [ˈɒːtʃəd] *noun* ■ el **huerto de árboles frutales**.

**orchestra** [ˈɔːkɪstrə] *noun* ■ la **orquesta:** she plays in an orchestra toca en una orquesta.

**order** [ˈɔːdər] *(noun & verb)*
■ *noun*
**1. el orden:** the names are in alphabetical order las nombres están en orden alfabético; I hope everything is in order espero que todo esté en orden
**2. la orden** *(plural* las **órdenes)**: he gave me an order me dio una orden
**3. el pedido:** the waiter took our order el mesero nos tomó el pedido
➤ out of order fuera de servicio: the elevator is out of order el ascensor está fuera de servicio
➤ in order to para: he came back home in order to see his parents volvió a su casa para ver a sus padres
■ *verb*
**1. ordenar:** she ordered me to leave me ordenó que me fuera
**2. pedir:** Oliver ordered fish Oliver pidió pescado.

**ordinary** [ˈɔːdənrɪ] *adjective* ■ **normal:** it was an ordinary day fue un día normal
➤ Austin's just an ordinary guy Austin es un tipo del montón
➤ out of the ordinary fuera de lo común: I didn't notice anything out of the ordinary no noté nada fuera de lo común.

**organ** [ˈɔːgən] *noun* ■ el **órgano**.

**organic** [ɔːˈgænɪk] *adjective* ■ **orgánico:** I always buy organic food siempre compro comida orgánica.

**organization** [ˌɔːgənaɪˈzeɪʃn] *noun* ■ la **organización** *(plural* las **organizaciones)**: the Red Cross is an international organization la Cruz Roja es una organización internacional.

**organize** [ˈɔːgənaɪz] *verb* ■ **organizar:** we're organizing a trip to Canada estamos organizando un viaje a Canadá.

**original** [ɒˈrɪdʒənl] *adjective*
**1. original:** it's an original idea es una idea original
**2. primero:** who were the original inhabitants of the country? ¿quiénes eran los primeros habitantes del país?

**originally** [əˈrɪdʒənəlɪ] *adverb* ■ **en un principio:** the house was originally painted white en un principio, la casa estaba pintada de blanco.

**ornament** [ˈɔːnəmənt] *noun* ■ el **adorno:** there were many ornaments on the Christmas tree había muchos adornos en el árbol de Navidad.

**orphan** [ˈɔːfn] *noun* ■ el **huérfano,** la **huérfana:** she's an orphan es huérfana.

**orphanage** [ˈɔːfənɪdʒ] *noun* ■ el **orfanato,** el **orfanatorio** *Mexico*.

**ostrich** [ˈɒstrɪtʃ] la **avestruz** *(plural* las **avestruces)**.

**other** [ˈʌðər] *adjective & pronoun* ■ **otro:** the other shirt is dirty la otra camisa está sucia; I saw Darren the other day vi a Darren el otro día; they had other problems tenían otros problemas
➤ the other one el otro: I'll take the other one me llevo el otro
➤ the others los otros: the others are not coming los otros no vienen.

**otherwise** [ˈʌðəwaɪz] *(conjunction & adverb)*
■ *conjunction*
**si no:** go now, otherwise you'll miss your train váyanse ahora, si no van a perder el tren
■ *adverb*
**aparte de eso:** we couldn't do otherwise aparte de eso, no pudimos hacer otra cosa.

**ouch** [aʊtʃ] *exclamation* ■ ¡ay!: ouch, that hurts! ¡ay, eso duele!

**ought** [ɔːt] *verb*

"Ought" is translated by the verb **deber** in the conditional tense:

you ought to go to the dentist deberías ir al dentista; they ought to be here soon deberían llegar pronto.

**ounce** [aʊns] la **onza:** there are 16 ounces in a pound hay 16 onzas en una libra.

**our** [ˈaʊəʳ] *possessive adjective* ■ **nuestro**

In Spanish the possessive adjective agrees in number (singular or plural) with the noun that follows:

our dog is called Sammy nuestro perro se llama Sammy; our cousins live in Canada nuestros primos viven en Canadá

Use the definite article (el, la, los or las), not the possessive adjective, with parts of the body:

we brushed our teeth nos lavamos los dientes.

**ours** [ˈaʊəz] *possessive pronoun*
1. **nuestro**

In Spanish the possessive pronoun agrees in gender (masculine and feminine) and number (singular or plural) with the noun it replaces:

their house is big, ours is small la casa de ellos es grande, la nuestra es chica; their books are new, ours are old sus libros son nuevos, los nuestros, viejos

2. **nuestro:** this book isn't ours este libro no es nuestro; he's a friend of ours es nuestro amigo.

**ourselves** [aʊəˈselvz] *pronoun*
1. **nos:** we're enjoying ourselves nos estamos divirtiendo
2. **nosotros mismos:** we asked him ourselves nosotros mismos le preguntamos
➤ by ourselves solos.

**out** [aʊt] *adverb & preposition*
1. **afuera:** it's hot out afuera está caluroso; they're out in the garden están afuera en el jardín; come out here ven aquí afuera
2. **pasado de moda:** long skirts are out las faldas largas están pasadas de moda
➤ the lights are out se apagaron las luces
➤ she's out no está
➤ I'm going out voy a salir
➤ he ran out se escapó

**out of** *preposition*
1. *With verbs of motion* he walked out of the room salió del cuarto; get out of here! ¡salgan de aquí!; she jumped out of bed se levantó de la cama de un salto
2. **por:** she did it out of love lo hizo por amor
3. **de:** ten out of every twenty diez de cada veinte
➤ we drank out of china cups tomamos en tazas de porcelana.

**outdoor** [ˈaʊtdɔːʳ] *adjective*
1. **al aire libre:** outdoor sports deportes al aire libre
2. **descubierto:** an outdoor swimming pool una piscina descubierta, una alberca descubierta *Mexico*.

**outdoors** [aʊtˈdɔːz] *adverb* ■ **al aire libre:** we had lunch outdoors almorzamos al aire libre.

**outer** [ˈaʊtəʳ] *adjective* ■ **externo:** the outer layer is made of metal la capa externa es de metal
➤ outer space espacio exterior.

**outfit** [ˈaʊtfɪt] *noun* ■ el **conjunto:** that's a nice outfit ése es un conjunto bonito.

**outgrow** [ˈaʊtɡrəʊ] *(past participle* outgrow, *past tense* outgrew) *verb*
■ babies outgrow their clothes so quickly a los bebés la ropa les queda chica muy rápidamente.

**outing** [ˈaʊtɪŋ] *noun* ■ la **excursión** *(plural* las **excursiones***):* we're going on an outing to the museum vamos a salir de excursión al museo.

**outlaw** [ˈaʊtlɔː] *noun* ■ el **forajido,** la **forajida**.

**outlet** [ˈaʊtlet] *noun* ■ la **toma de corriente:** plug the computer into the nearest outlet enchufa la computadora en la toma de corriente más cercana.

**outline** [ˈaʊtlaɪn] *noun* ■ el **contorno:** you can see the outline of the tower puedes ver el contorno de la torre.

**outrageous** [aʊtˈreɪdʒəs] *adjective*
1. **escandaloso:** his behavior has been outrageous su comportamiento ha sido escandaloso
2. **exorbitante:** they charge outrageous prices cobran unos precios exorbitantes
3. **extravagante:** an outrageous hat un sombrero extravagante.

**outside** [aʊtsaɪd, ˌaʊtˈsaɪd] *(adjective, adverb, noun & preposition)*
■ *adjective*
**exterior:** the outside walls las paredes exteriores
■ *adverb*
[ˌaʊtˈsaɪd] **afuera:** wait for me outside espérame afuera
■ *noun*
el **exterior:** the outside of the box is red el exterior de la caja es rojo
■ *preposition*
**afuera de:** she lives outside the city vive afuera de la ciudad.

**outskirts** [ˈaʊtskɜːts] *noun* ■ las **afueras:** they live on the outskirts of Boston viven en las afueras de Boston.

**oval** [ˈəʊvl] *(adjective & noun)*
■ *adjective*
**ovalado:** an oval window una ventana ovalada

■ *noun*
el **óvalo.**

**oven** [ˈʌvn] *noun* ■ el **horno:** put the chicken in the oven mete el pollo en el horno.

**over** [ˈəʊvəʳ] *(adjective, adverb & preposition)*
■ *adjective*
➤ to be over terminar: finals are over on Friday los exámenes finales terminan el viernes
■ *adverb*
**más:** you have to be 5 feet or over to go on the ride tienes que medir 5 pies o más para subirte a los juegos
➤ I invited him over lo invité a casa
■ *preposition*
1. **encima de:** there's a light over the table hay una luz encima de la mesa
2. **por encima de:** he jumped over the fence saltó por encima de la cerca
3. **más de:** she's over forty tiene más de cuarenta
4. **durante:** it happened over the Christmas holidays esto sucedió durante las vacaciones de Navidad
➤ over here aquí: the store is over here la tienda queda aquí
➤ over there ahí: look over there miren ahí
➤ all over por todo: there were papers all over the floor había papeles por todo el piso
➤ it's all over now ya pasó todo.

**overalls** [ˈəʊvərɔːlz] *plural noun* ■ el **overol,** el **mameluco** *Southern Cone:* he wears overalls at work usa un overol para trabajar.

**overcame** *past tense* ➤ overcome.

**overcome** [ˌəʊvəˈkʌm] *(past tense* overcame [ˌəʊvəˈkeɪm]*, past participle* overcome) *verb* ■ **superar:** she tried to overcome the problem trató de superar el problema.

**overlook** [ˌəʊvəˈlʊk] *verb*
1. **dar a:** our room overlooks the sea nuestro cuarto da al mar
2. **pasar por alto:** she overlooked an important detail pasó por alto un detalle importante.

**overnight** [,əʊvə'naɪt] *adverb*

1. **durante la noche: we traveled overnight** viajamos durante la noche
2. **de la noche a la mañana: she changed overnight** cambió de la noche a la mañana
➤ **he stayed overnight** se quedó a pasar la noche.

**overseas** ['əʊvəsiːz] *(adjective & adverb)*

■ *adjective*
**extranjero: they are overseas students** son estudiantes extranjeros

■ *adverb*
**en el extranjero: she lives overseas** vive en el extranjero.

**oversleep** [,əʊvə'sliːp] *(past tense & past participle* oversleft*) verb* ■ **quedarse dormido: I overslept this morning** esta mañana me quedé dormido.

**overslept** *past tense & past participle* ➤ oversleep.

**overtime** ['əʊvətaɪm] *noun* ■ **las horas extra: she's doing overtime** está haciendo horas extra.

**overweight** [,əʊvə'weɪt] *adjective* ■ **demasiado gordo: being overweight is bad for your health** estar demasiado gordo es perjudicial para la salud.

**owe** [əʊ] *verb* ■ **deber: I owe him fifty bucks** le debo cincuenta dólares.

**owl** [aʊl] *noun* ■ **el búho, el tecolote** *Mexico.*

**own** [əʊn] *(adjective & verb)*

■ *adjective*
**propio: do you have your own bike?** ¿tienes tu propia bicicleta?; **I saw it with my own eyes** lo vi con mis propios ojos
➤ **on one's own** solo: **I'll do it on my own** lo haré solo

■ *verb*
**ser dueño de: she owns a car** es dueña de un coche

**own up** *phrasal verb* ■ **admitir tener la culpa**
➤ **own up to something** admitir algo: **he**

owned up to taking the money admitió que había robado el dinero.

**owner** ['əʊnər] *noun* ■ **el dueño, la dueña**.

**ox** [ɒks] *(plural* oxen ['ɒksn]*) noun* ■ **el buey**.

**oxygen** ['ɒksɪdʒən] *noun* ■ **el oxígeno**
➤ **an oxygen mask** una máscara de oxígeno.

**oyster** ['ɔɪstər] *noun* ■ **la ostra, el ostión** *(plural* los **ostiones***) Mexico.*

**oz.** ➤ ounce ε ounces.

**ozone** ['əʊzəʊn] *noun* ■ **el ozono**
➤ **the ozone layer** la capa de ozono.

**pace** [peɪs] *(noun & verb)*

■ *noun*
1. **el paso: she walked at a brisk pace** caminaba con paso enérgico
2. **el ritmo: he couldn't take the pace** no pudo mantener el ritmo

■ *verb*
➤ **to pace up and down** pasearse de arriba para abajo.

**Pacific** [pə'sɪfɪk] *noun* ■ **the Pacific** el Pacífico; **the Pacific Ocean** el océano Pacífico.

**pacifier** ['pæsɪfaɪəʳ] *noun* ■ el **chupe-te**, el **chupón** *(plural* los **chupones)** *Latin America except Southern Cone,* el **chupo** *Colombia*: **the baby dropped his pacifier** se le cayó el chupete al bebé.

**pack** [pæk] *(noun & verb)*
■ *noun*
1. el **paquete: a pack of cigarettes** un paquete de cigarrillos
2. la **manada: a pack of wolves** una manada de lobos
➤ **a six-pack** un paquete de seis: **I bought a six-pack of soda** compré un paquete de seis refrescos
■ *verb*
1. **hacer la maleta: he packed his bags** hizó las maletas
2. **abarrotar: the crowd packed into the stadium** la muchedumbre abarrotaba el estadio.

**package** ['pækɪdʒ] *noun* ■ el **paque-te: the mailman left a package for you** el cartero dejó un paquete para ti.

**packed** [pækt] *adjective* ■ **abarrotado: the train was packed today** el tren iba abarrotado.

**packet** ['pækɪt] *noun* ■ el **paquete: she bought a packet of seasoning mix** compró un paquete de condimentos variados.

**pad** ['pæd] *(noun & verb)*
■ *noun*
1. la **almohadilla: the seat has a thick pad for comfort** la silla tiene una almohadilla gruesa que la hace cómoda
2. el **bloc**
➤ **a pad of paper** un bloc de papel
■ *verb*
**acolchar: I padded the bottom to make it more comfortable** acolché la parte de abajo para hacerla más cómodo.

**paddle** ['pædl] *(noun & verb)*
■ *noun*
el **remo: he dropped his paddle into the water** se le cayó el remo al agua

■ *verb*
**remar**
➤ **to paddle a canoe** remar una canoa: **he was paddling the canoe** estaba remando la canoa.

**padlock** ['pædlɒk] *noun* ■ el **candado: he put a padlock on his bike** le puse un candado a la bici.

**page** [peɪdʒ] *noun* ■ la **página: turn the page** pasa la página.

**paid** [peɪd] *past tense & past participle*
➤ **pay.**

**pain** [peɪn] *noun*
1. el **dolor: I felt a sharp pain in my side** sentí un dolor agudo en el costado
2. la **lata** *informal* : **what a pain to have to do it again** ¡qué lata tener que hacerlo otra vez!
➤ **to be in pain** estar adolorido: **she's in a lot of pain** está muy adolorida
➤ **a pain in the neck** un pesado: **my little sister is a pain in the neck** mi hermanita es una pesada.

**painful** ['peɪnfʊl] *adjective* ■ **doloro-so: sunburn is very painful** la quemadura de sol es muy dolorosa.

**paint** [peɪnt] *(noun & verb)*
■ *noun*
la **pintura: wet paint** pintura fresca
■ *verb*
**pintar: he paints landscapes** pinta paisajes.

**paintbrush** ['peɪntbrʌʃ] *noun* ■ el **pincel**.

**painter** ['peɪntəʳ] *noun* ■ el **pintor,** la **pintora: Vincent's a painter** Vincent es pintor.

**painting** ['peɪntɪŋ] *noun*
1. la **pintura: she likes painting** le gusta la pintura
2. el **cuadro: it's a painting by Monet** es un cuadro de Monet.

**pair** [peəʳ] *noun* ■ el **par: a pair of shoes** un par de zapatos
➤ **a pair of pants** unos pantalones.

**pajamas** [pə'dʒɑːməz] *plural noun* ■ el **pijama**: he was still in his pajamas estaba todavía en pijama
➤ a pair of pajamas un pijama.

**pal** [pæl] *noun* ■ *informal* el **amigo**, la **amiga**.

**palace** ['pælɪs] *noun* ■ el **palacio**.

**pale** [peɪl] *adjective*
1. **pálido**: I was so pale at the end of the winter estaba tan pálido al final del invierno
2. **claro**: her dress was pale blue su vestido era azul claro.

**palm** [pɑːm] *noun*
1. la **palma**: she was holding an egg in the palm of her hand tenía un huevo en la palma de la mano
2. la **palmera**: a palm tree una palmera.

**pamphlet** ['pæmflɪt] *noun* ■ el **folleto**.

**pan** [pæn] *noun* ■ el **sartén** *(plural* los **sartenes)*: put the bacon in the pan pon el tocino en el sartén.

**Panama** [pænəmɑː] *noun* ■ **Panamá** *(masculine)*.

**pancake** ['pænkeɪk] *noun* ■ el **panqueque**, la **crepa** *Mexico*, el **panqué** *Central America, Colombia*, la **panqueca** *Venezuela*: I made pancakes for breakfast preparé panqueques para el desayuno.

**panda** ['pændə] *noun* ■ el/la **panda**.

**pane** [peɪn] *noun* ■ el **vidrio**: a pane of glass un vidrio.

**panic** ['pænɪk] *(noun & verb)*
■ *noun*
el **pánico**
■ *verb (past tense & past participle* panicked)
he panicked when the car broke down le entró el pánico cuando el coche se descompuso; **don't panic!** ¡tranquilos!

**pant** [pænt] *verb* ■ **jadear**: the dog was panting in the heat el perro jadeaba por el calor.

**panties** ['pæntɪz] *plural noun* ■ los **calzones**, las **pantaletas** *Mexico, Venezuela*: a pair of panties unos calzones.

**pants** [pænts] *plural noun* ■ los **pantalones**: a pair of pants unos pantalones.

**pantyhose** ['pæntɪhəʊz] *plural noun* ■ los **pantis**, las **pantimedias** *Mexico*, las **medias bombachas** *River Plate*, las **medias pantalón** *Colombia*.

**paper** ['peɪpər] *noun*
1. el **papel**: he wrote the number on a piece of paper escribió el número en un pedazo de papel; a paper bag una bolsa de papel
2. el **periódico**: David was reading the paper David estaba leyendo el periódico.

**paperback** ['peɪpəbæk] *noun* ■ el **libro en rústica**.

**paper clip** ['peɪpərklɪp] *noun* ■ el **clip** *(plural* los **clips**).

**parachute** ['pærəʃuːt] *noun* ■ el **paracaídas** *(plural* los **paracaídas)*: he came down in a parachute bajó en paracaídas.

**parade** [pə'reɪd] *noun* ■ el **desfile**: we watched the New Year's Day parades vimos el desfile del día de Año Nuevo.

**paradise** ['pærədaɪs] *noun* ■ el **paraíso**.

**paragraph** ['pærəgrɑːf] *noun* ■ el **párrafo**.

**Paraguay** ['pærəgwaɪ] *noun* ■ **Paraguay** *(masculine)*.

**parallel** ['pærəlel] *adjective* ■ **paralelo**: parallel lines líneas paralelas.

**paralyzed** ['pærəlaɪzd]          *adjective* ■ **paralítico**: she was paralyzed in a riding accident quedó paralítica en un accidente de equitación.

**pardon** ['pɑːdn] *noun*
➤ pardon? ¿cómo?, ¿mande? *Mexico*: pardon? — I said it's that way ¿cómo? - dije que era en esa dirección.

**parentheses** [pəˈrenθisiːz] *plural noun* ▪ el **paréntesis** *(plural* los **paréntesis)*: in parentheses entre paréntesis.

**parents** [ˈpeərənts] *plural noun* ▪ los **padres**.

**park** [paːk] *(noun & verb)*
- *noun*
  el **parque**: let's go to the park vayamos al parque
- *verb*
  **estacionar**: where can we park? ¿dónde podemos estacionar?; I parked the car estacioné el auto.

**parking** [ˈpaːkɪŋ] *noun* ▪ el **estacionamiento**
➤ no parking prohibido estacionar
➤ a parking lot el estacionamiento: the car is in the parking lot el coche está en el estacionamiento
➤ a parking meter el parquímetro
➤ a parking ticket una multa por estacionamiento indebido.

**parliament** [ˈpaːləmənt] *noun* ▪ el **parlamento**.

**parrot** [ˈpærət] *noun* ▪ el **loro**.

**parsley** [ˈpaːslɪ] *noun* ▪ el **perejil**.

**part** [paːt] *(noun & verb)*
- *noun*
  1. la **parte**: I like parts of the book me gustaron algunas partes del libro
  2. el **papel**: he plays a big part in the play tiene un papel importante en la obra
  3. la **pieza**: I bought some spare parts for the car compré unas piezas de repuesto para el coche
  4. la **raya**: she has a center part tiene la raya al medio
➤ to take part in something participar en algo: he took part in the race participó en la carrera
- *verb*
  **separarse**: they parted at the gates se separaron en los portones
➤ to part your hair peinarse con raya: she parts her hair in the middle se peina con raya al medio

**part with** *phrasal verb* ▪ **desprenderse de**: I had to part with my favorite sweater tuve desprenderme de mi suéter favorito.

**participle** [ˈpaːtɪsɪpl] *noun* ▪ el **participio**: the past participle el participio pasado.

**particular** [pəˈtɪkjʊləʳ] *adjective*
1. **en particular**: why do you need that particular book? ¿por qué necesitas ese libro en particular?
2. **exigente**: she's very particular about her clothes es muy exigente con la ropa
➤ in particular en particular: are you looking for something in particular? ¿estás buscando algo en particular?

**particularly** [pəˈtɪkjʊləlɪ] *adverb*
▪ **particularmente**: I'm not particularly interested in going no estoy particularmente interesada en ir.

**partner** [ˈpaːtnəʳ] *noun* ▪ el **socio**, la **socia**
➤ a business partner un socio comercial.

**part-time** [paːttaɪm] *adjective & adverb*
▪ **a tiempo parcial**: he has a part-time job tiene un trabajo a tiempo parcial; she works part-time trabaja a tiempo parcial.

**party** [ˈpaːtɪ] *(plural* parties) *noun*
1. la **fiesta**: we're having a party vamos a dar una fiesta; a birthday party una fiesta de cumpleaños
2. el **partido**: the Democratic party el partido demócrata
3. el **grupo**: how many people are in your party? ¿cuánta gente hay en tu grupo?

**pass** [paːs] *(noun & verb)*
- *noun*
  1. el **pase**: you need a pass to get in necesitas un pase para poder entrar; he made a pass to Owen le hizo un pase a Owen
  2. el **abono**: a bus pass un abono de autobús
  3. el **paso**: a mountain pass el paso de montaña
➤ a boarding pass la tarjeta de embarque, el pase de abordar *Mexico*

■ *verb*

1. **pasar:** can you pass me the salt? ¿podrías pasarme la sal?; **they played cards to pass the time** jugaron a las cartas solo para pasar el tiempo; **the evening passed quickly** la tarde pasó rápido; **what's the capital of Poland? — pass!** ¿cuál es la capital de Polonia? - ¡paso!

2. **pasar por:** I pass the museum on my way to school paso por el museo de camino a la escuela

3. **adelantar a, rebasar a** *Mexico*: he passed the car in front adelantó al coche de delante

4. **aprobar:** he passed his driving test aprobó el examen de manejar; **the law was passed last year** la ley fue aprobada el año pasado

**pass on** *phrasal verb* ■ **pasar:** can you pass the message on? ¿puedes pasar el mensaje?

**pass out** *phrasal verb* ■ **desmayarse:** she passed out se desmayó.

**passage** ['pæsɪdʒ] *noun*

1. **el pasaje:** it's an interesting passage from the book es un pasaje interesante del libro

2. **el callejón** *(plural* **los callejones***):* he walked along the passage caminó por el callejón.

**passenger** ['pæsɪndʒər] *noun* ■ **el pasajero, la pasajera.**

**passerby** [ˌpɑːsə'baɪ] *(plural* passersby [ˌpɑːsəz'baɪ]*) noun* ■ **el/la transeúnte.**

**passion** ['pæʃn] *noun* ■ **la pasión:** she has a passion for music siente pasión por la música
➤ **passion fruit** el maracuyá.

**passive** ['pæsɪv] *(adjective & noun)*
■ *adjective*
**pasivo**
■ *noun*
la **voz pasiva:** in the passive en voz pasiva.

**Passover** ['pɑːsˌəʊvər] *noun* ■ **la Pascua judía.**

**passport** ['pɑːspɔːt] *noun* ■ **el pasaporte.**

**password** ['pɑːswɜːd] *noun* ■ **la contraseña:** what's the password? ¿cuál es la contraseña?

**past** [pɑːst] *(adjective, noun & preposition)*
■ *adjective*
1. **último:** during the past few days durante los últimos días
2. **pasado:** the past tense el tiempo pasado
■ *noun*
el **pasado:** she often thinks about the past piensa a menudo en el pasado
➤ **in the past** en el pasado: there are more students now than in the past hay más estudiantes ahora que en el pasado
■ *preposition*
**por delante de:** we drove past the school pasamos en el coche por delante de la escuela
➤ **it's just past the church** queda pasando la iglesia
➤ **half past** y media: it's half past eight son las ocho y media.

**pasta** ['pæstə] *uncountable noun* ■ **la pasta:** pasta with tomato sauce pasta con salsa de tomate.

**pastime** ['pɑːstaɪm] *noun* ■ **el pasatiempo:** my favorite pastime is swimming mi pasatiempo preferido es la natación.

**pastry** ['peɪstrɪ] *noun*
1. *(plural* pastries*)* el **pastel:** we offer a selection of pastries ofrecemos una variedad de pasteles
2. **la masa:** she's making pastry for an apple tart está haciendo la masa para una tarta de manzana.

**pat** [pæt] *(past tense & past participle* patted*) (noun & verb)*
■ *noun*
la **palmadita:** he gave the boy a friendly pat on the shoulder le dio al niño una palmadita amistosa en el hombro
■ *verb*
**darle palmaditas a:** can I pat your dog? ¿puedo darle unas palmaditas al perro?

**183**

**patch** [pætʃ] (plural patches [pætʃɪz])
(noun & verb)
■ noun
1. el **parche**: his jeans had patches on the
knees sus jeans tenían parches en las rodillas
2. la **zona**: there were icy patches on the
road había zonas con hielo en la carretera
➤ to be going through a bad patch pasar
por una mala racha
■ verb
ponerle un parche a: she patched the
holes in her sweater le puso un parche a los
agujeros del suéter.

**path** [pɑːθ] noun ■ el **sendero**: this
path leads to the river este sendero lleva al
río.

**pathetic** [pəˈθetɪk] adjective ■ **malísi-
mo**: that's a pathetic excuse es una excusa
malísima.

**patience** [ˈpeɪʃns] noun ■ la **paciencia**: she has a lot of patience tiene mucha
paciencia.

**patient** [ˈpeɪʃnt] (adjective & noun)
■ adjective
**paciente**: he's very patient with the children es muy paciente con los niños
■ noun
el/la **paciente**.

**patiently** [ˈpeɪʃntlɪ] adverb ■ **pacientemente**: he waited patiently for her la
esperó pacientemente.

**patriotic** [ˌpeɪtrɪˈɒtɪk] adjective ■ **pa-
triótico**.

**patrol** [pəˈtrəʊl] noun ■ la **patrulla**:
the soldiers are on patrol los soldados
andan de patrulla
➤ a patrol car un coche patrulla, una patrulla
Mexico, un patrullero Peru, Southern Cone.

**pattern** [ˈpætən] noun ■ el **estampado**: I like the pattern on your dress me
gusta el estampado de tu vestido.

**pause** [pɔːz] (noun & verb)
■ noun
la **pausa**: there was a slight pause between songs hubo una breve pausa entre las
canciones

■ verb
**detenerse**: I paused before entering the
room me detuve antes de entrar al cuarto.

**pavement** [ˈpeɪvmənt] noun ■ el **pavimento**: the car skidded on the icy
pavement el coche patinó en el pavimento
cubierto de hielo.

**paw** [pɔː] noun ■ la **pata**: the dog
scratched himself with his paw el perro se
rascaba con la pata.

**pay** [peɪ] (past tense & past participle
paid) verb ■ **pagar**: I'll pay the bill pagaré
la cuenta; he's paid by the week le pagan
por semana
➤ to pay attention prestar atención: I
wasn't paying attention no estaba pres-
tando atención

**pay back** phrasal verb ■ **devolver el
dinero**: I'll pay you back later te devolveré
el dinero después.

**pay for** phrasal verb ■ **pagar**: I've already paid for the meal ya pagué la cena;
he paid 30 dollars for that shirt pagó
treinta dólares por esa camisa.

**paycheck** [peɪtʃek] noun ■ el **cheque
del sueldo**.

**payment** [ˈpeɪmənt] noun ■ el **pago**:
my car payments are $239 a month el pa-
go mensual por el coche es de 239 dólares.

**pay phone** [ˈpeɪfəʊn] noun ■ el **teléfono público**.

**PC** [ˌpiːˈsiː] (abbreviation of personal
computer) noun ■ la **PC**.

**pea** [piː] noun ■ la **arveja**, el **chícharo**
Central America, Mexico.

**peace** [piːs] noun ■ la **paz** (plural las
paces): they made peace hicieron las paces
➤ to leave somebody in peace dejar a
alguien en paz
➤ peace and quiet paz y tranquilidad: I came
here looking for peace and quiet vine
aquí buscando paz y tranquilidad.

**peaceful** ['piːsfʊl] *adjective*

1. **tranquilo:** it's a very peaceful town es un pueblo muy tranquilo
2. **pacífico:** we took part in a peaceful demonstration participamos en una manifestación pacífica
➤ it's very peaceful in the country hay mucha tranquilidad en el campo.

**peach** [piːtʃ] *(plural* peaches [piːtʃɪz]) *noun* ■ el **durazno**.

**peacock** ['piːkɒk] *noun* ■ el **pavo real**.

**peak** [piːk] *noun*

1. la **cumbre:** he reached the peak of the mountain llegó a la cumbre de la montaña
2. el **auge:** she died at the peak of her movie career murió en el auge de su carrera en el cine.

**peanut** ['piːnʌt] *noun* ■ el **maní** *(plural* los **maníes***) Central America, South America,* el **cacahuate** *Mexico*
➤ peanut butter mantequilla de maní, mantequilla de cacahuate.

**pear** [peəʳ] *noun* ■ la **pera**.

**pearl** [pɜːl] *noun* ■ la **perla:** she wore a pearl necklace tenía puesto un collar de perlas.

**pebble** ['pebl] *noun* ■ el **guijarro**.

**peculiar** [pɪ'kjuːljəʳ] *adjective* ■ **raro:** it has a peculiar smell tiene un olor raro.

**pedal** ['pedl] *(noun & verb)*

■ *noun*
el **pedal:** put your foot on the pedal pon el pie en el pedal

■ *verb*
**pedalear:** you have to pedal harder when you go up a hill tienes que pedalear más fuerte cuando vas de subida.

**pedestrian** [pɪ'destrɪən] *noun* ■ el **peatón** *(plural* los **peatones***):* this street is for pedestrians only esta calle es sólo para peatones
➤ a pedestrian area un área peatonal.

**pee** [piː] *verb* ■ *informal* hacer pipí *informal,* hacer del uno *Mexico, Peru:* I have to pee! ¡tengo que hacer pipí!

**peek** ➤ peep.

**peel** [piːl] *(noun & verb)*

■ *noun*
la **cáscara:** he ate the orange with the peel on se comió la naranja con cáscara
➤ take the peel off before you eat the fruit pela la fruta antes de comértela

■ *verb*
1. **pelar:** he's peeling the potatoes está pelando las papas
2. **despellejarse:** my skin is peeling me estoy despellejando

**peel off** *phrasal verb* ■ **despegar:** peel the label off despega la etiqueta.

**peep, peek** [piːp, piːk] *(noun & verb)*

■ *noun*
el **vistazo**
➤ to take a peep echar un vistazo: I took a peep into the kitchen to see how dinner was coming along eché un vistazo en la cocina para ver cómo iba la cena

■ *verb*
**espiar**
➤ no peeping! ¡no miren!

**peg** [peg] *noun* ■ el **gancho:** put your coat on the peg pon tu abrigo en el gancho.

**pen** [pen] *noun* ■ el **bolígrafo,** la **pluma atómica** *Mexico:* can I borrow a pen? ¿me prestas un bolígrafo?

**penalty** ['penltɪ] *(plural* penalties) *noun*
1. la **pena:** the death penalty la pena de muerte
2. *In sports* el **penalty,** el **penal**.

**pencil** ['pensl] *noun* ■ el **lápiz** *(plural* los **lápices***):* write your name in pencil escribe tu nombre con lápiz
➤ a pencil case un estuche de lápices
➤ a pencil sharpener un sacapuntas.

**pendant** ['pendənt] *noun* ■ el **colgante:** she's wearing a pendant tiene puesto un colgante.

**penguin** ['peŋgwɪn] *noun* ■ el **pingüino**.

**penknife** ['pennaɪf] *(plural* penknives [pennaɪvz]*) noun* ■ la **navaja**.

**penny** ['penɪ] *noun* ■ *(plural* **pennies***)* el **centavo**: do you have a couple of pennies? ¿tienes algunos centavos?

**pension** ['penʃn] *noun* ■ la **pensión** *(plural* las **pensiones***)*: the company will contribute to your pension la empresa va a hacer aportes para tu pensión.

**Pentagon** ['pentəgən] *noun* ■ the Pentagon el Pentágono

THE PENTAGON

El edificio del Pentágono, nombrado así por su forma, y que se encuentra en las afueras de la ciudad de Washington, es la sede de la secretaría de la defensa estadounidense. Muchas veces se habla del Pentágono para referirse al poder militar de los Estados Unidos en general. Parte del Pentágono fue destruida en los ataques terroristas del 11 de septiembre del 2001.

**penthouse** ['penthaʊs] *noun* ■ el **penthouse**.

**people** ['piːpl] *plural noun*
1. la **gente**

Gente is a singular noun and is used with a verb in the singular:

they're nice people es gente agradable; there are a lot of people here hay mucha gente aquí
2. las **personas**: there's enough room for ten people hay espacio suficiente para diez personas
➤ people say that... dicen que ...: people say that he's mean dicen que es tacaño
➤ English people los ingleses.

**pepper** ['pepər] *noun*
1. la **pimienta**: salt and pepper sal y pimienta
2. el **pimiento**: I'd like green peppers and mushrooms on the pizza me gusta la pizza con pimientos verdes y champiñones.

**peppermint** ['pepəmɪnt] *noun* ■ la **menta**.

**per** [pɜːr] *preposition* ■ **por**: it costs $10 per person cuesta $10 por persona.

**percent** [pɜːrsent] *adverb* ■ **por ciento**: 20 percent of the students are absent today hoy faltó el 20 por ciento de los alumnos.

**perfect** ['pɜːfɪkt] *adjective* ■ **perfecto**: the weather is perfect el tiempo está perfecto.

**perfectly** ['pɜːfɪktlɪ] *adverb* ■ **perfectamente**: she speaks Spanish perfectly habla español perfectamente
➤ I'm perfectly happy estoy muy contento.

**perform** [pəfɔːm] *verb*
1. **actuar**: he's performing in a play está actuando en una obra de teatro
2. **realizar**: a computer can perform several tasks at once una computadora puede realizar varias tareas a la vez.

**performance** [pəfɔːməns] *noun*
1. la **función** *(plural* las **funciones***)*: the performance lasts two hours la función dura dos horas
2. la **actuación**: the team's performance was excellent la actuación del equipo fue excelente
3. el **rendimiento**: the student's performance has been good el rendimiento de los alumnos ha sido bueno.

**perfume** ['pɜːfjuːm] *noun* ■ el **perfume**: she's wearing perfume tiene puesto perfume.

**perhaps** [pəhæps] *adverb* ■ **quizás**: perhaps you're right quizás tengas razón
➤ perhaps not quizás no.

**period** ['pɪərɪəd] *noun*
1. el **periodo**: a long period of drought un largo periodo de sequía
2. la **clase**: I have history next period la próxima clase es de historia
3. la **regla**: she has her period está con la regla

4. el **punto:** don't forget the period at the end of the sentence no olviden poner el punto al final de la frase.

**perm** [pɜːm] noun ■ la **permanente,** el **permanente** *Mexico:* she's going to get a perm se va a hacer la permanente.

**permanent** ['pɜːmənənt] *(adjective & noun)*
■ *adjective*
**permanente:** it's part of the museum's **permanent collection** es parte de la colección permanente del museo
■ *noun*
la **permanente,** el **permanente** *Mexico:* I'm getting a permanent me voy a hacer la permanente.

**permission** [pə'mɪʃn] noun ■ el **permiso:** she gave me permission to leave me dio permiso para irme.

**permit** *(noun & verb)*
■ *noun*
['pɜːmɪt] el **permiso:** his work permit has expired se le venció el permiso de trabajo
■ *verb*
[pə'mɪt] *(past tense & past participle **permitted**)* **permitir:** her parents won't permit her to travel alone sus padres no le van a permitir viajar sola
➤ smoking is not permitted no está permitido fumar.

**person** ['pɜːsn] *(plural **people**)* noun ■ la **persona:** there's room for one more person hay espacio para una persona más; it's $20 per person es $20 por persona
➤ in person en persona: she came to see me in person vino a verme en persona.

**personal** ['pɜːsənl] *adjective* ■ **personal:** it's a personal letter es una carta personal
➤ a personal stereo un walkman.

**personality** [ˌpɜːsə'næləti] *(plural **personalities**)* noun ■ la **personalidad:** he has a strong personality tiene una personalidad fuerte.

**persuade** [pə'sweɪd] *verb* ■ **convencer:** I persuaded him not to go out lo convencí de que no saliera.

**pessimistic** [ˌpesɪ'mɪstɪk] *adjective* ■ **pesimista.**

**pet** [pet] noun
1. el **animal doméstico:** do you have any pets? ¿tienes algún animal doméstico?
2. el **preferido,** la **preferida:** he's the teacher's pet es el preferido de la maestra
➤ a pet store una tienda de animales.

**petal** ['petl] noun ■ el **pétalo.**

**pharmacy** ['fɑːməsi] *(plural **pharmacies**)* noun ■ la **farmacia:** the pharmacy is open until 8 la farmacia está abierta hasta las 8.

**pheasant** ['feznt] noun ■ el **faisán** *(plural los **faisanes**).*

**philosopher** [fɪ'lɒsəfər] noun ■ el **filósofo,** la **filósofa:** Plato was a Greek philosopher Platón fue un filósofo griego.

**philosophy** [fɪ'lɒsəfi] noun ■ la **filosofía:** she's studying philosophy estudia filosofía.

**phobia** ['fəʊbjə] noun ■ la **fobia:** she has a phobia about spiders le tiene fobia a las arañas.

**phone** [fəʊn] *(noun & verb)*
■ *noun*
el **teléfono:** where's the phone? ¿dónde está el teléfono?
➤ to be on the phone estar hablando por teléfono: Fred's on the phone Fred está hablando por teléfono
➤ the phone book la guía telefónica, el directorio telefónico *Latin America except Southern Cone:* look up the number in the phone book busca el número en la guía telefónica
➤ a phone booth una cabina telefónica
➤ a phone call una llamada telefónica
➤ a phone number un número de teléfono: what's your phone number? ¿cuál es tu número de teléfono?
■ *verb*
**llamar por teléfono:** I have to phone my parents tengo que llamar por teléfono a mis papás

**187**

**phone back** *phrasal verb* ■ **volver a llamar**: I'll phone back tonight te vuelvo a llamar esta noche.

**phony, phoney** ['fəʊnɪ] *adjective* ■ **falso**: she gave a phoney name dio un nombre falso.

**photo** ['fəʊtəʊ] *noun* ■ la **foto**: he took a photo sacó una foto
➤ to take a photo sacarle una foto: he took a photo of me me sacó una foto.

**photocopy** ['fəʊtəʊ,kɒpɪ] *(noun & verb)*
■ *noun*
la **fotocopia**: I'll make a photocopy of the article voy a hacer una fotocopia del artículo
■ *verb*
*(past tense & past participle* **photocopied***)* fotocopiar: I photocopied the letter fotocopié la carta.

**photograph** ['fəʊtəgrɑːf] *noun* ■ la **fotografía**: she was taking photographs estaba sacando fotografías
➤ to take a photograph sacarle una fotografía: he took a photograph of the bridge le sacó una fotografía al puente.

**photographer** [fə'tɒɡrəfər] *noun* ■ el **fotógrafo**, la **fotógrafa**: she's a photographer es fotógrafa.

**photography** [fə'tɒɡrəfɪ] *noun* ■ la **fotografía**.

**phrase** [freɪz] *noun* ■ la **frase**
➤ a phrase book una guía de bolsillo para el viajero.

**physical** ['fɪzɪkl] *adjective* ■ **físico**: he does a lot of physical exercise hace mucho ejercicio físico
➤ physical education educación física.

**physician** [fɪ'zɪʃn] *noun* ■ el **médico**, la **médica**: he's a physician es médico.

**physics** ['fɪzɪks] *uncountable noun* ■ la **física**: physics is my favorite subject mi materia favorita es física.

**pianist** ['pɪənɪst] *noun* ■ el/la **pianista**: Mary's a pianist María es pianista.

**piano** [pɪ'ænəʊ] *noun* ■ el **piano**: Pete plays the piano Pete toca el piano.

**pick** [pɪk] *(noun & verb)*
■ *noun*
➤ go ahead, take your pick! ¡vamos, adelante, elige la que quieras!
➤ an ice pick un punzón para el hielo
■ *verb*
1. **elegir**: I picked the green shirt elegí la camisa verde
2. **recoger**: we went to pick apples fuimos a recoger manzanas
3. **cortar**: she's picking flowers está cortando flores
➤ to pick a fight buscar camorra
➤ to pick one's nose meterse los dedos en la nariz

**pick on** *phrasal verb* ■ **meterse con**: they're always picking on him in school siempre se están metiendo con él en la escuela.

**pick up** *phrasal verb*
1. **recoger**: he bent down and picked up the coin se agachó y recogió la moneda; I'll pick you up at the station te recogeré en la estación
2. **aprender**: she picked up a bit of Italian aprendió un poco de italiano.

**pickpocket** ['pɪk,pɒkɪt] *noun* ■ el/la **carterista**: beware of pickpockets ten cuidado con los carteristas.

**picnic** ['pɪknɪk] *noun* ■ el **picnic** *(plural* los **picnics***)*: we're going on a picnic nos vamos de picnic
➤ to have a picnic tener un picnic.

**picture** ['pɪktʃər] *noun*
1. el **cuadro**: she's drawing a picture está haciendo un cuadro
2. la **ilustración** *(plural* las **ilustraciones***)*: are there any pictures in this book? ¿hay ilustraciones en este libro?
3. la **foto**: I took a picture of him le saqué una foto.

**pie** [paɪ] *noun* ■ la **tarta**, el **pay**: I baked an apple pie hice una tarta de manzana.

**piece** [piːs] *noun*

1. el **pedazo**: a piece of bread un pedazo de pan; it fell to pieces se hizo pedazos
2. la **pieza**: I lost a piece of the jigsaw puzzle perdí una pieza del rompecabezas
➤ to take something to pieces desarmar algo
➤ a piece of furniture un mueble
➤ a piece of advice un consejo.

**pierced** [pɪəst] *adjective* ■ **perforado**: she has pierced ears tiene las orejas perforadas.

**pig** [pɪg] *noun*

1. el **cerdo**, el **chancho** *Andes, River Plate*: they keep pigs on the farm crían cerdos en la granja
2. el **glotón** *(plural los* **glotones**)*, la* **glotona**: you greedy pig! ¡mira que eres glotón!

**pigeon** ['pɪdʒɪn] *noun* ■ la **paloma**.

**piggyback** ['pɪgɪbæk] *adjective*
➤ to give someone a piggyback ride llevar a alguien a caballo: he gave me a piggyback ride me llevó a caballo.

**piggybank** ['pɪgɪbæŋk] *noun* ■ la **alcancía**, el **chanchito** *Andes, River Plate*, el **cochinito** *Mexico, Venezuela*.

**pigtail** ['pɪgteɪl] *noun* ■ la **coleta**: she wears her hair in pigtails usa coletas.

**pile** [paɪl] *(noun & verb)*

■ *noun*
el **montón** *(plural los* **montones**)*: she left her clothes in a pile on the floor dejó su ropa en un montón en el suelo; there was a pile of books on his desk había un montón de libros en su escritorio
■ *verb*
**apilar**: he neatly piled his clothes on the bed apiló cuidadosamente la ropa sobre la cama

**pile into** *phrasal verb* ■ **meterse**: we all piled into the van todos nos metimos en la furgoneta.

**pile up** *phrasal verb* ■ **amontonarse**: the dirty plates are piling up in the sink los platos sucios se están amontonando en el fregadero.

**pill** [pɪl] *noun* ■ la **píldora**: he swallowed the pill tragó la píldora.

**pillar** ['pɪlər] *noun* ■ el **pilar**: tall marble pillars held up the roof grandes pilares de mármol sostenían el techo.

**pillow** ['pɪləʊ] *noun* ■ la **almohada**.

**pillowcase** ['pɪləʊkeɪs] *noun* ■ la **funda**.

**pilot** ['paɪlət] *noun* ■ el/la **piloto**: Ted's father is a pilot el papá de Ted es piloto.

**pimple** ['pɪmpəl] *noun* ■ el **grano**: oh, no! there's a pimple on my nose! ¡ay, no! ¡tengo un grano en la nariz!

**pin** [pɪn] *(noun & verb)*

■ *noun*
el **alfiler**: she pricked her finger with a pin se pinchó el dedo con una alfiler
■ *verb*
**prender**: he had a rose pinned in his buttonhole tenía una rosa prendida en el ojal
➤ she pinned a sign on the bulletin board puso un letrero en el tablero de anuncios.

**PIN** [pɪn] *(abbreviation of* personal identification number*) noun* ■ el **número de identificación personal**.

**pinch** [pɪntʃ] *verb* ■ **pellizcar**: she pinched me on the arm me pellizcó el brazo.

**pine** [paɪn] *noun* ■ el **pino**
➤ a pine tree un pino.

**pineapple** ['paɪnæpl] *noun* ■ la **piña**, el **ananá** *River Plate*.

**pink** [pɪŋk] *adjective* ■ **rosa**: she's wearing a pink skirt tiene puesta una falda rosa
➤ bright pink rosa brillante.

**pint** [paɪnt] *noun* ■ la **pinta**: there are 2 pints in a quart hay dos pintas en una cuarto de galón.

**pipe** [paɪp] *noun*

1. la **cañería**: the pipes are frozen las cañerías están congeladas
2. la **pipa**: he smokes a pipe fuma pipa.

**pirate** ['paɪrət] *noun* ■ el/la **pirata**.

**pistol** ['pɪstl] *noun* ■ la **pistola**.

**pitch** [pɪtʃ] *(plural* pitches) *(noun & verb)*
■ *noun*
el **lanzamiento**: the mayor will throw the first pitch el alcalde va a hacer el primer lanzamiento
■ *verb*
**lanzar, pichear**: he pitched the ball to the catcher le lanzó la pelota al receptor.

**pitcher** ['pɪtʃər] *noun*
1. la **jarra**: I made a pitcher of tea hice una jarra de té
2. el **lanzador**, la **lanzadora**, el/la **pitcher** *(plural* los/las **pitchers**): the Mets have a new pitcher los Mets tienen un nuevo lanzador.

**pity** ['pɪtɪ] *(noun & verb)*
■ *noun*
1. la **compasión**: she did it out of pity lo hizo por compasión
2. la **lástima**: what a pity! ¡qué lástima!; it's a pity you didn't see it es una lástima que no lo hayas visto

Use a verb in the subjunctive after **lástima que**.

➤ she took pity on them se compadeció de ellos
■ *verb*
**compadecer**: I pity him lo compadezco.

**pizza** ['piːtsə] *noun* ■ la **pizza**
➤ a pizza parlor una pizzería.

**place** [pleɪs] *(noun & verb)*
■ *noun*
el **lugar**: can you save me a place? ¿podrías guardarme el lugar?; what is your place of birth? ¿cuál es su lugar de nacimiento?; a parking place un lugar para estacionar
➤ my place mi casa
➤ to change places cambiar de lugar: can I change places with you? ¿puedo cambiar de lugar con usted?
➤ to take place tener lugar: when did the game take place? ¿cuándo tuvo lugar el juego?
➤ all over the place por todas partes: he spilled milk all over the place derramó leche por todas partes

■ *verb*
**poner**: place your hands on the table pon las manos sobre la mesa.

**plain** [pleɪn] *(adjective & noun)*
■ *adjective*
1. **sencillo**: he's wearing a plain blue tie tiene puesta una sencilla corbata azul; he likes his food plain le gusta la comida sencilla
2. **liso**: a plain blue blouse una blusa azul lisa
3. **claro**: it's plain that he's lying es claro que está mintiendo
4. **poco agraciado**: she's rather plain es bastante poco agraciada
➤ plain yogurt yogurt natural
■ *noun*
la **llanura**: the battle took place on the plain la batalla tuvo lugar en la llanura.

**plan** [plæn] *(noun & verb)*
■ *noun*
1. el **plan**: what are your plans for the future? ¿qué planes tienes para el futuro?
2. el **plano**: she drew a plan of the house dibujó un plano de la casa
➤ to go according to plan salir según lo previsto: everything went according to plan todo salió según lo planeado
■ *verb*
**planear**: they're planning a surprise party están planeando una fiesta sorpresa
➤ to plan to do something tener planeado hacer algo: I'm planning to go to Europe tengo planeado ir a Europa.

**plane** [pleɪn] *noun* ■ el **avión** *(plural* los aviones): John has his own plane John tiene su propio avión.

**planet** ['plænɪt] *noun* ■ el **planeta**.

**plant** [plɑːnt] *(noun & verb)*
■ *noun*
la **planta**: I forgot to water the plants olvidé regar las plantas
■ *verb*
**plantar**: we are going to plant an apple tree vamos a plantar un manzano.

**plaster** ['plɑːstər] *noun* ■ el **yeso**
➤ his arm is in a plaster cast tiene el brazo enyesado.

**plastic** ['plæstɪk] *(adjective & noun)*

■ *adjective*
**de plástico: a plastic bag** una bolsa de plástico

■ *noun*
**el plástico: it's made out of plastic** es de plástico.

**plate** [pleɪt] *noun* ■ **el plato: the plates are in the cabinet** los platos están en el armario.

**platform** ['plætfɔːm] *noun*
1. **el andén** *(plural* los andenes*):* **the passengers are waiting on platform 2** los pasajeros esperan en el andén 2
2. **la tarima: there was a platform for the band** había una tarima para la banda.

**play** [pleɪ] *(noun & verb)*

■ *noun*
1. **la obra de teatro: she's acting in the school play** actúa en la obra de teatro de la escuela
2. **la jugada: that was a great play by the quarterback** fue una gran jugada del corebac

■ *verb*
1. **jugar: they're playing in the park** están jugando en el parque; **do you want to play chess?** ¿quieres jugar ajedrez?
2. **tocar: can you play the guitar?** ¿tocas la guitarra?
3. **poner: let's play a CD** pongamos un CD
➤ **to play a part in something** desempeñar un papel en algo: **she played an important part in the negotiations** desempeñó un papel importante en las negociaciones.

**player** ['pleɪəʳ] *noun* ■ **el jugador, la jugadora: he's a football player** es jugador de futbol americano
➤ **a piano player** un pianista.

**playful** ['pleɪfʊl] *adjective* ■ **juguetón** *(feminine* juguetona*):* **the kitten is very playful** el gatito es muy juguetón.

**playground** ['pleɪgraʊnd] *noun* ■ **el área de juegos**

> Feminine noun that takes **un** or **el** in the singular.

**we went to the playground in the park** fuimos al área de juegos del parque.

**plead** [pliːd] *(past tense* pleaded o pled) *verb* ■ **suplicar: I pleaded with him not to go** le supliqué que no fuera
➤ **to plead guilty/not guilty** declararse culpable/inocente: **the prisoner pled guilty to murder** el preso se declaró culpable del asesinato.

**pleasant** ['pleznt] *adjective* ■ **agradable: we spent a pleasant day at the beach** pasamos un día agradable en la playa.

**please** [pliːz] *(adverb & verb)*

■ *adverb*
**por favor: can you tell me the time, please?** ¿puede decirme la hora, por favor?; **please, tell me!** ¡por favor, dímelo!

■ *verb*
**complacer: you can't please all the people all the time** no puedes complacer a todo el mundo todo el tiempo.

**pleased** [pliːzd] *adjective* ■ **contento: she's not very pleased** no está muy contenta
➤ **pleased to meet you!** ¡encantado de conocerlo!

**pleasure** ['pleʒəʳ] *noun* ■ **el placer: she knits for pleasure** teje por placer
➤ **my pleasure!** ¡no hay de qué!: **thank you for your help — my pleasure!** gracias por la ayuda - ¡no hay de qué!

**plenty** ['plentɪ] *pronoun* ■ **de sobra: we have plenty of time** hay tiempo de sobra
➤ **there's plenty to eat** hay mucha comida
➤ **that's plenty** es suficiente.

**pliers** ['plaɪərz] *noun* ■ **los alicates: use the pliers to bend the end of the wire** usa los alicates para doblar la punta del alambre.

**plot** [plɒt] *(noun & verb)*

■ *noun*
1. **la conspiración** *(plural* las conspiraciones*):* **the plot to kill the president failed** fracasó la conspiración para matar al presidente
2. **el argumento: the film has a complicated plot** la película tiene un argumento complejo

■ *verb*
**conspirar: they're plotting against the king** están conspirando contra el rey.

**plow** [plaʊ] *(noun & verb)*
■ *noun*
el **arado**
■ *verb*
**arar**.

**plug** [plʌg] *noun*
1. el **enchufe**: put the plug back in the socket mete el enchufe en la toma de corriente
2. el **tapón** *(plural* los **tapones***)*: I pulled the plug out of the sink le saqué el tapón al fregadero

**plug in** | *phrasal verb* ■ *(past tense & past participle* **plugged in***)* **enchufar**: she plugged the television in enchufó la televisión.

**plum** [plʌm] *noun* ■ la **ciruela**.

**plumber** ['plʌməʳ] *noun* ■ el **plomero**, la **plomera**, el **fontanero** *Central America,* la **fontanera** *Central America,* el/la **gásfiter** *Chile:* he's a plumber es plomero.

**plural** ['plʊərəl] *noun* ■ el **plural**: in the plural en el plural.

**plus** [plʌs] *preposition* ■ **más**: 10 plus 5 equals 15 10 más 5 es igual a 15
➤ a **plus sign** el signo de más.

**p.m.** [ˌpiː'em] *adverb*
➤ at 3 p.m. a las 3 de la tarde
➤ at 8 p.m. a las 8 de la noche.

**pocket** ['pɒkɪt] *noun* ■ el **bolsillo**, la **bolsa** *Mexico:* she had her hands in her pockets tenían las manos en los bolsillos.

**poem** ['pəʊɪm] *noun* ■ el **poema**.

**poet** ['pəʊɪt] *noun* ■ el **poeta**, la **poetisa**.

**poetry** ['pəʊɪtrɪ] *noun* ■ la **poesía**: do you like poetry? ¿te gusta la poesía?

**point** [pɔɪnt] *(noun & verb)*
■ *noun*
1. la **punta**: she found a stick with a sharp point encontró un palo con una punta afilada
2. el **punto**: the point where the river divides el punto donde el río se divide; a meeting point un punto de encuentro; you get two points for each correct answer obtienes dos puntos por cada respuesta correcta
3. el **momento**: at that point, the police arrived en ese momento, llegó la policía
4. el **sentido**: what's the point of the game? ¿qué sentido tiene este juego?; I don't see the point of going no veo qué sentido tiene ir
➤ what's the point? ¿para qué?
➤ two point seven dos coma siete
➤ point of view punto de vista: what's your point of view? ¿cuál es tu punto de vista?
➤ to have a point tener un poco de razón: you have a good point there tienes un poco de razón en lo que dices
➤ to make a point of doing something asegurarse de hacer algo: I made a point of saying hello to her me aseguré de saludarla
➤ to get to the point ir al grano
➤ to miss the point no entender
■ *verb*
**señalar con el dedo**: she pointed at the tower señaló la torre con el dedo
➤ he pointed the gun at the guard apuntó al guardia con el arma

**point out** | *phrasal verb* ■ **señalar**: he pointed out the opera house to me me señaló el teatro de ópera; he pointed out that no one had paid señaló que nadie había pagado.

**pointed** ['pɔɪntɪd] *adjective* ■ **puntiagudo**: he's wearing pointed shoes tiene puestos unos zapatos puntiagudos.

**pointless** ['pɔɪntlɪs] *adjective* ■ **inútil**: it's pointless to try again es inútil intentarlo de nuevo.

**poison** ['pɔɪzn] *(noun & verb)*
■ *noun*
el **veneno**: arsenic is a poison el arsénico es un veneno
■ *verb*
**envenenar**: she poisoned her husband envenenó a su marido.

**poisonous** ['pɔɪznəs] *adjective* ■ **venenoso**: these mushrooms are poisonous estos hongos son venenosos.

**poke** [pəʊk] *verb*
➤ she poked me in the ribs me dio un codazo en las costillas

➤ she poked me in the eye me metió un dedo en el ojo.

**polar bear** ['pəʊləᵇbeəʳ] *noun* ▦ el **oso polar**.

**pole** [pəʊl] *noun* ▦ el **palo**: he stuck a pole in the ground clavó un palo en el suelo
➤ the pole vault el salto con garrocha
➤ the North Pole el Polo Norte
➤ the South Pole el Polo Sur.

**police** [pə'liːs] *plural noun* ▦ la **policía**: the police are on their way la policía está en camino
➤ a police car un coche patrulla, una patrulla *Mexico*, un patrullero *Peru, Southern Cone*
➤ a police officer un policía
➤ the police station la comisaría.

**policeman** [pə'liːsmən] *(plural policemen* [pə'liːsmən]*) noun* ▦ el **policía**: he's a policeman es policía.

**policewoman** [pə'liːsˌwʊmən] *(plural policewomen* [pə'liːsˌwɪmɪn]*) noun* ▦ la **policía**: she's a policewoman es policía.

**polish** ['pɒlɪʃ] *(noun & verb)*
▪ *noun*
la **cera**
➤ nail polish esmalte de uñas
➤ shoe polish betún, grasa para los zapatos *Mexico*
▪ *verb*
**lustrar, bolear** *Mexico*: he's polishing his shoes se está lustrando los zapatos.

**polite** [pə'laɪt] *adjective* ▦ **educado**: he's very polite es muy educado.

**political** [pə'lɪtɪkl] *adjective* ▦ **político**

POLITICAL PARTIES

🖎   En los Estados Unidos existen básicamente sólo dos partidos políticos: el partido demócrata y el partido republicano. Los demócratas tienen tendencias más liberales, mientras que los republicanos son más bien conservadores.

**politician** [ˌpɒlɪ'tɪʃn] *noun* ▦ el **político**, la **política**: he's a politician es político.

**politics** ['pɒlətɪks] *noun* ▦ la **política**: she's interested in politics le interesa la política.

**poll** [pəʊl] *noun* ▦ la **encuesta**
➤ an opinion poll una encuesta de opinión.

**pollen** ['pɒlən] *noun* ▦ el **polen**.

**pollute** [pə'luːt] *verb* ▦ **contaminar**: they fine any factories that pollute the river multan a las industrias que contaminan el río.

**pollution** [pə'luːʃn] *uncountable noun* ▦ la **contaminación**: pollution is a serious problem in the city la contaminación es un problema serio en la ciudad
➤ air pollution contaminación del aire.

**pond** [pɒnd] *noun* ▦ el **estanque**.

**pony** ['pəʊnɪ] *(plural ponies) noun* ▦ el **poni**.

**ponytail** ['pəʊnɪteɪl] *noun* ▦ la **cola de caballo**: she put her hair in a ponytail se hizo una cola de caballo.

**poodle** ['puːdl] *noun* ▦ el/la **caniche**, el/la **poodle** *Chile, Mexico*.

**pool** [puːl] *noun*
1. la **piscina**, la **alberca** *Mexico*, la **pileta** *River Plate*: he's swimming in the pool está nadando en la piscina
2. el **charco**: a pool of water formed under the leak se formó un charco debajo de la gotera
3. el **pool**: they're playing pool están jugando pool.

**poor** [pɔːʳ] *adjective*
1. **pobre**: they are very poor son muy pobres; poor thing! I hope she'll be all right ¡pobre! espero que esté bien
2. **malo**: that's a poor excuse ésa es una mala excusa

Malo becomes mal before a masculine singular noun:

the weather has been poor ha hecho mal tiempo.

**pop** [pɒp] (adjective, noun & verb)

■ adjective

**pop: she used to be in a pop group** solía estar en un grupo de música pop

■ noun

la **música pop: she likes listening to pop** le gusta escuchar música pop

➤ **the balloon made a loud pop** el globo hizo ¡pum!

■ verb

(past tense & past participle **popped**) **reventar: he popped the balloon** reventó el globo

**pop by** phrasal verb ■ **Annie popped by last night** Annie pasó por casa anoche.

**pop in** phrasal verb ■ **pasar un momento: I'll pop in and see you** voy a pasar un momento a verte.

**popcorn** ['pɒpkɔːn] uncountable noun ■ las **palomitas de maíz,** el **pochoclo** Argentina, las **cabritas** Chile.

**pope** [pəʊp] noun

➤ **the Pope** el Papa.

**poppy** ['pɒpɪ] (plural **poppies**) noun ■ la **amapola**.

**popular** ['pɒpjʊlər] adjective ■ **popular: he's a very popular singer** es un cantante muy popular

➤ **Janet's very popular** Janet le cae bien a todo el mundo.

**population** [ˌpɒpjʊ'leɪʃn] noun ■ la **población** (plural las **poblaciones**): **what is the population of Uruguay?** ¿cuál es la población de Uruguay?

**porch** [pɔːtʃ] noun ■ el **porche: let's sit outside on the porch** sentémonos afuera en el porche.

**pork** [pɔːk] noun ■ el **cerdo,** el **puerco** Mexico, el **chancho** Peru, Southern Cone, el **cochino** Venezuela: **we're having pork chops tonight** hoy vamos a cenar chuletas de cerdo.

**port** [pɔːt] noun

1. el **puerto: New York is a port** Nueva York es un puerto

2. el **oporto: a glass of port** una copa de oporto.

**portable** ['pɔːtəbl] adjective ■ **portátil: a portable TV** un televisor portátil.

**porter** ['pɔːtər] noun ■ el **maletero: the porter took our luggage** el maletero nos llevó el equipaje.

**portion** ['pɔːʃn] noun ■ la **porción** (plural las **porciones**): **they serve large portions at this restaurant** sirven porciones abundantes en este restaurante.

**portrait** ['pɔːtreɪt] noun ■ el **retrato: he painted a portrait of his father** pintó un retrato de su padre.

**position** [pə'zɪʃn] noun

1. la **posición** (plural las **posiciones**): **he changed position** cambió de posición; **what position does Kidd play?** ¿en qué posición juega Kidd?

2. la **situación** (plural las **situaciones**): **I'm in a difficult position** estoy en una situación difícil

➤ **to be in position** estar en posición

➤ **to get into position** ponerse en posición.

**positive** ['pɒzətɪv] adjective

1. **positivo: he has a positive attitude** tiene una actitud positiva

2. **seguro: I'm positive about it** estoy seguro de eso.

**possession** [pə'zeʃnz] noun

➤ **she took all her possessions with her** se llevó todas sus pertenencias.

**possibility** [ˌpɒsə'bɪlətɪ] (plural possibilities) noun ■ la **posibilidad: that's a possibility** ésa es una posibilidad.

**possible** ['pɒsəbl] adjective ■ **posible: is it possible to change the tickets?** ¿es posible cambiar los boletos?

➤ **as soon as possible** lo antes posible: **come and see me as soon as possible** ven a verme lo antes posible.

**possibly** ['pɒsəblɪ] adverb ■ **posiblemente: will you finish today? — possibly** ¿vas a terminar hoy? - posiblemente

➤ I can't possibly accept your money me es imposible aceptar tu dinero.

**post** [pəʊst] *(noun & verb)*

■ *noun*
el **poste**: the net is fixed between two posts la red está atada a dos postes

■ *verb*
**fijar**: he posted a sign on the door fijó un letrero en la puerta.

**postcard** ['pəʊstkɑːd] *noun* ■ la **postal**: I got a postcard from my friend recibí una postal de mi amigo.

**poster** ['pəʊstər] *noun* ■ el **póster** *(plural* los **pósters***)*: they put up posters advertising the concert pusieron pósters anunciando el concierto.

**postpone** [ˌpəʊst'pəʊn] *verb* ■ **posponer**: the meeting has been postponed pospusieron la reunión.

**potato** [pə'teɪtəʊ] *(plural* potatoes*)* *noun* ■ la **papa**
➤ potato chips las papas fritas.

**pottery** ['pɒtərɪ] *noun* ■ la **cerámica**: I'm taking a pottery class this semester estoy tomando clases de cerámica este semestre; she had a collection of colorful pottery tenía una colección de cerámica de muchos colores.

**poultry** ['pəʊltrɪ] *noun* ■ las **aves de corral**.

**pound** [paʊnd] *noun* ■ *(abbreviation* lb.*)* la **libra**: it weighs about two pounds pesa alrededor de dos libras.

**pour** [pɔːr] *verb*
1. **echar**: she poured the water into the glass echó el agua en el vaso
2. **llover a cántaros**: it poured all day and all night llovió a cántaros todo el día y toda la noche.

**poverty** ['pɒvətɪ] *noun* ■ la **pobreza**.

**powder** ['paʊdər] *noun* ■ el **polvo**
➤ baby powder el talco de bebé.

**power** ['paʊər] *noun*
1. el **poder**: a new party is in power un nuevo partido ocupa el poder; they took power by force tomaron el poder por la fuerza
2. la **fuerza**: the power of the explosion knocked him off his feet la fuerza de la explosión lo tiró al suelo
3. la **electricidad**: there was a power cut hubo un corte de electricidad
➤ nuclear power la energía nuclear
➤ a power plant una central eléctrica.

**powerful** ['paʊəful] *adjective*
1. **poderoso**: a powerful nation una nación poderosa
2. **potente**: it's a very powerful computer es una computadora muy potente.

**practical** ['præktɪkl] *adjective* ■ **práctico**: she's very practical es muy práctica
➤ a practical joke una broma: he played a practical joke on his teacher le hizo una broma a la profesora.

**practice** ['præktɪs] *(noun & verb)*

■ *noun*
1. la **práctica**: she needs practice le falta práctica
2. el **entrenamiento**: I've got football practice tonight tengo entrenamiento de fútbol esta noche
3. el **bufete**: she joined our practice after law school pasó a ser parte de nuestro bufete después de recibirse de abogada
➤ out of practice fuera de práctica: she's out of practice está fuera de práctica

■ *verb*
1. **practicar**: she needs to practice more necesita practicar más
2. **entrenar**: the team practices every Saturday el equipo entrena todos los sábados.

**praise** [preɪz] *(noun & verb)*

■ *noun*
el **elogio**: you deserve all this praise te mereces todos estos elogios

■ *verb*
**elogiar**: they praised us for our hard work nos elogiaron por nuestro duro trabajo.

**pray** [preɪ] *verb* ■ **rezar**: they prayed to God le rezaron a Dios.

**prayer** [preə<sup>r</sup>] *noun* ■ la **oración** *(plural* las **oraciones**): she was saying her prayers estaba rezando sus oraciones.

**precaution** [prɪ'kɔːʃn] *noun* ■ la **precaución** *(plural* las **precauciones**): we must take precautions tenemos que tomar precauciones.

**precious** ['preʃəs] *adjective*
1. **valioso**: water is a precious resource el agua es un recurso valioso
2. **querido**: my children are very precious to me mis hijos son lo más querido para mí
➤ a precious stone una piedra preciosa.

**precise** [prɪ'saɪs] *adjective* ■ **preciso**: can you be more precise in describing the mugger? ¿puedes ser más preciso al describir al atracador?

**precisely** [prɪ'saɪslɪ] *adverb* ■ **exactamente**: tell us precisely what happened cuéntanos exactamente lo que sucedió.

**predict** [prɪ'dɪkt] *verb* ■ **predecir**: we can't predict the future no podemos predecir el futuro.

**prefer** [prɪ'fɜː<sup>r</sup>] *verb* ■ **preferir**: which one do you prefer? ¿cuál prefieres?; she prefers chicken to fish prefiere el pollo al pescado.

**pregnant** ['pregnənt] *adjective* ■ **embarazada**: she's seven months pregnant está embarazada de siete meses.

**prehistoric** [ˌpriːhɪ'stɒrɪk] *adjective* ■ **prehistórico**: prehistoric animals animales prehistóricos.

**prejudice** ['predʒʊdɪs] *noun* ■ el **prejuicio**: he has a prejudice against women tiene prejuicios contra las mujeres.

**prejudiced** ['predʒʊdɪst] *adjective*
➤ to be prejudiced against somebody tener prejuicios contra alguien: he was prejudiced against foreigners tenía prejuicios contra los extranjeros.

**preparation** [ˌprepə'reɪʃn] *noun* ■ la **preparación** *(plural* las **preparaciones**): it takes a lot of preparation to get to that level necesitas mucha preparación para llegar a ese nivel
➤ to make preparations for something hacer preparativos para algo: they're making preparations for their trip están haciendo preparativos para el viaje.

**prepare** [prɪ'peə<sup>r</sup>] *verb* ■ **preparar**: she's preparing dinner está preparando la cena; she's preparing for her exam se está preparando para el examen.

**prepared** [prɪ'peəd] *adjective* ■ **dispuesto**: are you prepared to do it? ¿estás dispuesto a hacerlo?; Harry was prepared for anything Harry estaba dispuesto a todo.

**preposition** [ˌprepə'zɪʃn] *noun* ■ la **preposición** *(plural* las **preposiciones**).

**prescription** [prɪ'skrɪpʃn] *noun* ■ la **receta**: the doctor gave me a prescription for the pills el médico me dio una receta para las pastillas
➤ by prescription con receta médica: this medicine is only available by prescription este medicamento sólo lo venden con receta médica.

**present** *(adjective, noun & verb)*
■ *adjective*
['preznt]
1. **actual**: in the present circumstances en las circunstancias actuales
2. **presente**: I was present at the meeting estaba presente en la reunión
➤ the present tense el tiempo presente: put the verb in the present tense pon el verbo en el tiempo presente
■ *noun*
['preznt]
1. el **regalo**: he gave me a birthday present me dio un regalo de cumpleaños
2. el **presente**: I try to enjoy the present trato de disfrutar el presente
➤ at present en este momento: that color is not available at present este color no está disponible en este momento
■ *verb*
[prɪ'zent]
➤ to present someone with something entregarle algo a alguien: they presented her with a medal le entregaron una medalla.

**president** ['prezɪdənt] *noun* ■ el **presidente, la presidenta: he's the president of the United States** es el presidente de los Estados Unidos

### PRESIDENT'S DAY

 **President's Day**, que se festeja el tercer lunes de febrero, es la fecha en que se conmemoran los cumpleaños de dos de los presidentes estadounidenses más destacados, George Washington y Abraham Lincoln. Dado que ambos hombres nacieron en el mes de febrero, se designó un día para celebrarlos a los dos.

**press** [pres] *(noun & verb)*

■ *noun*
la **prensa: the press followed her every move** la prensa le seguía todos sus movimientos

■ *verb*
**apretar: you have to press the button** tienes que apretar el botón; **the potter pressed down on the clay** el ceramista apretaba la arcilla.

**pressure** ['preʃər] *noun* ■ la **presión** *(plural* las **presiones): she's under pressure** está bajo presión

➤ **to put pressure on somebody** presionar a alguien.

**presume** [prɪ'zju:m] *verb* ■ **suponer: I presume you're right** supongo que tienes razón.

**pretend** [prɪ'tend] *verb* ■ **fingir: I was just pretending** sólo estaba fingiendo; **he pretended to be surprised** fingió estar sorprendido

⚠ La palabra inglesa **pretend** es un falso amigo, no significa "pretender".

**pretty** ['prɪtɪ] *(adjective & adverb)*

■ *adjective*
**bonito: what a pretty dress!** ¡qué vestido más bonito!

■ *adverb*
**bastante: the book was pretty good** el libro era bastante bueno.

**prevent** [prɪ'vent] *verb* ■ **impedir**

➤ **to prevent someone from doing something** impedir que alguien haga algo: **she tried to prevent me from coming in** trató de impedir que entrara

The verb following **impedir que** must be in the subjunctive.

**previous** ['pri:vjəs] *adjective* ■ **anterior: it happened the previous Tuesday** pasó el martes anterior.

**prey** [preɪ] *noun* ■ la **presa**
➤ **a bird of prey** un ave rapaz.

**price** [praɪs] *noun* ■ el **precio: what price did you pay?** ¿qué precio pagaste?
➤ **a price tag** una etiqueta de precio.

**prick** [prɪk] *verb* ■ **pincharse: she pricked her finger** se pinchó el dedo.

**prickly** ['prɪklɪ] *adjective* ■ **espinoso: this cactus is prickly** éste es un cactus espinoso.

**pride** [praɪd] *uncountable noun* ■ el **orgullo: she looked at her daughter with pride** miró a su hija con orgullo; **it hurt his pride** hirió su orgullo.

**priest** [pri:st] *noun* ■ el **sacerdote: he's a priest** es sacerdote.

**prime minister** [praɪm'mɪnɪstər] *noun* ■ el **primer ministro, la primera ministra.**

**prince** [prɪns] *noun* ■ el **príncipe.**

**princess** [prɪn'ses] *noun* ■ la **princesa.**

**principal** ['prɪnsəpl] *(adjective & noun)*

■ *adjective*
**principal: that's the principal reason** ésa es la razón principal

■ *noun*
el **director: the teacher sent him to the principal's office** la profesora lo mandó a la oficina del director.

**principle** ['prɪnsəpl] *noun* ■ el **principio: lying goes against all my principles** mentir va contra todos mis principios.

**print** [prɪnt] (noun & verb)

■ noun

1. la **letra**: the sign was written in large print el letrero estaba escrito con letra grande
2. la **copia**: I want to make a print from the negative quiero sacar una copia del negativo
3. la **huella**: the police took his prints la policía le tomó las huellas

■ verb

1. **imprimir**: I printed the letter imprimí la carta
2. **escribir con letra de imprenta**: print your name escriba su nombre con letra de imprenta.

**printer** ['prɪntər] noun ■ la **impresora**: turn the printer on enciende la impresora.

**prison** ['prɪzn] noun ■ la **cárcel**: he's in prison está en la cárcel

➤ they sent him to prison lo encarcelaron.

**prisoner** ['prɪznər] noun ■ el **prisionero**: he was taken prisoner lo hicieron prisionero

➤ a prisoner of war un prisionero de guerra.

**private** ['praɪvɪt] (adjective & noun)

■ adjective

**privado**: he doesn't talk much about his private life no habla mucho sobre su vida privada; he flew in on his private jet voló en su avión privado; can we discuss this somewhere more private? ¿podemos discutir esto en algún lugar más privado?

➤ a private detective un detective privado
➤ private property propiedad privada
➤ a private school un colegio privado

■ noun

el **soldado**: Private Jones el soldado Jones

➤ in private en privado: I need to talk to you in private tengo que hablarte en privado.

**privately** ['praɪvɪtlɪ] adverb ■ **en privado**: she told me privately me lo contó en privado.

**privilege** ['prɪvɪlɪdʒ] noun ■ el **privilegio**: sitting with the dean is a real privilege sentarse con el decano es un verdadero privilegio.

**prize** [praɪz] noun ■ el **premio**: she won first prize ganó el primer premio.

**probably** ['prɒbəblɪ] adverb ■ **probablemente**: he'll probably come tonight probablemente venga esta noche; are you going? — probably not ¿vas a ir? — probablemente no.

**problem** ['prɒbləm] noun ■ el **problema**: what's the problem? ¿algún problema?; the roadwork on I-10 is likely to cause problems es probable que las obras en la ruta I-10 causen problemas

➤ no problem! ¡no hay problema!

**process** ['prəʊses] (noun & verb)

■ noun

el **proceso**

➤ to be in the process of doing something estar haciendo algo
➤ she's in the process of painting the house está pintando la casa

■ verb

**procesar**: the computer can process a lot of data la computadora puede procesar muchos datos.

**produce** [prə'djuːs] verb ■ **producir**: these toys are produced in China en China producen estos juguetes.

**producer** [prə'djuːsər] noun ■ el **productor**, la **productora**: he's a television producer es productor de televisión.

**product** ['prɒdʌkt] noun ■ el **producto**: they're bringing out a new product van a sacar un nuevo producto.

**production** [prə'dʌkʃn] noun ■ la **producción** (plural las **producciones**): the new machines will increase production las nuevas máquinas aumentarán la producción; the film is a multinational production la película es una producción multinacional.

**profession** [prə'feʃn] noun ■ la **profesión** (plural las **profesiones**): what is your profession? ¿cuál es tu profesión?

**professional** [prə'feʃənl] (adjective & noun)

■ *adjective*
**profesional: he's a professional photographer** es fotógrafo profesional
■ *noun*
**el/la profesional: we hired a professional to install the lighting** contratamos a un profesional para instalar la iluminación.

**professor** [prə'fesəʳ] *noun* ■ el **catedrático, la catedrática: she's a professor at Yale** es catedrática en Yale.

**profit** ['prɒfɪt] *noun* ■ la **ganancia: they made a large profit** obtuvieron grandes ganancias.

**program** ['prəʊɡræm] *(noun & verb)*
■ *noun*
**el programa: a computer program** un programa de computadora; **a TV program** un programa de televisión; **I picked up a program before the performance** agarré un programa antes de la función
■ *verb*
*(past tense & past participle* **programmed)**
**programar: do you know how to program a computer?** ¿sabes programar una computadora?

**progress** ['prəʊɡres] *noun* ■ el **progreso: we made good progress on our science project** hicimos bastantes progresos en nuestro proyecto científico.

**project** ['prɒdʒekt] *noun* ■ el **proyecto: we're doing a project on rainforests** estamos haciendo un proyecto sobre las selvas tropicales
➤ **a housing project** un complejo de viviendas subvencionadas, un complejo de viviendas de interés social *Mexico*.

**prom** [prɑːm] *noun* ■ *baile de las escuelas secundarias*

PROM

✎ **Prom** es el baile formal que se celebra cada primavera en las escuelas secundarias de Estados Unidos. Es indudablemente el evento social más importante del año escolar. Muchos jóvenes gastan mucho dinero en sus vestidos y trajes y en el alquiler de limusinas para esa noche.

**promise** ['prɒmɪs] *(noun & verb)*
■ *noun*
**la promesa: Tanya kept her promise** Tania cumplió su promesa
■ *verb*
**prometer: I promised to help her** prometí ayudarla.

**promote** [prə'məʊt] *verb*
1. **promocionar: he's promoting his new movie** está promocionando su nueva película
2. **ascender**
➤ **to be promoted** ser ascendido: **I've been promoted to vice-president** me han ascendido a vicepresidente.

**promotion** [prə'məʊʃn] *noun* ■ el **ascenso: she got a promotion at work** obtuvo un ascenso en el trabajo.

**pronoun** ['prəʊnaʊn] *noun* ■ el **pronombre: "he" is a personal pronoun** "él" es un pronombre personal.

**pronunciation** [prə,nʌnsɪ'eɪʃn] *noun*
■ la **pronunciación** *(plural* las **pronunciaciones)**: **her pronunciation is very good** su pronunciación es muy buena.

**proof** [pruːf] *uncountable noun* ■ la **prueba: do you have any proof?** ¿tienes alguna prueba?

**proper** ['prɒpəʳ] *adjective* ■ **correcto: I'll show you the proper way to do it** te mostraré la manera correcta de hacerlo.

**properly** ['prɒpəlɪ] *adverb* ■ **correctamente: you're not doing it properly** no lo estás haciendo correctamente.

**property** ['prɒpətɪ] *(plural* **properties)** *noun* ■ la **propiedad: the sign says "private property"** el cartel dice "propiedad privada"
➤ **personal property** bienes personales
➤ **public property** propiedad pública.

**proposal** [prə'pəʊzl] *noun* ■ la **propuesta: she has a new building proposal** tiene una nueva propuesta de construcción; **she accepted his marriage proposal** aceptó su propuesta de matrimonio.

**propose** [prə'pəʊz] *verb* ■ **proponer:** he's proposing a new way of doing things propone una nueva manera de hacer las cosas

➤ to propose to someone proponerle matrimonio a alguien: he got down on one knee and proposed to her se puso en una rodilla y le propuso matrimonio.

**protect** [prə'tekt] *verb* ■ **proteger:** a helmet will protect you if you fall un casco te protegerá si te caes.

**protection** [prə'tekʃn] *noun* ■ la **protección:** he brought a gun for protection trajo un arma como protección.

**protein** ['prəʊtiːn] *noun* ■ la **proteína.**

**protest** *(noun & verb)*

■ *noun*
['prəʊtest] la **protesta:** she did it as a sign of protest lo hizo en señal de protesta

■ *verb*
[prə'test] **protestar:** many people are protesting against the new law mucha gente está protestando contra la nueva ley.

**Protestant** ['prɒtɪstənt] *adjective & noun* ■ el/la **protestante.**

**proud** [praʊd] *adjective* ■ **orgulloso:** he's proud of his son está orgulloso de su hijo.

**prove** [pruːv] *(past participle* proved, *past participle* proven) *verb* ■ **probar:** I can't prove he's lying no puedo probar que miente.

**proverb** ['prɒvɜːb] *noun* ■ el **proverbio.**

**provide** [prə'vaɪd] *verb*

➤ to provide something for someone proporcionarle algo a alguien: they provided a home for the orphans les proporcionaron un hogar a los huérfanos.

 **provided** [prə'vaɪdɪd] *conjunction* ■ **siempre que:** she'll do the work provided they pay her hará el trabajo siempre que le paguen

The verb following **siempre que** must be in the subjunctive.

**prune** [pruːn] *noun* ■ la **ciruela pasa.**

**pseudonym** ['sjuːdənɪm] *noun* ■ el **seudónimo.**

**psychiatrist** [saɪ'kaɪətrɪst] *noun* ■ el/la **psiquiatra:** she's a psychiatrist es psiquiatra.

**psychologist** [saɪ'kɒlədʒɪst] *noun* ■ el **psicólogo,** la **psicóloga:** he's a psychologist es psicólogo.

**public** ['pʌblɪk] *(adjective & noun)*

■ *adjective*
**público:** this is a public place éste es un lugar público
➤ **public opinion** la opinión pública
➤ **public school** la escuela pública

■ *noun*
➤ **the public** el público: the museum isn't open to the public today el museo no está abierto al público hoy
➤ **in public** en público: I don't like singing in public no me gusta cantar en público.

**publicity** [pʌb'lɪsɪtɪ] *uncountable noun* ■ la **publicidad:** her new video got a lot of publicity su nuevo video tuvo mucha publicidad.

**publish** ['pʌblɪʃ] *verb* ■ **publicar.**

**pudding** ['pʊdɪŋ] *noun* ■ el **budín** *(plural* los **budines):** chocolate pudding budín de chocolate.

**puddle** ['pʌdl] *noun* ■ el **charco.**

**puff** [pʌf] *verb* ■ **resoplar:** he was puffing and panting resoplaba y jadeaba.

**pull** [pʊl] *verb*

1. **tirar:** don't pull so hard no tires tan fuerte
2. **tirar de:** he pulled her hair le tiró del pelo; she was pulling on the rope tiraba de la cuerda

**pull down** | *phrasal verb*
1. **bajar:** pull the blind down baja la persiana
2. **derribar:** they pulled down the old building derribaron el viejo edificio.

**pull in** | *phrasal verb* ■ **llegar:** the train pulled into the station el tren llegó a la estación.

**pull out** | *phrasal verb* ■ **sacar:** he pulled something out of his pocket sacó algo del bolsillo; the dentist pulled his tooth out el dentista le sacó el diente.

**pull through** | *phrasal verb* ■ **recuperarse:** don't worry, she'll pull through no te preocupes, se recuperará.

**pull up** | *phrasal verb*
1. **subirse:** he pulled his socks up se subió los calcetines
2. **parar:** a car pulled up in front of the house un coche paró frente a la casa.

**pulse** [pʌls] *noun* ■ **el pulso:** the doctor took my pulse el doctor me tomó el pulso.

**pump** [pʌmp] *(noun & verb)*
■ *noun*
la **bomba:** a bicycle pump una bomba de bicicleta
➤ **a gas pump** un surtidor de gasolina
■ *verb*
**bombear:** he pumped the water out of the pond sacó bombeando el agua del estanque

**pump up** | *phrasal verb* ■ **inflar:** he's pumping up the tires está inflando las llantas.

**pumpkin** ['pʌmpkɪn] *noun* ■ la **calabaza,** el **zapallo** *Peru, Southern Cone*: a pumpkin pie una tarta de calabaza.

**punch** [pʌntʃ] *(noun & verb)*
■ *noun*
1. **el puñetazo:** he knocked me out with a single punch me noqueó de un sólo puñetazo

2. **el ponche:** a glass of punch un vaso de ponche
■ *verb*
1. **darle un puñetazo a:** she punched him le dio un puñetazo
2. **perforar, ponchar** *Mexico*: the inspector punched my ticket el inspector me perforó el boleto.

**punctuation** [ˌpʌŋktʃʊ'eɪʃn] *noun* ■ la **puntuación** *(plural* las **puntuaciones)**: punctuation marks signos de puntuación.

**punish** ['pʌnɪʃ] *verb* ■ **castigar:** they punished him for staying out all night lo castigaron por pasar toda la noche fuera.

**punishment** ['pʌnɪʃmənt] *noun* ■ el **castigo:** your punishment will be to do all the chores for a week tu castigo será hacer todos los quehaceres durante una semana.

**pupil** ['pjuːpl] *noun* ■ la **pupila:** the doctor looked at his pupils el médico le miró las pupilas.

**puppet** ['pʌpɪt] *noun* ■ el **títere:** a puppet show un espectáculo de títeres.

**puppy** ['pʌpɪ] *(plural* puppies) *noun* ■ el **cachorro:** our dog had puppies nuestra perra tuvo cachorros.

**purchase** ['pɜːtʃəs] *(noun & verb)*
■ *noun*
la **compra:** she showed me her newest purchase me mostró su última compra
■ *verb*
**comprar:** they purchased a new car compraron un coche nuevo.

**pure** [pjʊəʳ] *adjective* ■ **puro:** it's made of pure silk es de seda pura.

**purple** ['pɜːpl] *adjective* ■ **morado**.

**purpose** ['pɜːpəs] *noun* ■ el **propósito:** what is the purpose of your visit? ¿cuál es el propósito de su visita?

➤ **on purpose** a propósito: **I didn't do it on purpose** no lo hice a propósito.

**purr** [pɜːʳ] *verb* ■ **ronronear: the cat purred happily** el gato ronroneó alegremente.

**purse** [pɜːs] *noun* ■ el **bolso,** la **bolsa** *Mexico,* la **cartera** *South America:* **her purse matched her shoes** el bolso le combinaba con los zapatos.

**push** [pʊʃ] *verb*
1. **empujar: she pushed the door open** empujó la puerta para abrirla
2. **apretar: I pushed the button** apriete el botón.

**push-up** [pʊʃʌp] *noun* ■ la **flexión de brazos** *(plural* las **flexiones de brazos):* **he does 100 push-ups a day** hace 100 flexiones de brazos al día.

**put** [pʊt] *(past tense & past participle* put) *verb*
1. **poner: put the plates on the table** pon los platos en la mesa; **put it over there** ponlo allá
2. **decir: I don't know how to put it** no sé cómo decirlo
3. **invertir: Bob put a lot of money into the project** Bob invirtió mucho dinero en el proyecto
➤ **he put his arm around her** la rodeó con un brazo

**put away** *phrasal verb* ■ **guardar: she put all her things away** guardó todas sus cosas.

**put back** *phrasal verb* ■ **volver a poner en su lugar: put the scissors back when you're finished with them** vuelve a poner las tijeras en su lugar cuando hayas terminado.

**put down** *phrasal verb* ■ **soltar: he put the gun down** soltó el arma.

**put off** *phrasal verb* ■ **aplazar: the party has been put off** la fiesta ha sido aplazada; **she's putting off the decision** está aplazando la decisión

➤ **it put me off mussels for life** hizo que me dejaran de gustar los mejillones para siempre.

**put on** *phrasal verb*
1. **ponerse: she put her hat on** se puso el sombrero
2. **encender: I'll put the light on** voy a encender la luz
3. **presentar: we're putting on a Christmas show** estamos presentando un espectáculo de Navidad
4. *informal* **tomar el pelo: you're putting me on** me estás tomando el pelo
➤ **I've put on weight** he engordado
➤ **to put the brakes on** frenar.

**put out** *phrasal verb*
1. **apagar: put the lights out** apaga las luces
2. **tender: he put his hand out** tendió la mano
3. **sacar: I'll put out the garbage** voy a sacar la basura
4. **molestar: will it put you out if we change the meeting to Monday?** ¿te molesta si cambiamos la reunión para el lunes?

**put up** *phrasal verb*
1. **armar: where shall we put the tent up?** ¿dónde armamos la tienda?
2. **poner: Perry put some posters up on his bedroom wall** Perry puso algunos pósters en la pared de su dormitorio
➤ **can you put me up for the night?** ¿puedo quedarme a dormir en tu casa?

**put up with** *phrasal verb* ■ **aguantar: I won't put up with this kind of behavior** no voy a aguantar este tipo de comportamiento.

**puzzle** ['pʌzl] *noun*
1. el **misterio: her disappearance remains a puzzle** su desaparición sigue siendo un misterio
2. el **rompecabezas** *(plural* los **rompecabezas):** **he played with a puzzle on the floor** jugaba con un rompecabezas en el suelo
➤ **a crossword puzzle** un crucigrama
➤ **a jigsaw puzzle** un rompecabezas.

**puzzled** ['pʌzld] *adjective* ■ **perplejo:** I was puzzled by her comments me quedé perplejo con sus comentarios.

**pyramid** ['pɪrəmɪd] *noun* ■ la **pirámide.**

**qualification** [ˌkwɒlɪfɪ'keɪʃn] *noun* ■ el **título:** list your academic qualifications enumere sus títulos académicos.

**qualified** ['kwɒlɪfaɪd] *adjective* ■ **titulado:** he's a qualified teacher es un profesor titulado.

**qualify** ['kwɒlɪfaɪ] *(past tense & past participle* qualified*) verb* ■ **clasificarse, calificar** *Mexico*: our team qualified for the state championship nuestro equipo se clasificó para el campeonato estatal.

**quality** ['kwɒlətɪ] *(plural* qualities*) noun*

1. la **cualidad:** she has many good qualities tiene muchas buenas cualidades
2. la **calidad:** our products are of the finest quality nuestros productos son de la mejor calidad.

**quantity** ['kwɒntətɪ] *(plural* quantities*) noun* ■ la **cantidad:** he has a large quantity of books tiene una gran cantidad de libros.

**quarrel** ['kwɒrəl] *(noun & verb)*

■ *noun*
la **pelea:** they had a quarrel tuvieron una pelea
■ *verb*
*(past tense & past participle* quarreled*)* **pelear:** we quarreled all morning peleamos toda la mañana.

**quart** ['kwɔːt] *noun* ■ el **cuarto de galón.**

**quarter** ['kwɔːtər] *noun*

1. el **cuarto:** he ate a quarter of the cake se comió un cuarto del pastel; a quarter of an hour un cuarto de hora; three quarters of an hour tres cuartos de hora; it's a quarter after two son las dos y cuarto; it's a quarter to six son un cuarto para las seis, son las seis menos cuarto *River Plate*
2. la **moneda de veinticinco centavos:** I need some quarters for the soda machine necesito unas monedas de veinticinco centavos para la máquina de refrescos.

**quay** [kiː] *noun* ■ el **muelle.**

**queen** [kwiːn] *noun* ■ la **reina.**

**question** ['kwestʃn] *(noun & verb)*

■ *noun*
la **pregunta:** I asked the teacher a question le hice una pregunta al profesor; he answered all my questions contestó todas mis preguntas
➤ that's out of the question es imposible
➤ a question mark un signo de interrogación
■ *verb*
**interrogar:** the police want to question him la policía quiere interrogarlo.

**quick** [kwɪk] *(adjective & adverb)*

■ *adjective*
**rápido:** what's the quickest way back? ¿cuál es el camino de vuelta más rápido?; I have to make a quick phone call tengo que hacer una llamada rápida
➤ be quick! ¡apúrate!
■ *adverb*
**rápido:** quick, here he comes! ¡rápido, aquí viene!

**quickly** ['kwɪklɪ] *adverb* ■ **rápidamente:** he finished quickly terminó rápidamente.

**quiet** [ˈkwaɪət] *adjective*

1. **tranquilo:** a quiet street una calle tranquila; we had a quiet evening tuvimos una tarde tranquila
2. **bajo:** she spoke in a quiet voice habló en voz baja
➤ be quiet! ¡silencio!
➤ to keep quiet no decir nada: keep quiet about the party no digas nada sobre la fiesta.

**quietly** [ˈkwaɪətlɪ] *adverb*

1. **sin hacer ruido:** she left the room quietly dejó la habitación sin hacer ruido
2. **en voz baja:** he speaks very quietly habla en voz muy baja.

**quilt** [kwɪlt] *noun* ■ el **edredón** (*plural* los **edredones**).

**quit** [kwɪt] (*past tense & past participle* quit) *verb* ■ **dejar:** she quit her job dejó su empleo; I'm trying to quit smoking estoy tratando de dejar de fumar.

**quite** [kwaɪt] *adverb* ■ **bastante:** she's quite pretty es bastante bonita
➤ not quite no del todo: are you finished? — not quite ¿terminaste? — no del todo.

**quiz** [kwɪz] (*plural* quizzes [ˈkwɪzɪz]) *noun*

1. el **concurso:** he won the money on a TV quiz show se ganó el dinero en un programa concurso
2. la **prueba:** we had a math quiz today tuvimos una prueba de matemáticas hoy.

**quotation** [kwəʊˈteɪʃn] *noun* ■ la **cita:** it's a quotation from Shakespeare es una cita de Shakespeare
➤ quotation marks comillas
➤ in quotation marks entre comillas.

**quote** [kwəʊt] (*noun & verb*)

■ *noun*
la **cita:** it's a quote from Oscar Wilde es una cita de Oscar Wilde
➤ quotes comillas: his words were in quotes sus palabras estaban entre comillas
■ *verb*
**citar:** she quoted Homer citó a Homero.

**rabbi** [ˈræbaɪ] *noun* ■ el **rabino,** la **rabina:** he's a rabbi es rabino.

**rabbit** [ˈræbɪt] *noun* ■ el **conejo**.

**race** [reɪs] (*noun & verb*)

■ *noun*
1. la **carrera:** she won the race ganó la carrera
2. la **raza:** the human race la raza humana
➤ a race car un coche de carreras
➤ a race car driver un piloto de coches de carreras
■ *verb*
1. **correr:** she raced to the door corrió a la puerta
2. **echar una carrera, jugar una carrera** *River Plate:* I'll race you te echo una carrera.

**racehorse** [ˈreɪshɔːs] *noun* ■ el **caballo de carreras**.

**racetrack** [ˈreɪstræk] *noun* ■ el **circuito:** the cars sped around the racetrack los coches aceleraban por el circuito.

**racism** [ˈreɪsɪzm] *noun* ■ el **racismo**.

**racist** [ˈreɪsɪst] *adjective* ■ **racista**.

**rack** [ræk] *noun* ■ el **portaequipajes** (*plural* los **portaequipajes**)
➤ a towel rack un toallero.

**racket** [ˈrækɪt] *noun*

1. la **raqueta:** a tennis racket una raqueta de tenis
2. *informal* el **alboroto:** what's all the racket for? ¿a qué viene todo este alboroto?

**radiator** [ˈreɪdɪeɪtər] *noun* ■ el **radiador**.

**radio** [ˈreɪdɪəʊ] *noun* ▪ la **radio**: I heard it on the radio lo escuché en la radio
➤ a radio station una estación de radio.

**radish** [ˈrædɪʃ] *noun* ▪ el **rábano**.

**raft** [ræft] *noun* ▪ la **balsa**: they built a raft out of logs construyeron una balsa con troncos.

**rag** [ræg] *noun* ▪ el **trapo**: he wiped his hands on an oily rag se limpió las manos con un trapo aceitoso

**rags** *plural noun* ▪ el **harapo**: he was dressed in rags estaba vestido con harapos.

**rage** [reɪdʒ] *noun* ▪ la **rabia**: he was speechless with rage estaba mudo de rabia
➤ she flew into a rage when she heard the news se puso furiosa cuando escuchó la noticia.

**raid** [reɪd] *(noun & verb)*
■ *noun*
la **redada**: a police raid una redada policial
➤ a bombing raid un bombardeo aéreo
■ *verb*
1. **allanar**: the police raided their offices la policía allanó sus oficinas
2. **saquear**: he raided the fridge in the middle of the night saqueó el refrigerador en la mitad de la noche.

**rail** [reɪl] *noun*
1. el **pasamanos** *(plural* los **pasamanos**): hold onto the rail when you come down the stairs tómense del pasamanos al bajar la escalera
2. el **riel**: electrified rails rieles electrificados
➤ by rail en tren: she prefers to travel by rail ella prefiere viajar en tren
➤ the train went off the rails el tren se descarriló.

**railing** [ˈreɪlɪŋz] *noun* ▪ la **reja**: he leaned over the railing on the balcony se inclinó sobre la reja del balcón.

**railroad** [ˈreɪlrəʊd] *noun* ▪ la **vía férrea**
➤ a map of the railroad network un mapa de la red de vías férreas
➤ a railroad track una vía férrea

➤ a model railroad una maqueta de vía férrea.

**rain** [reɪn] *(noun & verb)*
■ *noun*
la **lluvia**: we're expecting rain today hoy esperamos lluvia
■ *verb*
**llover**: it's been raining all afternoon estuvo lloviendo toda la tarde.

**rainbow** [ˈreɪnbəʊ] *noun* ▪ el **arco iris** *(plural* los **arco iris**): how many colors are there in a rainbow? ¿cuántos colores tiene el arco iris?

**raincoat** [ˈreɪnkəʊt] *noun* ▪ el **impermeable**.

**rain forest** [ˈreɪnfɒrɪst] *noun* ▪ la **selva tropical**: the rain forests of Brazil las selvas tropicales de Brasil.

**raise** [reɪz] *(verb & noun)*
■ *verb*
1. **levantar**: she raised her hand levantó la mano
2. **aumentar**: they've raised their prices han aumentado sus precios
3. **mejorar**: we must raise standards debemos mejorar los niveles
4. **criarse**: the children were raised in Canada los niños se criaron en Canadá
➤ to raise your voice levantar la voz: she raised her voice to make herself heard levantó la voz para hacerse oír
➤ to raise money reunir dinero: the school is trying to raise money la escuela está tratando de reunir dinero
■ *noun*
el **aumento**: all the staff got a raise todo el personal tuvo un aumento.

**raisin** [ˈreɪzn] *noun* ▪ la **pasa**.

**rake** [reɪk] *noun* ▪ el **rastrillo**: he used a rake to gather all the leaves usó un rastrillo para juntar todas las hojas.

**ramp** [ræmp] *noun* ▪ la **rampa**: he pushed the cart up the ramp empujó el carrito por la rampa; the exit ramp was full of cars la rampa de salida estaba llena de automóviles.

**ran** [ræn] *past tense* ➤ run.

**ranch** [rɑːntʃ] *(plural* ranches) *noun*
■ la **hacienda**, el **rancho** *Mexico*, la **estancia** *River Plate*.

**random** ['rændəm] *adjective*
➤ at random al azar: **choose a number at random** elije un número al azar.

**rang** [ræŋ] *past tense* ➤ ring.

**range** [reɪndʒ] *(noun & verb)*
■ *noun*
1. la **gama**: **there is a wide range of sizes** hay una amplia gama de tamaños
2. el **alcance**: **the target is out of range** el objetivo está fuera de alcance
3. la **cocina**, la **estufa** *Colombia, Mexico*: **they bought a new range** compraron una cocina nueva
➤ **it's out of my price range** es más de lo que puedo pagar
➤ **a mountain range** una cordillera
■ *verb*
➤ **to range from ... to ...** oscilar entre .... y ....: **prices range from 50 to 500 dollars** los precios oscilan entre los 50 y los 500 dólares.

**rank** [ræŋk] *(noun & verb)*
■ *noun*
1. el **rango**: **the rank of colonel is above captain** el rango de coronel está por sobre del de capitán
2. la **fila**: **the soldiers broke ranks** los soldados rompieron filas
■ *verb*
**clasificar**: **he's ranked second in the world** está clasificado segundo en el mundo.

**rap** [ræp] *noun* ■ el **rap**: **a rap singer** un cantante de rap.

**rare** [reəʳ] *adjective*
1. **raro**: **this is a rare animal** éste es un animal raro
2. **poco cocido, a la inglesa** *Mexico*: **I'd like my steak rare** quiero el filete poco cocido.

**rarely** ['reəlɪ] *adverb* ■ **rara vez**: **they rarely go out** salen rara vez.

**rash** [ræʃ] *noun* ■ el **sarpullido**: **he broke out in a rash** le salió un sarpullido.

**raspberry** ['rɑːzbərɪ] *(plural* raspberries) *noun* ■ la **frambuesa**.

**rat** [ræt] *noun* ■ la **rata**.

**rate** [reɪt] *noun*
1. la **tasa**: **the birth rate** la tasa de nacimientos; **interest rates are low** las tasas de interés son bajas
2. la **tarifa**: **are there special rates for students?** ¿hay tarifas especiales para estudiantes?

**rather** ['rɑːðəʳ] *adverb* ■ **mejor**
➤ **rather than** en lugar de: **he did it alone rather than ask for help** lo hizo solo en lugar de pedir ayuda
➤ **I'd rather go now** preferiría irme ahora
➤ **she'd rather not talk to him** preferiría no hablar con él.

**rattle** ['rætl] *noun* ■ el **sonajero**, la **sonaja** *Mexico*: **the baby dropped its rattle** el bebé dejó caer el sonajero.

**rattlesnake** ['rætlsneɪk] *noun* ■ la **serpiente de cascabel**: **rattlesnakes are poisonous** las serpientes de cascabel son venenosas.

**raw** [rɔː] *adjective* ■ **crudo**: **a raw carrot** una zanahoria cruda
➤ **raw materials** materias primas.

**ray** [reɪ] *noun* ■ el **rayo**: **the sun's rays warmed the ground** los rayos de sol calentaron el suelo.

**razor** ['reɪzəʳ] *noun* ■ la **navaja**
➤ **a razor blade** una hoja de afeitar, una hoja de rasurar *Mexico*.

**reach** [riːtʃ] *(verb & noun)*
■ *verb*
1. **llegar a**: **we reached Savannah before dark** llegamos a Savannah antes del anochecer; **the snow reached the window** la nieve llegó a la ventana; **they've reached a decision** llegaron a una decisión
2. **alcanzar**: **I can't reach the book on the top shelf** no alcanzo el libro en la repisa más alta
3. **contactar**: **you can reach me on this number** puedes contactarme en este número

■ *noun*

➤ **within reach** al alcance: **the telephone is within reach** el teléfono está al alcance

➤ **within easy reach** muy cerca: **the school is within easy reach of my house** la escuela está muy cerca de mi casa

➤ **out of reach** fuera del alcance: **the radio was out of reach** el radio estaba fuera del alcance

**reach out** *phrasal verb* ■ **extender la mano: he reached out and touched her arm** extendió la mano y le tocó el brazo.

**react** [rɪ'ækt] *verb* ■ **reaccionar: he didn't react to her speech** no reaccionó ante su discurso.

**reaction** [rɪ'ækʃn] *noun* ■ **la reacción** *(plural* **las reacciones***): what was her reaction when you told her the news?* ¿cuál fue su reacción cuando le contaste la noticia?

**read** [ri:d] *(past tense & past participle* read [red]*) verb* ■ **leer: she's reading the newspaper** está leyendo el diario; **have you read this book?** ¿has leído este libro?

➤ **read out loud** leer en voz alta: **she read the story out loud to the class** leyó el cuento en voz alta para toda la clase.

**reading** ['ri:dɪŋ] *noun* ■ **la lectura: reading is my favorite hobby** la lectura es mi pasatiempo favorito.

**ready** ['redɪ] *adjective*

1. listo: **are you ready to go?** ¿estás listo para salir?

2. dispuesto: **she's always ready to help** siempre está dispuesta a ayudar

➤ **to get ready** prepararse: **she's getting ready to leave** se está preparando para irse

➤ **to get something ready** preparar algo: **he's getting lunch ready** está preparando el almuerzo.

**real** ['rɪəl] *adjective*

1. verdadero: **that's not the real reason** ése no es el verdadero motivo; **he's a real crook** es un verdadero sinvergüenza

2. auténtico: **it's made of real leather** es de cuero auténtico

3. real: **the real world** el mundo real

➤ **real estate** la propiedad inmobiliaria: **her father's in real estate** su padre trabaja en la propiedad inmobiliaria.

**realistic** [,rɪə'lɪstɪk] *adjective* ■ **realista: the movie shows a realistic vision of war** la película muestra una visión realista de la guerra.

**reality** [rɪ'ælətɪ] *noun* ■ **la realidad**.

**realize** ['rɪəlaɪz] *verb* ■ **darse cuenta de: he realized his mistake** se dio cuenta de su error; **I didn't realize what the time was** no me di cuenta de la hora que era.

**really** ['rɪəlɪ] *adverb* ■ **realmente: it's really late** es realmente tarde; **are you really going to Australia?** ¿realmente vas a Australia?

➤ **really?** ¿en serio?: **Ann won the lottery! — really?** Ann se ganó la lotería — ¿en serio?

➤ **do you want to go to the party? — not really** ¿quieres ir a la fiesta? — en realidad, no.

**rear** [rɪəʳ] *(adjective & noun)*

■ *adjective*

trasero: **please use the rear entrance** por favor, utilice la entrada trasera

■ *noun*

la **parte trasera: I was sitting at the rear of the bus** estaba sentado en la parte trasera del autobús.

**reason** ['ri:zn] *noun* ■ **la razón** *(plural* **las razones***): that's the reason she left** ésa es la razón por la que se fue.

**reasonable** ['ri:znəbl] *adjective* ■ **razonable: Alex is such a reasonable person usually** Alex suele ser una persona tan razonable; **the prices are reasonable in that store** en esa tienda los precios son razonables.

**reasonably** ['ri:znəblɪ] *adverb* ■ **bastante: she's reasonably happy** es bastante feliz

➤ **the food is reasonably good** la comida es bastante buena.

**reassure** [ˌriːəˈʃʊəʳ] *verb* ■ **tranquilizar**: I tried to reassure her traté de tranquilizarla.

**receipt** [rɪˈsiːt] *noun* ■ el **recibo**: I'd like a receipt, please quisiera un recibo, por favor.

**receive** [rɪˈsiːv] *verb* ■ **recibir**: I received a letter this morning recibí una carta esta mañana.

**receiver** [rɪˈsiːvəʳ] *noun* ■ el **auricular**: he picked up the receiver levantó el auricular.

**recent** [ˈriːsnt] *adjective* ■ **reciente**: we saw the most recent James Bond movie vimos la más reciente película de James Bond.

**recently** [ˈriːsntlɪ] *adverb* ■ **recientemente**: we hired Kim recently recientemente contratamos a Kim.

**reception** [rɪˈsepʃn] *noun* ■ la **recepción** *(plural* las **recepciones**): the reception will be held at the Waldorf la recepción se hará en el Waldorf; please sign in at the reception desk por favor firme el registro en recepción
➤ a wedding reception un banquete de bodas.

**receptionist** [rɪˈsepʃənɪst] *noun* ■ el/la **recepcionista**: she's a receptionist es recepcionista.

**recess** [ˈriːses] *noun* ■ el **recreo**: Timmy played with Connie at recess Timmy jugaba con Connie durante el recreo.

**recipe** [ˈresɪpɪ] *noun* ■ la **receta**: can I have your cookie recipe? ¿me das tu receta de galletas?

**recognize** [ˈrekəgnaɪz] *verb* ■ **reconocer**: I didn't recognize you no te reconocí.

**recommend** [ˌrekəˈmend] *verb* ■ **recomendar**: he recommended this book to me me recomendó este libro.

**record** *(noun & verb)*
■ *noun*
[ˈrekɔːd]
1. el **récord** *(plural* los **récords**): she has broken the world record batió el récord mundial
2. el **disco**: I like listening to old records me gusta escuchar discos viejos
➤ a criminal record antecedentes penales
➤ to keep a record of something llevar un registro de algo: you should keep a record of your expenses deberías llevar un registro de tus gastos
■ *verb*
[rɪˈkɔːd] **grabar**: I've recorded the movie grabé la película

**records** *plural noun* ■ el **historial**: get the patient's medical records busque el historial clínico del paciente.

**recording** [rɪˈkɔːdɪŋ] *noun* ■ la **grabación** *(plural* las **grabaciones**): this is a bad recording ésta es una mala grabación.

**recover** [rɪˈkʌvəʳ] *verb* ■ **recuperarse**: she's recovering from a cold se está recuperando de un resfriado.

**recovery** [rɪˈkʌvərɪ] *noun* ■ la **recuperación** *(plural* las **recuperaciones**): best wishes for a quick recovery! ¡los mejores deseos para una rápida recuperación!

**rectangle** [ˈrekˌtæŋgl] *noun* ■ el **rectángulo**.

**recycle** [ˌriːˈsaɪkl] *verb* ■ **reciclar**: we recycle bottles and newspapers reciclamos botellas y diarios
➤ recycled paper papel reciclado.

**recycling** [ˌriːˈsaɪklɪŋ] *uncountable noun* ■ el **reciclaje**: a recycling facility un centro de reciclaje.

**red** [red] *adjective* ■ **rojo**: a red apple una manzana roja; a bright red hat un sombrero rojo brillante
➤ she has red hair es pelirroja
➤ the Red Cross la Cruz Roja
➤ a red light un semáforo en rojo, un alto *Mexico*: he went through a red light se pasó un semáforo en rojo.

**redhead** ['redhed] *noun* ■ el **pelirrojo,** la **pelirroja:** Julie is a natural redhead Julie es pelirroja natural.

**redo** [,ri:'du:] *(past tense* redid, *past participle* redone) *verb* ■ **rehacer:** she had to redo her homework tuvo que rehacer sus tareas.

**reduce** [rɪ'dju:s] *verb* ■ **reducir:** they've reduced the price redujeron el precio.

**reduction** [rɪ'dʌkʃn] *noun* ■ la **reducción** *(plural* las **reducciones***):* we've seen a reduction in traffic in this area hemos visto una reducción del tráfico en esta zona.

**reef** [ri:f] *noun* ■ el **arrecife:** a coral reef un arrecife de coral.

**refer** [rɪ'fɜːr] *(past tense & past participle* referred) *verb* ■ **referirse:** I don't know what you're referring to no se a qué te refieres
➤ to refer to referirse a: she's referring to your son se refiere a tu hijo.

**referee** [,refə'ri:] *noun* ■ el **árbitro,** la **árbitra:** the referee blew his whistle el árbitro tocó el silbato.

**reference** ['refrəns] *noun*
1. la **referencia:** she made a reference to her family hizo referencia a su familia
2. las **referencias:** could you give me a reference for the job? ¿podría darme referencias para el trabajo?
➤ a reference book un libro de consulta
➤ a reference number un número de referencia.

**reflection** [rɪ'flekʃn] *noun* ■ el **reflejo:** I can see my reflection in the mirror veo mi reflejo en el espejo
➤ on reflection, I don't think it's a good idea pensándolo bien, no creo que sea una buena idea.

**reflex** ['ri:fleks] *noun* ■ el **reflejo:** he has good reflexes tiene buenos reflejos.

**refreshing** [rɪ'freʃɪŋ] *adjective* ■ **refrescante:** I took a refreshing shower me di una ducha refrescante.

**refrigerator** [rɪ'frɪdʒəreɪtər] *noun* ■ el **refrigerador,** la **heladera** *River Plate.*

**refugee** [,refjʊ'dʒi:] *noun* ■ el **refugiado,** la **refugiada**.

**refund** *(noun & verb)*
■ *noun*
['ri:fʌnd] el **reembolso:** we'll give you a refund if you are not satisfied le hacemos un reembolso si usted no está satisfecho
■ *verb*
[rɪ'fʌnd] **reembolsar:** they refunded my money me reembolsaron el dinero.

**refuse** [rɪ'fju:z] *verb* ■ **negarse:** I refuse to do it me niego a hacerlo.

**regard** [rɪ'gaːd] *verb* ■ **considerar:** I regard her as my sister la considero mi hermana; he's regarded as the best player in the world está considerado el mejor jugador del mundo.

**regards** [rɪ'gaːdz] *plural noun* ■ los **saludos:** give her my regards dale mis saludos; he sends his regards manda saludos.

**region** ['ri:dʒən] *noun* ■ la **región** *(plural* las **regiones***):* Tibet is a mountainous region el Tíbet es una región montañosa.

**register** ['redʒɪstər] *(noun & verb)*
■ *noun*
el **registro:** she signed the register firmó el registro
■ *verb*
**inscribirse:** she wants to register for a Spanish course quiere inscribirse en un curso de español.

**regret** [rɪ'gret] *(noun & verb)*
■ *noun*
do you have any regrets? ¿te arrepientes de algo?; I have no regrets no me arrepiento de nada
■ *verb*
**arrepentirse:** he regrets breaking up with her se arrepiente de haber terminado con ella.

**regular** ['regjʊlər] *adjective*
1. **regular:** we meet at regular intervals nos reunimos a intervalos regulares

**2. habitual:** I'll see you at the regular time te veo a la hora habitual; **he's a regular customer** es un cliente habitual

**3. mediano:** a regular portion of fries una porción mediana de papas fritas.

**regularly** ['regjələlı] *adverb* ■ **regularmente:** I go to the dentist regularly voy al dentista regularmente.

**regulation** [ˌregjʊ'leɪʃn] *noun* ■ **la norma:** it's against regulations va contra las normas.

**rehearsal** [rɪ'hɜːsl] *noun* ■ **el ensayo:** there's a rehearsal for the play tonight hay un ensayo de la obra esta noche.

**rehearse** [rɪ'hɜːs] *verb* ■ **ensayar:** the band is rehearsing this afternoon la banda ensaya esta tarde.

**reindeer** ['reɪnˌdɪəʳ] *(plural* reindeer*)* *noun* ■ **el reno.**

**reins** [reɪnz] *plural noun* ■ **las riendas:** she was holding the horse's reins llevaba las riendas del caballo.

**reject** [rɪ'dʒekt] *verb* ■ **rechazar:** they rejected my book rechazaron mi libro.

**related** [rɪ'leɪtɪd] *adjective* ■ **relacionado:** the two problems aren't related los dos problemas no están relacionados
➤ **how is Sam related to Ted?** ¿qué parentesco tiene Sam con Ted?
➤ **they are related** son parientes.

**relation** [rɪ'leɪʃn] *noun*
**1. el/la pariente:** Vicky has relations in Miami Vicky tiene parientes en Miami
**2. la relación** *(plural* las **relaciones***):* there's no relation between the two crimes no hay relación entre los dos crímenes; **the two countries have good relations** ambos países tienen buenas relaciones.

**relationship** [rɪ'leɪʃnʃɪp] *noun* ■ **la relación** *(plural* las **relaciones***):* they have a good relationship tienen una buena relación.

**relative** ['relətɪv] *noun* ■ **el/la pariente:** he has relatives in New Orleans tiene parientes en Nueva Orleans.

**relax** [rɪ'læks] *verb* ■ **relajarse:** a massage will help you relax un masaje te ayudará a relajarte
➤ **relax, everything will be fine** tranquilo, todo va a estar bien.

**relaxation** [ˌriːlæk'seɪʃn] *noun* ■ **el descanso:** a good place to find relaxation un buen lugar para el descanso.

**relaxed** [rɪ'lækst] *adjective* ■ **relajado:** he's very relaxed since he came back from vacation está muy relajado desde que volvió de las vacaciones.

**relaxing** [rɪ'læksɪŋ] *adjective* ■ **relajante:** she had a relaxing bath se dio un baño relajante
➤ **it was a relaxing weekend** fue un fin de semana de descanso.

**relay, relay race** ['riːleɪ, 'riːleɪreɪs] *noun* ■ **la carrera de relevos.**

**release** [rɪ'liːs] *(noun & verb)*
■ *noun*
**la liberación** *(plural* las **liberaciones***):* we've arranged for the release of the hostages hemos hecho arreglos para la liberación de los rehenes
➤ **a new release** un nuevo disco: **his new release is called "No Good Blues"** su nuevo disco se llama "No Good Blues"
➤ **a press release** un comunicado de prensa
■ *verb*
**1. liberar:** they released the prisoners liberaron a los prisioneros
**2. sacar a la venta:** they've just released a new album acaban de sacar a la venta un nuevo album.

**reliable** [rɪ'laɪəbl] *adjective*
**1. cumplidor:** he's very reliable es muy cumplidor
**2. fiable:** is this a reliable computer? ¿es fiable esta computadora?

**relief** [rɪ'liːf] *noun* ■ **el alivio:** what a relief! ¡qué alivio!

**relieve** [rɪ'liːv] *verb* ■ **alivar:** the aspirin will relieve the pain esta aspirina aliviará el dolor.

**religion** [rɪ'lɪdʒn] *noun* ■ **la religión** (*plural* las **religiones**).

**religious** [rɪ'lɪdʒəs] *adjective* ■ **religioso:** what are your religious beliefs? ¿cuáles son tus creencias religiosas?; she's very religious es muy religiosa.

**reluctant** [rɪ'lʌktənt] *adjective* ■ **reacio:** he was a reluctant candidate fue un candidato reacio

➤ to be reluctant to do something mostrarse reacio a hacer algo: I was reluctant to leave me mostraba reacio a irme.

**reluctantly** [rɪ'lʌktəntlɪ] *adverb* ■ **de mala gana:** he reluctantly went to bed se fue a la cama de mala gana.

**rely** [rɪ'laɪ] *(past tense & past participle* relied*) verb*

➤ to rely on someone or something depender de alguien o algo: I've always relied on my parents siempre he dependido de mis padres

➤ it's a car you can rely on es un coche en el que se puede confiar.

**remain** [rɪ'meɪn] *verb*

1. **quedarse:** he remained at home se quedó en casa

2. **permanecer:** the house remained abandoned for years la casa permaneció abandonada durante años.

**remaining** [rɪ'meɪnɪŋ] *adjective*

➤ we ate the remaining cake nos comimos el resto del pastel.

**remains** [rɪ'meɪnz] *plural noun* ■ **los restos:** they found human remains encontraron restos humanos; the remains of an ancient city los restos de una antigua ciudad.

**remark** [rɪ'maːk] *noun* ■ **el comentario:** she made a critical remark hizo un comentario crítico.

**remarkable** [rɪ'maːkəbl] *adjective* ■ **excepcional:** she's a remarkable woman es una mujer excepcional.

**remember** [rɪ'membər] *verb*

1. **acordarse de:** I remember what happened me acuerdo de lo que sucedió; she doesn't remember me no se acuerda de mí

2. **recordar:** I don't remember no recuerdo

➤ to remember to do something acordarse de hacer algo: remember to take your umbrella acuérdate de llevar tu paraguas.

**remind** [rɪ'maɪnd] *verb*

➤ you remind me of my brother me recuerdas a mi hermano

➤ remind me to call David recuérdame que llame a David

> The verb following **recordarle a alguien que** must be in the subjunctive.

**remote** [rɪ'məʊt] *adjective* ■ **remoto:** a remote mountain village un pueblo remoto en la montaña

➤ the remote control el control remoto.

**remove** [rɪ'muːv] *verb*

1. **retirar:** he removed the plates from the table retiró los platos de la mesa

2. **quitar:** it's the best thing for removing stains es lo mejor para quitar manchas.

**renew** [rɪ'njuː] *verb* ■ **renovar:** I have to renew my passport tengo que renovar mi pasaporte.

**rent** [rent] *(noun & verb)*

■ *noun*
el **alquiler,** la **renta** *Mexico*: how much rent do you pay? ¿cuánto pagas de alquiler?

■ *verb*
**alquilar, rentar** *Mexico*: they rented a house for the summer alquilaron una casa para el verano

➤ for rent se alquila, se renta *Mexico*.

**rental** ['rentl] *(noun & adjective)*

■ *noun*
el **alquiler,** la **renta** *Mexico*

■ *adjective*
**de alquiler, rentado** *Mexico*: a rental car un coche de alquiler.

**repair** [rɪ'peəʳ] (noun & verb)

■ noun
el **arreglo**: the repairs cost 50 dollars el arreglo cuesta 50 dólares

■ verb
**arreglar**: he repaired the television arregló la televisión.

**repeat** [rɪ'piːt] verb ■ **repetir**: can you repeat what you just said? ¿puedes repetir lo que acabas de decir?

**replace** [rɪ'pleɪs] verb
1. **cambiar**: I replaced the broken window cambié la ventana rota
2. **volver a colocar**: replace the book on the shelf vuelve a colocar el libro en la repisa.

**reply** [rɪ'plaɪ] (noun & verb)

■ noun
la **respuesta**: we're waiting for a reply estamos esperando una respuesta

■ verb
(past tense & past participle **replied**) **responder**: I have to reply to this e-mail tengo que responder a este e-mail.

**report** [rɪ'pɔːt] (noun & verb)

■ noun
1. el **informe**: I read the police report leí el informe de la policía
2. el **reportaje**: we read the report in the paper leímos el reportaje en el diario
➤ a report card el boletín de calificaciones: we're getting our report cards today hoy nos entregan los boletines de calificaciones

■ verb
1. **dar parte de**: we reported the accident to the police dimos parte del accidente a la policía
2. **divulgar**: the news was reported in the paper divulgaron la noticia en el diario
3. **presentarse**: please report to my office por favor, preséntese en mi oficina.

**reporter** [rɪ'pɔːtəʳ] noun ■ el/la **periodista**: she's a reporter es periodista.

**represent** [,reprɪ'zent] verb ■ **representar**: the dotted line represents the border la línea punteada representa el borde; Ms. Smith will represent the company at the convention la señora Smith representará a la compañía en la convención.

**representative** [,reprɪ'zentətɪv] noun ■ el/la **representante**: Scott is our representative in Texas Scott es nuestro representante en Texas.

**reptile** ['reptaɪl] noun ■ el **reptil**.

**republic** [rɪ'pʌblɪk] noun ■ la **república**.

**Republican** [rɪ'pʌblɪkən] (adjective & noun)

■ adjective
**republicano**: the Republican Party el Partido Republicano

■ noun
el **republicano**, la **republicana**: my parents are both Republicans mis papás son republicanos.

**request** [rɪ'kwest] (noun & verb)

■ noun
la **petición** (plural las **peticiones**): they made a request for help presentaron una petición de ayuda

■ verb
**pedir**: I'll have to request more supplies tendré que pedir más provisiones
➤ request that pedir que: we requested that they provide more information pedimos que nos proporcionaran más información

> The verb following **pedir que** must be in the subjunctive.

**require** [rɪ'kwaɪəʳ] verb ■ **requerir**: this work requires a lot of concentration este trabajo requiere mucha concentración.

**rescue** ['reskjuː] (noun & verb)

■ noun
el **rescate**: he came to my rescue vino en mi rescate
➤ a rescue operation una operación de rescate
➤ a rescue team un equipo de rescate

■ verb
**rescatar**: they rescued her from the fire la rescataron del incendio.

**research** [ˌrɪˈsɜːtʃ] *(noun & verb)*

■ *noun*
la **investigación** *(plural* las **investigaciones***):* he's doing research on genetics están haciendo una investigación en genética

■ *verb*
**investigar:** they're researching alternative energy sources están investigando fuentes de energía alternativa.

**resemblance** [rɪˈzembləns] *noun* ■ el **parecido:** I don't see the resemblance between you and your sister no veo el parecido entre tú y tu hermana.

**resemble** [rɪˈzembl] *verb* ■ **parecerse:** the baby resembles his father el bebé se parece a su papá.

**reservation** [ˌrezəˈveɪʃn] *noun* ■ la **reserva:** I made a reservation for dinner hice una reserva para la cena.

**reserve** [rɪˈzɜːv] *(noun & verb)*

■ *noun*
la **reserva:** our water reserves are getting low nuestras reservas de agua están bajando
➤ a nature reserve una reserva natural
■ *verb*
**reservar:** she reserved a table for six reservó una mesa para seis.

**residence** [ˈrezɪdəns] *noun* ■ la **residencia:** it's the president's official residence es la residencia oficial del presidente.

**resident** [ˈrezɪdənt] *noun* ■ el **vecino,** la **vecina:** local residents are opposed to the proposal los vecinos se oponen a la propuesta.

**resign** [rɪˈzaɪn] *verb* ■ **renunciar:** he resigned from his job renunció a su trabajo.

**resist** [rɪˈzɪst] *verb*

1. **resistir:** I couldn't resist his blue eyes no pude resistir sus ojos azules
2. **resistirse a:** she resisted their efforts to change her mind se resistió a sus esfuerzos de hacerla cambiar de idea.

**resort** [rɪˈzɔːt] *noun*

1. el **centro vacacional:** a very popular resort in Mexico un centro vacacional muy popular en México
2. el **recurso:** we can call Dad as a last resort podemos llamar a papá como último recurso
➤ a ski resort una estación de ski.

**resource** [rɪˈsɔːs] *noun* ■ el **recurso**
➤ natural resources recursos naturales.

**respect** [rɪˈspekt] *(noun & verb)*

■ *noun*
el **respeto:** he has no respect for his parents no tiene ningún respeto por sus padres
■ *verb*
**respetar:** everybody respects her todo el mundo la respeta.

**responsibility** [rɪˌspɒnsəˈbɪləti] *noun* ■ la **responsabilidad:** he has more responsibilities in his new job tiene más responsabilidades en su nuevo trabajo.

**responsible** [rɪˈspɒnsəbl] *adjective* ■ **responsable:** she's responsible for the accident es responsable del accidente.

**rest** [rest] *(noun & verb)*

■ *noun*
el **descanso:** you need a good rest necesitas un buen descanso
➤ the rest el resto: the rest of the book was more interesting el resto del libro era más interesante
➤ to have a rest descansar: let's have a rest for a while descansemos un rato
■ *verb*
1. **descansar:** sit down and rest your legs siéntate y descansa las piernas
2. **apoyar:** she rested her bike against the wall apoyó la bicicleta contra la pared.

**restroom** [ˈrestruːm] *noun* ■ el **baño**.

**restaurant** [ˈrestərɒnt] *noun* ■ el **restaurante**.

**result** [rɪˈzʌlt] *noun* ■ el **resultado:** the doctor has your test results el doctor tiene el resultado de sus análisis.

**résumé** [ˈrezjuːmeɪ] *noun* ■ el **currículum vitae**.

**retire** [rɪˈtaɪər] *verb* ■ **jubilarse:** she retired at 60 se jubiló a los 60 años.

**return** [rɪ'tɜːn] *(noun & verb)*
■ *noun*
la **vuelta**: I will call on my return from Denver llamaré a mi vuelta de Denver
■ *verb*
1. **volver**: she returned to the office at 3 volvió a la oficina a las 3
2. **devolver, regresar** *Latin America except Southern Cone*: he returned the book I lent him devolvió el libro que le presté.

**reunion** [ˌriː'juːnjən] *noun* ■ la **reunión** *(plural* las **reuniones***)*: a family reunion una reunión familiar.

**reveal** [rɪ'viːl] *verb* ■ **revelar**: she revealed my secret reveló mi secreto.

**revenge** [rɪ'vendʒ] *noun* ■ la **venganza**
➤ to get revenge **vengarse**: I swore I'd get revenge juré que me vengaría.

**reverse** [rɪ'vɜːs] *(adjective, noun & verb)*
■ *adjective*
**inverso**: the letters are in reverse order las letras están en orden inverso
■ *noun*
la **marcha atrás**, la **reversa** *Colombia, Mexico*: put the car in reverse mete marcha atrás
■ *verb*
**dar marcha atrás, meter reversa** *Colombia, Mexico*: watch out — he's reversing! ¡cuidado! –¡está dando marcha atrás!

**review** [rɪ'vjuː] *noun* ■ la **crítica**: his new movie got great reviews su nueva película tuvo críticas excelentes.

**revolting** [rɪ'vəʊltɪŋ] *adjective* ■ **asqueroso**: the soup was revolting la sopa estaba asquerosa.

**revolution** [ˌrevə'luːʃn] *noun* ■ la **revolución** *(plural* las **revoluciones***)*.

**revolver** [rɪ'vɒlvəʳ] *noun* ■ el **revólver**.

**reward** [rɪ'wɔːd] *(noun & verb)*
■ *noun*
la **recompensa**: they're offering a reward están ofreciendo una recompensa

■ *verb*
**recompensar**: he was rewarded for his efforts lo recompensaron por sus esfuerzos.

**rewind** [ˌriː'waɪnd] *(past tense & past participle* rewound [ˌriː'waʊnd]*) verb*
■ **rebobinar**: I'll rewind the tape voy a rebobinar la cinta.

**rhinoceros** [raɪ'nɒsərəs] *noun* ■ el **rinoceronte**.

**rhyme** [raɪm] *(noun & verb)*
■ *noun*
1. la **rima**: I need a rhyme for "rain" necesito una palabra que haga rima con "lluvia"
2. la **canción** *(plural* las **canciones***)*: a nursery rhyme una canción infantil
■ *verb*
**rimar**: "bad" rhymes with "mad" "bad" rima con "mad".

**rhythm** ['rɪðm] *noun* ■ el **ritmo**.

**rib** [rɪb] *noun* ■ la **costilla**.

**ribbon** ['rɪbən] *noun* ■ la **cinta**: the girl had a ribbon in her hair la niña tenía una cinta en el pelo.

**rice** [raɪs] *uncountable noun* ■ el **arroz**
➤ fried rice arroz frito
➤ rice pudding arroz con leche
➤ brown rice arroz integral.

**rich** [rɪtʃ] *adjective* ■ **rico**: he's one of the richest men in the world es uno de los hombres más ricos del mundo.

**rid** [rɪd] *(past tense & past participle* rid*) verb*
➤ to get rid of something **deshacerse de algo**: he got rid of his old toys se deshizo de sus viejos juguetes.

**ridden** ['rɪdn] *past participle* ➤ ride.

**riddle** ['rɪdl] *noun* ■ la **adivinanza**: he asked me a riddle me preguntó una adivinanza.

**ride** [raɪd] *(noun & verb)*
■ *noun*
el **paseo**: she went for a ride on her bike fue a dar un paseo en bicicleta

➤ **to give somebody a ride** llevar a alguien: **can you give me a ride to school?** ¿me llevas al colegio?

■ *verb*

*(past tense* **rode**, *past participle* **ridden)**
**andar: he can't ride a bicycle** no sabe andar en bicicleta; **we rode our horses on the beach** anduvimos a caballo en la playa

➤ **she rides her bike to school** va en bicicleta al colegio.

**ridiculous** [rɪ'dɪkjʊləs] *adjective* ■ **ridículo: you look ridiculous in that hat** te ves ridículo con ese sombrero.

**rifle** ['raɪfl] *noun* ■ **el rifle: a hunting rifle** un rifle de caza.

**right** [raɪt] *(adjective, adverb & noun )*

■ *adjective*

1. **derecho: give me your right hand** dame la mano derecha

2. **correcto: that's the right answer** ésa es la respuesta correcta; **is that the right size?** ¿es ésa la talla correcta?

3. **bien: it's not right to steal** no está bien robar

➤ **to be right** tener razón: **she was right to tell the truth** tenía razón en decir la verdad

➤ **that's right** así es: **are you going to Turkey? — yes, that's right** ¿vas a Turquía? — sí, así es

➤ **right?** ¿verdad?: **you're Kathy, right?** tú eres Kathy, ¿verdad?

➤ **a right angle** un ángulo recto

■ *adverb*

1. **a la derecha: turn right at the corner** dobla a la derecha en la esquina

2. **bien: she got the question right** entendió bien la pregunta

3. **derecho: go right to the end of the corridor** vaya derecho hasta el final del corredor

4. **justo: it happened right after Christmas** ocurrió justo después de Navidad

➤ **right now or right away** ahora mismo: **you have to go right now** tienes que ir ahora mismo

■ *noun*

1. **la derecha: look to the right** mira hacia la derecha

2. **el derecho: you have the right to remain silent** tiene derecho a permanecer en silencio

➤ **human rights** derechos humanos

➤ **he can't tell right from wrong** no distingue lo que está bien de lo que está mal

➤ **right of way** derecho de paso: **you have the right of way** tienes el derecho de paso.

**right-hand** [raɪthænd] *adjective*

➤ **it's on the right-hand side** está a mano derecha.

**right-handed** [raɪthændɪd] *adjective*
■ **diestro: she's right-handed** es diestra.

**ring** [rɪŋ] *(noun & verb)*

■ *noun*

1. **el anillo: she has a diamond ring on her finger** tiene un anillo de diamantes en el dedo

2. **el círculo: they formed a ring around him** formaron un círculo a su alrededor

3. **el ring** *(plural* **los rings): the boxers climbed into the ring** los boxeadores subieron al ring

4. **el timbre: there was a ring at the door** había un timbre en la puerta

➤ **an engagement ring** un anillo de compromiso

➤ **a wedding ring** un anillo de boda

➤ **a ring binder** un archivador

■ *verb*

*(past tense* **rang**, *past participle* **rung)** **sonar: the phone is ringing** está sonando el teléfono

➤ **to ring the doorbell** tocar el timbre: **somebody rang the doorbell** alguien tocó el timbre.

**rink** [rɪŋk] *noun*

➤ **an ice rink** una pista de hielo

➤ **a roller-skating rink** una pista de patinaje sobre ruedas.

**rinse** [rɪns] *verb* ■ **enjuagar: rinse with cool water** enjuague con agua fría.

**riot** ['raɪət] *noun* ■ **los disturbios: a riot broke out on the street** empezaron disturbios en la calle.

**rip** [rɪp] *(past tense & past participle* **ripped)** *verb*

1. **rasgarse: he ripped his shirt** se rasgó la camisa; **my coat has ripped** se me rasgó el abrigo

**2.** **arrancar:** he ripped the poster off the **wall** arrancó el póster de la pared.

**ripe** [raip] *adjective* ■ **maduro:** these bananas are very ripe estos plátanos están muy maduros.

**rise** [raiz] *(noun & verb)*

■ *noun*

el **aumento:** temperatures are on the rise las temperaturas van en aumento

■ *verb*

*(past tense* **rose**, *past participle* **risen)**

**1.** **subir:** prices are rising están subiendo los precios

**2.** **salir:** the sun rises in the east el sol sale por el este; smoke rose from the chimney el humo salió por la chimenea.

**risk** [risk] *noun* ■ **el riesgo:** he doesn't like taking risks no le gusta correr riesgos.

**risky** ['riski] *adjective* ■ **arriesgado:** it's too risky es demasiado arriesgado.

**rival** ['raivl] *noun* ■ **el rival:** the Bears defeated their rivals los Bears vencieron a sus rivales.

**river** ['rivər] *noun* ■ **el río:** the Missouri is the longest river in North America el Missouri es el río más largo de América del Norte

➤ the Mississippi River el río Mississippi.

**road** [rəud] *noun*

**1.** **la carretera:** we rode along an old country road anduvimos por una vieja carretera rural

**2.** **la calle:** she lives on the other side of the road vive al otro lado de la calle

➤ on the road de viaje: I was on the road all day estaba siempre de viaje

➤ a road map un mapa de carreteras

➤ roadworks las obras

➤ a road sign una señal de tránsito.

**roar** [rɔːr] *verb* ■ **rugir:** the lion roared el león rugió.

**roast** [rəust] *adjective* ■ **asado:** a roast chicken un pollo asado

➤ roast beef el rosbif.

**rob** [rɒb] *(past tense & past participle* **rob-bed)** *verb*

**1.** **robar:** I've been robbed me robaron

**2.** **asaltar:** somebody robbed the bank alguien asaltó el banco.

**robber** ['rɒbər] *noun* ■ **el ladrón** *(plural* los **ladrones)**

➤ a bank robber un asaltante de bancos.

**robbery** ['rɒbəri] *(plural* robberies*)* *noun* ■ **el robo:** there have been several robberies in the area ha habido varios robos en la zona

➤ a bank robbery un asalto a un banco.

**robin** ['rɒbin] *noun* ■ **el petirrojo.**

**robot** ['rəubɒt] *noun* ■ **el robot** *(plural* los **robots)**.

**rock** [rɒk] *noun*

**1.** **la roca:** they drilled through the rock perforaron la roca

**2.** **la piedra:** he threw a rock at me me tiró una piedra

**3.** **el rock:** Susie loves rock music a Susie le encanta la música rock

➤ rock and roll el rocanrol

➤ a rock band una banda de rock

➤ a rock star una estrella de rock.

**rocket** ['rɒkit] *noun* ■ **el cohete:** they sent a rocket into space enviaron un cohete al espacio.

**rocking chair** ['rɒkiŋtʃeər] *noun* ■ **la mecedora.**

**rocking horse** ['rɒkiŋhɔːs] *noun* ■ **el caballito de balancín.**

**rocky** ['rɒki] *adjective* ■ **pedregoso:** a rocky path un camino pedregoso

➤ the Rocky Mountains or the Rockies las Montañas Rocallosas or las Rocallosas

---

**ROCKY MOUNTAINS**

Las Rocky Mountains, o las Montañas Rocallosas, es la cordillera que corre desde Canadá hasta México y atraviesa los Estados Unidos de norte a sur en la zona oeste del país. Se les conoce por su gran belleza natural y son la sede de populares centros de esquí como Vail y Aspen.

**rod** [rɒd] *noun*
➤ a fishing rod una caña de pescar.

**rode** [rəʊd] *past tense* ➤ ride.

**role** [rəʊl] *noun* ■ el **papel** *(plural* los **papeles)*: he has an important role hace un papel importante.

**roll** [rəʊl] *(noun & verb)*

■ *noun*
1. el **rollo**: a roll of toilet paper un rollo de papel higiénico
2. el **panecito,** el **bolillo** *Mexico*: a bread roll un panecito

■ *verb*
1. **rodar**: the ball rolled under the chair la pelota rodó debajo de la silla
2. **hacer rodar**: they rolled the barrel all the way hicieron rodar el barril todo el camino
3. **tirar**: roll the dice tira los dados

**roll up** *phrasal verb*
1. **enrollar**: she rolled up the map enrolló el mapa
2. **remangarse**: Danny rolled up his sleeves Danny se remangó.

**roller** ['rəʊləʳ] *noun* ■ el **rulo,** el **chino** *Mexico*: her hair is in rollers tiene rulos en el pelo.

**Rollerblades**® ['rəʊləbleɪdz] *plural noun* ■ los **patines en línea**: a pair of Rollerblades® un par de patines en línea.

**rollerblading** ['rəʊləbleɪdɪŋ] *uncountable noun* ■ el **patinaje en línea**: she loves rollerblading le encanta el patinaje en línea.

**roller coaster** ['rəʊləʳkəʊstəʳ] *noun* ■ la **montaña rusa** *(plural* las **montañas rusas)*: let's go on the roller coaster vamos a la montaña rusa.

**roller skates** ['rəʊləʳskeɪts] *plural noun* ■ los **patines**: a pair of roller skates un par de patines.

**roller-skating** ['rəʊləʳskeɪtɪŋ] *uncountable noun* ■ el **patinaje sobre ruedas**: do you like roller-skating? ¿te gusta el patinaje sobre ruedas?

**Roman** ['rəʊmən] *(adjective & noun)*

■ *adjective*

Remember not to use a capital letter for the adjective in Spanish:

**romano**: Roman numerals números romanos
➤ the Roman empire el Imperio romano

■ *noun*
el **romano**: the Romans arrived in Britain in 55 B.C. los romanos llegaron a Gran Bretaña en 55 A.C.

**Roman Catholic** ['rəʊmən'kæθlɪk] *adjective & noun* ■ **católico**: he's Roman Catholic es católico
➤ the Roman Catholic Church la Iglesia Católica.

**romance** [rəʊ'mæns] *noun*
1. el **romance**: a fairytale romance un romance de cuento
2. el **encanto**: the romance of travel el encanto de viajar.

**romantic** [rəʊ'mæntɪk] *adjective* ■ **romántico**: he's very romantic es muy romántico.

**roof** [ruːf] *noun* ■ el **techo**: the cat climbed onto the roof el gato subió al techo.

**room** [ruːm, rʊm] *noun*
1. el **cuarto**: she went up to her room subió a su cuarto
2. el **dormitorio,** la **recámara** *Mexico*: go to your room! ¡vete a tu dormitorio!
3. el **espacio**: there isn't enough room no hay suficiente espacio; the boxes take up a lot of room las cajas ocupan mucho espacio.

**roommate** ['ruːmmeɪt] *noun* ■ el **compañero de cuarto** *(plural* los **compañeros de cuarto)*: we were roommates in college fuimos compañeros de cuarto en la universidad.

**root** [ruːt] *noun* ■ la **raíz** *(plural* las **raíces)*: the roots of the tree are very strong las raíces del árbol son muy fuertes.

**rope** [rəʊp] *noun* ■ la **soga**: I tied the rope to the tree amarré la soga al árbol.

**rose** [rəʊz] *(noun & verb form)*

■ *noun*
la **rosa**: he gave her a bouquet of red roses le dio un ramo de rosas rojas

■ *past tense*
➤ rise

**subir**: the balloon rose into the air el globo subió por el aire.

**rot** [rɒt] *(past tense & past participle* rotted) *verb* ■ **pudrirse**: this melon will rot if you don't eat it este melón se va a pudrir si no te lo comes.

**rotten** ['rɒtn] *adjective*

1. **podrido**: rotten bananas bananas podridas
2. *informal* **pésimo**: it was a rotten party fue una fiesta pésima
3. *informal* **horrible**: I feel rotten this morning me siento horrible esta mañana
➤ that was a rotten thing to do fue horrible lo que hiciste.

**rough** [rʌf] *adjective*

1. **áspero**: the table has a rough surface la mesa tiene una superficie áspera
2. **agitado**: the sea is rough today el mar está agitado hoy
3. **brusco**: he's very rough with his sister es muy brusco con su hermana
4. **duro**: he led a rough life tuvo una vida dura
5. **peligroso**: it's a rough neighborhood es un barrio peligroso
6. **vago**: I have a rough idea of what to do tengo una vaga idea de qué hacer
➤ a rough copy un borrador.

**round** [raʊnd] *(adjective & noun)*

■ *adjective*
**redondo**: a round window una ventana redonda
➤ a round trip un viaje de ida y vuelta, un viaje redondo *Mexico*
➤ a round trip ticket un pasaje de ida y vuelta, un boleto redondo *Mexico:* I bought a round trip ticket to Boston compré un pasaje de ida y vuelta a Boston

■ *noun*
1. *In boxing* el **round**: he was knocked out in the first round fue noqueado en el primer round

2. la **visita a domicilio**: the doctor is doing his rounds el doctor está haciendo visitas a domicilios
3. la **vuelta**: they lost in the first round of the tournament perdieron en la primera vuelta del torneo
➤ a round of ammunition un disparo
➤ a round of applause un aplauso: he got a huge round of applause recibió un gran aplauso.

**route** [ruːt] *noun*

1. el **camino**: what is the quickest route to Houston? ¿cuál es el camino más rápido a Houston?
2. la **ruta**: Route 66 la Ruta 66
➤ a paper route un reparto de periódicos: Billy has a paper route Billy hace un reparto de periódicos.

**routine** [ruːˈtiːn] *noun* ■ la **rutina**: exercise is part of my daily routine el ejercicio es parte de mi rutina diaria.

**row** *(noun & verb)*

■ *noun*
['rəʊ]
1. la **hilera**: a row of houses una hilera de casas
2. la **fila**: they are sitting in the second row están sentados en la segunda fila
➤ in a row seguido: he phoned her three times in a row la llamó tres veces seguidas

■ *verb*
[rəʊ]
**remar**: he rowed for three hours remó por tres horas
➤ to row across the river cruzar el río a remo.

**rowboat** ['rəʊbəʊt] *noun* ■ el **bote a remos**.

**rowdy** ['raʊdɪ] *adjective* ■ **bullicioso**: a rowdy class una clase bulliciosa.

**royal** ['rɔɪəl] *adjective* ■ **real**: the royal family la familia real.

**rub** [rʌb] *(past tense & past participle* rubbed) *verb*

1. **frotar**: don't rub so hard no frotes tan fuerte

2. **frotarse:** he rubbed his eyes se frotó los ojos.

**rubber** ['rʌbəʳ] *noun* ■ la **goma,** el **hule** *Mexico*: the ball is made of rubber la pelota es de goma
➤ a rubber ball una pelota de goma
➤ a rubber band una goma elástica, una liga *Mexico*.

**ruby** ['ruːbɪ] *noun* ■ el **rubí** (*plural* los **rubíes**): a ruby necklace un collar de rubíes.

**rude** [ruːd] *adjective*
1. **grosero:** she was rude to her mother fue grosera con su madre
2. **de mala educación:** it's rude to talk with your mouth full es de mala educación hablar con la boca llena.

**rug** [rʌg] *noun* ■ la **alfombra:** there's a rug in front of the fireplace hay una alfombra frente a la chimenea.

**ruin** ['ruːɪn] (*noun & verb*)
■ *noun*
la **ruina:** they found the ruins of an old castle encontraron las ruinas de un viejo castillo
➤ in ruins en ruinas: the city is in ruins la ciudad está en ruinas
■ *verb*
**arruinar:** he ruined my party arruinó mi fiesta; the crash ruined him el choque lo arruinó.

**rule** [ruːl] (*noun & verb*)
■ *noun*
la **regla:** what are the rules of the game? ¿cuáles son las reglas del juego?; he broke the rules rompió las reglas
➤ to be against the rules ir contra las reglas: smoking is against the rules fumar va contra las reglas
■ *verb*
**gobernar:** who is going to rule the country? ¿quién va a gobernar el país?

**rule out** *phrasal verb* ■ **descartar:** we can't rule out the possibility of rain no podemos descartar la posibilidad de que llueva.

**ruler** ['ruːləʳ] *noun*
1. la **regla:** use a ruler to measure the line usa una regla para medir la línea
2. el **gobernante:** the ruler of the country el gobernante de un país.

**rum** [rʌm] *noun* ■ el **ron.**

**rumor** ['ruːməʳ] *noun* ■ el **rumor** (*plural* los **rumores**): it's just a rumor sólo es un rumor.

**run** [rʌn] (*noun & verb*)
■ *noun*
1. she went for a five-mile run salió a correr cinco millas
2. la **carrera:** he scored 4 runs anotó 4 carreras; I have a run in my pantyhose tengo una carrera en la media
➤ in the long run a la larga: in the long run it won't really matter a la larga, no importará realmente
■ *verb*
(*past tense* **ran**, *past participle* **run**)
1. **correr:** she ran 5 miles corrió 5 millas; you left the water running dejaste el agua corriendo
2. **dirigir:** she runs a big company dirige una gran empresa
3. **gotear:** my nose is running me gotea la nariz
4. **marchar:** the bus runs on gas el autobús marcha a gasolina; the engine is running el motor está marchando
5. **circular:** the trains don't run on Sundays los trenes no circulan los domingos
6. **pasar:** she ran her hand through her hair se pasó la mano por el cabello
7. **ser candidato a:** Bush is running for president Bush es candidato a presidente

**run away** *phrasal verb* ■ **huir:** the thieves ran away los ladrones huyeron.

**run out** *phrasal verb* ■ **agotarse:** their supplies ran out se les agotaron las provisiones
➤ time is running out se está acabando el tiempo
➤ to run out of something quedarse sin algo: they ran out of milk se quedaron sin leche.

**run over** *phrasal verb* ■ **atropellar:** he was run over by a car lo atropelló un coche
➤ to get run over ser atropellado.

**rung** [rʌŋ] *past participle* ➤ ring.

**runner** ['rʌnəʳ] *noun* ■ el **corredor,** la **corredora:** there are ten runners in this race hay diez corredores en esta carrera.

**runner-up** ['rʌnəʳʌp] *noun* ■ el **sub-campeón** (plural los **subcampeones**), la **subcampeona:** she was runner-up in her category fue subcampeona en su categoría.

**running** ['rʌnɪŋ] *noun* ■ he took up running at 40 empezó a correr a los 40 años.

**runny** ['rʌnɪ] *adjective*
➤ to have a runny nose gotear la nariz: I have a runny nose me gotea la nariz.

**runway** ['rʌnweɪ] *noun* ■ la **pista de aterrizaje:** the plane is on the runway el avión está en la pista de aterrizaje.

**rush** [rʌʃ] (*noun & verb*)
■ *noun*
el **apuro:** what's the rush? ¿qué apuro hay?
➤ in a rush a la carrera: I did my homework in a rush hice mi tarea a la carrera
➤ to be in a rush estar apurado: I'm in a rush! ¡estoy apurado!
➤ rush hour hora pico: traffic is awful at rush hour el tráfico es terrible a la hora pico
■ *verb*
**apurarse:** you'll have to rush if you want to catch the train tendrás que apurarte si quieres alcanzar el tren.

**rust** ['rʌst] *noun* ■ el **óxido:** your bike is covered in rust tu bicicleta está cubierta de óxido.

**rusty** ['rʌstɪ] *adjective* ■ **oxidado:** a rusty old nail un viejo clavo oxidado
➤ my Italian is rusty tengo muy olvidado el italiano.

**rye** [raɪ] *noun* ■ el **centeno:** rye bread pan de centeno.

**sack** [sæk] *noun* ■ el **saco:** a sack of potatoes un saco de papas.

**sad** [sæd] *adjective* ■ **triste:** she looks very sad parece estar muy triste.

**saddle** ['sædl] *noun* ■ la **montura:** the jockey climbed into the saddle el jinete subió a su montura.

**sadly** ['sædlɪ] *adverb*
1. **con tristeza:** he looked at me sadly me miró con tristeza
2. **lamentablemente:** sadly she died lamen-tablemente murió.

**sadness** ['sædnɪs] *noun* ■ la **tristeza**.

**safe** [seɪf] (*adjective & noun*)
■ *adjective*
1. **sin peligro:** it's safe to swim here aquí se puede nadar sin peligro
2. **a salvo:** he's safe now ahora está a salvo
3. **seguro:** this ladder isn't very safe esta escalera no es muy segura
4. **prudente:** he's a safe pilot es un piloto prudente
➤ to feel safe sentirse seguro
➤ to be in a safe place estar en un lugar se-guro: the jewels are in a safe place las joyas están en un lugar seguro
➤ it's not safe no es seguro
■ *noun*
la **caja fuerte:** there's a lot of money in the safe hay mucho dinero en la caja fuerte.

**safety** ['seɪftɪ] *noun* ■ la **seguridad:** they say they do it for our safety dicen que lo hacen por nuestra seguridad
➤ a safety belt un cinturón de seguridad

➤ a safety pin un imperdible, un seguro *Mexico*.

**said** [sed] *past tense & past participle*
➤ say.

**sail** [seɪl] *(noun & verb)*

■ *noun*
la **vela**: a ship in full sail un barco con las velas desplegadas

➤ to set sail zarpar: they set sail at dawn zarparon al amanecer

■ *verb*

1. navegar: the boat is sailing to America el barco está navegando hacia Estados Unidos

2. ir en barco: it takes three hours to sail to the island ir en barco a la isla se tarda tres horas

3. zarpar: we sail tomorrow mañana zarpamos.

**sailboat** [seɪlbəʊt] *noun* ■ el **velero**.

**sailing** ['seɪlɪŋ] *uncountable noun* ■ navegar: he goes sailing on the weekends sale a navegar los fines de semana.

**sailor** ['seɪlər] *noun* ■ el **marinero**.

**saint** [seɪnt] *noun* ■ el **santo**, la **santa**: he's a saint es un santo

Before a man's name, **Santo** is shortened to **San**, except before Tomás and Domingo:

Saint Paul San Pablo; **Saint Thomas** Santo Tomás; **Saint Catherine** Santa Catalina
➤ **Saint Patrick's Day** el día de San Patricio.

**sake** [seɪk] *noun*

➤ for somebody's sake por alguien: do it for my sake hazlo por mí.

**salad** ['sæləd] *noun* ■ la **ensalada**
➤ salad dressing el aderezo de ensalada.

**salary** ['sælərɪ] *(plural salaries) noun*
■ el **sueldo**.

**sale** [seɪl] *noun* ■ la **rebaja**: Bloomingdale's is having a sale hay rebajas en Bloomingdale's

➤ on sale a precio rebajado: I bought this coat on sale compré este abrigo a precio rebajado

➤ for sale se vende: their house is not for sale su casa no se vende.

**salesman** ['seɪlzmən] *(plural salesmen* ['seɪlzmən]*) noun* ■ el **vendedor**: he's an insurance salesman es vendedor de seguros.

**salmon** ['sæmən] *noun* ■ el **salmón** *(plural* los **salmones**).

**salon** ['sælɒn] *noun* ■ el **salón** *(plural* los **salones**): a beauty salon un salón de belleza.

**salt** [sɒlt] *noun* ■ la **sal**.

**salty** ['sɔːltɪ] *adjective* ■ **salado**.

**salute** [sə'luːt] *verb* ■ **saludar**: the general saluted the troops el general saludó a las tropas.

**same** [seɪm] *adjective & pronoun* ■ **mismo**: she's wearing the same sweater as I am tiene puesto el mismo suéter que yo; we left at the same time nos fuimos al mismo tiempo

➤ the same el mismo: she has the same one as me tiene el mismo que yo, lo mismo: I'm going to have the same as you voy a pedir lo mismo que tú

➤ to look the same parecerse: they all look the same todos se parecen.

**sand** [sænd] *uncountable noun* ■ la **arena**

➤ a sand castle un castillo de arena
➤ a sand dune una duna de arena.

**sandal** ['sændl] *noun* ■ la **sandalia**, el **huarache** *Mexico*: she's wearing sandals tiene sandalias puestas.

**sandwich** ['sænwɪdʒ] *noun* ■ el **sándwich** *(plural* los **sándwiches**): a cheese sandwich un sándwich de queso.

**sang** [sæŋ] *past tense* ➤ sing.

**sanitary napkin** ['sænɪtrɪ'næpkɪn] *noun* ■ la **toalla higiénica**.

**sank** [sæŋk] *past tense* ➤ sink.

**Santa Claus** ['sæntə,klɔːz] *noun* ■ **Papá Noel**.

**sarcastic** [saːrˈkæstɪk] *adjective* ■ **sarcástico**.

**sardine** [saːˈdiːn] *noun* ■ **la sardina**.

**sat** [sæt] *past tense & past participle* ➤ sit.

**SAT** [ɜseɪtiː] *noun* ■ un examen

SAT

✎ El **SAT** (las siglas no tienen significado) es un examen de conocimientos generales que se ofrece a nivel nacional a los estudiantes que desean asistir a alguna universidad estadounidense. El examen se administra en ciertas fechas fijas a lo largo del año escolar, y se puede presentar más de una vez si es necesario para obtener un buen resultado. Aunque es una parte importante de la solicitud universitaria, el SAT no es el único criterio para admisión. También se consideran las calificaciones y actividades del estudiante.

**satellite** [ˈsætəlaɪt] *noun* ■ **el satélite**: satellite TV televisión por satélite
➤ a satellite dish una antena parabólica.

**satisfied** [ˈsætɪsfaɪd] *adjective* ■ **satisfecho**: I'm not satisfied with your work no estoy satisfecha con tu trabajo.

**Saturday** [ˈsætədɪ] *noun*

In Spanish the days of the week do not start with a capital letter:

el **sábado**: it's Saturday today hoy es sábado; next Saturday el próximo sábado; last Saturday el sábado pasado
➤ on Saturday el sábado: I'll see you on Saturday te veo el sábado
➤ on Saturdays los sábados: he comes to see me on Saturdays viene a verme los sábados.

**sauce** [sɔːs] *noun* ■ **la salsa**: apple sauce salsa de manzana.

**saucepan** [ˈsɔːspən] *noun* ■ **la cacerola**.

**sauna** [ˈsɔːnə] *noun* ■ **el sauna**.

**sausage** [ˈsɒsɪdʒ] *noun* ■ **la salchicha**.

**save** [seɪv] *verb*
1. **salvar**: she saved my life me salvó la vida
2. **ahorrar**: we must try and save water debemos tratar de ahorrar agua
3. **ahorrarse**: I saved a hundred dollars me ahorré cien dólares
4. **guardar**: he saved the cake for later guardó el pastel para más tarde; I saved my file onto a floppy guardé mi archivo en un diskette
➤ to save time ahorrar tiempo: that will save you a lot of time eso te ahorrará mucho tiempo

**save up** *phrasal verb* ■ **ahorrar**: he's saving up to buy a guitar está ahorrando para comprar una guitarra.

**savings** [ˈseɪvɪŋz] *plural noun* ■ **los ahorros**: she has spent all her savings se ha gastado todos sus ahorros.

**saw** [sɔː] *(noun, verb & verb form)*
■ *noun*
la sierra: a power saw una sierra eléctrica
■ *verb*
*(past tense* sawed, *past participle* sawed*)* **cortar**: he sawed the board in half cortó la tabla a la mitad
■ *past tense*
➤ see.

**saxophone** [ˈsæksəfəʊn] *noun* ■ **el saxofón** *(plural* los **saxofones***)*: she plays the saxophone toca el saxofón.

**say** [seɪ] *(past tense & past participle* said*)* *verb* ■ **decir**: what did you say? ¿qué dijiste?; I said I was tired dije que estoy cansado
➤ could you say that again? ¿podrías repetir lo que dijiste?

**saying** [ˈseɪɪŋ] *noun* ■ **el dicho**: it's a well-known saying es un dicho muy conocido.

**scale** [skeɪl] *noun*
1. la **escala**: this map has a scale of 1/100 este mapa tiene una escala de 1/100; she's practicing her scales está practicando las escalas
2. la **magnitud**: the scale of the damage la magnitud del daño

3. la **balanza**: put your luggage on the scale coloque su equipaje sobre la balanza
➤ a bathroom scale una báscula.

**scan** [skæn] *(past tense & past participle* scanned*) verb* ■ **escanear:** I scanned the photo escanée la foto.

**scandal** ['skændl] *noun* ■ **el escándalo:** it caused a scandal causó un escándalo.

**scanner** ['skænər] *noun* ■ **el escáner** *(plural* **los escáneres***)*: put the photo in the scanner pon la foto en el escáner.

**scar** [skaːr] *noun* ■ **la cicatriz** *(plural* **las cicatrices***)*.

**scare** [skeər] *(noun & verb)*
■ *noun*
el **susto:** you gave me a scare me diste un susto
➤ a bomb scare una amenaza de bomba
■ *verb*
**asustar:** Juan scares me Juan me asusta.

**scarecrow** ['skeəkrəʊ] *noun* ■ el **espantapájaros** *(plural* los **espantapájaros***)*.

**scared** ['skeəd] *adjective* ■ **asustado:** I was scared of him estaba asustada de él; I'm not scared of flying no me asusta volar.

**scarf** [skaːf] *(plural* scarfs [skaːfs] o scarves [skaːvz]*) noun*
1. la **bufanda:** a woolen scarf una bufanda de lana
2. el **pañuelo:** a silk scarf un pañuelo de seda.

**scary** [skeəri] *adjective*
➤ to be scary ser aterrador: it's a scary film es una película de terror.

**scarves** *plural* ➤ scarf.

**scene** [siːn] *noun*
1. la **escena:** there is a very funny scene in the film hay una escena muy divertida en la película
2. el **lugar:** the scene of the crime el lugar del crimen
➤ behind the scenes entre bastidores.

**scenery** ['siːnəri] *uncountable noun* ■ el **paisaje:** I love the scenery in this part of the country me encanta el paisaje en esta zona del país.

**schedule** ['skedʒʊl] *noun* ■ el **calendario:** I have a busy schedule tengo el calendario muy apretado
➤ we're on schedule estamos al día
➤ we're ahead of schedule estamos adelantados
➤ we're behind schedule estamos atrasados.

**scheme** [skiːm] *noun* ■ el **plan:** it's a scheme to make money es un plan para ganar dinero.

**scholarship** ['skɒləʃɪp] *noun* ■ la **beca:** he got a scholarship obtuvo una beca.

**school** [skuːl] *noun* ■ el **colegio:** all children have to go to school up to the age of 16 todos los niños tienen que ir al colegio hasta los 16 años
➤ a school bus un autobús escolar, un camión escolar *Mexico*
➤ the school year el año escolar

**SCHOOL**

El sistema educativo en los Estados Unidos se divide en dos niveles básicos: primaria y secundaria. La escuela primaria (**grade school**) abarca de 1 a 8 años. Los alumnos entran a high school, la etapa secundaria, aproximadamente a los 14 años. Este nivel abarca cuatro años (de 9 a 12); generalmente los estudiantes se gradúan a la edad de 18. El gobierno ofrece educación primaria y secundaria gratuita y obligatoria a todos los niños a través de las escuelas públicas (**public schools**), pero también existe la posibilidad de asistir a escuelas privadas (**private schools**).

**schoolbook** ['skuːlbʊk] *noun* ■ el **libro de texto:** don't forget your schoolbooks no te olvides de tus libros de texto.

**schoolchildren** ['skuːltʃɪldrən] *plural noun* ■ los **escolares**.

**science** ['saɪəns] *noun* ■ la **ciencia**: science and technology ciencia y tecnología; **Chris wants to study science** Chris quiere estudiar ciencias

➤ **science fiction** ciencia ficción: **it's a science fiction book** es un libro de ciencia ficción.

**scientific** [ˌsaɪən'tɪfɪk] *adjective* ■ **científico**.

**scientist** ['saɪəntɪst] *noun* ■ el **científico**, la **científica**.

**scissors** ['sɪzəz] *plural noun* ■ las **tijeras**

➤ **a pair of scissors** unas tijeras.

**scoop** [skuːp] *noun* ■ la **bola**: **three scoops of ice cream** tres bolas de helado.

**scooter** ['skuːtər] *noun*

1. la **Vespa®**, la **motoneta** *South America*: **a lot of people use scooters to get around** mucha gente usa Vespas® para trasladarse

2. la **patineta**, el **patín del diablo** *(plural* los **patines del diablo**) *Mexico*: **the child was playing on his scooter** el niño jugaba con su patineta.

**score** [skɔːr] *(noun & verb)*

■ *noun*
el **resultado**: **the final score was one nothing** el resultado final fue uno a cero
➤ **what's the score?** ¿cómo van?
■ *verb*
**marcar**: **he scored a goal** marcó un gol; **they haven't scored yet** no han marcado todavía.

**scorpion** ['skɔːpjən] *noun* ■ el **escorpión** *(plural* los **escorpiones**).

**Scotland** ['skɒtlənd] *noun* ■ **Escocia** *(feminine)*.

**Scottish** ['skɒtɪʃ] *adjective*

Remember not to use a capital letter for the adjective in Spanish:

**escocés**: **the Scottish countryside is beautiful** la campiña escocesa es hermosa.

**scrambled eggs** ['skræmbldegz] *plural noun* ■ los **huevos revueltos**.

**scratch** [skrætʃ] *(noun & verb)*
■ *noun*
1. el **rasguño**: **my legs are covered with scratches** tengo las piernas llenas de rasguños

2. el **rayón** *(plural* los **rayones**): **there's a scratch on this CD** este CD tiene un rayón
➤ **to start from scratch** empezar desde cero: **we'll just have to start from scratch** vamos a tener que empezar desde cero
■ *verb*
1. **rascar**: **can you scratch my back?** ¿me rascas la espalda?

2. **rascarse**: **don't scratch** no te rasques; **he was scratching his leg** se estaba rascando la pierna

3. **arañar**: **the cat scratched my hand** el gato me arañó la mano.

**scratch paper** [skrætʃ'peɪpər] *noun* ■ el **papel de borrador**.

**scream** [skriːm] *(noun & verb)*
■ *noun*
el **grito**: **I could hear screams** oía gritos
■ *verb*
**gritar**: **she screamed when the vampire appeared** gritó cuando apareció el vampiro.

**screen** [skriːn] *noun* ■ la **pantalla**: **it's a good film to see on the big screen** es una buena película para ver en pantalla grande; **the computer screen is very bright** la pantalla de la computadora está muy brillante
➤ **a screen saver** un protector de pantalla.

**screw** [skruː] *(noun & verb)*
■ *noun*
el **tornillo**: **he went to buy some screws** fue a comprar tornillos
■ *verb*
1. **atornillar**: **you have to screw the mirror to the wall** tienes que atornillar el espejo a la pared

2. **enroscar**: **I screwed the top on the bottle** enrosqué la tapa en la botella.

**screwdriver** ['skruːˌdraɪvər] *noun* ■ el **destornillador**, el **desarmador** *Mexico*.

**scroll** [skrəʊl] *verb* ■ **desplazarse:** scroll down to the end of the document desplácese hacia abajo, hasta el final del documento.

**sculptor** ['skʌlptər] *noun* ■ el **escultor,** la **escultora.**

**sculpture** ['skʌlptʃər] *noun* ■ la **escultura:** an exhibition of modern sculptures una exposición de esculturas modernas.

**sea** [si:] *noun* ■ el **mar: I** like swimming in the sea me gusta nadar en el mar
➤ by sea en barco
➤ by the sea a orillas del mar.

**seafood** ['si:fu:d] *uncountable noun* ■ los **mariscos.**

**seagull** ['si:gʌl] *noun* ■ la **gaviota.**

**seal** [si:l] *(noun & verb)*
■ *noun*
la **foca:** seals are mammals that live in cold waters las focas son mamíferos que viven en aguas frías
■ *verb*
**cerrar:** have you sealed the envelope yet? ¿ya cerraste el sobre?

**search** [sɜ:tʃ] *(noun & verb)*
■ *noun*
1. el **registro,** el **cateo:** the police carried out a search of the house la policía efectuó un registro domiciliario
2. la **búsqueda:** there was a search for the missing boy se hizo una búsqueda del chico desaparecido
➤ a search engine un buscador
➤ a search party un grupo de rescate
■ *verb*
1. **registrar, catear** *Mexico:* the police searched the apartment la policía registró el departamento
2. **buscar:** we searched the whole town buscamos por toda la ciudad; I searched my pockets busqué en mis bolsillos

**search for** *phrasal verb* ■ **buscar:** I'm searching for my keys estoy buscando mis llaves.

**seashell** ['si:ʃel] *noun* ■ la **concha marina.**

**seasick** ['si:sɪk] *adjective*
➤ to be seasick estar mareado: she was seasick estaba mareada
➤ to get seasick marearse.

**season** ['si:zn] *noun*
1. la **estación** *(plural* las **estaciones):** my favorite season is spring mi estación favorita es la primavera
2. la **temporada:** it's football season es temporada de fútbol
➤ a season ticket un abono: I'm going to get season tickets voy a comprar unos abonos.

**seat** [si:t] *noun*
1. el **asiento:** your book's on the back seat of the car tu libro está en el asiento de atrás del automóvil
2. el **escaño,** el **curul** *Colombia, Mexico,* la **banca** *Southern Cone:* he has a seat in Congress tiene un escaño en el Congreso
3. la **localidad:** I reserved two seats for the play reservé dos localidades para ver la obra
➤ a seat belt un cinturón de seguridad: **fasten your seat belts** ajústense los cinturones de seguridad.

**seaweed** ['si:wi:d] *uncountable noun* ■ el **alga marina**

> Feminine noun that takes **un** or **el** in the singular.

**second** ['sekənd] *(adjective & noun)*
■ *adjective*
**segundo:** that's the second time he has rung ésa es la segunda vez que toca el timbre
➤ it's June second today hoy es el dos de junio
➤ on the second floor en el segundo piso
➤ to come in second llegar segundo
■ *noun*
el **segundo:** wait a second! ¡espera un segundo!
➤ to have seconds repetir: may I have seconds? ¿puedo repetir?

**second-hand** [,sekənd'hænd] *adjective & adverb* ■ **de segunda mano:** it's a second-hand bike es una bicicleta de segunda mano; I bought it second-hand la compré de segunda mano.

**secret** ['siːkrɪt] *(adjective & noun)*

■ *adjective*
**secreto: it's a secret meeting place** es un lugar de encuentro secreto

■ *noun*
**el secreto: he can't keep a secret** no sabe guardar un secreto

➤ **we met in secret** nos encontramos en secreto.

**secretary** ['sekrətrɪ] *(plural* secretaries*) noun* ■ **el secretario, la secretaria**.

**section** ['sekʃn] *noun* ■ **la sección** *(plural* las **secciones***): there are three sections to the newspaper** hay tres secciones en el diario.

**security** [sɪ'kjʊərətɪ] *noun* ■ **la seguridad: security at the airport has been tightened** han reforzado la seguridad en el aeropuerto

➤ **a security guard** un guardia de seguridad.

**see** [siː] *(past tense* saw, *past participle* seen*) verb* ■ **ver: I saw Jack yesterday** ayer vi a Jack; **have you seen any good films recently?** ¿has visto alguna buena película últimamente?; **I can't see** no veo; **I'll see what I can do** veré lo que puedo hacer

➤ **we'll see** veremos
➤ **see you soon!** ¡hasta pronto!
➤ **see you!** ¡nos vemos!

**see off** *phrasal verb* ■ **despedir: he saw me off at the airport** me despidió en el aeropuerto.

**see to** *phrasal verb* ■ **encargarse de: I can't close the door — I'll see to it** no puedo cerrar la puerta — yo me encargo de eso.

**seed** [siːd] *noun* ■ **la semilla: she planted some sunflower seeds** plantó unas semillas de girasol.

**seek** [siːk] *(past tense & past participle* sought*) verb* ■ **buscar: we're seeking a solution** estamos buscando una solución.

**seem** [siːm] *verb* ■ **parecer: she seems sad** parece triste; **they seem bored** parecen estar aburridos; **you seem to be having problems** parece que tienes problemas;

**there seems to be a delay** parece que hay una demora.

**seen** [siːn] *past participle* ➤ see.

**seesaw** ['siːsɔː] *noun* ■ **el balancín** *(plural* los **balancines***)*.

**select** [sɪ'lekt] *verb* ■ **seleccionar: she selected the CD she wanted** seleccionó los CD que quería.

**selection** [sɪ'lekʃn] *noun*
1. **la selección** *(plural* las **selecciones***): you've made a good selection** hiciste una buena selección
2. **el surtido: there's a good selection of food in the market** hay gran surtido de comida en el mercado.

**self-confident** [ˌself'kɒnfɪdənt] *adjective* ■ **seguro de sí mismo: Kim's very self-confident** Kim es muy segura de sí misma.

**self-conscious** [ˌself'kɒnʃəs] *adjective* ■ **cohibido: I feel very self-conscious in my red hat** me siento muy cohibida con mi sombrero rojo.

**self-control** [ˌselfkən'trəʊl] *noun* ■ **el dominio de sí mismo: he lost his self-control** perdió el dominio de sí mismo.

**self-defense** [ˌselfdɪ'fens] *noun* ■ **la defensa personal: a self-defense course** un curso de defensa personal

➤ **in self-defense** en defensa propia: **she shot him in self-defense** le disparó en defensa propia.

**selfish** ['selfɪʃ] *adjective* ■ **egoísta**.

**sell** [sel] *(past tense & past participle* sold*) verb* ■ **vender: I sold him my bike** le vendí mi bici

**sell out** *phrasal verb* ■ **all the tickets are sold out** las entradas están agotadas; **we're sold out of coffee** se nos terminó el café.

**semester** [sɪ'mestər] *noun* ■ **el semestre**.

**semicircle** ['semɪsɜːkl] *noun* ■ el **semicírculo**.

**semicolon** [ˌsemɪ'kəʊlən] *noun* ■ el **punto y coma**.

**Senate** ['senɪt] *noun* ■ the Senate el Senado

SENATE

El Senado (**Senate**) constituye, junto con la Cámara de Representantes, el organismo legislativo estadounidense. Se elige a sus 100 miembros cada seis años. Cada uno de los 50 estados tiene 2 senadores. Todas las leyes nuevas deben ser ratificadas por ambas cámaras del Congreso.

**senator** ['senətəʳ] *noun* ■ el **senador**, la **senadora**: he's a New York senator es senador por Nueva York.

**send** [send] *(past tense & past participle* sent*) verb* ■ **mandar**: he sent me a letter me mandó una carta

➤ send them my love mándales saludos de mi parte

➤ to send somebody home mandar a alguien a casa

**send back** *phrasal verb* ■ **devolver, regresar** *Latin America except Southern Cone*: if you don't want it, you can send it back si no lo quieres, puedes devolverlo.

**send for** *phrasal verb* ■ **mandar a buscar**: I sent for the doctor mandé a buscar al médico.

**send off** *phrasal verb* ■ **despachar**: Ray sent off the package yesterday Ray despachó el paquete ayer.

**senior** ['siːnjəʳ] *(adjective & noun)*

■ *adjective*
**alto**: these are senior people in the government estos son altos personajes del gobierno

➤ a senior citizen una persona de la tercera edad

➤ senior year el último año de la universidad: Raul's in his senior year Raúl está en el último año de la universidad

■ *noun*
1. el/la **estudiante del último año**: the school's seniors are taking their final exams los estudiantes del último año están haciendo sus exámenes finales
2. la **persona de la tercera edad**: the seniors of the community decided to start a bingo club las personas de la tercera edad de la comunidad decidieron abrir un club de bingo

➤ he's my senior es mi superior

 Senior es un falso amigo, no significa "señor".

**sense** [sens] *noun*
1. el **sentido**: what you say doesn't make sense lo que dices no tiene sentido; the five senses los cinco sentidos
2. el **sentido común**: you have no sense no tienes sentido común

➤ that makes sense eso tiene sentido

➤ a sense of humor un sentido del humor: she doesn't have a sense of humor no tiene sentido del humor

➤ the sense of smell el sentido del olfato

➤ the sense of touch el sentido del tacto.

**sensible** ['sensəbl] *adjective* ■ **sensato**

⚠ La palabra inglesa **sensible** es un falso amigo, no significa "sensible".

**sensitive** ['sensɪtɪv] *adjective* ■ **sensible**: he's a sensitive boy es un muchacho sensible

➤ she's sensitive about her weight no le gusta que hagan comentarios sobre su peso.

**sent** [sent] *past tense & past participle* ➤ send.

**sentence** ['sentəns] *(noun & verb)*

■ *noun*
la **oración** *(plural* las **oraciones)**: a sentence should begin with a capital letter and end with a period una oración debe empezar con mayúscula y terminar con un punto

■ *verb*
**condenar**: he was sentenced to five years in prison lo condenaron a cinco años de prisión.

**separate** *(adjective & verb)*

■ *adjective*
['seprət]

1. **aparte:** put it in a separate envelope pon-lo en un sobre aparte

2. **diferente:** these are two separate issues estos son dos temas diferentes

3. **separado:** can we have separate receipts? ¿podría darnos recibos separados?

➤ she has a separate room tiene su propio cuarto

■ *verb*
['sepəreɪt]

1. **separar:** they separated the boys from the girls separaron a los niños de las niñas

2. **separarse:** they separated after ten years of marriage se separaron después de diez años de matrimonio.

**September** [sep'tembər] *noun*

In Spanish the months of the year do not start with a capital letter:

**septiembre** *(masculine)*: school starts in September las clases empiezan en septiembre; **next September** el próximo septiembre; **last September** el pasado septiembre.

**sequel** ['siːkwəl] *noun* ■ la **continuación** *(plural* las **continuaciones)*: have you seen the sequel to the film? ¿viste la continuación de la película?

**sergeant** ['saːdʒənt] *noun* ■ el/la **sargento:** he's a sergeant in the army es sargento de la armada; **he's a police sergeant** es sargento de policía.

**series** ['siəriːz] *(plural* series) *noun* ■ la **serie:** we've had a series of problems hemos tenido una serie de problemas

➤ The World Series La Serie Mundial.

**serious** ['siəriəs] *adjective*

1. **serio:** he always looks serious siempre se ve serio

2. **grave:** she has a serious illness padece una enfermedad grave.

**seriously** ['siəriəsli] *adverb*

1. **en serio:** seriously, what do you think? en serio, ¿qué crees tú?

2. **gravemente:** he was seriously injured estaba gravemente herido.

**serve** [sɜːv] *verb* ■ **servir:** dinner is served at 7 o'clock la cena se sirve a las 7 en punto

➤ that serves you right lo tienes bien merecido.

**service** ['sɜːvɪs] *noun*

1. el **servicio:** the service is good in this restaurant el servicio en este restaurante es bueno

2. la **revisión** *(plural* las **revisiones)*: I'm going to take the car for a service voy a llevar el coche para que le hagan la revisión

➤ a service station una estación de servicio.

**session** ['seʃn] *noun* ■ la **sesión** *(plural* las **sesiones)*: a recording session una sesión de grabación.

**set** [set] *(noun, adjective & verb)*

■ *noun*

1. el **juego:** a set of keys un juego de llaves; **a chess set** un juego de ajedrez

2. la **colección** *(plural* las **colecciones)*: a set of encyclopedias la colección de enciclopedias

3. el **set:** Sampras won the first set Sampras ganó el primer set

➤ a television set un televisor

■ *adjective*
**listo:** they were set to leave estaban listos para salir

➤ a set menu un menú del día

■ *verb*
*(past tense & past participle* set)

1. **poner:** she set the vase on the table puso el jarrón sobre la mesa; **he set his bike against the wall** puso su bici contra la pared; **I'll set the alarm for 6 a.m.** voy a poner el despertador a las 6 a.m.

2. **fijar:** let's set a time and a place fijemos una hora y lugar

3. **establecer:** he set a new world record estableció un nuevo record mundial

4. **ponerse:** the sun's setting el sol se está poniendo

➤ to set somebody free poner en libertad a alguien

➤ to set something on fire prenderle fuego a algo

➤ to set the table poner la mesa

➤ the film's set in Casablanca la película está ambientada en Casablanca

**set off** *phrasal verb*

1. **salir:** they set off at dawn salieron al amanecer
2. **tirar:** they set some fireworks off tiraron fuegos artificiales
3. **hacer explotar:** they set the bomb off hicieron explotar la bomba
4. **hacer sonar:** the burglar set the alarm off el ladrón hizo sonar la alarma.

**set out** *phrasal verb* ■ **proponerse:** he set out to find the buried treasure se propuso encontrar el tesoro enterrado.

**set up** *phrasal verb*

1. **montar:** he set up a new business montó un nuevo negocio
2. **instalar:** he set the computer up in his room instaló la computadora en su cuarto
3. **armar:** they set the tent up in the garden armaron la tienda en el jardín.

**settle** ['setl] *verb*

1. **resolver:** we settled the argument resolvimos la discusión
2. **pagar:** may I settle the bill now? ¿podría pagar la cuenta ahora?
3. **establecerse:** they settled in Canada se establecieron en Canadá
➤ that's settled queda decidido

**settle down** *phrasal verb*

1. **calmarse:** settle down! ¡cálmate!
2. **acomodarse:** she settled down in the armchair se acomodó en el sillón.

**seven** ['sevn] *number* ■ **siete:** the seven wonders of the world las siete maravillas del mundo; she's seven tiene siete años; he went out at seven salió a las siete.

**seventeen** [,sevn'tiːn] *number* ■ **diecisiete:** there are seventeen girls in the class hay diecisiete niñas en la clase; she's seventeen tiene diecisiete años.

**seventeenth** [,sevn'tiːnə] *number* ■ **decimoséptimo**
➤ it's her seventeenth birthday cumple diecisiete años
➤ it's May seventeenth today hoy es el 17 de mayo.

**seventh** ['sevnə] *number* ■ **séptimo:** on the seventh floor en el séptimo piso
➤ it's November seventh today hoy es el 7 de noviembre.

**seventy** ['sevntɪ] *number* ■ **setenta:** she's seventy tiene setenta años
➤ seventy-one setenta y uno
➤ seventy-two setenta y dos.

**several** ['sevrəl] *adjective & pronoun* ■ **varios:** she called me several times me llamó varias veces; he ate several of them se comió varios.

**sew** [səʊ] *(past tense* sewed, *past participle* sewn *o* sewed) *verb* ■ **coser:** do you know how to sew? ¿sabes coser?; she sewed the button on cosió el botón.

**sewing** ['səʊŋ] *uncountable noun* ■ **la costura**
➤ a sewing machine una máquina de coser.

**sewn** [səʊn] *past participle* ➤ sew.

**sex** [seks] *noun* ■ **el sexo:** there were young people of both sexes había jóvenes de ambos sexos
➤ to have sex with somebody tener relaciones sexuales con alguien.

**sexist** ['seksɪst] *adjective* ■ **sexista:** don't be sexist no seas sexista.

**sexy** ['seksɪ] *adjective* ■ **sexy** *(plural* sexy): she was wearing a sexy dress llevaba un vestido sexy.

**shade** [ʃeɪd] *noun*

1. **la sombra:** I was sitting in the shade estaba sentado a la sombra
2. **el tono:** choose another shade of green elige otro tono de verde.

**shadow** ['ʃædəʊ] *noun* ■ **la sombra:** I saw a shadow on the wall vi una sombra en la pared.

**shake** [ʃeɪk] *(past tense* shook, *past participle* shaken) *verb*

1. **sacudir:** shake the tree to make the apples fall sacude el árbol para que caigan las manzanas

**2.** **agitar:** you have to shake the bottle first tienes que agitar la botella primero

**3.** **temblar:** my legs are shaking me tiemblan las piernas; she's shaking with cold está temblando de frío

➤ to shake hands with somebody darle la mano a alguien: we shook hands nos dimos la mano

➤ to shake one's head negar con la cabeza: I asked if she was coming and she shook her head le pregunté si venía y lo negó con la cabeza.

**shaken** ['ʃeɪkn] *past participle*
➤ shake.

**shall** [ʃəl, ʃæl] *verb*

**1.** *The future tense* I shall see him tomorrow lo veré mañana

**2.** *Making suggestions* shall I open the window? ¿abro la ventana?; let's go, shall we? ¿qué les parece si vamos?

**shallow** ['ʃæləʊ] *adjective* ■ **poco profundo:** the river is shallow here el río es poco profundo aquí.

**shame** [ʃeɪm] *noun* ■ **la vergüenza:** he put me to shame me hizo pasar vergüenza

➤ it's a shame es una lástima: it's a shame that you lost es una lástima que hayas perdido

➤ what a shame! ¡qué lástima!

**shampoo** [ʃæm'puː] *noun* ■ **el champú** *(plural* los **champús***)*.

**shape** [ʃeɪp] *noun* ■ **la forma:** a cake in the shape of a heart un pastel en forma de corazón

➤ to be in good shape estar en buena forma: he's in good shape está en buena forma.

**share** [ʃeəʳ] *(noun & verb)*

■ *noun*
**la parte:** I didn't get my share no obtuve mi parte

■ *verb*
**compartir:** I share a room with him comparto un cuarto con él.

**shares** ['ʃeəʳz] *plural noun* ■ **las acciones:** we have shares in the company tenemos acciones en la compañía.

**shark** [ʃaːk] *noun* ■ **el tiburón** *(plural* los **tiburones***)*: these waters are full of sharks estas aguas están llenas de tiburones.

**sharp** [ʃaːp] *(adjective & adverb)*

■ *adjective*
**1.** **afilado:** a sharp knife un cuchillo afilado
**2.** **puntiagudo:** a sharp needle una aguja puntiaguda
**3.** **brusco:** a sharp rise in prices una subida brusca de los precios
**4.** **agudo:** he's very sharp es muy agudo
■ *adverb*
at eight o'clock sharp a las 8 en punto.

**shave** [ʃeɪv] *(noun & verb)*

■ *noun*
➤ you need a shave necesitas una afeitada, necesitas una rasurada *Mexico*
■ *verb*
**afeitarse, rasurarse** *Mexico*: he shaves every day se afeita todos los días; he shaved off his beard se afeitó la barba
➤ to shave one's legs afeitarse las piernas.

**shaving cream** ['ʃeɪvɪŋkriːm] *noun*
■ **la crema de afeitar,** la **crema de rasurar** *Mexico*.

**shawl** [ʃɔːl] *noun* ■ **el chal.**

**she** [ʃiː] *pronoun* ■ **ella**

The pronoun "she" is often not translated unless it is needed for emphasis or clarification:

she's called Eileen se llama Eileen; she came to see me vino a verme; she did it ella lo hizo; she doesn't know it but he does ella no lo sabe pero él sí
➤ there she is! ¡ahí está!

**shed** [ʃed] *noun* ■ **el cobertizo:** there's a shed in the garden hay un cobertizo en el jardín.

**she'd** [ʃɪd, ʃiːd] ➤ she had; ➤ she would.

**sheep** [ʃiːp] *(plural* sheep) *noun* ■ **la oveja.**

**sheet** [ʃiːt] *noun*

1. la **sábana**: the sheets are clean las sábanas están limpias
2. la **hoja**: give me a sheet of paper dame una hoja de papel.

**shelf** [ʃelf] *(plural* shelves [ʃelvz]*) noun* ▪ la **repisa**: I put the book on the shelf puse el libro en la repisa.

**shell** [ʃel] *noun*

1. la **concha**: there are lots of shells on the beach hay muchas conchas en la playa
2. el/la **caparazón** *(plural* los/las **caparazones**): the turtle has a very big shell la tortuga tiene un caparazón muy grande
3. la **cáscara**: the shell of the egg la cáscara del huevo
4. el **proyectil**: the shell exploded in the field el proyectil explotó en el campo.

**she'll** [ʃiːl] ➤ she will; she shall.

**shelter** [ˈʃeltər] *(noun & verb)*

▪ *noun*
el **refugio**: we were looking for shelter estábamos buscando refugio
➤ to take shelter refugiarse: he took shelter from the storm se refugió de la tormenta
▪ *verb*
**proteger**: he sheltered the girl with his body protegió a la niña con su cuerpo.

**shelves** *plural* ➤ shelf.

**shepherd** [ˈʃepəd] *noun* ▪ el **pastor**.

**sheriff** [ˈʃerif] *noun* ▪ el/la **sheriff**: he's the sheriff of Great Rock es el sheriff de Great Rock.

**she's** [ʃiːz]
➤ she is; she has.

**shield** [ʃiːld] *noun* ▪ el **escudo**: the soldiers used shields to protect themselves los soldados usaban escudos para protegerse.

**shin** [ʃin] *noun* ▪ la **espinilla**, la **canilla** *Argentina, Chile*.

**shine** [ʃain] *(past tense & past participle* shone) *verb* ▪ **brillar**: the sun was shining el sol brillaba.

**shiny** [ˈʃaini] *adjective* ▪ **brillante**.

**ship** [ʃip] *noun* ▪ el **barco**: the ship sank el barco se hundió
➤ we went by ship fuimos en barco.

**shipwreck** [ˈʃiprek] *noun* ▪ el **naufragio**.

**shipwrecked** [ˈʃiprekt] *adjective*
➤ to be shipwrecked naufragar.

**shirt** [ʃɜːt] *noun* ▪ la **camisa**: he was wearing a shirt and tie iba de camisa y corbata.

**shiver** [ˈʃivər] *verb*

1. **tiritar**: it's so cold she's shivering hace tanto frío que está tiritando
2. **temblar**: she heard the scream and shivered oyó los gritos y tembló.

**shock** [ʃɒk] *(noun & verb)*

▪ *noun*

1. el **shock**: I got a shock when I heard the news me llevé un shock cuando escuché las noticias
2. la **descarga**, el **toque** *Mexico*: he got an electric shock recibió una descarga eléctrica
▪ *verb*
**escandalizar**: his behavior shocked me or I was shocked by his behavior su comportamiento me escandalizó.

**shocking** [ˈʃɒkiŋ] *adjective* ▪ **escandaloso**: his attitude is shocking su actitud es escandalosa.

**shoe** [ʃuː] *noun* ▪ el **zapato**: put your shoes on! ¡ponte los zapatos!; I took my shoes off me quité los zapatos
➤ a pair of shoes un par de zapatos
➤ a shoe store una zapatería.

**shoelace** [ˈʃuːleis] *noun* ▪ el **cordón de los zapatos** *(plural* los **cordones de los zapatos**), la **agujeta** *Mexico*: your shoelace is undone tienes los cordones desamarrados.

**shone** [ʃɒn] *past tense & past participle*
➤ shine.

**shook** [ʃʊk] *past tense* ➤ shake.

**shoot** [ʃuːt] *(past tense & past participle shot) verb*

1. **disparar: where did you learn to shoot?** ¿dónde aprendiste a disparar?
2. **pegarle un tiro a: he was shot in the leg** le pegaron un tiro en la pierna
3. **fusilar: they shot him at dawn for his treachery** lo fusilaron al amanecer por su traición
4. **filmar: they shot the film in New Zealand** filmaron la película en Nueva Zelanda
➤ **he was shot dead in a robbery** lo mataron a tiros en el asalto.

**shop** [ʃɒp] *(noun & verb)*

■ *noun*
**la tienda: that shop sells used books** esa tienda vende libros usados
➤ **a shop window** un escaparate, una vitrina *Andes, Venezuela*, un aparador *Mexico*, una vidriera *River Plate*

■ *verb*
**hacer compras: we shop often at that mall** a menudo hacemos compras en este centro comercial.

**shopping** [ʃɒpɪŋ] *uncountable noun*
■ **las compras**
➤ **to go shopping** ir de compras: **he goes shopping every Friday** va de compras todos los viernes
➤ **a shopping bag** una bolsa de la compra
➤ **a shopping mall** un centro comercial, un shopping *River Plate*, un mall *Chile*.

**short** [ʃɔːt] *adjective*

1. **corto: Sam has short hair** Sam tiene pelo corto; **it's a short film** es una película corta
2. **bajo: he's very short** es muy bajo
➤ **Dan is short for Daniel** Dan es el diminutivo de Daniel
➤ **they call him Bob for short** lo llaman Bob para abreviar.

**shortcut** [ʃɔːtkʌt] *noun* ■ **el atajo: she took the shortcut** tomó el atajo.

**shortly** [ʃɔːtlɪ] *adverb* ■ **dentro de poco: I'll see you again shortly** te veré de nuevo dentro de poco.

**shorts** [ʃɔːts] *plural noun* ■ **los shorts: he was wearing shorts** iba de shorts.

**shot** [ʃɒt] *(noun & verb form)*

■ *noun*
1. **el disparo: we heard shots** oímos disparos
2. **la vacuna: the baby has had all his shots** el bebé ha recibido todas las vacunas
3. **la toma: this is a nice shot** ésta es una buena toma
➤ **good shot!** ¡buen tiro!
■ *past tense & past participle*
➤ **shoot**.

**shotgun** [ʃɒtgʌn] *noun* ■ **la escopeta**.

**should** [ʃʊd] *verb*

> "Should" is translated by the verb **deber** in the conditional tense:

**you should go** deberías irte; **she should be home soon** debería estar en casa pronto; **they should have won the match** deberían haber ganado el partido.

**shoulder** [ˈʃəʊldər] *noun* ■ **el hombro: he put his hand on her shoulder** le puso la mano en el hombro.

**shouldn't** [ʃʊdnt] ➤ should not.

**should've** [ʃʊdəv] ➤ should have.

**shout** [ʃaʊt] *(noun & verb)*

■ *noun*
**el grito: I heard a shout** oí un grito
■ *verb*
**gritar: he was shouting at me** estaba gritándome.

**show** [ʃəʊ] *(noun & verb)*

■ *noun*
1. **el espectáculo: we're going to see a show on Broadway** vamos a ver un espectáculo en Broadway; **an art show** un espectáculo artístico
2. **el programa: it's a live television show** es un programa de televisión en vivo
■ *verb*
*(past tense* **showed***, past participle* **shown** *or* **showed***)*
1. **mostrar: I showed them the photos** le mostré las fotos
2. **indicar: can you show me the way?** ¿puedes indicarme el camino?
3. **dar: they are going to show the film tomorrow** van a dar la película mañana

**show off** phrasal verb ■ **lucirse:** he's always showing off siempre se está luciendo.

**show up** phrasal verb ■ **aparecerse:** she hasn't shown up yet todavía no se ha aparecido.

**shower** ['ʃaʊəʳ] noun

1. la **ducha,** la **regadera** Colombia, Mexico, Venezuela: he's in the shower está en la ducha
2. el **chubasco:** it's not raining much, it's only a shower no está lloviendo mucho, es sólo un chubasco
➤ to take a shower ducharse: I'm going to take a shower voy a ducharme.

**shown** [ʃəʊn] past participle ➤ show.

**show-off** ['ʃəʊnf] noun ■ el **fanfarrón** (plural los **fanfarrones),** la **fanfarrona:** he's a show-off es un fanfarrón.

**shrank** [ʃræŋk] past tense ➤ shrink.

**shrimp** [ʃrɪmp] noun ■ el **camarón** (plural los **camarones).**

**shrink** [ʃrɪŋk] (past tense shrank, past participle shrunk) verb ■ **encoger:** this material shrinks esta tela encoge.

**shrug** [ʃrʌg] (past tense & past participle shrugged) verb
➤ to shrug one's shoulders encogerse de hombros: he shrugged his shoulders se encogió de hombros.

**shrunk** [ʃrʌŋk] past participle ➤ shrink.

**shuffle** ['ʃʌfl] verb
➤ to shuffle the cards barajar las cartas.

**shut** [ʃʌt] (adjective & verb)
■ adjective
**cerrado:** the window is shut la ventana está cerrada
■ verb
(past tense & past participle shut) **cerrar:** she shut the door cerró la puerta

**shut up** phrasal verb ■ **callarse:** will you shut up! ¿quieres callarte?

**shutter** ['ʃʌtəʳ] noun ■ el **postigo:** close the shutters cierra los postigos.

**shuttle** ['ʃʌtl] adjective ■ el **transbordador:** a space shuttle el transbordador espacial.

**shy** [ʃaɪ] adjective ■ **tímido.**

**sick** [sɪk] adjective ■ **enfermo:** he's not at school because he's sick no ha venido a la escuela porque está enfermo
➤ to be sick of something estar harto de algo: I'm sick of your lies estoy harto de tus mentiras.

**side** [saɪd] noun

1. el **lado:** the school is on the other side of the road la escuela está del otro lado de la calle; his dog stood by his side su perro estaba a su lado
2. la **orilla:** there's a house by the side of the river hay una casa a la orilla del río
3. el **equipo:** our side won the match nuestro equipo ganó el partido
➤ side by side uno al lado del otro: they were walking side by side caminaban uno al lado del otro
➤ to be on somebody's side estar de parte de alguien: are you on my side? ¿estás de mi parte?
➤ to take sides tomar partido.

**sideburns** ['saɪdbɜːnz] plural noun ■ las **patillas:** he has sideburns tiene patillas.

**sidewalk** ['saɪdwɔːk] noun ■ la **acera,** la **vereda** Andes, River Plate, la **banqueta** Mexico.

**sideways** ['saɪdweɪz] adverb ■ **de lado:** crabs walk sideways los cangrejos caminan de lado.

**sigh** [saɪ] (noun & verb)
■ noun
el **suspiro:** he gave a sigh of relief dio un suspiro de alivio
■ verb
**suspirar:** she sighed with frustration suspiró de frustración.

**sight** [saɪt] *noun* ■ **la vista:** I have good sight tengo buena vista; **I've lost sight of her** la perdí de vista; **at first sight** a primera vista

➤ he faints at the sight of blood se desmaya de sólo ver sangre

➤ to catch sight of something ver algo: I caught sight of the pyramids vi las pirámides

➤ I know him by sight lo conozco de vista

➤ what a funny sight! ¡qué espectáculo tan cómico!

**sights** [saɪts] *plural noun* ■ **los lugares de interés turístico:** we went to see the sights of New York visitamos los lugares de interés turístico de Nueva York.

**sightseeing** ['saɪt,siːɪŋ] *noun* ■ **let's go sightseeing** vamos a visitar los lugares de interés turístico.

**sign** [saɪn] *(noun & verb)*

■ *noun*

1. **la señal:** Harry made a sign to me Harry me hizo una señal; **the victory sign** la señal de la victoria

2. **el letrero:** follow the signs to the station sigue los letreros hacia la estación

■ *verb*

**firmar:** can you sign here, please? ¿puede firmar aquí, por favor?

**signal** ['sɪgnl] *noun* ■ **la señal:** the teacher gave them the signal to start la maestra les hizo una señal para que comenzaran.

**signature** ['sɪgnətʃər] *noun* ■ **la firma:** I can't read the signature no puedo leer la firma.

**significant** [sɪg'nɪfɪkənt] *adjective* ■ **significativo:** it's a significant discovery es un descubrimiento significativo.

**silence** ['saɪləns] *noun* ■ **el silencio:** a sudden noise broke the silence un ruido repentino rompió el silencio.

**silent** ['saɪlənt] *adjective* ■ **en silencio:** they kept silent se mantuvieron en silencio.

**silicon chip** [,sɪlɪkən'tʃɪp] *noun* ■ **el chip de silicio** *(plural* **los chips de silicio**).

**silk** [sɪlk] *noun* ■ **la seda:** it's made of silk es de seda

➤ a silk blouse una blusa de seda.

**silly** ['sɪlɪ] *adjective* ■ **tonto:** don't be silly! ¡no seas tonto!

**silver** ['sɪlvər] *adjective* ■ **la plata:** it's made of silver es de plata

➤ a silver bracelet una pulsera de plata.

**similar** ['sɪmɪlər] *adjective* ■ **parecido:** these two colors are similar estos dos colores son parecidos

➤ to be similar to something ser parecido a algo: her coat's similar to mine su abrigo es parecido al mío.

**simple** ['sɪmpl] *adjective* ■ **simple:** it's a simple question es una pregunta simple.

**sin** [sɪn] *noun* ■ **el pecado:** it's a sin to lie es pecado mentir.

**since** [sɪns] *(preposition, conjunction & adverb)*

■ *preposition*

**desde:** it's been raining since Sunday está lloviendo desde el domingo; **I've lived in France since 1990** vivo en Francia desde 1990; **she'd been waiting since 7 p.m.** esperaba desde las 7 de la tarde

➤ since then desde entonces

■ *conjunction*

1. **conocer:** I've known him since I was 10 lo conozco desde que tenía 10 años

2. **ya que:** since it's raining, we might as well stay at home ya que está lloviendo, más vale que nos quedemos en casa

■ *adverb*

**desde entonces:** I haven't seen her since no la he visto desde entonces.

**sincere** [sɪn'sɪər] *adjective* ■ **sincero.**

**sincerely** [sɪn'sɪəlɪ] *adverb*

➤ Sincerely yours Atentamente.

**sing** [sɪŋ] *(past tense* **sang***, past participle* **sung***) verb* ■ **cantar:** he sang a song cantó una canción.

**singer** ['sɪŋər] *noun* ■ **el/la cantante.**

**singing** ['sɪŋɪŋ] *uncountable noun* ■ **el canto:** singing lessons clases de canto.

**single** ['sɪŋgl] *(adjective & noun)*

■ *adjective*

1. **solo:** there isn't a **single** book in their house no hay ni un solo libro en su casa
2. **soltero:** she's **single** es soltera

■ *noun*
   el **single** *(plural* los **singles)**: their latest **single** is on the album su último single viene en el álbum

➤ a **single** bed una cama individual
➤ in **single** file en fila india: they were walking in **single** file caminaban en fila india
➤ a **single** parent un padre que cría a sus hijos sin pareja: she's a **single** parent es una madre que cría a sus hijos sin pareja
➤ the men's **singles** los individuales masculinos.

**singular** ['sɪŋgjʊləʳ] *noun* ■ **singular:** put this noun in the **singular** pon este sustantivo en singular.

**sink** [sɪŋk] *(noun & verb)*

■ *noun*
   el **fregadero,** el **lavaplatos** *(plural* los **lavaplatos)** *Chile, Mexico,* la **pileta** *River Plate*: the dishes are in the **sink** los platos están en el fregadero

■ *verb*
   *(past tense* **sank,** *past participle* **sunk) hundirse:** the Titanic **sank** in 1912 el Titanic se hundió en 1912; our feet **sank** into the mud se nos hundieron los pies en el barro.

**sir** [sɜːʳ] *noun* ■ **señor:** excuse me, **sir** disculpe, señor; yes, **sir!** sí, señor
➤ Dear **Sir,** … Estimado Señor,…

**sister** ['sɪstəʳ] *noun* ■ la **hermana:** he has two **sisters** tiene dos hermanas.

**sister-in-law** ['sɪstəʳɪnlɔː] *(plural* **sisters-in-law)** *noun* ■ la **cuñada**.

**sit** [sɪt] *(past tense & past participle* **sat)** *verb*

1. **sentarse:** come and **sit** here ven a sentarte aquí

➤ to be **sitting** estar sentado: Vicky was **sitting** on the floor Vicky estaba sentada en el piso

**sit down** *phrasal verb* ■ **sentarse:** **sit down!** ¡siéntate!; he **sat down** in the armchair se sentó en el sillón.

**site** [saɪt] *noun*

1. la **sede:** have you visited the CNN **site?** ¿visitaste la sede de la CNN?
2. la **obra:** Bill works on a building **site** Bill trabaja en una obra

➤ an archaeological **site** un yacimiento arqueológico.

**situation** [ˌsɪtjʊ'eɪʃn] *noun* ■ la **situación** *(plural* las **situaciones)**: we're in a difficult **situation** estamos en una situación difícil.

**six** [sɪks] *number* ■ **seis:** there are **six** states in Australia Australia tiene seis estados; he's **six** tiene seis años; we went out at **six** salimos a las seis.

**sixteen** [sɪks'tiːn] *number* ■ **dieciséis:** there are **sixteen** boys in the class hay dieciséis varones en la clase; he's **sixteen** tiene dieciséis años.

**sixteenth** [sɪks'tiːnə] *number* ■ **décimosexto**

➤ it's his **sixteenth** birthday cumple 16 años
➤ it's June **sixteenth** today hoy es 16 de junio.

**sixth** [sɪksə] *number* ■ **sexto:** on the **sixth** floor en el sexto piso

➤ it's January **sixth** today hoy es 6 de enero.

**sixty** ['sɪkstɪ] *number* ■ **sesenta:** she's **sixty** tiene sesenta años

➤ **sixty-one** sesenta y uno
➤ **sixty-two** sesenta y dos.

**size** [saɪz] *noun*

1. el **tamaño:** the two rooms are the same **size** las dos habitaciones tienen el mismo tamaño
2. la **talla,** el **talle** *River Plate*: what **size** are you? ¿qué talla usas?; I'm a **size** 40 uso la talla 40
3. el **número:** what shoe **size** do you take? ¿qué número de zapatos calzas?; I take a **size** 7 shoe calzo el número 7.

**skate** [skeɪt] *noun* ■ el **patín** *(plural* los patines): I'm getting some new skates me voy a comprar patines nuevos.

**skateboard** ['skeɪtbɔːd] *noun* ■ la **patineta**.

**skating** ['skeɪtɪŋ] *noun*
➤ to go skating ir a patinar: we go skating on the lake in winter vamos a patinar en el lago en invierno
➤ a skating rink una pista de patinaje.

**skeleton** ['skelɪtn] *noun* ■ el **esqueleto**: there's a skeleton in the grave hay un esqueleto en la tumba.

**sketch** [sketʃ] *(noun & verb)*
■ *noun*
el **bosquejo**: I drew a sketch dibujé un bosquejo
■ *verb*
**hacer un bosquejo**: he sketched the White House hizo un bosquejo de la Casa Blanca.

**ski** [skiː] *(noun & verb)*
■ *noun*
el **esquí**: he's wearing skis tiene puestos los esquís
➤ ski boots botas de esquí
➤ a ski lift un telesquí
➤ a ski pole el bastón de esquí
➤ a ski slope una pista de esquí
■ *verb*
*(past tense & past participle* skied, *present participle* skiing*)* esquiar: she's learning how to ski está aprendiendo a esquiar.

**skier** ['skiːəʳ] *noun* ■ el **esquiador**, la **esquiadora**: she's a good skier es buena esquiadora.

**skies** *plural* ➤ sky.

**skiing** ['skiːɪŋ] *uncountable noun* ■ el **esquí**: he's having skiing lessons está tomando clases de esquí
➤ to go skiing ir a esquiar: they go skiing every week van a esquiar todas las semanas.

**skill** [skɪl] *noun* ■ la **habilidad**: a surgeon needs great skill un cirujano necesita una gran habilidad.

**skillful** ['skɪlfʊl] *adjective* ■ **hábil**.

**skin** [skɪn] *noun* ■ la **piel**: she has fair skin tiene la piel blanca
➤ a banana skin una cáscara de plátano.

**skinny** ['skɪnɪ] *adjective* ■ **flaco**.

**skin-tight** [skɪntaɪt] *adjective* ■ **muy ceñido**: she was wearing skin-tight jeans tenía puestos unos jeans muy ceñidos.

**skip** [skɪp] *(past tense & past participle* skipped*) verb*
1. **saltarse**: she skipped breakfast se saltó el desayuno
2. **faltar**: he skipped his class faltó a clase.

**skirt** [skɜːt] *noun* ■ la **falda**, la **pollera** *Southern Cone*: Diana's wearing a red skirt Diana tiene puesta una falda roja.

**skull** [skʌl] *noun* ■ el **cráneo**.

**sky** [skaɪ] *(plural* skies [skaɪz]*) noun* ■ el **cielo**: the sky's blue el cielo está azul
➤ sky blue celeste: the walls are sky blue las paredes son celestes.

**skylight** ['skaɪlaɪt] *noun* ■ la **claraboya**.

**skyscraper** ['skaɪ,skreɪpəʳ] *noun* ■ el **rascacielo**.

**slam** [slæm] *(past tense & past participle* slammed*) verb* ■ **cerrar de un golpe**: I slammed the door cerré de un golpe la puerta
➤ the door slammed la puerta se cerró de un portazo.

**slang** [slæŋ] *noun* ■ el **argot**: it's a slang word es una palabra del argot.

**slap** [slæp] *(noun & verb)*
■ *noun*
la **palmada**: he gave me a slap on the back me dio una palmada en la espalda
➤ he gave me a slap in the face me dió una cachetada
■ *verb*
*(past tense & past participle* slapped*)* **darle una palmada a**: he slapped me on the back me dio una palmada en la espalda

➤ **I slapped him in the face** le di una cachetada.

**slave** [sleɪv] *noun* ■ el **esclavo**, la **esclava**: there were slaves at that time había esclavos en esa época.

**slavery** ['sleɪvəri] *noun* ■ la **esclavitud**: slavery was abolished in 1833 in Britain and in 1865 in the US la esclavitud fue abolida en Inglaterra en 1833 y en EE.UU. en 1865.

**sled** [sled] *noun* ■ el **trineo**: they came down the hill in a sled bajaron la colina en un trineo.

**sleep** [sliːp] *(noun & verb)*
■ *noun*
el **sueño**: it's the lack of sleep es la falta de sueño
➤ **I need some sleep** necesito dormir
■ *verb*
*(past tense & past participle* **slept***)* **dormir**: she's sleeping está durmiendo; we slept at the Imperial dormimos en el Imperial; he went to sleep straightaway se durmió enseguida
➤ **to go to sleep** dormirse

**sleep in** *phrasal verb* ■ **dormir hasta tarde**: I sleep in when I don't have to go to school duermo hasta tarde cuando no tengo que ir a la escuela.

**sleep over** *phrasal verb* ■ **quedarse a dormir**: I slept over at Patty's house me quedé a dormir en la casa de Patty.

**sleeping bag** ['sliːpɪŋbæg] *noun* ■ el **saco de dormir**, la **bolsa de dormir** *Argentina*, el **sobre de dormir** *Uruguay*.

**sleepy** ['sliːpi] *adjective*
➤ **to be sleepy or to feel sleepy** tener sueño: I feel sleepy tengo sueño.

**sleeve** [sliːv] *noun* ■ la **manga**
➤ he rolled up his sleeves se arremangó.

**slender** ['slendər] *adjective* ■ **delgado**.

**slept** [slept] *past tense & past participle*
➤ sleep.

**slice** [slaɪs] *(noun & verb)*
■ *noun*
la **rebanada**: he cut a slice of bread cortó una rebanada de pan
■ *verb*
**cortar**: can you slice the bread? ¿puedes cortar el pan?

**slide** [slaɪd] *(noun & verb)*
■ *noun*
1. el **tobogán** *(plural* los **toboganes**), la **resbaladilla** *Mexico*: the children are playing on the slide los niños están jugando en el tobogán
2. las **diapositivas**: they showed us their slides nos mostraron sus diapositivas
■ *verb*
*(past tense & past participle* **slid***)* **deslizarse**: he was sliding on the ice se deslizaba en el hielo.

**slight** [slaɪt] *adjective* ■ **leve**: there has been a slight improvement ha habido una leve mejoría.

**slightly** ['slaɪtli] *adverb* ■ **un poco**: I feel slightly better me siento un poco mejor.

**slim** [slɪm] *adjective* ■ **delgado**: Nicole's very slim Nicole es muy delgada.

**sling** [slɪŋ] *noun* ■ el **cabestrillo**: his arm is in a sling tiene el brazo en cabestrillo.

**slip** [slɪp] *(noun & verb)*
■ *noun*
la **combinación** *(plural* las **combinaciones***)*, el **fondo** *Mexico*, el **viso** *River Plate*: she needs to wear a slip with that dress necesita ponerse una combinación con ese vestido
➤ **a slip of paper** un papelito: I wrote it on a slip of paper lo escribí en un papelito
■ *verb*
*(past tense & past participle* **slipped***)*
1. **resbalarse**: I slipped me resbalé
2. **meter disimuladamente**: he slipped some money into my pocket me metió disimuladamente dinero en el bolsillo.

**slipper** ['slɪpər] *noun* ■ la **pantufla**: he put on his slippers se puso las pantuflas.

**slope** [sləʊp] *noun* ■ **la pendiente**: it's a very steep slope es una pendiente muy empinada.

**slot** [slɒt] *noun* ■ **la ranura**: put your money in the slot meta su dinero en la ranura.

➤ a slot machine una máquina tragamonedas.

**slow** [sləʊ] *(adjective, adverb & verb)*
■ *adjective*
**lento**: this bus is very slow este autobús es muy lento
➤ my watch is slow mi reloj se atrasa: my watch is five minutes slow mi reloj se atrasa cinco minutos
➤ in slow motion en cámara lenta
■ *adverb*
**despacio**: we're going slow vamos despacio
■ *verb*
**disminuir la velocidad**: she slowed to a stop fue disminuyendo la velocidad hasta detenerse

**slow down** *phrasal verb* ■ **disminuir la velocidad**: you're driving too fast, slow down estás manejando muy rápido, disminuye la velocidad.

**slowly** ['sləʊlɪ] *adverb* ■ **lentamente**: I was walking slowly caminaba lentamente.

**smack** [smæk] *(noun & verb)*
■ *noun*
**la palmada**: she gave him a smack le dió una palmada
■ *verb*
**dar una palmada**: she smacked him on the bottom le dió una palmada en el trasero, le dio una nalgada *Mexico*.

**small** [smɔːl] *adjective* ■ **pequeño, chico**: they live in a small village viven en un pueblo pequeño.

**smart** [smaːt] *adjective* ■ **inteligente**: his child is very smart su hijo es muy inteligente.

**smash** [smæʃ] *verb*
ɪ. **romper**: he smashed a window rompió una ventana

2. **romperse**: the glass smashed on the floor el vaso se rompió en el suelo.

**smell** [smel] *(noun & verb)*
■ *noun*
**el olor**: I love the smell of cut grass me encanta el olor del pasto cortado
➤ the sense of smell el sentido del olfato
■ *verb*
*(past tense & past participle* **smelled***)*
ɪ. **oler**: I can smell gas huelo gas; that cake smells good ese pastel huele bien
2. **oler mal**: your socks smell! ¡tus calcetines huelen mal!

**smile** [smaɪl] *(noun & verb)*
■ *noun*
**la sonrisa**: he gave me a big smile me sonrió de oreja a oreja
■ *verb*
**sonreír**: she smiled at me me sonrió.

**smoke** [sməʊk] *(noun & verb)*
■ *noun*
**el humo**: the room is full of smoke el cuarto está lleno de humo
■ *verb*
**fumar**: he was smoking a cigarette estaba fumando un cigarrillo.

**smoker** ['sməʊkəʳ] *noun* ■ **el fumador, la fumadora**
➤ he's a heavy smoker fuma mucho.

**smoking** ['sməʊkɪŋ] *noun*
➤ there is no cure for smoking el tabaquismo no tiene cura
➤ to give up smoking dejar de fumar
➤ no smoking prohibido fumar.

**smooth** [smuːð] *adjective* ■ **suave**: he has smooth skin tiene la piel suave.

**snack** [snæk] *noun*
➤ to have a snack tomarse un tentempié
➤ a snack bar una cafetería.

**snail** [sneɪl] *noun* ■ **el caracol**.

**snake** [sneɪk] *noun* ■ **la serpiente**.

**snap** [snæp] *(past tense & past participle* snapped*) verb*
ɪ. **cortarse**: the rope snapped la cuerda se cortó

2. **quebrar:** I snapped the branch in two quebré la rama en dos.

**snatch** [snætʃ] *verb* ■ **arrebatar:** he snatched my bag from my hands me arrebató la bolsa de las manos.

**sneakers** ['sniːkəz] *plural noun* ■ **las zapatillas de deportes,** los **tenis** *Central America, Cuba, Mexico*: **Ben's wearing sneakers** Ben tiene puestas zapatillas de deportes.

**sneeze** [sniːz] *verb* ■ **estornudar:** I sneezed estornudé.

**sniff** [snɪf] *verb* ■ **olfatear:** the dog sniffed the bone el perro olfateó el hueso.

**snob** [snɒb] *noun* ■ **el/la esnob** (*plural* los/las **esnobs**): you're a snob eres un esnob.

**snore** [snɔːʳ] *verb* ■ **roncar:** he snores at night ronca de noche.

**snorkel** ['snɔːkl] *noun* ■ **el esnórquel.**

**snorkeling** ['snɔːklɪŋ] *noun*
➤ to go snorkeling ir a bucear con esnórquel.

**snow** [snəʊ] (*noun & verb*)
■ *noun*
la **nieve:** there's snow on the top of the mountains hay nieve en la cima de las montañas
■ *verb*
**nevar:** it's snowing está nevando.

**snowball** ['snəʊbɔːl] *noun* ■ la **bola de nieve.**

**snowboard** ['snəʊˌbɔːd] *noun* ■ el **snowboard** (*plural* los **snowboards**).

**snowboarding** ['snəʊˌbɔːdɪŋ] *noun* ■ el **snowboard:** to go snowboarding hacer snowboard.

**snowman** ['snəʊmæn] (*plural* snowmen ['snəʊmen]) *noun* ■ el **muñeco de nieve:** they made a snowman hicieron un muñeco de nieve.

**so** [səʊ] (*adverb & conjunction*)

■ *adverb*
1. **tan:** she's so beautiful! ¡es tan bonita!; don't be so stupid! ¡no seas tan estúpido!
2. **también:** he's American and so is she él es americano y ella también; she has a dog and so do I ella tiene un perro y yo también
3. *With think, hope, say, suppose* I don't think so no creo; I think so creo que sí; I hope so espero que sí; I suppose so supongo que sí
➤ so far hasta ahora: so far I haven't made any mistakes hasta ahora no he cometido ningún error
➤ so many tantos: she has so many friends! ¡tiene tantos amigos!
➤ I've never seen so many people nunca había visto tanta gente
➤ so much tanto: I have so much work! ¡tengo tanto trabajo!; I've never seen so much money nunca había visto tanto dinero
I love you so much te quiero tanto
➤ or so más o menos: thirty or so treinta más o menos
■ *conjunction*
**así:** I'll be on vacation, so I won't be able to come estaré de vacaciones, así que no voy a poder venir; my bike was broken so I repaired it mi bici estaba rota, así que la arreglé
➤ so what's the point then? ¿para qué entonces?
➤ so what? ¿y qué?
➤ so long! adiós
➤ so that para que: he worked hard so that everything would be ready in time trabajó mucho para que todo estuviera listo a tiempo

> The conjunction **para que** is followed by a verb in the subjunctive in Spanish.

**soak** ['səʊk] *verb* ■ **dejar remojando:** she soaked the shirt in soapy water dejó la camisa remojando en agua jabonosa.

**soaking** ['səʊkɪŋ] *adjective* ■ **empapado:** I'm soaking or I'm soaking wet estoy empapado.

**soap** [səʊp] *noun* ■ el **jabón** (*plural* los jabones): a bar of soap una barra de jabón
➤ a soap opera la telenovela.

**soccer** ['sɒkə<sup>r</sup>] *noun* ■ el **fútbol**, el **futbol** *Mexico*: I play soccer every Saturday juego fútbol todas las sábados
➤ a soccer player un jugador de fútbol

> SOCCER
>
>  Soccer es la palabra que se utiliza en Estados Unidos para referirse al deporte mundialmente conocido como fútbol. Ha ganado mucha popularidad en años recientes y hoy en día muchos niños y niñas estadounidenses practican este deporte.

**social** ['səʊʃl] *adjective* ■ **social**: the social sciences las ciencias sociales; the social services los servicios sociales.

**society** [sə'saɪətɪ] *(plural* societies*) noun*
1. la **sociedad**: we live in a multicultural society vivimos en una sociedad multicultural
2. la **asociación** *(plural* las **asociaciones**): Chantal is in the drama society Chantal está en una asociación de teatro.

**sock** [sɒk] *noun* ■ el **calcetín** *(plural* los **calcetines**), la **media** *Colombia, River Plate*: he's wearing black socks tiene puestos calcetines negros.

**soda** ['səʊdə] *noun* ■ el **refresco**: Cheryl's drinking a soda Cheryl está tomando un refresco.

**sofa** ['səʊfə] *noun* ■ el **sofá**.

**soft** [sɒft] *adjective*
1. **suave**: the baby has soft skin el bebé tiene la piel suave
2. **blando**: the butter is soft la mantequilla está blanda; a nice soft bed una cama buena y blanda; a soft leather bag un bolso de cuero blando
➤ a soft drink un refresco.

**softly** ['sɒftlɪ] *adverb* ■ **bajo**: she was singing softly estaba cantando bajo.

**software** ['sɒftweə<sup>r</sup>] *uncountable noun* ■ el **software**: the computer comes with a lot of software la computadora viene con mucho software.

**soil** [sɔɪl] *noun* ■ la **tierra**: the soil is red in Australia la tierra es roja en Australia.

**solar** ['səʊlə<sup>r</sup>] *adjective* ■ **solar**: solar energy la energía solar.

**sold** [səʊld] *past tense & past participle*
➤ sell.

**soldier** ['səʊldʒə<sup>r</sup>] *noun* ■ el/la **soldado**.

**sole** [səʊl] *noun* ■ la **suela**: there's a hole in the sole of my shoe hay un agujero en la suela de mi zapato.

**solid** ['sɒlɪd] *adjective*
1. **sólido**: the bridge is very solid el puente es muy sólido
2. **macizo**: he wears a solid gold chain usa una cadena de oro macizo.

**solution** [sə'luːʃn] *noun* ■ la **solución** *(plural* las **soluciones**): we're trying to find a solution estamos tratando de encontrar una solución.

**solve** [sɒlv] *verb* ■ **resolver**: he has solved the problem ha resuelto el problema.

**some** [sʌm] *(adjective, pronoun & adverb)*
■ *adjective*
1.

> When "some" refers to something that is uncountable, it is often not translated:

do you want some coffee? ¿quieres café?; I bought some meat compré carne; he gave me some money me dió dinero
2. **alguno**: some swans are black algunos cisnes son negros; some people like his music a algunos les gusta su música

> **alguno** becomes **algún** before masculine nouns:

➤ some day algún día
■ *pronoun*
**alguno**: some are red, some are blue algunos son rojos, algunos son azules; I bought a pound of oranges, some of them were bad compré una libra de naranjas, algunas estaban en mal estado

➤ that cake looks nice, can I have some? este pastel se ve bueno ¿puedo comer un poco?

■ *adverb*
unos: there were some 7,000 people at the concert había unas 7.000 personas en el concierto.

**somebody, someone** ['sʌmbədɪ, 'sʌmwʌn] *pronoun* ■ alguien: somebody came to see you alguien vino a verte; he's somebody famous es alguien famoso; somebody else otra persona.

**someday** ['sʌmdeɪ] *adverb* ■ algún día: someday I'll be rich and famous algún día seré rico y famoso.

**somehow** ['sʌmhaʊ] *adverb* ■ de alguna manera: I'll do it somehow lo haré de alguna manera

➤ somehow, I don't think he'll come back no sé por qué, pero no creo que él vuelva.

**someone** *pronoun* ➤ somebody.

**someplace** ['sʌmpleɪs] *adverb* ■ algún lugar: they live someplace in Mexico viven en algún lugar de México; I'm looking for someplace to live estoy buscando algún lugar donde vivir

➤ someplace else otro lugar: let's go someplace else vamos a otro lugar.

**something** ['sʌmθɪŋ] *pronoun* ■ algo: I have something in my eye tengo algo en el ojo; don't just stand there, do something! ¡no te quedes ahí parado, haz algo!; something odd happened algo extraño pasó

➤ I'll have something else voy a tomar otra cosa

➤ that was something else! ¡eso fue genial!

➤ he's something else! ¡es fuera de serie!

**sometime** ['sʌmtaɪm] *adjective* ■ en algún momento: come and see me sometime ven a verme en algún momento; I'll see you sometime next week te veré en algún momento la semana que viene.

**sometimes** ['sʌmtaɪmz] *adverb* ■ a veces: she sometimes writes to me a veces me escribe; sometimes I make mistakes a veces cometo errores.

**son** [sʌn] *noun* ■ el hijo: they have three sons tienen tres hijos.

**song** [sɒŋ] *noun* ■ la canción (plural las canciones): he was singing a love song estaba cantando una canción de amor.

**son-in-law** ['sʌnɪnlɔ:] (plural sons-in-law) *noun* ■ el yerno.

**soon** [su:n] *adverb* ■ pronto: he'll soon be here estará aquí pronto; I'll see you soon! ¡te veré pronto!

➤ soon after poco después: she left soon after se fue poco después

➤ as soon as en cuanto, tan pronto como:

> En cuanto and tan pronto como, when used to express "as soon as" with an event that has not yet occurred, must be followed by a verb in the subjunctive:

I'll tell you as soon as he leaves te lo diré en cuanto él se vaya

➤ as soon as possible lo antes posible, cuanto antes: leave as soon as possible vete lo antes posible

➤ I'll be back soon! ¡volveré pronto!

**sooner** ['su:nə'] (comparative of soon) *adverb* ■ antes: you should have come sooner deberías haber venido antes

➤ sooner or later tarde o temprano: sooner or later you'll have to tell me tarde o temprano me lo tendrás que decir

➤ the sooner the better cuanto antes, mejor.

**sore** [sɔ:'] *adjective*

➤ this burn on my hand is really sore esta quemadura en la mano realmente me duele

➤ she has a sore throat le duele la garganta.

**sorrow** ['sɒrəʊ] *noun* ■ la pena: his death caused me great sorrow su muerte me causó una gran pena.

**sorry** ['sɒrɪ] *adjective*

➤ I'm really sorry, I have to go lo siento de veras, pero tengo que irme

➤ I'm sorry I'm late perdón por llegar tarde

➤ sorry? ¿perdón?, ¿mande? *Mexico*: sorry? what did you say? perdón ¿qué fue lo que dijo?

➤ sorry! ¡perdón!

➤ you'll be sorry! te vas a arrepentir

➤ **say you're sorry to your sister** pídele perdón a tu hermana

➤ **he said he was sorry** pidió perdón

➤ **to feel sorry for somebody** compadecer a alguien: **I feel sorry for him** lo compadezco.

**sort** [sɔːt] *(noun & verb)*

■ *noun*
el **tipo**: **there were all sorts of people** había todo tipo de gente

■ *verb*
**clasificar**: **the computer sorts the words in alphabetical order** la computadora clasifica las palabras por orden alfabético

**sort out** | *phrasal verb*

1. **ordenar**: **I'm going to sort out all my papers** voy a ordenar todos mis papeles
2. **solucionar**: **he managed to sort the problem out** logró solucionar el problema
3. **encargarse**: **I'll sort the tickets out** me voy a encargar de las entradas.

**sought** [sɔːt] *past tense & past participle*
➤ seek.

**soul** [səʊl] *noun* ■ el **alma**

> Feminine noun that takes **un** or **el** in the singular.

**sound** [saʊnd] *(noun & verb)*

■ *noun*
1. el **sonido**: **I recognized the sound of her voice** reconocí el sonido de su voz
2. el **volumen**: **turn the sound up** sube el volumen
3. el **ruido**: **I heard a sound** oí un ruido
➤ **sound effects** efectos sonoros

■ *verb*
1. **hacer sonar**: **they sounded the alarm** hicieron sonar la alarma
2. **sonar**: **this wall sounds hollow** esta pared suena hueca
3. **parecer**: **he sounds happy** parece contento; **it sounds as if they have a problem** parece que tuvieran un problema.

**soundtrack** ['saʊndtræk] *noun* ■ la **banda sonora**: **I bought the soundtrack to the film** compré la banda sonora de la película.

**soup** [suːp] *noun* ■ la **sopa**: **a bowl of onion soup** un tazón de sopa de cebollas.

**sour** ['saʊəʳ] *adjective* ■ **ácido**: **this yogurt tastes sour** este yogurt tiene sabor ácido

➤ **the milk has gone sour** la leche está cortada.

**source** [sɔːs] *noun* ■ la **fuente**: **the Internet is a good source of information** Internet es una buena fuente de información.

**south** [saʊθ] *(noun, adjective & adverb)*

■ *noun*
el **sur**: **Texas is in the south of the United States** Texas está en el sur de los Estados Unidos

■ *adjective*
**sur** *(plural* **sur**)*: **the prettiest beaches are on the south coast** las playas más hermosas están en la costa sur

■ *adverb*
**hacia el sur**: **a lot of birds fly south in the winter** muchos pájaros vuelan hacia el sur en el invierno

➤ **south of** al sur de: **Houston is south of Dallas** Houston está al sur de Dallas.

**South America** [ˌsaʊθəˈmerɪkə] *noun* ■ **América del Sur** *(feminine)*.

**South American** [ˌsaʊθəˈmerɪkən] *(adjective & noun)*

■ *adjective*

> Remember not to use a capital letter for the adjective in Spanish:

**sudamericano**: **I like South American music** me gusta la música sudamericana

■ *noun*

> In Spanish, a capital letter is not used for the inhabitants of a country or region:

el **sudamericano**, la **sudamericana**: **many South Americans speak Spanish or Portuguese** muchos sudamericanos hablan español o portugués.

**southeast** [ˌsaʊθˈiːst] *noun* ■ el **sureste**: **Georgia is in the southeast of the United States** Georgia está en el sureste de los Estados Unidos.

**southwest** [ˌsaʊθ'west] *noun* ▪ **el suroeste**: New Mexico is a part of the southwest of the United States Nuevo México es parte del suroeste de los Estados Unidos.

**souvenir** [ˌsuːvə'nɪər] *noun* ▪ **el recuerdo**: he bought a lot of souvenirs in Madrid compró muchos recuerdos en Madrid.

**soy sauce** [ˌsɔɪ'sɔːs] *noun* ▪ **la salsa de soya**.

**space** [speɪs] *noun*
1. **el espacio**: who was the first man in space? ¿quién fue el primer hombre en el espacio?; leave a space for corrections deja un espacio para las correcciones; there's not enough space for a bed no hay suficiente espacio para una cama
2. **el lugar**: can you make a space for me? ¿puedes hacerme un lugar?
➤ a parking space un lugar para estacionar
➤ to stare into space mirar al vacío
➤ a space shuttle un transbordador espacial.

**spaceship** ['speɪsʃɪp] *noun* ▪ **la nave espacial**.

**spacesuit** ['speɪssuːt] *noun* ▪ **el traje espacial**.

**spade** [speɪd] *noun* ▪ **la pala**: the children were playing with their buckets and spades on the beach los niños estaban jugando con sus baldes y palas en la playa
➤ the queen of spades la reina de picas

 **Spade** es un falso amigo, no significa "espada".

**spaghetti** [spə'getɪ] *uncountable noun* ▪ los **espaguetis**.

**Spain** [speɪn] *noun* ▪ **España** *(feminine)*.

**Spanish** ['spænɪʃ] *(adjective & noun)*
▪ *adjective*

Remember not to use a capital letter for the adjective or the language in Spanish:

**español**: sangria is a Spanish drink la sangría es una bebida española

▪ *noun*
el **español**, el **castellano**: she speaks Spanish habla español

In Spanish, a capital letter is not used for the inhabitants of a country or region:

➤ the Spanish los españoles.

**spare** [speər] *(adjective & verb)*
▪ *adjective*
1. **de más**: I've got a spare ticket tengo una entrada de más
2. **libre**: there's a spare seat at the back hay un asiento libre en el fondo
➤ a spare part un repuesto, una refacción *Mexico*
➤ a spare room un cuarto de huéspedes: we have a spare room tenemos un cuarto de huéspedes
➤ spare time tiempo libre: I don't have any spare time no tengo tiempo libre
➤ a spare tire una rueda de repuesto, una llanta de refacción *Mexico*
▪ *verb*
➤ can you spare a few minutes? ¿tienes unos minutos?
➤ I can't spare the time no tengo tiempo
➤ I arrived with a minute to spare llegué con un minuto de anticipación.

**sparkling** ['spaːklɪŋ] *adjective* ▪ **con gas**: a bottle of sparkling water una botella de agua con gas.

**sparrow** ['spærəʊ] *noun* ▪ **el gorrión** *(plural* los **gorriones***)*.

**spat** [spæt] *past tense & past participle*
➤ spit.

**speak** [spiːk] *(past tense* spoke, *past participle* spoken) *verb* ▪ **hablar**: do you speak English? ¿hablas inglés?; speak more slowly habla más despacio; I spoke to my parents about the party hablé con mis padres sobre la fiesta; can I speak to Henry, please? ¿podría hablar con Henry, por favor?
➤ who's speaking? ¿quién habla?
➤ this is Kate speaking habla Kate.

**speaker** ['spiːkər] *noun* ▪ **el parlante**, la **bocina** *Mexico*: don't put the speakers too close together no pongas los parlantes muy cerca el uno del otro

➤ **he's an English speaker** es hablante de inglés.

**special** ['speʃl] *adjective* ▪ **especial:** you need special shoes to run in necesitas zapatos especiales para correr; **this is a special case** es un caso especial; **this ring is very special to me** este anillo es muy especial para mí.

**specialist** ['speʃəlɪst] *noun* ▪ **el/la especialista.**

**specialty** ['speʃltɪ] (*plural* **specialties**) *noun* ▪ **la especialidad: steak is that restaurant's specialty** el filete es la especialidad de este restaurante.

**species** ['spɪːʃiːz] (*plural* **species**) *noun* ▪ **la especie: this species is extinct** esta especie está extinguida.

**spectacular** [spek'tækjʊlər] *adjective* ▪ **espectacular.**

**spectator** [spek'teɪtər] *noun* ▪ **el espectador, la espectadora.**

**sped** [sped] *past tense & past participle* ➤ **speed.**

**speech** [spɪːtʃ] *noun* ▪ **el discurso: he gave a speech** pronunció un discurso.

**speed** [spɪːd] (*noun & verb*)
▪ *noun*
**la velocidad: at the speed of light** a la velocidad de la luz
➤ **at top speed** a toda velocidad: **they were driving at top speed** manejaban a toda velocidad
➤ **the speed limit** el límite de velocidad: **the speed limit is 50 miles an hour** el límite de velocidad es de 50 millas por hora
▪ *verb*
(*past tense & past participle* **sped** *or* **speeded**)
**ir a exceso de velocidad: the driver was speeding** el conductor iba a exceso de velocidad

**speed up** *phrasal verb* ▪ **acelerar: can you speed up a bit?** ¿puedes acelerar un poco?

**speeding** ['spɪːdɪŋ] *uncountable noun*
▪ **el exceso de velocidad: he was fined for speeding** lo multaron por exceso de velocidad.

**speedometer** [spɪ'dɒmɪtər] *noun* ▪ **el velocímetro: his speedometer is broken** se le rompió el velocímetro.

**spell** [spel] (*noun & verb*)
▪ *noun*
➤ **to cast a spell on somebody** hechizar a alguien: **the sorcerer cast a spell on him** el brujo lo hechizó
▪ *verb*
(*past tense & past participle* **spelled**)
1. *In writing* **escribir: how do you spell that?** ¿cómo se escribe eso?
2. *Aloud* **deletrear: could you spell your name for me?** ¿podrías deletrearme tu nombre?

**spell-checker** ['speltʃekər] *noun* ▪ **el corrector ortográfico.**

**spelling** ['spelɪŋ] *noun* ▪ **la ortografía: a spelling mistake** una falta de ortografía.

**spend** [spend] (*past tense & past participle* **spent**) *verb*
1. **gastar: how much did you spend?** ¿cuánto gastaste?
2. **pasar: I'd like to spend a few days in New York** me gustaría pasar unos pocos días en Nueva York.

**spent** [spent] *past tense & past participle* ➤ **spend.**

**spice** [spaɪs] *noun* ▪ **la especia.**

**spicy** ['spaɪsɪ] *adjective* ▪ **picante, picoso** *Mexico*.

**spider** ['spaɪdər] *noun* ▪ **la araña.**

**spill** [spɪl] (*past tense & past participle* **spilled**) *verb*
1. **derramar: I spilled the water** derramé el agua
2. **derramarse: the milk spilled on the floor** la leche se derramó en el suelo.

**spin** [spɪn] (*past tense & past participle* **spun**) *verb*

1. **girar:** the planet spins on its axis el planeta gira sobre su eje
2. **hacer girar:** he spun the wheel hizo girar la rueda
➤ my head is spinning la cabeza me da vueltas

**spin around** *phrasal verb*

1. **dar vueltas:** the moon spins around the earth la luna da vueltas alrededor de la Tierra
2. **voltearse:** she suddenly spun around se volteó repentinamente.

**spinach** ['spɪnɪdʒ] *uncountable noun* ▧ las **espinacas**.

**spine** [spaɪn] *noun* ▧ la **columna vertebral:** the spine forms the central part of the skeleton la columna vertebral es la parte central del esqueleto.

**spit** [spɪt] *(past tense & past participle* spat *or* spit) *verb* ▧ **escupir:** she spit the mushroom out escupió el hongo.

**spite** [spaɪt] *noun*
➤ in spite of a pesar de: in spite of the rain, they went for a long walk a pesar de la lluvia, salieron a dar un largo paseo
➤ out of spite por despecho: she did it out of spite lo hizo por despecho.

**splash** [splæʃ] *(noun & verb)*
■ *noun*
➤ I heard a loud splash oí un fuerte ruido de algo al caer al agua
■ *verb*
**salpicar:** you splashed me me salpicaste.

**splendid** ['splendɪd] *adjective* ▧ **espléndido**.

**splinter** ['splɪntər] *noun* ▧ la **astilla**.

**split** [splɪt] *(past tense & past participle* split) *verb*
1. **partir:** he split some wood for the fire partió leña para el fuego
2. **romperse:** the frame has split se rompió el marco
3. **rajarse:** I've split my shorts se me rajaron los shorts

4. **dividir:** let's split the work dividamos el trabajo; he split the class into two groups dividió la clase en dos grupos

**split up** *phrasal verb* ▧ **separarse:** the band split up last year la banda se separó el año pasado.

**spoil** [spɔɪl] *(past tense & past participle* spoiled) *verb*
1. **echar a perder:** you spoiled my party me echaste a perder la fiesta
2. **mimar demasiado:** they've spoiled their daughter han mimado demasiado a su hija.

**spoiled** [spɔɪld] *adjective* ▧ **mimado:** he's a spoiled child es un niño mimado.

**spoke** [spəʊk] *(noun & verb form)*
■ *noun*
el **radio:** the spokes of a wheel los radios de la rueda
■ *past tense*
➤ speak.

**spoken** ['spəʊkn] *past participle*
➤ speak.

**sponge** [spʌndʒ] *noun* ▧ la **esponja:** she wiped the table with a sponge limpió la mesa con una esponja
➤ a sponge cake un bizcocho.

**spoon** [spuːn] *noun* ▧ la **cuchara**.

**spoonful** ['spuːnfʊl] *noun* ▧ la **cucharada:** add a spoonful of lemon juice agregue una cucharada de jugo de limón.

**sport** [spɔːt] *noun* ▧ el **deporte:** they play a lot of sports hacen mucho deporte
➤ he's a bad sport es un mal perdedor
➤ a sports car un coche deportivo.

**sportsman** ['spɔːtsmən] *(plural* sportsmen ['spɔːtsmən]) *noun* ▧ el **deportista**.

**sportswoman** ['spɔːtswʊmən] *(plural* sportswomen ['spɔːtswɪmən]) *noun* ▧ la **deportista**.

**spot** [spɒt] *(noun & verb)*
■ *noun*
1. la **mancha:** a grease spot una mancha de grasa

**245**

2. el **lunar**: a shirt with red spots una camisa con lunares rojos

3. el **lugar**: I know a nice spot where we can eat conozco un lindo lugar donde comer

■ *verb*

**ver**: I spotted her in the distance la vi en la distancia

➤ he spotted the mistake descubrió el error.

**spotlight** ['spɒtlaɪt] *noun* ■ el **foco**

➤ he's in the spotlight es el centro de atención.

**sprain** [spreɪn] *verb*

➤ to sprain one's ankle torcerse el tobillo: I've sprained my ankle me torcí el tobillo.

**spray** [spreɪ] *(noun & verb)*

■ *noun*

el **spray** *(plural* los **sprays)**: an insect spray un insecticida en spray

■ *verb*

1. **rociar**: she sprayed the leaves with a bit of water roció las hojas con un poco de agua

2. **fumigar**: they're spraying the crops están fumigando los cultivos

➤ she sprayed perfume in her hair se puso perfume en el pelo con un atomizador

➤ somebody has sprayed a poem on the wall alguien ha pintado un poema en la pared con pistola pulverizadora.

**spread** [spred] *(past tense & past participle* spread*) verb*

1. **untar**: he spread butter on the bread untó mantequilla en el pan

2. **desplegar**: the bird spread its wings el pájaro desplegó las alas

3. **divulgar**: we must spread the news debemos divulgar la noticia

4. **extenderse**: the fire is beginning to spread el fuego está comenzando a extenderse

**spread out** *phrasal verb* ■ **dispersarse**: the search party spread out el equipo de rescate se dispersó.

**spring** [sprɪŋ] *noun*

1. la **primavera**: plants begin to grow again in the spring las plantas comienzan a crecer nuevamente en primavera

2. el **resorte**: this bed has a spring mattress esta cama tiene un colchón de resortes

3. el **manantial**: the water comes from a mountain spring el agua viene de un manantial en la montaña.

**springtime** ['sprɪŋtaɪm] *uncountable noun* ■ la **primavera**: the swallows start to come back in springtime las golondrinas comienzan a volver en la primavera.

**sprouts** [spraʊts] *plural noun*

➤ Brussels sprouts las coles de Bruselas.

**spun** [spʌn] *past tense & past participle*
➤ spin.

**spy** [spaɪ] *(noun & verb)*

■ *noun*

el/la **espía**

➤ a spy film una película de espionaje

■ *verb*

**espiar**

➤ to spy on somebody espiar a alguien.

**square** [skweəʳ] *(adjective & noun)*

■ *adjective*

**cuadrado**: the box is square la caja es cuadrada; two square feet dos pies cuadrados

■ *noun*

1. el **cuadrado**: it's a square not a circle es un cuadrado, no un círculo

2. la **plaza**: the hotel is near the market square el hotel está cerca de la plaza del mercado

➤ the town square la plaza del pueblo.

**squash** [skwɒʃ] *(noun & verb)*

■ *noun*

1. el **squash**: they're playing squash están jugando squash

2. la **calabaza**: he doesn't like eating squash no le gusta comer calabaza

■ *verb*

**aplastar**: he squashed my hat aplastó mi sombrero; you're squashing me! ¡me estás aplastando!

**squeeze** [skwiːz] *verb*

1. **exprimir**: she squeezed the sponge exprimió la esponja; a glass of freshly squeezed orange juice un vaso de jugo de naranja recién exprimido

2. **apretar**: I squeezed her hand le apreté la mano

**3.** meter a la fuerza: I squeezed my things into the suitcase metí a la fuerza mis cosas en la maleta.

**squirrel** ['skwɜːrəl] *noun* ■ la **ardilla**.

**St**

**1.** *(abbreviation of* street*)* **calle:** 13 Barrow St el número 13 de la calle Barrow

**2.** *(abbreviation of* saint*)* **Sto., Sta.:** St Thomas Sto. Tomás.

**stab** [stæb] *(past tense & past participle* stabbed*) verb* ■ **apuñalar:** the robbers stabbed him los ladrones lo apuñalaron.

**stable** ['steɪbl] *noun* ■ el **establo:** the horses are in the stable los caballos están en el establo.

**stack** [stæk] *noun* ■ la **pila:** there's a stack of newspapers on the floor hay una pila de periódicos en el suelo.

**stadium** ['steɪdjəm] *(plural* stadiums *or* stadia ['steɪdjə]*) noun* ■ el **estadio**.

**staff** [staːf] *noun* ■ el **personal:** the staff of our firm el personal de nuesta empresa.

**stage** [steɪdʒ] *noun*

**1.** el **escenario:** the actors are on the stage los actores están en el escenario

**2.** la **etapa:** we are doing this in stages estamos haciendo esto en etapas

➤ at this stage a estas alturas.

**stagger** ['stægər] *verb* ■ **tambalearse:** he was so drunk he was staggering estaba tan borracho que se tambaleaba.

**stain** [steɪn] *(noun & verb)*

■ *noun*

la **mancha:** there's a stain on your jacket tienes una mancha en la chaqueta

■ *verb*

**manchar:** the wine stained my dress el vino me manchó el vestido.

**stair** [steər] *noun* ■ el **peldaño:** he's sitting on the bottom stair está sentado en el peldaño de más abajo.

**staircase** ['steəkeɪs] *noun* ■ la **escalera**.

**stairs** [steərz] *plural noun* ■ las **escaleras:** she went down the stairs bajó las escaleras.

**stale** [steɪl] *adjective* ■ **duro:** the bread is stale el pan está duro.

**stammer** ['stæmər] *verb* ■ **tartamudear:** she stammers tartamudea.

**stamp** [stæmp] *(noun & verb)*

■ *noun*

la **estampilla,** el **timbre** *Mexico*: he stuck on the stamp pegó la estampilla

■ *verb*

**sellar:** they stamped my passport sellaron mi pasaporte

➤ to stamp one's foot dar una patada en el suelo: she stamped her foot in rage dio una patada en el suelo de rabia.

**stand** [stænd] *(noun & verb)*

■ *noun*

**1.** el **stand** *(plural* los **stands***):* we have a stand at the exhibition tenemos un stand en la exposición

**2.** la **tribuna:** the stands in a stadium las tribunas de un estadio

➤ a newspaper stand un puesto de periódicos

■ *verb*

*(past tense & past participle* stood*)*

**1.** **estar de pie:** she's standing by the door está de pie al lado de la puerta

**2.** **ponerse de pie:** everyone stood when the judge came in todo el mundo se puso de pie cuando entró el juez

**3.** **estar:** the house stands in the valley la casa está en el valle

**4.** **soportar:** I can't stand racism no soporto el racismo

➤ stand still! ¡estáte quieto!

**stand for** *phrasal verb*

**1.** **significar:** what does FAQ stand for? ¿qué significa FAQ?

**2.** **tolerar:** I won't stand for this behavior! ¡no voy a tolerar esta conducta!

**stand out** *phrasal verb* ■ **destacarse:** the colors stand out against the background los colores se destacan sobre el fondo

➤ she stands out in a crowd sobresale en la multitud.

**stand up** *phrasal verb* ■ **ponerse de pie: she stood up when I came in** se puso de pie cuando entré.

**stand up for** *phrasal verb* ■ **defender: he stands up for his little brother** defiende a su hermano menor.

**standard** ['stændəd] *(noun & adjective)*
■ *noun*
el **nivel: the standard is very high** el nivel es muy alto
➤ **his parents have strict standards** sus padres tienen principios estrictos
➤ **the standard of living** el nivel de vida: **they have a high standard of living** tienen un alto nivel de vida
➤ **he has high standards** exige mucho
■ *adjective*
**estándar: it's a standard hotel room** es una habitación estándar; **this is the standard size** éste es el tamaño estándar.

**stank** [stæŋk] *past tense* ➤ stink.

**staple** ['steɪpl] *(noun & verb)*
■ *noun*
la **grapa: the staple has come out** se salió la grapa
■ *verb*
**engrapar: I stapled the papers together** engrapé los papeles.

**stapler** ['steɪplər] *noun* ■ la **engrapadora**.

**star** [stɑːr] *(noun & verb)*
■ *noun*
la **estrella: there are lots of stars tonight** hay muchas estrellas esta noche; **he's an international star** es una estrella internacional
■ *verb*
1. **tener como protagonista: the film stars Mel Gibson** la película tiene como protagonista a Mel Gibson
2. **protagonizar: Julia Roberts stars in the film** Julia Roberts protagoniza la película.

**stare** [steər] *verb* ■ **mirar fijamente: he stared at me** me miró fijamente.

**Stars and Stripes** [,stɑːrzənd'straɪps] *noun* ■ **the Stars and Stripes** la bandera de Estados Unidos

THE STARS AND STRIPES

**The Stars and Stripes** es el nombre que se le da a la bandera estadounidense a causa de que su diseño incluye 13 bandas blancas y rojas, representando las 13 colonias originales de la época en que se fundó el país, y un campo azul con 50 estrellas blancas que representan los 50 estados actuales.

**start** [stɑːt] *(noun & verb)*
■ *noun*
el **principio: it's a start** es un principio; **at the start of the film** al principio de la película
■ *verb*
1. **empezar: the movie starts at four o'clock** la película empieza a las cuatro; **he wants to start a business** quiere empezar un negocio
2. **arrancar: the car won't start** el coche no arranca
3. **prender: can you start the washing machine?** ¿podrías prender la lavadora?
➤ **to start again** empezar de nuevo
➤ **to start to do something or to start doing something** ponerse a hacer algo: **he started working** se puso a trabajar
➤ **she started crying or she started to cry** se puso a llorar

**start off, start out** *phrasal verb*
■ **salir: we started off at dawn** salimos al amanecer.

**startle** ['stɑːtl] *verb* ■ **sobresaltar: you startled me** me sobresaltaste.

**starve** [stɑːv] *verb* ■ **pasar hambre: millions of people are starving all over the world** millones de personas pasan hambre en el mundo
➤ **I'm starving** me muero de hambre.

**state** [steɪt] *noun*
1. la **condición** *(plural* las **condiciones)*: **she's not in any state to drive** no está en condiciones de manejar

**2.** el **estado:** the head of state el jefe del estado; **Alaska is the biggest state in the United States** Alaska es el estado más grande de Estados Unidos
➤ **the States** Estados Unidos: **Vic lives in the States** Vic vive en Estados Unidos.

**station** ['steɪʃn] *noun* ▪ la **estación** (*plural* **las estaciones**): **I'll meet you at the station** te voy a buscar a la estación
➤ **a radio station** una estación de radio
➤ **a bus station** una terminal de autobuses, una terminal de camiones *Mexico*
➤ **a train station** una estación de trenes
➤ **a subway station** una estación de metro
➤ **the police station** la comisaría, la estación de policía *Colombia,* una delegación de policía *Mexico*
➤ **a station wagon** una camioneta.

**stationery** ['steɪʃnərɪ] *uncountable noun* ▪ los **artículos de escritorio: I bought some stationery** compré algunos artículos de escritorio
➤ **a stationery store** una papelería.

**statue** ['stætʃuː] *noun* ▪ la **estatua**
➤ **the Statue of Liberty** la estatua de la Libertad

THE STATUE OF LIBERTY

Se trata de un monumento regalado por el gobierno de Francia a los Estados Unidos en 1886 en reconocimiento de la alianza forjada entre éstos durante la revolución americana. La estatua mide 93 metros de altura y se encuentra en una isla (**Liberty Island**) en el puerto de Nueva York. Con el tiempo se convirtió en un símbolo de bienvenida a los inmigrantes que llegaban al país provenientes de todo el mundo. Actualmente es una popular atracción turística.

**stay** [steɪ] (*noun & verb*)
■ *noun*
la **estadía,** la **estancia** *Mexico*: **I enjoyed my stay in Mexico** disfruté mi estadía en México
■ *verb*
**quedarse: stay here!** ¡quédate aquí!; **I'll stay at home** me voy a quedar en casa; **he**

**stayed for a week** se quedó una semana; **I stayed in a hotel** me quedé en un hotel; **quedarse: she stayed awake all night** se quedó despierta toda la noche
➤ **to stay the night** quedarse a dormir: **do you want to stay the night?** ¿quieres quedarte a dormir?

**stay away** *phrasal verb* ▪ **mantenerse alejado:** **stay away from the door** mantente alejado de la puerta.

**stay out** *phrasal verb*
➤ **he stayed out all night** pasó toda la noche afuera.

**stay up** *phrasal verb* ▪ **quedarse levantado:** **she stayed up all night** se quedó levantada toda la noche.

**steady** ['stedɪ] *adjective*
**1.** **firme: the chair isn't very steady** la silla no es muy firme; **he has steady hands** tiene el pulso firme
**2.** **fijo: she has a steady job** tiene un empleo fijo
➤ **we're making steady progress** seguimos mejorando.

**steak** [steɪk] *noun* ▪ el **bistec** (*plural* los **bistecs**).

**steal** [stiːl] (*past tense* stole, *past participle* stolen) *verb* ▪ **robar: someone stole my wallet** alguien me robó la cartera.

**steam** [stiːm] *noun* ▪ el **vapor:** a steam engine** una máquina de vapor.

**steel** [stiːl] *uncountable noun* ▪ el **acero**.

**steep** [stiːp] *adjective*
**1.** **empinado: the stairs are steep** las escaleras son empinadas
**2.** **escarpada: it's a steep hill** es una montaña escarpada.

**steering wheel** ['stɪərɪŋwiːl] *noun* ▪ el **volante**.

**step** [step] (*noun & verb*)
■ *noun*
**1.** el **paso: she took one step backwards** dio un paso atrás

**2.** el **escalón** (plural los **escalones**): he was sitting on the step estaba sentado en el escalón

■ verb
(past tense & past participle **stepped**) **pisar**: he stepped on an ant pisó una hormiga

**step forward** phrasal verb ■ **dar un paso adelante**: can you step forward? ¿podrías dar un paso adelante?

**stepbrother** ['step,brʌðər] noun ■ el **hermanastro**.

**stepdaughter** ['step,dɔːtər] noun ■ la **hijastra**.

**stepfather** ['step,faːðər] noun ■ el **padrastro**.

**stepmother** ['step,mʌðər] noun ■ la **madrastra**.

**stepsister** ['step,sɪstər] noun ■ la **hermanastra**.

**stepson** ['stepsʌn] noun ■ el **hijastro**.

**stereo** ['sterɪəʊ] noun ■ el **estéreo**: he bought a new stereo compró un nuevo estéreo.

**stew** [stjuː] noun ■ el **guiso**: a beef stew un guiso de carne de vaca.

**stick** [stɪk] (noun & verb)

■ noun
**1.** el **palo**: he hit the tree with a stick golpeó el árbol con un palo
**2.** el **bastón** (plural los **bastones**): she was walking with a stick caminaba con un bastón

■ verb
(past tense & past participle **stuck**)
**1.** **pegar**: I stuck the stamps on the envelope pegué las estampillas en el sobre
**2.** **pegarse**: the label won't stick la etiqueta no se pega
**3.** **clavar**: he stuck the penknife into the wood clavó la navaja en la madera
**4.** informal **poner**: stick your bag over there pon tu bolso allá

**stick out** phrasal verb ■ **asomarse**: your shirt is sticking out se te asoma la camisa

➤ to stick one's tongue out sacar la lengua: he stuck his tongue out sacó la lengua.

**sticker** ['stɪkər] noun ■ el **adhesivo**: her case is covered in stickers su maleta está cubierta de adhesivos.

**sticky** ['stɪkɪ] adjective
**1.** **pegajoso**: my hands are sticky tengo las manos pegajosas
**2.** **adhesivo**: a sticky label una etiqueta adhesiva.

**stiff** [stɪf] adjective ■ **duro**: stiff cardboard cartón duro
➤ to be stiff estar agarrotado: I'm stiff all over estoy todo agarrotado
➤ to have a stiff neck tener tortícolis
➤ he's bored stiff informal se aburre como ostra
➤ she's scared stiff informal está muerta de miedo.

**still** [stɪl] (adverb & adjective)

■ adverb
**1.** **todavía**: are you still at this address? ¿todavía vives en esta dirección?; that's better still eso es todavía mejor
**2.** **aún así**: he's very lazy but she still likes him es muy flojo pero aún así ella lo quiere

■ adjective
**quieto**: the lizard was very still la lagartija estaba muy quieta
➤ to keep still quedarse quieto: she won't keep still no se queda quieta
➤ sit still! ¡quédate quieto!

**sting** [stɪŋ] (noun & verb)

■ noun
la **picadura**, el **piquete** Mexico: a bee sting una picadura de abeja

■ verb
(past tense & past participle **stung**) **picar**: a bee stung me me picó una abeja.

**stink** [stɪŋk] (past tense **stank**, past participle **stunk**) verb ■ **apestar**: it stinks in here! ¡apesta aquí adentro!

**stir** [stɜːr] (past tense & past participle **stirred**) verb ■ **mezclar**: you stir the eggs and sugar together mezclas los huevos con el azúcar.

**stitch** [stɪtʃ] *(noun & verb)*

■ *noun*

1. la **puntada:** you can see the stitches on the hem se ven las puntadas en el dobladillo
2. el **punto:** he had three stitches in his arm le pusieron tres puntos en el brazo

■ *verb*
**coser:** she stitched the button back on cosió el botón.

**stock** [stɒk] *noun*

1. la **reserva:** we have a stock of canned food at home tenemos una reserva de comida enlatada en casa
2. el **caldo:** chicken stock caldo de pollo
➤ **in stock** en existencia
➤ **they are out of stock** están agotados
➤ **the stock market** el mercado de valores.

**stocking** ['stɒkɪŋ] *noun* ■ la **media:** she's wearing silk stockings tiene puestas medias de seda.

**stole** [stəʊl] *past tense* ➤ steal.

**stolen** ['stəʊln] *past participle* ➤ steal.

**stomach** ['stʌmək] *noun* ■ el **estómago**.

**stomachache** ['stʌməkeɪk] *noun* ■ el **dolor de estómago**
➤ **I've got a stomachache** me duele el estómago.

**stone** [stəʊn] *noun* ■ la **piedra:** she threw a stone at the window tiró una piedra a la ventana.

**stood** [stʊd] *past tense & past participle* ➤ stand.

**stool** [stuːl] *noun* ■ el **taburete:** she's sitting on a stool está sentada en un taburete.

**stop** [stɒp] *(noun & verb)*

■ *noun*
la **parada:** where's the next stop? ¿dónde es la próxima parada?; a bus stop una parada de autobús
➤ **to come to a stop** detenerse: the train came to a stop el tren se detuvo

■ *verb*
*(past tense & past participle* **stopped**)

1. **frenar:** she stopped the car frenó el coche

2. **parar:** the bus stopped in front of the school el autobús paró enfrente de la escuela
3. **pararse:** my watch has stopped se me paró el reloj
➤ **to stop doing something** dejar de hacer algo: it has stopped raining at last finalmente ha dejado de llover

> **Impedir que** must be followed by a verb in the subjunctive:

➤ **to stop somebody from doing something** impedir que alguien haga algo: I tried to stop him from leaving traté de impedir que se fuera.

**store** [stɔːʳ] *(noun & verb)*

■ *noun*
la **tienda:** he went into the store on the corner entró en la tienda de la esquina

■ *verb*

1. **guardar:** we store wine in the cellar guardamos vino en la bodega
2. **almacenar:** the latest computers can store even more information las últimas computadoras pueden almacenar aún más información.

**stork** [stɔːk] *noun* ■ la **cigüeña**.

**storm** [stɔːm] *noun* ■ la **tormenta**.

**stormy** ['stɔːmɪ] *adjective* ■ **tormentoso:** it's stormy today hoy está tormentoso.

**story** ['stɔːrɪ] *(plural* stories) *noun*

1. la **historia:** she told us a story nos contó una historia
2. el **piso:** the building has ten stories el edificio tiene diez pisos.

**straight** [streɪt] *(adjective & adverb)*

■ *adjective*

1. **recto:** draw a straight line dibuja una línea recta
2. **lacio:** he has straight hair tiene pelo lacio
3. **franco:** he's always very straight with me siempre es muy franco conmigo

■ *adverb*

1. **directamente:** he went straight to the police fue directamente a la policía
2. **derecho:** walk straight ahead camina todo derecho

**3. inmediatamente:** it happened straight after that sucedió inmediatamente después de eso.

**strain** [streɪn] *verb*

➤ **to strain a muscle** hacerse un esguince: **he strained a muscle** se hizo un esguince

➤ **to strain one's eyes** forzar la vista: **don't strain your eyes** no fuerces la vista.

**strange** [streɪndʒ] *adjective*

1. **raro:** it's strange that she's late es raro que no haya llegado todavía; **she's a strange woman** es una mujer rara

2. **desconocido:** there are a lot of strange faces hay un montón de caras desconocidas; **in a strange town** en un pueblo desconocido.

**stranger** ['streɪndʒəʳ] *noun* ■ el **desconocido,** la **desconocida:** he's a complete stranger es un perfecto desconocido.

**strangle** ['stræŋgl] *verb* ■ **estrangular:** the murderer strangled her el asesino la estranguló.

**strap** [stræp] *noun*

1. el **tirante,** el **bretel** *Southern Cone:* **my bra strap is broken** se me rompió el tirante del sostén

2. la **correa:** there's a strap around my suitcase hay una correa alrededor de mi valija; **my purse strap is too long** la correa de mi bolso es demasiado larga.

**straw** [strɔ:] *noun*

1. la **paja:** there's straw all over the floor hay paja tirada por todo el piso

2. la **pajita,** el **popote** *Mexico:* he was drinking through a straw estaba tomando con una pajita.

**strawberry** ['strɔ:bəri] *(plural* strawberries*) noun* ■ la **fresa,** la **rutilla** *Andes, River Plate*

➤ **strawberry jam** mermelada de fresa.

**stream** [stri:m] *noun* ■ el **arroyo:** we crossed the stream cruzamos el arroyo.

**street** [stri:t] *noun* ■ la **calle:** cross the street at the lights cruza la calle en los semáforos

➤ **a street lamp** or **a street light** un farol.

**streetwise** ['stri:twaɪz] *adjective* ■ **pillo:** these kids are very streetwise estos chicos son muy pillos.

**strength** [streŋθ] *noun* ■ la **fuerza:** I don't have the strength to get up no tengo fuerzas para levantarme.

**stress** [stres] *noun* ■ el **acento:** the stress is on the first syllable el acento recae sobre la primera sílaba

➤ **he's under a lot of stress** está muy estresado.

**stressed** [stresd] *adjective* ■ **estresado:** she's stressed está estresada.

**stretch** [stretʃ] *verb*

1. **estirarse:** she woke up and stretched se despertó y se estiró

2. **estirar:** they stretched the net between the two poles estiraron la red entre los dos palos; **stretch your arms towards the ceiling** estira los brazos hacia el techo

➤ **to stretch one's legs** estirar las piernas: **I went outside to stretch my legs** salí afuera a estirar las piernas

**stretch out** *phrasal verb*

1. **estirar:** she stretched her hand out to take it estiró la mano para tomarlo; **he stretched his legs out** estiró las piernas

2. **tenderse:** they stretched out on the grass se tendieron en el césped.

**stretcher** ['stretʃəʳ] *noun* ■ la **camilla:** they carried her on a stretcher la llevaban en una camilla.

**strict** [strɪkt] *adjective* ■ **estricto:** his parents are very strict sus padres son muy estrictos.

**strike** [straɪk] *(noun & verb)*

■ *noun*
la **huelga**

➤ **to be on strike** estar en huelga

➤ **to go on strike** declararse en huelga

■ *verb*
*(past tense & past participle* struck*)*

1. **pegar:** someone struck me alguien me pegó

**2.** **dar:** the clock struck six el reloj dio las seis

**3.** **llamar la atención:** I was struck by her beauty me llamó la atención su belleza

**4.** **chocar contra:** the car struck a tree el coche chocó contra un árbol

➤ to strike a match encender un fósforo: she struck a match encendió un fósforo.

**string** [strɪŋ] *noun* ▪ **la cuerda:** I tied the package with string amarré el paquete con cordel; the guitar has a broken string la guitarra tiene una cuerda rota

➤ a piece of string un cordel.

**strip** [strɪp] *(noun & verb)*

▪ *noun*
la **tira: a strip of paper** una tira de papel

▪ *verb*
*(past tense & past participle* **stripped***, present participle* **stripping)** **desnudarse:** he stripped and had a shower se desnudó y se duchó.

**stripe** [straɪp] *noun* ▪ la **raya:** there are red and green stripes on her dress su vestido tiene rayas verdes y rojas.

**striped** [straɪpt] *adjective* ▪ **rayado:** Don's wearing a striped shirt Don tiene puesta una camisa rayada.

**stroke** [strəʊk] *(noun & verb)*

▪ *noun*

**1.** el **trazo:** he made several strokes on the canvas with his brush dibujó diferentes trazos en el lienzo con el pincel

**2.** el **derrame cerebral:** he had a stroke tuvo un derrame cerebral

➤ a stroke of luck un golpe de suerte

▪ *verb*
**acariciar:** she was stroking the cat estaba acariciando al gato.

**stroll** [strəʊl] *(noun & verb)*

▪ *noun*
el **paseo: we're going for a stroll** vamos a dar un paseo

▪ *verb*
**pasear:** they were strolling through the park estaban paseando por el parque.

**stroller** ['strəʊlə'] *noun* ▪ la **silla de paseo,** el **changuito** *Argentina,* la **carreola** *Mexico:* she was pushing the baby in the stroller empujaba al bebé en la silla de paseo.

**strong** [strɒŋ] *adjective* ▪ **fuerte:** she likes her coffee strong le gusta el café fuerte; as strong as an ox fuerte como un toro.

**struck** [strʌk] *past tense & past participle*
➤ strike.

**structure** ['strʌktʃər] *noun* ▪ la **estructura.**

**struggle** ['strʌgl] *(noun & verb)*

▪ *noun*
la **lucha: a struggle to survive** una lucha para sobrevivir

▪ *verb*

**1.** **luchar:** he struggled to survive in the jungle luchó para sobrevivir en la selva

**2.** **forcejear:** she struggled to get free forcejeó para escaparse

**3.** **tener problemas:** he's struggling to finish his homework está teniendo problemas para terminar las tareas.

**stubborn** ['stʌbən] *adjective* ▪ **terco**

➤ as stubborn as a mule terco como una mula.

**stuck** [stʌk] *(adjective & verb form)*

▪ *adjective*
**atascado:** the window is stuck la ventana está atascada; we're stuck in a snowstorm estamos atascados en una tormenta de nieve

➤ to get stuck atascarse: my arm got stuck se me atascó el brazo

▪ *past tense & past participle*
➤ stick.

**stuck-up** [stʌk'ʌp] *adjective* ▪ *informal* **creído:** she's really stuck-up es muy creída.

**student** ['stjuːdnt] *noun* ▪ el/la **estudiante.**

**studio** ['stjuːdɪəʊ] *noun*

**1.** el **estudio: a television studio** un estudio de televisión

**2.** el **taller: a painter's studio** el taller de un pintor

➤ a studio apartment un estudio.

**study** ['stʌdɪ] (noun & verb)

■ noun
(plural **studies**) los **estudios**: he wants to continue his studies quiere continuar sus estudios

■ verb
**estudiar**: Flora's studying Spanish Flora está estudiando castellano

➤ to study for an exam estudiar para un examen: I'm studying for my exam estoy estudiando para el examen.

**stuff** [stʌf] informal (noun & verb)

■ noun
1. la **cosa**: what's that stuff you're eating? ¿qué es esa cosa que estás comiendo?; what's all this stuff on the table? ¿qué hacen todas estas cosas en la mesa?
2. las **cosas**: don't forget to take your stuff with you no olvides de llevarte tus cosas

■ verb
**meterse**: he stuffed the keys into his pocket se metió las llaves en el bolsillo.

**stuffy** ['stʌfɪ] adjective ■ **mal ventilado**: the room is stuffy el cuarto está mal ventilado.

**stumble** ['stʌmbl] verb ■ **tropezarse**: she stumbled down the stairs se tropezó bajando las escaleras.

**stung** [stʌŋ] past tense & past participle ➤ sting.

**stunk** [stʌŋk] past tense ➤ stink.

**stunned** [stʌnd] adjective ■ **pasmado**: he was stunned by the news las noticias lo dejaron pasmado.

**stunning** ['stʌnɪŋ] adjective
1. **asombroso**: it's stunning news es una noticia asombrosa
2. **impresionante**: the scenery is stunning el paisaje es impresionante.

**stunt** [stʌnt] noun ■ el **truco**
➤ a stunt man un doble.

**stupid** ['stjuːpɪd] adjective ■ **estúpido**.

**stutter** ['stʌtəʳ] verb ■ **tartamudear**: she stutters tartamudea.

**style** [staɪl] noun
1. la **moda**: a new style of sportswear una nueva moda en ropa deportiva
2. el **estilo**: James Bond has a lot of style James Bond tiene mucho estilo.

**subject** ['sʌbdʒekt] noun
1. el **tema**: what's the subject of the book? ¿cuál es el tema del libro?
2. la **asignatura**: history is my favorite subject historia es mi asignatura preferida.

**submarine** [ˌsʌbməˈriːn] noun ■ el **submarino**.

**subscription** [səbˈskrɪpʃn] noun ■ la **suscripción** (plural las **suscripciones**)
➤ to have a subscription to a magazine estar suscrito a una revista.

**substance** ['sʌbstəns] noun ■ la **sustancia**: a sticky substance una sustancia pegajosa.

**substitute** ['sʌbstɪtjuːt] noun ■ el **sustituto**, la **sustituta**: the teams can have three substitutes los equipos pueden tener tres sustitutos.

**subtitle** ['sʌbˌtaɪtl] noun ■ el **subtítulo**.

**subtle** ['sʌtl] adjective ■ **sutil**.

**subtract** [səbˈtrækt] verb ■ **restar**: subtract 78 from 100 resta 78 de 100.

**suburb** ['sʌbɜːb] noun ■ el **barrio residencial en las afueras**: Jersey Village is a suburb of Houston Jersey Village es un barrio residencial en las afueras de Houston
➤ the suburbs los barrios de las afueras.

**subway** ['sʌbweɪ] noun ■ el **metro**.

**succeed** [səkˈsiːd] verb
1. **tener éxito**: you have to work hard to succeed tienes que trabajar duro para tener éxito
2. **conseguir**: he succeeded in getting into Yale consiguió entrar a Yale.

**success** [səkˈses] noun ■ el **éxito**: it's a great success es un gran éxito

 Success es un falso amigo, no significa "suceso".

**successful** [sək'sesfʊl] *adjective* ■ **exitoso: it was a successful evening** fue una tarde exitosa

➤ **to be successful** tener éxito: **she's successful in whatever she does** tiene éxito en todo lo que hace.

**successfully** [sək'sesfʊlɪ] *adverb* ■ **con éxito**.

**such** [sʌtʃ] *adjective & adverb*

1. **tal: such situations are common** tales situaciones son frecuentes; **in such cases** en tales casos

2. **tanto: he has such a lot of books** tiene tantos libros; **I waited such a long time** esperé tanto tiempo

3. **tan: it's such a beautiful view!** ¡es una vista tan bonita!; **he's such a clever man** es un hombre tan inteligente; **I'd never seen such a big dog** nunca había visto un perro tan grande

➤ **it's such a pity** es una lástima

➤ **there's no such thing** no existe tal cosa

➤ **such as** como: **animals such as lions and tigers** animales como los leones y los tigres.

**suck** [sʌk] *verb* ■ **chuparse: he's sucking his thumb** se está chupando el pulgar.

**sudden** ['sʌdn] *adjective* ■ **repentino: there was a sudden shower** hubo un chubasco repentino

➤ **all of a sudden** de repente: **all of a sudden she got angry** de repente se enojó.

**suddenly** ['sʌdnlɪ] *adverb* ■ **de repente: suddenly he left** de repente se fue.

**suede** [sweɪd] *uncountable noun* ■ **el ante**.

**suffer** ['sʌfər] *verb* ■ **sufrir: he's really suffering** está sufriendo de verdad

➤ **to be suffering from a cold** estar resfriado.

**sugar** ['ʃʊgər] *noun* ■ **el/la azúcar**.

**suggest** [sə'dʒest] *verb*

1. **sugerir: what do you suggest?** ¿qué sugieres?

2. **aconsejar: I suggest you leave now** te aconsejo que te vayas ahora

> **Aconsejar que** must be followed by a verb in the subjunctive.

**suggestion** [sə'dʒestʃn] *noun* ■ **la sugerencia: can I make a suggestion?** ¿puedo hacer una sugerencia?

**suicide** ['sʊɪsaɪd] *noun* ■ **el suicidio**

➤ **to commit suicide** suicidarse: **she committed suicide** se suicidó.

**suit** [suːt] *(noun & verb)*

■ *noun*

1. **el traje: he's wearing a suit** tiene puesto un traje

2. **el traje de chaqueta: she's wearing a suit** tiene puesto un traje de chaqueta

■ *verb*

1. **quedar bien: that skirt suits you** esa falda te queda bien

2. **convenir: does Monday suit you?** ¿te conviene el lunes?

➤ **suit yourself!** ¡haz lo que quieras!

**suitable** ['suːtəbl] *adjective* ■ **apropiado: that dress isn't suitable for the occasion** este vestido no es apropiado para la ocasión.

**suitcase** ['suːtkeɪs] *noun* ■ **la maleta, la valija** *River Plate*: **I'm going to pack my suitcase** voy a hacer la maleta.

**suite** [swiːt] *noun* ■ **la suite: they have a suite at the Ritz** tienen una suite en el Ritz.

**sulk** [sʌlk] *verb*

➤ **she's sulking** está enfurruñada.

**sum** [sʌm] *(noun & verb)* *noun* ■ **la suma: that's a large sum of money** ésa es una gran suma de dinero

**sum up** *phrasal verb* ■ **resumir: let's sum up what we've done so far** resumamos lo que hemos hecho hasta el momento.

**summary** ['sʌmərɪ] *(plural summaries)* *noun* ■ **el resumen** *(plural* **los resúmenes***)*.

**summer** ['sʌmər] noun ■ el **verano**: in the summer en el verano; **they go to Corsica every summer** se van a Córcega todos los veranos
➤ a summer camp un campamento de verano
➤ summer clothes ropa de verano
➤ summer vacation vacaciones de verano.

**summertime** ['sʌmətaɪm] uncountable noun ■ el **verano**: it happened in the summertime sucedió en el verano.

**summit** ['sʌmɪt] noun ■ la **cumbre**: Edmund Hillary and Tenzing Norgay reached the summit of Everest in 1953 Edmund Hillary y Tenzing Norgay llegaron a la cumbre del Everest en 1953.

**sun** [sʌn] noun ■ el **sol**: the sun's shining el sol está brillando
➤ in the sun al sol: I don't want to go out in the sun no quiero salir al sol.

**sunbathe** ['sʌnbeɪð] verb ■ **tomar el sol**: she was sunbathing on the beach estaba tomando el sol en la playa.

**sunburn** ['sʌnbɜːn] uncountable noun ■ las **quemaduras de sol**: I have a sunburn on my arms tengo quemaduras de sol en los brazos.

**sunburned** ['sʌnbɜːnd] adjective
➤ to be sunburned estar bronceado: look how sunburned he is mira qué bronceado está.

**Sunday** ['sʌndɪ] noun ■

In Spanish the days of the week do not start with a capital letter:

el **domingo**: it's Sunday today hoy es domingo; next Sunday el próximo domingo; last Sunday el domingo pasado
➤ on Sunday el domingo: I'll see you on Sunday te veo el domingo
➤ on Sundays los domingos: he comes to see me on Sundays viene a verme los domingos
➤ to be in one's Sunday best ir vestido de domingo.

**sundown** ['sʌndaʊn] uncountable noun ■ el **atardecer**: they stopped work at sundown dejaron de trabajar al atardecer.

**sunflower** ['sʌn,flaʊər] noun ■ el **girasol**.

**sung** [sʌŋ] past participle ➤ sing.

**sunglasses** ['sʌn,glaːsɪz] plural noun ■ los **lentes de sol**.

**sunk** [sʌŋk] past participle ➤ sink.

**sunlight** ['sʌnlaɪt] uncountable noun ■ la **luz del sol**: in the sunlight a la luz del sol.

**sunny** ['sʌnɪ] adjective ■ **soleado**: it was a sunny day era un día soleado
➤ it's sunny hace sol.

**sunrise** ['sʌnraɪz] noun ■ la **salida del sol**: I woke up before sunrise me desperté antes de la salida del sol.

**sunset** ['sʌnset] noun ■ la **puesta del sol**: I came home after sunset llegué a casa después de la puesta del sol.

**sunshine** ['sʌnʃaɪn] uncountable noun ■ el **sol**: there isn't much sunshine today no hay mucho sol hoy.

**suntan** ['sʌntæn] noun ■ el **bronceado**: she has a nice suntan tiene un bonito bronceado
➤ suntan lotion bronceador.

**super** ['suːpər] adjective ■ informal **genial**: it's a super film es una película genial
➤ the Super Bowl el Supertazón

THE SUPER BOWL

El Super Bowl es un partido de fútbol americano en el que se enfrentan los campeones de las dos ligas o **conferences** más importantes del fútbol profesional en Estados Unidos. Tiene lugar al final de la temporada de juegos - a fines de enero de cada año - y una gran cantidad de gente en Estados Unidos y otros países presencian este encuentro por televisión.

**superhighway** ['suːpə,haɪweɪ] noun ■ la **autopista**
➤ the information superhighway la autopista de la información.

**superior** [su:'pɪərɪəʳ] *adjective* ■ **superior**.

**supermarket** ['su:pə,ma:kɪt] *noun* ■ el **supermercado**.

**supernatural** [,su:pə'nætʃrəl] *adjective* ■ **sobrenatural**.

**superstitious** [,su:pə'stɪʃəs] *adjective* ■ **supersticioso**.

**supper** ['sʌpəʳ] *noun* ■ la **cena**: supper time la hora de la cena
➤ to have supper cenar: we had fish for supper cenamos pescado.

**supply** [sə'plaɪ] *(noun & verb)*
■ *noun*
(plural supplies) el **suministro**: the supplies are running out se están acabando los suministros
➤ supply and demand la oferta y la demanda
■ *verb*
(past tense & past participle supplied) **suministrar**: the school supplies pencils la escuela suministra los lápices
➤ to supply someone with something facilitarle algo a alguien: I supplied him with the details le facilité los detalles.

**support** [sə'pɔ:t] *(noun & verb)*
■ *noun*
el **apoyo**: thanks to their support, he was elected mayor gracias a su apoyo, fue elegido alcalde
■ *verb*
1. **apoyar**: I will always support you siempre te apoyaré
2. **ser hincha de**: she supports the Miami Dolphins es hincha de los Miami Dolphins.

**supporter** [sə'pɔ:təʳ] *noun*
1. el **partidario**, la **partidaria**: he's a supporter of feminism es partidario del feminismo
2. el/la **hincha**: he's a Chicago Bears supporter es hincha de los Chicago Bears.

**suppose** [sə'pəʊz] *verb*
1. **suponer**: I suppose he'll come tomorrow supongo que vendrá mañana

2. **creer**: do you suppose he'll pass his exam? ¿crees que aprobará el examen?
➤ suppose you were rich ... imagínate que eres rico ...
➤ I suppose so supongo que sí
➤ we are supposed to wait here se supone que tenemos que esperar aquí.

**sure** [ʃʊəʳ] *adjective* ■ **seguro**: are you sure she'll come? ¿estás seguro que va a venir?; I'm not sure no estoy seguro
➤ they are sure to be late con toda seguridad van a llegar tarde
➤ to make sure asegurarse: make sure you don't forget! ¡asegúrate de no olvidarte!

**surely** ['ʃʊəlɪ] *adverb* ■ **seguro**: surely she didn't do that seguro que ella no hizo eso; slowly but surely lento pero seguro.

**surf** [sɜ:f] *verb* ■ **surfear**
➤ he surfs the Net for hours at a time navega por Internet durante horas seguidas.

**surface** ['sɜ:fɪs] *noun* ■ la **superficie**: I can see something on the surface of the water veo algo en la superficie del agua.

**surfboard** ['sɜ:fbɔ:d] *noun* ■ la **tabla de surf**.

**surfing** ['sɜ:fɪŋ] *uncountable noun* ■ el **surfing**: to go surfing hacer surfing; he goes surfing every weekend hace surfing todos los fines de semana.

**surgeon** ['sɜ:dʒən] *noun* ■ el **cirujano**, la **cirujana**.

**surprise** [sə'praɪz] *(noun & verb)*
■ *noun*
la **sorpresa**: what a surprise! ¡qué sorpresa!
■ *verb*
**sorprender**: that surprises me eso me sorprende.

**surprised** [sə'praɪzd] *adjective* ■ **sorprendido**: he was surprised to see me estaba sorprendido de verme.

**surprising** [sə'praɪzɪŋ] *adjective* ■ **sorprendente**: that's not surprising eso no es sorprendente.

**surrender** [sə'rendə$^r$] *verb* ■ **rendirse**: the soldiers surrendered los soldados se rindieron.

**surround** [sə'raʊnd] *verb* ■ **rodear**: the house is surrounded by a wall la casa está rodeada de un muro; the police surrounded the building la policía rodeó el edificio.

**survey** ['sɜːveɪ] *noun* ■ **la encuesta**.

**survive** [sə'vaɪv] *verb* ■ **sobrevivir**: two people survived sobrevivieron dos personas.

**survivor** [sə'vaɪvə$^r$] *noun* ■ **el/la sobreviviente**.

**suspect** *(noun & verb)*

■ *noun*
['sʌspekt] el **sospechoso**, la **sospechosa**: he's a suspect es sospechoso

■ *verb*
[sə'spekt] **sospechar**: they suspect her of stealing the diamond sospechan que robó el diamante.

**suspense** [sə'spens] *uncountable noun* ■ **el suspenso**: the film was full of suspense la película tenía mucho suspenso.

**suspicion** [sə'spɪʃn] *noun* ■ **la sospecha**: do you have any suspicions? ¿tienes alguna sospecha?

**suspicious** [sə'spɪʃəs] *adjective*

1. **desconfiado**: he became suspicious se volvió desconfiado

2. **sospechoso**: she looks very suspicious actúa de manera muy sospechosa

➤ **to be suspicious of somebody** desconfiar de alguien.

**swallow** ['swɒləʊ] *(noun & verb)*

■ *noun*
la **golondrina**: swallows migrate to Africa in the winter las golondrinas emigran a África en el invierno

■ *verb*
**tragarse**: she swallowed the pill se tragó la píldora.

**swam** [swæm] *past tense* ➤ **swim**.

**swamp** [swɒmp] *noun* ■ **el pantano**: there are alligators in this swamp hay caimanes en este pantano.

**swan** [swɒn] *noun* ■ **el cisne**.

**swap** [swɒp] *(past tense & past participle* swapped, *present participle* swapping*) verb*

1. **cambiarse**: let's swap jackets cambiémonos las chaquetas

2. **cambiar**: I swapped my bike for a scooter cambié mi bici por una Vespa®.

**swear** [sweə$^r$] *(past tense* swore, *past participle* sworn*) verb*

1. **decir malas palabras**: don't swear no digas malas palabras

2. **jurar**: I swear I'm telling the truth juro que estoy diciendo la verdad

➤ **to swear at somebody** insultar a alguien.

**swearword** ['sweəwɜːd] *noun* ■ **la mala palabra**: don't say that, it's a swearword no digas eso, es una mala palabra.

**sweat** [swet] *(noun & verb)*

■ *uncountable noun*
el **sudor**: I'm covered in sweat estoy cubierta de sudor

■ *verb*
**sudar**: I'm sweating estoy sudando.

**sweater** ['swetə$^r$] *noun* ■ **el suéter**: he's wearing a red sweater tiene puesto un suéter rojo.

**sweatshirt** ['swetʃɜːt] *noun* ■ **la sudadera**: she's wearing a green sweatshirt tiene puesta una sudadera verde.

**sweep** [swiːp] *(past tense & past participle* swept*) verb* ■ **barrer**: he's sweeping the floor está barriendo el suelo.

**sweet** [swiːt] *(adjective & noun) adjective*
■ **dulce**: the cake is too sweet el pastel es demasiado dulce; she's very sweet es muy dulce

➤ **sweet dreams!** ¡dulces sueños!

➤ **a sweet potato** una batata, un camote *Andes, Mexico*.

**swell** [swel] *(past tense* swelled, *past participle* swollen) *verb* ■ **hincharse:** my lip started to swell se me empezó a hinchar el labio

**swell up** *phrasal verb* ■ **hincharse:** her face has swollen up se le hinchó la cara.

**swept** [swept] *past tense & past participle*
➤ sweep.

**swerve** [swɜːv] *verb* ■ **virar bruscamente, dar un volantazo** *Mexico:* she swerved to avoid the child viró bruscamente para no atropellar al niño.

**swim** [swɪm] *(noun & verb)*

■ *noun*
➤ to go for a swim ir a nadar
■ *verb*
*(past tense* swam, *past participle* swum) **nadar:** can you swim? ¿sabes nadar?

**swimmer** ['swɪmər] *noun* ■ **el nadador, la nadadora:** he's a good swimmer es buen nadador.

**swimming** ['swɪmɪŋ] *uncountable noun* ■ **la natación:** I love swimming me encanta la natación
➤ to go swimming ir a nadar
➤ a swimming pool una piscina, una alberca *Mexico,* una pileta *River Plate*
➤ swimming trunks el traje de baño.

**swimsuit** ['swɪmsuːt] *noun* ■ **el traje de baño, la malla de baño** *River Plate.*

**swing** [swɪŋ] *(noun & verb)*

■ *noun*
**el columpio, la hamaca** *River Plate:* there are swings in the park hay columpios en el parque
■ *verb*
*(past tense & past participle* swung)
1. **balancearse:** the monkeys were swinging in the trees los monos se balanceaban en los árboles
2. **balancear:** he was swinging his arms balanceaba los brazos.

**switch** [swɪtʃ] *(noun & verb)*

■ *noun*
*(plural* switches) **el interruptor, el switch** *Colombia, Mexico:* where's the light switch? ¿dónde está el interruptor de la luz?

■ *verb*
**cambiar de:** let's switch places cambiemos de lugar

**switch off** *phrasal verb* ■ **apagar:** I switched off the light apagué la luz; he switched off the engine apagó el motor.

**switch on** *phrasal verb* ■ **prender:** she switched the light on prendió la luz; I switched the engine on prendí el motor.

**swollen** ['swəʊln] *(adjective & verb form)*
■ *adjective*
**hinchado:** she has a swollen arm tiene el brazo hinchado
■ *past participle*
➤ swell.

**sword** [sɔːd] *noun* ■ **la espada.**

**swore** [swɔːr] *past tense* ➤ swear.

**sworn** [swɔːn] *past participle* ➤ swear.

**swum** [swʌm] *past participle* ➤ swim.

**swung** [swʌŋ] *past tense & past participle*
➤ swing.

**syllable** ['sɪləbl] *noun* ■ **la sílaba:** "happiness" has three syllables "happiness" tiene tres sílabas.

**syllabus** ['sɪləbəs] *(plural* syllabuses or syllabi) *noun* ■ **el programa:** Spanish isn't on the syllabus any more castellano no está más en el programa.

**symbol** ['sɪmbl] *noun* ■ **el símbolo:** the white dove is a symbol of peace la paloma blanca es un símbolo de paz.

**sympathetic** [ˌsɪmpə'θetɪk] *adjective*
■ **comprensivo:** they were very sympathetic after hearing of our problem fueron muy comprensivos después de escuchar nuestro problema

 Sympathetic es un falso amigo, no significa "simpático".

**sympathy** ['sɪmpəθɪ] *uncountable noun*
■ **la compasión:** he has no sympathy for them no siente ninguna compasión por ellos.

**synagogue** ['sɪnəgɒg] *noun* ■ **la sinagoga.**

**syrup** ['sɪrəp] *uncountable noun* ■ **el jarabe**: a cough syrup un jarabe para la tos
➤ maple syrup jarabe de arce, miel de maple *Mexico*
➤ peaches in syrup duraznos en almíbar.

**system** ['sɪstəm] *noun* ■ **el sistema**.

**table** ['teɪbl] *noun* ■ **la mesa**: the guests are sitting at the table los invitados están sentados a la mesa
➤ to set the table poner la mesa: should I set the table? ¿pongo la mesa?
➤ table tennis ping-pong: they're playing table tennis están jugando ping-pong.

**tablecloth** ['teɪblklɒθ] *noun* ■ **el mantel**.

**tablespoon** ['teɪblspuːn] *noun* ■ **la cuchara de servir**
➤ a tablespoon of sugar una cucharada de azúcar.

**tablet** ['tæblɪt] *noun* ■ **la pastilla**: take one tablet every four hours tome una pastilla cada cuatro horas.

**tackle** ['tækl] *verb*
1. *In rugby and American football* **taclear**
2. *In soccer* **hacerle una entrada a**
➤ to tackle a problem enfrentar un problema.

**tadpole** ['tædpəʊl] *noun* ■ **el renacuajo**.

**tag** [tæg] *noun* ■ **la etiqueta**: what's the price on the tag? ¿cuál es el precio en la etiqueta?

**tail** [teɪl] *noun* ■ **la cola**: the dog's wagging its tail el perro está moviendo la cola
➤ heads or tails? ¿cara o cruz?, ¿águila o sol? *Mexico*.

**take** [teɪk] *(past tense* **took**, *past participle* **taken**) *verb*
1. **tomar**: let's take the bus tomemos el autobús; I haven't taken my medicine no he tomado mi medicina
2. **llevarse**: he took my bike while I wasn't watching se llevó mi bici cuando yo no estaba mirando
3. **sacar**: take the book off the shelf saca el libro del estante; I took a lot of photos saqué muchas fotos
4. **llevar**: take the chairs into the garden lleva las sillas al jardín; they took her some flowers le llevaron flores; he took me to the movies me llevó al cine
5. **hacer, dar** *Southern Cone*: to take an exam hacer un examen
6. **aceptar**: they don't take credit cards no aceptan tarjetas de crédito
7. **soportar**: he can't take criticism no soporta la crítica
8. *When "take" means "require"* it takes patience hace falta paciencia; it takes two hours to get there lleva dos horas llegar allí; how long will it take? ¿cuánto tiempo va a tardar?; it took us two days to finish nos llevó dos días terminar
➤ what size do you take? ¿qué talla usas?
➤ what shoe size do you take? ¿qué número de zapatos calzas?

**take after** *phrasal verb* ■ **parecerse a**: she takes after her grandmother se parece a su abuela.

**take apart** *phrasal verb* ■ **desarmar**: Jack took the car apart Jack desarmó el coche.

**take away** *phrasal verb*
1. **llevarse**: she took the plates away se llevó los platos

**2. quitar:** he was afraid they would take his car away from him tenía miedo que le quitaran el coche.

**take back** *phrasal verb* ■ **devolver, regresar** *Latin America except Southern Cone*: I took the jeans back to the shop devolví los jeans en la tienda.

**take down** *phrasal verb*

1. **desarmar:** they took the tent down desarmaron la carpa
2. **quitar:** she took the poster down quitó el póster
3. **anotar:** he took down her name and address anotó su nombre y dirección.

**take off** *phrasal verb*

1. **despegar:** the plane takes off at 5 a.m. el avión despega a las 5 de la mañana
2. **quitarse:** she took her shoes off se quitó los zapatos
➤ to take one's clothes off quitarse la ropa: he took his clothes off se quitó la ropa.

**take out** *phrasal verb* ■ **sacar:** I'm going to take some money out of the bank voy a sacar dinero del banco
➤ to take somebody out to dinner invitar a alguien a cenar afuera.

**take up** *phrasal verb* ■ **ocupar:** that box takes up too much room esa caja ocupa demasiado espacio
➤ he's taken up golf ha empezado a jugar golf.

**take-off** ['teɪkɒf] *noun* ■ **el despegue:** passengers must wear their seatbelts during take-off los pasajeros deben usar los cinturones de seguridad durante el despegue.

**tale** [teɪl] *noun* ■ **el cuento:** she likes fairy tales le gustan los cuentos de hadas.

**talent** ['tælənt] *noun* ■ **el talento**.

**talk** [tɔːk] *(noun & verb)*

■ *noun*

1. la **conversación** *(plural* las **conversaciones)**, la **plática** *Central America, Mexico*: I had a talk with my dad tuve una conversación con mi papá

2. la **charla,** la **plática** *Central America, Mexico*: he gave a talk on the environment dio una charla sobre el medio ambiente
■ *verb*

**hablar, platicar** *Central America, Mexico*: he's talking to his girlfriend está hablando con su novia; we talked about the future hablamos sobre el futuro.

**tall** [tɔːl] *adjective* ■ **alto:** Thomas is very tall Thomas es muy alto; the building is tall el edificio es alto
➤ how tall are you? ¿cuánto mides?

**tambourine** [tæmbə'riːn] *noun* ■ la **pandereta:** she plays the tambourine toca la pandereta.

**tame** [teɪm] *adjective* ■ **domesticado**.

**tan** [tæn] *noun* ■ el **bronceado:** what a great tan! ¡qué bronceado tan sensacional!
➤ to have a tan estar bronceado.

**tangerine** [ˌtændʒə'riːn] *noun* ■ la **tangerina**.

**tank** [tæŋk] *noun* ■ el **tanque:** the fuel tank is empty el tanque de combustible está vacío; there are a lot of tanks on the border hay muchos tanques en la frontera
➤ a fish tank una pecera.

**tanned** [tænd] *adjective* ■ **bronceado:** you're very tanned estás muy bronceado.

**tap** [tæp] *(noun & verb)*

■ *noun*

1. la **llave,** la **paja** *Central America,* la **pluma** *Colombia, Venezuela,* el **caño** *Peru,* la **canilla** *River Plate*: turn the tap on abre la llave; turn the tap off cierra la llave

2. el **golpecito:** I felt a tap on my arm sentí un golpecito en el brazo
■ *verb*

*(past tense & past participle* **tapped)** **darle un golpecito a:** someone tapped me on the shoulder alguien me dio un golpecito en el hombro
➤ he was tapping his fingers on the table tamborileaba con los dedos en la mesa

 Tap es un falso amigo, no significa "tapa".

**tape** [teɪp] *(noun & verb)*
- *noun*
1. **la cinta**: do you have a blank tape to record this film? ¿tienes una cinta virgen para grabar esta película?; **we listened to a Beatles tape** escuchamos una cinta de los Beatles
2. **la cinta adhesiva**: stick this down with tape pega esto con una cinta adhesiva
➤ **on tape** grabado: **I've got some good music on tape** tengo grabada buena música; **I've got "Star Wars" on tape** tengo grabada "La guerra de las galaxias"
- *verb*
**grabar**: **I taped the film** grabé la película.

**tape measure** [teɪp'meʒəʳ] *noun* ▧ **la cinta métrica**.

**target** ['tɑːgɪt] *noun* ▧ **el blanco**.

**task** [tɑːsk] *noun* ▧ **la tarea**: **it's a difficult task** es una tarea difícil.

**taste** [teɪst] *(noun & verb)*
- *noun*
**el sabor**: **this fish has a funny taste** el pescado tiene un sabor raro
➤ **have a taste!** ¡pruébalo!
➤ **to have good taste** tener buen gusto
- *verb*
1. **probar**: **taste this delicious soup** prueba esta sopa deliciosa
2. **saber**: **it tastes delicious** sabe delicioso
➤ **to taste like something or to taste of something** saber a algo: **it tastes like honey** sabe a miel.

**tasteless** ['teɪstlɪs] *adjective*
1. **desabrido**: **this soup is tasteless** esta sopa está desabrida
2. **de mal gusto**: **a tasteless joke** un chiste de mal gusto.

**tasty** ['teɪstɪ] *adjective* ▧ **sabroso**.

**tattoo** [tə'tuː] *noun* ▧ **el tatuaje**.

**taught** [tɔːt] *past tense & past participle*
➤ **teach**.

**tax** [tæks] *noun* ▧ **el impuesto**: **we all have to pay tax** todos tenemos que pagar impuestos.

**taxi** ['tæksɪ] *noun* ▧ **el taxi**: **let's take a taxi** tomemos un taxi
➤ **a taxi driver** un taxista
➤ **a taxi stand** una parada de taxis, un sitio de taxis *Mexico*.

**tea** [tiː] *uncountable noun* ▧ **el té**: **I'd like a cup of tea** me gustaría una taza de té.

**teach** [tiːtʃ] *(past tense & past participle* **taught**) *verb* ▧ **enseñar**: **my brother is teaching me Spanish** mi hermano me está enseñando castellano
➤ **to teach somebody to do something** enseñar a alguien a hacer algo: **she taught me to ski** me enseñó a esquiar.

**teacher** ['tiːtʃəʳ] *noun*
1. **el profesor, la profesora**: **he's a teacher** es profesor
2. **el maestro, la maestra**: **she's a teacher in a primary school** es maestra de una escuela primaria.

**team** [tiːm] *noun* ▧ **el equipo**.

**tear**¹ [tɪəʳ] *noun* ▧ **la lágrima**
➤ **he was in tears** estaba llorando.

**tear**² *(noun & verb)*
- *noun*
[teəʳ] **la rotura**: **can you mend this tear?** ¿puedes arreglar esta rotura?
- *verb*
*(past tense & past participle* **torn**)
1. **romper**: **I tore the page** rompí la página
2. **rasgarse**: **this cloth tears very easily** esta tela se rasga muy fácilmente

**tear down** *phrasal verb* ▧ **derribar**: they're going to tear the old factory down van a derribar la vieja fábrica.

**tear out** *phrasal verb* ▧ **arrancar**: **I tore the page out** arranqué la página.

**tear up** *phrasal verb* ▧ **hacer pedazos**: **he tore up the letter** hizo pedazos la carta.

**tease** [tiːz] *verb* ▧ **tomarle el pelo a**: **he's always teasing his little brother** siempre le está tomando el pelo a su hermano menor.

**teaspoon** ['tiːspuːn] *noun* ■ la **cucharita:** I need a teaspoon for my coffee necesito una cucharita para mi café
➤ add one teaspoon of sugar agregue una cucharadita de azúcar.

**technical** ['teknɪkl] *adjective* ■ **técnico.**

**technique** [tek'niːk] *noun* ■ la **técnica.**

**technological** [ˌteknə'lɒdʒɪkl] *adjective* ■ **tecnológico.**

**technology** [tek'nɒlədʒɪ] *noun* ■ la **tecnología.**

**teddy bear** ['tedɪbeəʳ] *noun* ■ el **oso de peluche.**

**teen** [tiːn] *noun* ■ el/la **adolescente**
➤ a teen magazine una revista para adolescentes.

**teenage** ['tiːneɪdʒ] *adjective* ■ **adolescente:** he has a teenage son tiene un hijo adolescente.

**teenager** ['tiːnˌeɪdʒəʳ] *noun* ■ el/la **adolescente.**

**teens** [tiːnz] *plural noun*
➤ to be in one's teens ser adolescente: he's in his teens es adolescente.

**teeth** *plural* ➤ tooth.

**telephone** ['telɪfəʊn] *noun* ■ el **teléfono:** the telephone's ringing está sonando el teléfono; he answered the telephone contestó el teléfono
➤ to be on the telephone estar hablando por teléfono: she's on the telephone at the moment está hablando por teléfono en este momento
➤ the telephone book or the telephone directory la guía telefónica, el directorio telefónico *Latin America except Southern Cone*
➤ a telephone booth una cabina telefónica, una caseta telefónica *Mexico*
➤ a telephone call una llamada telefónica
➤ a telephone number un número de teléfono: what's your telephone number? ¿cuál es tu número de teléfono?

**telescope** ['telɪskəʊp] *noun* ■ el **telescopio.**

**television** ['telɪˌvɪʒn] *noun* ■ la **televisión:** I watched it on television lo ví en la televisión.

**tell** [tel] *(past tense & past participle* told*)* *verb* ■ **decir:** I told him I would be late le dije que llegaría tarde
➤ I can tell he's really angry me doy cuenta de que está realmente enojado
➤ to tell lies decir mentiras: he often tells lies a menudo dice mentiras
➤ to tell a story contar una historia: I'm going to tell you a story te voy a contar una historia
➤ to tell the difference between distinguir entre: she can't tell the difference between me and my brother no distingue entre mi hermano y yo
➤ to tell somebody about something contarle a alguien de algo: I told her about my trip le conté de mi viaje
➤ to tell somebody to do something decirle a alguien que haga algo: he told me to wait for him here me dijo que lo esperara aquí.

**temper** ['tempəʳ] *noun* ■ el **genio:** she has an awful temper tiene muy mal genio
➤ to lose one's temper perder los estribos: I lost my temper perdí los estribos.

**temperature** ['temprətʃəʳ] *noun*
1. la **temperatura:** what is the temperature outside? ¿qué temperatura hay afuera?; I took her temperature le tomé la temperatura
2. la **fiebre:** he has a temperature tiene fiebre.

**temple** ['templ] *noun* ■ el **templo.**

**temporary** ['tempərərɪ] *adjective* ■ **temporal.**

**tempt** [tempt] *verb* ■ **tentar**
➤ I'm tempted to say no estoy tentado a decir que no.

**tempting** ['temptɪŋ] *adjective* ■ **tentador** (*feminine* **tentadora**): it's very tempting es muy tentador.

**ten** [ten] *number* ■ **diez:** the Ten Commandments los Diez Mandamientos; she's ten tiene diez años; he went out at ten salió a las diez.

**tenant** [ˈtenənt] *noun* ■ **el inquilino,** la inquilina.

**tend** [tend] *verb*
➤ to tend to do something tener tendencia a hacer algo: she tends to exaggerate tiene tendencia a exagerar.

**tender** [ˈtendər] *adjective* ■ **tierno:** the meat is nice and tender la carne está buena y tierna.

**tennis** [ˈtenɪs] *noun* ■ **el tenis:** she's playing tennis está jugando tenis; a game of tennis un juego de tenis
➤ a tennis ball una pelota de tenis
➤ a tennis court una cancha de tenis
➤ a tennis player un tenista
➤ a tennis racket una raqueta de tenis
➤ tennis shoes zapatillas de tenis.

**tension** [ˈtenʃn] *noun* ■ **la tensión** (*plural* **las tensiones**): there's a lot of tension between them hay mucha tensión entre ellos.

**tent** [tent] *noun* ■ **la tienda de campaña.**

**tenth** [tenθ] *number* ■ **décimo:** on the tenth floor en el décimo piso
➤ it's November tenth today hoy es el 10 de noviembre.

**term** [tɜːm] *noun* ■ **el término:** it's a technical term es un término técnico
➤ to be on good terms with somebody tener buenas relaciones con alguien
➤ to come to terms with something aceptar algo.

**terminal** [ˈtɜːmɪnl] *noun* ■ **la terminal:** there are three terminals at the airport hay tres terminales en el aeropuerto
➤ the bus terminal la terminal de autobuses, la terminal de camiones *Mexico*.

**terrace** [ˈterəs] *noun* ■ **la terraza.**

**terrible** [ˈterəbl] *adjective* ■ **terrible.**

**terribly** [ˈterəblɪ] *adverb* ■ **terriblemente:** he's terribly disappointed está terriblemente decepcionado
➤ I'm terribly sorry lo siento muchísimo.

**terrific** [təˈrɪfɪk] *adjective* ■ **estupendo.**

**terrified** [ˈterɪfaɪd] *adjective* ■ **aterrorizado**
➤ to be terrified of tenerle terror a: she's terrified of the dentist le tiene terror al dentista.

**territory** [ˈterətrɪ] (*plural* **territories**) *noun* ■ **el territorio.**

**terrorism** [ˈterərɪzm] *noun* ■ **el terrorismo.**

**terrorist** [ˈterərɪst] *noun* ■ **el/la terrorista:** a terrorist attack un ataque terrorista.

**test** [test] (*noun & verb*)
■ *noun*
la prueba: we had a test this morning tuvimos una prueba esta mañana; they are doing tests on the new drug están haciendo pruebas con la nueva droga
➤ I'm taking my driving test voy a hacer el examen de manejar, voy a hacer el examen de manejo *Mexico*
➤ a blood test un análisis de sangre
➤ nuclear tests pruebas nucleares
➤ a test tube un tubo de ensayo
➤ an eye test un examen de la vista
■ *verb*
1. probar: I'd like to test the computer before I buy it me gustaría probar la computadora antes de comprarla
2. hacerle una prueba a: the teacher tested us on irregular verbs la maestra nos hizo una prueba sobre los verbos irregulares.

**text** [tekst] *noun* ■ **el texto:** a text file un archivo de texto.

**textbook** [ˈtekstbʊk] *noun* ■ **el libro de texto:** a biology textbook un libro de texto de biología.

**than** [ðən, ðæn] *conjunction*

1. **que:** Tina's taller than Ted Tina es más alta que Ted; **I've got less than you** or **I've got less than you have** tengo menos que tú

2. *With quantities* **de:** it costs less than $50 cuesta menos de $50; **he stayed more than three months** se quedó más de tres meses.

**thank** [θæŋk] *verb* ■ **agradecer:** I'd like to thank you for your help quiero agradecerle su ayuda

➤ **thank you!** ¡gracias!: **thank you very much!** ¡muchas gracias!; **thank you for your help!** ¡gracias por tu ayuda!

➤ **thank God!** ¡gracias a Dios!

**thanks** [θæŋks] *exclamation & noun*

➤ **thanks!** ¡gracias!: **thanks a lot!** ¡muchas gracias!

➤ **thanks for everything!** ¡gracias por todo!

➤ **thanks for coming!** ¡gracias por venir!

➤ **thanks to** gracias a: **I succeeded thanks to you** lo logré gracias a ti.

**Thanksgiving** ['θæŋks,gɪvɪŋ] *noun* ■ la **Acción de Gracias**

THANKSGIVING

La fiesta de **Thanksgiving**, el cuarto jueves de noviembre, conmemora el establecimiento de los primeros colonos en lo que hoy son los Estados Unidos. La cena en familia que generalmente se celebra ese día consiste en un pavo con salsa de arándanos, acompañado por camotes (batatas) al horno, y el tradicional pay de calabaza (zapallo) como postre.

**that** [ðæt] (*adjective, pronoun, conjunction & adverb*)

■ *adjective*
(*plural* **those**)

A demonstrative adjective must agree in gender (masculine or feminine) and number (singular or plural) with the noun it precedes:

1. **ese:** give me that book dame ese libro; that soup is cold esa sopa está fría

2. **aquel**

Use **aquel** and **aquella** to express more distance between the speaker and the object:

I don't want that dress on the table, I want that dress over there no quiero ese vestido que está en la mesa, quiero aquel vestido

■ *pronoun*

A demonstrative pronoun must agree in gender (masculine or feminine) and number (singular or plural) with the noun to which it refers. If it does not refer to something that can be assigned gender, the neuter form is used:

1. **ése:** who's that? ¿quién es ése?; is that Janet? ¿es ésa Janet?; what's that? ¿qué es eso?; that's my brother ése es mi hermano; that's not true eso no es cierto; that one's mine ése es mío

2. **aquél**

Use **aquél**, **aquélla** or **aquello** to express more distance between the speaker and the object:

I don't want this, I want that over there no quiero éste, quiero aquél; this hat won't do, we must have that one over in the window este sombrero no es adecuado, debemos llevar aquél que está en la vidriera

➤ **is that you?** ¿eres tú?

■ *pronoun*

1. *Subject or object of the verb* **que:** where's the path that leads to the wood? ¿dónde está el camino que conduce al bosque?; the man that he saw el hombre que vió

2. *After a preposition* **el que**

The relative pronoun becomes **el que**, **la que**, **los que** or **las que** after a preposition, according to the gender (masculine or feminine) and number (singular or plural) of the noun to which it refers:

the chair that he was sitting on collapsed la silla en la que estaba sentado se vino abajo; the boys that he's talking to are his cousins los muchachos con los que está hablando son sus primos

■ *conjunction*

**que:** she said that she was coming dijo que venía

■ *adverb*

**tan:** it's not that bad no es tan malo.

**that's** [ðæts]

1. ➤ that is; that has.

**the** [ðə, ði:] *definite article* ■ **el**

> The definite article must agree in gender (masculine or feminine - **el, la**) and number (singular or plural - **los, las**) with the noun it precedes:

**give me the book** dame el libro; **look at the flower** mira la flor; **the man left** el hombre se fue; **where are the children?** ¿dónde están los niños?; **put the flowers in a vase** pon las flores en un florero

> When you say "of the" or "to the" in Spanish, the prepositions **de** and **a** combine with **el** to make one word: **de + el = del,** and **a + el = al:**

**I can't remember the name of the village** no puedo recordar el nombre del pueblo; **she gave the ball to the dog** le dió la pelota al perro.

**theater** ['θɪətər] *noun* ■ **el teatro.**

**theft** [θeft] *noun* ■ **el robo.**

**their** [ðeər] *possessive adjective* ■

> In Spanish the possessive adjective agrees in number (singular or plural) with the noun that follows:

**su:** their house is in the countryside su casa está en el campo; **their parents are doctors** sus padres son médicos

> Use the definite article (**el, la, los** or **las**), not the possessive adjective, with parts of the body and clothing when it's clear who the possessor is:

**they're brushing their teeth** se están lavando los dientes; **she put on her coat** se puso el abrigo.

**theirs** [ðeəz] *possessive pronoun*

> In Spanish the possessive pronoun agrees in gender (masculine or feminine) and number (singular or plural) with the noun it replaces:

1. **el suyo** (*feminine* **la suya**): our dog is big, theirs is small nuestro perro es grande, el suyo es pequeño; **your books are here, theirs are on the table** tus libros están aquí, los suyos están en la mesa
2. **suyo** (*feminine* **suya**): those books aren't theirs esos libros no son suyos; **she's a friend of theirs** es amiga suya.

**them** [ðəm, ðem] *pronoun*

1. *Direct object* **los** (*feminine* **las**): I can't see them no los puedo ver; **find them!** ¡encuéntralos!; **I saw them** los vi
2. *Indirect object* **les**: she gave them a kiss les dió un beso; **tell them to come** diles que vengan

> Instead of "les", use **se** as an indirect object when there is also a direct object pronoun:

**I gave it to them** se lo di a ellos

3. *After a preposition* **ellos** (*feminine* **ellas**): I'm going with them voy con ellos.

**themselves** [ðem'selvz] *pronoun*

1. **se:** the boys are washing themselves los muchachos se están lavando; **they're enjoying themselves** se están divirtiendo
2. **ellos mismos:** they made it themselves lo hicieron ellos mismos
3. **sí mismos:** they often talk about themselves a menudo hablan de sí mismos
➤ **by themselves** solos: they did it by themselves lo hicieron solos.

**then** [ðen] *adverb*

1. **entonces:** we lived in Boston then entonces vivíamos en Boston; **it's too sweet — don't drink it then** es muy dulce — entonces no lo tomes
2. **luego:** I had dinner then I went to bed cené y luego me fui a acostar.

**there** [ðeər] (*pronoun & adverb*)

■ *pronoun*
➤ **there is** or **there are** hay
➤ **there's a message for you** hay un mensaje para ti; **there are a lot of people here** hay mucha gente aquí; **there isn't any bread**

no hay pan; **there was a storm** hubo una tormenta
- *adverb*
1. **ahí: put it there** ponlo ahí
2. **allá: I'm going there next week** voy para allá la próxima semana; **there goes my teacher** allá va mi profesora
➤ **there he is!** ¡ahí está!
➤ **is Lance there?** ¿está Lance?

**therefore** ['ðeəfɔːʳ] *adverb* ■ **por lo tanto: he's only 15 and therefore can't drive** tiene sólo 15 años, por lo tanto no puede manejar.

**there's** [ðeəz]
1. ➤ there is; there has.

**thermometer** [θə'mɒmɪtəʳ] *noun* ■ el termómetro.

**these** [ðiːz] *(plural of this) (adjective & pronoun)*
- *adjective*

A demonstrative adjective must agree in gender (masculine or feminine) and number (singular or plural) with the noun it precedes:

**este** *(plural* **estos***)*: **these shoes are mine** estos zapatos son míos; **I prefer these flowers** prefiero estas flores
- *pronoun*

A demonstrative pronoun must agree in gender (masculine or feminine) and number (singular or plural) with the noun to which it refers:

**éstos** *(feminine* **éstas***)*: **these are my keys** éstas son mis llaves; **what are these?** ¿qué son éstos?; **which books do you want, these or those?** ¿qué libros quieres, éstos o aquéllos?

**they** [ðeɪ] *pronoun* ■ **ellos** *(feminine* **ellas***)*

"They" is not usually translated unless necessary for emphasis or clarification. Spanish nouns are either masculine or feminine. Remember to use **ellos** for masculine subjects and **ellas** for feminine subjects. When "they" includes male and female, use **ellos**:

**they're American** son norteamericanos; **where are my glasses? — they're on the table** ¿dónde están mis lentes? — están en la mesa; **they did it** ellos lo hicieron; **they don't know it but I do** ellos no lo saben pero yo sí
➤ **here they are!** ¡aquí están!

**they'd** [ðeɪd]
1. ➤ they had; they would.

**they'll** [ðeɪl] ➤ they shall; they will.

**they're** [ðeəʳ] ➤ they are.

**they've** [ðeɪv] ➤ they have.

**thick** [θɪk] *adjective* ■ **grueso: it's a thick book** es un libro grueso
➤ **the walls are ten inches thick** las paredes tienen diez pulgadas de espesor.

**thief** [θiːf] *(plural* thieves [θiːvz]) *noun* ■ el **ladrón** *(plural* los **ladrones***)*.

**thigh** [θaɪ] *noun* ■ el **muslo: skaters have muscular thighs** los patinadores tienen muslos musculosos.

**thin** [θɪn] *adjective*
1. **delgado: he's too thin** es muy delgado
2. **fino: a thin slice of lemon** una rodaja fina de limón.

**thing** [θɪŋ] *noun* ■ la **cosa: he has a lot of things to do** tiene muchas cosas que hacer; **what's this thing?** ¿qué es esta cosa?
➤ **my things** mis cosas
➤ **I can't see a thing** no veo nada
➤ **the poor thing!** ¡pobrecito!

**think** [θɪŋk] *(past tense & past participle* thought) *verb*
1. **pensar: what do you think?** ¿qué piensas?; **think carefully before you make a decision** piensa con cuidado antes de tomar una decisión; **I think you're mad** pienso que estás loco
2. **imaginar: think how life will be in ten years** imagina cómo será la vida dentro de diez años
➤ **I think so** eso creo
➤ **I don't think so** no creo

# third

**think about** *phrasal verb*

1. **pensar en:** what are you thinking about? ¿en qué estás pensando?; I'm thinking about the party estoy pensando en la fiesta; I'll think about what you said pensaré en lo que dijiste
2. **parecer:** what did you think about the movie? ¿qué te pareció la película?
➤ I'll think about it lo pensaré.

**think of** *phrasal verb* ■ **pensar de:** what do you think of her? ¿qué piensas de ella?

**third** [θɜːd] *(adjective & noun)*
■ *adjective*
**tercero**

> Tercero becomes "tercer" before masculine singular nouns:

the third Tuesday of each month el tercer martes de cada mes
➤ third time lucky la tercera es la vencida
➤ the Third World el Tercer Mundo
■ *noun*
el **tercio:** he ate a third of the cake se comió un tercio del pastel
➤ it's November third today hoy es el tres de noviembre.

**thirst** [θɜːst] *noun* ■ la **sed:** I'm dying of thirst estoy muerto de sed.

**thirsty** ['θɜːstɪ] *adjective*
➤ to be thirsty tener sed: I'm thirsty tengo sed.

**thirteen** [ˌθɜːˈtiːn] *number* ■ **trece:** thirteen is my lucky number el trece es mi número de la suerte; she's thirteen tiene trece años.

**thirteenth** [ˌθɜːˈtiːnθ] *number* ■ **décimo tercero**
➤ it's April thirteenth hoy es el trece de abril.

**thirtieth** ['θɜːtɪəθ] *number* ■ **trigésimo**
➤ it's December thirtieth hoy es treinta de diciembre.

**thirty** ['θɜːtɪ] *numeral* ■ **treinta:** she's thirty tiene treinta años
➤ thirty-one treinta y uno

➤ thirty-two treinta y dos.

**this** [ðɪs] *(plural* these*) (adjective, pronoun & adverb)*
■ *adjective*

> A demonstrative adjective must agree in gender (masculine or feminine) and number (singular or plural) with the noun it precedes:

**este** *(plural* estos*):* he left this morning se fue esta mañana; I prefer this CD prefiero este CD
■ *pronoun*

> A demonstrative pronoun must agree in gender (masculine or feminine) and number (singular or plural) with the noun to which it refers. If it does not refer to something that can be assigned gender, the neuter form is used:

**éste, esto:** this is for you esto es para ti; what's this? ¿qué es esto?; I don't want that dress, I want this one no quiero ese vestido, quiero éste
➤ who's this? ¿quién es?
➤ this is Jackie Brown
1. *Introducing somebody* **le presento a Jackie Brown**
2. *On the phone* **habla Jackie Brown**
■ *adverb*
➤ it was this big era así de grande
➤ I didn't know it was this far no sabía que era tan lejos.

**thorn** [θɔːn] *noun* ■ la **espina**.

**thorough** ['θʌrə] *adjective*
1. **riguroso:** they did a thorough test on the airplane hicieron una prueba rigurosa del avión
2. **meticuloso:** he's thorough in his work es meticuloso en su trabajo.

**thoroughly** ['θʌrəlɪ] *adverb*
1. **totalmente:** I thoroughly agree estoy totalmente de acuerdo
2. **minuciosamente:** he studied his case thoroughly estudió su caso minuciosamente.

**those** [ðəʊz] *(plural of* that*) (adjective & pronoun)*

■ *adjective*

> A demonstrative adjective must agree in gender (masculine or feminine) and number (singular or plural) with the noun it precedes:

ı. **esos**: those books are mine esos libros son míos; **I prefer those flowers** prefiero esas flores
2. **aquellos**

> Use **aquellos** and **aquellas** to express more distance between the speaker and the object:

she'd like those shoes over there a ella le gustarían aquellos zapatos de allá

■ *pronoun*

> A demonstrative pronoun must agree in gender (masculine or feminine) and number (singular or plural) with the noun to which it refers. If it does not refer to something that can be assigned gender, the neuter form is used:

ı. **ésos** (*feminine* **ésas**): those are my books ésos son mis libros; **what are those?** ¿qué son ésos?; **I don't want these books, I want those** no quiero estos libros, quiero ésos
2. **aquéllos** (*feminine* **aquéllas**)

> Use **aquéllos** and **aquéllas** to express more distance between the speaker and the object:

those flowers are nice, but those over there are nicer esas flores son lindas, pero aquéllas de allá son más lindas
➤ those who want to come should put their hand up los que quieran venir que levanten la mano.

**though** [ðəʊ] (*conjunction & adverb*)

■ *conjunction*
**aunque**: though the car's old, it's still in good condition aunque el auto es viejo, todavía está en buenas condiciones
■ *adverb*
**pero**: we lost! — it was a good game though ¡perdimos! — pero fue un buen juego.

**thought** [θɔːt] (*noun & verb form*)

■ *noun*
la **idea**: he had an interesting thought tuvo una idea interesante
➤ she was lost in her thoughts estaba abstraída en sus pensamientos
■ *past tense & past participle*
➤ think.

**thousand** ['θaʊznd] *number* ■ **mil**: it costs a thousand dollars cuesta mil dólares
➤ a thousand and one mil uno
➤ thousands of miles de: there were thousands of people había miles de personas.

**thread** [θred] *noun* ■ el **hilo**.

**threat** [θret] *noun* ■ la **amenaza**.

**threaten** ['θretn] *verb* ■ **amenazar**: she threatened to leave the team amenazó con retirarse del equipo.

**three** [θriː] *numeral* ■ **tres**: you get three chances tienes tres oportunidades; she's three tiene tres años; he went out at three salió a las tres.

**three-D,     three-dimensional**
[,θriː'diː, ,θriːdɪ'menʃənl] *adjective* ■ **tridimensional**: a three-dimensional object un objeto tridimensional
➤ a film in three-D una película en tres dimensiones.

**threw** [θruː] *past tense* ➤ throw.

**thrill** [θrɪl] (*noun & verb*)

■ *noun*
la **emoción** (*plural* las **emociones**): what a thrill! ¡qué emoción!
➤ seeing Everest was a real thrill ver el Everest fue verdaderamente emocionante
■ *verb*
**emocionar**: I was thrilled to see her again estaba emocionado de verla otra vez.

**throat** [θrəʊt] *noun* ■ la **garganta**: I have a sore throat me duele la garganta .

**throne** [θrəʊn] *noun* ■ el **trono**.

**through** [θruː] (*preposition & adverb*)

■ *preposition*
ı. **atravesar**: the bullet went through the wall la bala atravesó la pared; we went through the park atravesamos el parque

**2. por:** she was looking through the window estaba mirando por la ventana

**3. durante:** she talked all through the film habló durante toda la película

➤ I got the job through a friend conseguí el empleo gracias a un amigo

➤ to go through a red light pasar con la luz roja, saltarse un alto *Mexico*

➤ Monday through Friday de lunes a viernes

■ *adverb*

➤ the arrow went right through la flecha lo atravesó completamente

➤ to get through pasar: you'll have to move, I can't get through vas a tener que correrte, no puedo pasar

➤ to get through to somebody comunicarse con alguien: I can't get through to him on the phone no puedo comunicarme con él por teléfono

➤ to let somebody through dejar pasar a alguien.

**throughout** [θru:'aʊt] *preposition*

**1. durante:** he slept throughout the meeting durmió durante toda la reunión

**2. por todo:** throughout the house por toda la casa.

**throw** [θrəʊ] *(past tense* threw, *past participle* thrown) *verb* ■ **tirar, aventar** *Colombia, Mexico, Peru*: throw me the ball! ¡pásame la pelota!; they were throwing stones at the police le estaban tirando piedras a la policía

➤ to throw a party dar una fiesta

**throw away** *phrasal verb* ■ **tirar a la basura:** I threw my ticket away tiré mi boleto a la basura.

**throw out** *phrasal verb*

**1. tirar a la basura:** I'm going to throw this stale bread out voy a tirar este pan duro a la basura

**2. expulsar:** they threw him out lo expulsaron.

**throw up** *phrasal verb* ■ **vomitar:** he threw up vomitó.

**thrown** [θrəʊn] *past participle*
➤ throw.

**thumb** [θʌm] *noun* ■ **el pulgar**.

**thunder** ['θʌndər] *uncountable noun* ■ **el trueno**.

**thunderstorm** ['θʌndəstɔ:m] *noun* ■ **la tormenta eléctrica**.

**Thursday** ['θɜ:zdɪ] *noun* ■

In Spanish the days of the week do not start with a capital letter:

**el jueves:** it's Thursday today hoy es jueves; next Thursday el jueves próximo; last Thursday el jueves pasado

➤ on Thursday el jueves: I'll see you on Thursday te veré el jueves

➤ on Thursdays los jueves: he comes to see me on Thursdays viene a verme los jueves.

**ticket** ['tɪkɪt] *noun*

**1. el pasaje:** a plane ticket un pasaje de avión

**2. el boleto:** a train ticket un boleto de tren; I bought two tickets for the concert compré dos boletos para el concierto

➤ a parking ticket una multa de estacionamiento

➤ the ticket office la taquilla, la boletería.

**tickle** ['tɪkl] *verb* ■ **hacer cosquillas:** that tickles! ¡eso hace cosquillas!

**tide** [taɪd] *noun* ■ **la marea:** it's high tide or the tide is in la marea está alta; it's low tide or the tide is out la marea está baja.

**tie** [taɪ] *(noun & verb)*

■ *noun*

**1. la corbata:** he's wearing a tie tiene puesta una corbata

**2. el empate:** who won the game? — it was a tie ¿quién ganó el partido? — fue un empate

■ *verb*
*(present participle* tying)

**1. amarrar:** they tied his hands to the chair le amarraron las manos a la silla; tie the rope around the tree amarra la cuerda alrededor del árbol

**2. amarrarse:** tie your shoe laces amárrate los cordones de los zapatos

➤ he tied his scarf round his neck se envolvió el cuello con la bufanda

➤ **to tie a knot** hacer un nudo: **she tied a knot in her handkerchief** le hizo un nudo al pañuelo

**tie up** *phrasal verb* ■ **amarrar: she tied the package up with ribbon** amarró el paquete con una cinta; **they tied up the prisoner** amarraron al prisionero.

**tiger** ['taɪgəʳ] *noun* ■ **el tigre**.

**tight** [taɪt] *adjective*

1. **ajustado: this dress is too tight** este vestido es muy ajustado; **she was wearing tight jeans** tenía puestos unos jeans muy ajustados

2. **apretado: this knot is too tight** este nudo está muy apretado.

**tighten** ['taɪtn] *verb* ■ **apretar: he tightened the screw** apretó el tornillo.

**tightly** ['taɪtlɪ] *adverb* **she was holding my hand tightly** le tenía agarrada la mano con fuerza.

**tile** [taɪl] *noun*

1. **la teja: a tile fell off the roof** cayó una teja del techo

2. **el azulejo,** el **mosaico** *Mexico, River Plate*: **the floor and the walls in the bathroom are covered in blue tiles** el piso y las paredes del baño están revestidos de azulejos azules.

**till** [tɪl] *(noun, preposition & conjunction)*
■ *noun*
la **caja: pay at the till** pague en la caja
■ *preposition*
**hasta: we'll play till six** vamos a jugar hasta las seis
■ *conjunction*
**hasta que**

> The conjunction **hasta que** is followed by a verb in the subjunctive when referring to an event that has not yet happened:

**I'll stay here till he comes** me quedaré aquí hasta que llegue
➤ **till now** hasta ahora.

**time** [taɪm] *noun*

1. el **tiempo: I don't have time** no tengo tiempo; **take your time** tómate tu tiempo; **you're just in time for lunch** llegas justo a

tiempo para almorzar; **all the time** todo el tiempo; **most of the time** la mayor parte del tiempo

2. la **hora: what time is it?** ¿qué hora es?; **the train's on time** el tren viene a la hora

3. la **época: in Roman times** en la época romana

4. la **vez: how many times have you seen the film?** ¿cuántas veces has visto la película?; **the first time I saw you** la primera vez que te vi; **four times a year** cuatro veces al año

➤ **four at a time** de cuatro en cuatro
➤ **6 times 7 is 42** 6 por 7 es 42
➤ **from time to time** de vez en cuando
➤ **for the time being** por el momento
➤ **a long time** mucho tiempo: **we waited for a long time** esperamos mucho tiempo: **I've been here for a long time** he estado aquí mucho tiempo
➤ **it's time for bed** es hora de acostarse
➤ **it's time to go** es hora de irse
➤ **it's about time he left** ya es hora que se vaya
➤ **to have a good time** pasarlo bien: **I had a really good time at the party** lo pasé muy bien en la fiesta
➤ **in a week's time** dentro de una semana.

**timetable** ['taɪm,teɪbl] *noun* ■ el **horario: check the timetable to see when the next train is** revisa el horario para ver cuándo pasa el próximo tren.

**tin** [tɪn] *noun* ■ la **lata: it's made of tin** es de lata
➤ **a tin can** una lata.

**tinfoil** ['tɪnfɔɪl] *uncountable noun* ■ el **papel de aluminio**.

**tinsel** ['tɪnsl] *uncountable noun* ■ la **guirnalda navideña**.

**tiny** ['taɪnɪ] *adjective* ■ **diminuto**.

**tip** [tɪp] *(noun & verb)*
■ *noun*

1. la **punta: the tips of your fingers** la punta de tus dedos

2. la **propina: I gave the waiter a tip** le di propina al mozo

3. el **consejo: safety tips** consejos de seguridad

■ *verb*
(*past tense & past participle* **tipped**) **dar propina**: she tipped the waiter le dió propina
al mozo

**tip over** | *phrasal verb*
1. **volcar**: she tipped the bottle over volcó la
botella
2. **volcarse**: the glass tipped over se volcó el
vaso.

**tiptoe** ['tɪptəʊ] *noun*
➤ **on tiptoe** de puntillas, en puntas de pie
*Southern Cone*: he was walking on tiptoe
caminaba de puntillas.

**tire** ['taɪəʳ] *noun* ■ **el neumático**.

**tired** ['taɪəd] *adjective* ■ **cansado**: he's
very tired está muy cansado
➤ **to be tired of something** estar cansado de
algo: I'm tired of all these arguments
estoy cansado de todas estas discusiones
he's tired of waiting está cansado de esperar.

**tiring** ['taɪərɪŋ] *adjective* ■ **cansado**:
this work is tiring este trabajo es cansado.

**tissue** ['tɪʃuː] *noun* ■ **el kleenex**® (*plural* los **kleenex**®): can you give me a tissue? ¿me puedes dar un kleenex®?

**title** ['taɪtl] *noun* ■ **el título**: what's the
title of the film? ¿cuál es el título de la película?

**to** [tə] *preposition*
1. **a**: do you want to go to the beach? ¿quieres ir a la playa?; let's go to Seattle vamos a
Seattle; she wrote to her brother le escribió
a su hermano; from 9 to 5 de 9 a 5

When **a** combines with **el** it becomes **al**:

give these bones to the dog dale estos
huesos al perro
2. **hasta**: count to 10 cuenta hasta 10
3. *Telling the time* **para, menos** *River Plate*:
it's quarter to four es un cuarto para las
cuatro; it's ten to seven son diez para las
siete

4. *With infinitives*

When "to" is used as part of an infinitive
after certain verbs (begin to do, try to do),
it is usually translated by **a** or **de** depending on the verb used in Spanish:

she began to sing comenzó a cantar; he
tried to help me trató de ayudarme

When "to" is used after an adjective (easy
to do, hard to do), it is usually translated
by **de** when the infinitive has no object:

it's easy to understand es fácil de entender; it's hard to believe es difícil de creer

When the infinitive has an object, "to" is
not translated:

it's hard to understand him es difícil
entenderlo; it's not easy to talk to him no
es fácil hablar con él

When "to" means "in order to", it is
translated by **para**:

he worked hard to pass his exam trabajó
mucho para aprobar su examen; she went to
town to buy a coat fue al centro para comprar un abrigo.

**toad** [təʊd] *noun* ■ **el sapo**.

**toadstool** ['təʊdstuːl] *noun* ■ **el hongo**.

**toast** [təʊst] *noun* ■ **las tostadas, el
pan tostado** *Mexico*: I have toast for
breakfast comí tostadas en el desayuno
➤ **a piece of toast** una tostada, un pan tostado *Mexico*
➤ **to drink a toast to somebody** brindar por
alguien: let's drink a toast to Gary brinde-
mos por Gary.

**toaster** ['təʊstəʳ] *noun* ■ **la tostadora**.

**tobacco** [tə'bækəʊ] *noun* ■ **el tabaco**.

**today** [tə'deɪ] *adverb* ■ **hoy**: what did
you do today? ¿qué hiciste hoy?; what day
is it today? ¿qué día es hoy?

**toe** [təʊ] *noun* ■ **el dedo del pie**: I hurt
my toe me lastimé el dedo del pie.

**together** [tə'geðəʳ] *adverb* ■ **juntos:** they arrived together llegaron juntos
➤ **together with** junto con: **together with the CD, you get a booklet** junto con el CD, viene un folleto.

**toilet** ['tɔɪlɪt] *noun* ■ **el wáter**
➤ toilet paper el papel higiénico.

**toiletries** ['tɔɪlɪtrɪz] *plural noun* ■ los artículos de tocador.

**token** ['təʊkn] *noun* ■ la **muestra:** they gave her a gift as a token of their appreciation le dieron un regalo como muestra de su agradecimiento.

**told** [təʊld] *past tense & past participle* ➤ tell.

**toll** [təʊl] *noun* ■ el **peaje,** la **cuota** *Mexico*: **you have to pay a toll at the bridge** tienes que pagar peaje en el puente.

**toll-free** [təʊl'friː] *adverb*
➤ to call toll-free llamar gratis: **I called toll-free** llamé gratis.

**tomato** [tə'meɪtəʊ] *(plural tomatoes) noun* ■ el **tomate,** el **jitomate** *Mexico*
➤ tomato sauce la salsa de tomate.

**tomb** [tuːm] *noun* ■ la **tumba.**

**tomboy** ['tɒmbɔɪ] *noun* ■ la **niña poco femenina,** la **machetona** *Mexico*: **Claire's a real tomboy** Claire es de verdad poco femenina.

**tomorrow** [tə'mɒrəʊ] *adverb* ■ **mañana: I'll do it tomorrow** lo haré mañana
➤ tomorrow morning mañana en la mañana
➤ tomorrow evening mañana en la tarde
➤ the day after tomorrow pasado mañana: **I'll come over the day after tomorrow** pasaré por aquí pasado mañana.

**ton** [tʌn] *noun* ■ la **tonelada:** it weighs a ton pesa una tonelada
➤ tons of *informal* montones de: **she has tons of friends** tiene montones de amigos.

**tone** [təʊn] *noun* ■ el **tono:** don't speak to me in that tone no me hables en ese tono; the phone isn't working, there's no tone el teléfono no funciona, no tiene tono
➤ speak after the tone hable después del tono.

**tongue** [tʌŋ] *noun* ■ la **lengua:** she stuck her tongue out at me me sacó la lengua.

**tonight** [tə'naɪt] *adverb* ■ **esta noche.**

**tonsillitis** [ˌtɒnsɪ'laɪtɪs] *noun* ■ la **amigdalitis:** he has tonsillitis tiene amigdalitis.

**tonsils** ['tɒnslz] *plural noun* ■ las **amígdalas:** he had his tonsils out lo operaron de las amígdalas.

**too** [tuː] *adverb*
1. **también:** are you coming too? ¿vienes también?; I'm hungry — me too tengo hambre — yo también
2. **demasiado:** it's too late es demasiado tarde
➤ too many demasiados: **there are too many cars** hay demasiados coches
➤ there are too many people hay demasiada gente
➤ too much demasiado: **you drink too much coffee** tomas demasiado café.

**took** [tʊk] *past tense* ➤ take.

**tool** [tuːl] *noun* ■ la **herramienta**
➤ a tool box una caja de herramientas.

**tooth** [tuːθ] *(plural teeth [tiːθ]) noun* ■ el **diente:** she's brushing her teeth se está lavando los dientes.

**toothache** ['tuːθeɪk] *noun* ■ el **dolor de muelas**
➤ she has a toothache le duelen las muelas.

**toothbrush** ['tuːθbrʌʃ] *noun* ■ el **cepillo de dientes.**

**toothpaste** ['tuːθpeɪst] *noun* ■ la **pasta de dientes:** a tube of toothpaste un tubo de pasta de dientes.

**top** [tɒp] *(noun & adjective)*
■ *noun*
1. la **cima:** at the top of the mountain en la cima de la montaña

**2.** la **parte superior**: at the top of the page en la parte superior de la hoja

**3.** la **parte de arriba**: at the top of the stairs en la parte de arriba de la escalera

**4.** el **top** (plural los **tops**): she's wearing a pretty top tenía puesto un bonito top

**5.** el **tablero**: she polished the top of the table lustró el tablero de la mesa

**6.** el **tapón** (plural los **tapones**): put the top back on the bottle ponle el tapón a la botella

➤ **on top of** encima de: he was sitting on top of the table estaba sentado encima de la mesa

➤ **on top of that, he's stupid** más encima, es estúpido

➤ **he's at the top of the class** es el mejor de la clase

➤ **on top** encima: a cake with a cherry on top un pastel con una cereza encima

■ adjective

**1. de arriba**: the top drawer el cajón de arriba; the top stair la escalera de arriba

**2. destacado**: he's a top tennis player es un destacado tenista

➤ **the top floor** el último piso: they live on the top floor viven en el último piso.

**topic** ['tɒpɪk] noun ■ el **tema**: the main topic of conversation el tema principal de conversación.

**topping** ['tɒpɪŋ] noun

➤ what toppings do you want on your pizza? ¿con qué ingredientes quiere cubrir su pizza?

**top-secret** [,tɒp'si:krɪt] adjective ■ **secreto**: top-secret information información secreta.

**tore** [tɔːʳ] past tense ➤ tear.

**torn** [tɔːn] past participle ➤ tear.

**tornado** [tɔː'neɪdəʊ] (plural tornadoes o tornados) noun ■ el **tornado**.

**tortoise** ['tɔːtəs] noun ■ la **tortuga**.

**toss** [tɒs] verb ■ **tirar, aventar** Colombia, Mexico, Peru: he tossed me the ball me tiró la pelota

➤ to toss a coin echarlo a cara o cruz, echarlo a águila o sol Mexico: let's toss a coin echémoslo a cara o cruz

**toss out** phrasal verb ■ **tirar**: you can toss those old magazines out puedes tirar esas revistas viejas.

**total** ['təʊtl] (noun & adjective)

■ noun

el **total**: it costs a total of 200 dollars cuesta un total de 200 dólares

➤ **in total** en total

■ adjective

**total**: the total price el precio total.

**totally** ['təʊtəlɪ] adverb ■ **totalmente**.

**touch** [tʌtʃ] (noun & verb)

■ noun

el **tacto**: the sense of touch el sentido del tacto; it's soft to the touch es suave al tacto

➤ to keep in touch with somebody mantenerse en contacto con alguien

➤ to get in touch with somebody ponerse en contacto con alguien: I got in touch with him me puse en contacto con él

➤ to lose touch with somebody perder el contacto con alguien: I lost touch with them perdí el contacto con ellos

■ verb

**tocar**: I touched his hand le toqué la mano.

**touchdown** ['tʌtʃdaʊn] noun ■ el **touchdown** (plural los **touchdowns**): he scored a touchdown marcó un touchdown.

**tough** [tʌf] adjective

**1. duro**: the meat is tough la carne está dura; it's a tough life es una vida dura

**2. difícil**: it's a tough problem es un problema difícil

**3. peligroso**: this is a tough neighborhood éste es un barrio peligroso

➤ **tough luck!** ¡mala suerte!

**tour** [tʊəʳ] noun

**1.** el **viaje**: we went on a tour of Spain nos fuimos de viaje por España

**2.** la **visita**: I went on a tour of the museum hicimos una visita al museo

**3.** la **gira**: Jennifer López is on tour Jennifer López está de gira.

**tourism** ['tʊərɪzm] noun ■ el **turismo**.

**tourist** [ˈtʊərɪst] *noun* ▪ el/la **turista**
➤ a tourist office or a tourist information office una oficina de turismo or una oficina de información turística.

**tournament** [ˈtɔːnəmənt] *noun* ▪ el **torneo**: a chess tournament un torneo de ajedrez.

**toward, towards** [təˈwɔːd, təˈwɔːdz] *preposition*
1. **hacia**: he was walking toward me caminaba hacia mí
2. **con**: she was very kind toward us fue muy amable con nosotros.

**towel** [ˈtaʊəl] *noun* ▪ la **toalla**.

**tower** [ˈtaʊəʳ] *noun* ▪ la **torre**.

**town** [taʊn] *noun*
1. el **pueblo**: he lives in a small town vive en un pequeño pueblo
2. la **ciudad**: we went into town fuimos a la ciudad
➤ the town hall el municipio.

**toy** [tɔɪ] *noun* ▪ el **juguete**
➤ a toy store una juguetería.

**track** [træk] *noun*
1. el **camino**: a mountain track un camino en la montaña
2. la **pista**: he did three laps around the track dio tres vueltas alrededor de la pista
3. la **pieza**: can I listen to the next track? ¿puedo escuchar la siguiente pieza?
4. la **huella**: the tire tracks led to the river las huellas de las llantas conducían al río
➤ a railroad track una vía férrea.

**tractor** [ˈtræktəʳ] *noun* ▪ el **tractor**.

**trade** [treɪd] *noun*
1. el **oficio**: he's a chef by trade es chef de oficio
2. el **comercio**: international trade comercio internacional.

**trademark** [ˈtreɪdmaːk] *noun* ▪ la **marca**: a registered trademark una marca registrada.

**tradition** [trəˈdɪʃn] *noun* ▪ la **tradición** *(plural* las **tradiciones)**: it's a tradition

to kiss under the mistletoe es una tradición besarse debajo del muérdago.

**traditional** [trəˈdɪʃənl] *adjective* ▪ **tradicional**.

**traffic** [ˈtræfɪk] *uncountable noun* ▪ el **tráfico**: there's a lot of traffic hay mucho tráfico
➤ a traffic jam un embotellamiento: we got caught in a traffic jam nos agarró un embotellamiento
➤ traffic lights el semáforo: stop at traffic lights pare en el semáforo.

**tragedy** [ˈtrædʒədɪ] *(plural* tragedies) *noun* ▪ la **tragedia**.

**trail** [treɪl] *noun* ▪ el **rastro**: we are on their trail les estamos siguiendo el rastro.

**trailer** [ˈtreɪləʳ] *noun*
1. el **avance**: I liked the trailer for the film me gustó el avance de la película
2. el **remolque**: the car was pulling a trailer el coche llevaba un remolque
3. el **tráiler** *(plural* los **tráilers)**, el **cámper** *(plural* los **cámpers)** Chile, Mexico, la **casa rodante** Southern Cone, Venezuela: they live in a trailer viven en un tráiler
➤ a trailer park un estacionamiento para tráilers.

**train** [treɪn] *(noun & verb)*
▪ *noun*
el **tren**: I went to Chicago by train fui a Chicago en tren
▪ *verb*
1. **capacitar**: he is training the new assistant está capacitando al nuevo empleado
2. **estudiar**: she's training as a doctor está estudiando medicina
3. **entrenar**: he's training for the race está entrenando para la carrera.

**trainer** [ˈtreɪnəʳ] *noun* ▪ el **entrenador**, la **entrenadora**: the team has a new trainer el equipo tiene un nuevo entrenador.

**training** [ˈtreɪnɪŋ] *uncountable noun* ▪ la **capacitación**: he did his training in Spain hizo su capacitación en España
➤ to be in training estar entrenándose: he's in training for the tournament se está entrenando para el torneo

➤ **to be out of training** estar desentrenado
➤ **she's out of training now** está desentrenado en este momento.

**trampoline** ['træmpəliːn] *noun* ▇ **la cama elástica**, el **catre elástico** *Mexico*.

**translate** [træns'leɪt] *verb* ▇ **traducir: can you translate this letter into English?** ¿puedes traducir al inglés esta carta?

**translation** [træns'leɪʃn] *noun* ▇ la **traducción** (*plural* las **traducciones**).

**translator** [træns'leɪtəʳ] *noun* ▇ el **traductor**, la **traductora**.

**transparent** [træns'pærənt] *adjective* ▇ **transparente**.

**transportation** [ˌtrænspɔː'teɪʃn] *noun* ▇ el **transporte: we went by public transportation** fuimos en transporte público.

**trap** [træp] (*noun & verb*)
▇ *noun*
la **trampa: it's a trap** es una trampa
▇ *verb*
(*past tense & past participle* **trapped**)
1. **atrapado: I'm trapped, I can't get out** estoy atrapado, no puedo salir
2. **cazar con una trampa: the hunters trapped the lion** los cazadores cazaron al león con una trampa.

**trash** [træʃ] *uncountable noun* ▇ la **basura: there's a pile of trash in the corner** hay una pila de basura en el rincón
➤ **put it in the trash** tíralo a la basura
➤ **put the trash out** saca la basura.

**trashcan** ['træʃkæn] *noun* ▇ el **cubo de la basura**, el **bote de la basura** *Mexico*.

**travel** ['trævl] (*noun & verb*)
▇ *uncountable noun*
los **viajes: travel broadens the mind** los viajes amplían los horizontes
➤ **a travel agency** una agencia de viajes
▇ *verb*
(*past tense & past participle* **traveled**)
1. **viajar: he travels a lot** viaja mucho
2. **recorrer: I've traveled thirty miles** he recorrido treinta millas.

**traveler** ['trævləʳ] *noun* ▇ el **viajero**, la **viajera**
➤ **a traveler's check** un cheque de viajero.

**tray** [treɪ] *noun* ▇ la **bandeja**, la **charola** *Bolivia, Mexico, Peru*: **put the plates on a tray** pon los platos en una bandeja.

**treasure** ['treʒəʳ] *uncountable noun* ▇ el **tesoro: they found treasure on the shipwreck** encontraron un tesoro en los restos del naufragio.

**treat** [triːt] (*verb & noun*)
▇ *verb*
**tratar: she treats him well** lo trata bien
➤ **to treat somebody to something** invitar a alguien con algo: **he treated me to an ice-cream** me invitó a tomar un helado
▇ *noun*
el **gusto: I've bought you a treat** te compré algo para darte un gusto; **it was a treat to see you again** fue un gusto verte otra vez
➤ **it's my treat** yo invito.

**treatment** ['triːtmənt] *noun* ▇ el **tratamiento: he's having treatment at the hospital** está recibiendo tratamiento en el hospital.

**treaty** ['triːtɪ] (*plural* **treaties**) *noun* ▇ el **tratado: a peace treaty** un tratado de paz.

**tree** [triː] *noun* ▇ el **árbol**
➤ **a family tree** un árbol genealógico
➤ **a tree trunk** un tronco.

**tremble** ['trembl] *verb* ▇ **temblar: I was trembling all over** estaba temblando.

**trend** [trend] *noun*
1. la **moda: the latest trend** la última moda
2. la **tendencia: a new trend in music** una nueva tendencia musical.

**trendy** ['trendɪ] *adjective* ▇ *informal* **muy de moda: we went to a trendy club** fuimos a un club muy de moda.

**trial** ['traɪəl] *noun* ▇ el **juicio: he pleaded guilty at the trial** se declaró culpable en el juicio
➤ **to go on trial** ir a juicio.

**triangle** ['traɪæŋgl] *noun* ■ el **triángulo**.

**tribe** [traɪb] *noun* ■ la **tribu: an Amazonian tribe** una tribu amazónica.

**trick** [trɪk] *(noun & verb)*
■ *noun*
1. la **broma: he played a trick on his brother** le hizo una broma a su hermano
2. el **truco: there's a trick to opening the door** abrir la puerta tiene truco
■ *verb*
   **engañar: you tricked me** me engañaste.

**tried** [traɪd] *past tense & past participle*
➤ try.

**trigger** ['trɪgəʳ] *noun* ■ el **gatillo: she pulled the trigger** apretó el gatillo.

**trim** [trɪm] *(noun & verb)*
■ *noun*
   el **recorte**
➤ **to have a trim** recortarse el pelo
■ *verb*
   *(past tense & past participle* **trimmed)** **recortar: I need to trim my hair** necesito recortarme el pelo.

**trip** [trɪp] *(noun & verb)*
■ *noun*
1. el **viaje: they went on a trip to Italy** se fueron de viaje a Italia
2. el **paseo: we're going on a trip to the beach today** hoy nos vamos de paseo a la playa
■ *verb*
   *(past tense & past participle* **tripped)** **tropezar: I tripped and fell** tropecé y me caí.

**trombone** [trɒm'bəʊn] *noun* ■ el **trombón** *(plural* los **trombones)**: **he plays the trombone** toca el trombón.

**trophy** ['trəʊfɪ] *(plural* trophies) *noun* ■ el **trofeo**.

**tropical** ['trɒpɪkl] *adjective* ■ **tropical: a tropical rainforest** una selva tropical.

**trot** [trɒt] *(past tense & past participle* trotted) *verb* ■ **trotar: the horses were trotting round the field** los caballos trotaban por el campo.

**trouble** ['trʌbl] *(noun & verb)*
■ *uncountable noun*
1. el **problema: he made a lot of trouble for me** me causó muchos problemas; **that's the trouble** ése es el problema
2. la **molestia: he has gone to a lot of trouble to help me** se tomó mucha molestias para ayudarme
➤ **to be in trouble** estar metido en problemas: **he's in a lot of trouble** está metido en muchos problemas
➤ **to get into trouble** meterse en problemas: **I don't want to get into trouble** no quiero meterme en problemas
➤ **to have trouble doing something** tener problemas para hacer algo: **I had trouble writing my essay** tuve problemas para escribir mi trabajo
➤ **what's the trouble?** ¿qué pasa?
■ *verb*
   **molestar: I'm sorry to trouble you** siento molestarlo.

**trout** [traʊt] *noun* ■ la **trucha**.

**truck** [trʌk] *noun* ■ el **camión** *(plural* los **camiones)**: **the garbaje truck** el camión de la basura
➤ **a truck driver** el camionero.

**trucker** ['trʌkəʳ] *noun* ■ el **camionero**, la **camionera**.

**true** [truː] *adjective* ■ **verdadero: a true love** un amor verdadero
➤ **it's true** es verdad
➤ **to come true** hacerse realidad: **her dream came true** su sueño se hizo realidad.

**trumpet** ['trʌmpɪt] *noun* ■ la **trompeta: Louis plays the trumpet** Louis toca la trompeta.

**trunk** [trʌŋk] *noun*
1. el **tronco: a tree trunk** un tronco
2. la **trompa: elephants suck up water with their trunks** los elefantes succionan agua con la trompa
3. el **traje de baño: he packed his trunk** empacó su traje de baño
4. el **maletero**, la **cajuela** *Mexico*, el **baúl** *Colombia, River Plate*, la **maleta** *Chile, Peru*: **put your bags into the trunk of the car** pon tus maletas en el maletero del coche.

**trust** [trʌst] *(noun & verb)*
■ *uncountable noun*
la **confianza: she has a lot of trust in you**
tiene mucha confianza en ti
■ *verb*
**confiar: I trust you** confío en ti.

**truth** [tru:θ] *noun* ■ la **verdad: he's
telling the truth** está diciendo la verdad.

**try** [traɪ] *(noun & verb)*
■ *noun*
el **intento: I'll give it a try** haré el intento
■ *verb*
*(past tense & past participle* **tried***)*
1. **intentar: I tried to open the door** intenté
abrir la puerta
2. **probar: try a bit of this cake** prueba un poquito de este pastel
➤ **to try one's best** or **to try one's hardest**
hacer todo lo posible

**try on** *phrasal verb* ■ **probarse: try this
hat on** pruébate este sombrero.

**T-shirt** ['ti:ʃɜ:t] *noun* ■ la **camiseta,** la
**playera** *Mexico.*

**tube** [tju:b] *noun* ■ el **tubo: a tube of**
**toothpaste** un tubo de pasta de dientes.

**Tuesday** ['tju:zdɪ] *noun* ■

In Spanish the days of the week do not
start with a capital letter:

el **martes** *(plural* los **martes***)***: it's Tuesday
today** hoy es martes; **next Tuesday** el martes próximo; **last Tuesday** el martes pasado
➤ **on Tuesday** el martes: **I'll see you on
Tuesday** te veo el martes
➤ **on Tuesdays** los martes: **he comes to see
me on Tuesdays** viene a verme los martes.

**tulip** ['tju:lɪp] *noun* ■ el **tulipán** *(plural*
los **tulipanes***).*

**tummy** ['tʌmɪ] *noun* ■ *informal* la **barriga: I have a tummy ache** me duele la barriga.

**tuna** ['tu:nə] *(plural* **tuna** o **tunas***) noun*
■ el **atún** *(plural* los **atunes***).*

**tune** [tju:n] *noun* ■ la **melodía: I don't
know the words, but I'll sing you the
tune** no sé la letra, pero te cantaré la melodía
➤ **out of tune** desafinado: **he's singing out
of tune** está cantando desafinado.

**tunnel** ['tʌnl] *noun* ■ el **túnel**.

**turkey** ['tɜːkɪ] *noun* ■ el **pavo,** el **guajolote** *Mexico.*

**turn** [tɜːn] *(noun & verb)*
■ *noun*
1. el **turno**
2. la **curva: there's a turn in the road** hay
una curva en la carretera
➤ **it's my turn** me toca a mí
➤ **it's your turn to wash the dishes** te toca
a ti lavar los platos
➤ **to take turns at doing something** turnarse para hacer algo
■ *verb*
1. **doblar: turn left at the light** doble a la
izquierda en el semáforo
2. **girar: turn the knob to the right** gira la perilla hacia la derecha
3. **voltearse: he turned and spoke to me** se
volteó y me habló
4. **ponerse: she turned pale** se puso pálida;
**her face turned red** se le puso la cara colorada

**turn around** *phrasal verb*
1. **voltearse: he turned around when I came
in** se volteó cuando entré
2. **dar la vuelta: the car turned around** or **he
turned the car around** el coche dio la vuelta.

**turn back** *phrasal verb* ■ **regresar: we
walked for an hour and then turned back**
caminamos durante una hora y después re-
gresamos.

**turn down** *phrasal verb* ■ **rechazar:
they turned my offer down** rechazaron mi
oferta.

**turn into** *phrasal verb*
1. **convertir: the witch turned the prince into a frog** la bruja convirtió al príncipe en una
rana

**2. convertirse:** the caterpillar turned into a butterfly el gusano se convirtió en una mariposa.

**turn off** *phrasal verb* ■ **apagar:** turn the TV off apaga la televisión.

**turn on** *phrasal verb* ■ **prender:** turn the radio on prende la radio.

**turn over** *phrasal verb*

**1. voltear:** he turned his cards over volteó sus cartas

**2. voltearse:** she turned over and went back to sleep se volteó y se volvió a dormir.

**turn up** *phrasal verb*

**1. subir:** turn the music up sube la música

**2. aparecer:** he didn't turn up no apareció; don't worry, it'll turn up no te preocupes, ya aparecerá.

**turnip** ['tɜːnɪp] *noun* ■ el **nabo**.

**turquoise** ['tɜːkwɔɪz] *adjective* ■ **turquesa**.

**turtle** ['tɜːtl] *noun* ■ la **tortuga**.

**tusk** [tʌsk] *noun* ■ el **colmillo**.

**TV** [ˌtiːˈviː] *(abbreviation of* television*)* *noun* ■ la **televisión:** they're watching TV están viendo televisión; what's on TV? ¿qué hay en la televisión?

**twelfth** [twelfθ] *numeral* ■ **décimo segundo**

➤ on the twelfth floor en el piso doce

➤ it's November twelfth today hoy es el 12 de noviembre.

**twelve** [twelv] *numeral* ■ **doce:** the twelve apostles los doce apóstoles; she's twelve tiene doce años; I'll meet you at twelve nos encontramos a las doce; it's twelve o'clock at night son las doce de la noche.

**twentieth** ['twentɪəθ] *numeral* ■ **vigésimo:** in the twentieth century en el siglo veinte

➤ it's May twentieth today hoy es el 20 de mayo.

**twenty** ['twentɪ] *numeral* ■ **veinte:** it's twenty to four son veinte para las cuatro, son las cuatro menos veinte *River Plate;* she's twenty tiene veinte años

➤ twenty-one veintiuno

➤ the twenty-first century el siglo veintiuno.

**twice** [twaɪs] *adverb* ■ **dos veces:** I go swimming twice a week voy a nadar dos veces por semana; she earns twice as much as him ella gana el doble que él.

**twin** [twɪn] *noun* ■ el **mellizo**, la **melliza**, el **cuate**, la **cuata** *Mexico:* they are twins son mellizos; his twin brother su hermano mellizo; she's my twin sister es mi hermana melliza.

**twist** [twɪst] *verb*

**1. torcer:** he twisted my arm me torció el brazo

**2. girar:** I twisted the knob to the left giré la perilla hacia la izquierda

**3. enrollar:** twist the thread around the bobbin enrolla el hilo en la bobina

➤ to get twisted enroscarse: the cable has gotten twisted el cable se enroscó

➤ to twist one's ankle torcerse el tobillo: I twisted my ankle me torcí el tobillo.

**two** [tuː] *numeral* ■ **dos:** I cut the paper in two corté el papel en dos; she's two tiene dos años; he left at two se fue a las dos.

**type** [taɪp] *(noun & verb)*

■ *noun*

el **tipo:** there are different types of houses hay diferentes tipos de casas

■ *verb*

**escribir a máquina, tipear** *South America:* he typed the letter escribió la carta a máquina.

**typewriter** ['taɪpˌraɪtər] *noun* ■ la **máquina de escribir**.

**typical** ['tɪpɪkl] *adjective* ■ **típico**

➤ that's typical of him eso es típico de él.

**UFO** (abbreviation of unidentified flying object) noun ■ el **OVNI**.

**ugly** ['ʌglɪ] adjective ■ **feo**.

**UK** [ˌjuːˈkeɪ] (abbreviation of United Kingdom) noun ■ the UK el Reino Unido.

**umbrella** [ʌmˈbrelə] noun ■ el **paraguas** (plural los **paraguas**).

**umpire** ['ʌmpaɪəʳ] noun ■ el **árbitro, la árbitra**.

**UN** [juːˈen] (abbreviation of United Nations) noun ■ the UN la ONU.

**unable** [ʌnˈeɪbl] adjective
➤ to be unable to do something no poder hacer algo: he was unable to help me no pudo ayudarme
➤ she's unable to read no sabe leer.

**unbearable** [ʌnˈbeərəbl] adjective ■ **insoportable**.

**unbelievable** [ˌʌnbɪˈliːvəbl] adjective ■ **increíble**.

**uncle** ['ʌŋkl] noun ■ el **tío**.

**uncomfortable** [ˌʌnˈkʌmftəbl] adjective ■ **incómodo**
➤ to be uncomfortable ser incómodo: this chair is really uncomfortable esta silla es realmente incómoda
➤ to feel uncomfortable sentirse incómodo: I felt very uncomfortable at the party me sentí muy incómodo en la fiesta.

**under** ['ʌndəʳ] (preposition & adverb)
■ preposition
1. **debajo de**: the dog's under the sofa el perro está debajo del sofá
2. **menos de**: it weighs under 5 kilos pesa menos de cinco kilos
3. **menor de**: a game for children under five un juego para niños menores de cinco años
➤ it's under there está ahí debajo
➤ the road goes under the bridge el camino pasa por debajo del puente
■ adverb
1. **debajo**: he saw the bed and crawled under vió la cama y se metió debajo
2. **menos**: children of ten and under niños de diez años o menos.

**underground** ['ʌndəgraʊnd] (adjective & adverb)
■ adjective
**subterráneo**: an underground passage un pasaje subterráneo
■ adverb
**bajo tierra**: the animal went underground el animal se metió bajo tierra.

**underline** [ˌʌndəˈlaɪn] verb ■ **subrayar**: he underlined the heading subrayó el título.

**underneath** [ˌʌndəˈniːθ] (preposition & adverb)
■ preposition
**debajo de**: I looked underneath the chair miré debajo de la silla
■ adverb
**debajo**: I bent down and looked underneath me incliné y miré debajo.

**underpants** ['ʌndəpænts] plural noun ■ los **calzoncillos**: a pair of blue underpants unos calzoncillos azules.

**underpass** ['ʌndəpɑːs] noun ■ el **paso subterráneo**.

**undershirt** ['ʌndəʃɜːt] noun ■ la **camiseta**.

**understand** [ˌʌndəˈstænd] (past tense & past participle understood) verb ■ **entender**: do you understand? ¿entiendes?; I don't understand Spanish no entiendo español.

**understood** [ˌʌndəˈstʊd] *past tense & past participle* ➤ understand.

**underwater** [ˌʌndəˈwɔːtər] *(adjective & adverb)*
■ *adjective*
**submarino: an underwater camera** una cámara submarina
■ *adverb*
**por debajo del agua: he can swim underwater** puede nadar por debajo del agua.

**underwear** [ˈʌndəweər] *uncountable noun* ■ **la ropa interior.**

**undid** [ˌʌnˈdɪd] *past tense* ➤ undo.

**undo** [ˌʌnˈduː] *(past tense undid, past participle undone) verb* ■ **deshacer: I can't undo this knot** no puedo deshacer este nudo.

**undone** [ˌʌnˈdʌn] *adjective & past participle* ➤ undo.

**undress** [ˌʌnˈdres] *verb* ■ **desvestir**
➤ **to get undressed** desvestirse: **he got undressed** se desvistió.

**unemployed** [ˌʌnɪmˈplɔɪd] *adjective* ■ **desempleado**
➤ **the unemployed** los desempleados.

**unemployment** [ˌʌnɪmˈplɔɪmənt] *noun* ■ **el desempleo**
➤ **unemployment compensation** subsidio de desempleo.

**unexpected** [ˌʌnɪkˈspektɪd] *adjective* ■ **inesperado.**

**unexpectedly** [ˌʌnɪkˈspektɪdlɪ] *adverb* ■ **inesperadamente.**

**unfair** [ˌʌnˈfeər] *adjective* ■ **injusto.**

**unfortunately** [ʌnˈfɔːtʃnətlɪ] *adverb* ■ **lamentablemente: unfortunately, there isn't any cake left** lamentablemente, no queda más pastel.

**unfriendly** [ˌʌnˈfrendlɪ] *adjective* ■ **antipático.**

**unhappy** [ʌnˈhæpɪ] *adjective* ■ **infeliz** *(plural infelices).*

**unhealthy** [ʌnˈhelθɪ] *adjective*
1. **enfermizo: he looks really unhealthy** tiene un aspecto realmente enfermizo
2. **poco saludable: it's an unhealthy climate** es un clima poco saludable.

**unidentified flying object** [ˌʌnaɪˈdentɪfaɪdˌflaɪɪŋˈɒbdʒɪkt] *noun* ■ **el objeto volador no identificado.**

**uniform** [ˈjuːnɪfɔːm] *noun* ■ **el uniforme.**

**union** [ˈjuːnjən] *noun* ■ **el sindicato: they belong to a union** pertenecen al sindicato.

**unit** [ˈjuːnɪt] *noun* ■ **la unidad: a meter is a unit of measurement** el metro es una unidad de medida.

**United Kingdom** [juːˌnaɪtɪd ˈkɪŋdəm] *noun*
➤ **the United Kingdom** el Reino Unido.

**United Nations** [juːˌnaɪtɪdˈneɪʃnz] *plural noun*
➤ **the United Nations** las Naciones Unidas.

**United States** [juːˌnaɪtɪdˈsteɪts] *noun*
➤ **the United States** los Estados Unidos.

**universe** [ˈjuːnɪvɜːs] *noun* ■ **el universo.**

**university** [ˌjuːnɪˈvɜːsɪtɪ] *(plural universities) noun* ■ **el universidad: he goes to the university** va a la universidad.

**unkind** [ʌnˈkaɪnd] *adjective* ■ **descortés.**

**unleaded** [ˌʌnˈledɪd] *adjective* ■ **sin plomo: unleaded gas** la nafta sin plomo.

**unless** [ənˈles] *conjunction* ■ **a menos que, a no ser que**

The conjunctions a menos que and a no ser que are followed by a verb in the subjunctive:

**I'll stay here unless he comes** me quedaré aquí a menos que él venga.

**unlike** [ˌʌnˈlaɪk] *preposition* ■ **a diferencia de**: unlike other systems, this one is easy to install a diferencia de otros sistemas, este es fácil de instalar.

**unlikely** [ʌnˈlaɪklɪ] *adjective* ■ **poco probable, improbable**: he's unlikely to win es poco probable que él gane.

**unlock** [ˌʌnˈlɒk] *verb* ■ **abrir**: I will unlock the door voy a abrir la puerta.

**unlucky** [ʌnˈlʌkɪ] *adjective*
➤ to be unlucky tener mala suerte: he's so unlucky tiene tanta mala suerte
➤ it's unlucky to walk underneath a ladder pasar por debajo de una escalera trae mala suerte.

**unpack** [ˌʌnˈpæk] *verb* ■ **deshacer**: we unpacked our suitcases deshicimos las maletas
➤ I unpacked my clothes saqué la ropa de la maleta.

**unpleasant** [ʌnˈpleznt]          *adjective*
■ **antipático**: he was really unpleasant estuvo muy antipático.

**untie** [ˌʌnˈtaɪ] *(present participle* untying) *verb*
1. **deshacer**: I untied the knot deshice el nudo
2. **desatar**: they untied the prisoner desataron al prisionero.

**until** [ənˈtɪl] *(preposition & conjunction)*
■ *preposition*
**hasta**: we'll play until six o'clock vamos a jugar hasta las seis; until now hasta ahora
■ *conjunction*
**hasta que**

> The conjunction **hasta que** is followed by a verb in the subjunctive when referring to an event that hasn't yet occurred:

I'll stay here until he comes me quedaré aquí hasta que venga.

**unusual** [ʌnˈjuːʒl] *adjective*
1. **poco común**: an unusual color un color poco común

2. **raro**: she wears unusual clothes usa ropa rara

> The expression **es raro que** is followed by a verb in the subjunctive:

it's unusual for her to arrive late es raro que llegue tarde.

**unwilling** [ˌʌnˈwɪlɪŋ] *adjective*
➤ to be unwilling to do something no estar dispuesto a hacer algo: she was unwilling to come no estaba dispuesta a venir.

**unwrap** [ˌʌnˈræp] *(past tense & past participle* unwrapped) *verb* ■ **desenvolver**: she unwrapped her presents desenvolvió sus regalos.

**up** [ʌp] *(adverb, preposition & adjective)*
■ *adverb*
**arriba**: it's up here es aquí arriba
➤ don't look up no mires para arriba
■ *preposition*
1. **arriba de**: the house is up the hill la casa está arriba de la colina; the cat's up the tree el gato está arriba del árbol
2.

> When "up" is used with a verb of movement in English (to come up or to go up), you often use a verb alone in Spanish to translate it:

she went up the stairs subió las escaleras; they ran up the road corrieron por la calle
➤ their house is just up the road su casa queda un poco más adelante por esta calle
➤ up to hasta: the water came up to my knees el agua me llegaba hasta las rodillas
➤ up to 30 people hasta 30 personas
➤ it's up to you depende de ti
➤ I don't feel up to going out no me siento con ánimos para salir
➤ what's he up to? ¿qué está haciendo?
➤ he's up to something está tramando algo
■ *adjective*
**levantado**: I was up at dawn estaba levantado al amanecer; is she up? ¿está levantada?
➤ time's up! ¡ya es la hora!
➤ what's up? *informal* ¿qué pasa?

**update** [ˌʌpˈdeɪt] *verb* ■ **actualizar**: I updated the file actualicé el archivo.

**uphill** [ˌʌpˈhɪl] *adverb*
➤ to go uphill ir cuesta arriba: **the path goes uphill** el camino va cuesta arriba.

**upon** [əˈpɒn] *preposition* ➤ **on**.

**upper** [ˈʌpəʳ] *adjective* ■ **superior: the upper lip** el labio superior
➤ **the upper classes** las clases altas.

**upset** [ʌpˈset] *(adjective & verb)*
■ *adjective*
**afectado: she was very upset at the news** estaba muy afectada con las noticias
➤ **to be upset** disgustarse: **don't get upset at what I said** no te disgustes por lo que dice
➤ **to have an upset stomach** estar mal del estómago
■ *verb*
*(past tense & past participle* **upset***)*
1. **afectar: it upsets me to think about it** me afecta pensar en eso
2. **disgustar: this decision will upset a lot of people** esta decisión va a disgustar a mucha gente
3. **desbaratar: this has upset my plans** esto ha desbaratado mis planes
4. **tirar: I upset some coffee** tiré un poco de café.

**upside down** [ˌʌpsaɪdˈdaʊn] *adverb*
■ **al revés: the picture is upside down** el cuadro está al revés.

**upstairs** [ʌpˈsteəz] *(adverb & adjective)*
■ *adverb*
**arriba: wait for me upstairs** espérenme arriba
➤ **to come upstairs or to go upstairs** subir: **can you come upstairs?** ¿podrías subir?
■ *adjective*
**del piso de arriba: the upstairs rooms** los cuartos del piso de arriba.

**up-to-date** [ʌptəˈdeɪt] *adjective*
1. **al día: the data is up-to-date** la información está al día
2. **actualizado: an up-to-date computer** una computadora actualizada.

**urgent** [ˈɜːdʒənt] *adjective* ■ **urgente: I must speak to you, it's urgent** tengo que hablar contigo, es urgente.

**Uruguay** [ˈjurəgwaɪ] *noun* ■ **Uruguay** *(masculine).*

**us** [ʌs] *pronoun*
1. *As a direct or indirect object pronoun* **nos: she calls us every week** nos llama todas las semanas; **he gave the papers to us** nos dio los papeles
2. *After a preposition and the verb "to be"* **nosotros: is that for us?** ¿eso es para nosotros?; **you're coming with us** vienes con nosotros; **it's us** somos nosotros.

**US** [ˌjuːˈes] *(abbreviation of* United States*) noun*
➤ **the US** los EE.UU.

**USA** [ˌjuːesˈeɪ] *(abbreviation of* United States of America*) noun*
➤ **the USA** los EE.UU.

**use** *(noun & verb)*
■ *noun*
[juːs] el **uso: there's a ban on the use of certain products** está prohibido el uso de ciertos productos; **for my own use** para mi uso personal
➤ **directions for use** instrucciones de uso
➤ **to be of use** servir
➤ **to be in use** estar en uso
➤ **the elevator is out of use** el ascensor está fuera de servicio
➤ **it's no use** es inútil
➤ **what's the use?** ¿de qué sirve?
■ *verb*
[juːz] **usar: I used a new method** usé un método nuevo; **she uses vinegar to clean the windows** usa vinagre para limpiar los vidrios; **can I use your phone?** ¿puedo usar el teléfono?

**used** [juːzd] *adjective* ■ **usado: a used car** un coche usado
➤ **to be used to doing something** estar acostumbrado a hacer algo: **I'm used to going to bed late** estoy acostumbrada a acostarme tarde
➤ **to get used to doing something** acostumbrarse a hacer algo: **you'll get used to getting up early** te acostumbrarás a levantarte temprano

➤ **I used to live in Chile** antes vivía en Chile.

**useful** ['juːsfʊl] *adjective* ■ **útil: take the guidebook, it could be useful** llévate la guía, puede serte útil.

**useless** ['juːslɪs] *adjective*
1. **inservible: a useless piece of information** una información inservible
2. **inútil: he's completely useless** es totalmente inútil
➤ **it's useless** es inútil: **it's useless asking her** es inútil preguntarle.

**usual** ['juːʒəl] *adjective* ■ **de costumbre: we'll meet at the usual time** nos veremos a la hora de costumbre
➤ **as usual** como de costumbre: **she arrived early, as usual** llegó temprano, como de costumbre
➤ **later than usual** más tarde que de costumbre.

**usually** ['juːʒəlɪ] *adverb* ■ **normalmente: she usually leaves the house at nine** normalmente sale de la casa a las nueve.

**vacant** ['veɪkənt] *adjective* ■ **libre: is this seat vacant?** ¿está libre este asiento?

**vacation** [vəˈkeɪʃn] *uncountable noun* ■ **las vacaciones: they spent their vacation in Greece** pasaron las vacaciones en Grecia
➤ **on vacation** de vacaciones: **she's on vacation** está de vacaciones

➤ **where are you going on vacation?** ¿adónde vas a ir de vacaciones?

**vacuum** ['vækjʊəm] *(verb & noun)*
■ *verb*
**pasar la aspiradora: he's vacuuming the hall** está pasando la aspiradora en el vestíbulo
■ *noun*
**la aspiradora**
➤ **a vacuum cleaner** una aspiradora.

**vain** [veɪn] *adjective* ■ **vanidoso: he's very vain** es muy vanidoso
➤ **in vain** en vano: **I tried in vain to help him** intenté en vano ayudarlo.

**Valentine's Day** ['væləntaɪnzdeɪ] *noun* ■ **el día de San Valentín**.

**valid** ['vælɪd] *adjective* ■ **válido: your ticket isn't valid** su boleto no es válido.

**valley** ['vælɪ] *noun* ■ **el valle**.

**valuable** ['væljʊəbl] *adjective*
1. **de valor: a valuable necklace** un collar de valor
2. **valioso: your advice has been very valuable** tu consejo ha sido muy valioso.

**valuables** ['væljʊəblz] *plural noun* ■ **los objetos de valor: she keeps her valuables in a safe** guarda los objetos de valor en una caja fuerte.

**value** ['væljuː] *noun* ■ **el valor: the value of their house has doubled** se ha duplicado el valor de su casa.

**van** [væn] *noun* ■ **la furgoneta, la vagoneta** *Mexico*.

**vanilla** [vəˈnɪlə] *noun* ■ **la vainilla**.

**vanish** ['vænɪʃ] *verb* ■ **desaparecer: he vanished** desapareció.

**variety** [vəˈraɪətɪ] *(plural* varieties*)* *noun* ■ **la variedad: there are many different varieties of flowers** hay muchas variedades diferentes de flores
➤ **there's a wide variety of dishes on the menu** hay una amplia variedad de platos en el menú.

**various** ['veərɪəs] *adjective* ▦ **varios**: for various reasons por varias razones.

**vary** ['veərɪ] *(past tense & past participle* varied*) verb* ▦ **variar**: the weather varies from day to day el clima varía de día en día.

**vase** [veɪz] *noun* ▦ **el florero**: I put the flowers in the vase puse las flores en el florero

 Vase es un falso amigo, no significa "vaso".

**veal** [viːl] *uncountable noun* ▦ **la ternera**.

**vegetable** ['vedʒtəbl] *noun* ▦ **la verdura**.

**vegetarian** [ˌvedʒɪ'teərɪən] *noun* ▦ **el vegetariano** (*feminine* la **vegetariana**).

**vehicle** ['viːɪkl] *noun* ▦ **el vehículo**.

**veil** [veɪl] *noun* ▦ **el velo**: she's wearing a veil tiene puesto un velo.

**vein** [veɪn] *noun* ▦ **la vena**: veins carry blood to the heart las venas transportan la sangre al corazón.

**velvet** ['velvɪt] *noun* ▦ **el terciopelo**.

**vending machine** ['vendɪŋmə'ʃiːn] *noun* ▦ **la máquina expendedora**.

**Venezuela** [veniz'weɪlə] *noun* ▦ **Venezuela** (*feminine*).

**Venezuelan** [veniz'weɪlən] *(adjective & noun)*
▦ *adjective*

Remember not to use a capital letter for the adjective in Spanish:

**venezolano**: Venezuelan cuisine is very varied la cocina venezolana es muy variada
▦ *noun*

In Spanish, a capital letter is not used for the inhabitants of a country or region:

el **venezolano**, la **venezolana**: many Venezuelans live in the capital city muchos venezolanos viven en la capital.

**verb** [vɜːb] *noun* ▦ **el verbo**.

**verse** [vɜːs] *noun*
1. **el verso**: the poem has three verses el poema tiene tres versos
2. **el versículo**: a verse from the Bible un versículo de la Biblia.

**version** ['vɜːʃn] *noun* ▦ **la versión** (*plural* las **versiones**): there are two versions of the story hay dos versiones de la historia.

**versus** ['vɜːsəs] *preposition* ▦ **contra**: Dallas versus Washington Dallas contra Washington.

**vertical** ['vɜːtɪkl] *adjective* ▦ **vertical**: a vertical line una línea vertical.

**very** ['verɪ] *adverb* ▦ **muy**: he's very happy está muy contento
➤ **very much** mucho: I like him very much él me gusta mucho
➤ **the very same day** el mismo día.

**vest** [vest] *noun* ▦ **el chaleco**: he's wearing a suit and a vest tiene puesto un traje con un chaleco.

**vet, veterinarian** [vet, ˌvetərɪ'neərɪən] *noun* ▦ **el veterinario**, la **veterinaria**.

**via** ['vaɪə] *preposition* ▦ **vía**: you can go to Sydney via Los Angeles puedes ir a Sydney vía Los Angeles.

**vicious** ['vɪʃəs] *adjective*
1. **brutal**: a vicious attack una agresión brutal
2. **feroz** (*plural* **feroces**): a vicious dog un perro feroz
➤ **a vicious circle** un círculo vicioso.

**victim** ['vɪktɪm] *noun* ▦ **el/la víctima**.

**victory** ['vɪktərɪ] *(plural* victories*) noun* ▦ **la victoria**.

**video** ['vɪdɪəʊ] *noun* ▦ **el video**: they're watching a video están viendo un video
➤ **on video** en video: the film's out on video la película está en video
➤ **a video camera** una videocámara
➤ **a video cassette** un videocasete
➤ **a video game** un videojuego

**285**

➤ a video store un videoclub

➤ a video recorder un aparato de video.

**view** [vjuː] *noun*

1. la **vista**: there's a great view from the top of the Eiffel Tower hay una vista espectacular desde arriba de la Torre Eiffel

2. el **punto de vista**: what is your view on the subject? ¿cuál es tu punto de vista sobre el tema?

**viewer** ['vjuːəʳ] *noun* ▓ el **espectador, la espectadora**: the program attracts millions of viewers el programa atrae a millones de espectadores.

**village** ['vɪlɪdʒ] *noun* ▓ el **pueblo**.

**vine** [vaɪn] *noun* ▓ la **vid**: grapes grow on vines la uva crece en las vides.

**vinegar** ['vɪnɪgəʳ] *noun* ▓ el **vinagre**.

**vineyard** ['vɪnjəd] *noun* ▓ la **viña**.

**violence** ['vaɪələns] *noun* ▓ la **violencia**.

**violent** ['vaɪələnt] *adjective* ▓ **violento**: he's a violent man es un hombre violento.

**violin** [ˌvaɪə'lɪn] *noun* ▓ el **violín** *(plural* los **violines***)*: she plays the violin toca el violín.

**violinist** [ˌvaɪə'lɪnɪst] *noun* ▓ el/la **violinista**.

**virus** ['vaɪrəs] *noun* ▓ el **virus** *(plural* los **virus***)*.

**visa** ['viːzə] *noun* ▓ la **visa**: you need a visa to go to some countries necesitas visa para ir a algunos países.

**visit** ['vɪzɪt] *(noun & verb)*

▓ *noun*

la **visita**: I paid a visit to my uncle le hice una visita a mi tío

▓ *verb*

**visitar**: I visited my uncle visité a mi tío.

**visitor** ['vɪzɪtəʳ] *noun*

1. la **visita**: we have visitors tomorrow mañana tenemos visitas

2. el/la **visitante**: the park attracts a lot of visitors el parque atrae a muchos visitantes.

**vitamin** ['vaɪtəmɪn] *noun* ▓ la **vitamina**: citrus fruit is full of vitamin C los cítricos tienen mucha vitamina C.

**vocabulary** [və'kæbjʊlərɪ] *(plural* vocabularies*) noun* ▓ el **vocabulario**.

**voice** [vɔɪs] *noun* ▓ la **voz** *(plural* las **voces***)*: he has a deep voice tiene una voz grave

➤ she has a loud voice habla muy alto

➤ voice mail buzón de voz.

**volcano** [vɒl'keɪnəʊ] *(plural* volcanoes o volcanos*) noun* ▓ el **volcán** *(plural* los **volcanes***)*.

**volleyball** ['vɒlɪbɔːl] *noun* ▓ el **vóleibol**, el volibol *Colombia, Mexico, Venezuela*: they're playing volleyball están jugando vóleibol.

**volume** ['vɒljuːm] *noun* ▓ el **volumen** *(plural* los **volúmenes***)*: can you turn the volume up? ¿podrías subir el volumen?

**voluntary** ['vɒləntrɪ] *adjective* ▓ **voluntario**: she does voluntary work hace trabajo voluntario.

**volunteer** [ˌvɒlən'tɪəʳ] *(noun & verb)*

▓ *noun*

el **voluntario, la voluntaria**: they don't get paid, they're volunteers no les pagan, son voluntarios

▓ *verb*

➤ to volunteer to do something ofrecerse a hacer algo: he volunteered to help us se ofreció a ayudarnos.

**vomit** ['vɒmɪt] *verb* ▓ **vomitar**: he vomited vomitó.

**vote** [vəʊt] *(noun & verb)*

▓ *noun*

1. la **votación** *(plural* las **votaciones***)*: they organized a vote organizaron una votación

2. el **voto**: they won by 20 votes to 4 ganaron por 20 votos contra 4

3. el **derecho al voto**: women got the vote in Britain in 1888 las mujeres obtuvieron el derecho al voto en Inglaterra en 1888

■ *verb*
**votar: he voted for the Green party** votó por el Partido Verde.

**vowel** ['vaʊəl] *noun* ■ la **vocal: there are five vowels in English** en inglés hay cinco vocales.

**vulture** ['vʌltʃər] *noun* ■ el **buitre**.

**wade** [weɪd] *verb* ■ **vadear: they're wading in the stream** están vadeando el arroyo.

**waffle** ['wɒfl] *noun* ■ el **waffle**.

**wag** [wæg] *(past tense & past participle* wagged*) verb* ■ **menear: the dog's wagging its tail** el perro está meneando la cola.

**wage** [weɪdʒ] *noun* ■ el **sueldo: the wages are good** los sueldos son buenos.

**waist** [weɪst] *noun* ■ la **cintura: she has a small waist** tiene una cintura pequeña.

**wait** [weɪt] *(noun & verb)*

■ *noun*
la **espera: it was a long wait** fue una larga espera

■ *verb*
**esperar: we waited a long time** esperamos un rato largo; **wait a minute!** ¡espera un momento!; **I waited until he had left or I waited for him to leave** esperé hasta que se fuera

> The verb that follows **esperar hasta que** must be in the subjunctive.

➤ **I can't wait to see you** tengo muchas ganas de verte
➤ **to keep somebody waiting** hacer esperar a alguien: **I'm sorry to keep you waiting** perdón por hacerte esperar

**wait for** *phrasal verb* ■ **esperar: wait for me!** ¡espérenme!; **he's waiting for the bus** está esperando el autobús.

**waiter** ['weɪtər] *noun* ■ el **mesero**.

**waiting room** ['weɪtɪŋruːm] *noun* ■ la **sala de espera**.

**waitress** ['weɪtrɪs] *noun* ■ la **mesera**.

**wake** [weɪk] *(past tense* woke, *past participle* woken*) verb* ■ **despertar: wake me at six** despiértame a las seis

**wake up** *phrasal verb*
1. **despertar: can you wake me up in the morning?** ¿puedes despertarme en la mañana?
2. **despertarse: I woke up at seven** me desperté a las siete.

**walk** [wɔːk] *(noun & verb)*

■ *noun*
el **paseo: let's go for a walk** vamos a dar un paseo
➤ **it's a long walk** es una caminata larga
➤ **it's a five-minute walk** queda a cinco minutos a pie

■ *verb*
1. **ir a pie: I always walk to school** siempre voy a pie al colegio
2. **caminar: we walked along the beach** caminamos por la playa; **we've walked three miles** caminamos tres millas
➤ **to walk the dog** sacar a pasear al perro

**walk out** *phrasal verb* ■ **irse: he just got up and walked out** se levantó y se fue.

**walking** ['wɔːkɪŋ] *uncountable noun* ■ **walking is a good form of exercise** caminar es una buena forma de hacer ejercicio
➤ **walking shoes** zapatos para caminar
➤ **a walking stick** un bastón.

**Walkman®** [ˈwɔːkmən] *noun* ▪ el walkman® *(plural* los **walkman**): he's listening to his Walkman® está escuchando el walkman.

**wall** [wɔːl] *noun*

1. la **pared**: he put a poster on the wall of his **bedroom** puso un póster en la pared de su cuarto

2. el **muro,** la **barda** *Mexico*: he jumped over the wall saltó el muro.

**wallet** [ˈwɒlɪt] *noun* ▪ la **cartera**.

**wallpaper** [ˈwɔːlˌpeɪpəʳ] *noun* ▪ el **papel pintado,** el **papel tapiz** *Mexico*.

**walnut** [ˈwɔːlnʌt] *noun* ▪ la **nuez** *(plural* las **nueces)**, la **nuez de Castilla** *(plural* las **nueces de Castilla***) Mexico*.

**wand** [wɒnd] *noun* ▪ la **varita**: a magic wand una varita mágica.

**wander** [ˈwɒndəʳ] *verb* ▪ dar **vueltas**: we wandered around the town dimos vueltas por el pueblo.

**want** [wɒnt] *verb* ▪ **querer**: do you want some tea? ¿quieres té?; I want to go to the movies quiero ir al cine

➤ to want somebody to do something querer que alguien haga algo: she wants me to stay quiere que me quede

> The verb that follows **querer que** must be in the subjunctive.

**wanted** [ˈwɒntɪd] *adjective*

➤ he's wanted by the police lo busca la policía

➤ you're wanted in the kitchen te necesitan en la cocina.

**war** [wɔːʳ] *noun* ▪ la **guerra**: the Second World War la Segunda Guerra Mundial

➤ to be at war estar en guerra: the two countries are at war los dos países están en guerra.

**warehouse** [ˈweəhaʊs] *noun* ▪ el **almacén** *(plural* los **almacenes)**, la **bodega** *Chile, Colombia, Mexico*.

**warm** [wɔːm] *(adjective & phrasal verb)*
*adjective*

1. **templado**: the water is warm el agua está templado

2. **caluroso**: he got a warm welcome tuvo un recibimiento caluroso

➤ to be warm tener calor

➤ are you warm enough? ¿no tienes frío?

➤ it's warm today hoy hace calor

**warm up** *phrasal verb*

1. **calentar**: I'll warm up some apple pie voy a calentar un poco de tarta de manzana

2. **calentarse**: come and warm up in front of the fire ven a calentarte frente al fuego

3. **hacer ejercicios de calentamiento**: the athletes are warming up los atletas están haciendo ejercicios de calentamiento.

**warmth** [wɔːmθ] *noun* ▪ el **calor**.

**warn** [wɔːn] *verb* ▪ **advertir**: I warned you te lo advertí

➤ to warn somebody not to do something aconsejarle a alguien que no haga algo: I warned you not to go te aconsejé que no fueras

> The verb that follows **aconsejar que** must be in the subjunctive.

**warning** [ˈwɔːnɪŋ] *noun* ▪ la **advertencia**: this is my final warning ésta es mi última advertencia.

**warranty** [ˈwɒrəntɪ] *(plural* **warranties)** *noun* ▪ la **garantía**: the computer is still under warranty la computadora todavía está bajo garantía.

**wart** [wɔːt] *noun* ▪ la **verruga**.

**was** [wəz] *past tense* ➤ be.

**wash** [wɒʃ] *(noun & verb)*

▪ *noun*

➤ his shirt is in the wash su camisa está lavándose

▪ *verb*

1. **lavar**: he's washing his clothes está lavando la ropa

2. **lavarse:** I'm washing me estoy lavando; she washed her hands se lavó las manos; he's washing his hair se está lavando el pelo

**wash up** *phrasal verb* ■ **lavarse:** go and wash up before dinner ve a lavarte antes de comer.

**washing machine** ['wɒʃɪŋmə'ʃiːn] *noun* ■ la **lavadora.**

**wasn't** ['wɒznt] ➤ was not.

**wasp** [wɒsp] *noun* ■ la **avispa.**

**waste** [weɪst] *(noun & verb)*

■ *uncountable noun*

1. el **desperdicio:** what a waste! ¡qué desperdicio!

2. los **desechos:** industrial waste desechos industriales

➤ it's a waste of time es una pérdida de tiempo

■ *verb*

1. **derrochar:** he wastes money derrocha el dinero

2. **perder:** he wastes a lot of time pierde mucho tiempo.

**wastepaper basket** [ˌweɪst'peɪpər-ˌbɑːskɪt] *noun* ■ el **cesto de los papeles,** el **papelero** *Southern Cone.*

**watch** [wɒtʃ] *(noun & verb)*

■ *noun*

el **reloj:** my watch has stopped se me paró el reloj

■ *verb*

1. **ver:** they're watching television están viendo televisión

2. **cuidar:** I'm watching their luggage for them les estoy cuidando las maletas

**watch out** *phrasal verb* ■ **tener cuidado:** watch out, there's a car coming! ¡ten cuidado que viene un coche!

**water** ['wɔːtər] *(noun & verb)*

■ *uncountable noun*

el **agua**

Feminine noun that takes **un** or **el** in the singular.

■ *verb*

**regar:** remember to water the flowers no te olvides de regar las plantas

➤ my eyes are watering me lloran los ojos

➤ my mouth's watering se me hace agua la boca.

**waterfall** ['wɔːtəfɔːl] *noun* ■ la **catarata.**

**watermelon** ['wɔːtəˌmelən] *noun* ■ la **sandía.**

**waterproof** ['wɔːtəpruːf] *adjective*

1. **impermeable:** a waterproof jacket una chaqueta impermeable

2. **a prueba de agua:** a waterproof watch un reloj a prueba de agua.

**water-skiing** ['wɔːtərskiːɪŋ] *uncountable noun* ■ el **esquí acuático:** they go water-skiing often hacen esquí acuático con frecuencia.

**wave** [weɪv] *(noun & verb)*

■ *noun*

la **ola:** the waves are big today hoy las olas están grandes

➤ he gave me a wave me saludó con la mano

■ *verb*

1. **hacerle señas a:** he waved to me when he saw me me hizo señas cuando me vio

2. **agitar:** the children are waving flags los niños están agitando banderas

➤ to wave goodbye hacer adiós con la mano: I waved goodbye to them les hice adiós con la mano.

**wax** [wæks] *uncountable noun* ■ la **cera.**

**way** [weɪ] *noun*

1. la **manera:** I like the way she dresses me gusta la manera en que se viste; **in the same way** de la misma manera

2. el **camino:** the quickest way to the town el camino más rápido para llegar al centro; **it's on my way** me queda de camino; **we stopped on the way** paramos en el camino

➤ in a way en cierto modo

➤ can you tell me the way to the museum? ¿podría decirme cómo llegar al museo?

➤ **he got his own way** se salió con la suya
➤ **the way in** la entrada
➤ **the way out** la salida
➤ **to be in the way** estar bloqueando el camino: **you're in the way** estás bloqueando el camino
➤ **to get out of the way** quitarse del medio: **get out of the way!** ¡quítate del medio!
➤ **he's on his way** está en camino
➤ **it's a long way** está lejos
➤ **which way is it?** ¿por dónde es?
➤ **this way** por aquí: **the hotel's this way** el hotel está por aquí
➤ **that way** por allá: **he went that way** se fue por allá
➤ **is this the right way?** ¿está bien por aquí?
➤ **he went the wrong way** se equivocó de camino
➤ **no way!** ¡ni hablar!

**we** [wiː] *pronoun* ■ **nosotros, nosotras**

"We" is not usually translated unless necessary for emphasis or clarification:

**we live in Alabama** vivimos en Alabama; **we're going to the movies** vamos al cine

Spanish nouns are either masculine or feminine. Remember to use **nosotros** for masculine subjects and **nosotras** for feminine subjects. When "we" includes male and female, use **nosotros**:

**we did it** nosotros lo hicimos; **we know it but they don't** nosotros lo sabemos pero ellos no.

**weak** [wiːk] *adjective* ■ **débil**.

**wealthy** ['welθɪ] *adjective* ■ **rico**
➤ **the wealthy** los ricos.

**weapon** ['wepən] *noun* ■ **el arma**

Feminine noun that takes **un** or **el** in the singular.

**wear** [weər] (*past tense* **wore**, *past participle* **worn**) *verb*
1. **tener puesto: Carol's wearing a dress** Carol tiene puesto un vestido
2. **ponerse: what are you going to wear?** ¿qué te vas a poner?

**wear out** *phrasal verb*
1. **gastar: I've worn out my shoes** gasté los zapatos
2. **gastarse: my shoes wear out quickly** los zapatos se me gastan rápido
3. **agotar: that journey has worn me out** ese viaje me agotó.

**weather** ['weðər] *uncountable noun* ■ **el tiempo: what's the weather like?** ¿cómo está el tiempo?; **the weather is awful** el tiempo está horrible; **the weather is fine** hace buen tiempo
➤ **the weather forecast** el pronóstico del tiempo: **what's the weather forecast?** ¿cuál es el pronóstico del tiempo?

**web** [web] *noun*
➤ **the Web** el/la Web: **I found his address on the Web** encontré su dirección en el Web
➤ **a web page or a Web page** una página web.

**website** ['websaɪt] *noun* ■ **el sitio web: have you visited the Larousse website?** ¿entraste al sitio web de Larousse?

**we'd** [wiːd]
1. ➤ **we had; we would**.

**wedding** ['wedɪŋ] *noun* ■ **la boda**
➤ **a wedding anniversary** un aniversario de bodas
➤ **a wedding cake** una pastel de boda
➤ **a wedding dress** un vestido de novia
➤ **a wedding ring** un anillo de boda.

**Wednesday** ['wenzdɪ] *noun* ■

In Spanish the days of the week do not start with a capital letter:

**el miércoles** (*plural* **los miércoles**): **it's Wednesday today** hoy es miércoles; **next Wednesday** el próximo miércoles; **last Wednesday** el miércoles pasado
➤ **on Wednesday** el miércoles: **I'll see you on Wednesday** te veo el miércoles
➤ **on Wednesdays** los miércoles: **she has a Spanish class on Wednesdays** tiene una clase de español los miércoles.

**weed** [wi:d] *noun* ■ la **mala hierba: I'm going to dig up the weeds** voy a arrancar la mala hierba.

**week** [wi:k] *noun* ■ la **semana: in a week's time** dentro de una semana; **this week** esta semana; **next week** la próxima semana; **last week** la semana pasada

➤ **a week from Saturday** una semana a partir del sábado.

**weekend** [ˌwi:k'end] *noun* ■ el **fin de semana: what are you doing this weekend?** ¿qué vas a hacer este fin de semana?; **next weekend** el próximo fin de semana; **last weekend** el fin de semana pasado

➤ **on the weekend** el fin de semana: **I'll see you on the weekend** te veo el fin de semana.

**weep** [wi:p] *(past tense & past participle* wept) *verb* ■ **llorar: she started weeping** empezó a llorar.

**weigh** [weɪ] *verb* ■ **pesar: she weighs 140 pounds** pesa 140 libras; **can you weigh these apples?** ¿podría pesar estas manzanas?

**weight** [weɪt] *noun* ■ el **peso**

➤ **to put on weight** engordar: **I've put on weight** he engordado

➤ **to lose weight** adelgazar: **she lost weight** adelgazó.

**weird** [wɪəd] *adjective* ■ **raro**.

**welcome** ['welkəm] *(noun, verb & adjective)*

■ *noun*
la **bienvenida: they gave me a warm welcome** me dieron una calurosa bienvenida
■ *verb*
**recibir a alguien: they welcomed me with open arms** me recibieron con los brazos abiertos
■ *adjective*
**bienvenido: you're always welcome** siempre eres bienvenida

➤ **welcome!** ¡bienvenido!: **welcome to Chile!** ¡bienvenido a Chile!

➤ **thank you! — you're welcome!** ¡gracias! — ¡de nada!

**we'll** [wi:l] ➤ we shall; we will.

**well** [wel] *(adjective, adverb, noun & exclamation)*

■ *adjective*
*(comparative* better) **bien: I'm very well, thank you** estoy muy bien, gracias; **all is well** todo está bien
■ *adverb*
*(superlative* best) **bien: the party went well** la fiesta resultó bien; **she sings really well** canta realmente bien; **the work's well done** el trabajo está bien hecho

➤ **well done!** ¡muy bien!

➤ **as well** también: **he came as well** él vino también

➤ **as well as** además de: **they sell records as well as CDs** venden discos además de CDs
■ *noun*
el **pozo: an oil well** un pozo de petróleo
■ *exclamation*

1. **bueno: oh well, never mind!** ¡bueno, no importa!; **well, who was it then?** bueno ¿quién fue entonces?

2. **vaya: well, look who it is!** ¡vaya, miren quién es!

**well-behaved** [welbɪ'heɪvd] *adjective* ■ **que se porta bien**

➤ **the children were well-behaved** los niños se portaron bien.

**well-known** [ˌwel'nəʊn] *adjective* ■ **conocido: it's a well-known restaurant** es un restaurante conocido.

**went** [went] *past tense* ➤ go.

**wept** [wept] *past tense & past participle* ➤ weep.

**were** [wɜːʳ] *past tense* ➤ be.

**we're** [wɪəʳ] ➤ we are.

**weren't** [wɜːnt] ➤ were not.

**west** [west] *(noun, adjective & adverb)*

■ *noun*
el **oeste: the sun sets in the west** el sol se pone por el oeste
■ *adjective*
**oeste** *(plural* **oeste): San Francisco is on the west coast** San Francisco está en la costa oeste

■ *adverb*
**hacia el oeste: go west** vayan hacia el oeste
➤ **west of** al oeste de: **Chicago is west of De-troit** Chicago está al oeste de Detroit.

**western** ['westən] *(adjective & noun)*
■ *adjective*
**occidental: Western Europe** Europa Occidental
■ *noun*
el **western: he prefers westerns to thrill-ers** prefiere los westerns a las películas de suspenso.

**wet** [wet] *adjective*
1. **mojado: my hair's wet** tengo el pelo mojado
2. **lluvioso: the weather is wet** el tiempo está lluvioso
➤ **to get wet** mojarse: **I got wet** me mojé; **I got my shirt wet** me mojé la camisa.

**we've** [wiːv] ➤ we have.

**whale** [weɪl] *noun* ■ la **ballena**.

**what** [wɒt] *(adjective, pronoun & exclama-tion)*
■ *adjective*
**qué: what color is it?** ¿de qué color es?; **what time is it?** ¿qué hora es?; **what books do you want?** ¿qué libros quieres?; **what a pity!** ¡qué lástima!; **what lovely flowers!** ¡qué flores tan bonitas!
■ *pronoun*
1. *In questions*

> You generally translate "what" as **qué**:

**what's that?** ¿qué es eso?; **what's hap-pening?** ¿qué está pasando?; **what's wrong?** ¿qué pasa?; **what are you doing?** ¿qué estás haciendo?; **what are they talk-ing about?** ¿de qué están hablando?; **what are you thinking about?** ¿en qué estás pensando?

> Translate "what is" by **cuál es**:

**what's your address?** ¿cuál es tu direc-ción?; **what is your phone number?** ¿cuál es tu número de teléfono?

2. *In relative clauses*

> Translate "what" as **lo que**:

**I saw what happened** vi lo que pasó; **you can't always get what you want** no siem-pre puedes tener lo que quieres; **tell me what she said** dime lo que dijo
➤ **what about going out for a meal?** ¿qué tal si salimos a comer?
➤ **what about me?** ¿y yo qué?
➤ **what is it about?** ¿de qué se trata?
■ *exclamation*
**what!** ¡qué!; **what?** ¿qué?, ¿mande? *Mexi-co.*

**whatever** [wɒt'evəʳ] *(pronoun & adjec-tive)*
■ *pronoun*
1.

> When "whatever" means "no matter what", it's often translated by a repeti-tion of the verb in its subjunctive form:

**whatever happens, don't tell Joe** pase lo que pase, no le digas a Joe; **whatever he says, don't go with him** diga lo que diga, no vayas con él

2.

> When "whatever" means "everything", it's usually translated with **lo que** fol-lowed by a verb in the subjunctive:

**I'll do whatever I can** haré lo que pueda
■ *adjective*
**cualquiera que**

> **Cualquiera que** should be followed by a verb in the subjunctive:

**whatever decision you make, I'll support you** cualquiera que sea la decisión que to-mes, te apoyaré.

**wheat** [wiːt] *noun* ■ el **trigo**.

**wheel** [wiːl] *noun*
1. la **rueda: bicycles have two wheels** las bi-cicletas tienen dos ruedas
2. el **volante: who was behind the wheel?** ¿quién estaba al volante?

**wheelchair** ['wiːlˌtʃeəʳ] *noun* ■ la si-lla de ruedas.

**when** [wen] (adverb & conjunction)
- adverb
  **cuándo**: when are you going? ¿cuándo vas?; **tell me when you're coming** dime cuándo vienes
- conjunction
  **cuando**: he visited me when I lived in Paris me visitó cuando yo vivía en París; **he always gets annoyed when I sing** siempre se molesta cuando canto

> Cuando is followed by a verb in the subjunctive when it refers to the future:

I'll tell her when she gets here se le diré cuando llegue; I'll buy you a car when you are 18 te compraré un auto cuando tengas 18.

**whenever** [wen'evər] conjunction
1. **cuando**

> Cuando is followed by a verb in the subjunctive when it refers to an event that has not yet happened:

come whenever you like ven cuando quieras
2. **siempre que**: whenever I see them we argue discutimos siempre que nos vemos.

**where** [weər] (adverb & conjunction)
- adverb
  **dónde**: where is the station? ¿dónde queda la estación?; **tell me where you hid it** dime dónde lo escondiste
> where are you going? ¿adónde vas?
- conjunction
  **donde**: this is the town where I grew up este es el pueblo donde crecí.

**wherever** [weər'evər] conjunction
- **dondequiera que**: he followed her wherever she went la seguía dondequiera que ella iba

> Dondequiera que is followed by a verb in the subjunctive when it refers to an event that has not yet happened:

he'll follow you wherever you go te va a seguir dondequiera que vayas
> sit wherever you'd like siéntate donde quieras.

**whether** ['weðər] conjunction ■ **si:** I don't know whether she's coming no sé si va a venir.

**which** [wɪtʃ] (adjective & pronoun)
- adjective
  **qué**

> In questions, qué is often used before nouns to translate "which":

which bike is yours? ¿qué bici es la tuya?; which flowers do you like? ¿qué flores te gustan?
> which one? ¿cuál?: there are two bags, which one is yours? hay dos bolsas, ¿cuál es la tuya?
- pronoun
1. *In questions* **cuál**: out of the two dresses, which do you prefer? de los dos vestidos, ¿cuál prefieres?; **which of the shoes are yours?** ¿cuál de los zapatos son tuyos?
2. *In relative clauses* **que**: houses which are on the beach cost more las casas que están en la playa cuestan más; **the book which you lent me was good** el libro que me prestaste era bueno

> When "which" is used with a preposition it is translated by el que, la que, los que or las que depending on the gender (masculine or feminine) and the number (singular or plural) of the noun it refers to:

the chair on which he was sitting la silla en la que estaba sentado.

**while** [waɪl] (conjunction & noun)
- conjunction
1. **mientras**: I was reading while you were sleeping yo estaba leyendo mientras tú dormías
2. **mientras que**: he likes to go out while his brother prefers to watch TV le gusta salir mientras que a su hermano le gusta ver televisión
- noun
  **el rato**: let's stay here for a while quedémonos aquí un rato
> **after a while** después de un rato: after a while he got tired después de un rato, se cansó
> **for a while** un rato: he went to the party for a while, but then returned home fue

**293**

un rato a la fiesta, pero después volvió a la casa.

**whisper** ['wɪspər] *verb* ■ **susurrar: she whispered something to me** me susurró algo.

**whistle** ['wɪsl] *(noun & verb)*
■ *noun*
el **silbato: the referee blew his whistle** el juez tocó el silbato
■ *verb*
**silbar: can you whistle?** ¿sabes silbar?

**white** [waɪt] *adjective* ■ **blanco: a white shirt** una camisa blanca
➤ **a white lie** una mentira piadosa
➤ **the White House** la Casa Blanca

> WHITE HOUSE
>
> La Casa Blanca (**the White House**) es la residencia oficial y lugar de trabajo del presidente de los Estados Unidos. Se encuentra en Washington D.C., que además de ser la capital del país es la sede del gobierno federal. La Casa Blanca es un símbolo tanto de la presidencia, como del ramo ejecutivo del gobierno estadounidense.

**who** [hu:] *pronoun*
1. *In direct and indirect questions* **quién: who are you?** ¿quién eres?; **who are you talking about?** ¿de quién estás hablando?; **I don't know who she is** no sé quién es ella
2. *In relative clauses* **que: she's the woman who lives in that big house** es la mujer que vive en esa casa grande

> After a preposition, **que** becomes **el que**, **la que**, **los que** or **las que** depending on the gender (masculine or feminine) and the number (singular or plural) of the noun it refers to:

**the men who we were talking to disappeared** los hombres con los que estábamos hablando desparecieron.

**who'd** [hu:d]
➤ who had; who would.

**whoever** [hu:'evər] *pronoun*

1. **quien**

> When "whoever" means "anyone who", the verb that follows **quien** is in the subjunctive:

**you can invite whoever you like** puedes invitar a quien quieras
2. **quienquiera que**

> When "whoever" means "the one who", the verb that follows **quienquiera que** is in the subjunctive:

**whoever wins will get this cup** quienquiera que gane obtendrá esta copa.

**whole** [həʊl] *(adjective & noun)*
■ *adjective*
**entero: she ate the whole cake** se comió el pastel entero
■ *noun*
➤ **the whole of** todo: **the whole of the summer** todo el verano; **the whole of New York is talking about it** todo Nueva York está hablando de eso
➤ **on the whole** en general.

**who'll** [hu:l] ➤ who will; who shall.

**whom** [hu:m] *pronoun*
1. *In questions* **quién: with whom did she leave?** ¿con quién se fue?
2. *In relative clauses* **quien: the man whom she married** el hombre con quien se casó; **to whom it may concern** a quien corresponda.

**who're** ['hu:ər] ➤ who are.

**who's** [hu:z] *noun*
➤ who is; who has.

**whose** [hu:z] *(adjective & pronoun)*
■ *adjective*
1. **de quién: whose car is this?** ¿de quién es ese coche?
2. **cuyo**

> In Spanish the adjective agrees in gender (masculine or feminine) and number (singular or plural) with the noun to which it refers:

**that's the boy whose father is an astronaut** ése es el niño cuyo papá es astronauta; **the lady whose bags are in my car is gone** la mujer cuyas bolsas están en mi coche se ha ido

■ *pronoun*
**de quién: whose is it?** ¿de quién es esto?

**who've** [huːv] ➤ who have.

**why** [waɪ] *adverb* ■ **por qué: why did you lie?** ¿por qué mentiste?; **why don't you come too?** ¿por qué no vienes también?; **I don't know why he said that** no sé por qué dijo eso; **I haven't done my homework — why not?** no hice las tareas - ¿por qué no?; **do you want to go out? — OK, why not?** ¿quieres salir? - bueno, ¿por qué no?

**wicked** ['wɪkɪd] *adjective* ■ **malvado: he's a wicked man** es un hombre malvado.

**wide** [waɪd] *(adjective & adverb)*

■ *adjective*
1. **ancho: a wide road** una calle ancha; **how wide is the river?** ¿qué ancho tiene el río?, ¿qué tan ancho es el río? *Latin America except Southern Cone;* **it's ten feet wide** tiene diez pies de ancho
2. **gran: a wide variety** una gran variedad
■ *adverb*
➤ **open wide!** ¡abre bien la boca!
➤ **wide awake** completamente despierto: **she's wide awake** está completamente despierta
➤ **wide open** abierto de par en par: **the window's wide open** la ventana está abierta de par en par.

**widow** ['wɪdəʊ] *noun* ■ **la viuda**.

**widower** ['wɪdəʊəʳ] *noun* ■ **el viudo**.

**width** [wɪdθ] *noun* ■ **el ancho**.

**wife** [waɪf] *(plural* **wives** [waɪvz]*) noun* ■ **la esposa**.

**wig** [wɪg] *noun* ■ **la peluca**.

**wild** [waɪld] *adjective*
1. **salvaje: wild animals** animales salvajes
2. **silvestre: wild flowers** flores silvestres
3. **loco: that noise is driving me wild** ese ruido me está volviendo loco.

**will** ['wɪl] *(verb & noun)*
■ *verb (negative* **won't***)*
1. *The future tense* **I'll leave for Spain in the fall** me iré a España en el otoño; **when will you call?** ¿cuándo llamarás?

In Spanish you can use the present tense of the verb **ir** + infinitive to talk about the future:

**I'll do it now** lo voy a hacer ahora; **it will change everything** va a cambiar todo

You can also use the present tense to talk about the near future:

**will you help me?** ¿me ayudas?; **I'll go with you** yo voy contigo
2. *In invitations and requests* **querer: will you have some more cake?** ¿quieres más pastel?; **will you close the window?** ¿quieres cerrar la ventana?
➤ **he won't help me** no quiere ayudarme
➤ **the car won't start** el coche no arranca
➤ **that'll be your father** ése debe ser tu papá
■ *noun*
1. **la voluntad: I did it against my will** lo hice contra mi voluntad
2. **el testamento: to make a will** hacer un testamento
➤ **she has a strong will** tiene una gran fuerza de voluntad.

**willing** ['wɪlɪŋ] *adjective*
➤ **to be willing to do something** estar dispuesto a hacer algo: **I'm willing to help you** estoy dispuesto a ayudarte.

**win** [wɪn] *(past tense & past participle* **won***) verb* ■ **ganar: she won the race** ganó la carrera.

**wind** *(noun & verb)*
■ *noun*
[wɪnd] el **viento: there's a strong wind** hace un viento fuerte
➤ **a wind instrument** un instrumento de viento
■ *verb*
[waɪnd] *(past tense & past participle* **wound***)*
1. **enrollar: wind the rope around the pole** enrolla la cuerda alrededor del poste
2. **darle cuerda a: I forgot to wind the clock** me olvidé de darle cuerda al reloj

**wind up** *phrasal verb* ■ **terminar: he wound up in jail** terminó en la cárcel.

**windmill** ['wɪndmɪl] *noun* ■ **el molino de viento**.

**window** ['wɪndəʊ] *noun*

1. la **ventana: open the window** abre la ventana
2. el **vidrio: he's cleaning the car windows** está limpiando los vidrios del coche
3. el **escaparate,** la **vitrina** *Andes, Venezuela,* el **aparador** *Mexico,* la **vidriera** *River Plate:* **she's looking in the shop window** está mirando el escaparate.

**windshield** ['wɪndʃiːld] *noun* ▪ el **parabrisas** *(plural* los **parabrisas)**
➤ **windshield wipers** los limpiaparabrisas, los limpiadores.

**windsurfing** ['wɪnd,sɜːfɪŋ] *noun* ▪ el **windsurf: he goes windsurfing on weekends** hace windsurf los fines de semana.

**windy** ['wɪndɪ] *adjective*
➤ **it's windy** hace viento
➤ **it was a very windy day** era un día de mucho viento.

**wine** [waɪn] *noun* ▪ el **vino: a glass of red wine** una copa de vino tinto.

**wing** [wɪŋ] *noun* ▪ el **ala**

> Feminine noun that takes **un** or **el** in the singular.

**pelicans have large wings** los pelícanos tienen las alas grandes.

**wink** [wɪŋk] *verb* ▪ **guiñar el ojo: he winked at me** me guiñó el ojo.

**winner** ['wɪnər] *noun* ▪ el **ganador,** la **ganadora**.

**winter** ['wɪntər] *noun* ▪ el **invierno: it's cold in the winter** en invierno hace frío
➤ **winter sports** deportes de invierno.

**wintertime** ['wɪntətaɪm] *uncountable noun* ▪ el **invierno: in the wintertime** en el invierno.

**wipe** [waɪp] *verb* ▪ **limpiar: he's wiping the table** está limpiando la mesa

**wipe up** *phrasal verb* ▪ **limpiar: she wiped up the coffee from the floor** limpió el café del suelo.

**wire** ['waɪər] *noun*

1. el **alambre: a barbed wire fence** una valla de alambre de púas
2. el **cable: somebody cut the telephone wires** alguien cortó los cables del teléfono.

**wisdom** ['wɪzdəm] *noun* ▪ la **sabiduría**
➤ **a wisdom tooth** una muela del juicio.

**wise** [waɪz] *adjective* ▪ **sabio: he's a very wise man** es un hombre muy sabio.

**wish** [wɪʃ] *(noun & verb)*

▪ *noun*
el **deseo: his wish came true** su deseo se hizo realidad
➤ **best wishes on your birthday** muchas felicidades por tu cumpleaños
➤ **best wishes, Andrew** saludos, Andrew
▪ *verb*
**desear: you can stay here if you wish** puedes quedarte aquí si lo deseas; **he wished me a happy birthday** me deseó un feliz cumpleaños

> The verb that follows **ojalá** must be in the subjunctive:

➤ **I wish I had a yacht!** ¡ojalá tuviera un yate!
➤ **I wish you were here** ¡ojalá estuvieras aquí!

**witch** [wɪtʃ] *noun* ▪ la **bruja**.

**with** [wɪð] *preposition*

1. **con: I danced with Mary** bailé con Mary; **Tom came with us** Tom vino con nosotros; **with pleasure** con gusto; **I cut it with a knife** lo corté con un cuchillo
2. **de: the man with the hat** el hombre del sombrero; **she was trembling with fear** estaba temblando de miedo.

**within** [wɪ'ðɪn] *preposition*

1. **en menos de: the doctor came within ten minutes** el doctor vino en menos de diez minutos
2. **dentro de: the house is situated within a large property** la casa está situada dentro de una gran propiedad
3. **a menos de: we're within thirty miles of Chicago** estamos a menos de treinta millas de Chicago.

**without** [wɪð'aʊt] *preposition* ■ **sin: I won't go without you** no voy a ir sin ti; **he left without saying goodbye** se fue sin despedirse
➤ **to go without something or to do without something** arreglárselas sin algo: **we can't go without water** no podemos arreglárnoslas sin agua.

**witness** ['wɪtnɪs] *noun* ■ el/la **testigo**.

**witty** ['wɪtɪ] *adjective* ■ **ocurrente: he's very witty** es muy ocurrente.

**wives** *plural* ➤ wife.

**wizard** ['wɪzəd] *noun* ■ el **mago**.

**woke** [wəʊk] *past tense* ➤ wake.

**woken** ['wəʊkn] *past participle* ➤ wake.

**wolf** [wʊlf] *(plural* wolves ['wʊlvz]*) noun* ■ el **lobo**.

**woman** ['wʊmən] *(plural* women*) noun* ■ la **mujer**.

**won** [wʌn] *past tense & past participle* ➤ win.

**wonder** ['wʌndər] *(noun & verb)*
■ *noun*
la **maravilla: the seven wonders of the world** las siete maravillas del mundo
➤ **no wonder!** ¡con razón!: **no wonder you're tired!** ¡con razón estás cansado!
■ *verb*
**preguntarse: I wonder what he's doing** me pregunto qué estará haciendo.

**wonderful** ['wʌndəfʊl] *adjective* ■ **maravilloso**.

**won't** [wəʊnt] ➤ will not.

**wood** [wʊd] *noun* ■ la **madera: the table is made of wood** la mesa es de madera.

**wool** [wʊl] *noun* ■ la **lana**.

**word** [wɜːd] *noun*
1. la **palabra: she didn't say a word** no dijo ni una palabra; **what does this word mean?** ¿qué significa esta palabra?
2. la **letra: do you know the words to this song?** ¿sabes la letra de esta canción?

➤ **to give somebody your word** darle la palabra a alguien: **I gave you my word** te di mi palabra
➤ **to have a word with somebody** hablar con alguien: **I'm going to have a word with your teacher** voy a hablar con tu maestra.

**wore** [wɔːr] *past tense* ➤ wear.

**work** [wɜːk] *(noun & verb)*
■ *noun*
1. el **trabajo: I have a lot of work to do** tengo mucho trabajo que hacer; **she's not here, she's at work** no está aquí, está en el trabajo
2. la **obra: the complete works of Shakespeare** las obras completas de Shakespeare
➤ **a work of art** una obra de arte
➤ **to be out of work** estar sin trabajo
■ *verb*
1. **trabajar: where do you work?** ¿dónde trabajas?
2. **funcionar: the TV isn't working** la TV no funciona
3. **hacer funcionar algo: I can't work this machine** no puedo hacer funcionar esta máquina

**work out** *phrasal verb*
1. **encontrar: I've worked out the answer** encontré la respuesta
2. **resultar: everything worked out well** todo resultó bien
3. **hacer ejercicios: he works out every morning** hace ejercicios todas las mañanas.

**worker** ['wɜːkər] *noun* ■ el **trabajador,** la **trabajadora**
➤ **an office worker** un oficinista
➤ **a factory worker** un obrero.

**workman** ['wɜːkmən] *(plural* workmen ['wɜːkmən]*) noun* ■ el **obrero**.

**workshop** ['wɜːkʃɒp] *noun* ■ el **taller: a drama workshop** un taller de teatro.

**world** [wɜːld] *noun* ■ el **mundo**
➤ **the world champion** el campeón del mundo
➤ **the World Cup** el Mundial
➤ **the World Series** la Serie Mundial
➤ **the Second World War** la Segunda Guerra Mundial

WORLD SERIES

La **World Series** o Serie Mundial es un conjunto de hasta siete partidos de béisbol en los que se enfrentan, al final de la temporada, los campeones de las dos ligas principales: la National League y la American League. Se proclama campeón el primero en obtener cuatro victorias. Éste es uno de los acontecimientos deportivos anuales de mayor importancia en los Estados Unidos; la tradición marca que sea el presidente de la nación quien lance la primera bola del encuentro.

**worm** [wɜ:m] *noun* ■ el **gusano**.

**worn** [wɔ:n] *(adjective & verb form)*

■ *adjective*
**gastado: the carpet is worn** la alfombra está gastada
➤ **worn out** gastado: **my shoes are worn out** mis zapatos están gastados
■ *past participle*
➤ **wear**.

**worried** ['wʌrɪd] *adjective* ■ **preocupado: you look worried** te ves preocupado
➤ **to be worried about somebody or something** estar preocupado por alguien or algo: **I'm very worried about him** estoy muy preocupado por él
➤ **I'm worried sick** estoy preocupadísimo.

**worry** ['wʌrɪ] *(noun & verb)*

■ *noun*
*(plural* **worries***)* la **preocupación** *(plural* las **preocupaciones***)*: **he has a lot of worries** tiene muchas preocupaciones
■ *verb*
1. *(past tense & past participle* **worried***)* **preocuparse: he's worrying about the exams** se preocupa por los exámenes; **don't worry!** ¡no te preocupes!
2. **preocupar: the situation worries me** me preocupa la situación.

**worse** [wɜ:s] *(adjective & verb)*

■ *adjective*
*(comparative of* **bad***)* **peor: it could have been worse** podría haber sido peor; **the patient is worse today** el paciente está peor hoy
➤ **to get worse** empeorar: **things are getting worse** las cosas están empeorando
■ *adverb*
*(comparative of* **badly***)* **peor: he sings worse than I thought** canta peor de lo que yo pensaba.

**worst** [wɜ:st] *(adjective, adverb & noun)*

■ *adjective*
*(superlative of* **bad***)* **peor: it's the worst film I've ever seen** es la peor película que vi en mi vida; **it was the worst place to have a picnic** era el peor lugar para hacer un picnic
■ *adverb*
*(superlative of* **badly***)* **peor: he plays worst** es el que juega peor
■ *noun*
➤ **the worst** el peor, la peor: **of all the players I know, you're the worst** de todos los jugadores que conozco, tú eres el peor
➤ **at worst** en el peor de los casos: **at worst you'll be an hour late** en el peor de los casos llegarás una hora tarde.

**worth** [wɜ:θ] *(noun & adjective)*

■ *noun*
el **valor: a jewel of great worth** una joya de gran valor
➤ **I have 10 dollars' worth of change** tengo diez dólares en monedas
■ *adjective*
➤ **to be worth doing something** valer la pena hacer algo: **it's worth reading the book** vale la pena leer el libro; **it isn't worth waiting** no vale la pena esperar
➤ **it's worth it** vale la pena.

**would** [wʊd] *verb* ■ *(negative* **wouldn't***)*

"Would" is usually translated by a verb in the conditional tense in Spanish:

**if I won the lottery, I would buy a sports car** si ganara la lotería, compraría un auto deportivo; **if I were you, I wouldn't do it** si yo fuera tú, no lo haría; **we would have missed the train if we'd waited** habríamos perdido el tren, si hubiéramos esperado; **she said she would come** dijo que vendría
➤ **would you like another cookie?** ¿quieres otra galleta?
➤ **I'd like a cup of coffee** quisiera una taza de café

➤ **we'd really like to see you** nos gustaría mucho verte
➤ **the car wouldn't start** el coche no arrancaría.

**wouldn't** ['wʊdnt] ➤ would not.

**would've** ['wʊdəv] ➤ would have.

**wound** (noun, verb & verb form)
■ noun
[wuːnd] **la herida: he has a wound on his leg** tiene una herida en la pierna
■ verb
[wuːnd] **herir: she wounded him in the arm** lo hirió en el brazo
■ past tense & past participle
[waund] ➤ wind.

**wrap** [ræp] (past tense & past participle wrapped) verb
1. **envolver: he's wrapping the presents** está envolviendo los regalos
2. **envolverse: she wrapped herself in a blanket** se envolvió en una manta
➤ **he wrapped his scarf around his neck** se puso la bufanda alrededor del cuello.

**wreck** [rek] (noun & verb)
■ noun
**there was a wreck on the freeway** había restos de un vehículo accidentado en la autopista
■ verb
1. **destrozar: the bomb wrecked the village** la bomba destrozó el pueblo
2. **arruinar: the weather has wrecked all our plans** el tiempo arruinó todos nuestros planes.

**wrestler** ['reslər] noun ■ **el luchador, la luchadora.**

**wrestling** ['reslɪŋ] uncountable noun ■ **la lucha libre.**

**wrinkle** ['rɪŋkl] noun ■ **la arruga.**

**wrinkled** ['rɪŋkld] adjective ■ **arrugado.**

**wrist** [rɪst] noun ■ **la muñeca: she broke her wrist** se rompió la muñeca.

**write** [raɪt] (past tense wrote, past participle written) verb ■ **escribir: she's writing a letter** está escribiendo una carta
➤ **to write someone** escribirle a alguien: **you never write your grandmother** nunca le escribes a la abuela

**write back** phrasal verb ■ **contestar: I sent her a letter but she didn't write back** le mandé una carta pero no me contestó.

**write down** phrasal verb ■ **anotar: he wrote down everything I said** anotó todo lo que dije.

**writer** ['raɪtər] noun ■ **el escritor, la escritora: I'd like to be a writer** me gustaría ser escritor.

**writing** ['raɪtɪŋ] uncountable noun ■ **la letra: she has nice writing** tiene bonita letra
➤ **writing paper** papel de escribir.

**written** ['rɪtn] past participle ➤ write.

**wrong** [rɒŋ] (adjective & adverb)
■ adjective
1. **equivocado: that's the wrong answer** ésa es la respuesta equivocada; **it's the wrong address** es la dirección equivocada
2. **mal: it's wrong to lie** está mal mentir
3. **incorrecto: your calculations are wrong** tus cálculos son incorrectos
➤ **they went in the wrong direction** tomaron por donde no debían
➤ **to be wrong** estar equivocado: **you're wrong** estás equivocado
➤ **you have the wrong number** se ha equivocado de número
➤ **what's wrong?** ¿qué pasa?
➤ **there's something wrong with my bike** algo le pasa a mi bici
■ adverb
**mal: she wrote my name wrong** escribió mal mi nombre
➤ **to get something wrong** equivocarse en algo: **you've got the date wrong** te equivocaste en la fecha.

**wrote** [rəʊt] past tense ➤ write.

**299**

**Xmas** *(abbreviation of* Christmas*) noun*
■ la **Navidad,** la **Pascua** *Chile, Peru.*

**X-ray** ['eksreɪ] *(noun & verb)*
■ *noun*
la **radiografía: he needs to have an X-ray**
necesita hacerse una radiografía
■ *verb*
**hacer una radiografía: they X-rayed her**
**leg** le hicieron una radiografía de la pierna.

**xylophone** ['zaɪləfəʊn] *noun* ■ el
**xilófono**.

**yacht** [jɒt] *noun* ■ el **yate**.

**yard** [jaːd] *noun* ■ el **jardín** *(plural* los
**jardines**): **the house has a small yard** la
casa tiene un pequeño jardín.

**yawn** [jɔːn] *verb* ■ **bostezar: he's**
**yawning** está bostezando.

**year** [jɪəʳ] *noun* ■ el **año: we waited a**
**whole year** esperamos un año entero; **she's**
**21 years old** tiene 21 años
➤ **next year** el próximo año
➤ **last year** el año pasado
➤ **the New Year** el Año Nuevo.

**yell** [jel] *verb* ■ **gritar: she was yelling**
estaba gritando.

**yellow** ['jeləʊ] *adjective* ■ **amarillo:**
**she was wearing a yellow dress** llevaba un
vestido amarillo.

**yes** [jes] *adverb* ■ **sí: would you like**
**some cake? — yes, please** ¿quieres un poco de pastel? - sí, por favor; **aren't you hun-**
**gry? — yes, I am!** ¿no tienes hambre? - ¡sí!

**yesterday** ['jestədɪ] *adverb* ■ **ayer: I**
**saw her yesterday** la vi ayer
➤ **yesterday morning** ayer en la mañana
➤ **yesterday evening** ayer en la tarde
➤ **the day before yesterday** anteayer: **he**
**came home the day before yesterday** vino a casa anteayer.

**yet** [jet] *adverb*
1. **todavía: I haven't seen them yet** no los he
visto todavía
2. **ya: have they finished yet?** ¿ya terminaron?
➤ **not yet** todavía no: **has she arrived? — no,**
**not yet** ¿llegó? - no, todavía no.

**yoga** ['jəʊgə] *noun* ■ el **yoga: she**
**practices yoga** hace yoga.

**yogurt** ['jɒgət] *noun* ■ el **yoghourt**
*(plural* los **yoghourts**).

**you** [juː] *pronoun*

"You" as the subject of the verb is not
usually translated unless necessary for
emphasis or clarification:

1. *formal* **usted: what do you do?** ¿qué hace?; **you're always complaining** siempre
se está quejando; **you did it** usted lo hizo;
**you don't know it but he does** usted no lo
sabe pero él sí

2. *informal* **tú: are you coming with us?**
¿vienes con nosotros?; **you don't know it**
no lo sabes; **you said it** tú lo dijiste; **you are**
**ready but she is not** tú estás preparado pero ella no

3. *plural* **ustedes: do you all want to come?**
¿todos quieren venir?; **you two are late**
ustedes dos llegan tarde

4. *direct object of a verb: formal* **lo** (*femini-*
*ne* **la**): **do I know you?** ¿lo conozco?; **I can**
**take you in my car** la puedo llevar en mi
coche

5. *informal* **te: hello Jane, I called you yes-**
**terday** hola Jane, te llamé ayer; **I'll call you**
**tonight** te llamo esta noche

6. *plural* **los** (*feminine* **las**): **I remember you**
**all** los recuerdo a todos; **I'm watching you**
los estoy vigilando

7. *indirect object of a verb: formal* **le: I**
**gave you my address** le di mi dirección

> Use **se** instead of **le** when **you** is used with
> a direct-object pronoun:

**I gave it to you all** se la di a todos ustedes

8. *informal* **te: I told you yesterday** te lo dije
ayer

9. *plural* **les: children, I told you that it was**
**for today** niños, les dije que era para hoy

> Use **se** instead of **les** when **you** is used
> with a direct-object pronoun:

**I told you on Monday** se lo dije el lunes

10. *after a preposition: formal* **usted: this is**
**for you** esto es para usted; **I'll come with**
**you** voy con usted

11. *informal* **ti: thanks to you** gracias a ti

12. *plural* **ustedes: I've been thinking about**
**you all** he estado pensando en todos ustedes; **we're going without you all** nos vamos sin todos ustedes.

**you'd** [juːd]
1. ➤ you had; you would.

**you'll** [juːl] ➤ you will.

**young** [jʌŋ] *adjective* ∎ **joven** (*plural* **jó-**
**venes**)
➤ **young people** la gente joven.

**your** [jɔːʳ] *possessive adjective*

1.

> The possessive adjective must agree in
> number (singular or plural) with the noun
> that follows. Use **su** (or **sus**) to translate
> "your" when you are talking to somebody
> you don't know and use **tu** (or **tus**) when
> you are talking to somebody you know
> well, your family or friends:

**su: your dog bit me** su perro me mordió; **I**
**like your car** me gusta su coche; **pass me**
**your plate** páseme su plato

> Use the definite article (**el, la, los** or **las**),
> not the possessive adjective, with parts of
> the body:

**close your eyes** cierre los ojos

2. **tu: she likes your brother** le gusta tu hermano; **can I listen to your CDs?** ¿puedo
escuchar tus CDs?

> Use the definite article (**el, la, los** or **las**),
> not the possessive adjective, with parts of
> the body:

**have you washed your hands?** ¿te lavaste
las manos?

**you're** [jɔːʳ] ➤ you are.

**yours** [jɔːz] *possessive pronoun*

1.

> The possessive pronoun must agree in
> gender (masculine or feminine) and num-
> ber (singular or plural) with the noun it re-
> places. Use **suyo** (or **suya, suyos** or **suyas**)
> to translate "yours" when you are talking
> to somebody you don't know or **tuyo** (or
> **tuya, tuyos** or **tuyas**) when you are talk-
> ing to somebody you know well, your fam-
> ily or friends:

**suyo: is this yours?** ¿es suyo esto?; **my**
**surname is English, yours is Spanish** mi
apellido es inglés, el suyo es español; **her**
**shoes are red, yours are green** sus zapatos
son rojos, los suyos verdes

2. **tuyo: that bracelet is yours** esa pulsera es
tuya; **my bike has ten gears, yours has**
**twelve** mi bici tiene diez cambios y la tuya
doce

➤ **sincerely yours** atentamente.

**yourself** [jɔːˈself] *pronoun*

1.

> In Spanish there are two ways to translate "yourself". When you are talking to somebody you don't know, you use **se** or **usted mismo**. This is known as the polite form. When you are talking to somebody you know well, your friends or your family, you can use the informal form **te** or **tú mismo**:

**se:** don't cut yourself no se corte

2. **usted mismo:** did you make that yourself? ¿hizo eso usted mismo?

3. **te:** can you describe yourself in three words? ¿te puedes decribir con tres palabras?

4. **tú mismo:** did you do it yourself? ¿lo hiciste tú mismo?

➤ keep it for yourself quédese con él

➤ you were talking about yourself estabas hablando de ti mismo

➤ by yourself solo: were you by yourself? ¿estabas solo?

**yourselves** [jɔːˈselvz] *pronoun*

1.

> Use **se**, **ustedes mismos** or **ustedes mismas** when talking to more than one person:

**se:** did you enjoy yourselves? ¿se divirtieron?

2. **ustedes mismos:** do it yourselves! ¡háganlo ustedes mismos!

➤ help yourselves! ¡sírvanse!

➤ by yourselves solos: were you by yourselves? ¿estaban solos?

**you've** [juːv] ➤ you have.

**zebra** [ˈzebrə] *noun* ■ la **cebra**.

**zero** [ˈzɪərəʊ] *noun* ■ el **cero**: the temperature is below zero la tempertura está bajo cero; the Yankees won 16 to zero los Yankees ganaron 16 a cero.

**zip code** [zɪp] *noun* ■ el **código postal**.

**zipper** [ˈzɪpəʳ] *noun* ■ el **cierre**, el **zíper** *Central America, Mexico, Venezuela*.

**zone** [zəʊn] *noun* ■ la **zona**.

**zoo** [zuː] *noun* ■ el **zoológico**.

**zucchini** [zuːˈkiːnɪ] *(plural* zucchini*)* *noun* ■ el **calabacín** *(plural* los **calabacines**), la **calabacita** *Mexico*.

# Spanish Verbs

# Spanish Verbs

Key: A = present, B = imperfect, C = preterit, D = future,
E = conditional, F = present subjunctive, G = imperfect
subjunctive, H = imperative, I = gerund, J = past participle

## acertar

A acierto, acertamos, etc
F acierte, acertemos, etc
H acierta, acierte, acertemos, acertad, acierten

## adquirir

A adquiero, adquiere, adquirimos, etc
F adquiera, adquiramos, etc
H adquiere, adquiera, adquiramos, adquirid, adquieran

## AMAR

A amo, amas, ama, amamos, amáis, aman
B amaba, amabas, amaba, amábamos, amabais, amaban
C amé, amaste, amó, amamos, amasteis, amaron
D amaré, amarás, amará, amaremos, amaréis, amarán
E amaría, amarías, amaría, amaríamos, amaríais, amarían
F ame, ames, ame, amemos, améis, amen
G amara, amaras, amara, amáramos, amarais, amaran
H ama, ame, amemos, amad, amen
I amando
J amado, -da

## andar

C anduve, anduvo, anduvimos, etc
G anduviera, anduviéramos, etc

## avergonzar

A avergüenzo, avergüenza, avergonzamos, etc
C avergoncé, avergonzó, avergonzamos, etc
F avergüence, avergoncemos, etc
H avergüenza, avergüence, avergoncemos, avergonzad, avergüencen

## caber

A quepo, cabe, cabemos, etc
C cupe, cupo, cupimos, etc
D cabré, cabrá, cabremos, etc
E cabría, cabríamos, etc
F quepa, quepamos, cabed, etc
G cupiera, cupiéramos, etc
H cabe, quepa, quepamos, cabed, quepan

## caer

A caigo, cae, caemos, etc
C cayó, caímos, cayeron, etc
F caiga, caigamos, etc
G cayera, cayéramos, etc
H cae, caiga, caigamos, caed, caigan
I cayendo

## conducir

A conduzco, conduce, conducimos, etc
C conduje, condujimos, etc
F conduzca, conduzcamos, etc
G condujera, condujéramos, etc
H conduce, conduzca, conduzcamos, conducid, conduzcan

### conocer

A conozco, conoce, conocemos, etc
F conozca, conozcamos, etc
H conoce, conozca, conozcamos,
conoced, conozcan

### dar

A doy, da, damos, etc
C di, dio, dimos, etc
F dé, demos, etc
G diera, diéramos, etc
H da, dé, demos, dad, den

### decir

A digo, dice, decimos, etc
C dije, dijo, dijimos, etc
D diré, dirá, diremos, etc
E diría, diríamos, etc
F diga, digamos, etc
G dijéra, dijéramos, etc
H di, diga, digamos, decid, digan
I diciendo
J dicho, -cha

### dormir

A duermo, duerme, dormimos, etc
C durmió, dormimos, durmieron, etc
F duerma, durmamos, etc
G durmiera, durmiéramos, etc
H duerme, duerma, durmamos,
dormid, duerman
I durmiendo

### errar

A yerro, yerra, erramos, etc
F yerre, erremos, etc
H yerra, yerre, erremos, errad, yerren

### estar

A estoy, está, estamos, etc
C estuve, estuvo, estuvimos, etc
F esté, estemos, etc
G estuviera, estuviéramos, etc
H está, esté, estemos, estad, estén

### HABER

A he, has, ha, hemos, habéis, han
B había, habías, había, habíamos,
habíais, habían
C hube, hubiste, hubo, hubimos,
hubisteis, hubieron
D habré, habrás, habrá, habremos,
habréis, habrán
E habría, habrías, habría, habríamos,
habríais, habrían
F haya, hayas, haya, hayamos,
hayáis, hayan
G hubiera, hubieras, hubiera,
hubiéramos, hubierais, hubieran
H he, haya, hayamos, habed, hayan
I habiendo
J habido, -da

### hacer

A hago, hace, hacemos, etc
C hice, hizo, hicimos, etc
D haré, haremos, etc
E haría, haríamos, etc
F haga, hagamos, etc
G hiciera, hiciéramos, etc
H haz, haga, hagamos, haced, hagan
J hecho, -cha

### huir

A huyo, huye, huimos, etc
C huyó, huimos, huyeron
F huya, huyamos, etc
G huyera, huyéramos, etc
H huye, huya, huyamos, huid, huyan
I huyendo

## ir

A voy, va, vamos, etc
C fui, fue, fuimos, etc
F vaya, vayamos, etc
G fuera, fuéramos, etc
H ve, vaya, vayamos, id, vayan
I yendo

## leer

C leyó, leímos, leyeron, etc
G leyera, leyéramos, etc
I leyendo

## lucir

A luzco, luce, lucimos, etc
F luzca, luzcamos, etc
H luce, luzca, luzcamos, lucid, luz-can

## mover

A muevo, mueve, movemos, etc
F mueva, movamos, etc
H mueve, mueva, movamos, moved, muevan

## nacer

A nazco, nace, nacemos, etc
F nazca, nazcamos, etc
H nace, nazca, nazcamos, naced, nazcan

## oír

A oigo, oye, oímos, etc
C oyó, oímos, oyeron, etc
F oiga, oigamos, etc
G oyera, oyéramos, etc
H oye, oiga, oigamos, oíd, oigan
I oyendo

## oler

A huelo, huele, olemos, etc
F huela, olamos, etc
H huele, huela, olamos, oled, huelan

## parecer

A parezco, parece, parecemos, etc
F parezca, parezcamos, etc
H parece, parezca, parezcamos, pareced, parezcan

## PARTIR

A parto, partes, parte, partimos, partís, parten
B partía, partías, partía, partíamos, partíais, partían
C partí, partiste, partió, partimos, partisteis, partieron
D partiré, partirás, partirá, partire-mos, partiréis, partirán
E partiría, partirías, partiría, par-tiríamos, partiríais, partirían
F parta, partas, parta, partamos, partáis, partan
G partiera, partieras, partiera, par-tiéramos, partierais, partieran
H parte, parta, partamos, partid, partan
I partiendo
J partido, -da

## pedir

A pido, pide, pedimos, etc
C pidió, pedimos, pidieron, etc
F pida, pidamos, etc
G pidiera, pidiéramos, etc
H pide, pida, pidamos, pedid, pidan
I pidiendo

## poder

A puedo, puede, podemos, etc

# Spanish Verbs

C pude, pudo, pudimos, etc
D podré, podrá, podremos, etc
E podría, podríamos, etc
F pueda, podamos, etc
G pudiera, pudiéramos, etc
H puede, pueda, podamos, poded, puedan
I pudiendo

## poner

A pongo, pone, ponemos, etc
C puse, puso, pusimos, etc
D pondré, pondrá, pondremos, etc
E pondría, pondríamos, etc
F ponga, pongamos, etc
G pusiera, pusiéramos, etc
H pon, ponga, pongamos, poned, pongan
J puesto, -ta

## querer

A quiero, quiere, queremos, etc
C quise, quiso, quisimos, etc
D querré, querrá, querremos, etc
E querría, querríamos, etc
F quiera, queramos, etc
G quisiera, quisiéramos, etc
H quiere, quiera, queramos, quered, quieran

## reír

A río, ríe, reímos, etc
C rió, reímos, rieron, etc
F ría, riamos, etc
G riera, riéramos, etc
H ríe, ría, riamos, reíd, rían
I riendo

## saber

A sé, sabe, sabemos, etc
C supe, supo, supimos, etc
D sabré, sabrá, sabremos, etc

E sabría, sabríamos, etc
F sepa, sepamos, etc
G supiera, supiéramos, etc
H sabe, sepa, sepamos, sabed, sepan

## salir

A salgo, sale, salimos, etc
D saldré, saldrá, saldremos, etc
E saldría, saldríamos, etc
F salga, salgamos, etc
H sal, salga, salgamos, salid, salgan

## sentir

A siento, siente, sentimos, etc
C sintió, sentimos, sintieron, etc
F sienta, sintamos, etc
G sintiera, sintiéramos, etc
H siente, sienta, sintamos, sentid, sientan
I sintiendo

## ser

A soy, eres, es, somos, sois, son
B era, eras, era, éramos, erais, eran
C fui, fuiste, fue, fuimos, fuisteis, fueron
D seré, serás, será, seremos, seréis, serán
E sería, serías, sería, seríamos, seríais, serían
F sea, seas, sea, seamos, seáis, sean
G fuera, fueras, fuera, fuéramos, fuerais, fueran
H sé, sea, seamos, sed, sean
I siendo
J sido, -da

## sonar

A sueno, suena, sonamos, etc
F suene, sonemos, etc
H suena, suene, sonemos, sonad, suenen

# Spanish Verbs

## TEMER

A temo, temes, teme, tememos, teméis, temen
B temía, temías, temía, temíamos, temíais, temían
C temí, temiste, temió, temimos, temisteis, temieron
D temeré, temerás, temerá, temeremos, temeréis, temerán
E temería, temerías, temería, temeríamos, temeríais, temerían
F tema, temas, tema, temamos, temáis, teman
G temiera, temieras, temiera, temiéramos, temierais, temieran
H teme, tema, temamos, temed, teman
I temiendo
J temido, -da

## tender

A tiendo, tiende, tendemos, etc
F tienda, tendamos, etc
H tiende, tienda, tendamos, tended, tiendan

## tener

A tengo, tiene, tenemos, etc
C tuve, tuvo, tuvimos, etc
D tendré, tendrá, tendremos, etc
E tendría, tendríamos, etc
F tenga, tengamos, etc,
G tuviera, tuviéramos, etc
H ten, tenga, tengamos, tened, tengan

## traer

A traigo, trae, traemos, etc
C traje, trajo, trajimos, etc
F traiga, traigamos, etc
G trajera, trajéramos, etc
H trae, traiga, traigamos, traed, traigan
I trayendo

## valer

A valgo, vale, valemos, etc
D valdré, valdrá, valdremos, etc
F valga, valgamos, etc
H vale, valga, valgamos, valed, valgan

## venir

A vengo, viene, venimos, etc
C vine, vino, vinimos, etc
D vendré, vendrá, vendremos, etc
E vendría, vendríamos, etc
F venga, vengamos, etc
G viniera, viniéramos, etc
H ven, venga, vengamos, venid, vengan
I viniendo

## ver

A veo, ve, vemos, etc
C vi, vio, vimos, etc
G viera, viéramos, etc
H ve, vea, veamos, ved, vean
I viendo
J visto, -ta

# Verbos irregulares del inglés

## Verbos irregulares del inglés

| Infinitivo | Pasado simple | Participio pasado |
|---|---|---|
| arise | arose | arisen |
| awake | awoke | awoken |
| be | was/were | been |
| bear | bore | born(e) |
| beat | beat | beaten |
| begin | began | begun |
| bend | bent | bent |
| bet | bet/betted | bet/betted |
| bid | bid | bid |
| bind | bound | bound |
| bite | bit | bitten |
| bleed | bled | bled |
| blow | blew | blown |
| break | broke | broken |
| breed | bred | bred |
| bring | brought | brought |
| build | built | built |
| burn | burnt/burned | burnt/burned |
| burst | burst | burst |
| buy | bought | bought |
| can | could | – |
| cast | cast | cast |
| catch | caught | caught |
| choose | chose | chosen |
| come | came | come |
| cost | cost | cost |
| creep | crept | crept |
| cut | cut | cut |
| deal | dealt | dealt |
| dig | dug | dug |
| do | did | done |
| draw | drew | drawn |
| dream | dreamed/dreamt | dreamed/dreamt |
| drink | drank | drunk |
| drive | drove | driven |
| eat | ate | eaten |
| fall | fell | fallen |
| feed | fed | fed |
| feel | felt | felt |

# Verbos irregulares del inglés

| Infinitivo | Pasado simple | Participio pasado |
|---|---|---|
| fight | fought | fought |
| find | found | found |
| fling | flung | flung |
| fly | flew | flown |
| forget | forget | forgotten |
| freeze | froze | frozen |
| get | got | gotten |
| give | gave | given |
| go | went | gone |
| grind | ground | ground |
| grow | grew | grown |
| hang | hung/hanged | hung/hanged |
| have | had | had |
| hear | heard | heard |
| hide | hid | hidden |
| hit | hit | hit |
| hold | held | held |
| hurt | hurt | hurt |
| keep | kept | kept |
| kneel | knelt/kneeled | knelt/kneeled |
| know | knew | known |
| lay | laid | laid |
| lead | led | led |
| lean | leant/leaned | leant/leaned |
| leap | leapt/leaped | leapt/leaped |
| learn | learnt/learned | learnt/learned |
| leave | left | left |
| lend | lent | lent |
| let | let | let |
| lie | lay | lain |
| light | lit/lighted | lit/lighted |
| lose | lost | lost |
| make | made | made |
| may | might | - |
| mean | meant | meant |
| meet | met | met |
| mow | mowed | mown/mowed |
| pay | paid | paid |
| put | put | put |

# Verbos irregulares del inglés

| Infinitivo | Pasado simple | Participio pasado |
|---|---|---|
| quit | quit/quitted | quit/quitted |
| read | read | read |
| rid | rid | rid |
| ride | rode | ridden |
| ring | rang | rung |
| rise | rose | risen |
| run | ran | run |
| saw | sawed | sawn |
| say | said | said |
| see | saw | seen |
| seek | sought | sought |
| sell | sold | sold |
| send | sent | sent |
| set | set | set |
| shake | shook | shaken |
| shall | should | – |
| shed | shed | shed |
| shine | shone | shone |
| shoot | shot | shot |
| show | showed | shown |
| shrink | shrank | shrunk |
| shut | shut | shut |
| sing | sang | sung |
| sink | sank | sunk |
| sit | sat | sat |
| sleep | slept | slept |
| slide | slid | slid |
| sling | slung | slung |
| smell | smelt/smelled | smelt/smelled |
| sow | sowed | sown/sowed |
| speak | spoke | spoken |
| speed | sped/speeded | sped/speeded |
| spell | spelt/spelled | spelt/spelled |
| spend | spent | spent |
| spill | spilt/spilled | spilt/spilled |
| spin | spun | spun |
| spit | spat | spat |
| split | split | split |
| spoil | spoiled/spoilt | spoiled/spoilt |

# Verbos irregulares del inglés

| Infinitivo | Pasado simple | Participio pasado |
|------------|---------------|-------------------|
| spread | spread | spread |
| spring | sprang | sprung |
| stand | stood | stood |
| steal | stole | stolen |
| stick | stuck | stuck |
| sting | stung | stung |
| stink | stank | stunk |
| strike | struck | struck/stricken |
| swear | swore | sworn |
| sweep | swept | swept |
| swell | swelled | swollen/swelled |
| swim | swam | swum |
| swing | swung | swung |
| take | took | taken |
| teach | taught | taught |
| tear | tore | torn |
| tell | told | told |
| think | thought | thought |
| throw | threw | thrown |
| tread | trod | trodden |
| wake | woke/waked | woken/waked |
| wear | wore | worn |
| weave | wove/weaved | woven/weaved |
| weep | wept | wept |
| win | won | won |
| wind | wound | wound |
| wring | wrung | wrung |
| write | wrote | written |